SO-BZC-315

USED

USED

$46⁵⁰

PSYCHOLOGY

PSYCHOLOGY
THE SCIENCE OF BEHAVIOR

FOURTH EDITION

Neil R. Carlson

The University of Massachusetts

ALLYN AND BACON

Boston ■ London ■ Toronto ■ Sydney ■ Tokyo ■ Singapore

Editor-in-Chief, Social Sciences: Susan Badger
Developmental Editor: Elizabeth Brooks
Senior Editorial Assistant: Dana Hayes
Production Administrator: Annette Joseph
Editorial-Production Service: Woodstock Publishers' Services
Text Designer: Glenna Collett
Copyeditor: Carol I. Beal
Photo Researcher: Sue C. Howard
Composition Buyer: Linda Cox
Cover Administrator: Linda K. Dickinson
Cover Designer: Paradise Designs
Manufacturing Buyer: Megan Cochran

Copyright © 1993, 1990, 1987, 1984 by Allyn and Bacon
A Division of Simon & Schuster, Inc.
160 Gould Street
Needham Heights, MA 02194

All rights reserved. No part of the material protected by this copyright notice may be reproduced or utilized in any form or by any means, electronic or mechanical, including photocopying, recording, or by any information storage and retrieval system, without written permission from the copyright owner.

Library of Congress Cataloging-in-Publication Data

Carlson, Neil R.
    Psychology: the science of behavior / Neil R. Carlson. —4th ed.
        p.   cm.
    Includes bibliographical references and indexes.
    ISBN 0-205-14055-6
    1. Psychology.   I. Title.
BF121.C35   1993
150—dc20   92-23482
                                                  CIP

Printed in the United States of America

10 9 8 7 6 5 4 3 2 1   97 96 95 94 93 92

The credits continue on the pages following the index. They should be considered an extension of the copyright page.

Credits

Chapter 1
P. 5, NASA; p. 7, Fig. 1.1 Historical Picture Services, Chicago; p. 7, margin, National Library of Medicine; p. 8, National Library of Medicine; p. 9, National Library of Medicine; p. 11, National

CONTENTS

v

PREFACE

In this book I have tried to convey my own fascination with the pursuit of knowledge. I have tried to explain how psychologists go about discovering the causes of behavior, and, of course, I have summarized the important things we have learned. I have tried to integrate findings across different subdisciplines and show the student that all of what we do is related, even though different psychologists concern themselves with different phenomena, or with different levels of analysis of these phenomena.

MAJOR CONTENT CHANGES

When I began preparing the fourth edition of this book, I was pleased to have the opportunity to improve it. Aided by the helpful suggestions of students and instructors who had used the earlier editions, I had a clear plan for what should be done. The book now contains seventeen chapters. The material on social psychology is covered in one chapter. The chapter on child development has been expanded to include development throughout the life span. The chapter on emotion contains a new section on stress and health. The language chapter is now a chapter on language and thinking, and includes an expanded section on classifying, reasoning, and problem solving. I reorganized outlines that I thought could be clarified and generally tried to be sure that the text is as easy to read and understand as I could make it. The result is, I think, a significant improvement on previous editions.

As in previous editions, a section on descriptive and inferential statistics is included in the chapter on methods. Users of earlier editions were especially pleased with this chapter, because statistics is such an integral part of the experimental method. An appendix, entitled "Psychologists at Work," follows Chapter 17. This section, written by Robert Gifford of the University of Victoria, British Columbia, provides a practical guide to training and career opportunities in psychology.

PEDAGOGICAL AIDS

As in previous editions, I have provided summaries where they will do the most good: just after a sizable chunk of material. Each chapter contains several of these interim summaries, usually after each major heading. They provide students with a place to relax a bit and review what they have just read. Taken together, they provide a much longer summary than students would tolerate at the end of a chapter and will, I believe, serve them better. In addition, all figures are explicitly referred to in what I think are the best locations. These references are in boldface italic type so that the student can easily find his or her place in the text after examining the figure.

Each chapter of this edition also contains two new pedagogical features: a critical-thinking section called "Evaluating Scientific Issues" and an application section, which comes after the last interim summary. Examples of the issues covered in the critical thinking sections include subliminal self-help tapes, hypnosis and criminal investigation, the existence of a mid-life crisis, "physiological" versus "psychological" drug addiction, the cancer-prone personality, clinical versus actuarial diagnosis, and the existence of a language-acquisition device in the brain. The application sections illustrate how the concepts learned in the chapter can be applied to issues of a practical nature, such as conditioned flavor aversions in chemotherapy and in predator control, mnemonic systems, treatment of sleep disorders, integrity testing for personnel selection, lie detection in criminal investigations, and animal models of mental disorders.

ANCILLARY MATERIALS

Experience with the first three editions guided the revision of the supplements. The instructor's manual is now incorporated in the special *Annotated Instructor's Edition;* I think that it will serve as both a handy guide to the topical coverage in the text and a useful resource for teaching creatively and effectively. Allyn and Bacon also makes available to adopters a wide array of additional supplementary materials, including a new package of **overhead transparencies,** many in full color; a resource manual containing classroom activities and demonstrations; Allyn and Bacon's exclusive CNN videocassettes and videodisks, which include brief, up-to-the-minute segments on topics related to psychology, such as brain research; an extensive video library, including *The Brain* and *The Mind,* also available as teaching modules. Adopters can also obtain **PsychScience,** a program for MacIntosh or IBM-compatible computers that provides students with the opportunity to participate in online experiments. The **Study Guide** provides students with thorough studying and self-testing exercises. The learning objectives and practice test questions featured in the study guide are reflected in the **Test Bank,** which is also available in computerized form, for both MacIntosh and IBM computers. Questions of varying difficulty are provided for each learning objective. See your Allyn and Bacon representative for more information on these and other ancillary materials that are available with this book.

ACKNOWLEDGMENTS

As the writer I get to think of the book as "mine," but it belongs to many other people. I acknowledge their contributions and thank them. Susan Badger, my editor at Allyn and Bacon, found reviewers to read successive approximations of the final version of the text, and gathered a group of people to create the ancillary material, and convinced the management to put their best people to work on the production of the book. Elizabeth Brooks, developmental edi-

tor, discussed with me the changes I would make in this book and provided me with those necessary social reinforcers to keep my enthusiasm high during such a long project. Annette Joseph, the production editor, assembled the team that designed and produced the book. Barbara Gracia, of Woodstock Publishers' Services, managed the book's production and somehow managed to remain calm and collected (at least when I spoke with her) despite an extremely tight production schedule. Sue C. Howard, Annette Joseph, and Elizabeth Brooks read the manuscript and found photos to accompany the text. JAK Graphics drew the four-color anatomical art, and Precision Graphics prepared the graphs.

Many colleagues assisted me by reading drafts of chapters of the book, evaluating them, and suggesting changes. These people played an important part in shaping this edition. Their names are listed below. I also wish to acknowledge again my colleagues who read and evaluated the prior editions. Their names are listed on pages xiii–xiv.

But the writing was still not complete. My copy editor, Carol Beal, proved that there was still room for improvement. Her thoughtful, careful editing tightened and improved my prose.

I also want to thank the people who prepared the ancillary material for doing such a fine job. My wife Mary did the major part of the writing of the study guide and assembled the material for the Annotated Instructor's Edition, and Dennis Cogan, of Texas Tech University, wrote the Test Bank.

Finally, I thank my family for tolerating my spending so much time on the book and for putting up with my grouchiness when work seemed to be going slowly. Without their love and understanding I could never have finished this project.

REVIEWERS OF THE FOURTH EDITION

Daniel Ash
Jefferson Community College—Louisville

David Berger
State University of New York—Cortland

John Broida
University of Southern Maine

J. Timothy Cannon
University of Scranton

Dennis Cogan
Texas Tech University

Kim Dolgin
Ohio Wesleyan University

Robert Ennis
Golden West College

Edwin Fisher
Center for Health Behavior Research, St. Louis

Gabriel Frommer
Indiana University—Bloomington

James Holland
University of Pittsburgh

Janice Kennedy
Georgia Southern University

James Knight
Humboldt State University

Joseph Lowman
University of North Carolina

Jack Marr
Georgia Institute of Technology

Edmund Martin
Georgia Institute of Technology

Dale McAdam
University of Rochester

Linda Musun-Miller
University of Arkansas—Little Rock

Irvin Perline
Mesa Community College

Terry Steele
University of Wisconsin—Oshkosh

Robert Wallace
University of Hartford

Eric Zillmer
Drexel University

REVIEWERS OF PRIOR EDITIONS

Lewis Aiken
Pepperdine University

D. Chris Anderson
University of Notre Dame

Robert Arkin
University of Missouri

John F. Axelson
College of the Holy Cross

Ronald Baenninger
Temple University

Walter Beagley
Alma College

William Beatty
North Dakota State University

Paul Bell
Colorado State University

John Best
Eastern Illinois University

Michael Best
Southern Methodist University

Douglas Bloomquist
Framingham State College

John Bohannan
Virginia Technical University

J. Jay Braun
Arizona State University

Nancy Breland
Trenton State College

Diane Bukatko
Holy Cross College

Anthony Caggiula
University of Pittsburgh

Dennis Cannon
Indiana-Purdue University, Fort Wayne

J. Timothy Cannon
University of Scranton

Jack Carroll
Northeastern University

James Carroll
Central Michigan University

John Caruso
Southern Massachusetts University

Stephen J. Ceci
Cornell University

Brian Charter
University of Saskatchewan

Rachel Clifton
University of Massachusetts

Mark Covey
University of Idaho

Charles Crowell
University of Notre Dame

Sally Diveley
Trenton State University

David Dodd
University of Utah

John Donahoe
University of Massachusetts

Henry Ellis
University of New Mexico

Robert A. Emmons
University of California, Davis

Valeri Farmer-Dougan
Indiana University

Stanley Finger
Washington University in St. Louis

Mary Frances Farkas
Lansing Community College

Jeff Fisher
University of Connecticut

Leslie Fisher
Cleveland State University

Bruce Fogas
Arizona State University

Donald Forgays
University of Vermont

Paul Fox
University of Minnesota

Stephen L. Franzoi
Marquette University

Scott Fraser
University of Southern California

William Froming
University of Florida

Greg Gibson
Kearney State College

Arnold Glass
Rutgers College

Leonard Green
Washington University

Richard Griggs
University of Florida

Carl Gustavson
North Dakota State University

John Hall
The Pennsylvania State University

Renee Harrangue
Loyola-Marymount University

John Hazer
Indiana University

Ann Hempl
Arizona State University

Charles F. Hinderliter
University of Pittsburgh

Philip N. Hineline
Temple University

Larry A. Hjelle
State University of New York College at
   Brockport

Bartley Hoebel
Princeton University

Donald Hoffeld
Louisiana State University

David Hothersall
The Ohio State University

Lester Hyman
Michigan State University

Donald D. Jensen
University of Nebraska—Lincoln

Kent Johnson
Morningside Learning Center

William Johnson
University of Mississippi

Lawrence Kameya
Case Western Reserve University

Terry J. Knapp
University of Nevada

Marguerite Kermis
Canisius College

James Kilkowski
University of California

John Lamberth
Temple University

Marjorie Lewis
Illinois State University

Richard Lippa
California State University

William Mackavey
Boston University

Jane Maddy
University of Minnesota, Duluth

M. Jackson Marr
Georgia Institute of Technology

Dale W. McAdam
University of Rochester

David McDonald
University of Missouri at Columbia

Donald Meichenbaum
University of Waterloo

Gerald Mendelsohn
University of California, Berkeley

Steven Mewaldt
Marshall University

Harold L. Miller
WICAT Education Institute

Dick Miller
Western Kentucky University

David B. Mitchell
Southern Methodist University

James Mitchell
Kansas State University

Richard Morris
Trent University

Daniel Murphy
Indiana-Purdue University, Fort Wayne

Carnot Nelson
University of South Florida

Melinda Novak
University of Massachusetts

Edward F. O'Day
San Diego State University

Gayle A. Olson
University of New Orleans

Edgar O'Neal
Tulane University

Yvonne Hardaway Osborne
Louisiana State University

Marcia Ozier
Dalhousie University

Robert Payne
University of Victoria

Steven Anderson Platt
Northern Michigan University

Robert Plomin
The Pennsylvania State University

Merle Prim
Western Washington University

Janet D. Proctor
Purdue University

Jay R. Quinan
University of Georgia

Michael J. Renner
University of Wyoming

John Santelli
Farleigh Dickinson University

Michael Scheier
Carnegie-Mellon University

Lee Seecrest
University of Arizona

Lester Sdorow
Allentown College

Bryan Shepp
Brown University

Neil G. Simon
Lehigh University

Larry Smith
University of Maine—Orono

Robert F. Smith
George Mason University

Steven M. Smith
Texas A & M University

Paul Spear
California State University—Chico

H. J. Stanford
Trent University

Robert Stern
The Pennsylvania State University

Paul Tacon
York University

Joseph J. Tecce
Boston College

Michael Terman
Northeastern University

Ross Thompson
University of Nebraska, Lincoln

William Timberlake
Indiana University

Mary Trahan
Randolph-Macon College

Pat Tuntland
Pima Community College

Ko Van Denselaar
University of Saskatchewan

Joann Veroff
University of Michigan

Jean Volckmann
Pasadena City College

Susan A. Warner
University of Arizona

George E. Weaver
The Florida State University

Charles S. Weiss
Holy Cross College

Paul Wellman
Texas A & M University

Kipling Williams
Drake University

William C. Williams
Eastern Washington University

W. Jeffrey Wilson
Indiana University

Diana Woodruff-Pak
Temple University

Jay Wright
Washington State University

TO THE READER

You purchased this book because it was assigned to you, and this semester you will be spending a considerable amount of time reading it. I hope that you will enjoy it; learning about psychology can be fun. If it were not, I would never have finished writing this book, and I would long ago have tired of lecturing about it to my students.

When I took my first psychology course as an undergraduate, I was surprised to learn that psychological investigation was actually a scientific enterprise. I had thought that psychologists knew all there was to know about the real, often hidden, reasons for our behavior, and that I would now learn all their secrets. I had never really considered where this knowledge came from. I quickly learned that psychologists knew much less about the important questions than I thought they did, but their pursuit of knowledge was more interesting than I had suspected it could be.

It is the fascination and excitement of the pursuit of knowledge that I try to convey in my lectures, and which I have tried to convey in this book. The scientific method is an outstandingly successful intellectual achievement. It permits the practitioner to enjoy a mixture of speculation, logical deduction, and empirical data collection. Those of us who enjoy gadgets can spend time with computers and other hardware. Those of us who enjoy watching social interactions can design experiments that present interesting situations and observe our subjects' behavior. And afterward, we can teach our students about what we discovered, and how we discovered it.

There are some things you should know about the book before you start reading. Each chapter is preceded by a list of learning objectives. These objectives provide a quick summary of the topics that are covered and provide a focus for you to check your progress. The learning objectives are numbered, and you will find numbers in the text, enclosed in little boxes, that indicate the beginning of the material that is covered by the corresponding learning objective. The questions in the study guide are designed to help you master these objectives.

Because every discipline has its own vocabulary—and psychology is no exception—important terms are specially marked in the text. Each one appears in **boldface** where the definition or description is given. A list of these terms appears at the end of each chapter, with the appropriate page of text listed, in a section entitled "Key Terms." If, after reading a chapter, you find that some of these terms are unfamiliar to you, you can easily find them to review them. In addition, the study guide that accompanies this text has a set of flash cards at the end of each chapter with terms on the front and definitions on the back, which can help you learn new terms more efficiently.

The book contains tables, graphs, diagrams, drawings, and photographs. They are there to illustrate a point, and in some cases, to make a point that cannot be made with words alone. I am always annoyed when illustrations accompany text without a clear indication of when I should stop reading and consult them. If I look at the illustration too soon, I will not understand it. If I look at it too late, I will have struggled with text that I could have understood more clearly had I only looked at the illustration first. Therefore, I have added explicit references so that you will be spared this kind of annoyance. These are in boldface italics, like this: (See *Figure 5.10.*) If you wait until you see a figure or table reference before looking away from the text you will be consulting the illustration at the most appropriate time. Sometimes it is best to look at a figure more than once; in such cases I provide more than one reference to it. Some photographs that illustrate general rather than specific points are not numbered; you can look at these whenever you find a convenient stopping place.

Rather than provide a long summary at the end of each chapter I have provided *interim summaries*—reviews of the information that has just been presented. These summaries divide chapters into more easily managed chunks. When you reach an interim summary in your reading, take the opportunity to relax and think about what you have read. You might even want to take a five-minute break after reading the interim summary, then read it once again to remind yourself of what you just read, and go on to the next section. If you read the material this way, you will learn it with much less effort than you would otherwise have to expend.

The study guide that accompanies this text (consult your instructor regarding availability) is an excellent aid to actively learning the material in the book. By thinking about and answering the study questions you will be sure not to have missed some important points. In addition, each chapter in the study guide includes two short self-tests so you can assess your comprehension of the material.

I have not met you, but I feel as if I have been talking to you during the several years I have been writing and rewriting this book. Writing is an unsocial activity in the sense that it is done alone. It is even an antisocial activity when the writer must say, "No, I'm too busy writing to talk with you now." So as I wrote this book I consoled myself by imagining that you were listening to me. You will get to meet me, or at least do so vicariously, through my words, as you read this book. If you then want to make the conversation two-way, please write to me at the Department of Psychology, Tobin Hall, University of Massachusetts, Amherst, MA 01003. I hope to hear from you.

PSYCHOLOGY

1

THE SCIENCE OF PSYCHOLOGY

Henri Matisse, *The Sorrows of the King*
GIRAUDON/Art Resource, N.Y. © 1992 Succession H. Matisse/ARS, N.Y.

LEARNING OBJECTIVES

When you finish this chapter, you should be able to:

1. Describe the goal of psychological research and outline the philosophical roots of psychology.
2. Describe the biological roots of psychology.
3. Discuss the major trends in the early development of psychology: structuralism, the work of Ebbinghaus, functionalism, and the influence of Freud.
4. Outline the development of behaviorism, and describe the cognitive revolution.
5. Describe the different types of psychologists and the problems they study.

René, a lonely, intelligent young man of eighteen years, had secluded himself in Saint-Germain, a village to the west of Paris. He had recently suffered a nervous breakdown and chose the retreat to recover. Even before coming to Saint-Germain, he had heard of the fabulous Royal Gardens built for Henri IV and Marie de Médici, and one sunny day he decided to visit them. The guard stopped him at the gate; but when he identified himself as a student at the King's School at La Flèche, he was permitted to enter. The gardens consisted of a series of six large terraces overlooking the Seine, planted in the symmetrical, orderly fashion so loved by the French. Grottoes were cut into the limestone hillside at the end of each terrace; René entered one of them. He heard eerie music accompanied by the gurgling of water but, at first, could see nothing in the darkness. As his eyes became accustomed to the gloom, he could make out a figure illuminated by a flickering torch. He approached the figure, which he soon recognized as that of a young woman. As he drew closer, he saw that she was actually a bronze statue of Diana, bathing in a pool of water. Suddenly, the Greek goddess fled and hid behind a bronze rose bush. As René pursued her, an imposing statue of Neptune rose in front of him, barring the way with his trident.

René was delighted. He had heard about the hydraulically operated mechanical organs and the moving statues, but he had not expected such realism. As he walked back toward the entrance to the grotto, he saw the plates buried in the ground that controlled the valves operating the machinery. He spent the rest of the afternoon wandering through the grottoes, listening to the music and being entertained by the statues.

During his stay in Saint-Germain René visited the Royal Gardens again and again. He had been thinking about the relation between the movements of animate and inanimate objects, which had concerned philosophers for some time. He thought he saw in the apparently purposeful, but obviously inanimate, movements of the statues an answer to some important questions. Even after he left Saint-Germain, he revisited the grottoes in his memory; and he went so far as to name his daughter Francine after their designers, the Francini brothers of Florence.

Psychology is both a scientific discipline and a profession. Psychologists are probably the most diverse group of people in our society to share the same title. According to the latest census, there are 119,000 people in the United States employed as psychologists. They engage in research, teaching, counseling, and psychotherapy; they advise industry and governmental agencies about personnel matters, the design of products, advertising and marketing, and legislation; they devise and administer tests of personality, achievement, and ability. Psychologists study a wide variety of phenomena, including physiological processes within the nervous system, genetics, environmental events, mental abilities, and social interactions. And yet psychology is a new discipline; the first person to call himself a psychologist was still alive in 1920.

This chapter describes the nature of psychology, its history, and its goals.

THE SCIENCE OF PSYCHOLOGY: EXPLAINING BEHAVIOR

In this book we will study the science of psychology. The primary emphasis is on discovering the causes of human behavior. Of course, I shall describe the applications of these discoveries to treating mental disorders and improving society, but the focus will be on the way psychologists discover the facts that make these applications possible.

The goal of research in psychology is to understand human behavior: to explain why people do what they do. Different kinds of psychologists are interested in different kinds of behaviors and different levels of explanation. Therefore, before I describe the various types of psychologists, I must discuss the meaning of the term *explanation*.

How do psychologists "explain" behavior? In general, we discover its causes—those events that are responsible for its occurrence. If we can describe the events that caused the behavior to occur, we have "explained" it. Each type of psychologist looks for certain types of **causal events.** (Be careful; the word is *causal,* not *ca-su-al.*) Some look inside the organism in a literal sense, seeking physiological causes, such as the activity of nerve cells or the secretions of glands. Others look inside the organism in a metaphorical sense, explaining behaviors in terms of hypothetical mental states, such as anger, fear, or a need to achieve. Still others look only for environmental events that cause behaviors to occur.

The scientific search for the causes of behavior has been heavily influenced by the natural sciences, from which psychology emerged. A look at how psychology developed as a science will help us to appreciate some differences in approaches to explaining behavior.

The Goals of Psychological Research

Why do psychologists want to explain behavior? One good reason is intellectual curiosity. An essential part of human nature seems to be a need to understand what makes things work—and what could be more interesting than trying to understand our fellow human beings? But psychological research is more than an idle endeavor of curious scientists; it holds the promise of showing us how to solve our most important and pressing problems.

Human behavior is at the root of most of the world's problems: poverty, crime, overpopulation, drug addiction, bigotry, pollution, war. If the greenhouse phenomenon does adversely affect our planet, or if forests and lakes die because of acid rain, it will be because of our *behavior*—it is we who produce the chemicals and spew them into the atmosphere. Health-related problems—such as cardiovascular disease, some forms of cancer, and a large number of psychosomatic illnesses—are caused (or at least aggravated) by an individual's behavior.

Most problems faced by our species—such as global warming and the development of holes in the ozone layer—are the results of our own behavior.

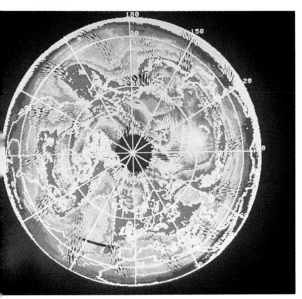

Smoking, obesity, lack of exercise, poor diet, unsanitary personal habits, and stressful lifestyles are responsible for much of the illness found around the world. Inappropriate agricultural practices, inefficient distribution of food, and wars and tribal conflicts—which you will note are the products of human *behaviors*—are responsible for much of the hunger and starvation that exists in the world today. If people's behavior could be changed, people's living conditions could be drastically improved.

Obviously, these problems are still with us; psychological research has not yet given us all the answers. In some cases we know what must be done, but we do not yet know how to change people's behavior. I hope that in reading this book and learning what psychologists have discovered about human behavior, you will think about what can be done. Perhaps you will be one of those who discover important principles of behavior or apply them to solving the problems that beset us—while there is still time.

THE RISE OF PSYCHOLOGY AS A SCIENCE

Although philosophers and other thinkers have been concerned with psychological issues for a long time, the science of psychology is comparatively young; it started in Germany in the late nineteenth century. In order to understand how this science came into being, we must first trace its roots back through philosophy and the natural sciences, because these disciplines provided the methods we use to study human behavior. These roots took many centuries to develop. Let us examine them now and see how they set the stage for the emergence of the science of psychology in the late nineteenth century.

Philosophical Roots of Psychology

Each of us is conscious of our own existence. Furthermore, we are aware of this consciousness. Although we often find ourselves doing things that we had not planned to do (or had planned *not* to do), by and large we feel that we are in control of our behavior. That is, we have the impression that our behavior is controlled by our consciousness. We consider alternatives, make plans, and then act. We get our muscles moving; we engage in behavior.

Consciousness is a private experience, and yet its study has a long history. At present, even though we can experience only our own consciousness directly, we assume that our fellow human beings are also conscious, and, to at least some extent, we attribute consciousness to other animals as well. To the degree that our behaviors are similar we tend to assume that our mental states, too, resemble one another. Much earlier in the history of our species, people were very generous in attributing a life-giving *animus,* or spirit, to anything that seemed to move or grow independently. Because they believed that the movements of their own bodies were controlled by their minds or spirits, they inferred that the sun, moon, wind, tides, and other moving objects were similarly animated. This primitive philosophy is called **animism** (from the Latin *animare,* "to quicken, enliven, endow with breath or soul"). Even gravity was explained in animistic terms: Rocks fell to the ground because the spirits within them wanted to be reunited with Mother Earth.

Obviously, our interest in animism is historical. No educated person in our society believes that rocks fall because they "want to." Rather, we believe that they fall owing to the existence of natural forces inherent in physical matter, even if we do not understand what these forces are. But note that different interpretations can be placed upon the same events. Surely, we are just as prone to subjective interpretations of natural phenomena, albeit more sophisticated ones, as our ancestors were. In fact, when we try to explain why people do what they do, we tend to attribute at least some of their behavior to the action of a motivating spirit—namely, a will. In our daily lives this explanation of behavior may often suit our needs. However, on a scientific level we need to base our explanations on phenomena that can be observed and measured objectively.

The best means we have to ensure objectivity is the scientific method (described in Chapter 2). Psychology as a science must be based on the assumption that behavior is strictly subject to physical laws, just as any other natural phenomenon is. The rules of scientific research impose discipline on humans whose natural inclinations might lead them to incorrect conclusions. It seemed natural for our ancestors to believe that rocks had spirits, just as it seems natural for people nowadays to believe that behavior can be affected by a person's will. In contrast, the idea that feelings, emotions, imagination, and other private experiences are the products of physical laws of nature did not come easily; it evolved through many centuries.

Although the history of Western philosophy properly begins with the ancient Greeks, we will begin here with René Descartes, a seventeenth-century French philosopher and mathematician. Descartes has been called the father of modern philosophy and of a biological tradition that led to modern physiological psychology. Descartes advocated a sober, impersonal investigation of natural phenomena using sensory experience and human reasoning. He assumed that the world was a purely mechanical entity that, having once been set in motion by God, ran its course without divine interference. Thus, to understand the world, one had only to understand how it was constructed. This stance challenged the established authority of the Church, which believed that the purpose of philosophy was to reconcile human experiences with the truth of God's revelations.

To Descartes, animals were mechanical devices; their behavior was controlled by environmental stimuli. His view of the human body was much the same: It was a machine. Thus, Descartes was able to describe some movements as automatic and involuntary. For example, the application of a hot object to a finger would cause an almost immediate withdrawal of the arm away from the source of stimulation. Reactions like this did not require participation of the mind; they occurred automatically. Descartes called these actions **reflexes** (from the Latin *reflectere,* "to bend back upon itself"). Energy coming from the outside source would be reflected back through the nervous system to the muscles, which would contract. The term is still in use today, but, of course, we explain the operation of a reflex differently. (See ***Figure 1.1.***)

What set humans apart from the rest of the world was their possession of a mind. The mind was a uniquely human attribute and was not subject to the laws of the universe. Thus, Descartes was a proponent of **dualism,** the belief that all reality can be divided into two distinct entities: mind and matter. He distinguished between "extended things," or physical bodies, and "thinking things," or minds. Physical bodies, he believed, do not think, and minds are not made of ordinary matter. Although Descartes was not the first to propose dualism, his thinking differed from that of his predecessors in one important way: He was the first to suggest that a link exists between the human mind and its purely physical housing. Although later philosophers pointed out that this theoretical link actually contradicted his belief in dualism, the proposal of an interaction between mind and

Figure 1.1 Descartes's diagram of a withdrawal reflex. (Historical Pictures Service, Chicago.)

nerves that connected them to the brain and spinal cord, just as water flowed through pipes to activate the statues. This inflation was the basis of the muscular contraction that causes us to move.

This story illustrates one of the first times that a technological device was used as a model for explaining how the nervous system works. In science a **model** is a relatively simple system that works on known principles and is able to do at least some of the things that a more complex system can do. For example, when scientists discovered that elements of the nervous system communicate by means of electrical impulses, researchers developed models of the brain based upon telephone switchboards and, more recently, computers. Abstract models, which are completely mathematical in their properties, have also been developed.

Although Descartes's model of the human body was mechanical, it was controlled by the nonmechanical (in fact, nonphysical) mind. Thus, humans were born with a special capability that made them greater than simply the sum of their parts; their knowledge was more than merely a physical phenomenon.

With the work of the English philosopher John Locke the mechanization of the whole world was complete. Locke did not exempt the mind from the mechanical laws of the material universe. Descartes's *rationalism* (pursuit of truth through reason) was replaced by **empiricism**—pursuit of truth through observation and experience. Locke rejected the notion that ideas were innately present in an infant's mind. Instead, all knowledge must come through experience. It is empirically derived. (In Greek, *empeira* means "experience.") His model of the mind was a tablet of soft clay, smooth at birth and ready to accept the writings of experience upon it.

Locke believed that our knowledge of complex experiences was nothing more than linkages of simple, primary sensations: simple ideas combined to form complex ones. In contrast, the Irish philosopher and mathematician George Berkeley believed that our knowledge of events in the world did not come simply from direct experience but instead was the result of inferences based upon the accumulation of past experiences. In other words, we must learn how to perceive. For example, our visual perception of depth involves several elementary sensations, such as observing the relative movements of objects as we move our head and the convergence of our eyes (turning inward toward each

John Locke (1632–1704)

matter was absolutely vital to the development of a psychological science.

Descartes reasoned that mind and body could interact. The mind controlled the movements of the body, while the body, through its sense organs, supplied the mind with information about what was happening in the environment. Descartes hypothesized that this interaction between mind and body took place in the pineal body, a small organ situated on top of the brain stem, buried beneath the large cerebral hemispheres of the brain. When the mind decided to perform an action, it tilted the pineal body in a particular direction, causing fluid to flow from the brain into the proper set of nerves. This flow of fluid caused the appropriate muscles to inflate and move. Let us see how Descartes came up with this mechanical concept of the body's movements.

Western Europe in the seventeenth century was the scene of great advances in the sciences. It was not just the practical application of science that impressed Europeans; it was the beauty, imagination, and fun of it as well. Craftsmen constructed many elaborate mechanical toys and devices during this period. As we saw in the opening vignette, the young René Descartes was greatly impressed by the moving statues in the Royal Gardens (Jaynes, 1970). These devices served as models for Descartes in theorizing about how the body worked. He conceived of the muscles as balloons. They became inflated when a fluid passed through the

other or away) as we focus on near or distant objects. Although our knowledge of visual depth seems to be immediate and direct, it is actually a secondary, complex response constructed from a number of simple elements. Our perceptions of the world can also involve integrating the activity of different sense organs, such as when we see, hear, feel, and smell the same object.

As you can see, the philosophers Locke and Berkeley were grappling with the workings of the human mind and the way in which people acquire knowledge. They were dealing with the concept of learning. (In fact, modern psychologists are still concerned with the issues that Berkeley raised.) As philosophers, they were trying to fit a nonquantifiable variable—reason—into the equation.

With the work of the Scottish philosopher James Mill the pendulum took its full swing from *animism* (physical matter animated by spirits) to **materialism** (mind composed entirely of matter). Mill worked on the assumption that humans and animals were fundamentally the same. Both humans and animals were thoroughly physical in their makeup and were completely subject to the physical laws of the universe. Essentially, he agreed with Descartes's approach to understanding the human body but rejected the concept of an immaterial mind. Mind, to Mill, was as passive as the body. It responded to the environment in precisely the same way. The mind, no less than the body, was a machine.

Biological Roots of Psychology

2 René Descartes and his model of muscular physiology provides a good beginning for a discussion of the biological roots of psychology. Descartes's concept was based on an actual working model (the moving statue) whose movements seemed similar to those of human beings. Recognition of that similarity served as "proof" of his theory; he did not have the means available to offer a scientific proof. But technological development soon made experimentation and manipulation possible. Truth need not only be reasoned; it could be demonstrated and verified. Descartes's hydraulic model of muscular movement was shown to be incorrect by Luigi Galvani (1737–1798), an Italian physiologist who discovered that muscles could be made to contract by applying an electrical current directly to them or to the nerve that was attached to them.

It is in the work of the German physiologist Johannes Müller that we note a very definite

transition from the somewhat sporadic, isolated instances of research into human physiology to the progressively more direct and precise exploration of the human body. Müller was a forceful advocate of applying experimental procedures to the study of physiology. He recommended that biologists should do more than observe and classify; they should remove or isolate animals' organs, test their responses to chemicals, and manipulate other conditions in order to see how the organism worked. His most important contribution to what would become the science of psychology was his **doctrine of specific nerve energies.** He noted that the basic message sent along all nerves was the same—an electrical impulse. And the impulse itself was the same, regardless of whether the message concerned, for example, a visual perception or an auditory one. What, then, accounts for the brain's ability to distinguish different kinds of sensory information? That is, why do we see what our eyes detect, hear what our ears detect, and so on? After all, the optic nerves and the auditory nerves both send the same kind of message to the brain.

The answer is that the messages are sent over different channels. Because the optic nerves are attached to the eyes, the brain interprets impulses received from these nerves as visual sensations. You have probably already noticed that rubbing your eyes causes sensations of flashes of light. When you rub your eyes, the pressure against them stimulates visual receptors located inside. The brain then interprets these messages as sensations of light.

Müller's doctrine had important implications. If the brain recognizes the nature of a particular sensory input by means of the particular nerve that brings the message, then perhaps the brain is similarly specialized, with different parts having different functions. In other words, if the messages sent by the nerves are anatomically distinct, then those regions of the brain that receive these messages must also be anatomically distinct. Müller's ideas have endured, forming the basis for investigations into the functions of the nervous system. For centuries, thinking or consciousness had been identified as the distinguishing feature of the human mind and had been localized as a function of the brain. Now the components of the nervous system were being identified and their means of operation were being explored.

Pierre Flourens, a French physiologist, provided experimental evidence for the implications of Müller's doctrine of specific nerve energies. He removed various parts of the nervous

*Johannes Müller
(1801–1858)*

system of animals and found that the resulting effects depended upon which parts were removed. He observed what the animal could no longer do and concluded that the missing capacity must have been the function of the part that he had removed. For example, if an animal could not move its leg after part of its brain was removed, then that region must normally control leg movements. This method, called **experimental ablation** (from the Latin *ablatus,* "carried away"), was soon adopted by neurologists, and it is still used by scientists today. Through experimental ablation Flourens claimed to have discovered the regions of the brain that control heart rate and breathing, purposeful movements, and visual and auditory reflexes.

The person to apply the logic of Flourens's method to humans was Paul Broca. In 1861 Broca, a French surgeon, performed an autopsy on the brain of a man who had had a stroke several years previously; the stroke had caused him to lose the ability to speak. Broca discovered that the stroke had damaged part of the cerebral cortex on the left side of the man's brain. He suggested that this region of the brain is a center for speech.

Although subsequent research has found that speech is not controlled by a single "center" in the brain, the area that Broca identified is indeed necessary for speech production. The comparison of postmortem anatomical findings with a patient's behavioral and intellectual deficits has become an important means of studying the functions of the brain. Psychologists can operate on the brains of laboratory animals, but

they obviously cannot operate on the brains of humans. Instead, they must study the effects of brain damage that occurs from natural causes.

In 1870 the German physiologists Gustav Fritsch and Eduard Hitzig introduced the use of electrical stimulation as a tool for mapping the functions of the brain. The results of this method complemented those produced by the experimental destruction of nervous tissue and provided some answers that the method of experimental ablation could not. For example, Fritsch and Hitzig discovered that applying a small electrical shock to different parts of the cerebral cortex caused movements of different parts of the body. In fact, the body appeared to be "mapped" on the surface of the brain. (See *Figure 1.2.*)

The work of the German physicist and physiologist Hermann von Helmholtz did much to demonstrate that mental phenomena could be explained by physiological means. This extremely productive scientist made contributions to both physics and physiology. He actively disassociated himself from natural philosophy, from which many assumptions about the nature of mind had been derived. Müller, under whom Helmholtz had conducted his first research, believed that human organs were endowed with a vital immaterial force that coordinated physiological behavior, a force that was not subject to experimental investigation. Helmholtz would allow no such assumptions about unproved (and unprovable) phenomena. He advocated a purely scientific approach, with conclusions based on objective investigation and precise measurement.

Paul Broca (1824–1880)

Hermann von Helmholtz (1821–1894)

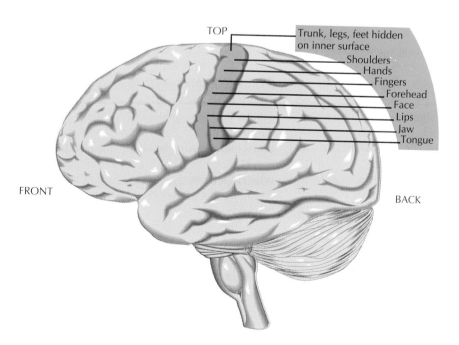

TOP

Trunk, legs, feet hidden on inner surface
Shoulders
Hands
Fingers
Forehead
Face
Lips
Jaw
Tongue

FRONT

BACK

Figure 1.2 Cortical motor map. Stimulation of various parts of the motor cortex causes contraction of muscles in various parts of the body.

Until Helmholtz's time scientists believed that the transmission of impulses through nerves was as fast as the speed of electricity in wires; under this assumption transmission would be virtually instantaneous, considering the small distances that impulses have to travel within the human body. Helmholtz successfully measured the speed of the nerve impulse and found that it was only about 90 feet per second, which is considerably slower than the speed of electricity in wires. This finding suggested to later researchers that the nerve impulse is more complex than a simple electrical current passing through a wire, which is indeed true.

Helmholtz also attempted to measure the speed of a person's reaction to a physical stimulus, but he abandoned this attempt because there was too much variability from person to person. However, this variability interested scientists who followed him; they tried to explain the reason for individual differences in behavior. Because both the velocity of nerve impulses and a person's reactions to stimuli could be measured, researchers theorized that mental events themselves could be the subject of scientific investigation. Possibly, if the proper techniques could be developed, one could investigate what went on within the human brain. Thus, Helmholtz's research was very important in setting the stage for the science of psychology.

In Germany a contemporary of von Helmholtz's, Ernst Weber, began work that led to the development of a method for measuring the magnitude of human sensations. Weber, an anatomist and physiologist, found that people's ability to tell the difference between two similar stimuli—such as the brightness of two lights, the heaviness of two objects, or the loudness of two tones—followed orderly laws. This regularity suggested to Weber and his followers that the study of perceptual phenomena could be as scientific as that of physics or biology. In Chapter 4 we will consider the study of the relation between the physical characteristics of a stimulus and the perceptions they produce, a field called **psychophysics,** or the physics of the mind.

INTERIM SUMMARY

The Rise of Psychology as a Science

We can see that by the mid–nineteenth century philosophy had embraced two concepts that would lead to the objective investigation of the human mind: the principles of materialism and empiricism. Materialism maintained that the mind was made of matter; thus, all natural phenomena, including human behavior, could be explained in terms of physical entities: the interaction of matter and energy. Empiricism emphasized that all knowledge was acquired by means of sensory experience; no knowledge was innate. By directing attention to the tangible, sensory components of human activity, these concepts laid the foundation for a scientific approach in psychology. At this time the divisions between science and philosophy were still blurred. But subsequent developments in the natural sciences, especially in biology and physiology, provided the necessary ingredients that, united with the critical, analytical components of philosophy, formed the scientific discipline of psychology. These ingredients were experimentation and verification.

To summarize our history thus far, we turn to the nineteenth-century French philosopher and mathematician Auguste Comte. His *law of three stages,* which traced human intellectual development, offers us an interesting analogy. Humans had moved from a theological stage (the world and human destiny explained in terms of gods and spirits), through a transitional stage (explanations given in terms of essences, final causes, and other abstractions), to the modern positive stage (explanations given in terms of natural laws and empirical data). We can relate the development of the study of the human mind to Comte's three stages. Beginning with animism, we moved through theology and philosophy, and from there into the arenas of biology and physiology. This progression led us to the laboratory of Ernst Weber and the development of psychophysics. ∎

MAJOR TRENDS IN THE DEVELOPMENT OF PSYCHOLOGY

3 Psychology began in Germany in the late nineteenth century with Wilhelm Wundt. Wundt was the first person to call himself a psychologist. He shared the conviction of other German scientists that all aspects of nature, including the human mind, could be studied scientifically. His book *Principles of Physiological Psychology* was the first textbook of psychology.

The fact that Germany was the birthplace of psychology had as much to do with social, political, and economic influences as with the abilities of its scientists and scholars. The German university system was well established, and professors were highly respected members of society. The academic tradition in Germany emphasized a scientific approach to a large number of subject areas, such as history, phonetics, archaeology, aesthetics, and literature. Thus, in contrast to French and British scholars, who adopted the more traditional, philosophical approach to the study of the human mind, German scholars were open to the possibility that the human mind could be studied scientifically. Experimental physiology, one of the most important roots of experimental psychology, was well established there. A more mundane and practical factor that favored Germany as the birthplace of psychology was that its universities were well financed; there was money to support researchers who wanted to expand scientific investigation into new fields. It was in this climate that Müller, Helmholtz, and Wundt conducted their research.

Structuralism

Wundt defined psychology as the "science of immediate experience," and his approach was called **structuralism.** Its subject matter was the *structure* of the mind, built from the elements of consciousness, such as ideas and sensations. Its raw material was supplied by trained observers who described their own experiences. The observers were taught to engage in **introspection** (literally, "looking within"); they observed stimuli and described their experiences. Wundt and his associates made inferences about the nature of mental processes by seeing how changes in the stimuli caused changes in the verbal reports of their trained observers.

Wundt was particularly interested in the problem that had intrigued George Berkeley: How did basic sensory information give rise to complex perceptions? His trained observers attempted to ignore complex perceptions and report only the elementary ones. For example, the sensation of seeing a patch of red is immediate and elementary, whereas the perception of an apple is complex.

Wundt was a very ambitious and prolific scientist who wrote many books and trained many other scientists in his laboratory. However, his method did not survive the test of time; structuralism died out in the early twentieth century. The major problem with his approach was the difficulty encountered by observers in reporting the raw data of sensation, data unmodified by experience. In addition, the emphasis of psychological investigation shifted from the study of the

human mind to the study of human behavior. More recently, psychologists have resumed the study of the human mind, but we now have better methods for studying it than were available to Wundt. Although structuralism has been supplanted, Wundt's contribution must be acknowledged. He established psychology as an experimental science, independent of philosophy. He trained a great number of psychologists, many of whom established their own laboratories and continued the evolution of the new discipline.

Ebbinghaus: Pioneer in Research on Human Memory

Most of the pioneers of psychology founded *schools,* groups of people with a common belief in a particular theory and methodology. (In this context the word *school* refers to a branch of a particular academic discipline, not a building or institution. For example, structuralism was a school of psychology.) The exception to this trend was Hermann Ebbinghaus. In 1876, after receiving his Ph.D. in philosophy but still unattached to an academic institution, Ebbinghaus came across a secondhand copy of a book by Gustav Fechner in which he described his mathematical approach to the measurement of human sensation. Intrigued by Fechner's research, Ebbinghaus decided to attempt to measure human memory: the processes of learning and forgetting.

Working alone, Ebbinghaus devised methods to measure memory and the speed with which forgetting occurred. He realized that he could not compare the learning and forgetting of two prose passages or two poems, because some passages would undoubtedly be easier to learn than others. Therefore, he devised a relatively uniform set of materials—nonsense syllables, such as *juz, bul,* and *gof.* He printed the syllables on cards and read through a set of them, with the rate of presentation controlled by the ticking of a watch. After reading the set, he paused a fixed amount of time, then read the cards again. He recorded the number of times he had to read the cards to be able to recite them without error. He measured forgetting by trying to recite the nonsense syllables on a later occasion—minutes, hours, or days later. The number of syllables he remembered was an index of the percentage of memory that had been retained.

Ebbinghaus's approach to memory was entirely empirical; he devised no theory of why learning occurs and was interested only in gathering facts through careful, systematic observa-

Wilhelm Wundt (1832–1920)

Hermann Ebbinghaus (1850–1909)

tion. However, despite the lack of theory, his work made important contributions to the development of the science of psychology. He introduced the principle of eliminating variable errors by making observations repeatedly on different occasions (using different lists each time) and calculating the average of these observations. **Variable errors** include errors caused by random differences in the subject's mood or alertness or by uncontrollable changes in the environment. He constructed graphs of the rate at which the memorized lists of nonsense syllables were forgotten, which provided a way to measure mental contents across time. As we will see in Chapter 7, Ebbinghaus's research provided a model of systematic, rigorous experimental procedures that modern psychologists still emulate.

Functionalism

After structuralism the next major trend in psychology was **functionalism.** This approach, which began in the United States, was in large part a protest against the structuralism of Wundt. Structuralists were interested in what they called the components of consciousness (ideas and sensations); functionalists focused on the process of conscious activity (perceiving and learning). Functionalism grew from the new perspective on nature supplied by Charles Darwin and his followers. Proponents of functionalism stressed the biological significance (the purpose, or *function*) of natural processes, including behaviors. The emphasis was on overt, observable behaviors, not on private mental events.

Charles Darwin proposed the theory of evolution in his book *On the Origin of Species by Means of Natural Selection.* As you know, his work, more than that of any other person, revolutionized biology. The concept of *natural selection* showed how the consequences of an animal's characteristics affect its ability to survive. Instead of simply identifying, describing, and naming species, biologists now began to look at the adaptive significance of the ways in which species differed.

Darwin's theory suggested that behaviors, like other biological characteristics, could best be explained by understanding their role in the adaptation of an organism to its environment. Thus, behavior has a biological context. Darwin assembled evidence that behaviors, like body parts, could be inherited. In *The Expression of the Emotions in Man and Animals* he proposed that the facial gestures that animals make in expressing emotions were descended from movements that previously had other functions. New areas of exploration were opened for psychologists by the ideas that an evolutionary continuity existed among the various species of animals and that behaviors, like parts of the body, had evolutionary histories.

The most important psychologist to embrace functionalism was William James. As James said, "My thinking is first, last, and always for the sake of my doing." That is, thinking was not an end in itself; its function was to produce useful behaviors. Although James was a champion of experimental psychology, he himself did not appear to enjoy doing research but spent most of his time reading, thinking, teaching, and writing during his tenure as professor of philosophy (later, professor of psychology) at Harvard University. His course entitled "The Relations Between Physiology and Psychology" was the first course in experimental psychology to be offered in the United States.

*Charles Darwin
(1809–1882)*

According to the functionalist tradition inspired by Darwin, behaviors, like other biological characteristics, can best be explained by understanding their role in adaptation to the environment.

James was a brilliant writer and thinker. Although he did not produce any important experimental research, his teaching and writing influenced those who followed him. His theory of emotion is one of the most famous and durable psychological theories. It is still quoted in modern textbooks of psychology. (Yes, you will read about it later in this book.) Psychologists still find it worthwhile to read James's writings; he supplied ideas for experiments that still sound fresh and new today.

Unlike structuralism, functionalism was not supplanted; instead, its major tenets were absorbed by its successor, behaviorism. One of the last of the functionalists, James Angell, described its basic principles:

1. Functional psychology is the study of mental *operations* and not mental *structures*. (For example, the mind remembers; it does not contain a memory.) It is not enough to compile a catalog of what the mind does; one must try to understand what the mind accomplishes by this doing.
2. Mental processes are not studied as isolated and independent events but as part of the biological activity of the organism. These processes are aspects of the organism's adaptation to the environment and are a product of its evolutionary history. The fact that we are conscious implies that consciousness has adaptive value for our species.
3. Functional psychology studies the relation between the environment and the response of the organism to the environment. There is no meaningful distinction between mind and body; they are part of the same entity.

Freud's Psychodynamic Theory

While psychology was developing as a fledgling science, an important figure, Sigmund Freud, was formulating a theory of human behavior that would greatly affect psychology and psychiatry and radically influence intellectuals of all kinds. Freud began his career as a neurologist, so his work was firmly rooted in biology. He soon became interested in behavioral and emotional problems and began formulating his psychodynamic theory of personality, which would evolve over his long career. Although his approach was based on observation of patients and not on scientific experiments, he remained convinced that the biological basis of his theory would eventually be established.

Freud and his theory are discussed in detail in Chapter 14; I mention him here only to mark his place in the history of psychology. His theory of the mind included structures, but his structuralism was quite different from Wundt's. He devised his concepts of ego, superego, id, and other mental structures through talking with his patients, not through laboratory experiments. His hypothetical mental operations included many that were unconscious and hence not available to introspection. And unlike Wundt, Freud emphasized function; his mental structures served biological drives and instincts and reflected our animal nature.

Behaviorism

4 The next major trend in psychology, behaviorism, directly followed from functionalism. It went further in its rejection of the special nature of mental events, denying that unobservable and unverifiable mental events were properly the subject matter of psychology. Because psychology is the study of observable behaviors, mental events, which cannot be observed, are outside the realm of psychology. **Behaviorism** is thus the study of the relation between people's environment and their behavior, without appeal to hypothetical events occurring within their heads.

One of the first behaviorists was Edward Thorndike, an American psychologist who studied the behavior of animals. His studies of the behavior of cats while they learned a task led him to formulate the law of effect. He placed cats in a cage equipped with a latch; the cats, who were hungry, had to operate the latch in order to leave the cage and eat the food placed in a dish outside. Thorndike observed that the cats' restless activity eventually resulted in their accidentally operating the latch. On subsequent trials the cats' behavior became more and more efficient, until they operated the latch as soon as they were placed in the cage. He called the process "learning by trial and accidental success."

Thorndike noted that some events, usually those that one would expect to be pleasant, seemed to "stamp in" a response that had just occurred. Noxious events seemed to "stamp out" the response, or make it less likely to occur. (Nowadays, we call these processes *reinforcement* and *punishment;* they are described in more detail in Chapter 6.) Thorndike defined the **law of effect** as follows:

> Any act which in a given situation produces satisfaction becomes associated with that situation, so that when the situation recurs the act is more likely than before to recur also. Conversely, any act which in a given situation

William James (1842–1910)

Sigmund Freud (1856–1939)

produces discomfort becomes disassociated from that situation, so that when the situation recurs the act is less likely than before to recur. (Thorndike, 1905, p. 203)

The law of effect is certainly in the functionalist tradition. It observes that the consequences of a behavior act back upon the organism, affecting the likelihood that the behavior that just occurred will occur again. The cat accidentally presses the latch, and the consequences of this act (being able to leave the cage and eat) make pressing the latch become more likely the next time the cat is put into the cage. This process is very similar to the principle of natural selection; just as organisms that successfully adapt to their environment are more likely to survive and breed, behaviors that cause useful outcomes become more likely to recur.

Although Thorndike insisted that the subject matter of psychology was behavior, his explanations contained mentalistic terms. For example, in his law of effect he spoke of "satisfaction," which is certainly not a phenomenon that can be directly observed. Later behaviorists threw out terms like "satisfaction" and "discomfort" and replaced them with more objective terms that reflected the behavior of the organism rather than any feelings it might have.

Another major figure in the development of the behavioristic trend was not a psychologist at all but a physiologist: Ivan Pavlov, a Russian who studied the physiology of digestion (for which he later received a Nobel Prize). In the course of studying the stimuli that produce salivation, he discovered that hungry dogs would salivate at the sight of the attendant who brought in their dish of food. Pavlov found that a dog could be trained to salivate at completely arbitrary stimuli, such as the sound of a bell, if the stimulus was quickly followed by the delivery of a bit of food into the animal's mouth.

Pavlov's discovery had profound significance for psychology. He showed that through experience an animal could learn to make a response to a stimulus that had never caused this response before. This ability, in turn, might explain how organisms learn cause-and-effect relations in the environment. In contrast, Thorndike's law of effect suggested an explanation for the adaptability of an individual's behavior to its particular environment. So from Thorndike's and Pavlov's studies two important behavioral principles had been discovered.

Behaviorism as a formal school of psychology began with the publication of a book by John B. Watson, *Psychology from the Standpoint of a Behaviorist.* Watson was a professor of psychology at Johns Hopkins University. He was a popular teacher and writer and was a very convincing advocate of behaviorism. Even after leaving Johns Hopkins and embarking on a highly successful career in advertising, he continued to lecture and write magazine articles about psychology.

According to Watson, psychology was a natural science whose domain was restricted to observable events: the behavior of organisms. He believed that the elements of consciousness studied by the structuralists were too subjective to lend themselves to scientific investigation.

The consequences of a behavior affect the likelihood that the behavior will occur again.

Ivan Pavlov (1849–1936) in his laboratory with some of his collaborators. His research revealed valuable, though unsought, information about the principles of learning.

He defined psychology as the objective study of stimuli and the behaviors they produced. Even thinking was reduced to a form of behavior—talking to oneself:

> Now what can we observe? We can observe *behavior—what the organism does or says*. And let us point out at once: that saying is doing—that is, *behaving*. Speaking overtly or to ourselves (thinking) is just as objective a type of behavior as baseball. (Watson, 1930, p. 6)

Behaviorism is still very much in evidence today in psychology. Its advocates included the late B.F. Skinner, one of the most influential psychologists of the twentieth century. Behaviorism has given birth to the technology of teaching machines (which have since been replaced by computers), the use of behavior modification in instructing the mentally retarded, and the use of behavior therapy to treat mental disorders. Research on the nature of the basic principles that were discovered by Thorndike and Pavlov still continues.

Psychologists, including modern behaviorists, have moved away from the strict behaviorism of Watson; mental processes such as imagery and attention are again considered to be proper subject matter for scientific investigation. But Watson's emphasis on objectivity in psychological research remains, so that the discipline is known to some as *methodological behaviorism*. Even those modern psychologists who most vehemently protest against the per-

ceived narrowness of behaviorism use the same principles of objectivity to guide their research. As research scientists, they must uphold the principles of objectivity that evolved from positivism to functionalism to behaviorism. A person who studies private mental events realizes that these events can only be studied indirectly, by means of behavior—verbal reports of inner experiences. Psychologists realize that these reports are not pure reflections of these mental events; like other behaviors, these responses can be affected by many factors. But as much as possible, they strive to maintain an objective stance to ensure that their research findings will be valid and capable of being verified.

Reaction Against Behaviorism: The Cognitive Revolution

The emphasis on behaviorism restricted the subject matter of psychology to observable behaviors. For many years concepts such as consciousness were considered to be outside the domain of psychology. As one psychologist put it, "psychology, having first bargained away its soul and then gone out of its mind, seems now . . . to have lost all consciousness" (Burt, 1962, p. 229). During the past two decades many psychologists have protested against the restrictions of behaviorism and have turned to the study of consciousness, feelings, dreams, and other private events. Much of *cognitive psychology* uses an approach called **information**

*John B. Watson
(1878–1958)*

processing; information received through the senses is "processed" by various systems of neurons in the brain. Some systems store the information in the form of memory, and other systems control behavior. Some systems operate automatically and unconsciously, while others are conscious and require effort on the part of the individual. Because the information-processing approach was first devised to describe the operations of complex physical systems such as computers, the modern model of the human brain is, for most cognitive psychologists, the computer. (As you will learn in Chapter 5, another model is beginning to replace the computer.)

Although cognitive psychologists now study mental structures and operations, they have not gone back to the introspective methods that were employed by structuralists such as Wundt. They still use objective research methods, just as behaviorists do. For example, several modern psychologists have studied the phenomenon of imagery. If you close your eyes and imagine what the open pages of this book look like, you are viewing a *mental image* of what you have previously seen. This image exists only within your brain, and it can be experienced by you and no one else. I have no way of knowing whether your images are like mine any more than I know whether the color red looks the same to you as it does to me. The *experience* of imagery cannot be shared.

But behaviors that are based upon images can indeed be measured. For example, Kosslyn (1973, 1975) asked a group of people to memorize several drawings. Then he asked them to imagine one of them, focusing their attention on a particular feature of the image. Next, he asked them a question about a detail of the image that was either "near" the point they were focusing on or "far" from it. For example, if they were picturing a boat, he might ask them to imagine that they were looking at its stern (back). Then he might ask them whether the boat had a rudder at the stern, or whether a rope was fastened to its bow (front). Because the bow is at the opposite end of the boat, it should be located at the "opposite end" of the image.

Kosslyn found that people could very quickly answer a question about a feature of the boat that was near the place they were focusing on, but they took longer to answer a question about a part that was farther away. It was as if they had to scan their mental image to get from one place to the other. (See **Figure 1.3.**)

Because we cannot observe what is happening within a person's head, the concept of

Figure 1.3 A drawing used in the imagery study by Kosslyn. (From Kosslyn, S.M. *Perception and Psychophysics*, 1973, *14*, 90–94. Reprinted with permission.)

imagery remains hypothetical. However, this hypothetical concept very nicely explains and organizes some concrete results—namely, the amount of time it takes for a subject to give an answer. Although the explanation for the results of this experiment is phrased in terms of private events (mental images), the behavioral data (how long it takes to answer the questions) are empirical and objective.

INTERIM SUMMARY

Major Trends in the Development of Psychology

We can see that psychology has come a long way in a relatively short time. The first laboratory of experimental psychology was established in 1879, not too much over a century ago. Nineteenth-century philosophers set the stage for psychology through the doctrine of positivism; the biologists provided the means to carry it out through the establishment of the science of experimental physiology. Wilhelm Wundt established psychology as a discipline that was independent of philosophy. At about the same time, Ebbinghaus contributed important methods for objectively measuring learning and forgetting. Even though Wundt's structuralism did not last, the interest in psychology continued to grow. It took on added breadth and scope with the emergence of functionalism, which grew out of Darwin's theory of evolution, with its stress on the adaptive value of biological phenomena. Functionalism gave rise to the objectivity of behaviorism, which, despite the reaction of many modern psychologists, still dominates the way we do research. ■

FIELDS OF PSYCHOLOGY

5 Psychologists come in many varieties. Some of us are scientists, trying to discover the causes of behavior. Some of us are practition-

Most applied psychologists work in the field of human services as school psychologists, psychotherapists, or counselors.

ers, applying what their scientific colleagues have learned to the solution of problems in the world outside the laboratory. (Of course, some psychologists perform both roles.) Some of us are clinical practitioners, helping people with mental disorders or problems of adjustment to daily life. Some of us work in schools as school psychologists or guidance counselors. Some of us help athletes achieve their highest potential. Some of us work for marketing and advertising firms. Some of us design equipment that people can operate more easily and reliably. The areas of **applied psychology** are described in the appendix to this book, "Psychologists at Work," that follows Chapter 17. If you want to know more about the kind of jobs psychologists hold, and if you want to know what training is needed to become a psychologist and what kinds of professional opportunities the field holds, you should read that section.

This section describes the various types of scientific research performed by psychologists. Most research psychologists are employed by colleges and universities or by private or governmental research laboratories. As the history of psychology shows, psychologists have differed from one another in how they explained behavior. Research psychologists differ from one another in two principal ways: in the types of *phenomena* they investigate and in the *causal events* they analyze. That is, they explain different types of behaviors, and they explain them in terms of different types of causes. For example, two psychologists might both be interested in the same psychological phenomenon of memory, but they might attempt to explain memory in terms of different causal events: physiological versus environmental, for example. Of course, not all psychologists are engaged in research.

Physiological psychologists study almost all behavioral phenomena that can be observed in nonhuman animals. They study such topics as learning, memory, sensory processes, emotional behavior, motivation, sexual behavior, and sleep. They look for causal events in the organism's physiology, especially the nervous system and its interaction with glands that secrete hormones. Physiological psychologists mostly study animals because physiological experiments cannot ethically be performed with humans.

Psychophysiologists generally study human subjects. They measure people's physiological reactions, such as heart rate, blood pressure, electrical resistance of the skin, muscle tension, and electrical activity of the brain. These measurements provide an indication of a person's degree of arousal or relaxation. Most psychophysiologists investigate phenomena such as stress and emotions. A practical application of their techniques is the lie detector test.

Comparative psychologists, like physiological psychologists, mostly study the behavior of animals other than humans. The behavioral phenomena they study are also similar to the behaviors that physiological psychologists study. However, comparative psychologists explain behavior in terms of evolutionary adaptation to the environment. They are more likely than most other psychologists to study inherited behavioral patterns, such as courting and mating, predation, defensive behaviors, and parental behaviors.

In the past the term **experimental psychologist** described a very large group of scientists in the mainstream of the behavioristic tradition. Today this term is usually applied to psychologists who are interested in the general principles of learning, perception, motivation, and memory. Some experimental psychologists investigate the behavior of animals, but most of them study human behavior. The causal events that they study are nearly all environmental.

Cognitive psychologists, the largest subcategory of experimental psychologists, almost exclusively study humans, although some of them have begun to study animal cognition as well. They study complex processes such as perception, memory, attention, and concept formation. To them, the causal events consist of functions of the human brain in response to environmental events, but most of them do not study physiological mechanisms. Their explanations involve characteristics of inferred mental processes, such as imagery, attention, and mechanisms of language.

Experimental neuropsychologists are closely allied with both cognitive psychologists and physiological psychologists. They are generally interested in the same phenomena studied by cognitive psychologists, but they attempt to discover the particular brain mechanisms responsible for cognitive processes. One of their principal research techniques is to study the behavior of people whose brains have been damaged by natural causes.

Developmental psychologists study physical, cognitive, emotional, and social development, especially of children. Some of them study phenomena of adolescence or adulthood—in particular, the effects of aging. The causal events they study are as comprehensive as all of psychology: physiological processes, cognitive processes, and social influences.

Social psychologists study the effects of people upon people. The phenomena they explore include perception (of oneself as well as others), cause-and-effect relations in human interactions, attitudes and opinions, interpersonal relationships, group dynamics, and emotional behaviors, such as aggression and sexual behavior.

Personality psychologists study individual differences in temperament and patterns of behavior. They look for causal events in a person's past history, both genetic and environmental. Some personality psychologists are closely allied with social psychologists; others work on problems related to adjustment to society and hence study problems of interest to clinical psychologists.

Psychometricians devise ways to measure human personality and ability. Psychometricians develop psychological tests, some of which you have taken during your academic career. These tests are used by school systems, counselors, clinical psychologists, and employers. In general, psychometricians are interested in the practical issues of measurement, and most of them do not seek causes in a person's hereditary or environmental history. However, their tests are often used by other psychologists to investigate the causes of behavior.

Most **clinical psychologists** are practitioners who attempt to help people solve their problems, whatever the causes. But some are scientists who do research on mental disorders and problems of adjustment. They look for a wide variety of causal events, including genetic factors, physiological factors, and environmental factors such as parental upbringing, interactions with siblings, and other social stimuli. They also do research on evaluating and improving methods of psychotherapy.

KEY TERMS AND CONCEPTS

**The Science of Psychology:
Explaining Behavior**

causal event *(4)*

The Rise of Psychology as a Science

animism *(6)*
reflex *(6)*
dualism *(6)*
model *(7)*
empiricism *(7)*
materialism *(8)*
doctrine of specific nerve energies *(8)*

experimental ablation *(9)*
psychophysics *(10)*

**Major Trends in the Development
of Psychology**

structuralism *(11)*
introspection *(11)*
variable error *(12)*
functionalism *(12)*
behaviorism *(13)*
law of effect *(13)*
information processing *(15)*

Fields of Psychology

applied psychology *(17)*
physiological psychologist *(17)*
psychophysiologist *(17)*
comparative psychologist *(17)*
experimental psychologist *(17)*
cognitive psychologist *(18)*

experimental neuropsychologist *(18)*
developmental psychologist *(18)*
social psychologist *(18)*
personality psychologist *(18)*
psychometrician *(18)*
clinical psychologist *(18)*

SUGGESTIONS FOR FURTHER READING

Butterfield, H. *The Origins of Modern Science: 1300–1800.* New York: Macmillan, 1959.

Whitehead, A.N. *Science and the Modern World.* New York: Macmillan, 1925.

The books by Butterfield and Whitehead describe the history of science in general. Whitehead's book is old, but it is a classic.

Benjamin, L.T. *A History of Psychology: Original Sources and Contemporary Research.* New York: McGraw-Hill, 1988.

Boring, E.G. *A History of Experimental Psychology.* New York: Appleton, 1950.

Schultz, D., and Schultz, S.E. *A History of Modern Psychology,* 4th ed. New York: Academic Press, 1987.

Viney, W. *Great Ideas in the History of Psychology.* Boston: Allyn and Bacon, 1993.

Several books describe the history of psychology, including its philosophical and biological roots, and you may wish to read one of them and then expand your reading from there to learn more. The books by Benjamin, Schultz and Schultz, and Viney are excellent introductions. Boring's book is the classic text, but it is rather heavy going for the casual reader.

2
THE WAYS AND MEANS OF PSYCHOLOGY

Henri Matisse, *The Snail*
Tate Gallery, London/Art Resource, N.Y. © 1992 Succession H. Matisse/ARS, N.Y.

LEARNING OBJECTIVES

When you finish this chapter, you should be able to:

1. Identify the four principal steps of the scientific method.
2. Discuss the importance of operational definitions and explain the meaning of reliability and validity.
3. Discuss the manipulation and control of independent variables.
4. Discuss the confounding of subject variables and the problem of subject expectations.
5. Describe observational studies, case studies, and problems encountered in generalizing their findings.
6. Discuss ethical issues involved in psychological research and describe the guidelines to promote the humane and ethical treatment of living subjects.
7. Describe measures of central tendency, measures of variability, and measures of relations.
8. Describe how to determine whether the results obtained in a study are statistically significant.

During her summer vacations Carlotta works for her parents, who own a small business employing about a dozen people. The employees place electronic components on circuit boards; the company works on orders too small to be done by large, automated factories. Last summer, after her first year of college, Carlotta decided to try to help increase the company's productivity. Naturally, if a worker could complete more boards in a day, the company would earn more money—and the worker would receive a larger bonus. One evening she spent a few hours working on a circuit board, adjusting the angle at which the board rested in a holder fastened to the workbench. Then after discussing the project with her parents, she designed an experiment, using the principles she had learned in her introductory psychology course.

That evening she adjusted all the holders to a new angle, which she thought would be better than the original one. The next morning she met with the employees before they began work. "As you can see, I have adjusted the circuit board holders. I think you'll find the new angle more comfortable, and I hope that you'll be able to finish more boards. I'll see how many you complete over the next few days, and if you're able to do more, then we'll know that the new angle is better." At the end of the day the workers, eager to know how they had done, gathered around Carlotta as she totaled the production figures. Suddenly, she grinned and said triumphantly, "It worked! We finished almost 20 percent more circuit boards." The workers, sharing her enthusiasm, congratulated her as they left for home.

Carlotta continued to collect data for the rest of the week and then met with her friend Paul, who had taken a statistics course. They used a statistical test to compare the production figures for the four days prior to the change with figures for the four days after the change, and they found that without a doubt the production had increased significantly. Unfortunately, a week later she discovered that production had fallen back to its earlier level. A week after that it was actually 5 percent lower! She consulted with her parents and then readjusted the angle of the holders back to the previous position. After a week, production was back to normal. "I can't understand what happened," she said. "I did everything right."

As soon as she returned to school in September, Carlotta sought out her psychology professor, Dr. P., and told him what had happened. She insisted that she had diligently applied the rules of the scientific method, so her experiment should have worked. Dr. P. smiled and said, "You've come across the Hawthorne effect."

"I've never heard of that. Who is Hawthorne?"

"Hawthorne is a place, not a person. Over forty years ago the managers of the Hawthorne Plant of Western Electric Company tried to see whether raising the level of lighting would increase productivity. They found that it did but that the changes were only temporary. They went on to do some more investigating and found that productivity went up even if they *lowered* the level of lighting. What was actually happening was this: The people knew that their performance was being monitored and that an experiment was being done. This knowledge probably made them work just a little harder. They may even have been pleased that management was trying to improve their working conditions and tried to return the favor. Of course, the effect didn't last indefinitely, and eventually, production returned to normal. When industrial psychologists design experiments, they must be careful not to obtain results contaminated by the Hawthorne effect."

"I get it. I thought I was manipulating only one independent variable—the angle of the circuit board holder—but I was introducing a new one: the fact of being observed."

"Exactly. People are not passive participants in an experiment. They have their own expectations and reactions to being observed."

Psychologists attempt to explain behavior—to understand its causes. As scientists, we believe that behaviors, like other natural phenomena, can be studied objectively. Like other scientists, psychologists must follow the procedures and principles of the scientific method, which is what this chapter is about.

The scientific method permits a person to discover the causes of a natural phenomenon, including an organism's behavior. The scientific method has become the predominant method of investigation for a very practical reason: It works better than any other method we have discovered. The generalizations obtained by following the scientific method are the ones that are most likely to survive the test of time.

In this chapter you will learn how the scientific method is used in psychological research. What you learn here will help you understand

Understanding the complexities of human behavior is a constant challenge to psychologists. For example, what motivates members of the Polar Bear club to subject their bodies to the frigid water in the middle of winter?

the studies described in the remaining chapters of the book. But understanding the scientific method is even more important than that, because what you learn here can be applied to everyday life. Knowing how a psychologist can be fooled by the results of an improperly performed study can help us all avoid being fooled by more casual observations.

Following the steps of the scientific method does not guarantee that the results of a study will be important. Not all properly performed experiments are worthwhile; some studies are trivial or have no relevance to what goes on in a more natural environment. All that the scientific method promises is that the particular question being asked of nature will be answered. If a scientist asks a trivial question, nature will return a trivial answer.

Note that no area of psychological investigation is inherently more "scientific" than any other. For example, the physiological analysis of hunger is not inherently more scientific than an investigation of the social factors affecting a person's willingness to help someone else. A scientist is a person who follows the scientific method while investigating natural phenomena. He or she does not necessarily need a laboratory or any special apparatus. Depending on the question being asked, a scientist might need no more than a pad of paper and a pencil and some natural phenomenon (such as another person's behavior) to observe.

THE SCIENTIFIC METHOD

What can a scientist hope to accomplish, and what rules must be followed? As we will see, a scientist attempts to discover *relations* among events and to phrase these relations in language that is precise enough to be understood by others but general enough to apply to a wide variety of phenomena. As we have already seen in Chapter 1, this language takes the form of "explanations," which are general statements about the events that cause phenomena to occur. But what is the nature of these general statements? The answer should become clear as we see how psychologists use the scientific method.

The **scientific method** consists of four major steps, listed below. Some new terms are introduced here without definition, but they will be described in detail later in this chapter.

1. *Identify the problem and formulate hypothetical cause-and-effect relations among variables.* This step involves classifying *variables* (different behaviors and different environmental and physiological events) into the proper categories and then describing the relations among variables in general terms. An example is the following *hypothesis*: "Loss of self-esteem increases a person's susceptibility to propaganda." This statement describes a relation between two events—loss of self-esteem and susceptibility to propaganda—and states that an increase in one causes an increase in the other.

2. *Design and execute a study.* There are two basic types of studies that scientists perform: experiments and observational studies. Experiments involve manipulating *independent variables* and observing *dependent variables.* For example, if we wanted to test the hypothesis I just suggested, we would have to do something to lower people's self-esteem (the independent variable) and see whether that experience altered their susceptibility to propaganda (the dependent variable). But how would we lower their self-esteem, and how would we measure their susceptibility to propaganda? Both variables must be *operationally defined,* and the independent variable must be *controlled* so that definitive conclusions can be made. The second type of study—the observational study—involves the simultaneous observation of two or more variables; there are no independent or dependent variables. Thus, no variables are manipulated.

3. Evaluate the hypothesis by examining the data from the study. Do the results support the hypothesis, or do they suggest that the facts are otherwise? This step often involves special mathematical procedures to determine whether an observed relation is *statistically significant.*

4. Communicate the results. Once a psychologist has learned something about the causes of a behavior from an experiment or observational study, he or she must tell others about the new information. In most cases this communication is accomplished by writing an article that includes a description of the procedure and results and a discussion of their significance. The article is sent to one of the many journals that publish results of psychological research. Thus, other psychologists will be able to incorporate these findings into their own thinking and hypothesizing.

Why do we have to follow rules when we do scientific research? The answer is that unless we do so, we are likely to be misled by our observations. As we shall see in Chapter 9 ("Language and Thinking"), we humans have a natural tendency to accept some types of evidence even though the rules of logic indicate that we should not. Our instinctive responses usually serve us well in our daily lives, but they can lead us to make the wrong conclusions when we try to understand the real causes of natural phenomena (including our own behavior).

The scientific method insists that the author of a study publish details about what he or she has done so that another investigator can repeat, or *replicate,* the study. **Replication** is one of the great strengths of science; it ensures that erroneous results and incorrect conclusions get weeded out. Before the development of the scientific method, people were reluctant to question the writings of eminent scholars. For example, although the Greek philosopher and naturalist Aristotle was a brilliant observer and thinker, some of his observations—and the conclusions he drew from them—were wrong. *Everyone* makes some mistakes. For many centu-

ries, however, secular and religious authorities persecuted anyone who dared to test Aristotle's conclusions about natural laws.

Nowadays, when scientists publish a study, they know that if the findings are important enough, their colleagues will try to replicate it (perhaps with some minor variations) to be sure that the results were not just a statistical fluke—or the result of some unsuspected errors in the design or execution of the study. You have undoubtedly read a newspaper article announcing some important new findings from scientific research. If the author of the newspaper article asks the opinion of experts in the field, they will almost always say something like this: "I think that these findings are very important, but I don't think we can be sure until we see whether they are confirmed by research in other laboratories." Experienced scientists know that all too often, interesting and provocative results fail to be replicated.

Now that I have presented an overview of the scientific method, let me describe its components and the rules that govern it.

Hypotheses

A hypothesis is the starting point of any study. It is an idea, phrased as a general statement, that the scientist wishes to test scientifically. In the original Greek *hypothesis* means "suggestion," and the word still conveys the same meaning. When a scientist forms a hypothesis, he or she is simply suggesting that a relation exists among various phenomena (like the one that might exist between loss of self-esteem and a person's susceptibility to propaganda). Thus, a **hypothesis** is a tentative statement about a relation between two or more events.

Hypotheses do not spring out of thin air; they occur to a scientist as a result of research or scholarship. Research breeds more research. That is, worthwhile research does not merely answer questions; it suggests new questions to be asked—new hypotheses to be tested. Productive and creative scientists formulate new hypotheses by thinking about the implications of studies that they have performed or that have been performed by others.

Theories

A **theory** is an elaborate form of hypothesis. In fact, a theory can be a way of organizing a system of related hypotheses to explain some larger aspect of nature. In addition, good theories fuel the creation of further hypotheses. (More accurately, a good scientist, contemplating a good theory, thinks of more good hypotheses to test.) For example, Einstein's theory of relativity states that time, matter, and energy are interdependent. Changes in any one will produce changes in the others. The hypotheses suggested by this theory revolutionized science; the field of nuclear physics largely rests on experiments arising from Einstein's theory.

The framework for most psychological research is larger in scope than a hypothesis but smaller in scope than a full-fledged theory. For example, a psychologist might publish an article that pulls together the results of many previous studies on a particular topic. The frustration-aggression hypothesis, which you will learn about in a later chapter, suggests that organisms have a tendency to become aggressive when they do not achieve a goal that they have been accustomed to achieving in a particular situation. This hypothesis makes a prediction that might fit a wide variety of situations. Indeed, many experiments have been performed to test this hypothesis under different conditions. Even though the frameworks that most psychologists construct fall short of constituting a theory, they serve a similar function by getting researchers to think about old problems in new ways and by showing how findings that did not appear to be related to each other can be explained by a single concept. There is even a scientific journal *(Psychological Review)* that is devoted to articles that the authors hope will have theoretical significance.

Variables

The hypothesis that I proposed earlier—"Loss of self-esteem increases a person's susceptibility to propaganda"—describes a relation between lowered self-esteem and susceptibility to propaganda. Scientists refer to these two components as **variables:** things that can vary. Variables are quantities, characteristics, or phenomena that a scientist either measures or manipulates when performing a study. *Manipulate* literally means "to handle," from *manus,* "hand." Psychologists use the word to refer to setting the value of a variable for experimental purposes. The results of this manipulation determine whether the hypothesis is true or false.

To test the "self-esteem" hypothesis in an experiment, we would set the value of people's self-esteem at a lower level and then measure their susceptibility to propaganda. The first variable—the one that the experimenter manipu-

lates—is called the **independent variable.** The second one, which the experimenter measures, is the **dependent variable.** An easy way to keep them straight is to remember that a hypothesis always describes how a dependent variable *depends* on the value of an independent variable. For example, susceptibility to propaganda (the dependent variable) depends on the level of a person's self-esteem (the independent variable). (See *Figure 2.1.*)

As we saw, hypotheses are expressed in general terms. Thus, the variables that hypotheses deal with are also general rather than specific. That is, we want to understand the behavior of people in general, not just one particular person in one particular situation. Hence, variables are *categories* into which various behaviors are classified. For example, if a person hits, kicks, or throws something at someone else, we can label all of these behaviors as "interpersonal aggression." Presumably, they would have very similar causes. Therefore, a psychologist must know enough about a particular type of behavior to be able to classify it correctly.

Although one of the first steps in psychological investigation involves naming and classifying behaviors, we must be careful to avoid committing the nominal fallacy. The **nominal fallacy** refers to the erroneous belief that one has explained an event simply by naming it. (*Nomen* means "name.") However, classifying a behavior does not explain it; classifying only prepares us to examine and discover events that cause a behavior. For example, suppose that we see a man frown and shout at other people without provocation, criticize their work when it is really acceptable, and generally act unpleasantly toward everyone around him. Someone says, "Boy, he's really angry today!" Does this statement explain his behavior?

It does not; it only *describes* the behavior. Instead of saying he is angry, we might better say that he is "engaging in angry or hostile behaviors." This statement does not pretend to

Figure 2.1 Independent and dependent variables.

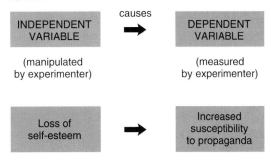

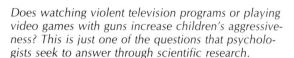

Does watching violent television programs or playing video games with guns increase children's aggressiveness? This is just one of the questions that psychologists seek to answer through scientific research.

explain why he is acting the way he is. To say he is angry suggests that an internal state is responsible for his behavior, that is, that anger is causing his behavior. But all we have observed is his behavior, not his internal state. Even if he is experiencing feelings of anger, these feelings still do not explain his behavior. What we really need to know is *what events made him act the way he did.* Perhaps he has a painful toothache. Perhaps he just learned that he was passed over for a promotion. Perhaps he had a terrible fight with his wife. Perhaps he just read a book that advised him to be more assertive. Events like these are causes of both the behavior and the feelings; and unless they are discovered, we cannot say that we have explained his behavior.

Of course, a large number of events precede any behavior. Many of these events are completely unrelated to the observed behavior. I get off the train because the conductor announces my stop, not because one person coughs, another turns the page of her newspaper, another crosses his legs, or another looks at her watch. The task of a psychologist is to determine which of the many events that occurred before a particular behavior caused that behavior to happen.

Operational Definitions

2 Hypotheses are phrased in general terms, but experiments and observational studies (step 2 of the scientific method) require that something *particular* be done. In order to lower the self-esteem of the subjects in our proposed experiment, the experimenter must arrange a particular situation that causes this event to occur. Similarly, the experimenter must measure the subjects' susceptibility to propaganda in a particular way, perhaps by testing their opinion on a

certain topic, then showing them a film that promotes a point of view on the topic, and finally, testing their opinion again. In other words, generalities such as "self-esteem" and "susceptibility to propaganda" must be translated into specific operations.

This translation of generalities into specific operations is called an **operational definition:** Independent variables and dependent variables are defined in terms of the operations an experimenter performs to set their values or to measure them. Here is an example of an operational definition of an independent variable:

> A subject's self-esteem was lowered by arranging for the subject to accidentally knock over a precariously placed pile of color slides. The experimenter responded politely but showed some distress, letting it be known that she had just spent a lot of time arranging them for a talk and now would have to do the work all over again.

The operational definition of the dependent variable "susceptibility to propaganda" would be "the degree of change in a person's opinion on a particular topic after having been exposed to propaganda on that topic." It would include a description of the opinion test used and the propaganda film the subjects watched. In subsequent chapters you will encounter many operational definitions when I describe studies performed by contemporary psychologists.

The importance of providing an operational definition of variables should be obvious. If research is to be understood, evaluated, and (possibly) replicated by other people (step 4 of the scientific method), the investigator must provide others with an adequate description of the procedures that were used. Communicating the results is as important a part of the scientific method as obtaining them.

There are many ways to translate a particular general concept into a set of operations. Using a particular operational definition, the experimenter may or may not succeed in manipulating the desired independent variable or in measuring the desired dependent variable. For example, there is certainly no single definition of self-esteem. Another investigator, using a different set of operations to lower a person's self-esteem, might obtain results that are different from our own. Which operational definition is correct? Which set of results should we believe?

Validity. The question of the "correctness" of an operational definition of a variable brings us to the issue of validity. Everyone knows the meaning of the word *valid*: well-grounded, fit, appropriate. Thus, the **validity** of an operational definition refers to how appropriate it is—how accurately it represents the variable whose value it sets or measures. Obviously, validity is very important; if an operational definition is not valid, a study that uses it cannot provide meaningful results.

How can the validity of an operational definition be determined? Unfortunately, there is no simple answer. Various techniques have been used, but none is foolproof. To begin with, an investigator examines the **face validity** of the operations, which is just a fancy way of saying that he or she thinks about them and decides whether they make sense. On the *face* of it, do the operations appear to manipulate or measure the variables in question? My earlier definition of lowered self-esteem—having someone accidentally cause a lot of extra trouble for a kind, hardworking experimenter—makes sense (at least to me), so it has some face validity. A psychologist trying to decide how to test a particular hypothesis must use his or her expertise (and common sense) to arrive at operations that have face validity. Given enough time, the validity of an operational definition will emerge (or so we hope). Investigators will compare the results of their research with those of others and will see whether they are compatible.

The question of validity is especially important when psychologists attempt to investigate something other than direct manifestations of behavior. Thus, this question will come up again in later chapters when we examine research on topics such as abilities, attitudes, and personality traits.

Reliability. Having carefully designed a study, the psychologist must then decide how best to conduct it. This brings us to the second part of step 2 of the scientific method: execute the study. The psychologist must decide what subjects will be used, what instructions will be given, and what equipment and materials will be used. He or she must ensure that the data collected will be accurate; otherwise, all effort will be in vain.

If the procedure described by an operational definition gives consistent results under consistent conditions, the procedure is said to have high **reliability.** Note, however, that it may or may not be *valid.* For example, suppose that I operationally define "susceptibility to propaganda" as the length of a person's thumb; the longer someone's thumb is, the more susceptible that person is to propaganda. Even though this measurement can be made accurately and reliably, it is still nonsensical. (Of course, most examples of reliable but invalid operational definitions are more subtle than this one.) Achieving reliability is usually much easier than achieving validity; reliability is mostly a result of care and diligence on the part of the researcher.

Let us look at an example. Suppose you want to measure people's reading speed. You select a passage of prose and see how much of it each person can read in five minutes. This operational definition of reading speed certainly has face validity, as long as you choose a passage that is reasonably easy for a normal adult to understand. But suppose you test people in a building that is located under the flight path of an airport. At times, the noise of planes flying overhead creates a terrible din. At other times, all is quiet. If people are tested when planes are roaring overhead, the distracting noise may very well disrupt their reading, producing low scores. The on-again, off-again noise will affect the accuracy of the measurement; it will lower its reliability.

An alert, careful experimenter can control most of the extraneous factors that could affect the reliability of his or her measurements. Conditions throughout the experiment should always be as consistent as possible. For example, the same instructions should be given to each person who participates in the experiment, all mechanical devices should be in good repair, and all assistants hired by the experimenter should be well trained in performing their tasks. Noise and other sources of distraction should be kept to a minimum.

Our definition of reading speed is *objective;* that is, even a nonexpert could follow our procedure and obtain the same results. All the person would have to do would be to count the number of words the subject read in five minutes. But researchers often attempt to study variables whose measurement is *subjective,* requiring judgment and expertise. For example, suppose a psychologist wants to count the number of friendly interactions that a child makes with other children in a group. This measurement requires someone to watch the child and count the number of times a friendly interaction occurs. But it is difficult to be absolutely specific about what constitutes a friendly interaction and what does not. What if the child looks at another child and their gazes meet? One observer may say that the look conveyed interest in what the other child was doing, so it should be scored as a friendly interaction. Another observer may deny that anything passed between them and say that a friendly interaction should not be scored.

The solution in this case is, first of all, to try to specify as precisely as possible the criteria for scoring a friendly interaction—to make the measurement as objective as possible. Then two or more people should watch the child's behavior and score it independently. That is, neither person should be aware of the other person's ratings. If their ratings agree, we can say that the scoring system has high **interrater reliability.** If they disagree, interrater reliability is low, and there is no point in continuing the study. Instead, the rating system should be refined, and the raters should be trained to apply it consistently. Any investigator who performs a study that requires some degree of skill and judgment in measuring the dependent variables must be sure that interrater reliability is sufficiently high.

INTERIM SUMMARY

The Scientific Method

The scientific method is a method of inquiry that allows us to determine the causes of natural phenomena. There are two basic forms of scientific research: experiments and observational studies. Only experiments permit us to be certain that a cause-and-effect relation exists. An experiment tests the truth of a hypothesis, which is a tentative statement about a cause-and-effect relation between an independent variable and a dependent variable. To perform an experiment, a scientist alters the value of the independent variable and looks for changes in the dependent variable. Because a hypothesis is stated in general terms, the scientist must spec-

ify the particular operations that he or she will perform to manipulate the independent variable and to measure the dependent variable. That is, the experimenter must provide operational definitions, which may require some ingenuity and hard work. Operational definitions are a necessary part of the procedure by which a hypothesis is tested; they also can eliminate confusion by giving concrete form to the hypothesis, thus making its meaning absolutely clear to other psychologists.

The validity of an operational definition refers to the degree to which it adequately produces a particular value of the independent variable or measures the value of the dependent variable. The reliability of an operational definition refers to its consistency and precision. A careful researcher achieves high reliability by paying attention to the conditions of the study and ensuring that the procedures are followed carefully and correctly. If a measurement involves some subjectivity, then the researcher should make sure that interrater reliability is high. ■

Control of Independent Variables

3 A hypothesis, you will recall, makes a tentative statement about a possible relation between two or more variables. An experiment is the procedure for testing the hypothesis to determine whether these variables *are* related. A scientist performs an experiment by altering the value of the independent variable (such as the level of a person's self-esteem) and then observing whether this change affects the dependent variable (in this case, susceptibility to propaganda). If an effect is seen, the scientist can conclude that there is a cause-and-effect relation between the variables. That is, changes in the independent variable cause changes in the dependent variable.

In designing an experiment, the experimenter must be sure that the procedure alters the value of the independent variable, and *only* the independent variable. In most experiments we are interested in the effects of a small number of independent variables (usually just one) on a dependent variable. For example, if we want to determine whether noise has an effect on people's reading speed, we must choose our source of noise carefully. If we use the sound from a television set to supply the noise and find that it slows people's reading speed, we cannot conclude that the effect was caused purely by "noise." We might have selected a very interesting program (as unlikely as that may seem), thus distracting the subjects' attention from the material they were reading. If we want to do this experiment properly, we should use noise that is neutral and not a source of interest by itself: noise like the *sssh* sound that is heard when an FM radio is tuned between stations.

In the example I just described, the experimenter intended to test the effects of an independent variable (noise) on a dependent variable (reading speed). By using a television to provide the noise, he or she was inadvertently testing the effects of other variables besides noise on reading speed. The experimenter had introduced extra, unwanted independent variables.

Confounding of Independent Variables. One of the meanings of the word *confound* is "to fail to distinguish," which is precisely the meaning that applies here. If an experimenter accidentally manipulates more than one independent variable, he or she cannot distinguish the effects of any one of them on the dependent variable. There are many ways in which **confounding of variables** can occur. The best way to understand the problems that can arise is to examine some of the mistakes that an experimenter can make.

When I was a graduate student, I accompanied several fellow students to hear a talk that was presented by a visitor to the Zoology Department. He described research he had conducted in a remote area of South America. He was interested in determining whether a particular species of bird could recognize a large bird that normally preys upon it. He had constructed a set of cardboard models that bore varying degrees of resemblance to the predator: from a perfect representation, to two models of noncarnivorous birds, to a neutral stimulus (a triangle, I think). The experimenter somehow restrained the birds that were being tested and suddenly presented the bird with each of the test stimuli, in decreasing order of similarity to the predator—that is, from predator to harmless birds to triangle. He observed a relation between the amount of alarm that the birds showed and the similarity that the model bore to the predator. The most predatorlike model produced the greatest response. (See *Figure 2.2.*)

As one of us pointed out—to the embarrassment of the speaker and his hosts—the study contained a fatal flaw that made it impossible to conclude whether a relation existed between the independent variable (similarity of the model to the predator) and the dependent variable (amount of alarm). Can you figure it out?

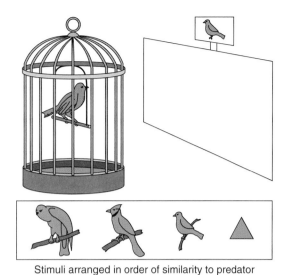

Stimuli arranged in order of similarity to predator

Figure 2.2 A schematic representation of the flawed "predator" experiment.

Reread the previous paragraph, consult Figure 2.2, and think about the problem for a while before you read on.

Here is the answer. To test the birds' responses to the models, the investigator presented them at different times, *and always in the same order.* Can we reasonably suppose that the presentation of one stimulus has an effect on the response produced by the next stimulus? Of course we can. Very likely, if the birds were shown the *same* model again and again, they would exhibit less and less of a response. We very commonly observe this phenomenon, called *habituation,* when a stimulus is presented repeatedly. The last presentation produces a much smaller response than the first. Consequently, we do not know whether the decrease in signs of alarm occurred because the stimuli looked less and less like the predator or because the birds' responses simply habituated to the stimuli. The investigator's trip to South America was a waste of time, at least insofar as this experiment was concerned.

Could the zoologist have carried out his experiment in a way that would have permitted a relation to be inferred? Yes, he could have; perhaps the solution has occurred to you already. (If it has not, think about it for a while.) Here is the answer: The experimenter should have presented the stimuli in different orders to different birds. Some birds would see the predator first, others would see the triangle first, and so on. Then he could have calculated the average amount of alarm that the birds showed to each of the stimuli, with the assurance that the results would not be contaminated by habituation. This

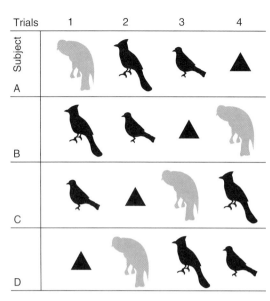

Figure 2.3 Counterbalancing in the "predator" experiment by changing the order of presentation of the models.

procedure is called **counterbalancing.** To *counterbalance* means to "weigh evenly," and counterbalancing would have been accomplished if the investigator had made sure that each of the models was presented equally often (to different birds, of course) as the first, second, third, or fourth stimulus. The effects of habituation would thus be spread equally among all the stimuli. (See *Figure 2.3.*)

Let us look at another example of an extra, unwanted independent variable intruding into an experiment. Suppose we want to determine whether watching violence on television increases a child's aggressiveness. We select two television shows, one violent and the other nonviolent. We will show the violent program to one group of children and the nonviolent one to another group, and then we will observe the behavior of both groups. We may place the children in a room full of toys and count the number of destructive acts they commit (such as knocking down towers of blocks, banging toy trucks into the furniture and walls, or fighting with other children). We will train our observers well and make sure that the interrater reliability of the measurement is high.

The design of this experiment is simple and straightforward. But to be able to conclude that watching the violent program affected the children's aggressive behavior, we must be sure that the treatment of both groups is identical in every way except for the amount of violence they see. How can we select, from the programs available on television, two that are identical except for the amount of violence they con-

tain? Obviously, we cannot. And the differences can be very important. Suppose that the children who watched the violent program found it to be very interesting, but the children who watched the nonviolent one found it to be extremely dull and boring. We might expect a group of angry and hostile children to emerge from watching the nonviolent program, after having been forced to undergo such a tedious experience.

If these events occurred, the results of our study might suggest that watching a violent program *reduced* the frequency of aggression in children. Of course, we would have really proved nothing of the kind. The higher level of violence in the group of children who watched the nonviolent program was caused by their having been forced to watch a program that bored them.

What can we do about this problem? One solution is to add another group of children who do not watch a television program. This group is called a control group. A **control group** is a no-treatment group; it is used to contrast the effects of manipulating an independent variable with no treatment at all. If we had used such a group, perhaps we would have seen that the children who watched the nonviolent program were more violent and aggressive than the children who did not watch television at all, and we would have realized that something was wrong. We would have seen that watching a nonviolent program was not the neutral experience we had thought it would be. (See *Figure 2.4.*)

Now that you know what a control group is, let us apply this term to the procedure of the "propaganda" experiment, described earlier. The experimental group consists of the subjects who are tricked into knocking over the slides; subjects in the control group simply chat with the experimenter. (See *Figure 2.5.*)

Figure 2.4 Possible outcome of an experiment testing the effects of watching a violent television program. This design includes a control group.

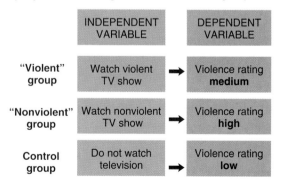

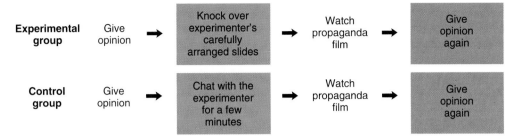

Figure 2.5 Design of the "propaganda" experiment.

4 Confounding of Subject Variables. My examples so far have dealt with the confounding of independent variables, which are manipulated by the experimenter. But there is another source of confounding: variables that are inherent in the subjects whose behavior is being observed. Here is an example of a study with confounded subject variables: Suppose a professor wants to determine which of two teaching methods works best. She teaches two courses in introductory psychology, one that meets at 8 A.M. and another that meets at 4 P.M. She uses one teaching method for the morning class and another for the afternoon class. At the end of the semester she finds that the final-examination scores were higher for her morning class. She concludes that from now on she will use that particular teaching method for all of her classes.

What is the problem? The two groups of subjects for the experiment are not equivalent. People who sign up for a class that meets at 8 A.M. are likely to be somewhat different from those who sign up for a 4 P.M. class. Perhaps the school schedules some kinds of activities (like long laboratory courses or athletic practice) late in the afternoon, which means that some students will not be able to enroll in the 4 P.M. class. In addition, people's learning efficiency may vary at different times of the day. For a variety of reasons the students in the two classes will probably not be equivalent. Therefore, we cannot conclude that the differences in their final-examination scores were solely a result of the different teaching methods.

Subjects must be carefully assigned to the various groups used in an experiment. The usual way to assign them is by **random assignment.** One way to accomplish random assignment is to assemble the names of the available subjects and then toss a coin for each one to determine the subject's assignment to one of two groups. (More typically, the assignment is made by computer or by consulting a list of random numbers.) We can expect people to have different abilities, personality traits, and other characteristics that may affect the outcome of the experiment. But if they are randomly assigned to the experimental conditions, the composition of the groups should be approximately the same.

A psychologist must remain alert to the problem of confounded subject variables even after he or she has designed the experiment and randomly assigned subjects to the various groups. Some problems will not emerge until the investigation is actually performed. Suppose that an experimenter was interested in finding out whether anger decreases a person's ability to concentrate. The experimenter acts very rudely toward the subjects, which presumably makes them angry. (A complete description of the rude actions would constitute the operational definition of anger.) Subjects in the control group are treated politely. Then, after the rude or polite treatment, the subjects watch a video screen that shows a constantly changing display of patterns of letters. The task is to press a button whenever a particular letter appears. This test shows how vigilant subjects are—how carefully they are paying attention to the letters on the screen.

The design of this experiment is sound. Assuming that the subjects are really angry and that our test is a valid measure of concentration, we should be able to make conclusions about the effects of anger on concentration. However, the experiment, as performed under real conditions, may not work out the way we want it to. Suppose that some of our "angry" subjects simply walk away. All experimenters are required to tell subjects that they are free to leave at any time—and some angry subjects might well do so. If they do, we will now be comparing the behavior of two groups of subjects of somewhat different character—a group of people who are willing to submit to the experimenter's rude behavior and a group of randomly selected people, some of whom *would have* left had they been subjected to the rude treatment. We have inadvertently added another variable to our original

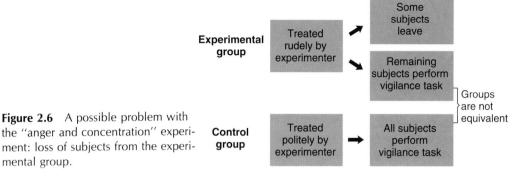

Figure 2.6 A possible problem with the "anger and concentration" experiment: loss of subjects from the experimental group.

hypothesis: People who will tolerate rude behavior may differ from other people in their ability to concentrate. (See *Figure 2.6.*)

The moral of this example? An experimenter must continue to attend to the possibility of confounded variables even after the experiment has been designed. The solution in this case? There probably is none. Because we cannot force subjects to continue to participate, there is a strong possibility that some of them will leave. Some psychological variables are, by their very nature, difficult to investigate.

The Problem of Subjects' Expectations. When subjects take part in an experiment, they are not simply passive participants whose behavior is controlled solely by the independent variables selected by the experimenter. In the opening vignette we saw that Carlotta learned this fact when she tried to improve production at her parents' company. Subjects who are participating in experiments know they are being observed by a psychologist, and this knowledge is certain to affect their behavior in some way. In fact, some subjects may try to outwit the psychologist by acting in a way that is opposite to what they think is expected. However, most subjects will try to cooperate because they do not want to ruin the experiment for the investigator. In fact, they may even try to figure out what question is being asked so that they can act accordingly. Because the study is being run by a psychologist, some subjects are unlikely to take what he or she says at face value and will look for devious motives behind an apparently simple task. Actually, most experiments are not devious at all; they are what they appear to be.

"Devious" studies do not always succeed in fooling the subjects. For example, suppose you are a participant in an experiment that was represented as being a learning study. On the table in front of you is an assortment of knives and pistols. The experimenter says, "Oh, ignore

them. Someone else left them here. They have nothing to do with this study." Do you believe her? Probably not, and you will undoubtedly try to figure out what the presence of these weapons is supposed to do to your behavior. You may suspect that the psychologist is trying to determine whether the presence of weapons will increase your hostility. With this suspicion in mind, you may (1) act naturally, so that you will not spoil the experiment, (2) act aggressively, to help the experimenter get the results you think she wants, or (3) act nonaggressively, to prove that you are immune to the effects of objects associated with violence. The results of this study may not show the effects of the presence of weapons on aggression but, rather, show the relative numbers of people who select strategy 1, 2, or 3.

An experimenter must always remember that subjects do not merely react to the independent variable in a simpleminded way. As you will see in Chapter 17, these considerations are especially important in social psychology experiments. In some of these studies the experimenter or the experimenter's assistants act out roles designed to provide a particular kind of social situation to which the subjects are exposed. Obviously, the subjects' interpretation of these situations affects their behavior.

Single-Blind Experiments. A special problem is posed by experiments in which a subject's behavior might be affected by his or her knowledge of the independent variable. For example, suppose we want to study the effects of a stimulant drug, such as amphetamine, on a person's ability to perform a task that requires fine manual dexterity. We will administer the drug to one group of subjects and leave another group untreated. (Of course, the experiment will have to be supervised by a physician, who will prescribe the drug.) We will determine how many times the subjects in each group can thread a needle in a ten-minute period (our operational definition of manual dexterity). We will then see whether taking the drug had any effect on the number of needle threadings.

But there is a problem in our design. For us to conclude that a cause-and-effect relation exists, the treatment of the two groups must be identical except for the single variable that is being manipulated. In this case the *mere administration* of a drug may have effects on behavior, independent of any pharmacological effects. If subjects know that they have just taken an amphetamine pill, their behavior is very likely to be affected by this knowledge, as well as by the drug circulating in their bloodstream.

The answer, of course, is to give pills to the members of both groups. People in one group will receive amphetamine, and those in the other group will receive an inert pill—a **placebo**. (The word comes from the Latin *placere*, "to please." A physician sometimes gives a placebo to anxious patients to placate them.) Subjects will not be told which pill they receive. By using this improved experimental procedure, we can infer that any observed differences in needle-threading ability of the two groups were produced by the pharmacological effects of amphetamine. The procedure is called a **single-blind** study; the subjects do not know what kind of pill they are taking.

Double-Blind Experiments. Now let us look at an example in which it is important to keep both the experimenter and the subjects in the dark. Suppose we believe that if patients with mental disorders take a particular drug, they will be easier to talk with. We give the drug to some patients and administer a placebo to others. We talk with all of the patients afterward and rate the quality of the conversation. But "quality of conversation" is a difficult dependent variable to measure, and the rating is therefore likely to be somewhat subjective. The fact that we, the experimenters, know which patients received the drug means that we may tend to give higher ratings to the quality of conversation with those patients. Of course, we would not intentionally cheat, but even honest people tend to perceive results in a way that favors their own preconceptions.

The solution to this problem is simple. Just as the patients should not know whether they are receiving a drug or a placebo, neither should the experimenter. Someone else should administer the pill, or the experimenter should be given a set of identical-looking pills in coded containers, so that both experimenter and patient are unaware of the nature of the contents. Now the ratings cannot be affected by experimenter bias. We call this method the **double-blind** procedure.

The double-blind procedure does not apply only to experiments that use drugs as the independent variable. Suppose that the experiment I just described attempted to evaluate the effects of a particular kind of psychotherapy, not a drug, on the ability of a therapist to communicate with a patient. (In fact, we will encounter such evaluations in Chapter 16.) If the same person did both the psychotherapy and the rating, that person might tend to see the results in a light that was most favorable to his or her own expectations. In this case, then, one person should perform the psychotherapy and another person should evaluate the quality of conversation with the patients. The evaluator will not know whether a particular patient has just received psychotherapy or is a member of the control (untreated) group.

Observational Studies

[5] If we want to be sure that a cause-and-effect relation exists, we must perform an experiment in which we ourselves manipulate the independent variable and look for effects on the dependent variable. But there are some variables—especially subject variables—that a psychologist cannot manipulate. For example, a person's sex, income, social class, family environment, and personality are obviously not under the psychologist's control. Nevertheless, because these variables affect people's behavior, they are often of interest. Because they cannot be altered by the psychologist, they cannot be investigated in an experiment. Therefore, a different approach is used; an observational study is performed.

The basic principle of an **observational study** is simple: In each member of a group of people we measure two or more variables as they are found to exist, and we determine whether the variables are related. Observational studies are often done to investigate the effects of personality variables. For example, we may ask whether shyness (a personality variable) is related to daydreaming. We decide how to assess a person's shyness and the amount of daydreaming that he or she engages in each day, and we then take the measure of these two variables for a group of people. If shy people tend to daydream more (or less) than people who are not shy, we can conclude that the variables are related.

Suppose we find that shy people spend more time daydreaming. Such a finding tells us that the variables are related—we say they are *correlated*—but it does not permit us to make any conclusions about cause and effect. Shyness may have caused the daydreaming, or excessive daydreaming may have caused the shyness, or perhaps some other variable that we did not measure caused both shyness and an increase in daydreaming. In other words, correlations do not necessarily indicate cause-and-effect relations. (See *Figure 2.7.*)

A good illustration of this principle is provided by an observational study that attempted to determine whether membership in the Boy Scouts would affect a person's subsequent participation in community affairs (Chapin, 1947). The investigator compared a group of men who had once been Boy Scouts with a group who had not. He found that the men who had been Boy Scouts tended to join more community affairs groups later in life.

The investigator wanted to conclude that the experience of being a Boy Scout increased a person's tendency to join community organizations. However, this conclusion is not warranted. All we can say is that people who join the Boy Scouts in their youth tend to join community organizations later in life. It could be that people who, for one reason or another, are "joiners" tend to join the Boy Scouts when they are young and community organizations when they are older. To determine cause and effect, we would have to perform an experiment. We would make some boys join the Boy Scouts and prevent others from doing so—and then see how many organizations they would voluntarily join later in life. Because we cannot interfere in people's lives in such a way, we can never be certain that being a Boy Scout increases peo-

Figure 2.7 An example of a correlation. Correlations do not necessarily indicate cause-and-effect relations: Daydreaming could cause shyness, or shyness could cause daydreaming.

Daydreaming keeps a person from making many contacts with other people; experiences in fantasies are more successful and gratifying than those in real life.

He does not know how to respond in the company of other people.

Person has poor social skills; finds contacts with other people uncomfortable.

He turns to daydreaming because he receives no gratification from social contacts.

ple's tendency to join community organizations.

There are some procedures that can be followed to reduce some of the uncertainty inherent in all observational studies. When attempting to study the effects of a variable that he or she cannot alter (such as sex, age, socioeconomic status, or personality characteristics), a psychologist can use a procedure called **matching.** Rather than select subjects randomly, the researcher *matches* the subjects in each of the groups on all of the relevant variables except the one being studied. For instance, if a psychologist wants to study the effects of shyness on daydreaming, he or she may gather two groups of subjects, shy and nonshy. The subjects in each group are selected in such a way that the effects of other variables are minimized: The average age, intelligence, income, and personality characteristics (other than shyness) of the two groups are the same.

If, after following this matching procedure, the investigator finds that shyness is still related to daydreaming, we can be somewhat more confident that the relation is one of cause and effect—that one variable is causing the other, and that the two variables are not simply being caused by another one. The limitation of the matching procedure is that a psychologist may not know all the variables that should be held constant. If, unbeknownst to the researcher, the two groups are not matched on an important variable, then the results will be misleading. In any case, even the matching procedure does not permit us to decide which is the cause and which is the effect; we still do not know whether shyness causes daydreaming or daydreaming causes shyness.

The strengths and limitations of observational studies will become evident in subsequent chapters in this book. For example, almost all studies that attempt to discover the environmental factors that influence personality characteristics or the relationship between these characteristics and people's behavior are observational.

Generality

When we carry out an experiment or an observational study, we are usually not especially interested in the particular subjects whose behavior we observe. Instead, we probably assume that our subjects are representative of the larger population. In fact, a representative group of subjects is usually referred to as a **sample** of the larger population. (The words *sample* and *example* have the same root.) If we study the behavior of a group of five-year-old children, we probably want to make conclusions about five-year-olds in general. That is, we want to be able to **generalize** our specific results to the population as a whole—to conclude that the results of our study tell us something about human nature in general, not simply about our particular subjects.

Many researchers recruit their subjects from introductory courses in psychology. Thus, the results of studies that use these students as subjects can be generalized only to other groups of students who are recruited in the same way. In the strictest sense, the results cannot be generalized to students in other courses, to adults in general, or even to all students enrolled in introductory psychology—after all, students who volunteer to serve as subjects may be very different from those who do not. Even if we used truly random samples of all age groups of adults in our area, we could not generalize the results to people who live in other geographical regions. You may now be thinking that if our ability to generalize is really so limited, it is hardly worthwhile to do psychological research.

But we are not so strict, of course. Most psychologists assume that a relation among variables that is observed in one group of humans will also be seen in other groups, as long as the relation is a relatively strong one and the sample of subjects is not especially unusual. (For example, we may expect data obtained from prisoners to have less generality than data obtained from college students.) Generalization from a particular sample of subjects to a larger population is one of those cases in which scientific practice usually does not rigorously follow scientific law.

The problem of generalizing occurs in observational studies just as often as it does in experiments. In one famous case the limitations of generalizing were demonstrated with a vengeance. During the United States presidential campaign of 1948 poll takers predicted, from a sampling of the populace, that Dewey would easily defeat Truman. Of course, they were wrong—embarrassingly so. The subjects in the sample group had been drawn from telephone directories. In 1948 a smaller percentage of Americans had telephones than have them today, and those who did have telephones tended to be wealthier than those who did not. A much higher proportion of this second group (people without telephones) voted for Truman; hence the samples drawn by poll takers were not representative of the population to which they wanted to generalize—United States voters.

Harry Truman, the winner of the 1948 U.S. presidential election, appears to enjoy the premature headline proclaiming Dewey's victory. The Chicago Daily Tribune *based its new story on the opinion polls instead of waiting for the verdict from the voting polls. Modern polling techniques are much more accurate, but they are still not infallible.*

Case Studies

Not all investigations make use of groups of subjects. **Case studies** investigate the behavior of individuals, and for some phenomena this method is very effective. Case studies can be experiments or they can be observational studies. Let us consider an experimental case study. Suppose we are investigating a potential food additive. We feed a small amount to a rat, who immediately has a convulsion and dies. We now strongly suspect that the compound is poisonous. Perhaps we will try it on one more rat to be sure that the first one was not about to die anyway. If the second rat dies, we probably will not bother to do further testing. The response is so closely tied to the administration of the compound that we are willing to conclude that one event caused the other. There is no point in carrying out a full-fledged testing procedure, with an experimental group given the drug and a control group given a placebo.

In another type of case study psychologists often take advantage of events that occur outside their control. For example, some colleagues and I studied a woman who had sustained a serious skull fracture in an automobile accident (Margolin, Marcel, and Carlson, 1985). The damage to her brain made it impossible for her to read, although her vision was almost normal. We gave her lists of words, such as *rose, violet, carrot, petunia, daffodil,* and asked her to choose the one that did not belong with the others. She would point to the word *carrot* even though she could not read it and had no idea why she chose the one she did. Her performance proves that people can have some idea of the meaning of words even though they cannot say the words to themselves.

Obviously, we cannot fracture the skulls of a group of people to study phenomena like this one experimentally. Instead, we carefully study patients whose brains have been damaged by accident or disease. We compare their performance before and after the brain damage occurred. Usually, we do not meet the patients until *after* the brain damage occurs, so we must compare their performance with *our estimate* of what it was previously. In some cases our estimate is certain to be reasonably accurate. For example, if we meet a patient who cannot read but who received a college education and had a job that required a high level of literacy, we can be sure that the inability to read was caused by the brain damage.

Case studies are also performed by clinical psychologists and other mental health professionals, who observe the behavior of their clients and listen to what they have to say about their lives. Often the clinician tries to correlate events that occurred in the client's past (perhaps in childhood) with the client's present behavior and personality. Studies like these are called **retrospective studies** ("backward looking"), and their validity depends heavily on the client's memory for past events. Because recollections are often faulty, one must be cautious about accepting the conclusions of retrospective studies whose results cannot be independently verified. And because these studies are observational and not experimental, we cannot be sure that the events that occurred in the past were the *causes* of the client's present behavior—any more than we can conclude that joining the Boy Scouts causes people to participate in community affairs later in life.

Retrospective case studies of the clients of clinical psychologists have yet another drawback: The people who are studied are not representative of the population as a whole. For example, many psychiatrists and clinical psychologists used to believe that homosexuality was a disorder, and that it was caused by unhealthy family relationships. They made this conclusion because they found that most of their homosexual clients reported that they had experienced such relationships when they were children. But this conclusion is not justified. People do not consult mental health professionals unless they have some sort of problem; thus, the professionals are unlikely to see happy, untroubled people in their practices. Instead, they see a nonrepresentative sample of the population. In fact, research has shown that mentally healthy homosexuals are no more likely to have had unhappy childhoods than anyone else. (The evidence is reviewed in Chapter 11.)

EVALUATING SCIENTIFIC ISSUES

Format for Critical Thinking

As we have seen, the scientific method provides a set of rules that help us design research that will provide accurate and unbiased results. In each of the subsequent chapters in this book you will find a section entitled "Evaluating Scientific Issues." Each of these sections presents a controversial issue or an unanswered question and then examines the quality of the evidence for or against the issue.

Each section begins with a statement of the controversy. In most cases the statement is in the form of an assertion that a certain state of affairs is true. For example, Chapter 4 evaluates the assertion that subliminal messages can be used in teaching or advertising, and Chapter 10 evaluates the assertion that most people have a mid-life crisis during their early to middle forties.

After presenting the assertion, the evidence in favor of the assertion is described. Next, contrary evidence is presented, along with a critique of the evidence in favor of the assertion. The critiques refer back to the rules of the scientific method. The assertion will then be accepted or rejected—or we will see that more evidence is needed before a decision can be made.

The point of these sections is to help you develop your ability to think critically—to learn to evaluate controversies by examining the nature and quality of the evidence and drawing from the evidence only those conclusions that logically follow from it. Unfortunately, many people misuse or misinterpret the findings of psychologists or misrepresent falsehoods as rigorous scientific findings in an attempt to alter our attitudes and opinions—or to sell us something. For example, they will cite the opinions of scientific "experts." But there is no certified board of experts who are always right; we need to know the basis for their opinions. That is, we need to know enough about the evidence that we can critically evaluate it.

People who try to convince us about something often use nonscientific arguments. They may say something like "Everyone knows that . . . " or "Contrary to what so-called 'experts' say, common sense tells us that . . ." (The rule seems to be: If you cannot find an expert to quote, then condemn experts as "living in an ivory tower" or being "out of touch with reality.") People trying to convince us of something will also cite their personal experiences or offer testimonials of other people. If the cases they cite are rich with personal details, it is difficult not to be swayed by them. Chapter 9 ("Language and Thought") and Chapter 17 ("Social Psychology") discuss this phenomenon.

Although some of you will eventually become psychologists, most of you will not. Nevertheless, I hope that after reading this book, you will come to appreciate the fact that being able to apply the scientific method to issues in psychological research will help you critically evaluate other issues that you will encounter in and out of the classroom. ∎

INTERIM SUMMARY

The Scientific Method

Psychologists are interested in explaining the causes of behavior in a scientific way. To do so, they perform experiments or observational studies. To carry out experiments, they form hypotheses, manipulate independent variables, and measure dependent variables. If this procedure is to work, they must be certain that other variables are controlled—they must prevent the occurrence of confounded variables. If an extra independent variable is inadvertently manipulated, and if this extra variable has an effect on the dependent variable, then the results of the experiment will be invalid. In addition, confounding of subject variables can be caused by improper assignment of subjects to the various groups or by treatments that cause some subjects to leave the experiment. Another possible problem involves subjects' expectations; most people who participate in psychological experiments try to figure out what the experimenter is trying to accomplish, and their conclusions can affect their behavior. If knowledge of the experimental condition could alter the subjects' behavior, the experiment should be conducted with a single-blind procedure. And if that knowledge might alter the experimenter's assessment of the subjects' behavior, a double-blind procedure should be used.

Observational studies involve assessing relations among variables that the researcher cannot readily manipulate, such as personality characteristics, age, or sex. The investigator attempts to isolate variables of interest by matching members in each of the groups on all relevant variables except for the one in question. The problem is that investigators may miss an important variable. And, of course, even a good observational study cannot determine which variable is the cause and which is the effect.

Researchers are almost never interested only in the particular subjects they study; they want to be able to generalize their results and conclusions to a larger population. The confidence a researcher can have in his or her generalizations depends on the nature of the variables being studied and on the composition of the sample group of subjects. ∎

Should animals be used in psychological research? Most psychologists and other researchers strongly believe that animal research, conducted humanely, is necessary and ethically justified. The American Psychological Association has established a strict set of guidelines for the use of animals in research.

ETHICS

6 Unlike many other scientists, psychologists must study living subjects. Thus, a psychologist must obey ethical rules as well as scientific rules. Great care is needed in the treatment of human subjects, because we can hurt people in very subtle ways. For example, let us reconsider the hypothetical experiment on anger and concentration. For the experiment to be scientifically valid, we must make the subjects angry. Exactly what would the experimenter do? How would the subjects be likely to react? Would the experimenter's rude behavior have long-lasting effects on the subjects?

In the United States, federal regulations state that all departments of psychology that engage in federally funded research must have a committee that reviews the ethics of all studies that use humans as subjects. The committee must review the studies before they can be performed, to ensure that subjects will be treated properly. In addition, the American Psychological Association has its own ethical guidelines for human research. Review committees are in everyone's interest; both the researchers and their subjects can be confident that the procedures are unlikely to produce harm. (See *Table 2.1.*)

Although most psychologists study the behavior of their fellow humans, some of them study the behavior of animals. Any time we use another species of animals for our own purposes, we should be sure that what we are doing is both humane and worthwhile. I believe that a good case can be made that psychological

Table 2.1 Rights and responsibilities of research participants

Rights

1. Participants should know the general purpose of the study and what they will be expected to do. Beyond this, they should be told everything a reasonable person would want to know in order to decide whether to participate.

2. Participants have the right to withdraw from a study at any time after beginning participation in the research. A participant who chooses to withdraw has the right to receive whatever benefits were promised.

3. Participants should expect to receive benefits that outweigh the costs or risks involved. To achieve the educational benefit, participants have the right to ask questions and to receive clear, honest answers. When participants do not receive what was promised, they have the right to remove their data from the study.

4. Participants have the right to expect that anything done or said during their participation in a study will remain anonymous and confidential, unless they specifically agree to give up this right.

5. Participants have the right to decline to participate in any study and may not be coerced into research. When learning about research is a course requirement, an equivalent alternative to participation should be available.

6. Participants have a right to know when they have been deceived in a study and why the deception was used. If the deception seems unreasonable, participants have the right to withhold their data.

7. When any of these rights is violated or participants object to anything about a study, they have the right and the responsibility to inform the appropriate university officials, including the chairpersons of the Psychology Department and the Institutional Review Board.

Responsibilities

1. Participants have the responsibility to listen carefully to the experimenter and ask questions in order to understand the research.

2. Be on time for the research appointment.

3. Participants should take the research seriously and cooperate with the experimenter.

4. When the study has been completed, participants share the responsibility for understanding what happened.

5. Participants have the resonsibility for honoring the researcher's request that they not discuss the study with anyone else who might be a participant.

From Korn, J.H. Students' roles, rights, and responsibilities as research participants. *Teaching of Psychology*, 1988, *15*, 74–78.

research with animals qualifies on both counts. Humane treatment is a matter of procedure. We know how to maintain laboratory animals in good health in comfortable, sanitary conditions. For those cases where the experiments involve surgery, we know how to administer anesthetics and analgesics so that animals do not suffer. Most industrially developed societies have very strict regulations about the care of animals and also require approval of the procedures that will be used in the experiments in which they participate. There is no excuse for mistreating animals in our care. In fact, the vast majority of laboratory animals *are* treated humanely.

Whether an experiment is *worthwhile* is more difficult to say. We use animals for many purposes. We eat their meat and their eggs and drink their milk; we turn their hides into leather; we extract insulin and other hormones from their organs to treat people with diseases; we train them to do useful work on farms or to entertain us. Even having a pet is a form of exploitation; it is we—not they—who decide that they will live in our homes. The fact is, we have been using other animals throughout the history of our species.

Pet owning causes much more suffering among animals than scientific research does. As Miller (1983) notes, pet owners are not required to receive permission from a board of experts including a veterinarian to house their pets, nor are they subject to periodic inspections to be sure that their home is clean and sanitary, that their pets have enough space to exercise properly, that their diets are appropriate; but scientific researchers are. Miller also notes that fifty times more dogs and cats are killed by humane societies each year because they have been abandoned by former pet owners than are used in scientific research.

The use of animals in research and teaching is a special target of animal rights activists. Nicholl and Russell (1990) examined 21 books written by such activists and calculated the number of pages devoted to concern for different uses of animals. Next, they compared the relative concern the authors showed for these uses to the numbers of animals actually involved in each of these categories. The results indicate that the authors showed relatively little concern for animals used for food, hunting, or furs or for those killed in pounds; but although only 0.3 percent of the animals were used for research and education, 63.3 percent of the pages are devoted to this use. In terms of pages per million animals used, the authors devoted 0.08 to food, 0.23 to hunting, 1.27 to furs, 1.44 to killing in pounds—and 53.2 to research and education. The authors showed 665 times more concern for research and education than for food, and 231 times more than for hunting. Even the use of animals for furs (which consumes two-thirds as many animals as research and education) attracted 41.9 times less attention per animal.

Our species is beset by medical, mental, and behavioral problems, many of which can be solved only through research that involves animals. In fact, research with laboratory animals has produced important discoveries about the possible causes or potential treatments of neurological and mental disorders, including Parkinson's disease, schizophrenia, manic-depressive illness, anxiety disorders, obsessive-compulsive disorders, anorexia nervosa, obesity, and drug addictions. Although much progress has been made, these problems are still with us and cause much human suffering. Unless we continue our research with laboratory animals, they will not be solved. Some people have suggested that instead of using laboratory animals in our research, we could use tissue cultures or computers. Unfortunately, tissue cultures or computers are not substitutes for living organisms. We have no way to study behavioral problems such as addictions in tissue cultures, nor can we program a computer to simulate the workings of an animal's nervous system. (If we could, that would mean we already had all the answers.)

DESCRIPTIONS OF OBSERVATIONS

7 In most of the examples I have cited so far, the behavior of several subjects was observed. I implied that the data obtained from them would be combined in some way to represent a particular value of a variable. That is, a single number would be used to represent the results of several observations. There is nothing novel about such a procedure. For example, I am sure that all of you know how to calculate the average of a set of numbers; an average is a common measure of central tendency. You might be less familiar with measures of variability, which tell us how groups of numbers differ from one another, or with measures of relations, which tell us how closely related two sets of numbers are.

These measures, which describe the results of experiments or observational studies, are called **descriptive statistics.** They are used for two reasons. First, the investigator cal-

culates them and uses their values to determine whether the results support the hypothesis (step 3 of the scientific method). Second, the investigator uses these values to communicate the results of the experiment accurately and succinctly to others (step 4 of the scientific method). In this section we will examine some of the descriptive statistics commonly used in psychological studies.

Measures of Central Tendency

When we say that the average weight of an adult male in North America is 173 pounds or that the average density of population in the United States is 63.9 people per square mile, we are using a **measure of central tendency,** a statistic that represents a number of observations. The most common measure of central tendency is the average, which psychologists and statisticians usually refer to as the mean. As you probably already know, the **mean** is calculated by adding the individual values of the sample and dividing by the number of observations. The

An observational study of preschoolers allows a researcher to measure interactions such as friendliness or competitiveness between the children, without influencing or interfering with their behavior.

mean is the most frequently used measure of central tendency in reports of psychological experiments.

Although the mean is usually selected to measure central tendency, it is not the most precise measure of that characteristic, especially if the sample contains a few especially high or low values. When we want to choose a measure for descriptive purposes that is the most representative of a sample of numbers, we should use the *median*, not the mean. For this reason we usually read "median family income" rather than "mean family income" in newspaper or magazine articles.

To calculate the **median** of a set of numbers, we arrange them in numerical order and find the midpoint. For example, the median of the numbers 1, 2, and 6 is 2. To understand why the median is the best representative of a sample that contains some extreme values, consider a small town that contains 100 families. Ninety-nine of the families, all of whom work in the local textile mill, make between $15,000 and $20,000 per year. However, the income of one family is $2 million per year (an extreme value, to be sure). This family consists of a novelist and her husband, who moved to the area because of its mild climate. The mean income for the town as a whole, considering the novelist as well as the mill workers, is $37,325 per year. In contrast, the median income for the town is $17,500 per year. Clearly, the median best represents the typical family income of the town.

Why, then, would we ever bother to use the mean rather than the median? As we will see later in this chapter, the mean is used to calculate other important statistics and has special mathematical properties that make it more useful than the median.

Measures of Variability

Many experiments produce two sets of numbers, consisting of the scores of subjects in the experimental and control groups. If the mean scores of these two groups differ, then the experimenter can conclude that the independent variable had an effect. As we will see in a later section of this chapter, the psychologist must decide whether the difference between the two groups is larger than what would probably occur by chance. To make this decision, he or she calculates a **measure of variability,** a statistic that describes the degree to which scores in a sample differ from each other. The psychologist then uses this measure as a basis for comparing the means of the two groups.

Two samples can have the same measure of central tendency and still be very different. For example, the mean and median of both sets of numbers listed in Table 2.2 are the same, but the samples are clearly different. The scores in sample B are more disparate. (See *Table 2.2.*)

One way of stating the difference between the two samples is to say that the numbers in sample A range from 8 to 12 and the numbers in sample B range from 0 to 20. The **range** of a sample is simply the largest number minus the smallest. Thus, the range of sample A is 4 and the range of sample B is 20.

The range is not used very often to describe the results of psychological experiments because another measure of variability—the standard deviation—has more useful mathematical properties, just as the mean does. To calculate the standard deviation of a sample of numbers, you first calculate the mean and then find the difference between each number and the mean. These difference scores are squared

Table 2.2 Two samples with the same mean and median but different ranges

Sample A		Sample B	
	8		0
	9		5
	10 ← Median		10 ← Median
	11		15
	12		20
Total:	50	Total:	50
Mean:	50/5 = 10	Mean:	50/5 = 10
Range:	12 − 8 = 4	Range:	20 − 0 = 20

Table 2.3 Calculation of the variance and standard deviation of two samples with the same mean

	Sample A				Sample B		
	Score	Difference Between Score and Mean	Difference Squared		Score	Difference Between Score and Mean	Difference Squared
	8	10 − 8 = 2	4		0	10 − 0 = 10	100
	9	10 − 9 = 1	1		5	10 − 5 = 5	25
	10	10 − 10 = 0	0		10	10 − 10 = 0	0
	11	11 − 10 = 1	1		15	15 − 10 = 5	25
	12	12 − 10 = 2	4		20	20 − 10 = 10	100
Total:	50	Total:	10	Total:	50	Total:	250
Mean:	50/5 = 10	Mean (variance):	10/5 = 2	Mean:	50/5 = 10	Mean (variance):	250/5 = 25
		Square root (standard deviation):	1.41			Square root (standard deviation):	5

(that is, multiplied by themselves) and added together. The mean of this total is called the *variance;* the **standard deviation** is the square root of the variance. (See **Table 2.3.**)

Measurement of Relations

In many studies, especially observational studies, the investigator wants to measure the degree to which two variables are related. For example, suppose that a psychologist has developed a new aptitude test and wants to sell the test to college admissions committees to use for screening applicants. Before they will consider buying the test, the psychologist must show that a person's score on the test is related to his or her subsequent success in college. To do so, the psychologist will give the test to a number of freshmen entering college and later obtain their average grades. The psychologist will then measure the relation between test scores and grades. But how does one measure a relation?

Let us suppose that we give the test to ten students entering college and later obtain their average grades. We will have two scores for each person, as shown in Table 2.4. (See **Table 2.4.**) We can examine the relation between these variables by plotting the scores on a graph. For example, student A.C. received a test score of 15 and earned an average grade of 2.8 (B minus). We can represent this student's score as a point on the graph shown in Figure 2.8. The horizontal axis represents the test score, and the vertical axis represents the average grade. We put a point on the graph that

corresponds to the score of student A.C. on both of these measures. (See **Figure 2.8.**)

We can construct a graph that contains the scores of all ten students and then look at the distribution of scores to determine whether they are related. Examination of this graph, called a **scatterplot,** shows that the points are not randomly distributed; instead, they tend to be located along a diagonal line that runs from the lower left to the upper right. (See **Figure 2.9.**)

The data shown in Figure 2.9 indicate that a rather strong relation exists between a student's test score and average grade. High scores are associated with good grades, low scores with poor grades. However, the psychol-

Table 2.4 Test scores and average grades of ten students

Student	Test Score	Average Grade[a]
A.C.	15	2.8
B.F.	12	3.2
G.G.	19	3.5
L.H.	8	2.2
R.J.	14	3.0
S.K.	11	2.6
P.R.	13	2.8
A.S.	7	1.5
J.S.	9	1.9
P.V.	18	3.8

[a] 0 = F; 4 = A.

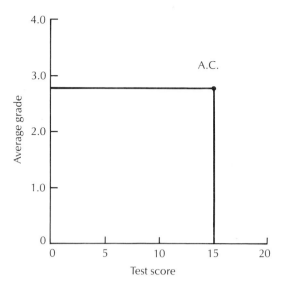

Figure 2.8 An example of graphing one data point: the test score and average grade of student A.C.

ogist who developed the test would want a more convenient way to communicate the results than showing the scatterplots, so he or she would probably calculate the **correlation coefficient,** a number that expresses the strength of a relation. Calculating this statistic for the two sets of scores in my example gives a correlation of +.9 between the two variables. (I will not bother you with the details of how this measure is calculated.) A correlation this high is indeed a strong one, and a psychologist would be delighted to have developed a test whose scores correlated with college grades this well. The value of a correlation coefficient can vary from 0 (no relation) to 1.0 (perfect relation). A perfect relation means that if we know the value of a

Figure 2.9 A scatterplot of the test scores and average grades of ten students.

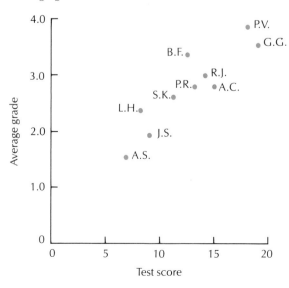

person's score on one measure, then we can determine precisely what his or her score will be on the other. Thus, a correlation of +.9 is very close to perfect; the hypothetical aptitude test of our example is indeed an excellent indicator of how well a student will do in college.

I should note that correlations can be negative as well as positive. A *negative* correlation indicates that high values on one measure are associated with low values on the other, and vice versa. An example of a negative correlation is the relation between the average score of a professional golfer and the amount of money he or she wins in a year. Because low golf scores indicate more skill, players with the lowest scores will tend to win the most money, and those with the highest scores will win the least.

For purposes of prediction a negative correlation is just as good as a positive one. A correlation of −.9 is an almost-perfect relation, but in this case high scores on one measure predict low scores on the other.

ASSESSING THE SIGNIFICANCE OF RELATIONS

8 Scientific investigations, whether they consist of experiments or observational studies, are concerned with relations. Sometimes, the investigator calculates the relation directly, by computing a correlation coefficient. Other times (for example, in an experiment), the investigator selects two or more values of the independent variable and measures the dependent variable. The results, usually expressed as means and standard deviations, indicate whether the independent variable had an effect on the dependent variable—that is, whether the mean values for the dependent variable differed from one another. The next step is to decide whether the difference observed between the group means reflects a real effect of the independent variable or whether the results are due to chance.

Statistical Significance

When we perform an experiment, we select a sample of subjects from a larger population—the one to which we want to generalize. In doing so, we hope that the results will be similar to those we might have obtained had we used all members of the population in the experiment. We assign the subjects to groups in an unbiased manner (usually by random assignment), alter only the relevant independent variables, and measure the dependent variable with a valid and reliable method. In other words, we put into practice the procedures I have outlined in this chapter. After we have completed the experiment, we must decide whether our results indicate that a relation exists between independent and dependent variables; that is, we must decide whether the results are **statistically significant.**

The concept of statistical significance is not an easy one to grasp, so I want to make sure you understand the purpose of this discussion. Suppose we wish to determine whether the presence of other people affects the speed at which a person can solve simple arithmetic problems. We test members of the experimental group with other people watching them; members of the control group work alone. We then calculate the mean number of problems solved by each group. If the means are different, we can conclude that the presence of an audience does affect the rate at which a person can solve arithmetic problems.

But how different is different? Suppose we tested two groups of people, *both* of whom performed alone. Would the mean scores be precisely the same? Of course not. *By chance,* they would be at least slightly different. Now back to our experiment. Suppose we find that the mean score for the group that worked in the presence of an audience is lower than the mean score for the group that performed alone. How much lower would it have to be before we could conclude that the presence of an audience disrupted our subjects' performance? In other words, how do we go about determining whether the difference between the mean scores is greater than can be accounted for by chance? These are the kinds of questions that every psychologist must ask when an experiment is finished.

Assessment of Differences Between Samples

The way to determine whether two group means differ significantly is to look at the size of the difference. If it is large, then we can be fairly confident that the independent variable had a significant effect. If it is small, then the difference is probably due to chance. What we need are guidelines to help us determine when a difference is large enough to be statistically significant.

The following example will explain how these guidelines are constructed. A few years ago, I distributed cards to students in one of my classes to collect some data that I could analyze to explain some statistical concepts. I will use the data I collected for that purpose here, too.

There were seventy-six students in the class. Their average height was 67.2 inches. I performed an observational study to test the following hypothesis: People whose first names end in a vowel will, on the average, be shorter than people whose first names end in a consonant. (I will tell you later why I expected this hypothesis to be confirmed.)

I divided the subjects into two groups: those whose first names ended in a vowel and those whose first names ended in a consonant. Table 2.5 contains a listing of these two groups. Indeed, the means for the two groups differed by 4.1 inches. (See *Table 2.5.*)

Table 2.5 Height (in inches) of selected sample of students

Name Ends in Consonant		Name Ends in Vowel
65	61	67
67	68	68
71	70	62
72	65	63
73	73	62
65	60	64
74	70	60
74	72	63
67	63	61
69	67	69
68	73	63
75	66	65
72	71	69
71	72	71
65	64	69
66	69	65
70	73	70
72	75	63
72	72	63
71	66	64
62	71	65
62	68	63
80	70	66
	75	62
Total: 3257		72
Mean: 3257/47 = 69.3		65
		66
		65
		65

Total: 1890

Mean: 1890/29 = 65.2

Difference between means: 69.3 − 65.2 = 4.1

A difference of 4.1 inches seems large, but how can we be sure that it is not due to chance? What we really need to know is how large a difference there would be if the means had been calculated from two groups that were randomly selected and not chosen on the basis of a variable that might be related to height. For comparison, I divided the class into two random groups by shuffling the cards with the students' names on them and dealing them out into two piles. Then I calculated the mean height of the people whose names were in each of the piles. This time, the difference between the means was 0.7 inch. (See *Table 2.6.*)

I divided the class into two random groups five more times, calculating the means and the difference between the means each time. The differences ranged from 0.2 to 0.7 inch. (See *Table 2.7.*) It began to look as though a mean difference of 4.1 inches was bigger than what one would expect by chance.

Next, I divided the class into two random groups 1000 times. (I used my computer to do the chore.) *Not once* in 1000 times was the difference between the means of the two randomly

Table 2.6 Height (in inches) of a random division of the class into two groups

Group A		Group B	
65	71	63	62
72	63	62	63
72	74	70	65
69	72	70	75
61	71	65	71
69	65	64	80
66	71	75	71
70	67	63	68
66	72	70	71
65	66	75	73
66	72	67	62
65	73	65	72
64	63	68	65
72	69	63	72
63	62	69	66
65	60	67	73
62	70	68	65
67	68	60	73
	69		61
	64		74
Total:	2561	Total:	2586
Mean:	67.4	Mean:	68.1
		Difference:	−0.7

Table 2.7 Mean heights (in inches) of five random divisions of the class into two groups

Group A	Group B	Difference
67.6	67.9	−0.3
68.1	67.4	0.7
67.8	67.6	0.2
67.9	67.5	0.4
68.0	67.4	0.6

chosen groups greater than 3.0 inches. Therefore, I can conclude that if the class is divided randomly into two groups, the chance that the means of their heights will differ by 4.1 inches is much less than one time in a thousand, or 0.1%. Thus, I can safely say that when I divided the students into two groups according to the last letter of their first names, I was dividing them on a basis that was somehow related to their height. The division was *not* equivalent to random selection; a person's height *is* related to the last letter of his or her first name.

Figure 2.10 presents a frequency distribution of the differences between the means of the two groups for 1000 random divisions of the class. The height of a point on the graph represents the number of times (the frequency) that the difference between the means fell into that particular range. For example, the difference between the means fell between −0.2 and +0.2 inch 170 times. (See *Figure 2.10.*)

Suppose the difference between the means in our observational study had been smaller than 4.1 inches. Suppose it had been only 2.3 inches. Would we conclude that the difference represented a real relation, or would we decide that the difference was due to chance? Figure 2.10 will help us decide.

We can see that only 15 out of 1000 times (1.5%) is the difference between the means of the two groups as large as or larger than 2.3 inches: 11 + 4 = 15. (See *Figure 2.10.*) Therefore, if we obtain a difference of 2.3 inches between the means of the groups and conclude that people whose first names end in vowels tend to be shorter than people whose first names end in consonants, *the likelihood of our being wrong is 1.5%.* The calculations show that we will obtain a difference of at least 2.3 inches between the means purely by chance only 1.5% of the time. Because 1.5% is a small likelihood, we can probably conclude that the relation is statistically significant.

The method I used to determine the statistical significance of my original findings from the

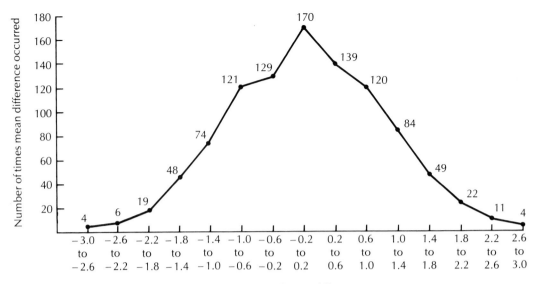

Figure 2.10 A frequency distribution. This distribution illustrates the number of occurrences of various ranges of mean differences in height. The group of 76 people was divided randomly into 2 samples 1000 times.

group of seventy-six students (a difference of 4.1 inches) employs the same principles that a psychologist uses to determine whether the results observed in a given experiment represent a real difference or are just due to chance. In my example we considered two possibilities: (1) the difference between the means was due to chance, and (2) the difference between the means occurred because the last letter of a person's first name is related to his or her height. We found that a difference of 4.1 inches would be expected less than one time in a thousand. Therefore, we rejected alternative 1 and concluded that alternative 2 was correct. My original hypothesis was right.

Ordinarily, psychologists who conduct experiments or observational studies like this one do not use their computers to divide their subject's scores randomly 1000 times. Instead, they calculate the mean and standard deviation for each group and consult a table that statisticians have already prepared for them. The table (which is based upon the special mathematical properties of the mean and standard deviation that I have alluded to) will tell them how likely it is that their results could have been obtained by chance—in other words, how likely it is that the last letter of a person's first name is not related to his or her height. If the likelihood is low enough, they will conclude that the results they obtained are statistically significant. Most psychologists consider a 5 percent probability to be statistically significant but are much more comfortable with 1 percent or less.

I must emphasize that statistical tests help us decide whether results are representative of the larger population but not whether they are

important. In general usage the word *significant* does mean "important," but in this context it simply means that the results appear not to be caused by chance. For example, suppose that a school system decides to perform an experiment to try a new teaching method. They find that the test scores of students who were taught by the new method are higher than those of students who were taught by the old method. The difference is statistically significant, but it is very small. (A small difference can be statistically significant if the variability within the groups is low enough or if the groups of subjects are very large.) Because changing all classes over to the new method is very expensive, the school system would probably decide to continue with the present method.

I should now tell you why I originally hypothesized that the last letter of a person's first name is related to his or her height. Females are more likely than males to have first names that end in a vowel (Paula, Anna, Marie, etc.). Because females tend to be shorter than males, I expected a group of students whose first names end in vowels would be shorter, on the average, than those whose first names end in consonants. Indeed, the data proved me correct.

INTERIM SUMMARY

Assessing the Significance of Relations

Psychologists need ways to communicate their results to others accurately and concisely. They typically employ three kinds of descriptive statistics: measures of central tendency, variability, and relations. The most common examples of these measures are the mean, the median, the standard deviation, and the correlation coefficient.

If a psychologist tests a hypothesis by comparing the scores of two groups of subjects, he or she must have some way of determining whether the observed difference in the mean scores is larger than what one would expect by chance. My example was an observational study; I certainly did not *manipulate* my students' names—they already had them when they came to my class. However, the procedure I followed is based upon the same logic that a psychologist would use in assessing the significance of the results of an experiment.

A psychologist performs an experiment by observing the performance of two or more groups of subjects who have been exposed to different conditions, representing different values of the independent variable. Next, the psychologist calculates the group means and standard deviations of the dependent variable. He or she uses a formula and consults a special table that statisticians have devised. The table gives the likelihood of getting such results when the independent variable actually has *no effect* on the dependent variable. If the probability of obtaining these results by chance is sufficiently low, the psychologist will reject the possibility that the independent variable had no effect and decide in favor of the alternative—that it really *did* have an effect on the dependent variable.

The scientific method consists of a logical system of inquiry with sensible rules that must be followed if a person wants to draw accurate conclusions about the causes of natural phenomena. These rules were originally devised by philosophers who attempted to determine how we can understand reality. Because by our natures we are all intuitive psychologists, trying to understand why other people do what they do, it is especially important to realize how easily we can be fooled about the actual causes of behavior. Thus, everyone, not just the professional psychologist, is well served by knowing the basic steps of the scientific method. ∎

APPLICATION

The Listerine Episode

The following article appeared in the *New York Times* of January 4, 1976. It demonstrates some of the practical difficulties that can occur when one tries to apply the double-blind method.

"Tests made over a 12-year period proved that people who gargled with Listerine full strength twice a day, every day, had fewer colds and milder colds than those who did not."

This statement and others like it have been used for years by the makers of nonprescription drugs in an attempt to persuade consumers that scientific evidence supports their advertising claims. Rarely, however, are the details of the cited research ever made public, even through scientific journals, so that the adequacy of the research methods can be evaluated.

Now, however, with the recent ruling by the Federal Trade Commission that Listerine's future advertising must deny past claims that it can prevent and cure the common cold, the F.T.C. has released documents describing the research in detail. After asking a number of eminent scientists to evaluate the research, the commission decided that the experiments were designed in such a way that they permitted biased results in favor of Listerine.

According to the F.T.C.'s documents, the 12-year tests that Warner-Lambert relied on were conducted during the winters of 1930 to 1942 on two groups of people—those who gargled with Listerine and those who did not.

Normally, drug testing observes standard rules intended to reduce any chance of subtle bias, such as selecting experimental and control groups to be evenly matched and keeping the subjects ignorant of what results are hoped for.

Instead of an independent scientist and a disinterested experimental group, Warner-Lambert conducted the Listerine research on its own employees in the factory. Employees were allowed to choose which group they would be in. Naturally, the F.T.C.'s experts said, those who believed in gargling joined that group, while those who did not remained nongarglers.

The garglers in the 12-year test, already believing in the usefulness of gargling, undoubtedly reported fewer cold symptoms than those who did not gargle.

Experts who testified at the F.T.C. hearings said that a properly designed study would have assigned people to the two groups randomly and given the control group a placebo, or similar-appearing dummy medication so that neither group would know which was getting the real thing. The placebo effect would thus be the same for both groups.

For 25 years, Warner-Lambert accepted the 12-year test as a

truly scientific experiment documenting the cold-fighting properties of Listerine. But, as the company's officials testified, doubts did creep up and it was decided to make a new test in 1967.

The company hired a pediatrician and sent him to St. Barnabas Catholic School in the Bronx. About 1,500 students were divided, this time randomly, into garglers and nongarglers and instructed to report to the pediatrician any morning they thought they had a cold.

The doctor, Benjamin W. Nitzberg, went to the school at 10 A.M. every day during the November-to-April test periods. To insure that the garglers participated in the test, they were made to gargle in school at 9 o'clock every morning using bottles labeled "Warner-Lambert Research Institute."

A proper experimental design, experts told the F.T.C., would keep the examining physician ignorant of which group any person belongs to. If the doctor knows which group a person is in and believes the drug to be effective and is in the pay of a manufacturer who would like favorable results, there is a good chance that at least borderline situations would be called in favor of the biases.

Students who wished to report to Dr. Nitzberg had to do so within an hour or so of gargling with Listerine. Thus, Dr. Nitzberg could hardly avoid smelling Listerine on the breath of those who gargled.

The F.T.C. also found that students were not kept ignorant of the expected outcome of the test. In fact, the purpose of the experiment was so well known that parents of nongarglers complained to school officials because they thought their children were being denied protection against colds.

Near the end of the four-year study, the Warner-Lambert researchers did recognize the lack of a placebo and thereafter had former nongarglers gargle with water colored to resemble Listerine.

However, F.T.C. investigators found that, since the placebo lacked Listerine's strong flavor and odor, by now well known to the entire school (which Dr. Nitzberg said smelled like a Listerine factory during the tests), few students were in doubt as to what they were gargling with.

If you were put in charge of a research project such as this one, what changes would you make in the experimental design?

KEY TERMS AND CONCEPTS

The Scientific Method

scientific method *(23)*
replication *(24)*
hypothesis *(24)*
theory *(24)*
variable *(25)*
independent variable *(25)*
dependent variable *(25)*
nominal fallacy *(25)*
operational definition *(26)*
validity *(27)*
face validity *(27)*
reliability *(27)*
interrater reliability *(28)*
confounding of variables *(29)*
counterbalancing *(30)*
control group *(30)*
random assignment *(31)*
placebo *(33)*
single-blind method *(33)*
double-blind method *(33)*

observational study *(33)*
matching *(35)*
sample *(35)*
generalization *(35)*
case study *(36)*
retrospective study *(36)*

Descriptions of Observations

descriptive statistics *(40)*
measure of central tendency *(40)*
mean *(40)*
median *(41)*
measure of variability *(41)*
range *(41)*
standard deviation *(42)*
scatterplot *(42)*
correlation coefficient *(43)*

Assessing the Significance of Relations

statistical significance *(44)*

Christensen, L.B. *Experimental Methodology,* 5th ed. Boston: Allyn and Bacon, 1991.

Several standard textbooks discuss the scientific method in psychological research. The Christensen book covers ethical and practical issues as well as theoretical ones.

Barber, T.X. *Pitfalls in Human Research.* New York: Pergamon Press, 1976.

McCain, G., and Segal, E.M. *The Game of Science,* 4th ed. Belmont, Calif.: Brooks/Cole, 1981.

Both of these books are rather entertaining accounts of the whys and wherefores of the scientific method. Most of us enjoy reading about the mistakes of others, perhaps thinking that we could have done things better. Barber's book allows us to indulge in this activity; it discusses specific instances of studies that were flawed.

Bell, J. *Evaluating Psychological Information: Sharpening Your Critical Thinking Skills.* Boston: Allyn and Bacon, 1991.

Bell's book provides what the title claims: an excellent way to sharpen your critical thinking skills. It is full of exercises to help you accomplish that goal.

3
BIOLOGY OF BEHAVIOR

Henri Matisse, Detail from "Icarus" from *Jazz*
Art Resource, N.Y. © 1992 Succession H. Matisse/ARS, N.Y.

LEARNING OBJECTIVES

When you finish this chapter, you should be able to:

1. Describe methods for studying the brain and for assessing brain damage.
2. Outline the basic structure of the nervous system.
3. Describe the primary sensory cortex, primary motor cortex, and association cortex and discuss the concept of lateralization of function.
4. Describe the functions of the four lobes of the cerebral cortex.
5. Describe the control of internal functions and automatic behaviors by the brain stem, the cerebellum, the thalamus, the hypothalamus, and the limbic system.
6. Describe the structures of the neuron.
7. Describe a synapse and the effects of synaptic transmission and explain how a simple neural circuit transmits messages.
8. Explain the steps of synaptic transmission and the effects of drugs and neuromodulators on this process.
9. Discuss the evidence for the interaction of hereditary and environmental factors on brain development.
10. Describe the effects of drugs that cause sedation, excitation, or alteration of perceptions and those that alleviate the symptoms of mental disorders.

Mrs. R. certainly did not look like a person who had just had a stroke. When a colleague and I asked whether we could talk with her about what had happened, she smiled and invited us into her hospital room. "I felt numb and dizzy and had trouble standing, so my husband drove me to the emergency room. The doctors did some tests and said I had a small stroke. I feel much better now, but I'm still a little disoriented. Sometimes, I'm not quite sure where I am, and I have trouble remembering the location of things in the room."

Having seen CT scans of Mrs. R.'s brain, we knew that she had had a stroke that damaged a small part of her brain, in a location that is involved in spatial relations—perceiving the relative location of things in her environment. Thus, we were not surprised to learn of her symptoms. We could hear that her speech was normal, and we found that she had no trouble reading or writing. Then we asked her to draw a simple picture of a house. "Now you've got me," she said with a wry expression. "Well, I'll try." And try she did, but without success. "I don't think a child in kindergarten would be pleased with this," she said as she slapped the pencil down in disgust. "I just can't picture where the lines are supposed to go."

"Were you good at drawing before your stroke?" I asked.

"Yes! That's what's so frustrating! I used to teach children to draw in my Sunday school classes."

We spent an hour testing Mrs. R. more carefully. We found that her difficulty extended to words that dealt with space. For example, although she could point to the ceiling and the floor if we asked her to, she could not say which was above the other. Similarly, although her perception of other people appeared to be normal, she could not say whether a person's head was at the top or bottom of the body. I wrote a set of multiple-choice questions that evening, and the next day I gave her a test. When a question contained a word that dealt with space, she failed to understand what it meant. For example, she chose the following statements:

A tree's branches are *under* its roots.

The sky is *down.*

But when a question did not deal with space, she had no trouble choosing the correct alternative. For example, she chose the following statements:

After exchanging pleasantries, they got *down* to business.

He got sick and threw *up.*

Consider the use of the word *up* in the last sentence. It does not refer to a direction (actually, when we vomit we usually point our mouths *down*). Instead, the word is simply part of a phrase. Similarly, getting *down* to business does not imply that the business has just gotten closer to the floor.

Mrs. R.'s case provided me with evidence that supported my belief that different types of memories are located in different regions of the brain. Because Mrs. R. had sustained damage to a part of the brain involved in spatial perception, she no longer knew the meanings of words that were related to space. However, if the same words had other, nonspatial meanings, she had no trouble understanding them, because those memories are located in other parts of the brain. Thanks to the cooperation of people such as Mrs. R., we are learning more about the workings of the human brain.

The brain has two roles: controlling the movements of the muscles and regulating the physiological functions of the body. Thus, the first role looks outward toward the environment, and the second looks inward. The outward-looking role includes several functions: perceiving events in the environment, learning about them, making plans, and acting. The inward-looking role requires the brain to control physiological processes in the body—to measure and regulate characteristics such as body temperature, blood pressure, and levels of nutrients. Psychologists are obviously more interested in the behavioral functions of the brain, but the regulatory functions are important, too, and both are described in this chapter.

STUDY OF THE BRAIN

Study of the brain and of the biology of behavior involves the efforts of many different types of scientists, including psychologists, physiologists, anatomists, pharmacologists, and biochemists. I will begin my discussion with a description of the types of research efforts that psychologists undertake in this quest.

Research Methods of Physiological Psychology

Physiological psychologists (also called *biopsychologists*) try to understand the physiology of behavior by performing experiments on laboratory animals. The most common research method involves correlating a behavioral deficit with the location of damage to the nervous system. The investigator produces a **brain lesion** (an injury to a particular part of the brain) and then studies the effects of the lesion on the animal's behavior. If particular behaviors are disrupted, then the damaged part of the brain must be involved in those behaviors.

To produce a brain lesion, the researcher anesthetizes an animal and prepares it for surgery, drills a hole in the skull, and destroys part of the brain. In most cases the region under investigation is located deep within the brain, so the investigator must use a special device called a **stereotaxic apparatus.** (The term *stereotaxic* refers to the ability to manipulate an object in three-dimensional space.) The researcher uses a stereotaxic apparatus to insert a fine wire into a particular location in the brain. He or she then passes electrical current through the wire, which destroys a small portion of the brain around the tip of the wire. After a few days the animal recovers from the operation, and the researcher can assess its behavior. (See *Figure 3.1.*)

A stereotaxic apparatus can also be used to insert wires for recording the electrical activity

Figure 3.1 A stereotaxic apparatus, used to insert a wire or metal tube into a specific portion of an animal's brain.

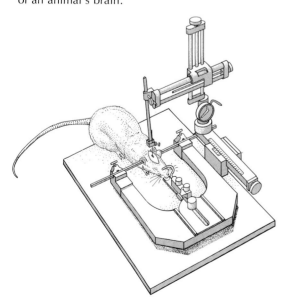

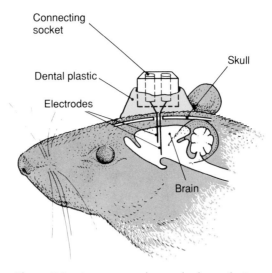

Figure 3.2 A permanently attached set of wires (electrodes) in an animal's brain, with a connecting socket cemented to the skull.

of nerve cells in particular regions of the brain. (As we will see later in this chapter, nerve cells transmit information from place to place by means of electrical charges; the wire in the brain detects these charges.) The wire is then attached to an electrical connector cemented to the animal's skull, and the scalp is sewed together. The connector is later attached to a wire leading to electronic devices that record the electrical activity of the brain while the animal is performing various behaviors. (See *Figure 3.2.*)

A wire placed in an animal's brain can be used to lead electrical current *into* the brain as well as out of it. The electrical connector on the animal's skull is attached to an electrical stimulator, and current is sent to a portion of the animal's brain. The experimenter then assesses the effects of this artificial stimulation on the animal's behavior. One example of an experiment that uses this technique is shown in Figure 3.3. A rat presses a lever attached to an electrical switch that turns on a stimulator. The stimulator sends a brief pulse of electricity through a wire placed in the rat's brain. If the tip of the wire is located in certain parts of the brain, the animal will press the lever again and again. (See *Figure 3.3.*) This finding suggests that these parts of the brain play a role in reward mechanisms. (Chapter 11 discusses this phenomenon in more detail.)

Physiological psychologists also use chemicals in their investigations of brain functions. Different drugs affect different types of nerve cells of the brain in different ways, and many of

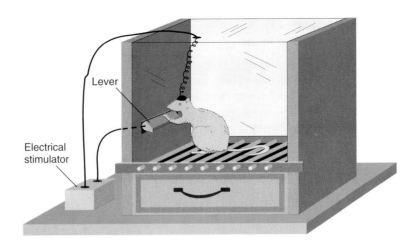

Figure 3.3 Electrical stimulation experiment. When the rat presses the switch, it receives a brief pulse of electricity to its brain, through wires like those shown in Figure 3.2.

the hormones produced by the glands of the body affect behavior by stimulating nerve cells. Therefore, physiological psychologists often administer drugs or hormones to laboratory animals in order to determine how their behavioral effects are produced. Administering chemicals can be even more precise: A researcher can use a stereotaxic apparatus to inject drugs or hormones directly into a particular part of the brain.

Although physiological psychologists regularly use many other techniques, lesion production, electrical recording, electrical stimulation, and the administration of drugs and hormones are the ones most frequently employed. They illustrate the basic types of approaches to research in physiological psychology.

Assessment of Damage to the Human Brain

Physiological psychologists know the approximate location of the lesions in the brains of their laboratory animals because they placed them there. In addition, they can confirm the precise location of the lesions by examining slices of the animals' brains under a microscope after the behavioral testing is completed. However, study of the human brain is a different matter. **Neuropsychologists** attempt to understand human brain functions by studying the behavior of people whose brains have been damaged. (For example, neuropsychologists carry out experiments such as the one I described in the opening vignette.) Most human brain lesions are the result of natural causes, such as a stroke. Strokes usually occur when a blood clot obstructs an artery in the brain and thus blocks the supply of oxygen and nutrients to a particular region, causing that region to die. In order to relate the brain damage to the behavioral

changes, neuropsychologists must know just where the damage is.

The development of several different diagnostic machines has revolutionized neuropsychological research. The machine most commonly used is the **CT scanner**. (*CT* stands for *computerized tomography. Tomos,* meaning "cut," describes the CT scanner's ability to produce a picture that looks like a slice of the brain.) The scanner sends a narrow beam of X rays through a person's head. The beam is moved around the patient's head, and a computer calculates the amount of radiation that passes through at various points along each an-

The CT scanner allows the operator to view a two-dimensional image of a "slice" of a person's brain. Imaging devices such as CT and MRI scanners have become an indispensable tool for neuropsychological research.

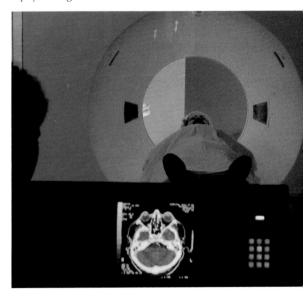

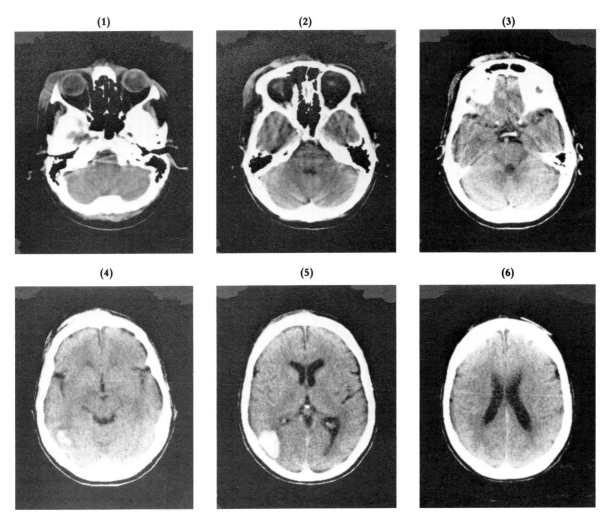

Figure 3.4 A complete set of CT scans from a patient with a lesion in the right occipital-parietal area. On CT scans left and right are reversed. (Courtesy of Dr. J.McA. Jones, Good Samaritan Hospital, Portland, Oregon.)

gle. The result is a two-dimensional image of a "slice" of the person's head, parallel to the top of the skull.

Although it was developed to assist neurologists and neurosurgeons to see tumors, regions destroyed by strokes, and other abnormalities within the brain, the CT scanner has become an indispensable tool for neuropsychological research. Now the investigator can determine the approximate location of a brain lesion in a living patient. Knowing the results of behavioral testing and the location of the brain damage, the neuropsychologist can compare them and make inferences about the normal function of the missing brain tissue. Figure 3.4 shows several CT scans of the brain of a patient with a lesion caused by a stroke. The scans are arranged from the bottom of the brain (scan 1) to the top (scan 6). You can easily see the lesion, a white spot, in the lower left corner of scan 5. (See *Figure 3.4.*)

Although the CT scanner is still the most commonly used brain-scanning device, two other machines, the *MRI scanner* and the *PET scanner* (for "magnetic resonance imagery" and "positron emission tomography," respectively), are becoming more common. At present the MRI scanner is much more expensive than the CT scanner, but it provides pictures of the brain that show much more detail, and it does so with the use of magnetic fields and radio waves rather than with X rays. Figure 3.5 shows an MRI scan of the head. As you can see, this image is extremely realistic and detailed. (See *Figure 3.5.*) The PET scan is used to investigate chemical processes within the brain. A person is given a harmless dose of a radioactive substance, which enters the brain. The chemical accumulates in particular regions of the brain; the locations depend on the specific nature of the chemical. Figure 3.6 shows PET scans after the use of a chemical that becomes concentrated

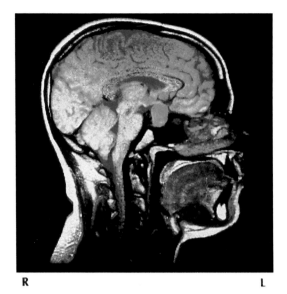

Figure 3.5 An MRI scan of a human brain. Color has been added by the computer to emphasize differences in density. (Mallinkrodt Institute of Radiology.)

Figure 3.6 PET scans of the left side of the brain, showing the regions with the highest amount of neural activity. The scans show that different regions of the brain are activated by different tasks. [*Discover*, 1989, *10(3)*, p. 61. Reprinted by permission of the publisher.]

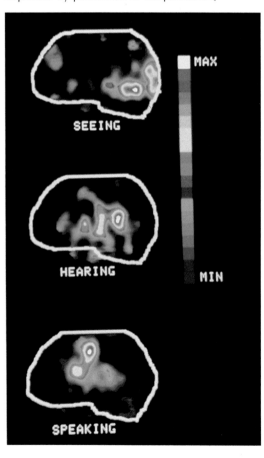

in regions of the brain that contain the most active nerve cells. As you can see, different regions become active when the person sees images, hears sounds, or talks. (See *Figure 3.6.*)

Structure of the Nervous System

2 The nervous system consists of two divisions: the **central nervous system** (the brain and spinal cord) and the **peripheral nervous system** (the nerves, which transmit information between the central nervous system and the rest of the body). (See *Figure 3.7.*)

The human brain has three major parts: the *brain stem*, the *cerebellum*, and the *cerebral hemispheres*. If the human brain is removed from the skull, it looks as if it has a handle or stem. The **brain stem** constitutes one of the most primitive regions of the brain, and its functions are correspondingly basic ones—primarily control of physiological functions and automatic behaviors. In fact, the brains of some animals, such as amphibians, consist primarily of a brain stem and a simple cerebellum. (See *Figure 3.8.*)

Figure 3.7 The central nervous system (brain and spinal cord) and the peripheral nervous system (cranial nerves and spinal nerves).

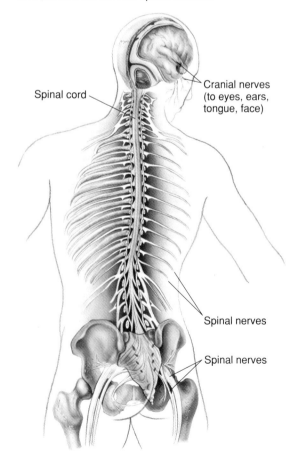

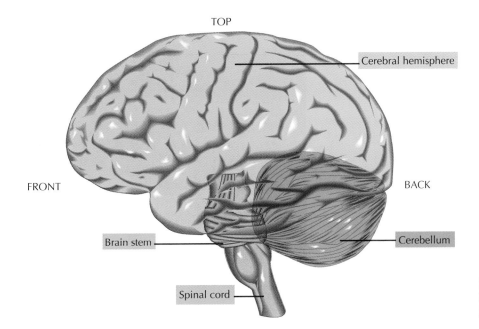

TOP

Cerebral hemisphere

FRONT

BACK

Brain stem

Cerebellum

Spinal cord

Figure 3.8 The three major parts of the brain: brain stem, cerebellum, and cerebral hemispheres.

The **cerebral hemispheres** constitute the largest part of the human brain. They contain the parts of the brain that evolved most recently; thus, this chapter will largely concern itself with the functions of the cerebral hemispheres. The **cerebellum** looks like a miniature version of the cerebral hemispheres, attached to the back of the brain stem. Its primary function is to control and coordinate movements. (See *Figure 3.8.*)

Because the central nervous system is so important, it is exceptionally well protected. The brain is encased in the skull, and the spinal cord runs through the middle of a column of hollow bones, the **vertebrae.** (Refer to *Figure 3.7.*) Both the brain and the spinal cord are enclosed by a three-layered set of membranes called the **meninges.** (*Meninges* is the plural of *meninx,* the Greek word for "membrane." You have probably heard of *meningitis,* which is an inflammation of the meninges.) The brain and spinal cord do not come into direct contact with the bones of the skull and vertebrae. Instead, they float in a clear liquid called **cerebrospinal fluid (CSF).** This liquid fills the space between two of the meninges, thus providing a liquid cushion that surrounds the brain and spinal cord and protects them from being bruised by the bones that encase them.

The central nervous system of a human embryo begins its existence as a hollow tube, and it maintains this basic shape even after it is fully developed. The brain contains four interconnected chambers called **ventricles** (from the Latin word for "belly"). The ventricles are filled with cerebrospinal fluid—in fact, they contain the tissue that produces it. Early in development the central nervous system contains three chambers. The tissue that surrounds them becomes the *forebrain,* the *midbrain,* and the *hindbrain.* (See *Figure 3.9a.*) Later, the front chamber expands, dividing into three ventricles, which are eventually surrounded by the cerebral hemispheres. The middle chamber contracts into a thin tube that connects the three ventricles of the forebrain with the one of the hindbrain. (See *Figures 3.9b* and *3.9c.*)

The surface of the cerebral hemispheres is covered by the **cerebral cortex.** (The word *cortex* means "bark" or "rind.") The cerebral cortex consists of a thin layer of tissue approximately 3 millimeters thick. It contains billions of nerve cells. It is here that perceptions take place, memories are stored, and plans are formulated and executed. The human cerebral cortex is very wrinkled; it is full of bulges separated by grooves. The bulges are called *gyri* (singular, *gyrus*), and the large grooves are called *fissures.* Fissures and gyri greatly increase the amount of surface area of the cortex. Thus, animals with the largest and most complex brains also have the most wrinkled brains.

The peripheral nervous system consists of the nerves that connect the central nervous system with sense organs, muscles, and glands. Nerves carry both incoming and outgoing traffic. The sense organs detect changes in the environment and send signals through the nerves to the central nervous system, and the brain sends signals through the nerves to the muscles (causing behavior) and the glands (producing adjustments in internal physiological processes).

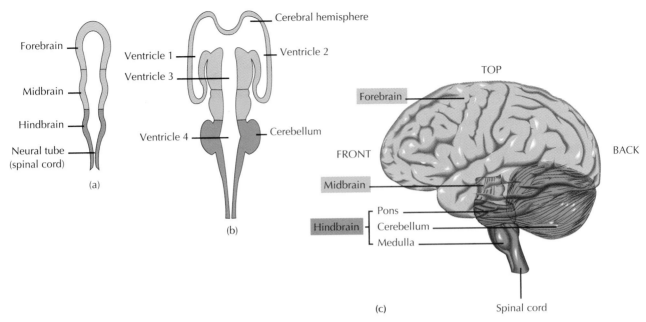

Figure 3.9 An outline of brain development. (a) Early development. (b) Late development, near the time of birth. (c) Adult brain.

Nerves are bundles of many thousands of individual fibers, all wrapped in a tough, protective membrane. Under a microscope nerves look something like telephone cables, with their bundles of wires. (See **Figure 3.10.**) Like the individual wires in a telephone cable, nerve fibers transmit messages through the nerve, from sense organ to brain or from brain to muscle or gland.

Some nerves are attached to the spinal cord. These *spinal nerves* serve all of the body below the neck, conveying sensory information from the body and carrying messages to muscles and glands. Other nerves are attached directly to the base of the brain; these *cranial nerves* primarily serve muscles and sense receptors in the neck and head. For example, when you taste food, the sensory information gets

Figure 3.10 Nerves. A nerve consists of a sheath of tissue that encases a bundle of individual nerve fibers (axons). BV, blood vessel; Fa, bundle of axons; A, individual axons; Ep and Pe, connective tissue. (From *Tissues and Organs: A Text-Atlas of Scanning Electron Microscopy.* By Richard G. Kessel and Randy H. Kardon. Copyright © 1979 by W.H. Freeman and Company. Reprinted by permission.)

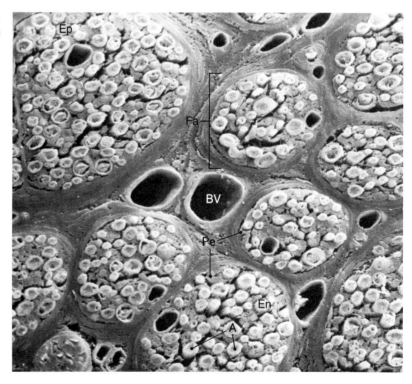

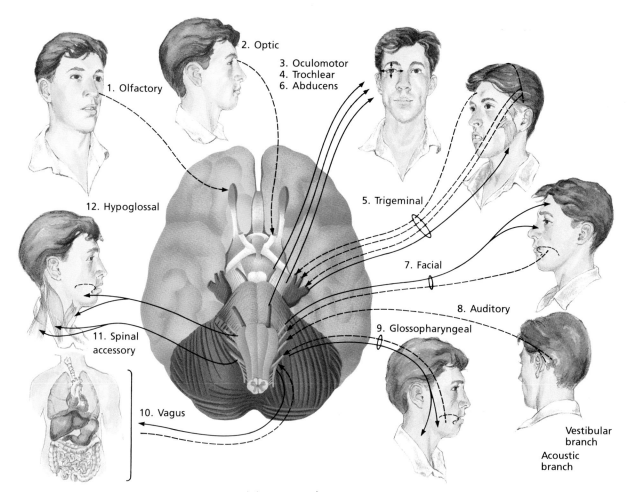

Figure 3.11 The twelve pairs of cranial nerves and the regions they serve.

from your tongue to your brain through one set of cranial nerves. And when you chew the food, the command to chew reaches your jaw muscles through another set of cranial nerves. (See *Figure 3.11.*)

INTERIM SUMMARY

Study of the Brain

The brain has two major functions: control of behavior and regulation of the body's physiological functions. Two groups of psychologists study the biology of behavior. Physiological psychologists usually study laboratory animals. They use a stereotaxic apparatus to destroy parts of the brain in animals or to place wires within an animal's brain in order to record electrical activity there or to stimulate it. They also investigate the effects of drugs or hormones on brain functions and behaviors. Neuropsychologists study people who have sustained brain

damage, correlating the person's behavioral deficits with the location of the lesion, usually determined by a CT scan or an MRI scan.

The central nervous system consists of the spinal cord and the three major divisions of the brain: the brain stem, the cerebellum, and the cerebral hemispheres. The cerebral hemispheres are wrinkled by the fissures and gyri and are covered by the cerebral cortex. The brain communicates with the rest of the body through the peripheral nervous system, which includes the spinal nerves and cranial nerves.

■

CONTROL OF BEHAVIOR

3 As we saw in the introduction to this chapter, the brain has two basic functions: controlling the movements of the muscles and regulating the physiological functions of the body. The first of these functions is, of course, of particular interest to psychology. So in this section we will examine the portions of the brain that control behavior.

Organization of the Cerebral Cortex

If we want to understand the brain functions most important to the study of behavior—perceiving, learning, planning, and moving—we should start with the cerebral cortex.

Regions of Primary Sensory and Motor Cortex. We become aware of events in our environment by means of the five major senses: vision, audition, olfaction, gustation (taste), and the somatosenses ("body" senses: touch, pain, and temperature). Three areas of the cerebral cortex receive information from the sensory organs. The **primary visual cortex,** which receives visual information, is located at the back of the brain, mostly hidden from view on the inner surfaces of the cerebral hemispheres. The **primary auditory cortex** is also mostly hidden from view on the inner surface of a deep fissure in the side of the brain. The **primary somatosensory cortex,** a vertical strip near the middle of the cerebral hemispheres, receives information from the body senses. As Figure 3.12 shows, different regions of the primary somatosensory cortex receive information from different regions of the body. In addition, the base of the somatosensory cortex receives information concerning taste. (See *Figure 3.12.*)

The three regions of primary sensory cortex in each hemisphere receive information from only one side of the body: the *opposite* side. Thus, the primary somatosensory cortex of the left hemisphere learns what the right hand is holding, the left primary visual cortex learns what is happening toward the person's right, and so on. The connections between the sensory organs and the cerebral cortex are said to be **contralateral** (*contra,* "opposite"; *lateral,* "side.")

The region of the cerebral cortex most directly involved in the control of movement is the **primary motor cortex,** located just in front of the primary somatosensory cortex. (Note that in this context *motor* is used in its original sense and refers to *movement,* not to mechanical engines.) Nerve cells in different parts of the primary motor cortex are connected to muscles in different parts of the body. The connections, like those of the posterior part of the brain, are contralateral; the left primary motor cortex controls the right side of the body, and vice versa. Thus, for example, if a surgeon electrically stimulates the "hand" region of the left primary motor cortex, the patient's right hand will move. (See *Figure 3.12.*) I like to think of the strip of primary motor cortex as the keyboard of a piano, with each key controlling a different movement. (We will see shortly who the "player" of this piano is.)

Association Cortex. The regions of primary sensory and motor cortex occupy only a small part of the cerebral cortex. The rest accomplishes what is done between sensation and action: perception, learning, planning, and acting. These processes take place in the *association areas* of the cerebral cortex.

The *central fissure* provides an important dividing line between the anterior (front) part of the cerebral cortex and the posterior (back) re-

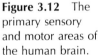

Figure 3.12 The primary sensory and motor areas of the human brain.

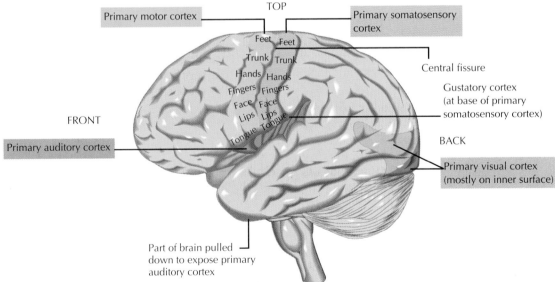

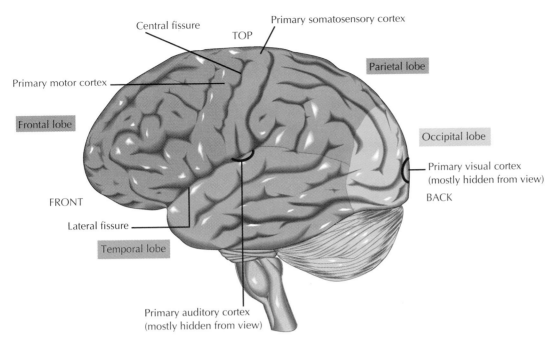

Central fissure
Primary somatosensory cortex
TOP
Parietal lobe
Primary motor cortex
Frontal lobe
Occipital lobe
Primary visual cortex
(mostly hidden from view)
FRONT
BACK
Lateral fissure
Temporal lobe
Primary auditory cortex
(mostly hidden from view)

Figure 3.13   The four lobes of the cerebral cortex.

gions. The anterior region is involved in movement-related activities, such as planning and carrying out behaviors. The posterior part is involved in perceiving and learning.

Discussing the various regions of the cerebral cortex is easier if we have names for them. In fact, the cerebral cortex is divided into four areas, or *lobes,* named for the bones of the skull that cover them: the frontal lobe, parietal lobe, temporal lobe, and occipital lobe. (Of course, the brain contains two of each lobe, one in each hemisphere.) The **frontal lobe** includes everything in front of the central fissure. The **parietal lobe** (the "wall") is located on the side of the cerebral hemisphere, just behind the central fissure, in back of the frontal lobe. The **temporal lobe** (the "temple") juts forward from the base of the brain, beneath the frontal and parietal lobes. The **occipital lobe** (*ob,* "in back of"; *caput,* "head") lies at the very back of the brain, behind the parietal and temporal lobes. (See *Figure 3.13.*)

Each primary sensory area of the cerebral cortex sends information to adjacent areas of the cortex, called the **sensory association cortex.** Circuits of nerve cells in the sensory association cortex analyze the information received from the primary sensory cortex; perception takes place there, and memories are stored there. The regions of sensory association cortex located closest to the primary sensory areas receive information from only one sensory system. For example, the region closest to the primary visual cortex analyzes visual information and stores visual memories. Regions of sensory association cortex located far from the primary sensory areas receive information from more than one sensory system; thus, they are involved in several kinds of perceptions and memories. (See *Figure 3.14.*)

Just as regions of the sensory association cortex of the posterior part of the brain are involved in perceiving and remembering, the frontal association cortex is involved in the planning and execution of movements. Thus, the anterior part of the frontal lobe is called the **motor association cortex.** This region controls the primary motor cortex; thus, it directly controls behavior. If the primary motor cortex is the keyboard of the piano, then the motor association cortex is the piano player. Obviously, we behave in response to events happening in the world around us. Therefore, the sensory association cortex of the posterior part of the brain sends information about the environment to the motor association cortex, which translates the information into plans and actions. (See *Figure 3.14.*)

Lateralization of Function

Although the two cerebral hemispheres cooperate with each other, they do not perform identical functions. Some functions are *lateralized—*

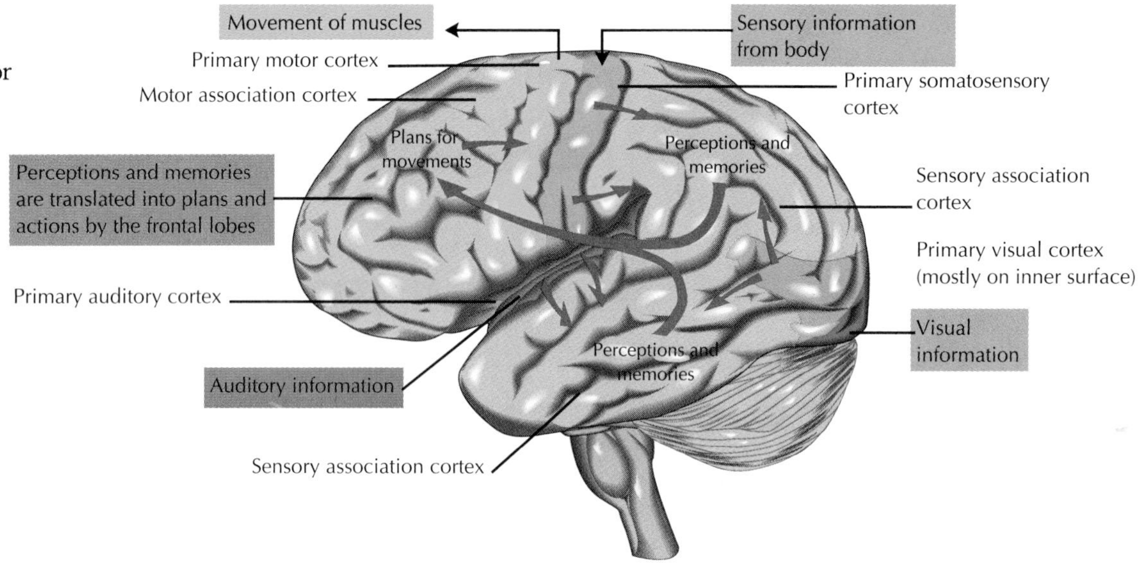

Figure 3.14 The relation between the regions of primary sensory and primary motor cortex and association cortex.

located primarily on one side of the brain. In general, the left hemisphere participates in the *analysis* of information—the extraction of the elements that make up the whole of an experience. This ability makes the left hemisphere particularly good at recognizing events whose elements occur one after the other and controlling serial behaviors. (In a few people the functions of the left and right hemispheres are reversed.) Included in the list of serial behaviors are verbal activities, such as talking, understanding the speech of other people, reading, and writing. These abilities are disrupted by damage to the various regions of the left hemisphere. (I will say more about this topic in Chapters 7 and 9.)

In contrast, the right hemisphere is specialized for *synthesis;* it is particularly good at putting isolated elements together to perceive things as a whole. Damage to the right hemisphere disrupts people's ability to draw sketches (especially of three-dimensional objects), read maps, and construct complex objects out of smaller elements.

The Occipital Lobe: Vision

4 The primary business of the occipital lobe is seeing. (Refer to *Figure 3.13.*) Total damage to the primary visual cortex produces blindness, but a small lesion in the primary visual cortex only produces a "hole" in the field of vision. A person with such a lesion can move his or her eyes around and eventually see everything in the environment. (Imagine looking at the world

through a cardboard tube that you have to move around in order to see everything.)

The effects of damage to the visual association cortex are more interesting, psychologically. Such damage will not cause blindness. In fact, visual acuity may be very good; the person may be able to see small objects and may even be able to read. However, he or she will not be able to recognize objects by sight. For example, when looking at a drawing of a clock, the person may say he or she sees a circle, two short lines forming an angle in the center of a circle, and some dots spaced along the inside of the circle, but will not be able to recognize what the picture shows. On the other hand, if the person is handed a *real* clock, he or she will immediately recognize it by touch. Similarly, the person may fail to recognize his or her spouse by sight but will be able to do so from the sound of the spouse's voice. This deficit in visual perception is called **visual agnosia** (*a-*, "without"; *gnosis,* "knowledge"). I will have more to say about it in Chapter 5.

The Temporal Lobe: Audition

The principal sensory function of the temporal lobe is hearing. (Refer to *Figure 3.13.*) Damage to the temporal lobe results in a variety of symptoms, depending on which region is destroyed and whether the left or right hemisphere is affected. Damage to the left auditory association cortex causes severe language deficits. People with such damage are no longer able to comprehend speech, presumably because they have lost the circuits of nerve cells that decode speech sounds. However, the deficit is more severe than that. They lose the ability to *produce* meaningful speech; their speech becomes a jumble of words. I will say more about the language deficits produced by brain damage in Chapter 9.

Damage to the auditory association cortex in the right hemisphere does not seriously affect speech perception or production, but it does affect the ability to recognize nonspeech sounds, including patterns of tones and rhythms. The damage can also impair a person's ability to perceive the location of sounds in the environment. As we will see later in this chapter, the right hemisphere is very important in the perception of space. The contribution of the right temporal lobe to this function is to participate in perceiving the placement of sounds.

The Parietal Lobe: Somatosensation and Spatial Perception

The primary sensory function of the parietal lobe is perception of the body. (Refer to *Figure 3.13.*) However, the association cortex of the parietal lobe is involved in much more than somatosensation. Damage to a particular region of the left parietal lobe can disrupt the ability to read or write without causing serious impairment in the ability to talk and understand the speech of other people. Damage to the parietal lobe also impairs a person's ability to draw. When the left parietal lobe is damaged, the primary deficit seems to be in the person's ability to make his or her hand go where it should. In contrast, the primary deficit produced by damage to the right parietal lobe is perceptual. The person can analyze the picture into its parts but has trouble integrating these parts into a consistent whole. Thus, he or she has difficulty drawing a coherent picture.

People with right parietal lobe damage also exhibit a symptom called *unilateral* (one-sided) *neglect.* People with unilateral neglect fail to pay attention to stimuli toward the left side of their body. For example, they will notice people standing to their right or straight in front of them but will ignore people standing to their left. Sometimes, they even fail to attend to the left side of their own body. They will shave or apply makeup only to the right side of their face, ignoring the left. If someone points to their left arm, they will then notice it but may deny that it belongs to them. Figure 3.15 shows unilateral neglect in a drawing of a clock by a man who had sustained damage to the right parietal lobe.

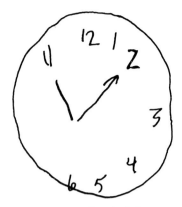

Figure 3.15 Drawing of a clock by a patient with damage to the right parietal lobe. (From Kaplan, E., and Velis, D.C. *The Neuropsychology of 10 after 11.* Paper presented at the International Neuropsychological Society Annual Meeting, Mexico City, 1983. Reprinted with permission.)

Once he drew the circle, he seemed to forget about its left side and neglected to include the numbers that should have gone there. (See *Figure 3.15.*)

Most neurologists and neuropsychologists believe that the left parietal lobe plays an important role in our ability to keep track of the location of the moving parts of our own body, whereas the right parietal lobe helps us keep track of the space around us. People with right parietal lobe damage usually have difficulty with tasks related to space, such as reading a map. People with left parietal lobe damage usually have difficulty with parts of their own body; for example, when asked to point to their elbow, they may actually point to their shoulder.

People with parietal lobe damage often have difficulty performing arithmetic calculations. This deficit is probably related to other spatially related functions of the parietal lobe. For example, try to multiply 55 by 12 without using pencil and paper. Close your eyes and work on the problem for a while. Try to analyze how you did it.

Most people report that they try to imagine the numbers arranged one above the other as they would be if paper and pencil were being used. They "write" the problem out mentally. Apparently, damage to the parietal lobes makes it impossible for people to keep the numbers in place and remember what they were.

The Frontal Lobe: Planning and Moving

The principal function of the frontal lobe is motor activity. (Refer to *Figure 3.13.*) However, the frontal lobe does much more. Its functions seem to be related to planning, changing strategies, being aware of oneself, attending to emotionally related stimuli, and performing a variety of spontaneous behaviors. It also contains a region involved in the control of speech.

Damage to the primary motor cortex produces a very specific effect: paralysis of the side of the body opposite to the brain damage. If a portion of the region is damaged, then only the corresponding parts of the body will be paralyzed. However, damage to the motor association cortex produces more interesting effects.

1. *Slowing of thoughts and behavior and loss of spontaneity.* The person will react to events in the environment, but he or she will not take much initiative. When a person with such damage is asked to say or write as many words as possible, he or she will have great difficulty coming up with more than a few, even though there is no problem in understanding words or identifying objects by name.

2. *Perseveration.* People with damage to the frontal lobes tend to have difficulty changing strategies. If given a task to solve, they may solve it readily; but then they will fail to abandon the strategy and learn a new one if the problem is changed.

3. *Loss of self-awareness and changes in emotional reactions.* People with damaged frontal lobes often have rather bland personalities. They react with indifference to events that would normally be expected to affect them emotionally. For example, they may show no signs of distress at the death of a close relative. They have little insight into their own problems and are uncritical of their performance on various tasks. They do not even seem to be bothered by pain, although they may say that they still *feel* it.

4. *Deficiencies in foresight and planning.* In terms of daily living the most important consequences of damage to the frontal lobes are probably lack of foresight and difficulty in planning. A person with frontal lobe damage might perform fairly well on a test of intelligence but be unable to hold a job. Presumably, planning is related to the general motor functions of the frontal lobes. Just as we can use the posterior regions of the brain to imagine something we have perceived, we can use the frontal region to imagine something we might do. Perhaps we test various possible actions by imagining ourselves doing them and guessing what the consequences of these actions might be. When people's frontal lobes are damaged, they often do things or say things that have unfavorable consequences because the ability to plan their actions is lost.

As we saw in Chapter 1, Paul Broca discovered that damage to a region of the left frontal lobe disrupts speech. This region, which we now call Broca's area, lies just in front of the "face" region of the primary motor cortex. (See *Figure 3.16.*) Thus, Broca's area controls the muscles used for talking. Circuits of neurons located in Broca's area appear to contain the memories of the sequences of muscular movements that are needed to pronounce words. I will have more to say about the effects of lesions of Broca's area in Chapter 9.

Figure 3.16 Broca's area, located just in front of the face region of the primary motor cortex.

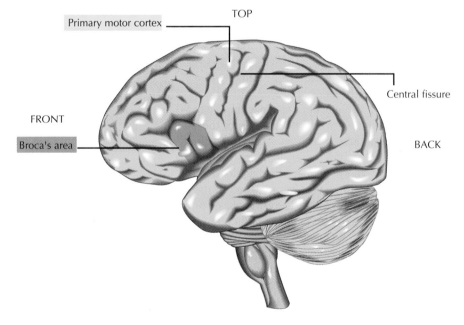

INTERIM SUMMARY
Control of Behavior

The cerebral cortex is organized into the three regions of the primary sensory cortex (visual, auditory, and somatosensory), the primary motor cortex, and the association cortex. Suppose you see a rose and then pick it and smell it. You see it because light reflected from it stimulates sensory receptors in the retinas of your eyes. The stimulation is transmitted through the optic nerves, one of the pairs of cranial nerves. The information reaches the primary visual cortex in the occipital lobe. Your perception of the rose causes you to remember how beautiful one looks in a vase on your desk. This memory, located in the visual association cortex, causes messages to be sent forward to the motor association cortex (the "piano player") in your frontal lobes. There, plans are made to pick the rose. Impulses are sent to your primary motor cortex and from there to the muscles that control your legs. As you move toward the rose, new sensory information received by the posterior lobes informs the frontal lobes about the appropriate movements. You reach for the rose and pick it.

When you pick the rose, you feel the stem with your fingers. The pressure of the stem on your skin stimulates touch receptors within your skin. This somatosensory information is transmitted to the spinal cord by means of a spinal nerve. It is then sent up through the spinal cord and is relayed to the primary somatosensory cortex. Next, your frontal lobes direct your hand to bring the rose under your nose and then command your muscles to make you breathe in some air. The aromatic molecules from the rose stimulate olfactory receptors embedded in the ceiling of your nasal cavity. The information is transmitted to your brain through the olfactory nerves, another pair of cranial nerves.

The right and left hemispheres are somewhat specialized. The left hemisphere is mostly concerned with details of perception and with events that occur one after the other, such as the series of sounds that constitute speech or the symbols that constitute writing. The right hemisphere is mostly concerned with the general form and shape of things.

The frontal lobes are concerned with motor functions, including planning and formulation of strategies. A region of the left frontal cortex is specialized for control of speech. The three lobes behind the central fissure are generally concerned with sensation: somatosenses in the parietal lobe, vision in the occipital lobe, and audition in the temporal lobe. The other functions of these lobes are related to these sensory processes; for example, the parietal lobes are concerned with perception of space as well as knowledge about the body. ■

CONTROL OF INTERNAL FUNCTIONS AND AUTOMATIC BEHAVIORS

5 So far, I have discussed brain functions involved in perceiving, remembering, planning, and acting. I have talked primarily about the role of the cerebral cortex in these activities. However, there is much more to the brain than the cerebral cortex; after all, the cortex consists of only the outer 3 millimeters of the surface of the cerebral hemispheres. We must still consider the brain stem, the cerebellum, and the interior of the cerebral hemispheres.

As we shall see, the primary function of the cerebellum is to help the cerebral hemispheres control movements and to initiate some automatic movements, such as postural adjustment. The brain stem and much of the interior of the cerebral hemispheres are involved in homeostasis and control of species-typical behaviors. **Homeostasis** (from the root words *homoio,* "similar," and *stasis,* "standstill") refers to maintaining a proper balance of physiological variables such as temperature, concentration of fluids, and the amount of nutrients stored within the body. **Species-typical behaviors** are the behaviors exhibited by most members of a species that are important to survival, such as eating, drinking, fighting, courting, mating, and caring for offspring.

The Brain Stem

The brain stem is divided into three structures: the *medulla,* the *pons,* and the *midbrain.* (See *Figure 3.17.*) These structures contain circuits of neurons that control functions and behaviors vital to the survival of the organism in general and of the species in particular. For example, circuits of neurons in the **medulla,** the part of the brain stem that is closest to the spinal cord, control heart rate, blood pressure, rate of respiration, and (especially in simpler animals) crawling or swimming motions. Circuits of neurons in the **pons,** the part of the brain just anterior to the medulla, control some of the stages of sleep. Circuits of neurons in the **midbrain** control movements used in fighting and sexual behavior and decrease sensitivity to pain while engaged in these activities.

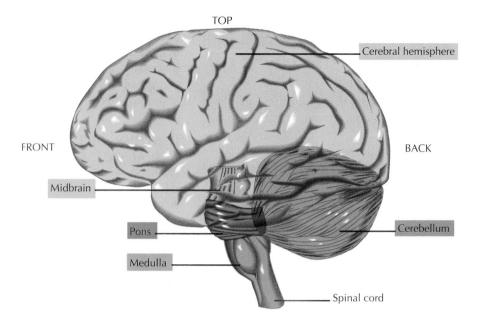

Figure 3.17 The divisions of the brain stem: the medulla, the pons, and the midbrain.

The Cerebellum

The cerebellum plays an important role in the control of movement. It receives sensory information, especially about the position of the body parts; thus, it knows what the parts of the body are doing. It also receives information from the cortex of the frontal lobes; thus, it knows what movements the frontal lobes intend to accomplish. The cerebellum is basically a computer that compares the location of the body parts with the intended movements and assists the frontal lobes in executing these movements. Without the cerebellum the frontal lobes would produce jerky, uncoordinated, inaccurate movements (which is exactly what happens when a person's cerebellum is damaged). Besides helping the frontal lobes accomplish their tasks, the cerebellum monitors information regarding posture and balance, to keep us from falling down when we stand or walk, and produces eye movements that compensate for changes in the position of the head.

Structures Within the Cerebral Hemispheres

The Thalamus. If you stripped away the cerebral cortex, you would find a layer of nerve fibers that connect the cortex with the rest of the brain. These fibers are referred to as **white matter** because of the shiny white appearance of the substance that coats and insulates them. If you then stripped away the white matter, you would reach the **thalamus,** located in the heart of the cerebral hemispheres. The thalamus has two parts, one in each cerebral hemisphere. Each part looks rather like a football, with the long axis oriented from front to back. (See *Figure 3.18.*)

The thalamus performs two basic functions. The first—and most primitive—is similar to that of the cerebral cortex. Parts of the thalamus receive sensory information, other parts integrate the information, and yet other parts control behaviors through their influence on circuits of neurons in the brain stem. However, the second role of the thalamus—that of a relay

The cerebellum plays an important role in the control of movement and in monitoring information regarding posture and balance.

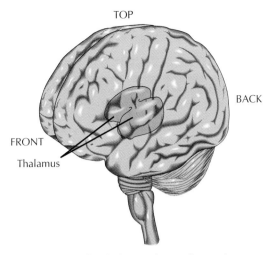

Figure 3.18 The thalamus, located near the center of the cerebral hemispheres.

station for the cortex—is even more important. As the cerebral hemispheres evolved, the cerebral cortex grew in size and its significance for behavioral functions increased. The thalamus took on the function of receiving sensory information from the sensory organs, performing some simple analyses, and passing the results on to the primary sensory cortex. Thus, all sensory information (except for olfaction, which is the most primitive of all sensory systems) is sent to the thalamus before it reaches the cerebral cortex.

The Hypothalamus. *Hypo-* means "less than" or "beneath," and as its name suggests, the **hypothalamus** is located below the thalamus, at the base of the brain. The hypothalamus

Figure 3.19 The hypothalamus and the pituitary gland.

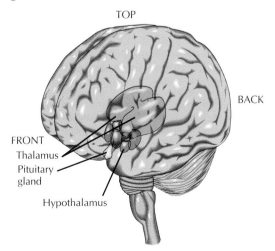

The hypothalamus regulates much of the activity of the autonomic nervous system, which controls functions involved in the regulation of body temperature such as sweating.

is a small region, consisting of less than 1 cubic centimeter of tissue (smaller than a grape). Its relative importance far exceeds its relative size. (See **Figure 3.19.**)

The hypothalamus, like the brain stem, participates in homeostasis and species-typical behaviors. The hypothalamus receives sensory information, including information from receptors inside the organs of the body; thus, it is informed about changes in the organism's physiological status. It also contains specialized sensors of its own that monitor various characteristics of the blood that flows through the brain, such as temperature, nutrient content, and amount of dissolved salts. In turn, the hypothalamus controls the **pituitary gland,** which is located on the end of a stalk attached directly to the base of the hypothalamus. (See **Figure 3.19.**)

The pituitary gland has been called the "master gland" because it controls the activity of the rest of the **endocrine glands,** which secrete hormones. Thus, by controlling the pituitary gland, the hypothalamus exerts control over the entire endocrine system. Some of the hormones secreted by the endocrine glands, such as the sex hormones, have important effects on behavior and will be discussed in later

Table 3.1 The major endocrine glands, the hormones they secrete, and their principal functions

Gland	Hormone	Function
Adrenal gland		
Cortex	Aldosterone	Excretion of sodium and potassium
	Androgens	Growth of pubic and underarm hair; sex drive (women)
	Cortisone	Metabolism; response to stress
Medulla	Epinephrine, norepinephrine	Metabolism; response to stress
Hypothalamus[a]	Releasing hormones	Control of anterior pituitary hormone secretion
Kidneys	Renin	Control of aldosterone secretion; blood pressure
Ovaries	Estradiol	Maturation of female reproductive system; secondary sex characteristics
	Progesterone	Maintenance of lining of uterus; promotion of pregnancy
Pancreas	Insulin, glucagon	Regulation of metabolism
Pituitary gland		
Anterior	Adrenocorticotropic hormone	Control of adrenal cortex
	Gonadotropic hormones	Control of testes and ovaries
	Growth hormone	Growth; control of metabolism
	Prolactin	Milk production
	Thyroid-stimulating hormone	Control of thyroid gland
Posterior	Antidiuretic hormone[b]	Excretion of water
	Oxytocin[b]	Release of milk; contraction of uterus
Testes	Testosterone	Maturation of male reproductive system; sperm production; secondary sex characteristics; sex drive (men)
Thyroid gland	Thyroxine	Energy metabolism; growth and development

[a] The hypothalamus, although it is part of the brain, secretes hormones; thus, it can be considered to be an endocrine gland.
[b] These hormones are produced by the hypothalamus but are transported to and released from the posterior pituitary gland.

chapters. *Table 3.1* lists some of the endocrine glands and the functions they regulate; and *Figure 3.20* shows their location in the body.

The hypothalamus also controls much of the activity of the **autonomic nervous system,** which consists of nerves that control the functions of the glands and internal organs. Thus, the autonomic nervous system controls activities such as sweating, shedding tears, salivating, secreting digestive juices, changing the size of blood vessels (thus altering blood pressure), and secreting some hormones. The autonomic nervous system has two branches, the sympathetic branch and the parasympathetic branch. The **sympathetic branch** directs activities that involve the expenditure of energy; the **parasympathetic branch** controls quiet activities such as digestion of food. Psychophysiologists monitor many of the responses produced by these two branches; in doing so, they can measure the activity of the autonomic nervous system and its relation to psychological phenom-

ena such as emotions. For example, when a person is angry, his or her heart rate and blood pressure rise. The lie detector (which is described in Chapter 12) works by recording emotional responses controlled by the autonomic nervous system. (See *Table 3.2.*)

The homeostatic functions of the hypothalamus can involve either internal physiological changes or behaviors. For example, the hypothalamus is involved in the control of body temperature. It can directly lower body temperature by causing sweating to occur, or it can raise it by causing shivering to occur. If these measures are inadequate, it can send messages to the cerebral cortex that will cause the person to engage in a learned behavior, such as turning on an air conditioner or putting another log on the fire. Damage to the hypothalamus can cause impaired regulation of body temperature, changes in food intake, sterility, or stunting of growth. Obviously, the hypothalamus is a very important structure.

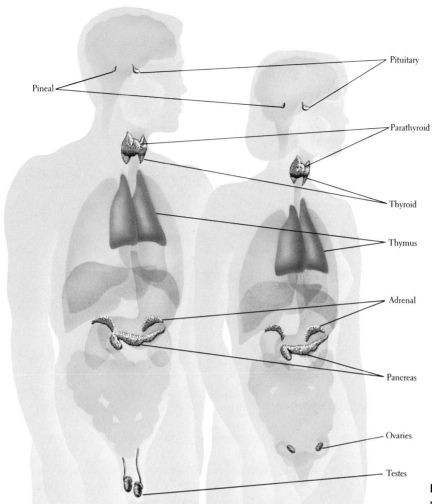

Figure 3.20 The location of the principal endocrine glands.

Table 3.2 Major functions of the autonomic nervous system

	Effect of Activity of Autonomic Nerve Fibers	
Organ	*Sympathetic*	*Parasympathetic*
Adrenal medulla	Secretion of epinephrine and norepinephrine	
Bladder	Inhibition of contraction	Contraction
Blood vessels		
Abdomen	Constriction	
Muscles	Dilation	Constriction
Skin	Constriction or dilation	Dilation
Heart	Faster rate of contraction	Slower rate of contraction
Intestines	Decreased activity	Increased activity
Lacrimal glands	Secretion of tears	
Liver	Release of glucose	
Lungs	Dilation of bronchi	Constriction of bronchi
Penis	Ejaculation	Erection
Pupil of eye	Dilation	Constriction
Salivary glands	Secretion of thick, viscous saliva	Secretion of thin, enzyme-rich saliva
Sweat glands	Secretion of sweat	
Vagina	Orgasm	Secretion of lubricating fluid

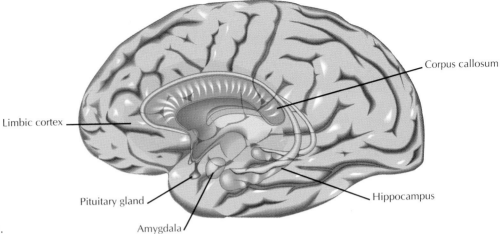

Figure 3.21 The principal structures of the limbic system.

The Limbic System. The **limbic system,** a set of structures located in the cerebral hemispheres, plays an important role in learning and in the expression of emotion. The limbic system consists of several regions of the **limbic cortex**—the cerebral cortex located around the edge of the cerebral hemispheres, where they join with the brain stem. (The word *limbus* means "border"; hence the term *limbic* system.) Besides the cortex, the most important components of the limbic system are the *amygdala* and the *hippocampus*. The amygdala and hippocampus get their names from their shapes; *amygdala* means "almond" and *hippocampus* means "sea horse." (See *Figure 3.21.*)

Damage to the **amygdala,** a cluster of nerve cells in the depth of the temporal lobe, affects emotional behaviors. Some of the effects of lesions of the amygdala in laboratory animals include indiscriminate sexuality (attempts to copulate with everything in sight) and loss of aggressive and defensive behaviors. The amygdala may also be responsible for some of the control the brain exerts on the immune system. As we shall see in Chapter 12, both physical and mental stress can decrease the activity of the immune system, lowering a person's defenses against infectious diseases and (perhaps) the growth of cancer cells.

The **hippocampus,** a collection of structures located just behind the amygdala, plays an important role in memory. People with lesions of the hippocampus lose the ability to learn anything new. For them, "yesterday" is always the time before their brain damage occurred; everything after that slips away, just as the memory of dreams often slips away from a person soon after awakening. I will have more to say about this phenomenon in Chapter 7, which discusses human memory.

INTERIM SUMMARY

Control of Internal Functions and Automatic Behaviors

The more primitive parts of the brain control homeostasis and species-typical behaviors. The brain stem, which consists of the medulla, the pons, and the midbrain, contains neural circuits that control vital physiological functions and produce automatic movements such as those used in locomotion, fighting, and sexual behavior. The cerebellum assists the cerebral cortex in carrying out movements; it coordinates the control of muscles, resulting in smooth movements. It also regulates postural adjustments.

Within the cerebral hemispheres the thalamus controls some primitive behaviors and relays sensory information to the cerebral cortex. The hypothalamus receives sensory information from sense receptors elsewhere in the body and also contains specialized receptors of its own, such as those used to monitor body temperature. It controls the pituitary gland, which in turn controls most of the endocrine glands of the body; and it also controls the internal organs through the nerves of the autonomic nervous system. The hypothalamus can control homeostatic processes directly and automatically, through its control of the pituitary gland and the autonomic nervous system, or it can cause neural circuits in the cerebral cortex to execute more complex, learned behaviors.

The amygdala and the hippocampus, both located within the temporal lobe, are important parts of the limbic system. The amygdala is involved in emotions and emotional behaviors, such as defense and aggression, and may play a role in the brain's control of the immune system. The hippocampus is involved in learning and memory; people with damage to this structure can remember their old memories but are unable to learn anything new. ∎

NEURONS

6 So far in this chapter I have been referring somewhat vaguely to "circuits of nerve cells" and "transmission of information" from place to place within the nervous system. Now that you have been introduced to the structure of the nervous system and have learned something about the functions of its parts, it is time to turn our attention to the elements that actually do the work of the nervous system: neurons.

Structure

Neurons, or nerve cells, are the elements of the nervous system that bring sensory information to the brain, store memories, reach decisions, and control the activity of the muscles. A neuron is shown in Figure 3.22; it has four principal parts.

1. The **soma,** or cell body, is the largest part of the neuron and contains the mechanisms that control the metabolism and maintenance of the cell. The soma also receives messages from other neurons. (See *Figure 3.22.*)
2. The **dendrites,** the treelike growths attached to the soma, function principally to receive messages from other neurons. (*Dendron* means "tree.") They transmit the information they receive down their "trunks" to the soma. (See *Figure 3.22.*)

3. The nerve fiber, or **axon,** carries messages away from the soma toward the cells with which the neuron communicates. (See *Figure 3.22.*) The message carried by the axon involves an electrical current, but it does not travel down the axon the way electricity travels through a wire. For one thing, electricity travels through a wire at the rate of 186,000 miles per second (the speed of light), or almost 300 million meters per second. As we saw in Chapter 1, Helmholtz discovered that the axon transmits information at a much slower rate—less than 100 meters per second.

The message carried by the axon resembles that of a fuse used for explosives. When one end of a fuse is lit, the flame travels to the opposite end, where the explosive is located. Similarly, when an axon is stimulated at one end, it sends an electrical message called the **action potential** down to the other end. (Of course, there is no explosion.) These action potentials follow all of the branches of the axon, down to their terminal buttons. But unlike an explosive fuse, the axon is reusable; messages can be sent down it repeatedly. For convenience, I will often refer to an action potential as the *firing* of an axon.

4. The **terminal buttons** are located at the ends of the "twigs" that branch off the ends of axons. (See *Figure 3.22.*) Terminal buttons secrete a chemical called a **transmitter substance** whenever an action potential is sent down the axon (whenever the axon fires). The transmitter substance affects the activity of the other cells with which the neuron communi-

Figure 3.22 A neuron.

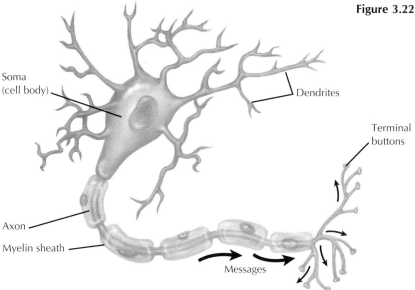

Soma
(cell body)

Dendrites

Terminal
buttons

Axon

Myelin sheath

Messages

cates. Thus, the message is conveyed from one neuron to another by a chemical. Most drugs that affect the nervous system (and hence alter a person's behavior) do so by affecting these chemical transmissions of messages from cell to cell.

Many axons, especially long ones, are insulated with a substance called *myelin*. The white matter located beneath the cerebral cortex gets its color from the **myelin sheaths** around the axons that travel through these areas. Myelin, part protein and part fat, is produced by special cells that individually wrap themselves around segments of the axon, leaving small bare patches of the axon between them. (See *Figure 3.22.*) The principal function of myelin is to insulate axons from each other and thus prevent the scrambling of messages. It also increases the speed of the action potential.

Synapses

7 Neurons communicate by means of synapses. A **synapse** is the conjunction of a terminal button of one neuron and a dendrite or the soma of another. (See *Figure 3.23 inset.*) A neuron receives messages from many terminal buttons that form synapses with it, and in turn it forms synapses with many other neurons. The drawing in Figure 3.23 is much simplified; an individual neuron can have tens of thousands of synapses on it.

Figure 3.24 illustrates the relation between a motor neuron and a muscle. A **motor neuron** is one that forms synapses with a muscle. When its axon fires, all the muscle fibers with which it forms synapses will contract with a brief twitch. (See *Figure 3.24.*) A muscle consists of thousands of individual muscle fibers. It is controlled by a large number of motor neurons, each of which forms synapses with different groups of muscle fibers. The strength of a muscular contraction, then, depends on the rate of firing of the axons that control it. If they fire at a high rate, the muscle contracts forcefully; if they fire at a low rate, the muscle contracts weakly.

Effects of Synaptic Transmission.   There are basically two types of synapses: *excitatory synapses* and *inhibitory synapses*. Excitatory synapses do just what their name implies. When the axon fires, they release a transmitter substance that excites the neurons with which they form a synapse. The effect of this excitation is to make it more likely that *these* neurons will fire. (The neuron that sends the message is called the **presynaptic neuron;** the one that receives the message is called the **postsynaptic neuron.**)

Inhibitory synapses do just the opposite. When they are activated, they lower the likelihood that the axon of the postsynaptic neuron will fire. Thus, the rate at which a particular axon fires is determined by the activity of the

Figure 3.23   *Synapses between several neurons.*

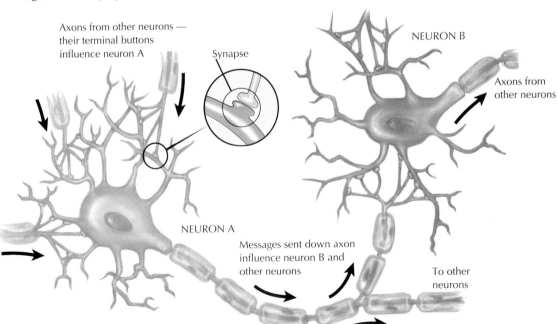

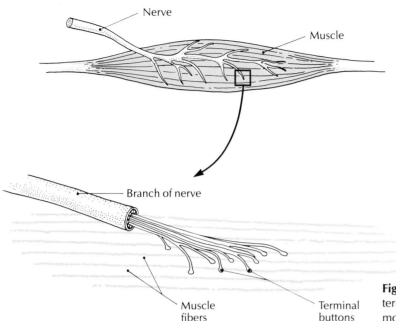

Figure 3.24 Synapses between terminal buttons of the axon of a motor neuron and a muscle.

synapses on the dendrites and soma of the cell. If the excitatory synapses are more active, the axon will fire at a high rate. If the inhibitory synapses are more active, it will fire at a low rate or, perhaps, not at all. (See *Figure 3.25.*)

A Simple Neural Circuit. The contest between excitatory and inhibitory synapses is the neural mechanism that takes place during decision making. The interconnections of the billions

Figure 3.25 Interaction between the effects of excitatory and inhibitory synapses. The rate of firing of the axon of Neuron C is controlled by these two factors.

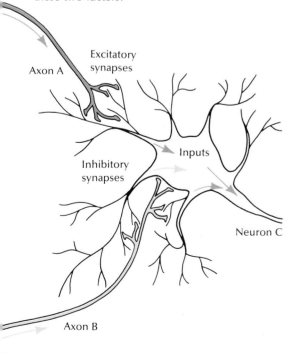

of neurons in our central nervous system provide us with the capacities for perception, decision making, memory, and action. Although we do not yet know enough to draw a "neural wiring diagram" for such complex functions, we can do so for some of the simpler reflexes that are triggered by certain kinds of sensory stimuli. For example, when your finger is pricked by a pin, your hand withdraws. When your eye is touched, your eyes close and your head draws back. When a baby's cheek is touched, it turns its mouth toward the object, and if the object is of the appropriate size and texture, the baby begins to suck. All these activities occur quickly, without requiring thought.

A simple withdrawal reflex, which is triggered by a noxious stimulus (such as a pinprick), requires three types of neurons. **Sensory neurons** detect the noxious stimulus and convey this information to the spinal cord. **Interneurons** receive the sensory information and in turn stimulate the motor neurons that cause the appropriate muscle to contract. (See *Figure 3.26.*) The sequence is simple and straightforward. A noxious stimulus applied to the skin produces a burst of action potentials in the sensory neurons. Their axons fire; and their terminal buttons, located within the spinal cord, release an excitatory transmitter substance. The chemical stimulates the interneurons and causes them to fire. They excite the motor neurons, and these neurons cause the muscle to contract. (See *Figure 3.26.*)

The next example adds a bit of complexity to the circuit. Suppose that someone picks a

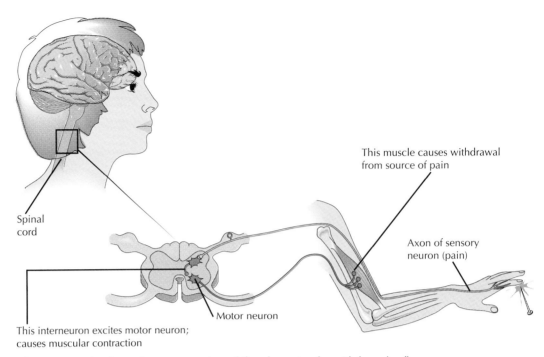

Figure 3.26 A schematic representation of the elements of a withdrawal reflex.

rose, but then her finger gets pricked by a thorn. The pain caused by the thorn triggers a withdrawal reflex that tends to make her drop the rose. And yet she manages to keep hold of it. What prevented the withdrawal reflex from occurring?

As we saw earlier, the activity of a neuron depends on the relative activity of the excitatory and inhibitory synapses on it. The pain caused by the thorn increases the activity of a number of excitatory synapses on the motor neurons, which would tend to cause the hand to open. However, this excitation is counteracted by inhibition from another source—the brain. Figure 3.27 shows an axon from a neuron in the brain that forms a synapse with an interneuron, which in turn forms a synapse with a motor neuron that causes the hand to open. The effect of the interneuron is *inhibitory;* when this neuron is active, its terminal buttons inhibit the firing of

Figure 3.27 A schematic representation of a withdrawal reflex being inhibited by the brain.

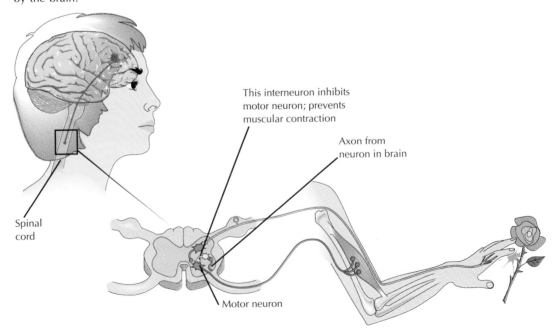

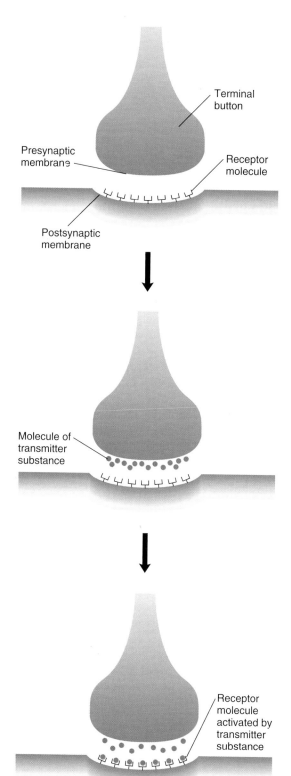

Figure 3.28 The release of a transmitter substance from a terminal button. *Top:* Before the arrival of an action potential. *Middle:* Just after the arrival of an action potential. Molecules of transmitter substance have been released. *Bottom:* Activation of receptor molecules. The molecules of transmitter substance diffuse across the synaptic cleft and some of them activate receptor molecules in the postsynaptic membrane.

the motor neuron and hence prevent the hand from opening. Thus, the circuit provides an example of competing tendencies: to drop the rose and to hold on to it. Complex decisions about behaviors are made within the brain by much more complicated circuits of neurons, but the basic principles remain the same. (See *Figure 3.27.*)

8 **Transmission of Messages at Synapses.** Terminal buttons excite or inhibit postsynaptic neurons by releasing transmitter substances. When an axon fires, the action potential travels to all its terminal buttons. When the action potential reaches a terminal button, it causes the terminal button to release a small amount of the transmitter substance into the fluid-filled space between the terminal button and the membrane of the postsynaptic cell (the *synaptic cleft*). The transmitter substance causes reactions in the postsynaptic neuron that either excite or inhibit it. These reactions are triggered by special submicroscopic protein molecules embedded in the postsynaptic membrane called **receptor molecules.** (See *Figure 3.28.*)

A molecule of a transmitter substance acts upon a receptor molecule like a key upon a lock. When a terminal button releases a transmitter substance, molecules find their way to the receptor molecules and activate them. In turn, the receptor molecules produce excitatory or inhibitory effects on the postsynaptic neuron. (See *Figure 3.29.*) Many drugs that have effects on behavior produce these effects by stimulating or blocking postsynaptic receptor molecules.

Figure 3.29 Detailed view of receptor molecules in the postsynaptic neuron. When activated by molecules of a transmitter substance, the receptor molecules excite or inhibit the postsynaptic neuron. (Adapted from Changeux, J.-P., Devillers-Thièry, A., and Chemouilli, P. *Science,* 1984, *225,* 1335–1345.)

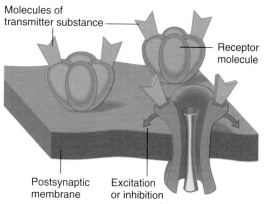

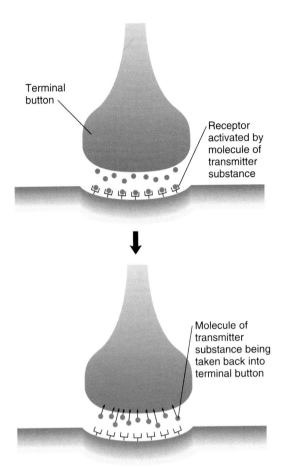

Figure 3.30 Reuptake of molecules of transmitter substance.

The excitation or inhibition produced by a synapse is brief; the effects soon pass away, usually in a fraction of a second. At most synapses the effects are terminated by a process called **reuptake.** The transmitter substance is released by the terminal button and is quickly taken up again, so that it has only a brief time to stimulate the postsynaptic receptor molecules. (See *Figure 3.30.*) The rate at which the terminal button takes back the transmitter substance determines how prolonged the effects of the chemical on the postsynaptic neuron will be. As we will see, some drugs affect the nervous system by slowing down the rate of reuptake.

Effects of Drugs on Synapses

Although the action potential consists of an electrical charge, most of the important events that take place within the nervous system are chemical. Communications between neurons, between sensory receptor and neuron, and between neuron and muscle take place chemically. A terminal button secretes a transmitter substance, which has an excitatory or inhibitory effect on another cell. There are many different kinds of transmitter substances in the brain, and various drugs affect their production or release, mimic their effects on the receptor molecules, block these effects, or interfere with their reuptake once they are released. Through these mechanisms a drug can alter the perceptions, thoughts, and behaviors controlled by a particular transmitter substance. In this section we will examine some of the ways drugs can affect the nervous system and, hence, behavior.

Stimulating or Inhibiting the Release of Transmitter Substances. Some drugs cause the terminal buttons to continuously release their transmitter substance. Others prevent the terminal buttons from releasing their transmitter substance when the axon fires. The effects of most of these drugs are more or less specific to one transmitter substance. Therefore, because different classes of neurons release different transmitter substances, the drugs affect only a selected set of neurons. An example of a stimulating drug is the venom of the black widow spider, which causes the release of **acetylcholine,** an important transmitter substance. In contrast, botulinum toxin, a poison that is sometimes present in improperly canned food, prevents the release of acetylcholine. An extremely small amount—less than a millionth of a gram—can kill a person. (See *Figure 3.31.*)

Acetylcholine plays a role in several important functions in the brain, including dreaming and memory. The stage of sleep during which dreaming occurs is controlled by neurons that secrete acetylcholine. Also, one of the earliest symptoms of a fatal illness called Alzheimer's disease is deterioration in memory, which ap-

Figure 3.31 The effects of black widow spider venom and botulinum toxin. Black widow spider venom causes the transmitter substance to be released. Botulinum toxin prevents the release of a transmitter substance from the terminal buttons.

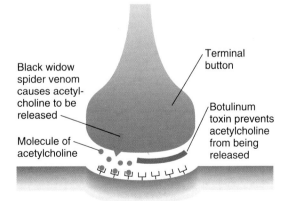

pears to occur because of degeneration of neurons that secrete acetylcholine.

Stimulating or Blocking Postsynaptic Receptor Molecules.

Transmitter substances produce their effects by stimulating postsynaptic receptor molecules, which in turn excite or inhibit the postsynaptic neurons. Some drugs *duplicate* the effects of particular transmitter substances by directly stimulating particular kinds of receptor molecules. For example, nicotine stimulates acetylcholine receptors and thus serves as a potent poison. (See *Figure 3.32.*) Other drugs *block* receptor molecules, making them inaccessible to the transmitter substance and thus inhibiting synaptic transmission.

If we use the lock-and-key analogy to describe the effects of a transmitter substance on a receptor molecule, then a drug that stimulates receptor molecules works like a master key, turning the receptor molecules on even when

Curare, used by South American natives on their darts, causes paralysis by blocking the acetylcholine receptors that control muscles.

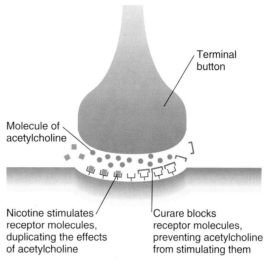

Figure 3.32 The effects of nicotine and curare. Nicotine directly stimulates the receptor molecules. Curare blocks receptor molecules and thus prevents acetylcholine from activating them.

the transmitter substance is not present. In contrast, a drug that blocks receptor molecules "plugs up" the lock so that the key will no longer fit into it. An example of a receptor blocker is the poison called curare, which was discovered by South American Indians, who use it on the darts of their blowguns. This drug blocks acetylcholine receptors, many of which are located on muscles. The curare prevents synaptic transmission in muscles, causing paralysis. The victim is unable to breathe and consequently suffocates. (See *Figure 3.32.*)

Some medically useful chemicals work by blocking receptor molecules. For example, antipsychotic drugs alleviate the symptoms of a mental disorder called *schizophrenia* by blocking receptor molecules in the brain that are normally stimulated by dopamine. (The antipsychotic drugs are discussed later in this chapter and then in more detail in Chapters 15 and 16.)

Inhibiting Reuptake. Most transmitter substances are taken back into the terminal buttons soon after they are released. Reuptake thus keeps the effects of synaptic transmission brief. Some drugs inhibit the process of reuptake so that molecules of the transmitter substance continue to stimulate the postsynaptic receptor molecules for a longer time. Therefore, inhibition of reuptake *increases* the effect of the transmitter substance. The excitatory effects of cocaine and amphetamine are produced by their ability to inhibit the reuptake of certain transmitter substances, including dopamine. (See *Figure 3.33.*)

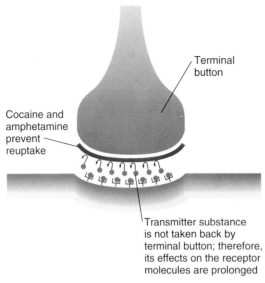

Terminal
button

Cocaine and
amphetamine
prevent
reuptake

Transmitter substance
is not taken back by
terminal button; therefore,
its effects on the receptor
molecules are prolonged

Figure 3.33 The effects of cocaine and amphetamine. Both drugs prevent reuptake of certain transmitter substances, thus prolonging their effects on the receptor molecules in the postsynaptic membrane.

Neuromodulators: Action at a Distance

As you just learned, terminal buttons excite or inhibit the postsynaptic neuron by releasing transmitter substances. These chemicals travel a very short distance and affect receptor molecules located on a small patch of the postsynaptic membrane. But some neurons release chemicals that get into the general circulation of the brain and stimulate receptor molecules on many thousands of neurons, some located a consider-

The release of endorphins inhibits the tigers' pain if they should injure each other while fighting. Territorial aggression is an important species-typical behavior.

able distance away. The chemicals these neurons release are called **neuromodulators,** because they modulate the activity of the neurons they affect.

The best-known neuromodulator is a category of chemicals called *endorphins,* or **opiods** ("opiumlike substances"). These chemicals are released while an animal is engaging in important species-typical behaviors, such as mating or fighting. The chemicals stimulate receptor molecules located on neurons in several parts of the brain and thus produce several effects, including a decreased sensitivity to pain, increased arousal, and a tendency to persist in ongoing behaviors. These effects ensure that a mating animal or an animal fighting to defend itself or its territory is less likely to be deterred by pain; thus, babies are more likely to be born and a defense is more likely to be successful.

Many years ago, people discovered that eating or smoking the sap of the opium poppy decreased a person's sensitivity to pain; thus, people began using it to relieve pain. They also discovered that the sap produced pleasurable effects; people who took it enjoyed the experience and wanted to take more. In recent times chemists have discovered that the sap contains a class of chemicals called *opiates* (from the word *opium*). They also learned how to extract and concentrate them and to produce synthetic versions with even greater potency. In the mid-1970s neurobiologists learned that opiates produce their effect by stimulating special receptor molecules located on neurons in the brain (Pert, Snowman, and Snyder, 1974). Soon after that, they discovered the brain's opioids themselves (Terenius and Wahlström, 1975). Thus, opiates mimic the effects of a special category of neuromodulators that the brain uses to regulate some types of species-typical behaviors. I will say more about opiates later in this chapter.

The brain produces other neuromodulators. Only a few have been identified, but others are undoubtedly waiting to be discovered.

EVALUATING SCIENTIFIC ISSUES

Nature or Nurture?

[9] The nature-nurture issue is one of the oldest questions in psychology. Normally, the controversy revolves around the origins of a particular behavior, talent, or personality trait. People ask, "Is it caused by biological or social factors?" "Is it innate or learned?" "Is it a result of heredi-

tary or cultural influences?" "Should we look for an explanation in the brain or in the environment?" Almost always, biology, innateness, heredity, and the brain are placed on the "nature" side of the equation. Society, learning, culture, and the environment are placed on the "nurture" side. Rarely does one question whether these items really form a true dichotomy.

Common Beliefs About Physiology. As you will see throughout the rest of this book, most modern psychologists consider the nature-nurture issue to be a relic of the past. That is, *all* behaviors, talents, and personality traits are the products of *both* types of factors: biological and social, hereditary and cultural, physiological and environmental. The task of the modern psychologist is not to find out which one of these factors is more important but to discover the particular roles played by each of them and to determine the ways in which they interact. But too often, physiology is assumed to be entirely determined by heredity.

As you know, the body develops according to a program established by the genes. The only way that heredity can influence our personality and behavior is through its effect on our bodies. Although the most important changes occur in the structure and connections of the brain, our behavior is affected by the endocrine system and by the structure of other parts of our bodies. For example, having a male or female body certainly influences our behavior and affects the way we are treated by other people.

Most people believe heredity is the sole influence on normal brain development. Many people are familiar with the fact that brain development can be disrupted by drugs taken by a pregnant woman or by diseases that she contracts. But few people consider the possibility that environmental factors have important influences on the *normal* development of the brain.

Evidence for Environmental Effects on Brain Development. Studies with humans and laboratory animals show that interactions between hereditary and environmental factors—between nature and nurture—begin very early in life. For example, more than twenty-five years ago, Rosenzweig and his colleagues began a research program designed to see what effects environmental stimulation would have on the development of the brain (see Rosenzweig, 1984, for a review). The experimenters divided litters of rats and placed the animals into two kinds of environments: enriched and impoverished. The enriched environment contained

such things as running wheels, ladders, slides, and "toys" that the animals could explore and manipulate. The experimenters changed these objects every day to maximize the animals' experiences and thus ensure that they would learn as much as possible. The impoverished environments were plain cages in a dimly illuminated, quiet room.

Rosenzweig and his colleagues found many differences in the brains of animals raised in the two environments. The brains of rats raised in the enriched environment had a thicker cerebral cortex, a better capillary supply, more protein content, and more acetylcholine (a transmitter substance that appears to play an important role in learning). Subsequent studies have found changes on a microscopic level as well. Turner and Greenough (1985) found that synapses in the cerebral cortex were larger and that more synapses were found on each neuron, and Greenough and Volkmar (1973) found that neurons had larger and more complex dendritic trees. Changes occur even in the adult brain. Sirevaag, Black, Shafron, and Greenough (1988) found that when rats were placed in an enriched environment between the ages of thirty and sixty days (young adulthood), the capillaries in their visual cortex grew more branches and their surface area increased, presumably to accommodate the growth that was stimulated by the experience.

Environmental stimulation does not begin at birth. While in the uterus, fetuses feel the movements of their mothers' bodies and hear the sounds of their mothers' voices—and even sounds from the external environment that pass through the abdominal wall. After they are born, infants receive much environmental stimulation when they are nursed, when they are bathed, when their diapers are changed, and when they are simply held and cuddled. This stimulation clearly contributes to normal development. When infants are born prematurely and must be placed in isolators, they are deprived of the stimulation that occurs in the uterus and receive less handling than a normal full-term infant. Several studies have found that gentle stroking can reduce the effects of the environmental deprivation; it increases growth rates and rates of motor development of premature infants (Solkoff et al., 1969; Solkoff and Matuszak, 1975). According to evidence from experiments with infant rats reviewed by Schanberg and Field (1987), stroking and handling an infant may stimulate the release of hormones necessary for normal growth and development (including that of the brain).

Specific types of experiences can affect the development of specific parts of the brain. For example, Nobel laureates David Hubel and Torsten Wiesel found that if one eye of a young animal is closed during a critical period of brain development that occurs shortly after birth, the normal neural connections are not established between that eye and the visual cortex—a fact that can easily be seen by microscopic examination of the brain. The eye effectively becomes blind (Wiesel, 1982). Even simple learning tasks can affect brain development. Spinelli and his colleagues (Spinelli and Jensen, 1979; Spinelli, Jensen, and DiPrisco, 1980) trained young animals to move one of their forelegs whenever they saw a particular visual stimulus. The training caused significant changes in the development of the visual cortex and in the part of the somatosensory cortex that analyzed information coming from the animals' wrists, where a tactile stimulus was presented.

As we shall see in Chapter 10, development of the male and female sex organs is controlled by the secretion of particular sex hormones during fetal development. These hormones also affect the development of the brain and influence sex-related behavior in the adult. Research by Moore and her colleagues (reviewed by Moore, 1987) indicates that at least some of the effects of heredity on sexual behavior are indirect. Female rats spend a considerable amount of time licking the genital region of their offspring. This behavior is very useful, because it stimulates urination and permits the mother to ingest the water and minerals that are released so they can be recycled in her milk.

Moore and her colleagues discovered that mothers spent much more time licking their male offspring and wondered whether this licking could have any effects on their sexual behavior later in life. Indeed, it did. First, the experimenters found that a male sex hormone was responsible for the presence of an odor in the male pups' urine, which was attractive to the mothers. Next, they found that if the mothers could not smell the odor, they failed to give the males special attention—and that the males showed decreases in their sexual behavior in adulthood. But if the experimenters stroked the genitals of the male pups with a small brush each day, the animals showed normal sexual behavior when they grew up.

In this example there are several steps between heredity and behavior. The genes are responsible for the presence of the male sex hormone in the rat, which has the effect of making the urine of male pups especially attractive to the mother. She spends more time licking their genitals, which somehow affects their sexual development. Whether the licking affects the development of the brain or the genitals (or both) has not yet been determined.

What Conclusions Can We Make? I have reviewed only a few of the many effects of environment on physiological development that researchers have discovered so far. It is clear that the body (and, in particular, the brain) does not develop in a vacuum. For example, the genes contain a program for the development of the visual system of the brain, but this program depends on the eyes' receiving visual stimulation. The genes also contain a program for the development of sex organs and the neural circuits necessary for sexual behavior. But normal development in rats depends on the responsiveness of the mother to an odor produced only in pups whose bodies contain male sex organs.

Not only has the nature-nurture issue become a relic of the past, but so has the assumption that physiology is solely a product of heredity. Interactions between genes and environment begin to occur early in development and undoubtedly continue throughout the life span. ∎

INTERIM SUMMARY

Neurons

The basic element of the nervous system is the neuron, with its soma, dendrites, axon, and terminal buttons. One neuron communicates with another (or with muscle or gland cells) by means of synapses. A synapse is the junction of the terminal button of the presynaptic neuron with the membrane of the postsynaptic neuron. This communication is chemical; when an action potential travels down an axon (when the axon "fires"), it causes a transmitter substance to be released by the terminal buttons. Molecules of the transmitter substance stimulate the receptor molecules on the postsynaptic neuron, which then either excite or inhibit the firing of the postsynaptic neuron. The combined effects of excitatory and inhibitory synapses on a particular neuron determine the rate of firing of that neuron. As we have seen, the reflex is the simplest element of behavior, and it serves to illustrate the contest between excitation and inhibition.

The nervous system contains neurons that release a wide variety of transmitter substances, many of which participate in several different functions. For example, acetylcholine is involved in memory and in control of muscles. Dopamine is involved in motor control and in mechanisms of reward (and hence produces pleasurable feelings).

Drugs can facilitate or interfere with synaptic activity. Facilitators include drugs that cause the release of a transmitter substance (such as the venom of the black widow spider); drugs that directly stimulate postsynaptic receptor molecules, thus duplicating the effects of the transmitter substance itself (such as nicotine); and drugs that inhibit the reuptake of a transmitter substance (such as amphetamine and cocaine). Drugs that interfere with synaptic activity include those that inhibit the release of a transmitter substance (such as botulinum toxin) and those that block receptor molecules (such as curare, which paralyzes the muscles).

Neuromodulators resemble transmitter substances, but they work at a greater distance. They are released into the general circulation and stimulate the receptor molecules of neurons located throughout the brain. The best-known neuromodulators are the opioids, which are released during times when the animal is engaged in important behaviors. The opiates, extracted from the sap of the opium poppy or produced in a laboratory, stimulate the brain's opiate receptors.

The nature-nurture controversy was important in the past, when psychologists asked whether particular behaviors, talents, or personality traits were caused by hereditary factors ("nature") or by experience ("nurture"). The controversy is now over, because psychologists realize that almost all characteristics are affected by *both* of these factors. What is less generally recognized is that the normal development of the brain—which was generally assumed to be programmed solely by hereditary factors—is also affected by the environment.

■

DRUGS THAT AFFECT BEHAVIOR

10 Long ago, people discovered that the sap, fruit, leaves, bark, or roots of various plants could alter their perceptions and behavior, could be used to treat diseases, or could be used as poisons to kill animals for food. Many of the chemicals found in plants are still used for their behavioral effects, and many others have been artificially produced in modern chemical laboratories. This section describes drugs that cause sedation or excitation, modify perceptions or cause hallucinations, or are used to treat mental disorders.

Drugs That Cause Sedation

Some drugs depress behavior, causing relaxation, sedation, or even loss of consciousness. In most cases the depression is caused by stimulation of a class of receptor molecules that is normally activated by neuromodulators produced by the brain. **Barbiturates** depress the activity of the brain, in part by unknown means, and in part by stimulating neuromodulator receptors. In low doses barbiturates have a calming effect. In progressively higher doses they produce difficulty in walking and talking, unconsciousness, coma, and death. Barbiturates are abused by people who want to achieve the relaxing, calming effect of the drugs, especially to counteract the anxiety and irritability that can be produced by stimulants. They are occasionally prescribed as sleep medications, but they are a very poor choice for this purpose, because they suppress dreaming and produce a particularly unrefreshing sleep.

Many **antianxiety drugs** are members of a family known as the **benzodiazepines,** which include the well-known tranquilizer Valium *(diazepam).* These drugs, too, stimulate some sort of neuromodulator receptors. The benzodiazepines are very effective in reducing anxiety and are sometimes used to treat people with anxiety disorders. In addition, some benzodiazepines serve as sleep medications. These behavioral effects suggest that they mimic the effects of neuromodulators involved in the regulation of mood and the control of sleep.

In the United States alone many tons of benzodiazepines are prescribed each year. Undoubtedly, this quantity is too high. Although these drugs are very safe—a lethal dose is extremely high—there is no disorder that they can cure. Indeed, people with anxiety disorders are very likely to become dependent on the drugs.

By far, the most commonly used depressant drug is ethyl alcohol, the active ingredient in alcoholic beverages. This drug has effects similar to those of the barbiturates; larger and larger doses of alcohol reduce anxiety, produce motor incoordination, and then cause unconsciousness, coma, and finally death. The effects of alcohol and barbiturates are *additive:* A moderate dose of alcohol plus a moderate dose of barbiturates can be fatal.

Figure 3.34 The effects of a recently discovered alcohol antagonist. Both rats received an injection of alcohol, but the one in the back also received an injection of the alcohol antagonist. (Photo courtesy of Steven M. Paul, National Institute of Mental Health, Bethesda, Md.)

The primary effect of alcohol appears to be similar to that of the benzodiazepines; it stimulates some type of neuromodulator receptor. Recently, Suzdak et al. (1986) discovered a drug that reverses alcohol intoxication, presumably by blocking some type of neuromodulator receptor. Figure 3.34 shows two rats who received injections of enough alcohol to make them pass out. The one facing us also received an injection of the antialcohol drug and appears completely sober. (See *Figure 3.34.*) The drug does *not* reverse the intoxicating effects of barbiturates; so although alcohol and barbiturates have similar—and additive—effects, these effects are not identical. Presumably, more than one class of receptor molecule is involved.

This wonder drug is not likely to reach the market soon. Although the behavioral effects of alcohol may be mediated by neuromodulator receptors, alcohol has other, potentially fatal effects on all cells of the body. Alcohol destabilizes the membrane of cells, interfering with their functions. Thus, a person who takes some of the newly discovered antialcohol drug could then go on to drink himself or herself to death, without becoming drunk in the process. Drug companies would obviously be afraid of possible liability suits stemming from such occurrences.

Alcohol is a dangerous drug because of its high potential for addiction. The problem of addiction (to alcohol, opiates, cocaine, tobacco, and other drugs) is discussed in further detail in Chapter 11.

Drugs That Cause Excitation

Several categories of drugs stimulate the central nervous system and thus activate behavior. Be-

cause of the effects some of these drugs have on the neural circuits involved in reinforcement (reward), they tend to be abused.

Two very popular stimulating drugs, amphetamine and cocaine, have almost identical effects: They inhibit the reuptake of dopamine and thus strengthen the effects of synapses that use this transmitter substance. As we shall see in Chapter 11, reinforcing stimuli—such as food to a hungry animal, water to a thirsty one, or sexual contact to a sexually aroused one—exert their behavioral effects largely by increasing the activity of a circuit of dopamine-secreting neurons. Thus, amphetamine and cocaine mimic the effects of reinforcing stimuli. In particular, free-base cocaine (crack) has an immediate effect on the reuptake of dopamine and produces such a profound feeling of euphoria and pleasure that the person wants to repeat the experience again

Free-base cocaine "crack" produces profound pleasure, euphoria, and a desire to repeat the experience again and again. Thus, this drug is extremely addictive.

and again. Thus, the drug is very addictive. Chapter 11 discusses the physiological and psychological aspects of drug addiction in detail.

Cocaine and amphetamine, if taken in large enough doses for a few days, can produce the symptoms of paranoid schizophrenia—a serious mental disorder. Heavy users of these drugs will suffer from hallucinations and their thoughts will become confused and difficult to control. They may come to believe that they are being attacked or plotted against. In fact, an experienced clinician cannot distinguish the drug-induced symptoms from those that occur in people who really have the psychosis. This fact has suggested to some investigators that schizophrenia may be caused by overactivity of dopamine-secreting synapses; this hypothesis will be discussed in more detail in Chapter 15.

Drugs That Modify Perceptions or Produce Hallucinations

Throughout history people have enjoyed changing their consciousness now and then by taking drugs, fasting, meditating, or chanting. Even children enjoy spinning around and making themselves dizzy—presumably for the same reasons. Chemicals found in several different plants produce profound changes in consciousness. Behaviorally, these changes are difficult to specify. Large doses of drugs such as marijuana or LSD tend to make laboratory animals become sedated, but they give no sign of having their consciousness altered. But then, how could they? Only humans can describe the consciousness-altering effects of the drugs.

Undoubtedly, drugs can affect consciousness in several different ways. The only one that we have any understanding of is the effect of drugs that affect synapses that utilize the transmitter substance called **serotonin.** Many consciousness-altering drugs, such as LSD, psilocybin, and DMT (dimethyltryptamine) produce hallucinations, which often are interesting and even awe inspiring but which sometimes produce intense fear and anxiety. Normally, we dream only when we are asleep, in a particular stage called *REM sleep* (for the rapid eye movements that occur then). During the rest of the day circuits of serotonin-secreting neurons inhibit the mechanisms that are responsible for dreaming, thus preventing them from becoming active. However, when a drug such as LSD suppresses the activity of serotonin-secreting neurons, the dream mechanisms become active, and hallucinations result.

Not all hallucinogenic drugs interfere with serotonin-secreting synapses. As you learned in the previous section, cocaine and amphetamine, which affect dopamine-secreting synapses, also produce hallucinations. However, the hallucinations produced by cocaine and amphetamine take some time to develop, and they are primarily auditory, whereas LSD-induced hallucinations are primarily visual (as dreams are). Therefore, the two types of hallucinations undoubtedly occur for different reasons.

Investigators still do not have an explanation for the behavioral effects of *phencyclidine* (PCP, or angel dust) and THC (tetrahydrocannibinal), which is the active ingredient of marijuana. Because both drugs stimulate special receptor molecules located on certain neurons in the brain, most researchers believe that they mimic the effects of some unidentified neuromodulators.

Psychotherapeutic Drugs

The symptoms of schizophrenia and the affective disorders (severe disturbances of mood) can be reduced or even eliminated by various psychotherapeutic drugs. As we already saw, cocaine and amphetamine—drugs that stimulate synapses that utilize dopamine—can induce the symptoms of schizophrenia. In contrast, drugs that block dopamine receptors can be used to reduce or even eliminate these symptoms. These antipsychotic drugs, which were discovered in the 1950s, have made it possible to discharge people from mental hospitals who would otherwise have been unable to care for themselves.

Another important category of psychotherapeutic drugs includes the antidepressant medications. Depression can result from tragedies in a person's life, but it can sometimes arise without any obvious external cause, presumably as a result of biochemical abnormalities within a person's brain. The antidepressant medications, which relieve depression, tend to stimulate synapses that use serotonin. They have saved many lives that otherwise would have been lost through suicide.

Yet another drug is also used to treat a special category of depression in which the person's mood fluctuates between periods of severe depression and periods of *mania,* a state of excited, unrealistic elation. This drug is a simple inorganic compound called *lithium carbonate.* The biochemical cause of its therapeutic effects is unknown.

INTERIM SUMMARY

Drugs That Affect Behavior

Many chemicals found in nature have behavioral effects, and many more have been synthesized in the laboratory. Alcohol, barbiturates, and tranquilizers depress the activity of the brain by stimulating various types of receptor molecules. Amphetamine and cocaine stimulate the brain, primarily by retarding the reuptake of dopamine. The opiates duplicate the effects of the brain's opioids, decreasing sensitivity to pain and producing an intensely enjoyable "rush." Although the physiological basis for the effects of marijuana is not known, we know that LSD, mescaline, and related drugs inhibit the activity of synapses that use serotonin. Perhaps the hallucinogenic effects of these drugs are related to dreaming, which is controlled by circuits of serotonin-secreting neurons.

Not all drugs with behavioral effects are abused; some are very useful in treating mental disorders. Psychotherapeutic drugs include those that reduce the symptoms of schizophrenia and those that relieve depression. Antischizophrenic drugs block dopamine receptors, and antidepressant drugs generally facilitate the action of serotonin. ∎

APPLICATION

The neural circuits in the brain must maintain a close balance between excitation. If there is too much inhibition, the brain cannot do its work. If there is too much excitation, neural activity gets out of control and causes a *seizure disorder* (otherwise known as "epilepsy"). During a seizure the neurons in the brain fire wildly and uncontrollably, disrupting normal brain functions. Most seizure disorders can be controlled by drugs, but occasionally neurosurgeons must perform an operation known as *seizure surgery*.

Most seizure disorders are caused by the presence of one or more *seizure foci* in the brain—regions of scar tissue that irritate the brain tissue surrounding them. From time to time excitation spreads throughout the brain, causing a seizure. Seizure surgery involves removing the abnormal brain tissue that contains a seizure focus. One of the pioneers of seizure surgery, the late Wilder Penfield, developed the operation, which has provided us with some interesting information about the functions of the human brain (Penfield and Jasper, 1954). The patients' heads are first shaved. Then under local anesthesia, the surgeon cuts the scalp and saws through the skull so that a piece of bone can be removed and the brain itself can be exposed. *The patient is conscious throughout the entire procedure.*

When removing the damaged part of the brain, the surgeon wants to cut away all the abnormal tissue—including the seizure focus—while sparing healthy neural tissue that performs important functions, such as the comprehension and production of speech. For this reason, Penfield first stimulated parts of the brain to determine what functions they performed, so he could decide which regions he could safely remove. Penfield touched the tip of a metal electrode to various parts of the brain and observed the effects of stimulation on the patient's behavior. For example, stimulation of one part of the brain produced movement, and stimulation of another part produced sensations of sounds. Stimulation of parts of the brain involved in verbal communication stopped the patient's ongoing speech and disrupted the ability to understand what the surgeon and his associates were saying.

Besides giving patients relief from their epileptic attacks, the procedure provided interesting data about brain function. As Penfield stimulated various parts of the brain, he noted the effect and placed a sterile piece of paper, on which a number was written, on the point stimulated. When various points had been stimulated, Penfield photographed the exposed brain with its numbered locations before removing the slips of paper and proceeding with the surgery. After the operation, he could then compare the recorded notes with the photograph of the patient's brain showing the location of the points of stimulation.

Because seizure surgery often involves the removal of a substantial amount of brain tissue (usually, from one of the temporal lobes), we might expect it to cause behavioral deficits. But in most cases the reverse is true; people's performance on tests of neuropsychological functioning usually *increases*. How can the removal of brain tissue improve a person's performance?

The answer is provided by looking at what happens in the brain not *during* seizures but *between* them. Between seizures, the excitatory activity caused by a seizure focus is

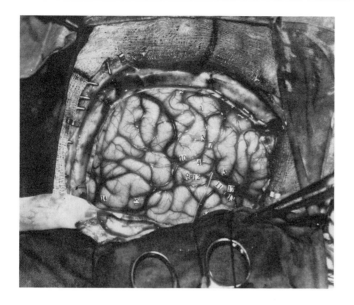

The appearance of the cortical surface of a conscious patient whose brain has been stimulated. The points of stimulation are indicated by the numbered tags placed there by the surgeon. (From Case, M.M., in Wilder Penfield, The Mystery of the Mind: A Critical Study of Consciousness and the Human Brain, with Discussions by William Feindel, Charles Hendel, and Charles Symonds. Copyright © 1975 by Princeton University Press. Figure 4, p. 24, reprinted by permission of Princeton University Press and the Literary Executors of the Penfield Papers.)

held in check by a compensatory increase in inhibitory activity. That is, inhibitory synapses in the region surrounding the seizure focus become more active. (This phenomenon is known as *interictal inhibition*; *ictus* means "stroke" in Latin.) A seizure occurs when the excitation overcomes the inhibition.

The problem is that the compensatory inhibition does more than hold the excitation in check; it also suppresses the normal functions of a rather large region of brain tissue surrounding the seizure focus. Thus, even though the focus may be small, its effects are felt over a much larger area—even between seizures. Removing the seizure focus and some surrounding brain tissue eliminates the source of the irritation and makes the compensatory inhibition unnecessary. Freed from interictal inhibition, the brain tissue located near the site of the former seizure focus can now function normally, and the patient's neuropsychological abilities will show an improvement.

Many seizure foci are caused by brain damage that occurs around the time of birth, but some can be caused by head injury later in life. Often, the seizures begin only after a delay of several months. The cause of the delay is related to some properties of neurons that make learning possible. Goddard (1967) placed metal wires in the brains of rats and administered a brief, weak electrical stimulus once a day. At first, the stimulation produced no effects, but after several days the stimulation began to trigger small, short seizures. As days went by, the seizures became larger and longer until the animal was finally having major convulsions. Goddard called the phenomenon *kindling*, because it resembled the way a small fire can be kindled to start a larger one.

Kindling appears to be analogous to learning, and it presumably involves increases in the strength of synapses. The probable reason for the delayed occurrence of seizures after a head injury is that it takes time for kindling to occur. The irritation produced by the brain injury eventually causes increased synaptic strength in excitatory synapses located nearby.

Kindling has become an animal model of focal-seizure disorders, and it has proved useful in research on the causes and treatment of these disorders. For example, Silver, Shin, and McNamara (1991) produced seizure foci in rats through kindling and compared the effects of some commonly used medications on both *seizures* (the uncontrolled firing of the neurons within the brain) and *convulsions* (the thrashing movements caused by the seizures). They found that one of the drugs they tested prevented the convulsions but had no effect on the seizures, whereas another prevented both seizures and convulsions. Because each seizure can produce some brain damage through overstimulation of neurons, the goal of medical treatment should be the elimination of seizures, not simply the convulsions that accompany them. Research with the animal model of kindling will undoubtedly assist in the search for more effective drugs for treating focal-seizure disorders.

KEY TERMS AND CONCEPTS

Study of the Brain

physiological psychologist *(53)*
brain lesion *(53)*
stereotaxic apparatus *(53)*
neuropsychologist *(54)*
CT scanner *(54)*
central nervous system *(56)*
peripheral nervous system *(56)*
brain stem *(56)*
cerebral hemisphere *(57)*
cerebellum *(57)*
vertebra *(57)*
meninges *(57)*
cerebrospinal fluid (CSF) *(57)*
ventricle *(57)*
cerebral cortex *(57)*

Control of Behavior

primary visual cortex *(60)*
primary auditory cortex *(60)*
primary somatosensory cortex *(60)*
contralateral *(60)*
primary motor cortex *(60)*
frontal lobe *(61)*
parietal lobe *(61)*
temporal lobe *(61)*
occipital lobe *(61)*
sensory association cortex *(61)*
motor association cortex *(61)*
visual agnosia *(62)*

Control of Internal Functions and Automatic Behaviors

homeostasis *(65)*
species-typical behavior *(65)*
medulla *(65)*
pons *(65)*
midbrain *(65)*

white matter *(66)*
thalamus *(66)*
hypothalamus *(67)*
pituitary gland *(67)*
endocrine gland *(67)*
autonomic nervous system *(68)*
sympathetic branch *(68)*
parasympathetic branch *(68)*
limbic system *(70)*
limbic cortex *(70)*
amygdala *(70)*
hippocampus *(70)*

Neurons

neuron *(71)*
soma *(71)*
dendrite *(71)*
axon *(71)*
action potential *(71)*
terminal button *(71)*
transmitter substance *(71)*
myelin sheath *(72)*
synapse *(72)*
motor neuron *(72)*
presynaptic neuron *(72)*
postsynaptic neuron *(72)*
sensory neuron *(73)*
interneuron *(73)*
receptor molecule *(75)*
reuptake *(75)*
acetylcholine *(76)*
neuromodulator *(78)*
opiod *(78)*

Drugs That Affect Behavior

barbiturate *(81)*
antianxiety drug *(81)*
benzodiazepine *(81)*
serotonin *(83)*

SUGGESTIONS FOR FURTHER READING

Gardner, H. *The Shattered Mind.* New York: Vintage Press, 1975.

Gardner's book describes the effects of strokes on intellectual and verbal abilities. The book is full of detailed descriptions of patients studied by Dr. Gardner. If you are interested in this topic, you will enjoy this book.

Gazzaniga, M.S., and LeDoux, J.E. *The Integrated Mind.* New York: Plenum Press, 1978.

This book, which sounds like the counterpart to Gardner's book, describes studies of people whose brains have been surgically disconnected into two rela-tively independent cerebral hemispheres. These studies permit interesting inferences to be made about differences in the functions of the two sides of the brain. The book is somewhat more formal than Gardner's, but it is clearly written.

Valenstein, E. *Brain Control.* New York: Wiley-Interscience, 1973.

Many people have been concerned about problems that might arise from our discoveries about human brain functions. For example, is it possible to control people's thoughts and behaviors by artificially stimulating their brains with electrical current? Are there potential abuses of psychosurgery, such as prefrontal lobotomies? Valenstein confronts these issues in his book.

Julien, R.M. *A Primer of Drug Action: A Concise, Nontechnical Guide to the Actions, Uses, and Side Effects of Psychoactive Drugs.* San Francisco: W.H. Freeman, 1992.

Grilly, D.M. *Drugs and Human Behavior.* Boston: Allyn and Bacon, 1989.

If you are interested in learning more about the effects of drugs that are often abused, you may want to read one of these books, both of which contain much helpful information about the effects of popular drugs and their use and abuse in society.

Carlson, N.R. *Foundations of Physiological Psychology*, 2nd ed. Boston: Allyn and Bacon, 1992.

My introductory textbook of physiological psychology discusses the topics presented in this chapter in more detail.

4
SENSATION

Henri Matisse, *Frutta e Bronzo*
SCALA/Art Resource, N.Y. © 1992 Succession H. Matisse/ARS, N.Y.

LEARNING OBJECTIVES

When you finish this chapter, you should be able to:

1. Describe how sensory organs detect environmental events and convert the information into sensory codes.
2. Describe the basic principles of psychophysics.
3. Describe and evaluate the usefulness of subliminal self-help instruction.
4. Describe the anatomy of the eye.
5. Describe the transduction of light by photoreceptors, adaptation to light and dark, and the nature and function of eye movements.
6. Describe the physical and perceptual dimensions of color and compare color mixing and pigment mixing.
7. Describe coloring coding by cones and ganglion cells in the retina, negative afterimages, and genetic defects in color vision.
8. Describe the structure and functions of the auditory system.
9. Describe receptor cells on the tongue, their role in transducing gustatory stimuli, and the four qualities of taste.
10. Describe the anatomy of the olfactory system and some of the problems of studying the dimensions of odor.
11. Describe the somatosenses, the internal senses, and the vestibular senses.

Nine-year-old Sara tried to think of something else, but the throbbing pain from her thumb was relentless and unremitting. Earlier in the day, her brother had slammed the car door on it, injuring it badly.

"Why does it have to hurt so much, Daddy?" she asked piteously.

"I wish I could help you, sweetheart," he answered. "Pain may be useful, but it sure isn't fun."

"What do you mean, useful?" she said with astonishment. "You mean it's good for me?" She looked at her father reproachfully.

"Well, this probably isn't the time to tell you about the advantages of pain, because it's hard to appreciate them when you're suffering." A glimmer of interest began to grow in her eyes. For as long as she could remember, Sara loved to have her father explain things to her, even when his explanations got a little confusing. It was comforting to know that someone close to her knew all about the world.

"You know," he said, "there are some people who never feel any pain. They are born that way."

"Really?" Her eyes widened. "They're lucky!"

"No, they really aren't. Without the sense of pain they keep injuring themselves. When they touch something hot, they don't know enough to let go, even when their hand is getting burned. If the water in the shower gets too hot, they don't realize they're getting scalded. If their shoes don't fit right, they will get huge blisters and never know what is happening. If they fall and sprain their ankle—or even break a bone—they don't feel that something bad has happened to them, and their injury will just get worse. Some people without the ability to feel pain have died when their appendix burst because they didn't know that something bad was happening inside them."

Sara looked thoughtful. Her father's explanation seemed to be distracting her from her pain.

"Parents with children who can't feel pain say that it's difficult to teach them to avoid danger. When a child does something that causes pain, she quickly learns to avoid repeating her mistake. Remember when you were three years old and walked on the grill of the heater in the cabin floor? You had just gotten out of the shower, and you burned the bottoms of your feet."

"I *think* so," she said slowly. "Yes, you bought me a bag of candy corn to make me forget how much it hurt."

"That's right. Your mom and I had told you that the grill was dangerous when the heater was on, but it took an actual experience to teach you to stay away. We feel pain when parts of our body are damaged. The injured cells make a chemical that's picked up by nerve endings, and the nerves send messages to our brain to warn it that something bad is happening. Our brain automatically tries to get us away from whatever it is that hurts us—and we also learn to become afraid of it. After you burned your feet on the grill, you stayed away from it even when you were wearing shoes.

"Kids who can't feel pain can learn to stay away from dangerous things, but it's not an automatic, gut-level kind of learning. They have to pay attention all the time, and if they let down their guard, it's easy for them to injure themselves. Pain isn't fun, but it's hard to survive without it."

"I guess so," said Sara reluctantly. She looked at her bandaged thumb, and the sudden realization of how much it hurt brought tears to her eyes again. "But the pain could go away now, because it's already taught me everything I need to know."

Behavior does not exist in a vacuum, nor do our thoughts and emotions. Our actions are provoked, informed, and guided by events occurring in our environment, and we think about—and have feelings about—what is happening there. Our senses are the means by which we experience the world; everything we learn is detected by sense organs and transmitted to our brains by sensory nerves. Without sensory input a human brain would be utterly useless; it would learn nothing, think no thoughts, have no experiences, and control no behaviors. This chapter describes our sense organs and discusses how sensory information is organized into experience.

Vision, to most people, is the most important sense modality. Through it we recognize family and friends, see their facial expressions and gestures, learn to read, perceive objects that are beyond our touch, and find our way around our environment. It provides us with information about the size, shape, color, and movement of objects nearby and at a distance. Through vision we receive some of our most powerful aesthetic experiences, in the form of art and other beautiful images—experiences rivaled only by music.

The other senses also contribute to the richness of experience. Because of the role that speech plays in human culture, audition is extremely important for social behavior. Along with vision, it provides information about distant events. Except for the sense of smell, which can tell us about sources of aromatic molecules far upwind, the other senses deal with things near our body, including such sensations as the taste of our favorite food or the touch of a loved one. The body senses are closely tied to our own movements. When we feel an object, we do not feel it passively; we move our hands over it to determine its shape, texture, and temperature. And information from specialized organs in the inner ear and from receptors in the muscles and joints is actually produced by our own movements. This information helps us maintain our balance as we engage in our everyday activities.

SENSORY PROCESSING

Experience is traditionally divided into two classes: sensation and perception. Most psychologists define **sensation** as the awareness of simple properties of stimuli, such as brightness, color, warmth, or sweetness. **Perception** is the awareness of more complex characteristics of stimuli. According to these definitions, seeing the color red is a *sensation,* but seeing an apple is a *perception.* Psychologists used to believe that perceptions depended heavily on learning, whereas pure sensations involved innate, "prewired" physiological mechanisms. However, neither behavioral nor physiological research has been able to establish a clear boundary between "simple" sensations and "complex" perceptions. Indeed, research has shown that experience is essential to the development of some of the most elementary features of sensory systems.

This chapter describes our sensory mechanisms: the visual, auditory, gustatory, olfactory, and somatosensory systems. According to tradition, we have five senses, but in fact, we have several more. For example, the somatosensory system includes separate components that are able to detect touch, warmth, coolness, vibration, physical damage (pain), head tilt, head movement, limb movement, muscular contraction, and various events occurring within our bodies. Whether we choose to call each of these components "senses" is a matter of terminology.

In any event, this chapter describes the basic processes by which these mechanisms oper-

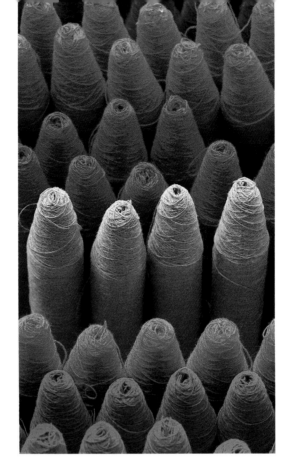

Humans are capable of distinguishing among approximately 7.5 million different colors.

ate. The next chapter deals with a closely related topic: visual perception. This topic receives a chapter of its own (separate from the discussion of the anatomy of the eye and the basic functions of the visual system of the brain) because psychologists have devoted so much attention to the topic.

Transduction

Sense organs can detect the presence of environmental stimuli provided by light, sound, odor, taste, or mechanical contact, but the brain cannot. Information about the environment must be gathered by sense organs and then introduced to the brain through neural impulses—action potentials carried by the axons in sensory nerves. To serve as an effective stimulus, an environmental event must cause a unique pattern of neural activity that the brain can distinguish from all other patterns.

Transduction (literally, "leading across") is the process by which the sense organs convert energy from environmental events into neural activity. Each sense organ responds to a particular form of energy given off by an environmental stimulus and translates that energy into neural firing to which the brain can respond.

Table 4.1 The types of transduction accomplished by the sense organs

Sense Organ	Nature of the Stimulus Transduced
Eye	Light (radiant energy)
Ear (cochlea)	Rapid, periodic changes in air pressure (mechanical energy)
Vestibular system	Tilt of head; rotation of head (mechanical energy)
Tongue (taste)	Recognition of molecular shape
Nose (odor)	Recognition of molecular shape (?)
Skin, internal organs	Touch: movement of skin (mechanical energy)
	Warmth and coolness: thermal energy
	Vibration: movement of skin (mechanical energy)
	Pain: damage to body tissue (chemical reaction)
Muscle	Stretch, changes in muscle length (mechanical energy)

The means of transduction are as diverse as the kinds of stimuli we can perceive. In most senses specialized neurons called **receptor cells** release chemical transmitter substances that stimulate other neurons, thus altering the rate of firing of their axons. In the somatosenses ("body senses"), neurons respond directly to physical stimuli, without the intervention of specialized receptor cells. However, some of these neurons do have specialized endings that enable them to respond to particular kinds of sensory information. Table 4.1 summarizes the types of transduction accomplished by our sense organs. (See *Table 4.1.*)

Sensory Coding

As we saw in Chapter 3, nerves are bundles of axons, each of which can do no more than transmit action potentials. These action potentials are fixed in size and duration; they cannot be altered. Thus, different stimuli cannot be translated into different types of action potentials. Yet we can detect an enormous number of different stimuli with each of our sense organs. For example, we are capable of discriminating among approximately 7.5 million different colors. We can also recognize touches to different parts of the body, and we can further discriminate the degree of pressure involved and the sharpness or bluntness, softness or hardness, as well as the temperature of the object touching us. Thus, our sense organs must respond differently to a multitude of stimuli, and the nerves conveying the information to the brain must carry many different kinds of messages. Because the action potentials themselves cannot be altered, differences in stimuli must be encoded by other means.

A *code* is a system of symbols or signals representing information. Spoken English, written French, semaphore signals, magnetic fields on a recording tape, and the electrical zeros and ones in the memory of a computer are all codes. As long as we know the rules of a code, we can convert a message from one medium to another without losing any information. Although we do not know the precise rules by which the sensory systems transmit information to the brain, we do know that they take two general forms: *anatomical coding* and *temporal coding*.

Anatomical Coding. Since the early 1800s, when Johannes Müller formulated his doctrine of specific nerve energies (discussed in Chapter 1), we have known that the brain learns what is happening through the activity of specific sets of neurons. Sensory organs are located in different places in the body and send their information to the brain through different nerves. Because the brain has no direct information about the physical energy impinging on a given sense organ, it uses **anatomical coding;** that is, it interprets the location and type of sensory stimulus according to which incoming nerve fibers are active. For example, if you rub your eyes and thus mechanically stimulate their light-sensitive receptors, you will see stars and flashes. Experiments performed during surgery have shown that electrical stimulation of the nerves that convey taste produces a sensation of taste, electrical stimulation of the auditory nerve produces a buzzing noise, and so forth.

We use forms of anatomical coding to distinguish not only among the sense modalities themselves but also among stimuli of the same sense modality. Obviously, sensory coding for the body surface is anatomical: Different nerve fibers innervate different parts of the skin. Thus, we can easily discriminate a touch on the arm from a touch on the knee. As we saw in Chapter 3, the primary somatosensory cortex contains a neural "map" of the skin; that is, receptors in the skin in different parts of the body send information to different parts of the primary somatosensory cortex. In addition, the primary visual cortex maintains a map of the visual field.

Temporal Coding. **Temporal coding** is the coding of information in terms of time. The simplest form of temporal code is *rate*. By firing at a faster or slower rate according to the intensity of a stimulus, an axon can communicate quantitative information to the brain. For example, a light touch to the skin can be encoded by a low rate of firing and a more forceful touch by a high rate. Thus, the firing of a particular set of neurons (an anatomical code) tells *where* the body is being touched; the rate at which these neurons fire (a temporal code) tells *how intense* that touch is. As far as we know, all sensory systems use rate of firing to encode the intensity of stimulation. The nervous system may use more complex forms of temporal codes, but this possibility has yet to be scientifically established.

Psychophysics

[2] As you learned in Chapter 1, nineteenth-century Europe was the birthplace of **psychophysics,** the systematic study of the relation between the physical characteristics of a stimulus and the perceptions they produce (the "physics of the mind"). To study perceptual phenomena, scientists had to find reliable ways to measure people's perceptions. We will examine some of these methods in the following subsections.

The Principle of the Just-Noticeable Difference. In Germany Ernst Weber (1795–1878), an anatomist and physiologist, investigated the ability of humans to discriminate between various stimuli, and he discovered a principle that held true for all sensory systems: the **just-noticeable difference (jnd).** For example, when he presented subjects with two metal objects and asked them to say whether they differed in weight, he found that people reported that two weights felt the same unless they differed by a factor of 1 in 40. That is, a person could just barely distinguish a 40-gram weight from a 41-gram weight, an 80-gram weight from an 82-gram weight, or a 400-gram weight from a 410-gram weight. Psychologically, the difference between a 40-gram weight and a 41-gram weight is equivalent to the difference between an 80-gram weight and an 82-gram weight: one jnd. Different senses had different ratios; for example, the ratio for detecting differences in the brightness of white light is approximately 1 in 60. These ratios are called **Weber fractions.**

Gustav Fechner (1801–1887), another German physiologist, used Weber's concept of the just-noticeable difference to measure people's perceptions. Assuming that the jnd was the basic unit of a perceptual experience, he measured the absolute magnitude of a perception in jnds.

Suppose we want to measure the strength of a person's perception of light of a particular

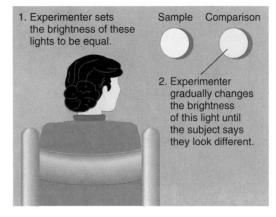

Figure 4.1   The method for determining a just-noticeable difference (jnd).

intensity. We seat the subject in a darkened room facing two disks of frosted glass with a lightbulb behind each one; the brightness of the lightbulb is adjustable. One of the disks serves as the sample stimulus, the other as the comparison stimulus. (See *Figure 4.1.*) We start with the sample stimulus turned off completely and increase the brightness of the comparison stimulus just until our subject can detect a difference. That value is one jnd. Then we set the sample stimulus to that intensity (one jnd) and again increase the brightness of the comparison stimulus just until our subject can again tell them apart. The new value of the comparison stimulus is two jnds. We continue making these measurements until our stimuli are as bright as we can make them or until they become uncomfortably bright for our subject. Finally, we construct a graph indicating the strength of a perception of brightness (in jnds) in relation to the intensity of a stimulus. The graph might look something like *Figure 4.2.*

Figure 4.2   A hypothetical range of perceived brightness (in jnds) as a function of intensity.

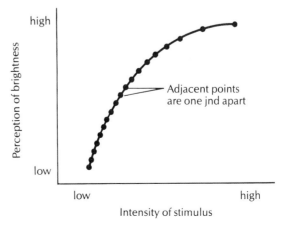

Our senses are the means by which we experience the world. What sensations are being experienced by this hang glider?

Signal Detection Theory. Psychophysical methods rely heavily on the concept of a **threshold,** in which an observer crosses from not perceiving to perceiving. The just-noticeable difference can also be called a **difference threshold**—the minimum detectable difference between two stimuli. An **absolute threshold** is the minimum value of a stimulus that can be detected—that is, discriminated from no stimulus at all. Thus, the first comparison in the experiment I just described, using a dark disk as the sample stimulus, measured an absolute threshold. The subsequent comparisons measured difference thresholds.

Even early psychophysicists realized that a threshold was not an absolutely fixed value. When an experimenter flashes a very dim light, a subject may report seeing it on some trials but not on others. By convention, the threshold is the point at which a subject detects the stimulus 50 percent of the time. This definition is necessary because of the inherent variability of the activity in the nervous system. Even when they are not being stimulated, neurons are never absolutely still; they fire every now and then. If a very weak stimulus occurs when neurons in the visual system happen to be quiet, the brain is likely to detect it. But if the neurons happen to be firing, the effects of the stimulus are likely to be lost in the "noise."

One effective method uses **signal detection theory** to measure a person's sensitivity to changes in physical stimuli (Green and Swets, 1974). According to this theory, every stimulus event requires discrimination between *signal* (stimulus) and *noise* (consisting of both background stimuli and random activity of the nervous system).

Suppose you are seated in a quiet room, facing a small warning light. The experimenter tells you that when the light flashes, you *may* hear a faint tone one second later. Your task is to say "yes" or "no" after each flash of the warning light, according to whether or not you hear the tone. At first the task is easy: Some flashes are followed by an easily heard tone; others are followed by silence. You are confident about your yes and no decisions. But as the experiment progresses, the tone gets fainter and fainter, until it is so soft that you have doubts about how you should respond. The light flashes. What should you say? Did you really hear a tone, or were you just imagining it?

At this point your *response bias*—your tendency to say "yes" or "no" when you are not sure whether you detected the stimulus—can have an effect. Suppose you want to be very sure that you are correct when you say "yes," because you would feel foolish saying you have heard something that is not there. Your response bias is to err in favor of making hits and avoiding false alarms, even at the risk of making misses. Alternatively, your response bias might be to err in favor of detecting all stimuli, even at the risk of making false alarms. According to the terminology of signal detection theory, *hits* are saying "yes" when the stimulus is presented; *misses* are saying "no" when it is presented; *correct negatives* are saying "no" when the stimulus is not presented; and *false alarms* are saying "yes" when the stimulus is not presented. Hits and correct negatives are correct responses; misses and false alarms are incorrect responses. (See **Figure 4.3.**)

A person's response bias can seriously affect an investigator's estimate of the threshold

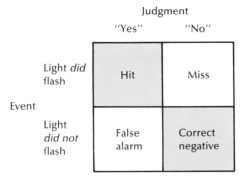

Figure 4.3 The four possibilities in judging the presence or absence of a stimulus.

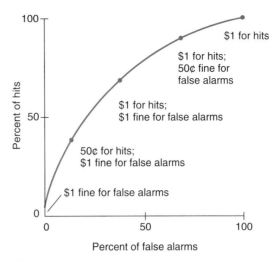

Figure 4.4 A receiver operating characteristic (ROC) curve: Percentage of hits and false alarms in judging the presence of a stimulus under several payoff conditions.

of detection. A conservative person will appear to have a higher threshold than someone who does not want to let a tone go by without saying "yes." Therefore, signal detection theorists have developed a method of assessing subjects' sensitivity, regardless of their initial response bias. They deliberately manipulate the response biases and observe the results of these manipulations on the subjects' judgments.

Suppose you are a subject in the experiment just described, and the experimenter promises you a dollar every time you make a hit, with no penalty for false alarms. I suspect you would tend to say "yes" on every trial, even if you were not sure you had heard the tone. In contrast, suppose the experimenter announced she would fine you a dollar every time you made a false alarm and give you nothing for making hits. You would undoubtedly say "no" every time, because you would have everything to lose and nothing to gain: You would be extremely conservative in your judgments.

Now consider your response bias under a number of intermediate conditions. If you receive a dollar for every hit but are also fined 50 cents for every miss, you will say "yes" whenever you are reasonably sure you heard the tone. If you receive 50 cents for every hit but are fined a dollar for each false alarm, you will be more conservative. But if you are sure you heard the tone, you will say "yes" to earn 50 cents. Figure 4.4 graphs your performance over this range of payoff conditions. (See *Figure 4.4.*)

The graph in Figure 4.4 is a **receiver operating characteristic curve** (ROC curve), named for its original use in research at the Bell Laboratories to measure the intelligibility of speech transmitted through a telephone system. The curve shows performance when the sound is difficult to detect. If the sound were louder, so that you rarely doubted whether you

heard it, you would make almost every possible hit and very few false alarms. The few misses you made would be under the low-payoff condition, when you wanted to be absolutely certain you heard the tone. The few false alarms would occur when guessing did not matter because the fine for being wrong was low or nonexistent. This new ROC curve (black) is shown with the original one (blue) in *Figure 4.5.* The difference between the two curves demonstrates that the louder tone is easier to detect. Detectability is measured by the relative heights of the peaks of the curves measured perpendicular to a 45-degree line.

Figure 4.5 Two ROC curves, obtained by presenting a more discriminable stimulus (black curve) and a less discriminable stimulus (blue curve).

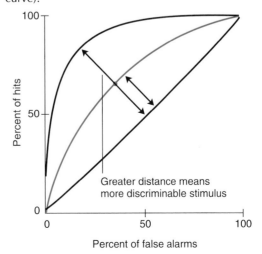

ROC curves can be obtained under a variety of conditions. They can measure one person's ability to detect two colors of light, to assess the sensitivity of his or her visual system to these stimuli; or they can measure the sensitivity of several people, to assess individual differences in their ability to detect stimuli. (I should note that there are other, less expensive ways to change people's response bias besides offering them payment, which is fortunate for researchers with limited budgets.)

The signal detection method I just described is the best way to determine a person's sensitivity to the occurrence of a particular stimulus. Note that the concept of threshold is not used; instead, a stimulus is more or less detectable. The subject *decides* whether a stimulus occurred, and the consequences of making hits or false alarms can bias this decision. Signal detection theory emphasizes that perception involves factors other than the activity of the sensory systems.

EVALUATING SCIENTIFIC ISSUES

Subliminal Self-Help

3 As you undoubtedly know, the market is full of self-help aids: books, audiocassettes, videocassettes, courses, and seminars on how to increase your productivity, improve your self-image, enhance your memory, reduce stress, quit smoking, become fit, and lose weight. If you are afraid that achieving these goals might take some effort on your part, don't worry—no work is necessary. Or so say the makers of subliminal self-help cassettes (that is, audio- or videocassettes with messages so faint that they cannot be consciously heard or seen).

The United States Armed Forces spend billions of dollars each year training their personnel, and they support research directed at developing more effective educational methods. In 1984 the Army Research Institute asked the National Academy of Sciences/National Research Council to investigate several methods purported to improve people's performance—including the use of subliminal self-help procedures. An investigation was carried out by qualified researchers in the appropriate fields of study, and two reports were published, one in 1988 and another in 1991. The latter study, reported in a book published by the National Academy Press (Druckman and Bjork, 1991) provides an objective, scientific, evaluation. The results of this evaluation are summarized in the following section.

What Is Being Asserted?   According to the vendor of a subliminal self-help audiocassette, *Building Self-Confidence,* the message provided by the tape reaches

> the subconscious mind, which is the seat of all memories, knowledge and emotions. The unconscious mind has a powerful influence on conscious actions, thoughts, feelings, habits, and behaviors, and actually controls and guides your life. If you want to make real, lasting changes and improvements in any area of your life, you must reach the subconscious mind where the changes begin. (Druckman and Bjork, 1991, p. 107)

The tape is rather pleasant to listen to; all one hears is the sound of surf washing on a beach, with the cries of sea gulls in the distance. But according to the manufacturer, the tape contains a voice making positive statements such as: "I am a secure person. I believe in myself more and more every day, and my confidence naturally rises to the surface in every situation." The voice is inaudible, masked by the sound of the surf. To profit from these messages, says a notice on the carton, "Simply play the tapes while you work, play, drive, read, exercise, relax, watch TV, or even as you sleep. No concentration is required for the tapes to be effective" (Druckman and Bjork, 1991, pp. 107–108).

Presently, there are at least 2000 vendors of subliminal self-help tapes in North America, with sales of more than $50 million a year (Oldenburg, 1990). One catalog of such tapes even promises to help restore hearing. Imagine, a deaf person restoring his or her hearing by listening to a subliminal message on an audiotape! What a remarkable achievement—to say the least.

Several vendors offer subliminal videotapes, in which they present visual information so briefly that it cannot be consciously detected. One manufacturer even supplies an electronic device that plugs into a television set and superimposes subliminal messages on ordinary programs, so that the viewer can effortlessly engage in self-improvement while watching reruns of, say, "The Love Boat" or "Mr. Ed."

What Evidence Supports the Assertion? How would one determine whether subliminal self-help tapes work? Having read Chapter 2, you know that one would perform a double-blind study. One group of subjects would listen to tapes that contained the message, while another group would listen to tapes that contained only the background noise. Measurements of the personal characteristics relevant to the tapes would be taken before and after the course of treatment. For example, if the tape helped people lose weight, we would weigh them. If it helped cure acne or helped people become better bowlers (no, I'm not making this up), we would count their pimples or record their bowling scores. You will probably not be surprised to learn that the vendors of subliminal self-help tapes have *not* performed studies such as these.

What kind of evidence do the manufacturers provide? They provide *testimonials*. "Bless you! I'm listening to my tape on pain reduction. It is marvelous. I had almost instant relief from pain on first using it a few days ago. It's much cheaper than a doctor and much better than medication. Phenomenal is what it has done for my spirits" (Druckman and Bjork, 1991, p. 113). Another satisfied customer got a new job, at three times the salary of his old one, after listening to a tape called *Wealth and Prosperity.*

We need not doubt the sincerity of the satisfied customers; vendors do not usually need to write their own testimonials. But can testimonials be taken as evidence that subliminal self-help really works? Let's evaluate the evidence.

Does the Evidence Support the Assertion? If a person is convinced that he or she received help from a subliminal tape, can we conclude that the system really works? Research—and simple logic—indicate that the answer is "no." At least three phenomena can account for the fact that some customers will say that they are satisfied. First, simply making a purchase indicates a commitment to self-improvement. In fact, some people with emotional or behavioral problems show improvements in their feelings and behavior as soon as they register for psychotherapy—even before the therapy actually begins (Rachman and Wilson, 1980). Second, social psychologists learned long ago that once people have expended some effort toward reaching a goal, they tend to justify their effort by perceiving positive results. (We will encounter experiments that provide several examples of this phenomenon in Chapter 17.) Finally, if a person expects an effect to occur, he or she is easily convinced that it really did.

The effect of expectation is demonstrated by a study carried out to follow up a famous hoax. In 1957 an advertising expert claimed that he had inserted subliminal visual messages in a showing of *Picnic,* a popular film. The messages, which said "Eat Popcorn" and "Drink Coke," supposedly caused people to rush to the refreshment stand and purchase these items. As you can imagine, this event received much attention and publicity. Several years later, the advertising expert revealed that he had invented the episode in an attempt to get some favorable publicity for his advertising firm (Weir, 1984); no subliminal messages were ever presented and no customers rushed out to buy popcorn and Coke.

In 1958, long before the advertising expert admitted his hoax, the Canadian Broadcasting Corporation commissioned a study to determine whether a subliminal message could really work (Pratkanis, Eskenazi, and Greenwald, 1990). At the beginning of a television show, an announcer described the alleged "Popcorn" study and told the viewers that a test of subliminal persuasion would follow, with an unspecified message appearing on the screen. In fact, the message was "Phone now." According to the telephone company, no increase in rate of phone calls occurred. But many viewers wrote to the television network to say that they had felt compelled to do *something,* such as eat or drink. Obviously, the specific message to "Phone now" did not get across to the viewers, but the expectation that they should feel some sort of compulsion made many of them report that they did.

Is there any objective, scientific evidence that subliminal perception can occur? The answer is yes, there is, but the information transmitted by this means is very scanty. *Subliminal* literally means "below threshold." The term **subliminal perception** refers to the behavioral effect of a stimulus that falls below the threshold of conscious detection. That is, although the subject denies having detected a stimulus, the stimulus has a measurable effect on his or her behavior. But the effects are subtle, and special procedures are required to demonstrate them. For example, if the word NURSE is first flashed on a screen, it becomes easier for the viewer to recognize a related word, such as DOCTOR, but not an unrelated word, such as CHAIR. This phenomenon, called *semantic priming,* occurs even when the priming stimulus (NURSE) is presented so rapidly that the subjects deny having seen it, meaning that it can occur subliminally (Marcel, 1983).

Results such as these simply indicate that perception is a complex process—that when a stimulus is too weak to give rise to a conscious perception, it may still be strong enough to leave some traces in the brain that affect people's perception of other stimuli. And this effect has a threshold of its own; if a word is presented *too* briefly, it has no effect at all on the perception of other words. The phenomenon is a real one that involves the sense receptors and normal physiological processes. It does not operate by magic. (The relation between consciousness, perception, and memories is described in more detail in Chapters 7 and 8.)

Psychologists have examined very few of the many thousands of different subliminal self-help tapes that are available, but those they have examined seem to be ineffective. Some, according to Merikle (1988), contain stimuli that are simply too weak for the human ear to detect, under any conditions. Others, when subjected to spectrographic analysis (which detects the presence of "voiceprints" in the sound track) were found to contain no message at all!

Perhaps this fact explains the results of the experiment by Pratkanis, Eskenazi, and Greenwald (1990). The experimenters recruited volunteers to listen to a subliminal tape designed to improve memory or one designed to improve self-esteem. After five weeks of listening to the tapes, the experimenters asked the subjects whether their memory or self-esteem had improved. About half of the subjects said that they had—but none of the objective tests of memory or self-esteem administered by the experimenters showed any effect. Besides, the experimenters had switched tapes for half of the subjects: some of those who thought they had received a memory tape actually received a self-esteem tape, and vice versa. The switch made no difference at all in the satisfaction ratings. Thus, a person's satisfaction is no indication that subliminal perception really took place.

What Should We Conclude?   Only one conclusion seems possible: If you have been thinking about purchasing subliminal self-help tapes, save your money—unless you think you will be content with a placebo effect caused by commitment to change, a need to justify your efforts, and expectation of good results. (But then, having read this section, your expectations may not be very high.)   ■

INTERIM SUMMARY

Sensory Processing

We experience the world through our senses. Our knowledge of the world stems from the accumulation of sensory experience and subse-

quent learning. All sensory experiences are the result of energy from events that is transduced into activity of receptors, which are specialized neurons. Transduction causes changes in the activity of axons of sensory nerves, and these changes in activity inform the sensory mechanisms of the brain about the environmental event. The information received from the receptors is transmitted to the brain by means of two coding schemes: anatomical coding and temporal coding.

To study the nature of experience scientifically, we must be able to measure it. In nineteenth-century Germany Weber and his successor Fechner began investigating the relation between the physical characteristics of stimuli and the perceptions they produced. Weber devised the concept of the just-noticeable difference, and Fechner used the jnd to measure the magnitude of sensations. In the twentieth century the signal detection theory gave rise to methods that enabled psychologists to assess people's sensitivity to stimuli despite individual differences in response bias. The methods of psychophysics apply to all sensory modalities, including sight, smell, taste, hearing, and touch.

The makers of subliminal self-help tapes suggest that material that is presented below the detection threshold can improve a variety of skills and attitudes. Evidence suggests, however, that the testimonials of satisfied customers are a result of phenomena well known to social psychologists: commitment to change, a need to justify one's efforts, and expectation of good results. In fact, subliminal perception does occur—as long as the stimulus is not *too* weak—but the effects are subtle and are unlikely to produce useful changes in people's behavior.   ■

VISION

The Eye and Its Functions

4 The eyes are important organs. Because they are delicate, they are well protected. Each eye is housed in a bony socket and can be covered by the eyelid to keep dust and dirt out. The eyelids are edged by eyelashes, which help keep foreign matter from falling into the open eye. The eyebrows prevent sweat on the forehead from dripping into the eyes. Reflex mechanisms provide additional protection: The sudden approach of an object toward the face or a touch on the surface of the eye causes automatic eyelid closure and withdrawal of the head.

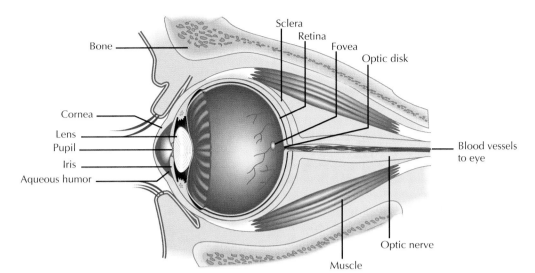

Figure 4.6 A cross section of the human eye.

Figure 4.6 shows a cross section of a human eye. The transparent **cornea** forms a bulge at the front of the eye and admits light. The rest of the eye is coated by a tough white membrane called the **sclera** (from the Greek *skleros,* "hard"). The **iris** consists of two bands of muscles that control the amount of light admitted into the eye. The brain controls these muscles and thus regulates the size of the pupil, constricting it in bright light and dilating it in dim light. The space immediately behind the cornea is filled with *aqueous humor,* which simply means "watery fluid." This fluid is constantly produced by tissue behind the cornea that filters the fluid from the blood. (If aqueous humor is produced too quickly or if the passage that returns it to the blood becomes blocked, the pressure within the eye can increase and cause damage to vision—a disorder known as *glaucoma.*) In place of blood vessels, the aqueous humor nourishes the cornea and other portions of the front of the eye, so that this fluid must circulate and be renewed. Because of its transparency, the cornea must be nourished in this unusual manner; our vision would be less clear if we had a set of blood vessels across the front of our eyes. (See *Figure 4.6.*)

The curvature of the cornea and of the **lens,** which lies immediately behind the iris, causes images to be focused on the inner surface of the back of the eye. The shape of the cornea is fixed, but the lens is flexible; a special set of muscles can alter its shape so that the eye can obtain images of either nearby or distant objects. This change in the shape of the lens to adjust for distance is called **accommodation.**

The **retina,** which lines most of the inner surface, performs the sensory functions of the eye. Embedded in the retina are over 130 million **photoreceptors**—specialized neurons that transduce light into neural activity. The information from the photoreceptors is transmitted to neurons that send axons toward one point at the back of the eye—the **optic disk.** All axons leave the eye at this point and join the optic nerve, which travels to the brain. (See *Figures 4.6* and *4.7.*) Because there are no photoreceptors directly in front of the optic disk, this portion of the retina is blind. If you have not located your own *blind spot,* you might want to try the demonstration shown in *Figure 4.8.*

Before the seventeenth century scientists thought that the lens sensed the presence of light. Johannes Kepler (1571–1630), the astronomer who discovered the true shape of the planets' orbits around the sun, is credited with the

Figure 4.7 A view of the back of the eye, showing the retina, the optic disk, and blood vessels. The fovea is located to the left of the topic disk, midway to the edge of the photograph. (Courtesy of Douglas G. Mollerstuen, New England Medical Center.)

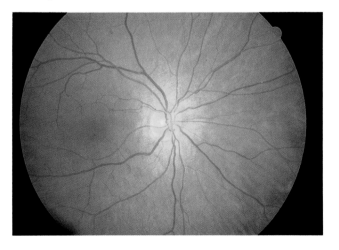

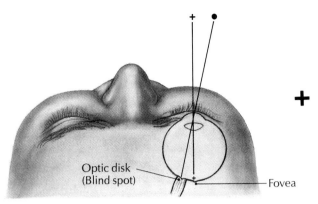

Figure 4.8   A test for the blind spot. With the left eye closed, look at the + with your right eye and move the page back and forth, toward and away from yourself. At about 20 centimeters the colored circle disappears from your vision because its image falls on your blind spot.

suggestion that the retina, not the lens, contained the receptive tissue of the eye. It remained for Christoph Scheiner (another German astronomer) to demonstrate in 1625 that the lens is simply a focusing device. (I suppose that astronomers had a special interest in vision and gave some thought to it during the long nights watching the sky.) Scheiner obtained an ox's eye from a slaughterhouse. After carefully peeling the sclera away from the back of the eye, he was able to see an upside-down image of the world through the thin, translucent membrane that remained. As an astronomer, he was familiar with the fact that convex glass lenses could cast images, so he recognized the function of the lens of the eye.

Figure 4.9 shows a cross section of the retina, with its three principal layers. Light passes successively through the *ganglion cell layer* (front), the *bipolar cell layer* (middle), and the *photoreceptor layer* (back). Early anatomists were surprised to find the photoreceptors in the deepest layer of the retina. As you might expect, the cells that are located above the photoreceptors are transparent. (See *Figure 4.9.*)

Photoreceptors respond to light and pass the information on by means of a transmitter substance to the **bipolar cells,** the neurons with which they form synapses. Bipolar cells transmit this information to the **ganglion cells,** neurons whose axons travel across the retina and through the optic nerves. Thus, visual information passes through a three-cell chain to the brain: photoreceptor → bipolar cell → ganglion cell → brain.

A single photoreceptor responds only to light that reaches its immediate vicinity, but a ganglion cell can receive information from many different photoreceptors. The retina also contains neurons that interconnect both adjacent photoreceptors and adjacent ganglion cells. (See *Figure 4.9.*) The existence of this neural circuitry indicates that some kinds of information processing are performed in the retina.

The human retina contains two general types of photoreceptors: 125 million **rods** and 6 million **cones,** so called because of their shapes. The **fovea,** a small pit in the back of the retina approximately 1 millimeter in diameter, contains only cones. (Refer to *Figure 4.6.*) Because

Figure 4.9   The cells of the retina. [Redrawn by permission of the Royal Society and the authors from Dowling, J.E., and Boycott, B.B. *Proceedings of the Royal Society (London)*, 1966, Series B, *166*, 80–111.]

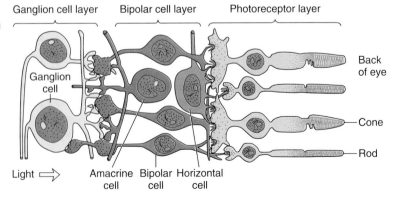

most cones are connected to only one ganglion cell apiece, the fovea is responsible for our finest, most detailed vision. When we look at a point in our visual field, we move our eyes so that the image of that point falls directly upon the cone-packed fovea. Thus, the fovea provides us with our greatest visual acuity. (*Acuity* derives from the Latin *acus,* meaning "needle." We use the same concept when we say that someone has "sharp eyes"; we mean he or she can see extremely small details.) Cones are also responsible for our ability to see colors, a topic discussed later in this chapter.

Farther away from the fovea the number of cones decreases and the number of rods increases. Up to 100 rods may converge on a single ganglion cell. A ganglion cell that receives information from so many rods is sensitive to very low levels of light. A small quantity of light falling on many rods can thus effectively stimulate the ganglion cell on which their information converges. Rods are therefore responsible for our sensitivity to very dim light but provide poor acuity.

Transduction of Light by Photoreceptors

5 Although light-sensitive sensory organs have evolved independently in a wide variety of animals—from insects to fish to mammals—the chemistry is essentially the same in all species: A molecule derived from vitamin A is the central ingredient in the transduction of the energy of light into neural activity. (Carrots are said to be good for vision because they contain a substance that the body easily converts to vitamin A.) In the absence of light this molecule is attached to another molecule, a protein. The two molecules together form a **photopigment.** The photoreceptors of the human eye contain four kinds of photopigments (one for rods and three for cones), but their basic mechanism is the same. When a photon (a particle of light) strikes a photopigment, the photopigment splits apart into its two constituent molecules. This event starts the process of transduction. The splitting of the photopigment causes a series of chemical reactions that stimulate the photoreceptor and cause it to send a message to the bipolar cell with which it forms a synapse. The bipolar cell sends a message to the ganglion cell, which then sends one on to the brain. (See *Figure 4.10.*)

Intact photopigments have a characteristic color. For example, **rhodopsin,** the photopigment of rods, is pink (*rhodon* means "rose" in Greek). However, once the photopigments are split apart by the action of light, they lose their color—they become bleached. Franz Boll discovered this phenomenon in 1876 when he removed an eye from an animal and pointed it toward a window that opened out onto a brightly lit scene. He then examined the retina under dim light and found that the image of the scene was still there. The retina was pink where little light had fallen and pale where the image had been bright. It was Boll's discovery that led investigators to suspect that a chemical reaction was responsible for the transduction of light into neural activity.

After light has caused a molecule of photopigment to become bleached (split), energy from the cell's metabolism causes the two molecules to recombine, and the photopigment is ready to be bleached by light again. Each photoreceptor contains many thousands of molecules of photopigment. The number of intact molecules of photopigment in a given cell depends upon the relative rates at which they are being split by light and being put back together by the cell's energy. The brighter the light, the more bleached photopigment there is—which leads us to the topic of the next section.

Adaptation to Light and Dark

The easiest way to introduce the phenomenon of visual adaptation is to ask you to remember how difficult it can be to find a seat in a darkened movie theater. If you have just come in from the bright sun, your eyes do not respond well to the

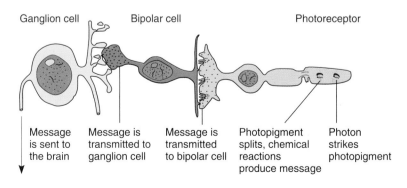

Ganglion cell   Bipolar cell   Photoreceptor

Message is sent to the brain

Message is transmitted to ganglion cell

Message is transmitted to bipolar cell

Photopigment splits, chemical reactions produce message

Photon strikes photopigment

Figure 4.10 Transduction of light into neural activity and the transmission of information to the brain.

low level of illumination. However, after a few minutes you can see rather well—your eyes have adapted.

In order for light to be detected, the photons must bleach (split) molecules of rhodopsin (or the other photopigments). When high levels of illumination strike the retina, the rate of regeneration of rhodopsin falls behind the rate of the bleaching process. With only a small percentage of the rhodopsin molecules intact, the rods are not very sensitive to light. If you enter a dark room after being in a brightly lit room or in sunlight, there are too few intact rhodopsin molecules for your eyes to respond immediately to dim light. The probability that a photon will strike an intact molecule of rhodopsin is very low. However, after a while the regeneration of rhodopsin overcomes the bleaching effects of the energy of light. The rods become full of unbleached rhodopsin, and a photon passing through a rod is likely to find a target. The eye has undergone **dark adaptation.**

Even before the development of electron microscopes, which permitted detailed examination of rods and cones, psychologists were able to demonstrate differences in their functions by studying the process of dark adaptation. Hecht and Schlaer (1938) exposed a subject's eyes to bright illumination and then completely darkened the room. At varying lengths of time they tested their subjects and determined the dimmest light that they were able to detect. As dark adaptation proceeded, the subjects' eyes became progressively more sensitive to light; they could detect fainter and fainter lights.

Figure 4.11 shows the results of the dark adaptation experiment. Each point on the vertical axis indicates the intensity of light necessary to produce a sensation. (Note that the scale on

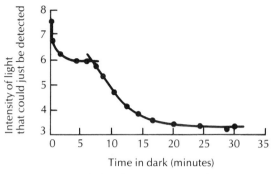

Figure 4.11 A dark adaptation curve showing a rod-cone break. (From Hecht, S., and Schlaer, S. *Journal of the Optical Society of America*, 1938, *28*, 269–275. Reprinted with permission.)

the vertical axis is logarithmic; a log value of 8 is 100,000 times greater than a log value of 3.) The figure shows clearly that the process of dark adaptation is not smooth and continuous; a break occurs after about seven minutes in the dark. (See *Figure 4.11.*)

The discontinuity in the dark adaptation curve is called the **rod-cone break.** The function is really composed of two curves, not one. Cones, which are less sensitive than rods, complete their regeneration of photopigments in five to seven minutes. The part of the curve before the break represents their activity. Rods are slower to regenerate rhodopsin, but they are more sensitive to light, so we see the effect of their adaptation only after the cones are completely dark-adapted.

How can we be sure that the break is due to differences in the rate of dark adaptation of rods and cones and that cones are responsible for the top curve and rods for the bottom one? A rather simple experiment provides the answer. Before I describe it, try to see whether you can think of

A rainbow contains colors that vary in their wavelength, which we see as a range of hues.

it yourself. Here is a hint: Remember that the fovea contains only cones.

The evidence can be obtained in the following way: If a subject looks directly at a small spot of light, only the fovea (which contains just cones) will be stimulated. A dark adaptation curve obtained in this way contains only the upper portion. However, if the spot of light appears off to the side, so that it stimulates more peripheral portions of the retina (where both rods and cones are located), the dark adaptation curve contains both portions.

Eye Movements

Our eyes are never completely at rest, even when our gaze is fixed upon a particular place (the *fixation point*). Three types of movements can be observed:

1. Fast, aimless, jittering movements occur, probably similar to the fine tremors we see in our hands and fingers when we attempt to keep them still.
2. Superimposed on these random tremors are slow, drifting movements that shift the image on the retina a distance of approximately twenty cone widths.
3. These slow drifts are terminated by quick movements that bring the image of the fixation point back to the fovea.

Although the small, jerky movements that the eyes make when at rest are random, they appear to have a definite purpose. Riggs, Ratliff, Cornsweet, and Cornsweet (1953) devised a way to project *stabilized images* on the retina; ones that remain in the same location on the retina. They mounted a small mirror in a contact lens worn by the subject and bounced a beam of light off it. They then projected the image onto a white screen in front of the subject, bounced it off several more mirrors, and finally directed it toward the subject's eye. (See *Figure 4.12*.) The path of the light was arranged so that the image on the screen moved in perfect synchrony with the eye movements. If the eye moved, so did the image; thus, the image that the experimenters projected always fell on precisely the same part of the retina despite the subject's eye movements. Under these conditions details of visual stimuli began to disappear. At first the image was clear, but then a "fog" drifted over the subject's field of view, obscuring the image. After a while some images could not be seen at all.

These results suggest that elements of the visual system are not responsive to an unchang-

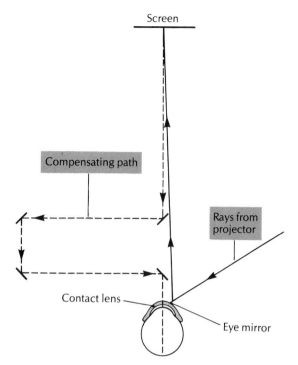

Figure 4.12 A procedure for stabilizing an image on the retina. (From Riggs, L.A., Ratliff, F., Cornsweet, J.C., and Cornsweet, T.N. *Journal of the Optical Society of America*, 1953, *43*, 495–501. Reprinted with permission.)

ing stimulus. The photoreceptors or the ganglion cells, or perhaps both, apparently cease to respond to a constant stimulus. The small, involuntary movements of our eyes keep the image moving and thus keep the visual system responsive to the details of the scene before us.

The eyes also make three types of "purposive" movements: conjugate movements, saccadic movements, and pursuit movements. **Conjugate movements** are cooperative movements that keep both eyes fixed upon the same target—or, more precisely, that keep the image of the target object on corresponding parts of the two retinas. If you hold up a finger in front of your face, look at it, and then bring your finger closer to your face, your eyes will make conjugate movements toward your nose. If you then look at an object on the other side of the room, your eyes will rotate outward, and you will see two separate blurry images of your finger. As you will learn in Chapter 7, conjugate eye movements assist in the perception of distance.

When you scan the scene in front of you, your gaze does not roam slowly and steadily across its features. Instead, your eyes make jerky **saccadic movements**—you shift your gaze abruptly from one point to another. When

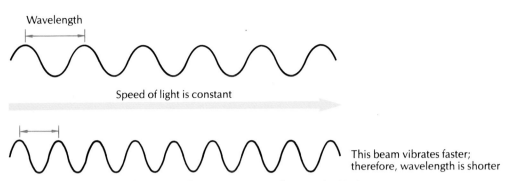

Wavelength

Speed of light is constant

This beam vibrates faster;
therefore, wavelength is shorter

Figure 4.13 Wavelength versus vibration. Because the speed of light is constant, faster vibrations produce shorter wavelengths.

you read a line in this book, your eyes stop several times, moving very quickly between each stop. You cannot consciously control the speed of movement between stops; during each *saccade* the eyes move as fast as they can. Only by performing a **pursuit movement**—say, by looking at your finger while you move it around—can you make your eyes move more slowly.

Color Vision

6 Among mammals, only primates have full color vision. A bull does not charge a red cape; he charges what he sees as an annoying gray object being waved at him. Among nonmammals, many birds and fishes also have excellent color vision; the brightly colored lure may really appeal to the fish as much as to the angler who buys it.

To understand color vision, we must know something about the physical nature of light. Wavelength is an important physical characteristic of light. Light from an incandescent source, such as the sun, consists of radiant energy similar to radio waves and contains a mixture of many frequencies. Because the speed of radiant energy is always constant (186,000 miles per second), the frequency of vibration determines the **wavelength** of the energy—the distance between adjacent vibrations. The faster the vibration, the shorter the wavelength is. (See *Figure 4.13.*)

The wavelength of visible light ranges from 380 through 760 nanometers (a nanometer, nm, is a billionth of a meter). Ultraviolet radiation, X rays, and gamma rays are also forms of radiant energy but have shorter wavelengths. Infrared radiation, radar, radio waves, and AC (alternating current) circuits have longer wavelengths. The entire range of wavelengths is known as the *electromagnetic spectrum;* the part our eyes can detect is called the *visual spectrum.* (See *Figure 4.14.*)

Experiments have shown that there are three types of cones in the human eye, each containing a different type of photopigment. Each type of photopigment is most sensitive to a particular wavelength of light; that is, light of a particular wavelength most readily causes a particular photopigment to split. Thus, different types of cones are stimulated by different wave-

Figure 4.14 The electromagnetic spectrum.

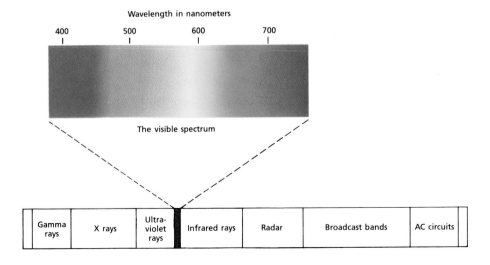

Wavelength in nanometers

400   500   600   700

The visible spectrum

| Gamma rays | X rays | Ultraviolet rays | Infrared rays | Radar | Broadcast bands | AC circuits |

Table 4.2 Physical and perceptual dimensions of color

Perceptual Dimension	Physical Dimension	Physical Characteristics
Hue	Wavelength	Frequency of oscillation of light radiation
Brightness	Intensity	Amplitude of light radiation
Saturation	Purity	Intensity of dominant wavelength, relative to total radiant energy

lengths of light. Information from the cones enables us to perceive colors.

Wavelength is related to color, but the terms are not synonymous. For example, the *spectral colors* (the colors we see in a rainbow, which contains the entire spectrum of visible radiant energy) do not include all colors that we can see, such as brown, pink, and the metallic colors silver and gold. The fact that not all colors are found in the spectrum means that differences in wavelength alone cannot account for the differences in the colors we can perceive.

The Dimensions of Color. Most colors can be described in terms of three physical dimensions: wavelength, intensity, and purity. Three perceptual dimensions—hue, brightness, and saturation—corresponding to these physical dimensions describe what we see. (See *Table 4.2.*) The **hue** of most colors is determined by

wavelength; for example, light with a wavelength of 540 nm is perceived as green. A color's **brightness** is determined by the intensity, or degree of energy, of the light that is being perceived, all other factors being equal.

The third perceptual dimension of color is saturation; **saturation** is roughly equivalent to purity. A fully saturated color consists of light of only one wavelength. Thus, the spectral colors of the rainbow are all fully saturated. White light consists of a mixture of all wavelengths of light; thus, although its components consist of light of all possible hues, we perceive it as being colorless. If white light is mixed with light of a particular wavelength, the result will be a desaturated color. For example, when red light (700 nm) is added to white light, the result is pink light. Pink is thus a less saturated version of red. Figure 4.15 illustrates how a color with a particular dominant wavelength (hue) can vary in its

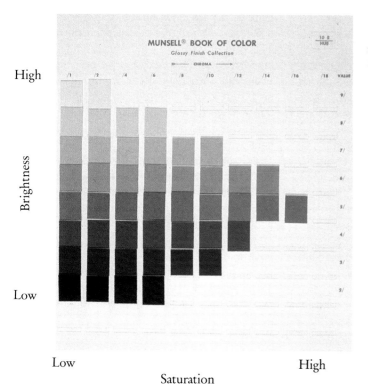

Figure 4.15 Hue, brightness, and saturation. These colors have the same dominant wavelength (hue) but different saturation and brightness. (Courtesy of Munsell Color Corporation.)

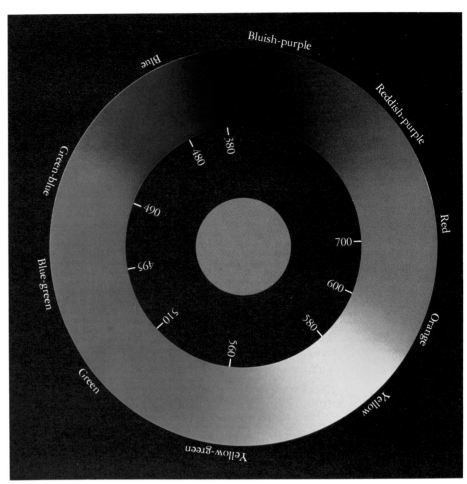

Figure 4.16 A color circle showing fully saturated hues of different wavelengths. The reddish-purple hues between 380 and 700 nm are not part of the spectrum but consist of mixtures of these two wavelengths. Pairs of hues on opposite sides of the circle are complementary; when added together, they produce a colorless gray.

brightness and saturation. Figure 4.16 illustrates a series of fully saturated colors of different hues. (See *Figures 4.15* and *4.16.*)

Color Mixing. The outer rim of the color circle shown in Figure 4.16 demonstrates that not all hues can be specified by wavelength; some hues are not found in the visual spectrum. There is a gap between red (700 nm) and violet (380 nm), but psychologically no gap exists. The colors blend, and there do not appear to be any sudden shifts in hue. (See *Figure 4.16.*) The colors on the circle between red and violet are not part of the spectrum; they are mixtures of various amounts of red and violet light. We perceive these mixtures as individual colors, intermediate in hue to the colors that produce them; we do not see the two component colors.

Vision is a *synthetic* sensory modality; that is, it synthesizes (puts together) rather than analyzes (takes apart). When two wavelengths of light are present, we see an intermediate color rather than the two components. (In contrast, the auditory system is *analytical.* If a high note and a low note are played together on a piano,

we hear both notes instead of a single, intermediate tone.) The addition of two or more lights of different wavelengths is called **color mixing.** This procedure is very different from paint mixing, and so are its results. If we pass a beam of white light through a prism, we break it into the spectrum of the different wavelengths it contains. If we recombine these colors by passing them through another prism, we obtain white light again. (See *Figure 4.17.*)

Color mixing must not be confused with pigment mixing—what we do when we mix paints. An object has a particular color because it contains pigments that absorb some wavelengths of light (converting them into heat) and reflect other wavelengths. For example, the chlorophyll found in the leaves of plants absorbs less green light than light of other wavelengths. Thus, when a leaf is illuminated by white light, it reflects a high proportion of green light and appears green to us.

When we mix paints, we are subtracting colors, not adding them. Mixing two paints yields a darker result. For example, adding blue paint to yellow paint yields green paint, which

Figure 4.17 Color mixing. White light can be split into a spectrum of colors with a prism and recombined through another prism.

certainly looks darker than yellow. But mixing two beams of light of different wavelengths always yields a brighter color. For example, when red and green light are shone together on a piece of white paper, we see yellow. In fact, we cannot tell a pure yellow light from a synthesized one made of the proper intensities of red and green light. To our eyes, both yellows appear identical.

To reconstitute white light, we do not even have to recombine all the wavelengths in the spectrum. If we shine a blue light, a green light, and a red light together on a sheet of white paper and properly adjust their intensities, the place where all three beams overlap will look perfectly white. (See **Figure 4.18.**)

7 Color Coding in the Retina. In 1802 Thomas Young, a British physicist and physician, noted that the human visual system can synthesize any color from various amounts of almost any set of three colors of different wavelengths. Young hypothesized that the eye contains three types of color receptors, each sensitive to a different hue, and that the brain synthesizes colors by combining the information received by each type of receptor. He suggested that these receptors were sensitive to three of the colors that people perceive as "pure": blue, green, and red. His suggestion was incorporated into a more elaborate theory of color vision by Hermann von Helmholtz.

Subsequent experiments in recent years have shown that the cones in the human eye do contain three types of photopigments, each of which preferentially absorbs light of a particular wavelength: 420, 530, and 560 nm. Although these wavelengths actually correspond to blue-violet, green, and yellow-green, most investigators refer to these receptors as *blue, green,* and *red* cones. To simplify the discussion here, I too will pretend that the three cones respond to these three pure hues. Red and green cones are present in about equal proportions, but there are far fewer blue cones.

Figure 4.19 helps explain the principle by which the three types of cones in the retina analyze the colors in a scene. Figure 4.19a

Figure 4.18 Additive color mixing and paint mixing. When blue, red, and green light of the proper intensity are all shone together, the result is white light. When red, blue, and yellow paints are mixed together, the result is a dark gray. (Courtesy of GATF.)

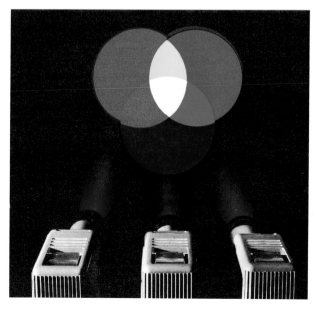

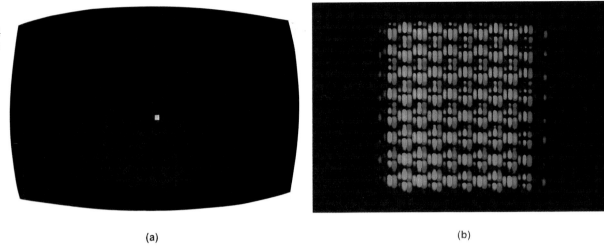

(a)   (b)

Figure 4.19 Color coding. The television screen demonstrates—in reverse—the principle of color coding by the three types of cones in the retina. (a) A small white rectangle shown in the middle of the screen. (b) An enlargement of the same white rectangle. Note that the screen displays only red, blue, and green spots of light. At a distance these colors blend and produce white light.

shows a color television screen displaying a white rectangle against a black background. Figure 4.19b shows a close-up of the center of the screen. You can see that the white rectangle is actually made of bright blue, green, and red spots of light; the screen contains absolutely no white spots. (See *Figure 4.19.*) When the screen displays various colors, it does so by varying the intensity of the spots. For example, in a patch of red, only the red spots will be illuminated.

The eye uses the principle of the color television screen but in reverse: Instead of displaying colors, it analyzes them. If a spot of white light shines on the retina, all three types of cones are stimulated equally, and we perceive white light. If a spot of pure blue, green, or red light shines on the retina, only one of the three classes of cones is stimulated, and a pure color is perceived. If a spot of yellow light shines on the retina, it stimulates red and green cones equally well but has little effect on blue cones. (You can see from Figure 4.16 that yellow is located midway between red and green.) Stimulation of red and green cones, then, is the signal that yellow light has been received.

Several scientists who came after Young and Helmholtz devised theories that took account of the fact that yellow is also a psychologically "pure" hue. Late in the nineteenth century Ewald Hering, a German physiologist, noted that the four primary hues appeared to belong to pairs of opposing colors: red/green and yellow/blue. We can imagine a bluish green or a yellowish green, or a bluish red or a yellowish red;

however, we cannot imagine a greenish red or a yellowish blue. Hering originally suggested that we cannot imagine these blends because there are two types of photoreceptors, one kind responding to green and red and the other kind responding to yellow and blue. (I will explain the reasoning behind this statement shortly.)

Hering's hypothesis about the nature of photoreceptors was wrong, but his principle does describe the characteristics of the retinal ganglion cells and hence of the axons that these neurons send to the brain. Two types of ganglion cells encode color vision: *red/green cells* and *yellow/blue cells*. Both types of ganglion cells fire at a steady rate when they are not stimulated. If a spot of red light shines on the retina, excitation of the red cones causes the red/green ganglion cells to begin to fire at a high rate. Conversely, if a spot of green light shines on the retina, excitation of the green cones causes the red/green ganglion cells to begin to fire at a slow rate. Thus, the brain learns about the presence of red or green light by the increased or decreased rate of firing of axons attached to red/green ganglion cells. Similarly, yellow/blue ganglion cells are excited by yellow light and inhibited by blue light. Because red and green light, and yellow and blue light, have opposite effects on the rate of axon firing, this coding scheme is called an *opponent process*.

Figure 4.20 provides a schematic explanation of the opponent-process coding that takes place in the retina. Stimulation of a red cone by red light excites the red/green ganglion cell, whereas stimulation of a green cone by green

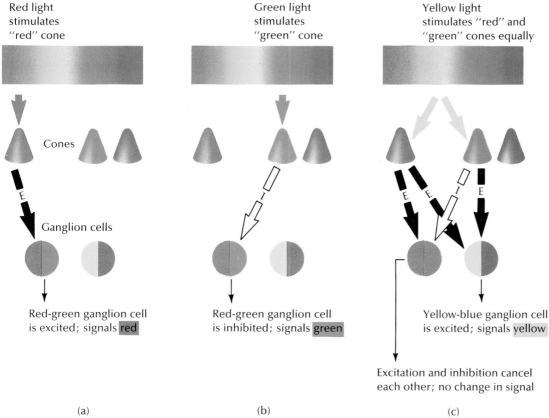

Red light stimulates "red" cone

Green light stimulates "green" cone

Yellow light stimulates "red" and "green" cones equally

Cones

Ganglion cells

Red-green ganglion cell is excited; signals red

Red-green ganglion cell is inhibited; signals green

Yellow-blue ganglion cell is excited; signals yellow

Excitation and inhibition cancel each other; no change in signal

(a)　　　　　　　　　　(b)　　　　　　　　　　(c)

Figure 4.20 Color coding in the retina. (a) Red light stimulating a "red" cone, which causes excitation of a red/green ganglion cell. (b) Green light stimulating a "green" cone, which causes inhibition of a red/green ganglion cell. (c) Yellow light stimulating "red" and "green" cones equally but not affecting "blue" cones. The stimulation of "red" and "green" cones causes excitation of a yellow/blue ganglion cell. The arrows labeled E and I represent neural circuitry within the retina that translates excitation of a cone into excitation or inhibition of a ganglion cell. For clarity, only some of the circuits are shown.

light inhibits the red/green ganglion cell. (See *Figures 4.20a* and *4.20b.*) If the photoreceptors are stimulated by yellow light, both the red and green cones are stimulated equally. Because of the neural circuitry between the photoreceptors and the ganglion cells, the result is that the yellow/blue ganglion cell is excited, signaling yellow. (See *Figure 4.20c.*)

The retina contains red/green and yellow/blue ganglion cells because of the nature of the connections between the cones, bipolar cells, and ganglion cells. The brain detects various colors by comparing the rates of firing of the axons in the optic nerve that signal red or green and yellow or blue. Now you can see why we cannot perceive a reddish green or a bluish yellow: An axon that signals red or green (or yellow or blue) can either increase or decrease its rate of firing; it cannot do both at the same time. A reddish green would have to be signaled by a ganglion cell firing slowly and rapidly at the same time, which is obviously impossible.

Negative Afterimages. Figure 4.21 demonstrates an interesting property of the visual system: the formation of a **negative afterimage.** Stare at the dot in the center of the flag on the left for approximately thirty seconds. Then quickly look at the dot in the center of the blank gray rectangle to the right. You will have a fleeting experience of seeing the red, white, and blue colors of an American flag—colors that are complementary, or opposite, to the ones on the left. (See *Figure 4.21.*) Complementary items go together to make up a whole. In this context, **complementary colors** are those that make white (or shades of gray) when added together.

The most important cause of negative afterimages is adaptation in the rate of firing of retinal ganglion cells. When some ganglion cells are excited or inhibited for a prolonged period of time, they later show a *rebound effect,* firing faster or slower than normal. For example, the green of the stripes in Figure 4.21 inhibits some red/green ganglion cells. When these regions of the

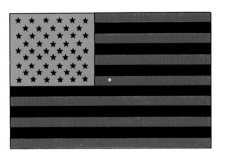 

Figure 4.21 A negative afterimage. Stare for approximately 30 seconds at the dot in the center of the left figure; then quickly transfer your gaze to the dot in the center of the right figure. You will see colors that are complementary to the originals.

retina are then stimulated with the neutral-colored light reflected off the gray-colored rectangle, the red/green ganglion cells—no longer inhibited by the green light—fire faster than normal. Thus, we see a red afterimage of the green stripes.

Defects in Color Vision. Approximately one in twenty males has some form of defective color vision. These defects are sometimes called *color blindness,* but the latter term should probably be reserved for the very few people who cannot see any color at all. Males are affected more than females because many of the genes for producing photopigments appear to be located on the X chromosome. Because males have only one X chromosome (females have two of them), a defective gene there will always be expressed.

There are many different types of defective color vision. Two of the three described here involve the red/green system. People with these defects confuse red and green. Their primary color sensations are yellow and blue; red and green both look yellowish. Figure 4.22 shows one of the figures from a commonly used test for defective color vision. A person who confuses red and green will not be able to see the 5. (See *Figure 4.22.*)

Figure 4.22 A figure commonly used to test for defective color vision. People with red/green color blindness will fail to see the 5.

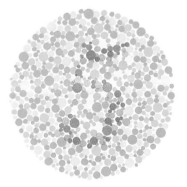

The most common defect, called **protanopia** (literally, "first-color defect"), appears to result from a lack of the photopigment for red cones. The fact that people with protanopia have relatively normal acuity suggests that they do have red cones but that these cones are filled with green photopigment (Boynton, 1979). (If red cones were missing, almost half of the cones would be gone from the retina, and hence vision would be less acute.) To a protanope, red looks much darker than green. The second form of red/green defect, called **deuteranopia** ("second-color defect"), appears to result from the opposite kind of substitution: Green cones are filled with red photopigment.

The third form of color defect, called **tritanopia** ("third-color defect"), involves the yellow/blue system and is much rarer: It affects fewer than 1 in 10,000 people. Tritanopes see the world in greens and reds; to them, a clear blue sky is a bright green, and yellow looks pink. The faulty gene that causes tritanopia is not carried on a sex chromosome; therefore, it is equally common in males and females. This defect appears to involve loss of blue cones. But because there are far fewer of these than of red and green cones to begin with, investigators have not yet determined whether the cones are missing or filled with one of the other photopigments.

INTERIM SUMMARY

Vision

You now have a better idea of how visual stimuli are detected and transmitted to the brain. The cornea and lens cast an image of the scene on the retina, which contains photoreceptors: rods and cones. The energy from light is transduced into neural activity when a photon strikes a molecule of photopigment, splitting it into its two constituents. This event causes the photoreceptor to send information to the ganglion cells by means of the bipolar cells. Adaptation to light and dark depends on the relative number of split and intact photopigment molecules in the photoreceptors. Rods are more sensitive to light but provide poor acuity; cones are less sensitive to light but provide excellent acuity and color vision.

Eyes make several kinds of movements. Vision, though popularly thought to be a passive experience (eyes being our windows on the world), requires the behavior of looking, which consists of moving our eyes and head. The eyes have a repertoire of movements that function for visual perception. Experiments with stabilized images show that the small, involuntary movements keep the image moving across the photoreceptors, thus preventing them from adapting to a constant stimulus. (As you will see later in this chapter, other sensory systems also respond better to changing stimuli than to constant ones.) When we are engaged in looking, we use other eye movements as well, including conjugate movements, saccadic movements, and pursuit movements.

When an image of the visual scene is cast upon the retina, each part of the image has a specific hue, brightness, and saturation. The red, blue, and green cones respond in proportion to the amount of each of these wavelengths contained in the light striking them. The encoded information is transmitted through red/green and yellow/blue ganglion cells, which send axons to the brain. The amount of activity in the red/green and yellow/blue axons from each part of the retina gives rise to the perception of an image, complete with color. Staring at a particular color for a while causes a negative afterimage to form, which contains the complementary color. Defects in color vision include two red/green confusions, in which red or green cones contain the wrong photopigment, and a blue/yellow confusion, caused by the absence of functioning blue cones. ■

AUDITION

8 Vision involves the perception of objects in three dimensions, at a variety of distances, and with a multitude of colors and textures. These complex responses may involve a single point in time or an extended period; they may also involve an unchanging scene or a rapidly changing one. The other senses analyze much simpler stimuli (such as an odor or a taste) or depend upon time and stimulus change for the development of a complex perception. For example, to perceive a solid object in three dimensions by means of touch, we must manipulate it—turn it over in our hands or move our hands over its surface. The stimulus must change over time for a full-fledged perception of form to emerge. The same is true for audition: We hear nothing meaningful in an instant.

Most people consider the sense of hearing second in importance only to vision. In some ways it is *more* important. A blind person can converse and communicate with other people almost as well as a sighted person. Deafness is much more likely to produce social isolation; a deaf person cannot easily join in the conversation of a group of people. Although our eyes can transmit much more information to the brain, our ears are used for some of our most important forms of social communication.

The Stimulus

Sound consists of rhythmical pressure changes in air. As an object vibrates, it causes the air around it to move. When the object is in the phase of vibration in which it moves toward you, it compresses molecules of air; as it moves away, it pulls the molecules farther apart. As a pressure wave arrives, it bends your eardrum in. The following wave of negative pressure (when the molecules are pulled farther apart) causes your eardrum to bulge out. (See ***Figure 4.23.***)

Sound waves are measured in frequency units of cycles per second called **hertz (Hz)**. The human ear perceives vibrations between approximately 30 and 20,000 Hz. Sound waves can vary in intensity and frequency. These

Figure 4.23 Sound waves. Changes in air pressure from sound waves move the eardrum in and out.

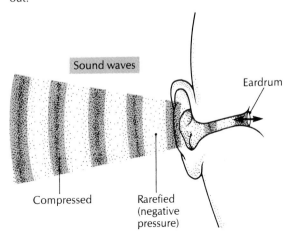

Physical dimension	Perceptual dimension				

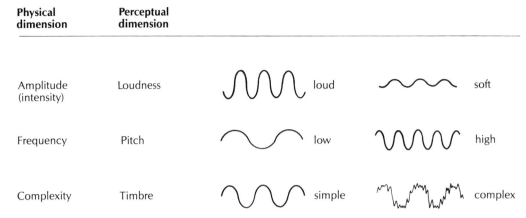

Figure 4.24   The physical and perceptual dimensions of sound waves.

variations produce corresponding changes in perception of loudness and pitch. (See **Figure 4.24.**) A third psychological dimension, *timbre,* corresponds to the complexity of the sound vibration. (I will discuss timbre in a later section of this chapter.)

Structure and Functions of the Auditory System

When people refer to the ear, they usually mean what anatomists call the *pinna*—the flesh-covered cartilage attached to the side of the head. (*Pinna* means "wing" in Latin.) But the pinna performs only a small role in audition; it helps funnel sound through the *ear canal* toward the middle and inner ear, where the business of hearing gets done. (See **Figure 4.25.**)

The *eardrum* responds to sound waves and passes the vibrations on to the receptor cells in the inner ear. The eardrum is attached to the first of a set of three middle ear bones called the **ossicles** (literally, "little bones"). The three ossicles are known as the *hammer,* the *anvil,* and the *stirrup,* because of their shapes. These bones act together, in lever fashion, to transmit the vibrations of the eardrum to the fluid-filled structure of the inner ear that contains the receptive organ.

The bony structure that contains the receptive organ is called the **cochlea** (*kokhlos* means "snail," which accurately describes its shape; see **Figure 4.25.**) A chamber attached to the cochlea (the *vestibule*) contains two openings, the oval window and the round window. The last of the three ossicles (the stirrup) presses against a membrane behind the **oval window** and transmits sound waves through it into the fluid inside the cochlea. The cochlea is divided into two parts by the **basilar membrane.** As the footplate of the stirrup presses back and forth against the membrane behind the oval window, pressure changes in the fluid above the basilar membrane cause it to vibrate back and

Figure 4.25   Anatomy of the auditory system.

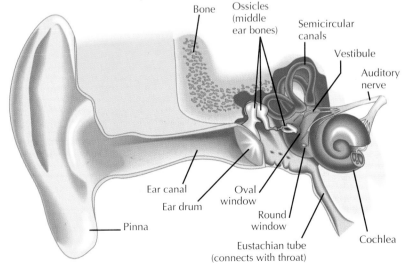

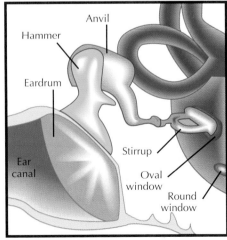

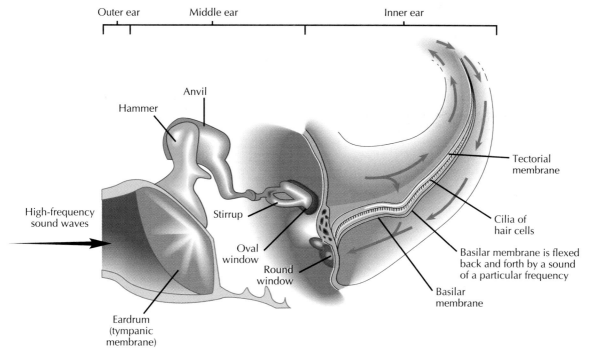

Outer ear   Middle ear   Inner ear

Anvil

Hammer

High-frequency
sound waves

Stirrup

Oval
window

Round
window

Eardrum
(tympanic
membrane)

Tectorial
membrane

Cilia of
hair cells

Basilar membrane is flexed
back and forth by a sound
of a particular frequency

Basilar
membrane

Figure 4.26   Responses to sound waves. When the stirrup pushes against the membrane behind the oval window, the membrane behind the round window bulges outward. Different high-frequency and medium-frequency sound vibrations cause flexing of different portions of the basilar membrane. Low-frequency sound vibrations cause the tip of the basilar membrane to flex in synchrony with the vibrations.

forth. Because the basilar membrane varies in its width and flexibility, different frequencies of sound cause different parts of the basilar membrane to vibrate. High-frequency sounds cause the end near the oval window to vibrate, medium-frequency sounds cause the middle to vibrate, and low-frequency sounds cause the tip to vibrate. (See *Figure 4.26.*)

In order for the basilar membrane to vibrate freely, the fluid in the lower chamber of the cochlea must have somewhere to go—unlike gases, liquids cannot be compressed. Free space is provided by the round window. When the basilar membrane flexes down, the displacement of the fluid causes the membrane behind the round window to bulge out; in turn, when the basilar membrane flexes up, the membrane behind the **round window** bulges in. (See *Figure 4.26.*) Some people suffer from a middle ear disease that causes the bone to grow over the round window. Because their basilar membrane cannot easily flex back and forth, these people have a severe hearing loss. However, their hearing can be restored by a surgical procedure called *fenestration* ("window making") in which a tiny hole is drilled in the bone where the round window should be.

Sounds are detected by special neurons known as auditory hair cells. **Auditory hair**

cells transduce mechanical energy caused by the flexing of the basilar membrane into neural activity. These cells possess hairlike protrusions called **cilia** ("eyelashes"). The ends of the cilia are embedded in a fairly rigid shelf (the **tectorial membrane**) that hangs over the basilar membrane like a balcony. When sound vibrations cause the basilar membrane to flex back and forth, the cilia are stretched. This pull on the cilia is translated into neural activity. (See *Figure 4.27.*)

When a mechanical force is exerted on the cilia of the auditory hair cells, the electrical charge across their membrane is somehow altered. The change in the electrical charge causes a transmitter substance to be released at a synapse between the auditory hair cell and the dendrite of a neuron of the auditory nerve. The release of the transmitter substance excites the neuron, which transmits messages through the auditory nerve to the brain. (See *Figure 4.27.*)

Perception of Pitch.   Scientists originally thought that the neurons of the auditory system represented pitch by firing in synchrony with the vibrations of the basilar membrane. However, they subsequently learned that axons cannot fire rapidly enough to represent the high frequencies that we can hear. A good, young ear

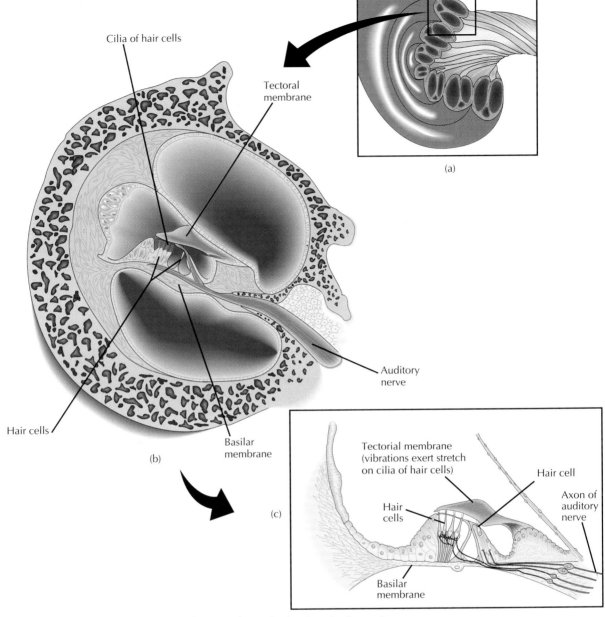

Cilia of hair cells

Tectoral
membrane

Auditory
nerve

Hair cells

Basilar
membrane

(b)

(a)

(c)

Tectorial membrane
(vibrations exert stretch
on cilia of hair cells)

Hair cell

Axon of
auditory
nerve

Hair
cells

Basilar
membrane

Figure 4.27   The transduction of sound vibrations in the auditory system.

can hear frequencies of more than 20,000 hertz, but axons cannot fire more than 1000 times per second. Therefore, high-frequency sounds, at least, must be encoded in some other way.

As we saw, high-frequency and medium-frequency sounds cause different parts of the basilar membrane to vibrate. Thus, sounds of different frequencies stimulate different groups of auditory hair cells located along the basilar membrane. At least for high-frequency and medium-frequency sounds, therefore, the brain is informed of the pitch of a sound by the activity of different sets of axons from the auditory nerve. (Refer to *Figure 4.26.*)

Two basic types of evidence indicate that pitch is detected in this way. First, direct observation of the basilar membrane has shown that the region of maximum vibration depends on the frequency of the stimulating tone (von Békésy, 1960). Second, experiments have found that damage to specific regions of the basilar membrane causes loss of the ability to perceive specific frequencies. The discovery that some antibiotics damage hearing (for example, deafness is one of the possible side effects of an antibiotic used to treat tuberculosis) has helped auditory researchers investigate the anatomical coding of pitch. Stebbins, Miller, Johnsson, and Hawkins

(1969) administered an antibiotic to different groups of animals for varying times. Afterward, they removed the animals' cochleas and examined them. The longer the exposure, the more hair cells that were killed. Damage started at the end of the basilar membrane nearer the oval window and progressed toward the other end. Tests of the animals' ability to perceive tones of different frequencies showed that as more and more hair cells were killed, the animals increasingly lost the ability to hear sounds, beginning with those of the highest frequencies. The animals' hearing loss exactly paralleled the death of the hair cells.

Although high-frequency and medium-frequency sounds are detected because they cause different regions of the basilar membrane to vibrate, low-frequency sounds are detected by a different method. Kiang (1965) recorded the electrical activity of single axons in the auditory nerve and found many that responded to particular frequencies. Presumably, these axons were stimulated by hair cells located on different regions of the basilar membrane. However, he did not find any axons that responded uniquely to particular frequencies lower than 200 Hz—and yet tones lower than 200 Hz are easily perceived. How, then, are the lower frequencies encoded?

The answer is this: Frequencies lower than 200 Hz cause the very tip of the basilar membrane to vibrate in synchrony with the sound waves. Neurons that are stimulated by hair cells located there are able to fire in synchrony with these vibrations, thus firing at the same frequency as the sound. The brain "counts" these vibrations (so to speak) and thus detects low-frequency sounds. As you may have recognized, this process is an example of temporal coding. (Refer to *Figure 4.26*.)

The best evidence that low frequencies are detected in this way comes from an experiment performed many years ago by Miller and Taylor (1948). These investigators used white noise as a stimulus. White noise consists of a random mixture of all the perceptible frequencies of sound—it sounds like the *sssh* heard when a television or FM radio is tuned between stations. White noise stimulates *all* regions of the basilar membrane because it contains all frequencies of sound.

Miller and Taylor presented human subjects with white noise that passed through a hole in a rotating disk. By spinning the disk at various speeds, the investigators could divide the noise into extremely brief pulsations, which could be presented at various time intervals. Thus, a "pitch" was artificially created by setting the pulsation of the white noise at a certain speed. When the frequency of the pulsation was less than 250 Hz, the subjects could accurately identify its pitch. However, above 250 Hz the perception of pitch disappeared. Obviously, because the white noise stimulated all parts of the basilar membrane, the low-frequency sounds must have been detected by neurons that fired in synchrony with the pulsations, whereas the medium-frequency and high-frequency sounds could not be differentiated by frequency of pulsation alone.

Perception of the Source of a Sound. When we hear an unexpected sound, we usually turn our head quickly to face its source. Even newborn infants can make this response with reasonably good accuracy. And once our face is oriented toward the source of the sound, we can detect changes in its location by as little as 1 degree. To do so, we make use of two qualities of sound: relative loudness and difference in arrival time.

Relative loudness is the most effective means of perceiving the location of high-frequency sounds. Acoustic energy, in the form of vibrations, does not in fact pass through solid objects. Low-frequency sounds can easily make a large solid object such as a wall vibrate, setting the air on the other side in motion and producing a *new* sound across the barrier. But solid objects effectively damp out high frequencies by casting a "sound shadow." Our head is one such solid object, damping out high-frequency sounds so that they appear much louder to the ear nearer the source of the sound. Thus, if a source on your right produces a high-frequency sound, your right ear will receive more intense stimulation than your left ear. (See *Figure 4.28*.)

Figure 4.28 The head casts a "sound shadow" for high-frequency sound vibrations.

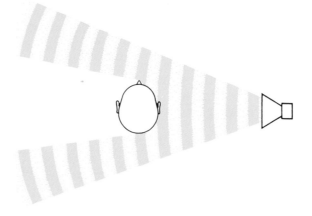

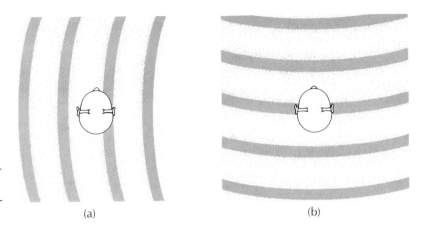

Figure 4.29 Detecting differences in arrival time. (a) Source of a 1000-Hz tone to the right. The pressure waves on each eardrum are out of phase; one eardrum is pushed in, while the other is pushed out. (b) Source of a sound directly in front. The vibrations of the eardrums are synchronized.

(a)

(b)

The second method, which works best for frequencies below approximately 3000 Hz, involves detecting differences in the arrival time of sound pressure waves at each eardrum. A 1000-Hz tone produces pressure waves approximately 1 ft apart. Because the distance between a person's eardrums is somewhat less than half that, a source of 1000-Hz sound located to one side of the head will cause one eardrum to be pushed in while the other eardrum is being pulled out. In contrast, if the source of the sound is directly in front of the listener, both eardrums will move in synchrony. (See **Figure 4.29.**)

Researchers have found that when the source of a sound is located to the side of the head, as in Figure 4.29a, axons in the right and left auditory nerves will fire at different times. The brain is able to detect this disparity, which causes the sound to be perceived as being off to one side. In fact, the brain can detect differences in firing times of a fraction of a millisecond (a thousandth of a second). The easiest stimuli to locate are those that produce brief clicks, which cause brief bursts of neural activity. Apparently, it is easiest for the brain to compare the arrival times of single bursts of incoming information.

Other animals can also detect the location of a sharp, short burst of sound more easily than a smooth, steady one. Birds capitalize upon this capability. When a male bird stakes out his territory, he sings with a very sharp, staccato song that is easy to localize. In effect, he is announcing, "Keep away, males, I am here and this place is mine!" In contrast, if a predator appears in the vicinity, many birds will emit alarm calls that warn others of the danger without endangering themselves by revealing their own location. An alarm call usually consists of steady whistles that start and end slowly. Because the

call has no sudden changes in loudness, it is more difficult to localize; it seems to be coming from everywhere. If you go for a walk in the woods sometime, try to listen for both types of calls.

Perception of Timbre. You can easily distinguish between the sounds of a violin and a clarinet, even if they are playing tones of the same pitch and loudness. So clearly, pitch and loudness are not the only characteristics of a sound. Sounds can vary greatly in complexity; they can start suddenly or gradually increase in loudness, be short or long, and seem thin and reedy or full and vibrant. The enormous variety of sounds that we can distinguish is in large part due to an important characteristic of sound called timbre.

The combining, or synthesis, of two or more simple tones, each consisting of a single frequency, can produce a complex tone. For example, an electronic synthesizer produces a mixture of sounds of different frequencies, each of which can be varied in amplitude (intensity). Thus, it can synthesize the complex sounds of a clarinet or violin or can assemble completely new sounds not produced by any other source. Conversely, complex sounds that have a regular sequence of waves can be reduced by means of analysis into several simple tones. Figure 4.30 shows a waveform produced by the sound of a clarinet (upper curve). The curves beneath it show the amplitude and frequency of the simple waves that can be shown, mathematically, to produce this waveform. (See **Figure 4.30.**)

An analysis like the one shown in Figure 4.30 specifies the timbre of a sound. We can tell a clarinet from another instrument because each instrument produces sounds consisting of a unique set of simple tones called **overtones.** Their frequencies are multiples of the **funda-**

Timbre, an important characteristic of sound, allows us to distinguish the tones of a violin, piano, and clarinet, even when these instruments are played at the same pitch and loudness.

Figure 4.30 The shape of a sound wave from a clarinet *(top)* and the individual frequencies into which it can be analyzed. (Copyright © 1977 by CBS Magazines. Reprinted from *Stereo Review,* June 1977, by permission.)

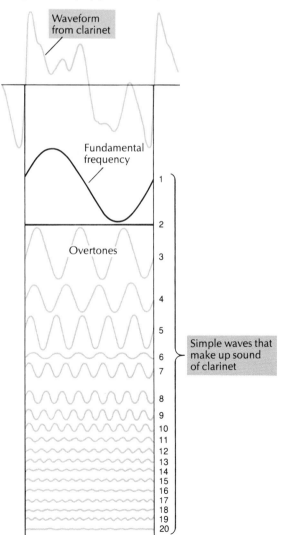

mental frequency, or the basic pitch of the sound. **Timbre** is the distinctive combination of overtones with the fundamental frequency. The fundamental frequency causes one part of the basilar membrane to flex, while each of the overtones causes another portion to flex. During a complex sound, then, many different portions of the basilar membrane are flexing simultaneously. Thus, the ear analyzes a complex sound, just as the person who devised Figure 4.30 did. Information about the fundamental frequency and each of the overtones is sent to the brain through the auditory nerve, and a complex tone with a particular timbre is perceived.

INTERIM SUMMARY

Audition

Were you to sit at a synthesizer, you would have at your fingertips the means to produce a vast array of sounds. You would also have at your disposal (in your head) an auditory system sophisticated enough to differentiate among these sounds. The physical dimensions of the synthesizer's sound—amplitude, frequency, and complexity—would be translated into the perceptual dimensions of loudness, pitch, and timbre for sounds ranging from 30 to 20,000 hertz. Sound pressure waves put the process in motion by setting up vibrations in the eardrum, which are passed on to the ossicles. Vibrations of the stirrup against the membrane behind the oval window create pressure changes in the fluid within the cochlea that cause the basilar membrane to flex back and forth. This vibration causes the auditory hair cells on the basilar membrane to move relative to the tectorial membrane. The resulting pull on the cilia of the hair cells stimulates them to secrete a transmitter substance that excites neurons of the auditory nerve. This process informs the brain of the presence of a sound.

Two different methods of detection enable the brain to differentiate the multitude of sounds that can be produced. Different high-frequency and medium-frequency sounds are perceived when different parts of the basilar membrane vibrate in response to these frequencies. Low-frequency vibrations are detected when the tip of the basilar membrane vibrates in synchrony with the sound, which causes the axons in the auditory nerve to fire at the same frequency. To locate the source of a sound (for example, if your synthesizer is hooked up to different speakers), you have available two means: Low-frequency sounds are located by differences in the arrival time of the sound waves in each ear, and high-frequency sounds are located by differences in intensity caused by the "sound shadow" cast by your head.

As you produce sounds of more and more complex timbre, the auditory system will analyze them into their constituent frequencies, each of which causes a particular part of the basilar membrane to vibrate. All these functions proceed automatically, so that when you press some keys on your synthesizer, your brain will then hear what you have played. ■

Taste buds viewed through a scanning electron micrograph.

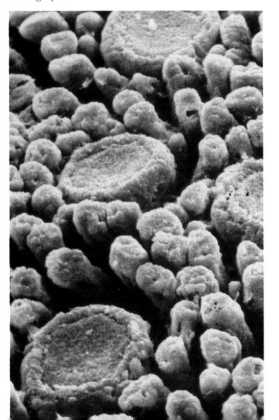

GUSTATION

9 Taste, or **gustation,** is the simplest of the sense modalities. We can perceive only four qualities of taste: *sourness, sweetness, saltiness,* and *bitterness.* Taste is not the same as flavor, which depends on odor as well as taste. You have probably noticed that the flavors of foods are diminished when you have a head cold. This loss of flavor occurs not because your taste buds are inoperative but because congestion with mucus makes it difficult for odor-laden air to reach your receptors for the sense of smell. Without their characteristic odors to serve as cues, onions taste much like apples (although apples do not make your eyes water). Even a steak tastes like, salty cardboard if we cannot smell it.

Receptors and Sensory Pathway

The tongue has a somewhat corrugated appearance, being marked by creases and bumps. The bumps are called **papillae** (from the Latin, meaning "nipple"). Each papilla contains a number of taste buds (in some cases as many as 200). A **taste bud** is a small organ that contains a number of receptor cells, each of which is shaped rather like a segment of an orange. The cells have hairlike projections called *microvilli* that protrude through the pore of the taste bud into the saliva that coats the tongue and fills the trenches of the papillae. (See *Figure 4.31.*) Molecules of chemicals dissolved in the saliva stimulate the receptor cells, probably by interacting with special receptors on the microvilli that are similar to the postsynaptic receptors found on other neurons. The receptor cells form synapses with dendrites of neurons that send axons to the brain through three different cranial nerves.

In the brain, gustatory information is closely related to that of the somatosenses (described in the last section of this chapter). Gustatory information is sent to the thalamus and is then relayed to the cerebral cortex, to a region adjacent to the one that receives somatosensory information from the head and face.

The Four Qualities of Taste

The surface of the tongue is differentially sensitive to taste. The tip is most sensitive to sweet and salty substances; the sides to sour substances; and the back of the tongue, the back of the throat, and the soft palate overhanging the back of the tongue to bitter substances. (See *Figure 4.32.*)

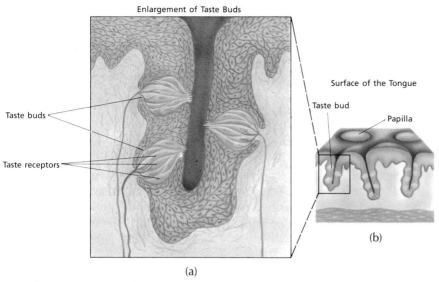

Enlargement of Taste Buds

Surface of the Tongue

Taste bud

Papilla

Taste buds

Taste receptors

(b)

(a)

Figure 4.31 The tongue. (a) Papillae on the surface of the tongue. (b) A taste bud.

The physical properties of the molecules that we taste determine the nature of the taste sensations. Different molecules stimulate different types of receptors. For example, all substances that taste *salty* ionize (break into charged particles) when they dissolve. The most important salty substance is, of course, table salt—sodium chloride (NaCl). Other chlorides, such as lithium or potassium chloride, and some other salts, such as bromides or sulfates, are also salty in taste; but none tastes quite as salty as sodium chloride. This finding suggests that the specific function of salt-tasting receptors is to identify sodium chloride. Sodium plays a unique role in the regulation of our body fluid. If the body's store of sodium falls, we cannot

Figure 4.32 Sensitivity of different regions of the tongue to different tastes.

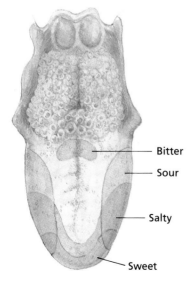

Bitter

Sour

Salty

Sweet

retain water, and our blood volume will fall. The result can be heart failure. Loss of sodium stimulates a strong craving for the salty taste of sodium chloride.

Both *bitter* and *sweet* substances seem to consist of large, nonionizing molecules. Scientists cannot predict, merely on the basis of shape, whether a molecule will taste bitter or sweet (or neither). Some molecules (such as saccharin) stimulate both sweet and bitter receptors; they taste sweet at the front of the tongue and bitter at the back of the palate and throat. Most likely, the function of the bitterness receptor is to avoid ingesting poisons. Many plants produce alkaloids that serve to protect them against being eaten by insects or browsing animals. Some of these alkaloids are poisonous to humans, and most of them taste bitter. In contrast, the sweetness receptor enables us to recognize the sugar content of fruits and other nutritive plant foods. When sweet-loving animals gather and eat fruit, they tend to disperse the seeds and help propagate the plant; thus, the presence of sugar in the fruit is to the plant's advantage as well.

Most *sour* tastes are produced by acids—in particular, by the hydrogen ion (H^+) contained in acid solutions. The sourness receptor probably serves as a warning device against substances that have undergone bacterial decomposition, most of which become acidic. In earlier times most wholesome, natural foods tasted either sweet or salty, not bitter or sour. (Nowadays, we can mix sweet-tasting and sour-tasting substances to make tasty beverages, such as lemonade.)

OLFACTION

[10] The sense of smell—**olfaction**—is one of the most interesting and puzzling of the sense modalities. For one thing, odors have a powerful ability to evoke old memories and feelings, even many years after an event. At some time in their lives most people encounter an odor that they recognize as having some childhood association, even though they cannot identify it. The phenomenon may occur because the olfactory system sends information to the limbic system, a part of the brain that plays a role in both emotions and memories. (The functions of the limbic system will be discussed in Chapter 12.)

Although other animals, such as dogs, have more sensitive olfactory systems, we should not underrate our own. We can smell some substances at lower concentrations than our most sensitive instruments can detect. One reason for the apparent difference in sensitivity between our olfactory system and those of other mammals is that they put their noses where the odors are the strongest—just above ground level. For example, watch a dog following an odor trail. The dog sniffs along the ground, where the odors of the passing animal will have clung. Even a bloodhound's nose would not be very useful if it were kept 5 feet above the ground, as ours is.

Odors play a very important role in the lives of most mammals. Although we do not make use of olfaction in identifying one another, we do use it to avoid some dangers, such as food that has spoiled. In fact, the odor of rotten meat will trigger vomiting—a useful response, if some of the rotten meat has been swallowed. Other animals recognize friend and foe by means of smell and use odors to attract mates and repel rivals. And the reproductive behavior of laboratory mammals—and even the menstrual cycles of women—can be influenced by the odors emitted by other animals of the same species.

Anatomy of the Olfactory System

Figure 4.33 shows the anatomy of the olfactory system. The receptor cells lie in the **olfactory mucosa,** 1-inch-square patches of mucous membrane located on the roof of the nasal sinuses, just under the base of the brain. (See *Figure 4.33.*) The receptor cells send axons up through small holes in the bone above the olfactory mucosa. The axons synapse on neurons in the **olfactory bulbs,** which are enlargements at the ends of the stalklike olfactory nerves. We do not yet know how olfactory receptor cells detect odors. The most widely accepted hypothesis is that the interaction between odor molecule and receptor is similar to that of transmitter substance and postsynaptic receptor on a neuron. Thus, similar mechanisms may detect the stimuli for taste and olfaction.

Unlike information from all other sensory modalities, olfactory information is not sent to the thalamus and then relayed to a specialized region of the cerebral cortex. Instead, olfactory information is sent directly to several regions of the limbic system, a set of brain structures involved in emotion, motivation, and memory. Olfaction is unlike other sensory modalities in two important ways: People have difficulty describing odors in words, and odors can often evoke vague memories and feelings that we are sure we experienced before but cannot easily describe. Undoubtedly, the connection between

Figure 4.33 The olfactory system.

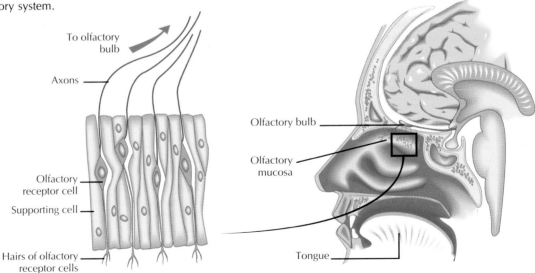

the olfactory system and the limbic system is responsible for these properties.

The Dimensions of Odor

We know that there are four taste dimensions and that a color can be specified by hue, brightness, and saturation, but we still do not know what the dimensions of odor might be. It seems reasonable to assume that there *are* dimensions, if only because the alternatives seem so implausible. We do not know how many odors we can identify, but the number is very large. We probably do not have separate receptors for each odor. Such a system would involve a phenomenal number of different receptors, and undoubtedly, more than a single receptor cell is needed to produce a sensation. Moreover, separate receptors would not explain how we can smell and learn to identify new, synthetic chemicals that were not in existence when our olfactory system was evolving. Thus, the hypothesis that we possess unique olfactory receptors for every new odor that exists or is yet to be synthesized by chemists does not seem likely.

Most people agree that some odors resemble one another. The smell of rotten eggs is not at all like the smell of lemons, but pine oil and cedar oil have a similar smell. Thus, a plausible assumption is that there are a limited number of "odor primaries" and that our olfactory system identifies an odor by determining the degree to which it resembles each of the primaries. The hue of a color can be specified by measuring the excitation produced in red, green, and blue receptors; perhaps the olfactory system works in a similar way.

The problem is to determine how many "odor primaries" there might be. Amoore (1970) studied the words that chemists used to describe the odors of chemicals and was able to reduce the descriptive adjectives to a list of seven: camphoraceous, ethereal, floral, musky, pepperminty, pungent, and putrid. Perhaps, he reasoned, the fact that people find these seven adjectives necessary means that there are seven odor primaries, just as there are four taste primaries.

Amoore also hypothesized that there were receptors on the cilia of the olfactory cells with specific shapes to accommodate odor molecules with particular three-dimensional configurations. According to this hypothesis, a particular molecule might fit the pepperminty receptors fairly well, the floral receptors a little less well, the ethereal receptors even less well, and the others not at all. Thus, the brain would receive signals of an odor that was strongly pepperminty, moderately floral, and slightly ethereal, combining these dimensions to produce the perception of a unique odor.

There is not enough supporting evidence to prove Amoore's theory and not enough contradictory evidence to disprove it. Some people appear to be unable to identify whole classes of odors, just as color-blind people cannot identify whole classes of colors. Perhaps these people lack one of the various types of odor receptors. However, the classes of odors that they cannot detect often do not correspond well with Amoore's hypothetical primaries. Furthermore, although there is some similarity between the three-dimensional shapes of molecules that are judged to be similar in odor, there are also some glaring discrepancies: Some similarly shaped molecules smell very different, and some differently shaped molecules smell similar. Finally, although we can synthesize sounds or colors, we cannot reproduce one odor by mixing several "simple" odors together.

Some scientists have rejected the notion that the shape of odor molecules is important and are investigating such characteristics as their vibration or emission of energy. Whatever the mechanism of odor recognition is, the answer appears to be a long way off.

INTERIM SUMMARY

Gustation and Olfaction

Both gustation and olfaction are served by cells with receptors that respond selectively to various kinds of molecules. Taste buds have four kinds of receptors, responding to molecules that we perceive as sweet, salty, sour, or bitter. To most organisms, sweet and moderately salty substances taste pleasant, whereas sour or bitter substances taste unpleasant. Sweetness and saltiness receptors permit us to detect nutritious foods and sodium chloride. Sourness and bitterness receptors help us avoid substances that might be poisonous.

Olfaction is a remarkable sense modality. We can distinguish countless different odors and can recognize smells from childhood even when we cannot remember when or where we encountered them. Although we recognize similarities between different odors, most seem unique. Unlike visual and auditory stimuli, odors do not easily blend; for example, when visiting a carnival, we can distinguish the odors of popcorn, cotton candy, crushed grass, and diesel oil in a single sniff. However, most investigators believe that there are odor primaries of some kind, even though they have not yet been discovered. ■

THE SOMATOSENSES

11 The body senses, or **somatosenses,** include our ability to respond to touch, vibration, pain, warmth, coolness, limb position, muscle length and stretch, tilt of the head, and changes in the speed of head rotation. The number of sense modalities represented in this list depends on one's definition of a sense modality. However, it does not really matter whether we say that we respond to warmth and coolness by means of one sense modality or two different ones; the important thing is to understand how our bodies are able to detect changes in temperature.

Many experiences require simultaneous stimulation of several different sense modalities. For example, taste and odor alone do not determine the flavor of spicy food; mild (or sometimes not-so-mild) stimulation of pain detectors in the mouth and throat gives Mexican food its special characteristic. Sensations such as tickle and itch are apparently mixtures of varying amounts of touch and pain. Similarly, our perception of the texture and three-dimensional shape of an object that we touch involves cooperation among our senses of pressure, muscle and joint sensitivity, and motor control (to manipulate the object). If we handle an object and find that it moves smoothly in our hand, we con-

clude that it is slippery. If, after handling this object, our fingers subsequently slide across each other without much resistance, we perceive a feeling of oiliness. If we sense vibrations when we move our fingers over an object, it is rough. And so on. If you close your eyes as you manipulate some soft and hard, warm and cold, and smooth and rough objects, you can make yourself aware of the separate sensations that interact and give rise to a complex perception.

The following discussion of the somatosenses groups them into three major categories: the skin senses, the internal senses, and the vestibular senses.

The Skin Senses

The entire surface of the human body is innervated (supplied with nerve fibers) by the dendrites of neurons that transmit somatosensory information to the brain. Cranial nerves convey information from the face and front portion of the head (including the teeth and the inside of the mouth and throat); spinal nerves convey information from the rest of the body's surface. All somatosensory information is detected by the dendrites of neurons; the system uses no separate receptor cells. However, some of these dendrites have specialized endings that modify the way they transduce energy into neural activity.

Figure 4.34 shows the sensory receptors found in hairy skin and in smooth, hairless skin (such as skin on the palms of the hands or the soles of the feet). The most common type is the **free nerve ending,** which resembles the fine roots of a plant. Free nerve endings infiltrate the middle layers of both smooth and hairy skin

Figure 4.34 Sensory receptors. (a) In hairy skin. (b) In hairless skin.

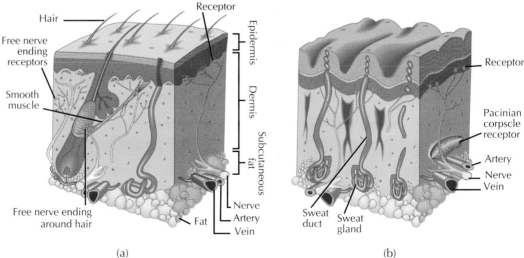

(a)

(b)

and surround the hair follicles in hairy skin. If you bend a single hair on your forearm, you will see how sensitive the free nerve endings are. (Try it; then see *Figure 4.34a.*)

The largest of the special receptive endings, called the **Pacinian corpuscle,** is actually visible to the naked eye. (See *Figure 4.34b.*) Pacinian corpuscles are very sensitive to touch; when they are moved, their axons fire a brief burst of impulses. Pacinian corpuscles are thought to be the receptors that inform us about vibration.

Other specialized receptors detect other sensory qualities, including warmth, coolness, and pain.

Temperature. There is general agreement that different sensory endings produce the sensations of warmth and coolness. Detectors for coolness appear to be located closer to the surface of the skin. If you suddenly place your foot under a stream of rather hot water, you may feel a brief sensation of cold just before you perceive that the water is really hot. This sensation probably results from short-lived stimulation of the coolness detectors located in the upper layers of the skin.

Our temperature detectors respond best to *changes* in temperature. Within reasonable limits the air temperature of our environment comes to feel "normal." Temporary changes in temperature are perceived as warmth or coolness. Thus, our temperature detectors adapt to the temperature of our environment. This adaptation can be easily demonstrated. If you place one hand in a pail of hot water and the other in a pail of cold water, the intensity of the sensations of heat and cold will decrease after a few minutes. If you then plunge both hands into a pailful of water that is at room temperature, it will feel hot to the cold-adapted hand and cold to the hot-adapted hand. It is mainly the change in temperature that is signaled to the brain. Of course, there are limits to the process of adaptation. Extreme heat or cold will continue to feel hot or cold, however long we experience it.

Pressure. Sensory psychologists speak of touch and pressure as two separate senses. They define *touch* as the sensation of very light contact of an object with the skin and *pressure* as the sensation produced by more forceful contact. Sensations of pressure occur only when the skin is actually moving, which means that the pressure detectors respond only while they are being bent. Just how the motion stimulates the neurons is not known. If you rest your fore-

arm on a table and place a small weight on your skin, you will feel the pressure at first, but eventually you will feel nothing at all, if you keep your arm still. You fail to feel the pressure not because your brain "ignores" incoming stimulation but because your sensory endings actually cease sending impulses to your brain. Studies that have measured the very slow, very minute movements of a weight sinking down into the skin have shown that sensations of pressure cease when the movements stop. With the addition of another weight on top of the first one, movement and sensations of pressure begin again (Nafe and Wagoner, 1941). A person will feel a very heavy weight indefinitely, but the sensation is probably one of pain rather than pressure.

Sensitivity to subtle differences in touch and pressure varies widely across the surface of the body. The most sensitive regions are the lips and the fingertips. The most common measure of the tactile discrimination of a region of skin is the **two-point discrimination threshold.** To determine this measure, the experimenter touches the subject with one or both legs of a pair of dividers and asks the person to say whether the sensation is coming from one or two points. (See *Figure 4.35.*) The farther apart the legs of the dividers must be before the person reports feeling two separate sensations, the lower the sensitivity of that region of skin is.

Pain. Pain is a complex sensation involving not only intense sensory stimulation but also an emotional component. That is, a given sensory input to the brain might be interpreted as pain in one situation and as pleasure in another. For example, when people are sexually aroused, they become less sensitive to many forms of pain and may even find such intense stimulation pleasurable.

Physiological evidence suggests that the sensation of pain is quite different from the emo-

Figure 4.35 The method for determining the two-point discrimination threshold.

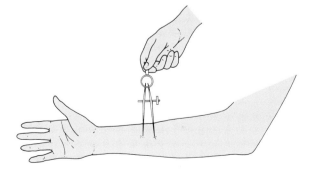

Information about the amount of force muscles exert is contained in special sensory endings found where the muscles and tendons connect to the bones. These receptors inhibit the strength of violent muscular contractions to prevent them from damaging the tendons or bones.

tional reaction to pain. Opiates such as morphine diminish the sensation of pain by stimulating opiate receptors on neurons in the brain; these neurons block the transmission of pain information to the brain. In contrast, some tranquilizers (such as Valium) depress neural systems that are responsible for the emotional reaction to pain but do not diminish the intensity of the sensation. Thus, people who have received a drug like Valium will report that they feel the pain just as much as they did before but that it does not bother them much.

Evidence from surgical procedures also supports the distinction between sensation and emotion. Prefrontal lobotomy (a form of brain surgery), like the use of tranquilizers such as Valium, blocks the emotional component of pain but does not affect the primary sensation. Therefore, operations similar to prefrontal lobotomy (but much less drastic) are sometimes performed to treat people who suffer from chronic pain that cannot be alleviated by other means.

Many noxious stimuli elicit two kinds of pain—an immediate sharp, or "bright," pain followed by a deep, dull, sometimes throbbing pain. Some stimuli elicit only one of these two kinds of pain. For example, a pinprick will produce only the superficial "bright" pain, whereas a hard blow from a blunt object to a large muscle will produce only the deep, dull pain. Different sets of axons mediate these two types of pain.

Pain—or the fear of pain—is one of the most effective motivators of human behavior. However, as the father in the opening vignette

pointed out to his child, it also serves us well in the normal course of living. As unpleasant as pain is, we would have difficulty surviving without it.

The Internal Senses

Sensory endings located in our internal organs, bones and joints, and muscles convey painful, neutral, and in some cases pleasurable sensory information. For example, the internal senses convey the pain of arthritis, the perception of the location of our limbs, or the pleasure of a warm drink entering our stomach.

Muscles contain special sensory endings. One class of receptors, located at the junction between muscles and the tendons that connect them to the bones, provides information about the amount of force the muscle is exerting. These receptors protect the body by inhibiting muscular contractions when they become too forceful. Some weight lifters receive injections of a local anesthetic near the tendons of some muscles to eliminate this protective mechanism and hence are able to lift even heavier weights. Unfortunately, if they use this tactic, some tendons may snap or some bones may break.

Another set of stretch detectors consists of spindle-shaped receptors distributed throughout the muscle. These receptors, appropriately called **muscle spindles,** inform the brain about changes in muscle length. People are not conscious of the specific information provided by the muscle spindles, but the brain uses the information from these receptors and from joint

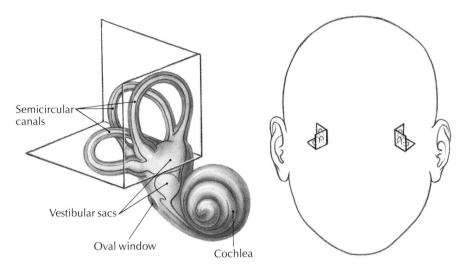

Semicircular
canals

Vestibular sacs

Oval window

Cochlea

Figure 4.36 The three semicircular canals and two vestibular sacs located in the inner ear.

receptors to keep track of the location of parts of the body and to control muscular contractions.

The Vestibular Senses

What we call our "sense of balance" in fact involves several senses, not just one. If we stand on one foot and then close our eyes, we immediately realize how important a role vision plays in balance. The **vestibular apparatus** of the inner ear provides only part of the sensory input that helps us remain upright.

The three **semicircular canals,** oriented at right angles to one another, detect changes in rotation of the head in any direction. (See *Figure 4.36.*) These canals contain a liquid, and rotation of the head makes the liquid flow, stimulating the nerve fibers that innervate them.

Another set of inner ear organs, the **vestibular sacs,** contain crystals of calcium carbonate that are embedded in a gelatinlike substance attached to receptive hair cells. In one sac the receptive tissue is on the wall; in the other it is on the floor. When the head tilts, the weight of the calcium carbonate crystals shifts, producing different forces on the cilia of the hair cells. (See *Figure 4.36.*)

The vestibular sacs are very useful in maintaining an upright head position. They also participate in a reflex that enables us to see clearly even when the head is being jarred. When we walk, our eyes are jostled back and forth. The jarring of the head stimulates the vestibular sacs to cause reflex movements of the eyes that partially compensate for the head movements. People who lack this reflex because of localized brain damage must stop walking in order to see things clearly—for example, to read a street sign.

The vestibular apparatus of the inner ear provides information necessary for these performers to keep their balance.

We know that the vestibular sacs provide the sensory input that can produce motion sickness, because slow, repetitive stimulation of the vestibular sacs can produce nausea and vomiting in a susceptible individual. What useful function this mechanism performs is difficult to imagine. It undoubtedly served our ancestors in some way unrelated to modern means of transportation.

INTERIM SUMMARY

The Somatosenses

The somatosenses gather several different kinds of information from different parts of the body. The skin senses of temperature, touch and pressure, vibration, and pain inform us about the nature of objects that come in contact with our skin. Imagine a man attempting to climb a rock cliff. As he reaches for a firm handhold overhead, the Pacinian corpuscles in his fingers detect vibration caused by movement of his fingers over the rock, which helps him determine its texture and find cracks into which he can insert anchors for his rope. Perhaps temperature receptors in his fingers tell him whether the rock is exposed to the sun and has warmed up or whether it is in the cool shade. If he cuts his skin against some sharp rock, free nerve endings give rise to sensations of pain. Presumably he is too intent on his task to notice sensations from his internal organs, although he would certainly feel a painful stimulus like a kidney stone; and if he thinks that he is slipping, he will most assuredly feel a queasy sensation caused by his internal reaction to a sudden release of adrenaline. As he climbs, he relies heavily on sensory receptors in his muscles and joints, which inform his brain of the movement and location of his arms and legs; and the vestibular senses help him keep his balance. When he reaches the top and enjoys a hot cup of tea, he can savor a comfortable, warm feeling going from his mouth and throat to his stomach. ∎

APPLICATION

Auditory Prostheses

Surgeons, engineers, and artisans have crafted many kinds of replacement parts for the human body; for example, they have made useful arms, legs, teeth, and heart valves. These parts are known as *prostheses* (literally, "attachments"). In recent years they have turned their attention to the development of prosthetic devices to replace the most important sensory organs: eyes and ears. The development of a functional artificial eye has just begun; and if success ever occurs, it is sure to be a long way off (Girvin, 1986). Electrical stimulation of the visual cortex does produce sensations of flashes of light (Bak et al., 1990), but we have no practical way to duplicate the patterns of activity present in the millions of neurons of the normal, functioning visual cortex.

Much more progress has been made in developing a prosthetic device to restore hearing in deaf people. There are two major types of deafness: *conduction deafness* and *sensorineural deafness*. Conduction deafness is caused by damage to the middle ear—usually to the ossicles—that makes it difficult for sound vibrations to reach the cochlea. Fortunately, surgeons have developed techniques to successfully treat most conduction problems. Middle ear operations, coupled with hearing aids if necessary, have restored hearing to many people. Sensorineural deafness involves damage to the sense organ or to the auditory nerve. If the damage is complete, no amount of amplification of the sound waves will restore hearing, because there is no way for the vibrations to be transformed into neural signals and transmitted to the brain. The only way to restore hearing to people with sensorineural deafness is to provide an artificial cochlea.

A common cause of sensorineural deafness is damage to the auditory hair cells, produced by meningitis, injury, ear infections, or the side effects of antibiotic drugs. People with this form of deafness have intact auditory nerves but lack the means to transduce acoustic information into neural information. If their auditory nerves are artificially stimulated with electrical current, impulses are transmitted to the brain and an acoustical sensation is produced. In 1790 Alessandro Volta, the Italian physicist who discovered that the nerves transmitted electrical information, inserted a metal rod into each of his ears and passed an electrical current through them. He reported that the current felt like a blow to his head and was followed by "a sound like the boiling of a viscous liquid" (Luxford and Brackmann, 1985). More than two hundred years later, much more sophisticated devices are providing useful acoustical sensations to formerly deaf people.

Today's artificial ear is known as a *cochlear implant.* The external part of a cochlear prosthesis consists of a microphone and a miniaturized electronic signal processor. The internal part consists of a very thin, flexible electrode, which the surgeon carefully inserts into the cochlea in such a way that it follows the snaillike curl and ends up resting along the entire length of the basilar membrane. The electrode is attached to a flat coil of wire placed under the skin just behind the ear. Another coil, attached to the external part of the prosthesis, transmits both electrical power and sensory signals to the internal part by means of electromagnetic coupling.

The most modern cochlear implants use an array of many electrodes, each of which stimulates groups of axons that innervate different parts of the basilar membrane. As you learned in this chapter, detection of tones with frequencies above 200 Hz is accomplished by the special mechanical properties of the basilar membrane: Different parts of the membrane vibrate in response to tones of different frequencies. The primary purpose of a cochlear implant is to restore a person's ability to understand speech. Because most of the important acoustical information in speech is much higher than 200 Hz, the multichannel electrode was developed in an attempt to duplicate the normal encoding of frequency on the basilar membrane (Loeb, 1990). The signal processor in the external device analyzes the sounds detected by the microphone and sends separate signals to the appropriate portions of the basilar membrane.

Obviously, the development of cochlear implants depends heavily on advances in surgery and engineering. But psychological issues are equally important, especially in guiding the design of the signal processor and choosing suitable candidates for surgery. Let us consider the signal processor first. Research in psychoacoustics has identified the aspects of the acoustical signal produced by the human voice that convey the information necessary to recognize the words and their intonation. For example, the information that permits us to distinguish the sounds of particular vowels is conveyed by four *formants*—bands of specific frequencies that originate in the resonance of different parts of the vocal tract. The signal processors of some cochlear implants analyze these formants and produce specific patterns of electrical pulses in different sets of electrodes in the cochlea. Research is presently under way to determine the best types of translation systems. Because the basilar membrane contains approximately 15,000 hair cells, it will never be possible to make an electrode with enough channels to duplicate the signal in the normal cochlea. Perhaps the best way to represent the acoustical signals of speech would be to produce unique and distinguishable patterns of stimulation of the cochlea and teach the patient to recognize them. The patient will hear patterns of complex sounds that do not resemble speech but will be able to learn which sounds correspond to which words—a task similar to learning the vocabulary of a new language. The job of the psychologist is to devise the best coding systems and the best methods to teach the patients.

A second consideration is patient selection. The most successful implants—which permit people to understand speech well enough to use a telephone—are those placed in adults who became deaf *after* having learned to speak. Placements of the devices in adults who were born deaf are generally unsuccessful (Tong, Busby, and Clark, 1988). The reason for this failure appears to lie in the development of the brain. As we saw in Chapter 3, brain development is affected by the environment and is not simply programmed by the genes. It appears that unless the auditory system of an infant's brain receives the information contained in speech sounds, it fails to develop the ability to analyze these sounds. And once the critical stage of brain development is past, the opportunity to develop this ability is lost (Fraser, 1985). For this reason, some investigators have suggested that children born with sensorineural deafness should receive a cochlear implant as soon as possible, so that the auditory system of the brain will develop the ability to analyze the information received from the prosthesis (Curtiss, 1989). As Loeb (1990) notes, this suggestion raises many technical, scientific, and ethical issues, which will not be resolved soon. One endeavor that will provide some of the information needed to resolve these issues will be psychological research on the development of the auditory system and the acquisition of language skills.

KEY TERMS AND CONCEPTS

Sensory Processing

sensation *(91)*
perception *(91)*
transduction *(91)*
receptor cell *(92)*
anatomical coding *(92)*
temporal coding *(92)*
psychophysics *(93)*
just-noticeable difference (jnd) *(93)*
Weber fraction *(93)*
threshold *(94)*
difference threshold *(94)*
absolute threshold *(94)*
signal detection theory *(94)*
receiver operating characteristic curve *(95)*
subliminal perception *(97)*

Vision

cornea *(99)*
sclera *(99)*
iris *(99)*
lens *(99)*
accommodation *(99)*
retina *(99)*
photoreceptor *(99)*
optic disk *(99)*
bipolar cell *(100)*
ganglion cell *(100)*
rod *(100)*
cone *(100)*
fovea *(100)*
photopigment *(101)*
rhodopsin *(101)*
dark adaptation *(102)*
rod-cone break *(102)*
conjugate movement *(103)*
saccadic movement *(103)*
pursuit movement *(104)*
wavelength *(104)*
hue *(105)*
brightness *(105)*

saturation *(105)*
color mixing *(106)*
negative afterimage *(109)*
protanopia *(110)*
deuteranopia *(110)*
tritanopia *(110)*

Audition

hertz (Hz) *(111)*
ossicle *(112)*
cochlea *(112)*
oval window *(112)*
basilar membrane *(112)*
round window *(113)*
auditory hair cell *(113)*
cilia *(113)*
tectorial membrane *(113)*
overtone *(116)*
fundamental frequency *(116)*
timbre *(117)*

Gustation

gustation *(118)*
papillae *(118)*
taste bud *(118)*

Olfaction

olfaction *(120)*
olfactory mucosa *(120)*
olfactory bulb *(120)*

The Somatosenses

somatosenses *(122)*
free nerve ending *(122)*
Pacinian corpuscle *(123)*
two-point discrimination threshold *(123)*
muscle spindle *(124)*
vestibular apparatus *(125)*
semicircular canal *(125)*
vestibular sac *(125)*

SUGGESTIONS FOR FURTHER READING

Bruce, V., and Green, P. *Visual Perception: Physiology, Psychology and Ecology.* London: Lawrence Erlbaum Associates, 1985.

Gregory, R.L. *Eye and Brain,* 3rd ed. New York: McGraw-Hill, World University Library, 1978.

Many books have been written about vision and visual perception. An excellent starting point is the inexpensive paperback by Gregory. Gregory knows his subject thoroughly and writes with wit and style. The book contains excellent illustrations, many in color. The book by Bruce and Green is also fine and discusses topics not covered in the Gregory book.

Gulick, W.L., Gescheider, G.A., and Frisina, R.D. *Hearing: Physiological Acoustics, Neural Coding, and Psychoacoustics.* New York: Oxford University Press, 1989.

Yost, W.A., and Nielsen, D.W. *Fundamentals of Hearing.* New York: Holt, Rinehart and Winston, 1977.

There are many excellent books on hearing. I can especially recommend these two.

Sternbach, R. *Pain: A Psychophysiological Analysis.* New York: Academic Press, 1968.

Sternbach's book about pain is old, but it contains many interesting examples.

Matlin, M., and Foley, H.J. *Sensation and Perception,* 3rd ed. Boston: Allyn and Bacon, 1992.

The book by Matlin and Foley is scholarly yet entertaining and has an excellent chapter on taste, with many applications for food and beverage tasting.

5
PERCEPTION

Henri Matisse, *Tetti a Collioure*
SCALA/Art Resource, N.Y. © 1992 Succession H. Matisse/ARS, N.Y.

LEARNING OBJECTIVES

When you finish this chapter, you should be able to:

1. Describe the primary visual cortex, the visual association cortex, and the effects of brain damage on visual perception.
2. Describe the distinction between figure and ground and the Gestalt laws of grouping.
3. Discuss current models of pattern perception.
4. Describe and evaluate serial and parallel models of mental functions.
5. Describe neural network models, compare them with serial models, and describe research on top-down and bottom-up perceptual processing.
6. Describe the binocular and monocular cues for the perception of distance.
7. Describe and discuss the phenomena of brightness and form constancy.
8. Discuss research on the perception of motion and the combining of information from successive fixations.

Dr. L., a young neuropsychologist, was presenting the case of Mrs. R. to a group of medical students doing a rotation in the neurology department at the medical center. The chief of the department had shown them Mrs. R.'s CT scans, and now Dr. L. was addressing the students. He told them that Mrs. R.'s stroke had not impaired her ability to talk or to move about, but it had affected her vision.

A nurse ushered Mrs. R. into the room and helped her find a seat at the end of the table.

"How are you, Mrs. R.?" asked Dr. L.

"I'm fine. I've been home for a month now, and I can do just about everything that I did before I had my stroke."

"Good. How is your vision?"

"Well, I'm afraid that's still a problem."

"What seems to give you the most trouble?"

"I just don't seem to be able to recognize things. When I'm working in my kitchen, I know what everything is as long as no one moves anything. A few times my husband tried to help me by putting things away, and I couldn't see them any more." She laughed. "Well, I could see them, but I just couldn't say what they were."

Dr. L. took some objects out of a paper bag and placed them on the table in front of her.

"Can you tell me what these are?" he asked. "No," he said, "please don't touch them."

Mrs. R. stared intently at the objects. "No, I can't rightly say what they are."

Dr. L. pointed to one of them, a wristwatch. "Tell me what you see here," he said.

Mrs. R. looked thoughtful, turning her head one way and then the other. "Well, I see something round, and it has two things attached to it, one on the top and one on the bottom." She continued to stare at it. "There are some things inside the circle, I think, but I can't make out what they are."

"Pick it up."

She did so, made a wry face, and said, "Oh. It's a wristwatch." At Dr. L.'s request, she picked up the rest of the objects, one by one, and identified each of them correctly.

"Do you have trouble recognizing people, too?" asked Dr. L.

"Oh, yes!" she sighed. "While I was still in the hospital, my husband and my son both came in to see me, and I couldn't tell who was who until my husband said something—then I could tell which direction his voice was coming from. Now I've trained myself to recognize my husband. I can usually see his glasses and his bald head, but I have to work at it. And I've been fooled a few times." She laughed. "One of our neighbors is bald and wears glasses, too, and one day when he and his wife were visiting us, I thought he was my husband, so I called him 'honey.' It was a little embarrassing at first, but everyone understood."

"What does a face look like to you?" asked Dr. L.

"Well, I know that it's a face, because I can usually see the eyes, and it's on top of a body. I can see a body pretty well, by how it moves." She paused a moment. "Oh, yes, I forgot, sometimes I can recognize a person by how he moves. You know, you can often recognize friends by the way they walk, even when they're far away. I can still do that. That's funny, isn't it? I can't see people's faces very well, but I can recognize the way they walk."

Dr. L. made some movements with his hands. "Can you tell what I'm doing?" he asked.

"Yes, you're mixing something—like some cake batter."

He mimed the gestures of turning a key, writing, and dealing out playing cards, and Mrs. R. recognized them without any difficulty.

"Do you have any trouble reading?" he asked.

"Well, a little, but I don't do too badly."

Dr. L. handed her a magazine, and she began to read the article aloud—somewhat hesitantly, but accurately. "Why is it," she asked, "that I can see the *words* all right but have so much trouble with *things* and with people's faces?"

Take a look around you—look around the room or out the window. Think of what you are seeing—shapes, figures, background, shadows, areas of light and dark—as you move and as your eyes move. Your knowledge of the objects and their relative location is extensive, and you have a good idea of what they will feel like, even if you have not touched them. If the lighting suddenly changes (if lamps are turned on or off or if a cloud passes in front of the sun), the amount of light reflected by the objects in the scene changes too, but your perception of the objects remains the same—you see them as having the same shape, color, and texture as before. Similarly, you do not perceive an object as increasing in size as you approach it, even though the image it casts upon your retina does get larger. These perceptions of form, movement, and space are the topics of this chapter.

Perception is a rapid, automatic, unconscious process. It allows us to organize and interpret sensory input in order to understand the world around us.

The visual system performs many remarkable tasks. The brain receives fragments of information from approximately 1 million axons in each of the optic nerves. It combines and organizes these fragments into the perception of a scene—objects with different forms, colors, and textures, residing at different locations in three-dimensional space. Even when our bodies or our eyes move, exposing the photoreceptors to entirely new patterns of visual information, our perception of the scene before us does not change. We see a stable world, not a moving one, because the brain keeps track of our own movements and those of our eyes and compensates for the constantly changing patterns of neural firing that these movements cause.

Perception is a rapid, automatic, unconscious process; it is not a deliberate one, in which we puzzle out the meaning of what we see. We do not first *see* an object and then *perceive* it; we simply perceive the object. Yes, occasionally we see something ambiguous and must reflect about what it might be or gather further evidence to determine what it is, but this situation is more problem solving than perception. If we look at a scene carefully, we can describe the elementary sensations that are present, but we do not become aware of the elements before we perceive the objects and the background of which they are a part. Our awareness of the process of visual perception comes only after it is complete; we are presented with a finished product, not the details of the process.

Whereas Chapter 4 described the basic features of the sensory systems, this chapter describes the more complex process of perception—in particular, *visual* perception. As I noted in Chapter 4, the distinction between sensation and perception is not easy to make; in some respects the distinction is arbitrary. Probably because of the importance we give to vision and because of the richness of the information provided by our visual system, psychologists make a more explicit distinction between visual sensation and perception than they do for any other sensory system. Hence visual perception earns a chapter of its own.

BRAIN MECHANISMS OF VISION

1 Although the eyes contain the photoreceptors that detect areas of different brightnesses and colors, perception takes place in the brain. As we saw in Chapter 3, the optic nerves send visual information to the thalamus, which relays the information to the primary visual cortex, located in the occipital lobe at the back of the brain. In turn, neurons in the primary visual cortex send visual information to two successive levels of visual association cortex. The first level, located in the occipital lobe, surrounds the primary visual cortex. The second level is divided into two parts, one in the middle of the parietal lobe and one in the lower part of the temporal lobe. (See *Figure 5.1.*)

Visual perception by the brain is often described as a hierarchy of information processing. According to this scheme, circuits of neurons analyze particular aspects of visual information and send the results of their analysis on to another circuit, which performs further analysis. At each step in the process successively more complex features are analyzed. Eventually, the process leads to the perception of the scene and of all the objects in it. The higher levels of the perceptual process interact with memories: The

Figure 5.1 The visual system of the brain. Sensory information from the eye is transmitted to the thalamus, and from there it is relayed to the primary visual cortex. The results of the analysis performed there are sent to the visual association cortex of the occipital lobe (first level) and then on to that of the temporal lobe and parietal lobe (second level). At each stage additional analysis takes place.

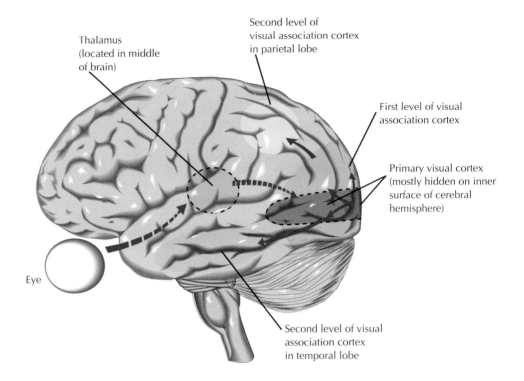

Thalamus (located in middle of brain)

Second level of visual association cortex in parietal lobe

First level of visual association cortex

Primary visual cortex (mostly hidden on inner surface of cerebral hemisphere)

Eye

Second level of visual association cortex in temporal lobe

viewer recognizes familiar objects and learns the appearance of new, unfamiliar ones.

The Primary Visual Cortex

Our knowledge about the characteristics of the earliest stages of analysis has come from investigations of the activity of individual neurons in the thalamus and primary visual cortex. For example, David Hubel and Torsten Wiesel have inserted *microelectrodes*—extremely small wires with microscopically sharp points—into various regions of the visual system of cats and monkeys to detect the action potentials produced by individual neurons (Hubel and Wiesel, 1977, 1979). The signals detected by the microelectrodes are electronically amplified and sent to a recording device so that they can be studied later.

After positioning a microelectrode close to a neuron, Hubel and Wiesel presented various stimuli on a large screen in front of the anesthetized animal. The anesthesia makes the animal unconscious but does not prevent neurons in the visual system from responding. The researchers moved a stimulus around on the screen until they located the point where it had the largest effect on the neuron. Next, they presented stimuli with various shapes to learn which ones produced the greatest response from the neuron.

From their experiments Hubel and Wiesel (1977, 1979) concluded that the geography of the visual field is retained in the primary visual cortex. That is, the surface of the retina is "mapped" on the surface of the primary visual cortex. However, this map on the brain is distorted, with the largest amount of area given to the center of the visual field, which projects on the fovea. The map is actually like a mosaic—a picture made of individual tiles or pieces of glass. Each "tile" consists of a block of tissue, approximately 0.5 x 0.7 mm and containing approximately 150,000 neurons. All of the neurons within a tile receive information from the same point on the retina. The primary visual cortex contains approximately 2500 of these tiles.

Because each tile in the visual cortex receives information from a small region of the retina, that means that it receives information from a small region of the visual field—the scene that the eye is viewing. If you would look at the scene before you through a soda straw, you would see the amount of information received by an individual tile. Hubel and Wiesel found that neural circuits within each tile analyzed various characteristics of their part of the visual field. Some circuits detected the presence of lines passing through the region and signaled the *orientation* of these lines (that is, the angle they made with respect to the horizon). Other circuits detected the thickness of these lines. Others detected movement and its direction. Still others detected colors.

Because each tile has information about only a restricted area of the visual field, the information must be combined somehow for perception to take place. This combination takes place in the visual association cortex.

The Visual Association Cortex

The first level of the visual association cortex, which surrounds the primary visual cortex, contains several subdivisions, each of which contains a map of the visual scene. Each subdivision receives—and combines—information from different types of neural circuits within the tiles of the primary visual cortex. One subdivision receives information about the orientation and widths of lines and edges and is involved in perception of shapes. Another subdivision receives information about movement and keeps track of the relative movements of objects (and may help compensate for movements of the eyes as we scan the scene in front of us). Yet another subdivision receives information concerning color (Livingstone and Hubel, 1988; Zeki and Shipp, 1988). (See *Figure 5.2.*)

The two regions of the second level of the visual association cortex put together the information gathered and processed by the various subregions of the first level. Information about shape, movement, and color are combined in the visual association cortex in the lower part of the temporal lobe. It is here that three-dimensional form perception takes place. The visual association cortex in the parietal lobe is responsible for perception of the *location* of objects; it

integrates information from the first level of visual association cortex with information from the body senses concerning movements of the eyes, head, and body (Ungerleider and Mishkin, 1982). (See *Figure 5.2.*)

The anatomy and functions of the visual association cortex have been studied in laboratory animals. The precise locations of comparable subregions in the human brain have not yet been determined, but advances in noninvasive methods of studying the living human brain will undoubtedly help researchers find them. As you will see in the next section, neuropsychologists have discovered that specific visual deficits can be caused by damage to various parts of the visual system, lending support to the conclusion that the organization of the visual association cortex of the human brain is similar to that of the laboratory animals studied so far.

Effects of Brain Damage on Visual Perception

The effects of damage to the primary visual cortex and to the visual association cortex support the general outline I have just described. When the primary visual cortex is damaged, the person becomes blind in some portion of the visual field. (The exact location depends on where the brain damage is.) However, even if the person loses a considerable amount of his or her sight, the person will be able to perceive objects and their backgrounds. This finding supports the

Figure 5.2 A schematic diagram of the types of analyses performed on visual information in the primary visual cortex and the various regions of the visual association cortex.

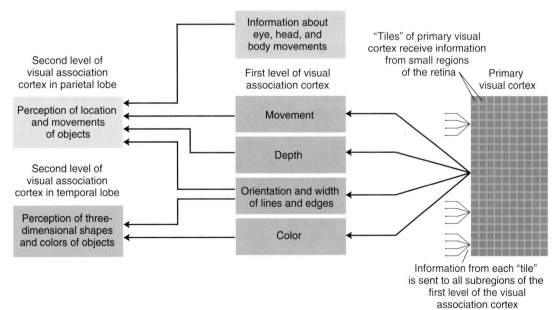

As long as the chameleon remains stationary, it blends in with the tree. Figure and ground are difficult to perceive in this image.

conclusion that perception takes place in the visual association cortex and not in the primary visual cortex.

You can try a simple demonstration that illustrates this principle. Roll up a piece of paper so that it forms a small tube and look through it as you would through a telescope. Move the tube around so that you can scan the scene in front of you. Although you see only a part of the scene at any one time, you have no difficulty perceiving what is present. Your experience is like that of a person with extensive damage limited to the primary visual cortex (but sparing the visual association cortex): a limited visual field but (eventually) good perceptual ability.

In contrast, damage to the visual association cortex does not disrupt the person's ability to see fine details, but it does produce varying amounts of difficulty in perceiving shapes and objects or in perceiving particular visual characteristics. For example, damage to part of the first region of visual association cortex can disrupt color vision—a condition known as **achromatopsia** (literally, "vision without color"). A person with achromatopsia can still see normally, but everything looks as if it had been filmed in black and white. Damage to another subregion can make it difficult for a person to perceive movements and keep track of moving objects. For example, Zihl, Cramon, Mai, and Schmid (1991) studied a woman who had sustained bilateral damage to the first level of the

visual association cortex. When she was shown a display with a moving stimulus, she never saw any movement but said that the stimulus suddenly jumped to a new position. Damage to yet another subregion disrupts depth perception.

Damage to the parietal lobe can make it difficult for a person to keep track of the location of objects in the visual scene. The person can recognize individual objects when he or she looks directly at them but is unable to see where they are located. The scene in front of them is a hopeless jumble of individual objects, arranged in no particular order. This visual deficit, known as *Balint's syndrome,* is discussed in more detail in Chapter 8.

Damage to the visual association cortex can produce a pure deficit in the ability to recognize objects without affecting the ability to see colors, movements, or fine details. This deficit is called **visual agnosia.** Mrs. R., the woman in the opening vignette, had visual agnosia. As we saw, she was able to make out details of objects that she looked at, but she could not perceive them as a whole. But she could recognize movements, and she could read.

One form of visual agnosia makes it difficult or impossible for the person to recognize particular faces—a disorder called **prosopagnosia** (from the Greek *prosopon,* meaning "face"). For example, a man with this disorder might be unable to recognize his wife by sight, but he will identify her as soon as he hears her voice. Most people with prosopagnosia have difficulty recognizing other complex visual stimuli as well (Damasio, Tranel, and Damasio, 1990). They can easily recognize *categories* of objects (such as automobiles, animals, or houses) but have difficulty distinguishing between particular *individuals* (their car, their dog, or their house). One woman with prosopagnosia could no longer distinguish between different makes of cars and so had to find her own in a parking lot by looking for the correct license plate. (Obviously, she could still distinguish numbers and letters.) Another, a farmer, could no longer tell his cows apart. As you may have concluded, Mrs. R. had prosopagnosia, as well as a visual agnosia for objects.

INTERIM SUMMARY

Brain Mechanisms of Vision

Visual information proceeds from the retina to the thalamus, and then to the primary visual cortex. The primary visual cortex is organized into approximately 2500 "tiles," each of which receives information from a small region of the retina. Neural circuits within each module analyze specific information from their part of the visual field, including the orientation and width of lines, color, and movement.

The different types of information analyzed by the neural circuits in the tiles of the primary visual cortex are sent to separate maps of the visual field in the first level of the visual association cortex. The information from these maps is combined in the second level of the visual association cortex: form perception in the base of the temporal lobe and spatial perception in the parietal lobe.

Damage to specific regions of the primary visual cortex causes blindness in corresponding parts of the visual field. Damage to parts of the first level of the visual association cortex causes achromatopsia (lack of color vision), lack of depth perception, or difficulty in perceiving movements. Damage to the visual association of the parietal lobe causes Balint's syndrome, a deficit in spatial perception. Damage to the visual association cortex can also disrupt form perception without affecting the ability to see colors, movements, or fine details—a condition called visual agnosia. ∎

PERCEPTION OF FORM

2 When we look at the world, we do not see patches of colors and shades of brightness; we see *things*. We see cars, streets, people, desks, books, trees, dogs, chairs, walls, flowers, clouds, televisions. We see where each object is located, how large it is, and whether it is moving. We recognize familiar objects and also recognize when we see something we have never seen before. Thus, the visual system is able to perceive shapes, determine distances, and detect movements; it tells us what something is, where it is located, and what it is doing. This section considers the first task: perceiving an object's form.

Figure and Ground

Most of what we see can be classified as either object or background. *Objects* are things with particular shapes and particular locations in space. (In this context people can be considered as objects.) *Backgrounds* are essentially formless and serve mostly to help us judge the location of objects we see in front of them. Psychologists use the terms **figure** and **ground** to label

Figure 5.3 A drawing in which figure and ground can be reversed. You can see either two faces against a white background or a wineglass against a dark background.

an object and its background, respectively. The classification of an item as a figure or as a part of the background is not an intrinsic property of the item; rather, it depends on the behavior of the observer. If you are watching some birds fly overhead, they are figures and the blue sky and the clouds behind them are part of the background. If, instead, you are watching the clouds move, then they become figures. If you are looking at a picture hanging on a wall, it is an object; if you are looking at a person standing between you and the wall, the picture is part of the background. Sometimes, we receive ambiguous clues about what is object and what is background. For example, does Figure 5.3 illustrate two faces or a wine goblet? (See *Figure 5.3.*)

What are the characteristics of the incredibly complex patterns of light, varying in brightness, saturation, and hue, that give rise to perceptions of figures, of *things?* One of the most important aspects of form perception is the existence of a *boundary*. If the visual field contains a sharp and distinct change in brightness, color, or texture, we perceive an edge. If this edge forms a continuous boundary, we will probably perceive the space enclosed by the boundary as a figure. (See *Figure 5.4.*)

Organization of Elements: Gestalt Laws of Grouping

As we just saw, most figures are defined by a boundary. But the presence of a boundary is not necessary for the perception of form. *Figure 5.5* shows that when small elements are ar-

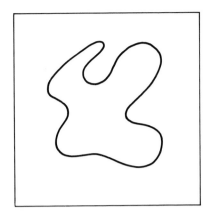

Figure 5.4 Form perception and boundaries. We immediately perceive even an unfamiliar figure when the outline is closed.

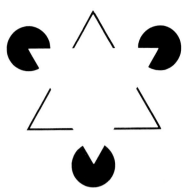

Figure 5.6 Illusory contours. Even when boundaries are not present, we can be fooled into seeing them. The triangle with its point down looks brighter than the surrounding area. (Reprinted with permission of Macmillan Publishing Co., Inc., from *An Introduction to Perception* by Irvin Rock. Copyright © by Irvin Rock.)

ranged in groups, we tend to perceive them as larger figures. And *Figure 5.6* demonstrates **illusory contours**—lines that do not exist. In this figure the orientation of the "pac men" and the three 45-degree segments make us perceive two triangles, one on top of the other. The one that looks like it is superimposed on the three black circles even appears to be brighter than the background.

The tendency to perceive elements as belonging together has been recognized for many years. Earlier in this century a group of psychologists organized a theory of perception called **Gestalt psychology.** *Gestalt* is the German word for "form," but Gestalt psychologists use the term to mean more than that. Their essential thesis is that in perception the whole is more than the sum of its parts. Because of the characteristics of the visual system of the brain, visual perception cannot be understood simply by analyzing the scene into its elements. Instead, what we see depends on the *relations* of these elements to one another.

Elements of a visual scene can combine in various ways to produce different forms. Gestalt psychologists have observed that several principles of grouping can predict the combination of these elements. The fact that our visual system groups and combines elements is useful because we can then perceive forms even if

they are fuzzy and incomplete. The real world presents us with objects partly obscured by other objects and with backgrounds that are the same color as parts of the objects in front of them. The outlines of objects are very often not distinct. As I look out the window of my office, I see a large bush against a background of trees. It is summer, and I see countless shades of green in the scene before me. I cannot distinguish the bush from the trees behind it simply by differences in color. However, I can clearly see the outline of the bush because of subtle differences in its texture (the leaves are smaller than those of the tree) and because the wind causes its branches to move in a pattern different from that of the tree branches. The laws of grouping discovered by Gestalt psychologists describe my ability to distinguish this figure from its background.

The **law of proximity** states that elements that are closest together will be perceived as belonging together. *Figure 5.7* demonstrates this principle. The pattern on the left looks like four vertical columns, whereas the one on the right looks like four horizontal rows.

The **law of similarity** states that elements that look similar will be perceived as part

Figure 5.5 Grouping. We tend to perceive a group of smaller elements as a larger figure.

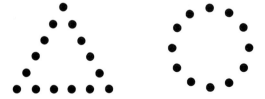

Figure 5.7 The Gestalt principle of proximity. Different spacing of the dots produces four vertical or four horizontal lines.

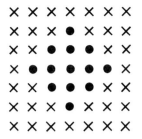

Figure 5.8 The Gestalt principle of similarity. Similar elements are perceived as belonging to the same form.

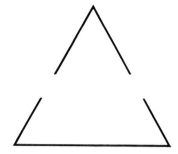

Figure 5.10 The Gestalt principle of closure. We tend to supply missing information to close a figure and separate it from its background. Lay a pencil across the gaps and see how strong the perception of a complete triangle becomes.

of the same form. We can easily see the diamond inside the square in *Figure 5.8.*

Good continuation refers to predictability or simplicity. Which of the two sets of colored dots best describes the continuation of the line of black dots in *Figure 5.9*? If you see the figure the way I do, you will choose the colored dots that continue the curve down and to the right. It is simpler to perceive the line as following a smooth course than as suddenly making a sharp bend.

Often one object partially hides another, but we nevertheless perceive the incomplete image. The **law of closure** states that our visual system often supplies missing information and "closes" the outline of an incomplete figure. For example, *Figure 5.10* looks a bit like a triangle, but if you place a pencil on the page so that it covers the gaps, the figure undeniably looks like a triangle.

The final Gestalt law of organization relies on movement. The **law of common fate** states that elements that move in the same direction will be perceived as belonging together and forming a figure. In the forest an animal is camouflaged if its surface is covered with the same elements found in the background—spots of brown, tan, and green—because its boundary is obscured. There is no basis for grouping the elements on the animal. As long as the animal is stationary, it remains well hidden. However, once it moves, the elements on its surface will move together, and the animal's form will quickly be perceived.

And how did I distinguish the bush from the trees? You will recall that the primary cues were differences in leaf size and in the movement induced by the wind, examples of similarity and common fate, respectively.

Models of Pattern Perception

[3] Most of the psychologists who are currently studying perception call themselves cognitive psychologists. They are interested in the mental processes responsible for perception—the steps that take place between the time the eye is exposed to a stimulus and the time a perception of the image is formed, ready for the person to act on. They collect behavioral data and try to make inferences about the nature of these mental processes. Let us examine some of the models they have devised to explain the process of pattern perception.

Templates and Prototypes. One possible explanation for our ability to recognize shapes of objects is that as we gain experience looking at things, we acquire **templates,** which are special kinds of memories utilized by the visual system. A *template* (pronounced *TEM plit*) is a type of pattern used to manufacture various types of objects. For example, a woodworker might use a sheet metal template in order to drill holes in the same locations when making several pieces

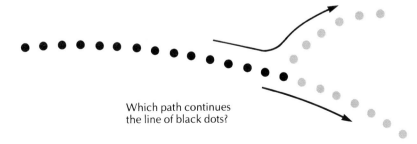

Figure 5.9 The Gestalt principle of good continuation. It is easier to perceive a smooth continuation than an abrupt shift.

Which path continues the line of black dots?

of furniture. Perhaps the visual system reverses the process; when a particular pattern of visual stimulation is encountered, it searches through its set of templates and compares each of them with the pattern provided by the stimulus. If it finds a match, it knows that the pattern is a familiar one. Connections between the appropriate template and memories in other parts of the brain could provide the name of the object and other information about it, such as its function, when it was seen before, and so forth.

The template model of pattern recognition has the virtue of simplicity. However, most psychologists do not believe that it could actually work—the visual system would have to store an unreasonably large number of templates. Consider a familiar object, such as a human hand. Hold your own hand out in front of you and look at it. Turn it around, wiggle your fingers, clench your fist, and see how many different patterns you can project on the retinas of your eyes. No matter what you do, you continue to recognize the pattern as belonging to your hand. How many different templates would your visual memory have to contain just to recognize a hand? And suppose the hand were more or less hairy, darker or lighter, with longer or shorter fingers, with or without rings—I think you get the point.

A more flexible model of pattern perception suggests that patterns of visual stimulation are compared with prototypes rather than templates. **Prototypes** are idealized patterns of a particular shape; they resemble templates but are used in a much more flexible way. The visual system does not look for exact matches between the pattern being perceived and the memories of shapes of objects but accepts a degree of disparity; for instance, it accepts the various patterns produced when we look at a particular object from different viewpoints.

Most psychologists believe that pattern recognition by the visual system does involve prototypes, at least in some form. For example, you can undoubtedly identify maple trees, fir trees, and palm trees when you see them. In nature each tree looks different from all the others, but maples resemble other maples more than they resemble firs, and so on. A reasonable assumption is that your visual system has memories of the prototypical visual patterns that represent these objects. Recognizing particular types of trees, then, is a matter of finding the best fit between stimulus and prototype.

Clearly, if the visual system contains prototypes, it contains many of them. Think of how many different people you can recognize by

Figure 5.11 Pattern recognition. Is a coffee mug recognized by the use of a single prototype, or are different prototypes required for different points of view?

sight, how many buildings in your town you can recognize, how many pieces of furniture in your house and in your friends' houses you are familiar with—the list may be very long. In fact, Standing (1973) showed people 10,000 color slides and found that they could recognize most of them weeks later. And do we have just one prototype for each object, or do we have different prototypes for radically different images produced by different points of view? For example, look at two views of the coffee mug shown in Figure 5.11. Are they represented by one prototype or two? (See *Figure 5.11.*)

I strongly suspect that many objects have to be represented by more than one prototype, such as profile and full-face views of a face. Perhaps there are even various levels of prototypes: generic ones such as maples or human faces and more specific ones such as the tree in your backyard or the face of a friend. In fact, evidence from studies with nonhuman primates suggests that familiarity with categories of objects may lead to the development of specific types of prototypes.

Humphrey (1974) showed monkeys pictures of other animals and used a phenomenon known as *habituation* to see how the monkeys categorized what they saw. The method he used was first developed to study the perceptual abilities of human infants, and it is described in more detail in Chapter 10. Briefly, if a monkey (or a baby) sees the same picture twice in succession, it spends less time looking at the picture the second time. Humphrey found that when monkeys were shown a series of pictures of different monkeys, they spent a considerable amount of time examining each one, as if each picture was novel and interesting. (After all, they were acquainted with monkeys and could certainly recognize different faces.) However, if the monkeys were shown a series of four-legged animals such as pigs and cows, they quickly lost interest; it was as if they were look-

$\mathcal{N}$ N N **N** N $\mathcal{N}$
N $\textit{N}$ N $\textit{N}$ ◫

Figure 5.12 Distinctive features. We easily recognize all of these items as the letter N.

ing at the same picture again and again. Over the next few months Humphrey showed the monkeys pictures of various species of animals. The experience seemed to sharpen the monkeys' ability to distinguish the animals. In fact, not only could they tell the difference between pigs and cows, but they could distinguish between one pig and another or one cow and another. It was as if the experience with many individuals led to the development of more and more specific prototypes of categories of four-legged animals.

Distinctive Features.   How complete does the information in a prototype have to be? Does a prototype have to contain a detailed representation of an image of the object it represents, or can the information be represented in some shorthand way? Some psychologists suggest that the visual system encodes images of familiar patterns in terms of **distinctive features**—collections of important physical features that specify particular items. For example, Figure 5.12 contains several examples of the letter N. Although the examples vary in size and style, you have no trouble recognizing them. (See *Figure 5.12.*) How do you do so? Perhaps your visual system contains a specification of the distinctive features that fit the criterion for an N: two parallel vertical lines connected by

GDOROC	IVEMXW
COQUCD	XVIWME
DUCOQG	VEMIXW
GRUDQO	WEXMVI
OCDURQ	XIMVWE
DUCGRO	IVMWEX
ODUCQG	VWEMXI
CQOGRD	IMEWXV
DUZORQ	EXMZWI
UCGROD	IEMWVX
QCUDOG	EIVXWM
RQGUDO	WXEMIV
DRGOQC	MIWVXE
OQGDRU	IMEVXW
UGCODQ	IEMWVX
ODRUCQ	IMWVEX
UDQRGC	XWMVEI
ORGCUD	IWEVXM
QOGRUC	VMIWEX

Figure 5.13   A letter-search task. Look for the letter Z hidden in each column. (Adapted from Neisser, U. *Scientific American*, 1964, *210*, 94–102.)

a diagonal line sloping downward from the top of the left one to the bottom of the right one.

An experiment by Neisser (1964) supports the hypothesis that perception involves analysis of distinctive features. Figure 5.13 shows one of the tasks his subjects were asked to do. The figure shows two columns of letters. Scan through them until you find the letter Z, which occurs once in each column. (See *Figure 5.13.*)

How does our visual system analyze the complex, distinctive features of the Brooklyn Bridge? Perception is not simply an assembly of individual features.

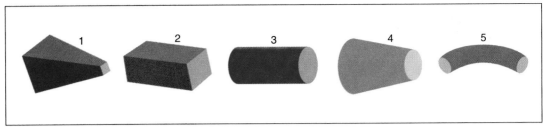

(a) Geons

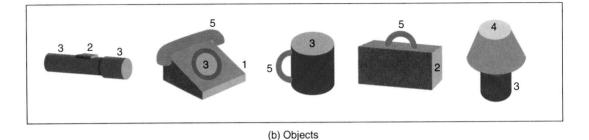

(b) Objects

Figure 5.14 Geons for perception. (a) Several different geons. (b) The combination of two or three geons into three-dimensional objects. (Adapted from Biederman, I., in *An Invitation to Cognitive Science. Vol. 2: Visual Cognition and Action,* edited by D.N. Osherson, S.M. Kosslyn, and J. Hollerbach. Cambridge, Mass.: MIT Press, 1990.)

Chances are good that you found the letter in the left column much faster than the one in the right column, just as Neisser's subjects did. Perhaps you guessed why: The letters in the left column have few features in common with those found in the letter Z, so the Z stands out from the others. In contrast, the letters in the right column have many features in common with the target letter, and thus the Z is camouflaged, so to speak. (See *Figure 5.13.*)

The distinctive-features model appears to be a reasonable explanation for the perception of letters, but what about more natural stimuli, which we encounter in places other than the written page? Biederman (1987, 1990) suggests that the forms we encounter can be constructed from a set of thirty-six different shapes that he refers to as **geons**. Figure 5.14 illustrates a few geons and some objects that can be constructed from them. (See *Figure 5.14.*) Perhaps, Biederman suggests, the visual system recognizes objects by identifying the particular sets and arrangements of geons that they contain.

There are some phenomena that cannot easily be explained by the distinctive-features model. The model suggests that the perception of an object consists of analysis and synthesis; the visual system first identifies the component features of an object and then adds up the features to determine what the object is. We might expect, then, that more complex objects, with more distinctive features, would take longer to

perceive. But often, the addition of additional features, in the form of contextual cues, *speeds up* the process of perception. Figure 5.15 contains two sets of four items. One item in each is different from the other three. Look at the two sets, and see which types of items are easier to distinguish. (See *Figure 5.15.*) As you can see, the patterns in both sets differ with respect to only one feature: the tilt of the diagonal line. But the addition of the horizontal and vertical lines make the perceptual task much easier. We see a triangle and three right angles bisected by a diagonal line; the triangle just pops out as being different. If we perceived individual features (such as the diagonal lines) before perceiving more complex figures (such as triangles and bisected right angles) that are composed of these features, then we should perceive simpler figures faster than more complex ones. The fact that we do not means that a perception is not simply an assembly of individual features.

Figure 5.15 Contextual cues. Perceiving a simple stimulus is facilitated by contextual cues.

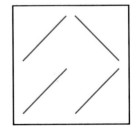
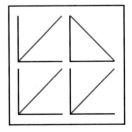

Is the Brain a Computer?

[4] As we saw in Chapter 1, when we try to understand something very complicated (such as the functions of the human brain), we tend to think in terms of things that are familiar to us. For example, René Descartes used the moving statues in the Royal Gardens as a basis for his hydraulic model of the nervous system. He saw an analogy between nerves-muscles-brain of the body and pipes-cylinders-valves of the statues, and he suggested that their principles of operations might be similar. Although cognitive psychology has a history that dates back to the early part of this century, most of its philosophy and methodology developed during the past twenty-five years. During this time the best-known physical device that performs functions similar to those of the human brain has been the general-purpose digital computer. Thus, it is the computer that provided (and still provides) much of the inspiration for the models constructed by cognitive psychologists.

How Does a Serial Computer Work? To understand the thought processes that guide the development of models inspired by computers, we must understand something about how modern general-purpose computers work. They consist of four major parts (and countless other parts that I will not talk about). *Input devices* and *output devices* (or, collectively, *I/O devices*) permit us to communicate with the computer: to give it instructions or data and to learn the results of its computations. *Memory* permits information to be stored in the computer. This information can contain instructions or data we have given it, or it can contain the intermediate steps and final results of its calculations. Finally, a *central processor* contains the electronic circuits necessary for the computer to perform its functions: to *read the information* received by the input devices and store it into memory, to *execute the steps* specified by the instructions contained in its programs, and to *display the results* by means of the output devices. (See *Figure 5.16.*)

Modern general-purpose computers can be programmed to store any kind of information that can be coded in numbers or words, can solve any logical problem that can be explicitly described, and can compute any mathematical equations that can be written. Therefore—in principle, at least—they can be programmed to

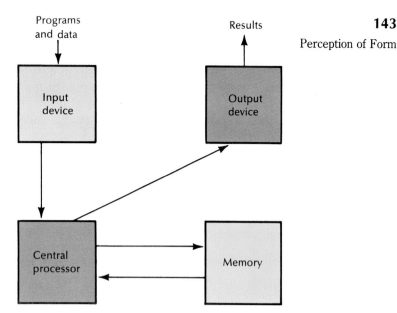

Figure 5.16 The basic features of a general-purpose serial computer.

do the things we do: perceive, remember, make deductions, solve problems. The power and flexibility of computers seem to make them an excellent basis for constructing models of mental processes. For example, psychologists, linguists, and computer scientists have constructed computer-inspired models of visual pattern perception, speech comprehension, reading, control of movement, and memory.

The construction of computer programs that simulate human mental functions is called **artificial intelligence.** Such an enterprise can help clarify the nature of the mental functions. For instance, to construct a program and simulate, say, perception and classification of certain types of patterns, the investigator is forced to specify precisely what is required by the task of pattern perception. (So far, no program is advanced enough to deal with more than a small fraction of the patterns a human can recognize.) If the program fails to recognize the patterns, then the investigator knows that something is wrong with the model or with the way it has been implemented in the program. The investigator revises the model, tries again, and keeps working until it finally works (or until he or she gives up the task as being too ambitious).

Ideally, the task of discovering what steps are necessary in a computer program to simulate some human cognitive abilities tells the investigator the kinds of processes the brain must perform. However, there is usually more than one way to accomplish a particular goal; critics of artificial intelligence have pointed out that it is entirely possible to write a program that performs a task that the human brain performs—and comes up with exactly the same results—but does the task in an entirely different way. In fact, some say, given the way that computers work and what we know about the structure of the human brain, the computer program is *guaranteed* to work differently.

When we base our models of complex processes (such as those that take place in the brain) on a physical device with which we are familiar (such as a computer), we enjoy the advantage of being able to think concretely about something that is difficult to observe. However, if the brain does not work like a computer, then our models will not tell us very much about the nature of cognitive processes. Such models are *constrained* ("restricted") by the computer metaphor; they will only be able to do things the way that computers can do them. If the brain can actually do some different sorts of things—things that computers cannot do—the models will never contain these features.

Let us examine the basic workings of modern general-purpose computers. Computers are **serial devices;** they work one step at a time. (*Serial,* from the Latin *serere,* "to join," refers to events that occur in order, one after the other.) Programs consist of a set of instructions read into memory through an input device. Instructions tell the computer to perform a logical or arithmetic calculation—for example, compare numbers, add them together, or print a message to the user. The central processor fetches an instruction from memory, does what it says, fetches the next instruction, and so on, until the program is finished.

Each step a computer performs takes time. A complicated program will contain more steps and therefore will take more time to execute. In this respect computers and brains are somewhat similar; in general, it takes us longer to solve a difficult problem than a simple one. But we do some things extremely quickly that computers take a very long time to do. One of the best examples (appropriately enough, given the subject of this chapter) is visual perception. We can recognize a complex figure about as quickly as a simple one; for example, it takes about the same amount of time to recognize a friend's face as it does to identify a simple triangle. The same is not true at all for a serial computer. A computer must "examine" the scene through an input device something like a television camera. Information about the brightness of each point of the picture must be converted into a number

and stored in a memory location. Then the program examines each memory location, one at a time, and does calculations that determine the locations of lines, edges, textures, and shapes; finally, it tries to determine what these shapes represent. Recognizing a face takes *much* longer than recognizing a triangle.

An Alternative: The Parallel Processor. By definition, serial computers do their work one step at a time. Because a modern computer can perform many millions of steps each second, it can do most complex tasks rather quickly. Even so, it is much slower than the brain at recognizing pictures. Thus, if the brain were a serial device like a computer, it would have to perform the steps even more rapidly than a computer does. But we know that it cannot; although the transistors inside a computer can be made to operate at millions of times per second, neurons are much slower. If the brain were a serial device, its maximum speed would probably be around ten steps per second (Rumelhart and McClelland, 1986). Obviously, when we perceive visual images, our brain does *not* act like a serial device.

Instead, the brain appears to be a **parallel processor,** in which many different modules (collections of circuits of neurons) work simultaneously at different tasks. A complex task is broken down into many smaller ones, and separate modules work on each of them. Because the brain consists of many billions of neurons, it can afford to devote different clusters of neurons to different tasks. With so many things happening at the same time, the task gets done quickly.

Another way that brains differ from serial computers is in the effects of damage. Consider what would happen if some memory locations of a computer were damaged. If the locations contained steps of a program, then the program would go awry; as computer experts succinctly put it, the program would "crash." Damage to the components of the central processor or the units that control the input or output devices would similarly be disastrous. But brain damage does not produce disastrous effects on brain functioning unless the damage is extensive. For example, a person who suffers from the early stages of a degenerative brain disease may have lost hundreds of millions of neurons scattered throughout the brain but will still be able to perform reasonably well on all sorts of tasks. The damage slows them down, makes them less efficient, impairs their ability to perceive, learn, and remember; but it does not cause their programs to "crash."

The effects of brain damage tell us something else: *There does not appear to be a single central processor.* Computers contain input and output devices, memory banks, and a central processor. The central processor is the executive that runs the show; if it is damaged, the computer cannot function. Studies of people with severe damage to particular parts of the brain (as opposed to widespread, moderate damage) have not suggested that any one part serves as a central processor. Neither have neuroanatomists found any brain structures that have the kinds of connections to "input/output devices" and "memory banks" that central processors would need to have. Instead, what we appear to have is a series of semi-independent systems that communicate with each other and share information but that can still function, more or less efficiently, with the loss of other parts of the brain.

5 The Emerging Model: Neural Networks. It is one thing to say that the brain consists of many different modules, all working in parallel on separate pieces of a complicated task (such as recognizing someone's face), and another thing to explain how these modules work. Recently, psychologists have begun to devise models of mental functions that are based, more or less, on the way the brain seems to be constructed. These models come under the heading of **neural networks.** (They have other names too, such as *adaptive neural nets;* and the approach has been called *connectionism* or *parallel distributed processing.)*

Investigators have discovered that when they construct a network of simple elements, interconnected in certain ways, the network does some surprising things. The elements have properties like those of neurons. They are connected to each other through junctions similar to synapses. Like synapses, these junctions can have either excitatory or inhibitory effects. When an element receives a critical amount of excitation, it sends a message to the elements with which it communicates, and so on. Some of the elements of a network have input lines that can receive signals from the "outside," which could represent a sensory organ or the information received from another network. Other elements have output lines, which communicate with other networks or control muscles, producing behavior. Thus, particular patterns of input can represent particular stimuli, and particu-

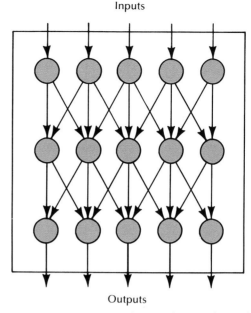

Figure 5.17 A very simple neural network, used as a model of brain function. The connections (arrows) can be excitatory or inhibitory, depending on the particular model.

lar patterns of output can represent responses. (See *Figure 5.17.*)

Neural networks can be taught to "recognize" particular stimuli. They are shown a particular stimulus, and their output is monitored. If the response on the output lines is incorrect, the network is given a signal indicating the correct response. This signal causes the strength of some of the junctions to be changed, just as learning is thought to alter the strength of synapses in the brain. After several trials the network learns to make correct responses.

Investigators do not construct actual networks; instead, they write computer programs that simulate them. The programs keep track of each element and the state of each of its inputs and outputs and calculate what would happen if a particular pattern of input is presented. If the network uses a sufficiently large number of elements, it can be trained to recognize several different patterns, producing the correct response each time one of the patterns is shown to it. In addition, it will even recognize the patterns if they are altered slightly, or if only parts of the patterns are shown. Thus, neural networks can recognize not only particular patterns but also variations on that pattern. Thus, they act as if they had learned general *prototypes,* not specific *templates.*

If some of the elements of a neural network are destroyed or if some of the connections between them are cut, the network will still function somewhat normally. That is, changes in the patterns of output will still reflect changes in the patterns of input, although a few minor errors will begin to occur. Thus, the network acts something like the brain: Widespread, moderate damage does not radically alter the way the system works; it just makes the system work less precisely.

Models that employ neural networks are very different from those that employ serial processing. Neural networks contain very large numbers of simple elements, all working at the same time. They do not contain a central processor or memory banks. Instead, the elements work cooperatively, all on the same level, and what the network has learned is reflected in the changes in strength of connections between the elements. Unlike serial devices, a sufficiently large neural network can recognize complex patterns about as quickly as simple ones, just as people can. Recall that in contrast to a serial computer, we can recognize a face about as quickly as a triangle.

Visual perception, then, consists of a series of analyses, beginning with simple features and progressing to more complex ones. Each level of analysis involves a different neural network. In the primary visual cortex the networks are small and local; each one analyzes simple features—such as orientation of lines and edges, color, and movement—within a restricted part of the visual field. In the subregions of the visual association cortex of the occipital lobes, larger networks process the information they receive from the primary visual cortex. For example, the region that receives information about orientation of lines and edges recognizes shapes and patterns: squares, circles, ice-cream cones, dogs, cats, faces. Other networks of neurons in the visual association cortex of the temporal lobes put all the information together and perceive the entire, three-dimensional scene, with objects having particular shapes, colors, and textures. The locations of the objects in the visual scene are determined by a network of neurons in the parietal lobes.

Psychologists are excited by the ability of neural networks to simulate mental functions and to do so with elements that so closely resemble neurons. In just a few years investigators have constructed models that recognize patterns, learn names of objects, control the finger movements used by a typist, read words, and learn the past tenses of English verbs, to name but a few tasks (Rumelhart, McClelland, and the PDP Research Group, 1986). Thus, this approach has relevance not only to perception but also to memory, to language, and to the control of movement. ∎

Top-Down Processing: The Role of Context

We must often perceive objects under conditions that are less than optimum; the object is in a shadow, camouflaged against a similar background, or obscured by fog. Nevertheless, we usually manage to recognize the item correctly. We are often helped in our endeavor by the context in which we see the object. For example, look at the four items in *Figure 5.18.* Can you tell what they represent? Now, look at *Figure 5.20* on page 148. With the aid of a context the items are easily recognized.

Palmer (1975) showed that even more general forms of context can aid in the perception of objects. He first showed his subjects familiar scenes, such as a kitchen. (See *Figure 5.19.*) Next, he used a device called a tachistoscope to show them drawings of individual items and asked the subjects to identify them. (The word comes from *takhistos,* "most swift," and *skopein,* "to see.") A **tachistoscope** can present visual stimuli very briefly, so that they are very difficult to perceive. Sometimes, the subjects saw an object that was appropriate to the scene, such as a loaf of bread. Other times, they saw an inappropriate but similarly shaped object, such as a mailbox. (See *Figure 5.19.*)

Palmer found that when the objects fit the context that had been set by the scene, the subjects correctly identified about 84 percent of them; but when they did not, performance fell to about 50 percent. Performance was intermediate in the no-context control condition, under which subjects did not first see a scene. Thus, compared with the no-context control condition, an appropriate context facilitated recognition and an inappropriate one interfered with it.

The context effects demonstrated by experiments such as Palmer's are not simply examples of guessing games. That is, subjects do not think to themselves, "Let's see, that shape could be either a mailbox or a loaf of bread. I just saw a picture of a kitchen, so I guess it's a loaf of bread." The process is rapid, unconscious, and automatic; thus, it belongs to the category of

Figure 5.18 Simple elements that are difficult to recognize without a context.

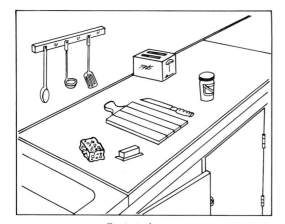

Contextual scene

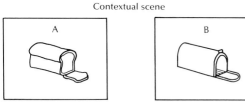

Target object (presented very briefly)

Figure 5.19 Stimuli from the experiment by Palmer (1975). After looking at the contextual scene, the subjects were shown one of the stimuli below it very briefly, by means of a tachistoscope. (From Palmer, S.E. *Memory and Cognition*, 1975, *3*, 519–526. Reprinted by permission of the Psychonomic Society, Inc.)

perception rather than to problem solving, which is much slower and more deliberate. Somehow, seeing a kitchen scene sensitizes the neural circuits responsible for the perception of loaves of bread and other items we have previously seen in that context.

Psychologists make distinctions between two general categories of information-processing models of pattern recognition: *bottom-up processing* and *top-down processing*. **Bottom-up processing** is also referred to as *data-driven processing;* the perception is constructed out of the elements—the bits and pieces—of the stimulus, beginning with the image that falls on the retina. The information is processed by successive levels of the visual system until the highest levels (the "top" of the system) are reached, and the object is perceived. **Top-down processing** refers to the use of contextual information—with the "big picture." Presumably, once the kitchen scene is perceived, information is sent from the "top" of the system down through lower levels. This information excites neural circuits responsible for perceiving those objects normally found in kitchens and inhibits others. Then when the subject sees a drawing of a loaf of bread, information starts coming up through

the successive levels of the system and finds the appropriate circuits already warmed up, so to speak.

Haenny and Schiller (1988) obtained direct evidence that watching for a particular stimulus can, indeed, "warm up" neural circuits in the visual system. They trained monkeys to look at a pattern of lines oriented at a particular angle, remember that pattern, and then pick it out from a series of different patterns presented immediately afterward. A correct response would be rewarded by a sip of fruit juice.

While the animals were performing the task, the experimenters recorded the activity of individual neurons in the visual association cortex. They found that watching for a pattern of lines with a particular orientation affected the responsiveness of the neurons. For example, if the monkeys were watching for a pattern containing lines oriented at 45 degrees, neurons that detected lines of that orientation responded more vigorously than normal when that pattern was presented again. Haenny, Maunsell, and Schiller (1988) found this enhancement could even be produced by letting the monkeys feel the orientation of a pattern of grooves in a metal plate they could not see; when a subsequent visual pattern contained lines whose orientation matched that of the grooves, a larger neural response was seen.

In most cases perception consists of a combination of top-down and bottom-up processing. Figure 5.21 shows several examples of objects that can only be recognized by a combination of both forms of processing. Our knowledge of the configurations of letters in words provides us

A tachistoscope. The woman on the right is looking at stimuli presented with this device, while the experimenter records her responses.

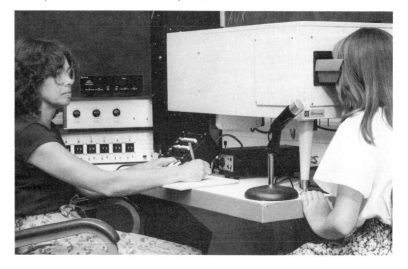

Figure 5.20 An example of top-down processing. The context facilitates our recognizing the items shown in Figure 5.18. (Adapted from Palmer, S.E., in *Explorations in Cognition*, edited by D.A. Norman, D.E. Rumelhart, and the LNR Research Group. San Francisco: W.H. Freeman, 1975.)

Figure 5.21 Examples of combined top-down/bottom-up processing. The effect of context enables us to perceive the letters despite the missing or ambiguous features. (From McClelland, J.J., Rumelhart, D.E., and Hinton, G.E., in *Parallel Distributed Processing. Vol. I: Foundations*, edited by D.E. Rumelhart, J.L. McClelland, and the PDP Research Group. © 1986 the Massachusetts Institute of Technology; published by The MIT Press, Cambridge, Mass.)

with the contexts that permit us to organize the flow of information from the bottom up. (See *Figure 5.21.*)

INTERIM SUMMARY

Perception of Form

Perception of form requires, first, recognition of figure and ground. The Gestalt organizational laws of proximity, similarity, good continuation, and common fate describe some of the ways in which we distinguish figure from ground even when the outlines of the figures are not explicitly bounded by lines.

Psychologists have advanced two major hypotheses about the mechanism of pattern perception, or visual recognition of particular shapes. The first hypothesis suggests that our brain contains "templates" of all the shapes we can perceive. We compare a particular pattern of visual input with these templates until we find a fit. But how many different patterns can the brain hold? The second hypothesis suggests that our brain contains "prototypes," which are more flexible than simple templates. Some psychologists believe that prototypes are collections of distinctive features (such as the two parallel lines and the connecting diagonal of the letter N). Others prefer the neural network approach, asserting that the ability of neural networks to learn to recognize patterns of input is the best explanation for form perception.

Until very recently, cognitive psychologists used the modern serial computer as the basis for constructing information-processing models of the operations of the human brain. In theory, all mental functions can be simulated by computer programs. However, just because a function can be *simulated* does not mean that the brain and the program perform the function in the same way. In fact, they do not. The brain consists of billions of interconnected elements that operate rather slowly. However, by doing many things simultaneously, the brain can perform complex operations in a brief amount of time. For example, we can recognize faces about as quickly as we can recognize simple figures such as triangles; in contrast, serial computers take an extremely long time to recognize complex figures.

Another difference between the human brain and serial computers is that damage to serial computers is disastrous. If parts of the central processor or memory elements containing vital instructions or data are destroyed, the program "crashes." However, widespread, *moderate* damage to the human brain simply reduces efficiency. Because of these differences, recent attempts to devise models of mental functions—especially those involving pattern recognition, which is an essential feature of perception—have employed neural networks. This approach uses assemblies of elements with properties similar to those of neurons. Although the approach is still quite new, it appears to be promising.

Perception involves both bottom-up and top-down processing. Our perceptions are influenced not only by the details of the particular stimuli we see but also by their relations to each other and our expectations. Thus, we may perceive a shape as a loaf of bread in the kitchen and as a mailbox alongside a country road. ■

PERCEPTION OF SPACE AND MOTION

6 Besides being able to perceive the forms of objects in our environment, we are able to judge quite accurately their relative location in space and their movements. Perceiving where things are and perceiving what they are doing are obviously important functions of the visual system.

Perception of Distance

We perceive distance by means of two kinds of cues: binocular ("two-eye") and monocular ("one-eye"). Only animals with eyes on the front of the head (such as primates, cats, and some birds) can obtain binocular cues. Animals with eyes on the sides of their heads (such as rabbits and fish) can obtain only monocular cues,

because the visual fields of their eyes do not overlap. One of the monocular cues involves movement and thus must be experienced in the natural environment or in a motion picture. The other monocular cues can be represented in a drawing or a photograph. In fact, most of these cues were originally discovered by artists and only later studied by psychologists. Artists wanted to represent the world realistically, and they studied their visual environments to identify the features that indicated distance of objects from the viewer. Art historians can show us the evidence of their discoveries.

Figure 5.22 shows the ten most important sources of distance cues (color terms). (See ***Figure 5.22.***)

Binocular Cues. An important cue about distance is supplied by **convergence.** Recall from Chapter 4 that the eyes make conjugate movements so that both look at (*converge* on) the same point of the visual scene. If an object is very close to your face, your eyes are turned inward. If it is farther away, they look more nearly straight ahead. Thus, the eyes can be used like range finders. The brain controls the extraocular muscles, so it knows the angle between them, which is related to the distance between the object and the eyes. (See ***Figure 5.23.***)

An even more important factor in the perception of distance is the information provided by **retinal disparity.** (*Disparity* means "unlikeness" or "dissimilarity.") Hold up a finger of one hand at arm's length and then hold up a finger of the other hand midway between your nose and the distant finger. If you look at one of the fingers, you will see a double image of the other

Figure 5.22 The principal monocular and binocular depth cues. (Adapted from Matlin, M.W., and Foley, H.J. *Sensation and Perception*, 3rd ed. Boston: Allyn and Bacon, 1992.)

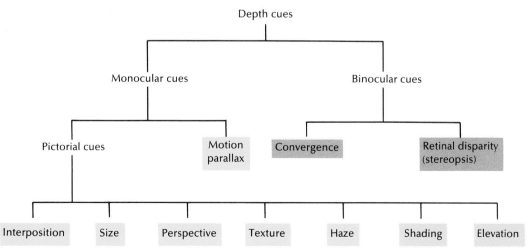

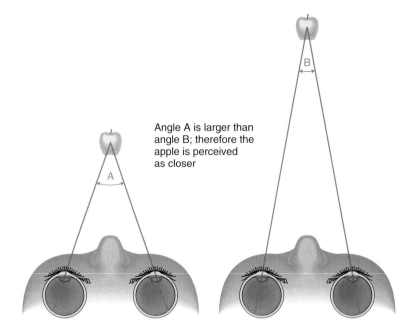

Angle A is larger than angle B; therefore the apple is perceived as closer

Figure 5.23 Convergence. When the eyes converge on a nearby object, the angle between them is greater than when they converge on a distant object. The brain uses this information in perceiving the distance of an object.

one. (Try it.) Whenever your eyes are pointed toward a particular point, the images of objects at different distances will fall on different portions of the retina in each eye. The amount of disparity produced by the images of an object on the two retinas provides an important clue about its distance from us.

The perception of depth from retinal disparity is called **stereopsis.** A *stereoscope* is a device that shows two slightly different pictures, one to each eye. The pictures are taken by a camera equipped with two lenses, located a few inches apart, just as our eyes are. When you look through a stereoscope you see a three-dimensional image. An experiment by Julesz (1965) demonstrated that retinal disparity is what produces the effect of depth. Using a computer, he produced two displays of randomly

positioned dots in which the location of some dots differed slightly. If some of the dots in one of the displays were displaced slightly to the right or the left, the two displays gave the impression of depth when viewed through a stereoscope.

Figure 5.24 shows a pair of these random-dot stereograms. If you look at them very carefully, you will see that some of the dots near the center have been moved slightly to the left. (See *Figure 5.24.*) Some people can look at these figures without using a stereoscope and see depth. If you want to try, hold the book at arm's length and look at the space between the figures. Now pretend you are looking "through" the book, into the distance. Each image will become double, since your eyes are no longer converged properly. If you try hard, you might

The Holmes-Bates stereoscope was invented by Oliver Wendell Holmes in 1861 and manufactured by Joseph Bates. It is a device that shows two slightly different pictures, one to each eye, producing a three-dimensional image by means of stereopsis.

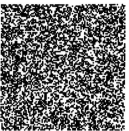

Figure 5.24 A pair of random-dot stereograms. (From Julesz, B. *Texture and visual perception. Scientific American*, 1965, *12*, 38–48. Copyright © 1965 by Scientific American, Inc. All rights reserved.)

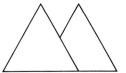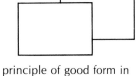

Figure 5.25 Use of the principle of good form in the perception of depth. The objects are perceived as identical pairs, but the one on the left in each pair looks closer than the one on the right.

make two of these images fuse into one, located right in the middle. If you keep looking, eventually you might see a small square in the center of the image, raised above the background.

Electrical recordings of individual neurons in the visual system of the brain have found a class of cells that receive information from both eyes and respond only when there is a slight disparity between the image of an object on both retinas. (This effect would occur if an object was slightly nearer or farther from you than the convergence point of the gaze of your eyes.) Thus, some neurons at this level apparently compare the activity of neurons with corresponding receptive fields for both eyes and respond when there is a disparity. Obviously, these neurons participate in stereopsis.

Monocular Cues. One of the most important sources of information about the relative distance of objects is **interposition** (*interposed* means "placed between"). If one object is placed between us and another object so that the closer object partially obscures our view of

the more distant one, we can immediately perceive which object is closer to us.

Obviously, interposition works best when we are familiar with the objects and know what their shapes should look like. But it even works with unfamiliar objects. Just as the Gestalt law of good continuation plays a role in form perception, the *principle of good form* affects our perception of the relative location of objects: We perceive the object with the simpler border as being closer. Figure 5.25 contains two drawings that can be seen either as complex two-dimensional figures sitting side by side or as two simple objects, one in front of the other. Because we tend to perceive an ambiguous drawing according to the principle of good form, we almost always see two objects. (See *Figure 5.25.*)

Another important monocular distance cue is provided by our familiarity with the *sizes* of objects. For example, if an automobile casts a very small image on our retinas, we will perceive it as being far away. Knowing how large cars are, our visual system can automatically compute the approximate distance from the size of the retinal image.

Figure 5.26 shows two columns located at different distances. The drawing shows **per-**

This young Nile crocodile can only utilize monocular cues of depth perception because the visual field of its eyes do not overlap.

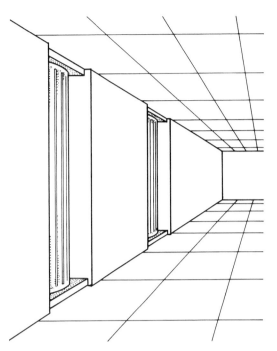

Figure 5.26 Principle of perspective. Perspective gives the appearance of distance and makes the two columns look similar in size.

spective: the tendency for parallel lines that recede from us to converge at a single point. Because of perspective, we perceive the columns as being the same size even though they produce retinal images of different sizes. (See *Figure 5.26.*)

Figure 5.27 Texture cues. Variations in texture can produce an appearance of distance. (Nancy Sheehan.)

Figure 5.28 Cues from atmospheric haze. Variation in detail, owing to haze, produces an appearance of distance.

In a natural environment that has not been altered by humans, we seldom see actual converging lines that denote perspective. For example, earlier in our evolutionary history people did not see streets, large buildings, and railroad tracks. Did we acquire the ability to use perspective cues only after producing these features of the landscape, or is there a counterpart of perspective to be found in nature?

Texture, especially the texture of the ground, provides another cue we use to perceive the distance of objects sitting on the ground. A coarser texture looks closer, and a finer texture looks more distant. (See *Figure 5.27.*) The earth's atmosphere, which always contains a certain amount of haze, can also supply cues about the relative distance of objects or parts of the landscape. Parts of the landscape that are farther away become less distinct because of haze in the air. Thus, **haze** provides a monocular distance cue. (See *Figure 5.28.*)

The patterns of light and shadow regions in a scene—its **shading**—can provide us with cues about the three-dimensional shapes of objects. Although the cues provided by shading do not usually tell us much about the absolute distances of objects from us, they can tell us which *parts* of objects are closer and which are farther. Figure 5.29 illustrates the power of this phenomenon. Some of the circles look as if they

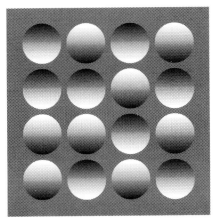

Figure 5.29 Depth cues supplied by shading. If the tops of the circles are dark, they look like depressions. If the bottoms are dark, they appear as bumps. (From Ramachandran, V.S. Perceiving shape from shading. *Scientific American,* 1988, *259*, 76–83. Copyright © 1988 by Scientific American, Inc. All rights reserved.)

bulged out toward us; others look as if they were hollowed out. The only difference is the direction of the shading. Our visual system appears to interpret such stimuli as if they were illuminated from above; thus, the top of a convex (bulging) object will be light and the bottom will be in shadow. (See *Figure 5.29.*)

When we are able to see the horizon, we perceive objects near it as being distant and

Figure 5.30 Depth cues supplied by elevation. The objects nearest the horizontal line appear farthest away from us. (Adapted from Matlin, M.W., and Foley, H.J. *Sensation and Perception,* 3rd ed. Boston: Allyn and Bacon, 1992.)

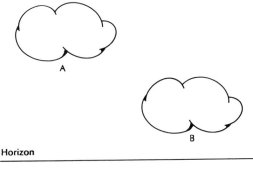

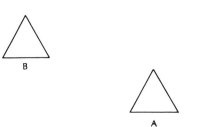

those above or below it as being nearer to us. Thus, an important monocular depth cue is provided by **elevation.** For example, cloud B and triangle B in *Figure 5.30* appear farther away from us than cloud A and triangle A.

So far, all the monocular distance cues discussed have been those that can be rendered in a drawing or captured by a camera. However, another important source of distance information depends on our own movement. If you focus your eyes on an object close to you and move your head from side to side, your image of the scene moves back and forth behind the nearer object. If you focus your eyes on the background while moving your head from side to side, the image of the nearer object passes back and forth across the background. Head and body movements cause the images from the scene before us to change; the closer the object, the more it changes, relative to the background. The information contained in this relative movement helps us perceive distance.

Figure 5.31 illustrates the kinds of cues supplied when we move with respect to features in the environment. The top part of the figure shows three objects at different distances from the observer: a man, a house, and a tree. The lower part shows the views that the observer will see from five different places (P_1–P_5). The changes in the relative locations of the objects provide cues to their distance from the observer. (See *Figure 5.31.*) The phenomenon is known as **motion parallax.** (*Parallax* comes from a Greek word meaning "change of position.")

Constancies of Visual Perception

[7] An important characteristic of the visual environment is that it is almost always changing as we move, as objects move, and as lighting conditions change. However, despite the changing nature of the image the visual environment casts on our retinas, our perceptions remain remarkably constant.

Brightness Constancy. Experiments have shown that people can judge the whiteness or grayness of an object very well, even if the level of illumination changes. If you look at a sheet of white paper either in bright sunlight or in shade, you will perceive it as being white, although the intensity of its image on your retina will vary. If you look at a sheet of gray paper in sunlight, it may in fact reflect more light to your eye than a white paper located in the shade, but you will still see the white paper as white and the gray

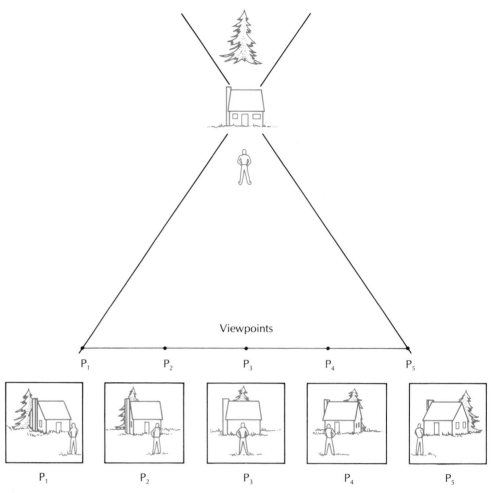

Viewpoints

P₁ P₂ P₃ P₄ P₅

Figure 5.31 Perception of distance. As we move, we make inferences about distance from the relative positions of objects in the environment. (From *The Psychology of Visual Perception* by Ralph H. Haber and Maurice Hershenson, copyright © 1973 by Holt, Rinehart & Winston, Inc., reprinted by permission of the publisher.)

Figure 5.32 Brightness constancy, demonstrated by the experiment by Katz (1935).

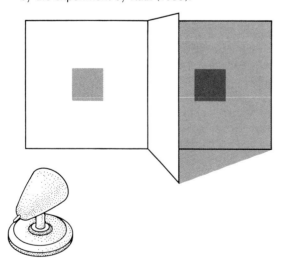

paper as gray. This phenomenon is known as **brightness constancy.**

Katz (1935) demonstrated brightness constancy by constructing a vertical barrier and positioning a light source so that a shadow was cast to the right of the barrier. In the shadow he placed a gray square card on a white background. In the lighted area on the left of the barrier he placed a number of shades of gray and asked subjects to choose one that matched the gray square in the shadow. (See *Figure 5.32.*) His subjects matched the grays not in terms of the light that the cards actually reflected but in terms of the light they *would have* reflected had both been viewed under the same level of illumination. In other words, the subjects compensated for the dimness of the shadow. The match was not perfect, but it was much closer than it would have been if perception of brightness had been made solely on the basis of the amount of light that fell on the retina.

The perception of white and gray, then, is not a matter of absolutes; rather, they are perceived relative to the surrounding environment. For example, you perceive a ceiling painted a rather dark off-white color as pure white unless a piece of white paper is placed next to it for comparison. When I lecture to my classes, I use an overhead projector that permits me to project notes and diagrams onto a screen at the front of the room. If I put a small piece of paper on the projector, point to the image it casts on the screen, and ask the students the color of the image, they invariably say "black." Then I turn off the projector, so that the entire screen has the color they just perceived as black. Now, they tell me, the screen is obviously white.

Form Constancy. When we approach an object or when it approaches us, we do not perceive it as getting larger. Even though the image of the object on the retina gets larger, we perceive this change as being due to a decrease in the distance between ourselves and the object. Our perception of the object's size remains relatively constant.

The unchanging perception of an object's size and shape when it moves relative to us is called **form constancy.** (People also refer to *size constancy,* but size is simply one aspect of form.) In the nineteenth century Hermann von Helmholtz suggested that form constancy was achieved by **unconscious inference**—a mental computation of which we are unaware. We know the size and shape of a familiar object; therefore, if the image it casts upon our retina is small, we perceive it as being far away. If the image is large, we perceive it as being close. (As we saw in the subsection on perception of

Figure 5.33 Form constancy. (a) This figure can be perceived as a trapezoid. (b) Because we recognize this figure as a window, we perceive its shape as rectangular.

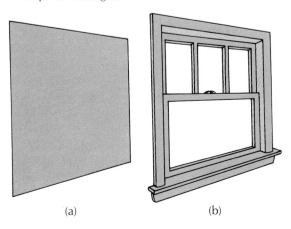

(a)   (b)

Figure 5.34 Effect of perceived distance. Although both mailboxes are exactly the same size, the upper one looks larger because of the depth cues (perspective and texture) that surround it. If you turn the book over and look at the picture upside down, thus disrupting the depth cues, the mailboxes look the same size.

distance, size is an important monocular cue.) In either case, we perceive the object itself as being the same size. Form constancy also works for rotation. The drawing of Figure 5.33a could be either a trapezoid or a rectangle rotated away from us. However, the extra cues clearly identify the drawing in Figure 5.33b as a window, and experience tells us that windows are rectangular rather than trapezoidal; thus, we perceive it as rectangular. (See *Figure 5.33.*)

The process I just described works for familiar objects. However, we often see unfamiliar objects, whose size we do not already know. If we are to perceive the size and shape of unfamiliar objects accurately, we must know something about their distance from us. An object that produces a large retinal image is perceived as big if it is far away and small if it is close. Apparently, the visual system performs this computation—another instance of unconscious inference. Figure 5.34 illustrates this phenomenon. Although the two mailboxes are exactly the same size, the one that appears to be farther away looks larger. (See *Figure 5.34.*) If you turn the book upside down and look at the figure again, the appearance of depth is greatly diminished, and the two mailboxes appear to be approximately the same size. (See *Figure 5.34.*)

Perception of Motion

8 Detection of movement is one of the most primitive aspects of visual perception. This ability is seen even in animals whose visual system

The combat soldier's survival depends on the ability to detect movement in the environment.

cannot obtain detailed images of the environment. Of course, our visual system can detect more than the mere presence of movement; we can see what is moving in our environment and can detect the direction in which it is moving.

Adaptation and Long-Term Modification. One of the most important characteristics of all sensory systems is that they show adaptation and rebound effects. For example, when you stare at a spot of color, the adaptation of neurons in your visual system will produce a negative afterimage if you shift your gaze to a neutral background; and if you put your hand in some hot water, warm water will feel cool to that hand immediately afterward.

Motion, like other kinds of stimuli, can give rise to adaptation and aftereffects. The first time I recorded an EEG, I remember watching the paper pass by the pens as they traced their record of the electrical activity of the subject's brain. I turned the machine off, and suddenly, the paper seemed to go backward. At first I thought that the paper was really going in reverse, but I realized that it never seemed to get anywhere. That is, I perceived the paper as moving, but at the same time I could see that it was clearly remaining in the same spot. The phenomenon is difficult to describe and must be experienced to be believed. You may not have an EEG machine available to you, but if you spend a minute or two watching a phonograph record turning around, it will appear to turn backward if you suddenly stop its movement.

A study by Ball and Sekuler (1982) suggests that even the long-term characteristics of the system that detects movement can be modified by experience. The experimenters trained people to detect extremely small movements. Each

subject sat in front of a display screen. A series of dots appeared, scattered across the face of the screen, and either all moved an extremely small distance or all remained stationary. The dots always moved in the same direction, but the direction was different for each person in the experiment. After several sessions the experimenters assessed the subjects' sensitivity to detecting movements of the dots. They found that each person was especially good at detecting movement *only in the direction in which he or she had been trained;* the training did not increase their detection of movements in other directions. The effect was still present when the subjects were tested again ten weeks later.

The fact that the subjects learned to detect a small movement in a particular direction, and not small movements in general, shows that particular aspects of their visual systems were modified by experience. Did they acquire new sets of feature detectors, or were parallel networks of neurons modified in some way? As yet, we have no way of knowing the nature of the changes to the visual system.

Interpretation of a Moving Retinal Image. As you read this book, your eyes are continuously moving. Naturally, the eye movements cause the image on your retina to move. You can also cause the retinal image to move by holding the book close to your face, looking straight ahead, and moving it back and forth. (Try it.) In the first case, when you were reading normally, you perceived the book as being still. In the second case you perceived it as moving. Why does your brain interpret the movement differently in these two cases? Try another demonstration. Pick a letter on this page, stare at it, and then move the book around, following the letter with your eyes. This time you will perceive the book as moving, even though the image on your retina remains stable. Thus, perception of movement requires coordination between movements of the image on the retina and those of the eyes.

Obviously, the visual system must know about eye movements in order to compensate for them in interpreting the significance of moving images on the retina. The source of the information is suggested by another simple demonstration. Close your left eye and look slightly down and to the left. Gently press your finger against the outer corner of the upper eyelid of your right eye and make your right eye move a bit. The scene before you appears to be moving, even though you know better. This sensation of movement occurs because your finger—not your eye muscles—moved your eye. When your eye moves normally, perceptual mechanisms in your brain compensate for this movement; thus, even though the image on the retina moves, you perceive the environment as being stationary. However, if the image moves because the object itself moves or because you push your eye with your finger, you perceive movement.

Besides perceiving absolute movements, we perceive the movements of objects relative to one another. Sometimes, we can be fooled. You may have sat in an automobile at a stoplight when the vehicle next to you started to roll backward. For a moment you were uncertain whether you were moving forward or the other vehicle was moving backward. Only by looking at nonmoving objects such as buildings or trees could you be sure.

In general, if two objects of different size are seen moving relative to each other, the smaller one is perceived as moving and the larger one as standing still. We perceive people at a distance moving against a stable background and flies moving against an unmoving wall. Thus, when an experimenter moves a frame that encloses a stationary dot, we tend to see the dot move, not the frame. This phenomenon is also encountered when we perceive the moon racing behind the clouds, even though we know that the clouds, not the moon, are moving.

Perception of movement can even help us perceive three-dimensional forms. Johansson (1973) demonstrated just how much information we can derive from movement. He dressed actors in black and attached small lights to several points on their bodies, such as their wrists, elbows, shoulders, hips, knees, and feet. He made movies of the actors in a darkened room

while they were performing various behaviors, such as walking, running, jumping, limping, doing push-ups, and dancing with a partner who was also equipped with lights. Even though observers who watched the films could only see a pattern of moving lights against a dark background, they could readily perceive the pattern as belonging to a moving human and could identify the behavior the actor was performing. Subsequent studies (Kozlowski and Cutting, 1977; Barclay, Cutting, and Kozlowski, 1978) showed that people could even tell, with reasonable accuracy, the sex of the actor wearing the lights. The cues appeared to be supplied by the relative amounts of movement of the shoulders and hips as the person walked.

Combining Information from Successive Fixations. As you saw in Chapter 4, when examining a scene, our eyes do not roam slowly around; rather, they make rapid steplike movements called *saccades*. After each saccade the eyes rest for a while, gathering information before moving again. These stops are called *fixations*. The visual system combines the information from each fixation and perceives objects too large or too detailed to see in a single glance. Obviously, in doing so, it must keep track of the locations of each of the fixations.

Figure 5.35 illustrates an *impossible figure*. That is, an artist can draw lines that, at first glance, represent a three-dimensional object. However, careful inspection shows that the object cannot possibly exist. (See **Figure 5.35.**) But the drawing in Figure 5.36 creates a very different impression; it does not look at all like a unified three-dimensional object. (See **Figure 5.36.**) The difference in the two impressions is that the details of the larger figure cannot be gathered in a single glance. Apparently, when we look from one end of the figure to the other, the information we gather from the first fixation is slightly modified to conform with the image of the second one. Of course, the two images do not exactly match, as a careful inspection shows.

Clearly, what we see during one fixation affects what we see in another. Long ago, psychologists discovered that if they presented two visual stimuli, one after the other, the second stimulus could sometimes erase the image of the first. That is, under the appropriate conditions the subject would fail to perceive the image that came first. The phenomenon is known as **backward masking** (Werner, 1935).

Backward masking normally can be demonstrated only in the laboratory, where the shape

Figure 5.35 An impossible figure. Only after carefully studying the figure do we see that it cannot be a drawing of a real three-dimensional object.

and intensity of the stimuli and the time interval between them can be carefully controlled. However, Breitmeyer (1980) suggests that the explanation for this phenomenon lies in the nature of the saccadic movements made by the eyes in gathering information about the visual environment. For example, consider the saccadic movements your eyes make as you read a line of text in this book. You do not stop and look at each letter or even at each word; instead, you make several fixations on each line. During each one your visual system gathers information and begins decoding the letters and words. Your eyes move on, and more words are perceived. Breitmeyer suggests that each saccade erases the image remaining from the previous fixation, leaving only the information that has been analyzed by the visual system. Figure 5.37 illustrates what might happen if this erasure did not occur. (See *Figure 5.37.*)

Perception of Movement in the Absence of Motion. If you sit in a darkened room and watch two small lights that are alternately turned on and off, your perception will be that of a single light moving back and forth between two different locations. You will not see the light turn off at one position and then turn on at the second position. If the distance and timing are just right, the light will appear to stay on at all times, quickly moving between the positions. This response is known as the **phi phenomenon.** Theater marquees and "moving" neon signs make use of it.

This characteristic of the visual system accounts for the fact that we perceive the images in motion pictures and on television as continuous rather than separate. The images actually jump from place to place, but we see smooth movement.

Figure 5.36 An unconvincing impossible figure. When the legs are short enough so that the entire figure can be perceived during a single fixation, the figure does not look paradoxical.

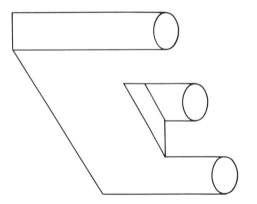

Figure 5.37 The role of backward masking. If each saccade did not erase the remaining image from the previous fixation, we probably would not be able to read. (From Margaret W. Matlin, *Sensation and Perception,* Second Edition. Copyright © 1988 by Allyn and Bacon. Reproduced with permission.)

You can read this sentence clearly

(a) If material from every fixation pause were retained during the later fixation pauses, a sentence might look like this at the third fixation pause.

You can read this sentence clearly

(b) Fortunately, masking prevents the persistence of earlier material, and so we see a sentence that looks like this.

INTERIM SUMMARY

Perception of Space and Motion

Our visual system accomplishes a remarkable feat: It manages to perceive the brightness, size, and shape of objects accurately even in the face of movement and changes in levels of illumination. We perceive the brightness of an object relative to that of objects around it; thus, objects retain a constant brightness under a variety of conditions of illumination. Because the size and shape of a retinal image vary with the location of an object relative to the eye, accurate form perception requires perception of an object's location in space. Binocular cues (from convergence and retinal disparity) and monocular cues (from the principle of good form, perspective, texture, shading, elevation, and the effects of head and body movements) help us perceive distance and thus maintain form constancy.

Because our bodies may well be moving while we are visually following some activity in the outside world, the visual system has to make further compensations. It keeps track of the commands to the eye muscles and compensates for the direction in which the eyes are pointing. Movement is perceived when objects move relative to one another. In particular, the smaller object is likely to be perceived as moving across the larger one. Movement is also perceived when our eyes follow a moving object, even though its image remains on the same part of the retina.

Movement supplies important cues about an object's three-dimensional shape. In fact, we are much more sensitive to complex movements than we commonly realize, as illustrated by the demonstration with the movies of actors wearing lights. Sometimes, we can even recognize a friend at a distance by the way that person walks.

Because a complex scene, covering a large area, cannot be seen in a single glance, the visual system must combine information from successive fixations. The phenomenon of backward masking suggests that the image received from the previous fixation is erased immediately after a saccade so that blurring does not occur.

The phi phenomenon describes our tendency to see an instantaneous displacement of an object from one place to another as movement of that object. Because of the phi phenomenon, we perceive television shows and movies as representations of reality, not as a series of disconnected images. ∎

APPLICATION

Designing Visual Displays

Engineering psychologists are concerned with improving the interface between people and machines. An important goal is to make visual displays easy to read so that people will make the right responses, and make them as quickly as possible. The control panels of nuclear power plants, the displays in aircraft cockpits, and the radar screens of air traffic controllers are complex and contain much information. If these displays are not well designed, the operators might not notice critical events quickly enough to take appropriate action, or they may misperceive the information being displayed and do something inappropriate. In either case, the results can be disastrous.

When designing visual displays, engineering psychologists obviously apply their knowledge of the principles of perception. In addition, they evaluate their designs by performing experiments in which subjects monitor the displays and respond to the information that is presented. The most elaborate experiments are *simulations,* in which the novel displays are incorporated into models of control panels or cockpits, and the subjects' reactions to both routine situations and simulated emergencies can be evaluated. Several journals (such as *Human Factors, Ergonomics,* and *Applied Ergonomics*) are devoted to reporting the results of such experiments.

In the past, visual displays meant rows of dials, gauges, and lights. Nowadays, these displays usually incorporate computer-controlled video screens, which can present both graphical displays and words. Some investigators have studied the variables that affect legibility of these displays. For example, Luria, Neri, and Schlichting (1989) found that subjects preferred using video screens that presented green letters and symbols (compared with amber, yellow, red, blue, and white), but that they made fewer errors when the letters and symbols were presented in yellow.

New instruments and new ways to display information are constantly being developed for the cockpits of commercial airplanes. Ellis, McGreevy, and Hitchcock (1987) tested an experimental display panel that shows a pilot other traffic in the vicinity. The new display used computerized techniques to show the location of the other aircraft in perspective. They found that pilots responded faster to the new display than to the traditional display, and that they were more likely to make the appropriate maneuvers to avoid getting too close to other aircraft.

Because operators of complex instrument panels must keep track of so many items, some designers have suggested that critical events should be presented by means of speech synthesizers. Presumably, the operators can keep their ears open even while they are watching the instrument panel. However, Robinson and Eberts (1987) found that subjects responded faster to information presented in a visual display than to information presented in speech. In addition, when they were required to perform a visual-tracking task while simultaneously monitoring another display, they performed better when the both displays were visual. The subjects responded more slowly to a voice than to a visual display in simulated emergencies, and they were more likely to make errors.

Most of us will never have the opportunity to pilot a commercial aircraft, control a nuclear power plant, or control air traffic, but most of us will drive a car. Most automobile instrument panels contain traditional dials and gauges, but computerized electronic displays will become more commonplace in the future. One display that is being tested by engineering psychologists is the *heads-up display,* in which information is projected onto the inside of the windshield, where it appears as a bright reflection. Drivers can look through the display to the road in front of them and only need to make a slight eye movement to see, for example, how fast they are going. They need not glance away from the road. Sojouner and Antin (1990) tested the driving performance of subjects in a simulation study that presented subjects with videotapes of a road trip. They found that the subjects did not believe that the heads-up display was more useful than the traditional instrument panel. However, their ability to maintain the proper speed, to navigate along the route, and to notice relevant events was superior when the heads-up display was in use.

Experience tells us that accidents are often the result of human error. If psychologists can contribute their knowledge and expertise to present information in ways that maximize speed of response and minimize errors, then they will have contributed to making our lives even safer.

KEY TERMS AND CONCEPTS

Brain Mechanisms of Vision

achromatopsia *(136)*
visual agnosia *(136)*
prosopagnosia *(136)*

Perception of Form

figure *(137)*
ground *(137)*
illusory contour *(138)*
Gestalt psychology *(138)*
law of proximity *(138)*
law of similarity *(138)*
good continuation *(139)*
law of closure *(139)*
law of common fate *(139)*
template *(139)*
prototype *(140)*
distinctive feature *(141)*
geon *(142)*
artificial intelligence *(143)*
serial device *(144)*
parallel processor *(144)*

neural network *(145)*
tachistoscope *(146)*
bottom-up processing *(147)*
top-down processing *(147)*

Perception of Space and Motion

convergence *(149)*
retinal disparity *(149)*
stereopsis *(150)*
interposition *(151)*
perspective *(151)*
texture *(152)*
haze *(152)*
shading *(152)*
elevation *(153)*
motion parallax *(153)*
brightness constancy *(154)*
form constancy *(155)*
unconscious inference *(155)*
backward masking *(157)*
phi phenomenon *(159)*

SUGGESTIONS FOR FURTHER READING

Matlin, M.W., and Foley, H.J. *Sensation and Perception,* 3rd ed. Boston: Allyn and Bacon, 1992.
Sekuler, R., and Blake, R. *Perception,* 2nd ed. New York: McGraw-Hill, 1990.

Two of the books that I recommended at the end of Chapter 4 discuss visual perception as well as sensory processes.

6
BASIC PRINCIPLES OF LEARNING

Henri Matisse, *The Painter's Family*
SCALA/Art Resource, N.Y. © 1992 Succession H. Matisse/ARS, N.Y.

HABITUATION

CLASSICAL CONDITIONING

The Work of Ivan Pavlov ▪ The Biological Significance of Classical Conditioning ▪ What Is Learned? ▪ Extinction ▪ Conditioned Emotional Responses ▪ Interim Summary

INSTRUMENTAL/OPERANT CONDITIONING

Reinforcement and Punishment ▪ Extinction ▪ Conditioned Reinforcement and Punishment ▪ Finding Effective Reinforcers: The Premack Principle ▪ Intermittent Reinforcement ▪ Interim Summary

PHENOMENA OF LEARNING

Discrimination ▪ Generalization ▪ Aversive Control ▪ Superstitious Behavior ▪ Conditioned Flavor Aversions ▪ Observation and Imitation ▪ *Evaluating Scientific Issues: What Is Insight?* ▪ Interim Summary

APPLICATION: CONDITIONED FLAVOR AVERSIONS

LEARNING OBJECTIVES

When you finish this chapter, you should be able to:

1. Define *learning*, and describe short-term and long-term habituation.
2. Describe the discovery of classical conditioning by Pavlov, discuss its characteristics, and describe conditioned emotional responses.
3. Describe instrumental conditioning, the nature of reinforcement and punishment, and the phenomenon of extinction.
4. Describe conditioned reinforcement and punishment, the role of classical conditioning in instrumental conditioning, the conditioning of complex behaviors, and the procedure called shaping.
5. Describe and discuss the Premack principle.
6. Describe intermittent reinforcement and its resistance to extinction.
7. Describe the phenomena of discrimination and generalization.
8. Describe the nature of punishment and negative reinforcement and the limitations of aversive control in instrumental conditioning.
9. Discuss the development of superstitious behavior and conditioned flavor aversions, and describe the learning that occurs through observation and imitation.
10. Discuss the nature of insightful behavior.

Ahmad Wahl, a successful lawyer, wanted to get rid of a bad habit. He was an excellent speaker and writer, and when he heard someone make a grammatical error, he was quick to point it out. Afterward, he regretted doing so, because he either embarrassed the other person or made them angry at him. He liked to think of himself as friendly, kind, and tolerant; and his habit of correcting people's grammar conflicted with this aspect of his self-image.

One day he was discussing a real estate transaction with a client, a psychologist. The client happened to commit a grammatical error, and before Ahmad could stop himself, he corrected her. He apologized immediately and said that he had tried to stop the bad habit but never seemed to think of remaining silent until afterward, when it was too late.

"If you really want to break that habit, I know how to do it," said the psychologist, May Lin Lee. "In fact, I'd be willing to bet that you can get rid of it within two weeks."

"Really? I thought psychoanalysis took a long time. That's why I never tried to find a psychologist to help me."

"I'm not a psychoanalyst; in fact, hardly any psychologists are. I'm a behavior analyst. I use some basic principles of learning that psychologists have discovered to help people change their behavior. Your little habit will be easy to get rid of."

"If you can really help me, I'll exchange my professional services for yours. How about a swap? If you succeed, I won't bill you for the closing on your house."

May Lin smiled. "It's a deal." She took a piece of paper and wrote a few lines. "Here," she said. "Read this contract, and then sign it."

Ahmad read what she had written and then looked at her suspiciously. "That's all there is to it? I have to burn a ten-dollar bill every time I correct someone's grammar?" She nodded. "Don't you want to talk to me to find out if I've got some kind of complex that's making me criticize others?"

"No, that's all you have to do. And I want you to make a note on your appointment calendar every time you have to burn a ten-dollar bill. Oh, make sure you carry a good supply of them with you—and a lighter or a pack of matches. You have to burn the money right away."

Ahmad looked unconvinced, but he signed the paper.

A week later he called May Lin, as he had agreed to do. "I can't understand it," he said. "I really think it's working. I had to burn one bill·

the first day, two the second, none the third, one the fourth, and one the fifth. That was the last. This morning, I talked with a client who made more grammatical errors than I could count, and I didn't correct any of them. But I can't understand this—if I can make myself burn ten-dollar bills, why couldn't I exercise enough willpower before to stop correcting people?"

"Breaking a habit is not really a matter of willpower—that's a misconception most people have. What you need to do is arrange the contingencies in your environment so that they reinforce desirable behaviors or, as in your case, punish undesirable ones. Psychologists have learned that behaviors are changed most effectively when they are reinforced or punished *immediately*. Somehow—and for our purposes it really doesn't matter how—you had acquired the habit of correcting people. Later in life, you began feeling bad about the effect this behavior had on other people and on your own self-image. But the immediate effect of correcting someone was probably a reinforcing one—a feeling that you had demonstrated your superiority, perhaps. The bad feeling you had afterward came too late to have a direct effect on your behavior. So I had you do something that was certain to have an unpleasant effect on you. The immediate punishing effect of the loss of the money outweighed the reinforcing effect of your demonstrating your superiority. And once you started realizing you were beating your habit, the satisfaction you derived from that accomplishment started reinforcing your remaining silent."

"You know, you're right. The past few days I've almost been hoping that people will make grammatical errors so that I can pride myself on keeping quiet."

When Ahmad called May Lin a week later, he reported that his stack of ten-dollar bills was still intact.

We are what we are because of history—both our ancestors' history and the history of our own lives. The evolution of our species was shaped by the process of natural selection: Mutations introduced variability, and those changes that produced favorable consequences were maintained. Our behaviors are similarly selected: Behaviors that produce favorable consequences are repeated, but those that produce unfavorable consequences tend not to recur. In other words, we learn from experience.

Learning refers to relatively long-lasting changes in an individual's behavior that are produced by environmental events. The process is one of adaptation; the changes in behavior are the result of interactions with the environment. As conditions change, new behaviors are learned, and old ones are eliminated.

Because an individual can learn something without showing an immediate change in behavior, many psychologists make a distinction between learning and performance. For them *learning* is defined as the changes within the individual that have been brought about by experience. Undoubtedly, learning takes place within the nervous system: Experiences alter the structure and chemistry of the brain, and these changes affect the individual's subsequent behavior. *Performance* is the behavioral change (or new behavior) produced by the internal change. Performance occurs only when the situation is appropriate. For example, a person may have learned a new dance, but unless the right music is playing and a suitable partner is available, the performance of what the person learned will not take place. Performance can also depend upon motivation; a rat taught by a psychologist to run through a maze for a piece of food will do so only if it is hungry.

This chapter considers three kinds of learning: habituation, classical conditioning, and operant conditioning. All three involve discovering the nature of cause-and-effect relations in the environment. We learn which stimuli are trivial and which are important, and we learn to make adaptive responses and avoid maladaptive ones. We learn to recognize conditions under which a particular response is useful and those under which another response is more appropriate. The types of learning described in this chapter are fundamental; they serve as the building blocks for more complex behaviors, including problem solving and thinking, which are described in later chapters.

HABITUATION

Many events may cause us to react automatically. For example, a sudden, unexpected noise causes an **orienting response**—we become alert and turn our head toward the source of the sound. However, if the noise occurs again and again, we gradually cease to respond to it—we eventually ignore it. **Habituation**, learning *not* to respond to an event that occurs repeatedly, is the simplest form of learning. We first encountered habituation in Chapter 2, where I described the zoologist's unfortunate experiment with South American birds. Even animals with very primitive nervous systems are capable of habituation. For example, if we tap the shell of a land snail with the point of a pencil, it will withdraw its body into its shell. After half a minute or so it will extend its body out of its shell and continue with whatever it was doing. If we tap it again, it will again withdraw, but this time it will stay inside its shell a shorter time. Another tap will cause it to withdraw again, but for even less time. Eventually, it will stop responding to the tap. The withdrawal response will have habituated.

From an evolutionary perspective habituation makes sense. If a once-novel stimulus occurs again and again without any important result, the stimulus has no significance to the organism. Obviously, it is a waste of time and energy to keep responding to a stimulus that has no importance. Consider what would happen to a land snail in a rainstorm if its withdrawal response never habituated—it would be obliged to remain in its shell until the drops stopped falling. And consider how distracting it would be to have your attention diverted every time a common household noise occurred.

The simplest form of habituation is temporary, known as *short-term habituation.* Suppose

When a child writes letters that look the way they should, seeing them reinforces her efforts.

we tap a snail's shell again and again until the withdrawal response habituates. If we tap it again the next day, we will find that it withdraws into its shell again and continues to do so for several more taps. It takes just as long for habituation to occur as it did the day before. And if we repeat our experiment every day afterward, the same thing will happen; the snail does not remember what happened previously.

Animals with more complex nervous systems are capable of *long-term habituation*. For example, a hunting dog may be frightened the first few times it hears the sound of a shotgun, but it soon learns not to respond to it. This habituation carries across from day to day or even from one hunting season to the next.

Certainly, habituation is the least interesting form of learning, but it is a useful one: It permits us to get more important things done and to remain relatively free from distraction by petty events. And as we shall see in Chapter 10, psychologists have put the phenomenon of habituation to practical use in studying the perceptual abilities of very young human infants.

CLASSICAL CONDITIONING

2 In contrast to habituation, which occurs when nothing important happens, **classical conditioning** involves learning about the conditions that predict that an event with some personal significance will occur. Many of your behaviors have been acquired through this learning process. For example, if you are hungry and smell (or perhaps even think about) some tasty food, your mouth is likely to water. If you see someone you just had a serious argument with, you are likely to experience again some of the reactions of your autonomic nervous system (the unpleasant feelings in your stomach) that occurred during the encounter. If you hear a song that you used to listen to with a loved one, you are likely to experience a feeling of nostalgia.

Let us examine how classical conditioning takes place. Suppose you are seated in a small room with a balloon located directly in front of your face. Someone starts inflating the balloon with an electric pump until the rubber begins to look very thin and taut. What are you likely to do? It is a pretty safe bet that you will grimace and squint your eyes partly shut. Why? You recognize that the balloon is ready to burst and explode in your face. You undoubtedly learned about balloons early in childhood; in fact, you probably cannot remember your first encounter with one.

Let us analyze how a person learns to flinch defensively at the sight of a thinly stretched balloon. Suppose we inflate a balloon in front of a young boy who has never seen one before. The child will turn his eyes toward the enlarging balloon, but he will not flinch. When the balloon finally explodes, the noise and the blast of air will cause a defensive startle reaction: The boy will squint, grimace, raise his shoulders, and suddenly move his arms toward his body. A balloon that bursts near someone's face provides an important stimulus, one that causes an automatic, unlearned defensive reaction. Figure 6.1 presents a schematic diagram of what I have discussed so far. (See ***Figure 6.1.***)

We will probably not have to repeat the experience many times for our subject to learn to react the way you do—by flinching defensively before the balloon actually bursts. A previously neutral stimulus (the overinflated balloon), followed by an important stimulus (the explosion that occurs when the balloon bursts), can now trigger the response by itself. The defensive flinching response has been *classically conditioned* to the sight of an overinflated balloon. (See ***Figure 6.2.***)

The Work of Ivan Pavlov

Ivan Pavlov, a Russian physiologist, carried out the pioneering studies in classical conditioning. (He performed such an impressive and authori-

Figure 6.1 Classical conditioning. The child watches the balloon grow large until it bursts, which causes a defensive startle reaction.

Figure 6.2 Conditioned response. After the child's first experience with a bursting balloon, the mere sight of an inflating balloon elicits a defensive reaction.

tative series of experiments over his long career that this form of learning is called "classical" out of respect for his work. It is sometimes also referred to as *Pavlovian conditioning.*) Pavlov's research interest was originally in the physiology of the digestive process, not in behavior. His interest led him to study the neural control of salivation and secretion of digestive juices in dogs. He inserted a small tube in a duct in the animal's mouth and collected drops of saliva as they were secreted by the salivary gland.

During his studies Pavlov noticed that after a dog had participated in an experiment for a while, it would begin to salivate as soon as he or one of his assistants entered the room. He had expected salivation to occur when the dogs received their food during the course of the experiment; he was surprised that it began earlier than that. At first, Pavlov regarded this anticipatory secretion of saliva as an annoying complication. However, he soon realized that the phenomenon had important implications. He knew that both dogs and humans begin to salivate at the beginning of a meal, even before food enters their mouth: The sight of the food is sufficient to stimulate salivation. Previously, scientists believed that this salivation was nothing more than an automatic, reflexive response. But Pavlov's dogs had obviously *learned* to salivate when they saw him or one of his assistants. Therefore, the salivation that normally occurs at the beginning of a meal may also be learned.

Pavlov devised a new apparatus to investigate this phenomenon, which he called "psychic secretion." He struck a tuning fork to make a sound, and half a second later he gave the dog some food. He found that salivation very quickly became conditioned to the tone. (See ***Figure 6.3.***) In later studies he used an electrical bell as a noise source and varied the time interval between the presentation of the sound and the food. Conditioning occurred only when the food

Figure 6.3 Pavlov's original procedure for classical conditioning. The experimenter strikes the tuning fork and then presents the food. Saliva is collected in the tube.

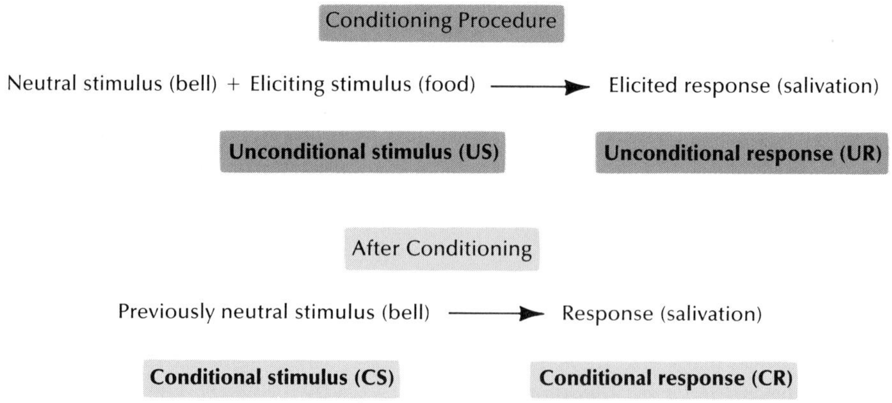

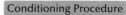

Conditioning Procedure

Neutral stimulus (bell) + Eliciting stimulus (food) ⟶ Elicited response (salivation)

Unconditional stimulus (US)   **Unconditional response (UR)**

After Conditioning

Previously neutral stimulus (bell) ⟶ Response (salivation)

Figure 6.4 The process of classical
conditioning.

Conditional stimulus (CS)   **Conditional response (CR)**

followed the sound within a short time. If there was a long delay between the sound and the food, or if the sound *followed* the food, the animal never learned to salivate to it. Thus, the sequence and timing of events are important factors in classical conditioning. Classical conditioning provides us with a way to learn about cause-and-effect relations. We are able to learn about the stimuli that warn us that an important event is about to occur. Obviously, warning stimuli must come *before* the event they are warning about.

The original eliciting stimulus is referred to as the **unconditioned stimulus (US)**. The response it elicits is called the **unconditioned response (UR)**. Classical conditioning occurs when a neutral stimulus, called the **conditioned stimulus (CS)**, is paired with the unconditioned stimulus (and thus with the unconditioned response). Once learning occurs, the conditioned stimulus produces the response by itself; and the response is now called the **conditioned response (CR)**. (See *Figure 6.4.*)

The easiest way to keep these terms straight is to remember that *unconditioned* comes first, and that *conditioned* comes only after learning has taken place. From the very beginning the *unconditioned* stimulus automatically produces the *unconditioned* response; no conditions have to be met. Once the conditions of pairing have been met, the *conditioned* stimulus elicits what is now called the *conditioned* response. The basic form of the response in both instances is the same; what differs is the stimulus that elicits it.

The Biological Significance of Classical Conditioning

Classical conditioning is an important form of learning, and it accomplishes two functions. First, the ability to learn to recognize stimuli that predict the occurrence of an important event allows the learner to make the appropriate response faster and perhaps more effectively. For example, hearing the buzz of a wasp near your head may make you duck and avoid being stung. Seeing a rival increases an animal's heart rate and flow of blood to its muscles, makes it assume a threatening posture, and causes the release of hormones that prepare it for vigorous exercise. Indeed, Hollis (1982) found that male Siamese fighting fish were more likely to win fights if they were given a warning stimulus that indicated that an intruding male would soon enter their territory. She and her colleagues also found that male blue gouramis (another species of fish) were more likely to mate and less likely to attack when they received a stimulus warning them of the approach of a female (Hollis, Cadieus, and Colbert, 1989).

The second function of classical conditioning is even more important. Through classical conditioning, stimuli that were previously unimportant take on some of the properties of the important stimuli with which they have been associated and thus become able to shape and modify behavior. A neutral stimulus becomes desirable when it is associated with a desirable stimulus, or it becomes undesirable when it is associated with an undesirable one. In a sense, the stimuli take on symbolic value. For example, we respond differently to the sight of a stack of money and, say, a stack of paper napkins. The reason for the special reaction to money is that money has, in the past, been associated with desirable commodities. I will have more to say about this role of classical conditioning later in this chapter.

What Is Learned?

Classical conditioning can occur only when an automatic relation exists between an unconditioned stimulus and an unconditioned response. These relations are wired into the brain, in the form of defensive or appetitive reflexes. *Defensive reflexes* protect the organism against harmful stimuli—or at least, help minimize the harm they produce. For example, if you touch something hot, your hand will automatically withdraw; if an object suddenly approaches your face, you will close your eyes, grimace, and duck your head (as the boy did when the balloon exploded in his face). *Appetitive reflexes* are part of behaviors that involve approach responses—that organisms *like* to do—and help prepare the body to perform these behaviors. For example, the taste of food causes salivation (and aids swallowing and digestion), and sexual contact causes genital arousal (and makes sexual intercourse possible).

Both defensive and appetitive reflexes can involve either overt movements or reactions of the parts of the body controlled by the autonomic nervous system. As you will remember from Chapter 3, the autonomic nervous system controls the activity of the internal organs and regulates such processes as heart rate, blood pressure, sweating, salivation, genital arousal, and the secretion of most hormones. All of the responses controlled by the autonomic nervous system can be classically conditioned. As we will see later in this chapter, the autonomic nervous system plays a particularly important role in conditioned emotional responses.

Extinction

The pairing of a neutral stimulus with an eliciting stimulus leads to classical conditioning; the previously neutral stimulus becomes a conditioned stimulus that is able to produce the conditioned response. However, classical conditioning is not necessarily permanent. Although the response will occur when the conditioned stimulus is presented by itself, the unconditioned stimulus must occur occasionally, or the conditioned stimulus will lose its ability to elicit the response.

For example, suppose we train a dog to salivate (conditioned response) to the sound of a bell (conditioned stimulus) by following the sound with a squirt of food (unconditioned stimulus) into the dog's mouth. After several repetitions of the stimuli the sound of the bell will elicit salivation even when no food is squirted. Now suppose that we permanently disconnect the device that squirts the food into the dog's mouth but continue to ring the bell every few minutes. For a while the dog will salivate whenever the bell is rung, but eventually, it will secrete less and less saliva; finally, the dog will stop re-

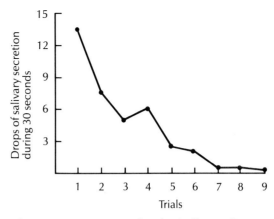

Figure 6.5 Extinction of a classically conditioned salivation response. (From Hall, J.F. *An Invitation to Learning and Memory*. Boston: Allyn and Bacon, 1982. Reprinted with permission. Based on data from Pavlov, 1927.)

sponding. Extinction has taken place; the response has been *extinguished*. (Note that responses, not organisms, are extinguished; obviously, an "extinguished" animal is a dead one.) **Extinction** occurs when the conditioned stimulus is repeatedly presented without being followed by the unconditioned stimulus.

Figure 6.5 presents data obtained for one of Pavlov's dogs during extinction. The dog had previously been trained to salivate in response to a noise. Pavlov then presented the noise (CS) every three minutes without the food (US) and counted drops of saliva (CR). By the ninth presentation of the noise alone the response was completely extinguished. (See *Figure 6.5*.)

Extinction is usually not permanent. Given a rest period after a series of presentations of the conditioned stimulus alone, the organism will once again emit the conditioned response when the conditioned stimulus is presented. This phenomenon is appropriately called **spontaneous recovery**. However, unless the unconditioned stimulus is also presented, the response will extinguish even more quickly than it did the first time.

Conditioned Emotional Responses

Many stimuli are able to arouse emotional responses, such as feelings of disgust, contempt, fear, anger, sadness, tenderness, longing, or sexual desire. Many of these stimuli—such as a particular location, a particular set of words, a particular song, or someone's voice and face—were originally neutral. Because these words were paired with other stimuli that evoked strong emotional reactions, they came, through classical conditioning, to take on the same properties.

If you read or hear words such as *enemy, ugly, bitter,* or *failure,* you are likely to experience at least a weak negative emotional response. However, *gift, win, happy,* and *beauty* evoke positive responses. Obviously, these words had no effect on you before you learned what they meant; thus, they took on their power through being paired with pleasant or unpleasant events (or perhaps with descriptions of such events). Staats and Staats (1957) found that if subjects read neutral nonsense words such as *yof* or *laj* while hearing positive or negative words, they later said that they liked those that had been associated with the positive words and disliked those that had been associated with the negative ones. They found that this procedure could even affect people's ratings of the pleasantness of names such as *Tom* or *Bill* or nationalities such as *Italian* or *Swedish* (Staats and Staats, 1958). Berkowitz (1964) found that when people had received unpleasant electrical shocks while in the company of another person, they later acted in a hostile manner toward them. Thus, classical conditioning may play a role in the development of ethnic prejudices and personal dislikes (and, of course, more positive reactions). Often we are not aware of the reason for our emotional reactions; we simply feel them and conclude that there is something "nice" or something "nasty" about the stimulus (or the person).

Many people are troubled by behaviors that they wish they could stop or by thoughts and fears that trouble them. **Phobias** are unreasonable fears of specific objects or situations, such as spiders, automobiles, or enclosed spaces.

Presumably, at some time early in life, the person was exposed to the now-fearsome object in conjunction with a stimulus that elicited pain or fear. For example, being stuck in a hot, overcrowded elevator with a group of frightened and sweating fellow passengers might be expected to lead to a distrust of elevators afterward and perhaps even to produce a full-fledged phobia.

Classical conditioning can occur even without direct experience with the conditioned and unconditioned stimuli. For example, if a child has a parent who has a dog phobia, he or she can develop the same fear simply by observing signs of fear in his or her parent; the child need not be attacked or menaced by a dog. In addition, people can develop phobias vicariously—by hearing about or reading stories that vividly describe unpleasant episodes. The imaginary episode that we picture as we hear or read the story can provide imaginary stimuli that lead to conditioned emotional responses. I will say more about imitation and observational learning later in this chapter.

Fetishes are abnormal sexual attachments to objects, such as articles of clothing. They probably occur because of the prior association of some stimulus—that most people find neutral—with sexual stimuli. One possible scenario is a teenage boy looking at sexually arousing pictures of women wearing high-heeled shoes. His arousal may become conditioned to the shoes worn by the women, and the boy will subsequently become a shoe fetishist. (Of course, fetishism cannot be that simple; there must be other factors operating, too. Some people are undoubtedly more susceptible than others to developing fetishes; for example, women very rarely develop them. Neverthe-

Therapists have used the principles of classical conditioning to reduce irrational fears. This man is learning to walk a tightrope in order to conquer his fear of heights.

less, the process by which the attachment occurs most likely involves classical conditioning.)

In a rather unusual study of fetishes Rachman and Hodgson (1968) conditioned a sexual response to an object popular among fetishists, women's knee-length boots. Their subjects, young single males, were shown first a color slide of the boots, then a slide of an attractive, naked woman. Sexual arousal was measured by a device called a *plethysmograph,* which measures changes in an object's size. In this case it was attached to the subjects' penises, to make an accurate record of their erections.

The experiment worked. The pairing of the boots as a conditioned stimulus and the pictures of naked women as unconditioned stimuli did result in classical conditioning: The subjects' penises enlarged somewhat in response to the picture of the boots alone. The subjects even responded to color slides of shoes. Repeated presentation of the conditioned stimulus alone (without the naked women) eventually led to extinction. (The experiment did not turn the subjects into shoe and boot fetishists.)

If classical conditioning is responsible for the development of phobias and fetishes, then perhaps a knowledge of the principles of learning can be used to eliminate them. In fact, therapists have done exactly that; the procedures they have devised will be discussed in Chapter 16.

INTERIM SUMMARY

Habituation and Classical Conditioning

I have so far discussed two forms of learning that help modify behavior: habituation and classical conditioning. Habituation screens out stimuli that experience has shown to be unimportant. This mechanism allows organisms to respond to more important stimuli, such as those related to survival and propagation.

Classical conditioning takes place when a neutral stimulus occurs just before an unconditioned stimulus, which elicits a behavior. The response that an organism makes to the unconditioned stimulus is already a natural part of its behavior; what the organism learns is to make it in response to a new stimulus (the conditioned stimulus). When conditioned stimuli are presented alone, the conditioned response eventually extinguishes.

The range of behaviors that can be classically conditioned is limited to those automati-

cally elicited by unconditioned stimuli; for example, we will learn to duck when we see someone make a throwing motion toward us. However, through classical conditioning, stimuli that were previously neutral with respect to an organism's behavior can be made to be important, and this importance can have profound effects on a limitless variety of behaviors. For example, the importance of money, established through classical conditioning, certainly affects our behavior.

Classical conditioning of physiological responses can play a role in feelings of emotion. The responses occur when we encounter a person, place, or object that was previously associated with a pleasant or unpleasant situation, and our perception of these responses constitutes an important part of feelings of emotions. Classical conditioning can also establish various classes of stimuli as objects of fear (phobias) or of sexual attraction (fetishes). ■

INSTRUMENTAL/OPERANT CONDITIONING

3 Habituation and classical conditioning teach us about stimuli in the environment: We learn to ignore unimportant ones, and we learn about those that predict the occurrence of important ones. These forms of learning deal with relations between one stimulus and another. In contrast, the process of **instrumental conditioning** (also called *operant conditioning*) teaches us the relations between environmental stimuli and *our own behavior.* The principle behind instrumental conditioning is already familiar to you: When a particular action has good consequences, the action will tend be to be repeated; conversely, when a particular action has bad consequences, the action will tend *not* to be repeated. Having read Chapter 1, you may recognize this principle as Thorndike's law of effect.

The essence of instrumental conditioning is the occurrence of a rewarding or punishing event immediately after an organism performs a particular behavior. The occurrence of the event is said to be *contingent* upon the organism's behavior. (A **contingency** is another name for a cause-and-effect relation; in this case the event occurs only when the behavior does.) The effect of the event is to increase or decrease the probability that the organism will perform that behavior again. In a general sense, instrumental conditioning is a description of the ways in which the consequences of an organism's actions cause its behavior to adapt to its environment.

The term *instrumental conditioning* reflects the fact that the behavior of the organism is *instrumental* in determining whether the reinforcing or punishing event occurs. As we shall see, reinforcing and punishing events can involve either an **appetitive stimulus** (one that an organism tends to approach) or an **aversive stimulus** (one that an organism tends to avoid).

Reinforcement and Punishment

Instrumental conditioning provides a way for a response to be either strengthened or weakened by its consequences. That is, the consequences of a response can either *reinforce* or *punish* the response.

Because it has fewer connotations, most psychologists prefer the term *reinforcement* to *reward*. A stimulus that increases the probability of a response that precedes it is called a **reinforcing stimulus** (also called a *reinforcer*). The phenomenon itself—that is, the increase in the probability of the response—is called **reinforcement**. In common usage the term *reward* implies that an organism has done something "good" and deserves a special treat. But the process of reinforcement is neutral—it is simply one of the natural consequence of a behavior. Sometimes, we deliberately set up a contingency between response and reinforcer; for ex-

A prize serves as a reinforcing stimulus because it indicates the recognition of a job well done.

ample, we might train a pet to do a trick by giving it some food it especially likes. But most reinforcement contingencies that occur in life outside the laboratory are unintentional. Suppose that a large, friendly dog jumps up on a small child with a candy bar who is playing in a park. The child takes fright, drops the candy bar, and runs away. The dog sees the candy bar and eats it. Suppose further that the dog now tends to jump up on small children playing in the park. We conclude that the first child inadvertently reinforced the dog's behavior by dropping the candy bar. However, we do not want to say that the child intended to *reward* the dog for its behavior.

Punishment refers to a decrease in the probability of a response caused by the stimuli that follow it. If a child touches a hot stove and burns its finger, it is unlikely to touch the stove again (at least, when the stove is hot). The response—touching the stove—is punished by the **punishing stimulus** (also called the *punisher*).

Whether or not a particular stimulus is reinforcing or punishing depends on the needs and previous experience of the organism. Suppose a busy mother decides to punish her child's whining. Every time the child whines, she says sternly, "Stop whining!" and delivers a lecture on the subject. Unfortunately, the child continues to whine several times a day and, in fact, seems to do so even more frequently than before the mother began the course of "punishment." Without intending to, the mother has actually reinforced the whining. Although the rebuke was meant to punish the whining, the attention she gave the child was apparently reinforcing enough to increase the frequency of the behavior. She should have paid attention to him at other times—for example, when he was playing nicely.

Most often, reinforcement occurs because a response is followed by an appetitive stimulus. But reinforcement can involve aversive stimuli, as well. Suppose you have to walk barefoot across a large asphalt parking lot on a hot, sunny day. As you walk, your feet get hotter and hotter. The pain becomes intense, and you look around for some relief. You see a puddle of water in a patch of shade provided by a large truck. You step into the puddle and find it to be delightfully cool on your feet. This stimulus change—removal of an aversive stimulus—is certainly reinforcing.

The type of reinforcement I just described—in which the behavior is reinforced by removal of an aversive stimulus—is called **neg-**

The threat of a fine can deter an undesirable behavior; it indicates that the behavior may be followed by a punishing stimulus—the loss of money.

ative reinforcement. (The other form of reinforcement—in which the behavior is reinforced by the occurrence of an appetitive stimulus—is sometimes called *positive* reinforcement, but most psychologists simply call it reinforcement, as I do in this book.) Many people confuse negative reinforcement with punishment, but the terms refer to entirely different phenomena. The most common use of the term *punishment* refers to the suppressing effect on behavior of an aversive stimulus that occurs right after the particular behavior. In contrast, negative reinforcement is a particular kind of reinforcement; it refers to the reinforcing effect caused by terminating an aversive stimulus immediately after a particular behavior. These contingencies are clearly different: *Punishment causes a behavior to decrease, whereas negative reinforcement causes a behavior to increase.* (That is a good rule to memorize.)

Just as the termination of an aversive stimulus is reinforcing, the termination of an appetitive stimulus is punishing. Suppose you meet a person to whom you find yourself attracted. You engage the person in conversation and enjoy the friendly attention that you receive. You talk for a while and are pleased to find that the other person also seems to be attracted to you. Then you make a disparaging remark about a well-known politician, and your new friend's smile disappears. You quickly change the subject and never

bring it up again. The behavior (disparaging remark) is followed by removal of an appetitive stimulus (a warm, friendly smile). The removal of the smile punishes the behavior.

This type of punishment is called **response cost**; a particular response (behavior) costs the organism the loss of a reinforcing stimulus. Just as negative reinforcement involves the removal of an aversive stimulus, punishment (in the form of response cost) involves the removal of an appetitive stimulus. Thus, there are four types of instrumental conditioning—two kinds of reinforcement and two kinds of punishment—caused by the administration or termination of appetitive or aversive stimuli. (See *Figure 6.6*.)

The following examples describe stimuli that can serve as reinforcers or punishers. See whether you can identify the response that is reinforced or suppressed, the reinforcing or punishing stimulus, and the type of instrumental conditioning: *reinforcement, negative reinforcement, punishment,* or *response cost.*

1. A woman staying in a rented house cannot get to sleep because of the unpleasant screeching noise made by the furnace. She goes to the basement, tries to discover the source of the noise, and finally kicks the side of the oil burner. The noise ceases. The next time the

Figure 6.6 Reinforcement and punishment produced by the onset or termination of appetitive or aversive stimuli.

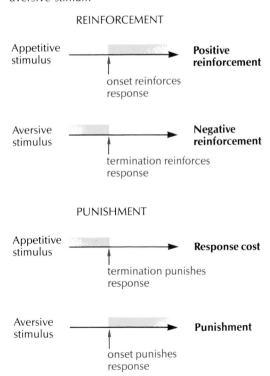

furnace makes the noise, she immediately goes to the basement and kicks the side of the oil burner.

2. A man decides to iron his pants while watching an important football game. During a time-out he brings the iron and ironing board into the living room and plugs in the iron. Immediately, the television screen goes blank; he has blown a fuse. By the time he gets the superintendent of the apartment building to unlock the room that contains the fuse box, he has missed two touchdowns. He never again tries to iron his clothes while watching television.

3. A woman returns home from work and discovers that her dog has soiled the carpet. The dog runs to greet her, and she says, "Naughty boy!" and slaps him. When she comes home the next day, she calls her dog; but he stays where he is, hiding under the sofa.

4. A little boy goes for a walk down the street and sees a strange dog. He says, "Hi, doggy!" The dog runs over to him, wagging its tail exuberantly, jumps on him, and knocks him down. The dog attempts to lick his face, but he squirms away and runs home. The next time he sees the dog, he turns away from it.

5. A man visits the lunch counter of a new restaurant and is served by an attractive, friendly waitress. He visits the restaurant for lunch several times during the next week.

Example 1 illustrates negative reinforcement. The unpleasant noise (aversive stimulus) is terminated when the woman kicks the side of the oil burner (response). Example 2 illustrates response cost. The football game (appetitive stimulus) disappears from the screen of the television set when the man plugs the iron into the wall socket (response); thus, the act of plugging in the iron is punished. Example 3 illustrates punishment, but not of the response that the woman intends. She slaps the dog, delivering an aversive stimulus, but the response she punishes is the one that the dog has just made: running up to her when she enters the door. Because the dog soiled the rug some time ago, that response is not punished. Example 4 is a straightforward illustration of punishment. The response of saying "Hi, doggy!" is punished by the fall to the ground. Example 5 illustrates reinforcement. Entering the restaurant and sitting at the lunch counter is reinforced by a friendly interaction with a pleasant, attractive woman.

Reinforcement and punishment occur only when a stimulus *immediately* follows the behavior, within a second or two. This principle was illustrated above, in the case of the woman who unsuccessfully tried to punish her dog for soiling the carpet. We also saw it illustrated in the opening vignette, in which the psychologist helped the lawyer arrange some contingencies that punished a behavior he was trying to get rid of. It may occur to you that many organisms—particularly humans—can tolerate a long delay between their work and the reward they receive for it. This ability appears to contradict the principle that reinforcement must occur immediately. However, the apparent contradiction can be explained by a phenomenon called *conditioned reinforcement,* which I will discuss later in this chapter.

An experiment by Logan (1965) illustrates the importance of the immediacy of reinforcement. Logan trained hungry rats to run through a simple maze in which a single passage led to two corridors. At the end of one corridor the rats would find a small piece of food. At the end of the other corridor they would receive much more food, but it would be delivered only after a delay. Although the most intelligent strategy would be to enter the second corridor and wait for the larger amount of food, the rats chose to take the small amount of food that was delivered right away. Immediacy of reinforcement took precedence over quantity.

Why is immediacy of reinforcement (or of punishment, for that matter) essential for learning? The answer is found by examining the function of instrumental conditioning: learning about the consequences of our own behavior. Normally, causes and effects are closely related in time; you do something, and something happens, good or bad. The consequences of the actions teach us whether to repeat that action, and events that follow a response by more than a few seconds were probably not caused by that response.

There is a notable exception to the rule I just outlined. Some behaviors have consequences that do not occur immediately. For example, if an animal eats something toxic (such as a poisonous plant or food that has been tainted by bacteria), it will get sick, but not until many minutes have passed. In fact, if it survives the illness, the animal is unlikely to eat that type of food again. Obviously, if learning could occur only with a brief interval between a response and its consequences, animals could never learn not to eat foods that make it sick. I will discuss this phenomenon in more detail later in this chapter, in the section entitled "Conditioned Flavor Aversions."

Extinction

Successful responses—those that produce an appetitive stimulus or that terminate an aversive stimulus—get reinforced. But sometimes, the environment changes, so that the contingency between response and reinforcement no longer exists. In that case continuing to respond would be unproductive. In fact, if a reinforcer no longer follows a response, the organism will eventually stop responding. That is, the response will *extinguish.*

Extinction is not the same as forgetting. Forgetting, when it occurs, requires the simple passage of time. Extinction takes place only when the organism actually makes unreinforced responses. The animal does not forget the response; it *learns not to make it.* Suppose a hungry rat is trained to press a lever that causes pieces of food to be delivered. If the animal is taken out of the chamber for a few days, its behavior will not extinguish; the rat will continue to respond when it is placed into the operant chamber again. For extinction to occur, the animal must be placed in the operant chamber where it will press the lever and not receive food for doing so.

When an animal's behavior is no longer reinforced, its rate of responding will usually increase at first. The increase is soon followed by a slowdown and finally by a long pause in responding. Periodically, at irregular intervals, the animal will respond again, usually in bursts. Finally, responding will cease. Figure 6.7 illustrates the extinction in a rat of a lever-pressing response that was formerly reinforced with small pieces of food. (See *Figure 6.7.*)

If an animal's behavior is extinguished on a particular day, it will usually make a few responses if it is put into the operant chamber on a subsequent day. That is, it will show *spontaneous recovery.* However, unless the animal's behavior is reinforced again, it does not respond for very long; the response soon extinguishes once more. (Recall from the section on classical conditioning that extinguished conditioned responses also show spontaneous recovery.)

Extinction makes good sense in a natural environment. If a response no longer "works," there is no point in persisting in making it. Doing so expends energy unnecessarily and keeps the organism from discovering a different response that *will* work. Similarly, spontaneous recovery makes good sense. Perhaps conditions have changed again, and the response will produce the reinforcer once more. It is worth a try.

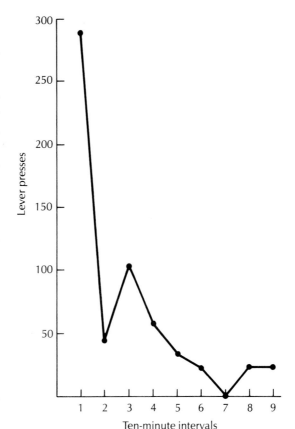

Figure 6.7 Extinction of an instrumentally conditioned lever-pressing response in a rat. (Based on data from Reynolds, G.S. *A Primer of Operant Conditioning.* Glenview, Ill.: Scott, Foresman, 1968.)

Behaviors we engage in outside the laboratory often become extinguished. For instance, suppose an angler catches many fish in a particular place one day and comes back to try again. Even if the angler has no luck, he or she will probably still try the spot a few more times, spending less time there on each subsequent visit. Sometimes, we deliberately extinguish another person's behavior. If you do not enjoy someone's company, you will probably stop smiling, nodding, and showing the signs of interest that serve as social reinforcers, hoping that the person will leave you alone.

Extinction of a response that was consistently reinforced in the past does more than reduce the probability of that response; it also increases the probability of other responses, especially aggressive ones. When an organism suddenly stops receiving reinforcers after making a previously reinforced response, it may attack other animals. The relation between extinction and aggression is discussed in more detail in Chapter 11.

Conditioned Reinforcement and Punishment

4 Some reinforcers and punishers have obvious biological significance; they are important to an individual's survival or to the survival of its species. For example, food, warmth, and sexual contact are reinforcing; and stimuli that cause pain are punishing. These stimuli are called **primary reinforcers** and **primary punishers**. Other classes of reinforcers and punishers are not so obvious. For humans, stimuli like money, admission tickets, the smell of delicious food, or parking tickets can serve as reinforcers or punishers, but only if the person has learned something about them. These stimuli are called **conditioned reinforcers** and **conditioned punishers**. (Sometimes, they are called *secondary reinforcers* and *secondary punishers,* to contrast with primary reinforcers and primary punishers.)

The Role of Classical Conditioning in Instrumental Conditioning. A stimulus becomes a conditioned reinforcer or punisher by means of classical conditioning. That is, if a neutral stimulus occurs regularly just before an appetitive or aversive stimulus, then the neutral stimulus itself becomes an appetitive or aversive stimulus. Once it does, the stimulus can reinforce or punish behaviors by itself. For example, money is a relatively neutral stimulus to a young child who has had no experience with it; paper money is not very good for drawing on, and coins do not make interesting toys. However, adults respond very differently, because for them money has regularly been associated with appetitive stimuli (those things that money will buy). Money, for most people, is an appetitive stimulus that can serve as a conditioned reinforcer. In contrast, the sight of a flashing light on top of a police car serves as a conditioned punisher to a person who is driving too fast, because such a sight precedes an unpleasant set of stimuli: a lecture by a police officer and a speeding ticket. The ticket itself is also a conditioned punisher, because it signals the loss of an appetitive stimulus: money.

The phenomena of conditioned reinforcement and punishment are extremely important. They permit an organism's behavior to be affected by stimuli that are not biologically important in themselves but that are regularly associated with the onset or termination of biologically important stimuli. Indeed, stimuli can even become conditioned reinforcers or punishers by being associated with *other* conditioned reinforcers or punishers. (The speeding ticket is just such an example.) If an organism's behavior could only be controlled by primary reinforcers and punishers, then that behavior would not be very flexible. The organism would never learn to perform behaviors that had only long-range benefits; instead, its behavior would be controlled on a moment-to-moment basis by a very limited set of stimuli. Conditioned reinforcers and punishers (such as money, grades, smiles, and frowns) allow for behavior to be altered by a wide variety of contingencies.

Conditioning of Complex Behaviors. So far, the examples of reinforced behaviors I have described are rather elementary. But people (and other animals, as well) are able to learn very complex behaviors. Consider the behavior of a young girl who is learning to print letters. She sits at her school desk, producing long rows of letters. What kind of reinforcing stimulus maintains her behavior? Why is she devoting her time to a task that appears to involve so much effort? The answer is that her behavior produces stimuli (the printed letters) that serve as conditioned reinforcers. In previous class sessions the teacher demonstrated how to print the letters and praised the girl for printing them herself. The act of printing was reinforced, and thus, the printed letters that this act produces come to serve as conditioned reinforcers. The child prints a letter, sees that it looks approximately the way it should, and her efforts are reinforced by the sight of the letter. *Doing something correctly,* or making progress toward that goal, can provide effective reinforcement.

This fact is often overlooked by people who take a limited view of the process of reinforcement, thinking that it has to resemble the delivery of a small piece of food to an animal being taught a trick. Some people even say that because reinforcers are rarely delivered to humans immediately after they perform a behavior, instrumental conditioning must not play a major role in human learning. This assertion misses the point that, especially for humans, reinforcers can be very subtle events.

It is true that most of the phenomena of instrumental conditioning have been discovered in experiments with nonhuman animals, but the process of reinforcement in real life is similar to what is observed in the laboratory. Psychologists sometimes unintentionally emphasize what they do rather than the process that occurs in nature; they say that a reinforcer is *delivered,* because in the controlled circumstances of experiments psychologists do deliver reinforcers

Doing something well can provide conditioned reinforcers that we label as "satisfaction."

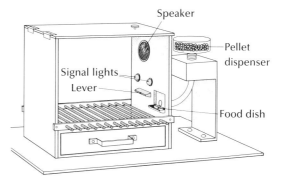

to their subjects. However, the overwhelming majority of reinforcers are not delivered by another agent; they are *obtained* by the organism that is doing the behaving. The reinforcement occurs as a natural consequence of the behavior. For example, a chimpanzee shakes the tree and eats the ripe fruit that falls down. In general, only in the laboratory, in some social situations, or in the classroom does a person *deliver* a reinforcer to another person.

An everyday term for the conditioned reinforcement that shapes and maintains our behavior when we perform a behavior correctly is *satisfaction*. Usually, we work hard at some task because it "gives us satisfaction." An artist who produces a fine painting gains satisfaction from the image that emerges as she works on it and receives even stronger satisfaction from looking at the finished product. This satisfaction derives from a lifetime of experience. The artist has learned to recognize good pieces of art; and when she produces one herself, she provides her own conditioned reinforcer.

Reinforcing Unlikely Responses: Shaping. Laboratory experiments have shown the importance of conditioned reinforcers in the instrumental conditioning of behaviors. You already know that reinforcement increases the probability that a particular response will occur again. But suppose you want to train an animal to perform a completely new response—one that you have never seen it make. How can you do so, when a behavior must occur before it can be reinforced? The answer is to use the procedure of **shaping**, which consists of reinforcing a succession of responses that are increasingly similar to the one you want the animal to perform.

Psychologists who study instrumental conditioning often use hungry rats as subjects and require them to press a small lever attached to a wall in order to obtain food. They generally use an apparatus called an **operant chamber**. (See *Figure 6.8*.) The device is also referred to as a "Skinner box," after the late B.F. Skinner of Harvard University, who invented it and pioneered the modern study of instrumental conditioning. (Skinner himself disliked that term.)

The lever on the wall of the chamber is attached to an electrical switch wired to electronic control equipment or a computer. A mechanical dispenser can automatically drop molded pellets of food, about the size of a very small pea, into a dish in the chamber. Thus, the delivery of a food pellet can be made contingent upon the rat's pressing the lever. The operant chamber shown in Figure 6.8 contains two lights and a loudspeaker mounted on the wall near the lever so that both visual and auditory stimuli can be presented. (See *Figure 6.8*.)

If we put a hungry rat into the apparatus, the animal will explore the chamber and may even depress the lever, perhaps while attempting to climb the wall. But we would probably have to wait a long time for the lever-pressing behavior to be reinforced by the delivery of the food. Reinforcement must be *immediate;* and unless the rat finds the food right after pressing the lever, some other behavior, not lever pressing, will be reinforced. Most likely, the delivery of the food pellet after an accidental lever press

Figure 6.8 An operant chamber.

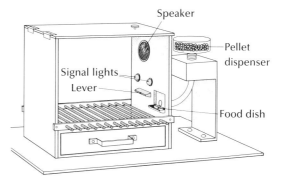

will reinforce the rat's approach to the dish, so the animal will tend to remain in its vicinity.

The solution is to deliver a reinforcer that has an immediate effect. To do so, we establish an auditory stimulus as a conditioned reinforcer. An auditory stimulus is best for our purpose because the rat will perceive it from any part of the cage. In this particular case a buzzer or other noise-making device is not necessary, because the pellet dispenser makes a noise of its own when it delivers a piece of food. So to begin with, we operate the pellet dispenser and let the rat find the pellet. After it eats the food, we deliver a few more pellets while the rat is in the vicinity of the food dish, until the noise of the pellet dispenser itself becomes an appetitive stimulus. Then we wait until the rat leaves the food dish and turns in the direction of the lever. As soon as the animal turns toward the lever, we operate the dispenser. The rat hears the noise and returns to the dish to eat the piece of food. Because the noise, now a conditioned reinforcer, was presented immediately after the turning movement, the turning movement is reinforced. The rat soon turns away from the food dish and toward the lever, and we activate the dispenser again.

Once the behavior of turning away from the food dish and toward the lever is firmly established, we reinforce a behavior that more closely resembles lever pressing. We wait until the rat turns even farther away from the dish and almost touches the lever before we activate the dispenser. (It is still the *noise,* not the food, that reinforces the behavior. The food simply serves to maintain the noise as a conditioned reinforcer.) Soon the rat is rapidly shuttling between lever and food dish. Now we wait until it touches the lever with any part of its body— most commonly, with its nose. Next, we require it to put its front feet on the lever, and finally, we activate the dispenser only when the rat actually presses the lever down hard enough to operate the switch. Now we can connect the switch to the dispenser and let the device operate automatically.

The formal name for shaping is the **method of successive approximations**. A reinforcer (almost always a conditioned reinforcer) is delivered immediately after responses that at first only approximately resemble the response that is to be conditioned (the **target behavior**). Successive responses must resemble the target behavior even more closely to be reinforced, until the goal is finally reached.

The method of successive approximations can be used to train an animal to perform just about any response that it is physically capable of doing. The tricks of performing dolphins and trained seals are developed by reinforcing a succession of responses that are increasingly similar to the desired one. The trainers usually reinforce the animals' behavior by producing a noise (such as the sound of a whistle) that has been paired with the delivery of food.

Shaping is a formal training procedure, but something like it also occurs in the world outside the laboratory. A teacher praises poorly formed letters produced by a child who is just beginning to print, but as time goes on, only more accurately drawn letters bring approval. The method of successive approximations can also be self-administered. Consider the acquisition of skills through trial and error. To begin with, you must be able to recognize the target behavior—that is, the behavior displayed by a person with the appropriate skill. Your first attempts produce behaviors that vaguely resemble those of a skilled performer, and you are satisfied by the results of these attempts. In other words, the stimuli that are produced by your behavior serve as conditioned reinforcers for that behavior. As your skill develops, crude approximations to the final behavior become less reinforcing; you are satisfied only when your behavior improves so that it more closely resembles the target behavior. Your own criteria change as you become more skilled. This process is perfectly analogous to the use of changing criteria in training an animal to perform a complex behavior.

Finding Effective Reinforcers: The Premack Principle

5 Some stimuli—food to a hungry animal, water to a thirsty one, warmth to a cold one—are obviously reinforcing. Other stimuli, not related to survival, are not as easy to predict. Sometimes, when trying to teach children or to change people's behavior, we must identify an effective reinforcer. Premack (1965) has suggested that an assessment of an individual's preferences can be used to determine whether a stimulus will serve as a reinforcer or punisher. The most accurate assessment is made by observing the individual's behavior; for infants or nonhuman animals this kind of assessment is the *only* one that can be made. For example, an animal can be put into an apparatus that is divided into two compartments. The stimulus to be tested can be made available in one of the compartments but not in the other. Or two different stimuli can be presented, one on one

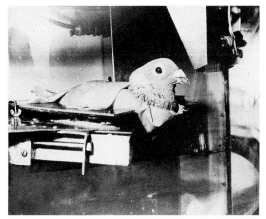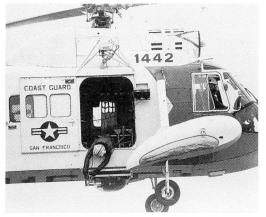

The Coast Guard used shaping to train pigeons to locate people lost at sea. The pigeons were trained to recognize the color orange, the international color of life jackets. In a search mission, pigeons were placed in chambers beneath a helicopter. When a pigeon spotted an orange object, it pecked a key that buzzed the pilot. Pigeons are better suited than humans for spotting distant objects at sea, because they can stare over the water for extended periods of time without suffering eye fatigue, have excellent color vision, and can focus on a 60– to 80–degree area, whereas a human can only focus on a 2– to 3–degree area.

side, a second on the other side. The relative amount of time that the animal spends in the two compartments reveals its preference. As you would expect, a hungry animal will stay where the food is, and a thirsty animal will stay where the water is. Similarly, if an animal stays in a compartment containing a window that permits it to look out, then we know that the opportunity to look outside is reinforcing.

Sometimes, an organism surprises us with its choice. Countless numbers of children have participated in learning experiments that required them to work a knob on a device resembling a pinball machine in order to receive an M&M candy (Premack, 1965). In other words, a response was reinforced with the delivery of M&Ms. (M&Ms, sugar-coated chocolate candies, are widely used because they are of a small, uniform size and can easily be dispensed, one at a time, by an automatic dispensing machine.) Premack found that some children, if given the choice, would play with the knob rather than eat an M&M: It was more fun to play the "game" than to eat an M&M. Premack turned the contingency around; he offered these children an M&M, and if they ate it, they got a chance to play with the knob for a while. The children quickly learned to eat M&Ms so that they could get a chance to play. Again, it is clear that the *subject,* and not the *experimenter,* determines which stimuli will serve as reinforcers.

The first part of the **Premack principle** states that an organism has different preferences for performing different behaviors. A large list of behaviors can be assembled, ranked in order of preference from low to high. (Such a list is called a **preference hierarchy**.) Some behaviors are very high on the list, some are neutral, and some are so low on the list that they will be avoided. (Screaming in response to the pain caused by having one's foot pounded by a sledge hammer is a behavior that is low on most people's list.) The second part of the Premack principle states that an organism will perform a behavior that is low in the hierarchy in order to gain the opportunity to perform a preferred behavior. Thus, if a child prefers playing with the knob to eating M&Ms, he or she can be trained to eat M&Ms if this behavior is reinforced by the opportunity to play with the knob. If a rat prefers eating food to running through a maze, it can be trained to run through the maze by reinforcing this behavior with the opportunity to eat food.

A case reported by Tyson (1980) illustrates this principle. The sole pleasure of a severely retarded man appeared to be making other residents' beds in the ward of the institution in which he lived. This resident also resisted bathing; so whenever he became so dirty and smelly that the attendants and fellow residents could not stand it, he was forcibly stripped, put into a bathtub, and washed. The ordeal was unpleasant both for the resident and for the attendants who had to wash him. Tyson decided to make use of the Premack principle. After obtaining permission from the ethics review board of the institution, he made bed making contingent on bathing; that is, the resident was permitted to make beds only after he bathed. The contingency worked; within a few days he was bathing regularly.

Stimuli, then, are reinforcing when they permit a particular behavior to occur; and each organism has its own set of preferences for engaging in a particular behavior. In addition, preferences can change from moment to moment, as we get bored with a particular behavior or as our physiological state changes. For example, a hungry animal prefers eating to most other behaviors; for this animal food is reinforcing because it permits eating. Obviously, it is futile to label stimuli as reinforcers or punishers without taking the organism's preference into account. Who could have predicted that the opportunity to make beds would serve as a reinforcer?

I should note that although the practical value of the Premack principle is unassailable, several learning theorists have discovered qualifications that must be made and conditions under which it does not work. Nevertheless, the concept of a preference hierarchy is an important one, and the Premack principle reminds us that reinforcers and punishers are effective to the extent that they cause us to engage in behaviors.

Intermittent Reinforcement

6 So far, we have considered situations in which a reinforcing stimulus is presented after each response (or, in the case of extinction, not at all). But usually, not every response is reinforced. Sometimes, a kind word is ignored; sometimes, it is appreciated. Not every fishing trip is rewarded with a catch, but some are, and that is enough to keep a person trying. As we shall see, the effects of intermittent reinforcement on behavior are very different from those of continuous reinforcement.

Schedules of Reinforcement. The term **intermittent reinforcement** refers to situations in which not every occurrence of a response is reinforced. The relation between responding and reinforcement usually follows one of two patterns: Each response has a certain probability of being reinforced, or responses are reinforced during particular intervals of time. Probability-based patterns require a variable number of responses for each reinforcer. For example, consider the performance of an archer shooting arrows at a target. Suppose the archer hits the bull's-eye one-fifth of the time. Thus, on the average he will have to make five responses

for every reinforcement (bull's-eye); the ratio of responding to reinforcement is five to one. The number of reinforcers the archer receives is directly proportional to the number of responses he makes. If his rate of responding increases, he will receive more reinforcers (assuming that he does not get tired or careless).

The best example of the second type of pattern is fishing. One form of fishing consists of casting a lure into the water and retrieving it in such a way that it resembles a minnow (the bait). If no fish are present, none will be caught; thus, during these times responses will not be reinforced. But every now and then, a hungry, eager-to-bite fish will swim by. If a lure is moving through the water at the same time, the angler may get a fish. After a fish is caught, another may come by soon or not for a long time. The only way to find out is to cast the lure. Clearly, the number of reinforcers an angler receives is not proportional to the number of casts made; casting the lure more often will not necessarily mean catching a larger number of fish, because the opportunities for catching one come only every now and then. Of course, if the angler waits too long between casts, he or she may miss catching a fish when it swims by.

Psychologists refer to the first pattern of intermittent reinforcement (the archer) as a **ratio schedule of reinforcement**. In the laboratory the apparatus controlling the operant chamber may be programmed to deliver a response after every fifth response (a ratio of five), every tenth, every two hundredth, or after any desired number. If the ratio is constant (a *fixed-ratio schedule*), the animal will respond rapidly, receive the reinforcer, pause a little while, then begin responding again. If the ratio is *variable* (averaging around a particular number, but varying from trial to trial), the animal will respond at a steady, rapid pace. A slot machine is programmed to deliver money on a variable-ratio schedule of reinforcement. *Variable* means that the person cannot predict how many responses will be needed for the next payoff.

The second pattern of intermittent reinforcement (the angler) is called an **interval schedule of reinforcement**. After various intervals of time a response will be reinforced. If the time intervals are fixed, the animal will stop responding after each reinforcement (it learns that responses made immediately afterward are never reinforced); then it will begin responding a little while before the next reinforcer is available. If the time intervals are variable, the animal (like the angler) will respond at a slow, steady rate. That way it will not waste energy

"One-armed bandits" are programmed to pay money to the gambler on a variable-ratio schedule of reinforcement. The gambler does not know how many pulls of the handle are required before the next payoff occurs.

on useless responses, but it will not miss any opportunities for reinforcement, either.

Various schedules of reinforcement are important because they show us that different reinforcement contingencies affect the pattern and rate of responding. Think about your own behavior. How would you perform differently in classes where your grades were determined by a midterm and a final, or by weekly quizzes, or by unannounced quizzes that occur at variable time intervals? What kind of schedule of reinforcement is a salesperson on while visiting potential customers? Some people work at a slow, steady rate, but others work furiously after long periods of inactivity. Can it be that their work habits were shaped by different schedules of reinforcement in the past?

Intermittent Reinforcement and Resistance to Extinction. Suppose that we train two pigeons to peck at a plastic disk by reinforcing these responses with the opportunity to eat a small amount of food. We train the animals for twenty daily sessions of thirty minutes each, but we train the two animals differently. We give the first animal some food every time it pecks the disk. We train the second animal the same way at first, but then we begin reinforcing every third response, on the average. (That is, we institute a variable-ratio schedule of three to

one.) Each day, we increase the number of responses required for reinforcement, until the bird is making an average of fifty responses to earn each reinforcer.

Now we stop reinforcing responding altogether; we put both birds on an extinction schedule. We find that the behavior of the first bird, accustomed to receiving food each time it responds, soon extinguishes. However, the second bird persists and makes thousands of responses before it finally quits. Why?

The behavior of the birds follows the rule that a response that has been reinforced intermittently is resistant to extinction; in other words, *it takes longer to extinguish a response that has been reinforced intermittently.* The more responses an organism has had to make for each reinforcement, the longer it will respond during extinction. Most psychologists would explain the phenomenon this way: Continuous reinforcement (that is, reinforcement after every response) is quite different from extinction; the very first nonreinforced response signals that conditions have changed. In contrast, intermittent reinforcement and extinction are much more similar. An organism whose behavior has been reinforced intermittently has had a lot of experience making nonreinforced responses. Thus, it cannot readily detect the fact that responses are no longer being reinforced. Therefore, the behavior extinguishes more slowly.

As you know, some people keep trying, even if they have difficulty succeeding. Other people seem to give up when they encounter the smallest difficulty. Perhaps one of the reasons for differences in people's perseverance is their past experience with different types of schedules of reinforcement. This possibility will be explored further in Chapter 11, which considers the variables that affect motivation.

INTERIM SUMMARY

Instrumental/Operant Conditioning

Instrumental conditioning involves a change in the likelihood of a response that is followed by the onset or termination of an appetitive or aversive stimulus. If the response becomes more likely, it is said to have been reinforced; if it becomes less likely, it is said to have been punished. Except in the special case of sickness produced by a novel food, the reinforcing or punishing stimulus must follow the behavior almost immediately if it is to be effective.

The major difference between classical conditioning and instrumental conditioning is in the nature of the contingencies: Classical conditioning involves a contingency between stimuli (CS and US), whereas instrumental conditioning involves a contingency between the organism's behavior and an appetitive or aversive stimulus. The two types of conditioning complement each other. The pairings of neutral stimuli with appetitive and aversive stimuli (classical conditioning) determine which stimuli become conditioned (secondary) reinforcers and punishers. Through the process of instrumental conditioning the contingencies between an organism's behavior and these stimuli adapt the organism's behavior to its environment. Complex responses, which are unlikely to occur spontaneously, can be reinforced by the method of successive approximations (shaping). Teachers use this process to train their students to perform complex behaviors; and something similar occurs when, in the course of learning a new skill, we become satisfied only when we detect signs of improvement.

The Premack principle helps identify reinforcing situations: The opportunity to perform a more preferred activity can be used to reinforce the performance of a less preferred one. ■

PHENOMENA OF LEARNING

7 Classical and instrumental conditioning involve different types of contingencies. Classical conditioning involves a contingency between two stimuli, and instrumental conditioning involves a contingency between a stimulus and a response. However, these two forms of learning share many features in common, and they interact with each other. This section discusses some of their common features and some of their interactions.

Discrimination

So far in this chapter we have encountered five types of stimuli: *unimportant stimuli,* to which orienting responses become habituated; *unconditioned stimuli,* which produce unconditioned responses; *conditioned stimuli,* which through association with unconditioned stimuli produce conditioned responses; *reinforcing stimuli,* which strengthen responses; and *punishing stimuli,* which suppress responses. Another category of stimuli—*discriminative stimuli*—guides responding by indicating that a particular response will be reinforced or punished on that occasion.

Discriminative stimuli indicate the nature of the current contingency between response and reinforcement (or punishment). That is, the stimuli say whether responses will be reinforced or punished, or whether there will be no consequences at all. *Every* instance of instrumental conditioning involves some sort of discriminative stimulus. First, let us look at a clear-cut example. Suppose you want to teach your dog to bark whenever you say "Speak!" You get a few pieces of food that the dog likes. Then you attract its attention and say, "Speak!" while waving a piece of food in front of it. The dog begins to show signs of excitement at the sight of the food and finally lets out a bark. Immediately, you give it the food. Then you bring out another piece of food and again say "Speak!" This time the dog probably barks a little sooner. After several trials the dog will bark whenever you say "Speak!" even if no food is visible.

You do not reinforce barking whenever it occurs but only when you first present the stimulus "Speak!". At all other times you ignore barking or perhaps even scold the dog for barking. In this way the dog learns to **discriminate** between the two conditions and to respond appropriately. The command "Speak!" serves as the discriminative stimulus.

Our daily behavior is guided by many different kinds of discriminative stimuli. If our telling of funny jokes has been reinforced by other people's laughter, we will tell them only when there are other people present; we will not tell jokes in an empty room. The presence of other people serves as the discriminative stimulus for the behavior of joke telling. Similarly, a rat that has been trained to press a lever in an operant chamber will not make pressing movements with its paws unless there is a lever to push. And an angler will not cast a lure into a swimming pool. We all learn that there are some conditions under which responding is worthwhile and some conditions under which it is useless.

Our ability to discriminate the stimuli provided by the behavior of other people is a very important skill. For example, we usually talk about different things with different people. We learn that some friends do not care for sports, so we do not talk about this topic with them because we will receive few reinforcers (such as nods or smiles). Instead, we discuss topics that have interested them in the past. A person with good social skills is one who is particularly adept at observing signs of interest in someone he or she has just met and who selects topics of conversation, even conversational styles, that elicit signs of interest.

To demonstrate discrimination in the laboratory, we might place a hungry rat in an operant chamber and train it to press a lever. Once the rat learns the response, we alternately turn a light located just above the lever on and off, for periods of a minute or two. When the light is on, the lever "works": Responses are reinforced. When the light is off, responses are not reinforced. Eventually, the rat learns the discrimination task, and it responds vigorously when the light comes on and responds very little (or not at all) when it goes off. (See *Figure 6.9.*)

Discrimination tasks permit us to assess an animal's perceptual abilities. Suppose we are interested in knowing whether fish have color vision. If they do, then perhaps the color of a fishing lure makes a difference to the fish, not just to the angler who buys it. We construct a lever that can be pushed by a fish (yes, we really can) and put it into a fish tank. We train the fish to push against the lever by reinforcing responses with a few grains of fish food. Then we turn on colored lights or place colored squares of plastic behind the lever and reinforce responding only when a particular color is present. If the fish learns the discrimination task, it has color vision. (In case you are interested, the experiment has been performed; and yes, fish *do* have color vision.)

Classical conditioning can also involve discrimination. For example, suppose that we classically conditioned an eyeblink response in a rabbit. The US would be a puff of air blown toward the rabbit's eye, which would make the animal blink. The CS would be a 1200-hertz tone; every time we present this tone, we follow it 0.5 second later by the US. But we also present another stimulus from time to time: a 2400-hertz tone. This stimulus is *never* followed by the US.

The procedure I just described—presenting one neutral stimulus that is always followed by a US and another neutral stimulus that is never followed by a US—is called **differential classical conditioning.** The two neutral stimuli are called the CS$^+$ and the CS$^-$. Obviously, the CS$^+$ is the one that is followed by the US. What happens when we follow this procedure? After several trials the rabbit will begin to blink its eye just after we present *either* the CS$^+$ or the CS$^-$. The animal makes conditioned responses, but it makes them indiscriminately. Then, eventually, the responses to the CS$^-$ drop out; the animal discriminates between the two stimuli. (See *Figure 6.10.*)

Generalization

Discrimination involves the perception of a particular stimulus. But no two stimuli are precisely alike. If you say "Speak!" many times, the sounds you produce will be very similar; but

Figure 6.9 Responses of a rat that is pressing a lever on a discrimination schedule. When the light is on, some of the animal's responses are reinforced; when it is off, none of them are.

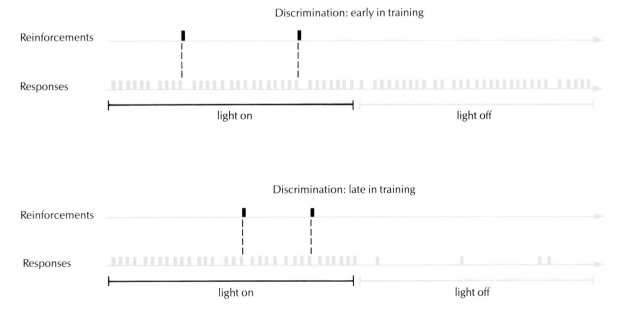

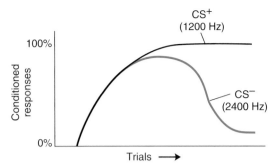

Figure 6.10 Acquisition of a differential classically conditioned response. The CS⁺ was always followed by the US (a puff of air directed toward the eye); the CS⁻ was always presented alone.

careful analysis will show that the word is pronounced somewhat differently each time. However, once your dog was trained, it would respond by barking every time you said the word, ignoring these slight differences. In other words, your dog would not discriminate among the slightly different sounds. Instead, it would show **generalization.** The word *general* comes from a Latin word that means "belonging to a kind or species." The definition fits precisely. Once an organism has learned to respond to a particular discriminative stimulus (through either classical or instrumental conditioning), it is said to be *generalizing* when it responds in the same manner to stimuli that are similar to the original one.

Let me give a more typical example of generalization. Honig, Boneau, Burstein, and Pennypacker (1963) trained pigeons to peck at a translucent plastic disk. When the disk contained a vertical line (projected onto the back of the disk), pecking was reinforced. When the disk did not contain a line, responses were not reinforced. After several sessions the pigeons learned the discrimination task; they pecked when a line was present but not when it was absent. Then they were tested for generalization: Lines with different orientations were projected onto the disk and the animals' responses were counted. Figure 6.11 shows the results. The circles below the horizontal axis illustrate the orientation of the line. Notice that the birds made the most responses when the vertical line was present and responded less and less when they saw lines tilted progressively farther away from the vertical. They responded according to the similarity between the original training stimulus and the test stimulus. (See ***Figure 6.11.***)

As you can see, discrimination and generalization go hand in hand. Discrimination involves

learning the significance of a particular stimulus; generalization involves recognizing similarities between the original discriminative stimulus and other stimuli. Organisms can be trained to recognize very complex similarities; that is, they can learn to recognize particular **concepts.** For example, Herrnstein and Loveland (1964) trained pigeons to respond to the concept of a human being. First, they trained the birds to peck at a translucent plastic disk. Then they assembled a set of more than a thousand 35-millimeter color slides. Some of the slides contained photographs of humans, depicted in a wide variety of scenes and poses. Other slides did not contain human figures. Herrnstein and Loveland selected a group of slides, with and without human figures, from the larger set and projected them on the translucent disk, where the birds could see them. Then they started discrimination training. When a human figure was projected, pecking was reinforced. When the projected image was that of a scene that did not contain a human, pecking was not reinforced; thus, a disk with no human figure was the discriminative stimulus that signaled extinction.

The birds quickly learned to respond to the concept of a human being. Their performance on the original set of slides generalized to slides

Figure 6.11 A generalization gradient of an instrumentally conditioned response. The pigeon was originally trained to peck at the disk when it contained a vertical line (90°). (From Honig, W.K., Boneau, C.A., Burstein, K.R., and Pennypacker, H.C. *Journal of Comparative and Physiological Psychology*, 1963, 56, 111–116. Copyright 1963 by the American Psychological Association. Reprinted by permission of the author.)

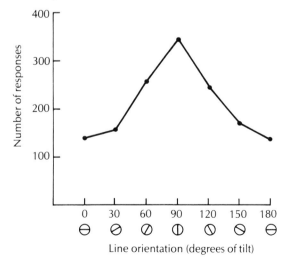

they had not seen before. The birds became as good as the experimenters at detecting whether a human figure was present in the image. In one instance the birds outperformed the humans. They pecked when they saw a slide that supposedly did not contain a human. When the experimenters looked at the slide more carefully, they discovered a tiny image of a person hidden away in the corner that they had missed when they had first sorted the slides.

Obviously, recognizing particular kinds of similarities between different categories of stimuli is a very important task in our everyday lives. When we encounter a problem to solve—for example, finding a justification for a legal argument, diagnosing a puzzling disease, improving a manufactured product, convincing a buyer that a particular purchase is advantageous, or coming up with an example that will make a point clear to students—we attempt to discover elements of the situation that are similar to those we have seen in others and try to apply the strategies that have been successful in the past. That is, we try to generalize old solutions to new problems.

A response that has been classically conditioned to a stimulus shows the same type of generalization as an instrumentally conditioned response. For example, you will recall the example of classical conditioning of a rabbit's eyeblink response that I described in the previous subsection. We would test for generalization by presenting some new tones of frequencies above and below 1200 hertz, the frequency of the CS⁺. We would find that the rabbit's eye would blink almost every time the 1200-hertz tone was sounded, but that tones of different frequencies would produce fewer responses. (See *Figure 6.12.*)

Aversive Control

8 As we saw, aversive stimuli can either punish or reinforce behavior; their occurrence punishes and their termination reinforces. Aversive stimuli have some special properties that make their effects different from those of appetitive stimuli, as we shall see in the following subsections.

The Nature of Punishment: The Role of Classical Conditioning. How does a punishing stimulus manage to suppress a behavior? Punishment, like reinforcement, usually involves a discriminative stimulus. Thus, a child's shouting is usually punished in the classroom but not outdoors during recess. A dog chases a por-

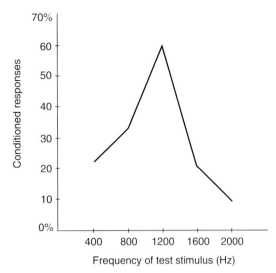

Figure 6.12 A generalization gradient of a classically conditioned response. The original CS⁺ was a tone of 1200 Hz. (Adapted from Moore, J., in *Classical Conditioning II: Current Research Theory,* edited by A.H. Black and W.F. Prokasy. Englewood Cliffs, N.J.: Prentice-Hall, 1972.)

cupine, gets stuck with quills, and never chases one again. However, it continues to chase the neighbor's cat.

Let us look at a possible explanation for punishment. Most aversive stimuli elicit some sort of protective or defensive response such as cringing, freezing, hiding, or running away. The response depends on the species of animal and, of course, on the situation. If you slap your dog for a misdeed, the dog will cower down and slink away, looking clearly "apologetic," because you are in a position of dominance. However, if the dog is struck by a stranger, it may very well react by attacking the person. Both types of behaviors are known as *species-typical defensive responses.*

Suppose a dog sees a porcupine for the first time. The sight of the animal evokes an approach response. The dog chases the porcupine, which stops, bristles its quills, and starts swinging its tail back and forth. (That is, the porcupine emits its own species-typical defensive responses.) The dog approaches and gets a faceful of quills, which hurts. The pain elicits a withdrawal response; the dog runs away. The next time the dog sees a porcupine, it runs toward it, seeing only a medium-sized animal that attracts its interest. But as soon as the dog gets close enough to see the porcupine clearly, it stops and then turns away.

Here is what might have happened. A stimulus (the sight of the porcupine) was present at

First Encounter

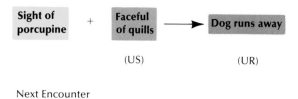

Next Encounter

Figure 6.13 A schematic diagram of the way an aversive stimulus can suppress (punish) a behavior by classical conditioning of a defensive withdrawal response.

the time the dog received a painful stimulus that evoked a species-typical defensive response. Through the process of classical conditioning the stimulus became linked to the response. Then the next time the dog spotted the porcupine, the sight of the animal elicited the defensive withdrawal response. (See *Figure 6.13.*)

Escape and Avoidance. Negative reinforcement teaches organisms to make responses that terminate an aversive stimulus. These responses can make the stimulus cease (for example, the woman kicked the oil burner and made the unpleasant noise stop), or the organism can simply run away. In either case psychologists call the behavior an **escape response**: The organism is subjected to the effects of the aversive stimulus until its behavior terminates the stimulus. In some cases the animal can do more than escape the aversive stimulus; it can learn to do something to *prevent* it from occurring. This type of behavior is known as an **avoidance response**.

Avoidance responses require discriminative stimuli. That is, there must be some warning that the aversive stimulus is about to occur in order for the organism to be able to make the appropriate response soon enough. Suppose you meet a man at a party who backs you against the wall and engages you in the most boring conversation you have ever had. Not only that, but his breath is so bad that you are afraid the plastic rims of your glasses will melt. You finally manage to break away from him (escape response). A few days later you attend another party. You begin walking toward the buffet table and see your tormenter (discriminative stimulus) standing nearby. You decide that you will get some food later and turn away to talk with some friends at the other end of the room (avoidance response).

Discriminative stimuli that produce avoidance responses can sometimes be internal rather than external. Suppose you are driving a car on a long trip when a leak develops in the radiator. You are not aware of the leak until the temperature gauge tells you that the engine has overheated. You pull over to the side of the road and find that the radiator is dry. Getting it filled again is a long, unpleasant task: You have to flag down another motorist, get a ride to a gas station, borrow a can of water, get a ride back to your car, put the water into the radiator, and drive back to the gas station to fill it up completely. Obviously, running out of water has unpleasant consequences. You do not have enough time to get the radiator repaired, so you realize that you will have to stop and refill the radiator periodically to keep the engine from overheating again. The internal discriminative stimulus that elicits this avoidance response is your estimate of the time that has elapsed since you last filled the radiator.

As we saw earlier, phobias can be considered to be conditioned emotional responses—fears that are acquired through classical conditioning. But unlike most classically conditioned responses, phobias are especially resistant to extinction. If we classically condition an eyeblink response in a rabbit and then repeatedly present the CS alone, without the US (puff of air), the response will extinguish. However, if a person has a phobia for dogs, the phobia will not extinguish even if the person encounters dogs and is never attacked or bitten by them. Why does the response persist?

Most psychologists believe that the answer lies in a subtle interaction between instrumental and classical conditioning. The sight of a dog makes a person with a dog phobia feel frightened; that is, he or she experiences an unpleasant conditioned emotional response. The person walks or runs away, leaving the dog behind and reducing the unpleasant feelings of fear. This reduction in an aversive stimulus reinforces the avoidance response—and perpetuates the phobia. (See *Figure 6.14.*)

Limitations of Aversive Control. As we just saw, aversive stimuli elicit species-typical defensive responses. Thus, punishment sometimes has undesirable consequences, and negative reinforcement cannot be used to train all types of behavior. Punishment can be a very effective way to suppress undesirable behaviors under some circumstances. For example, an ef-

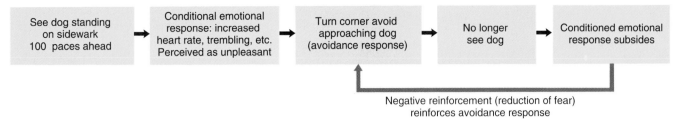

Figure 6.14 Maintenance of a phobia through negative reinforcement—reduction of fear by an avoidance response.

fective way to protect a child from a dangerous object may be to slap his or her hand when reaching for it. However, punishing stimuli can also elicit aggressive responses or withdrawal, neither of which is desirable in a child. And as you remember from the section on classical conditioning, emotional reactions tend to become attached to the people and objects present when they occur. If you make your child feel miserable by administering aversive stimuli, then you make it more likely that your presence elicits unpleasant reactions in the child.

Appetitive stimuli can reinforce a wide variety of responses, including unlikely ones that can be trained through the procedure of shaping. However, aversive stimuli can negatively reinforce only a small range of responses. For example, it is difficult to teach pigeons to peck at a plastic disk in order to turn off an aversive stimulus such as an electric shock, yet appetitive stimuli such as food or water can easily reinforce the same response. The reason for this discrepancy is that the species-typical defensive reactions elicited by aversive stimuli prevent the organism from emitting the response the experimenter is attempting to reinforce (Bolles, 1970). When threatened by a predator, a squirrel runs up a tree, a bird flies away, and a porcupine erects its quills. When a pigeon receives an electrical shock, it begins flapping its wings; it does not peck at the disk. Thus, you do not get the opportunity to reinforce the desired response.

Superstitious Behavior

[9] Whenever an organism encounters an appetitive stimulus, the behavior it just performed becomes more likely. Normally, the behavior is instrumental in obtaining the reinforcer; there is a cause-and-effect relation between response and reinforcement. We learn to press the button on a drinking fountain because the response makes the water flow. A duck learns to swim up to people on the shore because doing so often

results in their throwing food. But the response does not have to *cause* the appetitive stimulus for the behavior to be affected.

Consider the following example, based on an experiment by Skinner (1948). We place a hungry pigeon inside a small enclosure and program the apparatus to dispense a bit of food every fifteen seconds. After a few minutes we look in on the bird and find it spinning around frantically, counterclockwise. We remove the bird and replace it with another one. We find that after receiving several pieces of food, the second pigeon is standing in the middle of the floor, bobbing its head up and down like a mechanical toy. A third bird persists in flapping its wings.

As you might have guessed from the title of this section, the birds have acquired **superstitious behaviors**. Skinner explained them in the following way: When a reinforcer is intermittently given to an animal regardless of what the animal does, it will seldom just wait quietly for more. Instead, the animal will tend to persist in what it was doing when the reinforcement occurred. Perhaps the first pigeon was turning around when the food dispenser was first operated. The pigeon heard the noise, turned toward its source, and saw the food. It ate, waited in the vicinity of the food dispenser, and finally turned to go. Just then, another bit of food was delivered, so the bird went back to eat it. The next time, the pigeon turned away a little sooner and made a couple of revolutions before some food was dispensed again. From then on the pigeon went into a spin after each reinforcement. From the bird's point of view, the response was what brought the food. Similarly, head bobbing and wing flapping were accidentally reinforced in the other pigeons because these behaviors happened to occur immediately before food was delivered to them.

Apparently, we humans are not immune from acquiring superstitious behaviors. If you watch a baseball game, you will probably see some of them. Most baseball pitchers perform a

Superstitious behaviors, such as crossing one's fingers for luck, are social conventions. When psychologists refer to superstitious behaviors, they generally mean behaviors of an individual that have been accidentally reinforced.

little ritual before throwing the ball, such as scuffing the ground with a shoe, rubbing the ball, pulling at his hat, hunching his shoulders, rubbing his chest, or turning the ball in the glove. Each pitcher has a different routine. The same holds true for bowling, golf, or just about any other endeavor that requires performance of a skilled behavior. Whether they are relevant or irrelevant, those behaviors that preceded successful pitches, strikes, or golf strokes will tend to be repeated.

We can only speculate about the many taboos and rituals that are part of all human cultures and try to imagine which of these customs developed from behaviors that were inadvertently reinforced sometime long ago and then taught to subsequent generations. Once they become part of the culture, they become reinforced by the social behavior of other people.

Conditioned Flavor Aversions

Earlier in this chapter, I told you that an animal that eats poisoned food (and survives) will avoid eating that food again. But, of course, there is a long delay between the taste of the food and the symptoms of the illness. Thus, aversive stimuli (nausea, cramping, and other effects of the poison) are able to punish a behavior that occurred a relatively long time ago. The phenomenon is referred to as a **conditioned flavor aversion**. (Some psychologists call it a conditioned *taste* aversion, but the word *flavor* refers to a composite of taste and odor, and both sensory modalities contribute to this form of learning.)

It is certainly to an animal's advantage to be able to learn about the relation between a particular flavor and an illness that occurs later. Thus, the evolutionary process has selected for the neural circuits that can detect such a relation. In fact, different neural circuits appear to be involved in different types of learning. For example, Garcia and Koelling (1966) found that rats would learn to avoid a particular taste that was followed by illness or to avoid a particular noise that was immediately followed by a shock to the feet. However, they did not learn to avoid a particular *taste* followed by a *shock,* or a particular *noise* followed by *illness.* The results make good sense; after all, the animal has to taste the food that makes it sick, not hear it, and in the world outside the laboratory particular flavors do not usually signal painful stimuli.

Some animals have eating habits quite different from those of rats; they eat foods that they cannot taste or smell. For example, some birds eat seeds that are encased in a tasteless husk. They do not have teeth, so they cannot break open the husk and taste the inside of the seed. Thus, they cannot use odor or taste as a cue to avoid a poison. However, Wilcoxon, Dragoin, and Kral (1971) found that quail (a species of seed-eating birds) can form a conditioned aversion to the *sight* of food they eat before becoming sick.

Humans are also capable of the same kind of learning. A friend of mine often took trips on airplanes with her parents when she was a child. Unfortunately, she usually got airsick. Just before takeoff, her mother would give her some spearmint-flavored chewing gum to help relieve the pressure on her eardrums that would occur when the plane ascended. Yes, she developed a conditioned flavor aversion to spearmint gum. In fact, the odor of the gum still makes her feel nauseated. As we will see in the application section at the end of this chapter, conditioned flavor aversions present a real problem in the treatment of cancer patients with radiation or chemotherapy.

Conditioned flavor aversions are different from other forms of learning in two important ways. First, they occur even with a long delay between the two stimuli; an animal can taste the food several hours before it becomes ill, and conditioning will still take place. Second, they involve relations only between particular categories of stimuli—in most species of mammals, flavors and illness. Undoubtedly, the neural mechanisms responsible for conditioned flavor aversions differ from those responsible for other forms of learning.

Conditioned flavor aversions, like most learning situations, involve both classical and instrumental conditioning. From one point of view we can say that the aversive stimuli produced by the poison punish the behavior of eating a particular food. That is, the flavor serves as a *discriminative stimulus* for a *punishment contingency* (instrumental conditioning). But it also serves as a *conditioned stimulus* for a *classical conditioning* situation: The flavor is followed by an unconditioned stimulus (the poison) that elicits unpleasant responses of the autonomic nervous system, such as nausea, cramping, and retching. Then when the animal encounters the flavor at a later date, it experiences unpleasant reactions that cause it to leave the source of the stimulus and avoid the food.

Observation and Imitation

Normally, we learn about the consequences of our own behavior or about stimuli that directly affect us. But we can also learn by a less direct method: observing the behavior of others. Video game machines usually have instructions printed on them and often flash instructions on the screen. But it is much easier to learn how to play the game by watching someone who has had experience with it. Likewise, one of the best ways to improve your tennis game (besides taking lessons) is to watch experts play.

Humans are not the only animals who learn by imitation. A pigeon that watches another bird performing a complex operant task will learn the task much more quickly than one that has not had this opportunity. Why do organisms learn to imitate the behavior of others? Is this tendency innate?

Nature provides clear examples that imitation does seem to be an innate tendency. Many species of birds must learn to sing their characteristic song. If they are raised apart from other birds, they will never sing, or they will sing a peculiar song that bears little resemblance to that of normally raised birds. However, if they hear the normal song played over a loudspeaker, they will sing it properly when they become adults. They have learned the song, but clearly there were no external reinforcement contingencies; nothing in the environment reinforced their singing of the song. (This phenomenon is an excellent example of the distinction between learning and performance. A baby bird hears the proper song but does not sing it until adulthood. The changes that take place in its brain do not manifest themselves in behavior for many months.)

Classically conditioned behaviors, as well as instrumentally conditioned behaviors, can be acquired through observation. For example, suppose that a young girl sees her mother show signs of fear whenever she encounters a dog. The girl herself will likely develop a fear of dogs, even if she is never threatened or attacked by one. In fact, Bandura and Menlove (1968) reported that children who were afraid of dogs were likely to have a parent who feared dogs, but they usually could not remember having had unpleasant direct experiences with them. As we will see in Chapter 12, we tend to imitate—and feel—the emotional responses of people we observe. Perhaps when we see someone we know well show signs of fear, we imitate these responses ourselves; and the responses become classically conditioned to the salient stimulus—in this case, a dog.

Under normal circumstances learning by observation may not require external reinforcement; in fact, there is strong evidence that imitating the behavior of other organisms may be reinforcing in itself. However, in some cases in which this ability is absent, it can be learned through reinforcement. Baer, Peterson, and Sherman (1967) studied three severely retarded children who had never been seen to imitate the behavior of other people. When the experimenters first tried to induce the children to do what they themselves did, like clap their hands, the children were unresponsive. Next, the ex-

Imitation is an important form of learning.

perimenters tried to induce and reinforce imitative behavior in the children. An experimenter would look at a child, say "Do this," and perform a behavior. If the child made a similar response, the child was immediately praised and given a piece of food. At first, the children were physically guided to make the response. If the behavior to be imitated was clapping, the experimenter would clap his or her hands, hold the child's hands and clap them together, then praise the child and give him or her some food.

The procedure worked. The children learned to imitate the experimenters' behaviors. But even more importantly, the children had not simply learned to mimic a specific set of responses; they had acquired the *general tendency to imitate.* When the experimenters performed new behaviors and said "Do this," the children would imitate them.

Obviously, teaching retarded children is much more effective when they pay attention to their teachers and imitate their behaviors when requested to do so. The procedure I just described has proved to be extremely useful for teaching retarded children behaviors that will help them lead productive lives. But the theoretical significance of this demonstration is also important. The experiment indicates that imitation, as a general tendency, is subject to reinforcement (and presumably also to punishment). An organism can learn more than simply making a particular response to a particular stimulus; it can learn a strategy that can be applied to a variety of situations. Social learning theory emphasizes the importance of learning through observation and will be discussed in Chapter 17.

An interesting issue that remains controversial in psychology concerns the acquisition of language by children. Why do children learn to imitate the verbal behavior of older children and adults? Is this tendency innate, like the learning of songs by some species of birds, or is it subject to the contingencies of reinforcement and punishment? Chapter 9 discusses this topic in detail.

EVALUATING SCIENTIFIC ISSUES

What Is Insight?

[10] Many problems we have to solve in our daily lives require us to make responses that we have never made before and that we have never seen anyone else make, either. We often think about a problem, looking at the elements and trying to imagine various solutions. We try various responses in our heads, but none seem to work. Suddenly, we think of a new approach; maybe this one will work! We try it, and it does. We say that we have solved the problem through *insight.*

But what is insight? Some people see it as almost a magical process: a sudden flash of inspiration, a bolt from the blue, an answer coming from nowhere. Most people regard it is as a particularly human ability—or at least, an ability that belongs to our species and, perhaps, some of the higher primates.

Insight in Other Primates. During the early part of this century the German psychologist Wolfgang Köhler studied problem-solving behavior of chimpanzees. In one famous example (Köhler, 1927/1973) he hung some bananas from the ceiling of the animal's cage, just high enough to be out of reach. The cage also contained a large box. Sultan, one of the chimps, first tried to jump up to reach the bananas, then paced around the cage, stopped in front of the box, pushed it toward the bananas, climbed onto the box, and retrieved and ate the fruit. Later, when the bananas were suspended even higher, he stacked up several boxes. And on one occasion when no boxes were present, he grabbed Köhler by the hand, led him over to the bananas, and climbed on top of him. (Sorry, but I do not have a picture of that.)

Köhler believed that the insightful problem-solving behavior shown by the chimpanzees was different from the behavior of Thorndike's cats as they learned to escape the latch boxes. (These studies were described in Chapter 1.) The cats clearly showed trial-and-error behavior, coming upon the solution by accident. The escape from the box served as a reinforcing stimulus, and eventually the animals learned to operate the latch efficiently. But the behavior of the chimpanzees seemed very different. They suddenly came upon a solution, often after looking at the situation (and, presumably, thinking about it). Köhler saw no accidental trial-and-error behavior. Perhaps some processes other than instrumental conditioning are responsible for the kind of insight that primates can display. Perhaps insight is not a behavior that is subject to the principles of learning outlined in this chapter.

A Behavioral Analysis of Insight. More recent work suggests that insight may be less mysterious than it appears. Insight may actually be based on combinations of behaviors initially

Insightful behavior by a chimpanzee in an experiment similar to the one performed by Köhler. The chimpanzee piles boxes on top of each other to reach the banana hanging overhead. (Super Stock International, Inc.)

learned through trial and error. In one study (Epstein, Kirshnit, Lanza, and Rubin, 1984) the experimenters used instrumental procedures (with food as the reinforcer) to teach a pigeon two behaviors: (1) to push a box toward a target (a green spot placed at various locations on the floor) and (2) to climb onto a box and peck on a miniature model of a banana, which was suspended overhead. Once these behaviors had been learned, the experimenters confronted the pigeon with a situation in which the box was in one part of the chamber and the banana was in another. "At first, the bird appeared to be 'confused': It stretched toward the banana, turned back and forth from the banana to the box, and so on. Then, rather suddenly, it began to push the box toward the banana, sighting the banana and readjusting the path of the box as it pushed. Finally, it stopped pushing when the box was near the banana, climbed onto the box, and pecked the banana" (Epstein, 1985, p. 132). The pigeon acted much the way that Sultan did. In a subsequent experiment Epstein (1987) taught a pigeon to (1) peck at a model of a banana, (2) climb onto a box, (3) open a door, and (4) push a box toward a target. When the pigeon was confronted with a banana hanging above its head and a box behind a door, it combined all four behaviors: It opened the door, pushed the box out and moved it under the banana, climbed the box, and pecked the banana.

Insightful behavior generally involves combining and adapting behaviors in a new context. For example, Sultan had already had experience in sticking a bamboo rod out through the bars of its cage to retrieve bananas that were placed on the floor just out of reach. Then one day, Köhler gave Sultan two bamboo rods and placed a banana outside the cage far enough away so that it could not be reached with either of the rods. The chimpanzee tried unsuccessfully for an hour to reach the banana with the rods. This behavior was obviously useless, but it can be understood in terms of the animal's prior experience—it had worked in the past when the banana was just out of reach. Finally, the chimpanzee sat down and examined the sticks. "While doing this, it happens that [Sultan] finds himself holding one rod in either hand in such a way that they lie in a straight line; he pushes the thinner one a little way into the opening of the thicker, jumps up and is already on the run towards the railings . . . and begins to draw a banana towards him with the double stick" (Köhler, 1927/1973, p. 127).

We know from the experiments by Epstein and his colleagues that pigeons will show in-

Insightful behavior by a pigeon. The pigeon moves the box toward the banana overhead, pushes the box into position under the banana, mounts the box, and pecks the banana. (From Norman Baxley/© 1984 Discover Publications.)

sightful behavior only after they have learned the individual behaviors that must go together to solve a problem. For example, only if pigeons have learned to push a box toward a goal will they move it under a model banana hanging from the top of the cage. It is not enough to have learned to *push* a box; they must have learned to push it *toward a goal*. Presumably, the chimpanzees' experience with moving boxes around and climbing on them was necessary for them to solve the hanging banana problem.

What Should We Conclude? In Chapter 2 you learned about the pitfall called the nominal fallacy, in which we tend to think that we have explained a phenomenon simply by naming it. So, too, we must realize that simply labeling behavior as insightful does not help us understand it. If we do not know what behaviors the animal has already learned, a novel and complex sequence of behaviors that solves a problem seems to come from nowhere. In order to understand the necessary conditions for insight to occur, we need to know more than what is happening during the current situation; we also need to know what kinds of learning experiences the organism has encountered in the past.

The challenge to a scientist is to dissect even the most complex behaviors and try to understand their causes. Perhaps chimpanzees, like humans, are capable of solving problems by using some sort of mental imagery, testing possible solutions "in their heads" before actually trying them. But neither humans nor chimpanzees will be able to think about objects they have never seen or imagine themselves performing behaviors they have never performed (or seen others perform). Naturally, humans, chimpanzees, and pigeons will be able to perform different kinds of behaviors and perceive different kinds of relations in their environments, because of their different habitats and because of differences in the complexities of their brains. In addition, humans and chimpanzees are better able to learn through observation and imitation. For example, I suspect that a chimpanzee who had seen another animal put two bamboo rods together would be able to use that information to figure out how to reach the banana outside the cage. But the raw material for problem solving—including the thinking that may accompany some forms of insightful behavior—must come from previous experience. And that, of course, is what this chapter has been all about. ∎

INTERIM SUMMARY

Phenomena of Learning

Intermittent reinforcement occurs more often than continuous reinforcement. Researchers have developed various types of schedules of reinforcement, which have different effects on the rate and pattern of responding. When a response is reinforced intermittently, it is more resistant to extinction, probably because an intermittent reinforcement schedule resembles extinction more than a continuous reinforcement schedule does. Reinforcement may sometimes occur accidentally; many people—especially those who must perform highly skilled sequences of responses that can succeed or fail—may show superstitious behaviors.

Obviously, knowing how to perform a particular behavior is useless unless the organism also learns under what conditions the behavior should be performed; behaviors are guided by stimuli as well as reinforced or punished by them. Discrimination involves the detection of essential differences between stimuli or between situations so that responding occurs only when appropriate. Generalization is another necessary component of all forms of learning, because no two stimuli, and no two responses, are precisely the same. Thus, generalization embodies the ability to apply what is learned from one experience to similar experiences.

Punishment apparently occurs because stimuli present when an aversive stimulus occurs become classically conditioned to defensive responses, which interfere with—and thus punish—other responses. Aversive stimuli can also be used to negatively reinforce behaviors, but they bring with them some side effects: They tend to elicit species-typical defensive reactions that interfere with the response that is being taught.

Extinction occurs when responses are emitted but not reinforced—which makes sense, because organisms must be able to adapt to changing environments, with changing reinforcement contingencies. Intermittent reinforcement produces a resistance to extinction, probably because it is difficult to tell the difference between intermittent reinforcement and extinction. Various schedules of reinforcement, designed to study the principles of learning, have their counterparts in the world outside the laboratory.

The effects of reinforcing and punishing stimuli on behavior can be complex and subtle. We are able to acquire both instrumentally and classically conditioned responses through observation and imitation. In addition, we can learn to modify and combine responses learned in other contexts to solve new problems. That pigeons can too suggests that not all instances of insight learning require "thinking" in the sense of imagining the behavior before it is performed. Of course, pigeons are unlikely to learn the individual behaviors necessary for solving, say, the hanging banana problem unless someone deliberately teaches them. But chimpanzees' ability to manipulate objects and observe the behavior of others allows them to engage in much more flexible behaviors than most other species exhibit. ■

APPLICATION

Conditioned Flavor Aversions

As we saw earlier, conditioned flavor aversions occur when particular flavors are followed by feelings of nausea—even several hours later. This phenomenon has several implications for situations outside the laboratory.

An unfortunate side effect of chemotherapy or radiation therapy for cancer is nausea. Besides killing the rapidly dividing cells of malignant tumors, both the drugs and the radiation kill the rapidly dividing cells that line the digestive system—and cause nausea and vomiting. Therefore, knowing what we know about conditioned flavor aversions, we might predict that chemotherapy or radiation therapy would

cause a conditioned aversion for the foods a patient ate during the previous meal. Bernstein (1978) showed that this prediction is correct. She gave ice cream to some cancer patients who were about to receive a session of chemotherapy and found that several months later, 75 percent of these patients refused to eat ice cream with that flavor. In contrast, control subjects who did not taste it before their chemotherapy said that they liked it very much. Only one trial was necessary to develop the conditioned flavor aversion. Even when patients have a clear understanding that the drugs are responsible for their aversion and that the food is really wholesome, they still cannot bring themselves to eat it (Bernstein, 1991). Thus, a conditioned food aversion is not a result of cognitive processes such as reasoning or expectation.

Experiments such as the one I just cited indicate that cancer patients run a real risk of developing aversions to the foods they normally eat. And because cancer patients tend to have appetite problems and to lose weight, these aversions could have serious consequences. In fact, questionnaires and interviews reveal that cancer patients *do* develop aversions to the foods that they normally eat—even if their treatment sessions occur several hours after the previous meal (Bernstein, Webster, and Bernstein, 1982; Mattes, Arnold, and Boraas, 1987). When patients receive many treatment sessions, they are likely to develop aversions to a wide variety of foods.

Not all flavors are equally likely to become targets of aversions. In particular, people are likely to develop aversions to protein-rich foods or to foods with strong odors, such as chocolate or coffee. They are less likely to develop aversions to foods high in carbohydrates (Brot, Braget, and Bernstein, 1987).

Because a treatment that produces nausea may cause the development of a conditioned flavor aversion to the last thing a person has eaten, Broberg and Bernstein (1987) attempted to attach the aversion to a flavor other than one that patients encounter in their normal diets. The experimenters had cancer patients eat a coconut or root beer Lifesaver (a sugared candy) after the last meal before a chemotherapy session, with the hope that the unique flavor would serve as a scapegoat, preventing a conditioned aversion to the normal foods. The procedure worked; the patients were much less likely to show an aversion to the food eaten in the last meal before the treatment.

Conditioned flavor aversions can also have useful applications; therapists have used them to treat addictions. They have given people drugs that induce nausea in order to develop an aversion to the substance they are abusing. (Such drugs are called *emetic*—"vomit producing"—drugs.) The treatment has been found to be helpful in treating alcohol abuse (Howard and Jensen, 1990; Smith and Frawley, 1990) and cigarette smoking (Tiffany, Martin, and Baker, 1986). In the case of smoking the drugs contained in the cigarettes themselves can be used to produce the aversion. The subject is asked to smoke rapidly and continuously until he or she becomes nauseated.

Psychologists have even applied conditioned aversions to wildlife control. In regions where coyotes have been attacking sheep, they have left chunks of dog food, laced with an emetic drug, wrapped in pieces of fresh sheepskin. The coyotes eat the bait, get sick, and develop a conditioned aversion to the smell and taste of sheep (Gustavson and Gustavson, 1985). These methods can help protect

Naturalists have established specific conditioned flavor aversions in predators to protect livestock or members of endangered species.

endangered species, as well as livestock. Mongooses have been introduced into some islands in the Caribbean, where they menace the indigenous population of sea turtles. Nicolaus and Nellis (1987) found that a conditioned aversion to turtle eggs could be established in mongooses by feeding them eggs into which an emetic drug had been injected.

Evidence suggests that for some species conditioned flavor aversions can become cultural traditions. Gustavson and Gustavson (1985) reported that after adult coyotes had developed a conditioned aversion to a food, their offspring, too, avoided that food. Apparently, the young coyotes learned from their mothers what food was fit to eat. However, Nicolaus, Hoffman, and Gustavson (1982) found that adult raccoons with a conditioned aversion to chickens did *not* teach their offspring to avoid chickens. In fact, after seeing the young raccoons kill and eat chickens, the adults overcame their aversion and began preying on chickens again.

And sometimes wild animals find a way to outwit psychologists. Gustavson and Gustavson (1985) tell the story of the bears in Mount Rainier National Park in the northwestern United States who had developed a taste for the contents of the garbage cans in the campground. The psychologists sprayed the garbage several times each day with a mint-flavored emetic drug, hoping that the bears would leave the area after they developed an aversion to the garbage. The bears soon stopped eating the garbage, but then they began menacing campers who were preparing or eating their "mint-free" meals. The psychologists admitted defeat. The park rangers captured the bears and transported them to a remote part of the park.

The importance of the basic principles of learning is shown by the fact that all of them—including conditioned flavor aversions—have found applications to problems outside the laboratory.

Habituation

orienting response *(165)*
habituation *(165)*

Classical Conditioning

classical conditioning *(166)*
unconditioned stimulus (US) *(168)*
unconditioned response (UR) *(168)*
conditioned stimulus (CS) *(168)*
conditioned response (CR) *(168)*
extinction *(169)*
spontaneous recovery *(169)*
phobia *(170)*
fetish *(170)*

Instrumental/Operant Conditioning

instrumental conditioning *(171)*
contingency *(171)*
appetitive stimulus *(172)*
aversive stimulus *(172)*
reinforcing stimulus *(172)*
reinforcement *(172)*
punishment *(172)*
punishing stimulus *(172)*
negative reinforcement *(173)*

punishment *(173)*
response cost *(173)*
primary reinforcer *(176)*
primary punisher *(176)*
conditioned reinforcer *(176)*
conditioned punisher *(176)*
shaping *(177)*
operant chamber *(177)*
method of successive approximations *(178)*
target behavior *(178)*
Premack principle *(179)*
preference hierarchy *(179)*
intermittent reinforcement *(180)*
ratio schedule of reinforcement *(180)*
interval schedule of reinforcement *(180)*

Phenomena of Learning

discriminative stimulus *(182)*
discrimination *(182)*
differential classical conditioning *(183)*
generalization *(184)*
concept *(184)*
escape response *(186)*
avoidance response *(186)*
superstitious behavior *(187)*
conditioned flavor aversion *(188)*

SUGGESTIONS FOR FURTHER READING

Chance, P. *Learning and Behavior,* 2nd ed. Belmont, Calif.: Wadsworth, 1988.
Hall, J.F. *Learning and Memory.* Boston: Allyn and Bacon, 1989.
Reese, E.P. *Human Operant Behavior,* 2nd ed. Dubuque, Iowa: W.C. Brown, 1978.
Wilhite, S., and Payne, D. *Learning and Memory: The Basis of Behavior.* Boston: Allyn and Bacon, 1992.

All four books are useful for those who want to learn more about the basic principles of learning. They are well written and entertaining and contain many specific examples of human learning. Reese's book also contains examples of using operant techniques (instrumental conditioning) to change one's own behavior, such as studying or controlling one's diet more effectively.

7
MEMORY

Henri Matisse, *Entrance to the Casbah*
SCALA/Art Resource, N.Y. © 1992 Succession H. Matisse/ARS, N.Y.

LEARNING OBJECTIVES

When you finish this chapter, you should be able to:

1. Explain the difference between sensory memory, short-term/working memory, and long-term memory, and describe research on sensory memory.
2. Describe research on the encoding of information in short-term/working memory and on the process of proactive inhibition.
3. Discuss the behavioral and neurological evidence for the existence of phonological short-term memory.
4. Describe visual short-term memory, and explain how information is lost from short-term memory.
5. Discuss the consolidation hypothesis of learning and the effects of deep and shallow processing on remembering.
6. Discuss research on the distinction between episodic and semantic memory and the distinction between explicit and implicit memory.
7. Describe anterograde amnesia in humans and laboratory animals, and discuss the implications for the organization of long-term memory.
8. Explain how long-term memories may alter the structures of the brain, how information is remembered, and how information can be remembered more efficiently.
9. Describe the technique of hypnotic memory enhancement, and discuss the accuracy of induced memories.

I accompanied Fred, my graduate student, to the Veteran's Administration Hospital in a nearby town, where he had been studying several patients. We met Mr. P. in the lounge. Fred introduced us, and we walked to the room where he had set up his equipment. We sat down and chatted.

"How long have you been here?" Fred asked the man.

"Oh, about a week."

"Uh-huh. What brought you here?"

"I'm having some work done on my teeth. I'll be going back home in a couple of days. I have to help my father on the farm."

I knew that Mr. P. had actually been in the hospital for eleven years. He had been an alcoholic for a long time before that, and he was brought to the hospital in a severely malnourished condition. His father had died several years ago. Fred pointed to a slide projector and screen and asked Mr. P. whether he had seen them before. He looked at them and said, "No, I don't think so." Fred looked at me and said, "Say, have you met Dr. Carlson?" Mr. P. turned around, stood up, and extended his hand. "No, I don't believe I have. How do you do, sir?" he said. We shook hands, and I greeted him in return.

"Mr. P., a few days ago you saw some pictures here," said Fred. Mr. P. looked doubtful but said politely, "Well, if you say so." Fred dimmed the lights and showed him the first slide. Two pictures of two different automobiles were projected on the screen, side by side.

"Which one did you see before," Fred asked.

"Neither of them."

"Well," Fred persisted, "point to the one you *might* have seen." Mr. P. looked nonplused but pointed to the one on the right. Fred made a notation in his notebook and then showed the next slide, which showed views of two different trees.

"Which one?" he asked.

Silently, Mr. P. pointed to the one on the left. After showing eighteen pairs of slides, Fred said, "That's it, Mr. P. Thanks for helping me. By the way, have you met Dr. Carlson?" Mr. P. looked at Fred and then followed his gaze, turned around, and saw me. He stood up, and we shook hands and introduced ourselves.

As we left the hospital, I asked Fred how Mr. P. had done. "He got seventeen correct!" he exulted.

The behavioral approach to learning described in Chapter 6 investigates the relation between an organism's environment and its behavior. Behaviorists study generalization and discrimination, the effects of reinforcement and punishment contingencies on behavior, and so on. They do not try to infer what is going on within the subject's head. This chapter is entitled "Memory" rather than "Learning" because it describes an approach that does involve looking within the head, in an attempt to understand the *structure* of memory. In this context the word *structure* has two meanings, a literal one and a metaphorical one. Literally, some physiological psychologists (and other neuroscientists) are trying to discover the physiological changes in the brain that occur when an organism learns something. To them, the structure of memory refers to these physiological changes. Cognitive psychologists study the structure of memory in a metaphorical sense. In Chapter 5 we saw that psychologists have developed conceptual models to help them understand the nature of perception. Similarly, other psychologists have developed conceptual models of memory.

You have already studied the basic principles of learning; Chapter 6 described how classical conditioning and the contingencies of reinforcement and punishment can alter behavior. As far as we know, these principles apply to many species of vertebrates, including all mammals and birds, and even to some species of invertebrates. This chapter describes research on the nature of human memory; thus, most of the experiments reported here involve subjects of our own species. However, some questions—particularly those involving the physiological nature of memory—require the use of laboratory animals.

The ability to learn allows us to engage in an enormous variety of behaviors in response to an enormous variety of situations. The usefulness of memory, then, manifests itself in behavior. However, a lapse of time may occur between the act of learning and a change in behavior that results from this learning. For example, we may observe that a new restaurant has opened and then, some days later, visit that restaurant when we want to eat out. Presumably, the sight of the restaurant has induced some changes in our brain, which we refer to as a memory. Later, when we think about what restaurant we would like to go to, we think about the new restaurant (we *retrieve* the memory) and we act. This chapter describes both the formation and the retrieval of memories.

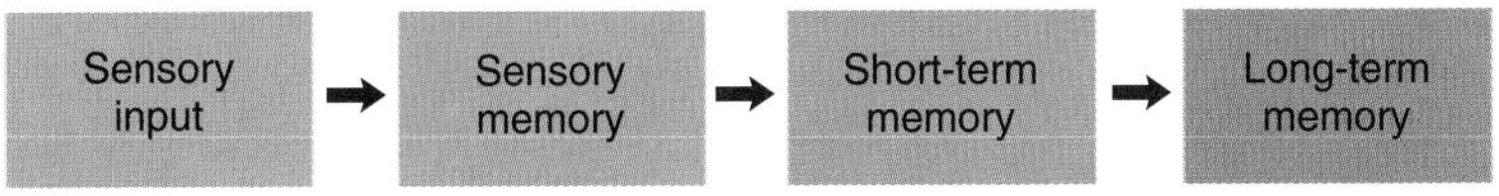

Sensory input → Sensory memory → Short-term memory → Long-term memory

Figure 7.1 Compartment model. This model of human memory is too simple.

AN OVERVIEW

[1] The learning process is selective. We perceive an enormous amount of information each day but can later remember only a portion of it. Research suggests that we possess at least three forms of memory: *sensory memory, short-term memory,* and *long-term memory* (Atkinson and Shiffrin, 1968). **Sensory memory** lasts for a very brief time—perhaps a second or less—and is difficult to distinguish from the act of perception. The information contained in sensory memory represents the original stimulus fairly accurately and contains all or most of the information that has just been perceived. For example, visual sensory memory contains a brief image of a sight we have just seen, and auditory sensory memory contains a fleeting echo of a sound we have just heard. Normally, we are not aware of sensory memory; no analysis seems to be performed on the information while it remains in this form. The function of sensory memory appears to be to hold onto information long enough for it to be transferred to the next form, *short-term memory.*

Short-term memory is an immediate memory for stimuli that have just been perceived. We can remember a new item of information (such as a telephone number) as long as we want to by engaging in a particular behavior: rehearsal. However, once we stop rehearsing the information, we may or may not be able to remember it later. That is, the information may or may not get stored in *long-term memory.*

Short-term memory can hold only a limited amount of information. To demonstrate this fact, read the following numbers to yourself just once, and then close your eyes and recite them back.

1 4 9 2 3 0 7

You probably had no trouble remembering them. Now, try the following set of numbers, and go through them *only once* before you close your eyes.

7 2 5 2 3 9 1 6 5 8 4

Very few people can repeat eleven numbers; in fact, you may not have even bothered to try, once you saw how many numbers there were. Thus, short-term memory has definite limits. Even if you practice, you will probably not be able to recite more than seven to nine *independent* pieces of information that you have seen only once. (As we will see in the application section at the end of this chapter, there are ways to organize new information so that you can remember more than seven to nine items, but in such cases they can no longer be considered independent.)

If you wanted to, you could recite the numbers again and again until you had memorized them; that is, you could rehearse the information in short-term memory until it was eventually stored in long-term memory. Unlike short-term memory, **long-term memory** has no known limits; and as its name suggests, it is relatively durable. Presumably, it occurs because of physical changes in the connections among neurons in the brain. If we stop thinking about something we have just perceived (that is, something contained in short-term memory), we may or may not remember the information later. However, information in long-term memory need not be continuously rehearsed; once we have learned something, we can stop thinking about it until we need the information at a future time.

Some psychologists argue that no real distinction exists between short-term and long-term memory; instead, they are seen as different phases of a continuous process. These psychologists object to the conception of memory as a series of separate units with information flowing from one to the next, as shown in *Figure 7.1.* And indeed, such a compartment model is too simple. But the purpose of this section is to provide you with an overview of the learning process; the complexities will come later.

SENSORY MEMORY

Under most circumstances we are not aware of sensory memory. Information we have just perceived remains in sensory memory just long enough to be transferred to short-term memory. In order for us to become aware of sensory memory, information must be presented very briefly so that we can perceive its aftereffects.

The image of a lightning bolt, and the scene it illuminates on a dark night, are briefly stored in iconic memory. Only part of the information will be transferred to short-term memory.

For example, a thunderstorm at night provides us with an opportunity to become aware of visual sensory memory. When a bright flash of lightning reveals a scene, we *see* things before we *recognize* them. That is, we see something first, then study the image left behind. Although we probably have a sensory memory for each sense modality, research efforts so far have focused on the two most important forms: iconic (visual) and echoic (auditory) memory.

Iconic Memory

Visual sensory memory is referred to as **iconic memory** (*icon* means "image"). To study this form of memory, Sperling (1960) presented visual stimuli to subjects by means of a tachistoscope (described in Chapter 5). Sperling flashed a set of nine letters, such as those shown below, on the screen for 0.05 second.

P Q B
C Z L
R K F

Sperling then asked the subjects to recall as many letters as they could (a method known as the *whole-report procedure*). On the average, they could remember only four or five letters, but they insisted that they could *see* more. However, the image of the letters faded too fast for the subjects to identify them all.

To determine whether the capacity of iconic memory accounted for this limitation, Sperling used a *partial-report procedure*. He asked the subjects to name the letters in only one of the three horizontal rows. Depending on whether a high, middle, or low tone was sounded, they were to report the letters in the top, middle, or bottom line. When people are warned beforehand which line they should pay attention to, they have no difficulty naming all three letters correctly. But Sperling sounded the tone *after* he flashed the letters on the screen. The subjects had to select the line from the *mental image* that they still had; that is, they had to retrieve the information from iconic memory. With brief delays they recalled the requested line of letters with perfect accuracy. For example, after seeing all nine letters flashed on the screen they would hear the high tone, direct their attention to the top line of letters in their iconic memory, and "read them off." These results indicated that their iconic memory contained an image of all nine letters.

Sperling also varied the delay between flashing the nine letters on the screen and sounding the high, medium, or low tone. If the delay was longer than one second, the subjects could report only around 50 percent of the letters. This result indicates that the image of the visual stimulus fades quickly from iconic memory. It also explains why subjects who were asked to report *all* the letters failed to report more than four or five. They had to scan their visual sensory memory, identify each letter, and store each letter in short-term memory. This process took time, and during this time the image of the letters in iconic memory was fading. Although their iconic memory originally contained all nine letters, there was time to recognize and report only four or five before the mental image disappeared.

An entirely different procedure confirmed Sperling's conclusions. Eriksen and Collins

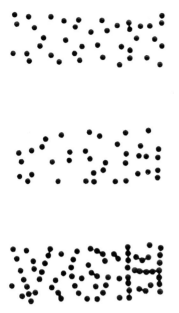

Figure 7.2 The stimuli used by Eriksen and Collins. The subjects saw the top and middle displays either simultaneously or separated by a delay. When the delay was less than 300 milliseconds, the subjects were able to see the letters in the composite display, shown at the bottom. (From Eriksen, C.W., and Collins, J.F. *Journal of Experimental Psychology*, 1967, *74*, 476–484. Copyright © 1967 by the American Psychological Association. Reprinted by permission.)

(1967) flashed pairs of dot patterns on a screen. When presented individually, each member of a pair of patterns looked meaningless. (See *Figure 7.2, top and middle.*) However, when the pairs were presented simultaneously, subjects could see an outline of three letters. (See *Figure 7.2, bottom.*) As you may have guessed, Eriksen and Collins actually flashed the pairs of patterns successively, with a delay between the first and second flash. If the delay was under 75 milliseconds (thousandths of a second), the subjects perceived a single flash. If the delay was greater than 75 milliseconds but less than approximately 300 milliseconds, the subjects saw two flashes, but they could still identify the letters. If the delay was greater than 300 milliseconds, the subjects did not perceive the letters. The most reasonable conclusion is that the image of a dot pattern remained in iconic memory for approximately 300 milliseconds. If the second pattern was presented within this interval of time, it would overlap with the first pattern, and the letters would be visible. If the second pattern occurred later, no overlap occurred, and no letters could be seen.

Echoic Memory

Auditory sensory memory, aptly called **echoic memory,** is necessary for comprehending many sounds, particularly those that constitute speech. When we hear a word pronounced, we hear individual sounds, one at a time. We cannot identify the word until we have heard all the sounds, so acoustical information must be stored temporarily until all the sounds have been received. For example, if someone says "mallet," we may think of a kind of hammer; but if someone says "malice," we will think of something entirely different. The first syllable we hear—*mal*—has no meaning by itself in English, so we do not identify it as a word. However, once the last syllable is uttered, we can put the two syllables together and recognize the word. At this point the word enters short-term memory. Echoic memory holds a representation of the initial sounds until the entire word has been heard.

Darwin, Turvey, and Crowder (1972) investigated echoic memory with a partial-report procedure similar to the one Sperling employed. On each trial they presented three different sets of numbers simultaneously, from three different locations (to the left and right of the subject and straight ahead). The numbers were spoken at a rate of three per second. After presenting the numbers, the experimenters presented a visual stimulus that indicated the location of the sounds the subjects should repeat. If the cue came soon after the numbers, subjects could accurately repeat what they had just heard from that direction. However, if the delay exceeded four seconds, the subjects did just as poorly as they did using the whole-report procedure. Thus, the experimenters concluded that echoic memory lasts less than four seconds.

INTERIM SUMMARY

An Overview and Sensory Memory

Memory exists in three forms: sensory, short-term, and long-term. The characteristics of each differ, which suggests that they differ physiologically, as well. Sensory memory is very brief; it provides temporary storage until the newly perceived information can be stored in short-term memory. Short-term memory is memory we are usually aware of; it contains a coded representation of information that has just been perceived, such as the item's name. The way information is encoded in short-term memory depends on what is already present in long-term memory. For example, if we have never before perceived a particular object, we have no name for it. Although the capacity of short-term memory is usually about seven to nine items of independent information, we can rehearse the information as long as we choose, thus increasing the likelihood that we will remember it indefinitely (that is, that it will enter long-term memory).

Information in sensory memory lasts for only a short time. The partial-report procedure shows that when a visual stimulus is presented in a brief flash, all of the information is available for a short time. If the viewer's attention is directed to one line of information within a few hundred milliseconds of the flash, the information can be transferred into short-term memory. Echoic memory appears to operate in a similar manner. ■

SHORT-TERM/WORKING MEMORY

2 Short-term memory has a very limited capacity, and most of the information that enters it is subsequently forgotten. What, then, is its function? Before I attempt to answer this question, let us examine its nature a little more closely.

Encoding of Information: Interaction with Long-Term Memory

So far, the story I have been telling has been relatively simple: Information in sensory memory enters short-term memory, where it may be rehearsed for a while. The rehearsal process keeps the information in short-term memory long enough for it to be transferred into long-term memory. After that the person can stop thinking about the information; it can be recalled later, when it is needed.

Clearly, this simple story is inaccurate. First of all, information does not simply "enter short-term memory." For example, read the letters below. Put them into your short-term memory, and keep them there for a few seconds while you look away from the book.

P X L M R

How did you keep the information in your short-term memory? You would probably tell me that you repeated the letters to yourself. You may even have whispered or moved your lips. You are able to say the names of these letters because many years ago you learned them. But that knowledge is stored in long-term memory. Thus, you *see* some letters, you retrieve information about their names from long-term memory, and then you *hear* yourself rehearse these names (out loud or silently, "within your head"). Clearly, the five letters you looked at contain only visual information; their names came from your long-term memory. That means that the information put into your short-term memory actually came from *long-term memory*. Perhaps Figure 7.3 more accurately represents the successive stages of the memory process than the box diagram I presented in Figure 7.1. I will discuss this issue again later in this chapter, in the section on long-term memory. (See **Figure 7.3**.)

You can see now that short-term memory is more than a simple way station between perception and long-term memory. For example, as I write this paragraph, I think not only about the words I have just written (which are stored in short-term memory) but also about *what I want to say next*. Obviously, this planning depends heavily on information stored in long-term memory. Even the act of remembering something can itself be a short-term memory. For example, think about the last time you mailed a letter. This information, and your awareness of thinking about it, are presently in your working memory, just as newly presented information would be. If I ask you later, "Do you remember thinking about the last time you mailed a letter?" you

Figure 7.3 Relations between iconic memory, short-term (working) memory, and long-term memory. Letters are read, transformed into their acoustic equivalents, and rehearsed as "sounds" in the head.

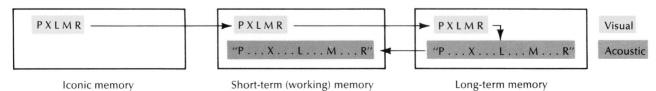

Iconic memory   Short-term (working) memory   Long-term memory

will undoubtedly be able to say "Yes." Thus, information can reach short-term memory *from the act of thinking and remembering* as well as from the sensory systems.

The fact that short-term memory contains both new information and information retrieved from long-term memory has led some psychologists to prefer the term **working memory** (Baddeley, 1986). Working memory does indeed seem to work on what we have just perceived. In fact, working memory represents a sort of behavior that takes place within our head; it represents our ability to remember what we have just perceived and to think about it in terms of what we already know. We use it to remember what a person says at the beginning of a sentence until we finally hear the end. We use it to remember whether any cars are coming down the street after looking left and right. We use it to think about what we already know and to come to conclusions on the basis of this knowledge.

What are the limits of working memory? Several pages ago, I asked you to try to repeat eleven numbers, which you were almost certainly unable to do. In fact, Miller (1956), in a paper entitled "The Magical Number Seven, Plus or Minus Two," demonstrated that people could retain, on the average, about seven pieces of information in their short-term memory: seven numbers, seven letters, seven words, or seven tones with a particular pitch. If we can remember and think about only seven pieces of information at a time, how can we manage to write novels, design buildings, or even carry on a simple conversation? The answer comes in a particular form of encoding of information that Miller called *chunking.*

A simple demonstration illustrates this phenomenon. Read the ten numbers printed below and see whether you have any trouble remembering them.

1 3 5 7 9 2 4 6 8 0

These numbers are easy to retain in short-term memory because we can remember a *rule* instead of ten independent numbers. In this case the rule concerns odd and even numbers. **Chunking** is Miller's term for the use of information already present in long-term memory to organize and simplify information just received in short-term memory. The actual limit of short-term memory is seven *chunks,* not necessarily seven individual items. Thus, the total amount of information we can store in short-term memory depends on the particular rules we use to organize it.

In the life outside the laboratory (and away from the textbook) we are seldom required to remember a series of numbers. The "rules" that organize our short-term memory are much more complex than those that describe odd and even numbers. But the principles I just described apply to more realistic learning situations. For example, say the group of words below, look away from the page, and try to recite the words from memory.

> along got the was door crept locked slowly he until passage the he to which

No doubt you found the task hopeless; there was just too much information to store in short-term memory. Now try the following group of words:

> He slowly crept along the passage until he got to the door, which was locked.

This time you were probably much more successful. Once the same fifteen words are arranged in a sequence that makes sense, they are not difficult to store in short-term memory.

Clearly, the size of short-term memory for verbal material is not measured in letters, syllables, or words. Instead, the limit depends on how much *meaning* the information has. The first set of words above merely contains fifteen different words. Because few people can immediately recite back more than seven to nine independent items, we are not surprised to find that we cannot store fifteen assorted words in short-term memory. However, when the items are related, we can store many more of them. We do not have to string fifteen words together in a meaningless fashion; instead, we can let the image of a man creeping down a passage toward a locked door organize the new information. Thus, we can read or hear a sentence such as the one above, understand what the sentence means, and think about that meaning.

Entry of Information into Short-Term Memory: Proactive Inhibition

As we have just seen, previously learned information can affect the entry of information into short-term memory. Sometimes, the effects can be inhibitory; old information can *interfere* with the retention of new information. For example, suppose you are asked to read lists containing the words *muskrat, beaver, weasel, ermine, rabbit,* and *opossum.* Soon afterward, you are given a list with the words *mink, otter,* and *badger* and are then asked to perform another verbal task, such as counting backward, in order to prevent rehearsal. After thirty seconds you are asked to recall the most recent words. You might forget some of the words on the most recent list and mistakenly say some of the words from the earlier lists. This effect is called **proactive inhibition;** previously learned information acts *forward in time* (or *proacts*), causing confusion when we attempt to learn more information later. As we will see, the effect is especially strong when the new information is similar to what we just learned.

What causes proactive inhibition? Experiments suggest that the most important cause is interference with the process of *retrieval*—with sorting out information already in short-term memory. Wickens (1972) presented subjects with lists of items and found that they became poorer and poorer at retaining information in short-term memory on successive trials. However, when the category of information was changed, the subjects suddenly performed as well as they had done on the first list. For example, the subjects became poorer and poorer at remembering lists of numbers, but when the experimenter switched to letters of the alphabet, their performance showed immediate improvement. Although the numbers had gotten difficult to remember, they had no trouble remembering letters. This phenomenon was called **release from proactive inhibition.**

Gardiner, Craik, and Birtwistle (1972) repeated Wickens's experiment but made a very subtle shift in the nature of the information presented to the subjects. On the first three trials the experimenters presented names of garden flowers such as *rose, tulip,* and *carnation.* On the fourth trial they switched to names of wildflowers such as *dandelion* and *daisy.* Control subjects were not told about the switch, nor did they appear to notice it; they showed no release from proactive inhibition. They confused the wildflower names with those of the garden flowers. In contrast, subjects who were told about the switch did show release from proactive inhibition, just as Wickens's subjects did. The important finding was that release from inhibition occurred when the subjects were told about the switch either beforehand or *after the fourth list had been presented.* In other words, the major cause of proactive inhibition must be interference with retrieval of information from short-term memory, not with its storage. Telling subjects about a subtle shift in category *after* they have heard the words cannot possibly affect the way the words are stored in short-term memory; they have already been stored. How-

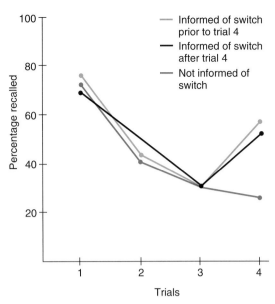

Figure 7.4 Release from proactive inhibition. The first three trials consist of names of garden flowers; performance declines because of proactive inhibition. On trial 4 subjects are presented with names of wildflowers. Those subjects who are told about the switch—either before or after the presentation of the items—perform better. (From Gardiner, J.M., Craik, F.I.M., and Birtwistle, J. *Journal of Verbal Learning and Verbal Behavior,* 1972, *11,* 778–783. Reprinted with permission.)

ever, it can affect the way the person attempts to retrieve them.

Figure 7.4 shows the evidence. As the subjects heard more and more lists, it became more difficult for them to remember a new one. But when the category switched, their performance improved dramatically. (See *Figure 7.4.*)

Varieties of Working Memory

3 So far, I have been referring to short-term (working) memory in the singular. But evidence suggests that working memory can contain a variety of sensory information: visual, auditory, somatosensory, gustatory, and olfactory. It can also contain information about movements that we have just made (*motor memories*), and it possibly provides the means by which we rehearse movements that we are thinking about making. Is all this information contained in a single system, or do we have several independent working memories?

How can we answer this question? The most common method is to take advantage of the limited capacity of working memory and see what kinds of tasks interfere with each other when they are performed simultaneously. For example, reciting one poem and simultaneously writing another is very difficult. But reciting a poem and simultaneously drawing a picture is easy. Thus, writing and talking appear to share some common processes, but talking and drawing have less in common. (These examples concern the use of information already in long-term memory, but they make the point.)

Most research on the nature of working memory has concentrated on visual or verbal material; few studies have investigated working memory for nonspeech sounds, touch, odors, or other types of information. Although each sensory modality may have a separate form of working memory associated with it, so far we have solid evidence for only two types of information in working memory: verbal and visual.

Phonological Short-Term Memory. Much of the information we receive can be encoded verbally. For example, we can see or smell a rose and think the word *rose;* we can feel the prick of a thorn and think the word *sharp;* and so on. Thus, seeing a rose, smelling a rose, and feeling a thorn can all result in words running through our working memory. How is verbal information stored in working memory? Evidence suggests that the short-term storage of words, whether originally presented visually or acoustically, occurs in **phonological short-term memory.** The Greek word *phone* means both "sound" and "voice"; thus, phonological coding could involve either the auditory system of the brain or the system that controls speech. (As we shall see, it involves both.)

Behavioral Evidence. An experiment by Conrad (1964) showed how quickly visually presented information becomes encoded acoustically. He briefly showed lists of six letters to his subjects and then asked them to write the letters. The errors the subjects made were almost always acoustical rather than visual. For instance, people sometimes wrote *B* when they had seen *V* (these letters sound similar), but they rarely wrote *F* when they had seen *T* (these letters look similar). The results imply that the subjects read the letters, encoded them acoustically ("heard them in their minds"), and remembered them by rehearsing the letters as sounds. During this process they might easily mistake a *V* for a *B*.

The fact that the errors seem to be acoustical may reflect a form of acoustical coding in

working memory. That is, phonological memory may be produced by activity in the auditory system—say, circuits of neurons in the auditory association cortex. However, we say words as well as hear them. Thus, as Hintzman (1967) suggested, the coding may be *articulatory*. (In this context *articulation* refers to coordinated movements of the muscles involved in speech.) That is, rather than hearing words echo in our heads, we may be feeling ourselves say them.

People often talk to themselves. Sometimes, they talk aloud; sometimes, they whisper or simply move their lips. At other times, no movements can be detected, but they can still report that they are thinking about saying the words; they are engaging in **subvocal articulation.** (*Subvocal articulation* means "unvoiced speech utterance.") For example, read the sentence below and rehearse it a few times, as if you were trying to memorize it. (It is the beginning of the poem "Jabberwocky" from *Through the Looking-Glass* by Lewis Carroll.)

> 'Twas brillig, and the slithy toves
> Did gyre and gimble in the wabe.

If you pay close attention to what you are doing, you will probably find that you not only "hear" the words but also say them to yourself. In fact, you may even make small movements of your tongue and lips. Studies have shown that actual movements are not necessary for verbal rehearsal; people can learn to keep their tongues and lips absolutely still while retaining verbal information in short-term memory (Garrity, 1977). But even though no actual movement may occur, it is still likely that activity occurs in the neural circuits in the brain that normally control speech. When we close our eyes and imagine seeing something, the mental image is undoubtedly caused by the activity of neurons in the visual association cortex. Similarly, when we imagine saying something, the "voice in our head" is probably controlled by the activity of neurons in the motor association cortex.

Conrad (1970) attempted to determine whether subvocal articulation played a role in phonological working memory by repeating his 1964 experiment and using deaf children as subjects. The children had been deaf from birth; thus, they obviously could not confuse the letters because of their sounds. Nevertheless, some of the children made "acoustical" errors. The children who made these errors were those who were rated by their teachers as being the best speakers. Therefore, the results suggested that the deaf children who could speak the best encoded the letters they saw in terms of the movements they would make to pronounce them.

The evidence from the second study provided clear evidence for an articulatory code in working memory. Of course, people who can both hear and speak may use both acoustic *and* articulatory codes: They may simultaneously hear the word and feel themselves saying it in their heads.

Salame and Baddeley (1982) obtained evidence that auditory coding, as well as articulatory coding, plays a role in phonological working memory. They showed subjects sequences of nine digits, presented one at a time on a computer terminal. After the digits had been presented, the subjects wrote as many of them as they could remember. Under control conditions the digits were presented silently or with a burst of noise. Under the experimental conditions subjects heard spoken words (such as *bid* or *pot*) or meaningless syllables (such as *pid* or *bot*). The subjects were told to ignore the sounds and concentrate on remembering the digits. The noise had little effect, but the sound of the words or meaningless syllables interfered with working memory; under the experimental conditions, subjects made approximately 40 percent more errors. Presumably, the presentation of the speech sounds interfered with an acoustical storage of the digits. Thus, we have evidence for both articulatory and acoustical coding in phonological working memory: for an "inner voice" and an "inner ear," as Baddeley puts it.

Baddeley (1986) suggests that the auditory system and the articulatory system of the brain cooperate in a looplike fashion. For example, when we see a printed word, we say it, out loud or silently. Suppose that we say it to ourselves, silently. Doing so obviously involves activity of circuits of neurons that control articulation. Information concerning this activity is communicated within the brain to circuits of neurons in the auditory system, and the word is "heard." Information is then transmitted back to the articulatory system, where the word is silently repeated again. The loop continues until the person's attention turns to something else or until it is replaced with new information. (See *Figure 7.5.*)

Neurological Evidence. The best neurological evidence for the existence of phonological short-term memory comes from a disorder called conduction aphasia. **Conduction aphasia,** usually caused by damage to a region of the left parietal lobe, appears as a profound deficit in phonological working memory. People with conduction aphasia can talk and comprehend what others are saying, but they are very poor at repeating precisely what they hear. When they attempt to repeat words that other people say, they often get the meaning correct but use different words. The examples below were attempts of a patient with mild conduction aphasia to repeat what the examiner read to him.

Examiner: Bicycle
Patient: Bicycle

Figure 7.5 A hypothetical explanation of phonological working memory: The articulatory loop.

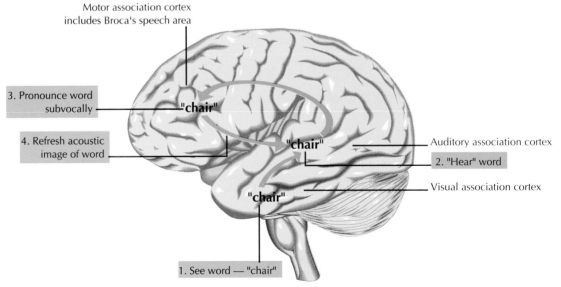

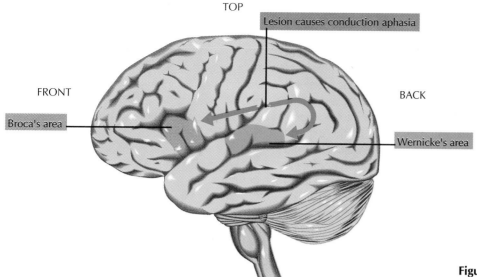

TOP

Lesion causes conduction aphasia

FRONT

BACK

Broca's area

Wernicke's area

Figure 7.6 A diagrammatic explanation of conduction aphasia.

Examiner: Hippopotamus

Patient: Hippopotamus

Examiner: Up and down.

Patient: Up and down.

Examiner: Look, car, house.

Patient: I didn't get it.

Examiner: Save your money.

Patient: Save your money.

Examiner: Yellow, big, south.

Patient: Yellen . . . Can't get it.

You will recall from an earlier example in this chapter that you could not repeat fifteen unrelated words but you could repeat them if they were arranged in a meaningful sentence. The patient described above had a much more limited phonological working memory: He could repeat single words or three-word phrases but not three independent words.

Most investigators believe that conduction aphasia is caused by brain damage that disrupts the connections between two regions of the cerebral cortex that play important roles in people's language ability. These two regions are *Wernicke's area,* which is concerned with the perception of speech, and *Broca's area,* which is concerned with the production of speech. (These areas are described in more detail in Chapter 9.) As we saw, phonological working memory appears to involve both articulatory and acoustical coding. Because the brain damage that produces conduction aphasia disconnects regions of the brain involved in speech perception and production, perhaps the damage disrupts acoustical short-term memory by making

such subvocal verbal rehearsal difficult or impossible. (See *Figure 7.6.*)

4 Visual Short-Term Memory. Verbal information can be received by means of the visual system or the auditory system. As we saw in the previous section, both forms of input produce acoustic and articulatory codes in phonological working memory. But much of the information we receive from the visual system is nonverbal. We recognize objects, perceive their locations, and find our way around the environment. We can look at objects, close our eyes, and then sketch or describe them. Alternatively, we can think about things we saw in the past and sketch or describe them. Thus, we apparently possess a working memory that contains visual information, either obtained from the immediate environment by means of the sense organs or retrieved from long-term memory.

Although most psychologists interested in short-term memory have employed verbal material, the chunking of information in working memory does not have to consist of words. Much of what we see is familiar; we have seen the particular items—or similar items—before. Thus, our visual working memory does not have to encode all the details, the way a photograph copies all the details in the scene gathered by the lens of a camera. For example, our short-term memory of the sight of a dog does not have to store every visual feature we saw, such as four legs, whiskers, ears, a tail. Instead, we already have mental images of dogs (probably a variety of different types) in our long-term memory; and when we see one, we can select a prototype that fits the bill, filling in a few features to represent the particular dog we just saw.

DeGroot (1965) performed an experiment that provides a nice example of the power of encoding visual information in working memory. He showed chessboards to expert players and to novices. If the positions of the pieces represented an actual game in progress, the experts could glance at the board for a few seconds and then look away and report the position of each piece. However, if the same number of pieces had been placed haphazardly on the board, the experts recognized immediately that their positions made no sense, and they could not remember their positions any better than a nonexpert could. Thus, their short-term memories for the positions of a large number of chess pieces depended on organizational rules stored in long-term memory as a result of years of experience playing chess. (Novices could not remember the location of the pieces in either situation because they lacked long-term memories for patterns of chess pieces on a board.)

Humans have a remarkable ability to manipulate visual information in working memory. For example, Shepard and Metzler (1971) presented subjects with pairs of drawings that could be perceived as three-dimensional constructions

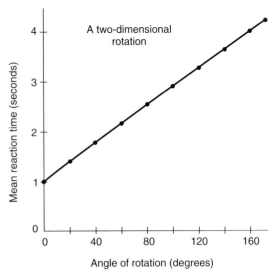

Figure 7.8   Mental rotation. Mean reaction time is shown as a function of angle of rotation. (From Shepard, R.N., and Metzler, J. *Science*, 1971, *171*, 701–703. Copyright 1971 by the American Association for the Advancement of Science.)

made of cubes. The subject's task was to see whether the shape on the right was identical to the one on the left; some were, and some were not. Even when the shapes were identical, the one on the right was sometimes drawn as if it had been rotated. For example, in Figure 7.7a the shape on the right has been rotated clockwise 80 degrees, but in Figure 7.7b the two shapes are different. (See **Figure 7.7.**)

Shepard and Metzler found that their subjects were very accurate in judging whether the pairs of shapes were the same or different. However, subjects took longer to decide when the right-hand shape was rotated. The subjects reported that they formed an image of one of the drawings in their heads and rotated it until it was aligned the same way as the other one. If their rotated image coincided with the drawing, they recognized them as having the same shape. If they did not, they recognized them as being different. (Look at Figure 7.7 to see whether you would use the same strategy.) The data supported what the subjects said: The decision time was a linear function of the degree of rotation. The more the shape was rotated, the longer it took for them to rotate the image of one of the shapes in working memory and compare it with the other one. (See **Figure 7.8.**)

This study (and many others like it) indicates that we can manipulate images just as we can manipulate physical objects. A very important human trait is the ability to build things: houses, tools, machines, bridges. The planners of these objects must be able to picture the

Figure 7.7   The mental rotation task. (a) The shape on the right is identical to the one on the left but rotated 80 degrees clockwise. (b) The two shapes are different. (Adapted from Shepard, R.N., and Metzler, J. *Science*, 1971, *171*, 701–703.)

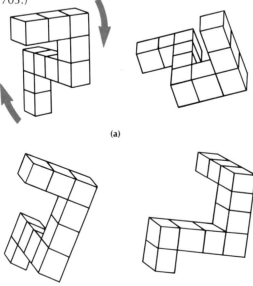

shapes of the parts and how they will together. An architect, a designer, or an engineer can make drawings to supplement his or her visual working memory, but most drawings serve to refine and elaborate images that are already at least somewhat developed. When a mason builds a wall from fieldstones, he looks at the rocks and imagines how they should be put together so that they will fit tightly; surely, this task involves rotating images of three-dimensional objects.

Loss of Information from Short-Term Memory

The essence of short-term memory is its transience (hence its name). Information enters from the environment and from long-term memory, is rehearsed, thought about, modified, and then leaves. Some of the information controls ongoing behavior and some of it causes changes in long-term memory, but ultimately, it is lost. What causes it to leave? The simplest possibility is that it simply decays—that it fades away. (Of course, rehearsal allows one to refresh information indefinitely, thus preventing the process of decay from eliminating the information.) However, the most important cause appears to be displacement. As you already know, short-term memory has a capacity of around seven independent items. Therefore, once this capacity is reached, either additional information will have to be ignored or some information already in short-term memory will have to move aside (be displaced) to make room available for the new.

One of the best examples of displacement of information in short-term memory comes from an experiment by Waugh and Norman (1965). The subjects heard lists of sixteen digits. The last one, accompanied by a tone, was called the *probe digit*. When the subjects heard it, they had to think back to the previous occurrence of the same digit and tell the experimenter the digit that followed that one.

That description is probably not very clear. Look at the sequence of numbers listed below. The last one, a 9, was accompanied by a tone, which told the subject that it was the probe. If you examine the list, you will see that the earlier occurrence of a 9 was followed by a 4. Thus, the correct response (the *target*) was "four."

2 6 7 5 1 3 7 2 6 3 9 4 5 8 1 <u>9</u>

Notice that the 4 is separated from the second 9 by three numbers. Waugh and Norman presented many different lists in which the location of the correct response varied; the distance between the target and the probe ranged from one to twelve items.

The experimenters ran two conditions in their study. In one condition the lists were presented rapidly, at four digits per second. In the other they were presented slowly, at only one digit per second. The reason for this manipulation was to determine whether any effects they observed were caused by the mere passage of time, rather than by displacement. Figure 7.9 shows the results. Clearly, the more items that came between the target and the probe, the less likely it was that the target would be remembered. Furthermore, the curves looked approximately the same for either the fast or the slow rate of presentation. Thus, the critical variable seems to be the number of items between the

If we are introduced to many people at a party, we soon find the limits of short-term memory; new information begins to displace old information.

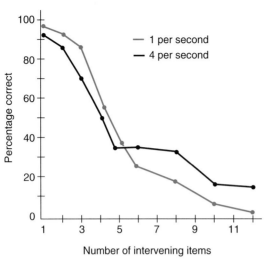

Figure 7.9 Displacement of information in short-term memory. The graph shows the percentage correct as a function of intervening items presented at two different rates. (Adapted from Waugh, N.C., and Norman, D.A. *Psychological Review,* 1965, *72,* 89–104.)

target and the probe, not the time that had elapsed. (See *Figure 7.9.*)

The results clearly indicate that new information displaces old information in short-term memory. If you look carefully at the graph again, you will also see some evidence for decay. At the longest delays (six or more intervening items), subjects performed more poorly when the items were presented slowly. Perhaps information in short-term does decay, but the effect is obviously much less important than displacement. (See *Figure 7.9.*)

INTERIM SUMMARY

Short-Term/Working Memory

Information in short-term memory is encoded according to previously learned rules; thus, information in long-term memory determines the nature of the coding. Because short-term memory contains information retrieved from long-term memory as well as newly perceived information, many investigators conceive of it as a "working" memory. Working memory is not simply a way station between sensory memory and long-term memory; it is where thinking is accomplished.

Not all information that enters short-term memory subsequently enters long-term memory. Some is lost by proactive inhibition from previously learned material. Studies suggest that the primary reason for this inhibition is interference with retrieval.

Although each sensory system probably has a working memory associated with it, psychologists have devoted most of their attention to two kinds: phonological and visual working memory. The existence of acoustical errors (rather than visual ones) in the task of remembering visually presented letters suggests that the information is represented phonologically in short-term (working) memory. Because deaf people (but only those who can talk) also show this effect, the code appears to be articulatory. But the sounds of words interfere with phonological working memory more than simple noises; thus, phonological working memory is coded acoustically as well. The best hypothesis is that this form of memory consists of an internal loop: an "inner voice" and an "inner ear," so to speak.

Visual working memory is also important and in the laboratory has been demonstrated by the ability of chess masters to remember a board and by the ability to perform mental rotation of meaningless shapes. The mental manipulation of shapes is an important component of our ability to design and construct tools, buildings, bridges, and other useful objects.

Physiological studies have supported the distinction between phonological and visual working memories. People with conduction aphasia show a specific deficit in phonological short-term memory, apparently because their brain damage interrupts direct communication between Wernicke's area and Broca's area.

As the Waugh and Norman study showed, the loss of information from short-term memory appears to be primarily a result of displacement; new information pushes out old information. However, as they found, a small amount of simple decay may also occur. ∎

LONG-TERM MEMORY

⑤ Information that is present in short-term (working) memory may or may not be available later; but once information has successfully made its way into long-term memory, it remains relatively stable. Of course, we do forget things, but our brains have the remarkable ability to store a vast amount of information for a very long time.

What kinds of information can be stored in long-term memory? To answer this question, let us consider the kinds of things we can learn.

First, we can learn to recognize things: objects, sounds, odors, textures, and tastes. Thus, we can remember perceptions received by all of our sensory systems, which means that we have visual memories, auditory memories, olfactory memories, somatosensory memories, and gustatory memories. These memories can be combined and interconnected, so that hearing a soft "meow" in the dark evokes an image of a cat. Sensory memories can also be combined in temporal order, so that we can remember the plot of a movie we saw or "hear" the melody of a song in our heads.

The second major type of learning involves making overt responses. We can learn to make new responses, as when we learn to operate a new machine, ride a bicycle, or say a new word, or we can learn to make old responses in new situations. Sensory memories presumably involve alterations in circuits of neurons in the sensory association cortex of the brain: visual memories in the visual cortex, auditory memories in the auditory cortex, and so on. Memories that involve combinations of sensory information

Long-term memory has no known limits. Shakespearean actors may remember their parts long after the performance is over.

presumably involve the establishment of connections between different regions of association cortex. For example, the sound of a "meow" evokes the memory of the cat's image by means of connections between auditory and visual association cortexes previously established by learning. Motor memories (memories for particular behaviors) presumably involve alterations in circuits of neurons in the motor association cortex of the frontal lobes. Thus, learning to perform particular behaviors in particular situations presumably involves the establishment of connections between the appropriate regions of sensory and motor cortexes.

The Act of Learning

Learning involves both active and passive processes. Sometimes, we use deliberate strategies to remember something (put the information into long-term memory), as when we rehearse the lines of a poem or memorize famous dates for a history course. At other times, we simply observe and remember without any apparent effort, as when we tell a friend about an interesting experience we had. And learning can even take place without our being aware of having learned something. Just what does learning involve, and what factors determine whether we can eventually remember an experience? In this section we will examine some hypotheses and some evidence gathered to date.

The Consolidation Hypothesis. The traditional view of learning is that it consists of a two-stage process (not counting sensory memory). That is, information enters short-term memory from the environment, where it is stored temporarily. Then if the material is rehearsed long enough, it is transferred into "cold storage": long-term memory. Once the information is in long-term memory, we can safely stop thinking about the material. The transfer of information from short-term memory into long-term memory has been called **consolidation** (Hebb, 1949). Presumably, short-term memory consists of activity of neurons that encodes the information received from the sense organs. Once this activity subsides, the information is forgotten. Through rehearsal (for example, by means of the articulatory loop), the neural activity can be sustained; and if enough time passes, the activity causes structural changes in the brain. These structural changes are more or less permanent and *solid* (hence the term *consolidation*). They are responsible for long-term memory.

Some of the best evidence in favor of the consolidation hypothesis comes from events that disrupt brain functioning. From the earliest times people have observed that a blow to the head can affect memory. Let us consider an imaginary case.

> José, a baseball player, is standing on first base. The pitcher begins his windup, and José takes a few steps toward second base. The pitch is wild, and the catcher loses his balance while reaching for it. Taking advantage of the momentary confusion, José runs for second base. The catcher sees him running, jumps to his feet, and throws the ball to second base just as José arrives there. José's foot touches the base in time, but his head comes between the ball, which has been thrown a bit high, and the second baseman's glove. The ball hits José just above the ear, and he crumples to the ground. He regains consciousness in the dugout, sees his teammates gathered around him, and sits up slowly.
>
> "What happened to me?" he asks. He sits for a while, dazed, then shakes his head tentatively and decides that he will be all right.
>
> "I'm OK. I'll go back on base." He leaves the dugout and heads for first base.
>
> "Hey!" one of his teammates yells. "You were on second—you stole second base."
>
> José looks at him incredulously but notes that the other teammates are nodding. It must be true. He walks to second base, puzzled.

In many similar incidents people have been hit on the head and have forgotten what happened immediately before the injury. A blow to the head makes the brain bump against the inside of the skull, and this movement apparently disrupts its normal functioning. The blow disrupts short-term memory but not long-term memory. A lack of memory for events that occurred just before an injury is called **retrograde amnesia.** (*Retro-* means "backward": in this case, backward in time.) José, the baseball player, had stood on first base long enough to form a long-term memory for having been there. He saw the wild pitch, ran to second base, and got hit on the head. His memory of the run to second base was in short-term storage and was destroyed when the normal functioning of his brain was temporarily disrupted.

I must note that my example is an uncomplicated one, chosen to illustrate some important principles. Actually, head injury often disrupts people's memories for a period of time afterward; and if the injury is severe enough, retrograde amnesia can extend back for a period of

days or even weeks. Obviously, the loss of memories in that case involves more than short-term memories. Why recent long-term memories are more vulnerable to injury than older long-term memories is a mystery.

Events like those in my simple story support two of the assumptions of the consolidation hypothesis. Because only recently perceived information is disrupted by a minor head injury, (1) short-term memory and long-term memory appear to be physiologically different, and (2) the transfer of information from short-term memory to long-term memory seems to take time. Information stored in fragile short-term memory is eventually consolidated into more stable long-term memory.

Elaboration: Levels of Processing. The consolidation hypothesis makes several assertions about the learning process. It asserts that, physiologically, short-term memory and long-term memory are different. The evidence I presented in the previous section supports this assertion, and few investigators doubt that information that has just been perceived is stored in the brain in a different way than information that was perceived some time ago. However, some other features of the original consolidation hypothesis have been challenged by recent evidence. First, the hypothesis asserts that all information gets into long-term memory only after passing through short-term memory. Second, it asserts that the most important factor determining whether a particular piece of information reaches long-term memory is the amount of time it spends in short-term memory.

Craik and Lockhart (1972) have pointed out that the act of rehearsal may effectively keep information in short-term memory but not necessarily result in the establishment of long-term memories. They suggested that people could engage in two different types of rehearsal: *maintenance rehearsal* and *elaborative rehearsal*. **Maintenance rehearsal,** which applies mostly to verbal material, consists of simple repetition of information—the kind we use to remember a telephone number long enough to dial it. This behavior serves to maintain the information in short-term memory but does not necessarily result in lasting changes. In contrast, when a person engages in **elaborative rehearsal,** he or she thinks about the information and relates it to what he or she already knows. Thus, elaborative rehearsal does not simply represent the new information; it elaborates upon it by causing the recollection of related information already in long-term memory.

The effectiveness of elaboration in remembering was nicely demonstrated in an experiment by Craik and Tulving (1975). The investigators gave subjects a set of cards, each containing a printed sentence with a missing word, denoted by a blank line, such as "The _____ is torn." After reading the sentence, the subjects looked at a word flashed on a screen, then pressed a button as quickly as possible to signify whether or not the word fit the sentence. In this example *dress* will fit, but *table* will not.

The sentences varied in complexity. Some were very simple:

She cooked the _____.

The _____ is torn.

Others were complex:

The great bird swooped down and carried off the struggling _____.

The old man hobbled across the room and picked up the valuable _____.

The sentences were written so that the same word could be used for either a simple or a complex sentence: "She cooked the *chicken*" or "The great bird swooped down and carried off the struggling *chicken*." All subjects who participated saw a given word once, in either a simple or a complex sentence.

No mention was made of a memory test, so there was no reason for the subjects to try to remember the words. However, after responding to the sentences, they were presented with them again and were asked to recall the words they had used. The investigators found that subjects were twice as likely to remember a word if it had previously fit into a sentence of medium or high complexity than if it had fit into a simple one.

These results suggest that a memory is more effectively established if the item is presented in a rich context—one that is likely to make us think about the item and imagine an action taking place. Consider the different images conjured up by these two sentences (also from Craik and Tulving, 1975):

He dropped the *watch*.

The old man hobbled across the room and picked up the valuable *watch*.

The second sentence provides much more information. The word *watch* is remembered in the vivid context of a hobbling old man, and the word *valuable* suggests that the watch is interesting. Perhaps, because the man is old, the

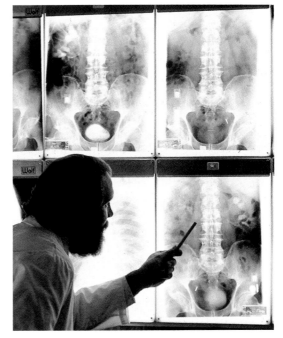

This radiologist relies on a large store of visually coded information in long-term memory to make his diagnoses.

watch is too; it might be a large gold pocket watch, attached to a gold chain. The image that is evoked by the more complex sentence provides the material for a more complex memory. This complexity makes the memory more distinctive and thus helps us pick it out from all the other memories we have. When the incomplete sentence is presented again, it easily evokes a memory of the image of the old man and of the watch.

Craik and Lockhart (1972) proposed a framework for understanding the process by which information entered long-term memory. They suggested that memory is a by-product of perceptual analysis. A central processor, analogous to the central processing unit of a computer, can analyze sensory information on several different levels. (This central processor can be thought of as a control mechanism involved in working memory.) They conceived of the levels as being hierarchically arranged, from shallow (superficial) to deep (complex). A person can control the level of analysis by paying attention to different features of the stimulus. If the person focuses on the superficial sensory characteristics of a stimulus, then these features will be stored in memory. If the person focuses on the meaning of a stimulus and the ways in which it relates to other things the person already knows, then these features will be stored in memory. For example, consider the word written below.

tree

You can see that the word is written in black type, that the letters are lowercase, that the bottom of the stem of the letter *t* curves upward to the right, and so on. Craik and Lockhart referred to these characteristics as surface features and to their analysis as **shallow processing.** In contrast, consider what the word *tree* means. You can think about how trees differ from other plants, what kinds and varieties of trees you have seen, what kinds of foods and what kinds of wood they provide, and so on. These features are called *semantic features,* and their analysis is called **deep processing.** In this context *semantic* refers to a word's meaning. In general, according to Craik and Lockhart, deep processing leads to better retention than surface processing does.

Among the evidence cited by Craik and Lockhart to support their model were the results from a study by Hyde and Jenkins (1969). These investigators asked subjects to analyze lists of words. Some subjects were asked to analyze surface features—to count the letters in each word or to see whether the word contained the letter *e.* Other subjects were asked to analyze deeper features—to think

Figure 7.10 Mean number of words recalled after performing tasks that required shallow or deep processing. (Based on Craik, F.I.M., and Lockhart, R.S. *Journal of Verbal Learning and Verbal Behavior,* 1972, *11,* 671–684.)

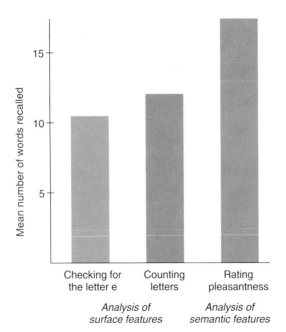

about the word and decide how pleasant or unpleasant they found it to be. As you can see in Figure 7.10, the subjects who engaged in a deeper level of processing remembered more words. (See *Figure 7.10.*)

The concept of processing depth has been useful in guiding research efforts to understand how we learn and remember. However, many psychologists have noted that the distinction between "shallow" and "deep" has never been rigorously defined. The difference between looking at the shape of the letters of a word and thinking about its meaning is clear, but most instances of learning cannot be so neatly categorized. The term *depth* seems to be a metaphor; it roughly describes the fact that information is more readily learned and remembered when we think about it in relation to what we already know, but it is not exact and specific enough to satisfy most memory theorists.

Psychologists have also criticized the assertion that tasks that encourage subjects to focus on superficial features of stimuli inevitably lead to poorer memory than tasks that encourage them to focus on "deeper" features. For example, after reading something new, people can often remember exactly where the information appeared on a page (Rothkopf, 1971). (I have had students tell me, after failing to answer a question on a test, that they could picture the page on which the answer could be found, but they could just not remember what the words said. This example indicates good retention of information that had undergone "shallow" processing but poor retention of information that had undergone "deep" processing.)

Most psychologists no longer believe that the original depth-of-processing model accurately describes the learning process. But the model did encourage researchers to investigate the possibility that different kinds of information were learned differently and organized differently in long-term memory.

The Organization of Long-Term Memory

6 As we just saw, consolidation is not simply a passive process; thinking about different aspects of newly perceived information can affect the learning process. Many investigators believe that long-term memory consists of more than a simple pool of information. Instead, it is *organized*—different kinds of information are encoded differently and stored in different ways.

Episodic and Semantic Memory. Long-term memory does not simply contain records

Experienced roller skaters use implicit (procedural) memories. The skill is performed automatically, without the need of deliberate, conscious recall.

describe in words. For example, suppose that someone asks us which is larger, a boat or a bee? We have probably never answered that question before. But we can easily do so, perhaps by picturing both of these objects and comparing their size.

In contrast, implicit memory is not something we answer questions about. Suppose we learn to ride a bicycle. We do so quite consciously and develop episodic memories about our attempts: who helped us learn, where we rode, how we felt, how many times we fell, and so on. But we also *learn to ride*. We learn to make automatic adjustments with our hands and bodies that keep our center of gravity above the wheels. Most of us cannot describe the rules that govern our behavior. For example, what do you think you must do if you start falling to the right while riding a bicycle? Many cyclists would say that they compensate by leaning to the left. But they are wrong; what they really do is turn the handlebars to the right. Leaning to the left would actually make them fall faster, because it would force the bicycle even farther to the right.

The point is that although they have learned to make the appropriate movements, they cannot necessarily describe in words what these movements are.

Evidence for the distinction between explicit and implicit memory comes from both behavioral and physiological studies. Let us consider the behavioral evidence first.

Learning Without Awareness. A large and growing body of evidence indicates that we can learn something without being aware that we have done so. That is, when we are asked questions about the information we encountered previously, we fail to answer them correctly. However, when we are tested in other ways, we indicate that learning has actually taken place.

The acquisition of specific behaviors and skills is probably the most important form of implicit learning. Driving a car, turning the pages of a book, playing a musical instrument, dancing, throwing and catching a ball, sliding a chair backward as we get up from the dinner table—all these skills involve coordination of movements with sensory information received from the environment and from our own moving body parts. Although these skills are very important, most memory theorists have not paid as much attention to them as they have to verbal tasks performed in the laboratory. Nevertheless, our ancestors were able to adapt their behavior to their environment long before they were able to talk. Thus, implicit memories may actually represent a majority of the contents of long-term memory.

A good example of learning without awareness is provided by an experiment by Graf and Mandler (1984). These investigators showed subjects a list of six-letter words and had some of them engage in a task that involved elaborative processing: to think about each word and decide how much they liked it. Other subjects were given a task that involved processing superficial features; they were asked to look at the words and decide whether they contained particular letters. (As you can see, the procedure was similar to one I described in the previous subsection.) Later, the subjects' explicit and implicit memories for the words were assessed. In both cases the basic task was the same, but the instructions to the subjects were different. The subjects were shown the first three letters of each word. For example, if one of the words had been DEFINE, they would have been shown a card on which was printed DEF. Several different six-letter words besides *define* begin with

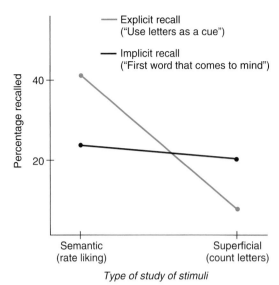

Figure 7.12 Explicit versus implicit memory. The graph shows the percentage of words recalled as a function of the type of study procedure. (Based on data from Graf and Mandler, 1984.)

the letters DEF, such as *deface, defame, defeat, defect, defend, defied,* and *deform,* so there are several possible responses. The experimenters assessed *explicit memory* by asking the subjects to try to remember the words they had previously seen, using the first three letters as hints. They assessed *implicit memory* by asking the subjects to say the first word that came to mind that started with the three letters on the card.

Figure 7.12 shows that deliberate processing (elaborative or superficial) had a striking effect on the explicit memory task but not on the implicit memory task. When subjects used the three letters as cues for deliberate retrieval, they were much more successful if they had thought about whether they liked the word than if they simply paid attention to the occurrence of particular letters. However, when subjects simply said the first word that came to mind, the way they had studied the words had no effect on the number of correct words that "popped into their heads." (See *Figure 7.12.*)

The results indicate that actively thinking about a word makes it easier to remember that word later. However, simply looking at the word makes it more likely that a person will later think of it, even if the person does not remember seeing it. As Figure 7.12 shows, when people simply looked at the words, they were able explicitly to remember only 7.8 percent of them afterward.

7 *Human Anterograde Amnesia.* Damage to particular parts of the brain can permanently impair people's ability to form new long-term memories, a phenomenon known as **anterograde amnesia.** The brain damage can be caused by the effects of long-term alcoholism, severe malnutrition, stroke, head trauma, or surgery. In general, the memory of these people for events that occurred prior to the damage still remains. They can talk about things that happened before the onset of their amnesia, but they cannot remember what happened since. They never learn the names of people they subsequently meet, even if they see them daily for years. As we saw in the opening vignette, Mr. P. had been in the hospital for eleven years, but he thought he had actually been there for about a week.

One of the most famous cases of anterograde amnesia is that of patient H.M. (Scoville and Milner, 1957; Milner, 1970; Corkin, Sullivan, Twitchell, and Grove, 1981). H.M.'s case is interesting because his amnesia is both severe and relatively pure, uncontaminated by other neuropsychological deficits. In 1953, when H.M. was 27, a neurosurgeon removed part of his temporal lobe on both sides of the brain. The surgery was performed to alleviate his very severe epilepsy, which was not responding to drug treatment. The surgery cured the epilepsy, but unfortunately, it caused anterograde amnesia. (Obviously, this type of operation is no longer performed.)

H.M. can carry on conversations, talking about general topics not related to recent events. He can also talk about his life prior to the surgery. However, he cannot talk about anything that has happened since 1953. He lives in an institution where he can be cared for and spends most of his time solving crossword puzzles and watching television. H.M. is aware he has a memory problem. For example, here is his response to an investigator's question.

> Every day is alone in itself, whatever enjoyment I've had, and whatever sorrow I've had. . . . Right now, I'm wondering. Have I done or said anything amiss? You see, at this moment everything looks clear to me, but what happened just before? That's what worries me. It's like waking from a dream; I just don't remember. (Milner, 1970, p. 37)

Clearly, H.M.'s problem lies in his ability to store new information in long-term memory, not in his short-term memory. His verbal short-term (working) memory is normal; he can repeat seven numbers forward and five numbers backward, which is about average for the general population. At first, investigators concluded that the problem was in memory consolidation and that the part of the brain that was destroyed during surgery was essential for carrying out this process. But subsequent evidence suggests that the brain damage disrupts *explicit memory* without seriously damaging *implicit memory.*

Many studies performed with H.M. and with other people with anterograde amnesia have shown that implicit learning can still take place. For example, Figure 7.13 shows two sets of drawings. Almost no one can recognize these drawings when they see version I or II. However, once they have seen the complete drawings, they can recognize the elephant and the umbrella if they later see only the incomplete versions. So can H.M.; seeing the complete

Figure 7.13 Two sets of the different versions of broken drawings presented to patient H.M. (Reproduced with permission of author and publisher from Gollin, E.S. Developmental studies of visual recognition of incomplete objects. *Perceptual and Motor Skills*, 1960, *11*, 289–298.) © Perceptual and Motor Skills, 1960.

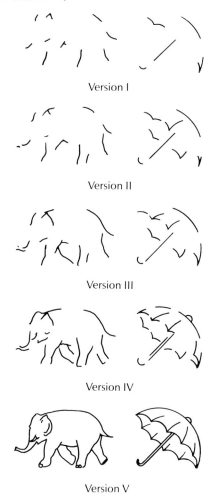

Version I

Version II

Version III

Version IV

Version V

versions leads to a long-term memory that aids his recognition (Milner, 1970). (See *Figure 7.13.*)

Other investigators have found that people with anterograde amnesia can learn to solve puzzles, perform visual discriminations in a human version of an operant chamber (with pennies as reinforcers), and make skilled movements that require hand-eye coordination (Squire, 1987). Obviously, their brains are still capable of undergoing the kinds of changes that constitute long-term memory. But in all cases *the people do not remember having performed the tasks previously.* For example, they may learn the task on one occasion. The next day, the experimenter brings them to the experimental apparatus and asks if they have ever seen it before. The subjects say no, they have not; thus, they have no explicit, episodic memory for having spent some time learning the task. But then they go on to perform the task well, clearly demonstrating the existence of implicit long-term memory.

Graf, Squire, and Mandler (1984) performed an experiment similar to the one by Graf and Mandler that I described in the previous subsection. They showed lists of six-letter words to amnesic and nonamnesic subjects and asked them to rate how much they liked them. (As you will recall, this task maximizes the formation of explicit memory but has no effect on implicit memory.) They then administered two types of memory tests. In the *explicit memory* condition they simply asked the subjects to recall the words they had seen. In the *implicit memory* condition they presented cards containing the first three letters of the words and asked the subjects simply to say the first word that started with those letters that came into their minds. As Figure 7.14 shows, the amnesic subjects explicitly remembered fewer words than the control subjects, but both groups performed well on the implicit memory task. (See *Figure 7.14.*)

What kinds of tasks can people with anterograde amnesia learn to do? In general, the task cannot be one that requires them to learn a complex set of verbal rules. The words will never be learned, so the rules cannot possibly be followed. In addition, the learning task and the task used to assess the people's memory must be identical, just as they would have to be if laboratory animals were being trained. For example, we can train many animals, including people, to operate a complicated latch. (You will recall from Chapter 1 that Thorndike taught cats such a task in his studies of learning.) Suppose we

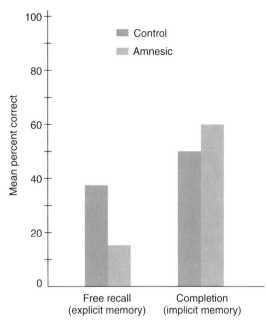

Figure 7.14 Explicit and implicit memory of amnesic patients and control subjects. The performance of amnesic patients was impaired when they were instructed to try to recall the words they had previously seen but not when they were asked to say the first word that came into their minds. (Based on data from Graf, Squire, and Mandler, 1984.)

want to see whether the subject still remembers how to operate the latch several days later. If the subject is a laboratory animal, the only way we can test it is to present the animal with the task and see whether it can still solve it. If the subject is a human, we can do the same thing; or we can simply ask him or her to describe how to open the latch. But clearly, these are two different types of tasks: Having them open the latch is a test of implicit memory, but asking them to talk about their ability is a test of explicit, episodic memory.

The evidence I have presented so far suggests that the brain damage causing anterograde amnesia disrupts the formation of new explicit memories but spares the ability to form new implicit memories. (The fact that amnesic patients can remember facts and describe experiences that occurred before the brain injury indicates that their ability to *recall* explicit memories acquired earlier is not severely disrupted.) What parts of the brain are involved in the functions necessary for establishing new explicit memories? The most important part seems to be the **hippocampus,** a structure located deep within the temporal lobe that forms part of the limbic system. (See *Figure 7.15.*)

The hippocampus receives information from all association areas of the brain and sends information back to them. In addition, the hippocampus has two-way connections with many regions in the interior of the cerebral hemispheres. Thus, the hippocampal formation is in a position to know—and to influence—what is going on in the rest of the brain. Presumably, it uses this information to influence the establishment of explicit long-term memories.

Anterograde Amnesia in Laboratory Animals. Why do we seem to have two different systems of long-term memory? Given that the difference between these systems seems to be whether or not we are able to talk about the memories, can we conclude that only humans have an explicit memory system? The answer seems to be no; damage to the hippocampus produces memory impairments in animals that resemble those that occur in humans. Of course, animals other than humans cannot talk, so the term *explicit,* or *declarative, memory* does not make much sense. When we understand the phenomena better, an imaginative psychologist will surely come up with better names.

As we saw, people with anterograde amnesia can learn to perform a variety of tasks as long as the tasks do not involve explicit memories. Therefore, it should come as no surprise that similar brain damage in laboratory animals does not interfere with most tests of memory. But suppose that we tried to devise a task that involved learning similar to what the human explicit memory system is capable of. As we saw earlier, the explicit memory system contains both semantic and episodic information. The term *semantic* refers exclusively to verbal information; because nonhuman animals cannot talk, we could hardly design a task to assess their semantic memory. But perhaps animals are able

Figure 7.15 The human hippocampus.

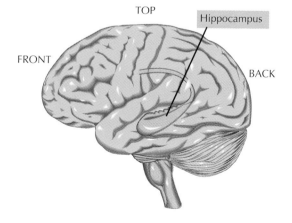

to remember episodes. What distinguishes episodic information from semantic information? The primary distinction seems to be that episodic information is organized in a *context*. In fact, I think I will underline that word to show how important it is: context.

In an earlier section I gave some examples of episodic memories—this morning's breakfast, my fifteenth birthday party, and the first time I went skiing. Episodic memories consist of collections of perceptions of events organized in time and identified by a particular *context*. For example, consider my memory of this morning's breakfast. I put on my robe, walked downstairs, filled the coffee maker with ten cups of water, put the coffee grinder on the counter and plugged it in, went to the cupboard and took out the container of coffee beans, . . . well, you probably are not interested in all the details. The point is that the memory contains many events, organized in time. But how do I know that I am talking about today's breakfast, not yesterday's? My memory contains many details about many breakfasts, and if I want to, I can describe a good number of them. The distinguishing feature among them is the context: today's breakfast, yesterday's breakfast, the first breakfast we had in a hotel room in Paris, and so on.

Can animals perform tasks that require them to learn the order in which events occur and to distinguish between different contexts? The answer seems to be yes. Olton and Samuelson (1976) devised a task that requires an animal to remember a recent episode. They constructed a maze consisting of a central octagonal platform with eight arms radiating away from it. They placed a small piece of food at the end of each arm and then put a hungry rat on the central platform. The animal began exploring the arms of the maze, finding and eating the food. As soon as all eight pieces of food were eaten, the experimenters removed the rat and ended the trial. (See *Figure 7.16.*) After twenty sessions most animals foraged for the food efficiently, entering each arm only once. Even when a series of doors was used to prevent the animals from visiting the arms in a particular order (say, simply working their way clockwise around the maze), the animals avoided retracing their steps (Olton, Collison, and Werz, 1977). Clearly, this performance required them to retain a particular episode in memory—the arms of the maze that have been visited *that day*. Yesterday's sequence was different and must not be confused with today's. (You can see that this task is similar to our abil-

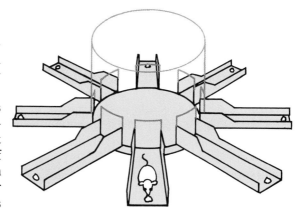

Figure 7.16 The eight-arm radial maze used by Olton and his colleagues.

ity to remember exactly where we parked our car on a given day.)

Olton and Samuelson found that surgical destruction of the hippocampus impaired the rats' performance. These rats learned that food was to be found at the ends of the arms of the maze and would eagerly run out to the ends of the arms. However, they visited the arms in an aimless fashion, often entering arms that they had already visited during the trial. Thus, damage to the hippocampus appears to disrupt an animal's ability to remember episodic information, just as it does in humans.

The foregoing studies with humans and laboratory animals suggest that the distinction between explicit and implicit memory identifies some important characteristics of the process of learning and remembering. The hippocampus and, perhaps, other parts of the brain are involved in some way in establishing explicit memories in humans and their analogues in other animals.

The Physical Basis of Long-Term Memory

[8] Psychologists agree that long-term memory involves more or less permanent changes in the structure of the brain. Most likely, the connections between neurons become altered in such a way that they form circuits that encode the information. As we saw in Chapter 5 ("Perception"), recent work with neural networks suggests that networks of simple elements that have properties similar to those of neurons can be taught to recognize stimuli or to connect the recognition of a stimulus with the production of a particular response. Learning in these networks is accomplished when the strength of the inhibitory or excitatory connections between the ele-

ments increases or decreases. Thus, learning in real circuits of neurons could be accomplished by changes in the synapses that connect them. For example, synapses could become larger or smaller, entirely new synapses could be established, or more transmitter substance could be produced and released by some synapses.

Let us consider some of the phenomena we have studied so far in this chapter. Short-term memory appears to consist of some sort of neural activity that provides a temporary representation of information that has just been perceived. As we saw, we can maintain a greater amount of information in short-term memory if it is meaningful to us—that is, if it relates to information that is already in long-term memory. Perhaps what this result really means is that short-term (working) memory actually consists of activated circuits of long-term memory. When you read a series of seven digits, you are not actually *learning* the numbers, because you already know them. Reading them might cause the neural circuits involved with seeing them (and hearing them, as well) to become activated and somehow temporarily linked together in order.

Let us take a more realistic—and perhaps more interesting—example. Read the following sentences.

> He rowed the boat to the dock, laid down the oars, and reached for the rope coiled on the floor behind him. He tossed the rope to his girlfriend, who was waiting for him. She held it fast while he climbed onto the boat's wooden seat and began to step onto the dock. Suddenly, the rotten wood gave way, and his foot went crashing down—through the seat and through the hull of the boat. He looked down at his leg, which projected through a splintered hole. Water began to fill the boat.

Now you have something in your short-term memory. I could ask you to repeat the story to me, and although the words would probably be somewhat different, your story would be the same as mine. You probably have some images representing the events. These images would not be precisely the same as mine, because we have had different experiences with boats, oars, and docks. Although I never stepped through the bottom of a boat, I once stepped through a rotten plank on a dock, and my image of the scene described above resembles my memory of having my foot stuck in the hole it had made in the wood. Obviously, the exact form of the images evoked by the words written above depend on the reader's existing long-term memories.

Suppose I ask you tomorrow to tell me about the story of the man in the rowboat. Chances are good that you will remember it; it will have entered your long-term memory. What will this memory involve? Will the experience of reading the story and thinking about it have established new circuits of neurons that encode each of the details? More likely, the memory for the episode will, for the most part, consist of connections between memories that already exist. Let us suppose that you remember the story as if it had happened to you. (Alternatively, you could remember the story from the point of view of the woman, who caught and held the rope and watched the man step through the bottom of the boat.) You have memories (firsthand or acquired from watching other people) of rowing boats, of throwing ropes, of stepping up onto things, of breaking through something supporting your weight, and so on. Perhaps remembering the episode is accomplished by linking these memories together in order and attaching to this linkage a label that corresponds to the context: an imaginary story you read about and thought about in this book on this occasion. As you will see in the next section, this account is not implausible. What psychologists have learned about remembering suggests that we do, indeed, base new memories on old ones. (In fact, we sometimes confuse the two later.) We also link items together; tricks for improving one's memory depend on that ability.

Of course, few of the experiences we have are simply rearrangements of familiar elements; most of them contain some entirely new information. Thus, besides linking together items that already exist in long-term memory, learning involves establishing some entirely new items. But as we have seen, if a situation contains a large number of novel, unfamiliar elements, we are not able to remember many of them.

Remembering

So far, I have described research and theorizing on the act of learning and the nature of long-term memory. But what about remembering—getting information *out* of long-term memory? Actually, we know less about remembering than we do about learning. What we do know can be summed up in two statements: *Remembering is automatic,* and *remembering is a creative process.*

Remembering and Recollecting. I just said that remembering is an automatic process. The word *automatic* means "acting by itself." But this definition implies that no special effort is involved. Thinking about examinations you may have taken—and the efforts you made to remember what you had studied—you may want to dispute that statement. Of course you are right; sometimes, we work very hard to try to remember something. What is automatic is the retrieval of information from memory in response to the appropriate stimulus; what is sometimes effortful is the attempt to come up with the thoughts (the internal stimuli) that cause the information to be retrieved.

Clearly, the retrieval of *implicit* memories is automatic: When the appropriate stimulus occurs, it automatically evokes the appropriate response. For example, when we open our car door, we do not have to think about how the latch works; our hand moves to the appropriate place, the fingers move into the proper position, and we make the necessary movements. But explicit memories, too, are retrieved automatically. Whisper your name to yourself. How did you manage to remember what your name is? How did you retrieve the information needed to move your lips in the proper sequence? Those questions simply cannot be answered by introspection. The information just "pops out" at us when the proper question is asked (or, more generally, when the appropriate stimulus is encountered).

Reading provides a particularly compelling example of the automatic nature of memory retrieval. When an experienced reader looks at a familiar word, the name occurs immediately, and so does the meaning. In fact, it is difficult to look at a word and *not* think of its name. Figure 7.17 contains a list of words that can be used to demonstrate a phenomenon known as the *Stroop effect* (Stroop, 1935; Dyer, 1973). Find them

and, as quickly as you can, say the names of the colors in which the words are printed; do not read the words themselves. (See *Figure 7.17.*)

Most people cannot completely ignore the words and simply name the colors; they find the tendency to think of the words and pronounce them is difficult to resist. The Stroop effect indicates that even when we try to suppress a well-practiced memory, it tends to be retrieved automatically when the appropriate stimulus occurs.

But what about the fact that some memories seem to be difficult to recall? For example, suppose that you have temporarily forgotten the name of someone you met recently. You might say to yourself, "He's Beth's husband. . . . It was a long name . . . rather unusual . . . more like a last name . . . Beth and . . . Beth and . . . Beth and Richmond! That's it, Richmond!" What is going on? You seem to be engaging in a behavior designed to produce a stimulus that will cause the required information to be retrieved. The information has not been learned very well, so the sight (or the thought) of the person is not sufficient to cause it to be recalled. You then try to think about other things that occurred during the episode in which you met him. You recall that the name was long, that it was unusual, and that is seemed more suitable as a surname—at least that much information came out automatically. Still, the name does not come to you. You remember that a mutual friend has said the couple's names to you, so you say "Beth and . . ." and that does it: The name "Richmond" suddenly pops out. This active search for stimuli that will evoke the appropriate memory has been called *recollection* (Baddeley, 1982).

Figure 7.17 The Stroop effect. Name the color of the words as quickly as you can; you will find it difficult to ignore what the words say.

blue blue blue green green yellow red yellow

yellow blue red green yellow yellow green

yellow yellow red yellow green blue yellow

red blue green green blue blue green green

yellow yellow blue yellow yellow red blue

yellow red blue red yellow blue red blue red

Reconstruction: Remembering as a Creative Process. Much of what we recall from long-term memory is not an accurate representation of what actually happened previously; it is a plausible account of what might have happened or even of what we think *should* have happened. An experiment by Bartlett (1932) called attention to this fact. He had his subjects read a story or essay or look at a picture; then he asked them on several later occasions to retell the prose passage or draw the picture. Each time, the subjects "remembered" the original a little differently. If the original story had contained peculiar and unexpected sequences of events, the subjects tended to retell it in a more coherent and sensible fashion, as if their memories had been revised to make the information accord more closely with their own conceptions of reality. Bartlett concluded that people remember only a few striking details of an experience and that during recall they *reconstruct* the missing portions in accordance with their own expectations. (These expectations would, of course, be contained in semantic memory.)

Many studies have confirmed Bartlett's conclusions and have extended his findings to related phenomena. An experiment by Spiro (1977, 1980) illustrated that people will remember even a rather simple story in different ways, according to their own conceptions of reality. Two groups of subjects read a story about an engaged couple in which the man was opposed to having children. In one version the woman was upset when she learned his opinion, because she wanted to have children. In the other version the woman also did not want to have children.

After reading the story, the subjects were asked to fill out some forms. While collecting the forms, the experimenter either said nothing more about the story or "casually mentioned" that the story was actually a true one and added one of two different endings: The couple got married and have been happy ever since, or the couple broke up and never saw each other again.

Two days, three weeks, or six weeks later, the subjects were asked to recall the story they had read. If at least three weeks had elapsed, the subjects who had heard an ending that contradicted the story tended to "remember" information that resolved the conflict. For example, if they had read that the woman was upset to learn that the man did not want children but were later told that the couple was happily married, the subjects were likely to "recall" something that would have resolved the conflict, such

as that the couple had decided to adopt a child rather than have one of their own. If subjects had read that the woman also did not want children but were later told that the couple broke up, then they were likely to "remember" that there was a difficulty with one set of parents. In contrast, the subjects who had heard an ending that was consistent with the story they had read did not remember any extra facts; they did not need them to make sense of the story. For example, if they had heard that the couple disagreed about having a child and later broke up, no new "facts" had to be added.

When asking subjects to recall details from the story, Spiro also asked them to indicate how confident they were about the accuracy of particular details. He found that subjects were most confident about details that had actually not occurred but had been added to make more sense of the story! Thus, a person's confidence in the accuracy of a particular memory is not necessarily a good indication of whether the event actually occurred.

Loftus and her colleagues have investigated the variables that affect the recall of details from episodic memory (Loftus, 1979). Their research indicates that the kinds of questions used to elicit the information can have a major effect on what the subjects remember. In courts of law, attorneys are not permitted to ask witnesses *leading questions*—questions that suggest what the answer should be. Loftus's research showed that even subtle changes in the question can affect people's recollections. For example, Loftus and Palmer (1974) showed subjects films of car accidents and asked them to estimate vehicles' speed when they *contacted, hit, bumped,*

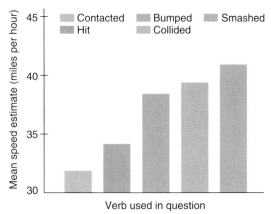

Figure 7.18 Mean estimated speed of the vehicles as recalled by the subjects in the study by Loftus and Palmer. (Based on data from Loftus, E.F., and Palmer, J.C. *Journal of Verbal Learning and Verbal Behavior,* 1974, 13, 585–589.)

Leading questions using words such as hit, bumped, or smashed often lead eyewitnesses to remember events differently. Eyewitness accounts are often inaccurate descriptions of what actually occurred.

collided, or *smashed* each other. As Figure 7.18 shows, the subjects' estimate of the vehicles' speed was directly related to the force of the impact suggested by the verb that appeared in the sentence. (See **Figure 7.18.**) In a similar experiment, when subjects were asked a week after viewing the film whether they saw any broken glass (there was none), the subjects in the *smashed* group were most likely to say "yes." Thus, a leading question that encouraged them to remember the vehicles going faster also encouraged them to remember that they saw nonexistent broken glass. The question appears to have modified the memory itself.

Another experiment indicates that even very subtle leading questions can affect people's recollections. Loftus and Zanni (1975) showed people short films of an accident involving several vehicles. Some subjects were asked, "Did you see a broken headlight?"; others were asked, "Did you see the broken headlight?" The particular question biased the subjects' responses: Although the film did not show a broken headlight, twice as many people who heard the article *the* said they remembered seeing one.

Experiments such as these have important implications for eyewitness testimony in courts of law. A judge can prevent an attorney from asking leading questions during a trial, but he or she cannot undo the effects of leading questions put to the witness during pretrial investigations.

A phenomenon first described by Colegrove (1899) suggests that events that produce strong emotional reactions can facilitate the storage of vivid episodic memories. He found that most of the people he questioned were able to describe in great detail what they were doing and what

was happening around them when they heard the news of the assassination of Abraham Lincoln. Brown and Kulik (1977) obtained the same results when they questioned people about important events during the twentieth century, such as the assassination of John F. Kennedy. They called the phenomenon **flashbulb memory,** because it was as if the emotional event firmly imprinted the details of the episode in people's memories.

Are flashbulb memories different from other types of episodic memory? Does a powerful emotion really cause the details of an episode to be recorded indelibly and accurately? Neisser (1982) suggests not. He describes a "flashbulb" memory of his own, which occurred when he learned that Pearl Harbor was bombed in December 1941. For many years he assumed that his memory was a faithful reflection of the events that he witnessed; but when he later thought about the episode in more detail, he discovered inconsistencies that proved that his memory was inaccurate. Once again, we see that the vividness of a memory is not a reliable indication of its accuracy.

Experiments like the ones I have cited in this section indicate that learning new information and recalling it later are not the passive processes implied by the terms *storage* and *retrieval;* we do not simply place an item of information in a filing cabinet and pick it up later. We organize and integrate information in terms of what we already know about life and have come to expect about particular experiences. Thus, when we recall the memory later, it is likely to contain information that was not part of the original experience. At first, this phenomenon may appear to be maladaptive, because it means that

Where were you when you heard the news of the Challenger explosion? An emotional event such as this one often produces a vivid memory that we remember all of our life.

eyewitness testimony cannot be regarded as infallible, even when the witness is trying to be truthful. However, it probably reflects the fact that information about an episode can be more efficiently stored by means of a few unique details. The portions of the episode that are common to other experiences, and hence resemble information already stored in long-term memory, need not be retained. If every detail of an experience had to be encoded uniquely in long-term memory, perhaps we would run out of storage space. Unfortunately, this process sometimes leads to instances of faulty remembering.

Memories can be used in creative, constructive ways to derive information that is not stored in a direct fashion. For example, if I ask you whether you know how many windows your house has, you probably will not know the answer. But you can probably imagine each room, count the number of windows in it, and keep a running total as you take a mental tour of the house. In cases like this, construction can lead to a useful result.

EVALUATING SCIENTIFIC ISSUES

Hypnosis and Criminal Investigation

9 In many criminal investigations—particularly those in which little or no physical evidence is available—the memory of witnesses becomes particularly important. Their ability to remember events and faces can determine the success or failure of the investigation—and of the subsequent prosecution, should a suspect be brought to trial. But memories of eyewitnesses are fallible, especially when the events in question are fast-paced, confusing, and frightening. It is not surprising that many criminal investigators have turned to hypnosis in an attempt to improve the recollection of crime witnesses.

The Technique of Hypnotic Memory Enhancement. Some police departments employ officers trained in hypnosis or hire professionals as consultants. If victims of crime or witnesses to crimes cannot supply the investigators with sufficient details to identify the criminal, they may be hypnotized to help them recollect facts that they are unable to recall. Several methods are used in this effort. The most common is to ask the witness to relax and to imagine himself or herself back at the scene of the crime, where he or she tries to see things as they were and describe all that happens. Almost always, the witness is told that hypnosis is a significant aid to memory and that he or she will become aware of information that was previously available only to the subconscious mind.

Sometimes, the hypnotist uses a method called the *television technique,* so named because of its resemblance to the methods used when broadcasting sporting events or events in the news. Witnesses are told to "zoom in" on details they have forgotten (such as the criminal's face or the license plates of the car involved in an accident) or to "freeze the frame" to examine fleeting details at their leisure (Reiser and Nielsen, 1980).

Police hypnotists have reported some successes with their techniques. One of the most famous was the capture and conviction of the kidnappers in the Chowchilla case (Kroger and Doucé, 1979). In July 1976 three masked men kidnapped a busload of children in Chowchilla, California, and transferred them to a subterranean chamber they had prepared in an abandoned quarry. Eventually, the bus driver and two of the older boys managed to dig their way out, and the children were rescued. The driver had seen the license plates on the two vans the criminals used to transport him and the children, but the most he could remember during the subsequent investigation was three numbers (out of seven) from one of them.

Under hypnosis the bus driver suddenly remembered the two license plate numbers, which the police investigated. It turned out that one of the numbers was completely wrong, but the other one was correct except for one digit. The police found the kidnappers, who were arrested, convicted, and sentenced to life imprisonment.

How Can Hypnosis Assist Memory?

Some advocates of hypnotic memory enhancement have made outrageous claims about its efficacy. But what can hypnosis actually do? First of all, it cannot possibly help people remember events that they did not witness; it can only help people recollect information that they have already learned and are having trouble recalling. In other words, hypnosis only helps if the information has been perceived and has left a trace in the brain. It cannot enhance memories themselves; it can only enhance their *recollection*. The bus driver in the Chowchilla case was able to remember three more numbers from one of the license plates only because he had actually seen the plates—and had, in fact, tried to memorize them at the time.

As we shall see in Chapter 8, hypnosis does not enable a person to do anything that he or she could not do, if properly motivated, when *not* hypnotized. That is, hypnosis does not give a person any special powers or abilities that he or she does not already possess. The same thing is true for recalling memories. In fact, some investigators have developed methods for improving recall of memories that do not involve hypnosis but are based on the research findings of cognitive psychologists interested in memory. These

methods appear to work just as well as hypnosis. The *guided memory* method of Malpass and Devine (1981) instructs witnesses to visualize the original environmental setting in which the events occurred and to try to imagine their mood, thoughts, and feelings at the time. Such a reconstruction often provides cues that help the witnesses recall details they thought they had forgotten. The *cognitive interview* of Geiselman et al. (1984) also encourages a re-creation of the original environment and, in addition, has the witness try to describe the episode from different perspectives.

The Dangers of Hypnotic Memory Enhancement. Even if hypnosis does not endow someone with special powers, perhaps it should be used routinely just in case it helps a witness to remember some unreported information. However, as Orne et al. (1988) point out, hypnosis does more than help people recollect memories; it can modify existing memories, increase people's confidence in their recollections, and even implant false memories. In one case a hypnotist interviewing a victim who had been raped by a masked man asked her to mentally "take off" his mask and report what his face looked like. She did, and the authorities even attempted to convict a man on the basis of her "eyewitness identification" (Orne et al., 1988). Obviously, since the victim never saw the man's face, her hypnotic visualization of it was completely imaginary.

Most witnesses to a crime want very much to help the police in their investigation. The eagerness of the witness (who may even be the victim of the crime), along with a belief in the mythical powers of hypnosis and the expertise of the hypnotist, sometimes leads the witness to "see" details that were never present at the scene of the crime. In one case, after being hypnotized, a witness to a murder identified a person as the murderer. However, testimony later showed that the witness was 270 feet away. Under the lighting conditions present at the time, this witness could not possibly have seen the murderer's face beyond 25 feet (*People v. Kempinski,* 1980).

Laurence and Perry (1983) demonstrated that through suggestion hypnosis can induce false memories that the subjects later sincerely come to believe. They hypnotized subjects and asked whether they had been awakened by some loud noises on a particular night. (They first ascertained that, in fact, the subjects had not been awakened then.) Most of the subjects reported that yes, they had heard some loud noises. When the subjects were interviewed by another experimenter later, in a nonhypnotized condition, 48 percent said that they had heard some loud noises on the night in question. Even after the experimenter told these subjects that the hypnotist had suggested that the noises had occurred, almost half of them still insisted that the noises had occurred. One said, "I'm pretty certain I heard them. As a matter of fact, I'm pretty damned certain. I'm positive I heard these noises" (Laurence and Perry, 1983, p. 524).

The results of this and other studies (Laurence and Perry, 1988) strongly suggest that the testimony of people who have been hypnotized by an investigator to "help refresh their memory" is not necessarily trustworthy. Fuzzy details become clear memories of events, and the witnesses become convinced that these events actually occurred. As we saw in the previous section of this chapter, research on eyewitness testimony has shown that leading questions can affect the memories of people who are not hypnotized. Hypnosis magnifies this effect; under hypnosis people are especially suggestible, and subtle hints by the examiner can inadvertently change the way they recollect an episode.

Because of some characteristics of human nature (which will be explored in more detail in Chapter 17), the eyewitness testimony of a person who appears to sincerely believe what he or she is saying is extremely compelling. Thus, it has a strong effect on a jury. If, in addition, the person's testimony is full of precise details about the episode, the effects on a jury are even more powerful. Because an interview under hypnosis tends to fill in missing details (often with events that never really happened) and increases the witness's confidence in what he or she remembers, the potential dangers of permitting a previously hypnotized witness to testify before a jury should be obvious.

What Should We Conclude? The Council on Scientific Affairs of the American Medical Association (1985) concludes that although hypnosis may be useful in providing leads to guide further investigation, the dangers of contaminating the recollection of witnesses are very real. In fact, most courts in North America do not permit witnesses to testify once they have been hypnotized. Thus, if the police hypnotize a witness, they run the risk of rendering the person's testimony inadmissible. Even if the only goal of hypnosis is to provide clues, the police must be wary of the results of the interview. If they

place too much credence in the statements of a hypnotized witness, they may end up following false leads and neglecting more productive ones. They may even be deliberately misled by a witness who stands to gain by doing so. Contrary to popular belief, there is no way to be sure that a person is hypnotized and not merely pretending to be; and even genuinely hypnotized people can lie. Justice would probably best be served if, instead of interviewing people under hypnosis, the police pursued methods based on scientific research on the memory process. ∎

INTERIM SUMMARY

Long-Term Memory

Long-term memory appears to consist of physical changes in the brain—probably within the sensory and motor association cortexes. Data from head injuries provide evidence that long-term and short-term memory are physiologically different: Short-term memories probably involve neural activity (which can be prolonged by rehearsal), whereas long-term memories probably involve permanent structural changes.

Craik and Lockhart's model of memory points out the importance of elaboration in learning. Maintenance rehearsal (simple rote repetition) is usually less effective than elaborative rehearsal, which involves deeper processing. These theorists assert that long-term memory is a by-product of the perceptual process. The level of processing (performed by a "central processor") is controlled by changes in attention. If information is analyzed at a superficial level, then superficial memories will be formed, and they will enter episodic memory. If information is analyzed at a deep level, it will enter semantic memory, where it will be connected with other information that we already know. Having read a description of one of their experiments, you can probably remember the end of the sentence "The great bird swooped down and carried off the struggling _____."

Critics point out that shallow processing sometimes produces very durable memories, and anyway, the distinction between "shallow" and "deep" has proved to be impossible to define explicitly. However, they agree that the kind of thinking that takes place when information is received plays an important role in the kind of learning that takes place.

Episodic and semantic memory refer to different degrees of specificity in long-term memories: We can remember the time and place we learned an episodic memory but not a semantic memory. The study by Sachs (with the "Galileo" sentences) provided behavioral evidence in support of this distinction. Most psychologists believe that the distinction is important but do not believe that episodic and semantic memories are parts of different systems.

Another distinction—between explicit and implicit memory—has received much attention recently. Psychologists have begun investigating the nature of automatic, nonverbal memories as well as those that we are able to talk about. Anterograde amnesia appears to be a deficit of explicit memory, without major impairment of implicit memory. People with anterograde amnesia cannot talk about events that took place after their brain damage occurred, but they can learn to perform many tasks that do not require verbal rules, such as recognizing fragmentary pictures. The behavior of laboratory animals also demonstrates this distinction.

If a rat's hippocampus has been destroyed, the animal cannot remember which arm of a maze it has just entered to eat a piece of food. The important feature appears to be the ability to use the present *context* to organize information in memory.

Most long-term memories contain mixtures of new and old information, tied together by a thread that provides continuity. The little story about the rowboat provided an illustration of this process.

Remembering is an automatic process, although we may sometimes work hard at generating thoughts that will help this process along. Recalling a memory of a complex event does not simply involve replaying a tape that has been recorded in our brain; it entails a process of reconstruction that uses old information. Sometimes, the reconstruction introduces new "facts" that we perceive as memories of what we previously perceived. This reconstructive process undoubtedly makes more efficient use of the resources we have available for storage of long-term memories. ∎

APPLICATION

Mnemonic Systems

Some things are exceedingly easy to remember. Suppose you are walking down the street and see someone fall from the roof of a building. You will not have to rehearse this information verbally to remember it; you see it so vividly that the scene remains with you always. Similarly, you can probably remember the missing word in the sentence "The old man hobbled across the room and picked up the valuable _____." But often we must remember information that does not fit in such a tidy package. When the information is hard to learn, we usually employ a special word to identify the process: *memorization.*

When we can imagine information vividly and concretely, and when it fits into the context of what we already know, it is easy to remember later. People have known this fact for millennia and have devised systems for remembering things in order to take advantage of it. All **mnemonic systems** (from the Greek *mneme,* meaning "memory") make use of information already stored in long-term memory to make memorization an easier task.

Mnemonic systems do not simplify information; in fact, they make it more elaborate. *More* information is stored, not less. However, the additional information makes the material easier to recall. Furthermore, mnemonic systems organize new information into a cohesive whole, so that retrieval of part of the information ensures retrieval of the rest of it. These facts suggest that the ease or difficulty with which we learn new information depends not on *how much* we must learn but on *how well it fits with what we already know.* The better it fits, the easier it is to retrieve.

Method of Loci.   In Greece before the sixth century B.C. few people knew how to write, and those who did had to use cumbersome clay tablets. Consequently, oratory skills and memory for long epic poems (running for several hours) were highly prized, and some people earned a living by using them. Because people could not carry around several hundred pounds of clay tablets, they had to keep important information in their heads. To do so, the Greeks devised the method of loci. (The word *locus* means "place"; the plural is *loci,* pronounced "LO sigh.")

To use the **method of loci,** would-be mnemonists (memory artists) had to memorize the inside of a building. In Greece they would wander through public buildings, stopping to study and memorize various locations and arranging them in order, usually starting with the door of the building. After memorizing the locations, they could make the tour mentally, just as you could make a mental tour of your house to count the windows. To learn a list of words, they would visualize each word in a particular location in the memorized building and picture the association as vividly as possible. For example, for the word *love* they might imagine an embracing couple leaning against a particular column in a hall of the building. To recall the list, they would imagine each of the locations in sequence, "see" the word, and say it. To store a speech, they would group the words into concepts and place a "note" for each concept at a particular location in the sequence.

Mnemonists could use a single building as a "memory temple" to store many different sequences. Modern psychologists still cannot explain why sequences from different speeches or poems did not become confused with each other.

Narrative Stories. Another useful aid to memory is to organize information into a narrative. Bower and Clark (1969) showed that even inexperienced subjects can use this method. The investigators asked subjects to try to learn twelve lists of ten concrete nouns each. They gave some of the subjects the following advice:

A good way to learn the list of items is to make up a story relating the items to one another. Specifically, start with the first item and put it in a setting which will allow other items to be added to it. Then, add the other items to the story in the same order as the items appear. Make each story meaningful to yourself. Then, when you are asked to recall the items, you can simply go through your story and pull out the proper items in their correct order. (Bower and Clark, 1969, p. 181)

A typical narrative, described by one of the subjects, was as follows (list words are italicized): "A *lumberjack dart*ed out of the forest, *skate*d around a *hedge* past a *colony* of *ducks*. He tripped on some *furniture*, tearing his *stocking* while hastening to the *pillow* where his *mistress* lay."

Control subjects were merely asked to learn the lists and were given the same amount of time as the "narrative" subjects to study them. Both groups could remember a particular list equally well immediately afterward. However, when all the lists had been learned, recall of all 120 words was far superior in the group that had constructed narrative stories.

Rhythm and Rhyme. Information is often easier to remember when it is organized by rhythm and rhyme (or both). For example, when most people learn the alphabet, they do so to the tune of a little song. Because of this, when they recite the alphabet they say: A, B, C, D, E, F, G (pause), H, I, J, K (now go twice as fast), L-M-N-O-P (pause) . . . and so on. Somehow, the structure of the rhythm and the melody of a song facilitate the learning of a list of verbal material.

Sometimes, information can be cast into the form of a poem, which people find easy to remember. Perhaps you learned a rhyme similar to the following one: "I before E except after C, or when sounded as A, as in neighbor or weigh." And if you need to remember how many days there in December, do you say to yourself, "Thirty days have September, April, June, and November . . ."?

Another use of rhythm and rhyme is to keep the initial letters of a list of words to be remembered and replace them with words that will fit into a verse. For example, to keep track of the order of the names of the twelve cranial nerves, students learn, "On old Olympus' towering tops, a Finn and German viewed some hops" (with the intention of making beer, I suppose). The initial letters stand for *olfactory, optic, occulomotor, trochlear, trigeminal, abducens, facial, auditory, glossopharyngeal, vagus, spinal accessory, hypoglossal.* If the students need help remembering the order of the three nerves that begin with the letter O, they can remember that the second letters (L, P, and C) spell out "Lovers prefer caresses."

Obviously, mnemonic systems have their limitations. They are useful for memorizing information that can be reduced to a list of words, but not all information can easily be converted to such a form. For example, if you were preparing to take an examination on the information in this chapter, figuring out how to encode it into lists would probably take you more time than studying and learning it by more traditional methods, such as those suggested in the study guide.

KEY TERMS AND CONCEPTS

An Overview

sensory memory *(199)*
short-term memory *(199)*
long-term memory *(199)*

Sensory Memory

iconic memory *(200)*
echoic memory *(201)*

Short-Term/Working Memory

working memory *(203)*
chunking *(203)*
proactive inhibition *(204)*
release from proactive inhibition *(204)*
phonological short-term memory *(205)*
subvocal articulation *(205)*
conduction aphasia *(206)*

Long-Term Memory

consolidation *(211)*
retrograde amnesia *(212)*
maintenance rehearsal *(212)*
elaborative rehearsal *(212)*
shallow processing *(214)*
deep processing *(214)*
episodic memory *(215)*
semantic memory *(215)*
explicit memory *(216)*
implicit memory *(216)*
anterograde amnesia *(218)*
hippocampus *(220)*
flashbulb memory *(225)*
mnemonic system *(229)*
method of loci *(229)*

SUGGESTIONS FOR FURTHER READING

Luria, A.R. *The Mind of a Mnemonist.* New York: Basic Books, 1968.

Given the importance of learning and forgetting in almost everyone's life, it is not surprising that many popular books have been written about human memory. This book is the great Russian neurologist's account of a man with an extraordinary memory.

Neisser, U. *Memory Observed: Remembering in Natural Contexts.* San Francisco: W.H. Freeman, 1982.

This book consists of studies about remembering in natural contexts, rather than arbitrary ones contrived in the laboratory.

Loftus, E.F. *Memory.* Reading, Mass.: Addison-Wesley, 1980.
Wells, G.L., and Loftus, E.F. *Eyewitness Testimony: Psychological Perspectives.* Cambridge, England: Cambridge University Press, 1984.

The first book was written for the general reader and discusses the tricks our memories can play on us when we try to remember what we have seen. The second book contains chapters written by experts on topics related to eyewitness testimony, such as people's memory for faces, their confidence in their memories, and hypnotically refreshed testimony.

Ashcraft, M.H. *Human Memory and Cognition.* Glenview, Ill.: Scott, Foresman, 1989.
Baddeley, A. *Human Memory.* Boston: Allyn and Bacon, 1990.

Both books are interesting and well written. The authors know their subjects well and engage the reader in interesting discussions.

Pettinati, H.M. *Hypnosis and Memory.* New York: Guilford Press, 1988.

The book edited by Pettinati contains chapters written by experts on various topics related to the effects of hypnosis on memory.

Cermak, L.S. *Improving Your Memory.* New York: W.W. Norton, 1975.

If you are interested in improving your own memory, there are dozens of books to choose from. Cermak's is one of the best.

8
CONSCIOUSNESS

Henri Matisse, *Odalisque à la Culotte Rouge*
GIRAUDON/Art Resource, N.Y. © 1992 Succession H. Matisse/ARS, N.Y.

LEARNING OBJECTIVES

When you finish this chapter, you should be able to:

1. Define *consciousness*, and explain how it is a social behavior.
2. Describe attention, discuss its importance, and describe research on the factors that affect auditory and visual attention.
3. Explain the significance of the symptoms of isolation aphasia, visual agnosia, and the split-brain syndrome to our understanding of consciousness.
4. Outline the history of hypnosis, and describe its induction and its characteristics.
5. Describe and evaluate current theories of hypnosis, discuss people's susceptibility to hypnosis, and describe its uses and limitations.
6. Describe and evaluate evidence that hypnosis can induce people to perform antisocial acts, and describe beneficial uses of hypnosis.
7. Name and describe the stages of sleep, and indicate how they are measured.
8. Describe the universal nature of sleep, and discuss research on sleep deprivation to determine whether sleep is a necessary period of repair.
9. Explain how sleep is a different state of consciousness, and describe dreams and their possible symbolism.
10. Discuss the effects of REM sleep deprivation and some disorders associated with REM sleep.

Laverne J. had brought her grandfather to see Dr. M., a neuropsychologist. Mr. J.'s stroke had left him almost completely blind; all he could see was a tiny spot in the middle of his visual field. Dr. M. had learned about his condition from his neurologist and had asked him to come to his laboratory so that he could do some tests for his research project.

Dr. M. welcomed his guests into his laboratory, which was equipped with a large video monitor screen, a computer, and an apparatus for testing visual fields.

"What are you going to do with my grandfather?" asked Laverne. "The permission form said that you wanted to test his vision—but he's almost completely blind."

"Yes, I know," said Dr. M., "but from the description his neurologist gave me, I think that he may have a condition that I have been studying. That's why I asked him to come in."

Dr. M. helped Mr. J. find a chair and sit down. Mr. J., who walked with the aid of a cane, gave it to his granddaughter to hold for him. "May I borrow that?" asked Dr. M. Laverne nodded and handed it to him. "The phenomenon I'm studying is called blindsight," he said. "Let me see if I can show you what it is."

"Mr. J., please look straight ahead. Keep looking that way, and don't move your eyes or turn your head. I know that you can see a little bit straight ahead of you, and I don't want you to use that piece of vision for what I'm going to ask you to do. Fine. Now, I'd like you to reach out with your right hand and point to what I'm holding."

"But I don't see anything—I'm blind!" said Mr. J., obviously exasperated.

"I know, but please try, anyway."

Mr. J. shrugged his shoulders and pointed. He looked startled when his finger encountered the end of the cane, which Dr. M. was pointing toward him.

"Gramps, how did you do that?" asked Laverne, amazed. "I thought you were blind."

"I am!" he said, emphatically. "It was just luck."

"Let's try it just a couple more times, Mr. J.," said Dr. M. "Keep looking straight ahead. Fine." He reversed the cane, so that the handle was pointing toward Mr. J. "Now I'd like you to grab hold of the cane."

Mr. J. reached out with an open hand and grabbed hold of the cane.

"Good. Now put your hand down, please." He rotated the cane 90 degrees, so that the handle was oriented vertically. "Now reach for it again."

Mr. J. did so. As his arm came up, he turned his wrist so that his hand matched the orientation of the handle, which he grabbed hold of again.

"Good. Thank you, you can put your hand down." Dr. M. turned to Laverne. "I'd like to test your grandfather now, but I'll be glad to talk with you later."

After the formal test session was over, Dr. M. met with Laverne. "Let me tell you a little bit about blindsight. Your grandfather's stroke damaged the visual cortex of the brain and some of the nerve fibers that bring information to it from the eyes. He has lost almost all of what we could call the mammalian visual system—the visual system of the brain that began evolving when mammals split off from their ancestors. That system is primarily responsible for our visual processes. But the brain that primitive mammals inherited from their ancestors already had a visual system—the one found in amphibians and reptiles. That system still exists in our brain today. Mainly, it helps us detect movements that occur off to the side. It directs our attention to things that we're not looking at but that might be important to us. Your grandfather's stroke did not damage his primitive visual system. That system still works, as you saw. Although it can only detect simple shapes that are clearly isolated from their background, it can direct his hand movements toward objects in his blind field."

Laverne nodded. "Yes, I can understand that, but why did gramps say that he couldn't see the cane, when he obviously could?"

"Now you're getting to the interesting part. When we say that we can *see* something, we mean that we are conscious of having perceived it." Laverne nodded. "Research from the past few years—with people like your grandfather, whose brains have been damaged in some way—indicates that consciousness is a property of particular parts of the brain, not of the brain as a whole. We're not sure just what parts they are, or exactly how they work, but they seem to be related to our ability to communicate—with others and with ourselves. The primitive visual system evolved long before our ancestors had self-awareness, before the brain functions necessary for consciousness evolved. Therefore, the primitive visual system is not connected with the systems responsible for consciousness; only the new mammalian visual system is. When we see something with the newer system, we are aware of what we see. But when your grandfather's remaining visual system—the primitive one—detects something, he is not conscious of seeing anything, because that system is not connected with those responsible for awareness."

"I think I understand," said Laverne. She paused, looking reflective. "I've never thought of consciousness as something that you could study scientifically. Do you think your research can find out how it works?"

"Well, that will probably take a long time, but I like to think my research takes us a few steps in that direction."

This chapter explores the nature of human self-awareness: knowledge of our own existence, behavior, perceptions, and thoughts. This is the most common, and probably the most important, meaning of consciousness. Why are we conscious? How do we direct our consciousness from one event to another, paying attention to some stimuli and ignoring others? What is known about the brain functions responsible for consciousness? What is hypnosis—can another person really take control of our own thoughts and behavior? Why do we regularly undergo the profound alteration in consciousness called sleep? We do not yet have all the answers to these questions, but we have made much progress.

CONSCIOUSNESS AS A SOCIAL BEHAVIOR

1 Why are we aware of ourselves? What purpose is served by our ability to realize that we exist, that events occur, that we are doing things, and that we have memories? If we view consciousness as an adaptive trait of the human species, the most likely explanation lies in its relation to communication. Because of our ability to communicate, we are aware of ourselves. Thus, consciousness is primarily a social phenomenon.

Consciousness is a private experience: Each person can directly experience only his or her own consciousness. However, we all realize that other people are conscious, too, because they can *tell* us they are. In fact, the sole criterion for consciousness is verbal acknowledgment. For example, suppose that you see a friend performing some peculiar mannerism. You say, "Do you realize what you're doing?" Your friend says, "No, what?" You point out the behavior, and she says, "Oh, I wasn't aware of that." Assuming that your friend was not lying, you would conclude that she was, in fact, not conscious of performing the behavior. You would trust the verbal report. Indeed, the only way to assess someone's consciousness is to ask the person. Verbal behavior *defines* consciousness.

Language is a very useful social behavior. For example, it provides a means of enlisting help from other people. To ask another person to perform a particular action requires two conditions. First, we must be able to recognize our needs and express them verbally; that is, we must have **verbal access** to them. If we cannot recognize and talk about our needs, we cannot request assistance. Second, the behavior that we request from the other person must be under **verbal control;** that is, words must be capable of causing the person addressed to perform the behavior. If a verbal request cannot

When do we become aware of our own existence?

elicit the behavior (assuming the person is already willing to cooperate), the request is useless.

The concepts of verbal access and verbal control are important and require some elaboration. Many events occur in our bodies to which we have no *verbal access*. For example, we cannot tell another person whether our parathyroid gland is secreting its hormones. However, we do have verbal access to the physiological events that occur when we go for a prolonged time without food or water; we can tell someone else that we are hungry or thirsty. The selective advantage to having verbal access to the physiological conditions of hunger and thirst is that we can ask other people for help in obtaining food or water.

Verbal control refers to the effect of words on the behavior of other people. A person raised completely apart from other people would not have learned to talk, because there would have been no reason to do so; speech would have had no effect on his or her environment. Speech is useful to us because it can elicit behaviors from other people. When we can elicit specific behaviors from other people by the sounds we make or the marks we put on a piece of paper, the behaviors are said to be under verbal control. Consciousness, then, can be seen as a consequence of our ability to communicate—internally, with ourselves, and externally, with others. We are conscious of those events we can talk about, including our own feelings and memories.

Although we are conscious because of our ability to communicate, not all instances of communication involve consciousness. For example, when baby mice become cold, they automatically emit an ultrasonic cry that elicits behavior from their mother: The mother finds them and brings them back to the nest, where they can get warm again (Noirot, 1972). This kind of communication is automatic and apparently unlearned; we need not assume that the baby mice are conscious of the cold or that the mother is conscious of being called.

Although the principal benefit of communication is its capacity to affect the behavior of other people, it has other advantages as well. Through communication, one person's experience can be shared with others. We are not limited to learning about things that we have directly observed; we can profit from what other people have learned by listening to them speak or by reading what they have written. This ability allowed human culture to evolve.

While members of all species can profit from the innovations introduced by genetic mutations of their ancestors, we humans can also profit from the discoveries made by our ancestors and passed down to us through writing or through oral traditions. Each generation can start where the previous one left off.

In addition, we can communicate with ourselves. This capacity is another important consequence of having verbal access to our perceptions and feelings and verbal control over our behavior. We can make plans in words, think about the consequences of these plans in words, and use words to produce behaviors—all without actually *saying* the words but by thinking them. As we saw in Chapter 7, thinking in words appears to involve subvocal articulation. Thus, the brain mechanisms that permit us to understand words and produce speech are the same ones we use to think in words. In support of this hypothesis, investigators have noted that deaf people who use sign language to communicate with each other often make small movements with their hands when they are thinking to themselves, just as those of us who can hear and speak sometimes talk to ourselves under our breath. Apparently, we exercise our expressive language mechanisms, whatever they are, when we think.

Although consciousness may be synonymous with activity of the verbal mechanisms of the brain, we need not conclude that only humans are conscious. The evolutionary process is incremental: New traits and abilities build upon ones that already exist. As we just saw, some forms of communication among animals are automatic and probably do not involve consciousness. However, others can be learned, just as we learn our own language. Certainly, your dog can learn to communicate with you. The fact that it can learn to tell you when it wants to eat, go for a walk, or play suggests that it may be conscious, also. By comparison, we have much more verbal access to our needs and perceptions than dogs have, which means that our consciousness is better developed. But if the ability to communicate evolved, then we must conclude that consciousness evolved along with it and that other animals possess varying amounts of consciousness.

In some cases verbal activity is not synonymous with consciousness. As we will soon see, some people whose brains have been injured show no comprehension of speech but repeat everything that is said to them, rather like a parrot. Because their speech does not express their awareness of events in their memory or in the environment, we can regard it as a nonconscious phenomenon.

INTERIM SUMMARY

Consciousness as a Social Behavior

Consciousness, as it is defined here, can be viewed as being synonymous with verbal processes. Its physiological basis is the activity of language mechanisms of the brain. The private use of language (thinking to oneself) is clearly conscious. Private nonverbal processes are conscious if we can describe them—that is, if their activities are available to the neural mechanisms of language. In the same way, we are conscious of *external* events only if we can think (and verbalize) about them. *Verbal access* is the ability to describe, in words, private events such as perceptions, feelings, and plans. *Verbal control* is the capacity of verbal stimuli to elicit behaviors from other people.

This view of human self-awareness is not the only one. But it seems to be the most useful one, for it helps present a unified picture of a variety of phenomena related to consciousness. ∎

ATTENTION

2 We do not become conscious of all the stimuli detected by our sensory organs. For example, if an angler is watching a large trout circling underneath an artificial fly he has gently cast on the water, he probably will not notice the chirping of birds in the woods behind him or the temperature of the water surrounding his legs or the floating twigs drifting by with the current. His attention is completely devoted to the behavior of the fish, and he is poised ready to respond with the appropriate movements of his fly rod if the fish takes the bait. The selective process that controls our awareness of events in the environment is called **attention.**

As we saw in Chapter 7, sensory memory receives more information than can be transferred into short-term (working) memory. For example, the experiment by Sperling (1960) found that although people could remember only about four or five of the nine letters he flashed on the screen if they tried to remember them all, they could *direct their attention* to any of the three lines of letters contained in sensory mem-

ory and identify them with perfect accuracy. The topic of Chapter 7 was memory; in that chapter I discussed the nature of sensory memory and the fate of information that entered short-term memory. In this chapter I will discuss the nature of the process of attention and the fate of information that *does not* enter short-term memory.

Attention refers to our ability to gain verbal access to stimuli currently present. Thus, the process of attention determines which events we become conscious of. Attention may be controlled automatically, as when a very intense stimulus (such as a loud sound) captures our attention. It may be controlled by instructions ("Pay attention to that one over there!"). Or it may be controlled by the demands of the particular task we are performing. (For example, when we are driving a car, we pay special attention to other cars, pedestrians, road signs, and so on.) Our attentional mechanisms serve to enhance our responsiveness to certain stimuli and to tune out irrelevant information.

Attention plays a very important role in memory. By exerting control over the information that reaches short-term memory, it determines what information ultimately becomes stored in explicit long-term memory. (As you will recall, *explicit memory* is the portion of long-term memory that we can talk about—that we can become conscious of.) But the storage of information in *implicit memory* does not require conscious attention; this fact indicates that not all the information we do not pay attention to is lost.

Auditory Information

The first experiments that investigated the nature of attention took advantage of the fact that we have two ears. Cherry (1953) devised a test of selective attention called **dichotic listening** (*dichotic* means "divided into two parts"). He placed headphones on his subjects and presented recordings of different spoken messages to each ear. He asked the subjects to **shadow** the message presented to one ear; shadowing ensured that they would pay attention to the message—to continuously repeat what the voice was saying. (See *Figure 8.1.*)

The subjects were able to shadow the message, but they repeated it in a rather monotonous voice, probably because of the great demands this task places on working memory. Shadowing involves listening to the sounds in one ear, recognizing them as words, and re-

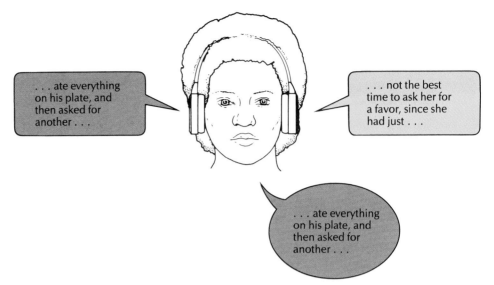

Figure 8.1 "Shadowing" a message presented dichotically by means of headphones.

membering them while repeating words that were heard a few seconds ago. These activities appear to keep the verbal system so busy that it can no longer also exert control over inflections in tone. The subjects generally do not realize how monotonous they sound; apparently, they are able to pay little attention to the sounds of their own voices.

What happened to the information that entered the unattended ear? In general, it appeared to be lost. When questioned about what that ear had heard, subjects responded that they had heard something, but they could not say what it was. Even if the voice presented to the unshadowed ear began to talk in a foreign language, they did not notice the change.

These results might suggest that a channel of sensory input (in this case, one ear) can simply be turned off. Perhaps neurons in the auditory system that detect sound from the unattended ear are inhibited so that they cannot respond to sounds presented to that ear. However, other data show that selective attention is not achieved by simply closing a sensory channel; some information, by its very nature, can break through into consciousness. For example, if the subject's name is presented to the unattended ear, he or she will very likely hear it and remember it later (Moray, 1959). Or if the message presented to the unattended ear contains sexually explicit words, subjects tend to notice them immediately (Nielsen and Sarason, 1981).

The fact that some kinds of information presented to the unattended ear, such as our name or particularly interesting words, can automatically grab our attention indicates that even unattended information undergoes some verbal anal-

ysis. If the unattended information is "filtered out" at some level, this filtration must not occur until *after* the sounds are identified as words.

Several studies have shown that information presented to the unattended ear can affect our behavior, if not our consciousness. To put it another way, the information can produce implicit memories. Von Wright, Anderson, and Stenman (1975) showed that words previously presented along with an unpleasant electrical shock would produce an emotional reaction when the words were presented to the unattended ear. Even when the subject was not attending to the voice in a verbal sense, the information produced a nonverbal response—an emotional reaction that had previously been classically conditioned to a particular word. Thus, the unattended information could produce a nonverbal implicit memory.

McKay (1973) showed that information presented to the unattended ear can influence verbal processing even when the information is not consciously noticed. In the attended ear subjects heard sentences like the following: *They threw stones toward the bank yesterday*. While this sentence was being presented, the subjects heard the word *river* or *money* in the unattended ear. Later, the subjects were asked which of the following sentences they had heard: *They threw stones toward the side of the river yesterday* or *They threw stones toward the savings and loan association yesterday*. Of course, the subjects had heard neither of these sentences. But as Sachs has shown (Chapter 7), people quickly forget the particular words a sentence contains, although they do remember its meaning much longer. McKay found that the subjects' choices were determined by whether the word *river* or *money* was presented to the unattended ear. They did not specifically remember hearing the words presented to the unattended ear, but obviously these words had affected their perception of the meaning of the word *bank*.

Besides being able to notice and remember some characteristics of information received by the unattended sensory channel, we are able to store information temporarily as it comes in. No doubt you have had the following sort of experience. You are intently reading or thinking about something, when you become aware that someone has asked you a question. You look up and say, "What?" but then answer the question before the other person has had a chance to repeat it. You first became aware that you had just been asked a question, but you did not know what had been asked. However, when you thought for a moment, you remembered what the question was—you heard it again in your mind's ear, so to speak. The information, held in temporary storage, was made accessible to your verbal system.

Treisman (1960) showed that people can follow a message that is being shadowed even if it switches from one ear to the other. Suppose a subject is shadowing a message presented to the left ear, while the message to the right ear is unshadowed. (See *Figure 8.2.*) In the example given in Figure 8.2, the subject will probably say *crept out of the swamp* and not *crept out of flowers*. Apparently, the switch occurs when the message begins to make no sense. However, by the time the subject realizes that *crept out of flowers* makes no sense, the rest of the message, *the swamp,* has already been presented to the right ear. Because the subject is able to continue the message without missing any words, he or she must be able to retrieve some

This stock exchange broker must keep track of several different conversations and selectively attend to each of them, one after the other.

words from memory. Thus, even though the unshadowed message cannot be remembered later, it produces some trace that can be retrieved if attention is directed to it soon after the words are presented.

The phenomenon of selective attention to auditory messages has practical significance outside the laboratory. For example, sometimes we have to sort out one message from several others without the benefit of such a distinct cue; we seldom hear one voice in one ear and another voice in the other. We might be trying to converse with one person while we are in a room with several other people who are carrying on their own conversations. Even in a situation like the one shown in Figure 8.3, we can usually sort out one voice from another—an example of the *cocktail-party phenomenon.* (See *Figure 8.3.*) In this case we are trying to listen to the person opposite us and to ignore the cross conversation of the people to our left and right. Our ears receive a jumble of sounds, but we are able to pick out the ones we want, stringing them together into a meaningful message and forgetting the rest. This task takes some effort; following one person's conversation in such circumstances is more difficult when what he or she is saying is not very interesting.

Figure 8.2 Switching from one ear to the other while shadowing a dichotically presented message.

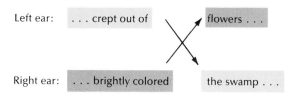

Figure 8.3 The cocktail-party phenomenon. Two conversations can be carried on simultaneously.

If we overhear a few words of another conversation that seems more interesting, it is hard to strain out the cross conversation.

Visual Information

More recent experiments have studied the nature of visual attention. These experiments have shown that we can successfully attend to the *nature* of the information (revealed by its physical form) or to the *location* of the information.

Let us consider first attention to particular locations. Sperling's studies on iconic memory were probably the first to demonstrate the role of attention in selectively transferring visual information into verbal short-term memory (or, for our purposes, into consciousness). Other psychologists have studied this phenomenon in more detail. For example, Posner, Snyder, and Davidson (1980) had subjects watch a computer-controlled video display screen. A small mark in the center of the screen served as a fixation point for the subjects' gaze. They were shown a warning stimulus near the fixation point followed by a target stimulus—a letter displayed to the left or the right of the fixation point. The warning stimulus consisted of either an arrow pointing right or left or simply a plus sign. The arrows served as cues to the subjects to expect the letter to occur either to the right or to the left. The plus sign served as a neutral stimulus, containing no spatial information. The subjects' task was to press a button as soon as they detected the letter.

Eighty percent of the time the arrow accurately pointed toward the location in which the letter would be presented. However, 20 percent of the time the arrow pointed *away from* the location in which it would occur. The results clearly indicated that advance warning had an effect on the subjects' response times: When they were correctly informed of the location of the letter, they responded faster; and when they were incorrectly informed, they responded more slowly. (See *Figure 8.4.*)

Posner and his colleagues (1980) showed that selective attention can affect the detection of visual stimuli. If a stimulus occurs where we expect it, we perceive it more quickly; if it occurs where we do *not* expect it, we perceive it more slowly. Thus, people can follow instructions to direct their attention to particular locations in the visual field. Because the subjects' gaze was fixed on the center of the screen in Posner's study, this movement of attention was independent of eye movement. However, visual attention for most events that occur outside the laboratory is controlled by eye movements: We see something interesting and direct our gaze to it. And if we expect to see something in a particular location, we turn our eyes toward that location, waiting to see what will happen.

Sometimes, two events happen in close proximity, but we can watch one of them while ignoring the other. Neisser and Becklen (1975) showed subjects a videotape that presented a situation similar to the one confronted by a person trying to listen to the voice of one person at

Figure 8.4 Mean reaction time in response to a letter displayed on a screen after receiving a cue directing attention toward the location in which the letter appears or away from it, or after receiving no cue. (Based on data from Posner, Snyder, and Davidson, 1980.)

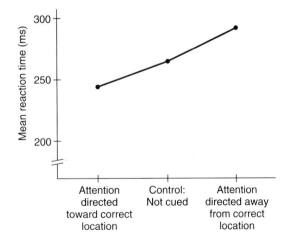

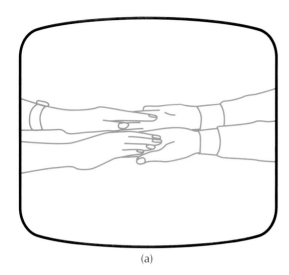

(a)

(b)

(c)

Figure 8.5 Drawings of the scenes from the videotapes. (a) The hand game. (b) The basketball game. (c) The two games superimposed. (From Neisser, U., and Becklen, R. *Cognitive Psychology,* 1975, *7,* 480–494. Reprinted with permission.)

a cocktail party. The videotape contained two different actions presented one on top of the other: a basketball game and a hand game, in which people try to slap the opponents' hands, which are resting on top of theirs. The subjects could easily follow one scene and remember what had happened in it; however, they could not attend simultaneously to both scenes. (See *Figure 8.5.*)

It is possible that the selective attention exercised by Neisser and Becklen's subjects was controlled by eye movements as their gaze followed the actions of one of the games. However, Rock and Gutman (1981) found that people can pay attention to one of two *shapes,* even when the shapes overlap. They presented overlapping outlines of shapes of familiar objects and meaningless forms, drawn in different colors (red and green). They asked the subjects to pay attention to only one of the colors. Afterward, on a recognition test, they showed the subjects all the forms they had seen. The subjects recognized only those shapes that they had been instructed to pay attention to. Even when the nonattended figures consisted of an easily recognized shape, they failed to notice them. (See *Figure 8.6.*)

What happens to visual information that people do not pay attention to? Is it simply "lost?" As we saw in the section on attention to auditory stimuli, some processing of unattended auditory information does occur, and implicit memories can be established to sounds we do not consciously notice. The same can be said of unattended visual information. For example, Neisser (1969) asked subjects to read lines of text printed in black but to ignore the lines of text printed in red, which appeared just below each black line. Afterward, the subjects could

Figure 8.6 Overlapping shapes. The subjects were told to pay attention to only one color. On a test later, they recognized only the ones they had paid attention to previously. (From Rock, I., and Gutman, D. *Journal of Experimental Psychology: Human Perception and Performance,* 1981, 7, 275–285. Copyright 1981 by the American Psychological Association.)

Figure 8.7 A demonstration of simultanagnosia. The patient can recognize the comb or the pencil, but not both simultaneously.

remember nothing of the text printed in red, unless their own name appeared there—these they noticed and remembered. Apparently, our own name tends to jump out at us in print, just as it shouts at us when presented acoustically to the unattended ear.

Brain Mechanisms of Selective Attention

You will recall from Chapter 3 that damage to the right parietal lobe produces a phenomenon known as *sensory neglect*. As we saw, people with such damage tend not to notice things that happen in the environment toward their left or in the left side of their body. For example, they tend not to shave or apply makeup to the left side of their face, and they fail to eat food on the left side of their plate. Similar effects are also seen in laboratory animals (Mesulam, 1985). Thus, neuropsychologists have suggested that the parietal lobes are involved in visual and spatial selective attention.

When the parietal lobe of *both sides* of the brain is damaged, people exhibit a deficit known as **Balint's syndrome.** One of the symptoms of this syndrome is **simultanagnosia,** the inability to perceive two objects at the same time. (Recall that *agnosia* means "failure to know.") A person with Balint's syndrome has difficulty controlling his or her eye movements. But if an examiner carefully places an object (such as a comb or a pencil) in the patient's line of sight, he

or she will be able to perceive it and report what it is. However, if two objects are placed together, the patient will report seeing one or the other, not both. (See *Figure 8.7.*)

Simultanagnosia reveals a very interesting fact about the perception of objects: Even when the images of two objects overlap on the retina (as shown in Figure 8.7), *the two images appear to be analyzed separately.* A person without parietal lobe damage can pay attention to (and thus be conscious of) both objects. However, people with simultanagnosia appear to have a severe deficit in attention that prevents them from being conscious of more than one object at a time.

INTERIM SUMMARY

Attention

As we saw in the first section of this chapter, consciousness can be analyzed as a social phenomenon, derived through evolution of the brain mechanisms responsible for our ability to communicate with each other (and, in addition, with ourselves). However, because our verbal mechanisms can contain only a limited amount of information at one time, we cannot be conscious of all the events that take place in our environment. The process of attention is the control mechanism that determines which stimuli will be noticed and which will be ignored. The factors that control our attention include novelty, verbal instructions, and our own assessment of the significance of what we are perceiving.

Dichotic listening experiments show that what is received by the unattended ear is lost within a few seconds unless something causes us to take heed of it; after those few seconds we cannot say what that ear heard. However, the study with the classically conditioned response to the electrical shock indicates that even unattended information can produce implicit (as opposed to explicit) memories.

Studies with visually presented information indicate that attention can focus on location or on shape. We can pay attention to particular objects or to stimuli that occur in a particular place.

The parietal lobes of the brain appear to play a special role in attention. Damage to the right parietal lobe causes a person to fail to notice objects and events in the left side of the environment and even to disregard the left side of his or her body. Damage to both parietal lobes leads to the inability to visually perceive more than one object at a time, a deficit known as simultanagnosia. ∎

CONSCIOUSNESS AND THE BRAIN

3 As we have already seen, brain damage can alter human consciousness. For example, in Chapter 7 I described the phenomenon of anterograde amnesia, caused by brain damage—particularly, to the hippocampus. You will recall that people with this defect cannot form new verbal memories, but they can learn some kinds of tasks. However, they remain unaware that they have learned something, even when their behavior indicates that they have. Thus, the brain damage does not prevent all kinds of learning, but it does prevent conscious awareness of what has been learned.

If human consciousness is related to speech, then it probably is related to the brain mechanisms that control comprehension and production of speech. This conclusion has an interesting implication: It suggests that for us to be aware of a piece of information, the information must be transmitted to neural circuits in the brain responsible for our communicative behavior. Several reports of cases of human brain damage support this suggestion.

Global Unawareness: A Case of Isolation Aphasia

Geschwind, Quadfasel, and Segarra (1968) described the case of a woman who had suffered severe brain damage from inhaling carbon monoxide from a faulty water heater. The damage spared the primary auditory cortex, the speech areas of the brain, and the connections between these areas. However, the damage destroyed large parts of the visual association cortex and isolated the speech mechanisms from other parts of the brain. In fact, the syndrome they reported is referred to as **isolation aphasia.** Thus, although the brain's speech mechanisms could receive auditory input and could control the muscles used for speech, they received no information from the other senses or from the neural circuits that contain memories concerning past experiences and the meanings of words.

The woman remained in the hospital for nine years, until she died. During this time she made few voluntary movements except with her eyes, which were able to follow moving objects. She gave no evidence of recognizing objects or people in her environment. She did not spontaneously say anything, answer questions, or give any signs that she understood what other people said to her. By all available criteria, she was not conscious of anything that was going on. However, the woman could *repeat* words that were spoken to her. And if someone started a poem she knew, she would finish it. For example, if someone said, "Roses are red, violets are blue," she would respond with "Sugar is sweet, and so are you." She even learned new poems and songs and would sing along with the radio. Her case suggests that consciousness is not simply activity of the brain's speech mechanisms; it is activity prompted by information received from other parts of the brain concerning memories or events presently occurring in the environment.

Lack of Verbal Access to Visual Perceptions: A Case of Visual Agnosia

The case I just described was that of a woman who appeared to have completely lost her awareness of herself and her environment. In other instances people have become unaware of particular kinds of information. For example, as we saw in the opening vignette of this chapter, people with a particular kind of blindness caused by brain damage can point to objects that they cannot see—or rather, that they are not aware of seeing. Two colleagues and I studied a young man with a different kind of disconnection between perception and awareness. His brain had been damaged by an inflammation of the blood vessels and he consequently suffered from visual agnosia (Margolin, Friedrich, and Carlson, 1985). The man had great difficulty identifying common objects by sight. For example, he could not say what a hammer was by looking at it, but he quickly identified it when he was permitted to pick it up and feel it. He was not blind; he could walk around without bumping into things, and he had no trouble making visually guided movements to pick up an object that he wanted to identify. The simplest conclusion was that his disease had damaged the neural circuits responsible for visual perception.

However, the simplest conclusion was not the correct one. Although the patient had great difficulty in visually identifying objects or pictures of objects, he often made hand movements that appeared to be related to the object he could not identify. For example, when we showed him a picture of a pistol, he stared at it with a puzzled look, then shook his head and said that he couldn't tell what it was. While continuing to study the picture, he clenched his right hand into a fist and began making movements with his index finger. When we asked him what he was doing, he looked at his hand, made a few tentative movements with his finger, then raised his hand in the air and moved it forward

each time he moved his finger. He was unmistakably miming the way a person holds and fires a pistol. "Oh!" he said. "It's a gun. No, a pistol." Clearly, he was not aware what the gun was until he paid attention to what his hand was doing. Similarly, once he looked at a picture of a belt and said it was a pair of pants. We asked him to show us where the legs and other parts of the pants were. When he tried to do so, he became puzzled. His hands went to the place where his belt buckle would be (he was wearing hospital pajamas) and moved as if he were feeling one. "No," he said. "It's not a pair of pants—it's a belt!"

The patient's visual system was not normal, yet it functioned better than we could infer from only his verbal behavior. That is, his perceptions were much more accurate than his words indicated. The fact that he could mime the use of a pistol or feel an imaginary belt buckle with his hands indicated that his visual system worked well enough to initiate appropriate nonverbal behaviors, though not the appropriate words. Once he felt what he was doing, he could name the object. The process might involve steps such as those shown in *Figure 8.8.*

Although the patient had lost his ability to read, speech therapists were able to teach him to use finger spelling to read. He could not say what a particular letter was, but he could learn to make a particular hand movement when he saw it. After he had learned the finger-spelling

Figure 8.8 Hypothetical exchanges of information within the brain of the patient with visual agnosia.

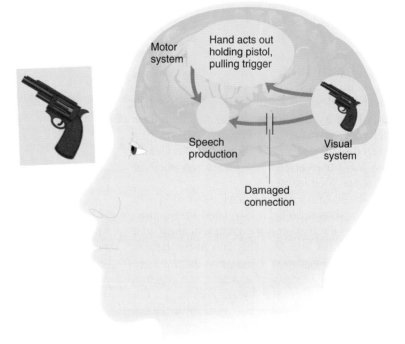

alphabet used by deaf people, he could read slowly and laboriously by making hand movements for each letter and feeling the words that his hand was spelling out.

This case supports the conclusion that consciousness is synonymous with a person's ability to talk about his or her perceptions or memories. In this particular situation disruption of the normal interchange between the visual perceptual system and verbal system prevented the patient from being directly aware of his own visual perceptions. It was as if his hands talked to him, telling him what he had just seen.

The Split-Brain Syndrome

One surgical procedure demonstrates dramatically how various brain functions can be disconnected from each other and from verbal mechanisms. It is used for people who have very severe epilepsy that cannot be controlled by drugs. In these people violent storms of neural activity begin in one hemisphere and are transmitted to the other by the **corpus callosum,** a large bundle of axons that connect corresponding parts of the cortex on one side of the brain with those on the other. Both sides of the brain then engage in wild neural firing and stimulate each other, causing a generalized epileptic seizure. These seizures can occur many times each day, preventing the patient from leading a normal life. Neurosurgeons discovered that cutting the corpus callosum (the **split-brain operation**) greatly reduced the frequency of the epileptic seizures. (See *Figure 8.9.*)

Sperry (1966) and Gazzaniga and his associates (Gazzaniga, 1970; Gazzaniga and LeDoux, 1978) have studied these patients extensively. After the two hemispheres are disconnected, they operate independently; their sensory mechanisms, memories, and motor systems can no longer exchange information. The effects of these disconnections are not obvious to the casual observer, for the simple reason that only one hemisphere—in most people, the left—controls speech. The right hemisphere of an epileptic person with a split brain can understand speech reasonably well, but it is poor at reading and spelling. And because Broca's speech area is located in the left hemisphere, it is totally incapable of producing speech.

Because only one side of the brain can talk about what it is experiencing, most observers do not detect the independent operations of the right side of a split brain. Even the patient's left brain has to learn about the independent existence of the right brain. One of the first things

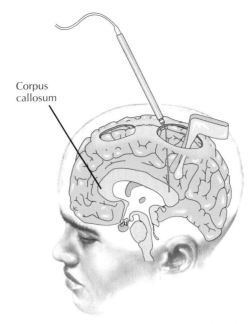

Corpus callosum

Figure 8.9 The split-brain operation. (Adapted from Gazzaniga, M.S. *Fundamentals of Psychology.* New York: Academic Press, 1973.)

that these patients say they notice after the operation is that their left hand seems to have a "mind of its own." For example, patients may find themselves putting down a book held in the left hand, even if they are reading it with great interest. At other times, they surprise themselves by making obscene gestures (with the left hand) at inappropriate times. Each side of the brain is connected to the opposite side of the body, controlling its movements and receiving sensations from it. Thus, the right hemisphere controls the movements of the left hand, and these unexpected movements puzzle the left hemisphere, the side of the brain that controls speech.

One exception to the crossed representation of sensory information is the olfactory system. When a person sniffs a flower through the left nostril, only the left brain receives a sensation of the odor. Thus, if the right nostril of a patient with a split brain is plugged up, leaving the left nostril open, the patient will accurately identify odors verbally. If the odor enters the right nostril, the patient will say that he or she smells nothing. But, in fact, the right brain has perceived the odor and can identify it. This ability is demonstrated by an experiment in which the patient is told to reach for some objects hidden from view by a partition. If asked to use the left hand, with the left nostril plugged up, he or she will select the object that corresponds to

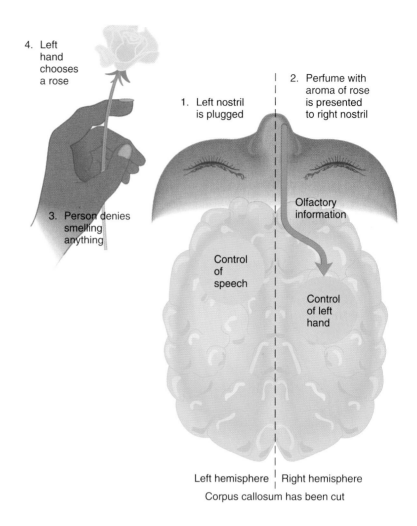

4. Left hand chooses a rose

1. Left nostril is plugged

2. Perfume with aroma of rose is presented to right nostril

3. Person denies smelling anything

Olfactory information

Control of speech

Control of left hand

Left hemisphere | Right hemisphere

Corpus callosum has been cut

Figure 8.10 Identification of an object in response to an olfactory stimulus by a person with a split brain.

the odor—a plastic flower for a floral odor, a toy fish for a fishy odor, a model tree for the odor of pine, and so forth. But if the left nostril is plugged up, the right hand fails this test, since it is connected to the left hemisphere, which did not smell the odor. (See *Figure 8.10.*)

Sometimes, the hands conflict, with one hand trying to put a book down while the other is trying to pick it up to read it. (Can you guess which hand is which?) One study even reported that a man with a split brain attempted to beat his wife with one hand and protect her with the other. Did he *really* want to hurt her? Yes and no, I guess.

As we saw in Chapter 3, the left hemisphere, besides giving us the ability to read, write, and speak, is good at other tasks that require verbal abilities, such as mathematics and logic. The right hemisphere excels at tasks of perception and has a much greater artistic ability. If a patient with a split brain tries to use his or her right hand to arrange blocks to duplicate a geometrical design provided by the experimenter, the hand will hopelessly fumble around

with the blocks. Often, the left hand (controlled by the right hemisphere) will brush the right hand aside and easily complete the task. It is as if the right hemisphere gets impatient with the clumsy ineptitude of the hand controlled by the left hemisphere.

The effects of cutting the corpus callosum reinforce the conclusion that consciousness depends on the ability of speech mechanisms in the left hemisphere to receive information from other regions of the brain. If such communication is interrupted, then some kinds of information can never reach consciousness.

INTERIM SUMMARY

Consciousness and the Brain

The suggestion that consciousness is a function of our ability to communicate with each other receives support from some cases of human brain damage. As we saw, people with isolation aphasia can perceive speech and talk without apparent awareness; and a patient with visual agnosia could nonverbally identify objects he saw, although he was not aware of what he was seeing. Thus, brain damage within the cerebral hemispheres can disrupt a person's verbal access to (awareness of) perceptual mechanisms without destroying these mechanisms. And although a person whose corpus callosum has been severed can make perceptual judgments with the right hemisphere, he or she cannot talk about them and appears to be unaware of them. ■

HYPNOSIS

4 Hypnosis is a specific and unusual form of verbal control that apparently enables one person to control another person's behavior, thoughts, and perceptions. Under hypnosis a person can be induced to bark like a dog, act like a baby, or tolerate being pierced with needles. Although these examples are interesting and amusing, hypnosis is important to psychology because it provides insights about the nature of consciousness and has applications in the fields of medicine and psychotherapy.

Hypnosis was discovered by Franz Anton Mesmer (1734–1815). Today hypnosis is used to decrease pain during childbirth, dentistry, and surgery and is used to help people break bad habits, such as smoking.

Hypnosis, or *mesmerism,* was discovered by Franz Anton Mesmer (1734–1815), an Austrian physician. He found that when he passed magnets back and forth over people's bodies (in an attempt to restore their "magnetic fluxes" and cure them of disease), they would often have convulsions and enter a trancelike state, during which almost miraculous cures could be achieved. As Mesmer discovered later, the patients were not affected directly by the magnetism of the iron rods; they were responding to his undoubtedly persuasive and compelling personality. We now know that convulsions and trancelike states do not necessarily accompany hypnosis, and we also know that hypnosis does not cure physical illnesses. Mesmer's patients apparently had psychologically produced symptoms that were alleviated by suggestions made while they were hypnotized.

The Induction of Hypnosis

A person undergoing hypnosis can be alert, relaxed, tense, lying quietly, or exercising vigorously. There is no need to move an object in front of someone's face or to say "You are getting sleepy"; an enormous variety of techniques can be used to induce hypnosis in a susceptible person. The only essential feature seems to be the subject's understanding that he or she is to be hypnotized. Moss (1965) reported having sometimes simply said to a well-practiced subject, in a normal tone of voice, "Please sit in that chair and go into hypnosis," and the subject complied in a few seconds. Sometimes, this approach even worked on volunteers who had never been hypnotized before. (Of course, these people had some expectations about what the word *hypnosis* means; their behavior conformed to their expectations.)

Obviously, soothing, friendly words are more persuasive than hostile ones; but most investigators agree that no special tricks are necessary to induce hypnosis. This is not to say that the words the hypnotist uses have no effect; if he or she emphasizes the word *sleep,* the subjects are more likely to enter a drowsy trance than a relatively alert one.

Characteristics of Hypnosis

Hypnotized people are very suggestible; they will do things in conformity with what the hypnotist says, even to the extent of appearing to misperceive reality. Under hypnosis people can be instructed to do things that they would not be expected to do under normal conditions, such as

Hypnosis is a popular nightclub entertainment. Hypnotized people can be instructed to do things they might not do under other circumstances. What ethical issue should be considered?

acting out imaginary scenes or pretending to be an animal. Hypnotized people can be convinced that an arm cannot move or is insensitive to pain, and they then act as if that is the case; hypnosis can thus be used to induce paralysis or anesthesia. They can also be persuaded to see things that are not there (**positive hallucinations**) or *not* to see objects that *are* there (**negative hallucinations**).

One of the most dramatic phenomena of hypnosis is **posthypnotic suggestibility,** in which a person is given instructions under hypnosis and follows those instructions after returning to a nonhypnotized state. For example, the hypnotist might tell a subject that he will become unbearably thirsty when he sees the hypnotist look at her watch. Usually, the hypnotist also admonishes the subject not to remember anything upon leaving the hypnotic state, so that **posthypnotic amnesia** is also achieved. After leaving the hypnotic state, the subject acts normally and professes ignorance of what he perceived and did during hypnosis, perhaps even apologizing for not having succumbed to hypnosis. The hypnotist later looks at her watch, and

the subject suddenly leaves the room to get a drink of water.

Studies indicate that when changes in perception are induced in hypnotized subjects, the changes occur not in the subjects' actual perceptions but in their verbal reports about their perceptions. For example, an experiment by Pattie (1937) indicates that local anesthesia induced by hypnotic suggestion is not the same as anesthesia produced by drugs. Pattie suggested to hypnotized subjects that they could feel nothing with one hand. He then had them cross their wrists so that their forearms formed an X, turn their palms together, interlace their fingers, and twist their hands toward their bodies until their thumbs pointed upward. (See *Figure 8.11.*) With the hands in this position, someone has difficulty telling which hand is being touched by another person. (Try it yourself; fold your hands as Figure 8.11 shows, have someone touch three or four fingers in rapid succession, and try to say to which hand the touched fingers belong.) Pattie touched several fingers on both of the subjects' hands and asked them to count the number of times they were touched. If, in fact,

Figure 8.11 The procedure used by Pattie (1937).

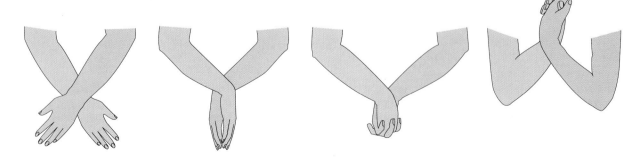

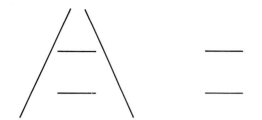

Figure 8.12 The Ponzo illusion. The short vertical lines are actually the same length.

they could not feel sensations from the "anesthetized" hand, they should not have counted the touches made to this hand; but they included many of these touches in the total count. Apparently, then, the hypnotized subjects were not anesthetized; they simply acted as if they were.

Many studies have also shown that hypnotically induced blindness or deafness does not take the same form it would if the sensory information was no longer being analyzed by the brain. For example, Miller, Hennessy, and Leibowitz (1973) used the *Ponzo illusion* to test the effects of hypnotically induced blindness. Although the two parallel horizontal lines in the left portion of Figure 8.12 are the same length, the top one looks longer than the bottom one. This effect is produced by the presence of the slanted lines to the left and right of the horizontal ones; if these lines are not present, the horizontal lines appear to be the same length. (See *Figure 8.12.*) Through hypnotic suggestion the experimenters made the slanted lines "disappear," but even though the subjects reported that they could not see the slanted lines (a negative hallucination), they still perceived the upper line as being longer than the lower one. This result indicates that the visual system continues to process sensory information during hypnotically induced blindness; otherwise, the subjects would have perceived the lines as being equal in length. The reported blindness appears to occur not because of altered activity in the visual system but because of altered activity in the verbal system (and in consciousness).

Explanations of Hypnosis

[5] Hypnosis has been called a special case of learning, a transference of the superego, a goal-directed behavior shaped by the hypnotist, a role-playing situation, and a restructuring of perceptual-cognitive functioning. In other words, no one yet knows exactly what it is. Hypnosis has been described as a state of enhanced suggestibility, but that is simply a description, not an explanation. Many people have advanced theories of hypnosis; a book by Sheehan and Perry (1976) describes six of them. I will discuss two theories that have been most influential.

Hilgard's Neodissociation Theory. Hilgard (1977, 1979) proposes that hypnosis represents a dissociation (division) of consciousness into separate channels of mental activity. He refers to his theory as **neodissociation** (*neo-* means "new") to distinguish it from earlier theories dating back to the turn of the century. Two examples of the types of dissociation described by Hilgard are hypnotically induced blindness, which involves a division between visual perception and consciousness, and hypnotically induced paralysis, which involves a division between consciousness and muscular control of particular parts of the body. Judging from the cases of brain damage I described in the previous section, the role of dissociation in hypnosis seems plausible. Perhaps hypnotic suggestion can induce neural inhibition that prevents transmission of some of the messages between the verbal system ("consciousness") and the perceptual and motor systems of the brain.

Hilgard (1973) discovered a hypnotic phenomenon that has become particularly important to his theory, a phenomenon called the hidden observer. Hilgard defined the **hidden observer** as a part of a hypnotized person's consciousness that has become dissociated from the rest. To bring forth the hidden observer, Hilgard used the following instructions:

> There are aspects of what is going on when you are deeply engrossed in hypnotic experiences that are unknown to you, but part of you is still registering what is happening. . . . When I place my hand on your shoulder I will be in communication with this hidden part, and we can talk together; but the hypnotized part of you, the part to which I am talking now, will not know that you are talking to me. . . . When I then remove my hand from your shoulder you will be back in the hypnotic state you are now in, and you will not know what you said or even that you were talking to me. . . . [When you] are out of hypnosis . . . [you will be able to] remember everything about the hidden part of yourself, what you said when I had my hand on your shoulder, and how you felt during the experiment when the events we talked about were taking place. (Hilgard, Hilgard, MacDonald, Morgan, and Johnson, 1978, p. 658)

Using such a technique, Hilgard found that

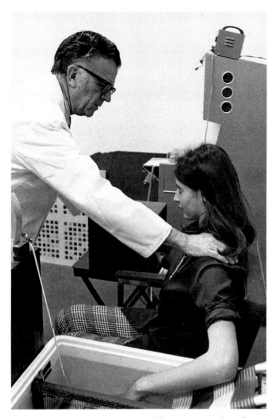

This woman was hypnotized by Ernest Hilgard. At first, she reported no feelings of pain when her arm was placed in an ice bath, but when special instructions brought out the "hidden observer," she reported intense pain.

the hidden observer was able to report pain that the hypnotized person denied feeling. The subjects were hypnotized and told that they would not feel any pain when a tourniquet was applied to their arm. (To produce pain without producing actual harm, experimenters employ two techniques: temporarily restricting the blood flow to an arm with a tourniquet, or immersing the arm in ice water. Both procedures eventually produce intense pain.) The suggestion worked; while under hypnosis the subjects reported much less intense pain than they did under control conditions. However, when the special instructions were used to bring forth the hidden observer, the subjects began reporting much more intense pain. The results indicated that during hypnosis part of the subjects' consciousness was dissociated from feelings of pain, but another part (the hidden observer) remained completely aware of the pain.

Many experiments have confirmed that the phenomenon of the hidden observer exists. However, as we will see in the next section, some investigators dispute its significance.

Barber's Social Role Theory. All the behavioral and perceptual phenomena discussed so far in this book have obvious survival value for the organism; that is, functional analysis of a behavioral phenomenon usually points to a plausible reason for the occurrence of the behavior. Therefore, if hypnotic phenomena occurred only when a person was hypnotized, it would be difficult to understand why the brain happened to evolve in such a way that people can be hypnotized. A theory of hypnosis by Barber (1979) indicates that at least some aspects of hypnosis are related to events that can happen every day.

Barber argues that hypnosis should not be viewed as a special state of consciousness, in the way that sleep is a state of consciousness that differs from waking; rather, the hypnotized person is acting out a social role. Thus, the phenomena of hypnosis are social behaviors, not manifestations of a special state of consciousness. Hypnotized subjects willingly join with the hypnotist in enacting a role expected of them. Some of the rules governing this role are supplied by the direct instructions of the hypnotist, others are indirectly implied by what the hypnotist says and does, and still others consist of expectations that the subjects already have about what hypnotized people do.

People's expectations about hypnosis do indeed play an important role in their behavior while under hypnosis. In lectures to two sections of an introductory psychology class, Orne (1959) told one section (falsely) that one of the most prominent features of hypnosis was rigidity of the preferred (that is, dominant) hand. Later, he arranged a demonstration of hypnosis during a meeting of students from both sections. Several of the students who had heard that the dominant hand became rigid showed this phenomenon when hypnotized, but none of the students who had not heard this myth developed a rigid hand. Similarly, if people become willing to follow a hypnotist's suggestions, perhaps they do so because they believe that this suggested behavior is what is supposed to happen. Perhaps people willingly follow a hypnotist's suggestion to do something silly (such as bark like a dog) because they know that hypnotized people are not responsible for their behavior.

If hypnosis can be described as role playing, then why are so many people willing to play this role? Barber (1975) submits that the suspension of self-control that occurs during hypnosis is very similar to our "participation" in the story of a movie or novel. When we go to a movie or read a book, we generally do so with the intent of becoming swept up in the story. We willingly let the filmmaker or author lead us through a fantasy. When we hear a story or read a book, we even imagine the scenes and the events that occur in them. We feel happy when good things happen to characters that we identify with and like, and we feel sad when bad things happen to them. Certainly, we express a full range of emotions while watching a good movie or reading a good book. In fact, one of the criteria we use to judge a movie or book is whether it causes us to enter this fantasy world; if it does not, we regard the work as a poor one. Perhaps these imagined events are similar to the positive hallucinations experienced during hypnosis.

The proposal that hypnosis is related to our ability to participate vicariously in a story provides at least a starting point for a functional explanation. One of the ways that we can affect other people's behavior verbally is to get them to imagine themselves in our place; this phenomenon is called *empathy*. It is easier to obtain assistance from others if they can imagine themselves in our place and thus see how important their help is to our well-being. Surely, the ability to think about another person's situation empathetically facilitates cooperation and assistance. Perhaps our moral codes owe their existence at least partly to this phenomenon.

Barber's description of his own thoughts while being hypnotized by a colleague demonstrates a striking similarity to participating vicariously in a story.

> The experimenter begins by asking me to clasp my hands together tightly with fingers interlaced. He then states, "Your hands are hard, solid, rigid. They are very rigid and solid. They are two pieces of steel that are welded together. They are rigid, solid, stuck together." He continues with these kinds of suggestions for about 30 seconds and finally states, "Try to take your hands apart. Notice that the harder you try, the more difficult it becomes. Try to take them apart; you can't." At the present time, I see this type of test situation as a valuable and useful experience. . . . I want to experience those things that are suggested. . . , and I believe or expect that I, and other investigators, can experience the suggested effects . . . if we temporarily put aside critical or analytical thoughts such as "It's impossible for my hands to become stuck together." . . . I cooperate and "think with" or "imagine" those things that are suggested. . . . I continue to focus my thoughts on the rigidity in the hands and to imagine that they are made of welded steel. I pull on the hands but they feel very tight, like a solid piece of metal. . . . Finally, the experimenter states,

"Now relax your hands. You can now easily unclasp them." After I relax the hands, I have a feeling of pleasant surprise to see how easily they now come apart. (Barber, 1975, p. 7)

Many hypnotic phenomena are striking and would seem impossible to achieve without hypnosis. However, researchers have successfully demonstrated all of them without hypnosis. If subjects are given carefully worded instructions that strongly motivate them to cooperate with the experimenter, they can learn to ignore painful stimuli, act as if they were a child, imagine themselves seeing nonexistent objects, fail to remember a list of words they have just read, and so on. The essential difference is that they realize that they are pretending, whereas hypnotized subjects generally believe that their behavior is involuntary. As Spanos, Gwynn, and Stam (1983) put it, "subjects must maintain control of their responding but, nonetheless, come to interpret and describe their goal-directed enactments as being involuntary 'happenings' " (p. 486).

As we saw earlier, the hidden observer appears to provide strong support for Hilgard's neodissociation theory. However, some experiments indicate that even this phenomenon is actually a role played according to a script supplied by the hypnotist. For example, Spanos, Gwynn, and Stam (1983) hypnotized people and had them place one of their arms in a bucket of ice water. They gave instructions that the subjects would not feel the pain, and indeed, the subjects reported that their arms felt numb. Then they gave two different sets of instructions designed to elicit the hidden observer. One set was similar to the instructions used by Hilgard, suggesting that the subject had a hidden part that "continued to remain aware of everything going on around it, and everything going on in [the subject's] body." Another set suggested that the hidden part was *"less aware* of everything going on around it, and everything going on in [the subject's] body" (italics mine). The experimenters then elicited ratings of pain from the subjects and from the subjects' hidden observers.

The results showed that, depending on the type of instructions the subjects were given, the hidden observer reported either more or less pain than the "rest" of the hypnotized person. (See ***Figure 8.13.***) As we saw, Hilgard explained the hidden observer in terms of a division of consciousness. Spanos and his colleagues proposed that the subject actually was playing two roles. In the condition used by Hilgard, the subject ignored the pain according

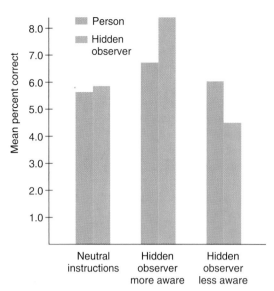

Figure 8.13 Pain ratings of the "person" and the "hidden observer" as a function of the experimenter's instructions regarding the nature of the hidden observer. (Based on data from Spanos, N.P., Gwynn, M.I., and Stam, H.J. *Journal of Abnormal Psychology*, 1983, *92*, 479–488.)

to the instructions that pain would not be felt and then paid attention to it when the hypnotist asked the hidden observer to come forth. According to this view, then, the hidden observer does not seem to be a part of a person's consciousness that remains aware of reality; instead, it, like the other aspects of a hypnotized person's consciousness, follows the instructions of the hypnotist.

Susceptibility to Hypnosis

Not everyone can be hypnotized. In fact, the ability to be hypnotized appears to be a stable trait; if a person can be hypnotized on one occasion, he or she probably can be hypnotized on another. However, attempts to relate personality traits to hypnotic susceptibility have yielded few definitive results. Susceptibility does not appear to be related strongly to any particular personality type (Hilgard, 1979). What does appear to be related to susceptibility to hypnosis is the ability to produce vivid mental images, a high capacity for becoming involved in imaginative activities, and a rich, vivid imagination (Kihlstrom, 1985). You can readily see that such people would be likely to participate vicariously in a story.

As we saw in Chapter 3, the left hemisphere is more involved in sequential tasks, including verbal tasks; and the right hemisphere is more involved in simultaneous tasks, including

picture perception and perception of space. In addition, several studies have indicated that the right hemisphere is more involved in social interactions (Kolb and Whishaw, 1990). There are some hints that hypnosis may be related to the functions of the right hemisphere. For example, Sackheim, Paulus, and Weiman (1979) found that people who are easily hypnotized tend to sit on the right side of the classroom. In this position they see most of the front of the room with their right hemispheres, so perhaps their choice represents a preference for right-hemisphere involvement in perceptual tasks. This preference may represent a generally increased sensitivity to social roles, including those involved in hypnosis. I hasten to add that this hypothesis is speculative and may very well be wrong, but at least it points the way to some hypotheses that can be tested experimentally.

EVALUATING SCIENTIFIC ISSUES

Can Hypnosis Cause Antisocial Behavior?

6 Dramatic demonstrations of the apparent power that a hypnotist exerts over the hypnotized subject have led some people to conclude that subjects can be induced to commit antisocial acts—even crimes—while under hypnosis. Most professionals assert quite the contrary: that people will never perform an act while hypnotized that violates their moral code. Who is right? How much freedom of action does a hypnotized person have while following the suggestions of the hypnotist?

Evidence for Hypnotic Coercion. Toward the end of the nineteenth century several experiments suggested that a hypnotized person can indeed be coerced into doing something dangerous or immoral. However, as Laurence and Perry (1988) note, the experiments are not very convincing, because the "harm" that the subjects caused was symbolic rather than real. A neurologist, Giles de la Tourette, gave a hypnotized subject a ruler, saying that it was in fact a pistol (Ladame, 1887). He implanted the posthypnotic suggestion that the next time the subject saw a certain person, she would shoot him. The victim then entered the room, and the subject "shot him." He fell to the floor, shouting "I am dead." Another subject was told that a piece of chalk was really a knife and that a door was a person. The subject willingly stabbed the door—that is, the person—to death (Liégois, 1889).

More recent experiments have induced subjects to perform much more convincing dangerous acts or acts of violence. For example, Rowland (1939) placed an agitated rattlesnake in a box and asked hypnotized subjects to reach inside and pick it up. Three of the four subjects tried to do so, banging their hands against an invisible sheet of glass that protected the front of the box; the fourth subject came out of hypnosis and refused to reach for the snake. The investigator also ordered two of the subjects to throw some sulfuric acid at him, and they did so. (Of course, he was protected by another invisible sheet of glass.) Rowland concluded that "persons in deep hypnosis will allow themselves to be exposed to unreasonably dangerous situations" and "will perform acts unreasonably dangerous to others" (p. 117).

Some reports of unethical use of hypnosis outside the laboratory provide further evidence for hypnotic coercion. For example, Kline (1972) reported the case of a physician who successfully used hypnosis to seduce some of his female patients. He hypnotized them repeatedly, establishing a close personal relationship and gradually introducing erotic suggestions. Several of his patients complied with his suggestions and had sexual relations with him. Eventually, however, he was caught when a patient who served as his unpaid assistant and mistress began talking about their sexual episodes in her sleep. Her husband made tape recordings of her descriptions and prosecuted the physician.

Evaluating the Evidence. The studies (and the case of seduction) I just cited may seem convincing, but we cannot necessarily conclude from them that a person may be coerced, through hypnosis, into doing something that he or she would not otherwise do. To begin with, how can we be sure that the subjects really perceive the act they are being asked to commit as dangerous? After all, they know that they are participating in an experiment being carried out by a respected scientist. Would that person really expose them to the danger of a rattlesnake bite or let himself receive a faceful of sulfuric acid? As Orne and Evans (1965) said about experiments like the one by Rowland (1939):

> If these actions are to be designated as antisocial or self-destructive it must be shown that they are perceived as such by subjects. . . . A subject is aware of certain realities imposed by the experimental situation. It is as clear to a subject as it is to any scientist that no reputable investigator can risk injuring a subject during the course of an experiment. . . . Consequently, any requested behavior which appears to a subject to be dangerous at face value may be reinterpreted in the context of a laboratory situation. (Orne and Evans, 1965, p. 191)

Orne and Evans performed an improved version of the experiment by Rowland. They told hypnotized subjects first to pick up a gecko (a small, harmless lizard), then a green tree snake (also harmless), and finally a red-bellied snake, which the subjects recognized as highly venomous. (The experiment was carried out at a university in Australia, where these animals are found.) Although the subjects could actually pick up the gecko and the green tree snake, an invisible sheet of glass was put in place in front of the red-bellied snake. Next, the experimenters asked the subjects to put their hand into a beaker of fuming concentrated nitric acid and pick up a coin that had just been placed there. In fact, the beaker *really did* contain concentrated nitric acid. As soon as a subject put his or her hand into the acid the experimenter grabbed it and submerged it in a basin of soapy lukewarm water, which washed off the acid before any harm could be done. (Before beginning the experiment, Orne practiced this "rescue operation" to be sure that the subjects would not get hurt. Nevertheless, I doubt that most review boards would permit such an experiment today.)

Five out of the six subjects complied with all of the experimenters' requests. (The sixth became terrified at the sight of the harmless gecko and dropped out of the experiment.) Thus, 83 percent of the subjects performed ostensibly dangerous acts. But did they really *perceive* them as dangerous? As the experimenters found out, they did not. When they were questioned afterward, they said that "they were quite convinced that they would not be harmed because the context was an experimental one, presumably being conducted by responsible experimenters. All subjects appeared to assume that some form of safety precautions had been taken during the experiment" (Orne and Evans, 1965, p. 199). And they were absolutely right; that is precisely what the experimenters had done.

Orne and Evans's experiment also contained two unhypnotized control groups. The subjects in one group were asked to pretend that they were hypnotized. All five subjects in this group attempted to pick up the snake and reached into the beaker of acid for the coin.

Subjects in another group were given no instructions concerning hypnosis but were simply asked to perform the tasks. *All five of them complied!* Thus, even though the tasks would seem to be convincingly dangerous, the subjects told themselves that they could not possibly be dangerous and did what the experimenters told them to. (As we saw in Chapter 2, subjects are not passive participants in experiments; what they do often depends on how they interpret the situation.)

But suppose that an experimenter could arrange a situation that really did convince subjects that they were being asked to perform an act that was truly antisocial or dangerous. Would hypnosis compel them to do so? Milgram (1963, 1974) instructed subjects to press a button that supposedly delivered an electric shock to a "trainee" (hidden behind a wall) whenever he made a wrong answer in a learning task. (In fact, the "trainee" never received a shock.) As the noises, pleas, and finally screams came through the wall, most of the subjects continued to press the button under the instructions of the experimenter. Even after silence suggested that the "trainee" had died, an overwhelming majority of the subjects continued to push the button while the experimenter turned up the voltage, demanding through the intercom that the apparently dead "trainee" respond.

Most of the button-pushing subjects actually were convinced that they were delivering a shock to the poor "trainee." They were upset and distressed by the "trainee's" cries. Some of them tried to stop the experiment, but they continued when the experimenter said that they had to go on. This experiment would seem to be a good demonstration of the power of hypnosis—except for the fact that none of the subjects were hypnotized! (The experiment is described in more detail in Chapter 17.)

Results such as these show why it is imperative that appropriate control groups be used in any experiment that attempts to determine whether hypnosis can induce people to commit antisocial acts. Even if hypnotized subjects perform acts that they believe to be antisocial or dangerous, how can we be sure that they would not have performed them *without* being hypnotized? An experiment by Coe, Kobayashi, and Howard (1973) found that several unhypnotized subjects were quite willing to become involved in a scheme to sell heroin. One subject later revealed that he had planned to attack a confederate of the experimenters (someone hired to play a role in the study) and steal the money involved in the transaction. Clearly, if people

commit an antisocial act when hypnotized, we cannot conclude that they did so *because* they were hypnotized unless the members of the control group fail to do so. And in the experiment by Coe et al. this was not the case.

What about the use of hypnosis for seduction? Again, without a control group we cannot conclude that hypnosis was necessary. For example, how can we be sure that the physician described by Kline (1972) would not have managed to seduce some women without hypnotizing them? After all, most seductions do not involve hypnosis.

What Can We Conclude?   I think it is unlikely that any experiment that follows proper ethical guidelines will be able to tell us whether hypnosis can be used to induce people to perform acts that violate their moral codes. First, the context of the experimental setting is a rather good guarantee that the subject will be protected from harm and prevented from harming another person. Second, it is difficult to determine just what a person's moral code is. Sometimes, people surprise us by their willingness to perform antisocial acts. And even if they believe that an act is harmful to someone else and that performing the act would violate their own moral code, they may tell themselves that whatever they do, it will be the experimenter's fault—and thus perform the act anyway. What they tell themselves will, of course, be absolutely correct. Suppose that an experimenter instructs a subject to do something that would seem to harm someone else. The subject complies, something goes wrong, and the other person really is hurt. Who is to blame? Obviously, it is the experimenter, not the subject.

The issue of hypnosis and antisocial behavior is an interesting one, but it will probably never be resolved. Even the scientific method cannot provide answers to every question we ask.   ■

Uses of Hypnosis

Hypnosis can play a useful role in medicine, dentistry, and psychotherapy. The analgesia (insensitivity to pain) produced by hypnosis is more effective than that produced by morphine, tranquilizers such as Valium, or acupuncture (Stern, Brown, Ulett, and Sletten, 1977). Thus, it can be used to suppress the pain of childbirth or of having one's teeth drilled or to prevent gagging when a dentist is working in a patient's mouth. It is also useful in reducing the nausea caused by the drugs used in chemotherapy for cancer.

However, because not all people can be hypnotized, and because the induction of hypnosis takes some time, few physicians or dentists use hypnosis to reduce pain—drugs are easier to administer. Hypnosis can also be used to help people break a bad habit such as smoking or overeating. As we have seen, hypnosis is a useful tool for research into human consciousness. Finally, hypnosis is often used in psychotherapy to help the patient discuss painful memories whose inaccessibility is impeding progress.

Reputable societies such as the American Medical Association and the American Psychological Association are opposed to the use of hypnosis for memory enhancement in criminal investigations. As we saw in the "Evaluating Scientific Issues" section of Chapter 7, hypnotic suggestions can alter people's memories or establish entirely new ones—which would render a witness's testimony invalid. But this characteristic of hypnosis has been exploited by clinicians to help their clients overcome the long-term effects of painful memories, such as those responsible for phobias (Baker, 1990). The therapist hypnotizes the client and has the client imagine the time and setting in which the traumatic event occurred. Then the therapist describes a different, more pleasant episode and suggests that the client will now remember the event differently. When this method successfully changes the memory, people often find that their phobia is eliminated.

INTERIM SUMMARY

Hypnosis

Hypnosis is a form of verbal control over a person's consciousness in which the hypnotist's suggestions affect some of the subject's perceptions and behaviors. Although some people have viewed hypnosis as a mysterious, trancelike state, investigations have shown its phenomena to be similar to many phenomena of normal consciousness. There is no single way to induce hypnosis, and the responses depend very much on what the hypnotist says. If the hypnotist stresses sleepiness, subjects will become sleepy; if the hypnotist tells the subjects to remain alert, they will do so.

Hilgard regards hypnosis as a form of dissociation, in which some streams of consciousness are divided from others. In this way perceptions can be separated from consciousness, and consciousness can be separated from motor con-

trol. The hidden observer phenomenon supports this conclusion. In contrast, Barber asserts that being hypnotized is similar to participating vicariously in a narrative, which is something we do whenever we become engrossed in a novel, a movie, a drama, or even the recounting of a friend's experience. When we are engrossed in this way, we experience genuine feelings of emotion, even though the situation is not "real." Studies by proponents of the hypothesis that hypnosis is the enactment of a social role have shown that the characteristics of the hidden observer can be affected by suggestion.

Although researchers have devised some ingenious experiments, we still do not know whether hypnosis can induce people to perform behaviors that they would not otherwise perform. For one thing, they will almost always assume that the experimenter has taken steps to protect them and prevent them from harming someone else. For another thing, many *unhypnotized* people perform what would appear to be antisocial acts; thus, the compliance rate is usually quite similar in experimental and control groups. Finally, even people who would not normally perform antisocial or distasteful acts may do so because they (correctly) assume that the experimenter is responsible for what they do.

Whatever its causes, hypnosis has been shown to be useful in reducing pain, eliminating bad habits, and helping people talk about painful thoughts and memories. However, as we saw in Chapter 7, most investigators distrust the use of hypnosis to refresh the memories of witnesses of crimes. ■

SLEEP

[7] Sleep is not a state of unconsciousness; it is a state of *altered* consciousness. During sleep we have dreams that can be just as vivid as waking experiences, and yet we forget most of them as soon as they are over. Our amnesia leads us to think—incorrectly—that we were unconscious while we were asleep. In fact, there are two distinct kinds of sleep—thus, two states of altered consciousness.

We spend approximately one-third of our lives sleeping—or trying to. Thus, you may think the reason we sleep is clearly understood by scientists who study this phenomenon. And yet, despite the efforts of many talented researchers, we are still not sure why we sleep. Many people are preoccupied with sleep or with the lack of it. Collectively, they consume tons of drugs each year in an attempt to get to sleep.

Figure 8.14 A subject prepared for a night's sleep in a sleep laboratory.

Advertisements for nonprescription sleep medications imply that a night without a full eight hours of sleep is a physiological and psychological disaster. Is this worry justified? Does missing a few hours—or even a full night—of sleep actually harm us? As we will see, the answer seems to be no.

The Stages of Sleep

Sleep is not uniform. We can sleep lightly or deeply; we can be restless or still; we can have vivid dreams or our consciousness can be relatively blank. Researchers who have studied sleep have found that its stages usually follow an orderly, predictable sequence.

Most sleep research takes place in a sleep laboratory. Because a person's sleep is affected by his or her surroundings, a sleep laboratory contains one or more small bedrooms, furnished and decorated to be as homelike and comfortable as possible. The most important apparatus of the sleep laboratory is the **polygraph,** a machine located in a separate room that records on paper the output of various devices that can be attached to the subject. For example, the polygraph can record the electrical activity of the brain (an **EEG,** or **electroencephalogram**) through small metal disks pasted to the scalp. It can record electrical signals from muscles (an **EMG,** or **electromyogram**) or from the heart (an **EKG,** or **electrocardiogram**). Or it can record eye movements (an **EOG,** or **electrooculogram**) through small metal disks attached to the skin around the eyes. Other special transducers can detect respiration, sweating, skin or body temperature, and a variety of other physiological states.

Let us look at a typical night's sleep of a female college student on her third night in the laboratory. (Of course, we would obtain similar results from a male, with one exception, which is noted later.) The EEG electrodes are attached to her scalp, EMG electrodes to her chin, EKG electrodes to her chest, and EOG electrodes to the skin around her eyes. (See *Figure 8.14.*) Wires connected to these electrodes are plugged into the amplifiers of the polygraph. The output of each amplifier causes a pen on the polygraph to move up and down while a long, continuous sheet of paper moves by.

The EEG record distinguishes between alert and relaxed wakefulness. When a person is alert, the tracing looks rather irregular, and the pens do not move very far up or down. The EEG in this case shows high-frequency (15–30 Hz), low-amplitude electrical activity called **beta activity.** When a person is relaxed and perhaps somewhat drowsy, the record shows **alpha activity,** a medium-amplitude, medium-frequency (8–12 Hz) rhythm. (See *Figure 8.15.*)

The technician leaves the room, the lights are turned off, and the subject closes her eyes. As she relaxes and grows drowsy, her EEG changes from beta activity to alpha activity. The first stage of sleep (stage 1) is marked by the presence of some **theta activity** (3.5–7.5 Hz). This stage is actually a transition between sleep and wakefulness; the EMG shows that her muscles are still active, and her EOG indicates slow, gentle, rolling eye movements. The eyes slowly open and close from time to time. Soon, the subject is fully asleep. As sleep progresses, it gets deeper and deeper, moving through stages

Awake

Alpha activity   Beta activity

Stage 1 sleep

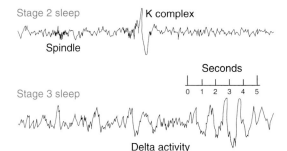

Theta activity

Stage 2 sleep   K complex

Spindle

Seconds

0 1 2 3 4 5

Stage 3 sleep

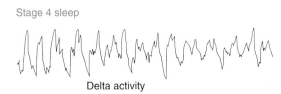

Delta activity

Stage 4 sleep

Delta activity

REM sleep

Theta activity   Beta activity

Figure 8.15 An EEG recording of the stages of sleep. (From Horne, J.A. *Why We Sleep: The Functions of Sleep in Humans and Other Mammals.* Oxford, England: Oxford University Press, 1988. Copyright 1988 Oxford University Press. By permission of Oxford University Press.)

2, 3, and 4. The EEG gets progressively slower in frequency and higher in amplitude. (See *Figure 8.15.*) Stage 4 consists mainly of **delta activity,** characterized by relatively high-amplitude waves occurring at less than 3.5 Hz. Our subject becomes less responsive to the environment, and it becomes more difficult to awaken her. Environmental stimuli that caused her to stir during stage 1 produce little or no reaction during stage 4. The sleep of stages 3 and 4 is called **slow-wave sleep.**

Stage 4 sleep is reached in less than an hour and continues for as much as a half hour. Then, suddenly, the EEG begins to indicate lighter levels of sleep, back through stages 3 and 2 to the activity characteristic of stage 1. The subject's heart becomes irregular and her respiration alternates between shallow breaths and sudden gasps. The EOG shows that the subject's eyes are darting rapidly back and forth, up and down. The EEG record looks like that of a person who is awake and active. Yet the subject is fast asleep. Although her EMG is generally quiet, indicating muscular relaxation, her hands and feet twitch occasionally. (See *Figure 8.15.*)

At this point the subject is dreaming. She has entered another stage of sleep, called **rapid eye movement (REM) sleep.** The first REM sleep lasts about twenty to thirty minutes and is followed by approximately one hour of slow-wave sleep. As the night goes on, the intervals of REM sleep get longer and the intervals of slow-wave sleep get shorter, but the total cycle remains at approximately ninety minutes. A typical night's sleep consists of four or five of these cycles. Figure 8.16 shows a record of a person's stages of sleep; the colored shading indicates REM sleep. (See *Figure 8.16.*)

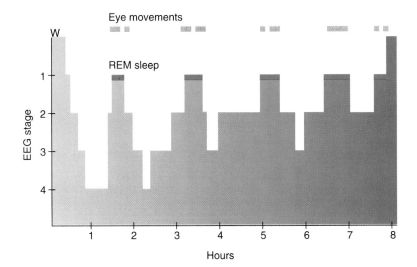

Figure 8.16 Typical progression of stages during a night's sleep. The colored shading indicates REM sleep. (From Hartmann, E. *The Biology of Dreaming,* 1967. Courtesy of Charles C. Thomas, Publisher, Springfield, Illinois.)

A person in REM sleep exhibits an EEG with irregular waves of low-voltage, rapid eye movements, brief twitches of the hands and feet, and rapid, irregular heart rate and breathing. The EMG shows that the facial muscles are still. In fact, physiological studies have shown that, aside from occasional twitching, a person actually becomes paralyzed during REM sleep. In addition, women's vaginal secretions increase at this time. Males are observed to have partial or full erections, which are usually not associated with sexual arousal—although both males and females sometimes have dreams of a sexual nature, occasionally ending with orgasm.

Functions of Sleep

8 Sleep is one of the few universal behaviors. All mammals, all birds, and some cold-blooded vertebrates spend part of each day sleeping. Sleep is seen even in species that would seem to be better off without sleep. For example, the Indus dolphin *(Platanista indi)* lives in the muddy waters of the Indus estuary in Pakistan (Pilleri, 1979). Over the years it has become blind, presumably because vision is not useful in the animal's environment. (It has an excellent sonar system, which it uses to navigate and find prey.) However, despite the dangers caused by sleeping, sleep has not disappeared. The Indus dolphin never stops swimming; doing so would result in injury, because of the dangerous currents and the vast quantities of debris carried by the river during the monsoon season. Pilleri captured two dolphins and studied their habits. He found that they slept a total of 7 hours a day, in very brief naps of 4–60 seconds each. If sleep did not perform an important function, we might

expect that it, like vision, would have been eliminated in this species through the process of natural selection.

Some other species of marine mammals have developed an extraordinary pattern of sleep: The cerebral hemispheres take turns sleeping, presumably because that strategy always permits at least one hemisphere to be alert. The bottlenose dolphin *(Tursiops truncatus)* and the porpoise *(Phocoena phocoena)* both sleep this way (Mukhametov, 1984). Figure 8.17 shows the EEG records from the two hemispheres; note that slow-wave sleep occurs independently in the left and right hemispheres. (See *Figure 8.17.*)

The universal nature of sleep suggests that it performs some important functions. But just what are they? The simplest explanation for sleep is that it serves to repair the wear and tear on our bodies caused by moving and exercising. Perhaps our bodies just get worn out by performing waking activities for sixteen hours or so.

One approach to the questions is the deprivation study. Consider, for example, the function of eating. The effects of starvation are easy to detect: The person loses weight, becomes fatigued, and will eventually die if he or she does not eat again. By analogy, it should be easy to discover why we sleep by seeing what happens to a person who goes without sleep.

Unfortunately, deprivation studies have not obtained persuasive evidence that sleep is needed to keep the body functioning normally. Horne (1978) reviewed over fifty experiments in which humans had been deprived of sleep. He reported that most of them found that sleep deprivation did not interfere with people's ability to perform physical exercise. In addition, they

Figure 8.17 Sleep in a dolphin. The two hemispheres sleep independently, presumably so that the animal remains behaviorally alert. (Adapted from Mukhametov, L.M., in *Sleep Mechanisms,* edited by A.A. Borbély and J.L. Valatx. Munich: Springer-Verlag, 1984.)

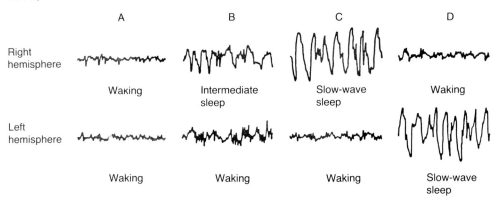

found no evidence of a physiological stress response to sleep deprivation. If people encounter stressful situations that cause illness or damage to various organ systems, changes can be seen in such physiological measures as blood levels of cortisol and epinephrine. (The physiology of stress is described in more detail in Chapter 12.) Generally, these changes did not occur.

Although sleep deprivation does not seem to damage the body, and sleep does not seem to be necessary for athletic exercise, sleep may be required for normal brain functioning. Several studies suggest that although sleep-deprived subjects are able to perform normally on most intellectual tasks, as long as the tasks are short, they perform more poorly on tasks that require a high level of cortical functioning after two days of sleep deprivation (Horne and Pettitt, 1985). In particular, they perform poorly on tasks that require them to be watchful, alert, and vigilant.

What happens to sleep-deprived subjects after they are permitted to sleep again? Most of them sleep longer the next night or two, but they never regain all of the sleep they lost. In one remarkable case a seventeen-year-old boy stayed awake for 264 hours so that he could obtain a place in the *Guinness Book of World Records* (Gulevich, Dement, and Johnson, 1966). After his ordeal the boy slept for a little less than 15 hours and awoke feeling fine. He slept slightly more than 10 hours the second night and just under 9 hours the third. Almost 67 hours were never made up. However, percentage of recovery was not equal for all stages of sleep. Only 7 percent of stages 1 and 2 were made up, but 68 percent of stage 4 slow-wave sleep and 53 percent of REM sleep were made up. This finding suggests that stage 4 sleep and REM sleep are more important than the other stages.

During stage 4 sleep the metabolic activity of the brain decreases to about 75 percent of the waking level (Sakai et al., 1979). Thus, stage 4 sleep appears to give the brain a chance to rest. In fact, people are unreactive to all but intense stimuli during slow-wave sleep and, if awakened, act groggy and confused—as if their cerebral cortex has been shut down and has not yet resumed its functioning. These observations suggest that during stage 4 sleep the brain is, indeed, resting.

Sleep deprivation studies with humans suggest that although the brain may need slow-wave sleep in order to recover from the day's activities, the rest of the body does not. Another way to determine whether sleep is needed for restoration of physiological functioning is to look at the effects of daytime activity on nighttime sleep. If the function of sleep is to repair the effects of activity during waking hours, then we should expect that sleep and exercise are related. That is, we should sleep more after a day of vigorous exercise than after a day spent quietly at an office desk.

In fact, the relation between sleep and exercise is not very compelling. For example, Ryback and Lewis (1971) found no changes in slow-wave or REM sleep of healthy subjects who spent six weeks resting in bed. If sleep repairs wear and tear, we would expect these people to sleep less. Adey, Bors, and Porter (1968) studied the sleep of *completely* immobile quadriplegics and paraplegics and found only a small decrease in slow-wave sleep as compared with uninjured people.

Horne (1981, 1988) reported that some studies have found that exercise increases slow-wave sleep but others have not. He noted that an important factor seems to be the climate in which the exercise occurs. If the temperature and the humidity are high, the exercise is likely to increase slow-wave sleep. Horne suggested that the important variable might be whether the exercise succeeded in heating the body.

To test this hypothesis, Horne and Moore (1985) had subjects exercise on a treadmill. Some subjects were cooled by electric fans, and their skin was periodically sprayed with water. Their body temperature rose only 1°C. That night, the slow-wave sleep of the "hot exercised" subjects rose by 25 percent, whereas that of the "cool exercised" subjects was unchanged. Horne (1988) now believes that the increased body temperature itself is not the significant factor but that an increase in brain temperature is. Perhaps, he says, an increase in brain temperature raises its metabolic rate and hence its demand for more slow-wave sleep. A preliminary study suggests that this hypothesis may have some merit. Horne and Harley (1988) warmed subjects' heads and faces with a hair dryer, which raised their brain temperature by an estimated 1°C. Four of the six subjects showed an increase in slow-wave sleep the next night. Clearly, further research is needed.

Although bodily exercise has little effect on sleep (as long as the brain remains cool), *mental* exercise seems to increase the demand for slow-wave sleep. In an ingenious study Horne and Minard (1985) found a way to increase mental activity without affecting physical activity and without causing stress. The investigators told subjects to show up for an experiment in which they were supposed to take some tests designed to test reading skills. In fact, when the subjects turned up, they were told that the plans had been changed. They were invited for a day out, at the expense of the experimenters. (Not surprisingly, the subjects willingly accepted.) They spent the day visiting an art exhibition, a shopping center, a museum, an amusement park, a zoo, and an interesting mansion. After a scenic drive through the countryside they watched a movie in a local theater. They were driven from place to place and certainly did not become overheated by exercise. After the movie they returned to the sleep laboratory. They said they were tired, and they readily fell asleep. Their sleep duration was normal, and they awoke feeling refreshed. However, their slow-wave sleep—particularly stage 4 sleep—was increased.

Dreaming

9 One of the most fascinating aspects of sleep is the fact that we enter a fantasy world several times each night during which we perceive imaginary events and perform imaginary behaviors. Why do we do so?

States of Consciousness During Sleep. A person who is awakened during REM sleep and asked whether anything was happening will almost always report a dream. The typical REM sleep dream resembles a play or movie—it has a narrative form. Conversely, reports of narrative, storylike dreams are rare among people awakened from slow-wave sleep. In general, mental activity during slow-wave sleep is more nearly static; it involves situations rather than stories and generally unpleasant ones. For example, a person awakened from slow-wave sleep might report a sensation of being crushed or suffocated.

Unless the sleep is heavily drugged, almost everyone has four or five bouts of REM sleep each night, with accompanying dreams. Yet if the dreamer does not happen to awaken while the dream is in progress, it is lost forever. Some people who claimed not to have had a dream for many years slept in a sleep laboratory and found that, in fact, they did dream. They were able to remember their dreams because the investigator awakened them during REM sleep.

Because we recall dreams only if we awaken during their progress, light sleepers tend to remember more dreams than heavy sleepers; we are also most likely to recall dreams that occur toward morning, just before awakening, when our sleep is lightest. Many

people in psychotherapy learn to remember their dreams so that they can discuss them with their therapists. Apparently, they are somehow able to awaken themselves during REM sleep.

The reports of people awakened from REM and slow-wave sleep clearly show that people are conscious during sleep, even though they may not remember any of their experiences then. Lack of memory for an event does not mean that it never happened; it only means that there is no permanent record accessible to conscious thought during wakefulness. Thus, we can say that slow-wave sleep and REM sleep reflect two different states of consciousness.

Why Do We Dream? There are two major approaches to the study of dreaming: a psychological analysis of the contents of dreams, and psychobiological research on the nature and functions of REM sleep. Let us consider the psychological analysis first.

Symbolism in Dreams. Since ancient times, people have regarded dreams as important, using them to prophesy the future, decide whether to go to war, or determine the guilt or innocence of a person accused of a crime. In this century Sigmund Freud proposed a very influential theory about dreaming. He said that dreams arise out of inner conflicts between unconscious desires (primarily sexual ones) and prohibitions against acting out these desires, which we learn from society. According to Freud, although all dreams represent unfulfilled wishes, their contents are disguised and expressed symbolically. The *latent content* of the dream (from the Latin word for "hidden") is transformed into the *manifest content* (the actual story line or plot). Taken at face value, the manifest content is innocuous, but a knowledgeable psychoanalyst can recognize unconscious desires disguised as symbols in the dream. For example, climbing a set of stairs or shooting a gun might represent sexual intercourse. The problem with Freud's theory is that it is not disprovable; even if it is wrong, a psychoanalyst can always provide a plausible interpretation of a dream that reveals hidden conflicts, disguised in obscure symbols.

Hall (1966), who agrees that symbols can be found in dreams, does not believe that they are usually hidden. For example, a person may plainly engage in sexual intercourse in one dream and have another dream that involves shooting a gun. Surely the "real" meaning of shooting the gun need not be hidden from a dreamer who has undisguised dreams of sexual intercourse at other times or who has an unin-

Marc Chagall's painting depicts images and symbols that could occur in a dream. Freud's assertion that dreams provide an opportunity for unconscious desires to be expressed symbolically is challenged by many psychologists today.

hibited sex life during waking. Why should this person disguise sexual desires while dreaming? As Hall says, people use their own symbols, not those of anyone else. They represent what the dreamer thinks, and therefore, their meaning is usually not hidden from the dreamer.

Sometimes, people dream about things that they avoid thinking about while awake, and these dreams may be filled with symbols whose significance they cannot recognize. In such cases a good psychotherapist may be able to use information from the dreams to understand what problems are bothering the client, in order to help the client with his or her difficulties. However, we cannot infer from these relatively rare situations that all dreams of all people are filled with symbols whose meanings can be understood only by a person with special training.

Hobson (1988) proposes an explanation for dreaming that does not involve unconscious conflicts or desires. Research has shown that REM sleep occurs when a circuit of acetylcholine-secreting neurons in the pons becomes active, stimulating rapid eye movements, activation of the cerebral cortex, and muscular paralysis. The activation of the visual system produces both eye movements and images. In fact, several experiments have found that the particular eye movements that a person makes during a dream correspond reasonably well with the content of a dream; that is, the eye movements are those that one would expect a person to make if the imaginary events were really occurring (Dement, 1974). The images evoked by the cortical activation often incorporate memories of episodes that have occurred recently or of things that a person has been thinking about lately. Presumably, the circuits responsible for these

memories are more excitable because they have recently been active. Hobson suggests that although the activation of these brain mechanisms produces fragmentary images, our brains try to tie these images together and make sense of them by creating a more or less plausible story.

We still do not know whether the particular topics we dream about are somehow related to the functions that dreams serve, or whether the purposes of REM sleep are fulfilled by the physiological changes in the brain—regardless of the plots of our dreams. Given that we do not really know for sure why we dream, this uncertainty is not surprising. But the rapid progress being made in most fields of brain research suggests that we will have some answers in the not-too-distant future.

10 *Effects of REM Sleep Deprivation.* There is considerable evidence that selective deprivation of REM sleep has effects on subsequent behavior. People who are sleeping in a laboratory can be selectively deprived of REM sleep; an investigator awakens them whenever the polygraph record indicates that they have entered REM sleep. The investigator must also awaken control subjects just as often at random intervals to eliminate any effects produced by being awakened several times.

If someone is deprived of REM sleep for several nights and is then allowed to sleep without interruption, the onset of REM sleep becomes more frequent. It is as if a need for REM sleep builds up, forcing the person into this state more often. When the subject is no longer awakened during REM sleep, a rebound phenomenon is seen: The subject engages in many more bouts of REM sleep than normal during the next night or two, as if catching up on something important that was missed.

Many studies with laboratory animals have shown that deprivation of REM sleep affects retention of new tasks learned during the previous day. For example, Rideout (1979) gave hungry mice one opportunity to run through a maze each day and find food at the end. After each day's trial he deprived some of them of REM sleep by putting them on a small platform in a cage filled with water. The mice who were deprived of REM sleep learned their way around the maze more slowly than the mice who were not deprived of REM sleep.

Deprivation of REM sleep in humans appears to have a greater effect on the assimilation of events that produce strong emotions than it does on simple learning. The saying "Things will look better in the morning" appears to be true. For example, Greenberg, Pillard, and Pearlman (1972) had subjects view a film of a very bloody and gruesome circumcision rite performed by a primitive tribe. This film produces anxiety when it is watched the first time; but if it is watched again on a later date, the anxiety effect is much smaller. Greenberg and his colleagues showed the film twice, on two separate days, to two groups of subjects. One group was permitted to sleep normally; the other group was deprived of REM sleep. The sleep-deprived subjects showed much less reduction in anxiety at the second viewing than the subjects who were permitted to obtain REM sleep. The results suggest that REM sleep may perform a role in reducing anxiety produced by events that occurred during the day; perhaps we really do "work things out" during REM sleep.

The calming effect of REM sleep appears to be contradicted by a puzzling phenomenon. The symptoms of people with severe depression are *reduced* when they are deprived of REM sleep. In addition, treatments that reduce the symptoms of depression, such as antidepressant drugs and electroconvulsive therapy, also suppress REM sleep. (These results will be discussed in more detail in Chapter 16.) If REM sleep helps people assimilate emotionally relevant information, why should REM sleep deprivation relieve the symptoms of people who are suffering from a serious emotional disorder? Unfortunately, we do not have an answer for this question yet.

Disorders Associated with REM Sleep. REM sleep is controlled by special circuits in the brain. When something goes wrong with these circuits, interesting symptoms can occur. As we saw, two important behavioral characteristics of REM sleep are dreaming and paralysis. The paralysis probably results from a mechanism that prevents us from acting out our dreams. We think of dreams as sensory events—as hallucinatory episodes—but very often the dreamer plays an active role in the dream. That is, the dreamer engages in imaginary action. In fact, the motor cortex and other regions of the brain involved in the control of movement become very active during REM sleep. Jouvet (1972) found that damage to a certain region in the pons of a cat's brain will prevent the animal from becoming paralyzed during REM sleep. The cat—still asleep—acts as if it were participating in the kind of a dream we would expect a cat to have: It walks around stalking imaginary prey and responding defensively to imaginary predators.

This phenomenon can occur in humans, too. A few years ago, Schenck, Bundlie, Ettinger, and Mahowald (1986) reported the existence of an interesting syndrome: **REM sleep behavior disorder.** Consider the following case:

> I was a halfback playing football, and after the quarterback received the ball from the center he lateraled it sideways to me and I'm supposed to go around end and cut back over tackle and—this is very vivid—as I cut back over tackle there is this big 280-pound tackle waiting, so I, according to football rules, was to give him my shoulder and bounce him out of the way . . . when I came to I was standing in front of our dresser and I had [gotten up out of bed and run and] knocked lamps, mirrors and everything off the dresser, hit my head against the wall and my knee against the dresser. (Schenck, Bundlie, Ettinger, and Mahowald, 1986, p. 294)

As we saw earlier in this chapter, studies with laboratory animals have shown that the neural circuitry that controls the paralysis that accompanies REM sleep is located in the pons. In humans, REM sleep behavior disorder seems to be produced by damage to this region (Culebras and Moore, 1989).

Dreams and muscular paralysis are fine when a person is lying in bed. But sometimes, a person is struck down by paralysis while actively going about his or her business. The person falls to the ground and lies there, paralyzed but fully conscious. These attacks of **cataplexy** (*kata-*, "down"; *plessein*, "to strike") generally last less than a minute. The attacks are usually triggered by strong emotional states, such as anger, laughter, or even lovemaking. People who have cataplectic attacks tend also to enter REM sleep as soon as they fall asleep, in contrast to the normal ninety-minute interval.

People who suffer from cataplexy also tend to have vivid **hypnagogic hallucinations** just before they fall asleep, during which they are paralyzed. The hallucinations, which are almost certainly premature dreams, are often continuations of events that have actually occurred. For example, a patient in a sleep laboratory experienced a hypnagogic hallucination in which the experimenter, who had just attached the electrodes, was attempting to cut off his ear with a scalpel (Dement, 1974). Thus, the disorder appears to involve overactive REM sleep mechanisms; the cataplexy is probably caused by inappropriate activity of the brain mechanism that keeps a person paralyzed during dreaming.

Cataplexy appears to be a biological disorder, probably involving inherited abnormalities in the brain. In fact, researchers have even developed breeds of dogs that are subject to attacks of cataplexy. (See *Figure 8.18.*) Cataplexy can be treated by drugs that increase the activity of neurons that use a particular transmitter substance (serotonin) to communicate with other neurons. In contrast, LSD and mescaline, drugs that produce visual hallucinations,

Figure 8.18 Dogs bred for vulnerability to cataplexy. (Top) Attack beginning. (Bottom) Attack complete; recovery is beginning. (Sleep Disorder Clinic, Stanford University.)

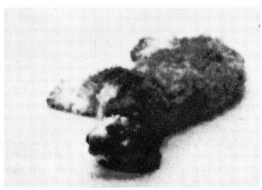

inhibit the activity of serotonin-secreting neurons. These findings suggest that there may be a relation between dreams and the hallucinations caused by LSD: Serotonin-stimulating drugs reduce them, whereas serotonin-inhibiting drugs make them more likely to occur.

INTERIM SUMMARY

Sleep

Sleep consists of several stages of slow-wave sleep, characterized by increasing amounts of delta activity in the EEG, and REM sleep, characterized by beta activity in the EEG, rapid eye movements, general paralysis (into which occasional twitching movements of the hands and feet intrude), and dreaming. Sleep is a behavior, not simply an altered state of consciousness. Although evidence suggests that sleep is not necessary for repairing the wear and tear caused by physical exercise, it may play an important role in providing an opportunity for the brain to rest.

Although narrative dreams occur only during REM sleep, people often are conscious of static situations during slow-wave sleep. Freud suggested that dreams provided the opportunity for unconscious conflicts to express themselves through symbolism in dreams. Hobson suggests that dreams are the attempts of the brain to make sense of hallucinations produced by the activation of the cerebral cortex. The function of REM sleep is uncertain, but it may be to integrate memories of events that happened during the preceding day. REM sleep also seems to play some role in sorting out emotionally significant memories.

Some disorders appear to be caused by malfunctions of the brain's sleep mechanisms. REM sleep behavior disorder is caused by damage to the neural circuits in the pons that produces paralysis during REM sleep; people with this disorder act out their dreams. Cataplectic attacks are caused by activation, at inappropriate times, of the mechanism that causes paralysis during REM sleep. Hypnagogic hallucinations are premature dreams. The REM sleep mechanisms appear to be under the control of neurons that secrete serotonin as a transmitter substance; drugs that stimulate this type of neuron are useful in treating cataplexy and hypnagogic hallucinations.

A final note: This chapter has explained consciousness in terms of verbal control, verbal mediation, and verbal access. It has also described the basic phenomena related to consciousness, including its dependence on the brain mechanisms of verbal behavior and its role in hypnosis, meditation, and sleep. Although consciousness is a private phenomenon, we can study it only through public phenomena—namely, the behaviors of other people. For this reason aspects of consciousness that do not manifest themselves in behavior (words, gestures, facial expressions of emotion, and the like) can never reveal themselves to us. This chapter suggests that study of these behaviors will reveal all that is essential to consciousness, because consciousness itself is a by-product of our ability to communicate with each other. In other words, thinking to ourselves and being aware of our own existence derive from our ability to talk about our existence and experiences to others. ∎

APPLICATION

Treatment of Sleep Disorders

Sleep does not always go smoothly, and some of the brain mechanisms responsible for sleep can malfunction, causing medical problems that manifest themselves while a person is awake. Fortunately, some of the things that sleep researchers have learned can help people with sleep-associated disorders.

Insomnia. Insomnia is a problem that is said to affect at least 20 percent of the population at some time (Raybin and Detre, 1969). However, I must emphasize that there is no single definition of insomnia that can apply to all people. The amount of sleep that individuals require is quite variable. A short sleeper may feel fine with 5 hours; a long sleeper may still feel unrefreshed after 10 hours of sleep. Insomnia must be defined in relation to a person's particular sleep needs. Some short sleepers have sought medical assistance because they thought that they were supposed to get more sleep, even though they felt fine. These people should be reassured that whatever amount of sleep seems to be enough *is* enough. Meddis, Pearson, and Langford (1973) reported the case of a seventy-year-old woman who slept approximately 1 hour each day (documented by sessions in a sleep laboratory). She felt fine and was of the opinion that most people "wasted much time" in bed.

Ironically, the most important cause of insomnia seems to be sleeping medication. Insomnia is not a disease that can be corrected with a medicine, in the way that diabetes can be treated with insulin. Insomnia is a symptom. If it is caused by pain or discomfort, the physical ailment that leads to the sleeplessness should be treated. If it is secondary to personal problems or psychological disorders, these problems should be dealt with directly. Patients who receive a sleeping medication develop a tolerance to the drug and suffer rebound symptoms if it is withdrawn (Weitzman, 1981). That is, the drug loses its effectiveness, so the patient requests larger doses from the physician. If the patient attempts to sleep without the accustomed medication or even takes a smaller dose one night, he or she is likely to experience a withdrawal effect: a severe disturbance of sleep. The patient becomes convinced that the insomnia is even worse than before and turns to more medication for relief. This common syndrome is called *drug dependency insomnia.* Kales, Scharf, Kales, and Soldatos (1979) found that withdrawal of some sleeping medications produced a rebound insomnia after the drugs were used for as few as three nights.

Most patients who receive a prescription for a sleeping medication are given one on the basis of their own description of their symptoms. That is, they tell their physician that they sleep very little at night, and the drug is prescribed on the basis of this testimony. Very few patients are observed during a night's sleep in a sleep laboratory; thus, insomnia is one of the few medical problems that physicians treat without having direct clinical evidence for its existence. But studies on the sleep of people who complain of insomnia show that most of them grossly underestimate the amount of time they actually sleep. The U.S. Institute of Medicine (1979) found that most insomniacs, even without sleeping medication, fall asleep in less than 30 minutes and sleep for at least 6 hours. *With* sleeping medication they obtained less than a 15-minute reduction in falling asleep, and their sleep length was increased by only about 30 minutes. Given the unfortunate side effects, sleeping medication should not be taken for more than a few days at a time.

A common cause of insomnia in older people is *sleep apnea* (*apnea* means "without breathing"): They cannot sleep and breathe at the same time. When they fall asleep, they stop breathing, the content of carbon dioxide in their blood builds up, and they awaken, gasping for air. After breathing deeply for a while, they go back to sleep and resume the cycle. Some people who suffer from sleep apnea are blessed with a lack of memory for this periodic sleeping

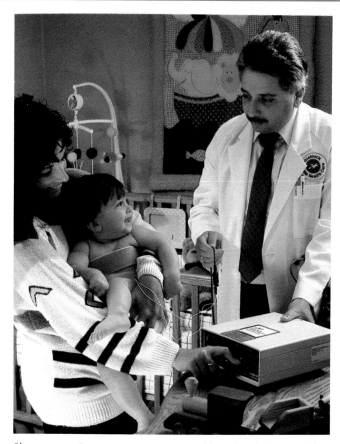

Sleep apnea *is temporary cessation of breathing during sleep. Children at risk for* sudden infant death syndrome *can be fitted with a sensor connected to an electronic infant monitoring system. An alarm will sound if the infant stops breathing for several seconds, thereby alerting the parents to wake the child.*

and awakening; others are aware of it and dread each night's sleep. Fortunately, some types of sleep apnea in adults can be corrected by throat surgery.

Many investigators have suggested that sleep apnea accounts for the *sudden infant death syndrome* ("crib death"), which mysteriously kills babies in their sleep. Evidence suggests that a susceptibility to SIDS is inherited; parents and siblings of some infants who have died of SIDS do not respond normally to increases in carbon dioxide (Kelly et al., 1980; Schiffman et al., 1980). Often infants who die of SIDS show signs of a low-grade illness, which may increase the tissue need for oxygen while simultaneously depressing respiratory mechanisms. Many infants' lives have been saved by monitoring devices that sound an alarm when a susceptible infant stops breathing during sleep, thus waking the parents in time for them to revive the child.

Some people suffer from an interesting, but unfortunate, form of "pseudoinsomnia": They dream that they are lying in bed—awake—trying unsuccessfully to fall asleep. In the morning their memories are of a night of insomnia,

and they feel as unrefreshed as if they really *had* been awake.

Insomnia can neither kill nor disable you. If a more basic problem, such as depression, seems to be causing your insomnia, get professional help. If there are no obvious causes and the insomnia is not severe, try doing your worrying (or whatever else it is that may interfere with sleep) *before* going to bed. Make bed a place where you sleep, not where you worry. Establish and follow a regular routine when you get ready for bed. If you do not fall asleep in a reasonable amount of time, do not lie there fretting. *Get up and do something else,* and do not go back to bed until you feel drowsy. Even if you are up most of the night, stay up until you feel sleepy enough to doze off as soon as you get into bed. Remember that you will survive even if you miss a night's sleep. Make yourself get up at a regular time each morning; if you do, you will eventually find it easier to fall asleep at night. Avoid taking naps; they make it more difficult to establish a strong daily pattern of sleep and wakefulness. Finally, remember that stimulants such as caffeine or depressants such as alcohol can be important sources of sleep disorders.

Disorders Associated with Slow-Wave Sleep. Several phenomena occur during the deepest phase (stage 4) of slow-wave sleep. These events include sleepwalking, sleeptalking, night terrors, and enuresis.

Sleepwalking can be as simple as getting out of bed and right back in again, or as complicated as walking out of a house and climbing into a car. (Fortunately, sleepwalkers apparently do not try to drive.) We know that sleepwalking is not the acting out of a dream, because it occurs during stage 4 of slow-wave sleep, when the EEG shows high-amplitude slow waves and the person's mental state generally involves a static situation, not a narrative. Sleepwalkers are difficult to awaken; and once awakened, they are often confused and disoriented. However, contrary to popular belief, it is perfectly safe to wake them up.

Sleepwalking is *not* a manifestation of some deep-seated emotional problem. Most sleepwalkers are children, who almost invariably outgrow this behavior. The worst thing to do, according to sleep researchers, is to try to get them treated for it. Of course, a house inhabited by a sleepwalker should be made as safe as possible, and the doors should be kept locked at night. For some reason sleepwalking runs in families; Dement (1974) tells of a family whose grown members were reunited for a holiday celebration. In the middle of the night they awoke to find that they had all gathered in the living room—during their sleep.

Sleeptalking sometimes occurs as part of a REM sleep dream, but it more usually occurs during other stages of sleep. Often one can carry on a conversation with the sleeptalker, indicating that the person is very near the boundary between sleep and waking. During this state sleeptalkers are sometimes very suggestible. So-called truth serums are used in an attempt to duplicate this condition, so that the person being questioned is not on guard against giving away secrets and is not functioning well enough to tell elaborate lies. Unfortunately for the interrogators (and fortunately for the rest of the population), there are no foolproof, reliable truth serums.

Night terrors, like sleepwalking, occur most often in children. In this disorder the child awakes, screaming with terror. When questioned, the child does not report a dream and often seems confused. Usually, the child falls asleep quickly without showing any aftereffects and seldom remembers the event the next day. Night terrors are not the same as nightmares, which are simply frightening dreams from which one happens to awaken. Apparently, night terrors are caused by sudden awakenings from the depths of stage 4 sleep. The sudden, dramatic change in consciousness is a frightening experience for the child. The treatment for night terrors, like that for sleepwalking, is no treatment at all.

The final disorder of slow-wave sleep, *enuresis,* or "bed-wetting," is fairly common in young children. Most children outgrow it, just as they outgrow sleepwalking or night terrors. Emotional problems can trigger enuresis, but bed-wetting does not itself indicate that a child is psychologically unwell. The problem with enuresis is that, unlike the other stage 4 phenomena, there are aftereffects that must be cleaned up. Parents dislike having their sleep disturbed and get tired of frequently changing and laundering sheets. The resulting tension in family relationships can make the child feel anxious and guilty and can thus unnecessarily prolong the disorder.

Fortunately, a simple training method often cures enuresis. A moisture-sensitive device is placed under the bed sheet; when it gets wet, it causes a bell to ring. Because a child releases only a few drops of urine before the bladder begins to empty in earnest, the bell wakes the child in time to run to the bathroom. In about a week most children learn to prevent their bladders from emptying and manage to wait until morning. Perhaps what they really learn is not to enter such a deep level of stage 4 sleep in which the mechanism that keeps the bladder from emptying seems to break down.

Key terms and concepts

Consciousness as a Social Behavior

verbal access (235)
verbal control (235)

Attention

attention (237)
dichotic listening (237)
shadowing (237)
Balint's syndrome (242)
simultanagnosia (242)

Consciousness and the Brain

isolation aphasia (243)
corpus callosum (245)
split-brain operation (245)

Hypnosis

positive hallucination (248)
negative hallucination (248)

posthypnotic suggestibility (248)
posthypnotic amnesia (248)
neodissociation (249)
hidden observer (249)

Sleep

polygraph (256)
electroencephalogram (EEG) (256)
electromyogram (EMG) (256)
electrocardiogram (EKG) (256)
electro-oculogram (EOG) (256)
beta activity (256)
alpha activity (256)
theta activity (256)
delta activity (257)
slow-wave sleep (257)
rapid eye movement sleep (REM sleep) (257)
REM sleep behavior disorder (262)
cataplexy (262)
hypnagogic hallucination (263)

Wallace, B., and Fisher, L.E. *Consciousness and Behavior,* 3rd ed. Boston: Allyn and Bacon, 1991.

This book provides more information about a variety of topics related to consciousness, including some that I did not discuss in this chapter, such as extrasensory perception (ESP).

Jaynes, J. *The Origin of Consciousness in the Breakdown of the Bicameral Mind.* Boston: Houghton Mifflin, 1976.

Jaynes's book presents the provocative hypothesis that human consciousness is a recent phenomenon that emerged long after the evolution of the human brain, as we know it now. You do not need to agree with Jaynes's thesis to enjoy reading this scholarly book.

Winson, J. *Brain and Psyche: The Biology of the Unconscious.* Garden City, N.Y.: Anchor Press/Doubleday, 1985.

Winson, a neurophysiologist, attempts to explain the physiology of unconscious phenomena.

Baker, R.A. *They Call It Hypnosis.* Buffalo, N.Y.: Prometheus Books, 1990.

Laurence, J.-R., and Perry, C. *Hypnosis, Will, and Memory: A Psycho-Legal History.* New York: Guilford Press, 1988.

Sheehan, P.W., and McConkey, K.M. *Hypnosis and Experience: The Exploration of Phenomena and Process.* Hillsdale, N.J.: Lawrence Erlbaum Associates, 1982.

Wallace, B. *Applied Hypnosis: An Overview.* Chicago: Nelson-Hall, 1979.

If you would like to learn more about hypnosis, you will enjoy reading any of these books. The Sheehan and McConkey book provides a more advanced, scholarly approach; and the Wallace book discusses applications of hypnosis.

Cohen, D.B. *Sleep and Dreaming: Origins, Nature and Functions.* New York: Pergamon Press, 1979.

Horne, J. *Why We Sleep: The Functions of Sleep in Humans and Other Mammals.* Oxford: Oxford University Press, 1988.

Both of these books about sleep are excellent and interesting.

9
LANGUAGE AND THINKING

Henri Matisse, *Conversation*
SCALA/Art Resource, N.Y. © 1992 Succession H. Matisse/ARS, N.Y.

LEARNING OBJECTIVES

When you finish this chapter, you should be able to:

1. Explain the functions of language and describe the recognition of individual speech sounds.
2. Describe research on recognition and comprehension of words in continuous speech.
3. Describe evidence about the nature of speech comprehension and production from the study of aphasia.
4. Describe the role of eye-tracking experiments in the study of reading and discuss research on the distinction between phonetic and whole-word recognition.
5. Describe research on the way that readers comprehend the meaning of words and sentences.
6. Describe the perception of speech sounds by infants, the stages of language acquisition, and the way that adults talk to children.
7. Describe children's acquisition of adult rules of grammar and their acquisition of the meanings of words.
8. Discuss the controversy about the existence of an innate language acquisition device and discuss the role of reinforcement in language acquisition.
9. Describe research on the abilities of other primates to communicate verbally.
10. Describe research on concepts and their role in thinking.
11. Describe research on deductive and inductive reasoning.
12. Describe the roles of spatial metaphors and heuristics in problem solving.

Dr. W. ushered Mr. and Mrs. V. into the office and introduced us. Most people would not guess that Mr. V. had suffered brain damage; he walked normally, had normal control of his hands, and spoke without difficulty. Well, his speech was sometimes hesitant, but it would be easy to attribute that to his personality; he was somewhat shy and seemed content to let his wife do most of the talking.

Several months earlier, Mr. V. had been savagely beaten on the head with a tire iron. While he was visiting a friend, a stranger broke into the apartment, attacked him, and fled. His skull was fractured, and surgery was necessary to remove bone fragments and stop the bleeding within his brain.

Mr. V. was in a coma for several days, but once he regained consciousness, his recovery was rapid. However, although his vision was only slightly impaired, he had lost the ability to read. His job as production supervisor in a factory obviously required him to read, so he could not go back to work. He continued to hope that his occupational therapist would be able to help him regain his ability, so he had not officially retired from his job. Remarkably—and this is why I was particularly interested in meeting him—he could still write. Mrs. V. told the story.

"It was about six months after F. got out of the hospital. We were standing in the kitchen, which is right next to the utility room. The washing machine had broken, and a repairman was there fixing it. F. wanted to tell me something he didn't want the repairman to overhear, so he picked up a pencil and a pad of paper and wrote me a note. I started reading it and all of a sudden we realized what had happened. F. could write! It nearly bowled us both over. How could he write if he couldn't read?"

We tested Mr. V. and found that his wife was correct. Mr. V. could not read even the simplest words. He would stare at them, take off his glasses and put them on again, and complain that his eyes were bothering him. However, when we showed him pictures of objects and designs, he had no trouble recognizing them and perceiving fine details. *Words* were what he had trouble with. But when we asked him to write, he was able to do so. His spelling was not very good, and his handwriting was even worse than mine, but we could certainly recognize what he had written. We asked him to write several sentences, each on a different piece of paper. We then shuffled the papers and asked him to try to read them. He could not.

Mr. V.'s condition was first reported in the late nineteenth century by a French neurologist, J. Dejerine. Dejerine concluded that damage to his patient's brain prevented information from the visual system from reaching structures in the left hemisphere that were involved with the comprehension of words. The right hemisphere was intact, so the patient could still perceive and recognize objects. Subsequent research proved him to be correct. Dejerine's observations provided the first proof that the left hemisphere was specialized for reading as well as for the production and comprehension of speech.

With the exception of sexual behavior (without which our species would not survive), communication is probably the most important of all human social behaviors. This chapter discusses

Communication is an important social behavior. Did the artists who created the paintings on the walls of the Lascaux caves in France intend to say something to those who would later see them?

verbal communication; nonverbal communication is examined in Chapter 12. Our use of language can be private—we can think to ourselves in words or write diaries that are meant to be seen by no one but ourselves—but language evolved through social contacts among our early ancestors. Speaking and writing are clearly social behaviors: We learn these skills from other people and use them to communicate with them.

Although the word *language* suggests a formal, impersonal system, the acts of speaking, listening, writing, and reading are behaviors and, like other behaviors, can be studied. Linguists have studied the "rules" of language and have described precisely what we do when we speak or write. On the other hand, researchers in **psycholinguistics** (a branch of psychology) are more concerned with human cognition than with the particular rules that describe language. Psycholinguists are interested in how children acquire language—how verbal behavior develops and how children learn to speak from their interactions with adults. They also investigate the role of cognitive development in the acquisition of language. These issues, rather than the concerns of linguists, are the focus of the first three parts of this chapter. The fourth part examines communication with other primate species.

The final part of this chapter describes an important function of verbal behavior: thinking. This section discusses what psychologists have learned about the ways we categorize things and events into concepts, the means by which we engage in deductive and inductive reasoning, and the processes we use to solve problems.

SPEECH AND COMPREHENSION

1 The ability to engage in verbal behavior confers decided advantages on our species. Through listening and reading we can profit from the experiences of others, even from those of people who died long ago, and through talking and writing we can share the results of our own experiences. We can request from other people specific behaviors and information that are helpful to us. We can give information to other people so that their behavior will change in a way that benefits them (or us). Consider the effects of the following sentences:

Please hold that knot for me while I tie another one.

Which way am I supposed to turn this?

Whenever you do that, I get very angry.

I want some milk, Mommy.

The sink is full of dirty dishes.

I love you.

Besides using language to communicate with others, we can use it as a tool in our own remembering and thinking. As we saw in Chapter 7, we often encode information in memory verbally. In fact, Schiano and Watkins (1981) determined that people could retain a longer series of pictures of objects in short-term memory when the things the pictures showed had short names and when the names sounded very different from one another. Presumably, shorter names took less "room" in short-term memory, and different-sounding names were less likely to be confused. In long-term memory we can use a verbal code to extend our memory for information by writing notes and consulting them later. Language also enables us to think about very complex and abstract issues by encoding them in words and then manipulating the words according to logical rules.

Perception of Speech

When we speak to someone, we produce a series of sounds in a continuous stream, punctuated by pauses and modulated by stress and changes in pitch. We write sentences as sets of words, with spaces between them. But we *say* sentences as a string of sounds, emphasizing some, quickly sliding over others, raising the pitch of our voice on some, lowering it on others. We maintain a regular rhythmic pattern of stress. We pause at appropriate times—for example, between phrases—but we do not pause after pronouncing each word. Thus, speech does not come to us as a series of individual words; we must extract the words from a stream of speech.

Recognition of Speech Sounds. The human auditory system performs a formidably complex task in enabling us to recognize speech sounds. These sounds vary according to the sounds that precede and follow them, the speaker's accent, and the stress placed on the syllables in which they occur. **Phonemes** are the elements of speech—the smallest units of sound that contribute to the meaning of a word. For example, the word *pin* consists of three phonemes: /p/ + /i/ + /n/. Thus, the first step in recognizing speech sounds appears to be the identification of phonemes.

Many experiments have investigated how we discriminate among phonemes. Let us consider just one distinction that we can detect: **voice-onset time.** The distinction between voiced and unvoiced consonants permits us to distinguish between /p/ and /b/, between /k/ and /g/, and between /t/ and /d/. Try to figure out the difference yourself by saying *pa* and *ba*. Pay attention to what the sounds are like, not to how you move your lips to make them.

The difference is very subtle. When you say *pa,* you first build up a little pressure in your mouth. When you open your lips, a puff of air comes out. The *ah* sound does not occur immediately, because the air pressure in your mouth and throat keeps air from leaving your lungs for a brief time. When you say *ba,* you do not first build up pressure. Your vocal cords start vibrating as soon as your lips open. The vibration of your vocal cords is called *voicing.* The delay in voicing that occurs when you say *pa* is very slight: only 0.06 second. Try saying *pa* and *ba* aloud a few more times and note the difference. Your vocal cords will start vibrating just a little later when you say *pa.*

Lisker and Abramson (1970) presented subjects with a series of computer-generated sounds consisting of a puff followed by an *ah.* The sounds varied only in one way: the amount of time between the puff and the *ah.* When we speak, we make a puff for *pa* but not for *ba.* However, even though the computer always produced a puff, subjects reported that they heard *ba* when the delay was short and *pa* when it was long. As Figure 9.1 shows, subjects discriminated between the phonemes /p/ and /b/ strictly according to the delay in voicing. (Negative delays mean that the *ah* sound started *before* the puff.) Note how sharp the discrimination

is. Obviously, the auditory system is capable of detecting very subtle differences. (See ***Figure 9.1.***)

Although the fundamental unit of speech—logically and descriptively—is the phoneme, research suggests that *psychologically* the fundamental unit is larger. For example, the two syllables *doo* and *dee* each consist of two phonemes. When we hear them spoken, we hear the same phoneme /d/ at the beginning. But Liberman, Cooper, Shankweiler, and Studdert-Kennedy (1967) analyzed the sounds of the syllables and found that the beginning phonemes were *not* the same. In fact, they could not cut out a section of a tape recording of the two syllables that would sound like /d/.

Results like these suggest that the fundamental unit of speech consists of groups of phonemes, such as syllables. An experiment by Ganong (1980) supports this suggestion. He found that the perception of a phoneme is affected by the sounds that follow. He used a computer to synthesize a sound between those of the phonemes /g/ and /k/. When the sound was followed by *ift,* the subjects heard the word *gift,* but when it was followed by *iss,* they heard *kiss.* These results suggest that we recognize speech sounds in pieces larger than individual phonemes.

2 **Recognition of Words in Continuous Speech: The Importance of Context.** The perception of continuous speech involves different mechanisms from those used in the perception of isolated syllables. Because speech is full of hesitations, muffled sounds, and sloppy pronunciations, many individual words are hard to recognize out of context. For example, when

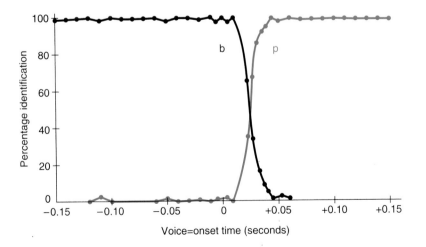

Figure 9.1 Identification of a sound as *ba* or *pa* as a function of voice-onset time. (From Lisker, L., and Abramson, A. *Proceedings of the Sixth International Congress of Phonetic Sciences, Prague, 1967.* Prague: Academia, 1970. Reprinted with permission.)

Pollack and Pickett (1964) isolated individual words from a recording of normal conversations and played them back to other people, those people correctly identified the words only 47 percent of the time. When they presented the same words in the context of the original conversation, the subjects identified and understood almost 100 percent of them. Miller, Heise, and Lichten (1951) found that subjects understood strings of words such as "who brought some wet socks" in a noisy environment but failed to understand strings such as "wet brought who socks some." These findings confirm that the context of speech provides important cues to our recognition of words.

The effect of context on the perception of words is an example of top-down processing. (This concept was discussed in Chapter 5, "Perception.") Other contexts also affect word perception. For example, although we tend to think of a conversation as involving only sounds, we also use other types of cues present in the environment to help us understand what someone is saying. If we are standing at a snack shop at a beach and someone says *I scream,* we are likely to hear it as *ice cream* (Reynolds and Flagg, 1983).

Understanding the Meaning of Speech

The meaning of a sentence (or of a group of connected sentences that are telling a story) is conveyed by the words that are chosen, the order in which they are combined, the affixes that are attached to the beginnings or ends of the words, the pattern of rhythm and emphasis of the speaker, and the knowledge about the world shared by the speaker and the listener. Let us examine some of these features.

Syntax. To get a listener to act upon speech, the speaker must follow the "rules" of language, using words with which the listener is familiar and combining them in specific ways. For example, if you say *The two boys looked at the heavy box,* you can expect to be understood; but if you say *Boys the two looking heavily the box at,* you will not be. Only the first sentence follows the rules of English grammar.

All languages have a *grammar;* that is, they follow certain principles, which linguists call **syntactical rules,** for combining words to form phrases, clauses, or sentences. (*Syntax,* like *synthesis,* comes from the Greek *syntassein,* "to put together.") Syntax provides important information. Consider the following sentence: *A*

little girl picked the pretty flowers. A linguist (or an English teacher) can analyze the sentence and identify the part of speech for each word. However, linguists and English teachers could *understand* sentences like this one while they were still children—even before they learned the names "articles," "noun phrases," and so on. Our understanding of syntax is automatic. We are no more conscious of this process than a child is conscious of the laws of physics when he or she learns to ride a bicycle.

The automatic nature of syntactical analysis is nicely illustrated by experiments performed with artificial grammars. For example, Reber and Allen (1978) devised a set of rules for combining the letters M, V, R, T, and X. For example, *MVRXR* and *VXTTV* were "grammatical" but *MXVTR* and *VMRTX* were "ungrammatical." (The rules were rather complex.) The subjects looked at twenty "grammatical" strings of letters, printed on index cards. They were told to "pay the utmost attention to the letter strings" but were not instructed to do anything else. Later, the subjects were presented with fifty different strings of letters, half of which were "grammatical" and half of which were not. Some of the "grammatical" strings were ones they had already seen, and some were new to them. The subjects were asked to indicate whether or not the strings were "grammatical."

The subjects did quite well; they correctly identified 81 percent of the strings of letters. Obviously, they had learned the rules, because they could recognize whether sequences they had never seen were correct. But despite their excellent performance, they could not express the rules verbally. The subjects made statements like the following: "The shapes of the items began to make sense." "While I know some things like the ok first and last letters, almost all my decisions are based on things looking either very right or very wrong. Sometimes for some reason things came out and glared at me saying, 'bad, bad, bad,' other times the letters just flowed together and I knew it was an ok item." "MXVR? MX? or XM? The MX hurts my eyes."

In Chapter 7 we saw that some memories (*implicit memories*) cannot be described verbally, whereas others (*explicit memories*) can. Apparently, the syntactic rules are learned implicitly. Later, we can be taught to talk about these rules and recognize their application (and, for example, construct diagrams of sentences), but this ability is not needed to speak and understand the speech of others. In fact, Knowlton,

Ramus, and Squire (1991) found that patients with anterograde amnesia were able to learn an artificial grammar, even though they had lost the ability to form explicit memories.

I have no intention of describing the syntactical rules of the English language; they are very complicated and would not tell you much about the psychology of verbal behavior. However, becoming acquainted with the types of cues we attend to in trying to understand things people say (or write) is useful. Syntactical cues are signaled by *word order, word class, function words, affixes, word meanings,* and *prosody.*

Word order is important in English. For example, if we say *The A Xs the B,* we are indicating that the agent is A, the object is B, and the thing being done is X. For example, in the sentences *The boy hit the ball* and *The ball hit the boy,* word order tells us who does what to whom.

Word class refers to the grammatical categories (such as noun, pronoun, verb, adjective) that we learn about in school. But a person need not learn to categorize these words deliberately in order to recognize them and use them appropriately. For example, when we hear a sentence containing the word *pretty,* we recognize that it refers to a person or a thing. Consider these two sentences: *The pretty girl picked the strawberries* and *The tablecloth was pretty.* Although the word *pretty* is used in two different ways, at the beginning or end of the sentence, we have no trouble identifying what the word refers to.

Words can be classified as function words or content words. **Function words** include determiners, quantifiers, prepositions, and words in similar categories: *a, the, to, some, and, but, when,* and so on. **Content words** include nouns, verbs, and most adjectives and adverbs: *apple, rug, went, caught, heavy, mysterious, thoroughly, sadly.* Content words express meaning; function words express the relations between content words and thus are very important syntactical cues. As we shall see later, people with a particular type of brain damage lose the ability to comprehend syntax. Included with this deficit is the inability to understand function words.

Affixes are sounds that we add to the beginning (*prefixes*) or end (*suffixes*) of words to alter their grammatical function. For example, we add the suffix *-ed* to the end of a regular verb to indicate the past tense *(drop/dropped);* we add *-ing* to a verb to indicate its use as a noun *(sing/ singing);* and we add *-ly* to an adjective to indicate its use as an adverb *(bright/brightly).* We are very quick to recognize the syntactical function of words with affixes like these. For exam-

ple, Epstein (1961) presented subjects with word strings such as the following:

> a vap koob desak the citar molent um glox nerf

> A vapy koob desaked the citar molently um glox nerfs.

Subjects could more easily remember the second string than the first, even though letters had been added. Apparently, the addition of the affixes *-y, -ed,* and *-ly* made the words seem more like a sentence and thus became easier to categorize and recall.

The *meaning* of a word provides important cues to the syntax of a sentence. For example, consider the following set of words: *Frank discovered a louse combing his beard.* The *syntax* of this sentence does not tell us whether Frank was combing Frank's beard, the louse was combing the louse's beard, or the louse was combing Frank's beard. But our knowledge of the world and of the usual meaning of words tells us that Frank was doing the combing, because people, not lice, have beards and combs.

Just as function words help us determine the syntax of a sentence, content words help us determine its meaning. For example, even with its function words removed, the following set of words still makes pretty good sense: *man placed wooden ladder tree climbed picked apples.* You can probably fill in the function words yourself and get *The man placed the wooden ladder against the tree, climbed it, and picked some apples.* We can often guess at function words, which is fortunate, because they are normally unstressed in speech and are therefore the most likely to be poorly pronounced.

The final syntactic cue is called prosody. **Prosody** refers to the use of stress, rhythm, and changes in pitch that accompany speech. As we already saw, people often use stress to emphasize the new information contained in a declarative sentence. In addition, prosody can emphasize the syntax of a word or group of words or even serve as the primary source of syntactic information. For example, in several languages (including English) a declarative sentence can be turned into a question by means of prosody. Read the following sentences aloud to see how you would indicate to a listener which is a statement and which is a question.

> You said that.

> You said that?

In written communication prosody is emphasized by punctuation marks. For example, a comma indicates a short pause, a period indicates a longer one along with a fall in the pitch of voice, and a question mark indicates an upturn in the pitch of voice near the end of the sentence. These devices serve as only a partial substitute for the real thing. Thus, because writers cannot rely on the cues provided by prosody, they must be especially careful to see that the syntax of their sentences is conveyed by other cues: word order, word class, function words, affixes, and word meaning.

Relation Between Semantics and Syntax. There is more than one way to say something, and sometimes, a particular sentence can mean more than one thing. In Chapter 7 I described an experiment by Sachs that showed that we soon forget the particular form a sentence takes but remember its meaning much longer. Noam Chomsky (1957, 1965), a noted linguist, suggested that newly formed sentences are represented in the brain in terms of their meaning, which he called their **deep structure.** The deep structure represents the kernel of what the person intended to say. In order to say the sentence, the brain must transform the deep structure into the appropriate **surface structure:** the particular form the sentence takes.

An example of a "slip of the tongue" recorded by Fromkin (1973) gives us some clues about the way a sentence's deep structure can be transformed into a particular surface structure.

> Rosa always date shranks.

The speaker actually intended to say *Rosa always dated shrinks* (psychiatrists or clinical psychologists). We can speculate that the deep structure of the sentence's verb phrase was something like this: *date* [past tense] + *shrink* [plural]. The words in brackets represent the names of the syntactical rules that are to be used in forming the surface structure of the sentence. Obviously, the past tense of *date* is *dated,* and the plural of *shrink* is *shrinks.* However, something went wrong during the transformation process. Apparently, the past tense rule got applied to the word *shrink,* resulting in *shrank.* The plural rule also got applied, making the nonsense word *shranks.* (See ***Figure 9.2.***)

Most psychologists agree that the distinction between surface structure and deep structure is important. In Chapter 7 we saw that conduction aphasia involves difficulty with surface structure more than deep structure, and later in this chapter we will encounter more neuropsychological evidence in favor of the distinc-

Rosa always date [past tense] shrink [plural]

(sentence formulated in posterior lobes)

Rosa always date shrink [past tense] [plural]

(error in transmission)

"Rosa always date shranks"

(result, as spoken)

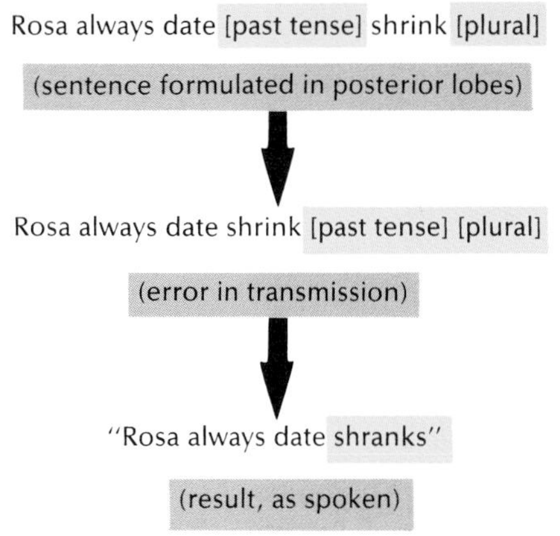

Figure 9.2 A possible explanation for the error in the sentence *Rosa always date shranks.*

tion. However, most psychologists disagree with Chomsky about the particular nature of the cognitive mechanisms through which deep structure is translated into surface structure (Tannhaus, 1988).

Knowledge of the World. Comprehension of speech also involves knowledge about the world and about particular situations that we may encounter. Schank and Abelson (1977) suggested that this knowledge is organized into **scripts,** which specify various kinds of events and interactions that people have witnessed or have learned about from others. Once the speaker has established which script is being referred to, the listener can fill in the details. For example, consider the following sentences (Hunt, 1985): *I learned a lot about the bars in town yesterday. Do you have an aspirin?* To understand what the speaker means, you must be able to do more than simply understand the words and analyze the sentence structure. You must know something about bars—for example, that they serve alcoholic beverages and that "learning about them" probably involves some drinking. You must also realize that drinking these beverages can lead to a headache and that aspirin is a remedy for headaches.

Hunt notes that when we describe an event to someone else, we usually do not spell out all the details. For example, consider this story: *Tony was hungry. He went to the restaurant and ordered a pizza. When he was finished, he found he had forgotten to take his wallet with him. He was embarrassed.* To understand it, you must know that after eating in a restaurant you are expected to pay, and because Tony had forgotten his wallet, he had no money with him.

Brain Mechanisms of Verbal Behavior

3 Studies of the verbal behavior of people with brain damage suggest that mechanisms involved in perceiving, comprehending, and producing speech are located in different areas of the cerebral cortex. These studies have furthered our understanding of the processes of normal verbal behavior. Let us examine some of these mechanisms.

Speech Comprehension: Evidence from Wernicke's Aphasia. The word **Aphasia** (literally, "without utterance") refers to a loss of ability to produce meaningful speech that is caused by brain damage. As we will see, several different types of aphasia can occur, depending on the location of the brain damage. In the late nineteenth century a German physician, Karl Wernicke, reported that a particular form of aphasia was caused by damage to a region of auditory association cortex located on the upper part of the temporal lobe of the left side of the brain (Wernicke, 1874). This region of the brain has come to be known as **Wernicke's area,** and the disorder is now called **Wernicke's aphasia.** (See "Wernicke's area" in *Figure 9.3;* the other details in this figure will be explained later.)

The most important symptoms of Wernicke's aphasia are very poor speech comprehension and fluent but meaningless speech. That is, people with this disorder fail to comprehend what others say to them, but they themselves talk, in an apparently effortless manner.

The problem is, what they say does not make much sense. For example, consider the following dialogue (from Kertesz, 1980):

> *Examiner:* Can you tell me a little bit about why you're here?
>
> *Patient:* I don't know whata wasa down here for me, I just don't know why I wasn't with up here, at all you, it was neva, had it been walked me today ta died.

The patient who spoke these words acted as if she had said something meaningful. She paused between phrases and dropped her voice at the end of "sentences." We can speculate that because she could not understand other people's speech, she could not realize that her own speech lacked meaning. Typically, the speech of people with Wernicke's aphasia retains some elements of grammar. It contains few content words but is full of function words, especially pronouns, conjunctions, and prepositions.

Most investigators believe that the primary deficit of Wernicke's aphasia is a loss of speech comprehension. Perhaps Wernicke's area contains memories of the sounds of words. These memories are necessary for two important functions: comprehending other people's speech and translating one's own thoughts into words.

Hemispheric specialization in auditory function is not limited to the human brain. Heffner and Heffner (1990) review a series of experiments from their laboratory indicating that the auditory system of the left hemisphere in monkeys also plays a special role in recognizing vo-

Figure 9.3   The functions and interconnections of Broca's area and Wernicke's area.

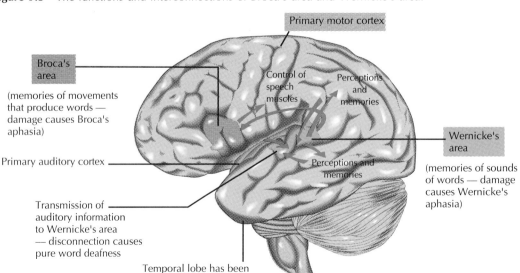

cal communications. Although Japanese macaques obviously cannot talk, they do have a repertoire of vocal calls that they use to communicate with each other. Heffner and Heffner found that lesions of the left auditory cortex produce a much more severe impairment in recognition of these calls than right-hemisphere lesions.

Speech Production: Evidence from Broca's Aphasia. As we saw in Chapter 1, Paul Broca, a French physician, discovered that damage to a region of the left frontal cortex caused a severe deficit in speech (Broca, 1861). The deficit is now referred to as **Broca's aphasia,** and the region of cortex is now called **Broca's area.** The symptoms of Broca's aphasia are quite different from those of Wernicke's aphasia. Whereas the speech of a person with Wernicke's aphasia is fluent, meaningless, and at least superficially grammatical, the speech of a person with Broca's aphasia is labored, meaningful, and ungrammatical. Consider the following sample of speech from a man with Broca's aphasia, who was explaining why he had come to the hospital. The dots indicate long pauses, during which the man was trying to find the proper words.

> Ah . . . Monday . . . ah Dad and Paul [patient's name] . . . and Dad . . . hospital. Two . . . ah doctors . . . , and ah . . . thirty minutes . . . and yes . . . ah . . . hospital. And, er Wednesday . . . nine o'clock. And er Thursday, ten o'clock . . . doctors. Two doctors . . . and ah . . . teeth. Yeah, . . . fine. (Goodglass, 1976, p. 278)

Most investigators believe that Broca's area contains memories of the sequences of muscular movements that must be performed to pronounce words. Thus, loss of this area makes it very difficult for people to speak. (See ***Figure 9.3.***)

In addition to its role in the production of words, Broca's area appears to perform some more complex functions. Damage to Broca's area often produces **agrammatism:** loss of the ability to comprehend or produce speech that employs complex syntactical rules. For example, the speech of a person with Broca's aphasia contains many content words but few function words. To test agrammatic subjects for speech comprehension, Schwartz, Saffran, and Marin (1980) showed them a pair of drawings, read a sentence aloud, and then asked them to point to the appropriate picture. The subjects heard forty-eight sentences such as *The clown applauds the dancer* and *The robber is shot by the cop.* For the first sample sentence one picture showed a clown applauding a dancer, and the other showed a dancer applauding a clown. On average, the brain-damaged subjects responded correctly to only 62 percent of the pictures (chance would be 50 percent). In contrast, the performance of normal people is around 100 percent on such a simple task. In another study Saffran, Schwartz, and Marin (1980) obtained evidence of the subjects' deficits in the use of syntactical rules by showing them simple pictures and asking them to say what was happening. Here are some of the responses:

> *Picture of a girl giving flowers to her teacher:* Girl . . . wants to . . . flowers . . . flowers and wants to. . . . The woman . . . wants to. . . . The girl wants to . . . the flowers and the woman.

> *Picture of a woman kissing a man:* The kiss . . . the lady kissed . . . the lady is . . . the lady and the man and the lady . . . kissing.

Given that the frontal lobes govern motor control and, more generally, planning, it is not surprising that damage to Broca's area impairs the production of proper syntax. Syntactical rules involve motor operations in the sense that they entail putting a word into its proper position, adding the correct ending to a verb, and so on. But damage to Broca's area also impairs comprehension. Thus, we cannot say that speech perception is strictly a function of Wernicke's area. Apparently, the mechanisms that permit us to translate meaning into syntax (in Chomsky's terms, deep structure into surface structure) are also necessary for us to extract meaning from syntax; encoding and decoding use the same brain mechanisms. This evidence supports the suggestion that in order to comprehend a sentence, listeners do the opposite of what speakers do: They transform a sentence's surface structure back to its deep structure.

If this explanation is true, we can understand why the speech of people with Wernicke's aphasia is full of function words: They have lost the neural circuits necessary for remembering the sounds and meanings of content words, but they retain the mechanisms that control utterances of function words. Their speech is controlled by neural mechanisms in Broca's area that have little meaningful input to guide them, and therefore, it consists mostly of function words.

INTERIM SUMMARY

Speech and Comprehension

Language, the second most important human social behavior, is an orderly system of communication. The recognition of words in continuous speech is a complex process. Phonemes are recognized even though their pronunciation is affected by neighboring sounds, by accents and speech peculiarities, and by stress. Studies have shown that we distinguish between voiced and unvoiced consonant phonemes such as /b/ and /p/ by means of voice-onset time, which consists of a 0.06-second delay in vibration of the vocal cords after opening the lips. Research has also shown that the primary unit of analysis is not individual phonemes but groups of phonemes—perhaps syllables.

Our recognition of words in continuous speech is far superior to our ability to recognize them when they have been isolated. We use contextual information in recognizing what we hear.

Meaning is a joint function of syntax and semantics. All users of a particular language observe syntactical rules that establish the relations of the words to one another. These rules are not learned explicitly. In fact, research indicates that people can learn to apply rules of an artificial grammar without being able to say just what these rules are. The most important features that we use to understand syntax are word order, word class, function words, affixes, word meanings, and prosody. Content words refer to objects, actions, and the characteristics of objects and actions and thus can express meaning even in some syntactically ambiguous sentences.

Chomsky has suggested that speech production entails the transformation of deep structure into surface structure. Most psychologists disagree with the details of Chomsky's explanation but consider the distinction between deep and surface structure to be an interesting and important insight.

The effects of brain damage suggest that memories of the sounds of words are located in Wernicke's area, and memories of the muscular movements needed to produce them are located in Broca's area. Thus, Wernicke's area is necessary for speech perception, and Broca's area is necessary for its production. Wernicke's aphasia is characterized by fluent but meaningless speech, scarce in content words but rich in function words. Presumably, function words and other syntactical features of speech related to motor operations involve mechanisms in the frontal lobes. As we saw, Broca's aphasia is characterized by nonfluent but meaningful speech, scarce in function words but rich in content words. Semantics, or meaning, requires other areas of the cortex, which contain memories of the relations between words and the concepts they denote. ∎

READING

4 The invention of writing was an important turning point in civilization. The first system of writing appears to have been developed around 4000 B.C. in ancient Sumeria (the location of present-day Iran and Iraq), apparently in response to the need to keep records of ownership and of business transactions. The earliest forms of writing were stylized drawings of real objects *(pictographs),* but most cultures soon developed symbols based on sounds. For example, Egyptian hieroglyphic writing used some symbols as pictographs but used others phonetically, to spell out people's names or words that denote concepts not easily pictured.

With the notable exception of Chinese (and other Oriental writing systems based on Chinese), most modern languages use an alphabetic

The earliest Egyptian hieroglyphs represented concepts as pictures. Later, the signs became stylized and could be used to represent the sounds of words.

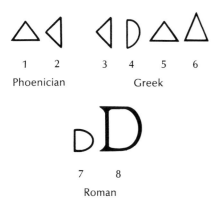

1 2 3 4 5 6
Phoenician   Greek

7 8
Roman

Figure 9.4 The evolution of the letter D. (Copyright © 1981 by Houghton Mifflin Company. Reprinted by permission from *The American Heritage Dictionary,* New College Edition.)

writing system in which a small number of symbols represent (more or less) the sounds used to pronounce words. For example, most European languages are represented by the Roman alphabet, originally developed to represent the sounds of Latin and subsequently adopted by tribes of people ruled or influenced by the Roman Empire. The Roman alphabet was adapted from the Greek alphabet, which in turn was adapted from the Phoenician alphabet. For example, the letter D has its origin in the Phoenician symbol *daleth,* which meant "door." At first, the symbol literally indicated a door, but later, it came to represent the phoneme /d/. The Greeks adopted the symbol and its pronunciation but changed its name to *delta.* Finally, the

Romans took it, altering its shape into the one we recognize in our own language today. (See *Figure 9.4.*)

Scanning of Text

As we saw in Chapter 5, our eyes make rapid jumps, called *saccades,* as we scan a scene. The same rapid movements occur while we read. In fact, a French ophthalmologist discovered saccadic eye movements while watching people read (Javal, 1879).

The study of eye movements made during reading have been greatly facilitated by the development of a device called an **eye tracker.** While reading, the subject is seated in front of a video display unit controlled by a computer. The computer also monitors the position of one of the subject's pupils through a video camera, which permits it to calculate the location of the subject's gaze.

We do not perceive things while the eyes are actually moving but during the brief **fixations** that occur between saccades. The average fixation has a duration of about 250 milliseconds (ms, 1/1000 s), but they can vary considerably. Figure 9.5 shows the pattern of fixations made by good and poor readers. The ovals above the text indicate the location of the fixations (which occur just below the ovals, on the text itself), and the numbers indicate their duration (in milliseconds). All of the good reader's fixations were made in the forward direction, whereas the poor reader looked back and

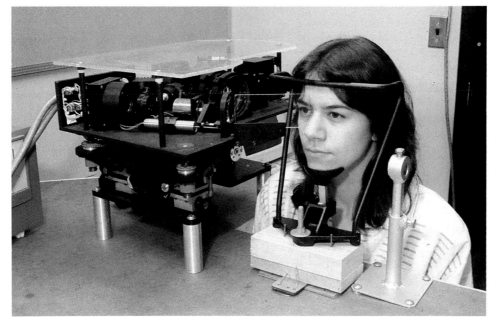

A subject seated in front of an eye tracker.

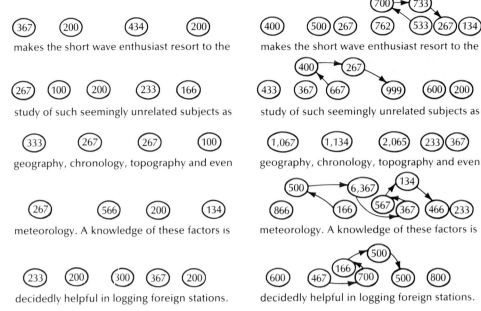

Figure 9.5 The pattern of fixations made by a reader. The ovals are placed above the locations of the fixations; the numbers within them indicate the duration of the fixation (in milliseconds). Arrows indicate backtracking to words already examined. (a) A good reader. (b) A poor reader. [From Marcel Adam Just and Patricia A. Carpenter, *The Psychology of Reading and Language Comprehension.* Copyright © 1987 by Allyn and Bacon. After Buswell (1937). Reproduced with permission.]

examined previously read words several times (indicated by the arrows). In addition, good readers took, on the average, considerably less time than poor readers did to examine each word. (See *Figure 9.5.*)

College students fixate on most words when they are asked to read text carefully enough to understand its meaning. They fixate on 80 percent of the content words but only 40 percent of the function words (Just and Carpenter, 1980). Of course, function words are generally shorter than content words, but the difference is not simply a matter of size; readers are more likely to skip over short function words such as *and* or *the* but not short content words such as *ant* or *run* (Carpenter and Just, 1983).

Eye movements provide an excellent window into the dynamics of the reading process. Apparently, as we read a sentence, we analyze it word by word. Of course, some words contribute more to our understanding than others. And sometimes, we must wait to see how a sentence turns out to understand the beginning. The more unusual a word is, the longer a reader fixates on it; presumably, unusual words take longer to recognize and understand. For example, the word *sable* receives a longer fixation than the word *table*. The word that follows an unusual word does not receive a longer-than-usual fixation, which indicates that the reader finishes processing the word before initiating the next saccade (Thibadeau, Just, and Carpenter, 1982).

Besides spending a longer time fixating on unusual words, readers spend more time fixating on *longer* words; in fact, if word familiarity is held constant, the amount of time a word receives is proportional to its length (Carpenter and Just, 1983). In addition, Just, Carpenter, and Wu (1983) found that the amount of time that Chinese readers spent fixating on a Chinese character was proportional to the number of brush strokes used to make it. All Chinese characters are of approximately the same size, so the increased fixation time appears to reflect the complexity of a word rather than the amount of space it occupies.

Phonetic and Whole-Word Recognition

Most psychologists who study the reading process believe that readers have two basic ways to recognize words: phonetic and whole-word recognition. Phonetic reading involves the decoding of the sounds that letters or groups of letters make. For example, I suspect that you and I would pronounce *praglet* in approximately the same way. Our ability to pronounce this

When people read Chinese, the amount of time they fixate on each character is proportional to its complexity—the number of brush strokes used to make it.

nonsense word depends on our knowledge of the relation between letters and sounds in the English language. We use such knowledge to "sound the word out." But do we have to "sound out" familiar, reasonably short words such as *table* or *grass?* It appears that we do not; we recognize the word as a whole.

If the reader is relatively inexperienced, he or she will have to sound out most words and, consequently, will read rather slowly. Experienced readers will have had so much practice looking at words that they will quickly recognize most of them as individual units. In other words, during reading, phonological and whole-word reading are engaged in a race. If the word is familiar, the whole-word method will win. If the word is unfamiliar, the whole-word method will fail, and the phonological method will have enough time to come to completion.

Whole-word recognition not only is faster than the phonological decoding but also is absolutely necessary in a language (such as English) in which spelling is not completely phonetic. Consider the following pairs of words: *cow/blow,* *bone/one, post/cost, limb/climb.* Obviously, no single set of phonological rules can account for the pronunciation of both members of each pair. But all these words are familiar and easy to read. If we did not have the ability to recognize words as a whole, we would not be able to read irregularly spelled words, which are rather common in our language.

Neuropsychological evidence supports the conclusion that phonetic reading and whole-word reading involve different mechanisms. Some colleagues and I (Margolin, Marcel, and Carlson, 1985) had the opportunity to study a woman whose left temporal lobe had been damaged in an automobile accident. The damage produced a severe **dyslexia**—a specific deficit in the ability to read. Although she was almost totally unable to read words, we discovered that she could still *perceive* them by the whole-word method. One day, when she was trying (without success) to read some words that I had typed, she suddenly said, "Hey! You spelled this one wrong." Indeed, I had. But even though she saw that the word was misspelled, she still could not say what it was, even when she tried very hard to sound it out. That evening I made up a list of eighty pairs of words, one spelled correctly and the other incorrectly. The next day she was able to go through the list quickly and easily, correctly identifying 95 percent of the misspelled words. She was able to *read* only five of them. Thus, brain damage that disrupts the ability to read words phonetically does not necessarily damage perceptual recognition of whole words.

Investigators have reported several types of dyslexia besides the one I just reported. For example, as we saw in the opening vignette, Mr. V. lost the ability to read even though he could still write. Dyslexias caused by brain damage that occurs after a person has already learned to read are called *acquired dyslexias.* In contrast, *developmental dyslexias* manifest themselves in childhood, when it becomes apparent that the child is having great difficulty learning to read, even though he or she is otherwise intelligent. Developmental dyslexias tend to occur in families, which suggests a genetic (and hence biological) component. In fact, several studies (Galaburda and Kemper, 1979; Galaburda et al., 1985; Galaburda, 1988) have found evidence that brain abnormalities in a portion of Wernicke's area may be responsible for their reading difficulty.

Geschwind and Behan (1984) have found that there is an association between dyslexia, left-handedness, and various immune disorders, such as thyroid and bowel diseases, diabetes, and rheumatoid arthritis. They suggest that a genetic abnormality, besides predisposing people for immune disorders, may also affect the development of parts of the left hemisphere of the brain. Their hypothesis is interesting and has some support, but much research has yet to be done to test it experimentally. And almost certainly, there are several types of developmental dyslexias, which means that the disorders may have several different causes.

Understanding the Meaning of Words and Sentences

5 Recognizing a word is a matter of perception. The primary task is a visual one; but as we saw in the previous section, when we encounter an unfamiliar word, we use phonological codes to "sound the word out." The next step in the reading process is understanding a word's meaning.

The meaning of words is learned through experience. The meaning of content words involves memories of objects, actions, and their characteristics; thus, meaning of content words involves visual, auditory, somatosensory, olfactory, and gustatory memories. For example, our understanding of the meaning of the word *apple* involves memories of the sight of an apple, the way it feels in our hand, the sound our teeth make when they bite into it, and the taste and odor we experience when we chew it. Our understanding of the meaning of the word *drop* involves memories of objects being released and falling. Our understanding of the meaning of adjectives such as the word *heavy* involves memories of objects that are difficult or impossible to lift. The image evoked by the phrase *heavy package* undoubtedly involves memories of our own experience with heavy packages, whereas the one evoked by the phrase *heavy rocket* (with which we have had no personal experience) is understood in terms of visual size and bulk.

What about the understanding of abstract content words, such as the nouns *honesty* and *justice?* These words are probably first understood as adjectives: An *honest student* is one who does not cheat on exams or plagiarize while writing papers; an *honest bank clerk* does not steal money; and so on. Our understanding of these words depends on our direct experience with such people or our vicarious experience with them through stories we read or hear about. By itself, the word *honesty* does not refer to much.

The understanding of most function words is also abstract. For example, the word *and* serves to link two or more things being discussed; the word *or* indicates a choice; the word *but* indicates that a contradiction will be expressed in the next phrase. The meanings of such words are difficult to imagine or verbalize, rather like the rules of grammar. The meanings of prepositions such as *in, under,* or *through* are more concrete and are probably represented by images of objects in relation to each other.

As we read (or hear) a sentence, the words and phrases we encounter activate memories that permit us to understand their meanings. Unless we deliberately pause to figure out an obscure allusion (which should not happen very often in the case of good writing and speaking), this activation is an automatic, unconscious process. When we read the sentence *She opened her mouth to let the dentist examine her aching tooth,* we very quickly picture a specific scene. Our understanding depends not only on the comprehension of the specific words but also on our knowledge of dental chairs, dentists, toothaches and their treatment, and so on.

A phenomenon known as semantic priming gives us some hints about the nature of activation of memories triggered by the perception of words and phrases. **Semantic priming** involves similarities in the *meanings* of words. If a person reads a particular word, then he or she can more easily read a second word that is related in meaning to the first. For example, if a person sees the word *bread,* he or she will be more likely to successfully recognize a fuzzy image of the word *butter* or an image that is presented very briefly by means of a tachistoscope (Johnston and Dark, 1986). Reading the word *bread* activates both neural circuits involved in visual perception of that word and neural circuits involved in memories of the word's meaning. Apparently, the activation spreads to circuits denoting related concepts, such as butter. Thus, our memories must be linked according to our experience regarding the relations between specific concepts.

Figure 9.6 suggests how neural representations of concepts may be linked. The concept *piano* has many different features, including the sounds it makes, its size, the shapes it can have, its components, the people who interact with it, and so on. Depending on the context in which it is perceived, the word *piano* can activate various subsets of these features. For example, the sentences *The piano was tuned* and *The piano was lifted* activate neural representations of different features. (See *Figure 9.6.*)

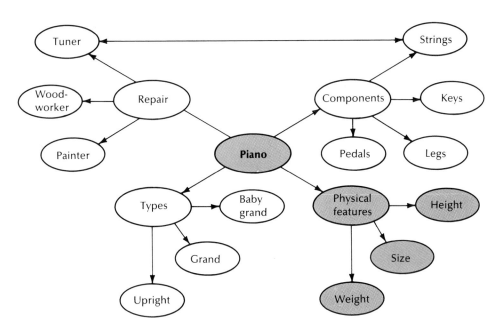

Figure 9.6 Linking neural representations of concepts. Recognizing the word *piano* activates neural representations of features related to pianos. The colored ovals indicate the concepts activated by the sentence *The piano was lifted.* (From Marcel Adam Just and Patricia A. Carpenter, *The Psychology of Reading and Language Comprehension.* Copyright © 1987 by Allyn and Bacon. Reproduced with permission.)

INTERIM SUMMARY

Reading

Writing allows people to communicate with other people they have never met—and who may not even be alive at the time the writing takes place. Recognition of written words is a complex perceptual task, however. The eye-tracking device allows researchers to study people's eye movements and fixations and to learn from these behaviors some important facts about the nature of the reading process. For example, we analyze a sentence word by word

as we read it, taking longer to move on from long words or unusual ones.

Once a word has been perceived, recognition of its pronunciation and meaning take place. Long or unfamiliar words are sounded out—that is, they are read phonologically. In contrast, short, familiar words are recognized as a whole. In fact, only whole-word reading will enable us to distinguish between words such as *cow* and *blow,* or *bone* and *one,* which have irregular spellings. In an experienced reader both processes take place simultaneously. If the word is recognized as a whole, the reader moves on to the next one; if not, he or she continues to decode it phonologically. The distinction between these two forms of recognition is supported by behavioral data and by the fact that some people with a particular type of acquired dyslexia can lose their ability to read phonologically but still recognize words by the whole-word method. Developmental dyslexias appear to be caused by abnormal development of parts of the left hemisphere, and they may be caused by a genetic defect that also affects the immune system and predisposes a person toward left-handedness.

The phenomenon of priming can be demonstrated for phonological similarity and for meaning. Thus, priming has been used to study the processes of word recognition and comprehension of meaning. ■

LANGUAGE ACQUISITION BY CHILDREN

6 How do children learn to communicate verbally with other people? How do they master the many rules needed to transform a thought into a coherent sentence? How do they learn the meanings of thousands of words? And *why* do they do all these things? Do other people shape their babble into words by appropriately reinforcing their behavior, or do innate mechanisms ensure the acquisition of language without reinforcement? This section addresses these and other questions related to children's verbal development.

Perception of Speech Sounds by Infants

An infant's auditory system is remarkably well developed. Wertheimer (1961) found that newborn infants in the delivery room can turn their head toward the source of a sound. Infants two or three weeks of age can discriminate the sound of a voice from nonspeech sounds. By the age of two months babies can tell an angry voice from a pleasant one: An angry voice produces crying, whereas a pleasant one causes smiling and cooing.

Psychologists have developed a clever technique to determine what sounds a very young infant can perceive. A special pacifier nipple is placed in the baby's mouth. The nipple is connected by a plastic tube to a pressure-sensitive switch that converts the infant's sucking movements into electrical signals. These signals can be used to turn on auditory stimuli; each time the baby sucks, a particular sound is presented. (See *Figure 9.7.*)

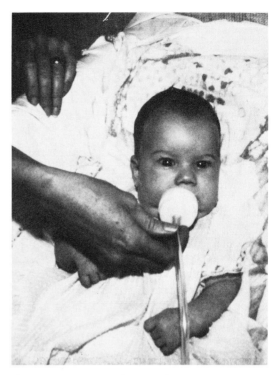

Figure 9.7 A procedure used to investigate auditory perception by infants. The baby's sucking action on the nipple turns on the tape recorder for a while.

If the auditory stimulus is novel, the baby usually begins to suck at a high rate. If the stimulus remains the same, its novelty wears off (habituation occurs) and the rate of sucking decreases. With another new stimulus the rate of sucking again suddenly increases, unless the baby cannot discriminate the difference. If the stimuli sound the same to the infant, the rate of sucking remains low after the change.

Using this technique, Eimas, Siqueland, Jusczyk, and Vigorito (1971) found that one-month-old infants could tell the difference between the sounds of the consonants *b* and *p*. Like Lisker and Abramson (1970) in the study discussed earlier, they presented the sounds *ba* and *pa,* synthesized by a computer. The infants, like the adult subjects in the earlier study, discriminated between speech sounds whose voice-onset time differed by only 0.02 second. Even very early during postnatal development, the human auditory system is ready to make very fine discriminations.

The Prespeech Period and the First Words

Kaplan and Kaplan (1970) have outlined the progression of early vocalizations in infants. The first sound that a baby makes is crying. As we will see in Chapter 10, this aversive stimulus serves a useful function; it is important in obtaining behaviors from the baby's caregivers. At about one month of age infants start making other sounds, including one that is called *cooing* because of the prevalence of the *oo* sound. Often during this period babies also make a series of sounds that resemble a halfhearted attempt to mimic the sound of crying.

At around six months a baby's sounds begin to resemble those that occur in speech. Even though its babbling does not contain words—and does not appear to involve attempts to communicate verbally—the sounds the infant makes, and the rhythm in which they are articulated, reflect the adult speech the baby hears. Boysson-Bardies, Sagart, and Durand (1984) had adult French people listen to recordings of the babbling of children from various cultures. The adults could easily distinguish the babbling of eight-month-old French infants from that of babies of different language backgrounds. Thus, even a prelinguistic child has begun to learn something about patterns of speech articulation from its environment.

A study by Kuhl et al. (1992) provides further evidence for the effect of a child's linguistic environment on its language development. Native speakers learn not to distinguish between

slight variations of sounds present in their language. In fact, they do not even *hear* the differences between them. For example, Japanese contains a sound that comes midway between /l/ and /r/. Different native speakers pronounce the sound differently, but all pronunciations are recognized as examples of the same phoneme. When native speakers of Japanese learn English, they have great difficulty distinguishing the sounds /l/ and /r/; for example, *right* and *light* sound to them like the same word. Presumably, the speech sounds a child hears alter the brain mechanisms responsible for analyzing them so that minor variations are not even perceived. The question is, When does this alteration occur? Most researchers have supposed that it happens only after children begin to learn the meanings of words, which occurs around ten to twelve months of age.

Kuhl and her colleagues studied six-month-old infants in the United States and Sweden. Each child was seated in its mother's lap, where it watched an experimenter sitting nearby, playing with a silent toy. Every 2 seconds, a loudspeaker located to the child's left presented the sound of a vowel. From time to time the sound was altered. If the child noticed the change and looked at the loudspeaker, the experimenter reinforced the response by activating a toy bear that pounded on a miniature drum. Thus, the procedure provided a test of children's ability to distinguish slight differences in vowel sounds.

The experimenters presented two different vowel sounds, one found in English but not in Swedish, and the other found in Swedish but not in English. From time to time they varied the sound slightly. The reactions of the Swedish infants and the American infants were strikingly different. Swedish children noticed when the English vowel changed but not when the Swedish vowel changed; and American children did the opposite. In other words, by the age of six months, the children had learned not to pay attention to slight differences in speech sounds of their own language, but they were still able to distinguish slight differences in speech sounds they had never heard. Even though they were too young to understand the *meaning* of what they heard, the speech of people around them had affected the development of their perceptual mechanisms.

At about one year of age a child begins to produce words. The first sounds children use to produce speech appear to be similar across all languages and cultures: The first vowel is usually the soft *a* sound of *father,* and the first consonant is a *stop consonant* produced with the

A baby's cooing seems to occur when it is showing signs of pleasure.

An American child being tested in the experiment by Kuhl and her colleagues.

lips—p or b. Thus, the first word is often *papa* or *baba.* The next feature to be added is *nasality,* which converts the consonants p or b into m. Thus, the next word is *mama.* Naturally, mothers and fathers all over the world recognize these sounds as their children's attempts to address them.

The development of speech sounds continues for many years. Some sequences are added very late. For example, the *str* of *string* and the *bl* of *blink* are difficult for young children to produce; they usually say *tring* and *link,* omitting the first consonant. Most children recognize sounds in adult speech before they can produce them. Consider this conversation (Dale, 1976):

> *Adult:* Johnny, I'm going to say a word two times and you tell me which time I say it right and which time I say it wrong: *rabbit, wabbit.*
>
> *Child: Wabbit* is wight and *wabbit* is wong.

Although the child could not pronounce the *r* sound, he clearly could recognize it.

The Two-Word Stage

At around eighteen to twenty months of age children start putting two words together, and their linguistic development takes a leap forward. It is at this stage that linguistic creativity really begins. Consider the creativity in *allgone outside,* said by a child when the door was closed.

Like first sounds, children's two-word utterances are remarkably consistent across all cultures that have been observed. Children use words in the same way, no matter what language their parents speak. Even deaf children who learn sign language from their parents put two words together in the same way as children who can hear (Bellugi and Klima, 1972). And deaf children whose parents do not know sign language invent their own signs and use them in orderly, "rule-governed" ways (Goldin-Meadow and Feldman, 1977). Thus, the grammar of children's language at the two-word stage appears to be universal.

For many years investigators described the speech of young children in terms of adult grammar, but researchers now recognize that children's speech simply follows different rules. Young children are incapable of forming complex sentences—partly because their vocabulary is small, partly because their short-term "working" memory is limited (they cannot yet encode a long string of words), and partly because their cognitive development has not yet reached a stage where they can learn complex rules of syntax.

How Adults Talk to Children

Parents do not talk to children the way they talk to adults; they use only short, simple, well-formed, repetitive sentences and phrases (Brown and Bellugi, 1964). In fact, such speech deserves its own label: **child-directed speech** (Snow, 1986). In a comprehensive review of the literature deVilliers and deVilliers (1978) found that adults' speech to children is characterized by clear pronunciation, exaggerated intonations, careful distinctions between similar-sounding phonemes, relatively few abstract words and function words, and a tendency to isolate constituents that undoubtedly enables young children to recognize them as units of speech.

Another important characteristic of child-directed speech is that it tends to refer to tangible objects the child can see, to what the child is doing, and to what is happening around the child (Snow et al., 1976). Words are paired with objects the child is familiar with, which is the easiest way to learn them. For example, caregivers make statements and ask questions about what things are called, what noises they make, what color they are, what actions they are engaging in, who they belong to, and where they are located (Snow, 1977).

Adults—particularly caregivers, who have a continuing relationship with a child—tend to act as tutors when talking with children. For example, Snow and Goldfield (1982) found that as a mother and child repeatedly read a book over a period of thirteen months, the mother's speech became more and more complex, especially when they were discussing a picture that they looked at again and again.

Adults often expand children's speech by imitating it but putting it into more complex forms, which undoubtedly helps the child learn about syntactical structure (Brown and Bellugi, 1964):

Child: Baby highchair.

Adult: Baby is in the highchair.

Child: Eve lunch.

Adult: Eve is having lunch.

Child: Throw daddy.

Adult: Throw it to daddy.

People make allowances for the age of the child with whom they are talking. Mothers talk differently to two-year-olds than to ten-year-olds (Snow, 1972a). Even four-year-old children talk differently to two-year-olds than they do to adults or other four-year-olds (Shatz and Gelman, 1973). It seems unlikely that these differentiated speech patterns are innately determined. Snow (1972a) compared the speech patterns of a mother talking to a child with her speech patterns when she only pretended to be talking to a child. The woman's speech when the child was absent was simpler than it would have been if addressed to an adult, but when the child was present, it was simpler still. Clearly, then, feedback from children is important.

The most important factor controlling adults' speech to children is the child's attentiveness. Both adults and children are very sensi-

tive to whether or not another person is paying attention to them. As Snow (1986) notes, people do not talk *at* children, they talk *with* them. When a child looks interested, we continue with what we are doing. When we notice signs of inattention, we advance or simplify our level of speech until we regain the child's attention. Stine and Bohannon (1983) found that when children give signs that they do not understand what an adult is saying, the adult's speech becomes simpler.

An experiment by Snow (1972b) showed that children pay more attention to a tape recording of speech directed to a child than to a recording of speech directed to an adult. Other researchers have found that children respond best to speech that is slightly more complex than their own (Shipley, Smith, and Gleitman, 1969). Interacting with someone who has achieved slightly greater competence appears to be an optimum strategy for most learning. For example, if you want to improve your tennis game, you should play with someone a bit better than you are. A poorer player is no challenge; and if you play with someone of professional quality, you will hardly get a chance to return the ball. Thus, children modify adults' speech, keeping it at the optimal level of complexity.

Acquisition of Adult Rules of Grammar

[7] The first words children use tend to be content words, probably because these words are emphasized in adult speech and because they refer to objects and actions that children can directly observe (Brown and Fraser, 1964). As children develop past the two-word stage, they begin to learn and use more and more of the grammatical rules that adults use. The first form of sentence lengthening appears to be the expansion of object nouns into noun phrases (Bloom, 1970). For example, *That ball* becomes *That a big ball*. Next, verbs get used more often, articles are added, prepositional phrases are mastered, and sentences become more complex. These results involve the use of inflections and function words. Function words, you recall, are the little words (*the, to, and,* and so on) that help shape the syntax of a sentence. **Inflections** are special suffixes we add to words to change their syntactical or semantic function. For example, the inflection *-ed* changes most verbs into the past tense (*change* becomes *changed*), *-ing* makes a verb into a noun (*make* becomes *making*), and *-'s* indicates possession (*Paul's truck*). Table 9.1 shows the approximate order in which children acquire

Table 9.1 The order in which children acquire some English inflectional suffixes and function words

Item	Example
1. Present progressive: *ing*	He is *sitting* down.
2. Preposition: *in*	The mouse is *in* the box.
3. Preposition: *on*	The book is *on* the table.
4. Plural: *-s*	The dog*s* ran away.
5. Past irregular: e.g., *went*	The boy *went* home.
6. Possessive: *-'s*	The girl*'s* dog is big.
7. Uncontractible copula *be*: e.g., *are, was*	*Are* they boys or girls? *Was* that a dog?
8. Articles: *the, a, an*	He has *a* book.
9. Past regular: *-ed*	He jump*ed* the stream.
10. Third person regular: *-s*	She run*s* fast.
11. Third person irregular: e.g., *has, does*	*Does* the dog bark?
12. Uncontractible auxiliary *be*: e.g., *is, were*	*Is* he running? *Were* they at home?
13. Contractible copula *be*: e.g., *'s, -re*	That*'s* a spaniel. They*'re* pretty.
14. Contractible auxiliary *be*: e.g., *-'s, -'re*	He*'s* doing it. They*'re* running slowly.

Source: Adapted from Table 9-3 from *Psychology and Language: An Introduction to Psycholinguistics* by Herbert H. Clark and Eve V. Clark, copyright © 1977 by Harcourt Brace Jovanovich, Inc., reprinted by permission of the publisher. After Brown (1973).

some of these inflections and function words. (See ***Table 9.1***.)

It is more difficult for children to add an inflection or function word to their vocabulary than to add a new content word, because the rules that govern the use of inflections or function words are more complex than those that govern the use of most content words. In addition, content words usually refer to concrete objects or activities. The rules that govern the use of inflections or function words are rarely made explicit. A parent seldom says, "When you want to use the past tense, add *-ed* to the verb"—nor would a young child understand such a pronouncement. Instead, children must listen to speech and figure out how to express such concepts as the past tense. Studies of children's speech have told us something about this process.

The most frequently used verbs in most languages are *irregular;* forming the past tense of such verbs in English does *not* involve adding *-ed.* (Examples are *go/went, catch/caught, throw/threw, buy/bought, be/was, see/saw,* and *can/could.*) The past tense of such verbs must be learned individually. Because irregular verbs get

more use than regular ones, children learn them first, producing the past tense easily in sentences such as *I came, I fell down,* and *She hit me.* Soon afterward, they discover the regular past tense inflection and expand their vocabulary, producing sentences like *He dropped the ball.* But they also begin to say *I comed, I falled down,* and *She hitted me.* Having learned a rule, they apply it to all verbs, including the irregular ones that they were previously using correctly. In fact, it takes children several years to learn to use the irregular past tense correctly again.

Acquisition of Meaning

How do children learn to use and understand words? The simplest explanation is that they hear a word spoken at the same time that they see (or hear, or touch) the object to which the word refers. After several such pairings they add a word to their vocabulary. Suppose we give a boy a small red plastic ball and say "ball." After a while, the child says "ball" when he sees it.

Yet we cannot conclude from this behavior that the child knows the meaning of *ball.* So far, he has encountered only one referent for the word: a small one made of red plastic. If he says "ball" when he sees an apple or an orange, or even the moon, we must conclude that he does not know the meaning of *ball.* This type of error is called **overextension.** If he uses the word to refer only to the small red plastic ball, his error is called an **underextension.** Table 9.2 lists some examples of children's overextensions in learning the meanings of new words. (See ***Table 9.2***.)

Both overextensions and underextensions are normal; a single pairing of a word with the object does not provide enough information for accurate generalization. Suppose someone is teaching you a foreign language. She points to a penny and says "pengar." Does the word mean "penny," "money," "coin," or "round"? You cannot decide from this one example. Without further information you may overextend or underextend the meaning of the word if you try to use it. If your teacher then points to a dollar bill and again says "pengar," you will deduce (correctly) that the word means "money."

Many words, including function words, do not have physical referents. For example, prepositions such as *on, in,* and *toward* express relations or directions, and a child needs many examples to learn how to use them appropriately. Pronouns are also difficult; for example, it takes a child some time to grasp the notion that *I*

Table 9.2 Some overextensions made by children while learning new words

Word	Original Referent	Application
mooi	moon	Cakes, round marks on windows, writing on windows and in books, round shapes in books, round postmarks, letter *o*
buti	ball	Toy, radish, stone sphere at park entrance
ticktock	watch	All clocks and watches, gas meter, firehose wound on spool, bath scale round dial
baw	ball	Apples, grapes, eggs, squash, bell clapper, anything round
mem	horse	Cow, calf, pig, moose, all four-legged animals
fly	fly	Specks of dirt, dust, all small insects, child's own toes, crumbs of bread, a toad
wau-wau	dog	All animals, toy dog, soft house slippers, picture of an old man dressed in furs

Source: Adapted from Table 13-2 from *Psychology and Language: An Introduction to Psycholinguistics* by Herbert H. Clark and Eve V. Clark, copyright © 1977 by Harcourt Brace Jovanovich, Inc., reprinted by permission of the publisher. After E. Clark (1975).

means the speaker: *I* means "me" when I say it, but *I* means "you" when you say it. In fact, parents usually avoid personal pronouns in speaking with their children; instead, they use sentences such as *Does baby want another one?* (meaning "Do you want another one?") and *Daddy will help you* (meaning "I will help you").

Abstract words such as *apparently, necessity, thorough,* and *method* have no direct referents and must be defined in terms of other words. Therefore, children cannot learn their meanings until after they have learned many other words. Explaining the meaning of *apparently* to a child with a limited vocabulary would be as hopeless a task as my using a Russian dictionary (not a *Russian-English* dictionary) to determine the meaning of a Russian word. Because I do not understand Russian, the definition would be just as meaningless to me as the word being defined.

EVALUATING SCIENTIFIC ISSUES

Is There a Language Acquisition Device?

8 The linguistic accomplishments of young children are remarkable. Even a child who later does poorly in school learns the rules of grammar and the meanings of thousands of words. Some children fail to work hard at school, but no normal child fails to learn to talk. What shapes this learning process, and what motivates it?

There is vigorous controversy about why children learn to speak and, especially, why they learn to speak grammatically. Noam Chomsky, the noted linguist, observed that the recorded speech of adults is not as correct as the dialogue we read in a novel or hear in a play; often it is ungrammatical, hesitating, and full of unfinished sentences. In fact, Chomsky (1965) character-

Preschoolers show remarkable linguistic accomplishments. They learn remarkably complex "rules" of grammar and the meanings of thousands of words.

ized everyday adult speech as "defective" and "degenerate." If this speech is really what children hear when they learn to speak, it is amazing that they manage to acquire the rules of grammar.

The view that children learn regular rules from apparently haphazard samples of speech has led many linguists and psycholinguists to conclude that the ability to learn language is innate; all a child has to do is to be in the company of speakers of a language. McNeill (1970) has proposed that a child's brain contains a "language acquisition device," which embodies rules of "universal grammar"; because each language expresses these rules in slightly different ways, the child must learn the details, but the basics are already there in the brain.

What Is Being Asserted? The assertion that an innate language acquisition device guides children's acquisition of a language is part of a general theory about the cognitive structures responsible for language and its acquisitions (Pinker, 1990). The most important components are as follows:

1. Children who are learning a language make hypotheses about the grammatical rules they need to follow. These hypotheses are confirmed or disconfirmed by the speech that they hear.
2. An innate language acquisition device (a part of the brain) guides children's hypothesis formation. Because they have this device, there are certain types of hypothetical rules they will never entertain and certain types of sentences they will never utter.
3. The language acquisition device makes reinforcement unnecessary; the device provides the motivation for the child to learn a language.
4. The language acquisition device works best during childhood; after childhood languages are difficult to learn and almost impossible to master.

What Evidence Supports the Assertion? (And Does It, Really?) At present, we have no way to evaluate the first assertion—that children make and test hypotheses about grammatical rules. No serious investigator believes that these hypotheses are conscious and deliberate; thus, we cannot simply ask children why they say what they do. We should probably consider the belief in children's hypothesis testing as a convenient metaphor for the fact that their speech sometimes follows one rule or another. For example, as we saw earlier, children often apply the regular past-tense rule even to irregular verbs, saying *I catched it* or *She hitted me* during one stage of language acquisition. Some researchers would say that the children are testing the hypothesis that all events in the past are expressed by adding *-ed* to the word that denotes the action.

A more important—and testable—assertion is that the hypothesis testing is guided by the language acquisition device. The most important piece of evidence in favor of this assertion is the discovery of **language universals:** characteristics that can be found in all languages that linguists have studied. Some of the more important language universals include the existence of noun phrases (*The quick brown fox . . .*); verb phrases (*. . . ate the chicken*); grammatical categories of words such as nouns and adjectives; and syntactical rules that permit the expression of subject-verb-object relations (*John hit Andy*), plurality (*two birds*), and possession (*Rachel's pen*). The fact that such characteristics exist in languages from all cultures suggests that they are the products of innate brain mechanisms.

Certainly, not all language universals can be attributed to innate brain mechanisms. For example, Hebb, Lambert, and Tucker (1973) observe that language universals may simply reflect realities of the world. When people deal with each other and with nature, their interactions often take the form of an agent acting on an object. Thus, the fact that all languages have ways of expressing these interactions is not surprising. Similarly, objects come in slightly different shapes, sizes, and colors, so we can expect the need for ways (such as adjectives) to distinguish among them. It is not unreasonable to suppose that the same kinds of linguistic devices have been independently invented at different times and in different places by different cultures. After all, archaeologists tell us that similar tools have been invented by different cultures all around the world. People need to cut, hammer, chisel, scrape, and wedge things apart, and different cultures have invented similar devices to perform these tasks. We need not conclude that these inventions are products of a "tool-making device" located in the brain.

But even if *some* language universals are dictated by reality, others could indeed be the result of a language acquisition device. For example, consider the following sentences (Pinker, 1990):

A1. *Irv drove the car* into the garage.

A2. Irv drove the car.

B1. *Irv put the car* into the garage.

B2. Irv put the car.

Someone (such as a child learning a language) who heard sentences A1 and A2 could reasonably infer that sentence B1 could be transformed into sentence B2. But the inference obviously is false; sentence B2 is ungrammatical. The linguistic rules that say that sentence A2 is acceptable but that sentence B2 is not are very complex; and their complexity is taken as evidence that they must be innate, not learned. As Pinker (1990) concludes, "The solution to the problem [that children do not utter sentence B2] must be that children's learning mechanisms ultimately do not allow them to make the generalization" (p. 206).

This conclusion rests on the assumption that children use rules similar to the ones that linguists use. How, the reasoning goes, could a child master such complicated rules at such an early stage of cognitive development unless the rules were already wired into the brain? But perhaps the children are *not* following such complex rules. Perhaps they learn that when you say *put* (*something*) you must always go on to say *where* you put something. Linguists do not like rules that deal with particular words, such as *put* (*something*) (*somewhere*); they prefer abstract and general rules that deal with clauses, prepositions, noun phrases, and the like. But children learn particular words and their meanings—why should they not learn that certain words must be followed (or must never be followed) by certain others? Doing so is certainly simpler than learning the complex and subtle rules that linguists have devised. It would seem that both complex and simple rules (or innate or learned ones) could explain the fact that children do not utter sentence B2.

The third assertion is that language acquisition occurs without the need of reinforcement—or even of correction. Brown and Hanlon (1970) recorded dialogue between children and parents and found that adults generally did not show disapproval when the children's utterances were ungrammatical and approval when they were grammatical. Instead, approval appeared to be contingent on the truth or accuracy of the children's statements. If there is no differential reinforcement, how can we explain the fact that children eventually learn to speak grammatically?

It is undoubtedly true that adults seldom say "Good, you said that right," or "No, you said that wrong." However, adults do distinguish between grammatical and ungrammatical speech of children. A study by Bohannon and Stanowicz (1988) found that adults are likely to repeat children's grammatically correct sentences verbatim but to correct ungrammatical sentences. For example, if a child says, "That be monkey," an adult would say "That is a monkey." Adults were also more likely to ask for clarifications of ungrammatical sentences. Thus, adults do tend to provide the information children need to correct their faulty speech.

As we saw in an earlier section, adults talk differently to children than they do to other adults; they speak in ways that would seem to be optimal for promoting learning. Chomsky's assertion about the defectiveness and degeneracy of adult speech is not true—at least as far as it applies to what children hear. In fact, according to Newport, Gleitman, and Gleitman (1977), almost all the speech that a young child hears (at least, in industrialized English-speaking societies) is grammatically correct. If that is so, why should we hypothesize that a language acquisition device exists? Because, say some researchers, not all children are exposed to child-directed speech. "In some societies people tacitly assume that children aren't worth speaking to and don't have anything to say that is worth listening to. Such children learn to speak by overhearing streams of adult-to-adult speech" (Pinker, 1990, p. 218). That is a very strong statement; it says that children in some cultures have no speech directed toward them until they have mastered the language. It implies that the children's mothers do not talk with them and ignores the fact that older children may not be quite so choosy about their conversational partners. To conclude that such an extreme statement is true would require extensive observation and documentation of child-rearing practices in other cultures.

In fact, children do *not* learn a language that they simply overhear. Bonvillian, Nelson, and Charrow (1976) studied children of deaf parents whose only exposure to spoken language was through television or radio. This exposure was not enough; although the children could hear and did watch television and listen to the radio, they did not learn to speak English. Thus, it takes more than "overhearing streams of adult-to-adult speech" to learn a language. The question is, Just how much instruction (in the form of child-directed speech) do children need? And the way that parents talk to their children is closely related to their language acquisition (Furrow, Nelson, and Benedict, 1979; Furrow and Nelson, 1986).

The fact that parents do not often reward their children's speech behaviors with praise or tangible reinforcers (such as candy) does not prove that reinforcement plays no role in learning a language. We humans are social animals; our behavior is strongly affected by the behavior of others. It is readily apparent to anyone who has observed the behavior of children that the attention of other people is extremely important to them. Children will perform a variety of behaviors that get other people to pay attention to them. They will make faces, play games, and even misbehave in order to attract attention. And above all, they will talk. Put yourself in the child's place. Adults or other children are likely to pay attention to you if you start talking to them. If they cannot understand your speech, you are unlikely to maintain their attention.

The final assertion—that the language acquisition device works best during childhood—has received the most experimental support. For example, Newport and Supalla (1987) studied the ability of people who were deaf from birth to use sign language. They found that the earlier the training began, the better the person was able to communicate. Also, Johnson and Newport (1989) found that native Korean and Chinese speakers who moved to the United States learned English grammar better if they arrived during childhood. The advantage did not appear to be a result of differences in motivation to learn a second language. Such results are consistent with the hypothesis that something happens to the brain after childhood that makes it more difficult to learn a language.

As you learned in Chapter 2, observational studies such as these do not prove that a cause-and-effect relation exists between the variables in question. The authors suggest that people's age (in particular, the age of their brain) affects their language learning ability. But other variables are also correlated with age. For example, the Korean and Chinese speakers who moved to the United States as children spent several years in school; and perhaps the school environment is a particularly good place to learn a second language. In addition, adults are generally more willing to correct children's grammatical errors than those made by adolescents or other adults; thus, children may get more tutoring. It is certainly possible that the investigators are correct, but their results cannot be taken as *proof* that the brain contains an innate language acquisition device.

What Should We Conclude? Does a language acquisition device exist? In one sense, yes, it does. The *human brain* is a language acquisition device, because without it, languages are not acquired. And regions such as Wernicke's area and Broca's area do seem to play especially important roles in verbal communication. The controversy is over the characteristics of this language acquisition device. Is it so specialized that it contains universal rules of grammar and provides innate motivation that makes reinforcement unnecessary?

The basic argument for innate rules of grammar is that the rules that guide a child's speech are so complicated that they could not

The earlier deaf children learn sign language the more fluent they become.

possibly be learned. But perhaps the rules are simpler than the ones that the researchers have proposed. If that is the case, then the argument loses its force.

What about the role of reinforcement? Certainly, we need not deliberately teach our children to speak. Some parents do, of course, but many do not; and their children still learn to talk. Does this fact make verbal behavior different from all other kinds of behavior? This issue will not be resolved until we know much more about the role of reinforcement in other types of behaviors that are learned through observation and imitation. Reinforcement need not be consciously and intentionally delivered; it can be provided by attention and other social stimuli, and it may even be provided by the satisfaction one gains by talking the way other people do.

In my opinion, the best strategy is to keep an open mind. The ease with which young children learn a language must be explained. The explanation will obviously involve some sort of interaction between the particular characteristics of the human brain and the information supplied by the environment. The precise nature of the brain mechanisms and the environmental contributions remain to be determined. ■

INTERIM SUMMARY

Language Acquisition by Children

Studies using the habituation of a baby's sucking response have shown that the human auditory system is capable of discriminating among speech sounds soon after birth. Human vocalization begins with crying, then develops into cooing and babbling, and finally results in patterned speech. During the two-word stage children begin to combine words creatively, saying things they have never heard.

Child-directed speech is very different from that directed toward adults; it is simpler, clearer, and generally refers to items and events in the present environment. As young children gain more experience with the world and with the speech of adults and older children, their vocabulary grows and they learn to use adult rules of grammar. Although the first verbs they learn tend to have irregular past tenses, once they learn the regular past-tense rule (add -ed), they apply this rule even to irregular verbs they previously used correctly.

Some researchers believe that a child learns language by means of a brain mechanism called the language acquisition device, which contains universal grammatical rules and motivates language acquisition. Although children's verbal performance can be described by complex rules, it is possible that simpler rules—which children could reasonably be expected to learn—can also be devised. Everyone agrees that deliberate reinforcement is not necessary for language learning, but a controversy exists about just how important child-directed behavior is. A critical period for language learning may exist, but the evidence is not yet conclusive. ■

COMMUNICATION WITH OTHER PRIMATE SPECIES

9 The members of most species can communicate with one another. Even insects communicate: A female moth that is ready to mate can release a chemical called a pheromone that will bring male moths from miles away. And a dog can tell its owner that it wants to go for a walk by bringing its leash in its mouth and whining at the door. But until recently, humans were the only species with *languages,* flexible systems that use symbols to express so many meanings.

In the 1960s Beatrice and Roger Gardner, of the University of Nevada, began Project Washoe (Gardner and Gardner, 1969, 1978), a remarkably successful attempt to teach sign language to a female chimpanzee named Washoe. Previous attempts to teach chimps to learn and use human language focused on speech (Hayes, 1952). These attempts failed because chimps lack the control of tongue, lips, palate, and vocal cords that humans have, and thus, they cannot produce the variety of complex sounds that characterize human speech.

Gardner and Gardner realized this limitation and decided to attempt to teach Washoe a *manual language*—one that makes use of hand movements. Chimps' hand and finger dexterity is almost as good as ours, so the only limitations in their ability would be cognitive ones. The manual language the Gardners chose was based on *Ameslan,* the *American sign langu*age used by the deaf. Ameslan is a true language: It contains function words and content words and has regular grammatical rules. People can communicate in Ameslan as fast as in spoken languages; they can even make puns based on similarities between signs, just as we make puns based on similarities between sounds of words.

Washoe was one year old when she began learning Ameslan; by the time she was four, she had a vocabulary of over one hundred thirty

The chimpanzee makes the sign for baby when shown a doll.

signs. Like children, she used single signs at first; then she began to produce two-word sentences such as *Washoe sorry, gimme flower, more fruit,* and *Roger tickle.* Sometimes, she strung three or more words together, using the concept of agent and object: *You tickle me.* She asked and answered questions, apologized, made assertions—in short, did the kinds of things that children would do while learning to talk. She showed overextensions and underextensions, just as human children do. Occasionally, she even made correct generalizations by herself. After learning the sign for the verb *open* (as in *open box, open cupboard*), she used it to say *open faucet,* in requesting a drink. She made signs to herself when she was alone and used them to "talk" to cats and dogs, just as children will do. Although it is difficult to compare her progress with that of human children (the fairest comparison would be with that of deaf children learning to sign), humans clearly learn language much more readily than Washoe did.

Inspired by Project Washoe's success, a number of other investigators have taught chimpanzees and other primate species to use sign language. For example, Patterson is teaching a gorilla (Patterson and Linden, 1981), and Miles (1983) is teaching an orangutan. Washoe's training started relatively late in her life, and her trainers were not, at the beginning of the project, fluent in Ameslan. Other chimpanzees, raised from birth by humans who are native speakers of Ameslan, have begun to use signs when they are three months old (Gardner and Gardner, 1975).

Many psychologists and linguists have questioned whether the behavior of these ani-

mals can really be classified as verbal behavior. For example, Terrace, Petitto, Sanders, and Bever (1979) argue that the apes simply learned to imitate the gestures made by their trainers, and that sequences of signs such as *please milk please me like drink apple bottle* (produced by a young gorilla) are nothing like the sequences that human children produce. Others have challenged these criticisms (Fouts, 1983; Miles, 1983; Stokoe, 1983), blaming much of the controversy on the method Terrace and his colleagues used to train their chimpanzee.

Certainly, the verbal behavior of apes cannot be the same as that of humans. If apes could learn to communicate verbally as well as children can, then humans would not be the only species to have developed language. The usefulness of these studies rests in what they can teach us about our own language and cognitive abilities. Through them we may discover what abilities animals need in order to communicate the way we do. They may also help us understand the evolution of these capacities.

These studies have already provided some useful information. For example, Premack (1976) taught chimpanzees to "read" and "write" by arranging plastic tokens into "sentences." Each token represents an object, action, or attribute such as color or shape, much the way words do. His first trainee, Sarah, whom he acquired when she was one year old, learned to understand complex sentences such as *Sarah insert banana in pail, apple in dish.* When she saw the disks arranged in this order, she obeyed the instructions.

Chimpanzees apparently can use symbols to represent real objects and can manipulate these symbols logically. These abilities are two of the most powerful features of language. For Premack's chimpanzees a blue plastic triangle means "apple." If the chimpanzees are given a blue plastic triangle and asked to choose the appropriate symbols denoting its color and shape, they choose the ones that signify "red" and "round," not "blue" and "triangular." Thus, the blue triangle is not simply a token the animals can use to obtain apples; it *represents* an apple for them, just as the word *apple* represents it for us.

Even though humans are the only primates that can pronounce words, several other species can *recognize* them. Savage-Rumbaugh (1990) taught Kanzi, a pigmy chimpanzee, to communicate with humans by pressing buttons that contained symbols for words. Kanzi's human companions talked with him, and he learned to understand them. Although the structure of his vocal apparatus prevented him from responding vocally, *he often tried to do so.* During a three-month period Savage-Rumbaugh and her colleagues tested Kanzi with 310 sentences, 302 of which the chimpanzee had never heard before. Only situations in which Kanzi could not have been guided by nonverbal cues from the human companions were counted; often, Kanzi's back was to the speaker. He responded correctly 298 times. Table 9.3 presents specific examples of these sentences and the actions that Kanzi took. (See **Table 9.3.**)

One conclusion that has emerged from the studies with primates is that true verbal ability is a social behavior; it builds upon attempts at nonverbal communication in a social situation. The most successful attempts at teaching a language to other primates are those in which the animal and the trainer have established a close relationship in which they can successfully communicate with each other nonverbally, by means of facial expressions, movements, and gestures. Apes and orangutans clearly perceive people as other beings, who can be loved, trusted, feared, or despised. Nonhuman primates (and humans, for that matter) learn a language best while inter-

Table 9.3   Distribution of semantic relations comprehended by Kanzi

Semantic Relations	N	Examples (Spoken)
Action-object	107	"Would you please carry the straw?" Kanzi looks over a number of objects on the table, selects the straw, and takes it to the next room.
Object-action	13	"Would you like to ball chase?" Kanzi looks around for a ball, finds one in his swimming pool, takes it out, comes over to the keyboard, and answers "Chase."
Object-location	8	"Would you put the grapes in the swimming pool?" Kanzi selects some grapes from among several foods and tosses them into the swimming pool.
Action-location	23	"Let's chase to the A-frame." Kanzi is climbing in trees and has been ignoring things that are said to him. When he hears this he comes down rapidly and runs to the A-frame.
Action-object-location	36	"I hid the surprise by my foot." Kanzi has been told that a surprise is around somewhere, and he is looking for it. When he is given this clue, he immediately approaches the speaker and lifts up her foot.
Object-action	9	"Kanzi, the pine cone goes in your shirt." Kanzi picks up a pine cone and puts it in his shirt.
Action-location-object	8	"Go the refrigerator and get out a tomato." Kanzi is playing in the water in the sink. When he hears this he stops, goes to the refrigerator, and gets a tomato.
Agent-action-object	7	"Jeannine hid the pine needles in her shirt." Kanzi is busy making a nest of blankets, branches, and pine needles. When he hears this, he immediately walks over to Jeannine, lifts up her shirt, takes out the pine needles, and puts them in his nest.
Action-recipient	13	"Kanzi, chase Kelly." Kanzi was chasing Liz when he heard this. He immediately stopped, ran over to Kelly and signed "Chase."
Action-object-recipient	19	"Kanzi please carry the cooler to Penny." Kanzi grabs the cooler and carries it over to Penny.
Other—object-action-recipient; action-recipient-location; etc.	69	

Source: From Savage-Rumbaugh, E.S. *Developmental Psychobiology,* 1990, *23,* 599–620. Reprinted with permission.

acting with others. Such interactions naturally lead to attempts at communication; and if signs (or spoken words) serve to make communication easier and more effective, they will most readily be learned.

One of the most interesting questions asked of researchers in this area is whether animals who learn to communicate by means of signs will teach those signs to their offspring. The answer appears to be, "Yes, they will." Fouts, Hirsch, and Fouts (1983) obtained a ten-month-old infant chimpanzee, Loulis, whom they gave to Washoe to "adopt." Within eight days the infant began to imitate Washoe's signs. To be certain that Loulis was learning the signs from Washoe and not from humans, the investigators used only the signs for *who, what, want, which, where, sign,* and *name* in his presence. As Fouts reported:

> [A] sign, *food* [which he now uses], was . . . actively taught by Washoe. On this occasion Washoe was observed to sign *food* repeatedly in an excited fashion when a human was getting her some food. Loulis was sitting next to her watching. Washoe stopped signing and took Loulis' hand in hers, molded it into the *food* sign configuration, and touched it to his mouth several times. . . . [E]vidence has [also] been found indicating very subtle tutorial activity on Washoe's part. For example, when Loulis was first introduced to Washoe, Washoe would sign *come* to Loulis and then physically retrieve him. Later she would sign *come* and approach him but not retrieve him, and finally she would sign *come* while looking and orienting toward him without approaching him. (Fouts, 1983, pp. 71–72)

INTERIM SUMMARY

Communication with Other Primate Species

Studies of the ability of other primates to learn language enable us to analyze some of the types of experiences necessary for acquiring the skills involved in producing and understanding speech. To the extent that apes can be taught at least some of the rudiments of language, their behaviors provide some hints about the ways humans acquire these skills. The studies also provide a way for us to ask other primates what they are thinking about. And even beyond the scientific value of these studies, they are fun and interesting. They provide a means for us to be-

come friends with fellow animals in a way that was heretofore impossible.

Our language provides us with a beautiful medium for thought and expression. We can appreciate fine prose and poetry, enjoy the sound of an actor's voice, converse with a loved one, listen to our children's first words, and think thoughts that could never occur without language. What we know about language so far is a pitifully small part of the entire picture. The quest for an understanding of verbal behavior, the most complex of all our activities, has just begun. ■

THINKING

Thinking is an activity that takes place where no one can see it—inside our heads. Because it is hidden, we can only infer its existence from people's behavior. When we think, we perceive, classify, manipulate, and combine information. When we are through, we know something we did not know before (although our "knowledge" may be incorrect).

The purpose of thinking is, in general, to solve problems. These problems may be simple classifications (*What is that, a bird or a bat?*). They may involve decisions about courses of actions (*Should I buy a new car or pay to fix the old one?*). Or they may require the construction, testing, and evaluation of complex plans of action (*How am I going to manage to earn money to support my family, help raise our children, and continue my education so that I can get out of this dead-end job—and still be able to enjoy life?*). Much, but not all, of our thinking involves language. We certainly think to ourselves in words, but we also think in shapes and images. And some of the mental processes that affect our decisions and plans take place without our being conscious of them. Thus, we will have to consider nonverbal processes as well as verbal ones.

This section discusses the important elements and goals of thinking: classification and concept formation, logical reasoning, and problem solving.

Classifying

10 When we think, we do not consider each object or each event as a completely independent entity. Instead, we learn to classify things—to categorize them according to their characteristics. Then, when we have to solve a problem involving a particular object or situation, we can use information that we have already learned about similar objects or situations. To take a very simple example: When we enter someone's house for the first time, we recognize chairs, tables, sofas, lamps, and other pieces of furniture, even though we may have never seen these particular items before. Because we recognize these categories of objects, we know where to sit, how to increase the level of illumination, and so on.

Concepts are categories of objects, actions, or states of being that share some attributes: cat, comet, team, destroying, playing, forgetting, happiness, truth, justice. Most thinking deals with the relations and interactions among concepts. For example, *The hawk caught the sparrow* describes an interaction between two birds; *Studying for an examination is fun* describes an attribute of a particular action; and *Youth is a carefree time of life* describes an attribute of a state of being. (There is no rule that says that thoughts have to be true!) Let us examine some features of concepts and concept formation.

Concepts can be described formally by listing their essential characteristics, as a dictionary definition does. For example, dogs have four legs, a tail, fur, and wet noses; are carnivores; can bark, growl, whine, and howl; pant when they are hot; bear live young; and so on. When a person understands a concept, he or she is acquainted with a sufficiently large number of characteristics to be able to say whether a particular item is or is not an example of the concept. Thus, a concept is a sort of category, which has rules about membership and nonmembership. However, as we shall see, formal dictionary definitions have little psychological reality; the concepts that guide our behavior are much fuzzier than dictionaries would suggest.

Concepts exist because the characteristics of objects have consequences for us. For example, *mean dogs* may hurt us, whereas *friendly dogs* may give us pleasure. *Mean dogs* tend to growl, bare their teeth, and bite; whereas *friendly dogs* tend to prance around, wag their tail, and accept our petting them. Thus, when we see a dog that growls and bares its teeth, we avoid it because it may bite us; but if we see one prancing around and wagging its tail, we may try to pet it. We have learned to avoid or approach dogs who display different sorts of behavior through direct experience with dogs or through the vicarious experience of watching other people interact with them. The point is, we can learn about mean and friendly dogs from the behavior of one set of dogs while we are young

and respond appropriately to other dogs later in life. Our experiences with particular dogs *generalize* to others.

Lumping things together in terms of characteristics important to us is obviously useful—we can predict how they will act, what value they will have for us, and so on. In the past psychologists investigated the nature of formally defined concepts, such as species of animals. For example, Collins and Quillian (1969) suggested that concepts are organized hierarchically in semantic memory. Each concept has associated with it a set of characteristics. For example, consider the hierarchy of concepts relating to animals. At the top is the concept *animal,* to which are associated the characteristics common to all animals, such as *has skin, can move around, eats, breathes,* and so on. Linked to the concept *animal* are groups of animals, such as *birds, fish,* and *mammals,* along with their characteristics. (See **Figure 9.8.**)

Collins and Quillian assumed that, for reasons of efficiency and economy in the organization of memory, the characteristics common to all members of a group of related concepts (such as all birds) were attached to the general concept (in this case *bird*) rather than to all the members. For example, all birds have wings. Thus, we need not remember that a canary, a blue jay, a robin, and an ostrich all have wings; we need only remember that each of these concepts belong to the category of *bird* and that birds have wings.

Collins and Quillian tested the validity of their model by asking people questions about the characteristics of various concepts. For example, consider the concept *canary.* The investigators asked people to say "true" or "false" to statements such as *A canary eats.* When the question dealt with characteristics that were specific to the concept (such as *can sing,* or *is yellow*), the subjects responded quickly. If the question dealt with a characteristic that was common to a more general concept (such as *has skin* or *breathes*), the subjects took a longer time in answering. Presumably, when asked a question about a characteristic that applied to all birds or to all animals, the subjects had to "travel up the tree" from the entry for *canary* until they found the level that provided the answer; the farther they had to go, the longer the process took. (See **Figure 9.8.**)

The model just presented has an appealing simplicity and logic to it, but it turns out that people's brains do not follow such tidy, logical schemes in classifying concepts and their characteristics. For example, although people may

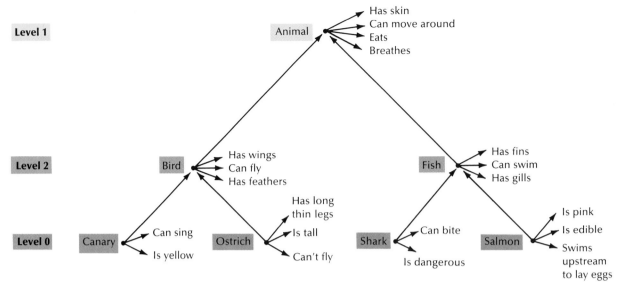

Figure 9.8 Collins and Quillian's model of the hierarchical organization of concepts in semantic memory. [From Robert L. Solso, *Cognitive Psychology,* Second Edition. Copyright © 1988 by Allyn and Bacon. After Collins and Quillian (1969). Reproduced with permission.]

indeed conceive of objects in terms of a hierarchy, a particular person's hierarchy of animals need not resemble that compiled by a zoologist. For example, Rips, Shoben, and Smith (1973) found that people said "yes" to *A collie is an animal* faster than they did to *A collie is a mammal.* According to Collins and Quillian's model, *animal* comes above *mammal* in the hierarchy, so the results should have been just the opposite.

Although some organization undoubtedly exists between categories and subcategories, it appears not to be perfectly logical and systematic. For example, Roth and Mervis (1983) found that people judged *Chablis* to be a better example of *wine* than *drink,* but they judged *champagne* to be a better example of *drink* than *wine.* This inconsistency clearly reflects people's experience with the concepts. Chablis is obviously a wine: It is sold in bottles that resemble those used for other wines, it looks and tastes similar to other white wines, the word *wine* is found on the label, and so on. By these standards, champagne appears to stand apart. A wine expert would categorize champagne as a particular type of wine. But the average person, not being particularly well acquainted with the fact that champagne is made of fermented grape juice, encounters champagne in the context of something to drink on a special occasion, something to christen ships with, and so on. Thus, its characteristics are perceived as being rather different from those of Chablis.

Rosch (1975; Mervis and Rosch, 1981) suggested that people do not look up the meaning of concepts in their heads the way they seek definitions in dictionaries. The concepts we use in everyday life are *natural concepts,* not arbitrary ones prescribed by experts who have examined characteristics we are not aware of; they are based on our own perceptions and interactions with things in the world. Thus, they are fuzzy, in contrast with precise dictionary definitions. For example, some things have wings, beaks, and feathers; and they fly, build nests, lay eggs, and make high-pitched noises. Other things are furry, have four legs and tails, and run around on the ground.

Rosch suggests that people's natural concepts are not idealized sets of rules but consist of collections of memories of *particular examples,* called **exemplars,** that share some similarities. Natural concepts are fuzzy—the distinction between a member and a nonmember is not always clear. Thus, not all members of a concept are equally good examples of that concept. A robin is a good example of *bird;* a penguin or ostrich is a poor one. We may acknowledge that a penguin is a bird because we have been taught that it is, but we often qualify the category membership by making statements such as *"Strictly speaking, a penguin is a bird."* Exemplars represent the important characteristics of a category—characteristics that we can easily perceive or that we encounter when we interact with its members.

Level of Concept

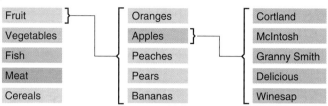

Examples

Figure 9.9 Examples of basic-level, subordinate, and superordinate concepts.

According to Rosch et al. (1976), natural concepts vary in their level of precision and detail; they are arranged in a hierarchy from very detailed to very general. When we think about concepts and talk about them, we usually deal with **basic-level concepts**—those that make important distinctions between different categories but do not waste time and effort with those that do not matter. For example, *chair* and *apple* are basic-level concepts. Concepts that refer to collections of basic-level concepts, such as *furniture* and *fruit,* are called **superordinate concepts**. Concepts that refer to types of items within a basic-level category, such as *lawn chair* and *McIntosh apple,* are called **subordinate concepts**. (See *Figure 9.9.*)

The basic-level concept tends to be the one that people spontaneously name when they see member of the category. That is, all types of chairs tend to be called "chair," unless there is a special reason to use a more precise label (for example, if you wanted to buy a particular kind of chair). People tend to use basic-level concepts for a very good reason: *cognitive economy.* The use of subordinate concepts wastes time and effort on meaningless distinctions, and the use of superordinate concepts loses important information. Rosch et al. (1976) presented subjects with various concepts and gave them 90 seconds to list as many attributes as they could for each of them. The subjects supplied few attributes for superordinate concepts but were able to think of many of them for basic-level concepts. Subordinate concepts evoked no more responses than basic-level concepts did. Thus, because they deal with a large number of individual items and their characteristics, basic-level concepts represent the most information in the most efficient manner. When people think about basic-level concepts, they do not have to travel up or down a tree to find the attributes that belong to the concept; the attributes are directly attached to the exemplars that constitute each concept.

Reasoning

11 Concepts are the raw material of thinking; they are what we think about. But thinking itself involves the manipulation and combination of concepts. Such thinking takes several forms, most of which come under two headings: deductive reasoning and inductive reasoning. This section explores these two types of thinking.

Deductive Reasoning. Deductive reasoning consists of inferring specific instances from general principles or rules. For example, the following two series of sentences express deductive reasoning:

> John is taller than Phil.
> Sue is shorter than Phil.
> Therefore, John is taller than Sue.

> All mammals have fur.
> A bat is a mammal.
> Therefore, a bat has fur.

Deductions consist of two or more statements from which a conclusion is drawn. The first group of sentences presented above involve the application of a simple mathematical principle. The second group of sentences presents a **syllogism,** a logical construction that consists of a major premise (*All mammals have fur*), a minor premise (*A bat is a mammal*), and a conclusion (*A bat has fur*). The major and minor premises are assumed to be true. The problem is to decide whether the conclusion is true or false.

People differ widely in their ability to solve syllogisms. For example, many people would agree with the conclusion of the following syllogism:

> All mammals have fur.
> A zilgid has fur.
> Therefore, a zilgid is a mammal.

These people would be wrong; the conclusion is not warranted. The major premise says only that all mammals have fur; it leaves open the possibility that some animals with fur are not mammals.

Why are some people better than others at solving syllogisms? Johnson-Laird (1985) notes that syllogistic reasoning is much more highly correlated with spatial ability than with verbal ability. Spatial ability includes the ability to visualize shapes and to manipulate them mentally. Why should skill at logical reasoning be related to this ability? Johnson-Laird suggests that people solve problems involving logical deduction by constructing **mental models** that represent the information. For example, read the following problem and answer it: *A is less than C. B is greater than C. Is B greater than A?* In order to compare A with B, you must remember the order of the three elements. One kind of mental model is an imaginary line going from small to large, in which you mentally place each item on the line as you encounter it. Then with all three elements in a row, you can answer the question. (See *Figure 9.10.*)

Figure 9.10 Mental modeling. Logical problems are often solved by imagining a physical representation of the facts.

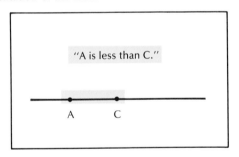

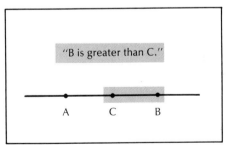

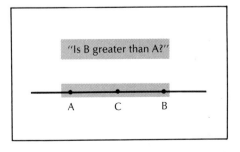

In fact, when we solve problems concerning comparisons of a series of items, we tend to think about our own mental model that represents the information rather than the particular facts given to us (Potts, 1972). For example, read the following passage:

> Although the four craftsmen were brothers, they varied enormously in height. The electrician was the very tallest, and the plumber was shorter than him. The plumber was taller than the carpenter, who, in turn, was taller than the painter. (Just and Carpenter, 1987, p. 202)

After reading this passage, people can more easily answer questions about pairs of brothers with large differences in height. For example, they are faster to answer the question "Who is taller, the electrician or the painter?" than the question "Who is taller, the plumber or the carpenter?" This finding is particularly important because the passage explicitly states that the plumber was taller than the carpenter, *but one must infer* that the electrician was taller than the painter. Thus, the result of an inference can be more readily available than information explicitly given. The most plausible explanation is that when people read the passage, they construct a mental model that represents the four brothers, arranged in order of height. The painter is clearly the shortest and the electrician is clearly the tallest; thus, a comparison between the extremes can be made very quickly. (See *Figure 9.11.*)

We use our spatial ability to construct models for representing and manipulating many types of information. For example, answer the following question and try to think about how you go about doing so: *What do you call your mother's sister's son?* Most people report that they answer the question by constructing a "mental family tree," with their mother above them, their mother's sister to the side, and her son below her. Then, comparing that location with their own, they can easily see that the answer is "cousin." Luria (1973) found that people with damage to the parietal lobes had difficulty answering such questions. As you learned in Chapter 3, the parietal lobes are involved with somatosensation and spatial abilities. Luria suggested that an impairment in spatial abilities makes it difficult for people with parietal lobe damage to construct a mental "family tree."

Many creative scientists and engineers report that they use mental models to reason logically and solve practical and theoretical problems (Krueger, 1976). For example, the late American physicist and Nobel laureate Richard

Figure 9.11 A "mental model" of the memory test. Subjects could judge the relative heights of the electrician and the painter faster than those of the plumber and the carpenter, even though they had never heard the heights of the electrician and the painter compared.

Feynman said that he used rather bizarre mental models to keep track of characteristics of complex mathematical theorems to see whether they were logical and consistent. Here is how Feynman described his thought processes:

> When I'm trying to understand . . . I keep making up examples. For instance, the mathematicians would come in with a . . . theorem. As they're telling me the conditions of the theorem, I construct something that fits all the conditions. You know, you have a set (one ball)—disjoint (two balls). Then the balls turn colors, grow hairs, or whatever, in my head as they [the mathematicians] put more conditions on. Finally, they state the theorem, which is some . . . thing about the ball which isn't true for my hairy green ball thing, so I say "False!" (Feynman, 1985, p. 70)

Such use of mental models by a talented and gifted scientist strengthens the conclusion that being able to convert abstract problems into tangible mental models is an important aspect of intelligent thinking.

Inductive Reasoning. As we saw, deductive reasoning involves applying the rules of logic to infer specific instances from general principles or rules. This type of reasoning works well when general principles or rules have already been worked out. But how does one accumulate new knowledge and formulate new general principles or rules? Having read Chapter 2 of this book, you already know the answer—by following the scientific method. But few people know the rules of the scientific method, and even those who do seldom follow them in their daily lives.

Inductive reasoning is just the opposite of deductive reasoning; it consists of inferring general principles or rules from specific facts. A well-known laboratory example of inductive reasoning works like a guessing game. The subjects are shown cards that contain figures differing in several dimensions, such as shape, number, and color. On each trial they are given two cards and are asked to choose the one that represents a particular concept. After they choose a card, the experimenter says "right" or "wrong." One trial is not enough to recognize the concept. For example, if the first trial reveals that card A is correct, then the concept could be *red,* or *four,* or *triangle,* or some combination of these, such as *red triangle, four red shapes,* or even *four red triangles.* Information gained from the second trial permits the subject to rule out some of these hypotheses—for example, now it appears that shape does not matter, but color and number do. The subject uses steps to solve the problem much the way a scientist does: Form a hypothesis on the basis of the available evidence and test that hypothesis on subsequent trials. If it is proven false, abandon it, try to think of a hypothesis consistent

 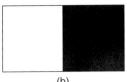 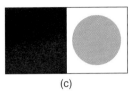 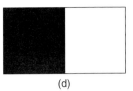

(a)   (b)   (c)   (d)

Figure 9.12   The cards used in one of the tasks of Johnson-Laird and Wason (1977).

with what went before, and test the new hypothesis.

Obviously, people can be trained to follow the rules of the scientific method. However, without special training they follow common-sense rules, some of which work and some of which do not. Psychologists interested in people's inductive reasoning ability have identified several tendencies that lead them astray. It is precisely because of such tendencies that we need to learn specific rules (such as those of the scientific method) so that we can have confidence in our conclusions.

People often fail to select the information they need to test a hypothesis. For example, consider the following task (Johnson-Laird and Wason, 1977):

> Your job is to determine which of the hidden parts of these cards you need to see in order to answer the following question decisively:
>
> FOR THESE CARDS IS IT TRUE THAT IF THERE IS A CIRCLE ON THE LEFT THERE IS A CIRCLE ON THE RIGHT?
>
> You have only one opportunity to make this decision; you must not assume that you can inspect the cards one at a time. Name those cards which it is absolutely essential to see.

The subjects were shown four cards like those shown in Figure 9.12. One-half of each card was covered so that the subject could not confirm the rule without removing some of the covers. Read the problem again, look at the cards, and decide which card (or cards) you would have to see. (See *Figure 9.12.*)

Most subjects say that they would need to see card (a), and they are correct. If there was not a circle to the right of the circle on card (a), then the rule is not correct. However, many subjects failed to realize that card (d) must also be inspected. True, there is no circle to the right of this card, but what if there is a circle to the left? If there is, then the rule is proved wrong. Many subjects also wanted to see card (c), but there is no need to do so, because the hypothesis says nothing about whether a circle can be on the right *without* there being one on the left.

Another problem in inductive reasoning occurs when people fail to consider a comparison group. Suppose you learn that 79 percent of the people with a particular disease get well within a month after taking a new, experimental drug (Stich, 1990). What would you conclude? Is the drug effective? The correct answer to this question is, "We cannot conclude anything—we need more information." What we need to know is what happens to people with the disease if they do *not* take the drug. If we find that only 22 percent of these people recover within a month, then we would conclude that the drug is effective; 79 percent is much greater than 22 percent. On the other hand, if we find that 98 percent recover without taking the drug, then we would conclude that the drug is worse than useless—it actually interferes with recovery. In other words, we need a control group. But most people are perfectly willing to conclude that because 79 percent seems like a high figure, that the drug must work. Seeing the necessity for a control group does not come naturally; unless people are deliberately taught about control groups, they will not realize the need for them.

Yet another tendency that interferes with people's ability to reason inductively is a disinclination to check evidence to see whether a hypothesis is false. Instead, people tend to seek evidence that might confirm their hypothesis; they exhibit the **confirmation bias.** For example, Wason (1968) presented subjects with the series of numbers "2, 4, 6" and asked them to try to figure out the rule to which they conformed. The subject was to test his or her hypothesis by making up series of numbers and saying them to the experimenter, who would reply "yes" or "no." Then, whenever the subject decided that enough information had been gathered, he or she could say what the hypothesis was. If the answer was correct, the problem was solved. If it was not, the subject was to think of a new hypothesis and test that one.

Several rules could explain the series "2, 4, 6." The rule could be "even numbers" or "each number is two more than the preceding one" or "the middle number is the mean of the first and third number." When people tested their hypotheses, they almost always did so by presenting several sets of numbers, *all of which were consistent with the hypothesis.* For example, if they thought that each number was two more than the preceding one, they might say "10, 12, 14" or "61, 63, 65." *Very few* subjects tried to test their hypothesis by choosing a set of numbers that did *not* conform to the rule, such as "12, 15, 22." In fact, the series "12, 15, 22" does conform to the rule. The rule was so simple that few subjects figured it out: Each number must be larger than the preceding one.

The confirmation bias is very strong. Unless people are taught to do so, they tend not to think of possible nonexamples of their hypothesis and see whether they might be true—the way that scientists do. But in fact, evidence that disconfirms a hypothesis is conclusive, whereas evidence that confirms it is not. Suppose that you thought that the answer to the problem I just described was "even numbers." You could give ascending lists of three even numbers hundreds of times, and each list would be correct. But, of course, your rule would still be wrong. If you gave just one nonexample—say, "5, 6, 7," the experimenter would say "yes" and you would immediately know that the answer was not "even numbers."

The confirmation bias in inductive reasoning has a counterpart in deductive reasoning. For example, consider the following sentences (Johnson-Laird, 1985):

All the pilots are artists.

All the skiers are artists.

True or false: All the pilots are skiers.

Many people say "true." They test the truth of the conclusion by imagining a person who is a pilot and an artist and a skier—and that person complies with the rules. Therefore, they decide that the conclusion is true. But if they would try to *disconfirm* the conclusion—look for an example that would fit the first two sentences but not the conclusion—they would easily find one. Could a person be a pilot but *not* a skier? Of course; the first two sentences say nothing to rule out that possibility. There are artist-pilots and there are artist-skiers, but nothing says there must be artist-pilot-skiers.

The tendency to seek (and pay more attention to) events that might confirm our beliefs is demonstrated by the way we have distorted the original meaning of the saying, "The exception proves the rule." Most people take this to mean that we can still consider a rule to be valid even if we encounter some exceptions. But that con-

clusion is illogical: If there is an exception, the rule is *wrong.* In fact, the original meaning of the phrase was, "The exception *tests* the rule," which it does. The word "prove" comes from the Latin *probare,* "to test."

Problem Solving

12 The ultimate function of thinking is to solve problems. People are faced with an enormous variety of them in their daily lives: fixing a television set, planning a picnic, choosing a spouse, navigating across the ocean, solving a math problem, tracking some game, designing a bridge, finding a job. The ability to solve problems is obviously related to academic and vocational success, so trying to understand how we do so is an important undertaking.

The Spatial Metaphor. According to Holyoak (1990), a problem is a state of affairs in which we have a goal but do not have a clear understanding of how it can be attained. As he notes, when we talk about problems, we often use spatial metaphors to describe them (Lakoff and Turner, 1989). We think of the solving of a problem as *finding a path to the solution.* We may have to *get around roadblocks* that we encounter or *backtrack* when *we hit a dead end.* If we *get lost,* we may try to *approach the problem from a different angle.* If we have experience with particular types of problems, we may know some *shortcuts.*

In fact, Newell and Simon (1972) have used the spatial metaphor to characterize the problem-solving process. At the beginning of their attempt to solve the problem, the *initial state* is different from the *goal state*—if it were not, there would be no problem. The person solving the problem has a number of *operators* available. Operators are actions that can be taken to change the current state of the problem; metaphorically, operators move the current state from one position to another. Not all people will be aware of the operators that are available; knowledge of operators depends on education and experience. In addition, there may be various costs associated with different operators; some may be more difficult, expensive, or time-consuming than others. The *problem space* consists of all the possible states that can be achieved if all the possible operators are applied. A *solution* is a sequence of operators (a "path") that moves from the initial state to the goal state. Of course, there may be more than one solution, and some solutions may be better than others. A good solution is one that uses the

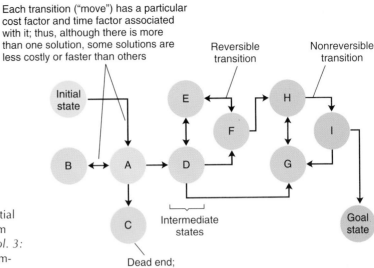

Each transition ("move") has a particular cost factor and time factor associated with it; thus, although there is more than one solution, some solutions are less costly or faster than others

Reversible transition

Nonreversible transition

Initial state

Intermediate states

Dead end; cannot return

Goal state

Figure 9.13 An illustration of Newell and Simon's spatial metaphor of the problem-solving process. (Adapted from Holyoak, K.J., in *An Invitation to Cognitive Science. Vol. 3: Thinking*, edited by D.N. Osherson and E.E. Smith. Cambridge, Mass.: MIT Press, 1990.)

smallest number of actions while minimizing the associated costs.

Figure 9.13 illustrates this process schematically. The circles represent the current or possible states of affairs while the problem is being solved. The arrows represent the operators—the actions that can be taken. Some actions are reversible (double arrows); others are not. A solution follows a path from the initial state to the goal state. (See **Figure 9.13.**)

As you can see, the problem shown in Figure 9.13 has more than one solution, but some are more costly and time-consuming than others. The relative importance of cost and speed determines which solution is best. For example, if the problem is to rescue a child who is up to her neck in quicksand, the best solution may be the most expensive one: Drive your $60,000 Mercedes into the pool of quicksand, climb up onto the roof, jump down to the hood, reach over the front of the car, pull her out—and then climb back over the top of the car and get to dry land before the car sinks. Finding a large object other than your valuable car would be cheaper, but it would take too much time.

Heuristics. Some problems are so simple that we can contemplate all the alternative actions at the same time and easily figure out the best solution. But many real-life problems are more complicated, and some of the alternatives do not reveal themselves until we take a particular action (that is, apply a particular operator). For example, during a game of chess we are presented with approximately thirty legal moves each time our turn comes around. The particular moves available to us depend not only on the moves we have made previously but also

Experienced chess players do not consider every possible move—they use heuristics to guide their choice.

on the moves our opponent makes. Thus, we cannot foresee all the possibilities at the beginning of the game.

When deciding what move to make, an expert chess player does *not* consider thirty possibilities. Instead, the player considers a few that seem to hold promise and then considers possible reactions by the opponent. How do experts know which possible moves are worthy of consideration? The answer is that they use *heuristics* to guide their search. **Heuristics** (pronounced *hyoo-RIS-tiks;* derived from the Greek *heuriskein,* "to discover") are general rules that are useful in guiding or furthering investigation. They tell us what to pay attention to, what to ignore, and what strategy to take in deciding how to act. For example, a heuristic principle in chess states that it is important to control the center of the board; thus, moves that help accomplish this subgoal are particularly useful.

Heuristic methods can be very specific (applying to the endgame in chess, when very few pieces are present), or they can be quite general, applying to large categories of problems. For example, management courses try to teach students problem-solving methods they can use in a wide variety of contexts. Newell and Simon (1972) suggest a general heuristic method that can be used to solve *any* problem: **means-ends analysis.** This principle behind this strategy is to look for differences between the current state and the goal state. The steps of this method are as follows (Holyoak, 1990, p. 121):

1. Compare the current state to the goal state and identify differences between the two. If there are none, the problem is solved; otherwise, proceed.
2. Select an operator that would reduce one of the differences.
3. If the operator can be applied, do so; if not, set a new *subgoal* of reaching a state at which the operator could be applied. Means-ends analysis is then applied to this new subgoal until the operator can be applied or the attempt to use it is abandoned.
4. Return to step 1.

Suppose the problem is to clear snow off our driveway. Rejecting several possible operators because they are too costly or too time-consuming (*dig the snow off with our hands,* or *melt the snow with a propane torch*), we decide to apply the operator *start the snowblower and run it up and down the driveway.* Unfortunately, we find that the snowblower will not start, which means that the operator we have chosen cannot

be applied. Thus, we set up a subgoal: *Fix the snowblower.*

One possible operator that will get us toward that subgoal is *put it in the car and bring it to a mechanic,* but the snow on our driveway precludes that option. Therefore, we decide to fix it ourselves. In order to fix it, we have to know what the problem is. We consider some possible actions, including *take the engine apart to see whether something inside is broken;* but we decide to try some simpler ones, such as *see whether the wire is attached to the spark plug* or *see whether there is gasoline in the tank.* We find the wire attached but the tank empty. The only operator that will get us to our subgoal is *fill the tank with gasoline.* But we have no gasoline. Therefore, we construct another subgoal: *Get some gasoline.*

What are the possible sources of gasoline? A gas station? No, we can't move the car. A neighbor? The snow is so deep that we do not want to fight our way through the drifts. The tank of our car? That's it. New subgoal: *Remove some gasoline from the car's fuel tank.* How do we get it out? New subgoal: *Find rubber hose to siphon the gasoline into the tank of the snowblower.* We do so, we start the engine, and we clear the snow off the driveway. The problem is solved.

The example I have just cited is obviously not very challenging, but it does illustrate the use of means-ends analysis. At all times, the person's activity is oriented toward reducing the distance between the current state and the goal state. If problems are encountered along the way (that is, if operators cannot be applied), then subgoals are created and means-ends analysis is applied to solving *that* problem—and so on, until the goal is reached.

Intelligent problem solving involves more than trying out various actions (applying various operators) to see whether they bring us closer to the goal; it also involves *planning.* When we plan, we act vicariously, "trying out" various actions in our heads. Obviously, planning requires that we know something about the consequences of the actions we are considering; experts are better at planning than novices are. If we do *not* know the consequences of particular actions, we will be obliged to try each action (apply each operator) and see what happens. Planning is especially important when many possible operators are present, when they are costly or time-consuming, or when they are irreversible. If we take an irreversible action that brings us to a dead end, then we have failed to solve the problem.

INTERIM SUMMARY

Thinking

Concepts are defined as lists of essential characteristics of objects and events, but research indicates that we deal with them in a rather informal way: Because of cognitive economy, our concepts appear to consist of collections of memories of particular examples, called exemplars. Concepts exist at the basic, subordinate, and superordinate level; we do most of our thinking about them at the basic level.

Deductive reasoning consists of inferring specific instances from general principles. That is, we take information that is already known and see whether particular occurrences are consistent with that information. One of the most important skills in deductive reasoning is the ability to construct mental models that represent the problem.

Inductive reasoning involves deducing general principles from particular facts. This form of thinking involves generating and testing hypotheses. Without special training (such as learning the rules of the scientific method) people often ignore relevant information, ignore the necessity of control groups, or show a confirmation bias—the tendency to only look for evidence that confirms one's hypothesis.

Problem solving is best represented spatially: We follow a path in the problem space from the initial state to the goal state, using operators to get to each intermediate state. Heuristics can guide us. The most general heuristic is means-ends analysis, which involves taking steps that reduce the distance from the current state to the goal. If obstacles are encountered, subgoals are created and attempts are made to reach them. ∎

APPLICATION

Expert Systems

The parallel advances in our understanding of human problem solving and our ability to design and write computer programs has led to the development of *expert systems:* computer programs that solve practical problems the way human experts do. These attempts represent one of the most interesting applications of the field of artificial intelligence.

Some kinds of problems can be solved by following a specific set of rules, called *algorithms*. For example, when you were taught to multiply numbers containing several digits (such as 3841×669), your teacher outlined a set of steps that you should follow: Write the numbers one above the other, with the right-hand digits lined up. Take the right-hand number in the bottom row and multiply it by each of the upper numbers, starting with the right. . . . And so on. The earliest attempts at developing expert systems employed algorithms. But it soon became apparent that people do not use a single, powerful strategy; they also use their *knowledge* to solve problems.

The game of chess provides a good example of the use of knowledge in problem solving. Expert chess players do not have to mentally imagine the consequences of each of the possible opening moves; they have memorized dozens of patterns of possible opening moves. These consequences of various patterns of opening moves have been tested by generations of expert chess players, and a player today uses that knowledge to guide the first dozen or so moves.

After that, the moves become less ritualized and the game takes on a personality of its own. Now, the players start thinking about the specific consequences of each move. Chess-playing computer programs work the same way: They have a "book" of openings that is used early in the game, and then they follow heuristics to generate a set of moves and countermoves by the opponent, whose consequences are then analyzed.

Once developers realized the importance of knowledge in problem solving, they began incorporating knowledge into their expert systems. One of the best-known expert systems is MYCIN, a computer program that can serve as a consultant to a physician trying to diagnose and prescribe antibiotic therapy for infections caused by bacteria in the blood and cerebrospinal fluid. The MYCIN project was started at Stanford University in the mid-1970s (Shortliffe, 1976).

MYCIN was given a knowledge base similar to the ones that human experts possess, represented in the form of IF . . . THEN rules. The following set of statements is an example of a MYCIN rule:

If: 1) The infection is meningitis and
    2) Organisms were not seen in the stain of the culture and
    3) The type of infection may be bacterial and
    4) The patient has been seriously burned,

Then: There is suggestive evidence that *Pseudomonas aeruginosa* is one of the organisms that might be causing the infection.

The MYCIN program consists of a network of about five hundred such rules, with the results of one rule feeding into others. The program asks questions of the physician, who sits at a computer terminal and answers them. Figure 9.14 shows some of the opening dialogue. The answers supplied by the physician are printed in color. (See *Figure 9.14.*)

As the program obtains more information, it "tests hypotheses" by requesting specific information until a tentative diagnosis is finally reached. Then, the program requests information about the patient in order to suggest a specific drug to treat the disease.

During the dialogue with the computer, the physician may type WHY or HOW to request further information. If he or she types WHY, the computer prints the rule that it is presently testing, for which it is requesting information. If the physician types HOW, the computer prints the rules that have been tested so far. The use of HOW and WHY makes the program more acceptable to physicians, because it lets them evaluate the computer's reasoning. In addition, these features make MYCIN a good tool for teaching medical students or for imparting new information to practicing physicians. (See *Figure 9.15.*)

MYCIN does an excellent job of diagnosing diseases. In one trial (Yu, Fagan, and Wraith, 1979) researchers found ten actual cases of meningitis and presented the symptoms to MYCIN. They gave the same information to a group of nine physicians of varying levels of experience and asked them to diagnose the disease and recommend antibiotic treatments. A group of experts performed a blind review of the diagnoses and recommendations (that is, they did not know who provided the diagnoses and recommendations).

Figure 9.14 Dialogue between a user and the MYCIN program. The user's responses are printed in color. (From Duda, R.O., and Shortliffe, E.H. *Science*, 1983, 220, 261–268. Reprinted with permission.)

```
Please enter information about the patient.
 1)  Name          Age           Sex          Race
     Pt219         42 YEARS      FEMALE       CAUCASIAN
 2)  Are there any positive cultures obtained
     from Pt219?
     NO
 3)  Are there any pending cultures of Pt219?
     YES
 4)  site          date          stain        method of
     collected     examined                   collection
                                              [urine, sputum only]
     CSF           3-Jun-75      YES          N/A
 5)  stain of smear              morph
     [type NONE if no organism was seen on the smear]
     NONE

                       .
                       .
                       .
             (more questions)
                       .
                       .
                       .
13)  Has Pt219 recently had symptoms of persistent headache
     or other abnormal neurologic symptoms (dizziness,
     lethargy, etc.?)
     YES
14)  Has Pt219 recently had objective evidence of abnormal
     neurologic signs (nuchal rigidity, coma, seizures,
     etc.) documented by physician observation or examina-
     tion?
     YES
The CSF cultures will be considered to be associated with
MENINGITIS.
```

Figure 9.15 Dialogue between a user and the MYCIN program, illustrating the program's responses to WHY and HOW. The user's responses are printed in color. (From Duda, R.O., and Shortliffe, E.H. *Science*, 1983, *220*, 261–268. Reprinted with permission.)

```
34) Is the meningitis a hospital-acquired infection?
    NO
35) Is Pt219's clinical history consistent with EPIGLOTTI-
    TIS?
    NO
36) Is Pt219's clinical history consistent with OTITIS-
    MEDIA?
    NO
37) Has the patient ever been to an area that is endemic
    for coccidiomycoses?
    UNKNOWN
38) Is Pt219 a burn patient?
    WHY

    [i.e. WHY is it important to determine whether Pt219
    has been seriously burned?]
     [4.0] This will aid in determining the organisms
           (other than those seen on cultures or smears)
           which might be causing the infection.
    It has already been established that
     [4.1] the infection which requires therapy is
           meningitis, and
     [4.2] organisms were not seen on the stain of the
           pending CSF culture (CULTURE-1), and
     [4.3] the type of the infection may be bacterial.
    Therefore, if
     [4.4] Pt219 has been seriously burned
    then
           there is suggestive evidence that Pseudomonas-
           aeruginosa is one of the organisms (other than
           those seen on cultures or smears) which might be
           causing the infection.
    Author: Yu
    [RULE 578]

    [back to question 38 . . .]
    HOW 4.3

    [i.e. HOW was it established that the type of the in-
    fection may be bacterial?]
                    Rule          Yes          No
          [4.5]     RULE 500     (.4)
          [4.6]     RULE 501                  (.17)
          [4.7]     RULE 502     (.1)
          [4.8]     RULE 524     (.42)
          [4.9]     RULE 504     (.28)
    Thus, it has been established that the type of the in-
    fection may be bacterial.
```

They gave the highest scores to MYCIN. Thus, the authors concluded that MYCIN could serve as a useful consultant for practicing physicians who did not have specific expertise in diagnosing and treating these particular diseases.

MYCIN is only one of several expert systems that have been developed. Other systems include DENDRAL, a pro-

gram that helps chemists figure out the chemical structure of unknown compounds; PROSPECTOR, which assists geologists in exploration for mineral ore deposits; and PUFF, which helps physicians diagnose lung diseases. Many more expert systems are being developed, and we can expect to see programs that will operate at the level of the very best human experts in the field, just as we have seen chess-playing programs that challenge all but the best human grand masters. A recent expert system based on neural networks rather than on explicit rules (the model "learns" from examples provided by human experts) did a better job of diagnosing heart attacks than the patient's physicians did (Baxt, 1991). What such programs will *not* do is find new strategies and invent new kinds of solutions; for creative solutions we will have to turn to human experts—at least for the time being.

KEY TERMS AND CONCEPTS

psycholinguistics *(271)*

Speech and Comprehension

phoneme *(271)*
voice-onset time *(272)*
syntactical rule *(273)*
function word *(274)*
content word *(274)*
affix *(274)*
prosody *(274)*
deep structure *(275)*
surface structure *(275)*
script *(275)*
aphasia *(276)*
Wernicke's area *(276)*
Wernicke's aphasia *(276)*
Broca's aphasia *(277)*
Broca's area *(277)*
agrammatism *(277)*

Reading

eye tracker *(279)*
fixation *(279)*
dyslexia *(281)*
semantic priming *(282)*

Language Acquisition by Children

child-directed speech *(286)*
inflection *(287)*
overextension *(288)*
underextension *(288)*
language universal *(290)*

Communication with Other Primate Species

Thinking

concept *(297)*
exemplar *(298)*
basic-level concept *(299)*
superordinate concept *(299)*
subordinate concept *(299)*
deductive reasoning *(299)*
syllogism *(299)*
mental model *(300)*
inductive reasoning *(301)*
confirmation bias *(302)*
heuristics *(305)*
means-ends analysis *(305)*

SUGGESTIONS FOR FURTHER READING

Osherson, D.N., and Lasnik, H. *An Invitation to Cognitive Science. Vol. 1: Language.* Cambridge, Mass.: MIT Press, 1990.

Osherson, D.N., and Smith, E.E. *An Invitation to Cognitive Science. Vol. 3: Thinking.* Cambridge, Mass.: MIT Press, 1990.

Tanenhaus, M.K. *Psycholinguistics: An Overview.* Cambridge: Cambridge University Press, 1988.

Just, M.A., and Carpenter, P.A. *The Psychology of Reading and Language Comprehension.* Boston: Allyn and Bacon, 1987.

Volumes 1 and 3 of An Invitation to Cognitive Science *contain chapters written by experts on various topics of language and thinking. The Tanenhaus book provides general information about psycholinguistics, and the book by Just and Carpenter focuses on written language.*

de Luce, J., and Wilder, H.T. *Language in Primates: Perspectives and Implications.* New York: Springer-Verlag, 1983.

This book describes attempts to teach language to non-human primates. It also describes the controversies about the success and significance of these attempts.

10
LIFE SPAN DEVELOPMENT

MATISSE, Henri.
The Piano Lesson. Issy-les-Moulineaux (late summer 1916).
Oil on canvas, 8'$\frac{1}{2}$" × 6'11$\frac{3}{4}$".
Collection, The Museum of Modern Art, New York. Mrs. Simon Guggenheim Fund.
© 1992 Succession H. Matisse/ARS, N.Y.

LEARNING OBJECTIVES

When you finish this chapter, you should be able to:

1. Describe the functions of chromosomes and genes, the processes of fertilization and differentiation, and the prenatal development of a human fetus.
2. Describe the physical and perceptual development of the human child.
3. Discuss the importance of a responsive environment, and describe and discuss the four periods of cognitive development proposed by Jean Piaget.
4. Describe the behaviors of infants that help establish the attachment between infant and caregiver.
5. Describe the variables that affect the nature of attachment between caregiver and infant, and discuss the importance of such attachment.
6. Assess the role of interactions with peers on a child's social development.
7. Define sexual identity, sex roles, and sex stereotypes, and describe the biological and social variables that affect their development.
8. Compare and contrast Piaget's and Kohlberg's theories of moral development, and discuss research on teaching morality to children.
9. Describe physical development during puberty and its behavioral effects.
10. Describe social development during adolescence.
11. Describe the physical changes that occur late in adult life and their consequences.
12. Describe the nature of personality development in adulthood.
13. Evaluate the evidence concerning the existence of a mid-life crisis.
14. Discuss the nature of cognitive changes in late adulthood and the variables that affect them.

One day a colleague of mine, Dr. D., approached me in the hall. He asked me how old my daughter was, and when I said she was six months old, he asked whether my wife and I would mind if he used her for a demonstration in his child development class. I said it would be fine with me, and I was sure my wife would agree also.

The next week, my wife brought our daughter to the psychology building at the appointed time. Dr. D. ushered them into a small room that contained a large square table. Part of the surface of the table was a strip of plywood about a foot wide, which ran along one edge. It was painted in a bright red-and-black checkerboard pattern. The rest of the table was topped with an enormous piece of glass. The floor under the glass, about 3 feet below, was painted in the same checkerboard pattern.

Dr. D. asked my wife to place our daughter at one corner of the table, on the end of the plywood platform. After my wife had done so, and after she had reassured our daughter that everything was all right, he asked her to go to the opposite corner of the table and stand there. He glanced up at the one-way glass that separated the room from the adjoining classroom, which contained a small group of students who were watching the procedure.

"Now ask her to come to you," he said.

"Come here, Kerstin," said my wife in a cheerful tone.

Kerstin grinned, made a happy noise, and scampered across the glass, making slapping sounds with her hands as she crawled. She seemed heedless of the 3-foot drop beneath the glass.

My wife picked her up, smiled at Dr. D., and realized from the expression on his face that something had gone wrong. He glanced at the one-way glass, cleared his throat, and said, "Let's try it again."

The second trial was like the first. In fact, this time Kerstin did not even wait for my wife to get to her corner before she started across the glass. Clearly, she knew how the game was played.

"Kerstin hasn't done this before, has she?" asked Dr. D.

"No, she hasn't," my wife replied. "But I think I know why she wasn't afraid of crawling onto the glass. That *was* what you expected, wasn't it?"

"Yes," he said.

"We have a glass-topped coffee table in the living room at home, and Kerstin likes to play there. She used to like to lie on the floor under it and look up through the glass, and the past couple of months we've put her on top of it and let her crawl around."

Dr. D. looked relieved. "That explains it," he said. "She has learned to trust her sense of touch, even though she undoubtedly could perceive that the floor under the glass was far away." He paused a few seconds. "Actually," he said, "this provides a nice demonstration of the interaction between experience and development. Although children change in predictable ways as they mature, their development is shaped by their encounters with their environment."

He thanked my wife and turned toward the classroom. He was obviously thinking about how he would take advantage of this unexpected happening in the rest of his lecture.

Human life is characterized by growth and change. We all begin existence as a single fertilized egg, and from that moment until the time we die we are continuously changing. Some of the changes are rapid and momentous; others are so slow that we do not notice them until we look back and see how different we are from the way we once were.

Developmental psychology is the study of these changes and of what causes them. Because developmental psychologists are concerned with physical, perceptual, cognitive, emotional, and social development, their research interests are closely related to every area of psychological inquiry described in this book, from physiological psychology to group dynamics.

This chapter begins at the beginning—conception—and continues to old age. The first six major sections deal with infancy and childhood; they describe prenatal development, physical and perceptual development, cognitive development, social development, development of sex roles, and moral development. The next major section describes adolescence, and the final section describes development in adulthood and old age.

Let us begin by examining basic processes that shape a child's physical development.

Chromosomes and Genes

[1] Our bodies consist of many trillions of cells, all descendants of a single fertilized egg that must contain the information necessary to construct a human being. This information resides in the nucleus of the cell in twenty-three pairs of chromosomes, and in the course of our physical development copies of these chromosomes will be included in every cell. This system must certainly be the most efficient means of information storage found anywhere in nature; a set of human chromosomes can easily fit on the point of a pin.

The functional unit of the chromosome is the **gene**; every chromosome consists of many thousands of genes, each of which contains the instructions necessary to produce a particular protein. Through their ability to direct the kinds and amounts of proteins manufactured, genes control an organism's development. In this regard, the most important class of proteins are *enzymes*.

When a pregnant woman eats, she ingests complex molecules in the form of animal or plant tissue, and her body then proceeds to break these molecules down to simple ones. Her body provides these simple nutrients to the cells of her developing offspring; each cell then combines these simple molecules into the complex ones it requires. This process is controlled by enzymes. **Enzymes** act as biological catalysts; they determine the kinds of chemical reactions that occur, without themselves becoming part of the final product. Thus, the types of enzymes present in a cell determine which complex molecules are produced by that cell and hence control the cell's structure and function.

Fertilization and Differentiation

Fertilization occurs when a man's sperm unites with a woman's ovum. Sperms and ova each contain twenty-three single chromosomes—one member of each pair. When an ovum is fertilized, the pairs are reconstituted in a single cell, with one member of each new pair coming from each parent. In this way each parent contributes half of a child's genetic material. (See *Figure 10.1.*)

A person's genetic sex is determined by the father's sperm at the time of fertilization. Twenty-two of the pairs of chromosomes determine the organism's physical development independent of its sex. The last pair consists of two **sex chromosomes,** which determine whether the offspring will be a boy or a girl. There are two types of sex chromosomes: **X chromosomes** and **Y chromosomes.** Females have two X chromosomes (XX); thus, all the ova that a woman produces will contain an X chromosome. Males have an X and a Y chromosome (XY). When a man's sex chromosomes divide, half the sperms contain an X chromosome and the other half a Y chromosome. A Y-bearing sperm produces an XY-fertilized ovum and, therefore, a male. An X-bearing sperm produces an XX-fertilized ovum and, therefore, a female. (See *Figure 10.2.*)

A fertilized human ovum is nothing more than a very large cell containing the twenty-three pairs of human chromosomes. This cell divides and redivides, with each division doubling the previous number of cells. Just before a cell divides, it duplicates all of its parts; it produces a duplicate set of chromosomes, with one set going to each of the two new cells. At first, the exact same cell is replicated, creating a mass of identical cells. Then, according to a spe-

Figure 10.1 Fertilization. Each parent contributes one-half of his or her child's chromosomes through the sperm or ovum.

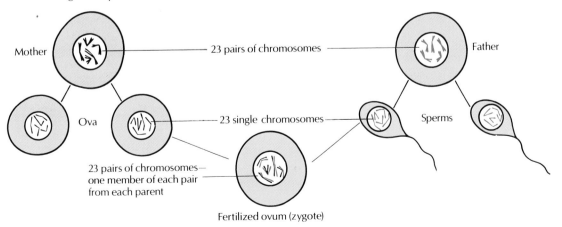

Mother

Ova

23 pairs of chromosomes

23 single chromosomes

Father

Sperms

23 pairs of chromosomes—
one member of each pair
from each parent

Fertilized ovum (zygote)

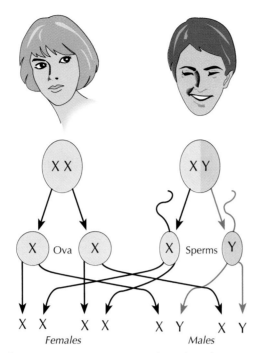

Figure 10.2 Determination of gender. The gender of the offspring depends on whether the sperm cell that fertilizes the ovum carries an X or a Y chromosome.

cial internal mechanism, the cells produced in this sequence of divisions undergo **differentiation** in which the various cells "specialize" by acquiring certain distinctive features. Thus, a single cell develops into a complex organism consisting of thousands of *different* kinds of cells.

Differentiation is accomplished by a process that deactivates most of the genes in a particular type of cell. Just as a cook keeps more recipes on file than are necessary for the preparation of a given meal, chromosomes contain more sets of instructions than any one cell will use in its lifetime. For example, a neuron contains the instructions for producing the enzymes that construct the enamel that covers teeth—instructions that it will never follow. Different types of cells use different sets of recipes in their daily activities. As the fertilized egg divides and redivides, some process, which we do not yet understand, deactivates some of the genes of the newly formed cells. Various sets of genes become deactivated in specific types of cells at certain stages of development, and thus, the cells take on different functions.

The factors that control the development of a human organism are incredibly complex. For example, the most complicated organ—the brain—consists of many billions of neurons (nerve cells), all of which are connected to other neurons. In addition, many of these neurons are connected to sensory receptors, muscles, or glands. During development these billions of neurons must establish the proper connections so that the eyes send their information to the visual cortex, the ears send theirs to the auditory cortex, and the nerve cells controlling movement connect with the appropriate muscles.

A pregnant woman's intake of various drugs can have disastrous effects on fetal development. For example, alcohol, opiates, cocaine, and the chemicals present in cigarettes can harm fetuses. In addition, diseases such as German measles produce toxins that can interfere with development of the fetal brain. Finally, several types of genetic abnormalities can harm development, causing brain damage and consequent mental retardation. All of these threats to fetal development are described in Chapter 13, which deals with intelligence.

Fertilization: an ovum surrounded by sperms.

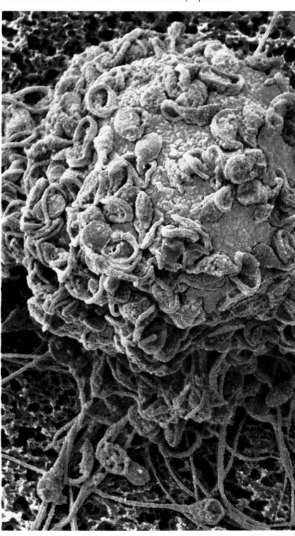

Development in the Uterus

The fertilized ovum begins to divide and redivide. Soon, it attaches itself to the wall of the uterus and begins to grow tendrils that intertwine with the rich supply of blood vessels located there. The mass of dividing cells begins to differentiate into various kinds of tissues. At this moment, when the cells begin to specialize, the organism becomes an embryo.

The embryo develops an **amniotic sac,** a membrane that completely encases it in a watery fluid. It also develops a **placenta,** which draws nourishment from the mother and passes waste products to her to be excreted. These transfers are conveyed by blood vessels in the umbilical cord, which connects the fetus to the placenta.

As we saw, gender is determined by the sex chromosomes. In fact, the deciding factor is the Y chromosome. If it is present, the embryo will become a male; if it is not, it will become a female. The process works like this: Early in prenatal development, the embryo develops a pair of gonads, which will become either ovaries or testes. (The word *gonad* comes from the Greek *gonos,* "procreation.") If a Y chromosome is present, a gene located on it causes the production of a chemical signal that makes the gonads develop into testes; otherwise, the gonads become ovaries.

The development of the other sex organs is determined by the presence or absence of testes. If testes are present, they begin secreting a class of sex hormones known as **androgens** (*andros* means "man"; *gennan* means "to produce"). The most important androgen is *testosterone.* Androgens bring about the development of the male internal sex organs, the penis, and the scrotum; thus, these hormones are absolutely necessary for the development of a male. In contrast, the development of female sex organs (uterus, vagina, and labia) simply occurs naturally; it does not need to be stimulated by a hormone. If the gonads completely fail to develop (a genetic disorder known as *Turner's syndrome*), the fetus becomes female, with normal female sex organs. Of course, lacking ovaries, such a person cannot bear children. (See *Figure 10.3.*)

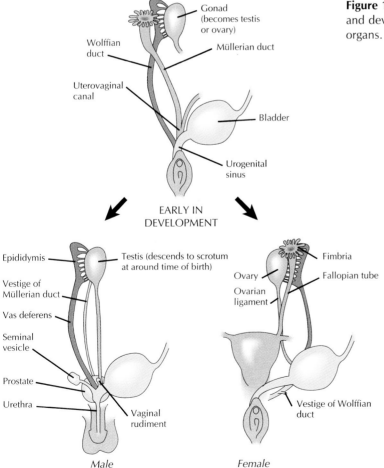

Figure 10.3 Differentiation and development of the sex organs.

By the time the embryo becomes a fetus (in approximately eight weeks), it is unmistakably human in appearance. When it is four months old, the mother can feel its movements. In another month it is capable of responding to the environment; it can swallow some of the amniotic fluid in which it floats, and sometimes, it even develops hiccups. The sucking reflex is well established before birth; pictures taken of fetuses by means of sonar have caught them in the act of sucking their thumbs. By the time the fetus is born, its organs have developed sufficiently so that it can sustain life on its own.

INTERIM SUMMARY

Prenatal Development

Fertilization of an ovum by a sperm determines the genetic blueprint for an individual. The eventual expression of this blueprint involves a complex interaction between the developing organism and its environment that begins long before the child is born. The importance of this interaction is underscored by the existence of genetically and environmentally produced defects.

Gender is determined by the sex chromosomes: XX produces a female, and XY produces a male. Male sex organs are produced by the action of a gene on the Y chromosome that causes the gonads to develop into testes. The testes secrete androgens, which stimulate the development of male sex organs. If testes are not present, the fetus develops as a female. ■

PHYSICAL AND PERCEPTUAL DEVELOPMENT IN INFANCY AND CHILDHOOD

2 The word *infant* comes from the Latin word meaning "unable to speak." By general agreement, the newborn baby is called an infant until two years of age, even though normal infants begin to speak during their second year. A newborn human infant is a helpless creature, absolutely dependent on adult care. But recent research has shown that newborns do not passively await the ministrations of their caretakers; they very quickly develop skills that shape the behavior of the adults with whom they interact.

Motor Development

At birth the infant's most important movements are reflexes—automatic movements in response to specific stimuli. The most important reflexes are the *rooting, sucking,* and *swallowing* responses. If a baby's cheek is lightly touched, he or she will turn the head so that the object reaches the lips (the **rooting** response). If the object is of the appropriate size, texture, and temperature, the baby will open the mouth and begin **sucking.** When the milk enters the mouth, the baby will automatically make **swallowing** movements. Obviously, these reflexes are important for the baby's survival. As we will see later in this chapter, these behaviors, along with cuddling, looking, smiling, and crying, are important for an infant's social development as well.

Newborn infants can also respond to noxious stimuli by withdrawing, but this reflex tends to be rather diffuse. Older children will pull their arm back if their hand strikes a hot or sharp object, but a baby's withdrawal reflex lacks such precision—the entire body participates in the movement. Because the baby's own organized movements are so limited, he or she must depend on adult intervention for protection from harm and for provision of food.

Normal motor development follows a distinct pattern, which appears to be dictated by maturation of the muscles and the nervous system. For example, Frankenberg and Dodds (1968) carried out a careful, thorough study of the stages of development of the ability to walk. Although individual children progress at different rates, their development follows the same basic pattern. ***Figure 10.4*** shows the results.

Development of motor skills requires two ingredients: maturation of the child's nervous system and lots of practice. Development of the brain is not complete at birth; considerable growth occurs during the first several months (Dekaban, 1970). In fact, some changes are still taking place in early adulthood. Particular kinds of movements must await the development of the necessary neuromuscular systems. But motor development is not merely a matter of using these systems once they develop; instead, physical development of the nervous system depends, to a large extent, on the baby's own movements while interacting with the environment.

Normal infants in stimulating and nonrestrictive environments will practice their developing motor skills. Practice is often hard work;

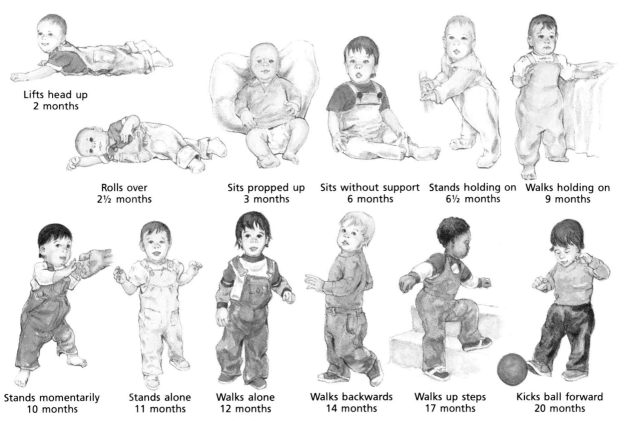

Lifts head up
2 months

Rolls over
2½ months

Sits propped up
3 months

Sits without support
6 months

Stands holding on
6½ months

Walks holding on
9 months

Stands momentarily
10 months

Stands alone
11 months

Walks alone
12 months

Walks backwards
14 months

Walks up steps
17 months

Kicks ball forward
20 months

Figure 10.4 Milestones in a child's motor development.

young children have to put real effort into mastering new skills. For example, infants expend much energy while learning how to walk. By the end of the first year of life babies can get from place to place very efficiently by crawling. However, they soon begin to struggle with standing upright and taking a few steps. When trying to get somewhere fast, a baby will drop to all fours and crawl. But when exploring in a more leisurely fashion, the baby will try to walk, even though locomotion is slow, tedious, and punctuated by frequent falls. For an infant, mastery of the skill of walking seems to serve as its own reward.

Studies have shown that children who have spent their infancy lying on their backs in cribs in institutional nurseries do not develop the normal motor skills of children who are raised in homes or in institutions that provide more stimulation and opportunity for movement and exploration (Dennis, 1960). Crawling and walking are among the skills that can be severely retarded. Fortunately, normal motor skills will develop in a wide range of environments; only the most restrictive ones produce severe motor impairments.

Perceptual Development

Almost everyone who has watched a newborn baby has wondered how infants view the world. What can they see? What can they hear? Until a few years ago, we could only speculate about the answers to these questions.

If we want to study how older children or adults perceive the world, we can simply ask them about their experiences. We can determine how large an object must be for them to see it or how loud a sound must be for them to hear it. But we cannot talk to infants and expect to get any answers; we must use their nonverbal behavior as an indicator of what they can perceive.

We have known for a long time that a newborn's senses function at least to a certain extent. We know that the auditory system can detect sounds, because the baby will show a startle reaction when presented with a sudden, loud noise. Similarly, a bright light will elicit eye closing and squinting. A cold object or a pinch will produce crying, so the sense of touch must be present. If held firmly and tilted backward, a baby will stiffen and flail his or her arms and legs, so we must conclude that babies have a sense of balance.

Research indicates that even an unborn fetus has a sense of taste. When a pregnant woman accumulates too much amniotic fluid, the condition can be corrected by injecting a sugar solution into the fluid. The fetus obviously detects the sweet taste, because it usually swallows enough fluid to eliminate the excess (Bookmiller and Bowen, 1967). The swallowed fluid enters the bloodstream of the fetus and is then transported through the placenta to the mother, who excretes it in her urine.

A newborn infant indicates its taste preference by facial expression and by choosing to swallow or not to swallow different liquids. When given a sweet liquid, an infant's face relaxes in an expression rather like a smile; but when it is given a sour or bitter liquid, its face indicates displeasure. Newborn infants also show signs of pleasure in response to the smells of foods such as chocolate or bananas, but the smell of rotten eggs causes them to spit and to turn down the corners of their mouth (Steiner, 1979). Newborn infants can even learn to recognize particular odors. Sullivan et al. (1991) presented one-day-old infants with a citrus odor and then gently stroked them. The next day, these infants (but not control infants) turned toward a cotton swab containing the odor that had been paired with the stroking.

Beyond these demonstrations, most recent investigations of the perceptual abilities of newborn infants have taken advantage of the fact that babies have good control of movements of their head, eyes, and mouth. We will look at the results of some of these studies next.

Perception of Patterns. Most investigations of infant perception have concentrated on vision, probably because it is such an important sense for humans. No careful observer ever doubted that a baby's eyes can respond to light; newborn infants will close their eyes and screw up their faces if the level of illumination is too high. But what about their ability to perceive objects?

The visual perceptual abilities of infants can be studied by observing their eye movements as visual stimuli are shown to them. A harmless spot of infrared light, invisible to humans, is directed onto the baby's eyes. A special television camera, sensitive to infrared light, records the spot and superimposes it on an image of the display that the baby is looking at. The technique is precise enough to determine which parts of a stimulus the baby is scanning. For example, Salapatek (1975) reported that a one-month-old infant tends not to look at the inside of a figure; instead, the child's gaze seems to be "trapped" by the edges. By the age of two months the baby scans across the border to investigate the interior of a figure. Figure 10.5 shows a computer-drawn reconstruction of the paths followed by the eye scans of infants of these ages. (The babies were looking at *real* faces, not the drawings shown in the figure. See *Figure 10.5.*)

The work by Salapatek and his colleagues suggests that at the age of one or two months babies are probably not perceiving complete shapes; their scanning strategy is limited to fixations on a few parts of the object they are looking at. However, by the age of five months they clearly perceive complete shapes; the combina-

Figure 10.5 The scanning sequence used by children viewing faces. (From Salapatek, P., in *Infant Perception: From Sensation to Cognition.* Vol. 1: *Basic Visual Processes,* edited by L.B. Cohen and P. Salapatek. New York: Academic Press, 1975. Reprinted with permission.)

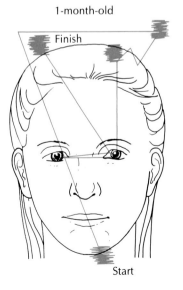

1-month-old

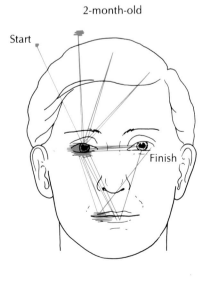

2-month-old

tion of maturation of the nervous system and practice looking at faces enables them to recognize a face they have seen before, even in a somewhat different pose (Fagan, 1976). Two months later, they are able to recognize a happy expression on an adult's face (Caron, Caron, and Myers, 1982).

Perception of Space.   The ability to perceive three-dimensional space comes at an early age. Gibson and Walk (1960) placed six-month-old babies on what they called a *visual cliff*—a platform containing a checkerboard pattern. The platform adjoined a glass shelf mounted several feet over a floor, which was also covered by the checkerboard pattern. (Yes, this is the device I described in the opening vignette.) Most babies who could crawl would not venture out onto the glass shelf. The infants acted as if they were afraid of falling. (Obviously, they had not had the experience my daughter had.)

Even infants too young to crawl appear to be able to perceive depth. Campos, Langer, and Krowitz (1970) found that two-month-old infants showed a decrease in heart rate when they are placed on the "deep" side of the visual cliff but not on the "shallow" side. One-month-old infants did not respond differentially. We cannot be sure whether the change in heart rate indicates fear or simply interest on the part of the infant, but we can conclude that the ability to perceive depth perception in this situation develops by the second month of life.

As you learned in Chapter 5, several different types of cues in the environment contribute to depth perception. One cue arises from the fact that each eye gets a slightly different view of the world (Poggio and Poggio, 1984). This form of depth perception, **stereopsis** ("solid appearance"), is the kind obtained from a stereoscope or a three-dimensional movie. As Hubel and Wiesel (1970) have shown, the brain mechanisms necessary for stereopsis will not develop unless animals have experience viewing objects with both eyes during a critical period early in life.

The term **critical period** refers to a very important concept in development: It is the specific time during which certain experiences must occur if an organism is to develop normally. Many behavioral, perceptual, and cognitive abilities are subject to critical periods. For example, as we shall see later in this chapter, if infants are not exposed to a stimulating environment and do not have the opportunity to interact with caregivers during the first two years of their lives, their cognitive development will be irreparably retarded. Human development is more than an unfolding of a genetically determined program; it consists of a continuous interaction between physical maturation and environmental stimulation.

The critical period in the development of stereopsis has important implications for the development of normal vision. If an infant's eyes do not move together properly—if they both are directed toward the same place in the environment (that is, if the eyes are "crossed")—the infant never develops stereoscopic vision, even if the eye movements are later corrected by surgery on the eye muscles. Banks, Aslin, and Letson (1975) studied infants whose eye movement deficits were later corrected surgically. Their results show that the critical period

A visual cliff. The child does not cross the glass bridge. (From a study conducted by Nancy Rader and Associates.)

ends sometime between one and three years of age; if surgery occurs before this time, stereoscopic vision will develop. If the surgery occurs later, it will not.

INTERIM SUMMARY

Physical and Perceptual Development in Infancy and Childhood

You now have a better idea of the importance of the interaction between hereditary and environmental factors in an infant's physical development and how crucial the timing between the two can be. Genetically, an infant has the potential to develop skills that coincide with the maturation of its nervous system. But in order for this potential to be realized, the infant's environment must supply the opportunity to test and practice these skills. If an infant is deprived of the opportunity to practice them at crucial times (during a critical period), these skills may fail to develop, which will affect his or her performance as an adult. As we will see in the section on social development, infants have certain innate behaviors that help ensure that they receive the proper attention and stimulation from their caregivers at the appropriate time. ∎

COGNITIVE DEVELOPMENT IN CHILDHOOD

As children grow, their nervous systems mature and they undergo new experiences. Perceptual and motor skills develop in complexity and competency. Children learn to recognize particular faces and voices, begin to talk and respond to the speech of others, and learn how to solve problems. In short, their cognitive capacities develop.

The Importance of a Responsive Environment

3 **Cognition** means "to get to know." The cognitive development of infants is therefore the process by which they get to know things about themselves and their world. Evidence suggests that one of the first steps in cognitive development is learning that events in the environment are often contingent on one's own behavior. Thus, the most stimulating environment—that is, the environment that is most effective in promoting cognitive development—is one in which the infant's behavior has tangible effects.

In an experiment testing this hypothesis Watson and Ramey (1972) presented three groups of infants with a mobile ten minutes per day for fourteen days. A pillow containing a pressure-sensitive switch was placed under the baby's head, and the mobile was suspended above the baby's face. For one group the mobile automatically rotated whenever the infant moved his or her head and activated the switch. For another group the mobile remained stationary. For the third group the mobile intermittently moved on its own (*not* in response to head movement).

Several weeks later, the babies were tested again. Those who had learned the contingency between head turning and mobile movement continued to turn their heads. In contrast, when the babies in the second and third groups were later given the opportunity to make the mobile move by turning their heads, they did *not* learn to control it. It was as if they had learned that nothing they could do would affect the movements of the mobile. (See ***Figure 10.6.***)

These results may have implications for infant-rearing practices. In some tragic cases babies have been raised in unresponsive, unstimulating institutions. In one institution infants were cared for physically but were raised in cribs that visually isolated them from each other. Although

Figure 10.6 The procedure and results of the experiment by Watson and Ramey (1972).

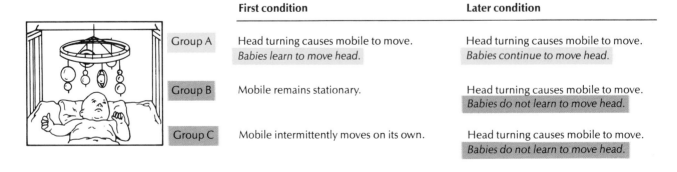

		First condition	**Later condition**
	Group A	Head turning causes mobile to move. *Babies learn to move head.*	Head turning causes mobile to move. *Babies continue to move head.*
	Group B	Mobile remains stationary.	Head turning causes mobile to move. *Babies do not learn to move head.*
	Group C	Mobile intermittently moves on its own.	Head turning causes mobile to move. *Babies do not learn to move head.*

their physical needs were fulfilled, they received no individual attention or personal interactions from their caregivers (Dennis, 1973).

The children raised under these conditions were extremely retarded in cognitive, language, and motor development. Dennis found that when children were adopted from the nursery and raised in a normal home environment, they showed significant gains in physical and intellectual development. However, there was evidence for a critical period. Children adopted before two years of age eventually achieved a normal level of development, whereas those who were adopted *after* the age of two years remained somewhat behind normally raised children. Thus, a nonstimulating environment may produce permanent damage if it persists through the child's first two years of life.

The Work of Jean Piaget

The most influential student of child development was Jean Piaget, a Swiss psychologist. Piaget formulated the most complete and detailed description of the process of cognitive development that we now have. His conclusions were based on his observations of the behavior of children—first, his own children at home and, later, other children at his Center of Genetic Epistemology in Geneva. He noticed that children of similar age tend to engage in similar behaviors and to make the same kinds of mistakes in problem solving. He concluded that these similarities are the result of a sequence of development that is followed by all normal children. Completion of each period, with its corresponding abilities, is the prerequisite for entering the next period.

According to Piaget, a child's cognitive development consists in the acquisition of **cognitive structures,** rules that are used for understanding and dealing with the world, for thinking about and solving problems. The two principal types of cognitive structures are schemas and concepts. A **schema** is a set of rules that define a particular category of behavior—how the behavior is executed and under what conditions. For example, the cognitive structure of an infant includes sucking schemas, reaching schemas, and looking schemas.

Piaget suggested that as a child acquires knowledge of the environment, he or she develops mental structures called concepts. **Concepts** are rules that describe properties of environmental events and their relations with other concepts. For example, concepts about the existence of various objects include what the ob-

Jean Piaget (1896–1980), a Swiss psychologist, was known for his detailed observations of the development of children's behavior and thought processes.

jects do, how they relate to other objects, and what happens when they are touched or manipulated. Thus, the cognitive structure of an infant includes concepts of such things as rattles, balls, crib slats, hands, and other people.

Infants acquire the rules that constitute their schemas and concepts by interacting with their environment. According to Piaget, two processes help the child adapt to its environment: assimilation and accommodation. **Assimilation** involves adding new items to a concept or a schema; **accommodation** involves changing them on the basis of new information. For example, suppose that little Erin's animal concept has three categories: doggies, kitties, and teddies. If she sees a picture of a deer and calls it a kitty, she has *assimilated* the new information into an existing concept. However, if she decides that a deer is a new kind of animal, she will *accommodate* her animal concept to include the new category. Now this concept consists of doggies, kitties, teddies, and deer.

Piaget's Four Periods of Cognitive Development

Although development is a continuous process, the cognitive structures of children vary enough from age to age to permit inferences about the rules used by children of certain ages to under-

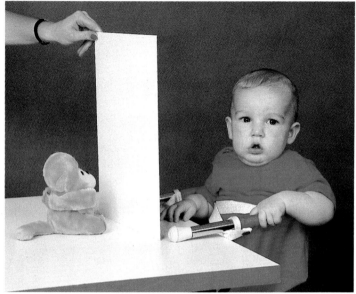

Early in the sensorimotor period, "out of sight" is "out of mind." A hidden object ceases to exist.

stand their environment and control their behavior. Piaget has divided cognitive development into four periods. What a child learns in one period enables that child to progress on to the next period.

The Sensorimotor Period. The **sensorimotor period** lasts for approximately the first two years of life. During this period cognition is closely tied to external stimulation. An important feature of the sensorimotor period is the development of the **object concept.** At first, the child appears to lose all interest in an object that disappears from sight; the proverb "Out of sight, out of mind" seems particularly appropriate. In addition, cognition consists entirely in behavior: Thinking is doing.

According to Piaget, the best way to investigate an infant's object concept is to see what the child does when an object disappears or is hidden. Piaget's observations include many descriptions of what his children did when he hid an interesting object. At first, infants do not appear to have a concept for objects. They can look at visual stimuli and will turn their head and eyes toward the source of a sound, but hiding an object elicits no particular response. At around three months they become able to follow moving objects with their eyes. If an object disappears behind a barrier, the infant will continue to stare at the place where the object disappeared but will not search for it. If the object does not soon reappear, the infant seems to lose interest. Piaget called this phenomenon **passive ex-**

pectation, because the baby appears to expect the object to reappear but does not actively search for it.

At around five months the infant can now grasp and hold objects and thus gains experience with manipulating and observing them. The infant can also anticipate the future position of a moving object. If a moving object passes behind a screen, the infant turns his or her eyes toward the far side of the screen; the child appears to anticipate the reappearance of the object on the other side.

During the last half of the first year the infant develops much more complex concepts concerning the nature of physical objects. He or she grasps objects, turns them over, and investigates their properties. By looking at an object from various angles, the infant learns that it can change its visual shape and still be the same object. In addition, if an object is hidden, the infant will actively search for it; the infant's object concept contains the rule of **permanence.** For an infant at this stage of development, a hidden object still exists. "Out of sight" is no longer "out of mind."

By early in the second year the object concept is well enough developed that infants will search for a hidden object in the last place they saw it hidden. However, infants at this stage can only keep track of changes that they can see in the hiding place. For example, if an adult picks up an object, puts it under a cloth, drops the object while his or her hand is hidden, closes the hand again, and removes it from the cloth, the infant will look for the object in the adult's hand. When the child does not find the object there, he or she looks puzzled or upset and does not search for the object under the cloth. (See *Figure 10.7.*)

According to Piaget, the infant begins to think during the middle of the second year. Thought is closely tied to motor schemas and concepts of the properties of objects, but the beginnings of symbolic representation are evident. For example, Piaget observed his sixteen-month-old daughter Lucienne use a motor schema (opening her mouth) to solve a problem (opening a box). A large match box held a chain that Lucienne liked to play with. She tried unsuccessfully to shake the chain out of the box, stopped, opened and shut her mouth several times, then put her finger into the opening of the box and enlarged it enough so that she could reach in for the chain.

Other cognitive structures develop by the end of the sensorimotor period. The infant begins to differentiate self from other objects in the environment and gains an appreciation of time and space. The child actively experiments with objects and discovers the consequences of these experiments. For example, the infant may learn what happens when a light switch is moved or when the knob of a television is turned. By

At this stage of development, "out of sight" is no longer "out of mind."

Figure 10.7 Sensorimotor development. An infant will not realize that the object has been left under the cloth.

the end of this period the infant has a good start acquiring language ability. The child knows the meaning of several dozen words and can produce a good number of his or her own.

The Preoperational Period. Piaget's second period of cognitive development, the **preoperational period,** lasts from approximately age two to age seven. This period is characterized by rapid development of language ability and of the ability to represent things symbolically—the **symbolic function.** The child arranges toys in new ways to represent other objects (for example, a row of blocks can represent a train), begins to classify and categorize objects, and starts learning to count and to manipulate numbers.

Piaget asserted that development of the symbolic function actually begins during the sensorimotor period, when an infant starts imitating events in his or her environment. For example, when Lucienne imitated the opening of the match box by opening her mouth, she was representing a concept symbolically by means of a behavioral schema that she possessed. Similarly, a child might represent a horse by making galloping movements with the feet or a bicycle by making steering movements with the hands. Symbolic representations like these are called **signifiers:** The motor act represents (signifies) the concept because it resembles either the movements the object makes or the movements the child makes when interacting with the object. Even a very young infant demonstrates the beginnings of this function; babies will often make shaking movements with their hand when they see a rattle.

Concepts can also be represented by words, which are symbols that have no physical resemblance to the concept; Piaget referred to such abstract symbols as **signs.** Signifiers are personal, derived from the child's own interactions with objects. Therefore, only the child and perhaps members of the immediate family will understand the child's signifiers. In contrast, signs are social conventions; they are understood by all members of society. A child who is able to use words to think about reality has made an important step in cognitive development.

Piaget's work demonstrated quite clearly that a child's representation of the world is different from that of an adult. For example, most adults realize that a volume of water remains constant when poured into a taller, narrower container, even though its level is now higher. However, early in the preoperational period children will fail to recognize this fact; they will say that the taller container contains more water. (See *Figure 10.8.*) The ability to realize that an object retains mass, number, or volume when it undergoes various transformations is called **conservation;** the transformed object *conserves* its original properties. (See *Figure 10.9.*)

Piaget concluded that the abilities to perceive the conservation of number, mass, weight, and volume are attributes of increasing development. His studies showed number to be conserved by age six, whereas conservation of volume did not occur until age eleven. Presumably, conservation of number comes first because children can verify the stability of number once they learn to count.

An important characteristic of the preoperational period is **egocentrism:** In this context the word does not mean selfishness; it refers to a child's belief that others see the world in precisely the way he or she does. For example, a child who is explaining a story or sequence of

Figure 10.8 Conservation. Early in the preoperational period a child does not recognize the conservation of a liquid quantity.

events to another person is likely to omit many important details, apparently because of the belief that other people know and understand what the child does. A child often uses pronouns without considering that another person might not understand to whom or what they refer.

The Period of Concrete Operations.
The **period of concrete operations** spans approximately ages seven to twelve; thus, its end marks the transition from childhood to adolescence. This period is characterized by the emergence of the ability to perform logical analysis, by an increase in the ability to empathize with the feelings and attitudes of others, and by an understanding of more complex cause-and-effect relations. The child becomes much more skilled at the use of symbolic thought. For example, even before the period of concrete operations children can arrange a series of objects in order of size and can compare any two objects and say which is larger. However, if they are shown that stick A is larger than stick B, and that stick B is larger than stick C, they cannot infer that stick A is larger than stick C.

During the early part of this period children become capable of such reasoning. However, although they can reason with respect to *concrete objects* such as sticks that they have seen, they cannot do so with *hypothetical objects*. For example, they cannot solve the following problem: "Judy is taller than Frank and Frank is taller than Carl. Who is taller, Judy or Carl?" The ability to solve such problems awaits the next period of cognitive development.

The Period of Formal Operations.
The final stage of cognitive development, the **period of formal operations,** begins at twelve years of age and includes the use of an essentially adult form of logic and symbolic representation. That is, in solving problems, the child learns to formulate a set of alternatives and to test these alternatives against reality. For example, the adolescent learns to reason with inductive and deductive logic and to consider several possible alternatives to a problem-solving situation and decide which is the most appropriate. This stage of development appears to depend heavily on a person's education; many adults never learn to reason formally, as defined by Piaget (Neimark, 1979). Formal operations are also culturally determined. In preliterate societies where formal schooling does not exist, *none* of the members are capable of formal reasoning (Dasen and Heron, 1981). We should probably view the period of formal operations as a product of our culture rather than an inevitable stage of human development. The issue of culture and intellectual abilities is explored in more detail in Chapter 13.

Figure 10.9 Various tests of conservation. (Adapted from *Of Children, an Introduction to Child Development,* Fourth Edition, by Guy R. Lefrancois. © 1983, 1980 by Wadsworth, Inc. Reprinted by permission of Wadsworth Publishing Company, Belmont, California 94002.)

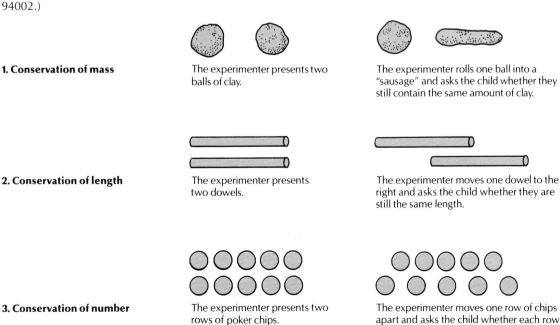

1. Conservation of mass

The experimenter presents two balls of clay.

The experimenter rolls one ball into a "sausage" and asks the child whether they still contain the same amount of clay.

2. Conservation of length

The experimenter presents two dowels.

The experimenter moves one dowel to the right and asks the child whether they are still the same length.

3. Conservation of number

The experimenter presents two rows of poker chips.

The experimenter moves one row of chips apart and asks the child whether each row still contains the same number.

Causes of Cognitive Development

Why does a child pass from one stage of cognitive development to the next? What motivates a child to change his or her way of reasoning and perceiving? According to Piaget, the important principle is **cognitive disequilibrium** (*disequilibrium* means "lack of balance"). Disequilibrium is produced when children encounter unexpected feedback from the environment as their developing ability to explore brings them in contact with new concepts that they cannot easily assimilate to their existing behavioral schemas. This disequilibrium requires the child to acquire new concepts and new behavioral schemas. For example, when an infant encounters another infant for the first time, he or she meets an object that is interesting to touch and grasp but can also move and do unexpected things, such as touch and grab. The infant must develop a concept for this new object and learn new ways of dealing with it.

In addition, if children who are at a particular stage of cognitive development observe an adult or older child solving a problem by rules that belong to another stage, they are put off balance because the other person's solution is different from their own. This disparity is motivating; the child seeks to reduce it by learning the new rules. A child who is sufficiently mature will learn to imitate the older model and will begin to pass on to the new stage. Thus, children can learn new concepts and behavioral schemas socially, by observing the behavior of other people.

Evaluation of Piaget's Contributions

Although Piaget's work has dominated twentieth-century child psychology, not all of his conclusions have been uncritically accepted. One criticism is that Piaget did not always define his terms operationally; consequently, it is difficult for others to interpret the significance of his generalizations. Many of his studies lack the proper controls that were discussed in Chapter 2. Thus, much of his work is not experimental, which means that cause-and-effect relations among variables cannot be identified with certainty.

Subsequent evidence has suggested that a child's ability to conserve various physical attributes occurs earlier than Piaget had supposed. Part of the problem might be in the child's understanding of words like *more* and *larger*. For an adult the word *more* means "containing a greater number." But suppose a child's concept of *more* is less restrictive than that of an adult. Perhaps *more*, for a young child, refers to a general concept of larger, longer, or occupying more space. If so, the response may then suggest that the child cannot conserve a particular property when in fact he or she actually can.

Gelman (1972) found that when the appropriate task is used, even three-year-old children are able to demonstrate conservation of number. She showed children two toy platters, each containing a row of toy mice. Instead of using the word *more*, Gelman called the platter with a larger number of mice the "winner," and she called the one with a smaller number of mice the "loser." The children were invited to play a game. They watched the experimenter hide the platters under two cans and then move the cans around the table. Each child had to point to the can that contained the "winner," which was then uncovered. If the uncovered plate contained the original number of mice, the children were satisfied that it was still the "winner," even if the experimenter tricked them by lengthening or shortening the row of mice. The children noticed that the mice had been moved but still identified the plate as the "winner." However, if mice were removed from the plate containing the larger number, the children were disturbed and asked where the missing mice were.

Clearly, the children were able to respond to the concept of number and recognized that a larger number of mice was still a larger number of mice even if the row was lengthened or shortened. Thus, the children seem to learn to conserve number before they learn the adult meaning of the word *more*. We must recognize that an estimate of a child's cognitive ability can be substantially affected by the testing method.

Piaget also appears to have underestimated the ability of young children to understand another person's point of view. In other words, they are less egocentric than he had thought. For example, Flavell, Everett, Croft, and Flavell (1981) found that even a three-year-old child realizes that a person looking at the opposite side of a card, which the child is examining, will not see the same thing; clearly, the child recognizes the other person's point of view. In addition, four-year-old children will use simpler speech when they talk with two-year-old children than when they talk with adults; thus, they take the other person's language ability into account (Gelman and Shatz, 1978).

Despite the fact that Piaget's method of observation led him to underestimate some important abilities, his meticulous and detailed observations of child behavior have been extremely important in the field of child development and have had a great influence on educational practice. His theoretical framework has provided a basis for more scientific studies and will undoubtedly continue to do so for many years.

INTERIM SUMMARY

Cognitive Development in Childhood

An important distinction between humans and other species is our cognitive abilities. The first step in children's cognitive development is learning that many events are contingent on their own behavior. This understanding occurs gradually and is controlled by the development of the nervous system and by increasingly complex interactions with the environment.

Jean Piaget divided a child's cognitive development into four periods—a system that is widely, if not universally, accepted. The periods are determined by the joint influences of the child's experiences and the maturation of the child's nervous system. They consist of the sensorimotor period, the preoperational period, the period of concrete operations, and the period of formal operations.

An infant's earliest cognitive abilities are closely tied to the external stimuli in the immediate environment; objects exist for the infant only when they are present. Gradually, infants begin to differentiate themselves from other objects in the environment and learn that objects exist even when hidden. The development of object permanence leads to the ability to represent things symbolically, which is a prerequisite for the use of language. Next, the ability to perform logical analysis and to understand more complex cause-and-effect relations develops. Around the age of twelve a child develops more adultlike cognitive abilities—abilities that may allow the child to solve difficult problems by means of abstract reasoning.

According to Piaget, children are motivated to advance in cognitive development by the cognitive disequilibrium caused by unexpected feedback from the environment. In addition, they may advance by observing adults or other children using strategies they do not yet possess.

Critics of Piaget point out that in some cases his tests of cognitive development underestimate children's abilities. For example, if tested appropriately, it is evident that they conserve various properties earlier than he

thought, and their egocentrism is less pronounced than his tests indicated. Nevertheless, his conclusions continue to have a profound impact on the field of child development. ∎

SOCIAL DEVELOPMENT IN CHILDHOOD

Development of Attachment

[4] Normally, the first adults with whom an infant interacts are the child's parents. In most cases one parent serves as the primary caregiver. As many studies have shown, a close relationship called *attachment* is extremely important for the infant's social development. **Attachment** refers both to the warm feelings that the parties have for each other and to the comfort and support they provide for each other, which becomes especially important during times of fear or stress. Because both parent and child are involved, the interactions must work both ways, with each of the participants fulfilling certain needs of the other. Formation of a strong and durable bond depends on the behavior of both people in the relationship.

Newborn infants are completely dependent upon their parents (or other caregivers) to supply them with nourishment, to keep them warm and clean, and to protect them from harm. But to most parents, the role of primary caregiver is much more than a duty; it is a source of joy and satisfaction. Nearly all parents anticipate the birth of their child with the expectation that they will love and cherish the child. And when the child is born, most of them do exactly that. As time goes on, and as parent and child interact, they become strongly attached to each other. What factors cause this attachment to occur? As we will see, the most important factors come from the behavior of the child.

Behaviors of the Infant That Foster Attachment

Evidence suggests that human infants are innately able to produce special behaviors that shape and control the behavior of their caregiver. As Bowlby (1969) noted, the most important of these behaviors are sucking, cuddling, looking, smiling, and crying.

Sucking. A baby must be able to suck in order to obtain milk. But not all sucking is related to nourishment. Piaget (1952) noted that infants often suck on objects even when they are not hungry. Nonnutritive sucking appears to be an

Not all sucking is related to nourishment; sucking on a pacifier seems to inhibit a baby's distress.

age, do not make the cuddling response and remain rigid in the adult's arms. Adults who hold such infants tend to refer to them as being not very lovable (Ainsworth, 1973).

A series of experiments with infant monkeys by Harry Harlow, the late director of the primate laboratory at the University of Wisconsin, showed that clinging to a soft, cuddly form appears to be an innate response (Harlow, 1974). Harlow and his colleagues isolated baby monkeys from their mothers immediately after birth and raised them alone in a cage containing two mechanical **surrogate mothers** (*surrogate* means "substitute"). One surrogate mother was made of bare wire mesh but contained a bottle that provided milk. The other surrogate was padded and covered with terry cloth but provided no nourishment.

The babies preferred to cling to the cuddly surrogate and went to the wire model only to eat. If they were frightened, they would rush to the cloth-covered model for comfort. These results indicate that close physical contact with a cuddly object is a biological need for a baby monkey, just as hunger and thirst are. A baby mon-

Cuddling behavior. An isolated infant monkey clings to its cuddly surrogate mother if it is frightened by novel stimuli.

innate behavioral tendency in infants that serves to inhibit a baby's distress. In modern society a human mother covers her breasts between feedings or feeds her baby with a bottle, so that a baby's nonnutritive sucking must involve inanimate objects or the baby's own thumb. In the Ganda society in Uganda mothers were observed to give their babies access to a breast when they were fussy, just as mothers in other cultures would give them a pacifier (Ainsworth, 1967).

Cuddling. The infants of all species of primates have special reflexes that encourage front-to-front contact with the mother. For example, a baby monkey clings to its mother shortly after birth. This clinging leaves the mother free to use her hands and feet. Human infants are carried by their parents and do not hold on by themselves. However, infants do adjust their posture to mold themselves to the contours of the parent's body. This response plays an important role in reinforcing the behavior of the caregiver. Some infants, perhaps because of hereditary factors or slight brain dam-

key clings to and cuddles with its mother because the contact is innately reinforcing, not simply because she also provides it with food.

Undoubtedly, physical contact with a soft object is also inherently reinforcing for human infants. As you know, many children become attached to soft objects such as blankets or stuffed animals. The name "security blanket" suggests that these objects are able to comfort their owner during times of distress. Indeed, children are most likely to ask for their special blanket or stuffed animal before going to bed, when they are ill, or when they are in an unfamiliar situation (Berk, 1989).

Looking.   Vision is not a passive sensory system; it is coupled with the behavior of looking. The eyes see best what is at the center of the gaze, so one must move one's eyes in order to see important visual features of the environment. Wolff (1966) showed that infants can con-

trol their eyes well enough to pursue a moving object visually within one day of birth.

Looking is more than an adjunct to vision; it serves as a signal to the parent. Even a very young infant seeks eye-to-eye contact with the parents. If a parent does not respond when eye contact is made, the baby usually shows signs of distress. Tronick, Als, Adamson, Wise, and Brazelton (1978) observed face-to-face interactions between mothers and their infants. When the mothers approached their babies, they typically smiled and began talking in a gentle, high-pitched voice. In return, they received a smile and an outreach of arms and legs from the infants. The mothers poked and gently shook their babies, making faces at them. The babies responded with facial expressions, wiggles, and noises of their own.

To determine whether the interaction was really two-sided, the experimenters had each mother approach her baby while keeping her

Figure 10.10   Reaction of an infant to the mother's expressionless face. Although each panel shows mother and infant side by side, they actually faced each other. The infant greets the mother with a smile and, getting no response, eventually turns away from her. (From Tronick, E., Als, H., Adamson, L., Wise, S., and Brazelton, T.B. *Journal of the American Academy of Child Psychiatry*, 1978, *17*, 1–13. © 1978 American Academy of Child Psychiatry.)

face expressionless, or masklike. At first, the infant made the usual greetings, but when the mother did not respond, the infant turned away. (See *Figure 10.10.*) From time to time the infant looked at her again, producing a brief smile but again turning away when the mother continued to stare without changing her expression. These interactions were recorded on videotape and were scored by raters who did not know the purpose of the experiment, so the results were not biased by the experimenters' expectations.

Each mother found it difficult to resist her baby's invitation to interact; in fact, some of the mothers broke down and smiled back. Most of the mothers who managed to hold out (for three minutes) later apologized to their babies, saying something like "I am real again. It's all right. You can trust me again. Come back to me" (Tronick et al., 1978, p. l0).

This study clearly shows that the looking behavior of an infant is an invitation for the mother to respond. If she does not, the infant is disturbed and avoids further visual contact.

Smiling. For almost any human, but especially for a parent, the smile of an infant is an exceedingly effective reinforcer. For example, the day after reading an article about imitation of facial expressions by newborn infants, I had a conversation with a woman who was holding her two-month-old daughter. The baby was alert, actively looking at the people around her. For approximately five minutes she made no particular facial expression. Then I remembered the article and mentioned it to the baby's father, who was also present. He suggested I see whether his daughter would imitate my facial expression. I stuck out my tongue, and immediately, the baby smiled, made a noise, and stuck out her tongue. I can still feel the delight that her smile gave me.

Wolff (1963) studied the development of smiling in infants and observed the stimuli that elicited it. During the first month the sound of a voice, especially a high-pitched voice, can elicit smiles. Moreover, people appear to recognize this fact; when they approach a baby and talk to him or her, they tend to raise the pitch of their voice (Tronick et al., 1978).

By the time an infant is five weeks old, visual stimuli begin to dominate as elicitors for smiling. A face (especially a moving one) is a more reliable elicitor of a smile than a voice is; even a moving mask will cause an infant to smile. Later (at approximately three months of age), specific faces—those of people to whom

the infant has become attached—will elicit smiles. The significance of these observations should be obvious. An infant's smile is very rewarding. Almost every parent reports that parenting becomes a real joy when the baby starts smiling as the parent approaches; the infant is now a "person." Once the infant begins smiling when seeing the parent's face, the parent becomes eager to spend time with his or her infant.

Crying. For almost any adult the sound of an infant's crying is intensely irritating or distressing. A young infant usually cries only when he or she is hungry, cold, or in pain (Wolff, 1969). In these situations only the intervention of an adult can bring relief. The stimulus that most effectively terminates crying is being picked up and cuddled. Because picking up the baby stops the crying, the parent learns to pick up the infant when he or she cries. Thus, crying serves as a useful means for a cold, hungry, or wet child to obtain assistance.

Wolff (1969) suggested that babies have different patterns of crying when they are hungry, in pain, or bored. Konner (1972), who was studying a hunter-gatherer tribe in Africa, found that a pain cry caused everyone in earshot to turn toward the infant and induced several of them to run toward the child. However, a hunger cry was responded to only by the child's caregivers. More recent evidence suggests that babies' cries do not fall into need-specific categories; instead, they simply vary in intensity, according to the level of the infant's distress. However, the *onset* of crying provides important information. If a baby suddenly begins crying intensely, mothers are more likely to assume that the baby is afraid or in pain. If the cry begins more gradually, mothers suspect hunger, sleepiness, or a need for a diaper change (Gustafson and Harris, 1990).

Everyone knows that children can be "spoiled"; when things are made too easy for them, they come to believe that their every whim will be (and should be) gratified. But research has clearly shown that a parent's attention does not necessarily "spoil" a very young infant. In the first few months of a baby's life, a parent should respond promptly when the baby cries. Bell and Ainsworth (1972) found that babies whose caregivers responded quickly to crying during the first three months actually cried *less* during the last four months of their first year than did infants with unresponsive caregivers. Instead of becoming spoiled, these babies learned to cry only when they needed attention from their caregiver. The infants with responsive caregivers also learned to communicate effectively by means of behaviors other than crying, such as prespeech sounds and facial gestures. Just as it is important for parents to interact with their infants to encourage their cognitive and social development, it is important for babies to learn that their communicative behaviors (such as crying) can affect the behavior of other people.

The Nature and Quality of Attachment

5 For an infant the world can be a frightening place. The presence of a primary caregiver provides a baby with considerable reassurance when he or she first becomes able to explore the environment. Although the unfamiliar environment produces fear, the caregiver provides a **secure base** that the infant can leave from time to time to see what the world is like.

Ainsworth's Strange Situation. Ainsworth and her colleagues (Ainsworth, Blehar, Waters, and Wall, 1978) have developed a test of attachment called the **Strange Situation.** This test provides a series of eight episodes, during which the baby is exposed to various events that might cause some distress. By noting the infant's reaction, researchers can evaluate the nature of the attachment.

The use of the Strange Situation has led Ainsworth and her colleagues to identify three patterns of attachment. **Secure attachment** is the ideal pattern. The infant shows a distinct preference for its mother over the stranger. The infant may cry when its mother leaves, but it stops as soon as she returns. Babies may also

form two types of *insecure attachments.* A baby with a **resistant attachment** shows tension in its relations with its mother. The infant stays close to her before she leaves but shows both approach and avoidance behaviors when she returns. The infant continues to cry for a while after she returns and may even push her away. **Avoidant attachment** is seen in about 20 percent of middle-class American infants. Infants who display this pattern generally do not cry when they are left alone. When the mother returns, they are likely to avoid or ignore her. These infants tend not to cling and cuddle when they are picked up.

The nature of an infant's attachment with its caregiver is affected by both the quality of the care provided and the characteristics of the infant. As I noted earlier, some infants are "difficult": They are irritable, do not cling and cuddle when they are picked up, and respond poorly to attempts to comfort them. Such children are more likely to form insecure types of attachment. Green, Fox, and Lewis (1983) found that mothers of difficult babies tended to spend less time playing with them.

Although an infant's personality certainly affects the nature of its interaction with its caregiver—and hence the nature of its attachment—the mother's behavior appears to be the most important factor in establishing a secure or insecure attachment (Ainsworth, Blehar, Waters, and Wall, 1978; Isabella and Belsky, 1991). Mothers of *securely* attached infants tend to be those who respond promptly to their crying and who are adept at handling them and responding to their moods. The babies apparently learned that the mothers could be trusted to react sensitively and appropriately. Mothers

Humans are not the only species to form attachments. Goslings learn to follow the first moving object they encounter after they hatch—normally, their mother. In this case it was an ethologist, Konrad Lorenz. This form of attachment is called imprinting.

who do not modulate their responses according to their infant's own behavior—who appear insensitive to their infants' changing needs—are most likely to foster *avoidant* attachment. It is as if the babies' avoidance is a defense against their mother's intrusive behavior. Mothers who are impatient with their infants and seem more interested in their own activities than in interacting with their offspring tend to foster *resistant* attachment.

The nature of the attachment between infant and caretaker appears to be related to the child's later social behavior. For example, Waters, Wippman, and Sroufe (1979) found that children who were securely attached at fifteen months were among the most popular and the most sociable children in their nursery school at three and one-half years of age. In contrast, insecurely attached infants had difficulties with social adjustment later in childhood; they had poor social skills and tended to be hostile, impulsive, and withdrawn (Erickson, Sroufe, and Egheland, 1985).

Of course, mothers are not the only people who can form close attachment with infants; so can fathers and other adults who interact with them. In fact, Parke and Tinsley (1981) observed that fathers are just as likely as mothers to touch, talk to, and kiss their babies. However, when the mother serves as the primary caregiver, fathers tend to play somewhat different roles. In general, they tend to engage in more physical games, lifting, tossing, and bouncing their babies. This difference may account for the fact that babies tend to seek out their mother when they are distressed but look for their father when they want to play (Clarke-Stewart, 1978).

Effects of Child Day Care. The importance of attachment inevitably leads to the question of whether child day care has deleterious effects on a child's development. In recent years many families have entrusted their infants to day care because both parents work. In the United States more than half of all mothers are employed outside the home (U.S. Bureau of the Census, 1990). Thus, because so many infants spend much of their waking hours away from their family, the question of the effects of day care is not simply academic.

Unfortunately, the question is not easily answered. Some studies (for example, Belsky and Rovine, 1988) have shown that infants—especially boys—whose mothers work outside the home during their first year of life are more likely to show insecure patterns of attachment

on the Strange Situation. Without question, the quality of care provided in a day-care center is critical. Studies during the 1970s found that day care had no effect on attachment; however, most of these studies were carried out in excellent facilities attached to universities (Clarke-Stewart and Fein, 1983). Obviously, high-quality day care is expensive, because of the expense of good facilities and good wages for people trained to provide excellent care. Therefore, the day care available to low-income families is generally of lower quality than that available to middle-class or upper-class families. Regrettably, infants who receive the poorest day care tend to be members of unstable households, often headed by a single mother; thus, they receive a double dose of less-than-optimal care. Day care need not impair a child's development, but the realities are that it sometimes does.

The age at which an infant enters child care appears to play an important role in the development of attachment. Several studies indicate that the children of both lower-class and middle-class families are more likely to develop insecure attachments if they enter day care during the first year of life (Shaffer, 1989). Entry after the first year is less likely to have deleterious effects.

Interactions with Peers

6 Although the attachment between an infant and its primary caregiver is the most important social interaction in early life, a child's social development must also involve other people. A normal infant develops attachments with other adults and with older siblings, if there are any. But interaction with peers—children of a similar age—is especially important to social development.

Studies by Harlow and his colleagues (Harlow, 1974) have shown that social contact with peers is essential to an infant monkey's social development; in fact, these interactions appear to be even more important than interactions with its mother. An infant monkey that is raised with only a cuddly surrogate mother can still develop into a reasonably normal adult. However, an isolated monkey that does not interact with other juveniles before puberty shows severe deficits. When a previously isolated adolescent monkey is introduced to a colony of normally reared age mates, it will retreat with terror and huddle in a corner in a desperate attempt to hide.

Apparently, social interaction helps young monkeys learn how to respond to each other—how to cope with fear, when to be dominant, and when not to challenge a more powerful and aggressive playmate. Young monkeys, like human children, engage in play, and this play appears to teach them what they need to know in order to form adult relationships.

Subsequent studies from Harlow's laboratory (such as Suomi and Harlow, 1972; Novak and Harlow, 1975) have shown that the pathological fearful behavior shown by a monkey that was raised in isolation can be eliminated. If there is a critical period during which monkeys learn to interact with their peers, it does not seem to be an absolute one. The important variable seems to be the abruptness with which a formerly isolated monkey is brought into social situations. If it is first placed with a younger, not-so-threatening "therapist" monkey, it can gradually learn how to interact normally with older monkeys. Thus, regardless of the specific stage of development at which socialization occurs, learning how to cope with a strange environment must be a gradual process.

An experiment by Fuhrman, Rahe, and Hartup (1979) demonstrates that research with nonhuman primates can have important implications for the understanding of human development. These researchers used the "juvenile therapist" technique that Harlow and his associates discovered to improve peer interactions among socially withdrawn children aged two and one-half to six and one-half years. The children appeared to be relatively isolated from their peers, spending less than a normal amount of time with them. Each child was paired with a partner for a series of ten play sessions of twenty minutes each. The partner was another child of the same age or twelve to twenty months younger. Interactions with peers were observed before, during, and after the play session. The play sessions were successful; they increased the amount of time that the isolated children spent with their peers. Furthermore, the children who were paired with younger "therapists" showed the greatest change. Control subjects, who did not participate in play sessions with another child, showed no change over the four-to-six-week periods.

INTERIM SUMMARY

Social Development in Childhood

Because babies are totally dependent upon their parents, the development of attachment between parent and infant is crucial to the infant's survival. A baby has the innate ability to shape and reinforce the behavior of the parent. To a large extent, the baby is the parent's teacher. Infant and parent reinforce each other's behavior, which facilitates the development of a durable attachment between them.

Some of the behaviors that babies possess innately are sucking, cuddling, looking, smiling, and crying. These behaviors promote parental responses and are instrumental in satisfying physiological needs. The smiling behavior develops as the child matures; the baby first smiles spontaneously, then in response to a high-pitched voice, and then in response to visual stimuli (especially the caregiver). The relationship between infant and caregiver develops

Programs such as Project Head Start provide opportunities for social interactions among children, which foster social development.

over several months; at least in humans, the time for bonding is not restricted to a few hours after birth.

Infants are normally afraid of novel stimuli, but the presence of their caregiver (or cuddly surrogate) provides a secure base from which they can explore a new environment. Ainsworth's Strange Situation allows an investigator to determine the nature of the attachment between infant and caregiver. By using this test, several investigators have identified some of the variables—some involving the infant and some involving the mother—that influence attachment. Fathers, as well as mothers, can form close attachments with infants. Excellent child care by outsiders will not harm a child's social development, but less-than-excellent child care, especially if it begins in the child's first year of life, can adversely affect attachment.

Development also involves the acquisition of social skills. Interaction with peers is probably the most important factor in social development. Research with monkeys has shown that deprivation of contact with peers has even more serious effects than deprivation of contact with the mother. ■

DEVELOPMENT OF SEX ROLES

[7] Physical development as a male or a female is only one aspect of sexual development; social development is also important. A person's **sexual identity** is an important part of his or her self-concept. It consists primarily of the acceptance of membership in a particular group of people: males or females. Acceptance of this membership does not necessarily indicate acceptance of the sex roles or sex stereotypes that may accompany it. For example, a dedicated feminist may fight to change the role of women in her society but can still clearly identify herself as a woman. **Sex roles** are collections of behaviors—and rules related to these behaviors—that a particular society considers appropriate for males or females. Closely related to them are **sex stereotypes,** beliefs about differences in the behaviors, abilities, and personality traits of males and females. Obviously, a society's sex stereotypes have an important influence on the behavior of its members. This section considers the nature of sex roles and their development.

Let us first examine the nature of sex stereotypes in Western society. In general, males are perceived as being *instrumental*—self-assertive, competent, and rational. Females are regarded as being *expressive*—warm, nurturing, and emotional (Parsons, 1955). Because they supposedly possess different characteristics, many people assume that men and women are best suited for different types of jobs. Although the women's movement has had a major impact on laws and on some social customs, sex stereotypes such as these still exist.

As Piaget's work on cognitive and moral development has shown, children readily accept adult assertions about the world and its rules. Thus, it should come as no surprise that children readily accept their statements about the ways boys and girls should behave. Their tendency to conform to sex stereotypes was nicely demonstrated in an experiment by Montemayor (1974), who invited children between the ages of six and eight years to play a game that involved tossing marbles into a clown's body. Some of the children were told that they were playing a "girl's game," some were told it was a "boy's game," and others were told nothing. Boys and girls both said that the game was more fun when it had been described as appropriate to their gender, and they even attained better scores when it was.

Both boys and girls learn about the characteristics of the masculine sex stereotype earlier than those of the feminine sex stereotype (Best et al., 1977). Presumably, this difference occurs because our society defines male sex roles more rigidly; a girl may engender some hostility for encroaching on male-related activities, but a boy is likely to receive ridicule from his peers for acting like "a sissy girl." For the same reasons, boys conform to the masculine sex stereotype at an earlier age than girls conform to the female stereotype (Williams, Bennett, and Best, 1975).

Now, let us examine the nature and causes of sex differences.

The Nature of Sex Differences

We have seen what people *believe* about sex differences and how readily children accommodate their behavior to sex stereotypes. But how accurately do these stereotypes reflect real differences in people's abilities, personality traits, and behavior?

Berk (1989) has reviewed recent research on sex differences and has concluded that the most reliable differences are the following: Girls show earlier verbal development, more effective expression and interpretation of emotional cues, and a higher tendency to comply with adults and peers. Boys show stronger spatial abilities, increased aggression, and greater tendency toward risk taking. Boys are also more likely to show developmental problems such as language disorders, behavior problems, or physical impairments. In addition, achievement motivation is related to the type of task that is being attempted; boys perceive themselves as being better at "masculine" tasks, while girls believe that they are better at "feminine" tasks.

Note that the existence of these differences does not mean they are biologically determined. In fact, socialization undoubtedly has a strong influence. Also, most sex differences are small. Deaux (1985) reports that on the average, only 5 percent of the variability in individual differences among children can be attributed to gender; the other 95 percent is due to individual genetic and environmental factors. Therefore, gender, by itself, is not a very good predictor of a person's talents, personality, or behavior.

The Causes of Sex Role Differences

As we have just seen, children readily learn sex stereotypes and adopt the roles deemed appropriate for their gender. Two factors—biology and culture—may be responsible for this acceptance.

Biological Causes. One possible explanation focuses on biological differences. Perhaps some of the observed differences between males and females can be attributed to chromosomal differences or to the effects of sex hormones. After all, these factors produce differences in the bodies of males and females, so perhaps they could affect their behavior, too.

A likely site of biologically determined sex differences is the brain. Studies with laboratory animals have shown that the exposure of a developing brain to male sex hormones has long-term effects; the hormones alter the development of the brain and produce changes in the animals' behavior, even in adulthood (Carlson, 1991). In addition, the human brain shows some sex differences, which are probably also caused by exposure to different patterns of hormones during development (Hofman and Swaab, 1991). The effects of these differences on the behavior of males and females are unknown.

Sex differences in two types of cognitive abilities may be at least partly caused by differences in the brain: verbal ability and spatial ability. Girls tend to learn to speak and to read sooner than boys, and boys tend to be better at tasks requiring spatial perception. Kimura (1987) suggests possible reasons for these sex differences. While the human brain was evolving

into its present form, our ancestors were hunter-gatherers, and men and women probably had different roles. Women were more likely to work near the home, performing fine manual skills with respect to objects within reach. Men were more likely to range farther from home, engaging in activities that involved coordination of body movements with respect to distant objects, such as throwing rocks or spears or launching darts toward other animals. In addition, men had to be able to keep track of where they were, so they could return home after following animals for long distances.

These specializations might favor the development of sex differences. In particular, women's movements might be expected to be better integrated with nearby objects, whereas men's movements might be expected to be better integrated with objects located at a distance. If Kimura's (1987) reasoning is correct, it is easy to see why men's spatial abilities are generally better than those of women. But why do girls learn to speak and read sooner than boys? Many researchers believe that our ancestors used hand gestures long before verbal communication developed. Kimura suggests that fine motor control and speech production are closely related—that the neural circuits that control the muscles we use for speech may be closely related to those we use to move our hands.

Of course, this account is very speculative and may be completely wrong. However, it provides a good example of the biological approach—in particular, the functional, evolutionary approach—to an understanding of human behavior.

Social Causes. Most psychologists believe that socialization plays the most significant role in the establishment of sex role differences. First adults and then peers teach, by direct instruction and by example, what is expected of boys and girls. These expectations are deeply ingrained in our culture and unconsciously affect our perceptions and our behavior. When someone announces the birth of a baby, most of us immediately ask, "Is it a boy or a girl?" Parents often dress their infants in clothing that makes it easy for strangers to quickly recognize their gender. And once we find out the baby's sex, we interact with the child in subtly (and not so subtly) different ways. For example, Condry and Condry (1976) showed college students a videotape of a baby crying. The subjects tended to see the crying as "angry" if they believed that the baby was a boy and "fearful" if they thought it was a girl. Obviously, these judgments were the result of their sex stereotypes and not their perceptions.

The effect of gender on adult's *perception* of infants is clear and has been confirmed in many studies. What about differences in the behaviors directed toward boys and girls? The strongest difference in the way parents socialize their sons and daughters is their encouragement of sex-typed play and the choice of "sex-appropriate" toys. Boys are encouraged to play with trucks, blocks, and other toys that can be manipulated, whereas girls are encouraged to play with dolls. However, a review of 172 studies conducted in North America, Australia, and Western Europe concluded that parents do not consistently treat their sons and daughters differently in any other important ways (Lytton and Romney, 1991).

Although parents do encourage "sex-appropriate" play, there is evidence that biological factors may play some role in children's preferences. Although fathers are less likely to give dolls to one-year-old boys than to one-year-old girls, the boys who do receive the toys are less likely to play with them (Snow, Jacklin, and Maccoby, 1983). Perhaps, as Lytton and Romney (1991) suggest, adults' expectations and encouragement build upon children's preferences, producing an amplifying effect. Then, because boys' toys provide more opportunity for devel-

Parents plan an important role in the development of their children's sexual identity and consciously or unconsciously encourage them to adopt behaviors that fit their sex roles.

oping motor skills, visuospatial skills, and inventiveness and girls' toys provide more opportunity for nurturance and social exchange, some important differences in sex roles may become established.

Once children begin to play with other children outside the home, peers have a significant influence on the development of their sex roles. In fact, Stern and Karraker (1989) found that the behavior of two-to-six-year-old children was even more influenced by the knowledge of a baby's gender than was the behavior of adults. By the time children are three years old, they reinforce sex-typed play by praising, imitating, or joining in the behavior. In contrast, they criticize sex-inappropriate behavior (Fagot, 1977; Langlois and Downs, 1980). Parents indirectly encourage sex-stereotyped play by seeking out children of the same sex as playmates for their own child (Lewis, Young, Brooks, and Michalson, 1975).

Of course, all the research I have cited in this section describes *tendencies* of parents and children to act in a particular way; in fact, I have probably used the words "tend to" or "tendency" more in this section than in any other section of the book. Many parents make a deliberate attempt to encourage their children's interest in both "masculine" and "feminine" activities, with the hope that doing so will help keep all opportunities for achievement and self-expression open to them, regardless of their gender. Almost everywhere, men and women are treated unequally. In most industrialized countries laws prohibit overt sexual discrimination, but despite these laws women have more difficulty obtaining prestigious jobs; and the higher levels of government and industry tend to be dominated by men. Our society may indeed be moving toward a time in which a person's gender neither hinders nor favors his or her aspirations, but clearly this time has not yet arrived.

INTERIM SUMMARY

Development of Sex Roles

Children's sex roles tend to conform to their society's sex stereotypes. Some of these differences may have biological roots; Kimura suggests that the different tasks performed by our ancestors shaped brain development and favored men with better spatial skills and women with better communication skills. But most sex differences in abilities and behaviors are small, and socialization undoubtedly plays a significant part in sex role differences.

Research has shown that both parents and peers tend to encourage children to behave in sex-appropriate ways—especially with regard to play activities and toys. However, scientific studies have revealed few other reliable differences in the ways parents treat young boys and girls. ■

MORAL DEVELOPMENT

8 The word *morality* comes from a Latin word that means "custom." Moral behavior is behavior that conforms to a generally accepted set of rules. Philosophers and theologians have argued about whether good and evil exist in any absolute sense, but we need not concern ourselves with this issue. Instead, we may accept the fact that morality is extremely useful to human society.

With very few exceptions (fortunately), by the time a person reaches adulthood, he or she has accepted a set of rules about personal and social behavior. These rules vary in different cultures—even in different individuals—but common themes are present in all of them. Let us begin by considering the way a child acquires a concept of morality. The pioneer in this field, as in cognitive development, was Jean Piaget.

Piaget's Description of Moral Development

Piaget studied the behavior of children from the ages of four to twelve years and interviewed them about their beliefs (Piaget, 1932). For example, he confronted them with stories about children who had committed various transgressions, and he asked them to give their opinions about the guilt of the children in the stories. According to Piaget, the first stage of moral development (ages five to ten years) is called **moral realism.** It is characterized by *egocentrism* ("self-centeredness") and blind adherence to rules. Guilt is determined almost solely by the effects a person's behavior has, not by his or her intentions.

An egocentric child can evaluate events only in terms of their personal consequences. The child's behavior is not guided by the effects it might have on someone else, because he or she is not capable of imagining himself or herself in the other person's place. Thus, a young child does not consider whether an act is right or wrong but only whether it is likely to have good

or bad consequences, *personally.* Punishment is a bad consequence, and the fear of punishment is the only real moral force at this age. A young child also believes that rules come from parents (or other authority figures, such as older children or God) and that rules cannot be changed.

Older children and adults judge an act by the intentions of the actor as well as by the consequences of the act. A young child considers only the objective outcomes, not the subjective intent that lay behind the act. For example, Piaget told two stories, one about John, who accidentally broke fifteen cups, and Henry, who broke one cup while trying to do something that was forbidden to him. When a young moral realist is asked which of the two children is the naughtiest, the child will say that John is, because he broke fifteen cups. The fact that the act was entirely accidental is not taken into account.

As a child matures, he or she becomes somewhat less egocentric and becomes capable of empathy; he or she can imagine how another person feels. This shift from egocentrism means that a child's behavior may be guided not merely by the effects acts have on himself or herself but also by the effects they have on others. Around ten years of age, the child enters the second stage of moral development: **morality of cooperation.** Rules also become more flexible as the child learns that many of them (such as those that govern games) are social conventions that may be altered by mutual consent.

Kohlberg's Description of Moral Development

Piaget's description of moral development has been considerably elaborated by Lawrence Kohlberg. Kohlberg studied somewhat older children (boys between ten and seventeen years of age), and he studied the same boys over a course of several years. He presented the children with stories that presented moral dilemmas. For example, one story described a man called Heinz whose wife was dying of a cancer that could only be treated by a medication discovered by a druggist living in the same town. The man could not afford the price demanded by the druggist, so the distraught man broke into the man's store and stole enough of the drug to save his wife's life. The children were asked what Heinz should have done and why he should have done it. On the basis of his research, Kohlberg decided that moral development consisted of six stages. These stages were tied to the child's cognitive development, as outlined by Piaget.

The first two stages belong to the *preconventional level,* during which morality is externally defined. During stage 1, *morality of punishment and obedience,* a child blindly obeys superior authority and avoids unpleasant punishment. When asked to decide what Heinz should do, children base their decisions on fears about being punished for letting one's wife die or for committing a crime. During stage 2, *morality of naive instrumental hedonism,* a child's behavior is guided by the pleasantness or unpleasantness of its consequences to him or her. The moral choice is reduced to a weighing of the probable risks and benefits of stealing the drug.

The next two stages belong to the *conventional level,* which includes an understanding that the social system has an interest in people's behavior. During stage 3, *morality of maintaining good relations,* the child wants to be regarded by people who know him or her as a good, well-behaved child. Moral decisions are based on perceived social pressure. Either Heinz should steal the drug because people would regard him as heartless, or he should not steal because they would regard him as a criminal. During stage 4, *morality of maintaining social order,* laws and moral rules are perceived as instruments to maintain social order and, as such, must be obeyed. Thus, both protecting a life and respecting people's property are seen as rules that help maintain social order.

Kohlberg also described a final level of moral development: the *postconventional, or principled, level.* At this level people realize that moral rules have some underlying principles that apply to all situations and societies. During stage 5, *morality of social contracts,* people recognize that rules are social contracts, that not all authority figures are infallible, and that individual rights can sometimes take precedence over laws. During stage 6, *morality of universal ethical principles,* rules and laws are perceived as being justified by abstract ethical values, such as the value of human life and dignity. As Kohlberg notes, not all people reach this level of moral development.

Critique of Piaget's and Kohlberg's Stages

Piaget's and Kohlberg's theories have greatly influenced research on moral development, but they have received some criticism. For example, Piaget's research indicated that children in the first stage (moral realism) respond to the magnitude of a transgression rather than the intent behind it. But even adults respond to the magnitude of a transgression—and rightly so. The theft of a few postage stamps by an office worker is not treated the same way as the embezzlement of thousands of dollars.

Kohlberg's conclusions have also been challenged. For example, Sobesky (1983) found that changes in the wording of Heinz's dilemma would drastically change people's responses. If the possibility of imprisonment was underscored, people tended to make more responses belonging to the preconventional level. Many researchers agree with Rest (1979), who concluded that Kohlberg's "stages" are not coherent entities but that they do describe a progression in the ability of children to consider more and more complex reasons for moral rules.

A different type of criticism was leveled by Gilligan (1977, 1982), who suggested that Kohlberg's theory is sex-biased. Some studies using Kohlberg's methods found that the development of moral reasoning of girls did not advance as rapidly as that of boys. However, Gilligan noted that Kohlberg's stages, which were based on studies that employed only boys as subjects and that used only stories about males in their moral dilemmas, are not representative of the population as a whole. According to her, these studies indicated that men (in general) adhered to universal ethical principles, whereas women (in general) preferred to base their moral judgments on the effects these judgments would have on the people involved. Men's judgments were based more on abstract ideas of *justice,* whereas women's judgments were based more on concrete considerations of *caring* and *concern for relationships.*

Gilligan's observations pointed out that abstract justice was not necessarily the highest form of morality. However, most researchers did *not* find that men's and women's moral judgments tend to be based on different types of values. For example, Donenberg and Hoffman (1988) found that boys and girls were equally likely to base their moral judgments on justice or caring, and that the sex of the main character in the moral dilemma had no effect on their judgments. Walker (1989) tested 233 subjects ranging in ages from 5 to 63 years and found no reliable sex differences. Thus, the available evidence does not appear to support the conclusion that such concern is related to a person's gender.

An interesting and promising alternative to Kohlberg's approach has been provided by Eisenberg and her colleagues (Eisenberg, 1982;

Eisenberg, Lennon, and Pasternack, 1986). This approach uses moral dilemmas that do not require children to consider having to break laws or defy authority figures. For example, one story asked whether a girl should help an injured child, even if doing so means that she will miss a birthday party. Eisenberg found that children's responses to dilemmas like this one above could be placed into five categories. As Berk (1989) notes, Eisenberg's stages, like those of Kohlberg, show a progression from selfishness to a need for social approval to empathy for others to internalized moral values. Because the decisions are not contaminated by fear of punishment, the stories find evidence of advanced moral reasoning at younger ages than does Kohlberg's method.

Teaching Morality to Children

In recent years research on moral development has been concerned less with describing its stages and more with discovering the factors that influence its course. Virtually all investigators believe that moral rules are first externally imposed on a child and then become internalized. The approaches of Piaget and Kohlberg attempt to describe children's ability to *understand* moral judgments; however, moral reasoning is only part of the story. After all, people often behave in ways that violate their own moral judgments.

Obviously, one important aspect of moral behavior is fear of punishment; people will avoid acts that might have aversive consequences for them, including pain, loss of money, loss of freedom, or social disapproval. But even in the absence of a direct threat of punishment, people avoid some acts because committing these acts would make them feel *guilty*. In other words, the avoidance of feelings of guilt can motivate moral behavior. Studies indicate that parents employ both punitive and guilt-inducing methods (*coercion* or *induction*) to correct their children's misbehavior. For example, a parent can say "Stop pushing her, or I'll spank you and send you to your room!" or "If you keep pushing her, she'll fall down and hurt herself, and it will be your fault."

Inductive methods of discipline require that a child be old enough to understand the reasoning that the parent provides; thus, these methods are less effective with preschoolchildren than with school-age children (Brody and Shaffer, 1982). However, even two-year-old children respond positively when they are told by their mother that their misbehavior makes her unhappy (Zahn-Waxler, Radke-Yarrow, and King, 1979).

Besides punishing bad acts (and attempting to make children feel guilty about not performing good acts), parents can reinforce good acts (and abstaining from committing bad ones). Parents can also act as models for their children. When children observe helpful or generous behavior, they are likely to imitate it—especially when the model explains his or her reasons for acting properly (Grusec, Kuczynski, Rushton, and Simutis, 1979).

INTERIM SUMMARY

Moral Development

Piaget suggested that moral development consists of two principal stages: moral realism, characterized by egocentrism and blind adherence to rules, and morality of cooperation, characterized by empathy and a realization that behavior is judged by the effects it has on others. Kohlberg suggested that moral development consists of three levels, each divided into two stages. During the first (preconventional) level morality is based on the personal consequences of an act. During the second level (morality of maintaining good relations), morality is based on the need to be well regarded and on sharing a common interest in social order. During the third (postconventional) level, which is achieved by only a minority of the population, morality becomes an abstract, philosophical virtue.

Critics of Piaget and Kohlberg point out that the stages of development are, to a certain degree, products of the measuring instruments. Although it does not appear, as Gilligan originally suggested, that females follow different moral rules, her work has sensitized researchers to the importance of including both sexes in studies of human development. Subtle changes in the way that moral dilemmas are posed can produce very different answers. In addition, dilemmas that do not require children to consider breaking laws are more likely to bring forth evidence of advanced moral reasoning.

Moral behavior can be taught to children by threat of punishment (and accompanying feelings of guilt); but inductive methods, which emphasize the reasons for behaving in a particular way, are more effective. Modeling—providing a good example—also teaches moral behavior. ■

ADOLESCENCE

After childhood comes adolescence, the threshold to adulthood. (In Latin, *adolescere* means "to grow up.") The transition between childhood and adulthood is as much a social as it is biological. In some societies people are considered to be adults as soon as they are sexually mature, at which time they may assume adult rights and responsibilities, including marriage. In most industrialized societies, where formal education often continues into the late teens and early twenties, adulthood officially comes several years later. Even then, it does not come all at once. Most often, the rights associated with adulthood—such as the ability to sign contracts, drive a car, marry, vote, and drink alcohol—are conferred at different ages.

Physical Development

9 **Puberty** (from the Latin *puber,* meaning "adult") marks the beginning of the transition from childhood to adulthood. Many physical changes occur during this stage: People reach their ultimate height, develop secondary sex characteristics (including breasts, increased muscle size, and body hair), and become capable of reproduction. There is also a change in social role. As a child, a person is dependent on parents, teachers, and other adults; as an adolescent, he or she is expected to assume more responsibility. Relations with peers also suddenly change; members of one's own sex become potential rivals for the attention of members of the other sex.

Sexual Maturation. The internal sex organs and genitalia do not change much for several years after birth, but they begin to develop again at puberty. When boys and girls reach about eleven to fourteen years of age, their testes or ovaries secrete hormones that begin the process of sexual maturation. This activity of the gonads is initiated by the hypothalamus, the part of the brain to which the pituitary gland is attached. The hypothalamus instructs the pituitary gland to secrete hormones that stimulate the gonads to secrete sex hormones. These sex hormones act on various organs of the body and initiate the changes that accompany sexual maturation. (See *Figure 10.11.*)

The sex hormones secreted by the gonads cause growth and maturation of the external genitalia and of the gonads themselves. In addition, these hormones cause the maturation of ova and the production of sperms. All these de-

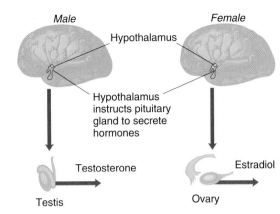

Figure 10.11 Sexual maturation. Puberty is initiated when the hypothalamus instructs the anterior pituitary gland to secrete hormones that cause the gonads to secrete sex hormones.

velopments are considered **primary sex characteristics,** because they are essential to the ability to reproduce. The sex hormones also stimulate the development of **secondary sex characteristics,** the physical changes that distinguish a male from a female. Before puberty boys and girls look much the same—except, perhaps, for their hairstyles and clothing. If their hairstyles and clothing are similar, it is difficult to determine their gender without looking at their genitalia. At puberty young men's testes begin to secrete **testosterone**; this hormone causes their muscles to develop, their facial hair to grow, and their voice to deepen. Young women's ovaries secrete estradiol, which is the most important **estrogen,** or female sex hormone. **Estradiol** causes women's breasts to grow and their pelvises to widen, and it produces changes in the layer of fat beneath the skin and in the texture of the skin itself.

Development of the adult secondary sex characteristics takes several years, and not all characteristics develop at the same time. The process begins in girls at around age eleven. The first visible change is the accumulation of fatty tissue around the nipples, followed shortly by the growth of pubic hair. The spurt in growth of height commences, and the uterus and vagina begin to enlarge. A pad of soft tissue above the pubic bone begins to grow, as do the labia—the lips that surround the vagina. The first menstrual period begins around age thirteen, just about the time the rate of growth in height begins to decline. In boys, sexual maturation begins slightly later. The first visible event is the growth of the testes and scrotum, followed by the first appearance of pubic hair. A few months later the penis begins to grow, and the spurt in growth of height starts. The larynx grows larger, which causes the voice to become lower. Sexual maturity—the ability to father a child—occurs at around age fifteen. The growth of facial hair usually occurs later; often a full beard does not grow until the late teens or early twenties.

In industrialized societies the average age at the onset of puberty has been declining. For example, the average age at the onset of menstruation was between fourteen and fifteen years in 1900 and is between twelve and thirteen years today. The most important reason for the decline is better childhood nutrition. It appears that the decline has leveled off in industrialized societies, but in many developing countries the age of the onset of puberty is beginning to fall as those countries enjoy increasing prosperity.

Behavioral Effects of Puberty. Changes that accompany sexual maturation have a profound effect on young people's behavior and self-concept. They become more sensitive about their appearance. Girls worry about their weight and about the size of their breasts and hips. Boys worry about their height, the size of their genitals, their muscular development, and the growth of their beard. Both boys and girls worry about their complexion. In addition, most adolescents display a particular form of egocentrism that develops early in the transition into the stage of formal operations: *self-consciousness*. Some developmental psychologists believe that self-consciousness results from the difficulty in distinguishing their own self-perception from the view other people have of them. As Elkind noted:

> When adolescents begin thinking about other people's thinking, they often assume that other people are thinking about them. They become, as a matter of fact, convinced that others are as concerned with them and their appearance as they are with themselves. Hence the "self consciousness" so characteristic of young adolescents has to be attributed, in part at least, to the appearance of formal operations. While the physical and physiological transformations undergone by the adolescent play a part in this self consciousness, its cognitive determination must also be recognized. (Elkind, 1976, p. 101)

Because the onset of puberty occurs at different times in different individuals, young adolescents can find themselves more mature or less mature than some of their friends, and this difference can have important social conse-

quences. An early study by Jones and Bayley (1950) found that early-maturing boys tended also to become more socially mature and were most likely to be perceived as leaders by their peers. Late-maturing boys tended to become hostile and withdrawn and often engaged in negative attention-getting behavior. Later studies have generally confirmed these findings and have found that behavioral differences extended into adulthood (Jones, 1965). The effect of age of maturity in girls is less clear. Some studies indicate that early-maturing girls may benefit from higher status and prestige, but they are also more likely to engage in norm-breaking behaviors such as stealing, cheating on exams, staying out late, or using alcohol (Jones, 1965; Brooks-Gunn, 1989). Brooks-Gunn suggests that the primary cause of the norm-breaking behaviors result from the fact that early-maturing girls are more likely to become friends with older girls.

Social Development

[10] During adolescence a person's behavior and social roles change dramatically. Adolescence is not simply a continuation of childhood; it marks a real transition from the dependency of childhood to the relative independence of adulthood.

The nature of friendship changes during adolescence, and it changes in different ways for boys and girls. For girls the most important function of childhood friendships is having someone to do things with—someone to share activities and common interests. At around the age of fourteen years girls begin to seek companions who can provide social and emotional support (Douvan and Adelson, 1966). As girls become aware of their growing sexuality and the changes in their relationships with boys, close friends serve as confidants—as sounding boards to help define their behavior and social roles. Adolescent boys' friendships are likely to be less intense than those of girls. Boys are more concerned with establishing and asserting their independence and defining their relation to authority; thus, groups of friends serve as allies—as mutual-aid societies, so to speak.

Sexuality has become a very evident component of modern culture in most industrialized societies. Displays of sexual attractiveness play an important role in advertisements in magazines and on television; sexual activities are portrayed in books and films; and personal sexual practices are discussed in print and during talk shows on radio and television. Sexuality was always a part of life (after all, our species has managed to propagate during all periods of history), but during the latter part of this century it has become much more open and evident than it was in previous years.

Sexual behavior during adolescence has increased in frequency during the past few decades. Fifty years ago, approximately 20 percent of the females and 40 percent of the males in the United States said that they had engaged in sexual intercourse by age twenty; now the figure for age nineteen is approximately fifty percent for both males and females (Brooks-Gunn and Furstenberg, 1989). The increase seems to have reached a peak in the late 1970s. Since then, the figures have declined slightly, and expressions of guilt feelings about sexual behavior have increased (Gerrard, 1986; 1987).

Adolescent boys and girls tend to react differently to their first intercourse. Sorenson (1973) found that boys were more likely to be excited, happy, satisfied, and thrilled by their experience, whereas girls were more likely to be afraid, worried, guilty, embarrassed, and sorry. (See *Table 10.1*.)

Table 10.1 Adolescents' immediate reactions to their first intercourse (%)*

	All	*Boys*	*Girls*
Excited	37	46	26
Afraid	37	17	63
Happy	35	42	26
Satisfied	33	43	20
Thrilled	30	43	13
Curious	26	23	30
Joyful	23	31	12
Mature	23	29	14
Fulfilled	20	29	8
Worried	20	9	35
Guilty	17	3	36
Embarrassed	17	7	31
Tired	15	15	14
Relieved	14	19	8
Sorry	12	1	25
Hurt	11	0	25
Powerful	9	15	1
Foolish	8	7	9
Used	7	0	16
Disappointed	6	3	10
Raped	3	0	6

* Percentages add up to more than 100% because most respondents reported more than one reaction.

Source: From Sorenson, 1973.

Along with sexual activity come the dangers of pregnancy and sexually transmitted diseases. Although the probability of contracting diseases such as gonorrhea, chlamydia, and genital herpes is higher than the probability of contracting AIDS (acquired immune deficiency syndrome), the threat of contracting a fatal illness has certainly increased young people's fears even if it does not always affect their behavior. Considering the impact that the fear of AIDS has had on our society, it is sometimes hard to believe that the first cases of this disease were not diagnosed until the late 1970s.

As adolescents begin to define their new roles and to assert them, they almost inevitably come into conflict with their parents. Some writers have claimed that changes in modern society have given rise to a "youth culture" apart from the rest of society and a "generation gap" that separates young people from their elders. However, research indicates that most of the differences between people of different generations are in style rather than in substance. Adolescents and their parents tend to have similar values and attitudes toward important issues (Youniss and Smollar, 1985). Unless serious problems occur, family conflicts tend to be provoked by relatively minor issues, such as messy rooms, loud music, clothes, curfews, and household chores. These problems tend to begin around the time of puberty; if puberty occurs particularly early or late, so does the conflict (Steinberg, 1987).

Adolescence is said to be a time of turmoil, a period characterized by unhappiness, stress, and confusion. While a few adolescents are unhappy most of the time (and most are unhappy some of the time), studies have found that the vast majority of teenagers generally feel happy and self-confident (Offer and Sabshim, 1984; Peterson and Ebata, 1987). But mood states do seem to be more variable during the teenage years than during other times of life. Csikszentmihalyi and Larson (1984) randomly sampled the mood states of a group of high school students. They gave them electronic beepers that sounded at random intervals that were, on the average, two hours apart. Each time the beeper sounded, the student stopped what he or she was doing and filled out a questionnaire that asked what they were doing, how they felt, what they were thinking about, and so on. The investigators found that the students' moods could swing from high to low and back again in the course of a few hours. The questionnaires also revealed conflicts between the subjects and other family members. Although the subjects of

Peer groups are especially important during adolescence.

the conflicts were usually trivial, they nevertheless concerned them deeply. As the authors noted:

> Asking a boy who has spent many days practicing a song on the guitar "Why are you playing that trash?" might not mean much to the father, but it can be a great blow to the son. The so-called "growth pains" of adolescence are no less real just because their causes appear to be without much substance to adults. In fact, this is exactly what the conflict is all about: What is to be taken seriously? (Csikszentmihalyi and Larson, 1984, p. 140)

INTERIM SUMMARY

Adolescence

Adolescence is the transitional stage between childhood and adulthood. Puberty is initiated by the hypothalamus, which causes the anterior pituitary gland to secrete hormones that stimulate the ovaries or testes to produce estradiol or testosterone. The sex hormones promote the development of secondary sex characteristics and cause the internal sex organs and external genitalia to assume their adult form and function. Because of improved nutrition and health care in industrialized countries, the age of puberty has declined over the past century, and it is beginning to decline in the more prosperous developing countries.

Puberty marks a significant transition, both physically and socially. Early maturity appears to be socially beneficial to boys, since early maturers are more likely to be perceived as leaders. The effects of early maturity in girls is mixed; although their advanced physical development may help them acquire some prestige, early-maturing girls are more likely to engage in norm-breaking behavior.

The nature of friendship changes during adolescence. Girls seek out confidants rather than playmates, and boys join groups that provide mutual support in their quest to assert their independence. Sexuality becomes important; most young people engage in sexual intercourse before they leave their teens. However, the increase in teenage sexual behavior seems to have peaked in the late 1970s; the figures have declined since then.

Although adolescence brings conflicts between parents and children, these conflicts tend to be centered on relatively minor issues. Most adolescents hold the same values and attitudes on important issues as their parents do. Mood swings during adolescence can be dramatic, but on the whole, teenagers report that they are generally happy and self-confident. ■

343

ADULT DEVELOPMENT

It is much easier to outline child or adolescent development than adult development; children and adolescents change faster, and the changes are closely related to age. Adult development is much more variable, because physical changes in adults are more gradual.

Mental and emotional changes during adulthood are more closely related to individual experience than to age. Some people achieve success and satisfaction with their careers, while some hate their jobs. Some marry and have happy family lives, while others never adjust to the role of spouse and parent. Crises occur at different times for different people, and they do not come in the same order. No single description of adult development will fit everyone.

Physical Development

11 Unlike the rapid physical changes that occur during prenatal development, childhood, and adolescence, the changes that occur during adulthood—except for sudden changes caused by accident or disease—are gradual. People are unlikely to notice these changes until they try to do something they have not done for several years and find it more difficult than it used to be, such as playing a sport that they have not practiced since their college days.

The effects of *looking* old can be more serious than the effects of declining physical abilities on a person's functional capacity. For example, the sex life of a person who is regarded as sexually unattractive because of age will suffer even if he or she is physiologically capable of vigorous sexual performance. Similarly, the intellectual and physical skills of an older person will go untested if he or she is regarded as "too old for the job." These age-related effects are purely social; they depend on society's attitudes toward older people.

Many physical changes in old age appear to be related to life-style. People who are active both physically and intellectually are likely to continue to be active and productive in old age. For example, the efficiency of the human respiratory system peaks at around age twenty-five and then steadily declines at approximately 1 percent a year. If, however, the person remains physically active and engages in a regular exercise program, the decline greatly diminishes (Kasch, Wallace, and Van Camp, 1985).

Muscular strength peaks during the late twenties or early thirties and then declines slowly thereafter as muscle tissue gradually deteriorates. By age seventy, strength has declined by approximately 30 percent in both men and women (Larsson, 1978; Young, Stokes, and Crowe, 1984). However, age has much less effect on *endurance* than on strength. Both laboratory tests and athletic records reveal that older people who remain physically fit show remarkably little decline in the ability to exercise for extended periods of time (Spirduso and MacRae, 1990).

Although it is easy to measure a decline in the sensory systems (such as vision or hearing), older people often show very little *functional* change in these systems. Most of them learn to make adjustments for their sensory losses, using additional cues to help them decode sensory information. For example, people with a hearing loss can learn to attend more carefully to other people's gestures and lip movements; they can also profitably use their experience to infer what was said.

Functional changes with age are also minimal in highly developed skills. For example, Salthouse (1984, 1988) found that experienced older typists continued to perform as well as younger ones, despite the fact that they performed less well on standard laboratory tests of sensory and motor skills, including the types of reaction time tests that one would expect to be important in typing. The continuous practice they received enabled them to develop strategies to compensate for their physical decline. For example, they tended to read farther ahead in the text they were typing, which enabled them to plan in advance the patterns of finger movements they would have to make.

With regular exercise and a flexible attitude, individuals can accommodate their interests and activities to the inevitable changes in physical abilities brought by aging. There is no reason why a reasonably healthy person of *any* age should stop enjoying life because of physical limitations.

Personality Development

12 Few theorists have attempted to describe personality development in adulthood, primarily because adult personality was assumed to be static and unchanging. As William James put it, an individual's personality was "set like plaster" by age thirty. Sigmund Freud's theory of personality development (described in Chapter 14) stops with young adulthood; the theory assumes that events that occur during early life determine a person's temperament and character, and it asserts that only psychoanalysis (which takes much time and effort) can produce significant changes.

One theorist who disagreed with the notion that adult personality is unchanging was Erik Erikson, a psychoanalyst who studied with Anna Freud, Sigmund Freud's daughter. Erikson's theory, which was based on his observations of patients in his psychoanalytical practice, divides human development into eight stages. As we shall see in Chapter 14, Freud believed that the important stages of development centered on changes in sexuality and thus were largely complete when a person reached young adulthood. In contrast, Erikson proposed that people encounter a series of crises in their social relations with other people. The ways people resolve these crises determine the character of their personality. Thus, Erikson's theory is one of *psychosocial development,* as opposed to Freud's *psychosexual development.* Because the nature of people's social relations change throughout life, their psychosocial development does not end when they become adults.

Erik Erikson with his wife Joan, an artist and author. Even in his nineties Erikson continued his scholarly writing.

At the age of 45, Nolan Ryan, considered by many as "over the hill" for a major league baseball player, became the first pitcher to achieve 5000 strikeouts.

Table 10.2 lists Erikson's eight stages of development, the nature of the crises, the social relationships involved in these crises, and the possible consequences—favorable or unfavorable—of these crises. (See *Table 10.2.*)

Erikson's theory of lifelong development has been very influential. In fact, the term *identity crisis,* which he coined, has become a familiar phrase in modern society. However, because the theory is phrased in global terms, it is difficult to make specific predictions from it that can be tested experimentally; thus, the theory has little empirical support.

Another, more recent attempt to identify and characterize stages of adult development is that of Daniel Levinson (Levinson et al., 1978). Levinson and his colleagues interviewed forty men—business executives, blue-collar workers, novelists, and biologists—spending ten to twenty hours with each of them. In addition, the investigators analyzed the biographies of famous men and examined stories of men's lives as portrayed in literature. They claimed to have discovered a pattern common to most men's lives. Instead of proceeding smoothly, their lives were characterized by several years of stability punctuated by crises. The crises were periods during which the men began to question their *life*

Table 10.2 Erikson's stages of psychosocial development

Life Crisis	Favorable Outcome	Unfavorable Outcome
First year Trust–mistrust	Hope: Trust in the environment and the future.	Fear of the future; suspicion.
Second year Autonomy–shame, doubt	Will: Ability to exercise choice as well as self-restraint; a sense of self-control and self-esteem leading to good will and pride.	Sense of loss of self-control or sense of external overcontrol; the result is a propensity for shame and doubt about whether one willed what one did or did what one willed.
Third through fifth years Initiative–guilt	Purpose: Ability to initiate activities, to give them direction, and to enjoy accomplishment.	Fear of punishment; self-restriction or overcompensatory showing off.
Sixth year through puberty Industry–inferiority	Competence: Ability to relate to the world of skills and tools, to exercise dexterity and intelligence in order to make things and make them well.	A sense of inadequacy and inferiority.
Adolescence Identity–confusion about one's role	Fidelity: Ability to see oneself as a unique and integrated person and to sustain loyalties.	Confusion over who one is.
Early adulthood Intimacy–isolation	Love: Ability to commit oneself, one's identity, to others.	Avoidance of commitments and of love; distancing of oneself from others.
Middle age Generativity–stagnation	Care: Widening concern for what has been generated by love, necessity, or accident; for one's children, work, or ideas.	Self-indulgence, boredom, and interpersonal impoverishment.
Old age Integrity–despair	Wisdom: Detached concern for life itself; assurance of the meaning of life and of the dignity of one's own life; acceptance that one will die.	Disgust with life; despair over death.

Source: From H. Gardner, *Developmental psychology* (2nd ed.). Boston: Little, Brown, 1982, p. 51. Reprinted with permission.

structures: their occupation, their relations with their families, their religious beliefs and practices, their ethnic identity, and the way they spent their leisure time. During times of transition—which caused considerable anxiety and turmoil—the men reevaluated the choices they had made and eventually settled on new patterns that guided them through another period of stability. Periods of transition lasted around

four or five years, whereas the intervening periods of stability lasted six or seven years.

For Levinson the most important crises occur early in adulthood, when choices must be made about career and marriage, and at mid-life (during the early to mid-forties), when realities about one's life structure must finally be faced. Although Levinson did not invent the notion of the mid-life crisis, he certainly helped bring it to the attention of the general public and helped make the phrase a part of everyone's vocabulary. (Gail Sheehy wrote her best-selling 1976 book, *Passages,* after discussing Levinson's ideas with him.) Levinson concluded that the mid-life crisis happened to all men. Men whose life structures do not yet meet their prior goals and expectations realize that the future will probably not bring the success that up until then has eluded them. Men who *have* succeeded begin to question whether the goals they had set for themselves were meaningful and worthwhile. All men, successful or not, also begin to confront the fact that they are getting older. They are starting to detect some signs of physical decline, and they are witnesses to the death of their parents or their parents' friends.

Figure 10.12 summarizes Levinson's periods of adult development. (See **Figure 10.12.**)

Levinson's work has been criticized for not having drawn a representative sample of the population. His range of occupational categories is very narrow. In addition, he interviewed only males, so his theory cannot necessarily address

Figure 10.12 Levinson's periods of adult development. (Adapted from Levinson, D.J., Darrow, C.N., Klein, E.B., Levinson, M.H., and McKee, B. *The Season's of a Man's Life.* New York: Alfred A. Knopf, 1978.)

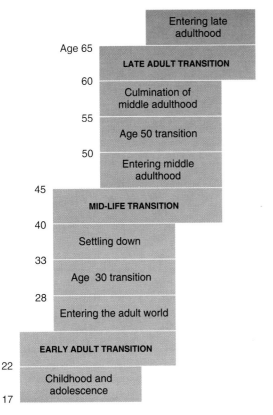

changes in *women's* lives. Even more fundamental criticisms are aimed at the method itself. (If the method is sound, it can be applied to other occupational groups and to women; if it is not, there is no point in doing so.) These criticisms, along with evidence concerning the search for the mid-life crisis, are discussed in the section that follows, "Evaluating Scientific Issues."

What is the present status of theories such as Erikson's and Levinson's, which assert that adult development consists of a series of stages? In one sense the notion of stages must be right: Our lives are marked by a series of important milestones, such as finishing formal education, embarking on a career, getting married, having children, getting divorced, having one's children grow up, having one's parents die, reaching a plateau in one's professional life, getting old, dying. Of course, not everyone encounters the same milestones, but all lives *do* have milestones. The question is, are the stages really universal? Do people's lives really *develop* according to a general plan? Are the stages that theorists describe a part of human nature, or do we simply react to milestones that are products of our culture and of chance events in our environments? Levinson insists that the stages are indeed part of human nature. According to him, they "have governed human development for the past five or ten thousand years . . ." (Levinson et al., p. 322) and fundamental change would come only after "hundreds of generations" (p. 340).

The word *development* implies change, and the two theories of adult development I have described assert that people change across the course of their lives. No one would disagree that the milestones we encounter change our life situations, but do they really change our *personalities?* According to the most recent evidence, gathered from thousands of people, they do not (Whitbourne, 1986). James may have exaggerated when he said that after thirty our personalities are "set like plaster," but he apparently was not far from wrong. Before thirty, the story is somewhat different. Many studies have shown that people's personality characteristics are still fluid and changeable until their mid-twenties (McCrae and Costa, 1990). According to Haan, Millsap, and Hartka (1986):

> Great shifts in personality organization are ordinarily thought to occur *during* adolescence, but [our] findings suggest that more marked shifts occur, not during adolescence, but at its end when most people make the profound role shifts entailed by entry into full-time work and marriage. (p. 225)

After age thirty, though, according to Mc-Crae and Costa (1990, p. 10), "personality change is the exception rather than the rule . . . ; somewhere in the decade between 20 and 30, individuals attain a configuration of traits that will characterize them for years to come." They base their conclusions on studies—their own and those of other investigators—that have measured people's personality traits at various ages. For example, they found that personality test scores obtained from over ten thousand black and white men and women aged thirty-five to eighty-four years were remarkably stable.

These data contrast with some earlier studies that showed large personality differences between young and old people. However, as Mc-Crae and Costa point out, the populations sampled by these studies varied according to age; for example, the oldest people were selected from nursing homes, whereas the youngest adults came from the colleges and universities in which the investigators worked. Thus, the oldest people were those whose weakness and ill health required them to live in an institution, whereas the youngest were among the most affluent and best-educated members of their age group. The fact that these studies found that older people were more rigid, more depressed, and more introverted certainly does not mean that the normal pattern of adult development is to become rigid, depressed, and introverted. When representative samples of various age groups are tested, the picture that emerges is stability of personality, not changeability or decline.

But what about life's milestones? Certainly, they provoke changes, but not necessarily changes in *personality*. In general, young extraverts become old extraverts, young pessimists become old pessimists, and so on. In fact, some studies suggest that people's *personalities* can affect their *life situations*. For example, Conley (1985) found that people who were rated high in neuroticism in 1935 were more likely to have an emotional disorder later; those who were low in impulse control were more likely to become alcoholics. Those who were open to experience were more likely to have artistic hobbies and watch public television; those who were closed to experience were more likely to prefer solitary, traditional hobbies and to watch game shows. Kelly and Conley (1987) found that patterns of personality traits measured early in life predicted the success of people's marriage. Low conscientiousness in husbands and high neuroticism in both husbands and wives predicted divorce, whereas introversion and dis-agreeability in husbands and high neuroticism in both husbands and wives predicted an unhappy marriage, but not divorce. Stressful life events, childhood histories, and other environmental variables had little effect on marital success.

You may find it discouraging to learn that research suggests that people's personalities are not likely to change drastically after their late twenties. But you should not confuse personality with life events; life is full of surprises for all of us, even if our temperaments remain relatively stable. And it should be reassuring to realize that if you marry a cheerful, open, optimistic, outgoing person, he or she is unlikely to become a crabby, closed, pessimistic introvert. (On the other hand, perhaps you should resist the temptation to marry someone with personality traits you do not like, with the intention of changing them after you get married.)

EVALUATING SCIENTIFIC ISSUES

Is There a Mid-Life Crisis?

[13] The belief that most people go through a special period of turmoil and self-examination during the early to mid-forties is currently prevalent in our society. The concept of a mid-life crisis plays a central role in Daniel Levinson's theory of adult development, and books are available to help people anticipate the problems that are sure to assail them when they reach that critical age. But the scientific method teaches us that the best way to evaluate the truth of a belief is to examine the evidence and not be swayed by the popularity of the belief or the eminence of its proponents.

What Is Being Asserted?   A mid-life crisis is a time when people—successful and unsuccessful—begin to reexamine their goals and priorities. Doing so is painful; the disillusionment that characterizes this period causes stress, turmoil, and depression. Unsuccessful or moderately successful people realize that they have not accomplished all they had set out to do with their lives. And successful people begin to doubt whether their goals are worthwhile and to suspect that their accomplishments are hollow and meaningless. This crisis happens to virtually everyone.

What Evidence Appears to Support the Assertion?   Although several theorists have obtained evidence for a mid-life crisis (Gould, 1978; Vaillant, 1977), the work of Levinson (Levinson et al., 1978) is best known. As we saw, Levinson based his conclusions on evidence gathered from interviews with forty men: novelists, business executives, biologists, and blue-collar workers. Obviously, he can be criticized for the limited range of occupations he studied and the fact that women were not represented at all. But what about his method? Levinson and his colleagues spent many hours with each subject, asking probing questions. As a result, they were able to get the subjects to talk about the crisis they were experiencing (or had experienced) during the critical years.

Does the Evidence Support the Assertion? Some of the principles of the scientific method were not followed in Levinson's observations. For one thing, the term *mid-life crisis* was not explicitly defined but was left to the judgment of the interviewer. Thus, what one person might consider to be a crisis might be regarded by someone else as an insignificant and transitory period of disturbance. The fact that no attempt was made to establish interrater reliability means that we cannot be sure just how many of the subjects experienced a genuine "crisis." Also, when a person spends several hours being interviewed by a charismatic, well-respected expert, one is likely to say things that appear to please the expert. Levinson himself said that the topic he chose to study "reflected a personal concern: at 46, I wanted to study the transition into middle age in order to understand what I had been going through myself" (Levinson et al., 1978, p. x). His words suggest that he expected people to have similar crises, and he probably showed interest and satisfaction when his subjects told him things that confirmed this belief.

Several investigators *have* defined objective criteria for the presence of a mid-life crisis and have looked for its presence in representative samples of subjects. For example, Costa and McCrae (1980) administered a *Midlife Crisis Scale* to 548 men aged thirty-five to seventy-nine years. The scale contained items asking whether the subjects were experiencing any of the symptoms of a mid-life crisis, such as dissatisfaction with job and family, a sense of meaninglessness, or a feeling of turmoil. They found absolutely no evidence for a mid-life crisis. Some people did report some of the symptoms, but they were no more likely to occur during the early to mid-forties than at any other age. A study of 60 women (Reinke, Holmes, and Harris, 1985) also found no evidence of a mid-life crisis.

Some people *do* have a mid-life crisis. But the evidence suggests that these crises are not isolated events, occurring at one particular stage of adult development. Instead, they seem to be part of a long-established pattern (Farrell and Rosenberg, 1981). McCrae and Costa (1990) report that people who score high on a test of neuroticism are more likely to report a "crisis" ten years later. They go on to suggest that "if we spoke to these men today, we might find them blaming all their troubles on recent events or on their age or health. But they had had more than their share of complaints many years earlier, and it begins to seem that they carried their troubles with them" (p. 166).

What Should We Conclude? We are faced with a choice of evidence gathered from intensive interviews with a few men or that gathered from objective questionnaires given to several hundred subjects. The interviews undoubtedly provide much more information about each individual. But because the interviewer *interacts* with each subject and consciously or unconsciously steers the course of the conversation, we cannot be sure about the accuracy or representativeness of the information gathered by this method. The lack of objective evidence for a mid-life crisis means that we should probably conclude that it is an interesting concept but that its existence is not yet proved. ■

Cognitive Development

14 One of the topics of adult development that has received the most attention is cognitive development. Psychologists have studied the effects of education and experience on intellectual abilities and have questioned whether intelligence inevitably declines with age. Most of us can conceive of a future when we can no longer run as fast as we do now or perform well in a strenuous sport, but we do not like to think of being outperformed intellectually by younger people. And, in fact, research indicates that people can get old without losing their intellectual skills.

Before I discuss the normal effects of aging in a healthy individual, I should discuss some changes caused by disease. As people get older, they have a greater risk of developing senile or presenile dementia—a class of diseases characterized by the progressive loss of cortical tissue and a corresponding loss of mental functions.

(*Senile* means "old"; *dementia* literally means "an undoing of the mind.") The distinction between senile and presenile dementia is not important, because the disease process is the same in both cases. The most prevalent form of dementia is **Alzheimer's disease,** which occurs in approximately 5 percent of the population above the age of sixty-five. It is characterized by progressive loss of memory and other mental functions. At first, the person may have difficulty remembering appointments and sometimes fails to think of words or people's names.

Figure 10.13 Alzheimer's disease. (a) A side view of the right side of the brain of a person who had Alzheimer's disease. Note that the sulci (grooves) of the temporal lobe and parietal lobe are especially wide, indicating degeneration of the neocortex (*arrows*). (Courtesy of A. D'Agostino, Good Samaritan Hospital, Portland, Oregon.) (b) A side view of the right side of a normal brain. (© Dan McCoy/Rainbow.)

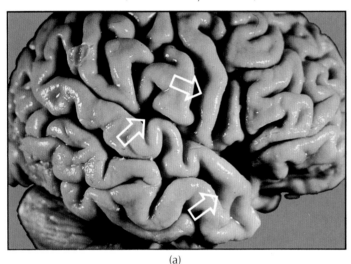

(a)

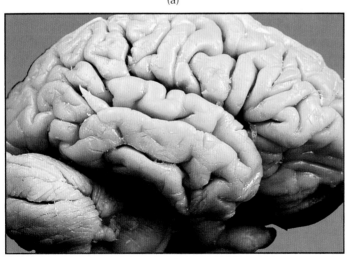

(b)

As time passes, he or she shows increasing confusion and increasing difficulty with tasks such as balancing a checkbook. In the early stages, the memory deficit involves recent events; but as the disease progresses, even old memories are affected. If the person ventures outside alone, he or she is likely to get lost. Eventually, the person becomes bedridden, completely helpless, and, finally, succumbs (Khachaturian and Blass, 1992; Terry and Davies, 1980).

Alzheimer's disease produces severe degeneration of the hippocampus and cerebral cortex, especially the association cortex of the frontal and temporal lobes. Figure 10.13 shows photographs of the brain of a patient with Alzheimer's disease and of a normal brain. You can see how much wider the sulci are in the damaged brain, especially in the frontal and temporal lobes, indicating substantial loss of cortical tissue. (See *Figure 10.13.*)

An even more common cause of mental deterioration in old age is depression, a psychological disorder. Some people find old age an unpleasant condition: They are declining physically; they no longer have jobs or family-related activities that confirm their usefulness to other people; and many old friends have died, are infirm, or have moved away. With this sense of loss or deprivation, some older people become depressed; they lose their appetite for food and for living in general, have trouble concentrating, and suffer losses in memory. Too often these symptoms of depression are diagnosed as dementia. Yet unlike dementia, depression is treatable with psychotherapy and drugs, as we will see in Chapters 15 and 16.

Studies have shown clearly that aging affects different intellectual abilities to different degrees. Schaie (1990), describing the results of the Seattle Longitudinal Study, reports that on the average, people's scores on five tests of intellectual abilities showed an increase until the late thirties or early forties, then a period of stability until the mid-fifties or early sixties, followed by a gradual decline. However, the decline was not uniform for all abilities. Figure 10.14 shows the percentage of subjects who maintained stable levels of performance on each of the tests over a seven-year period. As you can see, the performance of most of the subjects—even the oldest—remained stable. (See *Figure 10.14.*)

As we shall see in Chapter 13, many investigators believe that intelligence can be divided into two broad categories (Cattell, 1971). In general, old people in good health do well on tests of **crystallized intelligence**—abilities

People with Alzheimer's disease function best in a stable, structured environment. Strategically placed signs can remind them of simple tasks they should perform.

that depend on knowledge and experience. Vocabulary, the ability to see similarities between objects and situations, and general information are all aspects of crystallized intelligence. On the other hand, **fluid intelligence**—the capacity for abstract reasoning—appears to decline with age (Baltes and Schaie, 1974; Horn, 1982). The ability to solve puzzles, to memorize a series of arbitrary items such as unrelated words or letters, to classify figures into categories, and to change problem-solving strategies easily and flexibly are aspects of fluid intelligence.

The fact that older people excel in crystallized intelligence and younger people excel in fluid intelligence is reflected in the kinds of intellectual endeavors that the two age groups seem to be best suited for. For example, great mathematicians usually make their most important contributions during their twenties or early thirties; apparently, the ability to break out of the traditional ways of thinking and to conceive new strategies is crucial in such achievements. In contrast, great contributions to literature and philosophy, in which success depends heavily on knowledge and experience, tend to be made by older people.

At least three reasons may account for older people's apparent decline in fluid intelligence:

1. The abilities that constitute fluid intelligence may be especially sensitive to the inevitable deterioration in the brain that accompanies aging.

2. People's previous experience may cause them to adhere rigidly to particular problem-solving strategies, even when a more flexible approach would be more effective. In this case the decline would be due to experience rather than to a real loss of intellectual capacity.

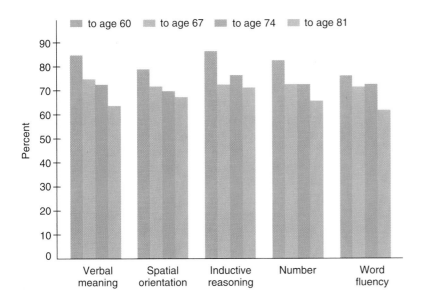

Figure 10.14 Percentage of subjects of various age groups who maintained stable levels of performance on each of five tests of intellectual ability over a seven-year period. (From Schaie, K.W., in *Handbook of the Psychology of Aging*, 3rd ed., edited by J.E. Birren and K.W. Schaie. San Diego: Academic Press, 1990. Reprinted by permission.)

3. People may learn so much and see so many relations among variables that they have difficulty focusing on the simple answer.

In support of the third suggestion, Kogan (1973) compared the strategies used by college students and members of a senior citizens club (average age seventy-three) to classify a number of objects and photographs. The older people were more likely to classify the items according to functional relations. For example, they might group pipes with matches. Younger people were more likely to classify objects according to physical characteristics (such as having handles) or according to a common general concept (such as kitchen utensils). Kogan attributed the difference to experience; the older subjects used a more subtle and less conventional scheme. Kogan noted that children who are rated as more creative also tend to classify according to functional relations rather than by type or physical characteristics. Thus, the behavior of the older people could be taken as evidence of a higher stage of cognitive development and not as evidence of intellectual deterioration.

In many societies, important decisions are left to the elder members of the family, perhaps because they have more experience and resist making hasty decisions.

Another aspect of intellectual ability is speed. Older people have difficulty responding and performing quickly. When time pressures prevail, their performance is worse than that of younger people. However, when time requirements are relaxed, the performance of older people improves much more than that of younger people (Arenberg, 1973; Botwinick and Storandt, 1974).

Part of the age-related decline in speed can be attributed to deterioration in sensory functions and to difficulty in changing strategies to meet new demands. But another important reason for decreased speed is caution; older people appear to be less willing to make mistakes. In some endeavors this caution is valuable. In fact, many societies reserve important decision-making functions for older people because they are less likely to act too hastily. A study by Leech and Witte (1971) illustrates the effect of caution on performance. The investigators found that older people who were paid for each response they made—correct or incorrect—learned lists of pairs of words faster than older people who were paid only for correct responses. The payment for incorrect responses increased their willingness to make a mistake, and this relaxation of their normal caution paid off in an increased speed of learning.

INTERIM SUMMARY

Adult Development

Up to the time of young adulthood, human development can reasonably be described as a series of stages: a regular sequence of changes that occur in most members of our species. However, development in adulthood is much more variable, and few generalizations will apply.

Aging brings with it a gradual deterioration in people's sensory capacities and changes in physical appearance that many people regard as unattractive. The effects of these changes can be minimized by vigorous participation in life's activities.

Erikson and Levinson have both proposed that people encounter a series of crises that serve as turning points in development. Erikson's stages span the entire life cycle, from infancy to old age, whereas Levinson's concentrate on mid-life development. Objective studies of personality development indicate that personality is remarkably stable after the late twenties. Even though people encounter milestones that affect their lives, these encounters do not significantly alter their basic personalities. The concept of the mid-life crisis, central to Levinson's theory, does not appear to have scientific support.

Although older people are more likely to develop dementing illnesses such as Alzheimer's disease, severe intellectual deterioration is often caused by depression, which can usually be treated successfully. Rather than undergoing sudden intellectual deterioration, older people are more likely to exhibit gradual changes, especially in abilities that require flexibility and learning new behaviors. Intellectual abilities that depend heavily on crystallized intelligence—an accumulated body of knowledge—are much less likely to decline than those based on fluid intelligence—the capacity for abstract reasoning. ■

APPLICATION

Children and Television

A child's cognitive development is influenced by many factors, including parents' education and occupational status, number of siblings, social class of playmates, nature of the neighborhood, availability in the home of educational resources such as books, opportunity for travel, and quality of schooling. These factors vary widely; a child from a privileged social milieu is much more likely to be exposed to situations that promote cognitive development. But almost all children in industrialized societies—even those in the poorest households—are exposed for several hours a day to a near-universal factor: television.

What are the effects of television on children? There are two issues—the *content* of programs and the general effects of the *medium*. Let us consider the content first. There is no question that television does not do the good it could, and it probably does some harm. The best example of the good it can do is demonstrated by "Sesame Street," an American program that was devised to teach school-readiness skills, such as counting, letter recognition, and vocabulary. Research indicates that the program has succeeded in its goals; children who watch "Sesame Street" have better vocabularies, have better attitudes toward school, adapt better to the classroom, and have more positive attitudes toward children of other races (Ball and Bogatz, 1970; Bogatz and Ball, 1982). ("Sesame Street" emphasizes multiculturalism in its choice of characters and the activities and interests they display.) Rice et al. (1990) studied a large sample of three-to-five-year-old children of a wide range of socioeconomic backgrounds and found that children of *all* backgrounds profited from watching "Sesame Street"—the advantages were not restricted to middle-class children.

On the other hand, many television programs are full of violence, and watching them may well promote aggressiveness and impatience with nonviolent resolution of disagreements in the children who watch such shows. (Research on this issue will be examined in Chapter 11.) In addition, commercial television affects consumer behavior. American children spent $6 billion of their own money in 1989, and sponsors target many of their commercial messages at these children (McNeal, 1990). Furthermore, sponsors produce commercials that encourage children to demand that their parents purchase particular snack foods, toys, and other items (Taras et al., 1989). We can ask ourselves whether sponsors are likely to find it in their interest to educate children to be informed consumers.

The second issue that people have raised about children and television regards the nature of the medium itself, and it is this issue that I will examine in the rest of this section. Many people who have written about the potential effects of television *as a medium* on children's cognitive development have concluded that the medium is generally harmful. Anderson and Collins (1988) summarize some of the criticisms these people have made:

1. Television has mesmerizing powers over children's attention; this power is exerted by the movement, color, and visual changes typical of television.
2. Children's comprehension of television is extremely poor; they remember only disconnected images.
3. Children do not think about television programs; that is, they do not engage in inferential and reflective thought while television viewing.
4. Children get overstimulated by television; by some accounts this leads to hyperactivity, and by other accounts this leads to passivity.
5. Television viewing displaces valuable cognitive activities, especially reading and homework.
6. Attention span is shortened, probably because of the rapidly paced visual images.
7. Creativity and imagination are reduced; in general, the child becomes cognitively passive.
8. Reading achievement is reduced. (Anderson and Collins, 1988, p. 4)

In a review of their own research and that of others, Anderson and Collins conclude that there is little evidence to support these criticisms. In fact, the evidence directly contradicts some of them. Let us examine four of the most important criticisms: that television mesmerizes, that it overstimulates children, that it displaces valuable cognitive activities, and that it reduces children's reading achievement.

Before we look at the evidence concerning these issues, we should ask just how much of a child's time is dominated by the medium. Estimates vary according to the method used. Generally, parents' estimates are higher than those of their children. The most objective measures have been obtained by placing a time-lapse video camera and videotape machine in people's homes next to their television sets so that the viewers can be recorded. Anderson et al. (1985) used this method to measure television viewing by members of ninety-nine families in a New England city. They found that children watched television around sixteen hours per week.

According to Anderson and Collins (1988), while watching television, children are often engaged in other activities; they eat, play with toys, draw or color pictures, read, play games, sleep, talk with others, or do their homework. They often enter and leave the room while the television is on. Thus, although the children do watch television a substantial amount of the time, it is probably inaccurate to say that the average North American child spends more time watching television than attending school.

Let us now examine the assertion that television mesmerizes children. Critics have said that television is "addictive" and "mesmerizing," that children who watch it have "glazed eyes," are "drugged" and "spaced out," are turned into "zombies" (Moody, 1980). Support for such terrible effects comes not from controlled experiments but from anecdotes and assertions of experts. In fact, studies that actually observe children who are watching television find no such effects. Children are rarely "glued" to the television set; they look away from it between 100 and 200 times each hour (Anderson and Field, 1983). They rarely look at the screen for much more than one minute at a stretch. Their viewing behavior is related to program content: They tend to pay attention when they hear other children's voices, interesting sound effects, and peculiar voices and when they see movement on the screen. They tend *not* to pay attention when they hear men's voices or see no signs of activity on the screen. Presumably, men's voices indicate that the program content is likely to be adult-oriented and thus more difficult to understand and less interesting (Anderson and Lorch, 1983).

The selectivity shown by young viewers is certainly not consistent with the behavior of someone who has been "mesmerized" or "drugged." The fact that the sound track of a television program has so much effect on their looking

behavior suggests that they have learned to use auditory cues to help them decide whether or not to watch, especially when *time-sharing*—alternating their attention between the television and another activity. If they hear certain categories of sounds, they turn their attention away from the alternate activity and look at the screen to see whether something interesting is happening.

What about the assertion that television overstimulates children? Moody (1980) states that "television is an intense kaleidoscope of moving light and sound. It can create extreme excitement in the brain and, after prolonged viewing, it can produce a 'drugged state' " (p. 18). Anderson and Collins found no good evidence to back up such claims. And the fact that children looking away from television so often suggests that if they found television too stimulating, they would have a simple means for reducing potential overarousal—simply looking away from the screen. Certainly, an exciting program can excite the viewer, but no evidence suggests that "kaleidoscopic images" act like drugs on the brains of young children.

Perhaps television takes up time that would otherwise be spent on activities that would stimulate children's cognitive development. Some evidence with respect to this possibility comes from observations made before and after television was available in remote towns (Hornik, 1981). In fact, television viewing primarily displaced other entertainment activities, such as listening to the radio, reading comic books, or going to movies. It had little effect on time spent reading or doing homework. As most parents undoubtedly know, many children do their homework in front of the television set, switching their attention back and forth between the screen and their books and papers. In general, children are more likely to use television as a backdrop for their math homework than for reading (Patton, Stinard, and Routh, 1983). Surprisingly, there is no evidence that the quality of the homework suffers.

The fact that children are less likely to watch television while doing homework that involves reading suggests that reading and viewing are at least somewhat incompatible. Indeed, one criticism of television—that it retards children's reading achievement—has received some support. Measurements of children's reading skills before and after television became available suggested that television viewing decreased the reading skills of young children (Corteen and Williams, 1986). However, the effects were slight and were not seen in older children. Perhaps, then, television viewing does interfere with reading achievement in young children (who tend to watch more than older children).

The survey of the scientific literature by Anderson and Collins (1988) certainly makes the medium of television look like less of a threat to children's cognitive development than many people believed. Studies that actually look at the viewing behavior of children rather than speculate about harmful effects show us that children are not passive recipients of whatever the medium offers them. They watch what interests them and look away at other times, and they engage in a variety of other behaviors while sitting in front of the set. Fortunately, children are more discerning in their watching than many people have believed.

KEY TERMS AND CONCEPTS

Prenatal Development

gene *(313)*
enzyme *(313)*
sex chromosome *(313)*
X chromosome *(313)*
Y chromosome *(313)*
differentiation *(314)*
amniotic sac *(315)*
placenta *(315)*
androgen *(315)*

Physical and Perceptual Development in Infancy and Childhood

rooting *(316)*
sucking *(316)*
swallowing *(316)*
stereopsis *(319)*
critical period *(319)*

Cognitive Development in Childhood

cognition *(320)*
cognitive structure *(321)*
schema *(321)*
concept *(321)*
assimilation *(321)*
accommodation *(321)*
sensorimotor period *(322)*
object concept *(322)*
passive expectation *(322)*
permanence *(322)*
preoperational period *(324)*
symbolic function *(324)*
signifier *(324)*
sign *(324)*
conservation *(324)*
egocentrism *(324)*

period of concrete operations *(325)*
period of formal operations *(325)*
cognitive disequilibrium *(326)*

Social Development in Childhood

attachment *(327)*
surrogate mother *(328)*
secure base *(331)*
Strange Situation *(331)*
secure attachment *(331)*
resistant attachment *(331)*
avoidant attachment *(331)*

Development of Sex Roles

sexual identity *(334)*
sex role *(334)*
sex stereotype *(334)*

Moral Development

moral realism *(337)*
morality of cooperation *(337)*

Adolescence

puberty *(340)*
primary sex characteristic *(340)*
secondary sex characteristic *(340)*
testosterone *(340)*
estrogen *(340)*
estradiol *(340)*

Adult Development

Alzheimer's disease *(350)*
crystallized intelligence *(350)*
fluid intelligence *(350)*

SUGGESTIONS FOR FURTHER READING

Berk, L.E. *Child Development,* 2nd ed. Boston: Allyn and Bacon, 1991.

Birren, J.E., and Schaie, K.W. *Handbook of the Psychology of Aging,* 2nd ed. San Diego: Academic Press, 1990.

Bukatko, D., and Daehler, M.W. *Child Development: A Topical Approach.* Boston: Houghton Mifflin, 1992.

McCrae, R.R., and Costa, P.T. *Personality in Adulthood.* New York: Guilford Press, 1990.

Whitbourne, S.K. *Adult Development,* 2nd ed. New York: Praeger Publishers, 1986.

11
MOTIVATION

Henri Matisse, *The Pink Studio*
SCALA/Art Resource, N.Y. © 1992 Succession H. Matisse/ARS, N.Y.

LEARNING OBJECTIVES

When you finish this chapter, you should be able to:

1. Define the terms *motivation* and *drive,* and describe and evaluate the drive reduction theory and the optimum-level theory.
2. Describe Murray's social needs and Maslow's hierarchy of needs.
3. Discuss how intermittent reinforcement, conditioned reinforcement, intrinsic motivation, and learned helplessness affect perseverance.
4. Discuss cultural and social influences on eating and the physiological mechanisms that begin a meal.
5. Discuss the physiological mechanisms that end a meal and the possible causes of obesity and anorexia nervosa.
6. Compare the responses of males and females to erotic imagery, and describe the effects of sex hormones on sexual behavior.
7. Discuss the factors that may influence sexual orientation.
8. Describe and discuss paraphilias, transvestism, and transsexualism.
9. Discuss the physiology of reinforcement and the reinforcing effects of addictive substances.
10. Discuss and evaluate the importance of physiological addiction in drug abuse.
11. Discuss the biological significance of aggressive behaviors and their physiological basis.
12. Discuss how environmental variables may influence human aggression.

In 1954 James Olds, a young assistant professor, designed an experiment to determine whether the reticular formation (located in the back part of the brain stem) might play a role in learning. Recent studies had suggested that the reticular formation was involved in arousal; when it was active, it would apparently increase an animal's attention and vigilance. Olds decided to place a small wire in the brains of rats in order to stimulate the reticular formation with electricity. Perhaps the stimulation would increase the rats' attention to their environment and facilitate their learning of a maze. If the stimulated animals learned the task faster than those that were not stimulated, his hypothesis would have strong support.

Olds enlisted the aid of Peter Milner, a graduate student who had experience with the surgical procedure needed to implant the electrodes in the brain. Because the procedure had only recently been developed and was not very accurate, one of the electrodes wound up in the wrong place—near the opposite end of the brain, in fact. This accident was a lucky one for the investigators because they discovered a phenomenon they would not have seen if the electrode had been located where they had intended it to be.

Olds and Milner had heard a talk by another physiological psychologist, Neal Miller, who reported that he had discovered that electrical stimulation of some parts of the brain could be aversive; the animals would work to avoid having the current turned on. The investigators decided that before they began their study, they would make sure that aversive stimulation was not occurring, because it might interfere with the animals' performance in the maze. The behavior of most of the animals was unremarkable, but here is Olds's report of what happened when he tested the rat with the misplaced electrode:

> I applied a brief train of 60-cycle sine-wave electrical current whenever the animal entered one corner of the enclosure. The animal did not stay away from that corner, but rather came back quickly after a brief sortie which followed the first stimulation and came back even more quickly after a briefer sortie which followed the second stimulation. By the time the third electrical stimulus had been applied the animal seemed indubitably to be "coming back for more." (Olds, 1973, p. 81)

Realizing that they had just seen something very important, Olds and Milner put more electrodes in rats' brains and allowed the rats to press a switch that controlled the current to the brain. The rats quickly learned to press the switch at a rate of over seven hundred times per hour. Subsequent studies obtained response rates of several thousand presses per hour. It turned out that the reinforcing effect of the electrical brain stimulation was very potent; when given a choice between pressing the lever and eating, drinking, or copulating, animals would choose the lever.

Olds and Milner's discovery probably had more impact on psychology than any other experiment performed by physiological psychologists. Articles in the popular press speculated on the nature of the "pleasure centers" in the brain. And some writers warned that a totalitarian society might someday control its population by putting electrodes in their brains and providing rewarding stimulation when they did what they were supposed to and withholding it when they did not. Such speculations prompted Eliot Valenstein to write a book demystifying the phenomenon, putting it in perspective (Valenstein, 1973).

The interest in reinforcing brain stimulation has peaked, but because the circuits discovered by Olds and Milner are responsible for the powerful addictive potential of drugs like cocaine, the research they began is still continuing. Many investigators are trying to understand the function these circuits play and how they relate to the effects of addictive drugs and the effectiveness of natural reinforcers. (By the way, it turns out that electrical stimulation of the reticular formation does *not* facilitate learning, but that is another story.)

When we investigate the causes of human behavior, we immediately encounter inconsistency. In a given situation different people act differently, and even a single individual acts differently at different times. There are many reasons for inconsistent behavior. A person eats or does not eat, depending on how recent his or her last meal was and how tasty the available food is. A person who usually picks up hitchhikers does not do so if he learns that a convict has just escaped from a nearby penitentiary. A person who likes to play tennis will probably turn down a game if she is suffering from a severe headache.

All these reasons for inconsistent behavior are aspects of *motivation* (derived from a Latin word meaning "to move"). Of course, once the reasons are known, the behaviors are no longer considered "inconsistent." In common usage **motivation** refers to a driving force that moves us to a particular action. For example, certain behaviors are likely to help us attain success, recognition, and financial well-being; other, more prosaic behaviors provide the next meal or drink of water. Motivation can affect the *nature* of an organism's behavior, the *strength* of its behavior, and the *persistence* of its behavior.

Motivation includes two types of phenomena. First, discriminative stimuli that were previously associated with reinforcement or punishment elicit approach behaviors toward reinforcers or avoidance behaviors away from punishers. For example, if something reminds you of an interesting person you met recently, you may try to meet that person again by consulting a telephone directory and making a telephone call. Second, being deprived of a particular reinforcer increases an organism's preference for a particular behavior. Besides obvious reinforcers such as food or water, this category includes more subtle reinforcers. For example, after spending considerable time performing routine tasks, we become motivated to go for a walk or meet with friends.

The first part of this chapter describes the nature of motivation and reinforcement and gives some theoretical explanations for these phenomena. The subsequent parts examine four important classes of motivated behaviors: eating, sexual behavior, addictive behavior, and aggression.

This chapter will not complete the discussion of motivation in this book. As you will see, motivation plays an especially important role in social behavior; thus, some topics dealing with social motivation will be discussed in Chapter 17.

WHAT IS MOTIVATION?

Motivation cannot be separated from reinforcement and punishment; we are motivated to perform a behavior to gain (or avoid losing) a reinforcer or to avoid (or escape from) a punisher. Some reinforcers and punishers are obvious, such as food or pain; others are subtle, such as smiles or frowns. This section describes the attempts by psychologists to identify the nature of reinforcement and to relate the process of reinforcement to motivation.

Biological Needs

Biological needs can be very potent motivators. Starving people have killed others for food. And you can undoubtedly imagine how hard you would struggle to breathe if something obstructed your windpipe. To survive, we all need air, food, water, various vitamins and minerals, and protection from extremes in temperature. All complex organisms possess physiological mechanisms that detect deficits or imbalances associated with these needs and mechanisms that permit them to engage in behaviors that can bring conditions back to normal, known as **regulatory behaviors.** Examples of regulatory behaviors include eating, drinking, hunting, shivering, building a fire, and putting on a warm coat. This process of detection and correction, which maintains physiological systems at their optimum value, is called **homeostasis** ("stable state"). Deficits or imbalances can be said to motivate an organism because they cause it to perform the appropriate regulatory behaviors.

A regulatory system contains four essential features: the **system variable** (the characteristic to be regulated), a **set point** (the optimal value of the system variable), a **detector** that monitors the value of the system variable, and a **correctional mechanism** that restores the system variable to the set point. A simple example of such a regulatory system is a room whose temperature is regulated by a thermostatically controlled heater. The system variable is the air temperature of the room, and the detector for

Motivation is a name we give to the factors that affect the nature, strength, and persistence of behavior. These factors vary, and so do people's behavior.

Figure 11.1 An example of a regulatory system.

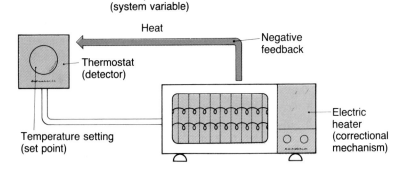

this variable is a thermostat. This device can be adjusted so that contacts of a switch will be closed when the temperature falls below a pre-set value (the set point). Closure of the contacts turns on the correctional mechanism—the coils of the heater. (See *Figure 11.1.*)

If the room cools below the set point of the thermostat, the thermostat turns the heater on, which warms the room. The rise in room temperature causes the thermostat to turn the heater off. Because the activity of the correctional mechanism (heat production) feeds back to the thermostat and causes it to turn the heater off, this process is called **negative feedback.** Negative feedback is an essential characteristic of all regulatory systems.

The earliest attempt to explain the nature of motivation and reinforcement stated that biological needs, caused by deprivation of the necessities of life, are unpleasant. According to this theory, the physiological changes associated with, say, going without food for several hours produce an unpleasant state called *hunger.* Hunger serves as a **drive,** energizing an organism's behavior. The organism then engages in behaviors that in the past have obtained food. The act of eating reduces hunger, and this **drive reduction** is reinforcing. Thus, we have the drive hypothesis of motivation and the drive reduction hypothesis of reinforcement. (See *Figure 11.2.*)

Not all drives are based on homeostasis—on biological needs like the ones for food and water. The most obvious example is the drive associated with sexual behavior. An organism can survive without sexual behavior; but the sex drive is certainly motivating, and sexual contact is certainly reinforcing. Similarly, most organisms placed in a featureless environment will soon become motivated to seek something new; they will work at a task that gives them a view of the world outside.

The drive reduction hypothesis of reinforcement has fallen into disfavor for two primary reasons. The first is that drive is almost always impossible to measure. For example, suppose you obtain pleasure from watching a set of color slides taken by a friend while on vacation. According to the drive reduction hypothesis, your "exploratory drive" or "curiosity drive" is high, and looking at vacation slides reduces it, providing reinforcement. Or consider a woman who very much enjoys listening to music. What drive induces her to turn on her stereo system? What drive is reduced by this activity? There is no way to measure "drive" in either of these examples and confirm that it actually exists; thus, the hypothesis cannot be experimentally tested.

The second problem is that if we examine our own behavior, we find that most events we experience as reinforcing are also exciting, or

Figure 11.2 The drive reduction theory of motivation and reinforcement.

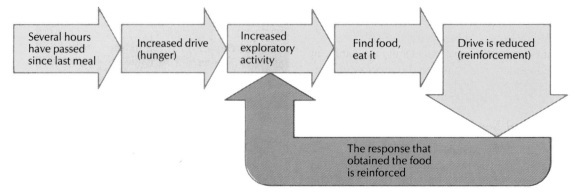

drive *increasing*. The reason a roller coaster ride is fun is certainly not because it *reduces* drive. The same is true for skiing, surfing, or viewing a horror film. Likewise, an interesting, reinforcing conversation is one that is exciting, not one that puts you to sleep. And people who engage in prolonged foreplay and sexual intercourse do not view these activities as unpleasant because they are accompanied by such a high level of drive. In general, the experiences we really want to repeat (that is, the ones we find reinforcing) are those that increase, rather than decrease, our level of arousal.

Learned Motivation

Drives can be learned as well as innate. We saw in Chapter 6 that neutral stimuli can become conditioned reinforcers through the process of classical conditioning. For example, money becomes a conditioned reinforcer through its association with desirable things. Similarly, organisms can acquire conditioned drives. Thus, a stimulus present while an animal experiences a primary drive can come to produce that drive itself. This phenomenon explains why the sight and smell of food can make a person become hungry and why the smile and tender words of a lover can arouse sexual desire.

Once learning has taken place, drives can be aroused through a process of anticipation—a phenomenon known as *incentive*. An **incentive** is an inducement to respond. It is aroused as an organism approaches a goal and anticipates performing the behavior that obtains the reinforcer. Certainly, we have all noticed that we feel more and more excited and enthusiastic as we approach something we very much enjoy. Anticipatory responses that we make in anticipation of the goal response also contribute to incentive. For example, we may salivate and lick our lips while approaching the table or imagine ourselves holding a loved one as we drive home from a long trip. Performing these small responses increases our motivation.

Optimum-Level Theory

Although events that increase our level of arousal are often reinforcing, there are times when a person wants nothing more than some peace and quiet; in this case avoidance of exciting stimuli is reinforcing. Negative reinforcement is also accomplished by the removal of aversive stimuli: Taking off a shoe that pinches reduces an unpleasant sensation and makes us feel much better. In an attempt to find a common explanation for both positive and negative reinforcement, some psychologists have proposed the **optimum-level hypothesis** of reinforcement and punishment. When the arousal level is too high, less stimulation is reinforcing; when it is too low, more stimulation is desired (Berlyne, 1966; Hebb, 1955). Berlyne hypothesized two forms of exploration: *Diversive exploration* is a response to understimulation (boredom) that increases the diversity of the stimuli the organism comes in contact with. *Specific exploration* is a response to overstimulation (usually because of a specific need) that leads to the needed item, thereby decreasing the organism's drive level.

The hypothesis that organisms seek an optimal level of arousal is certainly plausible. Any kind of activity—even the most interesting and exciting one—eventually produces satiety; something that was once reinforcing becomes bothersome. (Even the most avid video game player eventually moves on to something else.) Presumably, participation in an exciting behavior gradually raises an organism's arousal above its optimum level. However, the logical problem that plagues the drive reduction hypothesis also applies to the optimum-level hypothesis. Because we cannot measure an organism's drive or arousal, we cannot say what its optimum level should be.

Social Needs and Motives

2 At about the same time that drive theorists were developing their explanation of motivation, H. A. Murray and his colleagues were attempting to catalog the sources of human motivation, including those arising in social situations in which a person would be evaluated by other people (Murray, 1938/1962). Murray suggested that human behavior was motivated by two categories of needs: primary (physiological) and secondary (social). *Table 11.1* lists Murray's twenty-seven social needs.

Murray believed that all people had all of these social needs but that their levels varied from individual to individual. In addition, events occurring in the environment could interact with these needs. For example, if a person with a reasonably high level of need for recognition saw someone else receive an honor or an award, the observer's motivation to receive some sort of recognition would be increased. Or in a less competitive example, a person with a reasonably high level of need for nurturance would become motivated upon seeing someone who obviously needed care and attention.

Table 11.1 Murray's list of psychological needs

Major Category	Need	Representative Behavior
Ambition	n Achievement	Overcoming obstacles
	n Recognition	Describing accomplishments
	n Exhibition	Attempting to shock or thrill others
	n Acquisition	Obtaining things
	n Conservance	Repairing possessions
	n Order	Making things neat and orderly
	n Retention	Hoarding things
	n Construction	Building something
Defense of status	n Inviolacy	Keeping psychological distance
	n Infavoidance	Concealing a birthmark or handicap
	n Defendance	Giving an explanation or excuse
	n Counteraction	Retaliating for something
Response to human power	n Dominance	Directing others' behavior
	n Deference	Cooperating with, or obeying, someone
	n Similance	Imitating others
	n Autonomy	Standing up to authority
	n Contrariance	Being oppositional
	n Aggression	Attacking or belittling others
	n Abasement	Apologizing or confessing
	n Blame avoidance	Stifling blameworthy impulses
Affection between people	n Affiliation	Spending time with others
	n Rejection	Snubbing others
	n Nurturance	Taking care of someone
	n Succorance	Being helped by another
	n Play	Seeking diversion through others
Exchange of information	n Cognizance	Asking questions of others
	n Exposition	Delivering information to others

Source: From Charles S. Carver and Michael F. Scheier, *Perspectives on Personality.* Copyright © 1988 by Allyn and Bacon. Reprinted with permission. After Murray, 1962.

Although many psychologists found Murray's list of social needs to be reasonable, few of them have been operationally defined and studied. Three that have been most carefully studied are the *need for achievement,* the *need for dominance* (usually referred to nowadays as the *need for power*), and the *need for affiliation.*

Need for Achievement. The **need for achievement** was described by Murray as the tendency for people to strive to overcome obstacles—to do something difficult as well and as quickly as possible. This topic has been studied for over thirty years by McClelland, Atkinson, and their colleagues (McClelland, Atkinson, Clark, and Lowell, 1953; Atkinson, 1964; McClelland, 1985). According to these theorists, the strength of the motivation to perform a particular task is a product of three variables: motives, skills, and values. Motives are represented by the person's *need for achievement—* the concept outlined by Murray. Skills determine the person's *expectation of succeeding at a particular task.* Values are represented by the *perceived value of the goal*—the desirability of succeeding at the task.

It seems reasonable that motivation cannot be solely determined by any one of these factors. For example, even if a person ranks high in the need for achievement, he or she will not bother trying a task that is perceived as impossible, no matter how worthwhile the goal. For example, I would very much value winning a Nobel Prize, but I realize that the probability of my doing so is about as high as the likelihood of my getting hit by a meteorite. Therefore, the hope of winning a Nobel Prize cannot be said to motivate my behavior. Similarly, if a goal is perceived as worthless, a person is unlikely to try to perform a task that attains this goal, even if success on the task is perceived as being likely. I know that I would be able to count the names in my telephone directory; but because I would not obtain any gratification from doing so, I do not plan to try.

Need for Power. The **need for power** is the motive to assert authority and control the behavior of other people. Winter (1973) devised a coding scheme for a personality test (the TAT, described in Chapter 14) that permits its assessment. He found that people who score high on this need tend to seek positions of authority. They also tend to become friends with people who are not very popular, probably because such people are more easily dominated. Students who score high on the need for power are likely to make themselves more conspicuous by putting their names on the doors of their dormitory rooms and by enclosing term papers in fancy bindings.

An experiment by Fodor (1984) found that people who rate high in the need for power appear to become more aroused when a social situation calls for their leadership but does not seem to be responding to their efforts. Fodor told subjects that the experiment was a study of managerial ability. The subjects would be responsible for organizing and directing the activity of a group of high school students in the next room who were assembling some mechanical models. The subjects were to use all means at their disposal, including words of encouragement, reprimands, or promises of extra pay, in order to increase productivity. In fact, there were no workers; the voices the subject heard through the intercom had been prerecorded.

In the control condition things went smoothly; the "workers" performed well, and the "supervisor" had nothing to do. In the experimental condition the "workers" soon began having trouble; and as time went on, things got worse. Their complaints indicated that they wanted desperately to do well, but they perceived that their performance was not what it should have been. Obviously, nothing that the "supervisor" did or said had any effect.

Fodor predicted that exposure to the experimental condition, a situation that called for leadership but in which the subject apparently failed, would be particularly stressful for people who scored high on a need for power. Indeed, his prediction was fulfilled. After the experience with the industrial simulation the subjects were given a test that measures a person's self-reported level of activation (Thayer, 1967). This test requires subjects to rate themselves with respect to various adjectives denoting arousal, including *activated, energetic, lively,* and *wakeful.* As Figure 11.3 shows, people with a high need for power tended to become much more activated than people with a low need for power when their motivation to act was aroused but thwarted by a situation in which their efforts were futile. (See *Figure 11.3.*)

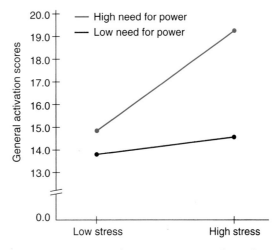

Figure 11.3 General activation scores of people rated high or low in the need for power in situations in which the groups they were leading performed well (*low stress*) or poorly (*high stress*). (From Fodor, E.M. The power motive and reactivity to power stress. *Journal of Personality and Social Psychology,* 1984, *47,* 853–859. Copyright 1984 by the American Psychological Association.)

Need for Affiliation. The **need for affiliation** is a need to maintain social relationships with other people. Shipley and Veroff (1952) have devised a method to assess this need. People with a need for affiliation tend to try to meet other people and establish friendships with them (Crouse and Mehrabian, 1977). In addition, they regard their social skills as important and are likely to become anxious when they are in a situation in which other people are able to assess these skills (Byrne, McDonald, and Mikawa, 1963).

As we saw in the introduction to this section, Atkinson, McClelland, and other theorists believe that the strength of the motivation to perform a particular task is a product of three variables: motives, skills, and values. Motives are stable personality variables, but skills and values depend on the particular task and the goal to which it leads. Constantian (1981) examined the interactions of two of these variables: motives and values. She measured people's need for affiliation (a motive) and the degree to which they valued solitude and being with others. She reasoned that people who scored high in need for affiliation and valued solitude more than being with others would spend more time than most people writing to friends, because this activity would permit them to strengthen their ties with other people while preserving their solitude.

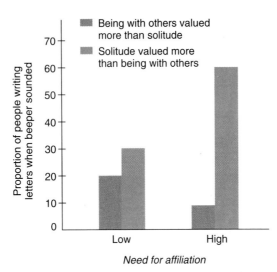

Figure 11.4 The results of the "beeper" study investigating the interaction between the need for affiliation and relative valuation of solitude and being with others. (Adapted from McClelland, 1985; based on data from Constantian, 1981.)

To test her hypothesis, she had people wear an electronic beeper on which they were paged seven times a day, at random intervals. When they were paged, they had to fill out a written report on what they were doing and thinking at the time. The results confirmed her hypothesis: People who had a strong need for affiliation but who valued solitude more than being with others did indeed spend significantly more time writing letters. (See *Figure 11.4*.)

A Hierarchy of Needs

Abraham Maslow (1908–1970) suggests that human behavior can be motivated by a hierarchy of needs. These needs are innate, although most of the ways in which they may be gratified must be learned. Failure to gratify a need will result in a psychological or physiological dysfunction; the need will remain important to the person until it is satisfied. Conversely, a need that is consistently gratified will cease to be important, and growth of the individual can occur, with other, less primitive needs becoming important. Healthy growth, then, is a shifting of the relative importance of needs from the most primitive to the most advanced—the most "human."

According to Maslow, the hierarchy contains five classes of basic needs. (See *Figure 11.5*.) *Physiological needs* include the needs for food, water, warmth, and sexual contact. Deprivation of physiological needs causes illness. Pre-

occupation with these needs (because of difficulty in gratifying them) blocks growth. For example, impoverished people living under conditions of near starvation will be unable to engage in higher forms of human activity, such as philosophy or art. *Safety needs* include the needs for security, dependency, freedom from fear, and a stable and structured environment. Insufficient gratification of safety needs will lead to a preoccupation with them and possibly to various forms of neurosis. *Needs for belongingness and love* include a striving for strong interpersonal relations with a lover and with a family group or clan. Prolonged deprivation of the needs for belongingness and love lead to feelings of rejection and loneliness. *Need for esteem* includes the need to feel competent and in control of one's own life (self-esteem) and a desire to be well regarded by other people. A person who fails to gratify the need for esteem will develop feelings of inferiority and helplessness.

Need for self-actualization is the final need, which can be fulfilled only if the others have been satisfied. This last need is the most difficult to define. In Maslow's own words, "What a man *can* be, he *must* be. He must be true to his own nature. [Self-actualization is a] desire to become more and more what one idiosyncratically is, to become everything that one is capable of becoming" (1970, p. 46). According to Maslow, a self-actualizing person has a more efficient perception of reality; demonstrates greater acceptance of self, others, and nature; is more spontaneous; pays more attention to problems outside himself or herself; is more comfortable with solitude and privacy; shows greater independence from culture and environment; appreciates a variety of experiences; identifies fully with humanity; engages in more profound interpersonal relationships; is more

Figure 11.5 Maslow's hierarchy of needs.

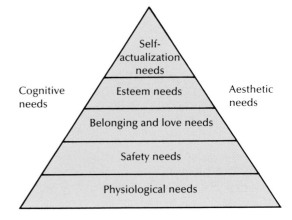

What factors are responsible for Mother Teresa's decision to dedicate her life to the poor people of India? Maslow would refer to her as a self-actualizing person.

creative; and has a more philosophical sense of humor.

As a prescription for living one's life, Maslow's description of the self-actualizing person has much to recommend it. All of us would like to have a more efficient perception of reality, a greater adaptation to the environment, greater spontaneity and creativity, and so on. Readers of Maslow's works are likely to come away feeling that they should try to make better persons of themselves.

However, Maslow's theory is inherently untestable; its concepts are not well defined and are not susceptible to experimental verification. We cannot predict from Maslow's theory how a particular person would behave in a particular situation. For example, Maslow asserts that a person must be true to his or her own nature. But exactly what is a person's true nature, and how can we ever know when it is achieved? Maslow and his followers would not be troubled by this uncertainty, because in their view experimentation is not an appropriate way to study human behavior. But if we cannot perform controlled observations, we cannot determine whether the theory is correct. Lacking specific definitions and criteria, we can never evaluate it.

3 Some people work hard even though the rewards for their work seem to occur very seldom; we refer to these people as well motivated. They exhibit **perseverance:** They continue to perform, even though their work is not regularly reinforced. Others give up easily or perhaps never try. Understanding the effects of reinforcement helps us explain why some people persevere and others do not.

Effects of Intermittent Reinforcement. We saw in Chapter 4 that when an organism's behavior is no longer reinforced, the behavior eventually ceases, or extinguishes. If the behavior was previously reinforced every time it occurred, extinction is very rapid. However, if it was previously reinforced only intermittently, the behavior persists for a long time. Intermittent reinforcement leads to perseverance, even when reinforcers are no longer received.

Many human behaviors are reinforced on intermittent schedules that require the performance of long sequences of behaviors over long intervals of time. A person's previous experience with various schedules of reinforcement probably affects how long and how hard the person will work between occasions of reinforcement. If all attempts at a particular endeavor are reinforced (or if none are), the person is unlikely to pursue a long and difficult project that includes the endeavor. If we knew more about a person's previous history with various schedules of reinforcement, we would probably know more about his or her ability to persevere when the going gets difficult (that is, when reinforcements become scanty).

The Role of Conditioned Reinforcement. Another phenomenon that affects the tendency to persevere is conditioned reinforcement. When stimuli are associated with reinforcers, they eventually acquire reinforcing properties of their own. For example, the sound of the food dispenser reinforces the behavior of a rat being trained to press a lever.

Motivation is not merely a matter of wanting to do well and to work hard. It also involves the ability to be reinforced by the immediate products of the work being done. If a person has regularly been exposed to particular stimuli in association with reinforcers, that person's behavior can be reinforced by those stimuli. In addition, if the person has learned how to recognize self-produced stimuli as conditioned reinforcers, the performance of the behaviors that produce them will be "self-reinforcing." For example, you will recall the schoolgirl I mentioned in Chapter 4 who tirelessly practiced writing the letters of the alphabet. She did so because she had learned to recognize the letters and had previously been praised by her teacher (and perhaps by her parents, as well) for producing letters that looked the way they should. Thus, the production of properly formed letters provided a conditioned reinforcer, which kept her working. As you learned earlier, the usual name for this process is *satisfaction*.

Intrinsic Motivation. Because most examples of reinforcement involve something that happens after an organism performs a task, people often tend to conceive of reinforcement as something separate from the task. However, as we saw in the previous section, performance of a task can be its own reward. This phenomenon is often referred to as **intrinsic motivation** because the reinforcement is an intrinsic part of the task itself. Some intrinsic reinforcers, such as the satisfaction the little girl derived from writing the letters properly, are conditioned reinforcers. Other intrinsic reinforcers are probably effective for other reasons, such as their novelty or the control they permit the organism to exert on its environment; video games and the authority to boss other people around are good examples of these. (As we will see, "making things happen" appears to be intrinsically reinforcing.)

Undermining of Intrinsic Motivation. Researchers have discovered that *extrinsic reinforcers*—those delivered to the subject after performing a task—can often make the task become less intrinsically reinforcing. That is, extrinsic reinforcement can often result in **undermining of intrinsic motivation.**

One of the most famous experiments demonstrating the undermining of intrinsic motivation was performed by Lepper, Greene, and Nisbett (1973). These investigators visited a nursery school and provided children with paper and a set of colored felt-tipped pens, which were not normally available. The children were tested individually. The experimenter gave the paper and pens to a child and watched the child draw for six minutes. Then some children were given an extrinsic reinforcer: a three-by-five-inch card with "Good Player Award" inscribed on it and containing a large gold star with a red ribbon. The experimenter wrote the child's name and school on the card and let the child place the card on a bulletin board for the rest of the class

to see. The children's behavior made it clear that the "Good Player Award" pleased them very much.

Some children received the extrinsic reinforcer as a surprise; they had no idea it would be presented. Other children were led to expect it; before they began to draw pictures with the felt-tipped pens, they were told someone had "brought along a few of these Good Player Awards to give to boys and girls who will help him out by drawing some pictures for him. See? It's got a big gold star and a bright red ribbon, and there's a place here for your name and your school."

The experiment consisted of three groups: children who were "bribed" to draw pictures, and two groups of children who drew pictures on their own accord, presumably because doing so was intrinsically reinforcing. One of these two groups received an unexpected reward, and the other did not. Several days later, the experimenters returned and unobtrusively watched the children to see whether they chose to play with the felt-tipped pens, which the teacher, under the experimenters' direction, placed on a table. The experimenters recorded the amount of time each child spent playing with the pens. The results are shown in *Figure 11.6.*

You can see from the figure that an unexpected award slightly increased the time the children spent using the pens in the follow-up session. However, the children who were "bribed" to draw appeared to have become

Figure 11.6 Percentage of time spent playing with felt-tipped pens as a function of expected or unexpected awards. (Based on data of Lepper, M.R., Greene, D., and Nisbett, R.E. *Journal of Personality and Social Psychology,* 1973, *28,* 129–137.

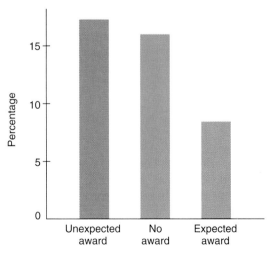

much less interested in the pens; that is, the extrinsic reinforcement undermined intrinsic motivation. The children who made drawings because they were being "bribed" to do so may have concluded (perhaps not consciously) that they did not much like drawing pictures with felt-tipped pens. After all, their previous experience told them that things you do for bribes are generally things you do not want to do. (This explanation is derived from *attribution theory*, which is described in more detail in Chapter 17.)

Because reinforcers are used to train children, pay workers, and change the behavior of people with behavior problems, the fact that extrinsic reinforcement can sometimes undermine intrinsic motivation has led to serious concern among researchers in the fields of education, management, and behavior therapy. Some investigators have even suggested that extrinsic reinforcement should be avoided, because it will make people work less hard. However, everyday observations reveal that extrinsic reinforcement can *increase* intrinsic motivation as well as decrease it. For example, if a person with a flair for telling jokes regularly gets laughs when he does so, the reinforcers (laughs) will certainly increase rather than decrease his interest in telling jokes. Subsequent research has confirmed such observations.

The most important characteristic of an extrinsic reinforcer is that it be *based on the person's performance*. That is, if reinforcers are given when the person's performance improves, the task will tend to become more intrinsically motivating. However, if the reinforcers are given merely for doing the task—regardless of whether the task is done poorly or well—then intrinsic motivation will be undermined. Deci (1975) suggested that reinforcement can imply that the subject is being controlled by the experimenter, which most people perceive as aversive, because people in general do not like to be controlled by others. However, when the reinforcement implies that a person is performing competently, it can increase intrinsic motivation. Deci (1971) found that verbal reinforcement ("that's very good; it's much better than average for this [puzzle]") led to large increases in the time people spent working on the puzzles during their free time.

Note that *most* reinforcement is contingent on people's performance. If we tell a story well, we are rewarded by signs of interest in other people. When we make something, the quality of the product is determined by how skillfully and diligently we work. And those things we do well we tend to enjoy. The undermining of in-

Reinforcement is usually contingent on our own performance; the quality of a product and the pride we derive from it is determined by a person's skill and diligence.

trinsic motivation appears to occur only when events imply that we are doing something because someone else is making us do it.

Preference for Free Choice. Even though scientists must assume that the world is a cause-and-effect system controlled by stable laws, most people (even scientists) feel as if they are able to choose what they do and resist feeling that they are being coerced. Suppose that we visit a restaurant and read the menu. We consider the alternatives and then decide what to order. We feel as if we are free to choose; and even after we place our order, we believe that we *could have chosen something different*. Scientific determinism says otherwise: Our choice was determined by the state of our nervous system at the time we placed our order, which reflects everything about our genetic makeup and our past history, including the foods we like and dislike, the foods we have eaten recently, the amount of money we have to spend, and so on.

Because people feel as if they are free to choose, it is up to the scientist to investigate the nature and possible causes of that feeling. Many studies have shown that we tend to value activities that we choose more than those chosen for us. Even the *illusion* of choice increases the value of an activity. For example, Swann and Pittman (1977) brought elementary schoolchildren into a room containing several interesting toys and games. Some children were simply instructed to begin playing a drawing game with felt-tipped pens; others were told that they could choose but were, in fact, subtly persuaded to play the drawing game. Later, when the children were permitted to play with whatever toy or game they chose, those in the "free-choice" group played with the felt-tipped pens more than those who had simply been instructed to do so. Having "chosen" to play with the pens, the children preferred this task when they actually were free to choose.

Failure to Persist: Learned Helplessness. A large body of evidence suggests that organisms can learn that they are powerless to affect their own destinies. Maier and Seligman (1976) reported a series of experiments demonstrating that animals can learn that their own behavior *has no effect* on an environmental event. This result is exactly the opposite of what has been assumed to be the basis of learning. All the examples of learning and conditioning cited so far have been instances in which one event predicts the occurrence of another. **Learned helplessness** involves learning that an aversive event *cannot* be avoided or escaped.

Overmeier and Seligman (1967) conducted the basic experiment. They placed a dog in an apparatus in which it received electrical shocks that could not be avoided; nothing the animal did would prevent the shocks. Next, they placed the dog in another apparatus in which the animal received a series of trials in which a warning stimulus was followed by an electrical shock. In this case the animal could avoid the shocks simply by stepping over a small barrier to the other side of the apparatus. Dogs in the control group learned to step over the barrier and avoid the shock, but dogs that had previously received inescapable shocks in the other apparatus failed to learn. They just squatted in the corner and took the shock, as if they had learned that it made no difference what they did. They had learned to be helpless.

Seligman (1975) has suggested that the phenomenon of learned helplessness has important implications for behavior. When people have experiences that lead to learned helplessness, they become depressed and their motivational level decreases. The change in motivation occurs because the helplessness training lowers their expectation that trying to perform a task will bring success. As we saw in the section on achievement motivation, the level of expectation of success is one of the variables that affects motivation; thus, a decrease in this expectation leads to a decrease in motivation to perform. Seligman also suggested that learned helplessness has the characteristics of a personality trait; that is, people who have had major experiences with insoluble tasks will not try hard to succeed in other types of tasks, including ones they could otherwise have solved.

Seligman's theory of learned helplessness has been challenged by other investigators, who have explained the phenomenon in other ways. The issue is whether learning to be helpless in a particular situation generalizes only to similar situations or to a wide variety of them. For example, McReynolds (1980) observed that when people experience a situation in which reinforcements are not contingent on their responding, their responding extinguishes. If the situation then changes to one in which responding will be reinforced, the people will continue not to respond *unless they perceive that the schedule of reinforcement has changed.* The more similar the second situation is to the first, the more likely it is that the person will act "helpless." This explanation describes the phenomenon of learned helplessness as a failure to discriminate between the condition under which responding is reinforced and the condition under which it is not. Further research will have to determine whether learned helplessness is, as Seligman asserts, a stable personality trait or whether it can be explained by the principles of instrumental conditioning.

INTERIM SUMMARY

What Is Motivation?

Motivation is a tendency to perform a class of behaviors that bring an organism in contact with an appetitive stimulus or move it away from an aversive one. Stimuli that alter motivation affect the nature, strength, and persistence of behavior. One important category of motivated behaviors are involved with internal regulation—with the maintenance of homeostasis. Regulatory systems include four features: a system variable (the variable that is regulated), a set point (the optimal value of the system variable), a detector to measure the system variable, and a correctional mechanism (in this case, a behavior) to change it. Formerly, psychologists believed that aversive drives were produced by deprivation and that reinforcement was a result of drive reduction. However, the fact that a large variety of stimuli could serve as reinforcers led to an unacceptable number of hypothetical drives. In addition, many reinforcers increase drive rather than reduce it. Thus, most psychologists doubt the validity of the drive reduction hypothesis of reinforcement.

Motivation obviously involves learning. In fact, stimuli that have been associated with reinforcing stimuli can themselves motivate and reinforce behavior. The anticipation of reinforcement, which serves also to motivate behavior, is referred to as incentive.

Because high levels of drive or arousal (such as those caused by painful stimuli) can be aversive, several investigators suggested the optimum-level theory of motivation and reinforcement. This theory suggests that organisms strive to attain optimum levels of arousal; thus, reinforcement and punishment are seen as two sides of the same coin. However, another problem remains: The optimum level can be determined only by observing the organism's behavior and therefore cannot be used as an *explanation* of that behavior.

Beginning with Murray's inventory of human needs and his development of the Thematic Apperception Test, theorists have tried to determine the role of social needs and motives. McClelland, Atkinson, and their students suggest that behavior is determined by the joint effects of motives, skills, and values. The needs for achievement, power, and affiliation have received the most study.

Maslow suggests that the various sources of motivation can be arranged hierarchically. Physiological needs are found at the most basic and primitive level, followed by safety needs, needs for belongingness and love, need for esteem, and finally, need for self-actualization. Although little research has been done on Maslow's theory, it does point out that the factors that motivate a person's behavior depend strongly on the person's economic, social, and occupational status. A person living in a society in which food, clothing, and housing are difficult to obtain or a person living in a region beset by civil strife will obviously be motivated by different needs than an upper-class resident of a highly industrialized country.

Perseverance, an important characteristic of motivation, has received much attention from psychologists. Two factors appear to control perseverance. One is the organism's previous history with intermittent reinforcement. The second factor is its opportunity to develop behaviors that produce conditioned reinforcers, such as the satisfaction we derive when we complete the little steps that constitute a long and difficult task. In addition, most people prefer behaviors they are free to choose, even if the freedom of choice is actually an illusion. Intrinsic motivation can be undermined by extrinsic reinforcers, but only if they are unrelated to the person's performance. If people receive reinforcers according to their level of accomplishment, such reinforcers will increase, not decrease, intrinsic motivation.

Some experiences can diminish an organism's perseverance and its ability to cope with new situations, as the phenomenon of learned helplessness demonstrates. Psychologists still dispute the causes of this phenomenon. However, learned helplessness is of practical importance because it may well be a factor in psychological disorders such as depression. ∎

EATING

4 Clearly, eating is one of the most important things we do—and it can also be one of the most pleasurable. Much of what an animal learns to do is motivated by the constant struggle to obtain food; thus, the need to ingest undoubtedly shaped the evolutionary development of our own species.

Simply put, motivation to eat is aroused when there is a deficit in the body's supply of stored nutrients, and it is satisfied by a meal that replenishes this supply. A person who exercises vigorously uses up the stored nutrients more rapidly and consequently must eat more food. Thus, the amount of food a person normally eats is regulated by need. But what, exactly, causes a person to start eating, and what brings the meal to an end? These are simple questions, yet the answers are complex. There is no single physiological measure that can tell us reliably whether a person should be hungry. Hunger is determined by a variety of conditions; so instead of asking what the *cause* of hunger is, we must ask what the *causes* are.

What Starts a Meal?

Although hunger and satiety appear to be two sides of the same coin, investigations have shown that the factors that cause a meal to begin are different from the ones that end it. Therefore, I will consider these two sets of factors separately.

Cultural and Social Factors.

Most of us in Western society eat three times a day. When the time for a meal comes, we get hungry and eat, consuming a relatively constant amount of food. The regular pattern of food intake is not determined solely by biological need; it is at least partially determined by habit. If you have ever had to miss a meal, you may have noticed that your hunger did not continue to grow indefinitely. Instead, it subsided some time after the meal would normally have been eaten, only to grow again just before the scheduled time of the next one. Hunger, then, can wax and wane according to a learned schedule.

Besides learning *when* to eat, we learn *what* to eat. Most of us would refuse to eat fresh clotted seal blood, but many Eskimos consider it a delicacy. What we accept as food depends on our culture. Our tastes are also shaped by habits acquired early in life. A child whose family eats nothing but simple meat-and-potato dishes will probably not become a venturesome gastronome.

Our immediate environment also affects our hunger. We are much more likely to feel hungry, and to consume more food, in the presence of companions who are doing the same. Even a chicken that has finished its meal will start eating again if it is placed among other chickens who are busily eating. Similarly, you may sometimes join some friends at their table just after you have eaten. You say, no, you don't want to eat . . . well, perhaps just a bite to keep them company—and you eat almost as much as they do.

Physiological Factors.

Cultural and social factors assuredly influence when and how much we eat. But everyone would also agree that the "real" reason for eating must be related to the fact that the body needs nourishment: If all other factors were eliminated, eating would be determined by some internal physiological state. What are the internal factors that cause us to eat?

Many years ago, Cannon and Washburn (1912) suggested that hunger resulted from an empty stomach. The walls of an empty stomach rubbed against each other, producing what we commonly identify as hunger pangs. (Cannon also suggested that thirst was produced by a dry mouth, because a loss of body fluid resulted in a decreased flow of saliva. Some skeptics called Cannon's explanation of hunger and thirst the "spit and rumble theory.") However, removal of the stomach does not abolish hunger pangs. Inglefinger (1944) interviewed patients whose stomach had been removed because of cancer or large ulcers; their esophagi had been attached directly to their small intestines. Because they had no stomachs to catch and hold food, they had to eat small, frequent meals. Despite their lack of a stomach, these people reported the same feelings of hunger and satiety that they had had before the operation.

A more likely cause of hunger is depletion of the body's store of nutrients. The primary fuels for the cells of our body are glucose (a simple sugar) and fatty acids (chemicals produced when fat is broken down). If our digestive system contains food, these nutrients are absorbed into the blood and nourish our cells. But the digestive tract is sometimes empty; in fact, most of us wake up in the morning in that condition. So there has to be a reservoir that stores nutrients to keep the cells of the body nourished when the gut is empty. Indeed, there are two reservoirs—one short-term and the other long-term. The short-term reservoir stores carbohydrates, and the long-term reservoir stores fats.

What and how we eat is determined by cultural factors.

The short-term reservoir is located in the cells of the muscles and the liver, and it is filled with a carbohydrate—a form of animal starch called **glycogen.** When glucose is received from a meal, some of it is used for fuel and some is converted into glycogen and stored in the liver. Our long-term reservoir consists of adipose tissue (fat tissue), which is found beneath the skin and in various locations in the abdomen. Adipose tissue consists of cells capable of absorbing nutrients from the blood, converting them to triglycerides (fats) and storing them. They can expand in size enormously; in fact, the primary physical difference between an obese person and a person of normal weight is the size of their fat cells, which is determined by the amount of triglycerides that these cells contain.

The long-term fat reservoir is obviously what keeps us alive during a prolonged fast.

Once the level of glycogen in our short-term carbohydrate reservoir gets low, fat cells start breaking down fats and releasing fatty acids and a carbohydrate called *glycerol.* The brain primarily lives on glucose, and the rest of the body lives on fatty acids. Glycerol is converted into glucose, so the brain continues to be nourished even after the short-term reservoir is depleted. (See *Figure 11.7.*)

Because glucose is such an important fuel, Mayer (1955a) proposed the **glucostatic hypothesis** of hunger. According to this hypothesis, hunger occurs when the level of glucose in the blood becomes low, presumably after the glycogen in the body's short-term reservoir has been used up. Mayer theorized that this decrease in blood sugar is detected by glucose-sensitive neurons in the brain called **glucostats.** (The term gluco*stat* is analogous to thermo*stat,* except that it refers to the measure-

Figure 11.7 Metabolic pathways when the digestive system contains food and when the digestive system is empty.

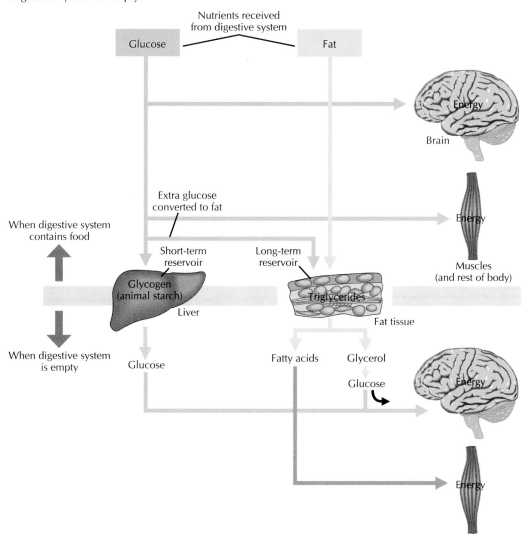

ment of glucose rather than temperature.) Mayer suggested that these detectors activate neural circuits that make a person hungry, thus stimulating the correctional mechanism, eating.

Subsequent evidence suggests that there are two different types of nutrient detectors, which measure the blood level of the two primary nutrients, glucose and fatty acids (Friedman, Tordoff, and Ramirez, 1986). The glucose detectors appear to be located in the liver, but the location of the fatty acid detectors is not yet known (Ritter and Taylor, 1989). Both sets of detectors send information to the brain, and activity of neural circuits there stimulates hunger.

What Stops a Meal?

5 Nutrient detectors sense the fact that the body's supplies of stored energy are getting low by measuring glucose and fatty acids in the blood. Through their connection with the brain these detectors are able to stimulate hunger. But what *ends* hunger? What brings a meal to its finish? Consider what happens when you eat. Your stomach fills with food, and the digestive process begins. However, for a good part of an hour no appreciable amounts of nutrients are absorbed from the intestines into the bloodstream. Therefore, the body's supply of fuel is not replenished until a rather long time after the meal begins. If you were to continue to eat until the nutrients actually entered the bloodstream, your stomach would burst. Therefore, some other detectors must be responsible for stopping the meal.

Although evidence suggests that the primary cause of hunger is not an empty stomach, the primary cause of satiety (that is, the cessation of hunger, caused by eating) seems to be a *full* stomach. Many studies have shown that satiety is caused by entry of a sufficient quantity of nourishing food into the stomach. Therefore, the stomach must contain detectors that sense the presence of food. We have known for a long time that hunger can be abolished by injecting food into an animal's stomach by means of a flexible tube. Even though the animal does not get to taste and smell the food, it will not subsequently eat. More recently, Davis and Campbell (1973) showed how precisely the stomach can measure its contents. The investigators allowed rats to eat their fill and then removed some food from their stomachs. When they let the rats eat again, they ate almost exactly as much as had been taken out.

The stomach appears to contain detectors that inform the brain about the chemical nature of its contents as well as the quantity. The ability to detect the chemical nature of food that has entered the stomach is important, because eating should stop relatively soon if the food is very nutritious but should continue for a longer time if it is not. Deutsch, Young, and Kalogeris (1978) injected either milk or a dilute salt solution into hungry rats' stomachs and thirty minutes later allowed them to eat. The rats that received injections of milk ate less than the ones that received the salt solution. Because the rats could not taste what was put in their stomachs, the effect had to come from detectors there. The nature of these detectors is not known, but they must respond to some chemicals present in food. You can try this experiment: Drink two glasses of water when you are very hungry and see whether they satisfy your appetite.

Obesity

The mechanisms that control eating generally do a good job. When people eat especially nutritious food, they soon learn to eat less. When they begin to exercise more, and hence burn up their store of nutrients faster, they soon start eating more. However, some people do *not* control their eating habits and become too fat or too thin. Does what we have learned about the normal regulation of food intake help us understand these disorders?

Obesity is extremely difficult to treat; the enormous financial success of diet books, fat farms, and weight reduction programs attests to the trouble people have losing weight. Kramer et al. (1989) reported that four to five years after participating in a fifteen-week behavioral weight loss program, fewer than 3 percent of the participants managed to maintain the weight loss they had achieved during the program. Even drastic means such as gastric and intestinal surgery (designed to limit the amount of food that the stomach can hold or to prevent food from being fully digested before it is eliminated) are not the answer. These procedures have risks of their own, often produce unpleasant side effects, and have a failure rate of at least 40 percent (Kral, 1989).

Many psychological variables have been suggested as causes of obesity, including lack of impulse control, poor ability to delay gratification, and maladaptive eating styles (primarily eating too fast). However, in a review of the literature Rodin, Schank, and Striegel-Moore (1989) found that none of these suggestions has received empirical support. Rodin and her colleagues also found that unhappiness and depression seem to be the *effects* of obesity, not its causes, and that dieting behavior seems to make the problem worse. (As we shall see later in this section, repeated bouts of weight loss and gain make subsequent weight loss more difficult to achieve.)

There is no single, all-inclusive explanation for obesity, but there are many partial ones. Four hypotheses are described below.

Habit. Habit plays an important role in the control of food intake. Early in life, when we are most active, we form our ideas about how much food constitutes a meal. Later in life we become less active, but we do not always reduce our food intake accordingly. We fill our plates according to what we think is a proper-sized meal (or perhaps the plate is filled for us), and we eat everything, ignoring the satiety signals that might tell us to stop before the plate is empty.

Metabolism. Some people appear to be destined for obesity; they become fat even though they eat less food than most thin people do. Rose and Williams (1961) studied pairs of people who were matched for weight, height, age, and activity. Yet some of these matched pairs differed by a factor of two in their intake of food (that is, one ate twice as much as the other). These results show clearly that some people convert their food into body tissue (principally fat) very efficiently but others do not. People with an efficient metabolism have difficulty keeping thin; people with an inefficient metabolism can eat large meals without getting fat. In fact, some people must live on a semistarvation diet to maintain their weight at normal levels. In a society that produces an abundance of food but admires thinness, inefficiency in producing fat is a definite advantage.

Differences in metabolism appear to have a hereditary basis. Griffiths and Payne (1976) found that the children of obese parents weighed more than other children, even though they ate less. Stunkard et al. (1986) found that the body weight of a sample of people who had been adopted as infants was highly correlated with their *biological* parents but not with their *adoptive* parents. Thus, a person's weight (presumably closely related to his or her metabolic efficiency) is influenced by genetic factors.

Why are there genetic differences in metabolic efficiency? James and Trayhurn (1981) suggest that under some environmental conditions metabolic efficiency is advantageous. That is, in places where food is only intermittently available in sufficient quantities, being able to stay alive on small amounts of food and to store up extra nutrients in the form of fat when food becomes available for a while is a highly adaptive trait. Therefore, the variability in people's metabolisms may reflect the nature of the environment experienced by their ancestors. For example, physically active lactating women in Gambia manage to maintain their weight on only 1500 calories per day (Whitehead, Rowland, Hutton, Prentice, Müller, and Paul, 1978). This efficiency, which allows people to survive in environments in which food is scarce, can be a disadvantage when food is readily available, because it promotes obesity.

Another factor—this one nonhereditary—can influence people's metabolism. Many obese people diet and then relapse, thus undergoing large changes in body weight. Some investigators have suggested that starvation causes the body's metabolism to become more efficient. For example, Brownell, Greenwood, Stellar, and Shrager (1986) fed rats a diet that made them become obese and then restricted their food intake until their body weights returned to normal. Then they made the rats fat again and reduced their food intake again. The second time, the rats became fat much faster and lost their weight much slower. Clearly, the experience of gaining and losing large amounts of body weight altered the animals' metabolic efficiency.

Steen, Oppliger, and Brownell (1988) obtained evidence that the same phenomenon (which we can call the "yo-yo" effect) takes place in humans. They measured the resting metabolic rate in two groups of high school wrestlers: those who fasted just before a meet and binged afterwards, and those who did not. (The motive for fasting just before a match is to qualify for a lower-weight group, where the competition is presumably less challenging.) The investigators found that wrestlers who fasted and binged had a resting metabolic rate 14 percent lower than those who did not. Possibly, these people will have difficulty maintaining a normal body weight as they get older.

Developmental Factors. Events that occur early in life can predispose a person toward obesity. Whatever its cause, obesity during childhood is a very strong predictor of obesity during adulthood (Stunkard and Burt, 1967). One suggestion is that juvenile obesity predisposes a person toward adult obesity through an increase in the number of fat cells. Obese people have, on the average, five times as many fat cells as

Obesity in childhood usually leads to obesity in adulthood.

nonobese people (Hirsch and Knittle, 1970). In addition, studies show that rats fed a fattening diet early in life will grow an increased number of fat cells. In contrast, if they are fattened up during adulthood, their fat cells will grow in size but not increase in number (Knittle and Hirsch, 1968). Perhaps juvenile obesity causes an increase in the number of fat cells, which makes it difficult for the person to lose weight later in life.

Another event that has been shown to predispose people toward obesity is early prenatal malnutrition. During the winter of 1944–1945 people in the Netherlands suffered a severe shortage of food. Even pregnant women received an extremely meager diet. A follow-up study of draftees in the Dutch armed forces showed that men whose mothers had been malnourished during the first two trimesters of pregnancy were twice as likely to become obese later in life (Ravelli, Stein, and Susser, 1976). These findings were later confirmed by a laboratory experiment using rats (Jones and Friedman, 1982). This phenomenon may help explain why obesity is seen more often in people of lower socioeconomic status (Goldblatt, Moore, and Stunkard, 1968); perhaps mothers in this group are more likely to receive inadequate nutrition during pregnancy.

Activity. Obviously, people who eat a constant number of calories each day will gain weight if they exercise less and lose weight if they exercise more. A study reported by Mayer (1955b) confirms that activity has a strong effect on eating and body weight. Mayer and his colleagues studied a group of men in a racially homogeneous community in India. They measured food intake and body weight and estimated the amount of energy the men expended in their jobs. People who expended at least moderate amounts of energy (such as clerks, mechanics, drivers, and carriers) all weighed about the same, although the carriers, who worked the hardest, ate more food than the clerks, who expended the least physical energy. These people matched their food intake to their expenditure of energy. (See *Figure 11.8.*)

However, the relation between food intake and physical activity broke down in the case of people with sedentary occupations: head clerks, supervisors, and shop owners. These people expended very little energy but ate almost as much as the carriers, who worked the hardest. Their weight was correspondingly higher: The shop owners weighed approximately 45 percent more than the carriers. (See *Figure 11.8.*)

The results suggest that relative inactivity leads to obesity. Of course, we must recognize that the most sedentary people also had the highest incomes, which could certainly influence their diet. An observational study like this one does not permit us to determine causes unequivocally.

Anorexia Nervosa

Most people, if they have an eating problem, tend to overeat. However, some people, especially young adolescent women, have the opposite problem: They suffer from **anorexia nervosa,** a disorder characterized by a severe decrease in eating. The literal meaning of the word *anorexia* suggests a loss of appetite, but people with this disorder generally do *not* lose their appetite. Their limited intake of food occurs despite intense preoccupation with food and its preparation. They may enjoy preparing meals for others to consume, collect recipes, and even hoard food that they do not eat. They have an intense fear of becoming obese, and this fear continues even if they become dangerously thin. Many exercise by cycling, running, or almost constant walking and pacing. Sometimes, their control of food intake fails, and they gorge themselves with food, a phenomenon known as **bulimia** (from *bous,* "ox," and *limos,* "hun-

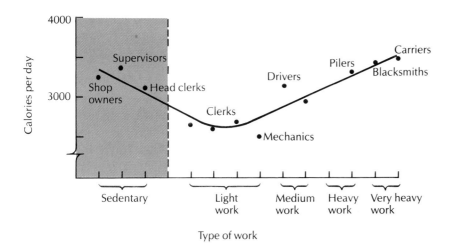

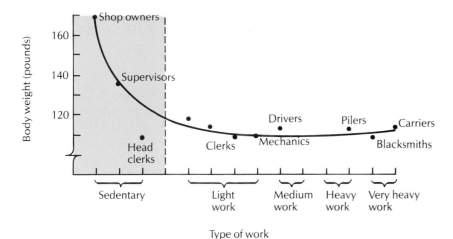

Figure 11.8 Food intake (calories per day) and body weight of people with various occupations in a town in India. (From Mayer, J., in *Weight Control: A Collection of Papers Presented at the Weight Control Symposium,* edited by E.S. Eppright, P. Swanson, and C.A. Iverson. Ames, Iowa: Iowa State College Press, 1955. Reprinted with permission.)

Karen Carpenter, shortly before she died of heart failure, apparently precipitated by her anorexia nervosa.

ger"). These episodes are usually followed by self-induced vomiting or use of laxatives, along with feelings of depression and guilt (Halmi, 1978; Mawson, 1974).

The fact that anorexia nervosa is seen primarily in young women has prompted both biological and social explanations. Most psychologists favor the latter, concluding that the emphasis our society places on slimness—especially in women—is responsible for this disorder. However, the success of psychotherapy is not especially encouraging (Patton, 1989). About one patient in thirty dies of the disorder. Many anorexics suffer from osteoporosis, and bone fractures are common. When the weight loss becomes severe enough, they cease menstruating. Two disturbing reports (Artmann et al., 1985; Lankenau et al., 1985) indicate that CT scans of anorexic patients show evidence of loss of brain tissue. Some of the loss, but not all, apparently returns to normal after recovery.

Another possibility is that changes in a young woman's endocrine status alter her metabolism or the neural mechanisms involved in feeding. Indeed, the female sex hormones progesterone and estradiol have been shown to affect food intake and body weight of laboratory animals through their interactions with receptors for these hormones located in various organs, including the brain and adipose tissue (Wade and Gray, 1979). However, no evidence yet shows that anorexia nervosa in humans is related to this phenomenon.

Many studies have found evidence of metabolic differences between anorexics and people of normal weight. But because prolonged fasting and the use of laxatives have many effects, interpreting these differences is difficult (Halmi, 1978).

Anorexia nervosa is a serious condition; understanding its causes is more than an academic matter. We can hope that research on the biological and social control of feeding and metabolism will help us understand this puzzling and dangerous disorder.

INTERIM SUMMARY

Eating

Hunger is the name we give to the feeling that precedes and accompanies an important regulatory behavior: eating. Eating begins for both social and physiological reasons. Physiologically, the most important event appears to be the detection of a lowered supply of nutrients available in the blood. When the digestive system is empty, these nutrients come from the short-term store of glycogen and the long-term store of fat. Detectors in the liver measure glucose level, and detectors elsewhere in the body measure the level of fatty acids. Both sets of detectors inform the brain of the need for food and arouse hunger. We stop eating for different reasons. Because it takes a considerable amount of time for a meal to be digested, another set of detectors must cause satiety. These detectors, which appear to be located in the walls of the stomach, are able to monitor both the quality and the quantity of the food that has just been eaten.

Sometimes, normal control mechanisms fail, and people gain too much weight. The one conclusion we can be sure about is that obesity has many causes. For any individual, genetic and environmental factors may interact to cause the person's weight to deviate from the norm. Thus, no single program can help all people lose weight. People differ genetically in the efficiency

of their metabolism; and in a society where food is cheap and plentiful, this efficiency easily leads to obesity. Particular eating habits, especially those learned during infancy, can override the physiological signals that would otherwise produce satiety. Experiences such as repeated fasting and refeeding (the yo-yo effect) or prenatal malnutrition can alter metabolism and thus affect hunger, and low levels of physical activity are often accompanied by overeating. More research on the causes of obesity may lead to ways of determining which factors are responsible for an individual's excessive weight.

Anorexia nervosa is a serious, even life-threatening, disorder. Most anorexic patients are young women. Although they avoid eating, they often remain preoccupied with food. Studies have found metabolic differences, but we cannot determine whether these differences are the causes or the effects of the disorder. Researchers are beginning to study possible abnormalities in the regulation of chemicals in the brain that seem to play a role in normal control of feeding to see whether medical treatments can be discovered. ∎

SEXUAL BEHAVIOR

[6] The motivation to engage in sexual behavior can be very strong (I doubt that most people need for me to tell them that). However, sexual behavior is not motivated by a physiological need, the way eating is. Because we must perform certain behaviors in order to reproduce, the process of natural selection has ensured that our brains are constructed in such a way as to cause enough of us to mate with each other that the species will survive.

Effects of Erotic Imagery in Men and Women

Men and women respond in basically the same way to visual and tactile sexual stimuli, but they appear to differ in the kinds of stimuli, imagery, and fantasies they consider erotic. Sigusch, Schmidt, Reinfeld, and Wiedemann-Sutor (1970) and Schmidt and Sigusch (1970) studied the attitudes and sexual responses of fifty men and women toward sexual stimuli. They measured sexual arousal by monitoring penile erections or vaginal lubrication with electronic sensing equipment.

The subjects looked at pictures of couples in romantic situations (showing affection and kissing) and in explicitly sexual situations (en-

Males usually prefer explicitly sexual pictures, whereas females generally prefer pictures of romantic situations.

gaging in intercourse). The women reported finding the pictures of romantic situations sexually arousing, and physiological measurements confirmed their statements. However, most of them reported finding the sexually explicit pictures distasteful. Presumably, women learn this distaste from their culture; many women are taught that it is not proper to show an interest in erotic materials. Thus, some women are likely

to avoid these materials, even though they can become as stimulated by them as men. The men reported the pictures of sexual behavior to be arousing (and the physiological measurements agreed); but unlike the women, they were not aroused by the romantic pictures.

Money and Ehrhardt (1972) described the kinds of stimuli to which men and women respond. If a man responds sexually to a picture of an attractive woman, he tends to imagine her as a sex object; figuratively, he takes her out of the picture and uses her. A woman may also respond to an erotic picture of another woman, but in her case she imagines herself in the woman's situation. In contrast, a picture of a naked man is generally not arousing to heterosexual men *or* women.

Masters and Johnson (1979) interviewed heterosexual and homosexual men and women and found that the subject matter of their sexual fantasies bore striking similarities, although the gender of the sex partner in the fantasies differed according to the person's orientation. (See ***Table 11.2.***)

Effects of Sex Hormones on Behavior

Effects of Androgens. As we saw in Chapter 10, androgens such as testosterone are necessary for male sexual development. During prenatal development (while still in the uterus), the testes of male fetuses secrete testosterone, which causes the male sex organs to develop. This hormone also affects the development of the brain. The prenatal effects of sex hormones are called **organizational effects** because

Table 11.2   The most prevalent types of sexual fantasies, by sex and sexual preference

Males	*Females*
Heterosexual	
Replacement of established partner	Replacement of established partner
Forced sexual encounter with female	Forced sexual encounter with male
Observation of sexual activity	Observation of sexual activity
Homosexual encounter	Idyllic encounter with unknown male
Group sex experience	Lesbian encounter
Homosexual	
Imagery of male sexual anatomy	Forced sexual encounter
Forced sexual encounter with male	Idyllic encounter with established partner
Heterosexual encounter	Heterosexual encounter
Idyllic encounter with unknown male	Recall of past sexual experience
Group sex experience	Sadistic imagery

Source: Adapted from Masters, W.H., and Johnson, V.E. *Homosexuality in Perspective.* Boston: Little, Brown, 1979.

they alter the organization of the sex organs and the brain. Studies with laboratory animals have shown that if the organizational effects of androgens on brain development are prevented, the animal later fails to exhibit male sexual behavior. In addition, males cannot have an erection and engage in sexual intercourse unless testosterone is present in adulthood. These effects are called **activational effects** because the hormone activates sex organs and brain circuits that have already developed.

Davidson, Camargo, and Smith (1979) performed a carefully controlled double-blind study of the activational effects of testosterone on the sexual behavior of men whose testes failed to secrete normal amounts of androgens. The men were given monthly injections of a placebo or one of two different dosages of a long-lasting form of testosterone. The effect of testosterone on total number of erections and attempts at intercourse during the month following the injection was large and statistically significant, in comparison with the performance of controls, and the larger dosage produced more of an effect than the smaller dosage. Thus, we may conclude that testosterone definitely affects male sexual performance.

If a man is castrated (has the testes removed, usually because of injury or disease), his sex drive will inevitably decline. Usually, he first loses the ability to ejaculate, and then he loses the ability to achieve an erection (Bermant and Davidson, 1974). But studies have shown that some men lose these abilities soon after castration, whereas others retain at least some level of sexual potency for many months. Injections or pills of testosterone quickly restore potency. Possibly the amount of sexual experience prior to castration affects performance afterward. Rosenblatt and Aronson (1958) found that male cats who had copulated frequently before castration were able to perform sexually for much longer periods of time after the surgery. Perhaps the same is true for men.

Environment can affect testosterone levels: Sexual activity raises the level, and stress lowers it. Even the *anticipation* of sexual activity can affect testosterone secretion. One careful observer (Anonymous, 1970) worked on a remote island, far from any women, and measured his beard growth every day by shaving with an electric razor and weighing the clippings. Just before his periodic trips to the mainland his beard grew faster. Because rate of beard growth depends upon testosterone level, the anticipation of sexual activity appears to have increased his testosterone production.

Testosterone affects sex drive, but it does not determine the *object* of sexual desire. A homosexual man who receives injections of testosterone will not suddenly become interested in women. If testosterone has any effect, it will be to increase his interest in sexual contact with other men.

Although evidence shows clearly that testosterone affects men's sexual performance, we humans are uniquely emancipated from the biological effects of hormones in a special way. Not all human sexual activity requires an erect penis. A man does not need testosterone to be able to kiss and caress his partner or to engage in other noncoital activities. Men who have had to be castrated and who cannot receive injections of testosterone for medical reasons report continued sexual activity with their partners. We must remember that for humans sexual activity is not limited to coitus.

Androgens appear to activate sex drive in women as well as men. Salmon and Geist (1943) reported that testosterone has a stimulating effect on sexual desire and on the sensitivity of the clitoris to touch. Persky et al. (1978) studied the sexual activity of eleven married couples ranging in age from twenty-one to thirty-one. The subjects kept daily records of their sexual feelings and behavior, and the experimenters measured their blood levels of testosterone twice a week. Couples were more likely to engage in intercourse when the woman's testosterone level was at a peak. In addition, the women reported finding intercourse more gratifying during these times.

Effects of Progesterone and Estrogen. In most species of mammals the hormones estradiol and progesterone have strong effects on female sexual behavior. The levels of these two sex hormones fluctuate during the menstrual cycle of primates and the **estrous cycle** of other female mammals. The difference between these cycles is primarily that the lining of the primate uterus—but not that of other mammals—builds up during the first part of the cycle and sloughs off at the end. A female mammal of a nonprimate species—for example, a laboratory rat—will receive the advances of a male only when the levels of estradiol and progesterone in the blood are high. This condition occurs around the time of ovulation, when copulation is likely to make her become pregnant. During this time the female will stand still while the male approaches her. If he attempts to mount her, she will arch her back and move her tail to the side, giving him access to her genitalia. In fact, an estrous female often does not wait for the male to take the initiative; she engages in seductive behaviors such as hopping around and wiggling her ears. These behaviors usually induce sexual activity by the male (McClintock and Adler, 1978).

A female rat whose ovaries have been removed is normally nonreceptive—even hostile—to the advances of an eager male. However, if she is given injections of estradiol and progesterone to duplicate the hormonal condition of the receptive part of her estrous cycle, she will receive the male or go after him. In contrast, women and other female primates are unique among mammals in their sexual activity: They are potentially willing to engage in sexual behavior at any time during their reproductive cycle. Some investigators have suggested that this phenomenon made monogamous relationships possible; because the male can look forward to his mate's receptivity at any time during her menstrual cycle, he is less likely to look for other partners. However, some species form monogamous-pair bonds even though they mate during only one season of the year, whereas most primate species are promiscuous.

Unlike that of most other female mammals, women's sex drive does not depend on the presence of ovarian hormones. During menopause, when the ovaries cease to secrete hormones, women often experience various uncomfortable symptoms, such as hot flashes, headaches, and depression, which can temporarily interfere with sex drive. The loss of estradiol tends to make the walls of the vagina thinner, and the decrease in vaginal secretions can make intercourse somewhat painful. However, with the use of a lubricant jelly, intercourse can be just as satisfying as it was before the ovaries ceased to function. Masters and Johnson (1966) reported that frequent intercourse itself tends to retard the effects of menopause on the vagina. In fact, with pregnancy no longer a possibility, many women report an *increase* in desire for sexual activity.

Sexual Orientation

[7] When people reach puberty, the effects of sex hormones on their maturing bodies and on their brains increase their interest in sexual activity. As sexual interest increases, most people develop a special interest in members of the other sex—they develop a heterosexual orientation. Why does opposite-sex attraction occur? And why does same-sex attraction sometimes occur? As we shall see, research has not yet provided definite answers to these questions, but it has provided some hints.

Homosexual behavior (engaging in sexual activity with members of the same sex; from the Greek *homos,* meaning "the same") is seen in male and female animals of many different species. The widespread occurrence of homosexual behavior means that we should not refer to it as "unnatural." However, humans are apparently the only species in which some members regularly exhibit *exclusive* homosexuality. Other animals, if not exclusively heterosexual, are likely to be bisexual, engaging in sexual activity with members of both sexes. In contrast, the number of men and women who describe themselves as exclusively homosexual exceeds the number who describe themselves as bisexual.

There is no evidence that homosexuality is a disorder. The problems that some homosexuals have in adjustment result because our society at large treats them differently. Therefore, even if we observe more neuroses in homosexuals than in heterosexuals, we cannot conclude that their maladjustment is directly related to their sexual orientation. In a society that was absolutely indifferent to a person's sexual orientation, homosexuals might be as well adjusted as heterosexuals. In fact, a large number of homosexuals are well adjusted and happy with themselves (Bell and Weinberg, 1978), suggesting that homosexuality is not necessarily associated with emotional difficulties.

Some researchers have suggested that homosexuality is an emotional disturbance caused by faulty child rearing. However, much of the data in these studies were gathered from people who went to a psychiatrist or clinical psychologist for help with emotional problems. Therefore, they were not necessarily typical of all homosexuals, and we cannot know whether their homosexuality was caused by an unhappy childhood, whether their unhappy childhood was caused by early manifestations of homosexual tendencies, or whether their emotional instability and homosexual orientation were purely coincidental.

An ambitious project reported by Bell, Weinberg, and Hammersmith (1981) studied a large number of male and female homosexuals, most of whom had not sought professional psychological assistance. The researchers obtained their subjects by placing advertisements in newspapers, approaching people in gay bars and bookstores, and asking known homosexuals to recommend friends. The study took place in San Francisco, where homosexuals form a large part of the population.

The subjects were asked about their relationships with their parents, siblings, and peers and about their feelings, gender identification, and sexual activity. The results provided little or no support for traditional theories of homosexuality. The major conclusions of the study follow.

1. Sexual orientation appears to be determined prior to adolescence and prior to homosexual or heterosexual activity. The most important single predictor of adult homosexuality was a self-report of homosexual feelings, which usually occurred three years before genital homosexual activity. This finding suggests that homosexuality is a deep-seated tendency. It also tends to rule out the suggestion that seduction by an older person of the same sex plays an important role in the development of homosexuality.

2. Most homosexual men and women have engaged in some heterosexual experiences during childhood and adolescence, but in contrast to their heterosexual counterparts, they found these experiences unrewarding. This pattern is also consistent with the existence of a deep-seated predisposition prior to adulthood.

3. There is a strong relation between gender nonconformity in childhood and the development of homosexuality. Gender nonconformity is characterized by an aversion in boys to "masculine" behaviors and in girls to "feminine" behaviors.

As the researchers admit, the results of the study are consistent with the hypothesis that homosexuality is at least partly determined by biological factors. That is, biological variables may predispose a child to behavior that is more typical of the other sex and eventually to sexual arousal by members of his or her own sex.

Is there evidence for what these biological causes of homosexuality may be? We can immediately rule out the suggestion that male homosexuals have insufficient levels of testosterone in their blood; well-adjusted male homosexuals have normal levels of testosterone (Tourney, 1980).

A more likely cause of male homosexuality is the pattern of exposure of the developing brain to sex hormones. Some experiments suggest that if a female rat is subjected to stress during pregnancy, the pattern of secretion of sex hormones is altered, and the sexual development of the male offspring is affected (Ward, 1972; Anderson et al., 1986). Two laboratories have studied the brains of deceased heterosexual and homosexual males and have found differences in the size of two different subregions of the hypothalamus (Swaab and Hofman, 1990; LeVay, 1991). One subregion was larger in homosexual males; the other was smaller. We cannot necessarily conclude that either of these regions is directly involved in people's sexual orientation, but the results do suggest that the brains may have been exposed to different patterns of hormones prenatally.

Although little research has been done on the origins of female homosexuality, Money, Schwartz, and Lewis (1984) found that the incidence of homosexuality was several times higher than the national average in women who had been exposed to high levels of androgens prenatally. (The cause of the exposure was an abnormality of the adrenal glands, which usually secrete very low levels of these hormones.) Thus, sexual orientation in females may indeed be affected by biological factors.

There is also some evidence that genetics may play a role in sexual orientation. Twin studies take advantage of the fact that identical twins have identical genes, whereas the genetic similarity between fraternal twins is, on the average, 50 percent. Bailey and Pillard (1991) studied pairs of male twins in which at least one member identified himself as homosexual. If both twins are homosexual, they are said to be *concordant* for this trait. If only one is homosexual, the twins are said to be *discordant*. Thus, if homosexuality has a genetic basis, the percentage of monozygotic twins concordant for homosexuality should be higher than that for dizygotic twins. And this is exactly what Bailey and Pillard found; the concordance rate was 52 percent for identical twins and 22 percent for fraternal twins.

As we have seen, there is evidence that two biological factors—prenatal hormonal exposure and heredity—can affect a person's sexual orientation. These research findings certainly contradict the suggestion that a person's sexual orientation is a moral issue. It appears that homosexuals are no more responsible for their sexual orientation than heterosexuals are. Ernulf, Innala, and Whitam (1989) found that people who believed that homosexuals were "born that way" expressed more positive attitudes toward them than people who believed that they "chose to be" or "learned to be" that way. Thus, we can hope that research on the origins of homosexuality will reduce prejudice based on a person's sexual orientation.

Variations in Sexual Behavior

[8] Variations refer to differences from a perceived norm, or "standard," and few issues are

as value-laden as the question of what constitutes "normal" sexual behavior. What one person regards as pleasurable and acceptable sexual activity another may regard as perverse or indecent, even in matters of the sexual relationship between husband and wife. Yet human sexual activity is limited only by a person's physical capacity and imagination. The behaviors discussed in this section are variations from our society's prevailing norms. Except for those that harm other people (such as sexual advances to young children), they have no inherent values, only the ones we attach to them.

Paraphilias. Paraphilias, "unusual loves," are directed at an astonishing variety of objects. People have been sexually attracted to animals, young children, dead people, specific parts of the body (especially feet or hair), or objects such as shoes or underwear. Many people who exhibit paraphilias are unable to function sexually in a more normal manner unless the object of their fixation is present.

Most people who develop paraphilias are men. As Money and Ehrhardt (1972) put it, "Nature makes more errors in the male" (p. 148). Apparently, male sexuality is more easily disrupted than female sexuality, perhaps because something must be *added* to make a male. As we saw in Chapter 10, a fetus develops into a female unless testosterone is present; the testosterone transforms the fetus into a male. If the additions are not accomplished properly, then abnormalities are likely to result. Of course, differences in socialization may also account for the higher incidence of paraphilias in men.

Like every other psychological abnormality, paraphilias have been blamed on improper child-rearing practices, but little or no progress has been made with this hypothesis. Another suggestion is that classical conditioning indelibly attaches a person's sexual response to unusual objects. As we saw in Chapter 4, this suggestion has some experimental support. However, the conditioning model does not explain why some people seem more susceptible than others to developing paraphilias, nor does it account for the higher incidence in men.

Transvestism (from *trans,* "across," and *vestire,* "to dress"), or cross-dressing, involves wearing clothes appropriate to the other sex. Like other paraphilias, transvestism is observed almost exclusively in men. Of course, society does not treat cross-dressing by men and women in the same way. A man who dresses in women's clothing is called abnormal; a woman who dresses in men's clothing is called fashionable. Often, one member of a lesbian couple will dress in masculine clothing, but the clothes themselves probably do not provide sexual stimulation, as they do for the transvestite. Similarly, some male homosexuals dress as women, but the clothes are usually a means to an end; they are worn to attract other men.

The true transvestite is almost always heterosexual and is often married. Many men are stimulated to some extent by the sight of women's underclothes. Superficially, at least, we can easily explain this phenomenon. Underclothes are seen in pictures of attractive, scantily clad women, and they are the last garments to come off when a woman undresses for intercourse. Thus, not surprisingly, underclothes themselves elicit a certain amount of sexual interest. It is only when a man receives all or most of his sexual gratification from wearing these garments himself that we would consider his behavior to be paraphiliac.

Transsexualism. The wish to be a member of the other sex is called **transsexualism.** Again, many more men than women are transsexuals, despite the obvious social and economic advantages men have in our society. Like transvestites, transsexuals want to dress in the

Transvestism ("cross-dressing") occurs almost exclusively among men. Most transvestites obtain sexual stimulation from wearing women's clothing.

clothes of the other sex, but for very different reasons. A transvestite man enjoys having a penis and derives sexual gratification from it. A transsexual man wants to become—indeed, feels that he really is—a woman. He despises his penis and wants to get rid of it. Some transsexuals have gone so far as to cut off their own penises (Money and Tucker, 1975).

From what we know of the organizational effects of hormones, we might speculate that an inadequate amount of testosterone during prenatal development causes transsexualism. However, there is no evidence for or against this hypothesis at present. Experts on transsexualism like John Money (see Money and Ehrhardt, 1972) believe that most instances of this disorder are results of child-rearing practices that do not encourage the person to be content and confident with his or her own sexuality. For example, if a child's parents really wanted a girl but got a boy, they might treat the child ambiguously and inconsistently. However, given that parents in most societies still tend to wish more for a boy than for a girl, this hypothesis does not explain the fact that most transsexuals are men.

INTERIM SUMMARY

Sexual Behavior

Although males and females are sometimes referred to as members of "opposite" sexes, there are many similarities in their sexual response. Men and women respond in similar fashion to erotic stimuli and engage in similar kinds of erotic fantasies, although social factors can have strong influences.

The sexual behavior of female mammals with estrous cycles depends on estradiol and progesterone, but these hormones have only a minor effect on women's sexual behavior. Their sexual desire, like that of men, is much more dependent on androgens. Testosterone has two major effects on male sexual behavior: organizational and activational. In the fetus testosterone organizes the development of male sex organs and of some neural circuits in the brain; in the adult testosterone activates these structures and permits erection and ejaculation to occur.

The development of sexual orientation appears to have its roots early in life—perhaps even in prenatal development. A large-scale study of homosexuals failed to find evidence that

particular child-rearing practices fostered homosexuality. Instead, the findings were consistent with the hypothesis that some events that occur during pregnancy may affect the later development of preference for a sexual partner of a particular gender. Studies have identified two different subregions of the hypothalamus that are of different sizes in homosexual and heterosexual males. This finding lends support to the suggestion that the brains of these two groups were exposed to different patterns of hormones early in life. In addition, twin studies indicate that homosexuality has a genetic component, as well. All the evidence gathered to date indicates that homosexuality is a biological phenomenon and not a moral issue.

Human sexual behavior includes many variations on the norm of heterosexual intercourse. Paraphilias have been explained in terms of classical conditioning, but we do not know why some people are more susceptible than others or why few women acquire them. Transvestism, or cross-dressing, is practiced mostly by heterosexual males and is distinct from transsexualism, which is a desire to be a member of the other sex.

Although an individual's sex life is a personal, private matter, scientific investigation into its nature in no way diminishes its quality. A thorough understanding of the social and biological determinants of sexual behavior will enable us to help those who experience sexual dysfunctions, thus enhancing at least some people's sex lives. ∎

ADDICTIVE BEHAVIOR

[9] For many centuries, people have ingested, smoked, or sniffed naturally occurring substances that contain drugs that affect the brain, such as tea, coffee, tobacco, alcohol, opiates, and coca leaves. More recently, people have learned to produce potent extracts of these substances and to synthesize entirely new compounds in the laboratory. Wars have been fought over trade routes between the sources of addictive drugs and the consumers. Lives have been ruined because of the physiological and social effects of addiction. Obviously, addictive drugs have very potent effects on motivation.

This section considers the motivating effects of addictive drugs and their relation to the physiology of reinforcement. Chapter 15 describes evidence concerning genetic and environmental causes of addiction.

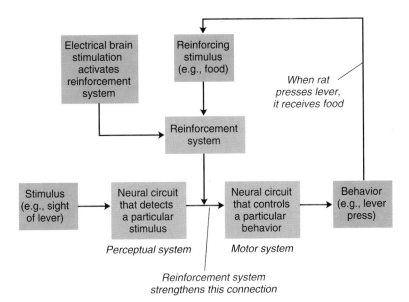

Figure 11.9 An overview of the functions of the reinforcement system and its activation by reinforcing electrical brain stimulation.

Physiology of Reinforcement

To understand the motivating properties of addictive drugs, we must understand something about the physiology of reinforcement. As we saw in the opening vignette of this chapter, in 1954 James Olds and Peter Milner discovered quite by accident that electrical stimulation of parts of the brain can reinforce an animal's behavior. The type of apparatus that they (and subsequent researchers) used was shown in Figure 3.3. (Refer to **Figure 3.3.**)

The neural circuits stimulated by the electricity are also responsible for the motivating effects of addictive drugs—and those of natural reinforcers, too, such as food, water, or sexual contact. Almost all investigators believe that the electrical stimulation of the brain is reinforcing because it activates the same system that is activated by natural reinforcers. The normal function of this system is to strengthen the connections between the neurons that detect the discriminative stimulus (such as the sight of a lever) and the neurons that produce the instrumental response (such as a lever press). The electrical brain stimulation activates this system directly. (See **Figure 11.9.**)

Researchers discovered that an essential component of the reinforcement system consists of neurons that release dopamine as their transmitter substance. Thus, all reinforcing stimuli trigger a release of dopamine in the brain.

Physiological Effects of Addictive Substances

Research by physiological psychologists indicates that all drugs that have the potential for being abused stimulate the release of dopamine, the transmitter substance involved in reinforcement (Carlson, 1992). Thus, these drugs reinforce the behaviors responsible for their delivery to the body: swallowing, smoking, sniffing, or injecting. The immediate consequences of these drugs are more powerful than the realization that in the long term bad things will happen. Table 11.3 lists some of the most important addictive drugs, along with their relative potential for abuse. (See **Table 11.3.**)

Opiates. Opium, derived from a sticky resin produced by the opium poppy, has been eaten and smoked for centuries. Morphine, one of the naturally occurring ingredients of opium, is sometimes used as a painkiller but has largely been supplanted by synthetic opiates. Heroin, a compound produced from morphine, is the most commonly abused opiate.

You learned in Chapter 3 that opiates such as morphine and heroin affect behavior because they mimic the effects of the brain's own opioids (the endorphins), which are released in times of stress or arousal. Opiates activate circuits of neurons in the brain by stimulating receptors located on neurons in many parts of the brain. One of the effects of such stimulation is analgesia: a decrease in sensitivity to stimuli that cause pain.

Another effect of opiates, more important to the topic of this chapter, is reinforcement. When an organism is aroused (for example, during fighting or sexual behavior), some cells in its brain secrete endorphins. These chemicals circulate throughout the brain and stimulate the appropriate receptors, activating neural systems that decrease pain. In addition, the endorphins also activate neural circuits involved in

Table 11.3 Toxic effects and addiction risk of the major psychoactive drugs

Drug Category	Acute Toxicity	Chronic Toxicity	Relative Risk of Addiction
Alcohol	Psychomotor impairment, impaired thinking and judgment, reckless or violent behavior; lowering of body temperature, respiratory depression	Hypertension, stroke, hepatitis, cirrhosis, gastritis, pancreatitis; organic brain damage, cognitive deficits; fetal alcohol syndrome; withdrawal effects: shakes, seizures, delirium tremens	3
Cocaine, amphetamine	Sympathetic overactivity: hypertension, cardiac arrhythmias, hyperthermia; acute toxic psychosis: delusions, hallucinations, paranoia, violence; anorexia	Unpleasant tactile sensations; stereotyped movements; seizures, withdrawal depression; chronic rhinitis, perforation of nasal septum	1
Caffeine	Cardiac arrhythmias; insomnia, restlessness, excitement; muscle tension, jitteriness; gastric discomfort	Hypertension; anxiety, depression; withdrawal headaches	5
Cannabis (marijuana, hashish)	Psychomotor impairment; additive effect with alcohol and sedatives	Apathy and mental slowing, impaired memory and learning (brain damage?); impaired immune response?	4
Nicotine	Nausea, tremor, tachycardia; high doses: hypertension, bradycardia, diarrhea, muscle twitching, respiratory paralysis	Coronary, cerebral, and peripheral vascular disease, gangrene; gastric acidity, peptic ulcer; withdrawal irritability, impaired attention and concentration; retarded fetal growth, spontaneous abortion; other substances in tobacco smoke: bronchitis, emphysema, lung cancer	2
Opiates	Sedation, analgesia, emotional blunting, dream state; nausea, vomiting, spasm of ureter and bile duct; respiratory depression, coma, additive effects with alcohol and sedatives; impaired thermoregulation; suppression of sex hormones	Disorders of hypothalamic and pituitary hormone secretion; constipation; withdrawal cramps, diarrhea, vomiting, gooseflesh, lacrimation	2
Hallucinogen (LSD, PCP)	Sympathetic overactivity; visual and auditory illusions, hallucinations, depersonalization; PCP: muscle rigidity, elevated body temperature, staggering gait, agitation, violence, stereotyped movements, convulsions	Flashbacks; depression, prolonged psychotic episodes	5

Source: From Goldstein, A., and Kalant, H. Drug policy: Striking the right balance. *Science,* 1990, *249,* 1513–1521. Copyright 1990 by the American Association for the Advancement of Science.

Note: Listed here are effects due to the drugs themselves. The effects are dose-related and subject to individual variation in sensitivity, so not all are expected to be seen in every user. Approximate rankings for relative risk of addiction are on a 5-point scale, where 1 is most severe.

reinforcement; thus, the endorphins *reinforce the organism's behavior.* The survival value of this system is obvious: A fighting or mating organism must continue what it is doing and not be easily inhibited by pain. A fighting organism that suddenly stops because of pain may be killed; a mating one will not reproduce.

When a person takes an opiate, the drug artificially stimulates the endorphin receptors in his or her brain and thus activates mechanisms of arousal, analgesia, and reinforcement. The activation of the reinforcement mechanisms strengthens the behaviors that have just occurred: preparing and taking the drug.

Opiate addiction has several high personal and social costs. First, because heroin is an illegal drug, an addict becomes, by definition, a criminal. Second, the behavioral response to opiates declines with continued use, which means that a person must take increasing amounts of the drug to achieve a "high." The habit thus becomes more and more expensive, and the person often turns to crime to obtain enough money to support his or her habit. (If the addict is a pregnant woman, her infant will also become dependent on the drug, which easily crosses the placental barrier. The infant must be given opiates right after being born and then be given gradually decreasing doses.) Third, an opiate addict often uses unsanitary needles; at present, a substantial percentage of people who inject illicit drugs have been exposed in this way to the AIDS virus. Fourth, the uncertainty about the strength of a given batch of heroin makes it possible for a user to receive an unusually large dose of the drug, with possibly fatal consequences. In addition, dealers typically dilute pure heroin with various adulterants such as milk sugar, quinine, or talcum powder; and dealers are not known for taking scrupulous care with the quality and sterility of the substances they use. Some heroin-induced deaths have actually been reactions to the adulterants mixed with the drugs.

Cocaine and Amphetamine. Cocaine and amphetamine have similar behavioral effects,

"Crack" cocaine, because its effects are so rapid and potent, has the highest abuse potential of any available drug.

because both directly increase transmission at synapses that utilize dopamine as a transmitter substance. "Crack," a particularly potent form of cocaine, is smoked and thus enters the blood supply of the lungs and reaches the brain very quickly. Because its effects are so potent and so rapid, it is probably the most effective reinforcer of all available drugs.

As you learned in Chapter 3, stimulants such as amphetamine and cocaine slow down the reuptake of dopamine. Because the dopamine is taken back into the terminal button more slowly, it is in contact with the receptor molecules in the postsynaptic neuron for a longer time and thus exerts a more profound effect. As we just saw, reinforcement appears to depend on the release of dopamine. Thus, drugs such as amphetamine and cocaine may be such effective reinforcers because they mimic the pharmacological effect of natural reinforcers.

When people take cocaine, they become euphoric, active, and talkative. They say that they feel powerful and alert. Some of them become addicted to the drug, and obtaining it becomes an obsession to which they devote more and more time and money. As we will see in Chapter 15, cocaine and amphetamine have a serious side effect: They cause the symptoms of schizophrenia, a serious mental disorder.

Humans are not the only species sensitive to the addictive effects of drugs such as cocaine. If a laboratory animal is permitted to press a lever that delivers cocaine through a plastic tube inserted into a vein, it will quickly learn to do so. The drug causes the animal to act excited and to show intense exploratory activity. If rats or monkeys are given continuous access to a lever that permits them to self-administer cocaine, they often self-inject so much cocaine that they die. In fact, Bozarth and Wise (1985) found that rats that self-administered cocaine were almost three times more likely to die than rats that self-administered heroin. (See *Figure 11.10.*)

Nicotine. A stimulant drug such as nicotine may seem rather tame after a discussion of opiates, cocaine, and amphetamine. Nevertheless, it, too, has addictive potential. Moreover, the combination of nicotine and other substances in tobacco smoke is carcinogenic and leads to cancer of the lungs, mouth, throat, and esophagus. Also, if the smoker is a pregnant woman, the development of her fetus is likely to be adversely affected. Although nicotine is less potent than the "hard" drugs, many more people who try it go on to become addicts. The addictive potential of nicotine should not be underes-

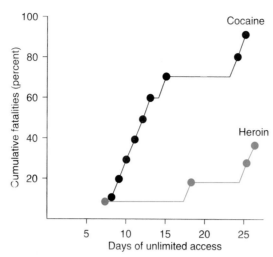

Figure 11.10 Cumulative fatalities in groups of rats self-administering cocaine or heroin. (From Bozarth, M.A., and Wise, R.A. *Journal of the American Medical Association*, 1985, *254*, 81–83. Copyright 1985, American Medical Association.)

timated; many people continue to smoke even when doing so causes serious health problems. For example, Sigmund Freud, whose theory of psychoanalysis stressed the importance of insight in changing one's behavior, was unable to stop smoking even after most of his jaw had been removed because of the cancer that this habit had caused (Brecher, 1972). He was in constant pain and knew that he was dying; nevertheless, he continued to smoke. His cancer finally killed him.

Ours is not the only species willing to self-administer nicotine; so will laboratory animals (Henningfield and Goldberg, 1983). As you learned in Chapter 3, nicotine acts like acetylcholine; it stimulates acetylcholine receptors. It also increases the release of dopamine in the brain (Damsma, Day, and Fibiger, 1989).

Wise (1988) notes that because nicotine stimulates the same neurons that are stimulated by cocaine and heroin, smoking could potentially make it more difficult for a cocaine or heroin addict to stop taking the drug. As several studies with laboratory animals have shown, if self-administration of cocaine or heroin is extinguished through nonreinforcement, an injection of drugs that stimulate the release of dopamine can reinstate the responding. A similar "cross-priming" effect from cigarette smoking could potentially contribute to a relapse in people who are trying to abstain from a more potent addictive drug. (As we shall see, alcohol also stimulates the release of dopamine, so drinking could present the same problem.)

Marijuana. Another drug that people regularly self-administer—almost exclusively by smoking—is THC, the active ingredient in marijuana. Recently, neuroscientists have discovered the presence of specific receptors for THC in the brain (Matsuda et al., 1990.) However, we still do not know what types of neurons contain these receptors, and we still do not know the physiological effects of THC. The fact that the brain contains THC receptors implies that the brain produces a chemical that can activate these receptors, just as it produces the endogenous opioids. What this chemical is and what functions it serves are yet to be discovered.

One thing we do now know about THC is that it, like other drugs with abuse potential, has an effect on neurons that secrete dopamine. Chen et al. (1990) injected rats with low doses of THC and measured the release of dopamine in the brain. Sure enough, they found that the injections caused the release of dopamine. (See *Figure 11.11.*) The hippocampus contains a large concentration of THC receptors. Marijuana is known to affect people's short-term memory; specifically, it impairs their ability to keep track of a particular topic—they frequently lose the thread of a conversation. As we saw in Chapter 7, the hippocampus plays an important role in learning and memory; perhaps, then, the drug affects memory by disrupting the normal functions of the hippocampus.

Alcohol. Alcohol costs society more than any other drug. A large percentage of deaths and injuries caused by motor vehicle accidents are related to alcohol use, and alcohol contributes to violence and aggression. Chronic alcoholics of-

Figure 11.11 Release of dopamine in the brain caused by injections of THC or an inert placebo. (From Chen, J., Paredes, W., Li, J., Smith, D., Lowinson, J., and Gardner, E.L. *Psychopharmacology*, 1990, *102*, 156–162. Reprinted with permission.)

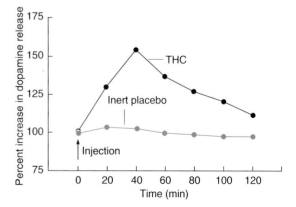

ten lose their jobs, their homes, and their families; and many die of cirrhosis of the liver, exposure, or diseases caused by poor living conditions and abuse of their body. Women who drink during pregnancy run the risk of giving birth to babies with fetal alcohol syndrome, which includes malformation of the head and the brain. In fact, the leading cause of mental retardation in the Western world today is alcohol consumption by pregnant women (Abel and Sokol, 1986). Thus, understanding the physiological and behavioral effects of this drug is an important issue.

At low doses alcohol produces mild euphoria and has an **anxiolytic effect**—that is, it reduces the discomfort of anxiety (*lysis* means "loosening"). At higher doses it produces incoordination and sedation. When they have had too much to drink, people often do things they normally would not do; the alcohol removes the inhibitory effect of social controls on their behavior.

Alcohol probably produces both positive and negative reinforcement. As you learned in Chapter 6, *positive* reinforcement is reinforcement caused by the presence of an appetitive stimulus, which, as we have seen, causes the release of dopamine in the brain. *Negative* reinforcement is reinforcement caused by the termination of an aversive stimulus. Negative reinforcement is provided by the anxiolytic effect of alcohol. If a person feels anxious and uncomfortable, then a drug that relieves this discomfort provides at least a temporary escape from an unpleasant situation. It is probably the unique combination of stimulating and anxiolytic effects—of positive and negative reinforcement—that makes alcohol so difficult for some people to resist.

Although the effects of heroin withdrawal have been exaggerated, those produced by alcohol withdrawal are serious and can even be fatal (Julien, 1981). Convulsions caused by alcohol withdrawal are considered to be a medical emergency and are usually treated with benzodiazepines ("tranquilizers").

EVALUATING SCIENTIFIC ISSUES

"Physiological" Versus "Psychological" Addiction

10 Many people believe that "true" addiction is caused by the unpleasant physiological effects that occur when an addict tries to stop taking the drug. For example, Eddy, Halbach, Isbell, and Seevers (1965) defined *physical dependence* as "an adaptive state that manifests itself by intense physical disturbances when the administration of a drug is suspended" (p. 723). In contrast, they defined *psychic dependence* as a condition in which a drug produces "a feeling of satisfaction and a psychic drive that requires periodic or continuous administration of the drug to produce pleasure or to avoid discomfort" (p. 723). Most people regard the latter as less important than the former. But, as we shall see, the reverse is true.

Evidence for Physiological Addiction. For many years, heroin has been considered as the prototype for drug addiction. People who habitually take heroin (or other opiates) become physically dependent on the drug; that is, they show *tolerance* and *withdrawal symptoms*. **Tolerance** is the decreased sensitivity to a drug that comes from its continued use; the drug user must take larger and larger amounts of the drug in order for it to be effective. Once a person has taken an opiate regularly enough to develop tolerance, that person will suffer **withdrawal symptoms** if he or she stops taking the drug. Withdrawal symptoms are primarily the opposite of the effects of the drug itself. That is, heroin produces euphoria; withdrawal from it produces *dysphoria*—a feeling of anxious misery. (*Euphoria* and *dysphoria* mean "easy to bear" and "hard to bear," respectively.) Heroin produces constipation; withdrawal from it produces nausea, cramping, and diarrhea. Heroin produces relaxation; withdrawal from it produces agitation.

Most investigators believe that the withdrawal symptoms are produced by the body's attempt to compensate for the unusual condition of heroin intoxication. That is, most systems of the body, including those controlled by the brain, are regulated so that they stay at an optimal value. When a drug artificially changes these systems for a prolonged time, homeostatic mechanisms begin to produce the opposite reaction, thus partially compensating for the disturbance from the optimal value. These compensatory mechanisms account for the fact that more and more heroin must be taken in order to achieve the effects that were produced when the person first started taking the drug (tolerance). They also account for the symptoms of withdrawal: When the person stops taking the drug, the compensatory mechanisms make themselves felt, unopposed by the action of the drug.

How Important Is Physiological Addiction? Heroin addiction has provided such a striking example of drug dependence that some authorities have concluded that "real" addiction does not occur unless a drug causes tolerance and withdrawal. Without doubt, withdrawal symptoms make it difficult for a person to stop taking heroin—they help keep the person hooked. But withdrawal symptoms do not explain why a person *becomes* a heroin addict; that fact is explained by the drug's reinforcing effect. Certainly, people do not start taking heroin so that they will become physically dependent on it and feel miserable when they go without it! Instead, they begin taking it because it makes them feel good.

Even though the withdrawal effects of heroin make it difficult to stop taking the drug, these effects alone are not sufficient to keep most people hooked. In fact, when the cost of the habit gets too high, some addicts stop taking heroin "cold turkey." Doing so is not as painful as most people believe; withdrawal symptoms have been described as similar to a bad case of the flu—unpleasant, but survivable. After a week or two, when their nervous system adapts to the absence of the drug, they recommence their habit. If their only reason for taking the drug was to avoid unpleasant withdrawal symptoms, they would never be capable of following this strategy. The reason that people take—and continue to take—drugs such as heroin is that the drugs give them a pleasurable "rush"; in other words, the drugs have a reinforcing effect on their behavior.

There are two other kinds of evidence that contradict the assertion that drug addition is caused by physical dependence. First, some very potent drugs, including cocaine, do not produce physical dependence. That is, people who take the drug do not show tolerance; and if they stop, they do not show any withdrawal symptoms. As a result, experts believed for many years that cocaine was a relatively innocuous drug, not in the same league as heroin. Obviously, they were wrong; cocaine is even more addictive than heroin. As we saw earlier, animals self-administering cocaine are more likely to die than those self-administering heroin. Second, some drugs produce physical dependence (tolerance and withdrawal symptoms) but are not abused (Jaffe, 1985). The reason they are not abused is that they do not have reinforcing effects on behavior.

What Should We Conclude? The most important lesson we can learn from the misguided distinction between "physiological" and "psychological" addiction is that we should never underestimate the importance of "psychological" factors. After all, given that behavior is controlled by circuits of neurons in the brain, even "psychological" factors involve physiological mechanisms. People often pay more attention to physiological symptoms than psychological ones—to consider them more *real*. But behavioral research indicates that an exclusive preoccupation with physiology can hinder our understanding of the causes of addiction. ∎

INTERIM SUMMARY

Addictive Behavior

Drug addiction is one of the most serious problems our society faces today. Apparently, all substances that produce addiction have an excitatory effect, although several addictive drugs, such as alcohol and the opiates, produce an inhibitory effect as well. The excitatory effect, correlated with reinforcement, appears to involve the release of dopamine in the brain. The circuits responsible for reinforcement were first identified through the discovery that electrical stimulation of some parts of the brain could be reinforcing.

Opiates produce tolerance and withdrawal symptoms, which make the habit become expensive and make quitting more difficult. But the primary reason for addiction is the reinforcing effect, not the unpleasant symptoms produced when an addict tries to quit. Tolerance appears to be produced by homeostatic mechanisms that counteract the effects of the drug. Cocaine and amphetamine are potent dopamine activators and thus serve as potent reinforcers—and substances with a high addictive potential. Nicotine and the active ingredient in marijuana also increase the release of dopamine in the brain. Alcohol has both excitatory and antianxiety effects and thus is able to produce both positive and negative reinforcement.

The distinction between "physiological" addiction (complete with tolerance and withdrawal effects) and "psychological" addiction (lacking these effects) has obscured the true cause of addiction: the reinforcing effect of the drug. Cocaine was once thought to be relatively harmless because it does not produce "real" (that is, physiological) addiction; obviously, we now know better. ∎

11 Aggression is a serious problem in human society; every day we hear or read about incidents involving violence and cruelty, and undoubtedly thousands more go unreported. If we are to provide a safe environment for everyone, we must learn more about the causes of aggressive behavior.

Probably many factors influence a person's tendency to commit acts of aggression, including childhood experiences, exposure to violence on television and in the movies, peer group pressures, hormones and drugs, and malfunctions of the brain. Various aspects of aggressive behavior have been studied by zoologists, physiological psychologists, sociologists, social psychologists, political scientists, and psychologists who specialize in the learning process. We will examine several of these aspects here.

Ethological Studies of Aggression

The Social Relevance of Intraspecific Aggression. The utility of species-typical behaviors such as sexual activity, parental behavior, food gathering, and nest construction is obvious; we can easily understand their value to survival. But violence and aggression are also seen in many species, including humans. If aggression is harmful, one would not expect it to be so prevalent in nature. Ethologists—zoologists who study the behavior of animals in their natural environments—have analyzed the causes of aggression and have shown that it, too, often has value for the survival of a species.

Intraspecific aggression involves an attack by one animal upon another member of its species. Ethologists have shown that intraspecific aggression has several biological advantages. First, it tends to disperse a population of animals, forcing some into new territories, where necessary environmental adaptations may increase the flexibility of the species. Second, when accompanied by rivalry among males for mating opportunities, intraspecific aggression tends to perpetuate the genes of the healthier, more vigorous animals.

Human cultures, however, are very different even from those of other species of primates. Perhaps intraspecific aggression has outlived its usefulness for humans and we would benefit from its elimination. Whatever the case may be, we must understand the causes of human aggression in order to eliminate it or direct it to more useful purposes.

Threat and Appeasement. Ethologists have discovered a related set of behaviors in many species: ritualized threat gestures and appeasement gestures. **Threat gestures** enable an animal to communicate aggressive intent to another before engaging in actual violence. For example, if one dog intrudes on another's territory, the defender will growl and bare its teeth, raise the fur on its back (presumably making it look larger to its opponent), and stare at the intruder. Almost always, the dog defending its territory will drive the intruder away. Threat gestures are particularly important in species whose members are able to kill each other (Eibl-Eibesfeld, 1980; Lorenz, 1966). For example, wolves often threaten each other with growls and bared teeth but rarely bite each other. Because an all-out battle between two wolves would probably end in the death of one and the serious wounding of the other, the tendency to perform ritualized displays rather than engage in overt aggression has an obvious advantage to the survival of the species.

To forestall an impending attack, one of the animals must show that it does not want to fight—that it admits defeat. The submissive animal makes an **appeasement gesture.** If a pair of wolves get into a fight, one usually submits to the other by lying down and exposing its throat. The sight of a helpless and vulnerable opponent presumably terminates the victor's hostility, and the fight ceases. The aggression of the dominant animal is *appeased.*

Appeasement gestures are even a part of human behavior. Suppose you are a male of average size standing at a bar next to a muscular, 280-pound male wearing a jacket with a skull and crossbones stenciled on the back. Would you stare directly at his face? And if he happened to stare at you, would you stand up tall and meet his gaze or slouch down a bit, displaying a diffident look on your face?

Hormones and Aggression

In birds and most mammals androgens appear to exert a strong effect on aggressiveness. You will recall from the section on sexual behavior that testosterone has an *organizational* effect on the development of sex organs and the brain and an *activational* effect during adulthood. Testosterone also appears to exert the same effects on some forms of aggressive behavior. If a male mouse is raised in isolation, it will fiercely attack other male mice. But if a male mouse is castrated early in life, before its brain has matured, it will not attack another male when it grows up,

Appeasement gesture (African hunting dogs). The submissive dog on the right is showing appeasement behavior by exposing its throat to the dominant animal.

even if it is given injections of testosterone (Conner and Levine, 1969). (See **Table 11.4.**)

Given that men are generally more aggressive than women (Maccoby and Jacklin, 1974) and that a man's sexual behavior depends on the presence of testosterone, perhaps this hormone also influences their aggressive behavior. Some cases of aggressiveness—especially sexual assault—have been treated with drugs that block androgen receptors and thus prevent androgens from exerting their normal effects. The rationale is based on animal research that indicates that androgens promote both sexual behavior and aggression in males. Clearly, treatment with drugs is preferable to castration, because the effects are not irreversible. However, the efficacy of treatment with antiandrogens has yet to be established conclusively (Bain, 1987).

Another way to determine whether androgens affect aggressiveness in humans is to examine the testosterone levels of people who ex-

hibit varying levels of aggressive behavior. However, even though this approach poses fewer ethical problems, it presents methodological ones. First, let me review some evidence. Dabbs, Frady, Carr, and Besch (1987) measured the testosterone levels of male prison inmates and found a significant correlation with several measures of violence, including the nature of the crime for which they were convicted, infractions of prison rules, and ratings of "toughness" by their peers. These relations are seen in female prison inmates too; Dabbs et al. (1988) found that women prisoners who showed unprovoked violence and had several prior convictions also showed higher levels of testosterone.

But we must remember that *correlation* does not necessarily indicate *causation*. A person's environment can affect his or her testosterone level. For example, losing a tennis match or a wrestling competition causes a fall in blood levels of testosterone (Mazur and Lamb, 1980; Elias, 1981). In a very elaborate study Jeffcoate et al. (1986) found that the blood levels of a group of five men confined on a boat for fourteen days changed as they established a dominance-aggression ranking among themselves: The higher the rank, the higher the testosterone level was. Thus, we cannot be sure in any correlational study that high testosterone levels *cause* people to become dominant or violent; perhaps their success in establishing a position of dominance increases their testosterone levels relative to those of the people they dominate.

A few studies have looked at the behavioral effects of administering androgens. Because of ethical concerns, people cannot be given androgen supplements merely to see whether they become more aggressive. First, excessive amounts of androgens have deleterious effects on a person's health. Second, it would be wrong to subject innocent people to possible harm from

Table 11.4 Organizational and activational effects of androgens on intraspecific aggression in male rats

	Treatment		
	Immediately After Birth	*When Rat Is Fully Grown*	*Results*
	Castrate	Inject with testosterone	Low aggressiveness
	Castrate—inject with testosterone	Inject with testosterone	High aggressiveness
	Castrate—inject with testosterone	No injection	Low aggressiveness
	Organizational effect	Activational effect	

the aggressive behavior of someone who receives androgens while participating in an experiment. Thus, the only evidence we have comes from case studies in which a person with abnormally low levels of testosterone is given the hormone to replace what would normally be present. For example, O'Carroll and Bancroft (1985) reported the case of an institutionalized, mentally retarded man who had lost his testes when he was seven years old. When he received an injection of testosterone, he became violent. Taken together, the findings reviewed in this section suggest (but still do not prove) that androgens play a role in stimulating aggression in humans.

Environmental Variables That Affect Human Aggression

12 Imitation of Aggression. Consider the significance of a conversation like this one:

Parent: I don't know what to do with Johnny. His teacher says he is simply impossible. He just can't keep from hitting and kicking other children.

Friend: Perhaps he needs more discipline.

Parent: But I spank him all the time!

Why does Johnny persist in being aggressive, even though this behavior is regularly punished? Some psychologists suggest that instead of suppressing his violent behavior, frequent spankings have *taught* him to be aggressive. When his parents become upset with his behavior, they resort to physical violence. And Johnny learns to imitate them. As we will see in Chapter 14, laboratory research by Albert Bandura has shown that children readily learn to imitate adults' aggressive behavior.

A large percentage of nonviolent people may have been spanked at least once when they were children, with no obvious harm. But when parents habitually resort to aggression, their children are likely to do the same. In the extreme case of child abuse, parents who beat their children usually turn out to have been victims of child abuse themselves; this unfortunate trait seems to be passed along like an unwanted family heirloom (Parke and Collmer, 1975).

Most parents do not beat their children or even spank them frequently, but there is another opportunity for imitation that is of concern to society: examples of violence on television or in movies. All too often, the heroes disdain peaceful solutions to their problems and instead seek to resolve them through fighting. Most people agree that it would be unfortunate if real people were as violent as the ones we see on television. Does the continued observation of violence in the mass media lead children to choose aggressive means to solve their problems? Or are the representatives for the television networks correct when they argue that children have no trouble separating fact from fancy, and that the networks only give us what we want anyway?

Field studies suggest, but do not prove, that long-term viewing of violence on television causes children to be more violent. For example, Lefkowitz, Eron, Walder, and Huesmann (1977) observed a correlation of .31 between boys' viewing of violence and their later behavior. They reported that the greater the boys' preference for violent television at age eight, the greater their aggressiveness was both at that age and ten years later, at age eighteen. (Girls were found to be much less aggressive, and no relation was observed between television viewing and violence.)

Feshbach and Singer (1971) carried out a bold and interesting field study in an attempt to manipulate directly the amount of violence seen by boys on television—and thus to determine whether the viewing would affect their later aggressiveness. With the cooperation of directors of various private boarding schools and homes for neglected children, half the teenage boys were permitted to watch only violent television programs, the other half only nonviolent ones. Six months later, no effect was seen on the behavior of the boys in the private schools. The boys in the homes for neglected children who had watched violent programs tended to be slightly *less* aggressive than those who had watched the nonviolent ones.

Two factors prevent us from concluding that violent television programs promote pacifism or at least have no effect. First, by the time people reach their teens, they may be too old to be affected by six months of television viewing; the critical period may come earlier. Second, some of the boys resented not being allowed to watch their favorite (in this case, violent) television programs, and this resentment may have made them more aggressive.

As with many other complex social issues, we lack definitive evidence that television violence makes members of our society more aggressive. However, the stakes in this particular issue are high enough that we should tolerate some uncertainty and choose what is clearly the lesser of two evils. Given both the possibility that violence on television has a harmful effect and the fact that no harm can come from reducing the amount of aggression on the airwaves, we should make every effort to provide a more peaceful and constructive model of human behavior to our children.

Frustration and Aggression. An influential hypothesis proposed by Dollard et al. (1939) stated that frustration causes aggression. In general usage the term *frustration* refers to an unpleasant feeling produced by an unfulfilled desire. However, Dollard and his colleagues defined **frustration** specifically as "an interference with the occurrence of an instigated goal-response at its proper time in the behavior sequence"—that is, as a condition that prevents the occurrence of an expected reinforcer. Expectation (implied by the term *goal-response*) plays a crucial role in the definition of frustration. For example, I cannot be said to be frustrated by not winning millions of dollars from my state's lottery. However, if I am very thirsty and put my last piece of change in a vending machine to get something to drink, my goal-response of drinking—which I expect to be able to do—is frustrated if the machine keeps my money but fails to deliver a beverage.

According to Dollard and his colleagues, frustration invariably increases an organism's tendency to engage in aggressive behavior and accounts for *all* instances of aggression. Their rationale was that frustration produces a drive that motivates the aggressive behavior; if this drive finds an outlet in the form of aggressive behavior, it will be reduced and the organism will no longer behave aggressively.

An analysis by Berkowitz (1978) disposes of the hypothesis that all aggressive acts are caused by frustration. Aggressive behaviors, like any other, can be reinforced. A dog can be trained to attack; an assassin can be hired to kill another person. Frustration does not play a causal role in either of these cases. Pain is also an effective agent in producing aggressive behavior. If two animals are placed in a small cage and receive electrical shocks to their feet, they are likely to fight.

Although some forms of aggression do not involve frustration, perhaps frustration invariably increases an organism's tendency to behave aggressively. To investigate this possibility, Berkowitz (1978) had subjects sit on a stationary bicycle and attempt to adjust their rate of pedaling to match that of a person in another room; if they succeeded, they would receive a reward. Near the end of the run, frustration was introduced in some subjects, who

suddenly received signals indicating that they were failing to match their partners' speed. Some subjects were told that a malfunction of the equipment had caused the failure; others were told that their partners were at fault. Subjects in both experimental groups reported that they were angry; subjects in a control group were not. Thus, frustration caused anger even when it was produced by factors apparently outside of anyone's control.

The next phase of the experiment tested actual aggression, by giving the subject an opportunity to punish the fictitious partner's behavior by pressing a button that allegedly delivered a loud, noxious noise. The perceived source of frustration did have an effect on aggressive behavior: Subjects who believed that the partner was to blame pressed the button more often and longer than did subjects who blamed the apparatus or control subjects who had not expected to receive a reward.

From the results of these and other experiments Berkowitz has suggested modifying the frustration-aggression hypothesis to account for the effects of other aversive stimuli, including pain. In our evolution pain became a potent elicitor for aggressive behavior; if an animal was in pain and another animal was present, the latter was likely to be the source of the pain. Thus, animals who attacked when in pain were more likely to survive than those who failed to respond.

Berkowitz and Frodi (1977) found that pain does elicit aggressive behavior in humans. They induced pain in volunteer subjects by having them place their hand in a tank of ice water. (The effect is painful but does not cause physical harm.) Control subjects placed their hand in cool water. After seven minutes the subjects were permitted to reward or punish the behavior of a (fictitious) person in the next room. Subjects who were experiencing pain administered more shocks than did control subjects. They also reported feeling annoyance, irritation, and anger, as well as pain and discomfort.

In conclusion, at least some forms of aggression appear to be produced by aversive stimuli, frustration being just one example.

Aggression and Catharsis. Dollard and his colleagues have accepted Freud's suggestion that aggression consists of response tendencies that are energized by a drive, and this hypothesis has been incorporated into many ethological theories. Various physiological and environmental influences increase the level of this drive. Once aroused, the aggressive drive must eventually find some sort of outlet in actual aggressive behavior or in some symbolic substitute; the Freudian and ethological models of aggression emphasize the importance of this **catharsis** (*katharsis* is Greek for "purge").

Experimental evidence suggests that acting out aggression tends to lead to even *more* aggression. Geen, Stonner, and Shope (1975) made some subjects angry by having a confederate unfairly give them an excessive number of electrical shocks while they were attempting to solve a problem. Afterward, some subjects were given the opportunity to punish their tormenter by supposedly delivering a shock whenever he made an error in a learning task. During a second learning task all subjects were given the same opportunity. However, this time they could turn a dial to determine how intense the shock would be. The subjects' blood pressure was taken several times during the experiment. According to the catharsis model, the subjects who were able to punish the confederate twice should have shown less anger during the second learning task, because their anger should have been released during the first task. In contrast, those who did not punish their tormenter during the first learning task should still have been angry, therefore causing them to set the shock intensity higher.

The blood pressure readings were in accord with the catharsis hypothesis: After each opportunity to punish the confederate, the subjects' blood pressure fell, presumably reflecting a decrease in anger. However, the *behavioral* effects were just the opposite: Subjects who had shocked the confederate during the first learning task shocked him even more during the second, and their responses on a questionnaire indicated that they felt more hostile toward him. Although aggression appeared to purge anger, it seemed also to increase aggressive tendencies.

The apparent reason for the increase is that the reduction of unpleasant feelings creates the conditions for *negative reinforcement,* which is achieved through the termination of an aversive stimulus. Thus, when a person gives vent to feelings of hostility and feels better afterward, the experience tends to increase the likelihood that aggressive behavior will recur.

INTERIM SUMMARY

Aggressive Behavior

Aggression serves useful purposes in the majority of species, yet most human societies attempt to suppress it in order to protect its victims. Studies of other species reveal the presence of mechanisms to avert violence: Threat gestures warn of an impending attack, and appeasement gestures propitiate the potential aggressor. In males of most species of animals, androgens have both organizational and activational effects on aggressive behavior. The same is probably true for humans, but definitive studies are impossible for ethical reasons.

Although some simple human aggressive behaviors may be innate, most are learned. Field studies on the effects of televised violence are not conclusive; observational studies have revealed a modest relation between preference for violent television shows and boys' aggressiveness, but we cannot be sure that the relation is causal. An attempt to manipulate aggression by forcing children to watch violent or nonviolent shows was inconclusive because many children resented their loss of choice.

The frustration-aggression hypothesis suggests that thwarting an organism's opportunity to obtain a reinforcer is the sole cause of aggression. However, some forms of aggression are not caused by frustration; for example, violence can be explicitly reinforced. Berkowitz suggested that unpleasant stimuli such as pain and the effects of frustration increase an organism's tendency to behave aggressively.

The catharsis hypothesis has received mixed support. Although the opportunity to engage in aggression may indeed relieve a person's *feelings* of anger, it is likely to increase further violence. ∎

Classical Conditioning and Opiate Addiction

Often people who are trying desperately to break a heroin addiction will see something that reminds them of their addiction and will suddenly feel a strong urge to inject themselves with heroin. For example, antidrug organizations have produced color posters featuring drug paraphernalia in full color: glassine envelopes with white powder spilling out of them, syringes, needles, a spoon and candle used to heat and dissolve the drug. The purpose of these posters is to frighten people away from experimenting with drugs. Unfortunately, the posters also may drive ex-addicts back to the drug.

The reason for this effect proceeds from the way the brain responds to long-term use of opiates. As we saw earlier in this chapter, tolerance (and the possibility of withdrawal effects) develops when compensatory mechanisms in the brain diminish the effects of the drug. In fact, there are two different types of compensatory mechanisms. The first mechanism takes place on a cellular level. Prolonged exposure to opiates causes a decrease in the responsiveness of neurons to opiates. The second mechanism—the one that can produce a relapse in an ex-addict—involves a phenomenon you are already familiar with: classical conditioning.

When a person takes heroin, the primary effects of the drug activate homeostatic compensatory mechanisms. These compensatory mechanisms are provided by neural circuits that oppose the effects of the drug. As Siegel (1978) has pointed out, the activation of these compensatory mechanisms is a response that can become classically conditioned to environmental stimuli that are present at the time the drug is taken. The stimuli associated with taking the drug—including the paraphernalia involved in preparing the solution of the drug, the syringe, the needle, the feel of the needle in a vein, and even the sight of companions who are usually present and the room in which the drug is taken—serve as conditioned stimuli. The homeostatic compensatory responses provoked by the effects of the drug serve as the unconditioned response, which becomes conditioned to the environmental stimuli. Thus, once classical conditioning has taken place, the sight of the conditioned stimuli will activate the compensatory mechanisms.

If an ex-addict sees a poster, the sight of the drug paraphernalia will act as a conditioned stimulus and will elicit the conditioned response—the compensatory mechanism. Because the person has not recently taken the drug, he or she will feel only the effect of the compensatory mechanism: dysphoria, agitation, and a strong urge to relieve these symptoms and replace them with feelings of euphoria.

Experiments with laboratory animals have confirmed that this explanation is correct. For example, Siegel et al. (1982) gave rats daily doses of heroin—always in the same

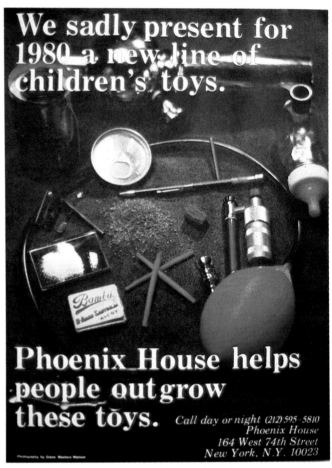

We sadly present for 1980 a new line of children's toys.

Phoenix House helps people outgrow these toys. *Call day or night (212) 595-5810*
Phoenix House
164 West 74th Street
New York, N.Y. 10023

Posters such as this one were designed to alert people to dangers of drug addiction. But they show stimuli associated with the taking of drugs, and addicts who are trying to quit their habit report that such posters make it difficult for them to stop taking the drug. Therefore, this type of poster is generally no longer used.

chamber—long enough for tolerance to develop. Then on the test day the experimenters gave the rats a large dose of the drug. Some of the animals received the drug in the familiar chamber, while others received it in a new environment. The investigators predicted that the animals receiving the drug in the familiar environment would have some protection from the drug overdose because the stimuli in that environment would produce a classically conditioned compensatory response. Their prediction was correct: Almost all the rats who received the overdose in the new environment died, whereas only slightly more than half of the rats who were injected in the familiar environment died. Siegel and his colleagues suggest that when human heroin addicts take the drug in an unfamiliar environment, they too run the risk of death from a drug overdose.

By the way, because so many heroin addicts trying to break their habit have reported that the sight of drug paraphernalia made it difficult for them to abstain, the agencies trying to combat drug addiction have stopped preparing posters that feature them.

KEY TERMS AND CONCEPTS

motivation *(358)*

What Is Motivation?

regulatory behavior *(359)*
homeostasis *(359)*
system variable *(359)*
set point *(359)*
detector *(359)*
correctional mechanism *(359)*
negative feedback *(360)*
drive *(360)*
drive reduction *(360)*
incentive *(361)*
optimum-level hypothesis *(361)*
need for achievement *(362)*
need for power *(362)*
need for affiliation *(363)*
perseverance *(365)*
intrinsic motivation *(366)*
undermining of intrinsic motivation *(366)*
learned helplessness *(368)*

Eating

glycogen *(371)*
glucostatic hypothesis *(371)*

glucostat *(371)*
anorexia nervosa *(374)*
bulimia *(374)*

Sexual Behavior

organizational effect *(377)*
activational effect *(378)*
estrous cycle *(378)*
paraphilia *(381)*
transvestism *(381)*
transsexualism *(381)*

Addictive Behavior

anxiolytic effect *(387)*
tolerance *(387)*
withdrawal symptom *(387)*

Aggressive Behavior

intraspecific aggression *(389)*
threat gesture *(389)*
appeasement gesture *(389)*
frustration *(392)*
catharsis *(393)*

SUGGESTIONS FOR FURTHER READING

Beck, R.C. *Motivation: Theories and Principles,* 3rd. ed. Englewood Cliffs, N.J.: Prentice-Hall, 1989.

Geen, R., Arkin, R., and Beatty, W. *Human Motivation: Physiological, Behavioral, and Social Approaches.* Boston: Allyn and Bacon, 1984.

Mook, D.G. *Motivation: The Organization of Action.* New York: W.W. Norton, 1987.

These texts describe the general principles of motivation as well as specific types of motivated behavior.

Olds, J. *Drives and Reinforcement.* New York: Raven Press, 1977.

Stellar, J.R., and Stellar, E. *The Neurobiology of Motivation and Reward.* New York: Springer-Verlag, 1985.

These books discuss the biology of reinforcement.

Logue, A.W. *The Psychology of Eating and Drinking,* 2nd ed. New York: W.H. Freeman, 1992.

This book covers alcohol abuse as well as eating and eating disorders.

Kelley, K., and Byrne, D. *Human Sexual Behavior.* Englewood Cliffs, N.J.: Prentice-Hall, 1991.

Masters, W.H., Johnson, V.E., and Kolodny, R.C. *Human Sexuality,* 2nd ed. Boston: Little, Brown, 1985.

Both books are well written and describe sexual behavior and the social and biological variables that affect it.

12
EMOTION, STRESS, AND HEALTH

Henri Matisse, *The Dream*
Art Resource, N.Y. © 1992 Succession H. Matisse/ARS, N.Y.

LEARNING OBJECTIVES

When you finish this chapter, you should be able to:

1. Define *emotion, mood,* and *temperament,* and describe how psychologists have attempted to classify emotions.
2. Discuss the production and control of conditioned emotional responses and the neural control of emotional behavior.
3. State Darwin's hypothesis of emotional expression, and describe cross-cultural studies and studies with the blind that support it.
4. Describe the social nature of emotional expression in humans and the display rules that influence emotional expression.
5. Describe research on monkeys' ability to learn how to display an emotion.
6. Discuss and evaluate the James-Lange theory of emotion.
7. Discuss Schachter's theory of emotion and research on the role of cognition and physiological responses on emotional states.
8. Explain why stress has harmful effects on health and the physiological response to stress.
9. Describe the variables that determine whether a particular situation will cause a stress reaction, and discuss how stress and personality factors affect cardiovascular disease and posttraumatic stress disorder.
10. Discuss how stress affects the immune system and the development of infectious diseases.

A few years ago, while I was on a sabbatical leave, a colleague stopped by my office and asked whether I would like to see an interesting patient. The patient, a seventy-two-year-old man, had suffered a massive stroke in his right hemisphere that had paralyzed the left side of his body. Three of us went to see him: Dr. W., an undergraduate psychology student who was on a summer internship, and me.

Mr. V. was seated in a wheelchair equipped with a large tray on which his right arm was resting; his left arm was immobilized in a sling, to keep it out of the way. He greeted us politely, almost formally, articulating his words carefully with a slight European accent.

Mr. V. seemed intelligent, and this impression was confirmed when we gave him some of the subtests of the Wechsler Adult Intelligence Test (WAIS-R). He could define rather obscure words, provide the meanings of proverbs, supply information, and do mental arithmetic. In fact, his verbal intelligence appeared to be in the upper 5 percent of the population. The fact that English was not his native language made his performance even more remarkable. But as we expected, he did poorly on even simple tasks that required him to deal with shapes and geometry. He failed to solve even the sample problem for the block design subtest, in which colored blocks must be put together to duplicate a pattern shown in a drawing.

The most interesting aspect of Mr. V.'s behavior after his stroke was his lack of reaction to his symptoms. After we had finished with the testing, we asked him to tell us a little about himself and his life-style. What, for example, was his favorite pastime?

"I like to walk," he said. "I walk at least two hours each day around the city, but mostly I like to walk in the woods. I have maps of most of the National Forests in the state on the walls of my study, and I mark all of the trails I've taken. I figure that in about six months I will have walked all of the trails that are short enough to do in a day. I'm too old to camp out in the woods."

"You're going to finish up those trails in the next six months?" asked Dr. W.

"Yes, and then I'll start over again!" he replied.

"Mr. V., are you having any trouble?" asked Dr. W.

"Trouble? What do you mean?"

"I mean physical difficulty."

"No." Mr. V. gave him a slightly puzzled look.

"Well, what are you sitting in?"

Mr. V. gave him a look that indicated he thought that the question was rather stupid—or perhaps insulting. "A wheelchair, of course," he answered.

"Why are you in a wheelchair?"

Now Mr. V. looked frankly exasperated; he obviously did not like to answer foolish questions. "Because my left leg is paralyzed!" he snapped.

Afterward, as we were discussing the case, Lisa, the student, asked why Mr. V. talked about continuing his walking schedule when he obviously knew that he couldn't walk. Did he think that he would recover soon?

"No, that's not it," said Dr. W. "He *knows* what his problem is, but he doesn't really *understand* it. The people at the rehab center are having trouble with him because he keeps trying to go outside for a walk. The first time, he managed to wheel his chair to the top of the stairs, but someone caught him just in time. Now they have a chain across the doorframe of his room so that he can't get into the hall without an attendant.

"Mr. V.'s problem is not that he can't verbally recognize what's going on; it's that he just can't grasp its significance. The right hemisphere is specialized in seeing many things at once: in seeing all the parts of a geometric shape and grasping its form, or in seeing all the elements of a situation and understanding what they mean. That is what's wrong. He can tell you about his paralyzed leg, about the fact that he is in a wheelchair, and so on, but he does not put these facts together and realize that his days of walking are over.

"As you could see, Mr. V. can still express emotions." We all smiled at the thought of the contemptuous look on Mr. V.'s face. "But the right hemisphere is especially important in assessing the significance of a situation and making conclusions that lead to our being happy or sad or whatever. People with certain right-hemisphere lesions are not bothered at all by their conditions. They can *tell* you about their problems, so I guess they verbally understand it, but their problems just don't affect them emotionally."

He turned to me. "Neil, do you remember Mr. P.?" I nodded. "Mr. P. had a left-hemisphere lesion. He had a severe aphasia and could hardly say a word. We showed him a picture of some objects and asked him to try to name them. He looked at them and started crying. Although he couldn't talk, he knew that he had a serious problem and that things would never be the same for him. His right hemisphere was still working. It could assess the situation and give rise to feelings of sadness and despair."

In a real sense emotions are what life is all about. Life without emotion would be bland and empty. When important things happen to us, they change our feelings. But emotions consist of more than feelings. They are evoked by particular kinds of situations, they tend to occur in association with approach or avoidance behaviors, and they are accompanied by expressions such as smiles and frowns that convey our feelings to other people. Most psychologists who have studied emotions have focused on one or more of the following questions: What kinds of situations produce emotions? What kinds of feelings do people say they experience? What kinds of behaviors do people engage in? What physiological changes do people undergo in situations that produce strong emotions?

Experimental research on human emotions is a difficult endeavor, primarily because ethical and practical considerations make it almost impossible to evoke strong emotions in subjects who volunteer to participate in experiments. Nevertheless, psychologists have learned much about the ways people express emotions and recognize their occurrence in others. Experiments with members of different cultural groups, with blind children, and with animals have shown that many emotions are expressed innately.

This chapter discusses research and theories on the nature of emotion, including the type of stimuli that elicit them and the nature of the feelings that accompany them. (One positive emotion—love—is not discussed in this chapter. Instead, it is discussed in Chapter 17, in a section on interpersonal attraction.) As you will see, the major conclusion that will be drawn in this chapter is that emotions, like consciousness and language, are social behaviors. That is, we display our feelings to others because it is usually advantageous to do so.

This chapter also examines the role of the body's stress reactions, which occur when the primitive flight-or-fight responses are evoked. Are the negative emotions associated with stress involved in physical illnesses, such as cardiovascular disease and cancer? Research on topics such as this one demonstrates how psychologists try to uncover the relations between environmental events and the behaviors, thoughts, and feelings they bring forth.

THE NATURE OF EMOTION

Although no general theory of emotion is available to give us a consistent definition, the term **emotion** is generally used by psychologists for a display of feelings that are evoked when important things happen to us. Emotions are relatively brief and occur in response to events in the environment (or their mental re-creation, as when we remember something embarrassing we did in the past and experience the feelings of embarrassment again). Emotions are closely tied to motivation; when we encounter reinforcing or punishing stimuli, we express and experience positive or negative emotions. The nature of the emotions depends on the nature of the stimuli—and on our prior experience with them.

In contrast, **moods** are longer-lived and are generally weaker than emotions. Behaviorally, moods consist of tendencies to react more strongly to situations that would be likely to evoke only mild emotional reactions in others. For example, if one day a person reacts with anger to situations that most people would ignore, we label the person's mood as *grouchiness*

When important events occur, our feelings and our facial expressions change: that is, we experience and express emotions.

or *irritability*. Much less is known about mood states than about emotions, because the conditions that control them are less distinct. Chapter 15 discusses mental disorders that consist of abnormal alterations in mood.

Temperament is similar to mood but is even longer-lived. Temperament refers to a person's general disposition, or typical pattern of reaction to various situations. Some people are especially sensitive to criticism and easily become angry or depressed; others are generally cheerful and tend to see the bright side of situations. Temperament is thus an aspect of personality, the topic of Chapter 14.

In this section we will consider the fundamental nature of emotions and the types of stimuli that elicit them.

Classification of Emotions

Just how many emotions are there, and what should we call them? Are emotions distinct and independent, or do some of them consist of combinations or blends of reactions? Psychologists have proposed several classification schemes, based on the stimuli that elicit them, the patterns of facial responses associated with them, and the adaptive significance of the behaviors that accompany them. The fact that emotions are elicited by reinforcing and punishing stimuli has suggested to several psychologists that emotions can be classified according to the presence (or the anticipated presence) of such stimuli.

Millenson (1967) suggested that three dimensions are basic to all emotions: fear, anger, and pleasure. These dimensions are all related to reinforcement or punishment: Fear is produced by anticipation of an aversive stimulus, anger by the removal of a reinforcer, and pleasure by anticipation (or actual experience) of reinforcement. A "pure" emotion consists of only one of these dimensions but can vary in intensity. For example, pleasure, elation, and ecstasy are all associated with reinforcement. "Mixed" emotions contain varying amounts of two or three of the factors. For example, Millenson suggests that a child who steals a cookie experiences both the pleasure of eating it and the fear caused by anticipation of punishment. The resulting compound emotion is usually labeled as *guilt*. (See *Figure 12.1.*) To this scheme, Rolls (1987) has added a fourth dimension, relief, which is produced by removal of an aversive stimulus.

Another theorist, (Tomkins, 1962, 1963, 1982), has proposed a classification scheme

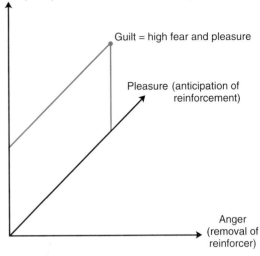

Figure 12.1   Millenson's model of emotion. When a child steals a cookie, the composite fear and pleasure cause the emotion of guilt.

based on the types of movements and expressions people exhibit. He asserts that there are nine innate emotions, three positive and six negative. The positive emotions are (1) *interest* (or *excitement*), expressed by a fixed or tracking stare (in the case of a moving object) with eyebrows down; (2) *enjoyment* (or *joy*), expressed by a smile; and (3) *surprise* (or *startle*), expressed with raised eyebrows and an eyeblink. The negative emotions are (1) *distress* (or *anguish*), expressed by crying; (2) *fear* (or *terror*), expressed by withdrawal, wide-open eyes, trembling, and pale, cold, and sweating skin; (3) *shame* (or *humiliation*), expressed by a lowering of the head and eyes; (4) *contempt*, expressed by raising the upper lip in a sneer; (5) *disgust*, expressed by protrusion and lowering of the lower lip; and (6) *anger* (or *rage*), expressed by a frown, clenched jaw, and reddening of the face.

Facial expressions of emotion communicate useful information to other members of the species. For instance, signs of surprise or fear alert other animals that something important or dangerous may be near. Signs of disgust suggest that something—perhaps a food that previously made the animal ill—is to be avoided. Signs of anger warn the recipient to retreat or be ready to fight. Signs of sadness (distress) invite sympathy and consolation. And signs of interest directed toward another animal suggest a willingness to engage in social interaction, perhaps including sexual activity. Some signs are used to reinforce or punish another animal's behavior: A smile (a sign of enjoyment) serves as a rein-

Table 12.1   Plutchik's categories of species-typical behaviors, functions, and emotional labels

Species-Typical Behaviors	Functions	Emotional Labels
Withdrawing, escaping	Protection	Fear
Attacking, biting	Destruction	Anger
Mating, courting	Reproduction	Joy
Crying for help	Reintegration	Sadness
Pair bonding, grooming	Affiliation	Acceptance
Vomiting, spitting out	Rejection	Disgust
Examining, mapping	Exploration	Expectancy
Stopping, freezing	Orientation	Surprise

Source: Adapted from Plutchik, R., Emotions: A general psychoevolutionary theory. In Scherer and Ekman (1984).

forcer, and an expression of contempt serves as a punisher. A sign of shame probably serves to prevent other animals from attacking a transgressor that acknowledges its wrongdoing. (The facial expression of emotions is discussed further in the next section of this chapter.)

Another approach to classifying emotions is based on the adaptive significance of various classes of species-typical behaviors (Plutchik, 1962, 1980). The functions of these behaviors include the following: *Protection* involves avoidance of danger or harm. *Destruction* involves attacking another animal or an inanimate source of danger. *Reproduction* involves courting, mating, and possessing another. *Reintegration* involves calling for assistance or sympathy because of a loss of something important. *Incorporation* (or *affiliation*) involves forming bonds with other members of the species. *Rejection* involves expelling harmful substances such as poisons. *Exploration* involves mapping the environment. And *orientation* involves turning toward a novel object or situation and paying attention to it. Table 12.1 shows the relation of these categories of functions to some representative species-typical behaviors that accomplish the functions; it gives some typical causes of the behaviors and also lists the emotions that accompany them. (See *Table 12.1.*)

Emotions as Response Patterns

2 All emotional responses, however we classify them, contain three components: behavioral, autonomic, and hormonal. The *behavioral* component consists of muscular movements that are appropriate to the situation that elicits them. For example, a dog defending its territory

against an intruder first adopts an aggressive posture, growls, and shows its teeth. If the intruder does not leave, the defender runs toward it and attacks. *Autonomic* responses—that is, changes in the activity of the autonomic nervous system—facilitate these behaviors and provide quick mobilization of energy for vigorous movement. As a consequence, the dog's heart rate increases, and changes in the size of blood vessels shunt the circulation of blood away from the digestive organs toward the muscles. *Hormonal* responses reinforce the autonomic responses. The hormones secreted by the adrenal glands further increase heart rate and blood flow to the muscles and also make more glucose available to them.

This section discusses research on the control of overt emotional behaviors and the autonomic and hormonal responses that accompany them. Special behaviors that serve to communicate emotional states to other animals, such as the threat gestures that precede an actual attack and the smiles and frowns used by humans, will be discussed in the second section of the chapter.

Conditioned Emotional Responses.   Emotional responses, like all other responses, can be modified by experience. For example, we can learn that a particular situation is dangerous or threatening. Once the learning has taken place, we will become frightened when we encounter that situation. This type of learning is called a **conditioned emotional response,** which is learned through the process of classical conditioning.

A conditioned emotional response is one that is produced by a neutral stimulus that has been paired with an emotion-producing stimulus. For example, a painful stimulus applied to an animal's paw will elicit a specific defensive reflex: The animal will withdraw its paw from the source of the pain. In addition, the painful stimulus will also elicit responses controlled by the autonomic nervous system: The animal's pupils will dilate, its heart rate and blood pressure will increase, it will breathe faster, and so on. The stimulus will also cause some stress-related hormones to be secreted. And depending on the animal's species and the nature of the aversive stimulus, it may run away or it may stop moving and "freeze" in place.

If an animal learns to make a specific response that avoids contact with the aversive stimulus (or at least minimizes its painful effect), most of the nonspecific "emotional" responses will eventually disappear. That is, if the animal learns a successful **coping response,** the emotional responses will no longer occur. For example, if an animal learns to retract its paw every time a warning stimulus occurs, thus avoiding a painful stimulus, the responses it showed earlier—the increased heart rate, blood pressure, and breathing—will no longer be seen. The situation is under control and no longer provokes an emotional reaction. (The role of coping responses in resistance to stress will be discussed in the final section of this chapter.) In contrast, if an aversive stimulus follows a warning stimulus *no matter what the animal does,* the animal will continue to display a conditioned emotional response. You can imagine your own emotional response to the buzzing sound of a flying wasp if on several occasions you were stung after hearing this sound, even though you tried to get away from the wasp.

Research by physiological psychologists indicates that a particular brain region plays an important role in the expression of conditioned emotional responses. It serves as a focal point between sensory systems and effector systems that are responsible for behavioral, autonomic, and hormonal components of conditioned emotional responses (Kapp et al., 1982; LeDoux, 1987). This region is the *amygdala,* which is

located in the temporal lobe, just in front of the hippocampus. (Refer to **Figure 3.21.**)

LeDoux and his colleagues have studied the role of the amygdala in conditioned emotional responses. They produced classically conditioned emotional responses in rats by pairing an auditory stimulus with a brief electrical shock delivered to the feet. They presented an 800-Hz (hertz) tone for 10 s (seconds), and then they delivered a brief (0.5 s) shock to the floor on which the animals were standing. (See **Figure 12.2.**) By itself, the shock produces an *unconditional* emotional response: The animal jumps into the air, its heart rate and blood pressure increase, and its adrenal glands secrete epinephrine, norepinephrine, and steroid stress hormones. The experimenters presented several pairings of the two stimuli, which established classical conditioning.

The investigators tested conditioned emotional responses the next day by presenting the 800-Hz tone several times and measuring the animals' blood pressure and heart rate and observing its behavior. (They did not present the shock.) When the rats heard this tone, their heart rate and blood pressure increased and they showed behavioral arrest—a species-typical defensive response called *freezing.* That is, the animals acted as if they were expecting to receive a shock.

LeDoux and his colleagues found that damage to the amygdala disrupts the behavioral, autonomic, and hormonal components of conditioned emotional responses (LeDoux, 1987; Van de Kar et al., 1991). Conversely, the injection of an excitatory drug into this region *produces* emotional responses, including increased heart rate and blood pressure (Iwata, Chida, and LeDoux, 1987). In fact, long-term stimulation of the central amygdala produces gastric ulcers (Henke, 1982), and its destruction helps *prevent* the development of ulcers when an animal is exposed to a stressful situation (Ray, Henke, and Sullivan, 1987). These observations suggest that the autonomic responses controlled by the central nucleus are among those responsible for the harmful effects of long-term stress, which are discussed in the final section of this chapter.

Researchers in several different laboratories have shown that individual neurons in the amygdala become active when emotionally relevant stimuli are presented. For example, these neurons are excited by such stimuli as the sight of a device that has been used to squirt either a bad-tasting or a sweet solution into the animal's mouth, the sound of another animal's vocaliza-

Figure 12.2 The procedure used to produce conditioned emotional responses.

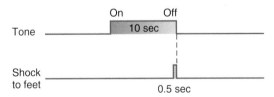

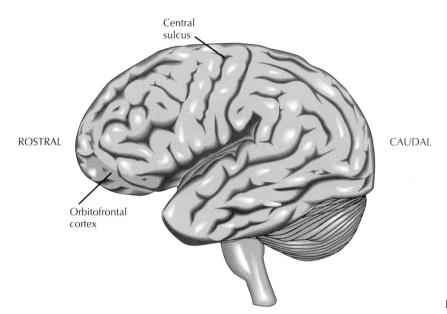

Central
sulcus

ROSTRAL

CAUDAL

Orbitofrontal
cortex

Figure 12.3   The orbitofrontal cortex.

tion, the sound of the opening of the laboratory door, the smell of smoke, or the sight of another animal's face (O'Keefe and Bouma, 1969; Jacobs and McGinty, 1972; Rolls, 1982; Leonard et al., 1985).

Emotions Produced by Social Situations. Although conditioned emotional responses can be elicited by very simple stimuli, our emotions are often reactions to very complex situations, especially those involving other people. Perceiving the meaning of social situations is obviously more complex than perceiving individual stimuli; it involves experiences and memories, inferences and judgments. In fact, the skills involved include some of the most complex ones we possess. These skills are not localized in any one part of the cerebral cortex, although research does suggest that the right hemisphere is more important than the left. But one region of the brain—the orbitofrontal cortex—plays a special role.

The **orbitofrontal cortex** is located at the base of the frontal lobes. It covers the part of the brain just above the *orbits*—the bones that form the eye sockets—hence the term *orbitofrontal*. (See *Figure 12.3.*) The orbitofrontal cortex receives information from the sensory system and from the regions of the frontal lobes that control behavior. Thus, it knows what is going on in the environment and what plans are being made to respond to these events. It also communicates extensively with the limbic system, which is known to play an important role in emotional reactions. In particular, its connections with the amygdala permit it to affect the activity of this structure.

The fact that the orbitofrontal cortex plays an important role in emotional behavior is shown by the effects of damage to this region. The first—and most famous—case comes from the mid-1800s. Phineas Gage, a dynamite worker, was using a steel rod to ram a charge of dynamite into a hole drilled in solid rock. Suddenly, the charge exploded and sent the rod into his cheek, through his brain, and out the top of his head. (See *Figure 12.4.*) He survived, but he was a different man. Before his injury he was serious, industrious, and energetic. Afterward,

Figure 12.4   A bust and skull of Phineas Gage. The steel rod entered his left cheek and exited through his left forehead. (Warren Museum, Harvard Medical School. Reprinted with permission.)

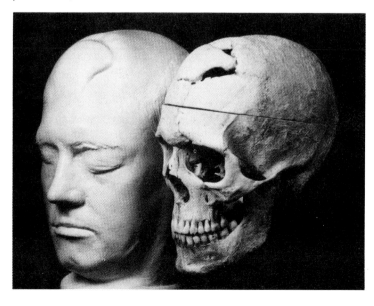

he became childish, irresponsible, and thought-less of others. He was unable to make or carry out plans, and his actions appeared to be capricious and whimsical. His accident largely destroyed the orbitofrontal cortex.

Over the succeeding years physicians reported several cases similar to that of Phineas Gage. In general, damage to the orbitofrontal cortex reduced people's inhibitions and self-concern; they became indifferent to the consequences of their actions. In addition, although they remained sensitive to noxious stimuli, the pain no longer bothered them—it no longer produced an emotional reaction. Then in 1935 the report of an experiment with a chimpanzee triggered events whose repercussions are still felt today. Jacobsen, Wolf, and Jackson (1935) tested various species of nonhuman primates on a *delayed response test*. While the animal watched, the experimenter hid a piece of food in one of two locations and then lowered an opaque screen in front of the animal. After a delay the opaque screen was raised, and the animal was given one chance to find the food. If it chose the wrong location, it got nothing and had to wait until the next trial. Obviously, this task required the animal to remember where the food was hidden during the delay period. Jacobsen and his colleagues described the case of one chimpanzee, Becky, who displayed a violent emotional reaction to this task.

> In the normal phase, this animal was extremely eager to work and apparently well motivated; but this subject was highly emotional and profoundly upset whenever she made an error. Violent temper tantrums after a mistake were not infrequent occurrences. She observed closely loading of the cup with food, and often whimpered softly as the cup was placed over the food. [When] the experimenter lowered . . . the opaque door to exclude the animal's view of the cups, she immediately flew into a temper tantrum, rolled on the floor, defecated and urinated. After a few such reactions during the training period, the animal would make no further responses. . . .
>
> [After a bilateral lesion of the frontal lobes was performed,] a profound change occurred. The chimpanzee offered its usual friendly greeting, and eagerly ran from its living quarters to the transfer cage, and in turn went properly to the experimental cage. The usual procedure of baiting the cup and lowering the opaque screen was followed. But the chimpanzee did not show any excitement and sat quietly before the door or walked around the cage. . . . If the animal made a mistake, it showed no evidence of emotional disturbance but quietly

awaited the loading of the cups for the next trial. (From C.F. Jacobsen, J.B. Wolf, and T.A. Jackson, *Journal of Nervous and Mental Disease, 82*, 9–10, © by Williams & Wilkins, 1935.)

These findings were reported at a scientific meeting in 1935, which was attended by Egas Moniz, a Portuguese neuropsychiatrist. Another report presented at that meeting indicated that radical removal of the frontal lobes in a human patient (performed because of a tumor) did not appear to produce intellectual impairment (Brickner, 1936). These two reports suggested that frontal lobotomy might reduce pathological emotional reactions and that the operation might not have serious consequences for the patient's intellect. One of Jacobson's colleagues, John Fulton, reported that after Jacobsen had described the results of Becky's surgery, "Dr. Moniz arose and asked if frontal-lobe removal . . . eliminates frustrational behavior, why would it not be feasible to relieve anxiety states in man by surgical means?" (Fulton, 1949, pp. 63–64). In fact, Moniz did persuade a neurosurgeon to do so, and approximately one hundred operations were eventually performed under his supervision. (In 1949 Moniz received the Nobel Prize for the development of this procedure.)

A few paragraphs ago I said that the repercussions of the 1935 meeting are still felt today. Since that time tens of thousands of people have received prefrontal lobotomies, primarily to reduce symptoms of emotional distress, and many of these people are still alive. At first the procedure was welcomed by the medical community because it provided their patients with relief from emotional anguish. Only after many years were careful studies performed on the side effects of the procedure. These studies showed that although patients did perform well on standard tests of intellectual ability, they showed serious changes in personality, becoming irresponsible and childish. They also lost the ability to carry out plans and most were unemployable. And although pathological emotional reactions were eliminated, so were normal ones. Because of these findings, and because of the discovery of drugs and therapeutic methods that relieve the patients' symptoms without producing such drastic side effects, neurosurgeons eventually abandoned the prefrontal lobotomy procedure (Valenstein, 1986).

What, exactly, does the orbitofrontal cortex do? One possibility is that it is involved in assessing the personal significance of whatever is currently happening. However, this suggestion does not appear to be correct. People whose orbitofrontal cortex has been damaged by disease or accident are still able to accurately assess the significance of particular situations, but only in a *theoretical* sense. For example, Eslinger and Damasio (1985) found that a patient with bilateral damage of the orbitofrontal cortex (produced by a brain tumor, which was successfully removed) displayed excellent social judgment. When he was given hypothetical situations that required him to make decisions about what the people involved should do—situations involving moral, ethical, or practical dilemmas—he always gave sensible answers and justified them with carefully reasoned logic. However, his own life was a different matter. He frittered away his life savings on investments that his family and friends pointed out were bound to fail. He lost one job after another because of his irresponsibility. He became unable to distinguish between trivial decisions and important ones, spending hours trying to decide where to have dinner but failing to use good judgment in situations that concerned his occupation and family life. (His wife finally left him and sued for divorce.) As the authors noted, "He had learned and used normal patterns of social behavior before his brain lesion, and although he could recall such patterns when he was questioned about their applicability, *real-life situations failed to evoke them*" (p. 1737). Thus, it appears that the orbitofrontal cortex is not directly involved in making judgments and conclusions about events (these occur elsewhere in the brain) but in *translating these judgments into appropriate feelings and behaviors.*

INTERIM SUMMARY

The Nature of Emotion

Several attempts to classify emotions have been based on a functional analysis of the biological significance of emotional displays. Millenson and Rolls relate emotions to the process of reinforcement and punishment; they suggest that emotions are produced by the presence or removal of aversive or appetitive stimuli. Tomkins suggests that there are nine primary emotions, based on innate patterns of body movement and facial expression. These expressions communicate useful information to other members of the species. Plutchik based his classification on various categories of species-typical behaviors, rea-

soning that emotional expressions and feelings would accompany each category of behavior.

The word *emotion* refers to behaviors, physiological responses, and feelings. This section has discussed emotional response patterns, which consist of behaviors that deal with particular situations and physiological responses (both autonomic and hormonal) that support the behaviors. The amygdala organizes behavioral, autonomic, and hormonal responses to a variety of situations, including those that produce fear or anger. Stimulation of the amygdala leads to emotional responses, and its destruction disrupts them. Electrical recordings of single neurons in the amygdala indicate that some of them respond when the animal perceives particular stimuli with emotional significance.

The orbitofrontal cortex plays an important role in emotional reactions. People with damage to this region are able to explain the implications of complex social situations but are unable to respond appropriately when these situations concern *them*. Thus, this region does not appear to be necessary for making judgments about the personal significance of social situations, but it does appear to be necessary for translating these judgments into appropriate actions and emotional responses. The orbitofrontal cortex receives information from the limbic system, the sensory system, and the brain regions that make plans and control movements. It produces emotional reactions through its connections with the amygdala and other parts of the limbic system.

Between the late 1930s and the late 1950s many people received prefrontal lobotomies, operations that damage the frontal lobes. Although the surgery affected many parts of the frontal lobes, the most important region was probably the orbitofrontal cortex. The operations often relieved emotional anguish and the suffering caused by pain. But it also made people become largely indifferent to the social consequences of their own behavior and to the feelings of others, and it interfered with their ability to make and execute plans. Prefrontal lobotomies are no longer performed. ∎

EXPRESSION AND RECOGNITION OF EMOTIONS

3 The previous section described emotions as organized responses (behavioral, autonomic, and hormonal) that deal with the existing situation in the environment, such as events that pose a threat to the organism. For our earliest premammalian ancestors that is undoubtedly all there was to emotions. But over time other responses, with new functions, evolved. Many species of animals (including our own) communicate their emotions to others by means of postural changes and facial expressions. These expressions serve useful social functions; they tell other individuals how we feel and—more to the point—what we are likely to do. For example, they warn a rival that we are angry or tell friends that we are sad and would like some comfort and reassurance.

This section reviews theories and research on the expression and recognition of emotions. As we will see, the available evidence indicates that emotional responses consist of particular patterns of movements, controlled by brain mechanisms that an organism inherits from its ancestors. If this conclusion is true, then emotions have been important enough to survival to affect the inheritance of these brain mechanisms. But natural selection cannot possibly operate on *feelings*—it must operate on some traits of the organism that affect its ability to survive and reproduce. The traits associated with emotions consist of behaviors important to survival and reproductive success, because they communicate vital messages to other members of the species.

Facial Expression of Emotions: Innate Responses

Charles Darwin (1872/1965) suggested that human expressions of emotion have evolved from similar expressions in other animals. He said that emotional expressions are innate, unlearned responses consisting of a complex set of movements, principally of the facial muscles. Thus, a man's sneer and a wolf's snarl are biologically determined response patterns, both controlled by innate brain mechanisms, just as coughing and sneezing are. (Of course, men can sneer and wolves can snarl for quite different reasons.) Some of these movements resemble the behaviors themselves and may have evolved from them. For example, a snarl shows one's teeth and can be seen as an anticipation of biting.

Darwin obtained evidence for his conclusion that emotional expressions were innate by observing his own children and by corresponding with people living in various isolated cultures around the world. He reasoned that if people all over the world, no matter how isolated, show the same facial expressions of emotion, then

these expressions must be inherited instead of learned. The logical argument goes like this: When groups of people are isolated for many years, they develop different languages. Thus, we can say that the words people use are arbitrary; there is no biological basis for using particular words to represent particular concepts. However, if facial expressions are inherited, then they should take approximately the same form in people from all cultures, despite their isolation from one another. And Darwin did, indeed, find that people in different cultures used the same patterns of movement of facial muscles to express a particular emotional state.

In 1967 and 1968 Ekman and Friesen carried out some interesting cross-cultural observations that validated those of Darwin (Ekman, 1980). They visited an isolated tribe in a remote area of New Guinea—the South Fore tribe. This group of 319 adults and children had never been exposed to Western culture. They had never seen a movie, lived in a Western town, or worked for someone from outside their culture. Therefore, if they were able to identify accurately the emotional expressions of Westerners as well as they could identify those of members of their own tribe, and if their own facial expressions were the same as those of Westerners, then the researchers could conclude that these expressions were not culturally determined.

Because translations of single words from one language to another are not always accurate, Ekman and Friesen told little stories to describe an emotion instead of presenting a single word. They told the story to a subject, presented three photographs of Westerners depicting three different emotions, and asked the subject to choose the appropriate one. Here are three examples of the stories:

> *Fear*—She is sitting in her house all alone and there is no one else in the village; and there is no knife, ax, or bow and arrow in the house. A wild pig is standing in the door of the house and the woman is looking at the pig and is very afraid of it. The pig has been standing in the doorway for a few minutes and the person is looking at it very afraid and the pig won't move away from the door and she is afraid the pig will bite her.
>
> *Happy*—Her friends have come and she is happy.
>
> *Anger*—She is angry and is about to fight. (Ekman, 1980, p. 130)

Now look at *Figure 12.5* to see whether you would have any trouble matching each of these

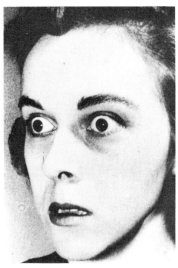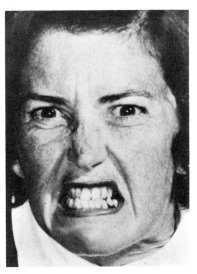

Figure 12.5 Emotional expression. In a study by Ekman and Friesen subjects were asked to match each story with the appropriate photograph. (From Ekman, P. *The Face of Man: Expressions of Universal Emotions in a New Guinea Village.* New York: Garland STPM Press, 1980. By permission of Silvan Tomkins. Photo by Ed. Gallob.)

stories with one of the photographs shown there.

I am sure that you did not have any trouble—and neither did the members of the Fore tribe. In a second study Ekman and Friesen asked Fore tribespeople to imagine how they would feel in situations that would produce various emotions, and the researchers videotaped their facial expressions. They showed photographs of the videotapes to American college students, who had no trouble identifying the emotions. Four of them are shown in Figure 12.6. The caption describes the story that was used to elicit the expression. (See *Figure 12.6.*)

Other researchers have compared the facial expressions of blind and normally sighted children. They reasoned that if the facial expressions of both groups are similar, then the expressions are natural for our species and do not require learning by imitation. (Studies of blind adults would not be conclusive, because adults would have heard enough descriptions of facial expressions to be able to pose them.)

In fact, the facial expressions of young blind and sighted children are very similar. However, as blind children grow older, their facial gestures tend to become somewhat less expressive (Woodworth and Schlosberg, 1954; Izard, 1971). This finding suggests that social reinforcement is important in maintaining our displays of emotion. However, the evidence clearly shows that we do not have to learn to smile, frown, or show other feelings with our facial gestures. Both the cross-cultural studies and

the investigations with blind children confirm the naturalness of these expressions.

The results of cross-cultural studies and studies with blind people suggest strongly that situations expected to have motivational relevance produce consistent patterns of contraction in the facial muscles. Thus, the patterns of movement are apparently inherited—wired into the brain, so to speak. The consistency of facial movements suggests an underlying consistency of emotional feeling throughout our species.

The neural circuits responsible for the pattern of movements that constitute facial expressions appear to be located in the brain stem. These circuits are controlled (that is, turned on or off according to what is happening to the person) by the frontal lobes. The best evidence for this proposition comes from a syndrome known as *pseudobulbar palsy*. Damage to the medulla (also known as the *bulb*) can cause a paralysis of the facial region known as *bulbar palsy*. **Pseudobulbar palsy** resembles this disorder but is caused by damage to the pathway between the frontal lobes and the regions of the brain stem that control movements of the facial muscles. People with pseudobulbar palsy cannot make voluntary movements of the facial muscles, but they can still show *automatic* movements such as yawning, coughing, and clearing the throat. More to the point, they can still smile, frown, laugh, and cry. In fact, seemingly trivial events can trigger a prolonged bout of uncontrollable laughing or crying, which the patient is helpless to stop. Apparently, once the brain stem mechanisms are deprived of their

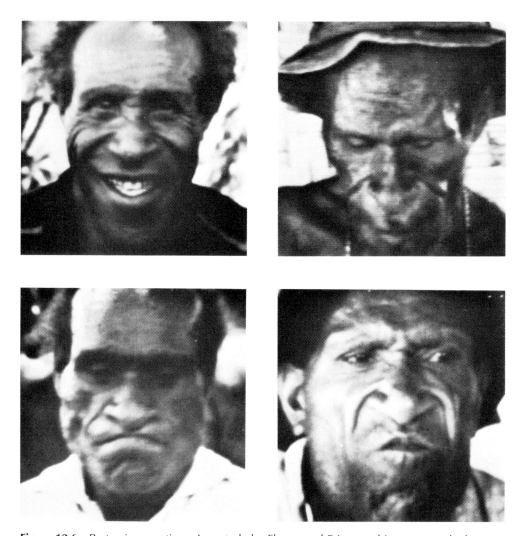

Figure 12.6 Portraying emotions. In a study by Ekman and Friesen subjects were asked to make faces (shown in the photographs) when they were told the stories. (a) "Your friend has come and you are happy." (b) "Your child had died." (c) "You are angry and about to fight." (d) "You see a dead pig that has been lying there a long time." (From Ekman, P. *The Face of Man: Expressions of Universal Emotions in a New Guinea Village.* New York: Garland STPM Press, 1980. Reprinted with permission.)

normal control by the frontal lobe, they are more easily aroused by the excitatory inputs from other parts of the brain.

The Social Nature of Emotional Expressions in Humans

4 A good case can be made that emotions exist because expressions of emotion communicate important information to other members of the species. An interesting study by Kraut and Johnston (1979) showed that people are more likely to express signs of happiness in the presence of other people than when they are alone. The investigators unobtrusively observed whether people smiled in three situations: while bowling and making a strike or missing one,

while watching a hockey game and seeing the home team score or be scored against, and while walking down a street on a beautiful day or a hot and humid one. They found that the happy situations (making a strike, seeing the home team score, or experiencing a beautiful day) produced only small signs of happiness when the people being observed were alone. However, when the people were interacting socially with other people, they were much more likely to smile. For example, bowlers who made a strike usually did not smile when the ball hit the pins. However, when the bowlers turned around to face their companions, they often smiled.

Of course, under some conditions, we suppress expressions of emotion, exaggerate them, or try to fake them, as we will see later in this chapter. But when we do express emotions, they tend to be displayed toward other people.

Situations That Produce Emotions: Role of Cognition

Emotions do not occur spontaneously; they are provoked by particular stimuli, as we saw in the section on conditioned emotional responses. For humans the eliciting stimuli and the emotions they produce can be far removed from each other in time, and they can involve cognitive processes. For example, we can experience emotions by remembering things that happened to us or things we did—or by imagining events that *might* occur. In addition, emotions can be the products of cognitive processes. For example, suppose that someone says something to you that, on the surface, appears to be complimentary. This event would probably make you feel pleased. But suppose you later think about the remark and realize that it was actually a disguised insult. This realization—a product of your cognitive processes—leads you to become angry.

Most investigators believe that humans do not differ substantially from most other mammals in their expressions and feelings of emotion. There are differences, of course, but the differences appear to be less important than the similarities. If you have ever had a dog, you know that it can express fear, anger, happiness, sadness, surprise, shame, and other emotions in ways that we can recognize as similar to ours. However, we do differ substantially from other animals in the *types of stimuli* that can evoke these emotions. For example, an animal may become frightened and embarrassed by the presence of a large group of strangers, but only humans can become frightened and embarrassed by having to perform in front of a television camera, because only humans realize that they are confronting an unseen audience. Similarly, only humans can experience feelings of love and longing while looking at a picture of an absent loved one.

In humans emotions are often produced by judging the significance of a particular situation. For example, after a performance a pianist may perceive the applause as praise for an outstanding performance, judging it to be a positive evaluation of her own worth. She feels pride and satisfaction. In this case her emotional state is produced by social reinforcement—the expression of approval and admiration by other people. However, if the pianist believes she has performed poorly, she may judge the applause as mindless enthusiasm of people who have no taste or appreciation for music, so that she feels only contempt. Furthermore, the person who turned the pages of the music is also present on the stage and thus also perceives the applause. However, because he does not evaluate the applause as praise for anything he did, he does not experience the emotions the pianist feels. The applause may even make him feel jealous. Clearly, a given set of stimuli does not always elicit the same emotion; in this case the judgments made about the significance of the stimuli determine the emotion the person feels.

Control of Emotional Expression: Display Rules

We all realize that our expressions of emotions can be read by other people. Consequently, we sometimes try to hide our true feelings, attempting to appear impassive or even to display an emotion different from what we feel. At other times, we may exaggerate our emotional response to make sure that others see how we feel. For example, if a friend tells us about a devastating experience, we make sure that our facial expression conveys appropriate sadness and sympathy.

Researchers have studied all these phenomena. Attempting to hide an emotion is called **masking.** Attempting to exaggerate or minimize the expression of an emotion is called **modulation.** And attempting to express an emotion we do not actually feel is called **simulation.** According to Ekman and Friesen (1975), the expression of emotions often follows culturally determined **display rules**—rules that prescribe under what situations we should or should not display signs of particular emotions. Although the patterns of muscular movements that accompany particular feelings are biologically determined, these movements can, to a certain extent, be controlled by display rules. (See *Figure 12.7.*)

Each culture has a particular set of display rules. For example, in Western society it is impolite for a winner to show too much pleasure and for a loser to show too much disappointment. The expression of these emotions is supposed to be modulated downward. Also, in many societies it is unmanly to cry or show fear and unfeminine to show anger.

Several studies have found that North American boys and girls differ in their facial expressions of emotion as they get older, presumably because they learn about their society's

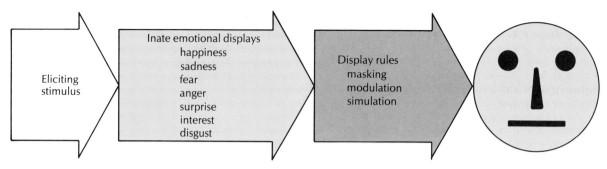

Figure 12.7 Controlled facial displays. Innate emotional displays can be modified by display rules. (Adapted from Ekman, P., and Friesen, W. *Semiotica*, 1969, *1*, 49–98.)

gender-specific display rules. Very young infants show no sex differences in facial expression (Field, 1982). However, by the time they are in nursery school, boys and girls begin to differ. Buck (1975, 1977) showed various types of color slides to nursery schoolchildren and unobtrusively videotaped their faces as they watched. Some slides were pleasant, some puzzling, and some unpleasant. He showed the videotapes of the children to adults (university students) and asked them to try to guess the nature of the children's emotional expressions. Buck assumed that the accuracy of the ratings would indicate the degree of emotional expression. Indeed, the adults could guess the girls' emotions more accurately than the boys'.

Ekman and his colleagues (Ekman, Friesen, and Ellsworth, 1972; Friesen, 1972) attempted to assess a different kind of culturally determined display rule. They showed a distressing film to Japanese and American college students, singly and in the presence of a visitor, who was described to the subjects as a scientist. Because the Japanese culture discourages public display of emotion, the researchers expected that the Japanese students would show fewer facial expressions of emotion in public than when alone.

The researchers recorded the facial expressions of their subjects with hidden cameras while the subjects viewed a film showing a gruesome and bloody coming-of-age rite in a primitive tribe. The results were as predicted. When the subjects were alone, American and Japanese subjects showed the same facial expressions. When they were with another person, the Japanese students were less likely to express negative emotions and more likely to mask these expressions with polite smiles. Thus, people from both societies used the same facial expressions of emotion but were subject to different social display rules.

When people attempt to mask the expression of a strongly felt emotion, they usually are not completely able to do so. That is, there is some **leakage,** or subtle sign of the emotion (Ekman and Friesen, 1969). Ekman and Friesen (1974) investigated this phenomenon. They showed an unpleasant film of burns and amputations to female nursing students. After watching the film, the subjects were interviewed by an experimenter, who asked them about the film. Some of the subjects were asked to pretend to the interviewer that they had seen a pleasant film. The experimenters videotaped the subjects during the interviews and showed these tapes to a separate group of raters, asking them to try to determine whether the people they were watching were being honest or deceptive. The raters were shown videotapes of the subjects' faces or bodies. The results indicated that the raters could detect the deception better when they saw the subjects' bodies than when they saw their faces; apparently, people are better at masking signs of emotion shown by their facial muscles than those shown by muscles in other parts of their body. Presumably, people recognize the attention paid to the face and learn to control their facial expressions better than the movements of the rest of the body.

Learning When to Display an Emotion

[5] A research project by Marler, Seyfarth, and Cheney (summarized by Marler, 1984) illustrates the adaptive value of emotional displays and shows how animals can learn to react appropriately to different stimuli. Vervet monkeys at Amboseli in Kenya are preyed upon by two species: leopards and martial eagles. If a leopard is in the area, the worst place for a monkey to be is in dense brush, where it might be attacked. The best place to be is up in a tree, perched on branches that are too small to bear the weight of a leopard. Conversely, if a martial eagle is nearby, then a tree is precisely the wrong place to be; the monkey should hide in dense cover

where an eagle cannot easily land. The most important value of a fear display is to warn other animals that danger is near. But for vervet monkeys of Amboseli a generalized display of fear that indicates the presence of a predator is not useful, because the other animals must know where to hide.

Indeed, Marler and his colleagues have found that when a vervet monkey detects the presence of a predator, it makes a particular type of alarm call. When a monkey sees a leopard, it emits loud, short, tonal sounds as it inhales and exhales. When a monkey sees a martial eagle, it emits a series of low-pitched, staccato grunts. In addition, when a monkey sees a snake (which does not prey on monkeys but can harm them), it emits a series of high-pitched "chutters." Even when they are played by a tape recorder, these three alarm calls cause different behaviors in the colony. Leopard alarm calls cause the monkeys to run up into trees; eagle alarm calls cause them to look up toward the sky and run into dense cover; and snake alarm calls cause them to look down at the ground, often while standing on their hind legs.

Adult vervet monkeys emit these alarm calls only when other monkeys are present; if

A vervet monkey from Kenya with her infant. Marler and his colleagues studied the development of vervet monkeys and their ability to learn to respond to appropriate stimuli with the appropriate signs of distress.

they are alone, they quickly and silently retreat to the best hiding place. This differentiation lends further support to the conclusion that the display is an important social behavior. In addition, the monkeys make the calls only when the appropriate predator is present. That is, they do not emit the eagle alarm call when they see a vulture or a stork or even another species of eagle, and they do not emit the leopard alarm call when they see other mammals. They may sometimes emit the leopard alarm call in response to a lion or a hyena, but such behavior is probably not a "mistake," because these animals can also be dangerous to monkeys and are best avoided by climbing a tree.

Young vervet monkeys act differently from adults. They, too, emit the three types of alarm calls. According to the observations of Marler (1984) and his colleagues, these calls appear to be innate responses. However, unlike adults, young monkeys make the calls in response to a wide range of stimuli. For example, they may emit the eagle alarm call when they see an owl. As they get older, their responses become more and more specific, until they are discriminating as well as the adults. In fact, their behavior resembles that of a human infant learning the precise meaning of a word. Marler and his colleagues suggest that the behavior of the rest of the colony reinforces correct discriminations. When an adult monkey emits an alarm call, the call is soon taken up by other monkeys. However, when an infant or a juvenile emits a call, the others join in only if they, too, see the predator. Thus, when an infant sees an owl and emits the eagle alarm call, the other monkeys, seeing only an owl, ignore it. However, when the response is appropriate, they join in chorus. Presumably, being ignored or joined in the alarm call extinguishes inappropriate responses and reinforces appropriate ones.

This impressive research project has interesting implications for the evolutionary development of both emotions and language. Clearly, the ability to learn to communicate with other individuals about particular classes of stimuli is not peculiar to our own species.

INTERIM SUMMARY

Expression and Recognition of Emotions

The effect of emotions on social behavior is seen in the facial gestures that we make to express our feelings to others. Darwin believed that expression of emotion by facial gestures was innate and that muscular movements were inherited behavioral patterns.

Subsequent experiments showed that Darwin was correct. Ekman and his colleagues performed a careful cross-cultural study with members of the Fore tribe. These people recognized facial expressions of Westerners and made facial gestures that were clear to Westerners. These results, along with observations of blind children, strongly suggest that emotional expressions are innate behavior patterns. A neurological disorder called pseudobulbar palsy indicates that facial expressions of emotion are organized by neural mechanisms in the brain stem but that the frontal lobes determine when these movements occur.

An observational study of humans indicated that smiles appear to occur most often when someone is interacting socially with other people. This finding supports the social nature of emotional expression. The fact that infants imitate people's facial expressions suggests that imitation is an innate tendency. Perhaps the function of this imitation is to permit the sender to evoke similar emotions in the receiver so that the receiver will engage in an appropriate behavior.

As we saw in the first section of this chapter, in the process of classical conditioning previously neutral stimuli can come to elicit emotions. Emotions can also be evoked by complex stimuli or situations or even in response to internal behaviors, as when we think about a situation and finally realize its significance.

Expressions of emotion are not always frank and honest indications of a person's emotional state; they can be masked, modulated, or simulated according to culturally determined display rules. For example, although male and female infants do not differ in their degree of emotional expression, children begin to acquire different patterns of responding during early childhood. Cultural differences also exist, as the study comparing Japanese and American people observed. Even when a person attempts to mask his or her expression of emotion, some leakage occurs, particularly in movements of the body. Presumably, we learn to control our facial expressions better because we are aware of the attention other people pay to these expressions.

Studies of vervet monkeys in their natural environment have shown that infants can be taught by adults to respond with the appropriate signs of distress to the appropriate eliciting stimuli. The alarm calls appear to be innate, but the monkeys must learn which stimuli are the appropriate elicitors of each. When a juvenile monkey makes an appropriate response, it is reinforced by the behavior of the rest of the colony. When the response is inappropriate, it is ignored. ∎

FEELINGS OF EMOTION

6 So far, we have examined two aspects of emotions: the patterns of responses—behavioral, autonomic, and hormonal—that deal with the situation that provokes the emotion, and the communication of emotional states with other members of the species. The next aspect of emotion to be examined in this chapter is the subjective component—feelings of emotion.

From very early times people have associated emotions with physiological responses. We can easily understand why. Strong emotions can cause increased heart rate, irregular breathing, queasy feelings in the internal organs, trembling, sweating, reddening of the face, or even fainting. The question is whether these physiological changes *constitute* emotions or are merely symptoms of some other underlying process. That is, do we feel frightened because we tremble, or do we tremble because we are frightened? In this section we will look at some theories that attempt to answer these questions.

The James-Lange Theory

William James (1842–1910), an American psychologist, and Carl Lange (1834–1900), a Danish physiologist, independently suggested similar explanations for emotion, which most people refer to collectively as the **James-Lange theory** (James, 1884; Lange, 1887). Basically, the theory states that emotion-producing situations elicit an appropriate set of physiological responses, such as trembling, sweating, and increased heart rate. The situations also elicit behaviors, such as clenching of the fists or fighting. The brain receives sensory feedback from the muscles and from the organs that produce these responses, and it is this feedback that constitutes our feelings of emotion. As James put it:

> *The bodily changes follow directly the perception of the exciting fact, and . . . our feelings of the same changes as they occur is the emotion.*
> Common sense says we lose our fortune, are sorry, and weep; we meet a bear, are frightened, and run; we are insulted by a rival, are angry, and strike. The hypothesis here to be

The expression of sadness is universal.

defended says that this order of sequence is incorrect, that the one mental state is not immediately induced by the other and that the bodily manifestations must first be interposed between. The more rational statement is that we feel sorry because we cry, angry because we strike, afraid because we tremble, and not that we cry, strike, or tremble because we are sorry, angry or fearful, as the case may be. (James, 1890, p. 449)

Chapter 17 describes a topic of research called *attribution,* by which process we make conclusions about the causes of other people's behavior. James's approach is closely related to the process of attribution; he suggests that our own emotional feelings are based on what we find ourselves doing and on the sensory feedback we receive from the activity of our muscles

Figure 12.8 A diagrammatic representation of the James-Lange theory of emotion. An event in the environment triggers behavioral, autonomic, and endocrine responses. Feedback from these responses produces feelings of emotions.

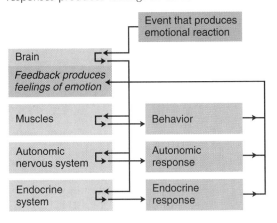

and internal organs. Thus, when we find ourselves trembling and feel queasy, we experience fear. Where feelings of emotions are concerned, we are self-observers. Thus, the two aspects of emotions reported in the first two sections of this chapter (patterns of emotional responses and expressions of emotions) give rise to the third—feelings. (See *Figure 12.8.*)

James's description of the process of emotion might strike you as being at odds with your own experience. Most of us feel that we experience emotions directly, internally. The outward manifestations of our emotions seem to us to be secondary events. But have you ever found yourself in an unpleasant confrontation with someone else and discovered that you were trembling, even though you did not think that you were bothered by the encounter? Or did you ever find yourself blushing in response to some public remark that was made about you? Or did you ever find tears coming to your eyes while watching a film that you did not think was affecting you? What would you conclude about your emotional states in situations like these? Would you ignore the evidence from your own physiological reactions?

A famous physiologist, Walter Cannon, criticized James's theory. For example, he said that the internal organs were relatively insensitive and that they could not respond very quickly, so feedback from them could not account for our feelings of emotions. In addition, he observed that cutting the nerves that provide feedback from the internal organs to the brain did not alter emotional behavior (Cannon, 1927). However, subsequent research indicated that Cannon's criticisms are not relevant. For example, although the viscera are not sensitive to some kinds of stimuli, such as cutting and burning, they provide much better feedback than Cannon suspected. Moreover, many changes in the viscera can occur rapidly enough so that they *could* be the causes of feelings of emotion.

Cannon cited the fact that cutting the sensory nerves between the internal organs and the central nervous system does not abolish emotional behavior in animals. However, this observation misses the point. It does not prove that *feelings* of emotion survive this surgical disruption. We do not know how the animals feel; we know only that they will snarl and attempt to bite if threatened. In any case, James did not attribute all feelings of emotion to the internal organs; he also said that feedback from muscles was important. The threat might make the animal snarl and bite, and the feedback from the facial and neck muscles might constitute a "feeling" of anger, even if feedback from the internal organs was cut off.

The suggestion that we experience our emotions indirectly, through feedback from emotional behaviors and autonomic reactions, receives some support from neuroanatomy. There are few direct connections between the parts of the brain that are involved in language and those that are involved in emotional reactions; thus, the communication between these regions is limited. As we saw in Chapter 8, the brain's verbal mechanisms appear to be respon-

sible for our self-awareness. Thus, indirect feedback through the sensory cortex may provide the richest source of information about our own emotional responses.

Hohman (1966) collected data from humans that directly tested James's hypothesis. He questioned people who had suffered damage to the spinal cord about how intense their emotional feelings were. If feedback is important, one would expect that emotional feelings would be less intense if the injury were high (that is, close to the brain) than if it were low, because a high spinal cord injury would make the person become insensitive to a larger part of the body. In fact, this result is precisely what Hohman found: The higher the injury, the less intense the feeling was. (See *Figure 12.9.*)

The comments of patients with high spinal cord injuries suggest that the severely diminished feedback does change their feelings but not necessarily their behavior.

> I sit around and build things up in my mind, and I worry a lot, but it's not much but the power of thought. I was at home alone in bed one day and dropped a cigarette where I couldn't reach it. I finally managed to scrounge around and put it out. I could have burned up right there, but the funny thing is, I didn't get all shook up about it. I just didn't feel afraid at all, like you would suppose.

Figure 12.9 The rationale for Hohman's investigation of the intensity of feelings of emotion in people with spinal cord damage.

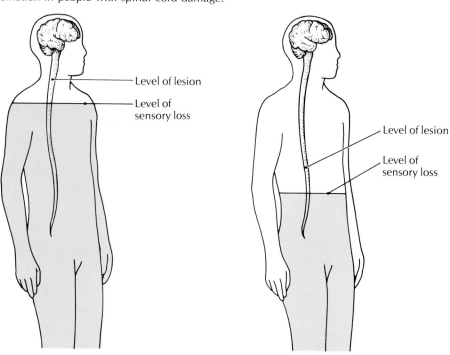

Now, I don't get a feeling of physical animation, it's sort of cold anger. Sometimes I act angry when I see some injustice. I yell and cuss and raise hell, because if you don't do it sometimes, I've learned people will take advantage of you, but it doesn't have the heat to it that it used to. It's a mental kind of anger. (Hohman, 1966, pp. 150–151)

These comments suggest that people do not necessarily engage in emotional behavior *because of* their feelings; lacking these feelings, people still engage in the same behaviors for "rational" reasons.

Feedback from Simulated Emotions

James stressed the importance of two aspects of emotional responses: emotional behaviors and autonomic responses. As we saw earlier in this chapter, a particular set of muscles—those of the face—helps us communicate our emotional state to other people. Several experiments suggest that feedback from the contraction of facial muscles can affect people's moods and even alter the activity of the autonomic nervous system.

Ekman and his colleagues (Ekman, Levenson, and Friesen, 1983; Levenson, Ekman, and Friesen, 1990) asked subjects to move particular facial muscles to simulate the emotional expressions of fear, anger, surprise, disgust, sadness, and happiness. They did not tell the subjects what emotion they were trying to make them produce but only what movements they should make. For example, to simulate fear, they told the subjects to "Raise your brows. While holding them raised pull your brows together. Now raise your upper eyelids and tighten the lower eyelids. Now stretch your lips horizontally." (You can see this expression if you examine the left photograph in Figure 12.5.) While the subjects made the expressions, the investigators monitored several physiological responses controlled by the autonomic nervous system.

The simulated expressions *did* alter the activity of the autonomic nervous system. In fact, different facial expressions produced somewhat different patterns of activity. For example, anger increased heart rate and skin temperature, fear increased heart rate but decreased skin temperature, and happiness decreased heart rate without affecting skin temperature.

Why should a particular pattern of movements of the facial muscles cause changes in mood or in the activity of the autonomic nervous system? Perhaps the connection is a result of

experience; in other words, perhaps the occurrence of particular facial movements along with changes in the autonomic nervous system leads to classical conditioning, so that feedback from the facial movements becomes capable of eliciting the autonomic response—and a change in perceived emotion. Or perhaps the connection is innate. As we saw earlier, the adaptive value of emotional expressions is that they communicate feelings and intentions to others. One of the ways we communicate feelings may be through imitation.

When people see someone expressing an emotion, they tend to imitate the expression. This tendency to imitate appears to be innate. Field, Woodson, Greenberg, and Cohen (1982) had adults make facial expressions in front of infants. The infants' own facial expressions were videotaped and were subsequently rated by people who did not know what expressions were being displayed by the adults. Field and her colleagues found that even newborn babies (with an average age of thirty-six hours) tended to imitate the expressions they saw. Clearly, the effect occurs too early in life to be a result of learning. Figure 12.10 shows three photographs of the adult expressions and the expressions they elicited in a baby. Can you look at them yourself without changing your own expression, at least a little? (See *Figure 12.10.*)

Perhaps imitation provides one of the channels by which organisms communicate their emotions. For example, if we see someone looking sad, we tend to assume a sad expression ourselves. The feedback from our own expression helps put us in the other person's place and makes us more likely to respond with solace or assistance. And perhaps one of the reasons we derive pleasure from making someone else smile is that their smile makes *us* smile and feel happy.

The Role of Cognition

7 One of the current controversies among psychologists interested in feelings of emotion is the relative importance of automatic processes (such as classical conditioning) and cognitive processes (especially those involving conscious thought). The person most responsible for directing researchers' attention to the possible interaction between cognition and activation of the autonomic nervous system is Stanley Schachter. Schachter (1964) proposed that feelings of emotions are determined *jointly* by perception of physiological responses and by cognitive

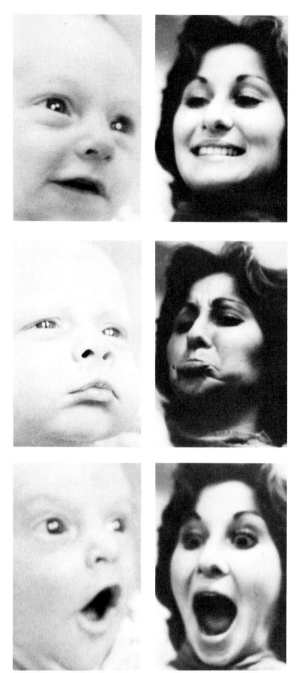

Figure 12.10 Photographs of happy, sad, and surprised faces posed by an adult, and the responses made by the infant. (From Field, T., in *Development of Nonverbal Behavior in Children*, edited by R.S. Feldman. New York: Springer-Verlag, 1982. Reprinted with permission.)

assessment of a specific situation. Thus, to Schachter, emotion is cognition plus perception of physiological arousal. Both are necessary.

Schachter and Singer (1962) tested this hypothesis by arranging to induce physiological arousal in groups of subjects placed in various situations. All subjects were told that they were part of an investigation on the effects of a vitamin called "suproxin" on visual perception. No such vitamin exists. The investigators gave some subjects injections of adrenaline, a hormone that stimulates a variety of autonomic nervous system effects associated with arousal, such as increased heart rate and blood pressure, irregular breathing, warming of the face, and mild trembling. Other subjects received a control injection of a salt solution, which has no physiological effects.

Next, the researchers placed some subjects in an anger-provoking situation in which they were treated rudely and subjected to obnoxious test questions such as the following: "How many men, besides your father, has your mother slept with? (a) one, (b) two, (c) three, (d) four or more." Others were treated politely and saw the antics of another "subject" (a confederate who was hired by the experimenters) who acted silly and euphoric. The experimenters hoped that these two situations, together with the physiological reactions produced by the injections of adrenaline, would promote either negative or positive emotional states.

Finally, some subjects were correctly informed that the injections they received would produce side effects such as trembling and a pounding heart. Others were told to expect irrelevant side effects or none at all. Schachter and Singer predicted that the subjects who knew what side effects to expect would correctly attribute their physiological reactions to the drug and would not experience a change in emotion. Those who were misinformed would note their physiological arousal and conclude that they were feeling especially angry or happy, as the circumstance dictated. All the subjects reported their emotional states in a questionnaire.

The results were not as clear-cut as the experimenters had hoped. The adrenaline did not increase the intensity of the subjects' emotional states. However, subjects who expected to experience physiological arousal as a result of the injection reported much less of a change in their emotional state than those who did not expect it, *regardless of whether they had received the adrenaline or the placebo;* in other words, no matter what their physiological state was, they felt less angry or happy after having been exposed to one of the emotional situations. These results suggest that we *interpret* the significance of our physiological reactions rather than simply experiencing them as emotions.

Nisbett and Schachter (1966) provided further evidence that subjects can be fooled into attributing their own naturally occurring physiological responses to a drug and thus into feeling less "emotional." First, they gave all subjects a placebo pill (one with no physiological effects). Half the subjects were told that the pill would make their hearts pound, their breathing increase, and their hands tremble; the other half (the control subjects) were told nothing about possible side effects. Then the researchers strapped on electrodes and gave the subjects electrical shocks. All subjects presumably experienced pain and fear, and consequently, their heart rate and breathing increased, they trembled, and so on. Yet the subjects who perceived their reactions as drug-induced were able to tolerate stronger shocks than the control subjects, and they reported less pain and fear. Thus, cognition can affect people's judgments about their own emotional states and even their tolerance of pain.

The precise nature of the interaction between cognition and physiological arousal has not been determined. For example, in the Nisbett and Schachter experiment, although the verbal instructions about effects of the placebo did affect the subjects' reaction to pain, it did not seem to do so through a logical, reasoned process. In fact, Nisbett and Wilson (1977) later reported that subjects did *not* consciously attribute their increased tolerance of pain to the effects of the pill. When subjects were asked whether they had thought about the pill while receiving the shocks or whether it had occurred to them that the pill was causing some physical effects, subjects typically gave answers such as "No, I was too worried about the shock." Even after the experimenters explained the experiment and its rationale in detail, subjects typically reported "that the hypothesis was very interesting and that many people probably would go through the process that the experimenter described, but so far as they could tell, they themselves had not" (Nisbett and Wilson, 1977, p. 237).

Some psychologists, such as Lazarus (1984), believe that emotions are produced only by cognitive processes. Others, such as Zajonc (1984), believe exactly the opposite, insisting that cognitive appraisal is not necessary and that emotions are automatic, species-typical responses heavily influenced by classical conditioning. Although the two sides of the debate appear to have been drawn sharply, it seems clear that both automatic processes and conscious deliberation play a role in the expression and feelings of emotion. As we saw earlier in this chapter, a person can become angry after realizing that someone's "kind words" actually contained a subtle insult; obviously, this anger is a result of cognition. Conversely, we also saw that through the process of classical conditioning, stimuli can evoke emotional reactions before we have time to realize what is happening. In some cases we may be acting hostile and angry without realizing what we are doing; if cognitive processes are responsible for our anger, they are certainly not conscious, deliberate ones.

Schachter's major contribution to the study of emotion was to make other psychologists consider the complex interactions between the automatic and conscious processes that are responsible for producing and perceiving emotional responses. As I said in the beginning of the chapter, emotions are what life itself is all about, so we should not be surprised that emotions are influenced by—and in turn have an influence on—so many different variables.

INTERIM SUMMARY

Feelings of Emotion

From the earliest times people recognized that emotions were accompanied by feelings that seemed to come from inside the body, which probably provided the impetus for developing physiological theories of emotion. James and Lange suggested that the physiological and behavioral reactions to emotion-producing situations were perceived by people as states of emotion, and that emotional states were not the *causes* of these reactions. Cannon criticized this theory, but many of the physiological data on which his criticisms were based were later shown to be incorrect. Hohman's study of people with spinal cord damage supported the James-Lange theory; people who could no longer feel the reactions from most of their body reported that they no longer experienced intense emotional states. However, the loss of feelings did not necessarily affect their behavior; thus, emotional feelings and behaviors may be at least somewhat independent.

Ekman and his colleagues have shown that even simulating an emotional expression causes changes in the activity of the autonomic nervous system. Perhaps feedback from these changes explains why an emotion can be "contagious"; we see someone smile with pleasure, we ourselves imitate their smile, and the internal feedback makes us feel at least somewhat happier.

The work environment that confronts air traffic controllers is often stressful; over time this stress increases the incidence of high blood pressure, diabetes, and ulcers.

Although emotional states are sometimes produced by automatic, classically conditioned responses, some psychologists have suggested that the perception of our own emotional state is not determined solely by feedback from our behavior and the organs controlled by the autonomic nervous system. It is also determined by cognitive assessment of the situation in which we find ourselves. Schachter and his colleagues found that information about the expected physiological effects of drugs (or placebos) influenced subjects' reports about their emotional state. In one study they even tolerated more intense electrical shocks because they had been told that their physiological reactions were the effects of a drug; hence they apparently discounted their own fear. Although these results do not support any single comprehensive theory of emotion, they do underscore the importance of cognitive factors in emotion and the complexity of this phenomenon. Emotions are undoubtedly not the products of automatic processes *or* conscious deliberations but involve both factors.

■

STRESS AND HEALTH

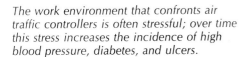 Aversive stimuli can produce more than negative emotional responses; they can also harm people's health. Many of these harmful effects are produced not by the stimuli themselves but by our reactions to them. Thus, the expression of negative emotions can have adverse effects on ourselves as well as on the people with whom we interact. Walter Cannon, the physiologist who criticized the James-Lange theory, introduced the term **stress** to refer to the physiological reaction caused by the perception of aversive or threatening situations. This section discusses the stress response and its effects on health.

Stress definitely can be hazardous to one's health. Some disease conditions, such as peptic ulcers, are often caused by the physiological responses that accompany negative emotions. Physical illnesses caused by stress are called **psychophysiological disorders.** (They are sometimes called *psychosomatic disorders*—"mind-body disorders.") Psychophysiological disorders are not imaginary illnesses; they are real and usually require medical treatment. Other disorders, such as heart attacks, strokes, asthma, menstrual problems, headaches, and skin rashes, can occur in the absence of stress but are aggravated by it.

As we saw in the first section of this chapter, emotional responses evolved because they are useful and adaptive. Why, then, can they harm our health? The answer appears to be that our emotional responses are designed primarily to cope with short-term events. The physiological responses that accompany the negative emotions prepare us to threaten rivals or fight them, or to run away from dangerous situations. Cannon also introduced the phrase **fight-or-flight response,** which refers to the physiological reactions that prepare us for the strenuous efforts required by fighting or running away. Normally, once we have bluffed or fought with an adversary or run away from a dangerous situation, the threat is over and our physiological condition can return to normal. The fact that the physiological responses may have adverse long-term effects on our health is unimportant as long as the responses are brief. But sometimes, the threatening situations are continuous rather than episodic, producing a more or less continuous stress response.

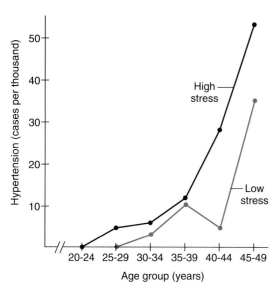

Figure 12.11 Incidence of hypertension in various age groups of air traffic controllers at high-stress and low-stress airports. (Based on data from Cobb and Rose, 1973.)

Several studies have demonstrated the deleterious effects of stress on health. For example, survivors of concentration camps, who were obviously subjected to long-term stress, have generally poorer health later in life than other people of the same age (Cohen, 1953). Air traffic controllers—especially those who work at busy airports where the danger of collisions is greatest—show a greater incidence of high blood pressure, which gets worse as the people grow older (Cobb and Rose, 1973). (See *Figure 12.11*.) They also are more likely to suffer from ulcers or diabetes.

Physiology of Stress

As we saw earlier in this chapter, emotions consist of behavioral, autonomic, and hormonal responses. The latter two components—autonomic and hormonal responses—are the ones that can have adverse effects on health. (Well, I guess the behavioral components can, too, if a person rashly gets into a fight with someone much bigger and stronger.) Because threatening situations generally call for vigorous activity, the autonomic and hormonal responses that accompany them help make the body's energy resources available. The sympathetic branch of the autonomic nervous system is active, and the adrenal glands secrete epinephrine, norepinephrine, and steroid stress hormones. Because the effects of sympathetic activity are similar to those of the adrenal hormones, I will limit my discussion to the hormonal responses.

Epinephrine releases the stored form of glucose that is present in the muscles, thus providing energy for strenuous exercise. Along with norepinephrine, the hormone also increases blood flow to the muscles by increasing the output of the heart. In doing so, they also increase blood pressure, which, over the long term, contributes to cardiovascular disease. The other stress-related hormone is *cortisol,* a steroid secreted by the *cortex* of the adrenal gland. Cortisol is called a **glucocorticoid** because it has profound effects on glucose metabolism, similar to those of epinephrine. In addition, glucocorticoids help break down protein and convert it to glucose, help make fats available for energy, increase blood flow, and stimulate behavioral responsiveness, presumably by affecting the brain. They have other physiological effects, too, some of which are only poorly understood. Almost every cell in the body contains glucocorticoid receptors, which means that few of them are unaffected by these hormones. (See *Figure 12.12.*)

The secretion of glucocorticoids does more than help an animal react to a stressful situation—it helps it survive. If a rat's adrenal glands are removed, it becomes much more susceptible to the effects of stress. In fact, a stressful situation that a normal rat would take in its stride may kill one whose adrenal glands have

Figure 12.12 Control of the secretion of epinephrine, norepinephrine, and cortisol by the adrenal gland.

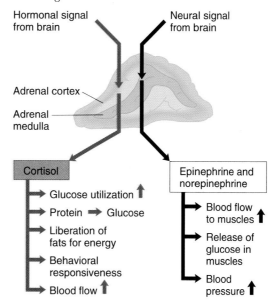

been removed. And physicians treating people whose adrenal glands have been damaged or removed know that if they are subjected to stress, they must be given additional amounts of glucocorticoid (Tyrell and Baxter, 1981).

A pioneer in the study of stress, Hans Selye, suggested that most of the harmful effects of stress were produced by the prolonged secretion of glucocorticoids (Selye, 1976). Although the short-term effects of glucocorticoids are essential, the long-term effects are damaging. These effects include increased blood pressure, damage to muscle tissue, a particular form of diabetes, infertility, inhibition of growth, inhibition of the inflammatory responses, and suppression of the immune system. High blood pressure can lead to heart attacks and stroke. Inhibition of growth in children subjected to prolonged stress prevents them from attaining their full height. Inhibition of the inflammatory response makes it more difficult for the body to heal itself after an injury, and suppression of the immune system makes an individual vulnerable to infections and (perhaps) cancer.

Several lines of research suggest that stress is related to aging in at least two ways. First, older people, even when they are perfectly healthy, do not tolerate stress as well as younger people (Shock, 1977). Second, stress may accelerate the aging process (Selye and Tuchweber, 1976). Sapolsky and his colleagues have investigated one rather serious long-term effect of stress: brain damage. As you learned in Chapter 7, the hippocampal formation plays a crucial role in learning and memory, and evidence suggests that one of the causes of memory loss that occurs with aging is degeneration of this brain structure. Research with animals has shown that long-term exposure to glucocorticoids destroys neurons located in a particular zone of the hippocampal formation. The hormone appears to destroy the neurons by making them more susceptible to the normal wear and tear that accompanies the aging process (Sapolsky, 1986; Sapolsky, Krey, and McEwen, 1986). Perhaps, then, the stress to which people are subjected throughout their lives increases the likelihood that they will have memory problems as they grow older.

Uno et al. (1989) found that if stress is intense enough, it can even cause brain damage in young primates. The investigators studied a colony of vervet monkeys housed in a primate center in Kenya. They found that some monkeys died, apparently from stress. Vervet monkeys have a hierarchical society, and monkeys near the bottom of the hierarchy are picked on by the others; thus, they are almost continuously subjected to stress. (Ours is not the only species with social structures that cause stress in some of its members.) The deceased monkeys had gastric ulcers and enlarged adrenal glands, which are signs of chronic stress. In addition, neurons in a particular region of their hippocampal formation were completely destroyed. Severe stress appears to cause brain damage in humans as well; Jensen, Genefke, and Hyldebrandt (1982) found evidence of brain degeneration in CT scans of people who had been subjected to torture.

People who have learned appropriate coping responses can work in a hostile environment without experiencing stress.

The Coping Response

[9] As we have seen, many of the harmful effects of long-term stress are caused by our own reactions—primarily the secretion of stress hormones. Some events that cause stress, such as prolonged exertion or extreme cold, cause damage directly. These stressors will affect everyone; their severity will depend on each person's physical capacity. The effects of other stressors, such as situations that cause fear or anxiety, depend on people's perceptions and emotional reactivity. That is, because of individual differences in temperament or experience with a particular situation, some people may find a situation stressful and others may not. In these cases it is the perception that counts.

One of the most important variables that determines whether an aversive stimulus will cause a stress reaction is the degree to which the situation can be controlled. As I mentioned earlier in this chapter, when an animal can learn a coping response that avoids contact with an aversive stimulus, its emotional response will disappear. Weiss (1968) found that rats who learned to minimize (but not completely avoid) shocks by making a response whenever they heard a warning tone developed fewer stomach ulcers than rats who had no control over the shocks. The effect was not caused by the pain itself, because both groups of animals received exactly the same number of shocks. Thus, being able to exert some control over an aversive situation reduces an animal's stress response. Hu-

mans react similarly. Situations that permit some control are less likely to produce signs of stress than those in which other people (or machines) control the situation (Gatchel, Baum, and Krantz, 1989). Perhaps this phenomenon explains why some people like to have a magic charm or other "security blanket" with them in stressful situations. Perhaps even the *illusion* of control can be reassuring.

According to Lazarus and Folkman (1984), there are two types of coping responses: problem-focused and emotion-focused. *Problem-focused coping* is directed toward the source of the stress. For example, if the stress is job-related, a person might try to change conditions at the job site or take courses to acquire skills that will enable him or her to obtain a different job. *Emotion-focused coping* is directed toward one's own reaction. For example, a person might try to relax and forget about the problem or find solace in the company of friends. Obviously, if the source of a stress-producing problem has a potential solution, problem-focused coping is the best strategy. If it does not, then emotion-focused coping is the only option.

Personality variables also affect people's reactions to stress. Some people are simply not bothered by situations that others perceive to be stressful. Because of this fact, researchers have tried to identify the nature of these individual differences. Knowing how people differ in their reactions to stress might provide practical benefits—it might even be possible to change their reactions through training. As we will see

This false color angiogram of blood vessels in the heart shows evidence of restricted blood flow caused by the buildup of atherosclerotic plaque. Stress hormones and a high level of cholesterol in the blood contributes to coronary artery disease.

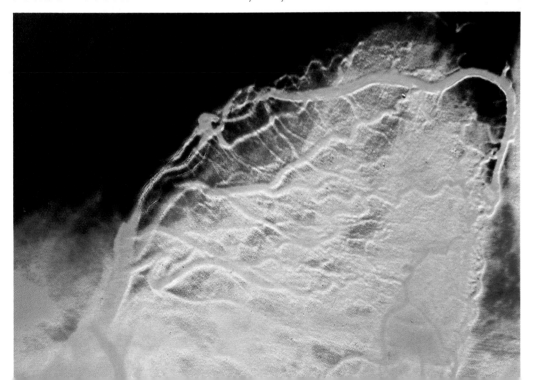

in a later section, clinicians have attempted to develop training programs to help reduce stress and its harmful effects.

Stress and Cardiovascular Disease

One of the most important causes of death is cardiovascular diseases—diseases of the heart and the blood vessels. Cardiovascular diseases can cause heart attacks and strokes; heart attacks occur when the blood vessels that serve the heart become blocked, while strokes involve the blood vessels in the brain. The two most important risk factors in cardiovascular disease are high blood pressure and a high level of cholesterol in the blood.

The degree to which people react to stress may affect the likelihood that they will suffer from cardiovascular disease. For example, Wood et al. (1984) examined the blood pressure of people who had been subjected to a *cold pressor test* in 1934, when they were children. The cold pressor test reveals how people's blood pressure reacts to the stress caused when their hand is placed in a container of ice water for one

Prolonged stress can suppress the immune system, increasing a person's susceptibility to infection or illness.

minute. Wood and his colleagues found that 70 percent of the subjects who hyperreacted to the stress when they were children had high blood pressure, compared with 19 percent of those who showed little reaction to the stress.

A study with monkeys showed that individual differences in emotional reactivity are a risk factor for cardiovascular disease. Manuck et al. (1983, 1986) fed a high-cholesterol diet to a group of monkeys, which increases the likelihood of their developing coronary artery disease. They measured the animals' emotional reactivity by threatening to capture the animals. (Monkeys avoid contact with humans, and they perceive being captured as a stressful situation.) Those animals who showed the strongest negative reactions eventually developed the highest rates of coronary artery disease. Presumably, these animals reacted more strongly to all types of stress, and their reactions had detrimental effects on their health.

Friedman and Rosenman (1959) identified a behavior pattern that appeared to be related to a person's susceptibility to cardiovascular disease. They characterized the disease-prone **type A pattern** as one of excessive competitive drive, impatience, hostility, fast movements, and rapid speech. People with the **type B pattern** were less competitive, less hostile, more patient, and more easygoing and tolerant, and they moved and talked more slowly; they were also less likely to suffer from cardiovascular disease. Friedman and Rosenman developed a questionnaire that distinguished these two types of people. The test is rather interesting, because the person who administers it is not a passive participant. The interviewer asks questions in an abrupt, impatient manner, interrupting the subject if he or she takes too much time to answer a question. The point of such behavior is to try to elicit type A behavior from the subject.

Researchers have devoted much attention to the relation between the type A personality and cardiovascular disease. The Western Collaborative Group Study (Rosenman et al., 1975), which studied 3154 healthy men for eight and one-half years, found that the type A behavior pattern was associated with twice the rate of coronary artery disease. Results such as these led an independent review panel to classify the type A behavior pattern as a risk factor for this disease (Review Panel, 1981). However, since then many contradictory results have been obtained. For example, one large study found that although people classified as type A were more likely to have a heart attack, the long-term survival rate after having a heart attack was higher for type A patients than for type B patients (Ragland and Brand, 1988). In this case it would seem better to be type A, at least after having a nonfatal heart attack. Other studies have failed to find a difference in cardiovascular disease in people with type A and type B personalities (Dimsdale, 1988).

Williams et al. (1980) suggested that one aspect of the type A personality—hostility—is of particular importance in cardiovascular disease. Several subsequent studies carried out in the early to mid-1980s confirmed that hostility was an important risk factor, but more recent studies have not. For example, Helmer, Ragland, and Syme (1991) studied 118 men who underwent angiography (X-ray inspection of the buildup of atherosclerotic plaque in the arteries of the heart that can ultimately cause a heart attack). They found no relation between either of two measures of hostility and the degree of coronary artery disease.

Although the relation between cardiovascular disease and hostility or the type A behavior pattern is unclear, several studies have found that personality variables are related to particular risk factors. For example, Howard, Cunningham, and Rechnitzer (1976) found that people who exhibited extreme type A behavior were more likely to smoke and to have high blood pressure and high blood levels of cholesterol. Weidner et al. (1987) confirmed the high level of cholesterol in a sample of men and women with the type A behavior pattern, and Irvine et al. (1991) confirmed the association between type A behavior and high blood pressure. Lombardo and Carreno (1987) found that type A smokers held the smoke in their lungs longer, leading to a high level of carbon monoxide in their blood.

What are we to conclude? Most investigators believe that personality variables *are* involved in susceptibility to heart attack but that we need a better definition of just what these variables are. In addition, it is possible that different personality variables are associated with different risk factors, which make it difficult to tease out the relevant variables. Personality factors certainly play an important role in cardiovascular disease, but at present the precise nature of this role is uncertain. This topic is important and clearly merits further research.

Posttraumatic Stress Disorder

The aftermath of tragic and traumatic events such as those that accompany wars and natural disasters often includes psychological symptoms that persist long after the stressful events are over. According to the American Psychiatric Association's *Diagnostic and Statistical Manual of Mental Disorders (Third Edition, Revised)*, **posttraumatic stress disorder** is caused by an event "outside the range of usual human experience . . . that would be markedly distressing to almost anyone." The symptoms produced by such exposure include recurrent dreams or recollections of the event, feelings that the traumatic event is recurring ("flashback" episodes), and intense psychological distress. These dreams, recollections, or flashback episodes lead the person to avoid thinking about the traumatic event, which often results in diminished interest in social activities, feelings of detachment from others, suppressed emotional feelings, and a sense that the future is bleak and empty. Particular psychological symptoms include difficulty falling or staying asleep, irritability, outbursts of anger, difficulty in concentrating, and heightened reactions to sudden noises or movements.

Posttraumatic stress disorder can strike people at any age. Children may show particular symptoms not usually seen in adulthood, such as loss of recently acquired language skills or toilet training, and somatic complaints such as stomachaches and headaches. Usually, the symptoms begin immediately after the traumatic event, but they are sometimes delayed for several months or years.

Some studies suggest that preexisting personality factors may play a role in the development of posttraumatic stress disorder. For example, Mikulincer and Solomon (1988) studied Israeli soldiers who suffered a combat stress reaction during the 1982 Lebanon war and found that those who tended to brood about their feelings were more likely to go on to develop posttraumatic stress disorder. The National Vietnam Veterans Readjustment Study carried out by the U.S. government found that four factors increased the likelihood that a soldier subjected to combat stress would develop posttraumatic stress disorder: being raised in a household with financial difficulty, having a history of drug abuse or dependency, having a history of affective disorders, and having a history of childhood behavior problems (Kulka et al., 1990).

The social support that a person receives (or does not receive) after being exposed to an unusually stressful situation can affect the likelihood of their developing posttraumatic stress disorder. As a result, mental health professionals try to seek out victims of natural disasters and crimes such as rapes or shooting sprees and provide them with treatment that might prevent future psychological disorders. As we shall see in Chapter 16, one of the goals of community psychology is to provide intervention of this kind.

Psychoneuroimmunology

10 As we have seen, long-term stress can be harmful to one's health and can even result in brain damage. The most important causes are elevated levels of glucocorticoids, epinephrine, and norepinephrine. But in addition, stress can impair the functions of the immune system, which protects us from assault from viruses, microbes, fungi, and other types of parasites. Study of the interactions between the immune system and behavior (mediated by the nervous system, of course) is called **psychoneuroimmunology.** This new field is described in the following section.

The Immune System.   The immune system is one of the most complex systems of the body. Its function is to protect us from infection; and because infectious organisms have developed devious tricks through the process of evolution, our immune system has evolved devious tricks of its own. The description I provide here is abbreviated and simplified, but it presents some of the important elements of the system.

The immune system derives from white blood cells that develop in the bone marrow and in the thymus gland. Some of the cells roam through the blood or lymphatic system; others reside permanently in one place. The immune reaction occurs when the body is invaded by foreign organisms, including bacteria, fungi, and viruses.

There are two types of specific immune reactions: *chemically mediated* and *cell-mediated.* Chemically mediated immune reactions involve antibodies. All bacteria have unique proteins on their surfaces, called **antigens.** These proteins serve as the invaders' calling cards, identifying them to the immune system. Through exposure to the bacteria the immune system learns to recognize these proteins. (I will not try to explain the mechanism by which this learning takes place.) The result of this learning is the development of special lines of cells that produce specific **antibodies**—proteins that recognize antigens and help kill the invading microorganism. One type of antibody is released into the circulation by **B lymphocytes,** which receive their name from the fact that they develop in bone marrow. These antibodies, called **immunoglobulins,** are chains of protein. Each type of immunoglobulin (there are five of them) is identical except for one end, which contains a unique receptor. A particular receptor binds with a particular antigen, just as a molecule of a hormone or a transmitter substance binds with its receptor. When the appropriate line of B lymphocytes detects an invading bacterium, the cells release their antibodies, which bind with the bacterial antigens. The antigens either kill the invaders directly or attract other white blood cells, which then destroy them. (See *Figure 12.13a.*)

The other type of defense by the immune system, cell-mediated immune reactions, is produced by **T lymphocytes,** which originally develop in the thymus gland. These cells also produce antibodies, but the antibodies remain attached to the outside of their membrane. T lymphocytes primarily defend the body against fungi, viruses, and multicellular parasites. When antigens bind with their surface antibodies, the cells either directly kill the invaders or signal other white blood cells to come and kill them. (See *Figure 12.13b.*)

In addition to the immune reactions produced by lymphocytes, **natural killer cells** continuously prowl through tissue; when they

Figure 12.13   Immune reactions. (a) Chemically mediated reaction. The B lymphocyte detects an antigen on a bacterium and releases a specific immunoglobulin. (b) Cell-mediated reaction. The T lymphocyte detects an antigen on a bacterium and kills it directly or releases a chemical that attracts other white blood cells.

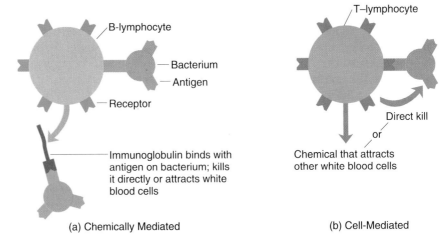

(a) Chemically Mediated   (b) Cell-Mediated

encounter a cell that has been infected by a virus or that has become transformed into a cancer cell, they engulf and destroy it. Thus, natural killer cells constitute an important defense against viral infections and the development of malignant tumors.

Although the immune system normally protects us, it can cause us harm, too. Allergic reactions occur when an antigen causes cells of the immune system to overreact, releasing a particular immunoglobulin that produces a localized inflammatory response. The chemicals released during this reaction can enter the general circulation and cause life-threatening complications. Obviously, allergic responses are harmful, and why they occur is unknown. The immune system can do something else that harms the body—it can attack its cells. **Autoimmune diseases** occur when the immune system becomes sensitized to a protein present in the body and attacks the tissue that contains this protein. Exactly what causes the protein to be so targeted is not known. What is known is that autoimmune diseases often follow viral or bacterial infections. Presumably, in learning to recognize antigens that belong to the infectious agent, the immune system develops a line of cells that treat one of the body's own proteins as foreign. Some common autoimmune diseases include rheumatoid arthritis, diabetes, lupus, and multiple sclerosis. As we shall see in Chapter 15, some researchers even believe that schizophrenia is caused by an autoimmune disorder.

Neural Control of the Immune System.

As we will see in the next subsection, stress can suppress the immune system, resulting in a greater likelihood of infectious diseases, and it can also aggravate autoimmune diseases. It may even affect the growth of cancers. What is the physiological explanation for these effects? One answer, and probably the most important one, is that (as you know) stress increases the secretion of glucocorticoids, and these hormones directly suppress the activity of the immune system. All types of white blood cells have glucocorticoid receptors, and suppression of the immune system is presumably mediated by these receptors (Solomon, 1987).

Because the secretion of glucocorticoids is controlled by the brain (through its secretion of ACTH-releasing hormone), the brain is obviously responsible for the suppressing effect of these hormones on the immune system. For example, in a study with rats Keller et al. (1983) found that the stress of inescapable shock decreased the number of lymphocytes (B cells, T cells, and natural killer cells) found in the blood. This effect was abolished by removal of the adrenal glands; thus, it appears to have been caused by the release of glucocorticoids triggered by the stress. (See *Figure 12.14a.*)

425

However, the same authors found that removal of the adrenal glands did *not* abolish the effects of stress on another type of immune response: stimulation of lymphocytes by an antigen. (See *Figure 12.14b.*) Thus, not all the effects of stress on the immune system are mediated by glucocorticoids; there must be other mechanisms as well.

These additional mechanisms may involve direct neural control. The bone marrow, the thymus gland, and the lymph nodes all receive neural input. Although researchers have not yet obtained direct proof that this input modulates immune function, it would be surprising if it did not. In addition, the immune system appears to be sensitive to chemicals produced by the nervous system. The best evidence comes from studies with the opioids produced by the brain. Shavit et al. (1984) found that inescapable intermittent shock produced both analgesia (decreased sensitivity to pain) and suppression of the production of natural killer cells. These effects both seem to have been mediated by endogenous opioids, because both effects were abolished when the experimenters administered a drug that blocks opiate receptors. Shavit et al. (1986) found that natural killer cell activity could be suppressed by injecting morphine directly into the brain; thus, the effect of the opiates appears to take place in the brain. The mechanism by which the brain affects the natural killer cells is not yet known.

Stress and Infectious Diseases. Often when a married person dies, his or her spouse dies soon afterward, frequently of an infection. In fact, a wide variety of stress-producing events in a person's life can increase the susceptibility to illness. For example, Glaser et al. (1987) found that medical students were more likely to contract acute infections—and to show evidence of suppression of the immune system—during the time that final examinations were given. In addition, autoimmune diseases often get worse when a person is subjected to stress, as Feigenbaum, Masi, and Kaplan (1979) found for rheumatoid arthritis. In a laboratory study Rogers et al. (1980) found that when rats were stressed by handling them or exposing them to a cat, they developed a more severe case of an artificially induced autoimmune disease.

Stone, Reed, and Neale (1987) attempted to see whether stressful events in people's daily lives might predispose them to upper respiratory infection. If a person is exposed to a microorganism that might cause such a disease, the

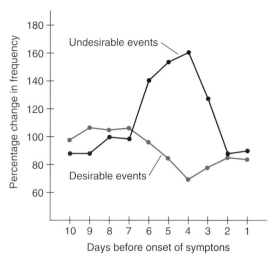

Figure 12.15 Mean percentage change in frequency of undesirable and desirable events during the ten-day period preceding the onset of symptoms of upper respiratory infections. (Based on data from Stone, Reed, and Neale, 1987.)

symptoms do not occur for several days; that is, there is an incubation period between exposure and signs of the actual illness. Thus, the authors reasoned that if stressful events suppressed the immune system, one might expect to see a higher likelihood of respiratory infections several days after such stress. To test their hypothesis, they asked volunteers to keep a daily record of desirable and undesirable events in their lives over a twelve-week period. The volunteers also kept a daily record of any discomfort or symptoms of illness.

The results were as predicted: During the three-to-five-day period just before showing symptoms of an upper respiratory infection, people experienced an increased number of undesirable events and a decreased number of desirable events in their lives. (See *Figure 12.15.*) Stone et al. (1987) suggest that the effect is caused by decreased production of a particular immunoglobulin that is present in the secretions of mucous membranes, including those in the nose, mouth, throat, and lungs. This immunoglobulin (known as IgA) serves as the first defense against infectious microorganisms that enter the nose or mouth. They found that this immunoglobulin is associated with mood; when a subject is unhappy or depressed, its levels are lower than normal. The results suggest that the stress caused by undesirable events may, by suppressing the production of IgA, lead to a rise in the likelihood of upper respiratory infections.

A direct relation between stress and the immune system was demonstrated by Kiecolt-

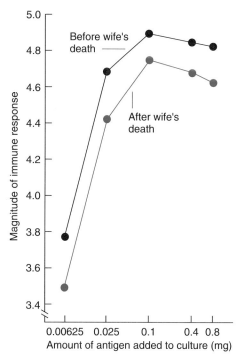

Figure 12.16 Stimulation of white blood cell (lymphocyte) production by an antigen in the blood of husbands before and after their wife's death. (Adapted from Schleifer, S.J., Keller, S.E., Camerino, M., Thornton, J.C., and Stein, M. *Journal of the American Medical Association,* 1983, 250, 374–377.)

Glaser et al. (1987). These investigators found that caregivers of family members with Alzheimer's disease—who certainly underwent considerable stress—showed weaker immune systems, based on several different laboratory tests. Bereavement, another source of stress, also suppresses the immune system. Schleifer et al. (1983) tested the husbands of women with breast cancer and found that their immune response was lower after their wives died. (See *Figure 12.16.*)

EVALUATING SCIENTIFIC ISSUES

Is There a Cancer-Prone Personality?

Many people—both professionals and laypeople—believe that psychological factors play a role in determining whether people develop cancers or, if they do, whether the cancers can be "beaten." Some professionals have even suggested that having a "cancer-prone personality" is a risk factor for the disease. Is there any truth to this assertion?

What Is Being Asserted? The idea that personality is related to the development of cancer is not a new one. During the second century A.D. Galen, the Greek anatomist and physician, concluded that melancholic women were more likely than optimistic women to develop cancer (Bastiaans, 1985). Physicians in more recent times have reported similar relations between cancer-proneness and personality, but it was not until the 1950s that investigators attempted to do systematic studies (Gil, 1989). Several studies (for example, LeShan and Worthington, 1956a, 1956b; Kissen, 1963) suggested that cancer-prone people had difficulty expressing emotions (especially anger and hostility) and had low self-esteem.

The concept of the "type C" (cancer-prone) personality was introduced in the 1980s (Morris, 1980). (As you may have guessed, the terminology is based on the type A and type B personality distinctions described earlier in this chapter in the section on cardiovascular disease.) According to Temoshok et al. (1985), the **type C pattern** is shown by a person "who is cooperative, unassertive, patient, who suppresses negative emotions (particularly anger), and who accepts/complies with external authorities" (p. 141). Temoshok and her colleagues conceive of the type C personality as the polar opposite of the type A pattern; thus, it "differs from the type B pattern, which is defined as the *absence* of type A characteristics" (p. 141).

Investigators who believe in the existence of a cancer-prone personality assert that there is a direct physiological connection between personality characteristics and cancer. That is, the maladaptive coping styles of people with the type C personality causes physiological events that favor the development of cancer. For example, Temoshok (1987) suggests that the chronically blocked expressions of emotions in people with the type C personality causes the release of certain chemicals in the brain (*neuropeptides*), which disrupt the body's homeostatic mechanisms and impair the body's ability to defend itself against the growth of cancer cells. Eysenck (1988) suggests that the negative emotions cause the release of glucocorticoids, which (as you know) suppress the immune system and interfere with its ability to destroy cancer cells.

What Evidence Supports the Assertion? Several studies have found a relation between personality variables and the presence or severity of cancer. For example, Temoshok et al. (1985) administered personality tests designed to measure type C personality characteristics to a group of patients who had been referred to a hospital for assessment and treatment of a malignant melanoma—a form of skin cancer that has a tendency to metastasize (spread to other parts of the body). They found that two personality variables were related to the thickness of the tumor: *faith* and *nonverbal type C*. People who scored high on *faith* agreed with statements such as "I'm placing my faith in God" (or "my doctor") and "Prayer can work miracles." People who scored high on *nonverbal type C* tended to be slow, lethargic, passive, and sad. Presumably, the existence of these personality variables favored the growth of the melanoma.

Most of the studies investigating the role of personality variables in cancer-proneness have assessed the personality characteristics of people who have *already been identified* as cancer patients. Some, like the one by Temoshok et al., have related the personality characteristics with severity of the disease; others have compared the personality variables of cancer patients with those of people without cancer. As we shall see in the next section, all such studies share some methodological problems. A more clear-cut approach is to administer personality tests to a large group of people and then follow them for several years, seeing who gets cancer and who does not. Grossarth-Maticek and his colleagues carried out an ambitious study on 1353 residents of a small town in Yugoslavia (Grossarth-Maticek, Bastiaans, and Kanazir, 1985). They administered psychological tests and questionnaires about current health status and habits such as smoking and drinking in 1966 and then followed the subjects for ten years. Their results showed that people with type C personality characteristics were most likely to develop cancer—especially lung cancer.

Grossarth-Maticek and his colleagues began an even more ambitious follow-up study in 1974, when they administered personality tests to 19,000 residents of Heidelberg, Germany. The study is still under way, and so far only a few small samples of the original group have been examined. However, the results so far indicate that the test successfully identifies people who are likely to develop cancer (Grossarth-Maticek and Eysenck, 1990). Examples of the questions that tend to be answered "yes" by people who later develop cancer include "I prefer to agree with others rather than assert my own views," "I am unable to express my feelings and needs openly to other people," and "I often feel inhibited when it comes to openly showing negative feelings such as hatred, aggression, or anger."

Does the Evidence Support the Assertion? Many of the studies that reported an association between personality variables and cancer can be criticized on methodological grounds. First, evidence from studies that test people who already have cancer cannot prove that personality variables play a role in the onset or progression of the disease. Physicians have known for a long time that malignancies can have physiological effects that alter people's emotions and personality, and these changes can occur even before the cancer is detected (Borysenko, 1982; Shakin and Holland, 1988). Thus, what may look like a *cause* of the disease can actually be an *effect*.

Because Grossarth-Maticek and his colleagues administered personality tests to healthy people and looked for the subsequent development of cancer, their studies are not subject to this criticism. Indeed, this approach is the very best way to see whether a cause-and-effect link exists between personality and cancer. However, even if the link exists, we cannot be sure that cancer-proneness is a direct result of people's emotional reactions—produced by suppression of the immune system, for example. Instead, the effect could be caused by differences in people's *behavior*. For example, people who are passive and who have faith that God or their doctor will take care of them might not take responsibility for their own health. Believing that someone else is responsible for their health, they might not bother to try to maintain a healthy life-style. They might not be alert for warning signs of cancer or might even disregard them until they become so blatant they cannot be ignored. Once the cancer is diagnosed, they might be less likely to comply with the treatment prescribed by their physician; after all, it is the *doctor's* responsibility to take care of them, not their own.

In any event, most investigators believe that if the immune system plays a role in the possible link between personality variables and cancer, it affects the *growth* of tumors, not their formation. Most of the studies with laboratory animals that have shown that stress can promote the growth of cancer have investigated tumors induced by viruses—and viruses do not appear to play a significant role in human tumors (Justice, 1987). Thus, this research may not be directly relevant to cancer in humans. The most important defense against the formation of tumors in humans appears to be carried out by mechanisms that help repair damaged DNA, and no one has yet shown a connection between stress and these mechanisms.

What Should We Conclude? The weight of the evidence suggests that personality variables, particularly those relevant to people's coping styles in dealing with unpleasant and stressful situations, can affect the development of cancer. What we do not know is whether these variables do so directly, by altering the activity of the immune system, or indirectly, by affecting people's health-related behavior.

If personality traits play a role in the development of cancer, then perhaps it would be possible to develop a form of psychotherapy that would alter these traits and hence help prevent or combat cancer. In fact, one careful study did find that psychotherapy can increase the survival rate of cancer patients. Spiegel, Bloom, and Yalom (1982) designed an experiment to see whether psychotherapy could help people cope with the anxiety, fear, and pain produced by their disease. (They did not intend the therapy to help the patients *survive* their disease.) The investigators randomly selected two groups of women with advanced breast cancer; one received psychotherapy and the other did not. All patients received standard medical treatment, including surgery, radiation, and chemotherapy. The psychotherapy did indeed help them cope with their cancer; they became less anxious and depressed and learned to reduce their pain. Thirteen years later, Spiegel and his colleagues decided to examine the medical records of the eighty-six subjects to see whether the psychotherapy had affected the course of their disease (Spiegel, Bloom, Kraemer, and Gottheil, 1989). They expected to find that it had not. But it had; those who received a year of therapy lived an average of thirty-seven months, compared with nineteen months for the control subjects. Three women were still alive, and all of them had received the psychotherapy.

According to Spiegel, we cannot necessarily conclude that the psychotherapy prolonged the patients' survival time simply because it reduced stress. Instead, the psychotherapy could have encouraged them to comply better with their physicians' orders concerning medication and diet, and the reduction in pain may have made it possible for them to exercise more and maintain their general health. But clearly, these findings are important; identifying the factors that helped retard the course of the illness could lead to the development of even more effective therapies.

Although Spiegel's report is encouraging, advocating and publicizing the belief that thinking negatively causes illnesses and thinking positively cures them has some harmful side effects. Even if the belief is true, variables such as heredity and exposure to carcinogens are by far the most important risk factors in tumor formation, and standard medical treatments provide by far the most effective forms of therapy. Some people may be tempted to forgo medical treatment, hoping that they can make their tumors wither away by thinking positively. Some therapists have advocated guided imagery, in which the patients visualize their white blood cells attacking their cancer cells. Such exercises may be harmless, but they seem to owe more to a belief in magic than an understanding of scientific evidence. Because early medical treatment is important, any delays in receiving such treatment may reduce the likelihood of a cure. If they cause a delay, even "harmless" exercises may threaten a patient's survival. In addition, a belief in the power of positive thinking can too easily turn into a game of "blame the victim." If someone tries to beat his or her cancer and fails to do so, then the implication is that the person simply did not try hard enough or had the wrong attitude. People dying of cancer should certainly not be led to believe that they are responsible for their condition; they do not need to be given an additional burden of guilt. ■

INTERIM SUMMARY

Stress and Health

People's emotional reactions to aversive stimuli can harm their health. The stress response, which Cannon called the fight-or-flight response, is useful as a short-term response to threatening stimuli but is harmful in the long term. This response includes increased activity of the sympathetic branch of the autonomic nervous system and increased secretion of hormones by the adrenal gland: epinephrine, norepinephrine, and glucocorticoids.

Although increased levels of epinephrine and norepinephrine can raise blood pressure, most of the harm to health comes from glucocorticoids. Prolonged exposure to high levels of these hormones can increase blood pressure, damage muscle tissue, lead to infertility, inhibit growth, inhibit the inflammatory response, and suppress the immune system. It can also damage the hippocampus, and some investigators believe glucocorticoids accelerate the aging process.

Because the harm of most forms of stress comes from our own response to it, individual differences in personality variables can alter the effects of stressful situations. The most important variable is the nature of a person's coping response. Research on the type A behavior pattern suggests that some of these variables—in particular, hostility—can predict the likelihood of cardiovascular disease. However, the research findings are mixed, and some suggest that health-related behaviors may be more important than patterns of emotional reactions. Investigators hope that research on this topic will foster the development of training methods to teach people behavior patterns that will reduce the incidence of the disease.

Posttraumatic stress disorder is a serious reaction to unusually intense stress, which sometimes does not occur until several months after the stressful event. Personality factors appear to affect an individual's susceptibility to this disorder only in cases where the stress is relatively mild. Research has demonstrated the beneficial effects of social support after the stressful event.

Psychoneuroimmunology is a new field of study that investigates interactions between behavior and the immune system, mediated by the nervous system. The immune system consists of several types of white blood cells that produce both nonspecific and specific responses to invading microorganisms. The nonspecific responses include the inflammatory response, the antiviral effect of interferon, and the action of natural killer cells against viruses and cancer cells. The specific responses include chemically mediated and cell-mediated responses. Chemically mediated responses are carried out by B lymphocytes, which release antibodies that bind with the antigens on microorganisms and kill them directly or target them for attack by other white blood cells. Cell-mediated responses are carried out by T lymphocytes, whose antibodies remain attached to their membranes. The immune system can produce harm when it triggers an allergic reaction or when it attacks the body's own tissues, in so-called autoimmune diseases.

A wide variety of stressful situations have been shown to increase people's susceptibility to infectious diseases. Animal research suggests that stress can even encourage the growth of malignant tumors, and allergies and autoimmune diseases can be exacerbated by stress. The most important mechanism by which stress impairs immune function is the increased blood levels of glucocorticoids. In addition, the neural input to the bone marrow, lymph nodes, and thymus gland may also play a role; and the endogenous opioids appear to suppress the activity of natural killer cells.

Several investigators have suggested that a type C ("cancer-prone") personality exists. Although the evidence is mixed, some careful, long-term studies suggest that cancerous tumors may develop faster in passive people who suppress the expression of negative emotions. A study on the effects of psychotherapy suggest that learning to cope with the pain and stress of cancer can increase survival rate. We do not know whether the personality variables affect the growth of cancer directly, through internal physiological processes, or whether they affect people's health-related behavior, such as exercise, avoidance of smoking, and compliance with medical treatment. ∎

Lie Detection in Criminal Investigation

In a criminal investigation where there is not enough physical evidence to indicate who is guilty and who is innocent, the authorities will interrogate witnesses and suspects and try to determine who is telling the truth. If we had a procedure that could tell when a person was lying, we could be sure that the guilty would be convicted and that the innocent would go free. Professional polygraphers (people who operate "lie detector" machines) say that we *do* have a method to detect deception. Are they right? What does a careful scientific analysis say?

In 1986 an American television network, CBS, hired four different polygraphers to find out which of four employees of a photography magazine (which the network owns) had stolen an expensive camera (Lykken, 1988). Each of the polygraphers were told that one of the four employees was suspected but that definite proof was lacking. Sure enough, the polygraphers identified the suspect—a different person in each case—as guilty. Needless to say, no camera was stolen; all the employees were innocent.

The fact that some polygraphers will supply the desired results for a client is certainly contemptible and unethical, but it does not necessarily follow that the practice of lie detection is invalid. After all, there are good and bad practitioners in every profession. How good are careful, well-run polygraph tests at detecting deception?

Before looking at the evidence, we should examine the methods that are used. A polygraph used for a lie detector test is simply a machine that records people's physiological reactions: heart rate, blood pressure, breathing, and skin conductance (a measure of sweating). The subject is hooked up to the machine, and the questioning begins. Polygraphers use two general methods of questioning: the *control question test* and the *guilty knowledge test.*

The control question test attempts to establish a pattern of physiological responding when the subject lies and when he or she tells the truth. In this test the examiner may instruct the subject to say "no" to simple yes-or-no questions about the day of the week. Obviously, the examiner will know when the subject is lying and can compare the pattern of responses with truthful and untruthful statements. Then, when the important questions are asked, the examiner can, theoretically, tell when the subject is lying. For this method to work, the subject must show an emotional reaction when he or she lies. Obviously, if the subject truly believes that the polygraph can detect lies, the reaction will be that much stronger. In fact, sometimes the examiner will trick the subject into this belief by having him or her choose a playing card from a deck, look at it, and then say "no" to every question the examiner asks about its identity. The examiner looks at the polygraph record and says, "I can see from your reactions that it is the queen of

hearts." The subject is impressed; now he or she is convinced that the polygraph works and is more likely to display an emotional reaction during an attempt to lie. (Of course, the examiner does not tell the subject that the cards are marked.)

The problem with the control question test is that even innocent people may react more strongly to a relevant question (that is, a crime-related question) than to a control question. First of all, stress is inevitable during a lie detector test. As Lykken (1988) notes, "Only someone who has actually had the polygraph attachments applied to one's body, and then been asked a series of intrusive questions by a stranger, can fully appreciate how vulnerable one feels in that situation" (p. 112). Even an innocent person can react emotionally when asked whether he or she stole the money or molested the little child.

Lykken (1988) reviewed the scientific literature on the validity of polygraph tests using the control question technique and found that although the studies correctly identified most of the cases of lying, the incidence of *false positives*—of incorrectly indicating that innocent people were lying—was almost 50 percent. And these studies were performed meticulously by well-trained examiners. You will understand why the laws of most countries do not permit polygraph tests to be used in court against people who are accused of crimes.

The second method of questioning—the guilty knowledge test—appears to be more reliable than the control question test. This method, developed by Lykken (1981), does not ask whether the subject committed a crime. Instead, it poses several multiple-choice questions about information that only the criminal could know. For example, suppose that a bank robber drops his hat in an alley after leaving the scene of a crime. The examiner will ask the following questions and note the reaction to each of the alternatives (Lykken, 1988, p. 121):

1. The robber in this case dropped something while escaping. If you are that robber, you will know what he dropped. Was it: a weapon? a face mask? a sack of money? his hat? his car keys?
2. Where did he drop his hat? Was it: in the bank? on the bank steps? on the sidewalk? in the parking lot? in an alley?
3. I'm going to show you five red hats or caps, one at a time. If one of them is your hat, you will recognize it. Which of these hats is yours? Is it: this one? this one? . . . etc.

If the subject knows nothing about the loss of the hat, the chances of showing the strongest reaction to the critical item on any one of the three multiple-choice questions is one in five. The chances of accidentally showing the strongest reaction to *all three* of the questions is eight in a thousand. Of course, if the examiner accidentally (or deliberately) asks the questions in such a way that the answer is obvious (for example, by pausing dramatically before mentioning the critical item), then the test is invalid. The best situation, according to Lykken, is for the examiner not to know which alternatives indicate the guilty knowledge. And the alternatives themselves must be well chosen; as you have undoubtedly learned through your own experience, the alternatives to some poorly written multiple-choice examination questions are simply not plausible. Studies have shown that the guilty knowledge test is much more accurate than the control question test; almost 90 percent of guilty subjects are correctly identified, and only around 3 or 4 percent of innocent people are incorrectly identified.

Not all criminal investigations can use the guilty knowledge test. For example, the test cannot use any of the information that has been presented to the public by the news media, because the subject may have learned of it that way. And if information about the details of the crime are not known to the authorities, it will not be possible to construct any test questions.

As Lykken (1988) notes, unlike Pinocchio, whose nose grew every time he told a lie, we do not emit a distinctive physiological response every time we try to deceive. Given that the overwhelming majority of polygraph tests use the control question procedure, they will inevitably misidentify innocent people as deceptive. Although the test results cannot be used in court, they can misdirect a police investigation by focusing suspicion on innocent people. The guilty knowledge test shows more promise, but more research will be needed to know whether it will find a useful place in criminal investigations.

KEY TERMS AND CONCEPTS

The Nature of Emotion

emotion *(399)*
mood *(399)*
temperament *(400)*
conditioned emotional response *(401)*
coping response *(402)*
orbitofrontal cortex *(403)*

Expression and Recognition of Emotions

pseudobulbar palsy *(407)*
masking *(409)*
modulation *(409)*
simulation *(409)*
display rule *(409)*
leakage *(410)*

Feelings of Emotion

James-Lange theory *(412)*

Stress and Health

stress *(418)*
psychophysiological disorder *(418)*
fight-or-flight response *(418)*
glucocorticoid *(419)*
type A pattern *(422)*
type B pattern *(422)*
posttraumatic stress disorder *(423)*
psychoneuroimmunology *(424)*
antigen *(424)*
antibody *(424)*
B lymphocyte *(424)*
immunoglobulin *(424)*
T lymphocyte *(424)*
natural killer cell *(424)*
autoimmune disease *(425)*
type C pattern *(427)*

Carlson, J.G., and Hatfield, E. *Psychology of Emotion*. Belmont, Calif.: Wadsworth, 1989.

Ekman, P. *The Face of Man: Expressions of Universal Emotions in a New Guinea Village*. New York: Garland STPM Press, 1980.

Frijda, N.H. *The Emotions*. Cambridge: Cambridge University Press, 1986.

James, W. *Principles of Psychology*. New York: Henry Holt, 1890.

Stein, N.L., Leventhal, B., and Trabasso, T. (eds.). *Psychological and Biological Approaches to Emotion*. Hillsdale, N.J.: Lawrence Erlbaum Associates, 1990.

The book by Carlson and Hatfield covers the field of emotion. The Ekman book discusses his cross-cultural studies on the expression and recognition of emotion. The Frijda book is a comprehensive review of the experimental literature and reviews several theories of emotion, including his own. William James's book provides insights into the history of our thinking about emotion. The book by Stein, Leventhal, and Trabasso is an edited volume that contains chapters by experts in the field of emotion.

Ader, R., Felten, D.L., and Cohen, N. (eds.). *Psychoneuroimmunology*, 2nd ed. San Diego: Academic Press, 1990.

Brown, M.R., Koob, G.F., and Rivier, C. (eds.). *Stress: Neurobiology and Neuroendocrinology*. New York: Dekker, 1990.

Gatchel, R.J., Baum, A., and Krantz, D.S. *An Introduction to Health Psychology*, 2nd ed. New York: Newbery Award Records, 1989.

These books describe the biological and psychological aspects of health and stress.

Ben-Shakhar, G., and Furedy, J.J. *Theories and Applications in the Detection of Deception*. New York: Springer-Verlag, 1990.

Gale, A. *The Polygraph Test: Lies, Truth and Science*. London: Sage Publications, 1988.

Lykken, D.T. *A Tremor in the Blood: Uses and Abuses of the Lie Detector*. New York: McGraw-Hill, 1981.

All three books provide a good review of the methods of lie detection and research on its reliability and validity. I particularly recommend the one by Lykken because of its informal style and its wealth of interesting details and vivid examples.

13
INTELLIGENCE

Henri Matisse, *Woman in a Kimono*
Art Resource, N.Y. © 1992 Succession H. Matisse/ARS, N.Y.

LEARNING OBJECTIVES

When you finish this chapter, you should be able to:

1. Describe Spearman's two-factor theory of intelligence and the results of intelligence research using factor analysis.
2. Discuss Sternberg's information-processing theory of intelligence.
3. Discuss Gardner's neuropsychological theory of intelligence.
4. Describe Galton's contributions to intelligence testing.
5. Describe the Binet-Simon Scale, the Stanford-Binet Scale, and Wechsler's tests, and discuss the reliability and validity of intelligence tests.
6. Discuss the use and abuse of intelligence tests.
7. Discuss the meaning of heritability, and describe the sources of environmental and genetic effects during development.
8. Discuss the results and implications of heritability studies of general intelligence and specific abilities.
9. Evaluate whether racial differences in intelligence are the result of heredity.

The syllogism, a form of deductive logic invented by Aristotle, is often found in tests of intelligence. (As you may recall, we already encountered the syllogism in Chapter 9.) Several studies suggested that illiterate, unschooled people in remote villages in various parts of the world were unable to solve syllogistic problems. Scribner (1977) visited two tribes of people in Liberia, West Africa, the Kpelle and the Vai. She found that, indeed, the tribespeople gave what Westerners would consider to be wrong answers.

But Scribner found that the people were not unable to reason logically; they simply approached problems differently. For example, she presented the following problem to a Kpelle farmer. At first glance, the problem appears to be a reasonable one even for an illiterate, unschooled person because it refers to his own tribe and to an occupation he is familiar with.

> All Kpelle men are rice farmers.
>
> Mr. Smith is not a rice farmer.
>
> Is he a Kpelle man?

The man replied:

> *Subject:* I don't know the man in person. I have not laid eyes on the man himself.
>
> *Experimenter:* Just think about the statement.
>
> *Subject:* If I know him in person, I can answer that question, but since I do not know him in person, I cannot answer that question.
>
> *Experimenter:* Try and answer from your Kpelle sense.
>
> *Subject:* If you know a person, if a question comes up about him you are able to answer. But if you do not know the person, if a question comes up about him it's hard for you to answer. (Scribner, 1977, p. 490)

The farmer's response did not show that he was unable to solve a problem in deductive logic. Instead, it indicated that as far as he was concerned, the question was unreasonable. In fact, his response contained an example of logical reasoning: "If you know a person . . . you are able to answer."

Luria (1977) received a similar answer from an illiterate Uzbekistanian woman, who was asked the following:

> In the far north all bears are white.
>
> Novaya Zemyla is in the far north.
>
> What color are the bears there?

The woman replied, "You should ask the people who have been there and seen them. We always speak of only what we see; we don't talk about what we haven't seen."

Scribner found that sometimes illiterate people would reject the premises of her syllogism, replace them with what they knew to be true, and then solve the new problem, *as they had defined it.* For example, she presented the following problem to a Vai tribesperson.

> All women who live in Monrovia are married.
>
> Kemu is not married.
>
> Does she live in Monrovia?

The answer was yes. The respondent said, "Monrovia is not for any one kind of people, so Kemu came to live there." The suggestion that only married women live in Monrovia was absurd, because the tribesperson knew otherwise. Thus, if Kemu wanted to live there, she could—and did.

Clearly, we cannot measure the intellectual ability of people in other cultures against our own standards. In the world of traditional tribal people, problems are solved by application of logical reasoning to facts gained through direct experience. Their deductive-reasoning ability is not necessarily inferior to ours—simply different.

We acknowledge that some people are more intelligent than others, but just what do we mean by that? In general, if people do well academically or succeed at tasks that involve their heads rather than their hands, we consider them to be intelligent. Thus, a critic who writes a witty, articulate review of an artist's exhibition of paintings is said to demonstrate his or her intelligence, whereas the painter is said to show his or her *talent.* Recently, psychologists have pointed out that any definition of intelligence depends on cultural judgments. Study of the types of skills that enable people to survive and flourish suggests that we should broaden our definition to include a wider range of abilities.

Traditionally, psychologists have followed two major approaches in their study of the nature of intelligence. The **differential approach** attempts to devise tests that identify and measure individual differences in people's abilities to solve problems—particularly those that utilize skills important in the classroom. These tests are important to all of us because they are used to screen applicants to schools and candidates for jobs. The **developmental approach** studies the ways in which infants

Different cultures have different definitions of intelligence. Members of the Abouai tribe from the Ivory Coast respect a person's ability to construct useful implements, including this canoe.

learn to perceive, manipulate, and think about the world. The most influential proponent of this approach was the Swiss psychologist Jean Piaget. Because his work was described in detail in Chapter 10, I will not discuss it further here. In the past few years cognitive psychologists have begun to use a third approach, the **information-processing approach,** which is based on research methods they developed to investigate the types of skills people use to think and to solve various types of problems.

THEORIES OF INTELLIGENCE

Differential (psychometric) approaches to the study of intelligence begin with the assumption that the nature of intelligence can best be investigated by studying the ways in which people differ in their performance on tests of intellectual abilities. There is no doubt that people vary widely in many ways, such as in their abilities to learn and use words, to solve arithmetic problems, and to perceive and remember spatial information. The question remains whether intelligence is a global trait or a composite of separate, independent abilities. The fact that psychometricians have devised tests yielding a single IQ score does not in itself mean that intelligence is a single, general characteristic. Some investigators have suggested that certain intellectual abilities are completely independent of one another; for example, a person can be excellent at spatial reasoning but poor at solving verbal analogies. Even investigators who believe that intelligence is a global trait acknowledge that people also have specific intellectual abilities and that these abilities are at least somewhat independent. But there is still disagreement between those who believe that specific abilities are totally independent and those who believe that one general factor influences them all.

Spearman's Two-Factor Theory

Charles Spearman (1927) proposed that a person's performance on a test of intellectual ability is determined by two factors: the **g factor,** which is a general factor, and the **s factor,** which is a factor specific to a particular test. Spearman did not call his *g* factor "intelligence"; he considered the term too vague. He defined the *g* factor as comprising three "qualitative principles of cognition": apprehension of experience, eduction of relations, and eduction of correlates. A common task on tests of intellectual abilities—solving analogies—requires all three principles (Sternberg, 1985). For example, consider the following analogy:

LAWYER:CLIENT::DOCTOR:_____

This problem should be read as "LAWYER is to CLIENT as DOCTOR is to _____." *Apprehension of experience* refers to people's ability to perceive and understand what they experience; thus, reading and understanding each of the words in the analogy requires this principle. *Eduction* (not "*education*") is the process of drawing or bringing out—that is, of figuring out from given facts. In this case, *eduction of relations* refers to the ability to perceive the relation between LAWYER and CLIENT—namely, that the lawyer works for, and is paid by, the client. *Eduction of correlates* refers to the ability to apply a rule inferred from one case to a similar case. Thus, the person whom a doctor works for and is paid by is obviously a PATIENT. Because analogy problems require all three of Spearman's principles of cognition, he advocated their use in intelligence testing.

Empirical evidence for Spearman's two-factor theory comes from correlations among various tests of particular intellectual abilities. The governing logic is as follows: Suppose we administer ten different tests to a group of people. If each test measures a separate, independent ability, the scores these people make on any one test will be unrelated to their scores on any other; the correlations among the tests will be approximately zero. However, if the tests measure abilities that are simply different manifestations of a single trait, the scores will be perfectly related; the intercorrelations will be close to 1.0. In fact, the intercorrelations among a group of tests are neither zero nor 1.0. Instead, most tests designed to measure specific intellectual abilities are at least moderately correlated, so that a person who scores well on a vocabulary test also tends to score better than average on other tests, such as arithmetic or spatial reasoning. The correlations among various tests of mental ability usually range from .30 to .70, which means that they have between 30 percent and 70 percent of their variability in common (Ozer, 1985).

Spearman concluded that a general factor (*g*) accounted for the common variability shared among different tests of ability. Thus, a person's score on a particular test depended upon two things: the person's specific ability (*s*) on the particular test (such as spatial reasoning) and his or her level of the *g* factor, or general reasoning ability.

Evidence from Factor Analysis

Factor analysis is a mathematical procedure developed by Spearman and Pearson that permits investigators to identify common factors—common sources of variability—among groups of tests. If tests in a group of individual tests tend to correlate with one another but not with other tests, we can conclude that the groups are measuring different factors. A factor analysis determines which particular tests form groups. For example, Birren and Morrison (1961) administered the Wechsler Adult Intelligence Scale (WAIS, described in the next section) to 933 people. They calculated the correlations each subtest had with every other subtest and then subjected these correlations to a factor analysis. The details of the procedure are not important to us here, but the results and their implications are.

Table 13.1 Three factors derived by factor analysis of scores on WAIS subtests

Subtest	Factors		
	A	*B*	*C*
Information	.70	.18	.25
Comprehension	.63	.12	.24
Arithmetic	.38	.35	.28
Similarities	.57	.12	.27
Digit span	.16	.84	.13
Vocabulary	.84	.16	.18
Digit symbol	.24	.22	.29
Picture completion	.41	.15	.53
Block design	.20	.14	.73
Picture arrangement	.35	.18	.41
Object assembly	.16	.06	.59

Source: Adapted from Morrison, D.F. *Multivariate Statistical Methods.* New York: McGraw-Hill, 1967.

Table 13.1 lists the results of a factor analysis on Birren and Morrison's data. The analysis revealed three factors, labeled A, B, and C. The numbers in the three columns in the table are called **factor loadings;** they are somewhat like correlation coefficients in that they express the degree to which a particular test is related to a particular factor. For the various subtests on factor A, the largest factor loading is for vocabulary, followed by information, comprehension, and similarities. (The subtests are described in Table 13.4, page 446.) In the middle range are picture completion, arithmetic, picture arrangement, and digit symbol. Digit span, object assembly, and block design are the smallest. (See *Table 13.1.*) Verbal subtests make the most important contribution, so we might be tempted to call this factor *verbal ability*. But almost all tests make at least a moderate contribution, so some people may prefer to call this factor *general intelligence*. Digit span loads very heavily on factor B (.84), whereas other tests register much lower on this factor, and arithmetic and digit symbol have moderate loadings. Factor B appears to be related to *maintaining information in short-term memory* and *manipulating numbers*. Factor C appears to be determined mainly by block design, object assembly, picture completion, and picture arrangement. A good name for this factor might be *spatial ability*.

Although factor analysis can give hints about the nature of intelligence, it cannot provide definitive answers. The names given to the factors are up to the investigator and are not prescribed by the mathematical analysis. Furthermore, factor analysis can never be more meaningful than the individual tests on which it is performed. To identify the relevant factors in human intelligence, one must include an extensive variety of tests in the factor analysis. For example, experience has shown that the WAIS is a useful predictor of scholastic performance and (to a lesser extent) of vocational success. Thus, it appears to measure some important abilities. But a factor analysis of the subtests will never reveal other important abilities that may *not* be measured by the WAIS. For example, the WAIS does not contain a test of musical ability. If it did, then a factor analysis would undoubtedly yield an additional factor. Whether musical ability is a component of intelligence depends on how we decide to define intelligence; this question cannot be answered by a factor analysis.

Many investigators have performed factor analyses on tests of intellectual abilities. For example, Louis Thurstone (1938) administered a battery of fifty-six tests to 218 college students and then performed a factor analysis and extracted seven factors, which he labeled *verbal comprehension, verbal fluency, number, spatial visualization, memory, reasoning,* and *perceptual speed.* At first, Thurstone thought that his results contradicted Spearman's hypothesized *g* factor. However, Eysenck suggested a few years later that a *second* factor analysis could be performed on Thurstone's factors. If the analysis found one common factor, then Spearman's *g*

Theories of
Intelligence

Figure 13.1 Five tests that correlate well with Cattell's g_f factor. (First four tests taken from the Culture Fair Intelligence Test, Scale 2, Form A test booklet. © 1949, 1960 R 1977, by the Institute for Personality and Ability Testing, Inc. Reproduced by permission of the copyright owner. Analogies test reproduced by permission of Raymond Cattell and of NFER-Nelson, Windsor, England.)

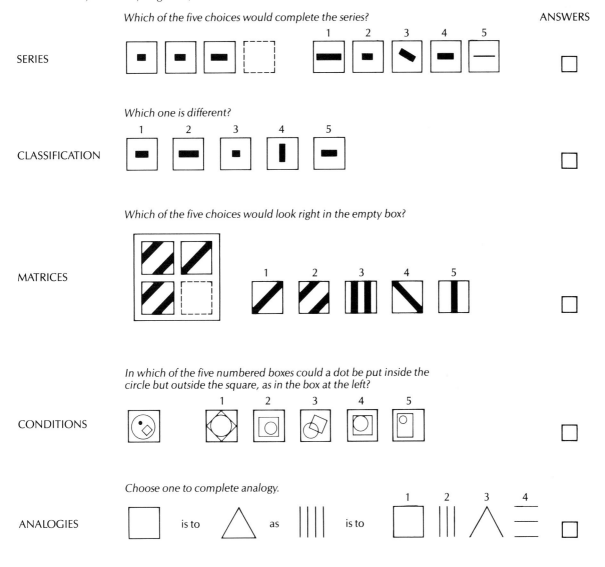

Table 13.2 Summary of tests with large factor loadings on g_f or g_c

Test	Approximate Factor Loadings	
	g_f	g_c
Figural relations: Deduction of a relation when this is shown among common figures	.57	.01
Memory span: Reproduction of several numbers or letters presented briefly	.50	.00
Induction: Deduction of a correlate from relations shown in a series of letters, numbers, or figures, as in a letter series test	.41	.06
General reasoning: Solving problems of area, rate, finance, and the like, as in an arithmetic reasoning test	.31	.34
Semantic relations: Deduction of a relation when this is shown among words, as in an analogies test	.37	.43
Formal reasoning: Arriving at a conclusion in accordance with a formal reasoning process, as in a syllogistic reasoning test	.31	.41
Number facility: Quick and accurate use of arithmetical operations such as addition, subtraction, and multiplication	.21	.29
Experiential evaluation: Solving problems involving protocol and requiring diplomacy, as in a social relations test	.08	.43
Verbal comprehension: Advanced understanding of language, as measured in a vocabulary or reading test	.08	.68

Source: Adapted from Horn, J.L. Organization of abilities and the development of intelligence. *Psychological Review*, 1968, *75*, 249. Copyright 1968 by the American Psychological Association. Adapted by permission of the author.

factor would receive support. In other words, if Thurstone's seven factors themselves had a second-order factor in common, this factor might be conceived of as general intelligence.

Cattell also performed a second-order factor analysis and found not one but two major factors. Horn and Cattell (1966) called these factors *fluid intelligence* (g_f) and *crystallized intelligence* (g_c). Fluid intelligence is defined by relatively culture-free tasks, whereas crystallized intelligence is defined by tasks that require people to have acquired information from their culture—particularly, vocabulary and the kind of information learned in schools. Cattell regards g_f as being closely related to a person's native capacity for intellectual performance; in other words, it represents a potential ability to learn and solve problems. In contrast, he regards crystallized intelligence as what a person has accomplished through the use of his or her fluid intelligence: what he or she has learned. Horn

differs with Cattell; he cites evidence suggesting that both factors are learned but are also based on heredity. He says that g_f is based on casual learning and g_c is based on cultural, school-type learning (Horn, 1978).

Figure 13.1 illustrates items from five subtests that load heavily on the g_f (fluid intelligence) factor. Although verbalization can help solve these problems, they are essentially nonverbal in form. In addition, the items differ from the types of problems encountered in school, and they do not appear to be closely tied to cultural experience. (See *Figure 13.1*.)

Tests that load heavily on the g_c (crystallized intelligence) factor include word analogies and tests of vocabulary, general information, and use of language. According to Cattell, g_c depends on g_f. Fluid intelligence supplies the native ability, whereas experience with language and exposure to books, school, and other learning opportunities develop crystallized intelligence. If two people have the same experiences, the one with the greater fluid intelligence will develop the greater crystallized intelligence. However, a person with a high fluid intelligence exposed to an intellectually impoverished environment will develop a poor or mediocre crystallized intelligence. Table 13.2 presents a summary by Horn (1968) of tests that load on g_f and g_c. (See *Table 13.2*.)

No two investigators agree about the nature of intelligence. However, most believe that a small number of common factors account for at least part of a person's performance on intellectual tasks.

An Information-Processing Theory of Intelligence

2 Sternberg (1985) has devised a theory of intelligence that derives from the information-processing approach used by many cognitive psychologists. Sternberg's theory is in three parts; he calls it a *triarchic* ("ruled by three") theory. The three parts of the theory deal with three aspects of intelligence: componential intelligence, experiential intelligence, and contextual intelligence.

Componential intelligence consists of the mental mechanisms people use to plan and execute tasks. The components revealed by the analyses of verbal ability and deductive reasoning that I just described come under this heading. Sternberg suggests that the components of intelligence serve three functions. *Metacompo-*

nents ("transcending" components) are the processes by which people decide the nature of an intellectual problem, select a strategy for solving it, and allocate their resources. For example, we saw earlier that good readers vary the amount of time they spend on a passage according to how much information they need to extract from it. This decision is controlled by a metacomponent of intelligence. *Performance components* are the processes actually used to perform the task—for example, lexical recognition and working memory. *Knowledge acquisition components* are those the person uses to gain new knowledge by sifting out relevant information and integrating it with what he or she already knows.

The second part of Sternberg's theory deals with experiential intelligence. According to the theory, a person with good **experiential intelligence** is able to deal more effectively with novel situations than an unintelligent person. He or she is better able to analyze the situation and bring mental resources to bear on the problem, even if one like it has never been encountered before. After encountering a particular type of problem several times, the intelligent person is also able to "automate" the procedure so that similar problems can be solved without much thought, freeing mental resources for other work. A person who has to reason out the solution to a problem every time it occurs will be left behind by people who can give the answer quickly and automatically. Sternberg suggests that this distinction is closely related to the distinction between fluid and crystallized intelligence (Horn and Cattell, 1966). According to Sternberg, tasks that utilize fluid intelligence are those that demand novel approaches, whereas tasks that utilize crystallized intelligence are those that demand mental processes that have become automatic.

The third part of Sternberg's theory deals with **contextual intelligence:** intelligence reflecting the behaviors that were subject to selective pressure in our evolutionary history. Contextual intelligence takes three forms. The first form, *adaptation,* consists in fitting oneself into one's environment by developing useful skills and behaviors. In different cultures adaptation will take different forms. For example, knowing how to distinguish between poisonous and edible plants is an important skill for a member of a hunter-gatherer tribe, and knowing how to present oneself in a job interview is an important skill for a member of an industrialized society.

The second form of contextual intelligence, *selection,* refers to the ability to find one's own niche in the environment. For example, Feldman (1982) studied some of the child prodigies who appeared on the "Quiz Kid" radio and television shows in the United States during the 1940s and 1950s. These children were selected for their ability to answer factual-knowledge questions quickly, and they had very high IQ scores. Feldman's follow-up study indicated that the ones with the most distinguished careers were those who had found something that interested them and had stuck to it. Those who failed to do so accomplished very little, despite their high IQs. According to Sternberg, the difference was a reflection of the selective aspect of contextual intelligence.

The third form of contextual intelligence is *shaping.* Sometimes, adapting to the environment or selecting a new one is not possible or profitable. In this case intelligent behavior consists in shaping the environment itself. For example, a person whose talents are not appreciated by his or her employer may decide to start his or her own business.

The importance of Sternberg's emphasis on practical intelligence is supported by observations of people with damage to their frontal lobes. Even after sustaining massive damage to the frontal lobes (for example, after an automobile or motorcycle accident), people often continue to score well on standard tests of intelligence; thus, we are tempted to conclude that their intelligence is unimpaired. But such people lose the ability to plan their lives or even their daily activities. I became familiar with the case of a formerly successful physician who had received a head injury that severely damaged his frontal lobes. Even though he still had a high IQ as measured by intelligence tests, he could no longer carry out his practice. He became a delivery truck driver for his brother, who owned a business. He was able to carry out this job only because his brother did all the planning for him, carefully laying out his route and instructing him to call the brother if he encountered any trouble. The man's behavior lost its flexibility and insightfulness. For example, if he found the front door locked at a business to which he was supposed to deliver an order, it would not occur to him to go around to the back; his brother would have to suggest that by telephone. Clearly, the man's behavior lacked a very crucial component of intelligence. The fact this component is not measured by most intelligence tests indicates that they are missing something important.

Robert J. Sternberg

Table 13.3 An outline of Sternberg's triarchic theory of intelligence

---

Componential Intelligence

Metacomponents (e.g., planning)

Performance components (e.g., lexical access)

Knowledge acquisition components (e.g., ability to acquire vocabulary words)

Experiential Intelligence

Novel tasks

Automated tasks

Contextual Intelligence

Adaptation (adapting to the environment)

Selection (finding a suitable environment)

Shaping (changing the environment)

Because so many categories and subcategories have been introduced in this section, I have collected the terms described here in **Table 13.3.**

A Neuropsychological Theory of Intelligence

[3] As we saw in the example I just presented, neuropsychological observations have provided us with some important insights about the nature of intelligence. Gardner (1983) has suggested a theory of intelligence based on a neuropsychological analysis of human abilities. As you have seen in previous chapters, localized brain damage can impair specific types of abilities. For example, damage to various parts of the left hemisphere can impair verbal abilities, and damage to various parts of the right hemisphere can impair the ability to orient well in space or to produce and recognize facial expressions of emotion. Gardner concludes that intelligence falls into seven categories: *linguistic intelligence, musical intelligence, logical-mathematical intelligence, spatial intelligence, bodily-kinesthetic intelligence,* and two types of *personal intelligence.* Bodily-kinesthetic intelligence includes the types of skills that athletes, typists, dancers, or mime artists exhibit. Personal intelligence includes awareness of one's own feelings *(intrapersonal intelligence)* and the ability to notice individual differences in other people and to respond appropriately to them—in other words, to be socially aware *(interpersonal intelligence).*

Three of Gardner's types of intelligence—verbal intelligence, logical-mathematical intelligence, and spatial intelligence—are not unusual, having been identified previously by many other researchers. But why include the others? According to Gardner, all seven abilities are well represented in the brain, in that specific brain damage can impair some of them but leave others relatively intact. For example, people with damage to the left parietal lobe can sustain an *apraxia,* an inability to perform sequences of voluntary skilled movements. In contrast, people with damage to the right parietal lobe "lose touch with themselves." For one thing, they are likely to ignore the left side of their bodies, failing to shave or apply makeup to the left side of their faces or to put on the left sleeve of their shirts or coats. In addition, they tend to become unaware of their physical condition; for instance, although they may have a paralyzed arm and leg, they do not take the disability into account when they make plans for the future. In another example of a neuropsychological relation, people with damage to the frontal or temporal lobes—especially of the right hemisphere—may have difficulty evaluating the significance of social situations. These examples illustrate bodily-kinesthetic intelligence and both intrapersonal and interpersonal intelligence.

Psychometric tests of intelligence emphasize the kinds of skills that can easily be tested at a desk or table, with paper and pencil or small puzzles. In general, we have tended not to consider skill at moving one's body as a measure of intelligence, although this talent was undoubtedly selected for during the evolution of our species. Individuals who could more skillfully prepare tools, hunt animals, climb trees, scale cliffs, and perform other tasks requiring physical skills were more likely to survive and reproduce. Psychometricians have indeed developed mechanical aptitude tasks, primarily to help employers select skilled prospective employees, but such skills have generally been regarded as representing something less than intelligence. If a person has good verbal skills, most people in Western cultures will not regard the person as less intelligent if he or she is also clumsy; similarly, they will not credit a person who has poor verbal skills with a measure of intelligence just because the person is physically skilled.

Gardner's theory has the advantage of being based on neuropsychological realities; it also accommodates the views of intelligence held by some non-Western cultures. For example, he would recognize the ability of a member of the Puluwat culture of the Caroline Islands to navigate across the sea by the stars as an example of intelligence (Gladwin, 1970).

INTERIM SUMMARY

Theories of Intelligence

Although intelligence is often represented by a single score, IQ, modern investigators do not deny the existence of specific abilities. What is controversial is whether a general factor also exists. Spearman thought so; he named the factor *g* and demonstrated that people's scores on a variety of specific tests of ability were correlated. However, he believed that specific factors (*s* factors) also existed. Thurstone performed a factor analysis on fifty-six individual tests that revealed the existence of seven factors, not a single *g* factor. Eysenck reasoned that because these factors were themselves correlated, a factor analysis on *them* was justified. Cattell performed such an analysis and obtained two factors, and he confirmed this result with factor analyses of tests of his own. The nature of the tests that loaded heavily on these two factors suggested the names *fluid intelligence* and *crystallized intelligence,* with the former representing a person's native ability and the latter representing what a person learns.

Sternberg's triarchic theory of intelligence is an ambitious attempt to integrate laboratory research using the information-processing approach along with an analysis of intelligent behavior in the natural environment. Gardner's neuropsychological theory of intelligence is based primarily on the types of skills that can selectively be lost by brain damage. Like Sternberg's theory, it emphasizes the significance of behaviors to the culture in which they occur. ■

INTELLIGENCE TESTING

4 Assessment of intellectual ability, or intelligence testing, is a controversial topic because of its importance in modern society. Unless people have special skills that suit them for a career in sports or entertainment, their economic success depends heavily on formal education; and admission to colleges and eligibility for scholarships are largely determined by the results of tests. In addition, many employers use specialized aptitude tests to help them select among job candidates. Because the scores achieved on these tests have major implications for the quality of people's adult lives, testing has become one of the most important areas of applied psychology. Today there are hundreds of tests of specific abilities, such as manual dexterity, spatial reasoning, vocabulary, mathematical aptitude, musical ability, creativity, and memory. There are also general tests of scholastic aptitude, some of which you have probably taken yourself. These tests vary widely in reliability, validity, and ease of administration.

From Mandarins to Galton

Undoubtedly, humans have been aware of individual differences in abilities since our species first evolved. Some people were more efficient hunters, some were more skillful at constructing tools and weapons, and some were more daring and clever warriors. As early as 2200 B.C., Chinese administrators tested civil servants (mandarins) periodically to be sure that their abilities qualified them for their jobs. But in Western cultures differences in social class were far more important than individual differences in ability until the Renaissance, when the modern concept of individualism came into being.

Although the term *intelligence* is an old one, deriving from the Latin *intellectus* (meaning "perception" or "comprehension"), its use in the English language dates only from the late nineteenth century, when it was revived by the philosopher Herbert Spencer and by the biologist-statistician Sir Francis Galton (1822–1911), the most important early investigator of individual differences in ability. Galton was strongly influenced by his cousin Charles Darwin, who stressed the importance of inherited differences in physical and behavioral traits related to a species's survival. Galton observed that there were family differences in ability and concluded that intellectual abilities were heritable. Having noted that people with low ability were poor at making sensory discriminations, he decided that tests involving such discriminations would provide valid measures of intelligence.

In 1884 Galton established the Anthropometric ("human-measuring") Laboratory at the International Health Exhibition in London. His exhibit was so popular that afterward his laboratory became part of the South Kensington Museum. He tested over nine thousand people on seventeen variables, including height and weight, muscular strength, and the ability to perform sensory discriminations. One task involved detecting small differences in the weights of objects of the same size and shape. The use of simple tests of sensory discrimination fell into disfavor among subsequent researchers in the field of intelligence, so Galton's program was not continued after his death.

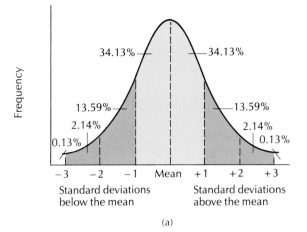

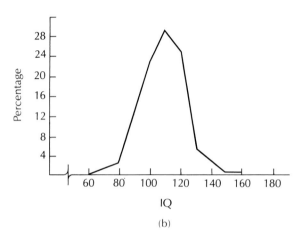

Figure 13.2 Curves used in intelligence testing. (a) A mathematically derived normal curve. (b) A curve showing the distribution of IQ scores of 850 children 2 ½ years of age. (From Terman, L.M., and Merrill, M.A. *Stanford-Binet Intelligence Scale.* Boston: Houghton Mifflin, 1960; material cited pertains to the 1960 edition and not to the Fourth Edition published in 1985. Reproduced by permission of The Riverside Publishing Company.)

Nevertheless, Galton made some important contributions to the study of individual differences. His systematic evaluation of large numbers of people and the methods of population statistics he developed served as models for the statistical tests now used in all branches of science. His observation that the distribution of most human traits closely resembles the normal curve developed by the Belgian statistician Lambert Quetelet is the foundation for many modern tests of statistical significance. (See *Figure 13.2.*)

Galton also outlined the logic of a measure he called *correlation*: the degree to which variability in one measure is related to variability in

another. From this analysis Karl Pearson derived the correlation coefficient *(r)* used today to assess the degree of statistical relation between variables. (I discussed this measure in Chapter 2.) In addition, Galton developed the logic of *twin studies* and *adoptive parent studies* to assess the heritability of a human trait. These methods are discussed later in the chapter.

The Binet-Simon Scale

[5] Alfred Binet, a French psychologist, disagreed with Galton's conception of human intelligence. He and a colleague (Binet and Henri, 1896) suggested that a group of simple sensory tests could not adequately determine a person's intelligence. They recommended measuring a variety of psychological abilities (such as imagery, attention, comprehension, imagination, judgments of visual space, and memory for various stimuli) that appeared to be more representative of the traits that distinguished people of high and low intelligence.

To identify children who were unable to profit from normal classroom instruction and needed special attention, Binet and a colleague, Theodore Simon, assembled a collection of tests, many of which had been developed by other investigators, and published the **Binet-Simon Scale** in 1905. The tests were arranged in order of difficulty, and the researchers obtained norms for each test. **Norms** are data from comparison groups that permit the score of an individual to be assessed relative to his or her peers. In this case the norms consisted of distributions of scores obtained by children of various ages. Binet and Simon also provided a detailed description of the testing procedure, which was essential for obtaining reliable scores. Without a standardized procedure for administering a test, different testers can obtain different scores from the same child.

Binet revised the 1905 test in order to assess the intellectual abilities of both normal children and those with learning problems. The revised versions provided a procedure for estimating a child's **mental age:** the level of intellectual development that could be expected for an average child of a particular age. For example, if a child of eight scores as well as average ten-year-old children, his or her mental age is ten years. Binet did not develop the concept of IQ (intelligence quotient). Nor did he believe that the mental age derived from the test scores expressed a simple trait called "intelligence"; rather, he conceived of the overall score as the average of several different abilities.

Test materials from the 1986 Stanford-Binet Intelligence Scale.

The Stanford-Binet Scale

Lewis Terman, of Stanford University, translated and revised the Binet-Simon Scale in the United States. The revised group of tests, published in 1916, became known as the **Stanford-Binet Scale.** Revisions by Terman and Maud Merrill were published in 1937 and 1960. In 1985 an entirely new version of the Stanford-Binet Scale was published. The scale consists of various tasks grouped according to mental age. Simple tests include identifying parts of the body and remembering which of three small cardboard boxes contains a marble. Intermediate tests include tracing a simple maze with a pencil and repeating five digits orally. Advanced tests

include explaining the difference between two abstract words that are close in meaning (such as *fame* and *notoriety*) and completing complex sentences.

The 1916 Stanford-Binet Scale contained a formula for computing the **intelligence quotient (IQ)**, a measure devised by Stern (1914). Its rationale is quite simple: If the test scores indicate that a child's mental age is equal to his or her chronological age (that is, calendar age), then the child's intelligence is average; if the child's mental age is above or below his or her chronological age, then the child is more or less intelligent than average. This relation is expressed as the quotient of mental age (MA) and chronological age (CA). The result is called the **ratio IQ:**

$$IQ = \frac{MA}{CA} \times 100$$

The quotient is multiplied by 100 to eliminate fractions. For example, if a child's mental age is ten and the child's chronological age is eight, then his or her IQ is $(10 \div 8) \times 100 = 125$.

The 1960 version of the Stanford-Binet Scale replaced the ratio IQ with the **deviation IQ.** Instead of using the ratio of mental age to chronological age, the new measure compared a child's score with those received by other children of the same chronological age. (The deviation IQ was invented by David Wechsler, whose work is described in the next section.) Suppose a child's score is one standard deviation above the mean for his or her age. (See Chapter 2 for a description of the standard deviation, a measure of variability.) The standard deviation of the ratio IQ scores is 16 points, and the score assigned to average IQ is 100 points; thus, the child's score is 100 + 16 (the standard deviation) = 116. A child who scores one standard deviation below the mean receives a deviation IQ of 84 (100 − 16). (See *Figure 13.3.*)

Figure 13.3   The rationale for calculating the deviation IQ score.

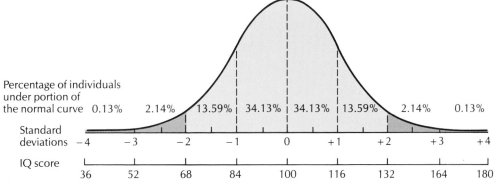

Percentage of individuals under portion of the normal curve	0.13%	2.14%	13.59%	34.13%	34.13%	13.59%	2.14%	0.13%
Standard deviations	−4	−3	−2	−1	0	+1	+2	+3	+4
IQ score	36	52	68	84	100	116	132	164	180

Wechsler's Tests

When David Wechsler was chief psychologist at New York City's Bellevue Psychiatric Hospital, he developed several popular and well-respected tests of intelligence. The Wechsler-Bellevue Scale, published in 1939, was revised in 1942 for use in the armed forces and was superseded in 1955 by the **Wechsler Adult Intelligence Scale (WAIS).** This test was revised again in 1981 (the WAIS-R). The **Wechsler Intelligence Scale for Children (WISC),** first published in 1949 and revised in 1974 (the WISC-R), closely resembles the WAIS. Wechsler also devised an intelligence test for preschoolchildren, a memory scale, and other measures of ability.

The WAIS-R consists of eleven subtests, divided into two categories: verbal and performance. Table 13.4 lists the subtests and a typical question or problem for each. (See *Table 13.4.*) The norms obtained for the WAIS-R permit the tester to calculate a deviation IQ score.

The block design subtest is part of both of Wechsler's Scales, the WISC-R and the WAIS-R.

Table 13.4 WAIS-R subtests and typical questions or problems

Subtest	Typical Question or Problem
Verbal	
Information	"What is the capital of France?"
Digit span	"Repeat these numbers back to me: 46239."
Vocabulary	"What does the word 'conventional' mean?"
Arithmetic	"Suppose you bought six postcards for thirteen cents each and gave the clerk a dollar. How much change would you receive?" (Paper and pencil cannot be used.)
Comprehension	"Why are we tried by a jury of our peers?"
Similarities	"How are goldfish and canaries similar to each other?"
Performance	
Picture completion	The tester shows the subject a picture with a missing part (such as a mouse without its whiskers) and says, "Tell me what's missing."
Picture arrangement	The tester shows a series of cartoon pictures (without words) and instructs the subject to arrange them in the proper sequence.
Block design	The tester shows a picture and four or nine blocks divided diagonally into red and white sections, then instructs the subject to arrange the blocks so that they match the design in the picture.
Object assembly	The tester gives the subject pieces of cardboard cut like a jigsaw puzzle and instructs him or her to assemble it. (When properly assembled, the pieces form the shape of a common object.)
Digit symbol	The tester presents a set of ten designs paired with the ten numerals and instructs the subject to write the corresponding symbols beneath each of a large series of numerals.

The WAIS-R has become the most popular individually administered adult intelligence test. Like the Stanford-Binet Scale, it is very reliable. An important advantage is that it tests verbal and performance abilities separately. Neuropsychologists often use it because people with brain damage tend to score very differently on the performance and verbal tests; thus, comparisons of performance and verbal test scores suggest the presence of undiagnosed brain damage. Because people who have had few educational and cultural opportunities often do worse on the verbal tests than on the performance tests, the WAIS-R is useful in estimating what their score might have been in a more favorable environment.

Reliability and Validity of Intelligence Tests

As you will recall from Chapter 2, the adequacy of a measure is represented by its reliability and validity. In the case of psychometric testing, reliability is assessed by the correlation between the scores people receive on the same measurement on two different occasions; perfect reliability is 1.0. High reliability is achieved by means of standardized test administration and objective scoring: All test takers are exposed to the same

Table 13.5 Verbal scores received on the Scholastic Aptitude Test (SAT) and freshman-year grade point averages of 250 American college students

	Freshman-Year Grade Point Average							
	F	*D*		*C*		*B*		*A*
SAT Verbal Score	*0.00–0.49*	*0.50–0.99*	*1.00–1.49*	*1.50–1.99*	*2.00–2.49*	*2.50–2.99*	*3.00–3.49*	*3.50–3.99*
750–799							1	2
700–749					2		5	4
650–699				1	8	3	4	2
600–649				4	10	7	5	1
550–599			6	12	16	13	2	
500–549		4	7	25	21	5	3	
450–499		5	10	14	7	2		
400–449	1	6	8	5	4	1		
350–399	2	5	4	2				
300–349	1							

Source: Adapted from Lewis R. Aiken, *Psychological Testing and Assessment,* Sixth Edition. Copyright © 1988 by Allyn and Bacon. Used with permission.

situation during testing, and all test givers score responses in the same way. The acceptable reliability of a modern test of intellectual ability should be at least .85.

Validity is the correlation between test scores and the **criterion:** an independent measure of the variable that is being assessed. For example, suppose you plan to estimate people's wealth by observing how many money-related words they use when describing a picture that illustrates a story. (This example is fictitious; no one has developed such a test—I think.) You can determine the validity of the test by seeing how accurately it estimates people's actual wealth (the criterion).

Because there is no single definition of intelligence, there is no single criterion measure. However, most tests of intelligence correlate reasonably well with measures like success in school (between .40 and .75). Thus, because intellectual ability plays at least some role in academic success, IQ appears to have some validity. Table 13.5 illustrates the relation between students' scores on the verbal subtest of the Scholastic Aptitude Test (SAT) and the grades they subsequently earned during their freshman year in college. (See *Table 13.5.*)

The Use and Abuse of Intelligence Tests

6 Many kinds of institutions use intelligence tests and tests of specific abilities. Schools that group students according to ability usually do so on the basis of test scores. Schools also administer tests to students who appear to be slow learners in order to assess educational needs that may require participation in a special program. At selective academic institutions test scores usually serve as an important criterion for admission. Similarly, many business organizations use ability tests to screen job candidates. Because test scores have such important consequences for so many people's opportunities, we must know whether intelligence tests are valid and whether they are being used appropriately.

Possible Problems. Critics of intelligence testing have argued that intelligence tests do not measure people's abilities at all; rather, they measure what people have learned. Therefore, people's educational opportunities in the home, neighborhood, and school directly influence their performance on intelligence tests. Consider the effects of a person's family background and culture on his or her ability to answer questions such as "Who wrote *Romeo and Juliet?*" "What is a hieroglyphic?" "What is the meaning of *catacomb?*" and "What is the thing to do if another boy (or girl) hits you without meaning to?" (Vernon, 1979, p. 22). Obviously, a child from a middle-class family is much more likely to be able to answer the first three questions than an equally intelligent child from a deprived environment. The answer given to the fourth question is also likely to be culturally determined.

Test constructors have responded to this criticism, and modern tests are much less likely to contain questions that are obviously culturally biased.

Unfortunately, the problem of cultural bias has not yet been solved. Even though questions with obvious cultural bias are no longer incorporated into intelligence tests, different experiences can lead to different test-taking strategies in nonobvious ways. For example, as we saw in the opening vignette, Kpelle tribespeople approach hypothetical logical problems very differently from people in literate societies. Their "failure" to solve such problems indicates cultural differences, not intellectual differences.

Another potential abuse of intelligence tests is to deprive low-scoring children of opportunities to receive an education that will make them competitive later in life. Children who discover that they have scored poorly on an intelligence test are likely to suffer feelings of inferiority and may become disinclined to try to learn, believing that they cannot. In addition, undue emphasis on testing may affect a school's curriculum and methods of teaching; teachers and administrators may try to teach information and skills that are measured by tests instead of basing their curriculum on the children's needs. Clearly, schools should use intelligence tests with great caution. If the results are not themselves used intelligently, such tests are actually harmful.

Identifying Specific Learning Needs. Intelligence testing has potential benefits when it is used in accordance with Binet's original purpose: to identify students who require special instruction. Children with severe learning problems are likely to develop a strong sense of inferiority if they are placed in classes with children whose academic progress is much faster than theirs; such children will probably benefit most from special teaching methods. These tests can also identify exceptionally bright students who are performing poorly because they are bored with the pace of instruction or who have been labeled as "troublemakers" by their teachers.

Many otherwise bright children suffer from various learning disabilities. Some have trouble learning to read or write; some perform poorly at arithmetic or motor skills. For example, some children have developmental dyslexias that make learning to read difficult for them. Dyslexic children are often frustrated by the contrast between their inability to read and their other abilities. They may act out this frustration through disruptive behavior at school and at home, or they may simply stop trying to excel at anything. As a result, they are sometimes stigmatized as mentally retarded and denied the opportunity for a good education. In this situation tests of intellectual abilities are extremely useful. By identifying a specific learning disability in an otherwise bright child, testing helps ensure remedial action and prevents mislabeling.

Identifying Degrees of Mental Retardation. Binet's original use of intelligence tests—to identify children who learn more slowly than most others and who therefore need special training—is still important. Some children are so deficient in intellectual abilities that they require institutional care. Intelligence tests are accepted means of evaluating the extent of a child's disabilities and, thus, of indicating the most appropriate remedial program.

The term **mental retardation** was originally applied to children with severe learning problems because they appeared to achieve intellectual skills and competencies at a significantly later age than most children. Their achievements came more slowly; thus, their developmental stages seemed to be retarded. Although most mentally retarded people were formerly relegated to a bleak and hopeless existence in institutions, many successful training programs have been initiated in recent years. The causes of mental retardation are discussed later in this chapter.

Mental retardation is often accompanied by deficits in physical and social skills. The most severe classification, *profound mental retardation,* designates people with a mental age of under three years and with IQ scores under 20. These people usually have severe brain damage, and they almost always also have physical defects. The next category is *severe mental retardation,* with a mental age of three to four years and with IQ scores between 20 and 35. Few of these people learn to read and write unless they are trained by special methods. Both groups need custodial care.

Moderate mental retardation designates people with mental ages ranging from four to seven and a half years and with IQ scores of 36 to 51. Many of these people also require custodial care. *Mild mental retardation* designates people with mental ages of seven and a half to eleven years and with IQ scores of 52 to 67. With adequate training most mildly mentally retarded people can lead independent lives and perform well at jobs that do not require a great deal of intellectual ability.

INTERIM SUMMARY

Intelligence Testing

Although the earliest known instance of ability testing was carried out by the ancient Chinese, modern intelligence testing dates from the efforts of Galton to measure individual differences. Galton made an important contribution to the field of measurement, but his tests of simple perceptual abilities were abandoned in favor of tests that attempt to assess more complex abilities, such as memory, logical reasoning, and vocabulary.

Binet developed a test that was designed to assess students' intellectual abilities in order to identify children with special educational needs. Although the test that superseded his, the Stanford-Binet Scale, provided for calculation of IQ, Binet believed that "intelligence" was actually a composite of several specific abilities. For him, the concept of mental age was a convenience, not a biological reality. Wechsler's two intelligence tests, the WAIS-R for adults and the WISC-R for children, are widely used today. The information provided by the verbal and performance scores helps neuropsychologists diagnose brain damage and can provide at least a rough estimate of the innate ability of poorly educated people.

Reliability of modern intelligence tests is excellent, but assessing their validity is still difficult. Because no single criterion measure of intelligence exists, intelligence tests are validated by comparing the scores with measures of achievement, such as scholastic success.

Intelligence testing can have both good and bad effects on the people who take them. The principal benefit is derived by identifying children with special needs (or special talents) who will profit from special programs. The principal danger lies in stigmatizing those who score poorly and depriving them of the opportunity for good jobs or further education. ■

THE ROLES OF HEREDITY AND ENVIRONMENT

7 Abilities of various kinds—intellectual, athletic, musical, and artistic—appear to run in families. Why? Are the similarities due to common heredity, or are they solely the result of a common environment, with similar educational opportunities and exposure to people with similar kinds of interests? As we will see, the evidence suggests that both hereditary and environmental factors play a role.

The Meaning of Heritability

When we ask how much influence heredity has on a given trait, we are usually asking what the heritability of the trait is. **Heritability** is a statistical measure that expresses the proportion of the observed variability in a trait that is a direct result of genetic variability. The value of this measure can vary from 0 to 1.0. The heritability of many physical traits in most cultures is very high; for example, eye color is affected almost entirely by hereditary factors and little, if at all, by the environment. Thus, the heritability of eye color is close to 1.0.

Heritability is a concept that many people misunderstand. It does not describe the extent to which the inherited genes are responsible for producing a particular trait; it measures the relative contributions of differences in genes and differences in environmental factors to the overall observed variability of the trait in a particular population. An example may make this distinction clear. Consider the heritability of hair color in the Eskimo culture. Almost all young Eskimos have black hair, whereas older Eskimos have gray or white hair. Because all members of this population possess the same versions of the genes that determine hair color, the genetic variability with respect to those genes is essentially zero. All the observed variability in hair color in this population is explained by an environmental factor: age. Therefore, the heritability of hair color in the Eskimo culture is zero.

As with hair color, we are forced to infer the heritability of a person's intelligence from his or her observed performance. Thus, looking at a person's IQ score is equivalent to looking at the color of a person's hair. By measuring the correlation between IQ score and various genetic and environmental factors, we can arrive at an estimate of heritability. Clearly, even if hereditary factors do influence intelligence, the heritability of this trait must be considerably less than 1.0, because so many environmental factors (such as the mother's prenatal health and nutrition, the child's nutrition, the educational level of the child's parents, and the quality of the child's school) can influence it.

When we consider studies that assess the heritability of intellectual abilities, we should be aware of the following considerations.

1. The heritability of a trait depends on the amount of variability of genetic factors in a given population. Because the ancestors of people living in developed Western nations came from all over the world, genetic variability is likely to be much higher there than in an isolated tribe of people in a remote part of the world. Therefore, if a person's IQ score is at all affected by genetic factors, the measured heritability of IQ will be higher in, say, North American culture than in an isolated tribe.

2. The relative importance of environmental factors in intelligence depends on the amount of environmental variability (EV) that occurs in the population. In a society with a low variability in environmental factors relevant to intellectual development—one in which all children are raised in the same way by equally skilled and conscientious caregivers, all schools are equally good, all teachers have equally effective personalities and teaching skills, and no one is discriminated against—the effects of EV would be small and those of GV (genetic variability) would be large. In contrast, in a society in which only a few privileged people receive a good education, environmental factors would be responsible for much of the variability in intelligence: The effects of EV would be large relative to those of GV.

3. Heritability is affected by the degree to which genetic inheritance and environment interact. For example, suppose that because of genetic differences some children are calm and others are excitable. Suppose that the excitable children will profit most from a classroom in which distractions are kept to a minimum and teachers are themselves calm and soothing. Further suppose that the calm students will profit most from an exciting classroom that motivates them to work their hardest. In this situation the actual performance of the students would be based on an *interaction* between heredity and environment. If all students were taught in a calm classroom, the excitable children would perform best and hence would learn more and obtain better IQ scores. If all students were taught in an exciting classroom, the calm children would do better and obtain the higher scores. (Ideally, a child's learning environment should match his or her hereditary predispositions.)

Sources of Environmental and Genetic Effects During Development

Both biological and environmental factors occurring before or after birth can affect intellectual abilities. Newborn infants cannot be said to possess any substantial intellectual abilities; rather, they are more or less capable of *developing* these abilities during their life. Therefore, prenatal influences can be said to affect a child's *potential* intelligence by affecting the development of the brain. Factors that impair brain development will necessarily also impair the child's potential intelligence.

The factors that control the development of a human organism are incredibly complex. For example, the most complicated organ—the brain—consists of many billions of neurons

Although heredity plays an important role in intelligence, children's home environments can determine whether they achieve their full potential.

(nerve cells), all of which are connected to other neurons. In addition, many of these neurons are connected to sensory receptors, muscles, or glands. During development these billions of neurons must establish the proper connections so that the eyes send their information to the visual cortex, the ears send theirs to the auditory cortex, and the nerve cells controlling movement connect with the appropriate muscles.

Experiments have shown that as the axons of developing neurons grow, they thread their way through a tangle of other growing cells, responding to physical and chemical signals along the way, much as a salmon swims upriver to the tributary in which it was spawned. During this stage of development, differentiating cells can be misguided by false signals. For example, if a woman contracts German measles during early pregnancy, toxic chemicals produced by the disease virus may adversely affect the development of the fetus. Sometimes, these chemicals can misdirect the interconnections of brain cells and produce mental retardation. Thus, although development of a human organism is programmed genetically, environmental factors can affect development even before a person is born.

Harmful prenatal environmental factors include physical trauma (perhaps through injury to the mother in an automobile accident) and toxic effects. A developing fetus can be exposed to toxins—for example, from diseases contracted by the mother during pregnancy (such as German measles). A pregnant woman's intake of various drugs can have disastrous effects on fetal development. For example, alcohol, opiates, cocaine, and the chemicals present in cigarettes can harm fetuses. There is some evidence that even a single alcoholic "binge" during a critical stage of pregnancy can cause permanent damage to the fetus. One of the most common drug-induced abnormalities, the **fetal alcohol syndrome,** is seen in many offspring of women who are chronic alcoholics. The children are much smaller than average, have characteristic facial abnormalities, and, more significantly, are mentally retarded. Figure 13.4 shows the face of a child with fetal alcohol syndrome, along with the face of a normal rat fetus and a rat fetus whose mother received alcohol during early pregnancy. (See *Figure 13.4.*)

Development can also be harmed by genetic abnormalities. Some of these abnormalities cause brain damage and consequently produce mental retardation. The best-known example of these abnormalities is **Down syndrome,** which is produced by a chromosomal abnormality consisting of an extra twenty-first chromosome, so that there are three, rather than a pair. Researchers believe that the harmful effects on brain development are related to excessive production of a special protein that also accumulates in the brains of people with Alzheimer's disease—a disorder that produces brain degeneration. Although Down syndrome is *genetic,* it is not caused by a faulty gene and is therefore not *hereditary.* The incidence of Down syndrome is related to the mother's age and, according to some researchers, possibly the father's as well.

Some children with Down syndrome are only moderately retarded; some score as well on tests of intelligence as people considered normal. Therefore, many such children remain with their families instead of living in an institution for mentally retarded children. However,

Figure 13.4 A child with fetal alcohol syndrome, along with magnified views of a rat fetus whose mother received alcohol during pregnancy (*left*) and a normal rat fetus (*right*). (Photograph courtesy of Katherine K. Sulik.)

Narrow forehead

Short palpebral fissures

Small nose

Long upper lip with deficient philtrum

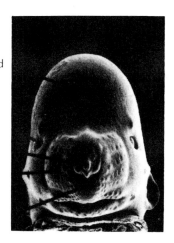

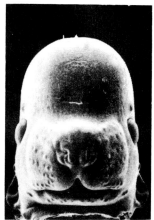

children with Down syndrome are more susceptible than normal children to a variety of physical disorders and therefore have a shorter life expectancy.

Another genetic disorder, **phenylketonuria** (PKU), is caused by a pair of faulty genes that fail to produce a particular enzyme. The enzyme normally causes one amino acid (phenylalanine) to be converted into another (tyrosine). In a baby with PKU the unconverted phenylalanine accumulates in the blood and damages the cells of the brain, causing mental retardation.

Fortunately, PKU can be treated. A special diet containing very little phenylalanine keeps the blood level of this amino acid low and allows the nervous system to develop normally. Once it is mature enough, the nervous system builds barriers that protect it from excessive levels of phenylalanine in the blood, and the dietary restriction can be relaxed somewhat. Early treatment is vital, however, because the brain damage is permanent. After the first twenty-five weeks of postpartum life, it is too late to prevent mental retardation. Reliable, valid tests for PKU are now available, and many countries require that all newborn infants be tested for the disorder.

From birth onward a child's brain continues to develop. Environmental factors can either promote or impede that development. Postnatal factors such as birth trauma, diseases that affect the brain, or toxic chemicals can prevent optimum development and thereby affect the child's potential intelligence. For example, encephalitis (inflammation of the brain), when contracted during childhood, can result in mental retardation. So can the ingestion of poisons such as mercury or lead.

Educational influences in the environment, including (but not limited to) schooling, enable a child to attain his or her potential intelligence. By contrast, a less-than-optimum environment prevents the fullest possible realization of potential intelligence. Experience with mentally retarded people demonstrates this point. Known causes account for only about 25 percent of observed cases of mental retardation. In addition, people whose mental retardation has no obvious physical cause are likely to have close relatives who are also mentally retarded. These findings strongly suggest that many of the remaining 75 percent of cases are caused by hereditary factors. However, environmental causes (such as poor nutrition or the presence of environmental toxins) can produce brain damage in members of the same family; thus, not all

cases of *familial* mental retardation are necessarily *hereditary.*

Clearly, the interactive effects of environmental and genetic factors are complex. The effects of hereditary factors on adult intellectual ability are necessarily indirect, and many environmental factors exert their effects throughout a person's life. Because an adult's intellectual abilities are the product of a long chain of events, we cannot isolate the effects of the earliest factors. The types of genetic and environmental factors influencing potential intelligence at each stage of development are summarized below.

Conception. A person's genetic endowment sets limits on his or her brain anatomy and thus on his or her potential intelligence.

Prenatal development. Good nutrition and a normal pregnancy result in optimum brain development and optimum potential intelligence. Drugs, toxic substances, poor nutrition, and physical accidents can impair brain development, thus lowering potential intelligence. Genetic disorders such as phenylketonuria and Down syndrome can impair brain development, thus lowering potential intelligence.

Birth. Anoxia (lack of oxygen) or head trauma can cause brain damage, thus lowering potential intelligence.

Infancy. The brain continues to develop and grow. Good nutrition continues to be important. Sensory stimulation and interaction with a responsive environment are important for cognitive development. An infant's environment and brain structure jointly determine his or her intelligence.

Later life. A person's intelligence continues to be jointly determined by environmental factors and brain structure and chemistry. Aging brings with it an increased chance of developing senile dementia—a class of diseases characterized by the progressive loss of cortical tissue and a corresponding loss of mental functions. (*Senile* means "old," *dementia* literally means "an undoing of the mind.") The most common causes of dementia are Alzheimer's disease (which was discussed in Chapter 10) and *multiple infarcts*— the occurrence of a large number of small strokes, each of which damages a small amount of brain tissue. In addition, as we saw in Chapter 10, mental deterioration can be produced by depression, a psychological disorder. Unlike Alzheimer's disease or multiple infarcts, depression can be treated with drugs and with psychotherapy.

Results of Heritability Studies

[8] Estimates of the degree to which heredity influences a person's intellectual ability come from several sources. The two most powerful methods are comparisons between identical and fraternal twins and comparisons between adoptive and biological relatives.

Because identical (monozygotic) twins share identical sets of chromosomes, they are genetically identical. They have also shared virtually the same environment in the uterus. For all practical purposes, they are two examples of the same person. Thus, the heritability of IQ in a given culture may be estimated by studying many sets of identical twins who were separated at birth and raised in different families. When identical twins are raised together, their postnatal environments are almost precisely the same. Thus, not surprisingly, the correlation between IQ scores of identical twins is extremely high. When identical twins are adopted and raised separately by different families, their environment obviously differs. If IQ scores were determined solely by heredity, the correlations between the scores of identical twins raised together or separately would be the same. In fact, they are not, which means that a person's environment affects his or her IQ score.

Other estimates of heritability have been made by comparing identical twins with fraternal (dizygotic) twins, both reared together. Whereas identical twins have the same genetic material, fraternal twins are no more closely related than any two siblings who were born at different times. On the average, 50 percent of the chromosomes of fraternal twins are identical (compared with 100 percent for identical twins). Because twins who are reared together share approximately the same environment, researchers have estimated heritability by observing the difference in correlation between the two types of twins.

General Intelligence. Table 13.6 presents correlations in intelligence between people of varying kinships and estimates based on these data of the relative contributions of genetic and environmental factors. The data in the table were obtained from a summary of several studies by Henderson (1982). As you can see, the correlation between two people is indeed related to their genetic similarity. (See **Table 13.6,** *top.*) For example, the correlation between identical twins is larger than that between fraternal twins. In addition, the correlation between parent and child is approximately the same regardless of whether or not the child is

Table 13.6 Correlations in intelligence between pairs of people with varying kinships and estimates of relative contributions of genetic and environmental factors

Relationship	Rearing	Percentage of Genetic Similarity	Correlation
Same individual	—	100	.87
Identical twins	Together	100	.86
Fraternal twins	Together	50	.62
Siblings	Together	50	.41
Siblings	Apart	50	.24
Parent-child	Together	50	.35
Parent-child	Apart	50	.31
Adoptive parent–child	Together	?	.16

Comparison	Estimates of Contributions of Genetics and Environment to Variability in Intelligence	
	Genetics	Environment
Identical twins together versus fraternal twins together	.58	.28
Parent-offspring together versus parent-offspring apart	.50	.04
Siblings together versus siblings apart	.25	.25

Source: Adapted from Henderson, N.D. A Human behavior genetics, pp. 403–440. Reproduced, with permission, from the *Annual Review of Psychology,* Volume 33. © 1982 by Annual Reviews Inc.

raised by the parent (.35 versus .31). This correlation, in turn, is higher than that between an adopted child and the parent who raises him or her (.16).

The bottom portion of Table 13.6 shows that estimates of the importance of common genetic and environmental factors vary considerably, depending on the type of comparison made. Estimates of genetic influence range from 25 to 58 percent. As Plomin (1988) notes, this finding means that if we know the IQ scores of the parents, we can predict the IQ of a child with a standard error of 12 points. Thus, heredity contributes substantially to the observed differences in IQ scores. (See **Table 13.6,** *bottom.*)

We should be careful not to misinterpret the meaning of estimates of genetic or environmental influences on IQ scores. These estimates only indicate how much of the variability of that trait *in that population* appears to be related to genetic or environmental differences. Suppose we were to raise some babies in stimulating, responsive environments, others in mediocre environments, and still others in environments so impoverished that words were never spoken.

The babies in the impoverished environments would never even learn to talk, and their IQs would be very low. In such a case we would find that environmental factors accounted for nearly 100 percent of the observed variability in this population, with genetic factors being almost negligible in comparison.

The fact that, by most estimates, genetic factors account for approximately 50 percent of the variability in IQ scores means that the other half of the variability is accounted for by environmental factors. However, when the data presented in Table 13.6 are used to estimate the contribution of environmental factors, the results suggest that this contribution is less than 25 percent. Some estimates, based on comparisons of parents and their offspring raised together or apart, suggest a value of only *4 percent*. Why are these figures so low?

Plomin (1988) suggests that estimates of the importance of environmental factors tend to be low because the environment in a given family is not identical for all its members. Some environmental variables within a family are shared by all members of the family, such as the number of books the family has, the examples set by the parents, the places the family visits on vacation, the noisiness or quietness of the home, and so on. But not all of the environmental factors that affect a person's development and behavior are shared in this way. For example, no two children are treated identically, even by family members; differences in their appearances and personalities affect the way other people treat them. Different members of a family will probably have different friends and acquaintances, attend different classes in school, and, in general, be exposed to different influences. And once people leave home, their environments become even more different.

Estimates of the contribution of environmental variability to intelligence based on measurements made during childhood tend to be higher than similar estimates based on measurements made during adulthood. The reason for this difference may be that during childhood family members share a more similar environment, whereas during adulthood their environments become less similar. As Plomin notes, recent studies of genetically unrelated children (with a mean age of under ten years), adopted and raised in the same family, suggest that up to 30 percent of the variability in IQ scores is due to common environmental factors. However, when the comparison is made of young adults, the figure drops to less than 3 percent. Thus, once children leave home and are exposed to different environmental variables, the effect of a common family environment almost disappears. (What is left, in the case of *related* individuals, is their common genetic heritage.)

Specific Abilities. So far, I have discussed the effects of genetic and environmental factors on tests of general intelligence. Scarr and Weinberg (1978) compared some specific intellectual abilities of parents and their adopted and biological children, and children and their biological and adopted siblings. To do so, they administered four of the subtests of the Wechsler Adult Intel-

Table 13.7 Correlations between parent and adoptive or biological child for four WAIS subscales

	Relationship		
WAIS Subscale	*Father-Offspring*	*Mother-Offspring*	*Sibling*
Adoptive family correlations			
Arithmetic	.07	−.03	−.03
Vocabulary	.24	.23	.11
Block design	.02	.13	.09
Picture arrangement	−.04	−.01	.04
Biological family correlations			
Arithmetic	.30	.24	.24
Vocabulary	.39	.33	.22
Block design	.32	.29	.25
Picture arrangement	.06	.19	.16

Source: Adapted from Scarr, S., and Weinberg, R.A. *American Sociological Review*, 1978, *43*, 674–692. Adapted with permission.

ligence Scale: arithmetic, vocabulary, block design, and picture arrangement. (The nature of these subtests was described in Table 13.4.) The results are shown in Table 13.7. As you can see, the correlations between biological relatives were considerably higher than those between adoptive relatives, indicating that genetic factors played a more significant role than shared environmental factors. In fact, with the exception of vocabulary, adopted children showed little resemblance to other members of their family. (See **Table 13.7.**)

These results suggest that a person's vocabulary is more sensitive to his or her home environment than other specific intellectual abilities. Presumably, such factors as the availability of books, parental interests in reading, and the complexity of vocabulary used by the parents has a significant effect on the verbal skills of everyone in the household, whether or not they are biologically related.

EVALUATING SCIENTIFIC ISSUES

The Issue of Race and Intelligence

[9] The fact that heredity appears to play an important role in people's innate intellectual capacities raises the question of whether people of some races are generally more intelligent than those of other races. Because of the harmful effects that racism has had on the lives of so many people, this question is not simply an academic one.

What Is Being Asserted? Many studies have established the fact that there are racial differences in scores on various tests of intellectual abilities. For example, people who are identified as "black" generally score an average of 85

on IQ tests, whereas people who are identified as "white" score an average of 100 (Lynn, 1978; Jensen, 1985). Thus, although many blacks score better than many whites, on the average whites do better on these tests.

The issue is not the facts themselves but what these facts *mean*. Some authors say that the racial differences in scores on the tests are caused by heredity. For example, Rushton (1988, 1990) suggests that the evolutionary history of Africans, Europeans, and Orientals is different. These races "emerged" at different times and were subjected to different kinds of selective pressures. As a result, their patterns of reproduction (referred to by evolutionary biologists as *reproductive strategies*) are different. The r strategy results in larger numbers of offspring and smaller brains, whereas the K strategy results in smaller numbers of offspring and larger brains. Rushton claims that Orientals are more K-selected and Africans are more r-selected; thus Orientals have the highest intelligence and Africans have the lowest intelligence, with Europeans in the middle.

Does the Evidence Support the Assertion? There are many reasons why we *cannot* conclude that the observed racial differences in average test scores are the result of heredity. I will examine the two most important ones here: the definition of race and the role of the environment. First, let us examine the concept of *race*. A biologist uses the term to identify a population of plants or animals that has some degree of reproductive isolation from other members of the species, with which it is perfectly capable of interbreeding. For example, collies, cocker spaniels, and beagles constitute different races of dogs (although we usually refer to them as *breeds*). In this case, reproductive isolation is imposed by humans; within obvious size limits, different breeds of dogs can readily mate with each other.

Scarr and Weinberg found that children raised in middle-class families have higher IQ scores than those raised in disadvantaged homes—regardless of the color of their skin.

Any isolated group of organisms will, as a result of chance alterations in genetic factors and differences in local environment, become genetically different over time. Groups of humans whose ancestors mated only with other people who lived in a restricted geographical region tend to differ from other groups on a variety of hereditary traits, including stature, hair color, skin pigmentation, and blood type. However, subsequent migrations and conquests caused the interbreeding of many different groups of people. As a result, human racial groups are much more similar than, say, breeds of dogs, so that classifying people on the basis of race is a difficult and somewhat arbitrary matter.

Many researchers have used the trait of skin pigmentation to classify people by race. Two chemicals, melanin and keratin, cause skin to be black and yellow, respectively; a combination produces brown skin, while lighter-colored skin contains little of either substance. Evidence suggests that the selective value of differing amounts of skin pigmentation is related to its ability to protect against the effects of sunlight (Loomis, 1967). Such protection was important near the equator, where the sun is intense all year, but was less important in temperate zones. Because vitamin D is synthesized primarily through the action of sunlight on deep layers of the skin, *lack* of pigmentation was advantageous to residents of northern latitudes, except to those living in Arctic regions, where vitamin D was readily available from fish and seal meat.

Thus, the selective advantage of differences in skin pigmentation is obvious; but there is no plausible reason to expect these differences to be correlated either with other physical measures or with measures of intellectual ability. Both the tallest people in the world (the Masai) and the shortest (the Pygmy) have black skin. Nor are shape of nose and forehead, hair texture, blood groups, and many other physical features well correlated with skin pigmentation. We would never classify varieties of dogs by color, assigning golden retrievers and Chihuahuas to one group and black Labrador retrievers and Scotties to another. Why, then, should we do so with humans?

The second reason why we cannot conclude that racial differences in test scores are caused by heredity is the existence of environmental differences. In North America racial membership is a cultural phenomenon, not a biological one. A man with three grandparents of European origin and one grandparent of African ori-

gin is defined as "black" unless he keeps this fact secret and "passes" (defines himself) as "white." Black people and white people are treated differently: The average black family is poorer than the average white one; blacks usually attend schools of lesser academic quality than whites; pregnant black women typically receive poorer medical care than their white counterparts, and their diet tends to be not as well balanced; and so on. In these circumstances we would expect people's IQ scores to differ in accordance with whether they had been raised as blacks or as whites—independent of their genetic background.

Some investigators have attempted to use statistical means to "remove" the effects of environmental variables, such as socioeconomic status, that account for differences in performance between blacks and whites. These efforts are subject to criticism on several grounds. On the other hand, a study by Scarr and Weinberg (1976) provides unambiguous evidence that environmental factors can substantially increase the measured IQ of a black child. Scarr and Weinberg studied ninety-nine black children who were adopted while they were young into white families of higher-than-average educational and socioeconomic status. The expected average IQ of black children in the same area who were raised in black families was approximately 90. The average IQ of the adopted group was observed to be 105.

What Should We Conclude? Some authors have flatly stated that there are no racial differences in biologically determined intellectual capacity. But this claim, like the one asserting that blacks are inherently less intelligent than whites, lacks scientific support. Although we know that blacks and whites have different environments, and that a black child raised in an environment similar to that of a white child will receive a higher IQ score, the question of whether or not any racial hereditary differences exist has not been answered. However, given that there is at least as much variability in intelligence between two people selected at random as there is between the average black and the average white, knowing a person's race tells us very little about how intelligent he or she may be.

Although the issue of race and intelligence as presently conceived does not appear to be meaningful, it would be scientifically interesting to study the effects of different environments on inherited intellectual capacity. One such investigation might involve human populations whose ancestors came from desert regions, cold regions, humid regions, regions with widely fluctuating temperatures, regions with a high level of diseases, regions where food is difficult to obtain, regions where food is easily available, regions where the last ice age affected the native population, regions where trade has been important, and regions that have been isolated and self-sufficient. Direct comparisons of the innate intellectual abilities of these people could tell us which environmental factors have been important in their selection. However, these factors would not be synonymous with racial differences.

The interesting and more valid questions concerning race are those addressed by social psychologists and anthropologists—questions concerning issues such as the prevalence of prejudice, ethnic identification and cohesiveness, fear of strangers, and the tendency to judge something (or someone) that is different as inferior. In fact, Chapter 17 discusses the topic of prejudice from the perspective of social psychology. ■

INTERIM SUMMARY

The Roles of Heredity and Environment

Variability in all physical traits is determined by a certain amount of genetic variability, environmental variability, and an interaction between genetic and environmental factors. The degree to which genetic variability is responsible for the observed variability of a particular trait in a particular population is referred to as the *heritability* of the trait. Heritability is not an indication of the degree to which the trait is determined by biological factors; rather, it reflects the relative proportions of genetic and environmental variability found in the population. As we saw, the heritability of hair color among Eskimos is close to zero because there is scarcely any genetic variability with respect to this trait. Obviously, this fact does not mean that hair color among Eskimos is not biologically determined.

Intellectual development is affected by many factors, both prenatal and postnatal. A person's heredity, because of its effect on brain development, determines his or her potential intelligence. This potential intelligence can be permanently reduced during prenatal or postnatal development by injury, toxic chemicals, poor nutrition, or disease. And in order for a person to achieve his or her potential intelligence, the person must have an environment that will foster the learning of facts and skills needed to function well in society.

Twin studies and studies comparing biological and adoptive relatives indicate that both genetic and environmental factors affect intellectual ability, which is probably not surprising. These studies also point out that not all of a person's environment is shared by other members of the family; each person is an individual and is exposed to different environmental variables.

Some people have suggested that racial differences in intellectual ability are the result of differences in heredity. However, the available data do not permit us to make this conclusion. First, race is almost always defined culturally, not genetically. Second, we cannot rule out the effects of environmental differences. It is impossible to measure people's inherited intellectual ability directly; all we can do is measure their *performance*—on tests, in school, or on the job. Because performance is determined by what people have learned, it reflects environmental factors as well as genetic ones. Therefore, because members of different racial groups have unequal opportunities to use their innate biological capacities to develop intellectual skills, no conclusions can be made about whether the racial differences are hereditary. The little evidence we do have suggests that when educational opportunities are equalized, so are test scores. ■

Project Head Start

As we have seen in this chapter, a person's intellectual abilities are determined by interactions between genetics and environment that begin even before birth. Because of environmental deficiencies, many people are unable to live up to their potential; their intellectual development is impaired.

Project Head Start, a program instituted by the United States government in 1965, was designed to enrich the intellectual and social environments of disadvantaged pre-schoolchildren (Zigler, 1985). The project was intended to provide basic health services and day care and to include activities to improve the children's social, emotional, motivational, and intellectual development. From the beginning, the project solicited the participation of parents and community leaders to be sure that the program was serving community needs. Currently, over 100,000 children participate each year in over 2000 locally administered programs. Unlike most other social welfare projects established during the 1960s' "war on poverty," Project Head Start has been endorsed by both liberal and conservative administrations. Approximately two-thirds of the children served by Project Head Start are members of minority groups.

Has Project Head Start met its goals? Reviews of studies evaluating the program have found that early interventions have immediate positive effects on a wide range of measures of intellectual abilities (Mann, Harrell, and Hurt, 1977; Greenspan and White, 1985). In comparison with disadvantaged children who have not had the benefit of an early intervention program, graduates of Head Start receive scores very close to national norms on measures of school readiness. They maintain this advantage during the first year of school, but in grades two and three their scores on tests of intellectual achievement resemble those of their peers. Thus, early gains in cognitive development are clear-cut, but long-term improvement is difficult to demonstrate.

When measures other than intelligence tests are used to evaluate the long-term effects of early intervention, the results are somewhat more promising. Several studies have shown that children who have participated in Project Head Start are less likely than their non-participant peers to be assigned to special education classes and are less likely to be held back in grade level for a second year. In addition, they have better self-images, and their parents express greater satisfaction with their academic progress (Zigler and Valentine, 1979; Cole and Washington, 1986).

According to Zigler (1979), during the 1960s, when Project Head Start was being developed, many experts believed that young children were especially susceptible to the effects of their environment. According to this belief, even a brief intervention program could produce significant, longlasting effects, so long as it occurred at the right time in a child's development. Thus, many experts held unrealistic expectations for the program. In large part, this belief was a reaction against the previously held position that IQ was basically unchangeable and environmental factors had only a minimal effect on cognitive development.

The short-term effectiveness of Project Head Start confirms that a positive change in a child's environment has beneficial effects on cognitive development, but it also shows that the enrichment must continue if permanent results are to occur. The greatest gains are shown when parents extend the remedial program in the home through their own efforts. In fact, Project Head Start has educated *parents* as well as children. Many parents who participated in the program had passively accepted the bleak futures that their children apparently faced. But once they took some responsibility for their children's education and saw that their own efforts could have positive effects, they began to take more control over their lives. The parents' increased self-esteem improved their relations with their children and their communities.

differential approach *(436)*
developmental approach *(436)*
information-processing approach *(437)*

Theories of Intelligence

g factor *(437)*
s factor *(437)*
factor loading *(438)*
componential intelligence *(440)*
experiential intelligence *(441)*
contextual intelligence *(441)*

Intelligence Testing

Binet-Simon Scale *(444)*
norm *(444)*
mental age *(444)*

Stanford-Binet Scale *(445)*
intelligence quotient (IQ) *(445)*
ratio IQ *(445)*
deviation IQ *(445)*
Wechsler Adult Intelligence Scale (WAIS) *(446)*
Wechsler Intelligence Scale for Children
  (WISC) *(446)*
criterion *(447)*
mental retardation *(448)*

The Roles of Heredity and Environment

heritability *(449)*
fetal alcohol syndrome *(451)*
Down syndrome *(451)*
phenylketonuria *(452)*

Suggestions for Further Reading

Aiken, L. *Psychological Testing and Assessment,* 6th
  ed. Boston: Allyn and Bacon, 1988.
Gardner, H. *Frames of Mind: The Theory of Multiple
  Intelligences.* New York: Basic Books, 1983.
Kaplan, R.M., and Saccuzzo, D.P. *Psychological
  Testing: Principles and Issues.* Pacific Grove,
  Calif.: Brooks/Cole, 1989.
Sternberg, R.J. *Beyond IQ: A Triarchic Theory of
  Human Intelligence.* Cambridge, England: Cam-
  bridge University Press, 1985.

Kamin, L. *The Science and Politics of IQ.* New York:
  John Wiley & Sons, 1974.
Scarr, S. *Race, Social Class, and Individual Differ-
  ences in IQ.* Hillsdale, N.J.: Lawrence Erlbaum As-
  sociates, 1981.
Vale, J.R. *Genes, Environment, and Behavior.* New
  York: Harper & Row, 1980.

*Gardner's book describes his theory, based on the exis-
tence of specific brain functions related to talents often
overlooked by traditional tests of intelligence. The
books by Aiken and by Kaplan and Saccuzzo provide
excellent discussions of the differential, or psychometric, approach to intelligence. Sternberg's book
describes his information-processing theory of
intelligence.*

*Kamin's book examines the history of the scientific
study of intelligence—in particular, its contamination
by racism and ethnocentrism. The books by Scarr and
by Vale provide excellent discussions of the interrela-
tions between environmental and hereditary influences
on intelligence.*

14
PERSONALITY

Henri Matisse, *Spanish Woman with a Tambourine*
SCALA/Art Resource, N.Y. © 1992 Succession H. Matisse/ARS, N.Y.

LEARNING OBJECTIVES

When you finish this chapter, you should be able to:

1. Distinguish between personality types and traits, and summarize the personality traits identified by Cattell, Eysenck, and the five-factor model.
2. Describe the psychobiological approach to personality: the effects of heredity and environment and the brain mechanisms that may be responsible for differences in personality traits.
3. Describe the behaviorist and social learning approaches to personality.
4. Evaluate the controversy about the relative importance of personality traits and environmental situations in predicting behavior.
5. Describe the historical background that led to Freud's psychodynamic theory of personality, and explain his hypothetical mental structures and defense mechanisms.
6. Explain Freud's psychosexual theory of personality, and explain how it influenced the theories of Jung, Adler, and Erikson.
7. Discuss modern research on the Freudian concepts of repression and self-deception.
8. Describe the rational and empirical strategies of test construction, and describe and evaluate the MMPI.
9. Explain the rationale of projective tests of personality, and describe and evaluate the Rorschach Inkblot Test and the Thematic Apperception Test.

The identical twin boys were separated at the age of thirty-seven days and were adopted by working-class families in Ohio. Both, coincidentally, were named Jim by their adoptive families. They did not meet each other again until the late 1970s, when the news of their reunion prompted Dr. Thomas Bouchard to begin the Minnesota Study of Twins Reared Apart.

Jim S. and Jim L. both liked math in school, but neither liked spelling. At ten years of age they both developed sinus headaches and a few years later developed migraine headaches as well—the so-called mixed-headache syndrome. They use the same terms to describe their head pain. Both twins have hemorrhoids and identical pulse rate and blood pressure, and both put on 10 pounds of weight at the same time in their lives. Both Jims are clerical workers who enjoy woodworking, serve as volunteers for police agencies, enjoy spending their vacations in Florida, have married and divorced women named Linda, chew their nails, owned dogs named Toy, and drive Chevrolets.

Bridget and Dorothy, identical twins, were thirty-nine years old when they were reunited. They came to their meeting wearing seven rings on their fingers, two bracelets on one wrist, and a watch and a bracelet on the other. Although the two women were raised by families with very different socioeconomic levels, their personalities were very similar. The most striking difference between them is that the one raised by the family of modest means has bad teeth.

Oskar and Jack were born in Trinidad. Their mother, a German, took Oskar back to Germany, where he was raised as a Catholic. He became a member of a Nazi youth group. His brother Jack was raised by his father in the Caribbean, as a Jew. He spent part of his adolescence on a kibbutz in Israel. Oskar now lives in Germany, and Jack lives in southern California. When the twins met at the airport, both were wearing wire-rimmed glasses and two-pocket shirts with epaulets. Both had mustaches. Questionnaires revealed that both like spicy foods and sweet liqueurs, tend to fall asleep while watching television, think it is funny to sneeze in a crowd of strangers, store rubber bands on their wrists, flush the toilet before using it, and read magazines from back to front. Although their backgrounds could not be much more different, their scores on the Minnesota Multiphasic Personality Inventory (the MMPI) are very similar.

These striking cases of identical twins reunited in adulthood suggest that heredity plays an important role in shaping personality. However, like all pieces of anecdotal evidence, they must be regarded as hints, subject to confirmation by careful scientific evaluation. The Minnesota Study of Twins Reared Apart is one of several projects designed to determine the roles of heredity and environment in the development of personality (Holden, 1980; Bouchard et al., 1981).

Psychologists who study human personality are, like the rest of us, interested in predicting behavior. They attempt to determine what behavioral characteristics people possess and to assess the value of these characteristics in predicting people's behavior in various situations. But another issue also interests psychologists: How and why do people differ from each other? As you will see, several very different types of theories have been proposed to explain individual differences in personality.

When studying personality, we must be careful to avoid the nominal fallacy; describing a personality characteristic is not the same as explaining it. However, identification is the first step on the way to explanation. What types of research efforts are necessary to study personality? Some psychologists devote their efforts to the development of tests that can reliably measure differences in personality. Others try to determine the events—biological and environmental—that cause people to behave as they do. Thus, research on human personality requires two kinds of efforts: identifying personality characteristics and determining the variables that produce and control them. In this chapter you will learn how psychologists have attempted to classify and measure differences in personality, and you will be introduced to the major approaches to the study of personality: trait, behavioral/cognitive, psychobiological, and psychodynamic.

TRAIT THEORIES OF PERSONALITY

1 According to a dictionary of psychological terms (Reber, 1985), the word *personality* is "so resistant to definition and so broad in usage that no coherent simple statement about it can be made—hence, the wise author uses it as the title of a chapter and then writes freely about it . . . " (p. 533). As you will see in this chapter, the term means different things to different people. The definition of personality that belongs to

*Psychologists who study personality study the
ways people differ from each other and try to
determine the causes of these differences.*

the trait approach is probably the closest to the
one we use in everyday speech: a set of personal characteristics that determine the ways
we act and react in a variety of situations.

Types and Traits

The fact that people differ in temperament—the
way they react in various situations—has long
been apparent. The earliest known explanation
for these individual differences is the *humoral
theory,* proposed by the Greek physician Galen
in the second century and based on then-com-
mon medical beliefs that had originated with the
ancient Greeks. The body was thought to contain four humors, or fluids: yellow bile, black
bile, phlegm, and blood. People were classified
according to the disposition supposedly produced by the predominance of one of these humors in their system. *Choleric* people, who had
an excess of yellow bile (*khole*), were bad-tem-
pered and irritable. *Melancholic* people, with an

excess of black bile (*melankhole*), had a gloomy
and pessimistic temperament. *Phlegmatic* people, whose bodies contained an excessive
amount of phlegm, were sluggish, calm, and un-
excitable. *Sanguine* people had a preponderance
of blood (*sanguis*), which made them cheerful
and passionate. (See *Figure 14.1.*)

Although later biological investigations dis-
credited the humoral theory, the notion that
people could be divided into different personality
types persisted long afterward. Theories of
personality type attempt to assign people to
different categories, which vary in accordance
with the theory. For example, Freud's theory,
which maintains that people go through several
stages of psychosexual development, predicts
the existence of different types of people who
have problems associated with each of these
stages.

Personality types are very useful in formulating hypotheses, because when a theorist is
thinking about personality variables, extreme

Figure 14.1   The effects of the four humors, according to a medieval artist. From left to
right: choleric, melancholic, phlegmatic, and sanguine.

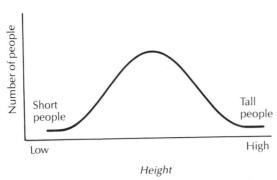

Figure 14.2 The distribution of height, which is continuous, not dichotomous.

cases—prototypes, so to speak—are easiest to think of. But the personality types outlined in some theories may have no validity. After identifying and defining the personality types, one must determine whether these types actually exist and whether knowing a person's personality type can lead to valid predictions about his or her behavior in a variety of situations. However, most modern investigators reject the notion that individuals can be assigned to discrete categories; instead, they generally conceive of individual differences as quantitative, not qualitative. Rather than classify people by categories, or types, most investigators prefer to measure the *degree* to which an individual expresses a particular **personality trait:** an enduring personal characteristic that reveals itself in a particular pattern of behavior in a variety of situations.

A simple example illustrates the difference between types and traits. We could classify people into two different *types:* tall people and short people. Indeed, we use these terms in everyday speech. But we all recognize that height is best conceived of as a *trait*—a dimension on which people can differ along a wide range of values. We can easily observe that people differ in height in a *continuous* rather than a *dichotomous* manner. If we measure the height of a large sample of people, we will find instances all along the distribution, from very short to very tall. (See *Figure 14.2.*)

Identification of Personality Traits

For centuries people have assessed other people's personality characteristics on a rather casual, informal basis. We assume that people tend to behave in particular ways: some are friendly, some are aggressive, some are lazy, some are timid, some are reckless. This type of categorization comes under the heading of *implicit psychology* and is discussed in more detail in

Chapter 17. Trait theories of personality fit this commonsense view.

Although personality theorists disagree about many issues, they all agree that personality traits are hierarchical. That is, broad traits can be subdivided into more narrow traits; these traits can in turn be subdivided into still more narrow traits; and so on. For example, Zuckerman (1991) notes that the trait of *fearfulness* (phobic anxiety) can be subdivided into four traits: *social anxiety; fear of injury; fear of travel, crowds, or strangers;* and *fear of small animals.* In turn, fear of small animals could be subdivided into fear of rats, or snakes, or spiders, or whatever. A fearful person is more likely than the average person to be afraid of social situations, injury, and so on, but he or she will have a unique pattern of fears. (See *Figure 14.3.*)

Personality traits are not simply patterns of behavior: They are factors that underlie these patterns and are responsible for them. In other words, *we carry our personality traits around with us in our heads*—or more exactly, in our brains. Please note that I am not saying that the acquisition of personality traits is strictly biological and that learning is not involved. Indeed, learning *is* involved in the development of personality traits. But once our personality traits are developed, they reside in our brains. And if they are changed by episodes and experiences in our lives, then changes occur in our brains.

Trait theories of personality do not pretend to be all-encompassing *explanations* of behavior—at least, not yet. Instead, they are still at the stage of discovering, describing, and naming the regular patterns of behavior that people exhibit. In all science, categorization must come before explanation; we must know what we are dealing with before we can go about providing explanations. The ultimate goal of the personality psychologist is to explain what determines people's behavior—which is the ultimate goal of *all* branches of psychology. Although we have some hopeful signs that this goal will be attained someday, that happy event will certainly not occur in the near future.

Many people are dissatisfied with an approach to personality that admits that explanations will come slowly, after we figure out what it is we want to explain. Freud's psychodynamic theory of personality (which is described later in this chapter) appeals to such people because it provides an explanation *now.* Unfortunately, because most aspects of Freud's theory are either untestable or have been contradicted by scientific evidence, a belief in Freud's theory remains a matter of faith.

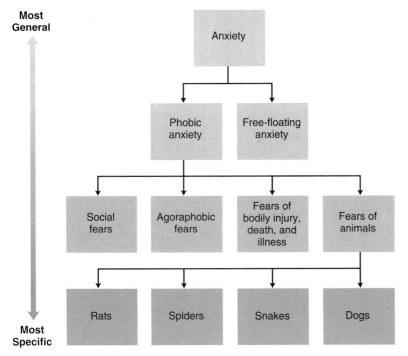

**Most
General**

Anxiety

Phobic
anxiety

Free-floating
anxiety

Social
fears

Agoraphobic
fears

Fears of
bodily injury,
death, and
illness

Fears of
animals

Rats

Spiders

Snakes

Dogs

**Most
Specific**

Figure 14.3 A hypothetical hierarchy of some important personality traits.

Cattell: Sixteen Personality Factors.
You will recall from Chapter 13 that factor analysis seeks out test items that tend to be correlated with each other. This method entails making a wide variety of observations of the behavior of a large number of people. Usually, the observations are limited to responses to a number of questions on a paper-and-pencil test, but occasionally, the investigator observes people's behavior in seminatural situations. Mathematical procedures then permit the investigator to determine which particular items tend to be answered in the same way by a given person, so as to infer the existence of common factors. For example, a shy person would tend to say "no" to statements such as "I attend parties as frequently as I can" and "When I enter a room full of people, I like to be noticed." In contrast, nonshy people would tend to say "yes" to these statements. However, the trait of shyness would probably not determine whether people would say "yes" or "no" to statements such as "I worry about my health a lot" or "I often get an upset stomach." The response to these statements would be related to the trait of hypochondriasis (excessive concern with one's health).

In practice, psychologists ask people hundreds of questions and mathematically identify the factors the different questions assess, such as shyness or hypochondriasis. To the degree that people possess orderly personality traits, they tend to answer certain clusters of questions in a particular way. Cattell (1946) began

with hypotheses he formulated by observing people's actual behavior. From analyses of these observations he devised thousands of questions, which he presented to subjects in the form of questionnaires. He performed factor analyses on the data and constructed new, improved tests. Eventually, he identified sixteen personality factors. Figure 14.4 illustrates a personality profile of a hypothetical individual, rated on Cattell's sixteen factors. The factors are listed in order of importance, from top to bottom. Look at the ratings to see whether you think they would help you predict the person's behavior. (See *Figure 14.4.*)

Eysenck: Three Factors. Eysenck also used the factor analytical method to devise his theory of personality (Eysenck, 1970; Eysenck and Eysenck, 1985). His analysis found three important factors: *extraversion, neuroticism,* and *psychoticism.* These factors are seen as bipolar dimensions: *Extraversion* is the opposite of *introversion, neuroticism* is the opposite of *emotional stability,* and *psychoticism* is the opposite of *self-control.* **Extraversion** refers to an outgoing nature and a high level of activity, whereas **introversion** refers to a nature that shuns crowds and prefers solitary activities. (The terms *extraversion* and *introversion* were originally coined by Jung, a contemporary of Freud's.) **Neuroticism** refers to a nature full of anxiety, worries, and guilt; whereas emotional stability refers to a nature that is relaxed and at

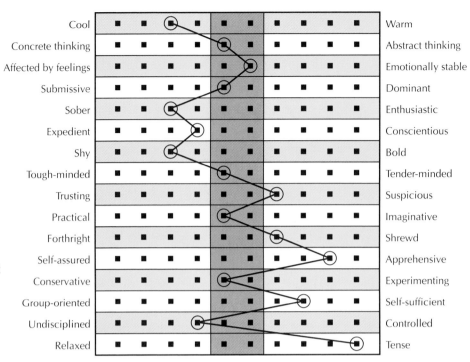

Figure 14.4 A hypothetical personality profile of a person on Cattell's sixteen personality factors. (Copyright © 1956, 1973, 1982, 1986 by the Institute for Personality and Ability Testing, Inc., P.O. Box 188, Champaign, Illinois, U.S.A. 61824–0188. Adapted and reproduced by permission.)

peace with oneself. **Psychoticism** refers to an aggressive, egocentric, and antisocial nature; whereas self-control refers to a kind and considerate nature, obedient of rules and laws. Eysenck's use of the term *psychoticism* is different from its use by most clinical psychologists; his term refers to antisocial tendencies and not to a mental illness. A person at the extreme end of the distribution of psychoticism (as defined by Eysenck) would receive the diagnosis of *antisocial personality disorder*. (This disorder is discussed in more detail in Chapter 15.)

Table 14.1 illustrates some questions that have high correlations (factor loadings) on Eysenck's three factors. The best way to understand the meaning of these traits is to read the questions and to imagine the kinds of people who would answer "yes" or "no" to each group. If a factor loading is preceded by a minus sign, it means that people who say "no" receive high scores on the trait; otherwise, high scores are obtained by those who answer "yes."

According to Eysenck, the most important aspects of a person's temperament are determined by the combination of the three dimensions of extraversion, neuroticism, and psychoticism—just as colors are produced by the combinations of the three dimensions of hue, saturation, and brightness. *Figure 14.5* illustrates the effects of various combinations of the first two of these dimensions—extraversion and neuroticism—and relates them to the four temperaments described by Galen.

Eysenck's theory has received considerable support, especially from his own laboratory, which has been especially productive. Most trait theorists accept the existence of his three factors because they have emerged in factor analyses performed by many different researchers.

Table 14.1 Some items from Eysenck's tests of extraversion, neuroticism, and psychoticism

Factor	Loading
Extraversion	
Do you like mixing with people?	.70
Do you like plenty of bustle and excitement around you?	.65
Are you rather lively?	.63
Neuroticism	
Do you often feel "fed-up"?	.67
Do you often feel lonely?	.60
Does your mood often go up and down?	.59
Psychoticism	
Do good manners and cleanliness matter much to you?	−.55
Does it worry you if you know there are mistakes in your work?	−.53
Do you like taking risks for fun?	.51

Source: Adapted from Eysenck, H.J., and Eysenck, M.W. *Personality and Individual Differences: A Natural Science Approach.* New York: Plenum Press, 1985.

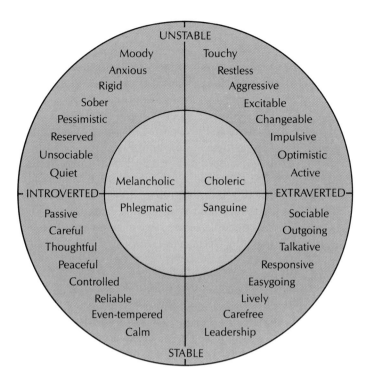

Figure 14.5 Eysenck's theory illustrated for two factors. According to Eysenck, the two dimensions of neuroticism (stable versus unstable) and introversion-extraversion combine to form a variety of personality characteristics. The four personality types based on the Greek theory of humors are shown in the center. (From Eysenck, H.J. *The Inequality of Man*. London: Temple Smith, 1973. Reprinted with permission.)

Five-Factor Model. An interesting approach to the study of the factors underlying personality differences has been to analyze the words we use to describe differences in temperament. Languages reflect the observations of a culture; that is, people invent words to describe distinctions they notice. Thus, theorists have performed factor analyses of ratings of words related to personality. An analysis by Tupes and Christal (1961), replicated by Norman (1963), has led to the **five-factor model** (McCrae and Costa, 1985, 1990); these factors are *neuroticism, extraversion, openness, agreeableness,* and *conscientiousness.* These factors are measured by the **NEO-PI**—the Neuroticism, Extraversion, and Openness Personality Inventory. (The name was chosen before the factors of agreeableness and conscientiousness were added.)

The NEO-PI consists of 181 items that potentially describe the person being evaluated, which can be the person answering the questions or someone he or she knows well (McCrae and Costa, 1990). (Studies have shown that self-ratings agree well with ratings of spouses and other people who know the subject well.) The test items are brief sentences, such as "I really like most people I meet" or (for ratings by someone else) "She has a very active imagination." The person taking the test rates the accuracy of each item on a scale of 1 to 5, from strong disagreement to strong agreement. The scores on each of the five factors consist of the sums of the answers to different sets of items.

You are already familiar with the first two factors, neuroticism and extraversion, which were identified by Eysenck. *Openness* is characterized by originality, imagination, and broad interests (McCrae and Costa, 1987). People who score high on the openness scale tend to regard themselves as intelligent (and tend to be rated as intelligent by other people), but openness is not synonymous with intelligence. *Agreeableness,* according to McCrae and Costa, is best understood by examining the negative end of the dimension: *antagonism.* Antagonistic people are mistrustful, unsympathetic, uncooperative, and rude. This dimension, they say, closely resembles Eysenck's psychoticism. However, not all antagonistic people are overtly aggressive; some may be polished manipulators. *Conscientiousness* refers to a tendency to be reliable, self-disciplined, rational, deliberate, and persevering. Thus, it resembles McClelland and Atkinson's *need to achieve,* described in Chapter 11. The opposite end of this dimension is called *undirectedness;* undirected people are those who tend to be disorganized and lazy.

When one reads a description of the five factors, it is tempting to conclude that one end of each dimension is good and the other is bad. For example, emotional stability seems better than neuroticism, extraversion seems better than introversion, openness seems better than closedness, agreeableness seems better than antagonism, and conscientiousness seems better than undirectedness. But as McCrae and

Costa (1990) note:

> All kinds of people are necessary: those who work well with others and those who can finish a task on their own; those who come up with creative new ways of doing things and those who maintain the best solutions of the past. There are probably even advantages to be found in neuroticism, since a society of extremely easy-going individuals might not compete well with other societies of suspicious and hostile individuals. Cultures need members fit for war as well as peace, work as well as play. . . . (p. 46)

Costa and McCrae (1988) performed a factor analysis comparing their five factors, measured by the NEO-PI, with a test of twenty-one of Murray's social needs (Jackson, 1984). (Murray's needs were described in Chapter 11.) The results of this analysis provide a good example of how various combinations of the five dimensions of neuroticism, extraversion, openness, agreeableness, and conscientiousness can form particular personality traits—just as various combinations of hue, saturation, and brightness can form particular colors. For example, *need for achievement* consists primarily of openness and conscientiousness; *need for affiliation* consists primarily of extraversion; *need for dominance* consists primarily of openness and antagonism (the opposite of agreeableness); and *need*

for nurturance consists primarily of extraversion and agreeableness.

McCrae, Costa, and Busch (1986) attempted to validate the five-factor model by performing a factor analysis on a list of adjectives contained in a test called the *California Q-Set*. This test consists of 100 brief descriptions (such as "irritable," "cheerful," "arouses liking," and "productive"). The items were provided by a large number of psychologists and psychiatrists who found the terms useful in describing people's personality characteristics. Thus, the terms are not restricted to a particular theoretical orientation. McCrae and his colleagues found that the factor analysis yielded the same five factors as the analysis based on everyday language: *neuroticism, extraversion, openness, agreeableness,* and *conscientiousness*. Table 14.2 lists some of the terms with the highest loadings on these factors. (See *Table 14.2*.)

The ultimate validity test of the five-factor model will be to see whether researchers eventually identify biological mechanisms (inherited, learned, or both) that are responsible for them. The psychobiological approach to personality, which will be used to settle the issue, is described in the next section.

INTERIM SUMMARY

Trait Theories of Personality

Personality characteristics can be conceived of as types or traits. The earliest theory of personality classified people into types according to their predominant humor, or body fluid. Today most psychologists conceive of personality differences as being represented by quantitative traits. Broad traits can be subdivided into more narrow ones.

Personality traits are the factors that underlie patterns of behavior; presumably, these factors are biological in nature, although they may be the products of learning as well as heredity. Several researchers developed their theories of personality through factor analysis. Cattell's analyses indicated the existence of sixteen personality factors. In contrast, Eysenck's research suggested that personality is determined by three dimensions: extraversion (versus introversion), neuroticism (versus emotional stability), and psychoticism (versus self-control). McCrae and Costa's five-factor model, based on an analysis of words used to describe people's behavioral traits, includes extraversion, neuroti-

Extraverts have outgoing personalities and exhibit a high level of activity, especially in social situations.

Factor	Low Scorer	High Scorer
Neuroticism (versus emotional stability)	Calm, relaxed Satisfied with self Clear-cut personality Prides self on objectivity	Thin-skinned Basically anxious Irritable Guilt-prone
Extraversion (versus introversion)	Emotionally bland Avoids close relationships Overcontrol of impulses Submissive	Talkative Gregarious Socially poised Behaves assertively
Openness (versus closedness)	Favors conservative values Judges in conventional terms Uncomfortable with complexities Moralistic	Values intellectual matters Rebellious, nonconforming Unusual thought processes
Agreeableness (versus antagonism)	Critical, skeptical Shows condescending behavior Tries to push limits Expresses hostility directly	Sympathetic, considerate Warm, compassionate Arouses liking Behaves in a giving way
Conscientiousness (versus undirectedness)	Eroticizes situations Unable to delay gratification Self-indulgent Engages in fantasy, daydreams	Behaves ethically Dependable, responsible Productive Has high aspiration level

Source: Adapted from McCrae and Costa (1990); after McCrae, Costa, and Busch (1986).

cism, agreeableness (versus antagonism), openness (versus closedness), and conscientiousness (versus undirectedness). The negative end of the agreeableness dimension appears to be the same as Eysenck's factor of psychoticism.

PSYCHOBIOLOGICAL APPROACHES

2 As I wrote earlier, we carry our personality traits around with us in our heads. Although we are far from understanding the psychobiology of personality, some progress has been made.

Zuckerman (1991) lists five criteria that will eventually have to be met in order to conclusively identify a basic personality dimension as a biological reality. None of the criteria have yet been met, but as we shall see, good progress is being made.

1. Reliable identification of the dimension across methods, genders, ages, and cultures.
2. Stability of dimensions in the same individuals over time.
3. Identification of similar kinds of behavioral traits in other species of animals, particularly mammals that live in social groups.
4. At least moderate heritability for the dimension.
5. The ultimate identification of the neural

mechanisms responsible for the dimension. (Adapted from Zuckerman, 1991, pp. 4–5)

Heritability of Personality Traits

Several trait theorists, including Cattell and Eysenck, have asserted that a person's genetic history has a strong influence on his or her personality, which implies that personality differences are, in large part, affected by biological differences—presumably, in the structure of the brain. Many studies have shown that most personality traits are strongly heritable.

As we saw in Chapter 13, the heritability of a trait can be assessed by comparing identical and fraternal twins, comparing twins raised together with twins raised apart, and comparing biological and adoptive relatives. Many studies have found that identical twins are more similar to each other than fraternal twins on a variety of personality measures, which indicates that these characteristics are heritable. (Identical twins have identical genes, whereas the genetic similarity between fraternal twins is, on the average, 50 percent.) Figure 14.6 shows the results of eleven studies using various tests of Eysenck's factors of extraversion, neuroticism, and psychoticism, compiled by Zuckerman (1991). The results of each study are shown as data points connected by straight lines. As you can see, every study found that identical twins

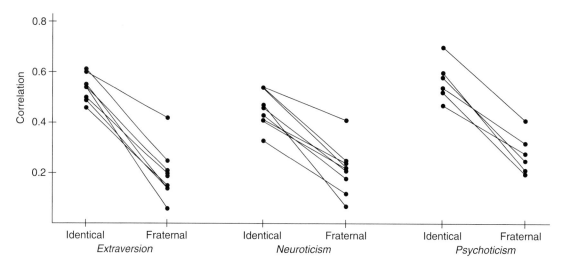

Figure 14.6 Correlations between members of pairs of identical and fraternal twins on tests of extraversion, neuroticism, and psychoticism. Individual pairs of data points come from different experiments. (Based on data from Zuckerman, M. *Psychobiology of Personality*. Cambridge: Cambridge University Press, 1991.)

were more similar than fraternal twins on every measure. (See *Figure 14.6.*) According to Zuckerman's calculations, the best estimates of the heritability of these three traits are extraversion, 70 percent; neuroticism, 48 percent; and psychoticism, 59 percent.

The results of the twin studies suggest that heredity is responsible for between 50 and 70 percent of the variability in these three personality traits. Thus, it would appear that the remaining 30 to 50 percent of the variability would be caused by differences in environment. In other words, some family environments should tend to produce extraverts, other should tend to produce introverts, and so on. But research indicates that the matter is not so simple.

Zuckerman (1991) reviewed several studies that measured the correlation in personality traits of pairs of identical twins raised together and raised apart. (One of the studies, by the way, was a product of the Minnesota Study of Twins Reared Apart mentioned in the opening vignette.) If family environment has a significant effect on personality characteristics, then the twins raised together should be more similar than those raised apart. But they were not; taken as a group, these studies found no differences. These results indicate that differences in family environment account for *none* of the variability of personality traits in the twins who were tested. Another approach, comparing the personality traits of parents with their adopted children, suggests that family environment may account for approximately 7 percent of the variability (Scarr et al., 1981). If 50 to 70 percent of

the variability in personality traits is caused by heredity and zero to 7 percent is caused by family environment, what is responsible for the remaining 23 to 50 percent of the variance? The answer is this: Heredity and environment *interact.*

As we saw in Chapter 13, heredity and environment can interact. In fact, the major source of the interaction seems to be the effect that a person's heredity has on the family environment he or she comes in contact with (Plomin and Bergeman, 1991). Figure 14.7 shows the correlations between the ratings of various characteristics of the family environment made by pairs of identical and fraternal twins. The family characteristics that they rated included cohesion, expressiveness, conflict, achievement, culture, activity, organization, and control. As you can see, the identical twins agreed on their ratings much more than the fraternal twins did; that is, they were much more likely to have experienced similar family environments. (See *Figure 14.7.*)

There are two possible explanations for these results: The family environments could have been more similar for identical twins than for fraternal twins, or the family environments could have been the same in all cases but were simply *perceived* as different by the fraternal twins. Evidence suggests that the first possibility is correct—the family environments really were different, and not just a matter of perception. How can this be? One might think that each family has a certain environment, and everyone in the household comes under its influence.

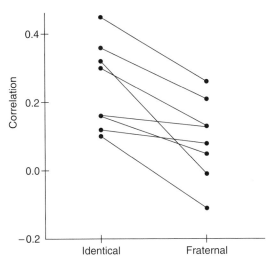

Figure 14.7 Correlations between members of pairs of twins on ratings of characteristics of their family environment. Individual pairs of data points represent ratings of cohesion, expressiveness, conflict, achievement, culture, activity, organization, and control. (Based on data from Plomin, R., and Bergemen, C.S. *Behavioral and Brain Sciences*, 1991, *14*, 373–427.)

In fact, although there are aspects of a family that are shared by the entire household, the factors that play the largest role in shaping personality development appear to come from social interactions between an individual and other family members. And these social interactions are different for different people. Because of hereditary differences, one child may be more sociable; this child will be the recipient of more social interactions. Another child may be abrasive and disagreeable; this child will be treated more coldly. Even physical attributes (which are largely hereditary) will affect a child's environment; a physically attractive child will receive more favorable attention than an unattractive child. In fact, studies that examined videotaped interactions between mothers and their children confirm that heredity does have an important influence on the nature of these interactions (Plomin and Bergeman, 1991). Thus, although a child's environment plays an important part in his or her personality development, *hereditary* factors play a large role in determining the nature of this environment.

One caution about this interpretation is in order. Although the studies I have cited have been replicated in several cultures, none of them have investigated the effects of the full range of cultural differences in family lives. That is, when comparisons have been made between twins raised together and those raised apart, almost all have involved family environments within the same culture. It is certainly possible that cultural differences in family environments could be even more important than the differences produced by a person's heredity; only cross-cultural studies will be able to test this possibility.

Are *all* personality traits a product, direct or indirect, of a person's heredity? The answer is no. Some personality characteristics show a strong effect of shared environment but almost no effect of genetics. For example, twin studies have found a strong influence of family environment, but not heredity, on belief in God, involvement in religion, masculinity/femininity, attitudes toward racial integration, and intellectual interests (Loehlin and Nichols, 1976; Rose, 1988). Thus, people tend to learn some important social attitudes from their family environment.

Biological Factors in Personality

As you will recall from Chapter 10 ("Life Span Development"), research has shown that personality traits are extraordinarily stable during adulthood. This evidence suggests that personality traits are determined primarily by brain development and by events that occur during childhood and adolescence. Remember that changes in life situations should not be confused with changes in personality. Losing one's job or winning a fortune from the lottery will certainly change a person's circumstances, but these events will not make an extravert become introverted, an antagonistic person become agreeable, or an undirected person become conscientious. The changed circumstances will change particular behaviors the person engages in but not the basic *pattern* of these behaviors. The pattern is, presumably, determined by characteristics of the brain that develop early in life.

There is no doubt that brain mechanisms are involved in personality traits. For example, brain damage can produce permanent changes in people's temperament, and drugs that affect particular transmitters can alter people's mood and anxiety level. But what particular brain mechanisms are involved in personality, and what personality traits do they affect? Several psychologists (for example, Eysenck and Eysenck, 1985; Gray, 1987; Zuckerman, 1991) have attempted to relate the three most basic dimensions of personality—extraversion, neuroticism, and psychoticism—to underlying physiological mechanisms. I will discuss the most recent of these proposals.

Zuckerman (1991) suggests that the personality dimensions of extraversion, neuroticism, and psychoticism are determined by the neural systems responsible for reinforcement, punishment, and arousal. People who score high on *extraversion* are particularly sensitive to reinforcement; perhaps their neural reinforcement system is especially active. As we saw in Chapter 11, this system involves neurons that secrete dopamine as a transmitter substance. Infants who later become extraverts show a higher activity level, whereas adults show more reinforcement-seeking behavior. Adults are not necessarily more physically active, but they engage in a greater number of different things. They participate in more social activities and tend to shift from one type of activity to another. They are optimistic; they expect that their pursuits will result in reinforcing outcomes. However, unlike people who score high on psychoticism, they are sensitive to punishment and can learn to act prudently.

People who score high on *neuroticism* are anxious and fearful. If they also score high on psychoticism, they are hostile as well. These people are particularly sensitive to the punishing effects of aversive stimuli; thus, Zuckerman suggests that the personality dimension of neuroticism is controlled by the sensitivity of the neural system responsible for punishment, which appears to involve the amygdala. As we saw in Chapter 12, an important function of the amygdala is to organize the behavioral, autonomic, and hormonal components of conditioned emotional responses—of classically conditioned defensive responses produced by aversive stimuli. If this system were oversensitive, a person would be expected to be especially fearful of situations in which he or she might encounter aversive stimuli. The amygdala is also involved in aggression, another form of defensive response. Thus, neurotics who also score high on psychoticism will tend to express their fear in the form of aggression.

People who score high on *psychoticism* have difficulty learning when not to do something. As

Zuckerman suggests, their punishment system is deficient. They also have a high tolerance for arousal and excitation; in other words, we could say that their optimal level of arousal is abnormally high. As we saw in Chapter 11, some theorists hypothesize that people seek situations that provide an optimal level of arousal: Too much or too little arousal is aversive. Therefore, a person with a high optimal level of arousal (a high tolerance for excitement) seeks out exciting situations and performs well in them. (A neurotic would find these situations aversive, and his or her behavior would become disorganized and inefficient.) A person with a high tolerance for excitement makes a good warrior but does not fit in well in civilized society.

In Chapter 15 we will examine people with antisocial personality disorder, which is characterized by an extremely high level of psychoticism. Such people habitually lie, cheat, steal, and commit other antisocial behaviors—without showing either excitement or remorse. The cold-blooded serial killer who tortures and dismembers his victims does not do so because of a high level of aggressiveness; he does so to provide himself with some excitement. Because his sensitivity to punishment is extremely low, nothing prevents him from hurting other people to obtain this excitement.

Table 14.3 summarizes Zuckerman's hypothetical explanations for the three major personality dimensions. (See *Table 14.3.*)

Research by physiological psychologists with laboratory animals has provided support for Zuckerman's suggestions concerning one personality dimension—neuroticism. A neurotic person avoids unfamiliar situations because he or she fears encountering aversive stimuli, whereas an emotionally stable person is likely to investigate the situation to see whether anything interesting will happen. The same is true for other species. For example, about 15 percent of kittens avoid novel objects, and this tendency persists when they become adults; some cats are "bold" while others are "timid." When

Table 14.3 Zuckerman's (1991) hypothetical biological characteristics that correspond to personality dimensions

Personality Trait	*Biological Characteristics*
Extraversion	High sensitivity to reinforcement
Neuroticism	High sensitivity to punishment
Psychoticism	Low sensitivity to punishment; high optimal level of arousal

the timid cats encounter a novel stimulus (such as a rat), the activity of the neural circuits in their amygdala responsible for defensive responses becomes more active (Adamec and Stark-Adamec, 1986).

Kagan, Reznick, and Snidman (1988) investigated the possibility that timidity in social situations (shyness) has a biological basis in humans. They noted that about 10 to 15 percent of normal children between the ages of two and three years become quiet, watchful, and subdued when they encounter an unfamiliar situation. In other words, like the kittens, they are shy and cautious in approaching novel stimuli. Childhood shyness seems to be related to two personality dimensions: a low level of extraversion and a high level of neuroticism (Briggs, 1988).

Kagan and his colleagues selected two groups of 21-month-old and 31-month-old children according to their reaction to unfamiliar people and situations. The *shy* group consisted of children who showed signs of inhibition, such as clinging to their mothers or remaining close to them, remaining silent, and failing to approach strangers or other novel stimuli. The *nonshy* group showed no such inhibition; these children approached the strangers and explored the novel environment. The children were tested for shyness several more times, up to the age of 7.5 years. The particular tests depended on the children's age, but all tests involved encounters with groups of strange adults or peers.

The investigators found that shyness was an enduring trait; children who were shy at the ages of 21 or 31 months continued to be shy at the ages of 7.5 years. At 7.5 years they avoided contact with other children and talked less with the examiner than the nonshy children did. In addition, the two groups of children showed differences in their physiological reactions to the test situation. Shy children were more likely to show increases in heart rate, their pupils tended to be more dilated, their urine contained more norepinephrine, and their saliva contained more cortisol. As you learned in Chapter 12, norepinephrine and cortisol are two hormones secreted during times of stress. Furthermore, their secretion in fearful situations is controlled by the amygdala. Obviously, the shy children found the situation to be stressful, whereas the nonshy children did not.

This study suggests that the biological basis of an important personality characteristic during childhood—shyness—may be the excitability of neural circuits that control avoidance behaviors.

Studies have shown that shyness is an enduring trait that begins at an early age and often continues for a lifetime.

Of course, the experimenters did not observe differences in the children's brains, so we cannot be sure about the nature of the biological difference between the two groups of children. Further research with both humans and laboratory animals may help us understand the biological differences responsible for personality characteristics.

INTERIM SUMMARY

Psychobiological Approaches

Studies of twins and adopted children indicate that personality factors—especially neuroticism, extraversion, and psychoticism—show a strong influence of genetics. However, there is little evidence for an effect of common family environment. The primary reason seems to be that an individual's environment is strongly affected by heredity factors, such as temperament and physical attributes. Some personal characteristics, such as social attitudes of religiousness and masculinity/femininity, appear to be learned from the family environment.

Several investigators believe that important personality traits are the products of neural systems responsible for reinforcement, punishment, and arousal. For example, Zuckerman believes that extraversion is caused by a sensitive reinforcement system (controlled by neurons that secrete dopamine), neuroticism is caused by a sensitive punishment system (which includes the amygdala), and psychoticism is caused by the combination of a deficient punishment system and an abnormally high optimal level of arousal.

Few studies have directly tested the hypothesis that personality differences can be accounted for by biological differences. One experiment, however, indicates that childhood shyness is a relatively stable trait that can be seen in the way infants react to strangers and strange situations. In addition, the differences between shy and nonshy children manifest themselves in physiological measures controlled by the amygdala that indicate the presence of stress. ■

BEHAVIORAL/COGNITIVE APPROACHES

3 Some psychologists, such as Cattell and Eysenck, are interested in the ways people differ with respect to their personality traits. Other psychologists are more interested in the ways people's behavioral characteristics are determined by what they encounter in their environment. This section considers the behaviorist and social learning approaches to personality.

Behaviorism

The most famous and influential behaviorist was the late B.F. Skinner (1904–1991), whose writings are either beautifully insightful and persuasive or infuriatingly wrong, according to the reader's point of view. Perhaps it is unfair to Skinner to call his view of human personality a "theory," because he disliked the term, at least as most psychologists use it. Skinner did not believe that most concepts dear to the hearts of personality theorists—those that deal with internal states and dispositions—are of any use in understanding human behavior. Instead, he believed that we must simply study an individual's behavior in response to his or her environment. According to Skinner, what we need to determine are the relations between stimuli and responses; nothing is gained by assuming the existence of personality structures within the

individual. Here is how Skinner put it:

> It is often said that a science of behavior studies the human organism but neglects the person or self. What it neglects is a vestige of animism, a doctrine which in its crudest form held that the body was moved by one or more indwelling spirits. When the resulting behavior was disruptive, the spirit was probably a devil; when it was creative, it was a guiding genius or muse. Traces of the doctrine survive when we speak of a *personality,* of an ego in ego psychology, or an *I* who says he knows what he is going to do and uses his body to do it, or of the role a person plays as a persona in a drama, wearing his body as a costume. (Skinner, 1974, p. 184)

Skinner said that human behavior is ultimately explainable in terms of the principles of instrumental conditioning. This approach is called **radical behaviorism.** *Radical* derives from the Latin word *radix,* meaning "root"; hence, radical behaviorism is behaviorism that is pure to the root.

Chapter 6 outlined the principles behind Skinner's views on human personality. We do what we do because in past situations some behaviors have been reinforced and others punished. We discriminate among various stimuli and respond appropriately. If we are reinforced for performing a particular behavior in the presence of a particular stimulus, we generalize our responding to similar stimuli. Sometimes, we behave superstitiously because a particular response was fortuitously followed by a reinforcing stimulus that would have occurred regardless of what we did. And, of course, we are reinforced by a much wider range of stimuli than food and water; our behavior is controlled by smiles and frowns, by our own self-appraisal, and by a variety of conditioned reinforcers. These conditioned reinforcers can be remote from the primary reinforcers with which they are associated, such as when a miser derives pleasure from a set of digits written in his or her bankbook.

In Skinner's view personality traits are best conceived of as behavioral tendencies produced by a person's history of reinforcement. For example, if a child's performance is reinforced on a variable-interval or variable-ratio schedule, he or she is likely to become industrious, because intermittent reinforcement leads to steady work and resistance to extinction. Conversely, if a child is given frequent, noncontingent reinforcers independent of his or her performance, the child will probably learn to be lazy. A child who is frequently punished will probably become timid and fearful or especially aggressive, depending on the schedule of punishment.

Skinner did not make a serious attempt to study enduring personality traits that might be a result of a person's heredity. Although he did not rule out hereditary factors in temperament, he viewed a person's conditioning history as more important and interesting. His goal was to be able to predict and control behavior, and non-modifiable behaviors did not hold much interest for him. He placed more stress on the role of genetics in the evolution of species than on its role in determining individual differences. In his view the role of natural selection is similar to that of reinforcement: The contingencies of the environment shape the behavioral repertoire of an individual organism through reinforcement and determine the behavioral capacities and tendencies of the species through natural selection.

Social Learning Theory

Social learning theory is derived from the behavioral approach to personality, but it differs from Skinner's radical behaviorism in its use of cognitive concepts, which are not directly observable. Social learning theorists believe that learning is the most important factor in personality development and that interactions with other people provide the most important experiences. Buss (1983), in discussing the types of reinforcing stimuli that can be provided by other people, describes two major types of social rewards. **Process rewards** involve social stimulation; they are pleasant in moderate amounts, but too much or too little is aversive. **Content rewards** involve relationships between individuals; they consist of bipolar dimensions, with one end being reinforcing and the other end being aversive. These two types of rewards (or punishers) have effects on personality traits. Process rewards are related to sociability; and content rewards are related to formality (politeness), self-esteem, and emotionality. (See *Table 14.4*.)

Social learning theorists emphasize the effects of the person on the environment as well as the effects of the environment on the person. These theorists attempt to understand covert behaviors such as planning and thinking, which cannot entirely be understood by examining the immediate environment, because they depend so much on the person's genetic makeup and earlier experiences. According to Mischel (1973), the most important personality characteristics are those that determine how people perceive and categorize various situations and how much value they place on particular social reinforcers and punishers. These characteristics lead them to perceive situations in particular ways and to form expectations about what might happen. These cognitions then determine their goals or plans and select which behaviors will take place in a particular situation.

Social learning theorists make much use of the term *self*. For example, they discuss people's self-concepts, their tendency to engage in self-praise or self-criticism, and their ability to exercise self-control. A **self-concept** is a person's perception of his or her own personality

Table 14.4   Nature and effects of process and content social rewards

Process Social Rewards (Reinforcing Only at Moderate Levels)			
Reward	*Deficiency*	*Excess*	*Associated Trait*
Mere presence of others	Isolation	Crowding	Loneliness
Attention from others	Shunning	Conspicuousness	Exhibitionism vs. shyness
Responsivity of others	Boredom	Overarousal	Sociability
Initiation of others	No interaction	Intrusiveness	Sociability and shyness
Content Social Rewards (Reinforcing at High Levels)			
Reward	*Its Opposite*		*Associated Trait*
Deference from others	Insolence, disrespect		Formality
Praise from others	Criticism		Self-esteem
Sympathy from others	Disdain		Emotionality
Affection from others	Hostility, rejection		Self-esteem

Source: Adapted from Buss, A.H. *Journal of Personality and Social Psychology*, 1983, *44*, 553–563.

and ability. **Self-praise** and **self-criticism** are responses people make after perceiving their own behavior and its consequences; obviously, these responses are learned by observing the behavior of others. For instance, in Chapter 6 I gave an example of a little girl learning how to write. When she succeeded in printing a letter that looked like the one her teacher made, she "praised herself" as her teacher had done in the past and experienced a feeling of satisfaction. As we saw, this process is an example of conditioned reinforcement. **Self-control** refers to people's ability to withhold a response normally elicited by a particular situation. For example, a child exercises a form of self-control called **delay of gratification** when he or she waits patiently for a larger reward rather than immediately taking a smaller one. Children differ in their ability to delay gratification; thus, the ability serves as an important personality trait (Bandura and Mischel, 1965; Mischel, 1977).

Bandura (1977a) developed a concept he calls *self-efficacy,* which consists of people's belief in their ability to succeed in the tasks they set out to accomplish. Thus, self-efficacy combines two issues important to social learning theorists: self-concept and self-control. Because Bandura has applied the concept of self-efficacy to psychotherapy, it will be described in more detail in Chapter 16.

Social learning theorists differ from behaviorists in the role they assign to the process of reinforcement in learning. According to behaviorists, reinforcement (or punishment) is crucial for learning; without it learning does not occur. Social learning theorists agree that reinforcement is very important, but they assert that learning can sometimes take place without it. Bandura (1977b) says that much social learning takes place through observation. People see what other people do and what happens as a result, and they learn new responses by watching this process take place. They do not have to engage in overt behaviors or to experience reinforcement or punishment directly.

A classic series of experiments reported by Bandura (1973) distinguished between the role of observation in learning a response and the role of reinforcement in determining whether the child performed it. In one set of experiments an adult attacked a large, inflated clown doll (a "Bobo doll"). One group of children witnessed the attack in person; others watched it on television. The control group watched the adult engage in innocuous behaviors. Later, the children were allowed to play in the room where the doll was kept.

All the children who had seen the adult beat Bobo, either in person or on television, imitated the adult's behavior, giving the doll a savage beating. The children who had watched innocuous behaviors did not display aggression toward the doll. It was also clear that the children's aggressive behavior was modeled on that of the adult. Those who had seen the adult kick the doll, use a hammer to hit it, or sit on top of it and pound its face did the same. Figure 14.8 shows the model behavior of the adult *(top)* and the imitative behavior of the children. (See *Figure 14.8.*)

In other experiments children watched a film of a person engaging in aggressive behavior and being subsequently rewarded or punished. Children who saw the person being rewarded were more aggressive; those who watched the person being punished made fewer attacks on the Bobo doll. When the experimenter later offered the children a reward for imitating the model, *both groups* started beating Bobo. Clearly, the children had learned the aggressive response through observation. However, the sight of the model being punished had inhibited the children's expression of the learned behaviors, so that they did not act out what they had learned until direct reinforcement of these behaviors removed the inhibition.

EVALUATING SCIENTIFIC ISSUES

Traits Versus Situations as Predictors of Behavior

[4] Both behaviorists and social learning theorists stress the importance of the environment on behavior. They tend to place less emphasis on the role of deep-seated personality traits. In contrast, trait theorists assume that people's dispositions are relatively stable, permitting others to predict how particular people will behave in various situations. The core beliefs of the personality psychologists are that traits are stable characteristics of individuals and that knowing something about these traits permits us to predict an individual's behavior.

The Case for Situationism.   Mischel (1968, 1976) has suggested that stable personality traits do not exist—or if they do, they are of little importance. He has suggested that situations, not traits, best predict behavior. He asks us to consider two situations: a party to celebrate someone's winning a large sum of money

Figure 14.8 Bandura's experiment. Aggressive behavior of the model is shown at the top. Imitative behavior by children is shown at the middle and bottom. (From Bandura, A., Ross, D., and Ross, S.A. *Journal of Abnormal and Social Psychology*, 1961, 66, 3–11. Copyright 1961 by the American Psychological Association. Reprinted by permission of the authors.)

in a lottery and a funeral. Certainly, people will be much more talkative, cheerful, and outgoing at the party than at the funeral. But suppose you know a person's score on a test of introversion-extraversion. How much will this knowledge enable you to predict whether he or she will be talkative and outgoing? In this case, knowing the situation has much more predictive value than knowing the test score.

Mischel cites several studies in support of his assertion that people tend to behave inconsistently in different situations. One of the first of these studies was performed over sixty years ago. Hartshorne and May (1928) designed a set of behavioral tests designed to measure the traits of honesty and self-control and administered them to over 10,000 students in elementary school and high school. The tests gave the children the opportunity to be dishonest—for example, to cheat on a test, to lie about the amount of homework they had done, to report inflated scores from their athletic performance, or to keep money they had been entrusted with. In all cases the experimenters had access to what the children had actually done, so they could determine whether the child acted hon-

estly or dishonestly. They found that, in general, the children acted inconsistently; a child that acted honestly (or dishonestly) in one situation did not necessarily act the same way in a different situation. The average correlation of a child's honesty from situation to situation—the **cross-situational consistency**—was below .30. The authors concluded that "honesty or dishonesty is not a unified character trait in children of the ages studied, but a series of specific responses to specific situations" (p. 243).

Mischel (1968) reviewed evidence from studies performed subsequent to the experiment by Hartshorne and May and found that most personal characteristics showed the same low cross-situational consistency—.30 or less. He concluded that the concept of personality traits was not useful. People's behavior was determined by the situations in which they found themselves, not by any intrinsic behavioral tendencies.

Evidence to the Contrary. Other psychologists responded to these results. For example, Epstein (1979) noted that personality traits are more stable than some of these measures had suggested. He noted that assessments of cross-situational consistency usually involve testing a group of people on two occasions and correlating their behavior in one situation with their behavior in the other. He showed that repeated measurements across several days yielded much higher correlations; the measures approached .80, which means that they account for 80 percent of the variability in the behavior. In a study of his own he had a group of twenty-eight undergraduates keep daily records of their most pleasant and most unpleasant experiences for a month. For each experience they wrote down the emotions they felt, their impulses to action, and their actual behavior. The correlation between a person's emotions, impulses, or behavior on any two days was rather low—on the order of .30. However, when he grouped measurements (that is, correlated the ratings obtained on odd-numbered days with those obtained on even-numbered days) the correlation rose dramatically—up to around .80.

Epstein also noted that the question "Which is more important in determining a person's behavior, the situation or his or her personality traits?" is similar to the question "Which is more important in determining a person's intelligence, heredity or environment?" And the answer to both questions is, "It depends." As we saw in Chapter 11, heritability depends on the particular population being considered. As I noted there, heritability of hair color is zero in a population homogeneous for this trait, such as Eskimos, but is high in heterogeneous populations. Similarly, the degree to which personality traits can be used to predict behavior depends on the variability of that trait within the population and on the variability of the situations.

Even though Mischel is skeptical about the value of the concept of personality trait, he has acknowledged that *particular* personality traits may be important as predictors of behavior (Mischel, 1977, 1979). He also points out that some situations by their very nature severely constrain a person's behavior, whereas others permit a wide variety of responses. He noted that some situations are "powerful," in that they largely determine people's responses, with little variability present. For example, red lights cause almost all motorists to stop their cars. In this case knowing the particular situation (the color of the traffic light) predicts behavior better than knowing something about the personality characteristics of the drivers. Conversely, some situations are "weak" and have little control over people's behavior. As Zuckerman (1991) points out, a yellow light is such a situation;

when drivers see a yellow light, some will stop if they possibly can and others will accelerate and rush through the intersection. The difference between the two behaviors is undoubtedly determined by individual personality traits.

Just as situations can be classified as strong or weak, we can probably classify personality variables as strong or weak in their predictive value. Consider a person who is so depressed that she will talk to no one; she just hangs her head, weeping quietly. She acts this way whether she is alone in her room or among a group of people at a party. Or consider a violent psychopath who attacks anyone who comes near him; he has to be restrained to keep him from hurting others. The behavior of these people is much less dependent on situations than is the behavior of most people. Although these cases are extreme, it seems likely that some personality variables predict behavior better than others in a variety of situations.

Personality and situations are usually conceived of as independent variables, but they are not always independent. In laboratory settings experimenters assign people to various situations; here situation and personality are truly independent. However, in real life our personality traits affect the situations we find ourselves in. For example, as we saw earlier, the way people act has a strong influence on the way other people act toward them. In addition, as Bem and Allen (1974) pointed out, people in life outside the laboratory are able to exert some choice over the situations they enter. For instance, a party is a moderately powerful situation and tends to produce extraverted behaviors. So introverted people may stay away from parties to avoid situations that encourage behaviors with which they are not comfortable. Similarly, extraverts may avoid situations in which they are alone. The fact that people choose their own situations means that personality traits *interact* with situations. Emmons, Diener, and Larsen (1986) found that people do, indeed, show consistent patterns in the types of situations they choose; and when circumstances force them to be in situations they do not normally choose, they feel uncomfortable.

What Should We Conclude? In acknowledgment of the stability of personality over a large number of situations and of the interaction between personality and situations, most psychologists agree that the original question, "Which is more important in determining a person's behavior, the situation or his or her personality traits?" has proved too simplistic. Some

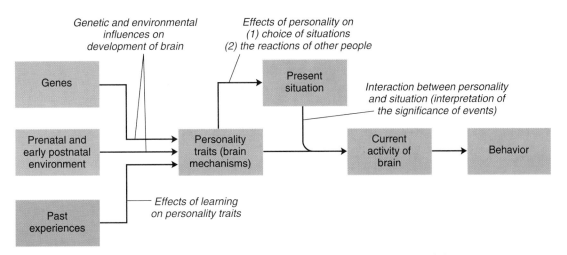

Figure 14.9 Interacting factors responsible for the development of personality and the occurrence of particular behaviors in a specific situation.

types of personality traits will prevail in most situations; some situations will dictate the behavior of most of the participants; but some interactions between situation and personality require the analysis of both variables.

Figure 14.9 illustrates some of the most important factors that control the development of an individual's personality traits. It also shows the interactions between these traits and situational factors in determining behavior. (See *Figure 14.9*.) ■

INTERIM SUMMARY

Behavioral/Cognitive Approaches

Skinner's approach to understanding the causes of behavior is based on the principles of reinforcement and punishment described in Chapter 6. His analysis consists in examining the reinforcement and punishment contingencies present in a person's environment, along with the discriminative stimuli signaling that these contingencies are operating. Skinner attributes the different patterns of behavior of different individuals (their personality traits) to their previous experience with different kinds of contingencies.

Behaviorism is also the parent of another important approach to the study of personality: social learning theory. This theory applies the principles of reinforcement to human motivation and social interactions. Social learning theory embraces concepts such as expectancy and emphasizes phenomena such as observational learning, which Skinner acknowledges but does not devote much attention to. Many investiga-

tors agree with Skinner about the importance of reinforcement but disagree with his insistence that intervening variables be abandoned; they hypothesize emotional and cognitive structures to which they assign explanatory functions. For example, Bandura developed the concept of self-efficacy, which he has applied to a particular form of psychotherapy.

Social learning theorists tend to emphasize the importance of imitation more than behaviorists do. Bandura's experiments on aggression suggest that a child may learn a response through observation and later, depending on the contingencies of reinforcement, exhibit this behavior or not exhibit it.

In the past, psychologists disagreed about the relative importance of situations and personality traits in determining a person's behavior. It now appears that personality traits are correlated with behavior, especially when multiple observations are made. In addition, some situations (such as a funeral or a stoplight) are more "powerful" than others, exerting more control on people's behavior. Also, traits and situations interact: Some people are affected more than others by a particular situation, and people tend to choose the types of situations in which they find themselves. In addition, people's personality traits affect the way others interact with them; therefore, these traits directly affect situational variables. ■

THE PSYCHODYNAMIC APPROACH

5 The work of Sigmund Freud has had a profound and lasting effect on twentieth-century society. Terms such as *ego, id, libido, repression, rationalization, Oedipus complex,* and *fixation* became as familiar to most Western laypeople as to clinicians. Before Freud formulated his theory, people believed that most behavior was determined by rational, conscious processes, although strong emotions might drive some to do irrational things. Freud was the first to claim that what we do is *often* irrational and that the reasons for our behavior are seldom available to our conscious mental processes. The mind, to Freud, was a battleground for the warring factions of instinct, reason, and conscience. The term **psychodynamic** refers to this struggle among the various aspects of personality.

Sigmund Freud (1856–1939) was a Viennese physician who acquired his early training in neurology, in the laboratory of Ernst Wilhelm von Brücke, an eminent physiologist and neuroanatomist. Freud's work in the laboratory consisted mostly of careful anatomical observation rather than experimentation. This approach also characterized his later work with human behavior; he made detailed observations of individual patients and attempted to draw inferences about the structure of the human psyche from these cases (*psyche,* from the Greek word for "breath" or "soul," refers to the mind). Freud did not try to carry out any psychological experiments. His disciples have continued in his tradition of observing and analyzing the verbal reports of patients.

Freud hoped to obtain a position at a university and continue his research, but the fact that he was Jewish made it impossible for him to obtain such a post. He therefore decided to set up a private medical practice of his own. Before doing so, he studied in Paris with Jean Martin Charcot, who was investigating the usefulness of hypnosis as a treatment for hysteria. Patients with hysteria often experience paralysis of some part of the body or loss of one of the senses, without any detectable physiological cause. The fact that hypnosis could be used either to produce or to alleviate these symptoms suggested that they were of psychological origin. Charcot proposed that hysterical symptoms were caused by some kind of psychological trauma. Freud was greatly impressed by Charcot's work and became even more interested in problems of the mind.

Freud returned to Vienna and opened his medical practice. He began an association with Josef Breuer, a prominent physician who helped him get his practice established. Freud and Breuer together published a book called *Studies on Hysteria,* and one of the cases cited in it, that of Anna O., provided the evidence that led to some of the most important tenets of Freud's theory.

The couch used by Freud for sessions of psychoanalysis with his patients.

Anna O. was treated by Breuer twelve years before he and Freud published their book. She suffered from an incredible number of hysterical symptoms, including loss of speech, disturbances in vision, headaches, and paralysis and loss of feeling in her right arm. Under hypnosis Anna was asked to go back to the times when her symptoms had started. Each of her symptoms appeared to have begun just when she was unable to express a strongly felt emotion. While under hypnosis she experienced these emotions again, and the experience gave her relief from her hysterical symptoms. It was as if the emotions had been bottled up, and reliving the original experiences uncorked them. This release of energy (which Breuer and Freud called *catharsis*) presumably eliminated the hysterical symptoms.

The case of Anna O. is one of the most frequently reported cases in the annals of psychotherapy. However, Breuer's original description appears to be inaccurate in some of its most important respects (Ellenberger, 1972). Apparently, the woman was not cured at all by Breuer's hypnosis and psychotherapy. Ellenberger discovered the existence of hospital records indicating that Anna O. (actually, Bertha Pappenheim) continued to take morphine for the distress caused by the disorders Breuer had allegedly cured. Freud appears to have learned later that the cure was a fabrication, but this fact did not become generally known until recently. However, Breuer's failure to help Anna O. with her problems does not mean that we must reject psychoanalysis. Although Breuer's apparent success inspired Freud to examine the unconscious, Freud's theory of personality must stand or fall on its own merits when evaluated by modern evidence.

The case of Anna O., along with evidence obtained from his own clinical practice, led Freud to reason that human behavior is motivated by instinctual drives, which, when activated, supply psychic energy. This energy is aversive, because the nervous system seeks a state of quiet equilibrium. According to Freud, if something prevents the psychic energy caused by activation of a drive from being discharged, psychological disturbances will result. (But as we saw in Chapter 11, not all psychologists agree that organisms invariably seek a state of reduced drive.)

Structures of the Mind: Id, Ego, and Superego

Freud was struck by the fact that psychological disturbances could stem from events a person apparently could no longer consciously recall, although they could be revealed during hypnosis. This phenomenon led him to conclude that the mind consists of both unconscious and conscious elements.

Freud divided the mind into three structures: the id, the ego, and the superego. The operations of the **id** are completely unconscious; its forces provide the energy for all psychic processes. The id contains the **libido,** which is the primary source of motivation; this force is insistent and is unresponsive to the demands of reality.

The **ego** is the self; it controls and integrates behavior. It acts as a mediator, negotiating a compromise among the pressures of the id, the counterpressures of the superego, and the demands of reality. The ego's functions of perception, cognition, and memory perform this mediation. The ego is driven by the **reality principle,** that is, the ability to delay gratification of a drive until an appropriate goal is located. To ward off the demands of the id when these demands cannot be gratified, the ego uses *defense mechanisms* (described later). Some of the functions of the ego are unconscious.

The **superego** is subdivided into the conscience and the ego-ideal. The **conscience** is the internalization of the rules and restrictions of society; it determines which behaviors are permissible and punishes wrongdoing with feelings of guilt. The **ego-ideal** is the internalization of what the person would like to be—his or her goals. The superego, like the id, is unconscious and is subject to irrational thought. For example, guilt feelings are not always rational.

Freud found the mind to be full of conflicts. A conflict might begin when one of the two primary drives, the *sexual instinctual drive* or the *aggressive instinctual drive,* is aroused. These drives demand gratification but are often held in check by internalized prohibitions against the behaviors the drives tend to produce. **Internalized prohibitions** are characteristics of the superego; they are rules of behavior learned in childhood that protect the person from the guilt he or she would feel if the instinctual drives were allowed to express themselves. The result of the conflict is **compromise formation,** in which a compromise is reached between the demands of the instinctual drive and the suppressive effects of internalized prohibitions. According to Freud, phenomena such as dreams, artistic creations, and slips of the tongue (we now call them *Freudian slips*) are examples of compromise formation.

For example, Freud believed that the *manifest content* of a dream—its actual story line—is only a disguised version of its *latent content* (its hidden message), which is produced by the unconscious. The latent content might be an unexpressed wish related to the sexual or aggressive instinctual drive. For example, a small boy might want to kill his father and sleep with his mother (thus satisfying both instinctual drives). However, if he acted out this scenario in a dream, he would experience very painful guilt and anxiety. Therefore, the nasty wishes of the unconscious are transformed into a more palatable form; the manifest content of the dream might be that his father became ill and that the boy helped his mother around the house, assuming some of his father's chores. These chores would substitute for the sexual activity his unconscious was really interested in. The manifest content of this dream manages to express, at least partly, the latent content supplied by the unconscious.

Defense Mechanisms

According to Freud, the ego contains **defense mechanisms**—systems that become active whenever unconscious instinctual drives of the id come into conflict with internalized prohibitions of the superego. The signal for the ego to utilize one of its defenses is the state of **anxiety** produced by an intrapsychic conflict. This unpleasant condition motivates the ego to apply a defense mechanism and thus reduce the anxiety. Six of the most important defense mechanisms are described below.

Repression is a means of preventing an idea, feeling, or memory from reaching consciousness. For example, Freud theorized that Anna O. had repressed the memories that caused the conflicts underlying her hysterical symptoms. Repression is the one phenomenon described by Freud that has received experimental attention.

Reaction formation involves replacing a threatening idea with its opposite. An often-cited example of a reaction formation is that of a person who is aroused and fascinated by pornographic material but whose superego will not permit this enjoyment. In consequence, he or she becomes a militant crusader against pornography. Reaction formation can be a very useful defense mechanism in this situation, permitting sexually acceptable interaction with the forbidden object. The crusader against pornography often studies the salacious material to see just how vile it is, so that he or she can better educate others about its harmful nature. Thus, enjoyment becomes possible without feelings of guilt.

Projection involves denial of one's own unacceptable desires and the discovery of evidence of these desires in the behavior of other people. For example, a man who is experiencing a great deal of repressed hostility may perceive the world as being full of people who are hostile to him. In this way he can blame someone else for any conflicts in which he engages.

Sublimation is the diversion of psychic energy from an unacceptable drive to an acceptable one. For example, a person may feel strong sexual desire but find its outlet unacceptable because of internalized prohibitions. Despite repression of the drive, its energy remains and finds an outlet in another drive, such as artistic or other creative activities. Freud considered sublimation to be an important factor in artistic and intellectual creativity. He believed that people have a fixed amount of drive available for motivating all activities; therefore, surplus sexual instinctual drive that is not expended in its normal way can be used to increase a person's potential for creative achievement.

Rationalization is the process of inventing an acceptable reason for a behavior that is really being performed for another, less acceptable reason. For example, a man who feels guilty about his real reasons for purchasing a magazine containing pictures of naked men or women may say, "I don't buy the magazine for the pictures. I buy it to read the interesting and enlightening articles it contains."

Conversion is the provision of an outlet for intrapsychic conflict in the form of a physical symptom. The conflict is transformed into blindness, deafness, paralysis, or numbness. (This phenomenon has also been called *hysteria,* which should not be confused with the common use of the term to mean "running around and shouting and generally acting out of control.") For example, a person might develop blindness so that he or she will no longer be able to see a situation that arouses a strong, painful intrapsychic conflict. In Chapter 15 we will examine the case of a man who became hysterically blind, apparently because he was overcome with jealousy watching his wife nurse their child. Anna O.'s problem would also be described as a conversion reaction.

Freud's Psychosexual Theory of Personality Development

6 Freud believed that the prime mover in personality development was the sexual instinctual drive, which is present in everyone from earliest childhood. In the healthy person this drive is expressed in certain specific ways at each level of physical development.

Because newborn babies can do little more than suck and drink, their sexual instinctual drive finds an outlet in these activities. Even as babies become able to engage in more complex behaviors, they continue to receive most of their sexual gratification orally. The early period of the **oral stage** of personality development is characterized by sucking and is passive. Later, as babies become more aggressive, they derive their pleasure from biting and chewing.

The **anal stage** of personality development begins during the second year of life; now babies begin to enjoy emptying their bowels (*anal* is derived from *anus,* the opening of the large intestine). During the early part of this stage, called the *expressive period,* babies enjoy expelling their feces. Later, in the *retentive period,* they derive pleasure from storing them up.

At around age three children discover that it is fun to play with their penis or clitoris, and they enter the **phallic stage.** (*Phallus* means "penis," but Freud used the term bisexually in this context.) Children also begin to discover the sex roles of their parents, and they attach themselves to the parent of the other sex. A boy's attachment to his mother is called the **Oedipus complex,** after the Greek king of mythology who unknowingly married his mother after killing his father. For a time Freud believed that a girl formed a similar attachment with her father, called the **Electra complex,** but he later rejected this concept. (In Greek mythology Electra and her brother killed her mother and her mother's lover to avenge her father's death.)

In boys the Oedipus complex normally becomes repressed by age five, although the conflicts that occur during the phallic stage continue to affect their personalities throughout life. A boy's wish to take his father's place is suppressed by his fear that his father will castrate him as punishment. (In fact, Freud believed that young boys regarded females as castrated males.) The conflict is finally resolved when the boy begins to model his behavior on that of his father, so that he achieves *identification* with the father.

Girls supposedly experience fewer conflicts than boys do during the phallic stage. According to Freud, the chief reason for their transfer of love from their mother (who provided primary gratification during early life) to their father is *penis envy.* A girl discovers that she and her mother lack this organ, so she becomes attached to her father, who has one. This attachment persists longer than the Oedipus complex, because the girl does not have to fear castration as revenge for usurping her mother's role. Freud believed that penis envy eventually becomes transformed into a need to bear children. The missing penis is replaced by a baby.

After the phallic stage comes a **latency period** of several years, during which the child's sexual instinctual drive is mostly submerged. At the onset of puberty the person begins to form adult sexual attachments to age mates of the other sex. Because the sexual instinctual drive now finds its outlet in heterosexual genital contact, this stage is known as the **genital stage.**

Freud's psychosexual theory of personality development has been extremely influential because of its ability to explain personality disorders in terms of whole or partial **fixation,** or "holding in place," at an early stage of development. For example, fixation at the oral stage may result from early (or delayed) weaning from breast to bottle to cup. Someone whose personality is fixated at the early oral stage might be excessively passive. "Biting" sarcasm or compulsive talking can represent fixation at the

later, aggressive phase of the oral stage. Other oral stage activities include habits like smoking and excessive eating.

Improper toilet training can result in fixation at the anal stage. People fixated at the anal expressive period are characterized as destructive and cruel; anal retentives are seen as stingy and miserly. Finally, people who do not successfully pass through the phallic stage may experience a variety of emotional problems. Freud believed that homosexuality stems from unresolved problems that occur during this stage.

Further Development of Freud's Theory: The Neo-Freudians

Freud had a number of disciples, known as neo-Freudians, who were strongly influenced by his theory. They accepted many of his ideas, such as the central role of the unconscious in personality development, but disagreed with the strong emphasis Freud placed on biological factors. They placed greater emphasis on social influences such as interpersonal relationships. Among the most influential of the neo-Freudians are Carl Gustav Jung, Alfred Adler, and Erik Erikson.

Jung. Carl Gustav Jung (1875–1961) believed strongly in the power of the unconscious but disagreed with Freud over its nature. Jung believed that Freud had overemphasized sexual motivation in his theorizing. He also believed that religious or spiritual concerns were more than sublimated sexual desires—they were fundamental aspects of human nature. He also distinguished between what he termed the personal unconscious and the collective unconscious, which he believed to be a universal storehouse of memories of our species' ancestral past (Jung, 1916). This unconscious, present at birth, contains myths, dreams, and symbols shared by all humans; and it also serves as the source of all creativity. As you might expect, this concept has not received empirical support.

Jung was the first to distinguish between introversion and extraversion, a concept that has endured and that *has* received empirical support.

Adler. In his theory of personality Alfred Adler (1870–1937) emphasized the social nature of human behavior. He believed that people strive for perfection in order to overcome feelings of inferiority, which originate in childhood. According to Adler, this feeling occurs when children discover that they cannot do all the things adults can do. After making this discovery, children begin to strive for superiority, which propels them to develop and grow. In addition, Adler believed that people have an innate interest in social interactions, which motivates them to strive to achieve goals that will contribute to a better society and to improve the quality of life.

Erikson. Erik Erikson (b. 1902) studied with Anna Freud, Sigmund Freud's daughter. He emphasized social aspects of personality development rather than biological factors. He also differed with Freud about the timing of personality development. For Freud the most important development occurs during early childhood; Erikson emphasized the ongoing process of development throughout the life span.

As we saw in Chapter 10, Erikson proposed that people's personality traits develop as a result of a series of crises they encounter in their social relations with other people. Because these crises continue throughout life, psychosocial development does not end when people become adults.

Erikson's theory of lifelong development has been very influential, and his term *identity crisis* has become a familiar one. However, because his theory does not make many empirically testable predictions, it has received little empirical support.

Modern Research on Psychodynamic Concepts

7 Freud's psychodynamic theory has had a profound effect on psychological theory, psychotherapy, and literature. His writing is lively and stimulating, and his ideas have provided many people with food for thought. However, his theory has received little experimental support, mainly because he referred to concepts that are poorly defined and that cannot be observed directly. How is one to study the ego, the superego, or the id? How can one prove (or disprove) that an artist's creativity is the result of a displaced aggressive or sexual instinctual drive? The writings of the neo-Freudians have had even less influence on modern research. Although the theories of Jung, Adler, and Erikson have their followers, scientific research on personality has largely ignored them.

The emphasis by Freud and his followers on the potentially harmful effects of particular types of childhood environment has led some psychotherapists to conclude that their patients' malad-

justments and mental disorders are, by and large, caused by their parents. Thus, many parents have blamed themselves for their children's disorders and have suffered severe feelings of guilt. As we shall see in Chapter 15, many forms of mental disorders—particularly the most serious ones—are largely a result of heredity and are not affected much by family environment. Hence, the teachings of Freud and his followers have compounded the tragedy of mental illness by causing parents to be accused unjustly of malfeasance.

Repression. The one Freudian phenomenon that has undergone experimental testing is repression. This phenomenon is very important to Freud's theory because it is one of the primary ego defenses and because it operates by pushing memories (or newly perceived stimuli) into the unconscious. Thus, experimental verification of repression would lend some support to Freud's notions of intrapsychic conflict and the existence of the unconscious.

However, the results have not been conclusive. Typically, the researchers in repression experiments ask subjects to learn some material associated with an unpleasant, ego-threatening situation, and they then compare their memory for the information with that of subjects who learned the material under nonthreatening conditions. If repression occurs, the threatened subjects should remember less of the material than the nonthreatened subjects. Some studies have reported positive results, but later experiments have shown that other, non-Freudian phenomena could explain them more easily. Perhaps the most important point here is that none of the experiments can really be said to have threatened the subjects' egos, producing the level of anxiety that would lead to the activation of a defense mechanism. Any experimental procedure that did so would probably be unethical.

One representative experiment on repression used a threat to the ego that has a certain amount of plausibility. D'Zurilla (1965) showed subjects ten pictures of inkblots, with two words beneath each inkblot, and asked the subjects to select the word that best described each inkblot. After making their ten choices, subjects in the experimental group were told that the task they had just performed was a test of latent homosexuality (homosexual tendencies that have not yet been fully expressed) and that they had chosen nine out of ten responses indicating this tendency. Control subjects were merely told that they were helping the experimenter develop a new psychological test. Five minutes later, both groups were tested to see how many of the twenty words they could remember. The experimental subjects remembered fewer of the words than the control subjects did, perhaps because they were repressing painful memories. The experimenter then told the experimental subjects that they had been deceived and that the test had nothing at all to do with homosexuality. In a subsequent memory test the experimental subjects did as well as control subjects. Perhaps the repression had been lifted; because the memories were no longer painful and ego threatening, the conscious was given free access to them.

But there is a simpler explanation. D'Zurilla asked the subjects what they had thought about during the five-minute period right after the first test. Most of the experimental subjects reported that they had been thinking about the test and brooding about the inkblots, their alleged homosexual tendencies, and related subjects. This response is quite the opposite of what Freud would have predicted; the subjects should have *avoided* these thoughts if they were painful. Perhaps the poor performance in the first recall test of the twenty words simply stemmed from interference; the subjects were preoccupied with thinking about what they had just been told about themselves. They were probably more interested in worrying about their scores on the test than in trying to remember the twenty words for the experimenter.

This experiment suggests the difficulty involved in testing even the most specific prediction of Freud's theory. It is very hard (perhaps impossible) to prove that a person's behavior is a result of unconscious conflicts.

Self-Deception. The details of Freud's psychodynamic theory of personality are not accepted by the overwhelming majority of experimental psychologists. As we just saw, tests of specific predictions of the theory are difficult to arrange. However, many of Freud's *ideas* have stimulated interesting and valuable research. One of the most important features of Freud's theory is the assertion that people often defend their egos by deceiving themselves, a process called **self-deception.** Many psychologists and philosophers have addressed the question of whether self-deception is possible. Gur and Sackheim (1979) have analyzed the process and reviewed experimental evidence on the subject. They conclude that self-deception requires that three conditions be met: (1) The person must simultaneously hold two contradictory beliefs,

(2) the person must be unaware of one of these beliefs, and (3) motivational factors must be responsible for determining which belief is conscious and which is not. If a person is conscious of having two contradictory beliefs, we can conclude that the person is indecisive but not that he or she is engaging in self-deception; thus, the person must not be conscious of one of these beliefs. And just as lying to another person is a motivated behavior, so is lying to oneself.

An interesting example of self-deception was demonstrated in an experiment by Quattrone and Tversky (1984). Some behaviors we engage in have direct effects on outcomes; for example, choosing whether or not to study for an examination will generally have an effect on a person's grade. Other behaviors are *diagnostic* of outcomes but do not cause them; for example, when students can sit wherever they choose in the classroom, a disproportionate number of those who receive good grades sit near the front. If the student has normal eyesight and hearing, sitting near the front probably has little effect on how well he or she will do on examinations. A more likely explanation for the phenomenon is that better students choose to sit near the front of the classroom because they enjoy academic work and identify more closely with the instructor or because they are pleased with their own self-image and want the instructor to be aware of them.

Quattrone and Tversky contrived a situation in which people could choose whether to perform a behavior that was diagnostic of a good outcome but could not possibly *cause* the outcome to be good. They were told by the experimenters that they were trying to determine whether athletes should take a cold shower after exercising in hot weather. Actually, the experimenters were not interested in "temperature change" but were measuring the subjects' tolerance of pain by having them immerse their arms in ice water as long as they could stand it.

First, the experimenters recorded how long the subjects could tolerate the pain of the cold water. Next, they had the subjects exercise on a stationary bicycle for one minute. Immediately afterward, they presented a lecture on the psychophysics of pain and mentioned that cold tolerance was affected by two variables: skin type and heart type. People with type 1 hearts were said to be frequently ill, to be prone to heart disease, and to have shorter life expectancies. People with type 2 hearts were said to be generally healthy, to have a low incidence of heart disease, and to have longer life expectancies. Half the subjects were told that having type 2 hearts (the "good" hearts) increased people's tolerance of cold after exercise, and the other half were told that having these hearts *decreased* people's tolerance of cold. Obviously, the stories told about type 1 and type 2 hearts were fictitious.

After hearing about these implications, the subjects took the cold tolerance test again. Afterward, they were asked what type of heart they believed they had. If, as the experimenters had suggested, tolerance to cold were in fact diagnostic of heart types, then differences in tolerance might indicate whether one had a type 1 or type 2 heart. But also consider that if there actually were two types of hearts, a person would already have one of them. Thus, there is no way that subjects could affect the type of heart they had by their performance on the cold tolerance test. "Cheating" on the test by increasing or decreasing one's tolerance makes as much sense as putting an ice cube in one's mouth before taking one's temperature: The ice cube may prevent the thermometer from registering a fever, but it does not produce good health. Nevertheless, Quattrone and Tversky (1984) found that the stories they told *did* alter people's pain tolerance. Most of the subjects kept their arms in the ice water for a longer or shorter time than they did before, depending on the version of the story they had heard. Only a few of those who did admitted that they had consciously tried to keep their arm in a longer or shorter time than in the first experiment. (As you learned in Chapters 4 and 8, many variables can affect people's perception of pain, including hypnotic and nonhypnotic suggestion.) In addition, most of the self-deceivers said that they believed they had type 2 hearts.

The results show, even in contrived laboratory situations, that some people do indeed engage in self-deception. Clearly, people's behavior can be affected by beliefs they do not admit to themselves.

INTERIM SUMMARY

The Psychodynamic Approach

Freud believed that the mind is full of conflicts between the primitive urges of the libido and the internalized prohibitions of the superego. According to Freud, these conflicts tend to be resolved through compromise formation and through ego defenses such as repression, sublimation, and reaction formation. His theory of

psychosexual development, a progression through the oral, anal, phallic, and genital stages, provided the basis for a theory of personality and personality disorders. Although Freud was a brilliant and insightful thinker, his theory has not been experimentally verified, primarily because most of his concepts are unobservable and, therefore, untestable. Even though many modern psychologists do not believe his psychodynamic theory to be correct, Freud made an important contribution to psychology with his realization that not all causes of our behavior are available to consciousness; many are unknown to us. In Chapter 16 we will examine psychoanalysis, the therapeutic technique based on his theory of personality.

Research on a factor common to all of Freud's proposed defense mechanisms—self-deception—shows that people do indeed deceive themselves. Self-deception implies the simultaneous holding of contradictory beliefs while not being aware of one of them for motivational reasons. Such conditions were met in the experiment on tolerance of pain caused by cold stress. ∎

ASSESSMENT OF PERSONALITY TRAITS

8 You have just learned about the many different types of theories that have been proposed to explain personality. Similarly, there are many different ways of measuring personality. This final section of the chapter explains how personality tests are constructed and describes some of the more useful and popular personality tests.

Test Construction

The Rational Strategy. The **rational strategy** of measurement requires prior definition of a trait, based on a theory of personality or on clinical observations. From this definition the investigators make predictions about the behavior of people who differ with respect to the trait. For example, to develop a test of "decisiveness," the investigators would list a number of ways in which the behavior of people at the extremes of the dimension would be expected to differ; they would then write items that are relevant to these differences. For instance, decisive people would be expected to answer "yes" to "I make up my mind quickly and have few regrets later" but "no" to "I usually rely on other people's advice when making important decisions." The test would consist of a number of items like these; a person's score would be the total number of "decisive" responses.

The success of this strategy depends on two important factors. First, the theory must be correct, at least with respect to the trait being assessed. Second, there must be good correspondence between a person's response and his or her behavior in the situation depicted in a particular question. If a person affirms that he or she relies on other people's advice but in fact never does so, then the question is not measuring what the test constructors think it is.

The Empirical Strategy. The second way to devise a test that measures a personality trait is the **empirical strategy;** investigators who use this method do not care whether a person's answer bears any relation to reality. For example, whether a person actually relies on other people's advice does not matter; what does matter is that a person tends to *answer this question in a particular way* and that the answer correlates with other measures of the trait in question. To devise a test of "decisiveness" by empirical means, a psychologist would write a large number of questions, much as the investigator using the factor analytical method would. After administering the test to a group containing a large number of decisive and indecisive people (the **criterion group**), the investigator would perform a statistical analysis of their answers, retaining those questions that were answered differently by the two groups of people and discarding all the others. The investigator would then devise a new test, using only the good questions, and administer it to a new group of decisive and indecisive people. The decision to retain a particular item would be completely empirical. For example, if decisive people answered "yes" to the item "I prefer oak trees to maples," the question would be used again. The lack of an apparent logical relation between the item and the trait being assessed does not matter. Once the best questions were selected and the worst ones weeded out, the investigator would publish the final form of the test.

The empirical method can be used only when the investigator *already knows* how to identify the traits to be measured; there must be some way to measure the criterion (in this case, decisiveness). Investigators generally use the empirical strategy of test construction when the usual way to measure a personality trait is difficult and expensive—for example, if the measurement requires hours of individual testing by a specially trained person. If a simple paper-and-pencil test can be devised that classifies people in the same way as the more expensive method, an obvious savings can be accomplished.

Objective Tests of Personality

Many kinds of tests have been devised to measure personality traits. The two major types are objective tests and projective tests. The responses that subjects can make on **objective tests** are severely constrained by the test design; the questions asked are unambiguous, and explicit rules for scoring the subjects' responses can be specified in advance. Responses are usually restricted to agreement or disagreement with a statement (yes/no or true/false) or to selection from a set of alternatives (multiple choice).

One of the oldest and the most widely used objective tests of personality is the **Minnesota Multiphasic Personality Inventory (MMPI)**, devised by Hathaway and McKinley in 1939. Their original purpose in developing the test was to produce an objective, reliable method for identifying various personality traits that were related to a person's mental health. The developers believed that this test would be valuable in assessing people for a variety of purposes. For instance, it would provide a specific

The Minnesota Multiphasic Personality Inventory Revised (MMPI-2) emphasizes personality traits rather than diagnostic categories.

means of determining how effective psychotherapy was; improvement in people's scores over the course of treatment would indicate that the treatment was successful.

Hathaway and McKinley used the empirical strategy to devise their test. They wrote 504 true/false items and administered the test to several groups of people in mental institutions in Minnesota who had been diagnosed as having certain specific disorders. These diagnoses had been arrived at through psychiatric interviews with the patients. Such interviews are expensive, so a simple paper-and-pencil test that accomplished the same result would be quite valuable. The control group consisted of relatives and friends of the patients, who were tested when they came to visit them. (Whether these people constituted the best possible group of normal subjects is questionable.) The responses were analyzed empirically, and the questions that correlated with various diagnostic labels were included in various scales. For example, if people who had been diagnosed as paranoid tended to say true to "I believe I am being plotted against," this question would become part of the paranoia scale.

The current revised version of the MMPI (the MMPI-2) has norms based on a sample of people that is much more representative ethnically and geographically than the original sample (Graham, 1990). It includes 550 questions, grouped into ten clinical scales and four *validity scales*. (See *Table 14.5.*) A particular item can be used on more than one scale. For example, both people who are depressed and those who are hypochondriacal tend to agree that they have gastrointestinal problems. The clinical scales include a number of diagnostic terms traditionally used to label psychiatric patients, such as *hypochondriasis, depression,* or *paranoia.*

The four **validity scales** were devised to provide the tester with some assurance that the subjects are answering questions reliably and accurately and that they can read the questions and pay attention to them. The *? scale* (cannot say) is simply the number of questions not answered. A high score on this scale indicates either that the person finds some questions irrelevant or that the person is evading issues that he or she finds painful.

The *L scale* (lie) contains items such as "I do not read every editorial in the newspaper every day" and "My table manners are not quite as good at home as when I am out in company." A person who disagrees with questions like these is almost certainly not telling the truth. A high score on the L scale suggests the need for

caution in interpreting other scales and also reveals something about the subject's personality. In particular, people who score high on this scale tend to be rather naive; more sophisticated people realize that no one is perfect and do not try to make themselves appear to be so.

The *F scale* (frequency) consists of items that are answered one way by at least 90 percent of the normal population. A high score on this scale indicates carelessness, poor reading ability, or very unusual personality traits. The usual responses are "false" to items such as "I can easily make other people afraid of me, and sometimes do for the fun of it" and "true" to items such as "I am liked by most people who know me."

The *K scale* (defensiveness) was devised to identify people who are trying to cover up their feelings to guard against internal conflicts that might cause them emotional distress. A person receives a high value on the K scale by answering "false" to statements such as "Criticism or scolding hurts me terribly" and "At periods my mind seems to work more slowly than usual." People who score very *low* on this scale tend to be in need of help or to be unusually immune to criticism and social influences.

Some psychologists argue that validity scales are useless or even harmful in most testing situations. For example, consider the following item: "Before voting, I thoroughly investigate the qualifications of all candidates." According to Crowne and Marlowe (1964), anyone who answers "yes" to such a question has to be lying. But as McCrae and Costa (1990) note, people taking tests do not necessarily respond passively to each item, taking it at face value. Instead their response is based on their interpretation of *what they think the question means.* They suggest that most people will say to themselves, " 'Surely these psychologists didn't mean to ask if I actually study the voting records of every single political candidate, from President to dogcatcher. No one does, so that would be a stupid question to ask. What they must have meant to ask was whether I am a concerned citizen who takes voting seriously. Since I am and I do, I guess I should answer *yes*' " (McCrae and Costa, 1990, p. 40).

There is evidence to support McCrae and Costa's suggestion. When psychologists calculate a person's score on the MMPI, they usually apply a correction factor derived from the validity scales. Several studies have shown that the use of the correction factors to the scores of normal subjects actually *reduces* the validity of these scores. McCrae and Costa suggest that

Table 14.5   Scales of the MMPI-2

489

Assessment of
Personality Traits

Scales	*Criteria*
Validity Scales	
? (Cannot say)	Number of items left unanswered
L (Lie)	15 items of overly good self-report, such as "I smile at everyone I meet" (answered true)
F (Frequency)	64 items answered in the scored direction by 10 percent or less of normals, such as "There is an international plot against me" (answered true)
K (Correction, or defensive-ness)	30 items reflecting defensiveness in admitting to problems, such as "I feel bad when others criticize me" (answered false)
Clinical Scales	
Hs (Hypochondriasis)	33 items derived from patients showing abnormal concern with bodily functions, such as "I have chest pains several times a week" (answered true)
D (Depression)	60 items derived from patients showing extreme pessimism, feelings of hopelessness, and slowing of thought and action, such as "I usually feel that life is interesting and worthwhile" (answered false)
Hy (Conversion hysteria)	60 items from neurotic patients using physical or mental symptoms as a way of unconsciously avoiding difficult conflicts and responsibilities, such as "My heart frequently pounds so hard I can feel it" (answered true)
Pd (Psychopathic deviate)	50 items from patients showing a repeated and flagrant disregard for social customs, emotional shallowness, and inability to learn from punishing experiences, such as "My activities and interests are often criticized by others" (answered true)
Mf (Masculinity-femininity)	60 items from patients showing homoeroticism and items differentiating between men and women, such as "I like to arrange flowers" (answered true, scored for femininity)
Pa (Paranoia)	40 items from patients showing abnormal suspiciousness and delusions of grandeur or persecution, such as "There are evil people trying to influence my mind" (answered true)
Pt (Psychasthenia)	48 items from neurotic patients showing obsessions, compulsions, abnormal fears, and guilt and indecisiveness, such as "I save nearly everything I buy, even after I have no use for it" (answered true)
Sc (Schizophrenia)	78 items from patients showing bizarre or unusual thoughts or behavior, frequent withdrawals, and delusions and hallucinations, such as "Things around me do not seem real" (answered true) and "It makes me uncomfortable to have people close to me" (answered true)
Ma (Hypomania)	46 items from patients showing emotional excitement, overactivity, and flight of ideas, such as "At times I feel very 'high' or very 'low' for no apparent reason" (answered true)
Si (Social introversion)	70 items from persons showing shyness, little interest in people, and insecurity, such as "I have the time of my life at parties" (answered false)

Source: Adapted from Aiken, L.R. *Psychological Testing and Assessment,* 4th ed. Boston: Allyn and Bacon, 1982. Copyright 1943, renewed 1970 by the University of Minnesota. Published by the University of Minnesota Press. All rights reserved.

when the MMPI is administered to normal subjects for research purposes, such corrections should not be made. However, validity scales may be useful in situations where subjects may be motivated to lie (for example, when a personality test is used to screen job applicants) or in cases where the test is being used clinically, to evaluate the possibility of mental illness or personality disorder.

Because the MMPI was devised by empirical means, the scales based on diagnostic categories can only be as valid as the original classification of the patients. Despite this potential drawback, the MMPI has proved to be very useful in clinical diagnosis. Research has shown that various patterns of responding on more than one scale are correlated with certain distinct psychological problems. For example, a person who suffers great emotional discomfort, against which he or she has few defenses, will probably score high on the Pt scale (psychasthenia) and low on the K scale (defensiveness). In contrast, a person who engages in antisocial behavior and harms other people tends to score high on both the Pt scale and the Ma scale (hypomania). Thus, the uses of the MMPI have been extended beyond its authors' original intentions.

As well as being used in clinical assessment, the MMPI has been employed extensively in personality research; and a number of other tests, including the California Psychological Inventory and the Taylor Manifest Anxiety Scale, are based on it. However, the MMPI has its critics. As we saw in the first section of this chapter, the five-factor model of personality has received considerable support. Some of its advocates have noted that the MMPI misses some of the dimensions measured by the NEO-PI, which includes tests of the five factors of neuroticism, extraversion, openness, agreeableness, and conscientiousness (Johnson et al., 1984). Thus, these factors will be missed by a clinician or researcher who relies only on this test. For this reason, many researchers—especially those interested in the psychobiology of personality—no longer use the MMPI.

Projective Tests of Personality

⑨ **Projective tests** of personality are quite different in form from objective ones; they are derived from psychodynamic theories of personality, which emphasize the importance of unconscious motives. Psychoanalytically oriented psychologists believe that behavior is determined by unconscious processes more than conscious ones. Thus, they believe that a test that asks straightforward questions is unlikely to tap the real roots of an individual's personality characteristics. Projective tests are designed to be ambiguous so that the person's answers will be more revealing than simple agreement or disagreement with statements provided by objective tests. The assumption of projective tests is that the subject will "project" his or her personality into the ambiguous situation and thus make responses that give clues to this personality. In addition, the ambiguity of the test makes it unlikely that subjects will have preconceived notions about which answers are socially desirable. Thus, it will be difficult for a subject to give biased answers in an attempt to look better (or worse) than he or she actually is.

The Rorschach Inkblot Test. One of the oldest projective tests of personality is the **Rorschach Inkblot Test,** published in 1921 by Hermann Rorschach, a Swiss psychiatrist. The test consists of ten pictures of inkblots, originally made by spilling ink on a piece of paper that was subsequently folded in half, producing an image that is symmetrical in relation to the line of the fold. Five of the inkblots are black and white, and five are in color. (See *Figure 14.10.*) The subject is shown each card and asked to describe what it looks like. Then the cards are shown again, and the subject is asked to point out the features he or she used to determine what was seen. The responses and the

Figure 14.10 An item similar to the one that appears in the Rorschach Inkblot Test.

nature of the features the subject uses to make them are scored on a number of dimensions.

In the following example described by Pervin (1975), a person's response to a particular inkblot (a real one, not the one shown in Figure 14.10) might be "Two bears with their paws touching one another playing pattycake or could be they are fighting and the red is the blood from the fighting." The classification of this response, also described by Pervin, would be as follows: *large detail* of the blot was used, *good form* was used, *movement* was noted, *color* was used in the response about blood, an *animal* was seen, and a *popular response* (two bears) was made. A possible interpretation of the response might be as follows:

> Subject starts off with popular response and animals expressing playful, "childish" behavior. Response is then given in terms of hostile act with accompanying inquiry. Pure color response and blood content suggest he may have difficulty controlling his response to the environment. Is a playful, childlike exterior used by him to disguise hostile, destructive feelings that threaten to break out in his dealings with the environment? (Pervin, 1975, p. 37)

Although, traditionally, the interpretation of people's responses to the Rorschach Inkblot Test was based on psychoanalytical theory, many investigators have used it in an empirical fashion. That is, a variety of different scoring methods have been devised, and the scores obtained by these methods have been correlated with clinical diagnoses, just as investigators have done with people's scores on the MMPI. When this test is used empirically, the style and content of the responses are not interpreted in terms of a theory (as Rorschach interpreted them) but are simply correlated with other measures of personality.

The Thematic Apperception Test. Another popular projective technique, the **Thematic Apperception Test (TAT)**, was developed by the American psychologists Henry Murray and C.D. Morgan to measure various psychological *needs*. People are shown a picture of a very ambiguous situation, such as the one in Figure 14.11, and are asked to tell a complete story about what is happening in the picture, explaining the situation, what led up to it, what the characters are thinking and saying, and what the final outcome will be. (See *Figure 14.11*.) Presumably, the subjects will "project" themselves into the scene, and their story will reflect their own needs. As you might imagine, scoring is difficult and requires a great deal of practice

Figure 14.11 An item from the Thematic Apperception Test. (Reprinted by permission of the publishers from *Thematic Apperception Test,* by Henry A. Murray, Cambridge, Mass.: Harvard University Press. Copyright © 1943 by The President and Fellows of Harvard College, © 1971 by Henry A. Murray.)

and skill. The tester attempts to infer the psychological needs expressed in the stories.

Phares (1979) has presented the responses of one woman to several TAT cards, along with a clinician's interpretation of these responses. The questions asked by the examiner are in parentheses.

> *Card 3BM.* Looks like a little boy crying for something he can't have. (Why is he crying?) Probably because he can't go somewhere. (How will it turn out?) Probably sit there and sob hisself to sleep.

> *Card 3GF.* Looks like her boyfriend might have let her down. She hurt his feelings. He's closed the door on her. (What did he say?) I don't know.

> *Card 10.* Looks like there's sorrow here. Grieving about something. (About what?) Looks like maybe one of the children's passed away.

> *Interpretation*: The TAT produced responses that were uniformly indicative of unhappiness, threat, misfortune, a lack of control over environmental forces. None of the test responses were indicative of satisfaction, happy endings, etc. . . . In summary, the test results point to an individual who is anxious and, at the same

time, depressed. Feelings of insecurity, inadequacy, and lack of control over environmental forces are apparent, as are unhappiness and apprehension. These factors result in a constriction of performance that is largely oriented toward avoiding threat and that hampers sufficient mobilization of energy to perform at an optimal level. (Phares, 1979, p. 273)

The pattern of responses in this case is quite consistent; few people would disagree with the conclusion that the woman is sad and depressed. However, not all people provide such clear-cut responses. As you might expect, interpreting differences in the stories of people who are relatively well adjusted is much more difficult. As a result, distinguishing among people with different but normal personality traits is hard.

Just as the Rorschach Inkblot Test has provided raw material for empirically determined scales, the TAT has been used to provide responses for a variety of personality tests. For example, the developers of the theory of achievement motivation have devised a special scoring system for the TAT to measure people's need to achieve, need for affiliation, and other motives.

Evaluation of Projective Tests. Most empirical studies have found that projective tests such as the Rorschach test and the TAT have poor reliability and little validity. For example, Eron (1950) found no differences between the scores of people who were in mental hospitals and college students. (No, I'm not going to make a joke about that.) Entwisle (1972) reported that "recent studies . . . yield few positive relationships between need achievement [measured by the TAT] and other variables" (p. 179). In a review of over three hundred studies, Lundy (1984) found that the validity of the TAT appears to be *lower* when it is administered by an authority figure, in a classroom setting, or when it is represented as a test. Lundy (1988) suggests that in such situations the subjects are likely to realize that they are talking about themselves when they tell a story about the cards and may be careful in what they say.

Even if people taking the TAT are not on their guard, their scores are especially sensitive to their mood (Masling, 1960). So the scores they receive on one day are often very different from those they receive on another day. But a test of personality is supposed to measure enduring traits that persist over time and in a variety of situations.

The reliability and validity of the Rorschach Test are also rather low. A recent study that used the most reliable scoring method found little or no correlation between subjects' scores on the Rorschach and their scores on six objective tests of personality (Greenwald, 1990). As the author notes, "With few exceptions, this attempt to validate selected Rorschach variables using self-report personality scales as external criteria did not provide support [for external construct validity]. Even when . . . relationships between Rorschach variables and self-report measures reached statistical significance, they typically did so at low levels" (Greenwald, 1990, p. 777).

If projective tests such as the Rorschach and the TAT have been found to be of low reliability and validity, why do so many clinical psychologists and psychiatrists continue to use them? The primary reason seems to be tradition. The use of these tests has a long history and the rationale for the tests is consistent with psychodynamic explanations of personality.

INTERIM SUMMARY

Assessment of Personality Traits

Tests of personality can be constructed by rational or empirical means. The rational strategy requires a detailed theory that can predict the behavior of people with various personality traits; the test is constructed in accordance with these predictions. The empirical strategy requires that the investigator first identify (perhaps by an expensive and time-consuming method) people who do or do not possess a particular personality trait. The investigator then assembles a criterion group consisting of a mixture of such people and gives them a test that includes a large number of items. Only those items answered differently by people with and without the trait are retained in the final form of the test.

Objective tests contain items that can be answered and scored objectively, such as true/false or multiple-choice questions. One of the most important objective personality tests is the Minnesota Multiphasic Personality Inventory, which was empirically devised to discriminate among people who had been assigned various psychiatric diagnoses. It has since been used widely in research on personality. Its validity scales have been challenged by researchers who suggest that most people's responses can be taken at face value. More recently, researchers interested in personality have turned to tests not based on people with mental disorders, such as the NEO-PI.

Projective tests, such as the Rorschach Inkblot Test and the Thematic Apperception Test, contain ambiguous items that presumably elicit answers that reveal aspects of the subjects' personalities. Because answers can vary widely, test administrators must receive special training to interpret them. Unfortunately, evidence suggests that the reliability and validity of such tests is not particularly high. ∎

APPLICATION

Integrity Testing for Personnel Selection

One of a company's most important resources is its employees. In today's competitive business environment, finding and hiring the right employee is an important—and costly—endeavor. Thus, preemployment testing has become a critical aspect of personnel selection. For years publishers have provided tests of specific aptitudes to help employers choose the most able job candidates. More recently, employers have been making use of personality tests to measure the characteristics that they believe are most important for particular positions. For example, they want extraverted salespeople and conscientious accountants.

A particularly important personality characteristic for employees is integrity. Dishonest employees may steal from the company or its customers, create dissension and poor morale among the rest of the employees, and cause other incidents that damage the employer's reputation. Detecting a dishonest employee is often difficult and occurs only after damage has been done; and firing an employee and finding and training a replacement is expensive. Thus, many employers have begun administering tests to job applicants to help screen out potentially dishonest candidates.

In the past some employers used polygraph testing to screen their candidates, but the expense of this procedure meant that it could be used only for candidates for especially sensitive positions. In 1986 the American Psychological Association passed a resolution stating that the validity of polygraph testing for employment screening had not been demonstrated scientifically. (The application section at the end of Chapter 12 reviewed the scientific evidence concerning lie detection by polygraphs and other electronic devices.) In 1988 the United States Congress passed the Employee Polygraph Protection Act, which prohibited employers from using such tests. (Security firms and companies manufacturing controlled drugs were exempted.) Other countries have adopted similar measures. Thus, the use of polygraph testing as a screening device has drastically declined; and the use of paper-and-pencil tests has increased.

In a review of published tests designed to assess employee integrity, Sackett, Burris, and Callahan (1989) note that the tests fall into two general categories: *overt integrity tests* and *personality-based measures*. Overt integrity tests ask the candidates about their attitudes toward theft, cheating, drug use, illegal gambling, and other undesirable acts, and inquire whether the candidates themselves have committed any of these acts. The questions on such tests are direct and obvious, and a person trying to look good would not have difficulty doing so. In fact, Ryan and Sackett (1987) found that a group of college students taking an integrity test scored very high when they were instructed to give answers that would make them appear honest; they had no difficulty figuring out what answers would give that impression. You might reasonably ask whether *anyone* applying for a job would admit to behaviors that would surely disqualify them. In fact, some do; in a study of 225,000 job applicants, Ash (1987) found that 6.1 percent admitted that they had been involved in investigations of theft in a previous job, 6.4 percent admitted that they had committed minor criminal acts, 4.4 percent admitted that they had committed a felony, and 4.5 percent admitted that they had frequently taken illegal drugs during working hours. But undoubtedly, many dishonest people simply portray themselves as honest.

Tests that belong to the second category, personality-based measures, do not contain obvious references to theft or other antisocial activities. Instead, such tests attempt to measure personality variables that correlate with "organizational delinquency," including "theft, drug and alcohol abuse, lying, insubordination, vandalism, sabotage, absenteeism, and assaultive actions" (Hogan and Hogan, 1989). The personality traits they attempt to identify include sociability, dependability, conscientiousness, self-restraint, and acceptance of convention (desirable traits) and thrill-seeking, hostility, nonconformity, and irresponsibility (undesirable traits). Sample items from these tests include the following: "You are more sensible than adventurous," "You work hard and steady at whatever you undertake," "You love to take chances," and "You never would talk back to a boss or a teacher" (Sackett, Burris, and Callahan, 1989, p. 493). Even though these items do not mention illegal acts, I suspect you can figure out which questions are best answered "yes" and which are best answered "no."

What evidence do we have about the validity of integrity tests? Sackett and his colleagues report studies that have employed several different types of criterion measures. Some studies correlated scores on particular tests with the results of a polygraph test; but since the validity of polygraph tests has not been established, the correlation is not a meaningful index. Other studies have looked for changes in statistics related to employee dishonesty after a company has adopted an integrity test as part of its hiring procedure. For example, Personnel Decisions Inc. (1985) reported that after a large retail chain adopted its test (the PDI Employment Inventory), terminations for theft fell from 2.5 percent to 1.3 percent. However, as Sackett and his colleagues note, studies such as this one do not contain a control group. Perhaps an economic downturn made employees act more prudently, because they feared that it would be difficult for them to find another job if they lost their present one. Perhaps the testing program simply communicated the fact that the employer was concerned about theft and dishonesty. In fact, some stores in the PDI study did *not* adopt the test, but the study did not report the termination rate for these stores. If these stores showed a similar decline in theft, we would have to conclude that factors other than the testing program were responsible. If the study had been reported in a peer-reviewed scientific journal, the reviewer would undoubtedly have insisted that such evidence be presented. But most studies evaluating commercial integrity tests are carried out and reported by the test's publisher, who obviously has a financial stake in the test's success.

The best evidence for validity comes from prospective studies, in which employees are given the integrity test but are hired regardless of their score. Then, after a sufficient amount of time has passed, the records are consulted to see whether employees who were found to be dishonest scored differently from those who were not. (These studies measure *predictive validity*—the ability of the test to predict who will and who will not commit dishonest acts.) Sackett, Burris, and Callahan (1989) found 16 such studies, most of which reported at least a modest degree of predictive validity.

Tests of integrity have been criticized as unfair to the individual; in fact, a substantial proportion of people who fail the tests would not commit dishonest acts if they were hired. The mean "failure rate" of honest employees in the prospective studies reported by Sackett and his colleagues was 44 percent, compared with 74 percent for those who turned out to be dishonest. The value of integrity tests to an employer depends on several factors. If the job is particularly sensitive (for example, if the person would be responsible for the safety of other people or would have an easy opportunity to steal from the company or its customers), then the advantages of such tests may outweigh any disadvantages. But in other cases they may not. The high failure rate of integrity tests means that an employer using one will screen out a large proportion of the applicants, many of whom would be good employees. Thus, an employer will have to interview and test a larger number of candidates, which will increase the associated costs. In addition, if candidates are scarce, positions may go unfilled for a long time.

Trait Theories of Personality

personality type *(463)*
personality trait *(464)*
extraversion *(465)*
introversion *(465)*
neuroticism *(465)*
psychoticism *(466)*
five-factor model *(467)*
NEO-PI (Neuroticism, Extraversion, and Openness Personality Inventory) *(467)*

Psychobiological Approaches

Behavioral/Cognitive Approaches

radical behaviorism *(474)*
process reward *(475)*
content reward *(475)*
self-concept *(475)*
self-praise *(476)*
self-criticism *(476)*
self-control *(476)*
delay of gratification *(476)*
cross-situational consistency *(477)*

The Psychodynamic Approach

psychodynamic *(480)*
id *(481)*
libido *(481)*
ego *(481)*
reality principle *(481)*
superego *(481)*
conscience *(481)*

ego-ideal *(481)*
internalized prohibition *(481)*
compromise formation *(481)*
defense mechanism *(481)*
anxiety *(482)*
repression *(482)*
reaction formation *(482)*
projection *(482)*
sublimation *(482)*
rationalization *(482)*
conversion *(482)*
oral stage *(482)*
anal stage *(482)*
phallic stage *(482)*
Oedipus complex *(483)*
Electra complex *(483)*
latency period *(483)*
genital stage *(483)*
fixation *(483)*
self-deception *(485)*

Assessment of Personality Traits

rational strategy *(486)*
empirical strategy *(487)*
criterion group *(487)*
objective test *(487)*
Minnesota Multiphasic Personality Inventory **(MMPI)** *(487)*
validity scale *(488)*
projective test *(490)*
Rorschach Inkblot Test *(490)*
Thematic Apperception Test (TAT) *(491)*

SUGGESTIONS FOR FURTHER READING

Carver, C.S., and Scheier, M.F. *Perspectives on Personality*, 2nd ed. Boston: Allyn and Bacon, 1992.

Pervin, L.A. *Personality: Theory and Research*, 4th ed. New York: John Wiley & Sons, 1984.

Personality testing and research on personality traits receive thorough coverage in these texts.

Skinner, B.F. *About Behaviorism.* New York: Vintage Press, 1976.

Bandura, A. *Social Learning Theory.* Englewood Cliffs, N.J.: Prentice-Hall, 1977.

B.F. Skinner presents his views about the causes of human behavior in his book, and Bandura presents an account of human behavior derived from the behaviorist tradition but heavily influenced by cognitive psychology.

Freud, S. *General Introduction to Psychoanalysis*, translated by J. Riviere. New York: Permabooks, 1957.

Jones, E. *The Life and Work of Sigmund Freud.* New York: Basic Books, 1953.

The best resource on Freud's general theories of personality is Freud himself. Jones provides an interesting discussion of Freud's life as well as his writings.

15

THE NATURE AND CAUSES OF MENTAL DISORDERS

Henri Matisse, *Liseuse sur Fond Noir*
GIRAUDON/Art Resource, N.Y. © 1992 Succession H. Matisse/ARS, N.Y.

CLASSIFICATION AND DIAGNOSIS
What Is "Abnormal"? ▪ The Value of Classification ▪ The DSM-III-R Classification Scheme ▪ *Evaluating Scientific Issues: Clinical Versus Actuarial Diagnosis* ▪ Interim Summary

NONPSYCHOTIC MENTAL DISORDERS
Anxiety Disorders ▪ Somatoform Disorders ▪ Dissociative Disorders ▪ Interim Summary

PERSONALITY AND PSYCHOACTIVE SUBSTANCE ABUSE DISORDERS
Antisocial Personality Disorder ▪ Psychoactive Substance Use Disorders ▪ Interim Summary

SCHIZOPHRENIC DISORDERS
Description ▪ Types of Schizophrenia ▪ Possible Causes ▪ Interim Summary

MOOD DISORDERS
Description ▪ Possible Causes ▪ Interim Summary

APPLICATION: ANIMAL MODELS OF MENTAL DISORDERS

LEARNING OBJECTIVES

When you finish this chapter, you should be able to:

1. Explain the meaning of abnormality, discuss the value of a classification system for mental disorders, and describe the most commonly used system.
2. Describe the nature of clinical and actuarial diagnosis, and discuss research on their reliability and validity.
3. Describe the symptoms and possible causes of the major anxiety disorders: panic disorder, phobic disorders, and obsessive compulsive disorder.
4. Describe the symptoms and possible causes of somatization disorder and conversion disorder.
5. Describe the symptoms and possible causes of the major dissociative disorders: psychogenic amnesia, psychogenic fugue, and multiple personality disorder.
6. Describe the symptoms and possible causes of antisocial personality disorder.
7. Describe the symptoms and possible causes of psychoactive substance abuse disorder.
8. Describe the characteristic symptoms of schizophrenia and the major types of schizophrenic disorders.
9. Evaluate research on the early predictors of schizophrenia, the role of heredity, the dopamine hypothesis, and the role of neurological disorders.
10. Describe the symptoms of bipolar disorder and major depression.
11. Explain cognitive theories of the causes of mood disorders, the role of heredity, research on biochemical factors, and the relation to sleep cycles.

"Bess is an attractive twenty-seven-year-old upper middle-class woman. She lives by herself in a well-kept apartment in one of the best sections in town. Yet, she had few friends, and social activities play a small role in her life. Most evenings, she works rather late and then comes home, fixes her own dinner, and reads or watches television until she gets ready to fall asleep. . . . Bess is a successful accountant for a large manufacturing firm and spends a lot of time with her work. She is a perfectionist, but this is generally functional in accounting.

"[At college] Bess slipped into the role of 'top student,' received many honors, and then easily moved into the consequent role of 'up-and-coming young career woman.' Her involvement in her job absorbed most of her time, and it was clear that she was a rising star in the firm. Bess continued to have vague anxieties about dating, marriage, having a family, and other related issues. She handled these anxieties by throwing herself even harder into her work. At the same time, however, she began to experience symptoms that focused around the issue of cleanliness. . . .

"This concern with cleanliness gradually evolved into a thoroughgoing cleansing ritual, which was usually set off by her touching her genital or anal area. In this ritual, Bess would first remove all of her clothing in a preestablished sequence. She would lay out each article of clothing at specific spots on her bed, and examine each one for any indications of 'contamination.' She would then thoroughly scrub her body, starting at her feet and working meticulously up to the top of her head, using certain washcloths for certain areas of her body. Any articles of clothing that appeared to have been 'contaminated' were thrown into the laundry. Clean clothing was put in the spots that were vacant. She would then dress herself in the opposite order from which she took the clothes off. If there were any deviations from this order, or if Bess began to wonder if she might have missed some contamination, she would go through the entire sequence again. It was not rare for her to do this four or five times in a row on certain evenings.

"As time passed, she began developing a variety of other rituals and obsessive thoughts, usually related to using the toilet, sexual issues, or the encountering of possible 'contamination in public places.' As her circle of rituals widened, her functioning became more impaired. She was aware of the absurdity of these behaviors, but at the same time felt compelled to go through with them and did not constantly question them. Fi-

nally, the behaviors began to intrude on her ability to work, the one remaining source of meaning and satisfaction in her world. It was then that she referred herself for help." (Excerpted from Robert G. Meyer and Yvonne Hardaway Osborne, *Case Studies in Abnormal Behavior,* Second Edition, pp. 41–43. Copyright © 1987 by Allyn and Bacon. Used with permission.)

Life is complex, and things do not always go smoothly. We are all beset by major and minor tragedies, but we usually manage to cope with them. Occasionally, we find ourselves behaving irrationally, having trouble concentrating on a single topic, or experiencing feelings that do not seem appropriate for the circumstances. Sometimes, we brood about imaginary disasters or harbor hurtful thoughts about people we love. For most of us, however, these problems remain occasional and do not cause much concern.

But the lives of some people are dominated by disordered thoughts, disturbed feelings, or inappropriate behaviors. Their problems become so severe that they cannot cope with life. Consequently, they either withdraw from it, seek the help of others, or are judged unfit by society and are placed in an institution. What goes wrong?

Some mental disorders—especially the less severe ones—appear to be caused by environmental factors, such as stress or unhealthy family interactions. For example, a boy who is constantly criticized by an overbearing, demanding parent may learn to be passive and nonresponding so that the attacks will cease as soon as possible. This strategy may be adaptive in interactions with his parent, but it would clearly be maladaptive if he were to use it too readily when he was stressed by other social situations. Many of the more severe mental disorders appear to be caused by hereditary biological factors, which disrupt normal thought processes or produce inappropriate emotional reactions.

This chapter describes the nature of some of the more important mental disorders and discusses research on their causes; Chapter 16 discusses the treatment of mental disorders and the efforts of clinical psychologists to help people with problems of daily living. The descriptions of mental disorders in this chapter necessarily make distinctions that are not always easy to make in real life; the essential features of the more important mental disorders are simplified here for the sake of clarity. Moreover, many of the cases that clinicians encounter are less clear-cut than the ones included here and are thus not so easily classified. Space does not permit coverage of features in our society—such as problems of marriage and family life, social inequities, war, and problems of personal adjustment—that cause mental stress in many people but do not lead to diagnosis of a specific mental disorder. Fortunately, more and more people are coming to realize that there is no sharp line dividing normal and abnormal behavior, and that they need not be "sick" to profit from professional advice concerning their feelings and behavior.

CLASSIFICATION AND DIAGNOSIS

What Is "Abnormal"?

1 Mental disorders are characterized by abnormal behavior, thoughts, and feelings. The term *abnormal* literally refers to any departure from the norm. Thus, a short or tall person is "abnormal," and so is someone who is especially intelligent or talented. Albert Einstein was "abnormal," and so was composer George Gershwin and baseball player Babe Ruth. But as you know, the term *abnormal* has taken on a pejorative connotation; we use it to refer to characteristics that we dislike or fear.

The most important feature of a mental disorder is not whether a person's behavior is "abnormal"—that is, different from that of most other people—but whether it is *maladaptive.* Mental disorders cause distress or discomfort and often interfere with people's ability to lead useful, productive lives. They often make it impossible for people to hold a job, or raise a family, or relate to others socially. But then, a person who holds an unpopular religious or political belief may be ostracized by the community and find it impossible to find employment or to make friends. Certainly in that society, the person's behavior is maladaptive. Should we say that the person has a mental disorder?

Of course not. Depending on our own point of view, we might be tempted to label the behavior as courageous and wise, or misguided and foolish. But simply disagreeing with the government, with established religious practices, or with popular beliefs is not sufficient evidence for mental illness. In the past many political dissidents in the Soviet Union who publicly disagreed with communist dogma were diagnosed as having a mental disorder and were sent to a prison camp for the "insane." Fortunately, these abuses appear to have ended with

the advent of *perestroika* and the dissolution of the Soviet Union, but they warn us of what can happen in a totalitarian system.

Although the diagnosis of mental disorders should be as objective as possible, it may never be completely free from social and political judgments. In societies like ours, receiving messages from God and being transported on mystical voyages to heaven would probably be labeled as hallucinations and delusions, whereas in other times and places they might be taken as signs of holiness and devotion. If historical records are accurate, the behavior of many people who are now venerated as prophets or saints would be regarded quite differently if they were presently alive. But the fact that the diagnoses are affected by the social context does not mean that they are invalid or futile. People *do* have mental disorders: They *do* have delusions and hallucinations, they *do* have thought disorders, they *do* experience inappropriate emotions. And these mental disorders bring pain and discomfort to the people and to their friends and families.

What causes mental disorders? In general, they are caused by an interaction between hereditary and environmental factors. In some cases the genetic component is strong; the person is likely to develop a mental disorder even in a very supportive environment. In other cases the environmental component is strong; as we

The Scream, by Edvard Munch

saw in Chapter 12, some situations are so stressful that most people exposed to them will develop a posttraumatic stress disorder. A complete understanding of mental disorders requires that scientists investigate both genetic and environmental factors. Once genetic factors are identified, the scientist faces the task of determining the physiological effects of the relevant genes and the consequences of these effects on a person's susceptibility to a mental disorder. And environmental factors do not simply mean a person's family history or present social interactions; they refer as well to the effects of prenatal health and nutrition, childhood diseases, and exposure to drugs and environmental toxins.

The Value of Classification

There are dangers in classifying a person's mental disorder. No classification scheme is perfect, and no two people with the same diagnosis will behave in exactly the same way. Yet once people are labeled, they are likely to be perceived as having all the characteristics assumed to accompany that label; their behavior will probably be perceived selectively and interpreted in terms of the diagnosis. Mental health professionals, like other humans, tend to simplify things by pigeonholing people.

An experiment by Langer and Abelson (1974) illustrated how labeling someone can affect clinical judgments. A group of psychoanalysts were shown a videotape of a young man who was being interviewed. Half of the psychoanalysts were told that the man was a job applicant, while the other half were told that he was a patient. Although both groups of clinicians watched the same man exhibiting the same behavior, those who were told that he was a patient rated him as being more disturbed—that is, less adjusted. (See *Figure 15.1.*)

Because labeling can have bad effects, some people have suggested that we should abandon all attempts to classify and diagnose mental disorders. However, proper classification has advantages for a patient. One advantage is that, with few exceptions, the recognition of a specific diagnostic category precedes the development of successful treatment for that disorder. Treatments for diseases such as diabetes, syphilis, tetanus, and malaria were found only after the disorders could be reliably diagnosed. A patient may have a multitude of symptoms; but before the cause of the disorder (and hence its treatment) can be discovered, the primary symptoms must be identified. For example,

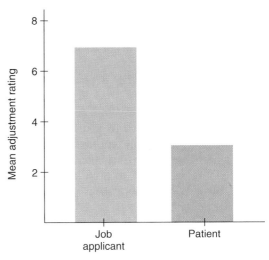

Figure 15.1 Adjustment ratings of the same person by psychoanalysts who were told he was a "job applicant" or a "patient." (Based on data from Langer, E.J., and Abelson, R.P. *Journal of Consulting and Clinical Psychology*, 1974, 42, 4–9.)

Graves's disease is characterized by irritability, restlessness, confused and rapid thought processes, and, occasionally, delusions and hallucinations. Little was known about the endocrine system during the nineteenth century when Robert Graves identified the disease, but we now know that this syndrome results from oversecretion of thyroxine, a hormone produced by the thyroid glands. Treatment involves prescription of antithyroid drugs or surgical removal of the thyroid glands, followed by administration of appropriate doses of thyroxine. Graves's classification scheme for the symptoms was devised many years before the physiological basis of the disease could be understood; but once enough was known about the effects of thyroxine, physicians were able to treat Graves's disease and strike it off the roll of mental disorders.

On a less dramatic scale, different kinds of mental disorders have different causes, and they respond to different types of behavioral treatments or drugs. If future research is to reveal more about causes and treatments of these disorders, we must be able to classify specific mental disorders reliably and accurately.

Another important reason for properly classifying mental disorders relates to their prognosis. Some disorders have a good prognosis; the patient is likely to improve soon and is unlikely to have a recurrence of the problem. Other disorders have progressive courses; the patient is less likely to recover from these disorders. In the first case the patient can obtain reassurance about his or her future; in the second case the patient's family can obtain assistance in making realistic plans.

The DSM-III-R Classification Scheme

Mental disorders can be classified in a number of ways, but the system most commonly used in North America today is the one presented in the American Psychiatric Association's **Diagnostic and Statistical Manual III-R** (DSM-III-R). (*Psychiatry* is a medical specialty devoted to the treatment of mental disorders. The corresponding specialty within psychology is called *clinical psychology*.) Table 15.1 lists these classifications, with several subclassifications omitted for the sake of simplicity. The ones described in this chapter are preceded by a colored dot. (See *Table 15.1.*)

The DSM-III-R is the latest version (published in 1987) of a classification scheme that was devised in an attempt to provide a reliable, universal set of diagnostic categories, with these criteria specified as explicitly as possible. The attempt appears to have paid off; in the area of the major diagnostic categories the DSM-III has proved itself more reliable than its predecessors (Grove et al., 1981).

EVALUATING SCIENTIFIC ISSUES

Clinical Versus Actuarial Diagnosis

[2] Clinical psychologists and other health professionals are often called upon to make diagnoses and predictions of people's future behavior. These decisions are important; for example, they can determine whether someone receives a treatment that has significant side effects, whether someone receives parole, whether someone stands trial for a crime, or whether someone is placed in a hospital. Two activities go into such decision: *collection* of information and *interpretation* of information. Both activities are essential; unreliable or irrelevant data cannot be interpreted, and good data can be spoiled through misinterpretation.

Mental health professionals have many ways to collect data. They can observe people and note the presence or absence of particular behaviors. They can order medical tests such as EEGs, X rays, or CT scans. They can interview people and make note of their facial expressions

and their responses to questions. They can administer objective and projective personality tests. They can examine a variety of documents that already exist, such as medical records, criminal records, or reports of behavior from mental or penal institutions.

Once the evidence is gathered, it can be interpreted in two ways: the *clinical method* or the *actuarial method*. Although a considerable amount of scientific research indicates that the actuarial method is superior, many mental health professionals still prefer to use the clinical method. In this section I will explain the difference between the two methods, summarize research that compares them, and discuss the reasons that the actuarial method is not more widespread.

How Do These Methods Differ? Clinical **judgments** are those based on the expert's experience. The information that is collected may come from a variety of sources; it is not the *source* of information that distinguishes the clinical method from the actuarial method—it is the *processing* of that information. Clinical judgments are based on experts' memories of similar cases and, of course, on their knowledge of the symptoms that predict particular types of outcomes.

Actuarial judgments are made by applying empirically derived rules that relate particular indications (symptoms, test scores, or personal characteristics such as age, gender, and medical history) with particular outcomes. Expert systems, which were described in Chapter 9, make use of the actuarial method. The actuarial method was first devised for the purposes of setting the rates for insurance policies. For example, an insurer can estimate a person's longevity by knowing his or her age, height, weight, sex, and health-related habits such as smoking. Although the insurer may be wrong about a particular person (for example, the person may be killed in a traffic accident or stop smoking), the predictions work very well when applied to a group of people.

What Is the Evidence? Of course, mental health professionals are asked to make predictions about an *individual,* not a group of people. Does the actuarial method work well in such a case? According to scientific research on the subject, the answer is yes.

For a fair comparison between clinical and actuarial judgments, both methods should make decisions about the same data. In addition, the eventual outcomes must be known—there must

Table 15.1 Classification of disorders in the DSM-III-R

Axis I, Clinical Syndromes

Disorders usually first evident in infancy, childhood, or adolescence
Disruptive behavior disorders
Anxiety disorders of childhood or adolescence
Eating disorders
Gender identity disorders
Tic disorders
Elimination disorders
Speech disorders not elsewhere classified
Other disorders of infancy, childhood, or adolescence

Organic mental disorders
Dementias arising in the senium and presenium
Psychoactive substance-induced organic mental disorders
[Other] organic mental disorders

* Psychoactive substance use disorders

* Schizophrenia
   * Catatonic
   * Disorganized
   * Paranoid
   * Undifferentiated
   Residual

* Delusional (paranoid) disorders

Psychotic disorders not elsewhere classified

Mood disorders
* Bipolar disorder
Depressive disorders
* Major depression
* Dysthymia
Depressive disorder not otherwise specified

Anxiety disorders (or anxiety and phobic neuroses)
* Panic disorder
   with agoraphobia
   without agoraphobia
* Agoraphobia without history of panic disorder
* Social phobia
* Simple phobia
* Obsessive-compulsive disorder
* Posttraumatic stress disorder
Generalized anxiety disorder
Anxiety disorder not otherwise specified

Somatoform disorders
Body dysmorphic disorder
* Conversion disorder (or hysterical neurosis, conversion type)
* Hypochondriasis (or hypochondriacal neurosis)
* Somatization disorder
Somatoform pain disorder
Undifferentiated somatoform disorder
Somatoform disorder not otherwise specified

Dissociative disorders (or hysterical neurosis, dissociative type)
* Multiple personality disorder
* Psychogenic fugue
* Psychogenic amnesia
Depersonalization disorder (or depersonalization neurosis)
Dissociative disorder not otherwise specified

Sexual disorders
Paraphilias
Sexual dysfunctions
Other sexual disorders

Sleep disorders
Dyssomnias
Parasomnias

Factitious disorders

Impulse control disorders not elsewhere classified

Adjustment disorder

Axis II, Developmental Disorders and Personality Disorders

Developmental disorders
Mental retardation
Pervasive developmental disorders
Specific developmental disorders
   Academic skills disorders
   Language and speech disorders
   Motor skills disorders

Personality disorder
Cluster A
   Paranoid
   Schizoid
   Schizotypal

Cluster B
   * Antisocial
   Borderline
   Histrionic
   Narcissistic

Cluster C
Avoidant
Dependent
Obsessive compulsive
Passive aggressive
Personality disorder not otherwise specified

be a way to determine which judgments are right and which are wrong (Meehl, 1954). Goldberg (1970) performed one of the first studies to make such a comparison in the realm of clinical psychology. He analyzed the relation between patients' scores on the MMPI and the diagnoses they finally received when they were discharged from mental institutions. (You will recall from Chapter 14 that the MMPI, or Minnesota Multiphasic Personality Inventory, is extensively used in the diagnosis of mental disorders.) Goldberg found that a single rule effectively discriminated between people who were judged psychotic and those who were judged neurotic: Add the scores from three of the scales of the MMPI (L, Pa, and Sc) and subtract the scores from two others (Hy and Pt). If the score exceeds 45 points, the person is diagnosed as psychotic.

Goldberg obtained the MMPI scores of 861 patients and sent them to 239 clinicians (experts and novices) who made a diagnosis based on the information. The judges were correct 62 percent of the time, on the average. The best judge was correct on 67 percent of the cases. The simple actuarial rule was superior; it was correct 70 percent of the time, which was better than the best of the expert human judges.

Leli and Filskov (1984) compared clinical and actuarial judgments on an important diagnosis—the presence of a progressive brain dysfunction, such as Alzheimer's disease. As you can imagine, telling a family that one of its members does or does not have such a disorder has important consequences. The investigators used statistical methods to predict the presence of the disorder from scores on tests of intellectual abilities and were able to correctly identify 83 percent of the cases. Experienced clinicians who used the same information to make clinical judgments were correct only 58 percent of the time.

According to Dawes, Faust, and Meehl (1989), over a hundred studies have compared actuarial and clinical judgments in the social sciences, and almost every one has shown actuarial judgment to be superior. The criterion measures predicted in these studies include college grades, parole violations, responses to particular forms of therapy, length of psychiatric hospitalization, and violent behavior. As Meehl (1986) notes, "There is no controversy in social science that shows such a large body of qualitatively diverse studies coming out so uniformly . . . as this one" (p. 373).

Why Is the Actuarial Method More Accurate? There are several reasons why actuarial judgments tend to be more accurate than clinical judgments. First, their reliability is always higher. Because a decision is based on a precise formula, the actuarial method always produces the same judgment for a particular set of data. On the other hand, an expert making a clinical judgment may make different decisions about the same set of data on different occasions (Fries et al., 1986). Experts may become tired, their judgment may be influenced by some recent cases they were involved in, or the order in which the information is presented to them may affect which items they consider in making their decision.

Another reason for inaccuracy in clinical judgment is the fact that the human brain has difficulty sifting through a mass of data and retaining useful information while discarding useless or unreliable information. Also, clinicians often do not receive feedback about the accuracy of their judgments; or if they do receive it, the feedback comes after a long period of time. Thus, they do not receive the information they need to decide which pieces of evidence they should consider in making their decisions. It is difficult for them to update their decision rules.

In Chapter 9 we saw that when people make decisions they usually follow heuristic rules. As we will see in Chapter 17, these rules can lead people astray. For example, we tend to pay too much attention to particularly striking cases and to underutilize valuable information about the incidence of particular pieces of evidence. Also, we all have a natural tendency to pay too much attention to information that is consistent with our own hypothesis and to ignore or minimize contradictory information (Greenwald et al., 1986). These tendencies interfere with our ability to make appropriate inferences.

Some advocates of clinical judgment assert that only an expert can detect those cases where the rules do not apply. For example, suppose that an actuarial method can use certain pieces of information to predict whether a person is likely to perform a particular behavior. Suppose further that we observe the person and notice that he or she currently has a broken leg. Knowing this, we declare that all bets are off; we know that certain types of behavior are now impossible (Meehl, 1957). But some experiments have permitted clinicians to use additional evidence to decide whether they will accept or contradict actuarial predictions. Such studies have shown that the accuracy of the experts' predictions goes down to the extent that they try to intervene; as Dawes, Faust, and Meehl

(1989) put it, "When operating freely, clinicians apparently identify too many 'exceptions' " (p. 1671).

Why Do Some Practitioners Prefer the Clinical Method? More and more mental health professionals are using the actuarial method for diagnosis. For example, consulting firms have developed actuarial methods for scoring tests such as the MMPI or the Rorschach. Clinicians can send the raw scores to these firms and receive a report, or they can purchase a program for their own computer that will analyze the data on the spot.

However, most mental health professionals still use clinical methods of prediction more than actuarial methods. According to a survey of psychologists involved in assessing the possibility that a patient has brain damage (Guilmette et al., 1989), most of the respondents prefer using tests and diagnostic procedures for which actuarial methods have *not* been developed. These findings suggest that some clinicians *avoid* the actuarial method. According to Dawes, Faust, and Meehl (1989), some clinicians simply do not know about the research showing the superiority of the actuarial method. Others consider it dehumanizing; they believe that the method ignores the fact that each person is unique. (Of course, if each person were absolutely unique, then even the clinical method would not work; an expert could make *no* predictions about an individual.) And perhaps experts prefer to use their own judgment for a perfectly understandable (and very human) reason: They find it difficult to believe that their diagnostic skills, developed through a long period of training and practice, can be duplicated by a formula (or by the operations of a computer program).

What Should We Conclude? Scientific studies have shown clinical judgments to be consistently inferior to actuarial judgments. What do these results say about the role clinicians should play in trying to make predictions? First, it is clear that clinicians play an essential role in making the measurements and in identifying new variables that may be important predictors. After all, the actuarial approach must have useful data if it is to work. For example, we humans are unexcelled in our ability to recognize complex visual patterns such as facial expressions, subtle indications of emotion in tones of voice and choice of words, and alterations in posture, gestures, or style of walking. Only humans are able to see these features, which often provide useful information for diagnostic purposes.

But perhaps experts should concentrate their efforts on what they do best and what a formula cannot do: observing people's behavior, developing new and useful measurements, and providing therapy. After all, helping people is a clinician's most important role. Perhaps routine diagnosis—a time-consuming activity—should be left to the actuarial method in those cases where it has been shown to be superior. ■

INTERIM SUMMARY

Classification and Diagnosis

Although clinical diagnosis is influenced by social norms, we should not abandon the attempt; the value of classification and diagnosis lies in the potential identification of disorders with common causes. Once disorders are classified, research can be carried out with the goal of finding useful therapies. The principal classification scheme in North America for mental disorders is the DSM-III-R, which provides explicit criteria for diagnosing these disorders.

Clinical judgments, such as diagnoses and predictions about a person's behavior, require the collection and interpretation of information. The interpretation can use the clinical method or the actuarial method. The clinical method is that of an expert who uses his or her experience and judgment to make a decision. The actuarial method is based on a statistical analysis of the relation between different items of information and clinical outcomes. Although research has consistently found the actuarial method to be superior, many clinicians do not use it. Some psychologists believe that clinicians should concentrate on developing new measures and making observations of behavior that only humans can make—and then employ actuarial methods to find the best ways to use the data they collect. ■

NONPSYCHOTIC MENTAL DISORDERS

Nonpsychotic mental disorders used to be called *neuroses*—and often still are. Most **neuroses** are strategies of perception and behavior that have gotten out of hand. They are characterized by pathological increases in anxiety and/or by defense mechanisms applied too rigidly, so that they have become maladaptive. Neurotic people are anxious, fearful, depressed, and generally unhappy. However, unlike people who are afflicted with psychoses, they do not suffer from delusions or severely disordered thought processes. Furthermore, *they almost universally realize that they have a problem;* most neurotics are only too aware that their strategies for coping with the world are not working.

Neurotic behavior is usually characterized by avoidance rather than confrontation of problems. People with neuroses turn to imaginary illnesses, oversleeping, or convenient forgetfulness to avoid having to confront stressful situations. Even normal people sometimes use these strategies. Any teacher can attest that a disproportionate number of students seem to be struck by illness and other emergencies just before examination time. But for most neurotic people avoidance is a way of life. People with serious neuroses tend to limit their functioning severely through overdependence on their maladaptive strategies, and the increasing hopelessness of their situation makes them cling even more tenaciously to self-defeating patterns of behavior. Eventually, they may turn to someone for help in their despair.

Anxiety Disorders

3 Several important types of mental disorders are classified as anxiety disorders, with fear and anxiety as the salient symptoms. Previously, these disorders were referred to as the *anxiety neuroses* and the *phobic neuroses.* However, research indicates that the primary characteristic of these disorders is anxiety. This section examines three important anxiety disorders: panic disorder, phobic disorders, and obsessive compulsive disorder.

Panic Disorder: Description. People with **panic disorder** suffer from episodic attacks of acute anxiety—periods of acute and unremitting terror that grip them for variable lengths of time, from a few seconds to a few hours. The estimated incidence of panic disorder is between 1 and 2 percent of the population (Robbins et al., 1984). Women are approximately twice as likely as men to suffer from panic disorder. The disorder usually has its onset in young adulthood; it rarely begins after age thirty-five (Woodruff, Guze, and Clayton, 1972).

Panic attacks include many physical symptoms, such as shortness of breath, clammy sweat, irregularities in heartbeat, dizziness, faintness, and feelings of unreality. The victim of a panic attack often feels that he or she is going to die. Leon (1977) described a 38-year-old man who suffered frequent panic attacks.

During the times when he was experiencing intense anxiety, it often seemed as if he were having a heart seizure. He experienced chest pains and heart palpitations, numbness, shortness of breath, and he felt a strong need to breathe in air. He reported that in the midst of the anxiety attack, he developed a feeling of tightness over his eyes and he could only see objects directly in front of him (tunnel vision). He further stated that he feared that he would not be able to swallow.

. . . The intensity of the anxiety symptoms was very frightening to him and on two occasions his wife had rushed him to a local hospital because he was in a state of panic, sure that his heart was going to stop beating and he would die. His symptoms were relieved after he was given an injection of tranquilizer medication. . . . He began to note the location of doctor's offices and hospitals in whatever vicinity he happened to be . . . and he became extremely anxious if medical help were not close by. (Leon, 1977, pp. 112, 117)

Between panic attacks, people with panic disorder tend to suffer from **anticipatory anxiety;** because attacks can occur without apparent cause, these people anxiously worry about when the next one might strike them. Sometimes, a panic attack that occurs in a particular situation can cause the person to fear that situation; that is, a panic attack can cause a phobia, presumably through classical conditioning. (As we shall see, most researchers believe that agoraphobia—described in the next section—is caused by fear of panic attacks.) Anxiety is a normal reaction to many stresses of life, and none of us is completely free from it. In fact, anxiety is undoubtedly useful in causing us to be more alert and to take important things seriously. However, the anxiety we all feel from time to time is obviously different from the intense fear and terror experienced by a person gripped by a panic attack.

Panic Disorder: Possible Causes. Of all the nonpsychotic disorders discussed in this chapter, panic disorder is the least adaptive, which makes it difficult to explain. Because the physical symptoms of panic attacks are so overwhelming, many patients reject the suggestion that they have a mental disorder, insisting that their problem is medical. In fact, they may be correct: A considerable amount of evidence suggests that panic disorder may have biological origins. First, the disorder appears to be hereditary; there is a higher concordance rate for the disorder between identical twins than between fraternal twins (Torgerson, 1983), and almost

30 percent of the first-degree relatives of a person with panic disorder also have panic disorder (Crowe et al., 1983). (*First-degree relatives* are a person's parents, children, and siblings.) According to Crowe et al., (1987), the pattern of panic disorder within a family tree suggests that the disorder is caused by a single, dominant gene.

Panic attacks can be triggered in people with a history of panic disorder by giving them injections of lactic acid (a by-product of muscular activity) or by having them breathe air containing an elevated amount of carbon dioxide (Woods et al., 1988; Cowley and Arana, 1990). People with a family history of panic attack are more likely to react to sodium lactate, even if they have never had a panic attack previously (Balon et al., 1989). Some researchers believe that what is inherited is a tendency to react with alarm to bodily sensations that would not disturb most other people. In any event, as we shall see in Chapter 16, panic disorder is often treated successfully with drugs.

Phobic Disorders: Description. Phobias—named after the Greek god *Phobos,* who frightened one's enemies—are irrational fears of specific objects or situations. Because phobias can be so specific, clinicians have coined a variety of inventive names. (See *Table 15.2.*)

Almost all of us have one or more irrational fears of specific objects or situations, and it is difficult to draw a line between these fears and phobic disorders. If someone is afraid of spiders but manages to lead a normal life by avoiding them, it would seem inappropriate to say that the person has a mental disorder. Similarly, many otherwise normal people are afraid of speaking in public. The term **phobic disorder** should be reserved for people whose fear makes their life difficult. One of the diagnostic criteria of the DSM-III-R is "significant distress because of the disturbance."

The DSM-III-R recognizes three types of phobic disorders: agoraphobia, social phobia, and simple phobia. **Agoraphobia** (*agora* means "open space") is the most serious of these disorders. Most cases of agoraphobia are considered to be caused by panic attacks and are classified along with them. Agoraphobia associated with panic attacks is defined as a fear of "being in places or situations from which escape might be difficult (or embarrassing) or in which help might not be available in the event of a panic attack. . . . As a result of this fear, the person either restricts travel or needs a companion when away from home." Agoraphobia can be

Table 15.2 Names and descriptions of some phobias

Name	Object or Situation Feared
Acrophobia	Heights
Agoraphobia	Open spaces
Ailurophobia	Cats
Algophobia	Pain
Astraphobia	Storms, thunder, lightning
Belonophobia	Needles
Claustrophobia	Enclosed spaces
Hematophobia	Blood
Monophobia	Being alone
Mysophobia	Contamination or germs
Nyctophobia	Darkness
Ochlophobia	Crowds
Pathophobia	Disease
Pyrophobia	Fire
Siderophobia	Railways
Syphilophobia	Syphilis
Taphophobia	Being buried alive
Triskaidekaphobia	Thirteen
Zoophobia	Animals, or a specific animal

severely disabling; some people with this disorder have stayed inside their houses or apartments for years, afraid to venture outside.

Social phobia is an exaggerated "fear of one or more situations . . . in which the person is exposed to possible scrutiny by others and fears that he or she may do something or act in a way that will be humiliating or embarrassing." Most people with social phobia are only mildly impaired. **Simple phobia** includes all other phobias, such as fear of snakes, darkness, or heights. They are often caused by a specific traumatic experience. Simple phobias are the easiest of all types of phobias to treat.

The incidence of agoraphobia is approximately 5 percent and that of simple phobia is approximately 10 percent (Robbins et al., 1984), but approximately a third of the population sometimes exhibit phobic symptoms (Goodwin and Guze, 1984). Both males and females are equally likely to exhibit social phobia, but females are more likely to develop agoraphobia or simple phobias. Phobias that begin to develop in childhood or early adolescence (primarily simple phobias) are likely to disappear, whereas those that begin to develop after adolescence are likely to endure. Social phobia tends to begin during the teenage years, whereas agoraphobia tends to begin during a person's middle or late twenties. These disorders rarely have their first appearance after age thirty.

Phobic Disorder: Possible Causes. Psychoanalytical theory attributes phobias to distress caused by intolerable unconscious impulses, such as an unresolved Oedipus or Electra complex. Whether or not this theory is true, almost all psychoanalysts and behaviorists believe that phobias are learned by means of classical conditioning—direct or vicarious. *Direct classical conditioning* occurs when a particular animal or object is present in an especially unpleasant situation. *Vicarious classical conditioning* occurs when a person observes another person (especially a parent or someone else to whom the person is closely attached) show fright in the presence of a particular animal or object. (Chapter 6 discussed classical conditioning at some length.)

To say that phobias are learned through classical conditioning does not explain this disorder completely. Many people have traumatic, frightening experiences, but few of them go on to develop phobic disorders; thus, it appears that not all people are likely to develop a phobia. Also, many people with phobias do not remember having had specific experiences with the objects they fear earlier in life. (Of course, they may have simply forgotten the experiences.) In addition, some objects are more likely to be feared than others; people tend to fear animals (especially snakes, spiders, dogs, or rodents), blood, heights, closed spaces, and air travel. They are less likely to fear automobiles or electrical outlets, which are potentially more dangerous than some of the common objects of phobias, such as snakes or spiders. Some investigators suggest that a tendency to develop a fear of certain kinds of stimuli may have a biological basis that reflects the evolution of our species. For example, chimpanzees raised in captivity will show signs of fear when they are shown a snake, even though they have had no previous experience with this animal. Öhman, Erixon, and Löfberg (1975) obtained results that support this suggestion. They showed subjects pictures of snakes, houses, and people's faces and gave them a painful electric shock after seeing one of the categories. All subjects showed a conditioned emotional response (change in skin resistance) when tested with the stimuli afterward. Next, they presented the pictures several times without the shock. The emotional responses conditioned to the houses or the faces quickly extinguished, but those conditioned to the snakes were relatively long lasting.

Lacey and Lacey (1962) suggested that some people's autonomic nervous systems are particularly reactive to unpleasant environmental stimuli and that this reactivity predisposes them to developing phobias. As we saw in the previous section, panic disorder, which often causes agoraphobia, appears to be a heritable trait. In contrast, simple or social phobias do not appear to run in families (Goodwin, 1983). The most important predisposing factor for developing these phobic disorders may be environmental; people who develop them tend to be from stable families with overprotective mothers (Goodwin and Guze, 1984).

As we will see in Chapter 16, the same classes of drugs useful in treating panic attacks also reduce the symptoms of agoraphobia. However, the most long-lasting results are obtained from behavior therapy.

Obsessive Compulsive Disorder: Description. As the name implies, people with an **obsessive compulsive disorder** suffer from **obsessions**—thoughts that will not leave them—and **compulsions**—behaviors that they cannot keep from performing. Unlike people with panic disorder, obsessive compulsives have a defense against anxiety—namely, their compulsive behavior. Unfortunately, the need

A person with acrophobia (fear of heights) would certainly not want this man's job.

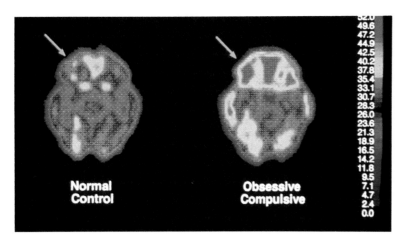

These PET scans indicate that the metabolism of the orbitofrontal cortex is higher in a person with an obsessive compulsive disorder than in a control subject.

to perform this behavior often becomes more and more demanding on their time, until it interferes with their careers and daily lives. Obsessions are seen in a variety of mental disorders, including schizophrenia. However, unlike schizophrenics, people with obsessive compulsive disorder recognize that their thoughts and behaviors are senseless and wish that they would go away.

The incidence of obsessive compulsive disorder is approximately 2 percent. Females are slightly more likely to have this diagnosis. Like panic disorder, obsessive compulsive disorder most commonly begins in young adulthood (Robbins et al., 1984). People with this disorder are unlikely to marry, perhaps because of the common obsessional fear of dirt and contamination or because the shame associated with the rituals they are compelled to perform causes them to avoid social contact (Turner, Beidel, and Nathan, 1985).

There are two principal kinds of obsessions: obsessive *doubt or uncertainty,* and obsessive *fear of doing something prohibited.* We all experience doubts about future activities (such as whether to look for a new job, eat at one restaurant or another, wear a raincoat or take an umbrella) and about past activities (such as whether one has turned off the coffeepot and whether one should have worn dressier clothes). But these uncertainties, both trivial and important, preoccupy some obsessive compulsives almost completely. Others are plagued with the fear that they will do something terrible—swear aloud in church, urinate in someone's living room, kill themselves or a loved one, or jump off a bridge—although they seldom actually do anything antisocial. And even though

they are often obsessed with thoughts of killing themselves, fewer than 1 percent of them actually attempt suicide.

Obsessions are thoughts; compulsions are actual behaviors. Klein and Howard (1972) described the following case:

> He felt a compulsive, irrational need to look into a mirror and stare into his eyes, feeling that they were "stiff." . . . Striving to cease staring at his eyes, he painted over all the mirrors in his house. But then he began to look for dirt in the indentations of his hands. When he no longer could tolerate this, he wore gloves, but became obsessed with the thought of the dirt that might be in the glove stitching. Then he had to stare at his trousers and shoes, check his socks and shoelaces, count the holes in his belt, straighten his underwear, and determine if his eyebrows were straight. The time spent performing these rituals increased from minutes to hours a day. He constantly thought about committing suicide. (Klein and Howard, 1972, p. 209)

Most compulsions fall into one of four categories: *counting, checking, cleaning,* and *avoidance.* For example, people might repeatedly check burners on the stove to see that they are off and windows and doors to be sure they are locked. Some people wash their hands hundreds of times a day, even when they become covered with painful sores. Other people meticulously clean their apartment or endlessly wash, dry, and fold their clothes. Some become afraid to leave home because they fear contamination and refuse to touch other members of their family. If they do accidentally become "contaminated," they usually have lengthy purification rituals. The case of Bess, described in the opening vignette, is a typical example.

Some investigators believe that the compulsive behaviors seen in obsessive compulsive disorder are forms of species-typical behavioral tendencies—for example, grooming, cleaning, and attention toward sources of potential danger—that are released from normal control mechanisms by a brain dysfunction (Wise and Rapoport, 1988).

Obsessive Compulsive Disorder: Possible Causes. Several possible causes have been suggested for obsessive compulsive disorder. Unlike simple anxiety states, this disorder can be understood in terms of defense mechanisms. Some investigators have suggested that obsessions serve as devices to occupy the mind and displace painful thoughts. This strategy is seen in normal behavior: A person who "psychs himself up" before a competitive event by telling himself about his skill and stamina is also keeping out self-defeating doubts and fears. Like Scarlett O'Hara in *Gone with the Wind,* who repeatedly told herself, "I'll think about it tomorrow," we all say, at one time or another, "Oh, I'll think about something else" when our thoughts become painful.

If painful, anxiety-producing thoughts become frequent, and if turning to alternative patterns of thought reduces anxiety, then the principle of reinforcement predicts that the person will turn to these patterns more frequently. Just as an animal learns to jump a hurdle to escape a painful foot shock, a person can learn to think about a "safe topic" in order to avoid painful thoughts. If the habit becomes firmly established, the obsessive thoughts may persist even after the original reason for turning to them—the situation that produced the anxiety-arousing thoughts—no longer exists. A habit can thus outlast its original causes.

Evidence is beginning to accumulate suggesting that obsessive compulsive disorder may have a genetic origin. Family studies have found that this disorder is associated with another disorder called Tourette's syndrome, which appears during childhood (Pauls et al., 1986). **Tourette's syndrome** is characterized by muscular and vocal tics, including making facial grimaces, squatting, pacing, twirling, barking, sniffing, coughing, grunting, or repeating specific words (especially vulgarities). Pauls and his colleagues believe that the two disorders are produced by the same single, dominant gene. It is not clear why some people with the faulty gene develop Tourette's syndrome early in childhood and others develop obsessive compulsive disorder later in life.

Not all cases of obsessive compulsive disorder have a genetic origin; the disorder sometimes occurs after brain damage caused by various means, such as birth trauma, encephalitis, and head trauma (Hollander et al., 1990). As we shall see in Chapter 16, obsessive compulsive disorder has been treated by psychosurgery, by drugs, and by behavior therapy. These treatments are sometimes effective, but the disorder often persists despite the efforts of experienced therapists.

Somatoform Disorders

[4] The primary symptoms of **somatoform disorder** are physical (*soma* means "body"). The two most important somatoform disorders are somatization disorder and conversion disorder.

Somatization Disorder: Description. **Somatization disorder** used to be called *hysteria.* The older term derives from the Greek word *hystera,* meaning "uterus," because of the ancient belief that various emotional and physical ailments in women could be caused by the uterus, which wandered around inside the body, searching for a baby. (As a remedy, Hippocrates recommended marriage.) It is true that somatization disorder is almost exclusively seen in women; however, modern use of the term *hysteria* does not imply any gynecological problems. Regier et al. (1988) found that the incidence of somatization disorder in a sample of over eighteen thousand people was less than 1 percent in women and nonexistent in men. In fact, almost all males who have been diagnosed as having somatization disorders have been involved in legal disputes about compensation for injuries or disability; thus, their symptoms may have been prompted by financial gain (Rounsaville, Harding, and Weissman, 1979). Somatization disorder is often chronic, lasting for decades.

Somatization disorder is characterized by complaints of symptoms for which no physiological cause can be found. Obviously, a proper diagnosis can be made only after medical examination and laboratory tests indicate the lack of disease. The DSM-III-R requires that the person have a history of complaining of physical symptoms for several years. The complaints must include at least thirteen symptoms from a list of thirty-five, which fall into the following categories: gastrointestinal symptoms, pain symptoms, cardiopulmonary symptoms, pseudoneurological symptoms, sexual symptoms, and female reproductive symptoms. These symptoms must also have led the person to take medication, see a physician, or substantially alter his or her life. Almost every woman who receives the diagnosis of somatization disorder reports that she does not experience pleasure from sexual intercourse. Obviously, everyone has one or more physical symptoms from time to time that cannot be explained through a medical examination, but few people chronically complain of at least thirteen of them. Although people with somatization disorder often make suicide attempts, they rarely actually kill themselves.

Somatization disorder resembles another somatoform disorder, **hypochondriasis** *(hypochondria* means "under the cartilage"). Greek physicians thought that the disorder occurred when black bile collected under the breastbone, which is made of cartilage. Unlike people with somatization disorder, who complain of specific physical symptoms, hypochondriacs demonstrate an excessive fear of illness. They interpret minor physical sensations as indications they may have a serious disease. They spend a lot of time in physicians' offices and in hospitals. Figure 15.2 shows the incidence of major operations performed on people with somatization disorder, medically ill control subjects, and healthy control subjects. As you can see, people with somatization disorder underwent an impressive number of operations, beginning after adolescence. (See *Figure 15.2.*)

Somatization Disorder: Possible Causes.
Somatization disorder is most common in poorly educated women of low socioeconomic status (Guze, Woodruff, and Clayton, 1971). The disorder also runs in families; Coryell (1980) found that approximately 20 percent of first-degree female relatives of people with somatization disorder also had the disorder. In addition, many studies have shown that somatization disorder is closely associated with antisocial personality disorder (which will be described in a later section). First-degree male relatives of women with somatization disorder have an increased incidence of alcoholism or antisocial behavior, and first-degree female relatives of convicted male criminals have an increased incidence of somatization disorder (Guze et al., 1967; Woerner and

Guze, 1968). These results suggest that a particular environmental or genetic history leads to different pathological manifestations in men and women. Hereditary factors appear to play at least a partial role; Cadoret (1978) observed a relation between somatization disorder and antisocial behavior in first-degree relatives who were raised in different households.

Conversion Disorder: Description. Conversion disorder (formerly called *hysterical neurosis, conversion type)* is characterized by physical complaints that resemble neurological disorders but have no underlying organic pathological basis. The symptoms include blindness, deafness, loss of feeling, and paralysis. Some investigators refer to these conditions as *pseudoneurological* disorders. According to the DSM-III-R, a conversion disorder must have some apparent psychological reason for the symptoms; they must occur in response to an environmental stimulus that produces a psychological conflict, or they must permit the person to avoid an unpleasant activity or to receive support and sympathy. Unlike somatization disorder, conversion disorder can afflict both men and women.

The term *conversion,* when applied to a mental disorder, derives from psychoanalytical theory, which states that the energy of an unresolved psychic conflict is converted into a physical symptom. Hofling (1963) described a case:

> The patient had taken the day off from work to be at home with his wife and [newborn] baby. During the afternoon, he had felt somewhat nervous and tense, but had passed off these feelings as normal for a new father. . . .
>
> . . . The baby awoke and cried. Mrs. L. said that she would nurse him. . . . As she put the baby to her breast, the patient became aware of a smarting sensation in his eyes. He had been smoking heavily and attributed the irritation to the room's being filled with smoke. He got up and opened a window. When the smarting sensation became worse he went to the washstand and applied a cold cloth to his eyes. On removing the cloth, he found that he was completely blind. . . .
>
> . . . Psychotherapy was instituted. . . . The visual symptoms disappeared rather promptly, with only very mild and fleeting exacerbations during the next several months. . . .
>
> . . . He had been jealous of the baby—this was a difficult admission to make—and jealous on two distinct counts. One feeling was, in essence, a sexual jealousy, accentuated by his

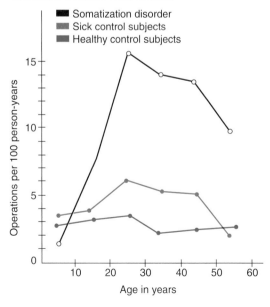

Figure 15.2 Major operations for healthy control subjects, sick control subjects, and people with somatization disorder. (From Cohen, M.E., Robins, E., Purtell, J.J., Altmann, M.W., and Reid, D.E. *Journal of the American Medical Association,* 1953, *151,* 977–986. Copyright 1953, American Medical Association.)

own sexual deprivation during the last weeks of the pregnancy. The other was . . . a jealousy of the maternal solicitude shown the infant by its mother. (Hofling, 1963, pp. 315–316)

Although the sensory deficits or paralyses of people with conversion disorders do not result from damage to the nervous system, these people are not faking their illnesses. People who deliberately pretend they are sick in order to gain some advantage (such as avoiding work) are said to be **malingering.** Malingering is not defined as a mental disorder by the DSM-III-R. Although it is not always easy to distinguish malingering from a conversion disorder, two criteria are useful. First, people with a conversion disorder are usually delighted to talk about their symptoms in great detail, whereas malingerers are reluctant to do so, for fear of having their deception discovered. Second, people with a conversion disorder usually describe the symptoms with great drama and flair but do *not* appear to be upset about them. This blasé attitude is so striking that it has been called *la belle indifférence,* ("fine unconcern").

Conversion disorders must also be distinguished from somatization disorder and psychophysiological disorders. As we just saw, somatization disorder consists of complaints of medical problems, but the examining physician is unable to see any signs that would indicate physical illness. In contrast, a patient with conversion disorder gives the appearance of having a neurological disorder such as blindness or paralysis. **Psychophysiological disorders** (also called *psychosomatic disorders*) are not the result of fictitious or imaginary symptoms; they are real organic illnesses caused or made worse by psychological factors. For example, stress can cause gastric ulcers, asthma, or other physical symptoms; ulcers caused by stress are real, not imaginary. Successful therapy would thus require reduction of the person's level of stress as well as surgical or medical treatment of the lesions in the stomach.

The particular physical symptoms of people with conversion disorders change with the times and with people's general sophistication. For example, around the turn of the century patients commonly developed "glove" or "stocking" anesthesias, in which the skin over their hands or feet would become perfectly numb. It is physiologically impossible for these anesthesias to occur as a result of nerve damage; the patterns of anesthesia produced by organic means would be very different. Today people seldom suffer such a naive disorder. (See *Figure 15.3.*)

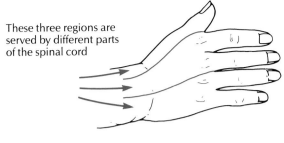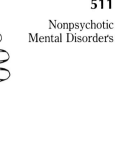

These three regions are served by different parts of the spinal cord

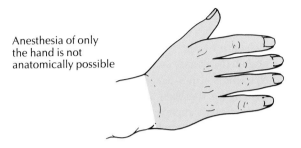

Anesthesia of only the hand is not anatomically possible

Figure 15.3 Glove anesthesia, a conversion disorder that was common many years ago.

Because conversion disorders can affect any part of the body, clinicians must distinguish between organic illness and conversion disorders. An organic illness can be mistaken for a conversion disorder, and there is nothing to prevent a person with a conversion disorder from also having an organic illness. Whitlock (1967) examined the subsequent medical history of patients diagnosed as having conversion disorders and found that more than 60 percent of them later were found to have organic diseases, in contrast to 5 percent of people with other types of mental disorders. The ailments of the people with conversion disorders included head injury (received before diagnosis), stroke, encephalitis, and brain tumors.

Conversion Disorder: Possible Causes. Psychoanalytical theory suggests that the psychic energy of unresolved conflicts (especially those involving sexual desires the patient is unwilling or unable to admit to having) becomes displaced into physical symptoms. In other words, psychoanalysts regard conversion disorders as primarily sexual in origin.

Behaviorists have suggested that conversion disorders can be learned for a variety of reasons. This assertion gains support from the finding that people with these disorders usually suffer from physical symptoms of diseases with which they are already familiar (Ullman and Krasner, 1969). A patient often mimics the symptoms of a friend. Furthermore, the patient must receive some kind of reinforcement for having the disability; he or she must derive some benefit from it.

Ullman and Krasner cited a case that was originally reported by Brady and Lind (1961). A soldier developed an eye problem that led to his discharge, along with a small disability pension. He worked at a series of menial jobs, returning periodically to the hospital for treatment of his eye condition. He applied for a larger disability pension several times but was turned down because his vision had not become worse. After twelve years the man, who was currently being forced by his wife and mother-in-law to spend his spare evenings and weekends doing chores around the house, suddenly became "blind." Because of his total disability, he was given special training for the blind and received a larger pension. He also received a family allowance from the community and no longer had to work around the house. In this case both criteria described by Ullman and Krasner were fulfilled: The patient was familiar with the disorder (indeed, he had a real eye disorder) and his symptoms were reinforced.

Dissociative Disorders

5 **Description.** Like *conversion disorder,* the term *dissociative disorder* comes from Freud; the original name of the disorder was *hysterical neurosis, dissociative type.* According to psychoanalytical theory, a person develops a **dissociative disorder** when a massive repression fails to keep a strong sexual desire from consciousness. As a result, the person resorts to dissociating one part of his or her mind from the rest.

The most common dissociative disorder is **psychogenic amnesia,** in which a person "forgets" all his or her past life, along with the conflicts that were present, and begins a new one. The term *psychogenic* means "produced by the mind." Because amnesia can also be produced by physical means—such as epilepsy, drug or alcohol intoxication, or brain damage—clinicians must be careful to distinguish between amnesias of organic and psychogenic origin. Any person with amnesia must undergo a complete neurological examination and appropriate laboratory tests.

A **psychogenic fugue** (pronounced *fyoog*) is a special form of amnesia in which the person leaves and starts a new life elsewhere (*fugue* means "flight"). Henderson and Gillespie (1950) reported the following case of psychogenic amnesia compounded by fugue:

A clergyman, the Rev. Ansell Bourne, disappeared from a town in Rhode Island. Eight weeks later a man calling himself A.J. Brown, who had rented a small shop six weeks previously in a town in Pennsylvania and had stocked it with confectionery, etc., woke up in a fright and asked who he was. He said he was a clergyman, that his name was Bourne, and that he knew nothing of the shop or of Brown. He was subsequently identified as the Rev. Ansell Bourne by his relatives, and remained terrified by the incident and unable to explain it. (Henderson and Gillespie, 1950, p. 192)

Multiple personality disorder is a very rare, but very striking, dissociative disorder. The DSM-III-R defines this condition as "the existence within the individual of two or more distinct personalities, each of which is dominant at a particular time." In addition, "each individual personality is complex and integrated with its own unique behavior patterns and social relationships." Only about a hundred cases of multiple personality have been documented, and some investigators believe that many, if not most of them, are simulations, not actual mental disorders. In one well-publicized case (the "Hill-

Kenneth Bianchi, the "Hillside strangler," was believed to be faking a multiple personality disorder to escape punishment for the murders he committed.

side strangler") the person was shown to be faking a multiple personality disorder in an attempt to escape punishment for having committed several brutal murders. In fact, the murderer had an antisocial personality disorder (described in the next section of this chapter). Multiple personality disorder has received much attention; people find it fascinating to contemplate several different personalities, most of whom are unaware of each other, existing within the same individual.

Bliss (1980) suggests that multiple personality disorder is a form of self-hypnosis, established early in life, which is motivated by painful experiences. In fact, the overwhelming majority of people diagnosed to have multiple personality disorder report having been physically abused when they were children (Kluft, 1984). These people also tend to be easily hypnotized (Bliss, 1983).

As we saw in Chapter 8, some psychologists believe that hypnosis is not a state but, rather, a form of social role playing. The same has been said for multiple personality disorder. Spanos, Weekes, and Bertrand (1985) found that when normal subjects were given appropriate instructions, they could easily simulate two different personalities. They adopted a new name for the new personality, and they gave different patterns of answers on a personality test when the second one was "in control." Although people are often impressed by the remarkable differences between the various personalities of someone with multiple personality disorder, the acting required for this task is within the ability of most people. That is not to say that everyone with multiple personality disorder is faking, but the results do suggest that such patients be approached with skepticism and caution.

Possible Causes. Dissociative disorders are usually explained as responses to severe conflicts resulting from intolerable impulses or responses to guilt stemming from an actual misdeed. Partly because they are rare, dissociative disorders are among the least understood of the mental disorders. In general, the dissociation is advantageous to the person. Amnesia enables the person to forget about a painful or unpleasant life. A person with fugue not only forgets but also leaves the area to start a new existence. And multiple personalities allow a person to do things that he or she would really like to do but cannot, because of the strong guilt feelings that would ensue. The alternate personality can be one with a very weak conscience.

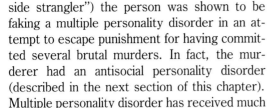

INTERIM SUMMARY

Nonpsychotic Mental Disorders

People with nonpsychotic mental disorders, previously called *neuroses,* have adopted strategies that have a certain amount of immediate payoff but in the long run are maladaptive. We can understand most of their problems as exaggerations of our own. Although their fears and doubts may be unrealistic, they do not seem bizarre and illogical. In contrast, psychoses involve obviously maladaptive features—delusions, hallucinations, disordered thought processes, and inappropriate emotional states.

Anxiety disorders include panic disorder, phobias, and obsessive compulsive disorder. All of them (except for simple phobia and social phobia) have a genetic component. Panic disorder is the least adaptive of all neurotic disorders; the person has no defense against his or her discomfort. In contrast, obsessive compulsive disorder provides thoughts or behaviors that prevent the person from thinking about painful subjects or that ward off feelings of guilt and anxiety.

Simple phobias can probably be explained by classical conditioning; some experience (usually early in life) causes a particular object or situation to become a conditioned aversive stimulus. The fear associated with this stimulus leads to escape behaviors, which are reinforced because they reduce the person's fear. Agoraphobia is a much more serious disorder, and it is apparently not caused by a specific traumatic experience. Social phobia is a fear of being observed or judged by others; in its mildest form it involves a fear of speaking in public.

Somatoform disorders include somatization disorder and conversion disorder. Somatization disorder comprises complaints of symptoms of illness without underlying physiological causes. Almost all people with this disorder are women, and almost all of them are indifferent to—or actively dislike—sexual intercourse. Conversion disorder includes specific neurological symptoms, such as paralysis or sensory disturbance, that are not produced by a physiological disorder. In most cases the patient derives some gain from his or her disability.

Dissociative disorders are rare but interesting. Psychogenic amnesia (with or without fugue) appears to be a withdrawal from a painful situation or from intolerable guilt. Because amnesia is a common symptom of brain injury or neurological disease, physical factors must be ruled out before accepting a diagnosis of psychogenic amnesia. Multiple personalities are even more rare and presumably occur because they permit a person to engage in behaviors contrary to his or her code of conduct. ∎

PERSONALITY AND PSYCHOACTIVE SUBSTANCE ABUSE DISORDERS

The DSM-III-R includes twelve personality disorders, which are abnormalities in behavior that impair social or occupational functioning. Examples include paranoid personality disorder, narcissistic personality disorder, compulsive personality disorder, and passive-aggressive personality disorder. Personality disorders are considered to be extreme forms of personality traits that lead to maladaptive behaviors or emotional distress. Psychoactive substance abuse disorders are closely related to personality disorders; in fact, many people who abuse alcohol and other drugs also have a personality disorder.

Antisocial Personality Disorder

[6] The only personality disorder I will specifically discuss here is the one that has the most impact on society: antisocial personality disorder.

Description. People have used many different terms to label what we now call **antisocial personality disorder.** Prichard (1835) used the term *moral insanity* to describe people whose intellect was normal but in whom the "moral and active principles of the mind are strongly perverted and depraved . . . and the individual is found to be incapable . . . of conducting himself with decency and propriety." Koch (1889) introduced the term *psychopathic inferiority,* which soon became simply *psychopathy* (pronounced *sy-KOP-a-thee*); a person who displayed the disorder was called a *psychopath.* The first version of the DSM (the DSM-I) used the term *sociopathic personality disturbance,* which was subsequently replaced by the present term, *antisocial personality disorder.* Most clinicians still refer to such people as *psychopaths* or *sociopaths,* and I will, too, in this section.

People with antisocial personality disorder cause a considerable amount of distress in society. Many criminals can be diagnosed as psychopaths, and most psychopaths have a record of criminal behavior. The diagnostic criteria of the DSM-III-R include evidence of at least three types of antisocial behavior before age fifteen and at least four after age eighteen. The adult forms of antisocial behavior include such things as inability to sustain consistent work behavior; lack of ability to function as a responsible parent; repeated criminal activity, such as theft, pimping, or prostitution; inability to maintain enduring attachment to a sexual partner; irritability and aggressiveness, including fights or assault; failure to honor financial obligations; impulsivity and failure to plan ahead; habitual lying or use of aliases; and consistently reckless or drunken driving. In addition to meeting at least four of these criteria, the person must have displayed a "pattern of continuous antisocial behavior in which the rights of others are violated, with no intervening period of at least five years without antisocial behavior." Clearly, these are people most of us do not want to get close to.

The incidence of antisocial personality disorder has been estimated at 4 percent among men and less than 1 percent among women (Robbins et al., 1984). However, we cannot be sure that this figure is accurate, because psychopaths do not voluntarily visit mental health professionals for help with their "problem." Indeed, most of them feel no need to change their ways. Psychopaths who are indicted for serious crimes will often be seen by psychiatrists in order to determine whether they are "sane," and some will feign mental illness so that they will be committed to a mental institution rather than to a prison. Once they reach the institution, they will quickly "recover" so that they can be released.

Cleckley (1976), one of the most prominent experts on psychopathy, has listed sixteen characteristic features of antisocial personality disorder. (See *Table 15.3.*) Cleckley's list of features provides a good picture of what most psychopaths are like. They are unconcerned for other people's feelings and suffer no remorse or guilt if their actions hurt them. Although they may be superficially charming, they do not form real friendships; thus, they often become swindlers or confidence artists. Both male and female psychopaths are sexually promiscuous from an early age, but these encounters do not seem to mean much to them. Female psychopaths tend to marry early, be unfaithful to their husbands, and soon become separated or divorced. They tend to marry other psychopaths, so their husbands' behavior is often similar to their own. Psychopaths habitually tell lies, even when there is no apparent reason for doing so, and even when the lie is likely to be discovered.

Table 15.3 Cleckley's primary characteristics of antisocial personality disorder

1. Superficial charm and good "intelligence"
2. Absence of delusions and other signs of irrational thinking
3. Absence of "nervousness" or [neurosis]
4. Unreliability
5. Untruthfulness and insincerity
6. Lack of remorse or shame
7. Inadequately motivated antisocial behavior
8. Poor judgment and failure to learn by experience
9. Pathologic egocentricity and incapacity for love
10. General poverty in major affective reactions
11. Specific loss of insight
12. Unresponsiveness in general interpersonal relations
13. Fantastic and uninviting behavior . . .
14. Suicide rarely carried out
15. Sex life impersonal, trivial, and poorly integrated
16. Failure to follow any life plan

Source: From Cleckley, H. *The Mask of Sanity,* 5th edition. St. Louis: C.V. Mosby, 1976, pp. 337–338. Reprinted with permission.

They steal things they do not need or even appear to want. When confronted with evidence of having lied or cheated, psychopaths do not act ashamed or embarrassed and usually shrug the incident off as a joke.

Psychopaths do not easily learn from experience; they tend to continue committing behaviors that get them into trouble. They also do not appear to be *driven* to perform their antisocial behaviors; instead, they usually give the impression that they are acting on a whim. When someone commits a heinous crime such as a brutal murder, normal people expect that the criminal had a reason for doing so. However, criminal psychopaths are typically unable to supply a reason more compelling than "I just felt like it." They do not show much excitement or enthusiasm about what they are doing and do not appear to derive much pleasure from life.

Psychopaths tend not to become emotionally involved with other people. The following report illustrates this lack of attachment:

> I can remember the first time in my life when I began to suspect I was a little different from most people. When I was in high school my best friend got leukemia and died and I went to his funeral. Everybody else was crying and

feeling sorry for themselves and as they were praying to get him into heaven I suddenly realized that I wasn't feeling anything at all. He was a nice guy but what the hell. That night I thought about it some more and found that I wouldn't miss my mother and father if they died and that I wasn't too nuts about my brothers and sisters for that matter. I figured there wasn't anybody I really cared for but, then, I didn't need any of them anyway so I rolled over and went to sleep. (McNeil, 1967, p. 87)

Possible Causes. Most investigators believe that the primary defects in people with antisocial personality disorder are their failure to learn to avoid aversive stimuli, their inability to form close social attachments, and their emotional unexcitability. Normal people learn not to perform behaviors that bring punishment; and if they do something that has been punished in the past, they will feel anxious and perhaps guilty. Psychopaths neither avoid these behaviors nor feel guilty about them. They are not indifferent to punishment; they simply do not change their behavior in order to avoid it. And although most psychopaths do not show signs of genuine guilt, they can make a show of remorse if they think that doing so will prevent them from being punished for their misdeeds. Normal people become attached to other people and empathize with them, sharing their moods. Although some psychopaths know how to act friendly, they do not appear to empathize with others and do not share other people's happiness or grief.

Cleckley (1976) suggested that the psychopath's defect "consists of an unawareness and a persistent lack of ability to become aware of what the most important experiences of life mean to others. . . . The major emotional accompaniments are absent or so attenuated as to count for little" (p. 371). Some investigators have hypothesized that this lack of involvement is caused by an unresponsive autonomic nervous system. If a person feels no anticipatory fear of punishment, then he or she is perhaps more likely to commit acts that normal people would be afraid to do. Similarly, if a person feels little or no emotional response to other people and to their joys and sorrows, he or she is unlikely to establish close relationships with them. Some investigators (for example, Quay, 1965) have even suggested that the criminal behavior displayed by so many psychopaths is also a result of their relative unresponsiveness; they seek thrills from criminal acts because only these acts provide enough stimulation to make them feel something.

Many experiments have found that psychopaths do show less reactivity in situations involving punishment. For example, Hare (1965) demonstrated that psychopaths show fewer signs of anticipatory fear. All subjects watched the numbers 1 through 12 appear in sequential order in the window of a device used to present visual stimuli. They were told that they would receive a very painful shock when the number 8 appeared. As Figure 15.4 shows, psychopathic subjects showed much less anticipatory responsiveness than did normal control subjects or nonpsychopathic criminals. (See *Figure 15.4.*)

A study by Schmauk (1970) showed that although psychopaths are poor at learning to avoid aversive stimuli, they readily learn to avoid a loss of an appetitive stimulus. Schmauk trained subjects on an avoidance task, using three types of aversive stimuli: a physical stimulus (a painful electrical shock), a social stimulus (the experimenter's saying "wrong"), and loss of money (the experimenter took a quarter from a pile that he had given to the subject). Control subjects, who were neither psychopaths nor criminals, readily learned the task in response to

all three types of aversive stimuli. Nonpsychopathic criminals also learned the task well, except when the motive was avoiding the aversive social stimulus; apparently, they were not very disturbed when the experimenter said "wrong." The psychopathic prisoners learned the task *only* when the motive was avoiding loss of money; they did not learn to avoid a painful electrical shock or hearing the experimenter say "wrong." Thus, we can conclude that psychopaths are perfectly capable of learning an avoidance task but that social stimuli or the fear of physical pain have little effect on their behavior.

We do not yet know what causes the deficits in emotion and empathy displayed by psychopaths. These people often (but not always) come from grossly disturbed families that contain alcoholics and other psychopaths. Christiansen (1970) found that the concordance rate for psychopathy was 36 percent for identical twins and only 12 percent for fraternal twins, which suggests a heritability of nearly 50 percent. Mednick, Gabrielli, and Hutchings (1983) examined the criminal records of men who had been adopted early in life and found that the likelihood of their being convicted of a crime was directly related to the number of convictions of their biological father. (See *Figure 15.5.*)

Psychoactive Substance Use Disorders

[7] According to the DSM-III-R, psychoactive substance use disorders include *psychoactive substance dependence,* or what is usually called "addiction," and *psychoactive substance abuse,* which is less severe but which still causes social, occupational, or medical problems.

Drug addiction is one of the most serious problems that presently faces us. Consider the disastrous effects caused by the abuse of humankind's oldest drug, alcohol: automobile accidents, fetal alcohol syndrome, cirrhosis of the liver, Korsakoff's syndrome, increased rate of heart disease, and increased rate of intracerebral hemorrhage. Smoking (nicotine addiction) greatly increases the chances of dying of lung cancer, heart attack, and stroke; and women who smoke give birth to smaller, less healthy babies. Cocaine addiction often causes psychosis, brain damage, and death from overdose; it produces babies born with brain damage and consequent psychological problems. Competition for lucrative drug markets terrorizes neighborhoods, subverts political and judicial systems, and causes many deaths. Addicts who take their drugs intravenously run a serious risk of contracting AIDS. Why do people use these

Figure 15.4 Changes in skin conductance in anticipation of a painful electric shock (at presentation of the number 8) of psychopathic prisoners, nonpsychopathic prisoners, and normal control subjects. (From Hare, R.D. *Journal of Abnormal Psychology,* 1965, 59, 367–370. Reprinted with permission of the Helen Dwight Reid Educational Foundation. Published by Heldref Publications, 1319 Eighteenth St., N. W., Washington, D.C. 20016. Copyright © 1965.)

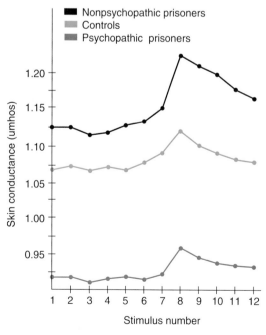

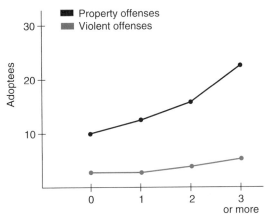

Figure 15.5 Percentage of male adoptees convicted of violent crimes or crimes against property as a function of the number of convictions of the biological father. (From Mednick, S.A., Gabrielli, W.F., and Hutchings, B., in *Prospective Studies of Crime and Delinquency,* edited by K.T. Van Dusen and S.A. Mednick. Hingham, Mass.: Martinus Nijhoff, 1983. Reprinted with permission.)

drugs and subject themselves to these dangers?

As we saw in Chapter 11 ("Motivation"), people abuse certain drugs because the drugs activate the reinforcement system of the brain, which is normally activated only by natural reinforcers, such as food, warmth, and sexual contact. Dopamine-secreting neurons are an important component of this system. Some drugs, such as crack cocaine, activate the reinforcement system rapidly and intensely, providing immediate and potent reinforcement. For many people the immediate effects outweigh the prospect of dangers that lie in the future. We also saw in Chapter 11 that although withdrawal symptoms make it more difficult for an addict to break his or her habit, these unpleasant symptoms are not responsible for the addiction itself.

Genetics of Addiction. Not everyone is equally likely to become addicted to a drug. Many people manage to drink alcohol moderately, and even many users of potent drugs such as cocaine and heroin use them "recreationally," without becoming dependent on them. There are only two possible sources of individual differences in any characteristic: heredity and environment. Obviously, environmental effects are important; people raised in a squalid environment without any real hope for a better life are more likely than other people to turn to drugs for temporary euphoria and escape from the unpleasant world that surrounds them. But

even in a given environment, poor or privileged, some people become addicts and some do not—and some of these behavioral differences are a result of genetic differences.

Most of the research on the effects of heredity on addiction have been devoted to alcoholism. One of the most important reasons for this focus—aside from the importance of the problems caused by alcohol—is that almost everyone is exposed to alcohol. Most people drink alcohol sometime in their lives and thus receive firsthand experience with its reinforcing effects. The same is not true for cocaine, heroin, and other drugs that have even more potent effects. In most countries alcohol is freely and legally available in local shops, whereas cocaine and heroin must be purchased illegally. From what we now know about the effects of addictive drugs on the nervous system, it seems likely that the results of studies on the heredity of alcoholism will apply to other types of drug addiction as well.

Alcohol consumption is not distributed equally across the population; in the United States 10 percent of the people drink 50 percent of the alcohol (Heckler, 1983). Both twin studies and adoption studies have shown that susceptibility to alcoholism is heritable. In a review of the literature on alcohol abuse Cloninger (1987) notes that there appear to be two principal types of alcoholics: those who cannot abstain but drink consistently, and those who are able to

An injection of heroin produces a euphoric "rush." The reinforcing effects of this rush can lead to addiction.

go without drinking for long periods of time but are unable to control themselves once they start. (For convenience, I will refer to these two groups as "steady drinkers" and "bingers.") Steady drinking is associated with antisocial personality disorder, discussed earlier in this chapter. Binge drinking is associated with emotional dependence, behavioral rigidity, perfectionism, introversion, and guilt feelings about one's drinking behavior. Steady drinkers usually begin their alcohol consumption early in life, whereas binge drinkers begin much later. (See *Table 15.4.*)

Steady drinking is strongly influenced by heredity. An adoption study carried out in Sweden (Cloninger et al., 1985) found that men with fathers who were steady drinkers were almost seven times more likely to become steady drinkers themselves than men whose fathers did not abuse alcohol. Family environment had no measurable effect; the boys began drinking whether or not the members of their adoptive family themselves drank heavily. Very few women become steady drinkers; the daughters of steady-drinking fathers instead tend to develop somatization disorder. Thus, the genes that predispose a man to become a steady-drinking alcoholic (antisocial type) predispose a woman to develop somatization disorder. The reason for this interaction with gender is not known.

Binge drinking is influenced *both* by heredity and by environment. The Swedish adoption study found that having a biological parent who was a binge drinker had little effect on the development of binge drinking unless the child was exposed to a family environment in which there was heavy drinking. The effect was seen in both males and females.

Causes of Addiction. When we find an effect of heredity on behavior, we have good reason to suspect the existence of a biological difference. That is, genes affect behavior only by affecting the body. A susceptibility to alcoholism could conceivably be caused by differences in the ability to digest or metabolize alcohol or by differences in the structure or biochemistry of the brain.

Most investigators believe that differences in brain physiology are more likely to play a role. Cloninger (1987) notes that many studies have shown that people with antisocial tendencies, which includes the group of steady drinkers, show a strong tendency to seek novelty and excitement. These people are disorderly and distractible (many have a history of hyperactivity as children) and show little restraint in their behavior. They tend not to fear dangerous situations or social disapproval. They are easily bored. On the other hand, binge drinkers tend to be anxious, emotionally dependent, sentimental, sensitive to social cues, cautious and apprehensive, fearful of novelty or change, rigid, and attentive to details. Their EEGs show little slow alpha activity, which suggests that they are aroused and anxious (Propping, Kruger, and Mark, 1981). When they take alcohol, they report a pleasant relief of tension (Propping, Kruger, and Janah, 1980). Perhaps, as Cloninger suggests, these personality differences are a result of differences in the sensitivity of neural mechanisms involved in reinforcement, exploration, and punishment.

For example, the brains of steady drinkers—like those of people with antisocial personality disorder—may contain an undersensitive punishment mechanism, which makes them unresponsive to danger and to social disapproval. They may also have an undersensitive reinforcement system, which leads them to seek more intense thrills (including those provided by alcohol) in order to experience pleasurable sensations. Thus, they seek the excitatory (dopamine-stimulating) effect of alcohol. On the other hand, binge drinkers may have an *oversensitive* punishment system. Normally, they avoid drinking because of the guilt they experience afterward; but once they begin, and once the sedative effect begins, the alcohol-induced suppression of the punishment system makes it impossible for them to stop.

Another approach to study of the physiology of addiction is through the use of animal models. At least two different strains of alcohol-preferring rats have been developed through selective breeding, and studies have shown that

Table 15.4 Characteristic features of two types of alcoholism

Feature	Type of Alcoholism	
	Steady	*Binge*
Usual age of onset (years)	Before 25	After 25
Spontaneous alcohol seeking (inability to abstain)	Frequent	Infrequent
Fighting and arrests when drinking	Frequent	Infrequent
Psychological dependence (loss of control)	Infrequent	Frequent
Guilt and fear about alcohol dependence	Infrequent	Frequent
Novelty seeking	High	Low
Harm avoidance	Low	High
Reward dependence	Low	High

Source: From Cloninger, C.R. *Science*, 1987, *236*, 410–416. Copyright 1987 by the American Association for the Advancement of Science.

these animals differ in interesting ways. Alcohol-preferring rats do just what their name implies: If given a drinking tube containing a solution of alcohol along with their water and food, they become heavy drinkers. The alcohol-nonpreferring rats abstain. Fadda et al. (1990) found that alcohol appeared to produce a larger release of dopamine in the brains of alcohol-preferring rats than in the brains of alcohol-nonpreferring rats, which suggests that the reinforcing effect of alcohol is stronger in these animals.

INTERIM SUMMARY

Personality and Psychoactive Substance Abuse Disorders

Antisocial personality disorder, also called *psychopathy* or *sociopathy,* is a serious problem. A large number of criminals are psychopaths, and many psychopaths become criminals. The hallmarks of psychopathy are an apparent indifference to the effects of one's behavior on other people, impulsiveness, failure to learn from experience, sexual promiscuity and lack of commitment to a partner, and habitual lying. Some psychopaths are superficially charming, and many find employment cheating others out of their money.

Psychopathy tends to run in families, and there is evidence from twin studies that heredity, as well as a poor environment, may contribute to its development. Unfortunately, the disorder is difficult to treat, because psychopaths do not see any reason for changing; they do not perceive themselves as being in need of improvement.

Drug addiction is one of the most serious problems our society faces today. Apparently, all substances that produce addiction do so by activating the reinforcement system of the brain, which involves the release of dopamine by terminal buttons.

Most people who are exposed to addictive drugs—even those with a high abuse potential—do not become addicts. Evidence suggests that the likelihood of addiction, especially to alcohol, is strongly affected by heredity. There may be two types of alcoholism: one related to an antisocial, pleasure-seeking personality (steady drinkers), and another related to a repressed, anxiety-ridden personality (binge drinkers). Some investigators believe that a better understanding of the physiological basis of reinforcement and punishment will help us understand the effects of heredity on susceptibility to addiction. Inbreeding has produced strains of laboratory animals that prefer to drink alcohol, and evidence suggests that this preference for alcohol may be related to differences in dopamine metabolism. ∎

SCHIZOPHRENIC DISORDERS

[8] *Schizophrenia,* the most common psychosis, includes several types, each with a distinctive set of symptoms. For many years a controversy has been brewing over whether schizophrenia is one disorder with various subtypes or whether each subtype constitutes a distinct disorder. Because the prognosis differs for the various subtypes of schizophrenia, they appear to differ at least in severity. However, a particular individual may, at different times, meet the criteria for different subtypes. As we will see later, recent evidence suggests that there are two basic types of schizophrenia, which do not correspond to the present DSM-III-R classifications.

Description

Schizophrenia affects approximately 1 percent of the world's population. Descriptions of symptoms in ancient writings indicate that the disorder has been around for thousands of years (Jeste et al., 1985). *Schizophrenia* is probably the most misused psychological term in existence. The word literally means "split mind," but it does *not* imply a split or multiple personality. People often say that they "feel schizophrenic" about an issue when they really mean that they have mixed feelings about it. A person who sometimes wants to build a cabin in Alaska and live off the land and at other times wants to take over the family insurance business may be undecided, but he or she is not schizophrenic. The man who invented the term, Eugen Bleuler, intended it to refer to a break with reality, caused by disorganization of the various functions of the mind, so that thoughts and feelings no longer worked together normally.

Schizophrenia is characterized by two categories of symptoms, positive and negative. **Positive symptoms** are those that make themselves known by their presence. These symptoms include thought disorders, hallucinations, and delusions. A **thought disorder**—disorganized, irrational thinking—is probably the most important symptom of schizophrenia.

Schizophrenics have great difficulty arranging their thoughts logically and sorting out plausible conclusions from absurd ones. In conversation they jump from one topic to another, as new associations come up. Sometimes, they utter meaningless words or choose words for their rhyme rather than for their meaning. *Delusions* are beliefs that are obviously contrary to fact. **Delusions of persecution** are false beliefs that others are plotting and conspiring against oneself. **Delusions of grandeur** are false beliefs in one's power and importance, such as a conviction that one has godlike powers or has special knowledge that no one else possesses. **Delusions of control** are related to delusions of persecution; the person believes (for example) that he or she is being controlled by others through such means as radar or tiny radio receivers implanted in his or her brain.

The third positive symptom of schizophrenia is **hallucinations,** which are perceptions of stimuli that are not actually present. The most common schizophrenic hallucinations are auditory, but they can also involve any of the other senses. The typical schizophrenic hallucination consists of voices talking to the person. Sometimes, they order the person to do something; sometimes, they scold the person for his or her unworthiness; sometimes, they just utter mean-

Catatonic schizophrenics may maintain bizarre postures for hours. Although they appear oblivious to events in their environment, they often later reveal that they were aware of what other people were doing and saying.

ingless phrases. Olfactory hallucinations are also fairly common; often they contribute to the delusion that others are trying to kill the person with poison gas.

In contrast to the positive symptoms, the **negative symptoms** of schizophrenia are known by the absence of normal behaviors: flattened emotional response, poverty of speech, lack of initiative and persistence, inability to experience pleasure, and social withdrawal (Crow, 1980; Andreasen and Olsen, 1982). Negative symptoms are not specific to schizophrenia; they are seen in many neurological disorders that involve brain damage, especially to the frontal lobes. As we will see later in this chapter, evidence suggests that these two sets of symptoms result from different physiological disorders. Positive symptoms appear to involve excessive activity in some neural circuits that include dopamine as a transmitter substance, and negative symptoms appear to be caused by brain damage. Many researchers suspect that these two sets of symptoms involve a common set of underlying causes, but these causes have yet to be discovered.

Types of Schizophrenia

Most cases of schizophrenia do not fit neatly into one of the categories described below. Many are diagnosed as **undifferentiated schizophrenia;** that is, the patients have delusions, hallucinations, and disorganized behavior but do not meet the criteria for catatonic, paranoid, or disorganized schizophrenia. In addition, some patients' symptoms change after an initial diagnosis, and their classification changes accordingly.

Catatonic schizophrenia (from the Greek *katateinein,* meaning "to stretch or draw tight") is characterized by various motor disturbances, including **catatonic postures**—bizarre, stationary poses maintained for many hours—and **waxy flexibility,** in which the person's limbs can be molded into new positions, which are then maintained. Contrary to popular assumptions, catatonic schizophrenics are often aware of all that goes on about them and will talk about what happened after the episode of catatonia subsides.

The preeminent symptoms of **paranoid schizophrenia** are delusions of persecution, grandeur, or control, although delusions can also occur in other forms of schizophrenia. The word *paranoid* has become so widely used in ordinary language that it has come to mean "suspicious." However, not all paranoid schizophrenics believe that they are being persecuted. Some believe that they hold special powers that can save the world or that they are Christ, or Napoleon, or the president of the United States.

Paranoid schizophrenics are among the most intelligent of psychotic patients, so not surprisingly, they often build up delusional structures incorporating a wealth of detail. Even the most trivial event is interpreted in terms of a grand scheme, whether it is a delusion of persecution or one of grandeur. The way a person walks, a particular facial expression or movement, or even the shapes of clouds can acquire special significance.

Disorganized schizophrenia is a serious disorder; usually, it is progressive and irreversible. People with disorganized schizophrenia often display signs of emotion, especially silly laughter, that are inappropriate to the circumstances. Also, their speech tends to be a jumble of words: "I came to the hospital to play, gay, way, lay, day, bray, donkey, monkey" (Snyder, 1974, p. 132). The speech of a seriously deteriorated hebephrenic is often referred to as a *word salad.*

Possible Causes

9 **Early Predictors.** Eugen Bleuler (1911/1950), one of the pioneers in the diagnosis and study of schizophrenia, divided the disorder into *reactive* and *process* forms. Patients with a general history of good mental health were designated as having **reactive schizophrenia,** on the assumption that their disorder was a *reaction* to stressful life situations. Typically, these patients soon recovered, and few experienced another episode. Patients with indications of mental illness early in life were designated as having **process schizophrenia** and were considered to have a chronic disorder.

If process schizophrenia does have its roots in early life, then an important task is to determine what the early signs are. The ability to identify people with a high risk of schizophrenia while they are still young will allow clinicians to institute some form of therapy before the disorder becomes advanced. The early signs may also indicate whether the causes of schizophrenia are biological, environmental, or both.

In fact, the results of many studies indicate that schizophrenia strikes people who were different from others even in childhood. However, they do not tell us whether these differences resulted from physiological disorders or from the behavior of other family members during the schizophrenics' infancy and early childhood. One remarkable study obtained home movies of people with adult-onset schizophrenia that showed them and their siblings when they were children (Walker and Lewine, 1990). Although the schizophrenia did not manifest itself until adulthood, viewers of the films (six graduate students and one professional clinical psychologist) did an excellent job of identifying the children who were to become schizophrenics. The viewers commented on the children's poor eye contact, relative lack of responsiveness and positive affect, and generally poor motor coordination. Clearly, something was different about the behavior of the schizophrenics even early in life.

Heritability. The heritability of schizophrenia—or more precisely, the heritability of a *tendency* toward schizophrenia—has now been firmly established by both twin studies and adoption studies. Identical twins are much more likely to be concordant for schizophrenia than fraternal twins, and the children of parents with schizophrenia are more likely to themselves become schizophrenic, even if they are adopted and raised by nonschizophrenic parents (Kety et al., 1968; Farmer, McGuffin, and Gottesman, 1987). Also, if a person has been diagnosed as schizophrenic, it is likely that other family members are, too. (See *Table 15.5.*) It is important to note that although the likelihood of developing schizophrenia increases significantly if a person has schizophrenic relatives, this disorder is not a simple trait like eye color that is inherited. Most people with schizophrenic relatives do *not* develop schizophrenia. Studies estimate that even if both parents are schizophrenic, the

Table 15.5   Summary of major European family and twin studies of the genetics of schizophrenia

Relation to Person Identifed as Schizophrenic	Percentage with Schizophrenia
Spouse	1.0
Grandchild	2.8
Niece/nephew	2.6
Child	9.3
Sibling	7.3
Fraternal twin	12.1
Identical twin	44.3

Source: Davison, G.C., and Neale, J.M. *Abnormal Psychology.* New York: John Wiley & Sons, 1990, after Gottesman, McGuffin, and Farmer (1987).

probability that their child will develop schizophrenia is 30 percent or less.

Most investigators believe that a person inherits a *predisposition* to become schizophrenic; in their view, most environments will foster normal development, whereas certain other environments will trigger various disorders, including schizophrenia. If the susceptibility hypothesis is true, then we would expect that some people carry a "schizophrenia gene" but do not express it; that is, their environment is such that schizophrenia is never triggered. One such person would be the nonschizophrenic member of a pair of monozygotic twins discordant for schizophrenia. The logical way to test this hypothesis is to examine the children of both members of discordant pairs. Gottesman and Bertelsen (1989) found that the percentage of schizophrenic children was nearly identical for both members of such pairs: 16.8% for the schizophrenic parents and 17.4% for the nonschizophrenic parents. For the dizygotic twins the percentages were 17.4% and 2.1%, respectively. These results provide strong evidence that schizophrenia is heritable, and they also support the conclusion that carrying a "schizophrenia gene" does not mean that a person will necessarily become schizophrenic. (See *Figure 15.6.*)

Many researchers have tried to discover the environmental factors that are responsible for triggering schizophrenia in a person with a hereditary predisposition for the disorder. Unfortunately, these attempts have not met with much success. Several studies have found that the likelihood of becoming schizophrenic is related only to a person's *biological* family history; it made no difference whether the person was raised by schizophrenic or nonschizophrenic foster parents. One study (carried out in Finland) obtained different results; it found evidence that suggests that being raised by a "mentally healthy" family helps protect against the development of schizophrenia (Tienari et al., 1987). The researchers examined the children of schizophrenic mothers who had been adopted away early in life. From interviews and psychological tests the families who adopted the children were classified as well-adjusted, moderately maladjusted, or severely maladjusted. The children adopted by the well-adjusted families were least likely to show signs of mental disturbance, including schizophrenia. These results are encouraging; but because several other studies found no such protective influence, more evidence is needed to be sure that the effects are real.

Although attempts to identify possible causes of schizophrenia in a person's social environment have not yet been successful, researchers have identified a social variable that affects the likelihood that a person with schizophrenia will recover. Brown and his colleagues (Brown et al., 1966; Brown, 1985) identified a category of behaviors of families of recovering schizophrenics that seemed to be related to the patient's rate of recovery. They labeled this variable *expressed emotion*. Patients living in family environments in which the level of expressed emotion was low were more likely to recover, whereas those in families in which it was high were likely to continue to exhibit schizophrenic symptoms. **Expressed emotion** consists of expressions of criticism, hostility, and emotional overinvolvement by the family members toward the patient.

Jenkins and Karno (1992) report that in the past decade over one hundred studies investigating expressed emotion have appeared. They found studies from North America, England, Denmark, Italy, France, Spain, Germany, Taiwan, India, Egypt, and Australia. In the United States, studies have been made of Anglo-Americans, Mexican-Americans, and African-Americans. The authors note that despite differences in the ways that people of different cultures perceive mental illness and express themselves, expressed emotion does not seem to be a culture-bound phenomenon. Two elements appear to be common to all cultures: critical comments

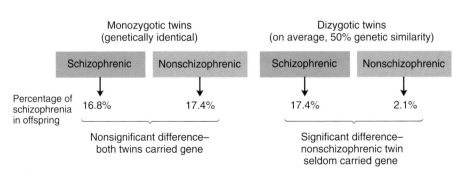

Figure 15.6 An explanation for evidence that people can have an unexpressed "schizophrenia gene."

and emotional overinvolvement. If these elements are present at a high level, patients are less likely to recover.

Biochemical Factors: The Dopamine Hypothesis. Two classes of drugs have been found to affect the symptoms of schizophrenia. Cocaine and amphetamine *cause* these symptoms, both in schizophrenics and in nonschizophrenics; antipsychotic drugs *reduce* them. Because both types of drugs affect neural communication in which dopamine serves as a transmitter substance, investigators have hypothesized that abnormal activity of these neurons is the primary cause of schizophrenia. That is, the **dopamine hypothesis** states that the symptoms of schizophrenia are produced by overactivity of synapses that use dopamine as a transmitter substance.

Earlier in this century, when cocaine was cheap and freely available without prescription, there was an epidemic of cocaine psychosis. Cocaine was outlawed, and its use became much more rare; also, because of its high price, it was usually taken in small amounts. Now that a particularly potent form of cocaine ("crack") is available on the illicit market, health care professionals are again encountering increasing numbers of cocaine-induced psychoses. Heavy users of cocaine develop a syndrome that closely resembles paranoid schizophrenia; they become suspicious and think that others are plotting against them, they hear voices talking to them, and they often have tactile hallucinations, such as the feeling that small insects have burrowed under their skin.

Amphetamine and related substances also make all kinds of naturally occurring schizophrenia worse: Paranoids become more suspicious, disorganized schizophrenics become sillier, and catatonics become more rigid or hyperactive. Davis (1974) injected an amphetaminelike drug into schizophrenic patients whose symptoms had abated. Within one minute each patient's condition changed "from a mild schizophrenia into a wild and very florid schizophrenia." One of them began to make a clacking noise, then pounded a pad of paper with a pencil until he shredded it. He said he had been "sending and receiving messages from ancient Egyptians."

People with a diagnosis of schizophrenia constitute the largest proportion of patients in mental hospitals. Until around 1955 the number of patients in mental hospitals grew steadily every year; then the number of patients began to decline. (See *Figure 15.7.*) Several factors led to this decrease, including a growing ten-

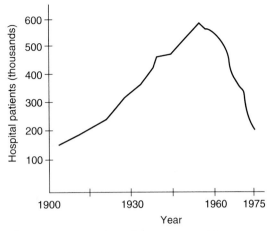

Figure 15.7 Number of patients in public mental hospitals from 1900 to 1975. (Redrawn from Bassuk, E.L., and Gerson, S. Deinstitutionalization and mental health services. *Scientific American*, 1978, *238*, 46–53. Copyright © 1978 by Scientific American, Inc. All rights reserved.)

dency to treat patients in community-based facilities. But one of the most important factors was the introduction of **chlorpromazine** (the trade name is Thorazine); chlorpromazine and other antipsychotic drugs are remarkably effective in alleviating the symptoms of schizophrenia. Hallucinations diminish or disappear, delusions become less striking or cease altogether, and the patients' thought processes become more coherent. These drugs are not merely tranquilizers; for example, they cause a patient with catatonic immobility to begin moving again, as well as causing an excited patient to quiet down. In contrast, true tranquilizers such as Librium or Valium only make a schizophrenic patient slow moving and groggy.

Amphetamine, cocaine, and the antipsychotic drugs act on synapses (the junctions between nerve cells) in the brain. As you may recall from Chapter 3, one neuron passes on excitatory or inhibitory messages to another by releasing a small amount of transmitter substance from its terminal button into the synaptic cleft. The chemical activates receptors on the surface of the receiving neuron, and the activated receptors either excite or inhibit the receiving neuron. Drugs such as amphetamine and cocaine cause the *stimulation* of receptors for dopamine, a transmitter substance. In contrast, antipsychotic drugs block dopamine receptors and *prevent* them from becoming stimulated. These findings led investigators to propose the dopamine hypothesis of schizophrenia.

Why, we might ask, should the increased activity of dopamine-secreting synapses cause the symptoms of schizophrenia? A possible explanation comes from the role of these synapses in reinforcement. As we saw, drugs that strongly reinforce behaviors (such as cocaine and amphetamine) also produce the positive symptoms of schizophrenia. Perhaps the two effects of the drugs are related. If reinforcement mechanisms were activated at inappropriate times, then inappropriate behaviors—including delusional thoughts—might be reinforced. At one time or another, all of us have had some irrational thoughts, which we normally brush aside and forget. But if neural mechanisms of reinforcement became active while these thoughts were occurring, we would tend to take them more seriously. In time, full-fledged delusions might develop.

Neurological Disorders. Although the dopamine hypothesis has for several years been the dominant biological explanation for schizophrenia, recent evidence suggests that it can offer only a partial explanation. Because antipsychotic drugs alleviate positive, but not negative, symptoms of schizophrenia (Angrist, Rotrosen, and Gershon, 1980), perhaps those patients who do not get better with medication have primarily negative symptoms.

Once investigators began paying more attention to negative symptoms, they discovered evidence for brain damage in patients exhibiting these symptoms. Several investigators have examined CT or MRI scans of patients with schizophrenia. For example, Weinberger and Wyatt (1982) found that the ventricles in the brains of schizophrenic patients were, on average, twice

as large as those of normal subjects. Similarly, Pfefferbaum et al. (1988) found evidence that the sulci (the wrinkles in the brain) were wider in the brains of schizophrenic patients. Enlargement of the hollow ventricles of the brain and widening of the sulci indicates the loss of brain tissue; thus, the evidence implied the existence of some kind of neurological disease.

Loss of brain tissue, as assessed by CT scans, appears to be related to negative symptoms of schizophrenia but not to positive ones (Johnstone et al., 1978). In addition, patients with loss of brain tissue respond poorly to antipsychotic drugs (Weinberger et al., 1980). These studies suggest that positive and negative symptoms of schizophrenia have different causes: Positive symptoms are a result of overactivity of dopamine synapses, whereas negative symptoms are produced by actual loss of brain tissue.

A study by Suddath et al. (1990) provided further evidence for the conclusion that the brain damage associated with schizophrenia is not caused directly by the patients' genes, but that heredity predisposes some people for the damaging effects of some environmental factors—perhaps a virus. The investigators examined MRI scans of monozygotic twins discordant for schizophrenia and found that in almost every case the twin with schizophrenia had larger lateral and third ventricles. In addition, the hippocampus was smaller in the schizophrenic twin, and the total volume of the gray matter in the left temporal lobe was reduced. Figure 15.8 shows a set of MRI scans from a pair of twins; as you can see, the lateral ventricles are larger in the brain of the twin with schizophrenia. (See *Figure 15.8.*)

Several studies have indicated that the cause of brain damage in schizophrenia may be a viral infection. No direct evidence for virally induced schizophrenia exists, but evidence reveals similarities between schizophrenia and known viral disorders. Stevens (1988) notes some interesting similarities between schizophrenia and multiple sclerosis, a neurological disorder. Multiple sclerosis appears to be an autoimmune disease—triggered by a virus—in which the patient's own immune system attacks the myelin sheaths that cover most axons in the central nervous system. The natural histories of multiple sclerosis and schizophrenia are similar in several ways. Both diseases are more prevalent and more severe in people who spent their childhood in latitudes far from the equator. Both diseases are more common in people with low socioeconomic status, who live in crowded,

Figure 15.8 MRI scans of the brains of twins discordant for schizophrenia. (a) Normal twin. (b) Twin with schizophrenia. (Courtesy of D.R. Weinberger, National Institute of Mental Health, Saint Elizabeth's Hospital, Washington, D.C.)

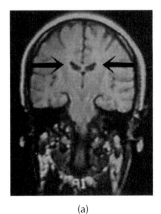
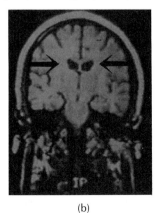

(a)   (b)

deprived conditions. Both diseases are characterized by one of three general courses: (1) attacks followed by remissions, many of which produce no residual deficits; (2) recurrent attacks with only partial remissions, causing an increasingly major deficit; or (3) an insidious onset with a steady and relentless progression, leading to permanent and severe deficits. These similarities suggest that schizophrenia, like multiple sclerosis, could be a virally induced autoimmune disease.

A second possible cause of schizophrenia is interference with normal prenatal brain development. Several studies show that people born during the winter months are more likely to develop schizophrenia later in life. Torrey, Torrey, and Peterson (1977) suggest that the causal factor could be seasonal variations in nutritional factors or—more likely—variations in toxins or infectious agents in air, water, or food. Several diseases known to be caused by viruses, such as measles, German measles, and chicken pox, show a similar seasonality effect. The seasonality effect is seen most strongly in poor, urban locations, where people are at greater risk for viral infections (Machon, Mednick, and Schulsinger, 1983).

A seasonally related virus could affect either a pregnant woman or her newborn infant. Two pieces of evidence suggest that the damage is done prenatally. First, brain development is more susceptible to disruption prenatally than postnatally. Second, a study of the offspring of women who were pregnant during an epidemic of type A2 influenza in Finland during 1957 showed an elevated incidence of schizophrenia (Mednick, Machon, and Huttunen, 1990). The increased incidence was seen only in the children of women who were in the second trimester of their pregnancy when the epidemic occurred. (See *Figure 15.9*.) Presumably, the viral infection produced toxins that interfered with the brain development of some of the fetuses, resulting in the development of schizophrenia later in life.

A third possible cause of schizophrenia is birth trauma. Schwarzkopf et al. (1989) found that if a schizophrenic person does not have relatives with a schizophrenic disorder—that is, if there is no evidence that the disease is a result of heredity—he or she is more likely to have had a history of complications at or around the time of childbirth. Thus, brain damage not related to heredity may also be a cause of schizophrenia.

In summary, researchers have suggested three possible causes of the brain damage—and

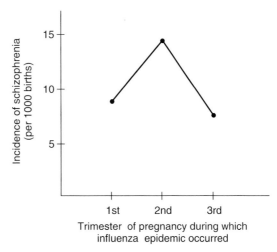

Figure 15.9 Incidence of schizophrenia in the offspring of women who were pregnant during the 1957 influenza epidemic in Finland. (Based on data of Mednick, S.A., Machon, R.A., and Huttunen, M.O. *Archives of General Psychiatry,* 1990, *47,* 292.)

the corresponding negative symptoms—that accompanies schizophrenia: a virus that triggers an autoimmune disease, which causes brain damage later in life; a virus that damages the brain early in life; and birth trauma. Heredity presumably interacts with the first two factors; many people may be exposed to the virus, but only in people with a genetic sensitivity will the virus go on to cause brain damage.

INTERIM SUMMARY

Schizophrenic Disorders

The principal positive symptoms of schizophrenia include thought disorders; delusions of persecution, grandeur, and control; and hallucinations. The principal negative symptoms include withdrawal, apathy, and poverty of speech. The DSM-III-R classifies schizophrenia into several subtypes, including undifferentiated, catatonic, paranoid, and disorganized; but the distinctions between process and reactive schizophrenia and between positive and negative symptoms seem to be more important.

People who develop chronic, process schizophrenia appear to be different from other people even as children, which suggests that the disorder takes root very early in life. Indeed, heritability studies have shown a strong genetic component in schizophrenia, although they do not rule out the possibility of interaction with adverse environmental situations as a causal factor. Recent research suggests that a low level of expressed emotion (including critical comments and emotional overinvolvement on the part of family members) facilitates the recovery of a patient with schizophrenia.

Positive symptoms of schizophrenia can be produced in normal people or made worse in schizophrenics by drugs that stimulate dopamine synapses (cocaine and amphetamine) and can be reduced or eliminated by those that block dopamine receptors (antipsychotic drugs). These findings have led to the dopamine hypothesis, which states that schizophrenia is caused by an inherited biochemical defect that causes dopamine neurons to be overactive, producing disorders in attentional mechanisms.

More recent studies indicate that schizophrenia can best be conceived of as two different disorders. The positive symptoms are produced by overactivity of dopamine neurons and can be treated with the antipsychotic drugs; but the negative ones, which do not respond to these drugs, are caused by brain damage. Investigators have found direct evidence of brain damage by inspecting slices of deceased patients' brains and CT scans of living patients' brains. Because most schizophrenic patients were born during late winter and early spring and because the disorder shows a particular geographical distribution, investigators have hypothesized that a neurological disease may be present. Perhaps the virus causes no brain damage in people with nonschizophrenic heredity but damages the brains of people with an inherited susceptibility to the disease. This pattern appears to be the case with multiple sclerosis.

Much more research will be necessary before investigators can determine whether, in fact, overactivity of dopamine synapses does produce positive symptoms of schizophrenia and whether a viral infection produces the brain damage that results in negative symptoms. But such biological explanations for schizophrenia will not lessen the usefulness of psychotherapy (discussed in the next chapter) in the treatment of this disorder. Experience has shown that it is not enough merely to medicate a schizophrenic patient with chlorpromazine. It is also important to teach the person how to structure a new life and how to cope with the many problems he or she will encounter in reentering society. In addition, psychotherapy is at present the only hope for patients with predominantly negative symptoms, who are not helped by antipsychotic drugs. ■

MOOD DISORDERS

Description

10 In contrast to schizophrenia, whose principal symptom is thought disorders, the **mood disorders** (formerly called the *affective disorders*) are primarily disorders of emotion. The most severe mood disorders are *bipolar disorder* and *major depression*. **Bipolar disorder** is characterized by alternating periods of mania (wild excitement) and depression; **major depression** is unrelieved by bouts of mania. The incidence of major depression is approximately 5 percent, and that of bipolar disorder is approximately 1 percent (Robbins et al., 1984). Although both sexes are equally likely to develop a bipolar disorder, females are at least twice as likely as males to suffer from major depression. Bipolar disorder tends to begin during the late twenties, and major depression tends to begin around age forty.

A less severe form of depression is called **dysthymic disorder.** (The term comes from the Greek words *dus,* "bad," and *thymos,* "spirit," and is pronounced *dis-THIGH-mik*). Dysthymic disorder used to be called *depressive neurosis.* The primary difference between this disorder and major depression is its lack of delusions and hallucinations and its relatively low severity. Similarly, **cyclothymic disorder** resembles bipolar disorder but is much less severe.

Mania. **Mania** (the Greek word for "madness") is characterized by wild, exuberant, unrealistic activity. During manic episodes people are usually elated and self-confident; however, contradiction or interference tends to make them very angry. Their speech (and, presumably, their thought processes) becomes very rapid. They tend to flit from topic to topic and are full of grandiose plans, but their thoughts are less disorganized than those of a schizophrenic. Manic patients also tend to be restless and hyperactive, often pacing around ceaselessly. They often have delusions and hallucinations—typically of a nature that fits their exuberant mood. Davison and Neale (1990) recorded a typical interaction:

> *Therapist:* Well, you seem pretty happy today.
>
> *Client:* Happy! Happy! You certainly are a master of understatement, you rogue! (Shouting, literally jumping out of seat.) Why I'm ecstatic. I'm leaving for the West coast today, on my daughter's bicycle. Only 3100 miles. That's nothing, you know. I could probably

walk, but I want to get there by next week. And along the way I plan to contact a lot of people about investing in my fish equipment. I'll get to know more people that way—you know, Doc, "know" in the biblical sense (leering at the therapist seductively). Oh, God, how good it feels. It's almost like a nonstop orgasm. (Davison and Neale, 1990, p. 222)

The usual response that manic speech and behavior evokes in another person is one of sympathetic amusement; in fact, when an experienced clinician finds himself or herself becoming amused by a patient, the clinician begins to suspect the presence of mania. Because very few patients exhibit only mania, the DSM-III-R classifies all cases in which mania occurs as bipolar disorder. Patients with bipolar disorder usually experience alternate periods of mania and depression. Each of these periods lasts from a few days to a few weeks, usually with several days of relatively normal behavior in between. Many therapists have observed that there is often something brittle and unnatural about the happiness during the manic phase, as though the patient is making himself or herself be happy to ward off an attack of depression. Indeed, some manic patients are simply hyperactive and irritable rather than euphoric.

One type of antidepressant drug, **lithium carbonate,** is effective in treating bipolar disorder, though as yet no one knows why. Lithium carbonate is a simple inorganic compound. Its active ingredient is the element lithium, a metal that is closely related to sodium, which is found in ordinary table salt. (In fact, lithium chloride was used as a sodium-free salt substitute until it was found to be toxic in large doses.) Lithium carbonate has been called the "wonder drug" of psychiatry; it is effective in most cases of bipolar disorder and it has few side effects as long as the dosage is carefully controlled. Many people who are being treated with lithium carbonate are leading perfectly normal lives.

Depression. Depressed people are extremely sad and are usually full of self-directed guilt. Beck (1967) identified five cardinal symptoms of depression: (1) a sad and apathetic mood, (2) feelings of worthlessness and hopelessness, (3) a desire to withdraw from other people, (4) sleeplessness and loss of appetite and sexual desire, and (5) change in activity level, to either lethargy or agitation. Most people who are labeled "depressed" have a dysthymic disorder; a minority of them have a severe mood disorder. Major depression must be dis-

tinguished from grief caused by death of a loved one. People who are grieving feel sad and depressed but do not fear losing their minds or have thoughts of self-harm. Because many people who do suffer from major depression or the depressed phase of bipolar disorder commit suicide, these disorders are potentially fatal. The fatality rate by suicide for major depression is estimated at 15 percent (Guze and Robins, 1970).

People with severe depression often have delusions, especially that their brains or internal organs are rotting away. Sometimes, they believe that they are being punished for unspeakable and unforgivable sins, as in the following dialogue, reported by Coleman (1976):

> My brain is being eaten away. . . . If I had any willpower I would kill myself . . . I don't deserve to live . . . I have ruined everything . . . and it's all my fault. . . . I have been unfaithful to my wife and now I am being punished . . . my health is ruined . . . there's no use going on . . . (sigh) . . . I have ruined everything . . . my family . . . and now myself . . . I bring misfortune to everyone. . . . I am a moral leper . . . a serpent in the Garden of Eden. (Coleman, 1976, p. 346)

Possible Causes

11 Faulty Cognition. Beck (1967) suggested that the changes in affect seen in depres-

Depression in the elderly often results from changes in their life situations.

sive psychoses are not primary but instead are secondary to changes in cognition. That is, the primary disturbance is a distortion in the person's view of reality. For example, a depressed person may see a scratch on the surface of his or her car and conclude that the car is ruined. Or a person whose recipe fails may see the unappetizing dish as proof of his or her unworthiness. Or a nasty dunning letter from a creditor is seen as a serious and personal condemnation.

In contrast with psychoanalytical theory, which emphasizes the role of the unconscious in the emergence of mental disorder, Beck's theory emphasizes the role of a person's judgment in contributing to his or her own emotional state. Though not yet proved correct, this theory has served a useful function in alerting therapists to the importance of considering the thought processes, as well as the feelings, of a patient with a severe mood disorder. Of course, if we observe an association between faulty cognition and depression, we cannot necessarily conclude that the faulty cognition causes the depression; in fact, the reverse could be true. In any event, Beck's method of treatment, based on his theory, has proved itself to be effective, as we shall see in Chapter 16.

Heritability. Like schizophrenia, the mood disorders appear to have a genetic component. People who have first-degree relatives with a serious mood disorder are ten times more likely to develop these disorders than are people without afflicted relatives (Rosenthal, 1970). Furthermore, the concordance rate for bipolar disorder is 72 percent for monozygotic twins, compared with 14 percent for dizygotic twins. For major depression the figures are 40 percent and 11 percent, respectively (Allen, 1976). Thus, bipolar disorder appears to be more heritable than major depression, and the two disorders appear to have different genetic causes.

Biochemical Factors. Two forms of medical treatment that have proved successful in alleviating the symptoms of severe depression are *electroconvulsive therapy* and *antidepressant drugs.* Their success indicates that physiological disorders may underlie these conditions. Because no one knows how electroconvulsive therapy works, it cannot yet provide information about the biochemical factors in mood disorders; discussion of this treatment is therefore deferred until Chapter 16. More is known about the biochemical effects of the **antidepressant drugs,** and this knowledge has led investigators to speculate that the mood disorders may have

physiological causes. Currently, two types of antidepressant drugs are in widespread use. The effects of lithium carbonate in relieving bipolar disorder were discussed earlier. The other class includes the **tricyclic antidepressant drugs,** such as imipramine. (*Tricyclic* refers to their molecular structure.) Experiments with laboratory animals have shown that these drugs have stimulating effects on synapses that utilize two transmitter substances, norepinephrine and serotonin.

Other drugs, including **reserpine,** which is used to treat high blood pressure, can *cause* episodes of depression. Reserpine lowers blood pressure by blocking the release of norepinephrine in muscles in the walls of blood vessels, thus causing the muscles to relax. However, because the drug also blocks the release of norepinephrine and serotonin in the brain, a common side effect is depression. This side effect strengthens the argument that biochemical factors in the brain play an important role in depression.

Several studies have found evidence for biochemical abnormalities in the brains of people with mood disorders. Taking samples of transmitter substances directly from the living brain is not possible. But when transmitter substances are released, a small amount gets broken down by enzymes in the brain, and some of the breakdown products accumulate in the cerebrospinal fluid or pass into the bloodstream and collect in the urine. Investigators have analyzed cerebrospinal fluid and urine for these substances.

For example, Träskmann et al. (1981) measured the level of a compound produced when serotonin is broken down in the cerebrospinal fluid of depressed people who had attempted suicide. The level of this compound (*5-HIAA*) was significantly lower than that of control subjects; this finding implies that there was less activity of serotonin-secreting neurons in the brains of the depressed subjects. In fact, 20 percent of the subjects with levels below the median subsequently killed themselves, whereas none of the subjects with levels above the median committed suicide. Taube et al. (1978) obtained evidence for decreased activity of neurons that secrete norepinephrine; they found low levels of a compound (*MHPG*) produced when this transmitter substance is broken down in the urine of patients with mood disorders. Thus, decreased activity of serotonin- and norepinephrine-secreting neurons appears to be related to depression. Presumably, the tricyclic antidepressant drugs alleviate the symptoms of depression by increasing the activity of these neurons.

Although the brain biochemistry of patients with mood disorders appears to be abnormal, we cannot be certain that a biochemical imbalance is the first event in a sequence that leads to depression. Environmental stimuli may cause the depression, which then leads to biochemical changes in the brain. For example, the brain levels of norepinephrine are lower in dogs who have been presented with an inescapable electrical shock and have developed learned helplessness (Miller, Rosellini, and Seligman, 1977). The dogs certainly did not inherit the low norepinephrine levels; they acquired them as a result of their experience. The findings so far suggest that a tendency to develop serious mood disorders is heritable and that low levels of norepinephrine and serotonin are associated with these disorders. However, the cause-and-effect relations have yet to be worked out.

Relation to Sleep Cycles. A characteristic symptom of mood disorders is sleep disturbances. Usually, people with a severe mood disorder have little difficulty falling asleep, but they awaken early and are unable to get back to sleep again. (In contrast, people with dysthymic disorder are more likely to have trouble falling asleep and getting out of bed the next day.) Kupfer (1976) reported that depressed patients tend to enter REM sleep sooner than normal people and spend an increased time in this state during the last half of sleep. Noting this fact, Vogel, Vogel, McAbee, and Thurmond (1980) deprived depressed patients of REM sleep by awakening them whenever the EEG showed signs that they were entering this stage. Remarkably, the deprivation decreased their depression. These findings are supported by the observation that treatments that alleviate depression, such as electroconvulsive therapy and the tricyclic antidepressant drugs, profoundly reduce REM sleep in cats (Scherschlicht et al., 1982).

Ehlers, Frank, and Kupfer (1988) have proposed an intriguing hypothesis that integrates behavioral and biological evidence. They suggest that depression is triggered environmentally, through loss of *social zeitgebers*. A **zeitgeber** (from the German word for "time giver") is a stimulus that synchronizes daily biological rhythms, which are controlled by an internal biological clock located in the hypothalamus. The most important zeitgeber is light; each morning, our biological clocks are synchronized ("reset to the time zero") by daylight. These clocks control sleep and waking cycles, cycles of hormone

secretion and body temperature, and many other physiological systems that fluctuate each day.

Ehlers and her colleagues note that in humans social interactions, as well as light, may serve as zeitgebers. For example, people tend to synchronize their daily rhythms to those of their spouses. After loss of a spouse, people's daily schedules are usually disrupted, and, of course, many of them become depressed. Flaherty et al. (1987) studied recently widowed people and found that the individuals who were the most depressed were those who had the greatest reduction in number of social contacts and regular daily activities. Ehlers et al. (1988) suggest that some people may be more susceptible to the disruptive effects of changes in social contacts and regular daily routines. This susceptibility represents the genetic contribution toward developing mood disorders. Almost everyone becomes depressed, at least for a period of time, after the loss of a loved one. Other events that change a person's daily routine, such as the birth of an infant or the loss of a job, can also precipitate a period of depression. Perhaps people who "spontaneously" become depressed are reacting to minor changes in their daily routine that disrupt their biological rhythms. Clearly, this interesting hypothesis deserves further research.

Yet another phenomenon relates depression to sleep and waking—or, more specifically, to the phenomena responsible for daily rhythms. Some people become depressed during the winter season, when days are short and nights are long. The symptoms of this form of depression, called **seasonal affective disorder,** are somewhat different from those of major depression; both forms include lethargy and sleep disturbances, but seasonal depression includes a craving for carbohydrate and an accompanying weight gain. (As you will recall, people with major depression tend to lose their appetite.)

Seasonal affective disorder can be treated by exposing people to bright light for several hours a day (Rosenthal et al., 1985). Possibly, people with seasonal affective disorder require a stronger-than-normal zeitgeber to synchronize their biological clock with the day-night cycle.

Several investigators have noticed that the symptoms of seasonal affective disorder resemble the behavioral characteristics of hibernation: carbohydrate craving, overeating and weight gain, oversleeping, and lethargy (Rosenthal et al., 1986). Animals who hibernate do so during the winter, and the behavior is triggered by a combination of short day length and cooler temperature. Thus, some of the brain mechanisms involved in hibernation may also be responsible for the mood changes associated with the time of year. This hypothesis has some support; Zvolsky et al. (1981) found that imipramine, an antidepressant drug, suppressed hibernation in hamsters.

As we saw, specific deprivation of REM sleep has an antidepressant effect. *Total* sleep deprivation also has an antidepressant effect. However, the effects are quite different. REM sleep deprivation takes several weeks to reduce depression and produces relatively long-lasting effects. Total sleep deprivation produces immediate effects—but the effects are short-lived (Wu and Bunney, 1990). Figure 15.10 shows the mood rating of a patient who stayed awake one night; as you can see, the depression was lifted by the sleep deprivation but returned the next day, after a normal night's sleep. (See ***Figure 15.10.***)

The data in Figure 15.11 are taken from eight different studies (cited by Wu and Bunney, 1990) and show self-ratings of depression of people who did and did not respond to sleep deprivation. (Total sleep deprivation improves the mood of patients with endogenous depression approximately two-thirds of the time.) People who responded to the sleep deprivation started the day depressed, but their mood gradually improved. This improvement continued through the sleepless night and during the following day. The next night they were permitted to sleep normally, and their depression was back the next morning. Wu and Bunney suggest that a *depressogenic* ("depression-producing") substance is produced during sleep but disappears during waking. (See ***Figure 15.11.***)

Why do some depressed people profit from total sleep deprivation while others do not? Although we cannot yet answer this question, an interesting study by Reinink et al. (1990) found that one can *predict* a person's responsiveness from his or her circadian pattern of mood. Most people feel better at a particular time of day—generally, either the morning or the evening. Depressed people, too, show these fluctuations in mood. Reinink and his colleagues found that the depressed people who were most likely to show an improvement in mood after a night of total sleep deprivation were those who felt worst in the morning and best in the evening. Perhaps these people are most sensitive to the hypothetical depressogenic substance produced during sleep. This substance makes them feel worst in the morning, and as the day progresses, the chemical is metabolized and they

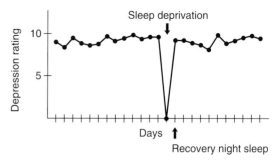

Figure 15.10 Changes in the depression rating of a depressed patient produced by a single night's total sleep deprivation. (From Wu, J.C., and Bunney, W.E. *American Journal of Psychiatry*, 1990, *147*, 14–21. Copyright 1990, the American Psychiatric Association. Reprinted by permission.)

start feeling better. A night without sleep simply prolongs this improvement in mood.

At the present time total sleep deprivation does not provide a practical way of reducing people's depression (people cannot stay awake indefinitely). But perhaps researchers can study the biochemistry of depressed people before and after sleep deprivation to see whether a "depressogenic" substance does exist. If it does, scientists may be able to identify the brain mechanisms responsible for depression and devise more effective therapies.

INTERIM SUMMARY

Mood Disorders

The serious mood disorders are primarily disorders of emotion, although delusions are also characteristically present. Bipolar disorder consists of alternating periods of mania and depression, whereas major depression consists of depression alone. The mood states are not precipitated by environmental events; there is no external reason for these people to feel sad or elated.

Freud suggested that fixation in the oral phase of psychosexual development was the cause of depression, but this explanation has not received empirical support. Beck has noted that although mood disorders involve emotional reactions, these reactions may at least in part be based on faulty cognition.

Heritability studies strongly suggest a biological component to mood disorders. This possibility receives support from the finding that biological treatments effectively reduce the

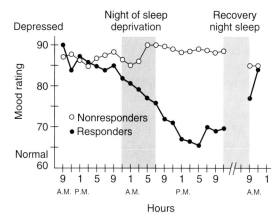

Figure 15.11 Mean mood rating of responding and nonresponding patients deprived of one night's sleep as a function of the time of day. (From Wu, J.C., and Bunney, W.E. *American Journal of Psychiatry*, 1990, *147*, 14–21. Copyright 1990, the American Psychiatric Association. Reprinted by permission.)

symptoms of these disorders, whereas reserpine can cause depression. Biological treatments include lithium carbonate (for bipolar disorder) and electroconvulsive therapy, tricyclic antidepressant drugs, and REM sleep deprivation (for depression). These findings, along with evidence from biochemical analysis of the breakdown products of norepinephrine and serotonin in depressed patients, suggest that depression results from underactivity of neurons that secrete norepinephrine or serotonin. However, the discovery that stress can reduce the amount of norepinephrine produced in an animal's brain warns us to be careful in making inferences about cause and effect.

Recent evidence suggests that the primary physiological disorder in mood disorders may manifest itself in terms of abnormalities in sleep/waking rhythms. Studies have shown that REM sleep deprivation alleviates the symptoms of depression, and all known biological treatments for depression themselves reduce REM sleep. Possibly, an important environmental trigger of depression may be events that disrupt a person's daily routine and social contacts. A specific form of depression, seasonal affective disorder, can be treated by exposure to bright light, the zeitgeber that synchronizes the biological clock with the day-night cycle. In addition, total sleep deprivation temporarily reduces the symptoms of depression, particularly in people who tend to feel less depressed at the end of the day.

A personal note to the reader: Besides having to simplify disorders that are typically complex, I have had to exaggerate the distinction between normalcy and mental disorder. I must emphasize again that there is no sharp line that divides normal from abnormal behavior. At the extremes, there is no mistaking a person with, say, a phobic disorder, schizophrenia, or a major affective disorder for a normal person. But most people do not fall at the extremes, and all of us recognize aspects of our own behavior in many of the descriptions of people with mental disorders. ■

APPLICATION

Animal Models of Mental Disorders

As we saw in Chapter 2, research with laboratory animals has led to the discovery of cures or treatments for many diseases. Such research has also helped scientists discover treatments for mental disorders. Most research with laboratory animals seeks to discover the basic principles of physiology and behavior and the relations between the two. Once we have such knowledge, we can try to understand why things go wrong and find ways to prevent or correct pathological conditions. For example, researchers have discovered a new drug to treat schizophrenia that apparently does not have the serious side effects that older drugs have (Kane et al., 1988). This drug was discovered by investigating the actions of various chemicals on the behavior of laboratory animals and on the activity and metabolism of neurons in particular regions of their brains.

Some research aims directly at finding ways to understand and treat diseases or mental disorders. An important feature of this research is the development of *animal models*—pathological conditions in animals that closely resemble those found in humans. Researchers can use these animals to study the disease process or to test drugs or other treatments designed to alleviate the pathological condition.

Some animal models occur naturally—that is, some animals are genetically susceptible to the same disorders found in the human population. For example, researchers have discovered genetic mutations in mice and rats that cause the animals to become obese. The metabolisms of these animals respond differently when they eat, and their cells respond differently to hormones related to the control of eating and body fat. And as I mentioned earlier in this chapter, researchers have also discovered that genetic variations in mice and rats can affect the animals' preference for alcohol. Most laboratory rodents will avoid drinking water to which some alcohol has been added, but animals in selected strains *prefer* alcohol and will drink a substantial amount each day if given the opportunity to do so. Genetically obese rodents and rodents who prefer to drink alcohol are used to help investigate the causes and treatment of obesity and alcoholism.

Sinclair (1990) describes a research project designed to find drugs that can help decrease alcohol drinking. He and his colleagues found that some drugs can reduce the reinforcing effects of alcohol by blocking certain receptor molecules in the brain. When rats of an alcohol-preferring strain are given such a drug and are permitted to drink for several days, their drinking eventually extinguishes. Perhaps such drugs can be used someday to diminish the reinforcing value of alcohol to recovering alcoholics and help them break their habit.

Some animal models are developed in the laboratory by exposing animals to particular situations. For example, Vogel, Neill, Hagler, and Kors (1990) have developed what they believe to be an animal model of depression, which may be useful in studying the physiological basis of this disorder. They gave young rats a series of injections of a drug that blocks the reuptake of serotonin. This early treatment appears to have affected the development of the brain. When the rats reached maturity, they showed many of the symptoms of endogenous depression: decreased sexual behavior, increased irritability, and decreased pleasure-seeking behavior (specifically, decreased willingness to work for reinforcing brain stimulation or for a taste of sucrose). The animals' sleep was also altered; the latency to the first bout of REM sleep was shorter, and the proportion of REM sleep was higher. The animals even responded to antidepressant treatment; if they were given imipramine or were deprived of REM sleep (treatments that help humans with depression), their sexual behavior increased. It will be interesting to see whether this model provides us with useful information about the physiology of depression.

Marczynski and Urbancic (1988) developed a similar animal model for the anxiety disorders. They gave pregnant cats injections of diazepam (Valium), which exposed their fetuses to the drug. When the offspring of these cats were one year old, the investigators tested their emotional reactions. They found that the animals showed restlessness and anxiety when they were placed in novel situations. This fearfulness could be reduced with an injection of diazepam. Later, they measured the level of benzodiazepine receptors in the animals' brains and found a decrease in several regions. Thus, fearfulness appears to be associated with a decreased number of benzodiazepine receptors. Most neuroscientists believe that the brain produces a neuromodulator that stimulates benzodiazepine receptors; if the brain has a deficiency of these receptors, this neuromodulator would have less effect on the animal's mood and behavior.

The development of animal models has become an important aspect of research in the treatment of neurological and mental disorders. Scientists believe that the future holds many treatments that will help alleviate human suffering.

KEY TERMS AND CONCEPTS

Further Reading

Classification and Diagnosis

Diagnostic and Statistical Manual III-R *(501)*
clinical judgment *(501)*
actuarial judgment *(501)*

Nonpsychotic Mental Disorders

neurosis *(504)*
panic disorder *(504)*
anticipatory anxiety *(505)*
phobic disorder *(506)*
agoraphobia *(506)*
social phobia *(506)*
simple phobia *(506)*
obsessive compulsive disorder *(507)*
obsession *(507)*
compulsion *(507)*
Tourette's syndrome *(509)*
somatoform disorder *(509)*
somatization disorder *(509)*
hypochondriasis *(509)*
conversion disorder *(510)*
malingering *(511)*
psychophysiological disorder *(511)*
dissociative disorder *(512)*
psychogenic amnesia *(512)*
psychogenic fugue *(512)*
multiple personality disorder *(512)*

Personality and Psychoactive Substance Abuse Disorders

antisocial personality disorder *(514)*

Schizophrenic Disorders

schizophrenia *(519)*
positive symptom *(519)*
thought disorder *(519)*
delusions of persecution *(520)*
delusions of grandeur *(520)*
delusions of control *(520)*
hallucination *(520)*
negative symptom *(520)*
undifferentiated schizophrenia *(520)*
catatonic schizophrenia *(520)*
catatonic posture *(520)*
waxy flexibility *(520)*
paranoid schizophrenia *(520)*
disorganized schizophrenia *(521)*
reactive schizophrenia *(521)*
process schizophrenia *(521)*
expressed emotion *(522)*
dopamine hypothesis *(523)*
chlorpromazine *(523)*

Mood Disorders

mood disorder *(526)*
bipolar disorder *(526)*
major depression *(526)*
dysthymic disorder *(526)*
cyclothymic disorder *(526)*
mania *(526)*
lithium carbonate *(527)*
antidepressant drug *(528)*
tricyclic antidepressant drug *(528)*
reserpine *(528)*
zeitgeber *(529)*
seasonal affective disorder *(529)*

SUGGESTIONS FOR FURTHER READING

Davison, G.C., and Neale, J.M. *Abnormal Psychology,* 5th ed. New York: John Wiley & Sons, 1990.

Goodwin, D.W., and Guze, S.B. *Psychiatric Diagnosis,* 4th ed. New York: Oxford University Press, 1989.

The book by Davison and Neale provides a survey of the field of abnormal psychology, including both diagnosis and treatment. The shorter book by Goodwin and Guze describes the characteristics of the most important mental disorders and what is known about their causes.

Meyer, R. *Case Studies in Abnormal Behavior,* 2d ed. Boston: Allyn and Bacon, 1987.

This book presents several accounts of specific cases of mental disorders and describes their diagnosis and treatment.

Rachman, S. *Obsessions and Compulsions.* Englewood Cliffs, N.J.: Prentice-Hall, 1975.

Rachman's book covers the range of obsessive compulsive behaviors, from the tunes that won't leave our minds to crippling disorders.

Cleckley, H. *The Mask of Sanity,* 5th ed. St. Louis: C.V. Mosby, 1976.

Cleckley's book is the definitive volume on antisocial personality disorder (psychopathy). Along with a thorough discussion of the disorder, it contains several detailed case studies.

Arieti, S., and Bemborad, J. *Severe and Mild Depression.* New York: Basic Books, 1978.

Bernheim, K., and Lewine, R. *Schizophrenia.* New York: W.W. Norton, 1979.

These books discuss the two most serious psychological disturbances.

16
THE TREATMENT OF MENTAL DISORDERS

Henri Matisse, *Goldfish*
SCALA/Art Resource, N.Y. © 1992 Succession H. Matisse/ARS, N.Y.

LEARNING OBJECTIVES

When you finish this chapter, you should be able to:

1. Describe the early treatment of the mentally ill, and outline the historical development of psychotherapy.
2. Explain and evaluate the treatment of mental disorders by means of psychoanalysis and humanistic/existential therapy.
3. Describe the use of classical and instrumental conditioning in behavior therapy.
4. Describe the use of modeling and cognitive restructuring in cognitive behavior therapy.
5. Evaluate behavior therapy, and describe the types of situations in which its use is appropriate.
6. Outline some of the benefits of group psychotherapy, and describe and evaluate family therapy and community psychology.
7. Describe and evaluate the treatment of mental disorders with antipsychotic, antidepressant, and antianxiety drugs.
8. Describe and evaluate the treatment of mental disorders with electroconvulsive therapy and psychosurgery.
9. Describe and discuss research on the effectiveness of therapies and therapists.

"Andrew was diagnosed as a catatonic schizophrenic. . . . He had been silent for 19 years. It was only by accident that the psychologist got the clue which enabled him to recondition Andrew's verbal behavior. . . . In one group session the attending psychologist . . . inadvertently dropped a stick of chewing gum on the floor. Andrew's eyes, which had normally been impassive and unresponsive, showed a glint of interest in the chewing gum. Later the psychologist thought about Andrew's behavior. If chewing gum had been effective in bringing Andrew out of his private world, perhaps it would also serve as a positive reinforcer.

"During the next two weeks, this hypothesis was discovered to be well founded. Periodically in the group sessions, a stick of gum was held before Andrew's face. The psychologist waited until Andrew's eyes moved toward it. When this occurred, he immediately relinquished the stick of gum to Andrew, who opened his mouth and chewed it with alacrity. . . . At the end of two weeks, Andrew cast his eyes toward the psychologist each time he produced a stick of gum.

"Having demonstrated that chewing gum was a positive reinforcer, the psychologist elected to use this simple but obviously powerful tool to reinstate verbal behavior in Andrew's life. . . . In accordance with the method of successive approximation [shaping], an initial response was selected for Andrew. Early in the third week, the experimenter saw Andrew make a slight movement of his lips. Immediately the psychologist pulled forth a stick of gum and reinforced this lip movement. By the end of that week, Andrew was regularly making both lip movements and eye contacts with the psychologist. At the beginning of the fourth week . . . , Andrew not only had to make contact with his eyes and move his lips, but he also was required to emit a vocal sound of one sort or another.

". . . By the end of the fourth week, Andrew was regularly making eye movements toward the experimenter, moving his lips, and making a vocal sound which resembled . . . a croak.

"At the beginning of the fifth week . . . , the psychologist waited until Andrew made a croaking sound and then he urged, 'Say gum, gum.'. . . The experimenter hesitated until the croaking sound faintly resembled the word 'gum' and then he gave Andrew his reinforcement. On the next occasion . . . , he withheld reinforcement until Andrew had all but approximated verbalizing 'gum.'

"During a session near the sixth week of the treatment, an exciting thing happened. . . . Andrew suddenly said quite clearly and distinctly, 'Gum, please.' Before the session had terminated, Andrew was answering questions about his name and his age and thereafter would answer any questions the psychologist directed to him. In the following days, Andrew continued to chat with the psychologist, both during the session and at other times and places within the institution." (From Donald L. Whaley/Richard W. Malott, *Elementary Principles of Behavior,* © 1971, pp. 79–82. Adapted by permission of Prentice Hall, Inc., Englewood Cliffs, New Jersey. Based on a case by Isaacs, Thomas, and Goldiamond, 1960.)

HISTORICAL BACKGROUND

Early Treatment of Mental Illness

1 Mental disorders have been with us since human existence began. For most of that time people afflicted with these disorders have been regarded, variously, with awe or fear. Sometimes, the delusions of people whom we would now probably classify as paranoid schizophrenics were regarded as prophetic; they were seen as instruments through whom gods or spirits were speaking. More often, they were considered to be occupied by devils or evil spirits and

The earliest known attempts to treat mental disorders involved trephining—producing holes in a person's skull to allow evil spirits to escape.

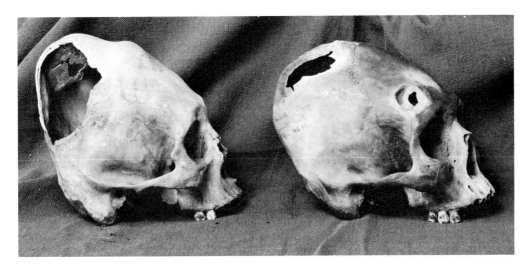

Figure 16.1 Prehistoric skulls showing trephining. (University Museum, University of Pennsylvania. Reprinted with permission.)

were made to suffer accordingly. The earliest known attempts to treat mental disorders involved **trephining,** or drilling holes in a person's skull. Presumably, the opening was made to permit evil spirits to leave the victim's head. In prehistoric times this procedure was performed with a sharp-edged stone; later civilizations, such as the Egyptians, refined the practice. Signs of healing at the edges of the holes in prehistoric skulls indicate that some people survived these operations. (See *Figure 16.1*.)

Many painful and degrading practices were directed at people's presumed possession by evil spirits. Those who were thought to be unwilling hosts for evil spirits were subjected to curses or insults designed to persuade the demons to leave. If this approach had no effect, exorcism was tried, to make the person's body an unpleasant place for devils to reside, through beatings, starving, near drowning, and the drinking of foul-tasting concoctions. Many people who were perceived as having accepted their condition voluntarily—as being in league with the devil—actively participated in their own prosecution and conviction. The delusional schemes of psychotics often include beliefs of personal guilt and unworthiness; and in a society that accepted the notion that there were witches and devils, these people were ready to imagine themselves as being evil and degraded. They "confessed" to unspeakable acts of sorcery and welcomed their own persecution and punishment. Consider the following case, which occurred during the Middle Ages:

> A certain woman was taken and finally burned, who for six years had an incubus devil [an evil spirit that has sexual intercourse with a sleeping woman] even when she was lying in bed at the side of her husband. . . . The homage she

has given to the devil was of such a sort that she was bound to dedicate herself body and soul to him forever, after seven years. But God provided mercifully for she was taken in the sixth year and condemned to the fire, and having truly and completely confessed is believed to have obtained pardon from God. For she went most willingly to her death, saying that she would gladly suffer an even more terrible death if only she would be set free and escape the power of the devil. (Stone, 1937, p. 146)

Until the eighteenth century many Europeans accepted the idea that devils and spirits were responsible for peculiar behaviors in some people. A few believed that these disorders reflected diseases and that they should be treated medically, with compassion for the victim. Johann Wier, a sixteenth-century physician, was among the first to challenge the entire concept of witchcraft. He argued that most people who were being tortured and burned for practicing witchcraft in fact suffered from mental illness. The Church condemned his writings as heretical and banned them until the twentieth century. However, even within the Church some people began to realize that the prevailing beliefs and practices were wrong. Saint Vincent de Paul, a seventeenth-century priest, wrote: "Mental disease is no different to bodily disease and Christianity demands of the humane and powerful to protect, and the skillful to relieve the one as well as the other" (cited in Coleman, 1976, p. 37).

As belief in witchcraft and demonology waned, the clergy, the medical authorities, and the general public began to regard people with mental disorders as ill; and torture and persecution eventually ceased. However, the lives of these people were not necessarily better as a result. Undoubtedly, many people with mental disorders were regarded as strange but harmless and managed to maintain a marginal existence in society. Others were sheltered by their families. The unfortunate ones were those who were consigned to the various "asylums" established for the care of the mentally ill. Most of these mental institutions were hideously inhumane. Patients were often kept in chains and sometimes wallowed in their own excreta. Those who displayed bizarre catatonic postures or who had fanciful delusions were exhibited to the public for a fee. Many of the treatments designed to cure mental patients were little better than the tortures that had previously been used to drive out evil spirits. Patients were tied up, doused in cold water, bled, made to vomit, spun violently in a rotating chair, and otherwise assaulted by the fruits of "modern science."

The mistreatment of the mentally ill did not go unnoticed by humanitarians. A famous and effective early reformer was Philippe Pinel (1745–1826), a French physician. In 1793 Pinel was appointed director of La Bicêtre, a mental hospital in Paris. Pinel believed that most mental patients would respond well to kind treatment. As an experiment, he removed the chains from some of the inmates, took them out of dungeons, and allowed them to walk about the hospital grounds. The experiment was a remarkable success; an atmosphere of peace and quiet replaced the previous noise, stench, and general aura of despair. Many patients were eventually discharged. Pinel's success at La Bicêtre was repeated when he was given charge

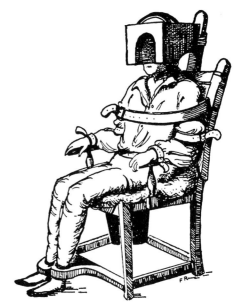

The "tranquilizing chair" devised by Benjamin Rush.

of Salpêtrière Hospital. From what we now know about psychoses, many patients eventually recover—or at least get much better—without any treatment at all. But if a person was put in one of the mental institutions that existed at that time, he or she never had a chance to show improvement; from our present perspective the conditions seem to have been designed to *prevent* recovery.

Pinel's success encouraged similar reforms elsewhere. In the United States the campaign for humane treatment of mental patients was led by Dorothea Dix (1802–1887), who raised millions of dollars for the construction of mental hospitals and spurred the reform of many mental health facilities. The process took a long time; until very recently, some large mental hospitals were little more than warehouses for severely affected patients, who received little or no treatment but were merely provided with the necessities of life. Today there is much greater emphasis on treatment in community-based facilities, and the discovery of the antipsychotic drugs has freed many patients who would otherwise have spent their lives in institutions.

The Development of Psychotherapy

The modern history of specific treatments for mental disorders probably began with Franz Anton Mesmer (1734–1815), an Austrian physician who practiced in Paris in the late eighteenth and early nineteenth centuries. As we saw in Chapter 8, he devised a theory of "magnetic fluxes" in which he attempted to effect cures by manip-

A rotating chair, used in the early nineteenth century to treat people with mental disorders.

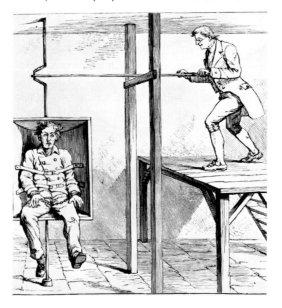

Philippe Pinel releasing the shackles from patients at Salpêtrière Hospital.

ulating iron rods and bottles of chemicals. What he actually did was hypnotize his patients, thereby alleviating some of their symptoms, especially those of psychological origin. Accordingly, hypnosis was first known as *mesmerism*.

A French neurologist, Jean Martin Charcot (1825–1893), began his investigations of the therapeutic uses of hypnosis when one of his students hypnotized a woman and induced her to display the symptoms of a conversion reaction (formerly called *hysteria*). Charcot examined her and concluded that she was a hysterical patient. The student then woke the woman, and her symptoms vanished. Charcot had previously believed that hysteria had an organic basis, but this experience changed his opinion, and he began investigating its psychological causes.

Just before Sigmund Freud began private practice, he studied with Charcot in Paris and observed the effects of hypnosis on hysteria. Freud's association with Charcot, and later with Breuer, started him on his life's study of the determinants of personality and the origins of mental illness. As we saw in Chapter 14, Freud formulated a psychodynamic theory of personality, which has proved to be one of the most influential attempts to explain human behavior. He also founded the practice of psychoanalysis, which many psychiatrists, and some psychologists, use today to treat patients with psychological problems.

The rest of this chapter describes four approaches to the treatment of mental disorders: insight psychotherapies, behavior therapy and cognitive behavior therapy, treatment of groups (including treatment of couples and the development of outreach programs that serve the community), and biological treatments. The insight psychotherapies include a variety of treatments that emphasize talk between the therapist and the client as a means of discovering the reasons for the client's problems. Insight into these reasons presumably helps the client solve the problems. In contrast, behavior therapies and cognitive behavior therapies downplay the importance of insight and concentrate on eliminating maladaptive behaviors (including maladaptive patterns of thinking) and replacing them with adaptive ones. Group therapies include both insight-oriented and behavior-oriented methods. Biological treatments attempt to change a person's behavior by altering the state of the nervous system medically, surgically, or through induction of a seizure. In practice, most clinical psychologists are not unalterably wedded to a particular system of therapy. Although each therapist discovers that he or she deals best with particular kinds of problems, most practitioners adopt a variety of techniques to achieve therapeutic results with their clients. The final section of the chapter considers research evaluating the usefulness of the various forms of therapy.

Chapter 15 was devoted to serious mental disorders. This chapter describes therapeutic practices in general. Although mental health professionals certainly treat clients with serious mental disorders such as schizophrenia, they also treat clients with much less profound difficulties. In fact, *treatment* is too strong a word for much of the work that clinicians do; more accurately, they advise their clients and help them find strategies for solving their problems. One need not have a mental disorder to profit from the advice and counsel of a mental health professional. People consult such professionals for help in breaking bad habits (from drug addiction to smoking to overeating to argumentativeness), for help in reducing anxiety, for help in improving marital relations, for help with a child with academic or behavioral difficulties—or for any of the other problems that confront all of us from time to time.

INSIGHT PSYCHOTHERAPIES

2 The case of Anna O., who was supposedly cured of hysteria by talking about various conflicts while under hypnosis (Chapter 14), probably marks the beginning of insight psychotherapy. **Insight psychotherapy** is based on the assumption that people are essentially normal but that they learn maladaptive thought patterns and behaviors. Once a patient understands the causes of his or her problems, they will cease; insight will lead to a cure.

Most forms of psychotherapy (those that are not based on biological treatment or on modification of the client's behavior) rely upon insight for behavioral change. Some therapies, such as psychoanalysis, emphasize causes in the patient's past. Others, such as client-centered therapy, emphasize the present; they attempt to get the patient to see the effects of his or her patterns of behavior and to find more adaptive ways of living.

Psychoanalysis

Description. Freud's psychodynamic theory of personality serves as the basis for psychoanalysis, the first formal psychotherapeutic procedure devised. **Psychoanalysis** means just what its name implies: A person's psyche, or mind, is analyzed. Freud asserted that psychopathology was caused by unconscious fears and motives. By bringing unconscious conflicts to consciousness, the client comes to understand the reasons for his or her behavior and realizes that the childhood conditions under which the causes developed no longer exist. Once this realization occurs, the conflicts can be resolved, and the person's behavior can come under the control of the ego, which is conscious and able to reflect, deliberate, and choose.

The first step, bringing the unconscious to light, involves relaxing or tricking the ego's defense mechanisms, which suppress unconscious thoughts. One technique used to accomplish this goal is **free association,** in which the client is encouraged to talk about anything and everything he or she thinks of. Before beginning free association, the psychotherapist says something like this:

> In ordinary conversation, you usually try to keep a connecting thread running through your remarks excluding any intrusive ideas or side issues so as not to wander too far from the point, and rightly so. But in this case you must talk differently. As you talk various thoughts will occur to you which you like to ignore because of certain criticisms and objections. You will be tempted to think, "that is irrelevant or unimportant, or nonsensical," and to avoid saying it. Do not give in to such criticism. Report such thoughts in spite of your wish not to do so. Later, the reason for this injunction, the only one you have to follow, will become clear. Report whatever goes through your mind. Pretend that you are a traveler, describing to someone beside you the changing views which you see outside the train window. (Ford and Urban, 1963, p. 168)

The alert psychotherapist notes the dominant themes in the client's narrative and attempts to interpret any symbolism that may represent disguised unconscious thoughts. The therapist also notes when the client shows **resistance** by acting uncomfortable, hesitating, abruptly changing the subject, or even "forgetting" to attend sessions. Resistance indicates that painful topics are being approached and provides important clues to the root of the person's problems.

Another source of data concerning the unconscious is dreams. Because the ego defenses are more relaxed during sleep, the content of dreams often suggests the nature of the client's conflicts. The latent (hidden) content of a dream is inferred from its manifest (apparent) content. Similarly, hypnosis may be used to uncover the client's unconscious thoughts.

As psychotherapy progresses, the therapist begins interpreting free associations and dreams for the client, in order to increase the person's insight. The interpretations must come at the proper stage of analysis. The client should be on the verge of his or her own discovery so that the explanations will be accepted; if they are presented prematurely, the client may rebel, and his or her resistance will increase.

During psychoanalysis the client generally forms a **transference neurosis,** transferring his or her feelings toward a dominant childhood figure—usually a parent—to the psychoanalyst.

Depending on the nature of the childhood relationship, the feelings may be positive and loving or negative and hostile. Transference is seen as essential for effective therapy; the psychoanalyst encourages its development by remaining a rather vague, shadowy figure seated behind the reclining client's head. Using the relationship that develops between client and therapist, the therapist can infer the childhood relationships that caused the conflicts to develop. However, the therapist must guard against the dangers of **countertransference,** which consists of the therapist's own feelings toward the client. All psychoanalysts must themselves receive a **training analysis** during their education, which permits them to understand their own conflicts and motivations, so as to avoid reacting inappropriately toward their clients.

According to Freud, therapists must not help their clients solve everyday problems. Solution of present problems is regarded by psychoanalysts as the easy way out, which should be avoided in the best interests of the client. (As we will see, most other types of therapists disagree with this belief.) In justifying their refusal to deal with their clients' present problems, psychoanalysts assert that the clients undoubtedly already received sympathy and advice from friends and family members. If such support was going to work, it already would have, and the clients would not have needed the services of a psychoanalyst. Instead, the clients must remain uncomfortable enough to be motivated to work on their repressed conflicts.

Evaluation. The scientific basis of psychoanalysis has not been established. As we saw in Chapter 14, the foundations of Freud's theory of personality remain unproved. But even though the theory cannot be confirmed, we should be able to assess the effectiveness of the psychoanalytical method—after all, it is results that count most. However, evaluating the effectiveness of psychoanalysis is difficult, because only a small proportion of people with mental disorders qualify for this method of treatment. They must be intelligent, articulate individuals who are motivated enough to spend three or more hours a week for several years working hard to uncover unconscious conflicts. In addition, they must be able to afford the psychoanalyst's fees, which are high. (Psychoanalysts maintain that it is in the interests of clients to make a financial sacrifice, because doing so encourages them to take the procedure seriously.) These qualifications rule out most psychotics, as well as people who lack the time or money to devote to such a long-term project. Furthermore, many who enter psychoanalysis become dissatisfied with their progress and leave; in other cases the therapist encourages a client to leave if he or she decides that the client is not cooperating fully. Thus, those who actually complete a course of psychoanalysis do not constitute a random sample, and we cannot conclude that psychoanalysis works just because a high percentage of this group is happy with the results. Those who have dropped out are not counted.

Another problem in evaluating psychoanalysis is the difficulty of explicitly defining the changes being sought in the client. For example, one of the goals is to lift unconscious repressions, but how can the therapist determine when this goal has been achieved? Perhaps a client's insight into his or her behavior demonstrates success. But some critics have argued that insight is no more than a client's acceptance of the therapist's belief system (Bandura, 1969). In fact, one critic (Levy, 1963) has asserted that the unconscious does not exist—that it is merely a disagreement between therapist and client about the causes of the client's behavior.

Yet another problem in evaluating psychoanalysis is that psychoanalysts have a way to "explain" their failures: They can blame them on the client. If the client appears to accept an insight into his or her behavior but the behavior does not change, the insight is said to be merely "intellectual." This escape clause makes the argument for the importance of insight completely circular and, therefore, illogical: If the client gets better, the improvement is due to insight; but if the client's behavior remains unchanged, real (as opposed to "intellectual") insight did not occur. An equivalent in logic is to argue that wearing a charm (and sincerely believing in it) will cure cancer. If some people who wear the charm get better, then the charm obviously works; if other people who wear the charm die, then they obviously were not sincere believers.

According to Luborsky and Spence (1978), evaluations of the results of psychoanalysis suggest that the method does not work very well with severe mental disorders, such as schizophrenia. This finding is to be expected, because psychoanalysis is based on verbalization and rationality, two responses impossible to achieve with extremely disturbed people. The method achieves better results with people who have anxiety disorders. Success appears to be best with highly educated clients.

Some clinicians have objected to the techniques used by psychoanalysts to encourage transference neurosis. For example, Wachtel

(1977) asserts that by remaining a vague, shadowy figure and refusing to respond to the client's pleas for guidance, the psychoanalyst causes frustration. The client then acts "childish" because of the psychoanalyst's behavior, not necessarily because of deep-seated unresolved conflicts that stem from experiences during childhood.

Many clinicians today practice *brief psychoanalysis,* a form of therapy that is based on psychoanalytical principles but that does not require clients to embark on a full-fledged program of intensive psychoanalysis over several years. This development recognizes that fact that not all psychological problems are so deep-seated that they require a complete psychological overhaul (so to speak). The therapists find that, sometimes, brief but intensive therapy is all that is needed to help clients solve their problems.

Humanistic Therapy

Psychoanalysis is not the only form of psychotherapy based on insight. Several other forms of therapy, grouped under the heading of *humanistic therapy,* have been developed. *Humanism* is a philosophy oriented toward human beings, their feelings, and their accomplishments rather than toward the abstractions of theology or the principles of science. The most important form of humanistic therapy is *client-centered therapy.*

Client-centered therapy was developed by Carl Rogers (1902–1987), an American psychologist. Rogers believed that people are basically good and that they all possess an innate drive toward self-actualization. Problems occur when people's concept of the *ideal self* begins to differ substantially from their concept of the *real self.* This discrepancy occurs when people fail to pay attention to their own internal evaluations of their self-concept, accepting the evaluations of others instead. The faulty self-concept inevitably conflicts with experience, and the person becomes unhappy and dissatisfied. Rogers asserted that the therapist must provide an environment of **unconditional positive regard** for the client; that is, the therapist must totally and unconditionally accept the client and approve of him or her as a person. In such an environment a client will follow his or her own instincts for goodness and will become a self-actualizing person without any psychological disturbances.

The primary objective of Rogers's therapeutic approach is to help the client pay attention to his or her own feelings so that these innate tendencies toward goodness can emerge. Only by using these feelings as guides can the person move toward a life-style that will be most gratifying for him or her as an individual.

The first requirement is that the therapist provide an atmosphere of unconditional positive regard so that the client can come to believe that his or her feelings are worthwhile and important. Once the client begins to pay attention to these feelings, a self-healing process begins. The therapist must be not only warm and friendly but also empathetic; he or she must use this empathy to try to help the client articulate these feelings. For example, a client usually has difficulty at first expressing feelings verbally. The therapist tries to understand the feelings underlying the client's confused state and help the client put them into words. Through this process the client learns to understand and heed his or her own drive toward self-actualization and goodness. Mental health automatically comes with an awareness of his or her own feelings; adaptive behaviors will then replace maladaptive ones. According to Rogers, the therapist should not manipulate events but should create conditions under which the client can make his or her own decisions independently. The following interaction illustrates this process:

> *Alice:* I was thinking about this business of standards. I somehow developed a sort of knack, I guess, of—well—habit—of trying to make people feel at ease around me, or to make things go along smoothly. . . .

Psychologist Carl Rogers (wearing glasses) developed a humanistic approach to psychotherapy. He believed that people are naturally motivated toward growth, fulfillment, and health. Here, Rogers facilitates a group therapy session in 1966.

Counselor: In other words, what you did was always in the direction of trying to keep things smooth and to make other people feel better and to smooth the situation.

Alice: Yes. I think that's what it was. Now the reason why I did it probably was—I mean, not that I was a good little Samaritan going around making other people happy, but that was probably the role that felt easiest for me to play. I'd been doing it around the home so much. I just didn't stand up for my own convictions, until I don't know whether I have any convictions to stand up for.

Counselor: You feel that for a long time you've been playing the role of kind of smoothing out the frictions or differences or what not. . . .

Alice: M-hum.

Counselor: Rather than having any opinion or reaction of your own in the situation. Is that it?

Alice: That's it. Or that I haven't been really honestly being myself, or actually knowing what my real self is, and that I've been just playing a sort of false role. Whatever role no one else was playing, and that needed to be played at the time, I'd try to fill it in. (Rogers, 1951, pp. 152–153)

According to Rogers, a good therapist is a spontaneous, open, authentic person who shows no phoniness or professional facade. A good therapist is self-disclosing and candid, which encourages the client to act in a similar fashion. (As we will see, behavior therapies and cognitive behavior therapies also rely heavily on the principle of *modeling,* or presenting a good example for the client to emulate.) Besides demonstrating unconditional positive regard, the therapist must truly understand how the client feels and show this empathy effectively.

Unlike many other clinicians, who prefer to rely on their own judgments concerning the effectiveness of their techniques, Rogers himself stimulated a considerable amount of research on the effectiveness of client-centered therapy. He recorded therapeutic sessions so that various techniques could be evaluated. One researcher, Charles Truax (1966), obtained permission from Rogers (and his clients) to record some therapy sessions, and he classified the statements made by the clients into several categories. One of the categories included statements of improving mental health, such as "I'm feeling better lately" or "I don't feel as depressed as I used to." After each of the patient's statements, Truax noted Rogers's reaction, to see whether he gave a positive response. Typical positive responses were "Oh, really? Tell me more" or "Uh-huh.

That's nice" or just a friendly "Mm." Truax found that of the eight categories of client statements, only those that indicated progress were regularly followed by a positive response from Rogers. Not surprisingly, during their therapy the clients made more and more statements indicating progress.

This experiment attests to the power of social reinforcement and its occurrence in unexpected places. Rogers was an effective and conscientious psychotherapist, but he had not intended to single out and reinforce his clients' realistic expressions of progress in therapy. (Of course, he did not uncritically reinforce exaggerated or unrealistic positive statements.) This finding does not discredit client-centered therapy. Rogers simply adopted a very effective strategy for altering a person's behavior. He used to refer to his therapy as *nondirective;* however, when he realized that he was reinforcing positive statements, he stopped referring to it as nondirective, because it obviously was not.

Davison and Neale (1982) point out an apparent shortcoming of client-centered therapy. Rogers assumed that once a person begins to heed his or her own feelings, maladaptive behaviors will automatically cease. But this assumption has by no means been proved. For example, once a person with a severe feeling of inferiority acknowledges that feeling, he or she may withdraw from the company of other people and hence never learn the social skills that we all develop through interactions with others. Even if therapy did improve the person's self-concept, he or she would still have problems in society. As Davison and Neale observe, a good psychotherapist must help people develop social skills as well as gain a better self-image; changes must occur in both behavior and self-concept to produce notable improvement.

One other limitation requires mention. Like psychoanalysis, client-centered therapy is not appropriate for serious problems such as psychoses. It is most effective for people who are motivated enough to want to change and who are intelligent enough to be able to gain some insight concerning their problems. In addition, Rogers's model of humans as being basically good may be wrong. For example, we might question whether a person with antisocial personality disorder should be provided with unconditional positive regard.

In defense of client-centered therapy, the method is much more affordable and less time-consuming than traditional psychoanalysis. Most ordinary, decent neurotic people would probably enjoy and profit from talking about their problems with a person as sympathetic as Carl Rogers. Although his theoretical formulation of human behavior is unlikely to have a lasting influence on the science of psychology, his insights into the dynamics of the client-therapist relationship have had a major impact on the field of psychotherapy.

INTERIM SUMMARY

Historical Background and Insight Psychotherapies

Insight psychotherapies are based primarily on conversation between therapist and client. The oldest form, psychoanalysis, was devised by Freud. Psychoanalysis attempts to discover the forces that are warring in the client's psyche and to resolve the inner conflicts by bringing to consciousness his or her unconscious drives and the defenses that have been established against them. Insight is believed to be the primary source of healing.

Whereas psychoanalysis regards human behavior as motivated by primitive, biologically determined urges, humanistic therapy emphasizes conscious, deliberate mental processes. Client-centered therapy is based on the premise that people are basically healthy and good and that their problems result from faulty learning. Instead of evaluating themselves in terms of their own self-concepts, they judge themselves by other people's standards. This tendency is rectified by providing an environment of unconditional positive regard in which clients can find their own way to mental health.

Existentialism teaches that individuals exist alone, that the world is indifferent to their fate, and that each person has free choice and is responsible for the consequences of his or her behavior. Existential therapy is designed to help people face these facts and to cope with existential anxiety. The goal is for the client to achieve authentic self-expression and to develop healthy and fulfilling interpersonal relations. ∎

BEHAVIOR AND COGNITIVE BEHAVIOR THERAPY

3 Insight psychotherapies are based on the assumption that understanding leads to behavioral change; once a person gains insight into the causes of his or her maladaptive behavior, that behavior will cease and will be replaced by adap-

tive behavior. However, insight is often *not* followed by behavioral change. In addition, some insight psychotherapies (particularly psychoanalysis) insist on explaining present difficulties as the result of conflicts dating from childhood. Behaviorally oriented therapists have decided that it is better to focus on a person's maladaptive behavior than to speculate on its causes. The *behavior itself* is the problem, not the historical reasons for its development. Consequently, the goal is to change the behavior by whatever means are found to be most effective.

Practitioners of behavior therapy employ a variety of techniques based on the principles of classical and instrumental conditioning (defined and described in Chapter 6). The emphasis in classical conditioning is on stimuli that elicit new responses contrary to the old, maladaptive ones. In instrumental conditioning (also called *operant conditioning*) the emphasis is on the responses made; adaptive responses are selectively reinforced, and maladaptive ones are ignored or punished.

The fact that behavior therapy is based on the results of experimental research does not make this approach easier to use, nor does it require less sensitivity or clinical experience on the part of the therapist. A successful behavior therapist must be able to determine what behaviors and emotional reactions need to be changed, find out what stimuli can serve as effective reinforcers, and successfully alter the client's environment in a way that produces desirable changes. Some skeptical insight therapists have tried behavioral methods and claimed that "rewards didn't work." Perhaps they never found effective reinforcers, or perhaps the procedures they followed were inadequate. Perhaps their clients derived more reinforcement from making the therapist look foolish than from experiencing the "reinforcing" effects of the stimuli they were expected to respond to. As we saw in Chapter 6, it is the individual who determines whether a particular stimulus is capable of reinforcing behavior. In any event, empirical research has proved the effectiveness of the techniques described in this section.

Classical Conditioning

Systematic Desensitization. One technique of behavior therapy has been especially successful in eliminating some kinds of neurotic fears and phobias. This technique, called **systematic desensitization,** was developed by Joseph Wolpe of the Temple University School of Medicine. Its goal is to remove the unpleasant emotional response produced by the feared object or situation and replace it with an incompatible one—relaxation.

First, the client is trained to achieve complete relaxation. The essential task is to learn to respond quickly to suggestions to feel relaxed and peaceful, so that these suggestions can elicit a relaxation response. Second, client and therapist construct a hierarchy of anxiety-related stimuli. Table 16.1 presents a hierarchy constructed with a subject who had an intense fear of spiders (Thorpe and Olson, 1990). The situations provoking least fear are at the top. (See *Table 16.1.*)

Finally, the conditional stimuli (fear-eliciting situations) are paired with stimuli that elicit the learned relaxation response. For example, a person with a fear of spiders is instructed to relax and then to imagine hearing from a neighbor that she saw a spider in her garage. If the client reports no anxiety, he or she is instructed to move to the next item and imagine hearing a neighbor say that there is a tiny spider across the street; and so on. Whenever the client begins feeling anxious, he or she signals to the therapist with some predetermined gesture— say, by raising a finger. The therapist instructs the client to relax and, if necessary, describes a less threatening scene. The client is not permitted to feel severe anxiety at any time. Gradually, over a series of sessions (the average is around eleven), the client is able to get through the entire list, vicariously experiencing even the most feared encounters.

Systematic desensitization is a very successful technique for people who have a specific phobia (as opposed to generalized fear and anxiety). Because this technique always has a specific goal, the therapist can assess its success or failure objectively. Of course, the therapist must first be sure that the client's anxiety is actually inappropriate. For example, several studies have demonstrated that systematic desensitization can effectively reduce students' anxiety about taking examinations. However, in some cases a student's test anxiety may be realistic, reflecting the fact that the student does not prepare well for examinations. In these cases therapeutic efforts should first be aimed at helping the students develop better study skills. Perhaps if the student learns to study more effectively, the test anxiety will disappear. In any event, reducing test anxiety in students who are not studying effectively will not improve their academic performance.

Scientific evaluations of systematic desen-

sitization have been positive, and several experiments have found that all elements of the procedure are necessary for its success. For example, a person will not get rid of a phobia merely by participating in relaxation training or by constructing hierarchies of fear-producing situations; only *pairings* of the anxiety-producing stimuli with instructions to relax will reduce the fear. One testimonial to this relation comes from a study by Johnson and Sechrest (1968), which attempted to reduce the fear of taking examinations in a group of college students. Students who underwent systematic desensitization received significantly higher grades on their final examination in a psychology course than did groups of control subjects who were also taking the course but who received either no treatment or relaxation training alone.

Systematic desensitization usually, but not always, involves imaginary encounters with the feared object or situation. In some cases the therapist arranges *in vivo* ("live") encounters. For example, a fear of snakes or spiders will be desensitized by actually approaching these objects. Similarly, a social phobia will be desensitized by having to talk in front of a group of strangers. The therapist generally begins systematic desensitization in the usual manner and then moves to actual encounters after progress

Table 16.1   Sample anxiety hierarchy: Phobia of spiders

1. Abbie [neighbor] tells you she saw one in her garage.
2. Abbie sees you, crosses the street, says there's a tiny one across the street.
3. Betty [at work] says there's one downstairs.
4. Friends downstairs say they saw one outside their apartment and disposed of it.
5. Carrie [daughter] returns from camp; says the restrooms were inhabited by spiders.
6. You see a small, dark spot out of the corner of your eye; you have a closer look; it isn't a spider.
7. You are with your husband. You see a tiny spider on a thread outside, but you can't see it very clearly.
8. You are alone. You see a tiny spider on a thread outside, but you can't see it very clearly.
9. You are reading the paper, and you see a cartoonist's caricature of a spider (with a human-like face and smile).
10. You are reading an article about the Brown Recluse.
11. You see a clear photograph of a spider's web in the newspaper.
12. You see a spider's web on the stairs at work.
13. You suddenly see a loose tomato-top in your salad.
14. You open a kitchen cabinet and suddenly see a large spider.

Source: G.L. Thorpe and S.L. Olson. *Behavior Therapy: Concepts, Procedures, and Applications.* Boston: Allyn and Bacon, 1990. Reprinted with permission.

has been made with imaginary ones. According to Wilson and O'Leary (1978), in vivo desensitization is almost always more effective and long lasting than vicarious desensitization.

Whereas practitioners of systematic desensitization are careful not to permit their clients to become too anxious, practitioners of a procedure called **implosion therapy** attempt to rid their clients of their fears by arousing them as intensely as possible. The therapist describes, as graphically as possible, the most frightening encounters possible with the object of the client's phobia. The client tries to vividly imagine the encounter and to experience intense fear. In some cases the client actually encounters the object of his or her fear, in which case the treatment is called *in vivo implosion therapy*. Of course, the client is protected from any adverse effects of the encounter (or the encounter is imaginary), so there are no dangerous consequences. Eventually, the fear response begins to subside, and the client learns that even the worst imaginable encounter can become tolerable. In a sense, the client learns not to fear his or her own anxiety attack, and avoidance responses begin to extinguish.

Although it may seem cruel to subject a client to a situation that produces anxiety, implosion therapy does appear to be an effective treatment for phobias. In fact, Chambless, Foa, Graves, and Goldstein (1979) found that agoraphobic subjects who were given an anxiety-reducing drug before being exposed to the situation they feared did not profit from treatment with the implosion technique; anxiety appears to be necessary for therapeutic effectiveness.

Aversive Classical Conditioning. Sometimes, people are attracted by stimuli that most of us would ignore, and they engage in maladaptive behavior as a result of this attraction. Fetishes (such as sexual attraction to women's shoes) are the most striking examples. The technique of **aversive classical conditioning** attempts to establish an unpleasant response (such as a feeling of fear or disgust) to the object that produces the undesired behavior. For example, a person with a fetish for women's shoes might be given painful electrical shocks while viewing color slides of women's shoes. Aversive classical conditioning has also been used to treat drinking, smoking, transvestism, exhibitionism, and overeating. This technique has been shown to be moderately effective (Kanfer and Phillips, 1970). However, because the method involves pain or nausea, the client's participation must be

voluntary, and the method should be employed only if other approaches fail or are impractical.

Instrumental Conditioning

Reinforcement of Adaptive Behaviors. Behavioral techniques are often used to alter the behavior of mentally retarded or emotionally disturbed people who are difficult to communicate with. The opening vignette describes a case reported by Isaacs, Thomas, and Goldiamond (1960) of a forty-year-old man with schizophrenia who had been admitted to a hospital nineteen years previously and had not spoken one word to anyone during those years. After discovering that the man loved to chew gum, the psychologist was able to reinforce speaking, using the method of successive approximations (shaping), which was described in Chapter 6.

Reinforcement can be a powerful method of behavioral change; it has been used in a wide variety of settings and for people with problems less dramatic and severe than that of the schizophrenic patient in the opening vignette. If the therapist has established a warm relationship with the client, he or she can use ordinary social reinforcers, such as signs of approval (friendly smiles and nods of the head), to encourage positive behavioral change. As we saw in the section on client-centered therapy, even nonbehavioral psychologists use reinforcement—deliberately or inadvertently—to effect behavioral change. And as we shall see in the section "Maintaining Behavioral Change," therapists often enlist the aid of friends and members of the client's family in seeing that appropriate behaviors are reinforced. Moreover, the client is often taught to arrange for the reinforcement of his or her own behavior by use of a technique called *self-control*.

Punishment of Maladaptive Behaviors. In general, punishment is not nearly as good a training method as positive reinforcement. For one thing, the person who is being punished may learn to fear or dislike the person who administers the punishment. If this person is the therapist, such an occurrence will probably interfere with other aspects of therapy. Second, there is a tendency to *overgeneralize*—to avoid performing a whole class of responses related to the one that is specifically being punished. For example, a child might not tell her father any more lies after being punished for doing so, but she might also stop sharing her fantasies with him. Unfortunately, it is usually easier to punish a response than it is to figure out how to reinforce other responses that will replace the undesirable one. And when we are angry, we often find that it is satisfying (reinforcing) to punish someone.

However, in some therapeutic situations, especially those in which the undesirable response is clearly harmful to the client, punishment is the most effective technique for eliminating an undesirable behavior. Cowart and Whaley (1971) reported the case of an emotionally disturbed child who persisted in self-mutilation. He banged his head against the floor until it was a swollen mass of cuts and bruises. As a result, he had to be restrained in his crib in a hospital for the mentally retarded. Obviously, the consequences of such confinement are serious for a child's development. After conventional techniques had failed, the therapist attached a pair of wires to the child's leg and placed him in a room with a padded floor. The child immediately began battering his head against the floor, and the therapist administered an electrical shock through the wires. The shock, which was certainly less damaging than the blows to the head, stopped the child short. He seemed more startled than anything else. He started banging his head against the floor again and received another shock. After very few repetitions of this sequence, the boy stopped his self-mutilation and could safely be let out of his crib.

The use of aversive methods does, of course, raise ethical issues, particularly when the individual is so severely impaired that he or she is unable to give informed consent to a particular therapeutic procedure. Carr and Lovaas (1983) state that aversive methods involving stimuli such as electric shock should be the last resort. They should be used only when the patient's behavior poses a serious threat to his or her own well-being and after the following methods have been employed unsuccessfully: reinforcing other behaviors, attempting to extinguish the maladaptive behaviors, temporarily removing the patient from the environment that reinforces the maladaptive behaviors (a method called *time-out,* described below), and trying to arrange for the patient to perform behaviors that are incompatible with the maladaptive ones.

As you will recall from Chapter 6, punishment can take two forms: the occurrence of an aversive stimulus and the removal of an appetitive one, otherwise known as *response cost.* Many therapists use a form of punishment that involves response cost: **time-out.** Rather than being subjected to an aversive stimulus, the individual is simply removed from the situation in which the behavior occurred. The person is placed in a small room in which he or she must remain for a short time with nothing to do and no one to interact with. This procedure is based on work with laboratory animals by Ferster and Skinner (1957); it has been found to be an effective method of reducing maladaptive, disruptive behaviors (Brantner and Doherty, 1983).

Sometimes, the appropriate response need not actually be performed in the presence of the therapist but can be practiced vicariously. Instead of experiencing an actual punishing stimulus after performing an actual behavior, the client imagines that he or she is performing an undesirable behavior and then imagines receiving an aversive stimulus. This method is called **covert sensitization.** For example, Thorpe and Olson (1990) describe the case of Frank, a man in his late twenties with a variety of social problems, including exhibitionism. He would drive far from his hometown and expose his genitals to unsuspecting strangers. Although he derived sexual pleasure from this practice, he was disturbed by it and wanted desperately to be able to stop this behavior.

The therapist used a variety of methods to help the client improve his social skills and reduce his anxiety. In addition, the therapist used covert sensitization to eliminate the exhibitionism. The client was encouraged to vividly imagine scenes such as the following:

> He was driving around in his car, looking for a suitable victim. A woman, walking alone, appeared. Frank stopped the car and got out. He began to loosen his clothing. He was feeling strongly aroused sexually. Suddenly a police car pulled up, its lights flashing and its siren wailing. The officers looked on Frank with contempt as they handcuffed him. At the same time one of Frank's workmates arrived on the scene. This workmate was the biggest gossip at the factory. News of Frank's arrest would soon be all over town. He would obviously lose his job. His crime would be reported in the local newspaper. Frank felt physically sick with shame. He thought ahead to the prospect of a long jail sentence in protective custody as a sex offender. (Thorpe and Olson, 1990, p. 17)

The client was indeed able to imagine scenes such as this one, and doing so made him feel very uncomfortable. Over several weeks his impulse to expose himself declined.

Token Economies.   The instrumental conditioning approach has been used on a large scale with generally good success in institutions that house people with serious problems, such as schizophrenia or severe mental retardation. In such institutions residents are often asked to do chores, both to keep operating costs low and to engage them in active participation in their environment. In some instances other specific behaviors are also targeted as desirable and therapeutic, such as helping residents who have more severe problems. To promote these behaviors, therapists have designed **token economies:** A list of tasks is compiled, and residents receive tokens as rewards for performing the tasks. Later, they can exchange these tokens for snacks, other desired articles, or various privileges. Thus, the tokens become conditioned reinforcers for desirable and appropriate behaviors. Figure 16.2 shows the strong effects of the contingencies of a pay scale used in a token economy established by Ayllon and Azrin (1968). The amount of time spent performing the desirable behaviors was high when reinforcement contingencies were imposed and low when they were not. (See *Figure 16.2.*)

Figure 16.2   The effects of a token economy system of reinforcement on performance of a group of patients on specified chores. (From Teodoro Ayllon and Nathan Azrin. *The Token Economy: A Motivational System for Therapy and Rehabilitation,* © 1968, pp. 249–250, 252. Reprinted by permission of Prentice-Hall, Inc., Englewood Cliffs, N.J.)

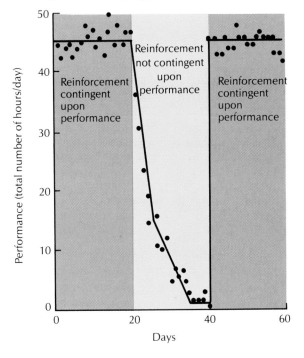

A comprehensive experiment by Paul and Lentz (1977) clearly demonstrated the effectiveness of a token economy. The patients had severe, chronic schizophrenia and had been in the hospital for many years. Some of them screamed wordlessly, some were mute and withdrawn, and some were violent. The experimenters set up a token economy designed to teach social skills such as self-grooming, good mealtime behavior, participation in classes, and socialization during free periods. The program lasted four and a half years. By the end of the treatment, more than 10 percent of the patients in the token economy had been discharged, but none of the control patients given routine treatment had been able to leave. In addition, many of the patients from the token economy ward were able to leave the hospital for community-based facilities such as halfway houses. These patients fared much better than control patients who were also moved to facilities in the community; more than 90 percent of the patients from the token economy ward were able to remain at these facilities during the eighteen-month follow-up period. The patients were not "cured" of their schizophrenia, but they obviously led much less disturbed lives.

Although token economies are based on a simple principle, they are very difficult to implement. A mental institution includes patients, caretakers, housekeeping staff, and professional staff. If a token economy is to be effective, all staff members who deal with residents must learn how the system is to work; ideally, they should also understand and agree with its underlying principles. A token economy can easily be sabotaged by a few people who believe that the system is foolish, wrong, or in some way threatening to themselves. If these obstacles can be overcome, token economies work very well.

Modeling

4   Humans (and many other animals) have the ability to learn without directly experiencing an event. As we have already seen, people's behavior can be punished vicariously, through covert sensitization. People can also imitate the behavior of other people, watching what they do and, if the conditions are appropriate, performing the same behavior. This capability provides the basis for the technique of modeling. Behavior therapists have found that clients can make much better progress when they have access to a model providing samples of successful behaviors to imitate. Bandura (1971) described a modeling session with people who had a phobic fear

of snakes:

> The therapist himself performed the fearless behavior at each step and gradually led subjects into touching, stroking, and then holding the snake's body with gloved and bare hands while the experimenter held the snake securely by head and tail. If a subject was unable to touch the snake following ample demonstration, she was asked to place her hand on the experimenter's and to move her hand down gradually until it touched the snake's body. After subjects no longer felt any apprehension about touching the snake under these secure conditions, anxieties about contact with the snake's head area and entwining tail were extinguished. The therapist again performed the tasks fearlessly, and then he and the subject performed the responses jointly; as subjects became less fearful, the experimenter gradually reduced his participation and control over the snake, until eventually subjects were able to hold the snake in their laps without assistance, to let the snake loose in the room and retrieve it, and to let it crawl freely over their bodies. Progress through the graded approach tasks was paced according to the subjects' apprehensiveness. When they reported being able to perform one activity with little or no fear, they were eased into a more difficult interaction. (Bandura, 1971, p. 680)

This treatment eliminated fear of snakes in 92 percent of the subjects who participated.

There are probably several reasons for the success of the modeling technique. Subjects learn to make new responses by imitating those of the therapist and are reinforced for doing so. When they observe a confident person approaching and touching a feared object without showing any signs of emotional distress, they probably experience a vicarious extinction of their own emotional responses. In fact, Bandura (1971) reports that "having successfully overcome a phobia that had plagued them for most of their lives, subjects reported increased confidence that they could cope effectively with other fear-provoking events" (p. 684), including encounters with other people. Bandura (1977) refers to this confidence as *self-efficacy*, a concept that will be discussed later.

Modeling has been used to establish new behaviors as well as eliminate fears. Sex therapists have used specially prepared films or videotapes showing explicit sexual acts to help clients overcome inhibitions that are interfering with their sexual relations with their spouses. Other therapists have acted out examples of useful, appropriate social exchanges for clients whose maladaptive behaviors usually prevent

such interactions. As we shall see in a later section, modeling is an important aspect of almost all forms of group therapy.

Maintaining Behavioral Change

One of the problems with behavior therapy is that behaviors learned under one set of conditions may fail to occur in different environments; that is, the behavioral change may not generalize to other situations. This problem is especially acute in the treatment of alcohol addiction; addicts may abstain from drinking in a treatment facility but go on a binge as soon as they leave the facility.

Behavior therapists have designed specific methods to ensure that positive behavioral change generalizes to situations outside the clinic. These methods include intermittent reinforcement, self-observation, and recruiting of other people to serve as "therapists." As we saw in Chapter 6, intermittent reinforcement increases resistance to extinction. Thus, it is more effective not to reinforce every desirable response the client makes but to reinforce desirable responses intermittently.

Another useful method that helps maintain behavioral change is *self-observation*, in which the client is taught to recognize when his or her behavior is appropriate. For example, Drabman, Spitalnik, and O'Leary (1973) rewarded a group of disruptive boys for performing desirable behaviors such as participating in classroom activities like reading. The reinforcement was effective; the frequency of disruptive behaviors declined and academic activity increased. To make the change as permanent as possible, the experimenters also rewarded the boys when the ratings of their own behaviors agreed with those of their teacher. In other words, they were trained to evaluate their behaviors in terms of those that should be reinforced and those that should not be. The assumption was that the self-evaluations would become conditioned reinforcers, because they would initially be paired with actual reinforcement. Thus, the process of self-evaluation would continue to reinforce the boys' behavior even after the period of training was over. Judging from the excellent results, the procedure succeeded.

Therapists also frequently ask friends and members of a client's family to become participants in the process of behavior therapy. These "adjunct therapists" are taught to encourage and reward desirable behaviors and to discourage or ignore undesirable ones. By these means a client does not shuttle back and forth between two different types of environments—one in which his or her therapist selectively reinforces good behaviors, and one in which reinforcement is haphazard or even inappropriate. For example, a person with behavioral problems may receive attention from the family only when he or she "acts up"; clearly, the best results will be obtained when other family members make an effort to ignore such outbursts and reinforce instances of good behavior instead.

Behavior therapists often employ methods of **self-control.** Although it may seem paradoxical that a person can reinforce or punish his or her own behavior, clients can indeed be taught methods to alter their own behavior or to maintain the behavioral changes accomplished in the clinic (Mahoney and Thoresen, 1974; Watson and Tharp, 1985). First, the client is taught the principles involved: the nature of reinforcement and punishment, the role of discriminative stimuli, and other information he or she will need to know for the method to work. Next, the therapist and client work out a program by which these principles may be applied to effect the desired behavioral changes.

For example, to punish unwanted behaviors—say, smoking or picking an argument with a co-worker—a client can make a contract with the therapist to send money to an organization he or she despises whenever the behavior occurs. To reinforce desirable behaviors, the client can treat himself or herself to an enjoyable activity, such as a telephone conversation with a friend or a snack (assuming that the client is not trying to eliminate a habit of overeating). The client and therapist help define the desirable and undesirable behaviors, set criteria for measuring them, and decide on the schedule of reinforcement or punishment that will be applied. As progress is made, the criteria and schedules are adjusted until the client's goals are met. The client may also be advised by the therapist to change his or her environment to eliminate discriminative stimuli that have in the past been present while the client performed the maladaptive behavior. Thus, a person who habitually has had a cigarette with a cup of coffee after dinner should forgo the cup of coffee (the discriminative stimulus) for a while if he or she is trying to quit smoking.

Cognitive Restructuring

Subsequent to the development of behavior therapy a group of behavior therapists began to adopt strategies based on cognitive models of human behavior. The focus of this method, called **cognitive behavior therapy,** is on behavioral change. Like behavior therapists—and unlike most insight psychotherapists—cognitive behavior therapists are not particularly interested in events that occurred in the client's childhood. They are interested in the here and now and in altering the client's behavior so that it becomes more functional. Although they employ many methods used by behavior therapists, they believe that when behaviors change, they do so because of changes in cognitive processes.

Most of the practitioners of cognitive behavior therapy use the methods of behavior therapy that I have just described. But in addition, they have developed some special methods designed to change the maladaptive patterns of cognition that they believe underlie maladaptive patterns of behavior. The attempt to change these patterns of cognition is referred to as **cognitive restructuring.**

Rational-Emotive Therapy. The first form of cognitive restructuring, called **rational-emotive therapy,** was developed in the 1950s by Albert Ellis, a clinical psychologist. In contrast to the other forms of cognitive behavior therapy, rational-emotive therapy did not grow out of the tradition of behavior therapy. For many years Ellis was regarded as being outside the mainstream of psychotherapy, but now his methods are being practiced by a substantial number of therapists. Like Carl Rogers, Ellis asserts that psychological problems are the result of faulty cognitions; therapy is therefore aimed at changing people's beliefs. But unlike Rogers, who believed that people will naturally abandon their irrational beliefs and adopt rational ones if given an environment of unconditional positive regard, Ellis is highly directive and confrontational. He tells his clients what they are doing wrong and how they should change.

According to Ellis and his followers, emotions are the products of cognition. A *significant activating event* (A) is followed by a highly charged *emotional consequence* (C), but it is not correct to say that A has caused C. Rather, C is a result of the person's *belief system* (B). Therefore, inappropriate emotions (such as depression, guilt, and anxiety) can be abolished only if a change occurs in the person's beliefs and perceptions. It is the task of the rational-emotive therapist to dispute the person's beliefs and to convince him or her that they are inappropriate.

The prevailing principle in rational-emotive theory is that the universe is logical and rational; the appropriate means of understanding it is the scientific method of controlled observation. Magic and superstition have no place in the belief system of a healthy, rational person. Therefore, the therapist attempts to get the client to describe his or her irrational beliefs so that these beliefs can be challenged and defeated. As Ellis puts it, the rational-emotive therapist is "an exposing and nonsense-annihilating scientist" (1979, p. 187).

Rational-emotive theory asserts that people have the capacity for rational understanding and thus possess the resources for personal growth. Unfortunately, they also have the capacity for self-delusion and acceptance of irrational beliefs. Rational-emotive therapy seeks to rid people of these illogical and counterproductive tendencies. In Ellis's form of cognitive restructuring people's faulty cognitions—including their misperceptions of events in the world and the incorrect assumptions they make about their own needs—are changed by the therapeutic process. Several types of faulty cognitions receive special emphasis: the tendency to perceive a desirable event as an absolute necessity, the need to be better than everyone else, and the perception of failure as a disaster.

Although rational-emotive therapy is much more directive than client-centered therapy, there are some similarities. Just as Rogers emphasized unconditional positive regard, Ellis and his followers attempt to engender a feeling of full self-acceptance in their clients. They teach that self-blame is the core of emotional disturbance and that people can learn to stop continuously rating their own personal worth and measuring themselves against an impossible standard. They emphasize that people will be happier if they can learn to see failures as unfortunate events, not as disastrous ones that confirm the lack of their own worth. Unlike a Rogerian therapist, a rational-emotive therapist will vigorously argue with his or her client, attacking beliefs that the therapist regards as foolish and illogical. This approach also differs from the client-centered approach in that the therapist does not need to be especially empathetic in order to be an effective teacher and guide.

In a recent review of research evaluating the effectiveness of rational-emotive therapy, Haaga and Davison (1989) concluded that the method has been shown to reduce general anxiety, test anxiety, and unassertiveness. It may help reduce excessive anger, depression, and antisocial behavior; it may help people learn to cope with everyday stress; and it may help to reduce type A behavior. (Type A behavior has been associated with coronary disease and was described in Chapter 12.) By itself, rational-emotive therapy is not particularly effective for treating phobias or sexual dysfunction.

Rational-emotive therapy has appeal and potential usefulness for those who can enjoy and profit from intellectual teaching and argumentation. The people who are likely to benefit most from this form of therapy are those who are self-demanding and who feel guilty for not living up to their own standards of perfection. People with serious anxiety disorders or with severe thought disorders, such as schizophrenia and the affective psychoses, are unlikely to respond to an intellectual analysis of their problems.

Many therapists who adopt an eclectic approach use some of the techniques of rational-emotive therapy with some of their clients. In its advocacy of rationality and its eschewal of superstition, the therapy proposes a common-sense approach to living. However, most psychotherapists disagree with Ellis's denial of the importance of empathy in the relationship between therapist and client.

Other Forms of Cognitive Restructuring. Many cognitive behavior therapists employ behavioral methods to change a particular form of private behavior, referred to as **self-talk.** Most of us silently "talk" to ourselves as we go about our daily activities, especially when we are working on a complex task that can be guided by verbal rules. For example, a person learning to drive a car with a manual transmission might say: "Let's see, push in the clutch, move the shift lever to the left and then down—there, it's in gear—now let the clutch come up—oh! It died—I should have given it more gas. Let's see, clutch down, turn the key. . . ." Maladaptive self-talk might include negative comments on one's own behavior or state of mind. Of course, self-talk does not have to be audible or even involve actual movements of the speech muscles; a person can think in words with neural activity that does not result in overt behavior.

Some cognitive behavior therapists have developed specific methods to alter people's self-talk in order to improve their psychological functioning. One of the best-known cognitive behavior therapists is Donald Meichenbaum. While he was still a graduate student, he attempted to establish some adaptive behaviors (including verbal behaviors) in a group of hospitalized schizophrenic patients. He discovered that some of them repeated his instructions to themselves, saying such things as "give healthy talk" and "be relevant." Indeed, the patients

Albert Ellis

seemed to be obeying their own self-talk and showed some lasting behavioral changes (Meichenbaum, 1977).

Encouraged by the apparent effectiveness of constructive self-talk, Meichenbaum developed special self-instructional methods. First, clients are trained to become aware of their own maladaptive self-statements. Many people make negative statements to themselves, either aloud or silently. These negative statements tend to be self-fulfilling prophecies, which serve to perpetuate maladaptive behaviors and interfere with the acquisition of adaptive ones. Once this training is complete, the therapist acts as a model, providing examples of appropriate behavior, while saying aloud the accompanying self-talk the clients can use to guide their own behavior. The clients then practice both the behavior and the verbalizations. For example, a client may find that a particular task produces so much anxiety that he or she cannot perform it. By having the client perform the task while verbalizing the details of each step, Meichenbaum helps the client avoid thinking about possible failure. The client therefore becomes more likely to complete the task successfully.

Meichenbaum has also developed a method designed to help people cope with problems yet to come, a method he calls *stress inoculation training*. During the first stage of this procedure—*education*—the client is told why maladaptive patterns of thinking are largely responsible for the occurrence of unpleasant emotional responses and counterproductive behaviors. During the second stage—*rehearsal*—the client engages in productive self-talk, making statements about coping with stressful events. During the third stage—*application*—the client uses the newly learned coping strategies to confront real stressors. For example, a client may be trained to withstand the discomfort caused by putting his or her hand into a bucket of ice water. Stress inoculation training enables clients to withstand the cold water for a longer time, and this success presumably gives them the confidence to face other forms of stress outside the clinic.

Another cognitive behavior therapist, Aaron Beck, believes that many maladaptive behaviors (particularly depression) are the result of maladaptive patterns of cognition (Beck, 1976; Beck and Emery, 1985). For example, disturbed people may show *selective abstraction,* focusing on a trivial negative aspect of a situation and concluding that things are worse than they really are. They may *overgeneralize,* perceiving a small failure as an indication of their own ineptitude. For example, they may misinterpret minor disagreements as signs that other people dislike them or are contemptuous of them. They may *maximize* the importance of negative events and *minimize* the importance of positive ones. They may perceive a task as too difficult to even begin to try—and consequently, they do not try.

Beck's therapy involves *collaborative empiricism.* The therapist works with the client and examines situations and the client's reactions to them. Together, they try to discover illogical perceptions and conclusions. The point of the exercise is to train the client not to automatically perceive situations in negative light, as he or she has been doing, but to come to realistic, logical conclusions about them. The client is often encouraged to perform empirical tests of his or her beliefs. For example, suppose that a client believes that one must perform all tasks perfectly or dreadful consequences will result. The therapist will encourage the client to do only a "satisfactory" job and see what happens. If the consequences are *not* dreadful, than clearly the belief was incorrect.

We saw in the section on modeling that when behavior therapy successfully reduces people's fear of specific objects, the people usually report that their fear of other objects and situations also decreases. Bandura (1977a) asserts that the reason for this generalized reduction in fear is the development of a cognitive concept he calls **self-efficacy.** By reducing a specific type of fear, behavior therapy enables a person to perform behaviors that he or she previously found impossible to do. The experience raises the person's self-efficacy—the degree to which the person believes he or she is able to cope with a difficult situation. Thus, when the person encounters other situations that have caused trouble, that person is much more willing to attempt acts previously avoided and, indeed, finds it possible to perform them. The greatest change in self-efficacy comes from experience; actually handling a spider gives clients a greater sense of self-efficacy than simply talking about handling them or imagining doing so.

Evaluation

[5] Psychotherapists with traditional orientations have criticized behavior therapy for its focus on the symptoms of a psychological problem to the exclusion of its roots. Some psychoanalysts even argue that treatment of symptoms is dangerous; in their view, the removal of one symptom of an intrapsychic conflict will simply

produce another, perhaps more serious, symptom. This hypothetical process is called **symptom substitution.**

However, there is little evidence that symptom substitution occurs. It is true that many people's behavioral problems are caused by conditions that existed in the past, and often these problems become self-perpetuating. Yet behavior therapy can, in many cases, eliminate the problem behavior without delving into the surrounding issues. For example, a child may (for one reason or another) begin wetting the bed. The nightly awakening irritates the parents, who must change the bedclothes and the child's pajamas. The disturbance often disrupts family relationships. The child develops feelings of guilt and insecurity and, as a result, wets the bed more often. Instead of analyzing the sources of family conflict, a therapist who uses behavior therapy would install a device in the child's bed that rings a bell when he or she begins to urinate. The child awakens and goes to the bathroom to urinate and soon ceases to wet the bed. The elimination of bed-wetting causes rapid improvement in the child's self-esteem and in the entire family relationship. Symptom substitution does not appear to occur (Baker, 1969).

There are some situations in which behavior therapy should not be used. For example, a person who is involuntarily confined to an institution should not be subjected to aversive techniques unless he or she clearly wants to participate or unless the benefits far outweigh the discomfort, as in the case of the child who stopped battering his head against the floor after he had received a few mild electrical shocks for doing so. The decision to use aversive techniques must not rest only with people who are directly in charge of the patients, lest the procedures eventually be used merely for the sake of convenience. The decision must involve a committee that includes people who serve as advocates for patients.

In other situations behavior therapy may not be appropriate because it raises unanswerable ethical issues. For example, a person may come to a therapist because his homosexuality causes him great anguish. The client asks for help and is willing to undergo whatever treatment is necessary; no coercion is involved. The therapist faces the dilemma of whether to embark on a course of treatment in which aversive stimuli are associated with other males or whether to try to help the client accept his sexual orientation and develop a better self-image. If the homosexuality is deep-seated, behavior therapy may simply make the client shun *all* sexual stimuli. It is not enough to learn the techniques of behavior therapy; one must also learn to recognize the circumstances in which these techniques are appropriate.

Although cognitive behavior therapists believe in the importance of unobservable constructs such as feelings, thoughts, and perceptions, they do not believe that good therapeutic results can be achieved by focusing on cognitions alone. They, like their behaviorist colleagues, insist that it is not enough to have their clients introspect and analyze their thought patterns. Instead, therapists must assist clients to change their behavior. Behavioral changes cause cognitive changes; for example, when a client observes that he or she is now engaging in fewer maladaptive behaviors and more adaptive behaviors, the client's self-perceptions are bound to change as a result. But cognitive behavior therapists say that therapy can be even more effective when specific attention is paid to cognitions as well as behaviors.

It is probably impossible to prove or disprove such assertions. After all, cognitions are not directly observable but must be inferred from people's behavior. If changing people's self-talk helps them function more effectively, we can conclude that the therapeutic method works. From a practical point of view, *why* the method works may not really matter. Emmelkamp, Kuipers, and Eggeraat (1978) make the following points:

> Giving a form of treatment a name is not the same as elucidating the therapeutic process involved. Whether the treatment "cognitive restructuring" does actually produce a modification of cognitive processes is a debatable point. On the other hand, the effects of prolonged exposure *in vivo* [a purely behavioral method] could at least partly be explained in terms of cognitive restructuring. During treatment with prolonged exposure *in vivo* clients notice, for example, that their anxiety diminishes after a time and that the events which they fear, such as fainting or having a heart attack, do not take place. This may lead them to transform their unproductive self-statements into more productive ones: "There you are, nothing will go wrong with me." (Emmelkamp, Kuipers, and Eggeraat, 1978, p. 40)

Whether behavioral methods are therapeutic because they change cognitive structure will undoubtedly continue to be a matter of debate. In a practical sense, because both types of therapists are firmly committed to using behavioral methodology and to evaluating their results empirically, it probably does not matter who is correct.

Because cognitive behavior therapists talk about unobservable cognitive processes, we must consider the differences between them and insight therapists, who also deal with unobservable processes. As Beck (1976) notes, unlike insight therapists, cognitive behavior therapists concern themselves with conscious thought processes, not unconscious motives. They are also more interested in the present determinants of the client's thoughts and behaviors, rather than his or her past history. And because they come from the tradition of experimental psychology, they use rigorous empirical methods to evaluate the effectiveness of their techniques and to infer the nature and existence of cognitive processes.

INTERIM SUMMARY

Behavior and Cognitive Behavior Therapy

Behavior therapists attempt to use the principles of classical and instrumental (operant) conditioning to modify behavior: to eliminate fears or replace maladaptive behaviors with adaptive ones. Systematic desensitization uses classical conditioning procedures to condition the response of relaxation to stimuli that were previously fear producing. In contrast, implosion therapy attempts to extinguish fear and avoidance responses. Aversive classical conditioning attempts to condition an unpleasant response to a stimulus with which the client is preoccupied, such as a fetish.

Whereas classical conditioning involves automatic approach and avoidance responses to particular stimuli, instrumental conditioning involves reinforcement or punishment of particular behaviors in particular situations. The most formal system involves token economies, which arrange contingencies in the environment of people who reside in institutions; in this case the system of payment and reward is obvious to the participants. But not all instances of reinforcement and punishment are overt; they can also be vicarious. With the guidance of therapists people can imagine their own behavior with its consequent reinforcement or punishment. Modeling has been used as an important adjunct to instrumental conditioning; therapists who use this effective technique provide specific examples of the desirable behaviors.

Although some people view behavior therapy as a simple and rigid application of the principles of conditioning, therapists must be well-trained, sensitive people if the techniques are to be effective. The major problem with behavior therapy is people's tendency to discriminate the therapeutic situation from similar ones in the outside world, thus failing to generalize their behavior to situations outside the clinic. Techniques to promote generalization include the use of intermittent reinforcement, self-observation training, and recruitment of outside "therapists."

With the exception of rational-emotive therapy, cognitive behavior therapies grew out of the tradition of behavior therapy. These therapies attempt to measure and change behavior, but they also pay attention to unobservable cognitive processes. The first form of cognitive restructuring, rational-emotive therapy, is based on the assumption that people's psychological problems stem from faulty cognitions. Its practitioners use many forms of persuasion, including ridicule, to get people to abandon these cognitions in favor of logical and healthy ones. According to these therapists, significant activating events give rise to emotional consequences, and the particular consequences that occur depend upon the person's belief system. Relief from distress is achieved by changing the belief system, not by reliving the past.

Other forms of cognitive behavior therapy involve systematic behavioral approaches to clients' problems, but the practitioners pay more attention to thinking and private verbal behavior than their behaviorist colleagues are likely to do. For example, Meichenbaum specifically focuses on self-talk and teaches his clients to adopt new forms of this behavior. He has also developed a method of stress inoculation training, which helps keep emotional and behavioral problems from developing. Beck has developed ways to help depressed people correct errors of cognition that perpetuate self-defeating thoughts. Bandura concentrates on changes in self-efficacy as well as in behavior, although he acknowledges that behavioral change is one of the most effective ways of achieving cognitive change; self-observation provides the most reliable evidence about oneself. ■

TREATMENT OF GROUPS

6 So far, I have been discussing individual forms of psychotherapy, in which a client meets with a therapist. But in many cases clients meet as a group, either because therapy is more effective that way or because it is more convenient or economical. In this section I will discuss group therapy, family therapy (including therapy specifically designed for couples), and community therapy.

Group Therapy

Group psychotherapy became common during World War II, when the stresses of combat produced psychological problems in many of the members of the armed forces, and the demand for psychotherapists greatly exceeded the supply. What began as an economic necessity became an institution, once the effectiveness of group treatment was recognized.

Because most psychological problems involve interactions with other people, treating these problems in a group setting may be worthwhile. Group therapy provides four advantages that are not found in individual therapy.

1. The group setting permits the therapist to observe and interpret actual interactions without having to rely on clients' descriptions, which may be selective or faulty.
2. A group can bring social pressure to bear on the behaviors of its members. If a person receives similar comments about his or her behavior from all the members of a group, the message is often more convincing than if a psychotherapist delivers the same comments in a private session.
3. The process of seeking the causes of maladaptive behavior in other people often helps a person gain insight into his or her own problems. Often, people can learn from the mistakes of others.
4. Knowing that other people have problems similar to one's own can bring comfort and relief. People discover they are not alone.

The structure of the group session varies widely. Some sessions are little more than lectures, in which the therapist presents information about a problem common to all members of the group, followed by discussion. For example, in a case involving a person with severe mental or physical illness, the therapist explains to family members the nature, treatment, and possible outcomes of the disorder. Then the therapist answers questions and allows people to share their feelings about what the illness has done to their family. Other groups are simply efficient ways to treat several clients at the same time. But most types of group therapy involve interactions among the participants.

In vivo desensitization is sometimes accomplished in groups. These clients will tour an airplane to overcome their fear of flying.

As we saw earlier, therapists often attempt to help their clients develop more productive social behaviors by modeling the behaviors for them and then having the clients copy and practice these behaviors. Obviously, social behaviors involve interactions among people, and a group provides an excellent setting for a behavior therapist to teach clients how to recognize adaptive and maladaptive interactions and to practice adaptive ones. For example, Lewinsohn, Weinstein, and Alper (1970) have used behavioral techniques to teach groups of depressed patients behaviors that would be likely to win them social reinforcement from other people.

Although most types of group therapy involve interactions among members of the group, at least one form of behavior therapy has lent itself to the treatment of noninteracting individuals in groups: systematic desensitization. As we saw, this technique involves imagining a series of increasingly threatening situations while remaining as relaxed as possible. Many behavior therapists (for example, Lazarus, 1961; Nawas, Fishman, and Pucel, 1970) have successfully performed systematic desensitization by assembling groups of people with the same type of phobia and providing group treatment.

Family Therapy and Couples Therapy

Family therapy and couples therapy have become important techniques for clinical psychologists. Very often, dealing with the problems of an individual is not enough. People are products of their environment, and the structure of a person's family is a crucial part of that environment. Consequently, helping an unhappy person frequently means also restructuring his or her relationship with other family members. In addition, problems in the relations between couples—with or without children—can often lead to stress and unhappiness.

In many cases a family therapist meets with all the members of a client's family and analyzes the ways individuals interact with each other. The therapist attempts to get family members to talk to each other instead of addressing all comments and questions to him or her. As much as possible, the family therapist tries to observe data about the interactions—how individuals sit in relation to each other, who interrupts whom, who looks at whom before speaking—in order to infer the nature of interrelationships within the family. For example, there may be barriers between certain family members; perhaps a father is unable to communicate with one of his children. Or two or more family members may be so "enmeshed" that they cannot function independently; they constantly seek each other's approval and, through overdependence, make each other miserable.

Salvador Minuchin (1974) has devised an approach called **structural family therapy.**

A psychologist watches a three-year-old child during a play therapy session.

He observes a family's interactions and draws simple diagrams of the relationships he infers from the behavior of family members. He identifies the counterproductive relationships and attempts to restructure the family in more adaptive ways. For example, he might diagram a family structure with father (F) on one side and mother (M) on the other side, allied with son (S) but estranged from daughter (D):

$$\frac{F}{MS|D}$$

He would then attempt to restructure the family as follows:

$$\frac{HW}{SD}$$

Husband (H) and wife (W) would replace mother and father, emphasizing that their primary relationship should be the one between spouses. The healthiest family interactions stem from an effectively functioning *marital subsystem,* consisting of husband and wife. A marriage that is completely child-oriented is always dysfunctional (Foley, 1979). And alliances between one parent and one or more children are almost always detrimental to the family.

After inferring the family structure, the therapist attempts to restructure it by replacing pathological interactions with more effective, functional ones. He or she suggests that perhaps all members of the family must change if the client is to make real improvement. The therapist gets family members to "actualize" their transactional patterns—that is, to act out their everyday relationships—so that the pathological interactions will show themselves. Restructuring techniques include forming temporary alliances between the therapist and one or more of the family members, increasing tension in order to trigger changes in unstable structures, assigning explicit tasks and homework to family members (for example, making them interact with other members), and providing general support, education, and guidance. Sometimes, the therapist visits the family at home. For example, if a child in a family refuses to eat, the therapist will visit during mealtime in order to see the problem acted out as explicitly as possible.

Behavior therapists have also applied their methods of analysis and treatment to families. This approach focuses on the social environment provided by the family and on the ways that family members reinforce or punish each other's behavior. The strategy is to identify the maladaptive behaviors of the individuals and the ways these behaviors are inadvertently reinforced by the rest of the family. Then the therapist helps the family members find ways to increase positive exchanges and reinforce each other's adaptive behaviors. A careful analysis of the social dynamics of a family often reveals that changes need to be made not in the individual showing the most maladaptive behaviors but in the other members of the family.

Not all problems that confront families involve all family members; for example, the parents may have sexual problems or problems involving finances that they do not want to discuss in front of their children. In addition, many couples do not have children or have children who have left the household. Thus, therapists have developed special methods to help couples with their problems.

All couples will find that they disagree on some important issues, and these disagreements necessarily lead to conflicts. For example, they may have to decide whether to move to accommodate the career of one of the partners, they will have to decide how to spend their money, and they will have to decide how to allocate household chores. Their ability to resolve conflict is one of the most important factors that affects the quality and durability of their relationship (Schwartz and Schwartz, 1980).

Therapists have used many different theoretical orientations to devise ways to treat the problems encountered by couples. For example, rational-emotive therapists try to convince their clients to rid themselves of irrational assumptions about the nature of their relationship. Often couples are dysfunctional because each of the partners holds an impossibly idealized image of how the other partner should be—and feels anger and disappointment when that person fails to live up to the image. In such cases the therapist tries to make these assumptions explicit so that they can be evaluated and modified.

When dealing with families and couples, which consist of people with long-established, ongoing personal relations, therapists have learned that changes in the nature of the relations can have unforeseen consequences—and that they must be alert for these consequences. For example, LoPiccolo and Friedman (1985) describe treatment of a couple with a sexual problem. At first, the problem appeared to belong to the man.

A woman listens as her husband talks to a marriage counselor.

> A couple with a marriage of twenty years duration sought treatment for the male's problem of total inability to have an erection. This had been a problem for over nineteen of their twenty years of marriage. Successful intercourse had only taken place in the first few months of the marriage. . . . [The wife] reported that she greatly enjoyed sex and was extremely frustrated by her husband's inability to have an erection. (LoPiccolo and Friedman, 1985, p. 465)

The therapists used techniques developed by Masters and Johnson (1970) to treat the man's impotence, which succeeded splendidly. Within ten weeks the couple were able to have sexual intercourse regularly, and both had orgasms. However, even though the problem appeared to have been cured, and despite the physical gratification they received from their sexual relations, they soon stopped having them. In investigating this puzzling occurrence, the therapists discovered

> . . . that the husband had a great need to remain distant and aloof from his wife. He had great fears of being overwhelmed and controlled by her, and found closeness to be very uncomfortable. . . . For him, the inability to have an erection served to keep his wife distant from him, and to maintain his need for privacy, separateness, and autonomy in the relationship. (LoPiccolo and Friedman, 1985, p. 465)

The therapists also found that the wife had reasons to avoid sexual contact. For one thing, she apparently had never resolved the antisexual teachings imparted to her as a child by her family. In addition,

> . . . over the nineteen years of her husband being unable to attain an erection, she had come to have a very powerful position in the

557

relationship. She very often reminded her husband that he owed her a lot because of her sexual frustration. Thus, she was essentially able to win all arguments with him, and to get him to do anything that she wanted. (LoPiccolo and Friedman, 1985, p. 465)

The therapists were able to address these issues and help the couple resolve them. Eventually, they were able to alter the structure of their marriage and resumed their sexual relations.

This case illustrates the fact that a couple is not simply a collection of two individuals. Long-standing problems bring adjustments and adaptations (not always healthy). And even if the original problems are successfully resolved, the adjustments to these problems may persist and cause problems of their own.

Community Psychology

So far, my discussion has been confined to therapists who wait for people with problems to approach them or who are hired to treat people committed to institutions. Another approach—followed by therapists who participate in various programs grouped under the heading of *community psychology*—actively seek out people with problems or even try to prevent problems before they begin. Community psychology deals with a range of problems and uses a range of approaches. It treats individuals and groups, establishes educational programs, and designs programs whose goal is to promote mental health by changing the environment.

Community mental health centers provide individual and group therapy and counseling to members of the communities in which they are located—most often, communities in which people are too poor to afford private mental health care. The goal of such centers is to provide immediate, accessible outpatient care for people who might otherwise find it difficult to find help. The centers are generally staffed by psychologists, psychiatrists, social workers, and nurses. Often they employ the services of paraprofessionals with roots in the community.

The use of paraprofessionals has many advantages. People from culturally deprived backgrounds frequently have difficulty relating to—and communicating with—middle-class therapists. However, if paraprofessionals with the same social and ethnic backgrounds are available, they may be able to gain the trust and confidence of the clients and enable them to profit from the help that is available. Also, having faced similar problems, the paraprofes-

Community psychologists help individuals and communities cope with a variety of challenges. They provide health education and organize support groups.

sionals may be able to provide useful advice and serve as role models for the clients; and modeling is more effective when the model resembles the client.

> Few models seem as plausible or relevant as people who have shared but overcome clients' own problems. This is critical if a client rejects staff members as reference figures because they appear too remote in age, education, status, ethnicity, and so on, for suitable comparisons with self, or are perceived as outsiders, lacking vivid conversance with the client's burdens and viewpoint. (Rosenthal and Bandura, 1978, p. 649)

Community psychology also tries to identify problems while they are small and prevent them from becoming more critical. For example, suicide prevention centers provide counselors—often paraprofessionals or volunteers—who can talk with people contemplating suicide. These services may be provided by a telephone hot line designed to dissuade people from committing suicide and to inform them of the sources of help that are available to them. Other centers provide counseling for the victims of rape or other forms of abuse, helping the victims with practical problems in dealing with law enforcement agencies and also trying to minimize psychological aftereffects of their ordeal.

Finally, community psychology includes attempts to prevent problems before they start. For example, community psychology may establish programs to provide educational enrichment for children from deprived families (such as the Head Start program in the United States). It may provide prenatal medical care and postnatal counseling for teenage mothers who are ill-equipped for the role they must fulfill. Or it may lobby for social changes to improve the living conditions in impoverished neighborhoods.

INTERIM SUMMARY

Treatment of Groups

Many types of group therapy have been developed in response to the belief that certain problems can be treated more efficiently and more effectively in group settings. Practitioners of family therapy, couples therapy, and some forms of group behavior therapy observe people's interactions with others and attempt to help them learn how to establish more effective patterns of responses. Treatment of groups permits the therapist to observe clients' social behaviors, and it uses social pressures to help convince clients of the necessity for behavioral change. It permits clients to learn from the mistakes of others and observe that other people have similar problems, which often provides reassurance.

Community psychology involves the attempts of psychologists to reach out to a community. It may try to establish readily available treatment facilities or provide crisis treatment to keep problems from becoming worse. It also tries to educate the public and promote social changes in order to prevent problems from occurring in the first place. ∎

BIOLOGICAL TREATMENTS

As we saw in Chapter 15, an important method for treating the symptoms of schizophrenia and the affective psychoses is medication. Besides drug therapy, there are two other forms of biological treatment: electroconvulsive therapy and psychosurgery.

Drug Therapy

7 **Antipsychotic Drugs.** The development of **antipsychotic drugs** has had a profound effect on the treatment of schizophrenia; although these drugs do not "cure" schizophrenia, they reduce the severity of its most prominent positive symptoms—delusions and hallucinations—apparently by blocking dopamine receptors in the brain. Drugs such as amphetamine, which excite dopamine synapses, produce symptoms of schizophrenia. Presumably, overactivity of these synapses is responsible for the positive symptoms of schizophrenia. Although dopamine-secreting neurons are located in several parts of the brain, most researchers believe that the ones involved in the symptoms of schizophrenia are located in the cerebral cortex and parts of the limbic system near the front of the brain.

A different system of dopamine-secreting neurons in the brain is involved in control of movement. Occasionally, this system of neurons degenerates spontaneously in older people, producing Parkinson's disease. Symptoms of this disorder include tremors, muscular rigidity, loss of balance, difficulty in initiating a movement, and impaired breathing that makes speech indistinct. In severe cases the person is bedridden.

The major problem with the antipsychotic drugs is that they do not discriminate between these two systems of dopamine-secreting neurons; the drugs interfere with the activity of both the circuit involved in the symptoms of schizophrenia and the circuit involved in the control of movements. Consequently, when a schizophrenic patient begins taking an antipsychotic drug, he or she often exhibits a movement disorder. Fortunately, the disorder is usually temporary and soon disappears. However, after taking the medication for several years, some patients develop a different—more serious—movement disorder known as **tardive dyskinesia** (*tardive* means "late developing"; *dyskinesia* refers to a disturbance in movement). The symptoms of this disorder include facial grimacing and involuntary movements of the tongue, mouth, and neck. Severely affected patients have difficulty talking, and occasionally, the movements interfere with involuntary breathing. The symptoms can temporarily be alleviated by *increasing* the dose of the antipsychotic drug, but doing so only serves to increase and perpetuate the patient's dependence on the medication (Baldessarini and Tarsy, 1980).

Fortunately, a new antischizophrenic drug has been developed that does not produce movement disorders. This drug, called *clozapine,* is also more effective than other antipsychotic drugs in helping hard-to-treat patients (Kane et al., 1988). Schizophrenic patients have not yet received clozapine for a long enough time for researchers to be sure that the drug will not eventually produce tardive dyskinesia, but the results so far seem promising.

Antidepressant Drugs. The uses of **antidepressant drugs**—the tricyclic antidepressants and lithium carbonate—were discussed in Chapter 15. As we saw, the tricyclic antidepressant drugs are most effective in the treatment of major depression, while lithium carbonate is most effective in the treatment of bipolar disorders or simple mania. Patients' manic symptoms usually decrease as soon as their blood level of lithium reaches a therapeutic level (Gerbino, Oleshansky, and Gershon, 1978). In bipolar disorder, once the manic phase is eliminated, the depressed phase does not return. People with bipolar disorder have remained free of their symptoms for years, as long as they continue taking lithium carbonate. This drug can have some side effects, such as a fine tremor or excessive urine production; but in general, the benefits far outweigh the adverse symptoms. However, an overdose of lithium is toxic, which means that the patient's blood level of lithium must be monitored regularly.

The major difficulty with treating bipolar disorder is that these patients often miss their "high." When medication is effective, the mania subsides, along with the depression. But most patients enjoy at least the initial phase of their manic periods, and some believe that they are more creative at that time. (In fact, they may be correct; many famous artists, writers, and composers were manic-depressives.) In addition, many of these patients say that they resent having to depend on a chemical "crutch." Unfortunately, the risk of death by suicide is particularly high during the depressive phase of bipolar disorder.

Unlike lithium carbonate, the tricyclic antidepressant drugs only work on a short-term basis. They are useful in treating episodes of severe depression, but evidence suggests that they are not useful when taken over a long period of time. In general, the tricyclic antidepressant drugs should be used when there is a family history of severe depression or when the person exhibits psychotic symptoms, lethargy, agitation, severe insomnia, expressions of feelings of hopelessness, or signs of suicidal tendencies (Reda, 1984). Once the severity of the symptoms subsides, psychotherapy should also be instituted.

A study by DiMascio et al. (1979) found that psychotherapy and the administration of a tricyclic antidepressant drug had independent therapeutic effects in the treatment of acute depression. The drug primarily improved sleep and appetite disturbances, whereas psychotherapy primarily improved mood, suicidal thoughts, ability to work, and apathy. Thus, the best results were obtained by simultaneous use of both drugs and psychotherapy.

Besides being effective in treating depression, the tricyclic antidepressant drugs have also been used successfully to treat several anxiety disorders, including panic disorder and agoraphobia (Klein, Zitrin, Woerner, and Ross, 1983). The drugs appear to reduce the incidence of panic attacks, including those that accompany severe agoraphobia. In addition, propranolol, a drug used to treat irregularities in heart rhythm, has proved helpful in reducing the changes in heart rate that accompany panic attacks (Granville-Grossman and Turner, 1966). The tricyclic antidepressant drugs do not reduce the anticipatory anxiety that the patient feels between panic attacks; this symptom can be reduced by antianxiety drugs, described in the next section.

Double-blind studies have found a particular tricyclic antidepressant drug, *clomipramine,* to be useful in treating obsessive compulsive disorder (Leonard et al., 1989). Because obsessive compulsive disorder is so difficult to treat, and because it can be so disabling, mental health practitioners are pleased to have a means of helping people whose lives have been disrupted. Other tricyclic antidepressant drugs, which alleviate the symptoms of depression, have no effect on obsessive compulsive disorder. Thus, the drug-induced biological changes that alleviate obsessive compulsive disorder are not the same as the ones that alleviate depression.

Although the tricyclic antidepressants and other drugs are useful in alleviating the symptoms of certain anxiety disorders, they do not "cure" any of these conditions. Because the disorders are at least partly heritable, as we saw in Chapter 15, they may thus have some biological causes at their root; yet the most permanent and long-lasting treatment is still behavior therapy. The drugs may be very useful in reducing the patients' symptoms so that they can participate effectively in therapy, but they do not provide a long-term solution.

Antianxiety Drugs. The **antianxiety drugs,** better known as tranquilizers, are the most prescribed of all drugs. Each year, North Americans consume many tons of drugs such as diazepam (Valium) and chlordiazepoxide (Librium) to combat the most common symptom of neurosis: anxiety. People with neuroses (or tendencies toward them) are especially prone to drug dependency in their search for a crutch to help them. Because some busy physicians find it easier to give a patient a prescription than to try to find out what is causing the anxiety, people rarely have trouble obtaining these drugs. If necessary, people hooked on tranquilizers will shop around until they find a physician who will oblige them.

Antianxiety drugs undoubtedly serve a useful purpose in helping people cope with transient crises. They are also effective in reducing the withdrawal symptoms of alcohol and opiate addictions. Sometimes, they are used as antidotes for overdoses of stimulant drugs. And as we just saw, they can be used in conjunction with the tricyclic antidepressant drugs to reduce the anticipatory anxiety suffered by people with panic disorder or with agoraphobia accompanied by panic attacks. However, there is no "disease state" that is alleviated by the antianxiety medications. Chronic, long-term use of tranquilizers is probably not in anyone's best interest (Baldessarini, 1977).

Electroconvulsive Therapy

8 Electroconvulsive therapy (ECT) involves applying a pair of metal electrodes to a person's head and then passing a brief surge of electrical current through them. (See *Figure 16.3.*) The jolt produces a storm of electrical activity in the brain (a seizure) that renders the person unconscious. The wild firing of neurons that control movement produces convulsions—muscular rigidity and trembling, followed by rhythmic movements of the head, trunk, and limbs. After a few minutes the person falls into a stuporous sleep. Today patients are anesthetized and temporarily paralyzed before the current is turned on. This procedure eliminates the convulsion but not the seizure, which is what delivers the therapeutic effect.

Electroconvulsive therapy has a bad reputation among many clinicians because it has been used to treat disorders such as schizophrenia, on which it has no useful effects, and because patients have received excessive numbers of ECT treatments—as many as hundreds. Originally, ECT was thought to alleviate the symptoms of schizophrenia, because schizophrenic people who also had epilepsy often appeared to improve just after a seizure. Subsequent research has shown that ECT has little or no effect on the symptoms of schizophrenia. However, it has been shown to be singularly effective in treating severe depression (Baldessarini, 1977). Although no one knows for certain why ECT alleviates depression, possibly it does so by reducing REM sleep. As we saw in Chapter 15, people with major depression engage in abnormally large amounts of REM sleep, and REM sleep deprivation is an effective antidepressant therapy.

A case report by Fink (1976) illustrates the response of a depressed patient to a course of ECT. A 44-year-old widow had been hospitalized for three months for severe depression. A course of three ECT treatments per week was prescribed for her by her therapist's supervisor. Unknown to her therapist (a trainee), the first twelve treatments were subthreshold; that is, the intensity of the electrical current was too low to produce seizures. (The treatments could be regarded as placebo treatments.) Although both patient and therapist expected the woman to show some improvement, none was seen. In the next fourteen treatments the current was raised to a sufficient level to produce seizures. After five actual seizures both patient and therapist noticed an improvement. The woman began to complain less about various physical symptoms, to participate in hospital activities, and to make more positive statements about her mood. She became easier to talk with, and the therapist's notes of their conversations immediately proliferated. The fact that these responses

Figure 16.3 A patient being prepared for electroconvulsive therapy.

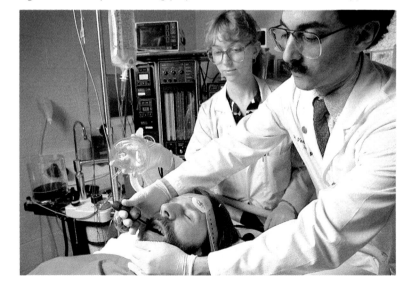

occurred only after several actual seizures suggests that improvement stemmed from the biological treatment and not simply from the therapist's or the patient's expectations.

Some patients with affective psychoses do not respond to antidepressant drugs, but a substantial percentage of these patients improve after a few sessions of ECT. Because antidepressant medications are generally slow acting, taking ten days to two weeks for their therapeutic effects to begin, severe cases of depression are often treated with a brief course of ECT to reduce the symptoms right away. The patients are then maintained on the antidepressant drug. Electroconvulsive therapy is also useful in treating pregnant women who have severe depression; because the procedure does not involve long-term administration of drugs, the danger to the fetus is minimized (Goodwin and Guze, 1984). Because a depressed person runs a 15 percent chance of dying by suicide, the use of ECT may be justified in such cases.

The second criticism of ECT, concerning the dangers inherent in repeated treatment, is quite true. An excessive number of ECT treatments will produce permanent loss of memory (Squire, Slater, and Miller, 1981) and probably also cognitive deficits. Nowadays, ECT is usually administered only to the right hemisphere, in order to minimize damage to people's verbal memories. Nevertheless, it is likely that even a small number of treatments causes at least some permanent brain damage. Therefore, the potential benefits of ECT must be weighed against its potential damage. Electroconvulsive therapy must be used only when the patient's symptoms justify it. Because ECT undoubtedly achieves its effects through the biochemical consequences of the seizure, pharmacologists may discover new drugs that can produce its rapid therapeutic effects without its deleterious ones. Once this breakthrough occurs, ECT can be discarded.

Psychosurgery

One treatment for mental disorders is even more controversial than electroconvulsive therapy: **psychosurgery,** which is the treatment of a mental disorder, in the absence of obvious organic damage, by means of brain surgery. In contrast, brain surgery to remove a tumor or diseased neural tissue or to repair a damaged blood vessel is *not* psychosurgery, and there is no controversy about these procedures.

As we saw in Chapter 12, a Portuguese neuropsychiatrist, Egas Moniz, was inspired by the report of the calming effects of prefrontal lobotomy on a violently emotional chimpanzee to propose trying this procedure on emotionally disturbed humans. Moniz personally supervised approximately one hundred prefrontal lobotomies, but neurosurgeons who followed him performed tens of thousands of them. (Ironically, a patient who had received a lobotomy later shot Moniz, and the bullet lodged in his spine, causing paralysis of the lower part of his body.)

Prefrontal lobotomies were found to have serious side effects, such as apathy and severe blunting of emotions, intellectual impairments, and deficits in judgment and planning. Nevertheless, the procedure was soon in common use for a variety of conditions, most of which were *not* improved by the surgery. Approximately forty thousand prefrontal lobotomies were performed in the United States alone; a simple procedure, called "ice pick" prefrontal lobotomy by its critics, was even performed on an outpatient basis. (See **Figure 16.4.**) The development of antipsychotic drugs and the increasing attention to the serious side effects of prefrontal lobotomy led to a sharp decline in the use of this procedure during the 1950s. Today it is no longer performed (Valenstein, 1986).

A few surgeons have continued to refine the technique of psychosurgery and now perform a procedure called a **cingulectomy,** which involves cutting the *cingulum bundle,* a small band of nerve fibers that connects the prefrontal cortex with parts of the limbic system (Ballantine et

Figure 16.4 "Ice pick" prefrontal lobotomy. The sharp metal rod is inserted under the eyelid and just above the eye, so that it pierces the skull and enters the base of the frontal lobe. [Adapted with permission from Freeman, W. *Proceedings of the Royal Society of Medicine,* 1949, *42 (suppl.),* 8–12.]

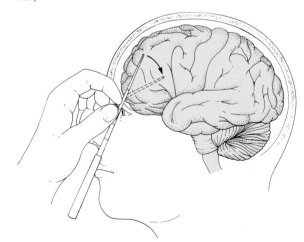

al., 1987). According to the National Commission for the Protection of Human Subjects of Biomedical and Behavioral Research (1977), these more restricted operations do not appear to produce the intellectual impairments or changes in personality that often occurred after prefrontal lobotomies. In fact, people's IQ test scores frequently improve after surgery, because their other problems are alleviated and they can devote more attention to the task at hand. The only reliable negative finding is an impairment in patients' ability to change their strategy in a problem-solving task. Another possible result is a mild, temporary blunting of affect.

Cingulectomies have been shown to be effective in helping people who suffer from severe compulsions. Tippin and Henn (1982) reported on five cases of people with obsessive compulsive disorder who received this form of surgery. Although the patients had had the disorder for between six and twenty years, all showed improvement. One was fully recovered, three were "much improved," and one was simply "improved." The following description illustrates the nature of the patients' problems:

> Ms. A . . . was psychiatrically well until the age of 27 years. Shortly after the birth of her first child, she became extremely fastidious in the care of her infant and unusually concerned about the child putting objects in its mouth that would "have germs all over them." Within a few weeks after the child's birth, Ms. A was refusing to leave the house because of her fear of coming into contact with germs. If she were to leave the house, upon returning she felt compelled to wash her hands and arms for hours. As her child developed into a toddler, Ms. A's obsessional behavior worsened. Her obsession with cleanliness progressed to the point that her husband felt it was easier for him to go to the restroom of a local gas station rather than subject his wife to the 1–2 hours she felt were necessary to properly clean and inspect the toilet after its use. (Tippin and Henn, 1982, p. 1602)

At age thirty-two, Ms. A was diagnosed as having obsessive compulsive disorder and was treated with an antianxiety drug and given behavior therapy, with little effect. The next year she was given a tricyclic antidepressant drug, electroconvulsive therapy, and more behavior therapy. She improved somewhat but soon relapsed. Finally, a cingulectomy was performed on Ms. A. Immediately afterward, she reported that her anxiety was much reduced, and she appeared more relaxed. When she went home, she found that her compulsive rituals had disappeared, but she admitted that she still had frequent obsessive thoughts about cleanliness. One year later, her obsessions, too, had disappeared, and she was working part time. Seven years later, she reported no difficulty with obsessive compulsive behavior or depression (Tippin and Henn, 1982).

According to the National Commission for the Protection of Human Subjects of Biomedical and Behavioral Research (1977), cingulectomy appears to be of most value in the treatment of affective disorders and compulsions; it does not substantially curtail thought disturbances. The report stresses the importance of carefully evaluating each case. In one flagrantly inadequate evaluation a surgeon noted that the surgery produced "no or little changes in intellect and discriminative ability," using as the only criterion the patient's ability to knit after the operation (Winter, 1972). Surgeons should not be expected to be able to perform a psychological evaluation.

I must stress that if psychosurgery is ever used, it must be used only as a last resort, and never on a patient who cannot consent to treatment. The effects of psychosurgery are permanent; there is no way to reverse a brain lesion. All mental health professions hope that more effective behavioral techniques and new drug treatments will make psychosurgical procedures obsolete.

INTERIM SUMMARY

Biological Treatments

Biological treatments for mental disorders include drugs, electroconvulsive therapy, and psychosurgery. Research has shown that treatment of the positive symptoms of schizophrenia with antipsychotic drugs, of major depression with the tricyclic antidepressant drugs, and of bipolar disorder with lithium carbonate are the most effective ways to alleviate the symptoms of these disorders. The tricyclic antidepressant drugs also can alleviate severe anxiety that occurs during panic attacks and agoraphobia and can reduce the severity of obsessive compulsive disorder. The antianxiety drugs help reduce anticipatory anxiety that occurs between panic attacks. Although electroconvulsive therapy is an effective treatment for depression, its use should be reserved for cases in which rapid relief is critical, because the seizures may produce brain damage. The most controversial treatment, psychosurgery, is rarely performed today. Its only presently accepted use, in the form of cingulectomy, is for treatment of crippling compulsions that cannot be reduced by more conventional means. ∎

EVALUATING SCIENTIFIC ISSUES

Assessing Psychotherapy

9 Evaluation of therapies and therapists is a very important issue. It has received much attention, but almost everyone who is involved agrees that too little is known about the efficacy of psychotherapeutic methods. In 1988 mental health problems in the United States alone (including substance abuse) cost *at least* $65.6 billion for treatment of these problems (National Clearinghouse for Alcohol and Drug Information, 1991). The consequences of mental problems—including lost productivity, law enforcement, crime, traffic accidents, and fires— amounted to *at least* $207.7 billion. Of the total, $129.3 billion is attributable to mental health problems other than substance abuse. Clearly, mental health problems cost a lot of money and produce much suffering. Is the money for treatment being well spent? Do the methods work? Unfortunately, we know less about the effectiveness of therapy than we should.

Why Is Psychotherapy Difficult to Evaluate? Several factors make it extremely difficult to evaluate the effectiveness of a particular form of therapy or an individual therapist. One is the problem of *measurement.* Measuring a person's dysfunction is difficult; there are no easily applied, commonly agreed-upon criteria for mental health. Therefore, one usually cannot make valid before-and-after measurements. Most studies rely on ratings of the clients or the therapists to determine whether the therapy has succeeded. These two measures are obviously correlated, because therapists primarily base their ratings on what the clients say to them. Few studies interview friends or family members to obtain independent evaluations of the clients' condition—and those that do generally find a poor correlation between these ratings and those of clients and therapists (Sloane et al., 1975).

Ethics also sometimes prevent clinicians from using a purely scientific method of evaluation, which requires that experimental and control groups be constituted in equivalent ways.

Leaving a person who appears to be suicidal untreated, so that comparisons can be made with similar people who receive therapy, presents risks that almost all therapists would consider unacceptable.

Self-selection involves clients' initial choices of a certain therapeutic approach. The resulting impossibility of establishing either a stable sample population or a control group also makes it difficult to compare the effectiveness of various kinds of therapies. Many patients change therapists or leave therapy altogether. What conclusions can we make about the effectiveness of the therapy by looking only at the progress made by the clients who remain?

Yet another problem with scientific evaluation of psychotherapy is the question of an appropriate *control group.* You may recall from Chapter 2 that the effects of therapeutic drugs must be determined through comparison with the effects of innocuous sugar pills (placebos), to be sure that the improvement has not occurred merely because the patient *thinks* that the pill has done some good. Placebo effects can also occur in psychotherapy; people know that they are being treated and get better because they believe that the treatment should lead to improvement. Most studies that evaluate psychotherapeutic techniques do not include control groups for placebo effects. To do so, the investigator would have to design "mock therapy" sessions, during which the therapist does nothing therapeutic but convinces the patient that therapy is taking place; obviously, this goal is not easily achieved.

What Evidence Is There? In a pioneering paper on psychotherapeutic evaluation Eysenck (1952) examined nineteen studies assessing the effectiveness of psychotherapy. He reported that of the people who remained in psychoanalysis as long as their therapists thought they should, 66 percent showed improvement. Similarly, 64 percent of patients treated eclectically showed an improvement. However, 72 percent of patients who were treated only custodially in institutions (receiving no psychotherapy) showed improvement. In other words, people got better just as fast by themselves as they did in therapy. This finding was obviously not favorable for psychotherapy.

Subsequent studies were not much more favorable. Some investigators (including Eysenck) concluded that it is unethical to charge a person for psychotherapy, because there is little scientific evidence that it is effective. Others say that the problems involved in performing scientific research are so great that we must abandon the attempt to evaluate therapies; validation of the effectiveness of therapy must rely on the therapist's clinical judgment. Many forms of therapy have never been evaluated objectively, because their practitioners are convinced that the method works and reject objective confirmation as unnecessary.

Critics point out that this argument is self-serving; it implies that practitioners of a particular approach should be able to continue to charge clients (or insurance companies or the welfare system) for their services while avoiding scrutiny that might reveal that the method is ineffective. These critics insist that a client (or someone paying the services provided to the client) has a right to demand that the method being used is an effective treatment for the client's problem.

Several more recent studies have compared the effectiveness of insight psychotherapies, behavior therapies, and drug treatments. The most comprehensive review was performed by Smith, Glass, and Miller (1980). The authors used a technique called **meta-analysis**, devised by Glass, McGaw, and Smith (1981); this procedure provides a statistical method for estimating the magnitude of experimental effects reported by published studies.

Smith and her colleagues found 475 studies that provided enough information to be analyzed. The overwhelming majority of the therapies being evaluated achieved significant positive results. Only 9 percent of the measures indicated that the people being treated got worse, indicating that the therapies were rarely harmful. Some studies included groups that received placebo therapy. In studies that evaluated psychotherapy, placebo therapy typically consisted of relaxation training without any attempt to address a patient's particular problems. In studies that evaluated drugs, placebos were simply inert pills or injections. Many of the studies demonstrated a significant placebo effect. Thus, when people believe they are receiving therapeutic attention, they tend to show some improvement.

In comparisons of insight therapies and behavior therapies, Smith and her colleagues found that behavior therapies produced consistently better results. However, the comparison is difficult to make directly, because studies of the two approaches tended to measure outcomes in different ways. The authors found that in treatment of both psychoses and neuroses psychotherapy combined with drug therapy was more effective than either approach by itself.

The authors concluded, "Psychotherapy is beneficial, consistently so and in many different ways. Its benefits are on a par with other expensive and ambitious interventions, such as schooling and medicine. The benefits of psychotherapy are not permanent, but then little is" (Smith, Glass, and Miller, 1980, pp. 183–188).

A Comparison of Psychotherapy and Drug Therapy. A very ambitious study sponsored by the U.S. National Institute of Mental Health compared the effectiveness of two forms of psychotherapy and drug treatment for treating depression (Elkin et al., 1985). The two forms of psychotherapy were Beck's cognitive therapy and a psychodynamic, insight-oriented approach known as interpersonal psychotherapy. The therapists were carefully selected and received additional training over the course of two years to be certain that the application of the therapeutic approaches was of the highest standard possible. The sessions were videotaped and scrutinized to be certain that the standard was maintained throughout the therapeutic sessions. The drug (imipramine, a tricyclic antidepressant medication) was not simply handed to the patient; the clients in this group met regularly with their physician, who provided a warm, supportive atmosphere—as should *always* be the case when someone consults a physician. However, the physicians did not specifically practice psychotherapy.

The control group was not exactly a "no-treatment" group. They were given a placebo, so that the effects of the antidepressant drug could be evaluated, but received the same type of support and encouragement that the drug group received. Thus, they were not simply left alone. A total of 250 patients participated in the study.

The participants were evaluated before treatment, at several points during treatment, at the end of treatment, and at 6-month, 12-month, and 18-month follow-up periods. The study permitted the comparison of two types of psychotherapy, a cognitive approach and a psychodynamic approach, applied under the best conditions possible, with drug treatment, also applied under the best conditions possible.

The results indicated that patients in all four groups, including the control group, improved over the course of the study (Elkin et al., 1989; Hirshfeld, 1990). Even the members of the control group improved. However, lacking a true "no-treatment" group, we cannot be sure whether the simple passage of time accounts for the improvement or whether the combination of placebo and warm, caring concern was responsible. The fact that nearly 60 percent of the participants had been depressed for more than six months before the study began suggests that time itself was not the only cause. Treatment with the antidepressant drug produced the most improvement, followed by the two psychotherapies. For moderately depressed patients the differences between the three active treatments was not statistically significant, but they *were* different for severely depressed patients. The recovery rate was approximately 70 percent for those who received imipramine, compared with 40 to 50 percent for those who received the psychotherapies and only 10 to 20 percent of the subjects in the control group. Further analyses and follow-up studies are in progress; it will be interesting to see whether the therapeutic methods differ in the protection they provide against recurrences of depression.

What Factors Influence Outcome? An interesting study by Luborsky, Chandler, Auerbach, Cohen, and Bachrach (1971) investigated the factors that influence the outcome of a course of psychotherapy, independent of the particular method used. They examined both patient variables and therapist variables. The important *patient variables* were psychological health at the beginning of the therapy, adequacy of personality, the patient's motivation for change, level of intelligence, level of anxiety (more anxious patients tended to do better), level of education, and socioeconomic status. Some of the variables seem to be self-confirming: If you are in fairly good psychological shape to begin with, you have a better chance of improving. In addition, if you are well educated and have adequate social and financial resources, your condition will probably improve. The finding that anxiety is a good sign probably indicates a motivation to improve.

Several *therapist variables* were significant. These variables were the number of years the therapist had been practicing, similarity in the personality of therapist and client, and the ability of the therapist to communicate empathy to the client. The finding that the more experienced therapists had more success with their clients is very encouraging; it suggests that therapists learn something from their years of experience, which in turn implies that *there is something to learn*. Thus, we have reason to believe that the process of psychotherapy is not futile.

The fact that the therapist's ability to express empathy is a significant variable has suggested to several investigators (such as Fix and Haffke, 1976) that a therapist's most important function is to change the client's thoughts and behaviors by social reinforcement. You will recall that Truax (1966) found that Carl Rogers was inadvertently reinforcing statements from his clients that indicated improvement. Therapists who demonstrate warmth and understanding are most successful in reinforcing desirable statements and behaviors of their patients. Cold, uninvolved therapists simply have less impact.

Several studies have suggested that the ability to form understanding, warm, and empathetic relationships is one of the most important traits that distinguish an effective therapist from an ineffective one. For example, Strupp and Hadley (1979) enlisted a group of college professors on the basis of their reputations as warm, trustworthy, empathetic individuals. The professors (from the departments of English, history, mathematics, and philosophy) were asked to hold weekly sessions to counsel students with psychological difficulties. Another group of students was assigned to professional psychotherapists, both psychologists and psychiatrists; and a third group received no treatment at all. Most of the students showed moderate depression or anxiety.

Although there was much variability, with some individual students showing substantial improvement, students who met with the professors did as well as those who met with the professional therapists. Both groups did significantly better than the control subjects who received no treatment. These results suggest that sympathy and understanding are the most important ingredients in the psychotherapeutic process, at least for treatment of mild neuroses. In such cases the therapists' theories of how mental disorders should be treated may be less important than their ability to establish a warm, understanding relationship with their clients.

What Should We Conclude? This chapter has tried to convey the ingenuity shown by clinicians in their efforts to help people with psychological problems. The magnitude of the task is formidable, and often the rewards are scanty, especially when objective research into the effects of their efforts shows so little. One encouraging outcome of evaluative research is its implication that what the therapist does can indeed have an effect on the outcome; experienced and empathetic therapists are more likely to help their clients get better. Another encouraging outcome is the general success achieved in behavior therapy, even though its goals are often circumscribed. Finally, although clinical psychologists are not responsible for the development of the biological therapies, they can take heart from several studies showing that psychotherapy significantly improves the mental health of clients who are also receiving drugs or electroconvulsive therapy. ■

INTERIM SUMMARY

Evaluation of Therapies and Therapists

The effectiveness of psychotherapeutic methods is difficult to assess, but given the immense expense of problems associated with mental disorders, we must do our best to evaluate them. Outcomes are difficult to measure objectively, ethical considerations make it hard to establish control groups for some types of disorders, and self-selection and dropouts make it impossible to compare randomly selected groups of subjects. However, what research there is suggests that some forms of psychotherapy—particularly behavior therapy and cognitive behavior therapy—are effective. The effectiveness of drug therapy is somewhat easier to demonstrate because experimenters can construct double-blind studies with placebos. Several experiments assessing both drug treatment and psychotherapy have found that a combined approach is the most beneficial. The most ambitious study found that antidepressant medication, delivered in a warm, caring atmosphere, was more effective than cognitive behavior therapy or interpersonal therapy in treating severe depression; no significant differences were seen in less severe cases. This study did not evaluate the effectiveness of drug treatment plus psychotherapy.

The most important characteristic of a good psychotherapist appears to be the ability to form a warm, understanding relationship with a client. Perhaps when the therapist is empathetic, the client grows to care about the therapist's opinions, which allows the therapist to administer social reinforcement. In addition, the client may be more willing to model his or her behavior on the behavior of a caring therapist. ■

APPLICATION

Finding Help

Chances are good that you or a close friend will become worried, anxious, or depressed. In most cases, people get through these low points in their lives by talking with sympathetic friends, relatives, teachers, or members of the clergy. But sometimes, problems persist despite their best efforts, and the person in distress thinks about seeking professional help. How can you tell that you need to consult a therapist, and how do you go about finding one?

In general, if you have a problem that makes you unhappy and that persists for several months, you should seriously consider getting professional advice. If the problem is very severe, you should not wait but should look for help immediately. For example, if you experience acute panic attacks, find yourself contemplating suicide, or hear voices that you know are not there, do not wait several months to see if the problems go away. You should also think about consulting a professional for specific problems, such as bad habits like smoking, or specific fears, such as fear of flying. You do not have to be "mentally ill" to seek help.

If you are a student at a college or university, the best place to turn is the counseling service. If you are not sure what mental health support is available on campus, someone in the psychology department will certainly be able to tell you where to go. In larger institutions the psychology department often operates its own clinic. If you are not a student, then you should ask your physician or call the local Mental Health Association and ask for advice. Or call the psychology department at a local college or university; you will surely find someone who will help you find professional help.

Once you have a list of names, how do you choose among them? The best approach is to be an informed consumer. You (or your insurance company) will be paying for someone's services, so make sure that these services meet your needs. First, check the therapist's credentials. Anyone can call himself or herself a "therapist"; the word has no legal significance. Although an advanced degree is no guarantee of competence, you should look for someone who has had several years of professional training. For example, a psychologist should be licensed by the appropriate government authority and should have a doctorate and specific training in psychotherapy.

You should talk with the therapist before committing yourself to a course of therapy. Do you like the person? Do you find the person sympathetic? If not, look elsewhere. Do not be impressed by an authoritative manner or glib assurances that he or she knows best what you need. Look for someone who asks good questions about your problems and needs and who helps you formulate a specific (and realistic) set of goals. Find out whether the therapist specializes in your type of problem. For example, if you want to overcome a specific fear or break a specific habit, you may not want to embark on a series of sessions in which you are expected to talk about the history of your relations with other family members. On the other hand, if your problem *is* with family relations, then a family therapist may be the best person to consult.

What about fees? As I mentioned earlier in this chapter, Freud thought that patients should pay substantial fees so that they would take the therapy seriously and be motivated to improve. However, research on this topic indicates that the amount a person pays has no relation to the benefits he or she receives. Ask the therapist about how much the services will cost. Find out whether your health insurance will cover the fees. If you will be paying yourself, do some comparison shopping. And be aware of the fact that therapists will often adjust their fees according to the ability of the client to pay.

How long should therapy continue? In some cases the therapist will suggest a fixed number of sessions. In other cases the duration is determined by the insurance company that pays for the services or by the policy of the clinic in which the therapist practices. But how do you decide when to quit in those cases where the duration is indefinite? Here are some guidelines. If you do not make progress within a reasonable amount of time, find someone else. If the therapist seems to be trying to exploit you—for example, by suggesting that sexual relations with him or her would benefit you—run, do not walk, away. The person is violating laws and ethical guidelines and is undoubtedly not someone who should be entrusted with your problems. If you find that therapy becomes the most important part of your life, or if you have become so dependent on your therapist that you feel unable to decide for yourself, think about quitting. If your therapist seems to want you to stay on even though your original problems have been solved, it is time to cut the cord.

Always remember that you are the consumer and that the therapist is someone you consult for professional advice and help. You do not owe the therapist anything other than frankness and a good-faith attempt to follow his or her advice. If you do not like the person or the advice, do not worry about hurting the therapist's feelings—look for someone else. Most people who consult a therapist are glad that they did so; they usually find experienced, sympathetic people that they can trust, who really *do* help them with their problems.

KEY TERMS AND CONCEPTS

Historical Background

trephining *(537)*

Insight Psychotherapies

insight psychotherapy *(540)*
psychoanalysis *(540)*
free association *(540)*
resistance *(540)*
transference neurosis *(540)*
countertransference *(541)*
training analysis *(541)*
client-centered therapy *(542)*
unconditional positive regard *(542)*

Behavior and Cognitive Behavior Therapy

systematic desensitization *(544)*
implosion therapy *(546)*
aversive classical conditioning *(546)*
time-out *(547)*
covert sensitization *(547)*
token economies *(548)*

self-control *(550)*
cognitive behavior therapy *(550)*
cognitive restructuring *(550)*
rational-emotive therapy *(550)*
self-talk *(551)*
self-efficacy *(552)*
symptom substitution *(553)*

Treatment of Groups

structural family therapy *(556)*

Biological Treatments

antipsychotic drugs *(559)*
tardive dyskinesia *(559)*
antidepressant drugs *(560)*
antianxiety drugs *(561)*
psychosurgery *(562)*
cingulectomy *(562)*

Evaluation of Therapies and Therapists

meta-analysis *(565)*

SUGGESTIONS FOR FURTHER READING

Davison, G.C., and Neale, J.M. *Abnormal Psychology,* 5th ed. New York: John Wiley & Sons, 1990.

Corsini, R.J., and Wedding, D. *Current Psychotherapies*, 3rd ed. Itasca, Ill.: R.E. Peacock, 1989.

These books do a good job of describing the full range of present-day treatments for mental disorders.

Minuchin, S. *Families and Family Therapy*. Cambridge, Mass.: Harvard University Press, 1974.

Minuchin describes his method of family therapy.

Thorpe, G.L., and Olson, S.L. *Behavior Therapy: Concepts, Procedures, and Applications*. Boston: Allyn and Bacon, 1990.

This book provides an excellent survey of the various techniques that have been used in behavior therapy.

17
SOCIAL PSYCHOLOGY

Henri Matisse, *Painter and His Model*
GIRAUDON/Art Resource, N.Y. © 1992 Succession H. Matisse/ARS, N.Y.

LEARNING OBJECTIVES

When you finish this chapter, you should be able to:

1. Describe the basic principles of attributional theory.
2. Discuss the common attributional biases and research on their causes.
3. Explain the use of heuristics in social cognition and the fallacies associated with them.
4. Discuss the formation of the affective, cognitive, and behavioral components of attitudes.
5. Describe Festinger's theory of cognitive dissonance, and discuss how and why induced compliance affects a person's attitude.
6. Describe the role of conflict resolution and expenditures on attitude change, and discuss Bem's theory of self-perception.
7. Summarize research on the origins of prejudice, some of its damaging consequences, and the reasons we have hope for change.
8. Describe research on the nature and effects of conformity and the conditions that facilitate or inhibit bystander intervention.
9. Discuss research on social facilitation and social loafing and the conditions under which each occurs.
10. Describe research on situations that require reciprocity and on the effects of making a commitment.
11. Discuss research on compliance with the requests of attractive people and authority figures and on the automatic nature of social influences.
12. Describe research on the effects of positive evaluation, similarity, physical appearance, and familiarity on interpersonal attraction.
13. Describe research on the role of negative reinforcement on feelings of romantic love.

Lamar and Roxanne Jones were driving home from work late Friday afternoon. The traffic was heavy and they were eager to get home. Suddenly, a slow-moving car switched lanes in front of them. Lamar braked hard and just avoided hitting the other car. Furious, he held the horn button down for several seconds.

"That idiot! That stupid jerk! If I hadn't been watching so carefully, we would have had an accident! Arrogant, rude, inconsiderate, thoughtless. . . ." Lamar was so angry that when the opportunity presented itself at a stoplight, he pulled alongside the other car and rolled down the window. He prepared some choice phrases to express his outrage; but just before he opened his mouth, he saw that the driver was his next-door neighbor, Frank.

Frank looked at Lamar and shrugged his shoulders sheepishly. "Sorry," he said. He started to say more, but the light changed, and the two cars drove off.

As they continued home, Lamar and Roxanne sat silently for a while. Lamar's temper had completely cooled, and he felt a little sheepish about having sounded his horn and wondered whether Frank had seen his angry expression.

"I didn't know it was Frank," he said. "I didn't recognize the car."

"Neither did I," said Roxanne. "Maybe they bought a new one."

When they reached their driveway, Frank had just pulled into his own. He came over to meet them as they got our of their car.

"I'm really sorry," he said. "I just picked this car up at the dealer today and I had forgotten to adjust the right side-view mirror. I didn't see you behind me."

"That's all right, no harm done," replied Lamar. "I was a little jumpy—I've had a bad week." He looked at Frank's new car. "That's a nice car," he said. The three walked over to it, glad to have something else to talk about.

During dinner that evening Lamar remarked to Roxanne, "You know, I was really mad at Frank. That is," he said, correcting himself, "I was mad at the driver until I realized who it was. Frank is one of the nicest, most considerate people I know."

"Yes, he is," said Roxanne. "And you know, if it hadn't been Frank, you'd still be thinking that the driver was a stupid, inconsiderate, rude, arrogant jerk."

"Uh, yeah, I guess so," he admitted.

"When you think about it, it really isn't fair to judge someone by a single act. Once we knew that it was Frank, we realized that there had to be a reason for what he did. We knew he wasn't stupid or careless, so it had to be something else." She paused and then smiled at Lamar innocently. "Do you remember last week when you pulled onto Route 9 from Harkness Road?"

"Yes, I remember," he said wryly.

"What do you think that driver would have said if someone asked him about your intelligence and judgment?"

"Never mind, I get the point."

This chapter examines the effects that people have on each other's behavior. Interactions with other people affect all aspects of human behavior, from infancy to old age. We learn from other people through instruction or example. The important people in our lives shape our emotions, thoughts, and personalities. Our perceptions—which we think of as private, solitary events—are affected by our interactions with others. Social psychologists have found that even the most personal and supposedly subjective aspects of human life, such as interpersonal attraction, can be studied objectively. We should not be disappointed that phenomena such as reinforcement play a role in determining with whom we fall in love. Instead, we should appreciate the intricate interplay of biological and social factors that con-

Human behavior is strongly influenced by social interactions.

trol behaviors that are important both to the survival of our species and to the individual happiness of its members.

This chapter is not the first to discuss some of the topics of social psychology; earlier chapters have discussed sexual behavior, aggressive behavior, the expression of emotion, the role of social reinforcement in learning and conditioning, and language.

The first three sections of this chapter are devoted to **social cognition**—the "knowing of people." They discuss three closely related topics: *attribution,* the means by which we attempt to understand the causes of other people's behavior; *attitudes,* the process by which ideas and events come to have particular emotional, behavioral, and cognitive significance for us; and *prejudice,* the social evil caused by a combination of particular human tendencies and the application of faulty heuristics. The final two sections discuss the nature of social interactions: social influences and interpersonal attraction.

ATTRIBUTION

1 In some ways we are all practicing (if not professional) social psychologists (Jones, 1990). Each of us uses certain principles to construct theories about the nature and causes of other people's behavior. We are confronted each day by many thousands of individual acts performed by other people. Some acts are important to us, because they provide clues about people's personality characteristics, how they are likely to interact with us, and how they are perceiving us. If we had to pay careful attention to each of these acts, to classify them, to think about their significance, and to compare them with other observations, we would be immobilized in thought. Instead, as a result of our previous experience, we pay attention to some types of behaviors and ignore others, and we make snap decisions about what categories various people and events belong to. We follow rules and strategies that often lead us to the correct conclusions. In doing so, we save time and effort.

However, as useful as these strategies and shortcuts may be, they sometimes lead us astray. In our reliance on our cherished rules of thumb we may focus on misleading information while ignoring useful information. We may unfairly categorize other people on the basis of superficial characteristics. We may uncritically adopt attitudes and prejudices we were taught, to the detriment of other people and of ourselves.

The process by which people infer the causes of other people's behavior is called **attribution.** The study of attribution has had a profound impact on social psychologists. And it has contributed to an increased understanding of persuasion, interpersonal attraction, group behavior, self-evaluation, and attitudes and opinions.

The Implicit Psychologist

As we saw in Chapter 9, everyone who is able to use a language knows a large set of complex rules of grammar, but few people know how to describe those rules. Similarly, although we all attribute causes to events every day, often without giving the matter much thought, the reasons for the choices we make are not always obvious to us. Our knowledge of human behavior is based on attributions; from them we construct theories of social behavior. These theories allow us to organize our observations and to predict the probable outcomes of our own behavior. If our theories are correct, we can affect the behavior of other people in ways that benefit us.

Implicit psychology involves both attribution and the formation of private theories of reality. Unlike the theories of psychologists, in which the methods, assumptions, and data are explicitly stated, implicit psychological theories are private and often cannot be explained by their owner. Indeed, people do not regard their implicit theories as theories at all, but as facts. Consequently, they tend not to revise the theories when provided with contradictory data. As we shall see in a later section, many prejudices and superstitions can best be understood as products of faulty implicit theories of human nature.

Disposition Versus Situation

The primary classification that we make concerning the causes of a person's behavior is the relative importance of situational and dispositional factors (Heider, 1958). **Situational factors** are stimuli in the environment; **dispositional factors** are individual personality characteristics. One of the tasks of socialization is to learn what behaviors are expected in various kinds of situations—to analyze the importance of various situational factors. In this way we learn both what to expect from others and how to behave so as not to elicit disapproval. Once we learn that in certain situations most people act in a specific way, we expect others to act similarly in those situations. For example, when people are introduced, they are expected to look at each other, smile, say something like "How do you do?" or "It's nice to meet you," and perhaps offer to shake the other person's hand. If people act in conventional ways in given situations, we are not surprised. Their behavior appears to be dictated by social custom—by the characteristics of the situation—and we therefore learn very little about them as individuals.

As we get to know other people, we also learn what to expect from them as individuals. We learn about their *dispositions*—the kinds of behaviors that they tend to engage in. We learn to characterize people as friendly, generous, suspicious, pessimistic, or greedy by observing their behavior in a variety of situations. Sometimes, we even make inferences from a single observation. If someone's behavior is seriously at variance with the way most people would act in a particular situation, we attribute his or her behavior to internal, or dispositional, causes (Jones and Davis, 1965). For example, if we see a person refuse to hold a door open for someone in a wheelchair, we assign that person some negative personality characteristics. Similarly, if a young boy gets some candy and shares it with his little sister, we attribute a generous nature to the child, because we assume that young children are typically selfish.

Sources of Information

Kelley has suggested that we attribute the behavior of other people to external (situational) or internal (dispositional) causes on the basis of three factors: *consensus, consistency,* and *distinctiveness* (Kelley, 1967; Kelley and Michela, 1980).

Consensual behavior—that is, a behavior shared by a large number of people—is usually attributed to external causes. The behavior is assumed to be demanded by the situation. For example, if someone asks an acquaintance for the loan of a coin to make a telephone call, we do not conclude that the person is especially kind and generous if he or she complies. The request is reasonable and costs little; lending the money is a consensual behavior. However, if a person has some change but refuses to lend it, we readily attribute dispositional factors such as stinginess or meanness to that person.

We also base our attributions on **consistency**—that is, on whether a person's behavior occurs reliably over time. For example, if you meet someone for the first time and notice that she speaks slowly and without much expres-

sion, stands in a slouching posture, and sighs occasionally, you will probably conclude that she has a sad and listless disposition. Now, suppose that after she has left, you mention to a friend that the young woman seems very passive and depressed. Your friend says, "No, I know her pretty well, and she's usually very cheerful and friendly." With this new evidence about her behavior you will reassess your conclusion and perhaps wonder what happened to make her act so sad. If a person's pattern of behavior is consistent, we attribute the behavior to internal causes; inconsistent behaviors lead us to seek external causes.

Finally, we base our attributions on **distinctiveness**—the extent to which a person performs a particular behavior only in a particular situation. Behaviors that are distinctively associated with a particular situation are attributed to situational factors; those that occur in a variety of situations are attributed to dispositional factors. For example, suppose a mother observes that her little boy is generally polite and well behaved; but whenever he plays with the child across the street, he comes home with his clothes dirty and acts sassy toward her until she has rebuked him a few times. She does not conclude that her boy has a rude or messy disposition; she probably concludes that the child across the street has a bad influence on him. Because her child's rude and messy behavior occurs only under a distinctive circumstance (the presence of the child across the street), she attributes it to external causes.

Attributional Biases

2 When we make attributions, we do not function as impartial, dispassionate observers. Our biases affect our conclusions about the actor (the person performing the behavior).

The Fundamental Attributional Error. When attributing the behavior of an actor to possible causes, an observer tends to *overestimate the significance of dispositional factors* and *underestimate the significance of situational factors.* For example, if we see a driver make a mistake, as Lamar and Roxanne did in the opening vignette, we are more likely to conclude that the driver is stupid and careless than to consider the fact that external factors may have temporarily distracted him. Ross (1977) calls this bias the **fundamental attributional error.** Many of the other attributional biases can be explained as consequences of this one.

The fundamental attributional error is remarkably potent. Even when evidence indicates otherwise, people seem to prefer dispositional explanations to situational ones. A study by Ross, Amabile, and Steinmetz (1977) demonstrates this tendency. Pairs of students played a contrived "quiz game" in which the questioner was permitted to ask any question he or she wanted to, no matter how obscure or esoteric. In this situation a person can easily stump someone else by choosing some topic that he or she knows more about than the average person. After the game the subjects were asked to rate both their own level of general knowledge and that of their opponent. Table 17.1 lists the ratings. Subjects who played the role of contestant tended to rate the questioner as much more knowledgeable than themselves. Apparently, they attributed the difficult questions to factors internal to their opponents rather than to the situation. When the subjects served as questioners, they did not make an internal attribution; they rated themselves as only slightly more knowledgeable than the person they questioned. (See **Table 17.1.**) Thus, a person is less likely to make the fundamental attributional error when he or she is the actor (the person who is performing the behavior—in this case, the questioner).

An experiment by Storms (1973) showed that the fundamental attributional error also plays a role when people witness their own behavior as an observer would. Storms had pairs of subjects carry on a discussion and videotaped one of them during the conversation. One group of subjects later watched a tape of the other subject (the same perspective that they had during the discussion). Another group saw themselves as their partners had. (See **Figure 17.1.**) After viewing the videotape, the subjects were asked to rate the degree to which their own behavior was due to dispositional versus situational causes. The results were as predicted. Subjects who did not see a tape of themselves attributed their own behavior to situational factors. Those who saw themselves as others would see them showed the fundamental attributional error: They judged their own behavior as being a consequence of dispositional factors.

Why do we make the fundamental attributional error when we observe the behavior of others but not when we explain the causes of our own behavior? Jones and Nisbett (1971) suggested two possible reasons. First, we have a *different focus of attention* when we view ourselves. When we ourselves are doing something, we see the world around us more clearly

Table 17.1 Ratings of general knowledge of self and opponent in a mock quiz game

Condition	Rating of Self	Rating of Opponent
Subjects Devised Questions		
Subject as questioner	53.5[a]	50.6[b]
Subject as contestant	41.3[a,c]	66.8[b,c]
Experimenter Prepared Questions		
Subject as questioner	54.1	52.5
Subject as contestant	47.0	50.3

Source: Adapted from Ross, L.D., Amabile, T.M., and Steinmetz, J.L. *Journal of Personality and Social Psychology,* 1977, *35,* 485–494. Copyright 1977 by the American Psychological Association. Adapted by permission of the author.
Note: Scores with the same superscripts differed significantly from each other.

than we see our own behavior. However, when we observe someone else doing something, we focus our attention on what is most salient and relevant: that person's behavior, not the situation in which he or she is placed.

A second possible reason for these differences in attribution is that *different types of information* are available to us about our own behavior and that of other people. We have more information about our own behavior—more than that of any other person. We are thus more likely to realize that our own behavior is often inconsistent. We also have a better notion of which stimuli we are attending to in a given situation. This difference in information leads us to conclude that the behavior of other people is consistent and thus is a product of their personality, whereas ours is affected by the situation in which we find ourselves.

False Consensus. The second attributional error is the tendency of an observer to perceive

Figure 17.1 The procedure used by Storms (1973).

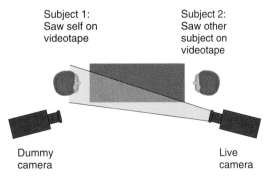

Subject 1: Saw self on videotape

Subject 2: Saw other subject on videotape

Dummy camera

Live camera

his or her own response as representative of a general consensus—an error called **false consensus.** For example, Sherman, Presson, and Chassin (1984) found that male high school students who smoke believe that a majority of their peers do so, too, whereas nonsmokers believe that a majority do *not* smoke. Obviously, both groups cannot be correct.

One explanation accounts for false consensus in terms of defense of ego or self-esteem. Presumably, people do not like to think of themselves as being too different from other people, so they prefer to think that most other people will act the way they do.

Another possible explanation is that people tend to place themselves in the company of others who are similar to themselves (Ross, 1977). As we will see later in this chapter, an important variable in interpersonal attraction is similarity in behavior and attitudes. Thus, when people conclude that other people are more similar to themselves than they actually are, the error may be a result of a sampling bias rather than of a need to minimize damage to their egos.

Motivational Biases. Both attributional biases discussed so far are logical, or intellectual. Other biases appear to be related to motivation—that is, to processes that have personal significance for the observer. We will examine three motivational biases here.

Credit for Success, Blame for Failure. People tend to attribute successful outcomes of their own behavior to internal causes, but they attribute their failures to external causes. For example, a person is likely to perceive a high score on a test as a reflection of his or her intelligence and motivation but to attribute a low score to an unfair examination, boring and trivial subject matter, or lack of opportunity to study properly. Similarly, football players and coaches tend to credit their wins to internal causes such as determination and skill but blame their losses on external causes such as luck or injuries (Lau and Russell, 1980).

Johnson, Feigenbaum, and Weiby (1964) enlisted students in an educational psychology course in a trial program of teaching mathematics to fourth-grade boys. The experimenters arranged the tests so that the performance of some boys would appear to improve during the teaching sessions, and the performance of others would stay the same or get worse. The "teachers" who had worked with boys whose test performance improved later cited their own teaching skills as the cause. Those who had worked with boys who did not improve blamed the poor performance on the low motivation or intelligence of the learner.

The perception of outside observers is quite different from the perception of a person who has personal involvement with the success or failure of an enterprise. Beckman (1970) performed an experiment similar to the one I just described but obtained attributional judgments both from the teachers and from observers. Unlike the teachers, the observers blamed the teachers for the students' poor performance but attributed good performance to the students' intelligence and motivation.

Motivational Relevance. Another element that influences our attributions of behavior to either dispositional or situational factors is the motivational relevance of the consequences of this behavior for the actor. Thibaut and Riecken (1955) arranged for undergraduates at Harvard University to make a request of both a person of higher status (a well-dressed, confident-acting man who had just received his Ph.D. and joined the faculty) and a person of lower status (a poorly dressed, self-deprecating undergraduate from a college that a Harvard student was likely to hold in low esteem). Both people (confederates of the experimenters) complied with the subjects' requests. When asked to explain why the people complied with their requests, the students attributed the compliance of the higher-status person to dispositional factors and that of the lower-status person to situational factors. Apparently, the subjects assumed that because the higher-status person had nothing to gain from agreeing to assist them, he must have done so because he was helpful and considerate. In contrast, because the lower-status person was perceived as being less free to choose, he complied because the subjects' request was persuasive.

The Illusion of Personal Causation. Independent of the tendency to take credit for our successes and to avoid blame for our failures is another motivational bias. We tend to assume that when we do something, our action will have an effect on subsequent events, even when logically these events cannot be related to our behavior. In other words, we have a fallacious belief in **personal causation.** In an experiment illustrating this phenomenon Langer (1975) allowed some subjects to select a 50-cent lottery ticket and simply handed one to others. When asked later how much money they would accept to sell their ticket, the subjects who had been given a ticket were willing to sell it for approximately $2, whereas those who had selected their ticket wanted nearly $9. The element of choice led to an illusion of personal causation; the chosen ticket was perceived as more likely to be a winner.

The illusion of personal causation may be an innate tendency. More likely, however, it is simply a generalization from our previous experience with reality. When we intend our behavior to have an effect on the environment, it often does. We push something and it moves; we say something and other people react. Thus, we come to regard our own efforts as causal. Because some people are more successful than others at making things happen, different people will have differing degrees of belief in the potency of their efforts.

Using Heuristics in Social Cognition

3 As Fiske and Taylor (1984) have observed, people act as *cognitive misers* much of the time. That is, we tend to follow general rules, or *heuristics*, when making decisions. This tendency is especially evident when we make social judgments; in fact, the rules of implicit psychology are examples of heuristics. Most of the time, these rules serve us well. However, sometimes they lead us astray. When they do, we refer to them as *biases* or *fallacies*. The two most important categories of heuristics are *representativeness* and *availability* (Tversky and Kahneman, 1982).

The Representativeness Heuristic. When we meet someone for the first time, we notice his or her clothes, hairstyle, posture, manner of speaking, grammar and vocabulary, hand gestures, and many other characteristics. From our previous experience we make tentative conclusions about other characteristics we cannot immediately discover. In doing so, we attempt to match the characteristics we can observe with stereotypes we have of different types of people. If the people we meet seem representative of one of these stereotypes, we conclude that they fit that particular category (Lupfer, Clark, and Hutcherson, 1990). In making this conclusion, we use the representativeness heuristic.

The **representativeness heuristic** is based on our ability to categorize and classify. We observe that some characteristics tend to go together (or we are taught that they do); and when we observe some of these characteristics, we conclude that the others are present, too.

Stereotypes can be misleading. Are you surprised to learn that the basketball player in this picture, Bill Bradley, is now a U.S. senator?

Most of the time this strategy works; we are able to predict people's behavior with a reasonable degree of accuracy. (If we could not, we could hardly use the term *heuristic.*)

Sometimes, the representativeness heuristic can mislead us. Consider the following example. I (a professor of psychology) have a friend who is also a professor. He likes to swim laps in the pool every lunch hour. He also likes to play tennis; and if he can find a willing opponent, he will even play in the dead of winter, if the court can be swept clear of snow. Which of the following is his field: (a) sports medicine or (b) psychology?

If you said "psychology," you were most likely to be right, because I am a professor of psychology and am therefore likely to have friends who are also professors of psychology. In addition, there are many more professors of psychology than professors of sports medicine. (In fact, my friend *is* a professor of psychology.) Yet you may have chosen alternative (a) or at least seriously considered it. The image of an athletic, tennis-playing person seems to be such a distinctive cue that it is difficult to "play the odds." Somehow, the image seems to be more representative of a person professionally involved in sports than in psychology. Paying too much attention to the image is an example of the **base-rate fallacy**—in this case, ignoring the relative numbers of professors of psychology and of sports medicine.

Learning to "play the odds" and avoid being misled by distinctive characteristics is particularly important in certain intellectual endeavors. For example, physicians who are experienced in making diagnoses of diseases teach their students to learn and make use of the probabilities of particular diseases and not to be fooled by especially distinctive symptoms. In fact, Zukier and Pepitone (1984) posed a problem to first-year medical students and to residents who had completed their clinical training. The inexperienced students were tricked by the base-rate fallacy but the residents played the odds, as they had been taught to do. Chapter 15 discussed a similar topic; it compared the accuracy of actuarial predictions (based on the odds) and clinical predictions.

The Availability Heuristic. When people attempt to assess the importance or the frequency of an event, they tend to be guided by the ease with which examples of that event come to mind—by how *available* these examples are to the imagination. This mental shortcut is therefore called the **availability heuristic.**

In general, the things we are able to think of most easily *are* more important and occur more frequently than things that are difficult to imagine. Thus, the availability heuristic serves us well—most of the time.

Some events are so salient and so vivid that we can easily picture their happening. For example, we can easily picture getting mugged while walking through the heart of a large city at night or being involved in an airplane crash, probably because such events are often reported in the news and because they are so frightening. Thus, people tend to overestimate the likelihood of such misfortunes happening to them. Tversky and Kahneman (1982) demonstrated the effect of availability by asking people to estimate whether English words starting with *k* were more or less common than words with *k* in the third position (for example, *kiss* versus *lake*). Most people said that more words started with *k*. In fact, more than twice as many words have *k* in the third position than have it first. But because thinking of words that start with a particular letter is easier than thinking of words that contain the letter in another position, people are misled in their judgment.

Many variables can affect the availability of an event or a concept and thus increase its effect on our decision making. For example, having recently seen a particular type of event makes it easier for us to think of other examples of that event. This phenomenon, discussed in Chapter 9, is called *priming*. Seeing a word even briefly makes it easier to perceive words related in meaning; thus, seeing the word *kitchen* makes us recognize the word *stove* more readily. Many first-year medical students demonstrate this phenomenon when, after learning the symptoms of various diseases, they start discovering these very symptoms in their own bodies.

Higgins, Rholes, and Jones (1977) demonstrated the effects of priming on judging the personality characteristics of strangers. They had subjects work on a task that introduced various descriptive adjectives. Next, the experimenters described an imaginary person, saying that he had performed such feats as climbing mountains and crossing the Atlantic Ocean in a sailboat. Finally, they asked the subjects to give their impressions of this person. Those subjects who had previously been exposed to words such as "adventurous" reported favorable impressions, whereas those who had been exposed to words such as "reckless" reported unfavorable ones. The priming effect of the descriptive adjectives had biased their interpretation of the facts.

The availability heuristic also explains why personal encounters tend to have an especially strong effect on our decision making. For example, suppose you have decided to purchase a new car. You have narrowed your choice down to two models, both available at local dealers for about the same price. You read an article in a consumer magazine that summarizes the experiences of thousands of people who have purchased these cars, and their testimony shows clearly that one of them has a much better repair record. You decide to purchase that brand and mention the fact to an acquaintance you happen to meet later that day. Your acquaintance says, "Oh, no! Don't buy one of those! I bought one last year, and it has been nothing but trouble. I was driving it on the highway two weeks after I bought it and it broke down. I was in the middle of nowhere and had to walk five miles to the nearest phone. I got it towed to a garage, and they had to order a part from the distributor. I ended up staying in that town for two days before it was fixed. Since then, I've had trouble with the cooling system, the transmission, and the brakes. So far, the car has been under warranty, but I'm worried about what will happen when I have to start paying for the repairs myself." Would this experience affect your decision to buy that brand of automobile?

Most people would take this personal encounter very seriously. Even though it consists of the experience of only one person, whereas the survey in the consumer magazine represents the experience of thousands of people, a vivid personal encounter is much more *available* than a set of statistics and tends to have a disproportionate affect on our own behavior. A study by Borgida and Nisbett (1977) confirms this principle. The experimenters provided college students with information about courses based on ratings of students who had previously enrolled in them. The information came from summaries of the ratings of many students and from face-to-face contact with a few students who had taken the courses. The students were then asked to choose the courses that they would like to take. Although the summaries provided the best information because they came from a large number of students, the face-to-face contacts had a stronger effect on the students' choices.

The availability principle, combined with the laws of probability, accounts for yet another source of error in our decision making: the **regression fallacy.** An anecdote by Kahneman and Tversky (1973) illustrates this fallacy. When some military flight instructors were urged to praise their students whenever they exhibited a good performance, they resisted doing so because of their previous experience. They had observed that whenever they praised an especially good performance, the student did worse, rather than better, the next time; reinforcement seemed to make the student try less hard. In contrast, whenever a student performed terribly, criticism led to improvement the next time. Assuming that their observations were correct, can you detect the error in the instructors' reasoning?

Consider what a student's performance would be if she received neither praise nor criticism. After exceptionally good or bad performance on one trial, you would predict that her performance on the next trial would, by chance, be less than exceptional. The tendency for an extreme event to be followed by one closer to the mean is called *regression toward the mean—* hence the term *regression fallacy.* If the instructor praises a fine performance and observes a more ordinary performance the next time, he is likely to conclude that his praise made the student's performance decline. Similarly, if the instructor criticizes especially poor performance and the student performs better the next time, he is likely to conclude that the criticism had a salutary effect. Thus, the instructors concluded that criticism was the best policy. But in both cases regression toward the mean, not praise or criticism, explains the change in behavior.

INTERIM SUMMARY

Attribution

The conclusions that people make about the causes of behavior of people around them have important effects on their own attitudes and behavior. We are all students of social behavior, because we are all members of society; and the ability to understand the causes of other people's behavior and predict what they are likely to do is an important skill. Only recently have psychologists begun to study the factors that govern the process of attribution.

Like scientists, people use the covariance method to determine cause and effect: Events that occur together are assumed to be causally related. We attribute particular instances of behavior to two types of causes: situational and dispositional. If a behavior is consensual (many people are acting the same way), we attribute it to situational factors. If a behavior is consistent (a person acts the same way in a variety of situations), we attribute it to dispositional factors. If a behavior is distinctive (occurring only under certain circumstances), we attribute it to situational factors.

Ross identified the fundamental attributional error as overreliance on dispositional factors and underreliance on situational factors. This tendency is best understood as the consequence of using a heuristic that saves time and mental energy, but it sometimes leads us astray. We are most likely to make the fundamental attributional error when trying to understand the causes of other people's behavior, because we are more aware of the environmental factors that affect our own behavior.

False consensus refers to the tendency to believe that others act and believe much as we do. We also tend to take credit for success and shun blame for failure, and many of us have an exaggerated belief in the efficacy of our own behaviors.

Because of the enormous amount of information we receive from the environment, we must utilize mental shortcuts in perceiving and making decisions and in determining what is going on around us. These mental shortcuts are rules or principles called heuristics. The representativeness heuristic describes our tendency to seize upon a few especially salient characteristics of a person or situation. Thus, we sometimes ignore other evidence and commit the base-rate error. The availability heuristic describes our tendency to judge the importance or the frequency of events by the ease with which examples come to mind. If we have recently been exposed to a particular concept, that concept becomes more available (through the phenomenon of priming) and thus biases our decisions. Personal encounters give rise to vivid memories of particular episodes, and the availability of these episodes, too, tends to outweigh less vivid—but more representative—evidence. Finally, the statistical tendency for unusual events to be followed by more ordinary ones often leads to the regression fallacy. ∎

ATTITUDES AND THEIR FORMATION

The study of attitudes and their formation constitutes an important part of the field of social psychology (Pratkanis, Breckler, and Greenwald, 1989). To a psychologist, the word *attitude* refers to three different components: *affective, behavioral,* and *cognitive* (Breckler, 1984). The affective component consists of the kinds of

feelings that a particular topic arouses. The behavioral component consists of a tendency to act in a particular way with respect to a particular topic. The cognitive component consists of a set of beliefs about a topic—beliefs that can be expressed in words. Social psychologists have studied all three aspects of attitudes, and we will examine their results in this section.

Formation of Attitudes

[4] The way we form an attitude is somewhat similar to the way we are persuaded to change it. Thus, the two phenomena are certainly related. However, people's attitudes are usually formed initially by implicit processes, whereas attempts to change people's attitudes are usually explicit and deliberate. Therefore, the two topics are discussed separately. Although the three components of attitudes have been described in an *ABC* order, I will discuss them in nonalphabetical order: affect, cognition, and behavior.

Affective Components of Attitudes. Affective components of attitudes can be very strong and pervasive. The bigot feels uneasy in the presence of people from a certain religious, racial, or ethnic group; the nature lover feels exhilaration from a pleasant walk through the woods. Like other emotional reactions, these feelings are strongly influenced by direct or vicarious classical conditioning (Rajecki, 1989).

Direct classical conditioning is straightforward. Suppose you meet someone who seems to take delight in embarrassing you. She makes clever, sarcastic remarks that disparage your intelligence, looks, and personality. Unfortunately, her remarks are so clever that your attempts to defend yourself make you appear even more foolish. After a few encounters with this person, the sight of her or the sound of her voice is likely to immediately evoke feelings of dislike and fear. Your attitude toward her will be negative.

Vicarious classical conditioning undoubtedly plays a major role in transmitting parents' attitudes to their children. People are skilled at detecting even subtle signs of fear, hatred, and other negative emotional states in other people, especially when they know them well. Thus, children perceive their parents' prejudices and fears even if these feelings are unspoken. Children who see their parents recoil in disgust at the sight of members of some ethnic group are likely to learn to react in the same way. We have a strong tendency to acquire classically conditioned responses when we observe them being elicited in other people by the conditional stimulus (Berger, 1962).

The affective component of attitudes tends to be rather resistant to change; it persists for some time even after a person has altered his or her opinion on a particular subject. For example, a person may successfully overcome a childhood racial prejudice and be completely fair and impartial in dealing with people of other races but may experience unpleasant emotional arousal at the sight of a racially mixed couple. This discrepancy between belief and feelings often makes people feel guilty.

Cognitive Components of Attitudes. We acquire most beliefs about a particular topic quite directly: We hear or read a fact or opinion, or other people reinforce our statements expressing a particular attitude. Someone may say to a child: "Blacks are lazy," "You can't trust whites," or "We Czechs are better than those Slovaks." A group of racially prejudiced people will probably ostracize a person who makes positive statements about the group or groups they are prejudiced against. Conversely, conscientious parents may applaud their child's positive statements about other ethnic groups or about social issues such as environmental conservation.

Children, in particular, form attitudes through imitating, or **modeling,** the behavior of people who play an important role in their lives. Children usually repeat opinions expressed by their parents. In the United States many children label themselves as Democrats or Republicans long before they know what these political parties stand for. Often they ask their parents, "What are we, Republicans or Democrats?" without considering whether they might have any choice in the matter. The tendency to identify with the family unit (and, later, with peer groups) provides a strong incentive to adopt the group's attitudes.

Behavioral Components of Attitudes. People do not always behave as their expressed attitudes and beliefs would lead us to expect. In a classic example LaPiere (1934) drove through the United States with a Chinese couple. They stopped at over two hundred fifty restaurants and lodging places and were refused service only once. Several months after their trip, LaPiere wrote to the owners of the places they had visited and asked whether they would serve Chinese people. The response was overwhelmingly negative; 92 percent of those who re-

Many people who consider themselves unprejudiced still feel uneasy at the sight of a racially mixed couple.

sponded said that they would not. Clearly, their behavior gave less evidence of racial bias than their expressed attitudes did. This study has been cited as proof that attitudes do not matter. However, more recent research indicates that there *is* a relation between attitudes and behavior, but that the relation is influenced by many factors. We will examine several of the factors in the following subsections.

Degree of Specificity. One important variable that affects the correspondence between a person's attitude and behavior is the degree of specificity. If you measure a person's general attitude toward a topic, you will be less likely to be able to predict his or her behavior; behaviors, unlike attitudes, are specific events. As the attitude being measured becomes more specific, the person's behavior becomes more predictable. For example, Weigel, Vernon, and Tognacci (1974) measured people's attitudes toward a series of topics that increased in specificity from "a pure environment" to "the Sierra Club" (an American organization that supports environmental causes). They used the subjects' attitudes to predict whether they would volunteer for various activities to benefit the Sierra Club.

Table 17.2 shows the results. A person's attitude toward environmentalism was a poor predictor of whether he or she would volunteer; his or her attitude toward the Sierra Club itself was a much better predictor. (See *Table*

581

Table 17.2 Correlation between willingness to join or work for the Sierra Club and various measures of related attitudes

Attitude Scale	Correlation
Importance of a pure environment	.06
Pollution	.32
Conservation	.24
Attitude toward the Sierra Club	.68

Source: Based on Wiegel, R.H., Vernon, D.T.A., and Tognacci, L.N. *Journal of Personality and Social Psychology,* 1974, *30,* 724–728.

17.2.) For example, a person might favor a pure environment but also dislike organized clubs or have little time to spare for meetings. This person would express a positive attitude toward a pure environment but would not join the club or volunteer for any activities to support it.

Motivational Relevance. Expressing a particular attitude toward a topic takes less effort than demonstrating that commitment with a time-consuming behavior. As the old saying puts it, "Talk is cheap." Even sincerely felt and expressed attitudes may not be acted on if the effects of a particular behavior do not have much personal significance. Sivacek and Crano (1982) demonstrated this phenomenon by asking students to volunteer their time to help campaign against a law pending in the state legislature that would raise the drinking age from eighteen to twenty. Although almost all of the students were opposed to the new drinking law, younger students, who would be affected by its passage, were much more likely to volunteer their time and effort. Thus, attitudes are more likely to be accompanied by behaviors if the effects of the behaviors have motivational relevance for the individual.

Self-Attribution. Another variable that affects the relation between attitude and behavior is the way the person formed his or her attitude. If a person has developed an attitude from the opinions or persuasive arguments of other people, the attitude will usually be a poor predictor of behavior. In contrast, an attitude formed through *self-attribution* is likely to be an excellent predictor of behavior.

Self-attribution occurs because we are all self-observers: We see how we behave in various situations and make attributions about our own dispositions, just as we make them about other people's. If we observe that someone else habitually avoids talking with fat people, we can conclude that the person has a negative attitude toward them. If we find ourselves avoiding fat people, we can make a similar self-attribution.

Several studies have found that when a person has had the opportunity to perform relevant behaviors, he or she is more likely to express attitudes consistent with subsequent behaviors. For example, Regan and Fazio (1977) had some subjects spend time playing with five puzzles; others merely heard descriptions of the puzzles. All subjects were asked to rate their interest in each puzzle.

Later, the subjects were given some "free time" during which they could play with the puzzles if they chose. The correlation between ratings and later activity with the puzzles was .54 for subjects who had actually played with the puzzles but only .20 for those who had merely heard them described. Therefore, we may conclude that attitudes based on people's previous behavior are better predictors of their future behavior. Personal experience forms the most consistent attitude-behavior relations.

Constraints on Behavior. Other more obvious factors, such as existing circumstances, also produce discrepancies between attitudes and behaviors. For example, a young man might have a very positive attitude toward a certain young woman. If he were asked, he might express a very positive attitude toward kissing her. However, he is never observed to engage in this behavior, because the young woman has plainly shown that she is not interested in him. No matter how carefully we measure the young man's attitudes, we cannot predict his behavior without additional information (in this case, from the young woman).

Cognitive Dissonance

[5] Although we usually regard our attitudes as causes of our behavior, our behavior also affects our attitudes. Two major theories attempt to explain the effects of behavior on attitude formation. The oldest theory, developed by Leon Festinger (1957; Cooper and Fazio, 1984), is that of **cognitive dissonance.** According to Festinger, when we perceive a discrepancy between our attitudes and behavior, between our behavior and self-image, or between one attitude and another, an unpleasant state of dissonance results. In an earlier example I described a person who feels uncomfortable in the com-

pany of racially mixed couples. The person experiences a conflict between the belief in his own lack of prejudice and the evidence of prejudice from his behavior. This conflict produces dissonance, which is aversive.

In Festinger's view an important source of human motivation is **dissonance reduction;** the aversive state of dissonance motivates a person to reduce it. (Because dissonance reduction involves the removal of an aversive stimulus, it serves as a reinforcer.) A person can achieve dissonance reduction by (1) reducing the importance of one of the dissonant elements, (2) adding consonant elements, or (3) changing one of the dissonant elements.

Suppose a student believes that he is very intelligent, but he invariably receives bad grades in his courses. Because the obvious prediction is that intelligent people get good grades, the discrepancy causes the student to experience dissonance. To reduce this dissonance, he may decide that grades are not important and that intelligence is not very closely related to grades. He is using strategy 1, reducing the importance of one of the dissonant elements—the fact that he received bad grades in his courses. Or the student can dwell on the belief that his professors were unfair or that his job leaves him little time to study. In this case he is using strategy 2, reducing dissonance by adding consonant elements—other factors can account for his poor grades and hence explain the discrepancy between his perceived intelligence and grades. Finally, the student can use strategy 3 to change one of the dissonant elements: He can either start getting good grades or revise his opinion of his own intelligence. Other factors (how hard he is willing to work, how important it is for him to feel he is intelligent) will determine which of these changes he makes in his opinions.

Induced Compliance. Most of us believe that although we can induce someone to do something, getting someone to change an opinion is much harder. However, Festinger's theory of cognitive dissonance and supporting experimental evidence indicate otherwise. Under the right conditions, when people are coerced into doing something or are paid to do so, the act of compliance causes a change in their attitudes.

Dissonance theory predicts that dissonance occurs when a person's behavior has outcomes harmful to self-esteem; there is a conflict between the person's belief in his or her own worth and the fact that he or she has done something that damages this belief. The person will then seek to justify the behavior. For example, suppose you are having a picnic at a park. While idly throwing stones, you happen to break a beer bottle that someone carelessly discarded. You think about retrieving the broken pieces of glass, but somehow, you never get around to doing it. Later, you hear the cries of a little girl who has been playing nearby and has cut her feet badly on the broken glass. You feel ashamed of yourself for not having picked up the pieces of broken glass, but you will probably try to lighten your share of the blame by saying to yourself, "The slob who left the bottle there is really responsible" or "Why weren't that girl's parents watching her more closely?"

Similarly, a poorly paid vacuum cleaner sales representative is likely to convince himself that the shoddy merchandise he sells is actually good. Otherwise, he must question why he works for a company that pays him poorly and requires him to lie to prospective customers about the quality of the product in order to make a sale. Conversely, an executive of one of the commercial television networks may know that the programs she produces are sleazy, mindless drivel, but she is so well paid that she does not feel bad about producing them. Her high salary justifies her job and probably also provides her with enough self-esteem that she has decided that the public "gets what it deserves" anyway.

Festinger and Carlsmith (1959) verified this observation by having subjects perform very boring tasks such as putting a number of spools on a tray, dumping them out, putting them on the tray again, dumping them out again, and so on. After they spent an hour on exercises like this, the experimenter asked each subject whether he or she would help out in the study by trying to convince the next subject that the task was interesting and enjoyable. Some subjects received $1 for helping out; others received $20. (In the late 1950s, $20 was a considerable sum for a student; in fact, it is not bad even today.) Control subjects were paid nothing; their assistance was presumably an expression of willingness to help the experimenter. The experimenters predicted that subjects who were paid only $1 would perceive the task as being relatively interesting. They had been induced to lie to a "fellow student" (actually, a confederate of the experimenters) for a paltry sum. Like the vacuum cleaner sales representative, they should convince themselves of the worth of the experiment so as to maintain their self-esteem. Figure 17.2 shows that poorly paid subjects did in fact rate the task better than control subjects or those who were well paid.

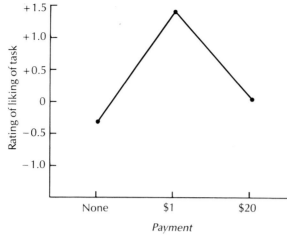

Figure 17.2 Ratings of liking of task by people who received no payment, payment of $1, or payment of $20. (Based on data from Festinger, L., and Carlsmith, J.M. *Journal of Abnormal and Social Psychology*, 1959, *58*, 203–210.)

(See *Figure 17.2.*) Clearly, our actions *do* have an effect on our attitudes; when faced with inconsistency between our behavior and our attitudes, we often change our attitudes to suit our behavior.

Steele and Liu (1981) obtained evidence supporting the suggestion that self-esteem plays a role in attitude changes motivated by cognitive dissonance. They induced subjects to write essays containing arguments against providing further state funding for facilities for the handicapped. We might reasonably expect that doing so would have negative effects on the subjects' self-esteem. The experimenters told some of the subjects that after they wrote the essay, they would be asked to help blind students by recording midterm and final exams onto cassettes. Presumably, this chance to help handicapped people would counteract any harm to self-esteem produced by writing an essay contrary to the interests of handicapped people. Indeed, Steele and Liu found that an opinion shift occurred only in those subjects who had not been told that they would be asked to help blind students.

Arousal and Attitude Change. Croyle and Cooper (1983) have obtained physiological evidence that induced compliance produces arousal. This finding is important because Festinger's theory hypothesizes that dissonance reduction is motivated by an aversive drive. The experimenters chose as their subjects Princeton University students who disagreed with the assertion "Alcohol use should be totally banned from the Princeton campus and eating clubs." The subjects were induced to write an essay containing strong and forceful arguments in favor of the assertion or in opposition to it. While the subjects were writing the essay, the experimenters measured the electrical conductance of their skin, which is known to be a good indicator of the physiological arousal that accompanies stress. Some subjects were simply told to write the essay. Other subjects were told that their participation was completely voluntary and that they were free to leave at any time; they even signed a form emphasizing the voluntary nature of the task. Of course, all subjects felt social pressure to continue the study, and all of them did. However, those who were simply told to write the essay should feel less personal responsibility for what they wrote and would therefore be expected to experience less cognitive dissonance than those who believed that they had exercised free choice in deciding to participate.

The results were as the experimenters had predicted: Subjects in the "free choice" condition who had written an essay contradicting their original opinion showed both a change in opinion and evidence of physiological arousal. Those subjects who were simply told to write the essay or who wrote arguments they had originally agreed with showed little sign of arousal or attitude change. (See *Figure 17.3.*)

6 **Conflict Resolution.** The theory of cognitive dissonance predicts that our decision-making behavior should have an effect on our attitudes. The effect should be strongest when we make a difficult decision based on conflicting tendencies. For example, suppose a young lawyer is offered two jobs. One is at a prestigious firm that pays well and offers good chances for advancement but expects only top-notch work from its employees; the firm has a reputation for firing even veteran employees if their performance lags. The other offer is from a less prestigious firm; if she takes this job, she will never fulfill her ambitions for recognition. However, the working conditions are pleasant, and the firm is very loyal to its employees; few employees are ever fired. Thus, the lawyer would be ensured of lifelong employment.

Suppose the young lawyer is initially torn between these two choices but finally decides to accept one of the job offers. Once the choice is made, her attitudes will probably undergo a change. If she chooses the high-powered firm, she is likely to perceive the practice of rewarding an employee's loyalty, as opposed to his or

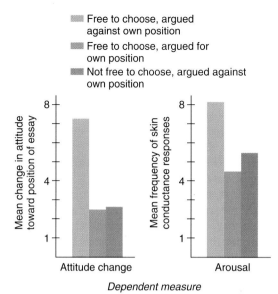

Figure 17.3 Mean change in attitude toward the position advocated by the essay and mean frequency of skin conductance responses (a physiological index of arousal) in subjects who argued for or against their own position. (Based on data from Croyle, R.T., and Cooper, J. *Journal of Personality and Social Psychology,* 1983, *45,* 782–791.)

her ability, as a weak and contemptible practice, because this belief will reduce any residual doubts about the wisdom of her choice. Conversely, if she chooses the other firm, she will probably tell herself that loyalty is an important virtue and that she is glad she did not commit herself to work in an inhumane place. Besides, since she will not have to worry about losing her job, she can concentrate on the task at hand and will actually become a better lawyer.

Attitudes and Expenditures. Festinger's theory of cognitive dissonance accounts for another relation between behavior and attitudes: our tendency to value an item more if it costs us something. For example, some people buy extremely expensive brands of cosmetics even though the same ingredients are used in much cheaper brands. Presumably, they believe that if an item costs more, it must work better. Following the same rationale, most animal shelters sell their stray animals to prospective pet owners, not only because the money helps defray their operating costs but also because they assume that a purchased pet will be treated better than a free pet.

Aronson and Mills (1959) verified this phenomenon. The experimenters subjected female college students to varying degrees of embar-

rassment as a prerequisite for joining what was promised to be an interesting discussion about sexual behavior. To produce slight embarrassment, they had the subjects read aloud five sex-related words (such as *prostitute, virgin,* and *petting*) to the experimenter, who was male. To produce more severe embarrassment, they had the women read aloud twelve obscene four-letter words and two sexually explicit passages of prose. The control group read nothing at all. The "interesting group discussion" turned out to be a tape recording of a very dull conversation. (When psychologists put their minds to it, they can produce excruciatingly boring material. Sometimes, they even produce it inadvertently.)

Festinger's theory predicts that the women who had to go through an embarrassing ordeal in order to join the group would experience some cognitive dissonance. They gave up something—some pride or self-esteem—to obtain a goal that they initially perceived to be worthwhile: the privilege of participating in an interesting discussion. This investment should make them view the "discussion" more favorably so that their effort would not be perceived as having been completely without value. The results were as predicted: The subjects who had been embarrassed the most rated the discussion higher than did the control subjects or the subjects who had experienced very slight embarrassment. Clearly, we value things at least partly by how much they cost us. (See ***Figure 17.4.***)

Figure 17.4 Ratings of a discussion by women who sustained varying amounts of embarrassment. (Based on data from Aronson, E., and Mills, J. *Journal of Abnormal and Social Psychology,* 1959, *67,* 31–36.)

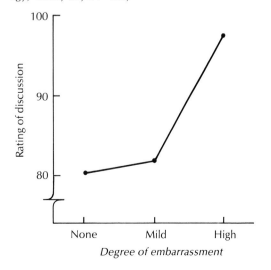

The effect of cognitive dissonance on attitude change does not always appear to depend on conscious deliberation; in this context *cognitive* does not necessarily mean *conscious*. Aronson (1975) reported that subjects apparently did not "decide" to like the discussion because of the embarrassment they had gone through. As he notes:

> We occasionally asked our subjects why they had responded as they did. The results were very disappointing. For example, in the [Aronson and Mills study] . . . , subjects did a lot of denying when asked if the [embarrassment] had affected their attitudes toward the group or had entered into their thinking at all. When I explained the theory [of cognitive dissonance] to the subjects, they typically said it was very plausible and that many subjects had probably reasoned just the way I said, but not they themselves. (Aronson, 1975)

Of course, the subjects may have been lying or may have forgotten their thought processes, but the conclusion that the influence occurred unconsciously is certainly a reasonable one. As you saw in the section on heuristics, our thoughts and behaviors are often affected by variables of which we are unaware.

Self-Perception

Daryl Bem (1972) proposed an alternative to the theory of cognitive dissonance. He defined **self-perception theory** in the following way:

> Individuals come to "know" their own attitudes, emotions, and other internal states partially by inferring them from observations of their own overt behavior and/or the circumstances in which this behavior occurs. Thus, to the extent that internal cues are weak, ambiguous, or uninterpretable, the individual is functionally in the same position as an outside observer, an observer who must necessarily rely upon those same external cues to infer the individual's inner states. (Bem, 1972, p. 2)

Bem noted that an observer who attempts to make judgments about someone's attitudes, emotions, or other internal states must examine the person's behavior for clues. For example, if you cannot ask someone why he or she is doing something, you must analyze the situation in which the behavior occurs to try to determine the motivation. Bem suggested that people analyze their own internal states in a similar way, making attributions about the causes of their own behavior.

You will recall the experiment by Festinger and Carlsmith (1959) in which students who were paid only $1 later rated a boring task as more interesting than did those who were paid $20. How does self-perception theory explain these results?

Suppose an observer watches a subject who has been paid $1 to deliver a convincing speech to another student about how interesting a task was. Because being paid such a small sum is not a sufficient reason for calling a dull task interesting, the observer will probably conclude that the student actually enjoyed the task. Lacking good evidence for external causes, the observer will attribute the behavior to a dispositional factor: interest in the task. Bem argued that the subject makes the same inference about himself or herself. Because the subject was not paid enough to tell a lie, he or she must have enjoyed the task. The principal advantage of self-perception theory is that it makes fewer assumptions than dissonance theory; it does not postulate a motivating aversive-drive state. But as Croyle and Cooper's (1983) experiment on essay writing showed, some conflict situations *do* produce arousal. Perhaps self-perception and cognitive dissonance occur under different situations, producing attitude changes for different reasons. Further evidence will be needed to determine whether the theories are competing or complementary.

INTERIM SUMMARY

Attitudes and Their Formation

The topic of attitudes fell into disrepute for several years. But we now understand the principal reasons for poor correspondence between attitudes and behavior: differences in degree of specificity of the attitude and behavior, the opportunity a person has had to observe his or her own attitude-related behavior, and external constraints that prevent a person's acting on his or her attitudes.

Attitudes have affective components, primarily formed through direct or vicarious classical conditioning, and cognitive components, formed through direct instruction or through instrumental conditioning or modeling.

Festinger's theory of cognitive dissonance suggests reasons for interactions between attitudes and behavior. It proposes that discrepancies between attitudes and behavior, between behavior and self-image, or between one attitude and another lead to the unpleasant state of cognitive dissonance. Reduction of this dissonance by changing the importance of dissonant elements, adding consonant ones, or changing one of the dissonant elements provides negative reinforcement. This theory explains why we place a higher value on things that cost us something; it also predicts that behaviors—even induced compliance—can lead to attitude changes.

Bem's alternative to cognitive dissonance—self perception theory—suggests that many of our attitudes are based on self-observation. When our motives are unclear, we look to the situation for the stimuli and probable reinforcers and punishers that cause us to act as we do. For example, subjects who are paid $1 to persuade fellow students to perform a boring task have a more favorable attitude toward it than those paid $20 or nothing at all because genuine interest is a more likely explanation for their own behavior than the receipt of such a small sum.

From the data presented in this section we see that no single theory can account for the formation of attitudes. Human behavior is complex; to understand it, we must evaluate a wide range of factors that may cause it to occur. ■

PREJUDICE

7 A **prejudice** is a particular form of attitude—an attitude toward a group of people defined by their racial, ethnic, or religious heritage, or by their gender, occupation, sexual orientation, level of education, or place of residence. A prejudice (literally, a "prejudgment") is a sort of mental shortcut through which people focus on a few salient features (such as a person's skin color, accent, family name, or manner of dressing) and assume that they possess other characteristics, too—mostly unfavorable. As you can see, a prejudice is an insidious example of the representativeness heuristic.

Prejudices are closely related to *stereotypes*. In fact, the meanings of the two terms overlap somewhat. But strictly speaking, a *prejudice* describes a negative attitude toward members of a particular group, whereas a **stereotype** describes a belief about their characteristics. (Occasionally, stereotypes can include favorable beliefs.) In addition, stereotypes refer to beliefs generally accepted within a particular culture,

whereas prejudices can be acquired by an individual through his or her experience.

Discrimination refers to behaviors, not to attitudes. In other contexts the word *discrimination* simply means "to distinguish." In the present context *discrimination* means treating people differently, according to their membership in a particular group. Thus, we can discriminate favorably or unfavorably, according to the nature of our attitudes and beliefs about the relative value of the groups.

The Origins of Prejudice

Unfortunately, prejudice seems to be an enduring characteristic of the human species. Prejudice is seen in all societies: rich and poor, literate and preliterate, agrarian and industrialized. History has shown that groups of people who have been oppressed go on to commit their own exploitation if they manage to overthrow their oppressors. Why is prejudice such a widespread trait?

Group Affiliation, Competition, and Self-Esteem.   Apparently, affiliation and prejudice are two sides of the same coin. That is, along with the tendency to identify with and feel close to members of our own group or clan goes the

Some prejudices are deliberately taught and passed along from generation to generation.

tendency to be suspicious of others. A classic experiment by Sherif et al., (1961) demonstrated just how easily intergroup mistrust and conflict can arise. The study took place at a remote summer camp. The subjects, eleven-year-old boys, were assigned to one of two cabins, isolated from each other. During the first week the boys in each cabin spent their time together as a group, fishing, hiking, swimming, and otherwise enjoying themselves. The boys formed two cohesive groups, which they named the Rattlers and the Eagles. They became attached to their groups and strongly identified with them. They even designed their own flags. (See *Figure 17.5*.)

Next, the experimenters sowed the seeds of dissension. They set up a series of competitions between the two groups. The best team was to win a trophy for the group and individual prizes for its members. As the competition progressed, the boys began taunting and insulting each other. Then the Eagles burned the Rattlers' flag, and in retaliation the Rattlers broke into the Eagles' cabin and scattered or stole their rivals' belongings. Although further physical conflict was prevented by the experimenters, the two groups continued to abuse each other verbally and seemed to have developed a genuine hatred for each other.

Figure 17.5 A map of the summer camp that served as the location of the experiment by Sherif, Harvey, White, Hood, and Sherif (1961). (From Robert A. Baron and Donn Byrne, *Social Psychology: Understanding Human Interaction*, Sixth Edition. Copyright © 1991 by Allyn and Bacon. Reproduced with permission.)

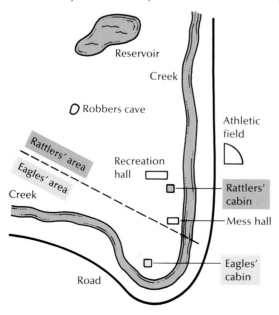

Eagles vs. Rattlers: A tug-of-war involved some of the boys who participated in the study on intergroup conflict.

Finally, the experimenters arranged for the boys to work together. They sabotaged the water supply for the camp and had the boys fix it; they had the boys repair a truck that had broken down; and they induced the boys to pool their money to rent a movie. After the boys worked on cooperative ventures, rather than competitive ones, the intergroup conflicts diminished.

The findings of this experiment suggest that when groups of people compete with each other, they tend to view their rivals negatively. Many other studies have confirmed these results. Note that the boys at the summer camp were racially and ethnically homogeneous; the assignment to one cabin or the other was arbitrary. Thus, a particular boy could have been either a Rattler-hating Eagle or an Eagle-hating Rattler, depending on chance assignment to a particular group.

Most social psychologists believe that competition is an important factor in the development of prejudice, if not the only one. The competition need not be for tangible goods; it can be motivated by a desire for social superiority. As we have seen many times in this book, the concept of self-esteem helps explain many different types of behavior. The tendency to perceive one's own group as superior and that of others as inferior may be based on a need to enhance one's own self-esteem. Thus, people who belong to groups that preach racial hatred tend to be those whose own social status is rather low.

An experiment by Meindl and Lerner (1985) supports this conclusion. The experimenters exposed English-speaking Canadians to a situation designed to threaten their self-esteem. They asked the subjects to walk across the room to get a chair. For members of the experimental group the chair was rigged in such a way that a pile of computer cards would be knocked over and scattered on the floor. In a situation like this most people feel clumsy and foolish—and also somewhat guilty about making trouble for the person who has to put the cards back in order. After this experience the subjects were asked to describe their attitudes toward French-speaking Canadians. As the experimenters predicted, subjects in the experimental group, who had toppled the cards, rated the "others" more negatively than those who had not. Presumably, by viewing the French-speaking Canadians as members of a group inferior to their own, the subjects partially compensated for the loss of their own self-esteem.

Social Cognition. In the section of this chapter on implicit psychology, I described some principles of social cognition that explain how, by following mental shortcuts that work most of the time *(heuristics),* we sometimes make errors of judgment. These mental shortcuts also play a role in the development of prejudice.

As we saw, *stereotypes* are conventional beliefs about the members of a particular group. These beliefs are convenient to the user, because they provide a way for a person to classify another individual quickly. The problem is, these beliefs are almost always wrong. Stereotypes are learned from family members, from friends, and from the mass media. The latter source is particularly dangerous, because it is both insidious and widespread. When members of minority groups are portrayed in television shows or movies as being criminals, as having low-status jobs, or as being rather comic and stupid, people acquire stereotypes that they may not even be aware of.

Dovidio, Evans, and Tyler (1986) showed how pervasive racial stereotypes can be. They presented white subjects with the words *white* and *black,* along with descriptive adjectives, both positive and negative, and asked the subjects to indicate whether the adjectives described the racial categories. They found that the subjects responded fastest when the word *white* was presented with positive adjectives and the word *black* was presented with negative ones. The results suggest that the concepts of the racial group are linked to negative or positive characteristics; thinking of the racial group automatically evokes thoughts of these characteristics.

As you will recall from the earlier discussion of social cognition, the availability heuristic describes our assuming that distinctive, easily imagined items are more important and more frequent. This phenomenon probably explains why people overestimate the rate of violent crime (because an act of violence is a frightening, distinctive event) and overestimate the relative numbers of violent crimes committed by members of a minority group (because members of minority groups tend to be more conspicuous). This tendency is an example of an **illusory correlation**—seeing a relation between two distinctive elements that does not actually exist (Spears, van der Pligt, and Eiser, 1985).

Another fallacy that promotes the formation of stereotypes is the **illusion of out-group homogeneity:** People tend to assume that groups other than their own are much more homogeneous than their own group. They recognize that members of their own group are very different from each other but perceive members of other groups as very similar (Linville, 1982). This tendency is even seen between the sexes: Men tend to perceive women as being more homogeneous than men, and women do the opposite (Park and Rothbart, 1982). The same is true for young and old people (Linville, Fischer, and Salovey, 1989). Most of us resist being stereotyped but nevertheless practice this activity when thinking about members of other groups.

Damaging Effects of Prejudice: Self-Fulfilling Prophecies

Prejudices and stereotypes have several unfortunate effects. They diminish and dishonor the person who possesses them, they promote discrimination against minority groups, and they influence the behavior of their subjects. It is the latter effect that we will consider in this section.

A **self-fulfilling prophecy** is "a *false* definition of the situation evoking a new behavior which makes the originally false conception come *true*" (Merton, 1948, p. 195). In the present context a self-fulfilling prophecy is a stereotype that causes the subject to act in a manner *consistent with that stereotype.* Such a tendency is insidious, because the behavior of the person who is the target of the stereotype then tends to confirm the stereotype.

One of the most memorable examples of the self-fulfilling prophecy was demonstrated in an experiment by Snyder, Tanke, and Berscheid (1977). The experimenters had male subjects carry on telephone conversations with female subjects. Just before each conversation took place, the male subjects were shown a photograph of the young woman they were to talk to. In fact, the pictures were not those of the partner but were photographs of attractive or unattractive women chosen by the experimenters. The conversations that took place were recorded, and the voices of the female subjects were played to independent observers, who rated their impressions of the young women.

The results indicated that believing that a woman was attractive made her act that way. That is, based on the sound of the female subjects' voices and what they said, the independent observers rated the women whose partners believed them to be attractive as being more friendly, likable, and sociable. Obviously, the male subjects talked differently to women they thought to be attractive or unattractive. Their words had either a positive or negative effect on the young women, which could be detected by the observers.

Stereotypes often cause selective perception in the people who hold them. For example, the same smile could be perceived as a friendly facial expression or as a contemptuous smirk, depending on the observer's preconceptions. And when a person is confronted by evidence contradictory to the stereotype, it can be attributed to alternative factors. For example, when a person whom we believe to be incompetent does a good job, we can say to ourselves that the person just happened to be lucky. And if a student's performance is better than a teacher's expectation, the teacher can attribute the performance to his or her own effectiveness or conclude that the student is an "overachiever." Either way, the stereotype can remain unchallenged (Miller and Turnbull, 1986).

Sometimes, people *misperceive* the evidence presented to them by the behavior of the target of a stereotype; in such cases the perceiver considers the prophecy to be fulfilled even when the evidence says otherwise. For example, Ickes, Patterson, Rajecki, and Tanford (1982) had subjects interact with partners they expected to be friendly or unfriendly. If the subjects expected the partners to be unfriendly, they rated them as being that way even when the partners actually acted in a friendly manner.

Hope for Change

Unfortunately, one of the primary reasons for racial or ethnic prejudice is that it can serve to justify exploitation of one group by another. If a particular group can be perceived as "stupid," "dependent," and "irresponsible," then another group can justify the exploitation of that group as being in their own best interest, or at least conclude that their treatment is the best that that group can reasonably expect. When prejudice and discrimination lead to material advantages in the form of cheap labor or unequal sharing of resources, the injustices will tend to persist. Such situations are not easily altered by the discoveries of social psychologists.

However, many instances of prejudice are inadvertent. Many people are unaware of their stereotypes and preconceptions about members of other groups; or if they are aware of them, they can be persuaded that their beliefs are unjustified. The best solution in this case is to teach people to become cognitively less lazy—that is, to give up some of their "cognitive miserliness" and take the time to reflect about their biases. For example, Langer, Bashner, and Chanowitz (1985) gave a group of sixth-grade children specific training in thinking about the problems of handicapped people. They thought about such problems as the ways that a handicapped person might drive a car and the reasons a blind person might make a good newscaster. After this training they were found to be more willing to go on a picnic with a handicapped person than children who did not receive the training. They were also more likely to see the specific consequences of particular handicaps rather than simply view handicapped people as "less fit." For example, they were likely to choose a blind child as a partner in a game of pin the tail on the donkey because they realized that the child would be likely to perform even better than a sighted child.

INTERIM SUMMARY

Prejudice

Prejudice is a negative attitude toward a group of people defined by such characteristics as race, ethnicity, religion, socioeconomic status, or sexual orientation. An important component of prejudice is the existence of a stereotype—a belief about the characteristics possessed by members of a particular group. Prejudices often lead to discrimination—actual behaviors injurious to the members of the group.

Prejudice seems to be an enduring human trait, and it is found in all societies. One of its important causes appears to be competition between groups for limited resources and the increased self-esteem that results from affiliating with a group perceived to be better than other groups. The study at the boy's camp indicates just how easily prejudices can form, even when the groups have similar types of individuals.

The principles of social cognition apply to the study of prejudice. In fact, stereotypes are examples of the mental shortcuts that guide us through many of our social encounters. One reason we tend to view minority group members negatively is our use of the availability heuristic: Negative behaviors are often more vivid than positive ones, and minority group members are more noticeable. Thus, when minority group members commit an illegal act, we are more likely to notice it and remember it. And we incorrectly conclude that the behavior is a characteristic of the group as a whole.

People also tend to apply the illusion of outgroup homogeneity. Although they realize that their own group contains members who are very different from each other, they tend to view members of other groups as rather homogeneous. Obviously, this tendency contributes to the formation of stereotypes.

Prejudices have many harmful effects, such as the self-fulfilling prophecy, in which being perceived as inferior leads the target of the prejudice to *act* that way. And even when the person does not, the observer may misperceive—or at least selectively perceive—the behavior. However, there is hope for the future. Many instances of prejudices are inadvertent. And when people are taught to think about members of other groups as individuals with specific characteristics, they can learn to avoid relying on some of their injurious mental shortcuts. ∎

SOCIAL INFLUENCES

The behavior of other people—or even their mere presence—exerts some powerful influences on our own thoughts and behavior. We are aware of some of these influences; for example, people's persuasive arguments make us think about issues or consider engaging in a particular behavior. The thoughts lead us to decide whether we will change our opinions or perform a particular behavior. Yet we are usually unaware of most social influences; and when they are pointed out later, we often find it difficult to believe that they could have affected our opinions or behavior.

This section discusses several ways social influences can control or alter a person's attitudes and behavior. As we will see, these influences make good sense; they are probably at the root of social organization and cooperation. Unfortunately, they can be exploited by unscrupulous people for their own selfish purposes. However, by understanding the nature of these influences, we may be able to resist influences that would lead us to attitude or behavior changes that are not in our best interest.

Imitation: Do As Others Do

[8] Probably the most powerful social influence on our behavior and attitudes is the behavior of other people. If we see people act in a particular way, we tend to act in that way, too. Sometimes, we observe that people are *not* performing a particular behavior; if so, we too tend not to perform that behavior.

Conformity. Most of us cherish our independence and like to think that we do what we do because *we* want to do it, not because others decree that we should. But none of us are immune to social influences, and most instances of conformity benefit us all. If we see someone whose face has been disfigured by an accident or disease, we do not stare at the person or comment about his or her appearance. If someone drops a valuable item, we do not try to pick it up and keep it for ourselves. If we lose a tennis match, we do not cry and pout; instead, we smile and congratulate the victor. If we have a cold, we try not to sneeze in someone else's face. Each society has developed norms that define the ways we should behave in various situations, and following these norms generally makes us feel more comfortable and also helps the group function smoothly.

Solomon Asch (1951) demonstrated just how powerful the tendency to conform can be, even while making simple perceptual judgments. He asked several groups of seven to nine students to estimate lengths of lines presented on a screen. A sample line was shown at the left, and the subjects were to choose which of the three lines to the right matched it. (See *Figure 17.6.*) The subjects gave their answers orally.

In fact, there was only one subject in each

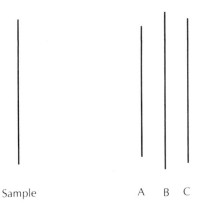

Sample   A B C

Figure 17.6 An example of the stimuli used by Asch (1951).

Conformity is a characteristic of all human societies.

group; all the others were confederates of the experimenter. The seating was arranged so that the subject answered last. Under some conditions the confederates made incorrect responses. When they made incorrect responses on six of the twelve trials in an experiment, 76 percent of the subjects went along with the group on at least one trial. Under control conditions, when the confederates responded accurately, only 5 percent of the subjects made an error.

Group pressure did not affect the subjects' perceptions; it affected their behavior. That is, the subjects went along with the group decision even though the choice still looked wrong to them—and even though the other people were complete strangers. When they were questioned later, they said that they had started doubting their own eyesight or had thought that perhaps they had misunderstood the instruc-

tions. The subjects who did not conform felt uncomfortable about disagreeing with the other members of the group. The Asch effect shows how strong the tendency to conform can be. Faced with a simple, unambiguous task in a group of strangers who showed no signs of disapproval when the subject disagreed with them, a large majority of subjects nevertheless ignored their own judgments and agreed with the obviously incorrect choice made by the other people.

People's tendency to imitate the behavior of others is a tool used by many people who are in the business of influencing others. Sometimes, the people setting the example are fictitious. For instance, bartenders and coatroom attendants often put folding money in the container they set out to solicit tips; presumably, they hope that customers will follow the example they themselves have established. Psychologists, too, have demonstrated the effectiveness of such a ploy. When Schofield (1975) merely asked twenty female college students to read and review some pamphlets, only seven agreed to do so. When she also said, to another group of twenty, that "she was pleased that most women in the previous groups" had complied with her requests, seventeen subjects agreed to help.

Sometimes, accomplices are enlisted to serve as examples, with the expectation that their behavior will influence that of others. For instance, Fuller and Sheehy-Skeffington (1974) showed that the canned laughter accompanying almost all comedy shows on television induces people to laugh more themselves and to rate the material as funnier, especially if it is not very funny to begin with (as seems to be the case for so many shows). This phenomenon occurs *despite* the fact that most people say that they detest canned laughter.

We might ask *why* people so readily conform. Baron and Byrne (1987) suggest that the two most important reasons are the desire to be liked and the desire to be right. As we will see later in this chapter, people tend to like other people who are similar to themselves, especially those who act like them and share their attitudes and opinions. Because most of us prefer to be liked, we tend to conform to the expectations of others. In addition, most of us prefer to be right rather than wrong. Yet many social issues cannot be settled decisively. For example, arguments can be made on both sides of political issues, and people can adopt a wide variety of clothing styles. When the people with whom we associate express particular political opinions or wear a particular style of clothing, we tend to assume that their opinions or styles are correct. And wanting to be correct ourselves, we tend to adopt them as our own.

Bystander Intervention. Conformity can sometimes have disastrous consequences. In 1964 in New York City a woman named Kitty Genovese was chased and repeatedly stabbed by an assailant, who took thirty-five minutes to kill her. The woman's screams went unheeded by at least thirty-eight people who watched from their windows. No one tried to stop the attacker; no one even made a quick, anonymous telephone call to the police. When the bystanders were questioned later, they could not explain their inaction. "I just don't know," they said.

As you can imagine, people were appalled and shocked by the bystanders' response to the Kitty Genovese murder. Commentators said that the apparent indifference of the bystanders demonstrated that American society, especially in urban areas, had become cold and apathetic. The reporter who first publicized the story agreed.

> It can be assumed . . . that their apathy was indeed one of the big-city variety. It is almost a matter of psychological survival, if one is surrounded and pressed by millions of people, to prevent them from constantly impinging on you, and the only way to do this is to ignore them as often as possible. Indifference to one's neighbor and his troubles is a conditioned reflex in life in New York as it is in other big cities. (Rosenthal, 1964)

Experiments performed by social psychologists suggest that this explanation is wrong— people in cities are not generally indifferent to the needs of other people. The fact that Kitty Genovese's attack went unreported is not remarkable because thirty-eight people were present; it is precisely because so many people were present that the attack was *not* reported.

Latané and Darley have extensively studied the phenomenon of **bystander intervention**—the actions of people witnessing a situation in which someone appears to require assistance. Their experiments have shown that in such situations the presence of other people who are doing nothing *inhibits* people from giving aid. For example, Darley and Latané (1968) staged an "emergency" during a psychology experiment. Each subject participated in a discussion about personal problems associated with college life with one, two, or five other people by means of an intercom. The experimenter ex-

Although many passersby may have noticed the person lying on the sidewalk, no one has stopped to help. Psychologists have studied the factors that determine when people try to intervene.

plained that the participants would sit in individual rooms so that they would be anonymous and hence would be more likely to speak frankly. The experimenter would not listen in but would get their reactions later in a questionnaire. Actually, only one subject was present; the other voices were simply tape recordings.

During the discussion one of the people, who had previously said that he sometimes had seizures, apparently had one. His speech became incoherent, and he stammered out a request for help.

> I—er—I—uh—I've got a—a one of the—er— sei——er—er—things coming on and— and—and I could really—er—use some help so if somebody would—er—give me a little h—help—uh—er—er—er—er—er—c— could somebody—er—er—help—er—uh— uh—uh (choking sounds). . . . I'm gonna die— er—er—I'm . . . gonna die—er—help— er—er—seizure—er—[chokes, then quiet]. (Darley and Latané, 1968, p. 379)

As Figure 17.7 shows, almost all subjects left the room to help the victim when they were the only witness to the seizure. However, when

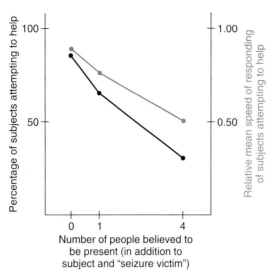

Figure 17.7 *Percentage of subjects attempting to help as a function of the number of other people the subject believed to be present. (Based on data from Darley, J.M., and Latané, B.* Journal of Personality and Social Psychology, *1968, 8, 377–383.)*

there appeared to be other witnesses, the subjects were much less likely to try to help. In addition, those who did try to help reacted more slowly if other people were thought to be present. (See *Figure 17.7.*)

Darley and Latané reported that the subjects who did not respond were not indifferent to the plight of their fellow student. Indeed, when the experimenter entered the room, they usually appeared nervous and emotionally aroused, and they asked whether the victim was being taken care of. The experimenters did not receive the impression that the subjects had decided not to act; rather, they were still in conflict, trying to decide whether they should do something. "On the one hand, subjects worried about the guilt and shame they would feel if they did not help the person in distress. On the other hand, they were concerned not to make fools of themselves by overreacting, not to ruin the ongoing experiment by leaving their intercom, and not to destroy the anonymous nature of the situation which the experimenter had earlier stressed as important" (Darley and Latané, 1968, p. 382).

These results have been replicated in other experimental settings, including incidents staged outside the laboratory. When a person is faced with a situation that *may* call for assistance, the person will tend to take his or her cue from other people; if they are doing nothing, then he or she, too, will probably not do anything. People tend to imitate the inaction of other bystanders. Presumably, people's thoughts go like this: "Well, no one else is doing anything, so I'd better not stick my neck out. I guess I don't understand what's going on." Thus, the fear of ridicule is one of the factors that deters a person from acting. As Cialdini (1988) points out, conditions that discourage bystander intervention are more often met in cities than in small towns or rural areas, and these conditions lead to the impression that city dwellers are apathetic and uncaring. Because more is happening in cities, people cannot always be sure that a particular situation actually represents an emergency. In addition, because cities have higher population densities, an emergency is more likely to be attended by a large group of bystanders.

If an emergency *clearly* requires bystander intervention, people are much more likely to render assistance, even if other bystanders are present. Clark and Word (1972, 1974) staged realistic "accidents" in a room adjacent to one in which individual subjects, or subjects in groups of two to five, were answering a questionnaire. The accidents involved a maintenance man who apparently fell from a ladder or a technician who apparently received a severe electrical shock. All of the groups of subjects came to the man's assistance.

Sometimes, people's failure to intervene results not from conformity but from ignorance: People may simply not know what to do in a particular situation. Shotland and Heinold (1985) staged an accident in which a person seemed to be bleeding. Bystanders who had received training in first-aid treatment were much more likely to come to the victim's aid, and they did so whether or not bystanders were present. Because they knew how to recognize an emergency and knew what to do, they were less likely to fear "doing the wrong thing."

Social Facilitation: When Someone Is Watching

9 As we just saw, the behavior of other people has a powerful effect on our own. But studies have shown that even the *mere presence* of other people can affect a person's behavior. Triplett (1897) published the first experimental study on **social facilitation:** the enhancement of a person's performance by the presence of other people. He had people perform a number of simple tasks, such as turning the crank of a fishing reel. He found that his subjects turned the crank faster and for a longer time if other people were present. Although many other studies found the same effect, some investigators reported just the opposite phenomenon: If the task was difficult and complex, the presence of an audience *impaired* the subjects' performance. You yourself have probably noticed that you have difficulty performing certain tasks if someone is watching you.

Robert Zajonc (1965) has suggested an explanation for the phenomenon of social facilitation. He claims that the presence of people who are watching a performer (or whom the performer *perceives* as watching) raises that person's arousal level. Presumably, the increase in arousal has the effect of increasing the probability of performing *dominant responses*: responses that are most likely to occur in a particular situation. When the task is simple, the dominant response is generally the correct one, so an audience improves performance. When the task is complex, a person can perform a number of different responses and must decide which one is appropriate. The presence of the audience makes the selection of the appropriate behavior more difficult, because the increased arousal tends to cause the person to perform the dominant response, which may not be the correct one. Suppose you are trying to assemble an intricate piece of machinery. A part is sticking. You want to bang on it, but you know that doing so will not help. You must be patient and gently manipulate it into place. Just then, a curious bystander approaches and stands close to you, asking if he or she can watch. You say yes and turn back to the task. The part seems to be giving you even more trouble than before, and you suddenly start banging on it.

Subsequent experiments have supported Zajonc's explanation. Martens (1969) tested the prediction that the presence of a group increases a person's level of arousal. While subjects performed a complex motor task alone or in the presence of ten people, the experimenter determined physiological arousal by measuring the amount of sweat present on the subjects' palms. The presence of an audience produced a clear-cut effect: The subjects who performed in front of other people had sweatier palms.

An experiment by Zajonc and Sales (1966) showed that the presence of an audience can raise the probability of dominant responses. The experimenters read aloud a list of fictitious Turkish words and had subjects pronounce each of them from one to sixteen times. Then they asked the subjects to watch a screen, on which the words would be flashed too rapidly to be seen clearly, and to guess which word had been presented. In fact, the experimenters flashed a

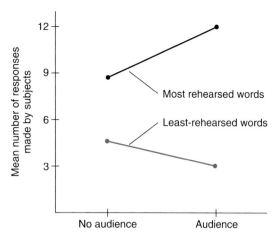

Figure 17.8 Number of responses of most rehearsed and least rehearsed words made by subjects in the presence or absence of an audience. (Based on data from Zajonc, R.B., and Sales, S.M. *Journal of Experimental Social Psychology,* 1966, 2, 160–168.)

meaningless jumble of shapes on the screen. Subjects who performed this part of the task alone guessed that they saw many of the words they had heard. They were more likely to say the words they had rehearsed more often, but they also chose a good number of the least practiced ones. Other subjects performed in the presence of two people who had supposedly asked the experimenter whether they could watch the procedure. With this audience present the subjects tended to stick with the words they had practiced the most; it was as if their increased arousal caused them to make only the dominant responses. Perhaps they found it harder to think of the words they had not rehearsed as often. (See *Figure 17.8.*)

Why does the presence of a group increase a person's arousal? One important factor seems to be whether the subjects perceive the group as observing (and thus evaluating) their performance. Cottrell, Wack, Sekerak, and Rittle (1968) had their subjects perform a task like the one used by Zajonc and Sales. During the word-guessing phase some subjects were tested alone; others were tested in the presence of two blindfolded or unblindfolded people. Only the subjects who were actually watched by other people showed the expected increase in dominant responses.

Another factor that affects social facilitation is the actor's perception of the audience. Sanna and Shotland (1990) found that subjects who believed that an audience would evaluate them positively performed better when the audience was present. Those who anticipated a negative evaluation performed worse when spectators were present.

Social Loafing: Share the Load

As we just saw, people usually try harder when other people are watching them. However, when the other people are co-workers rather than observers, the presence of a group sometimes results in a *decrease* in effort, or **social loafing.** Thus, the whole is often less than the sum of its individual parts. Many years ago, Ringelmann (cited by Dashiell, 1935) measured the effort that people made when pulling a rope in a mock tug-of-war contest against a device that measured the exerted force. Presumably, the force exerted by eight people pulling together in a simple task would be at least the sum of their individual efforts or even somewhat greater than the sum, because of the phenomenon of social facilitation. However, Ringelmann found that the total force exerted was only about half what would be predicted by the simple combination of individual efforts. The subjects exerted less force when they worked in a group.

More recent studies have confirmed these results and have extended them to other behaviors. For example, Latané, Williams, and Harkins (1979) asked subjects alone, in pairs, or in groups of six to shout as loudly as they could. The subjects wore blindfolds and headphones that played a loud noise. Thus, they could not hear the shouting of the other subjects nor could they see or be seen by the other people in their group. When subjects shouted alone, they made more noise than when they shouted in groups; their group effort was only 82 percent of their individual effort.

Several variables determine whether the presence of a group will produce social facilitation or social loafing. One of the most important of them is *identifiability*. Williams, Harkins, and Latané (1981) asked subjects to shout as loud as they could individually or in groups. Subjects who were told that the equipment could measure only the total group effort shouted less loudly than those who were told that the equipment could measure individual efforts. The latter shouted just as loudly in groups as they did alone. These results suggest that a person's efforts in a group activity are affected by whether or not other people can observe his or her individual efforts. If they can, social facilitation is likely to occur; if they cannot, then social loafing is likely to occur.

We can analyze the effect of identifiability on effort in terms of reinforcement. When a person's efforts can be measured by other people, that person can potentially receive social reinforcers such as approval or acknowledgment of a job well done. The person can also receive disapproval for failing to work hard enough. In other words, *contingencies of reinforcement* (cause-and-effect relations) are present. When a person's efforts are submerged in those of the group, these contingencies cannot apply, and the quality of individual effort declines.

Another variable that determines whether social facilitation or social loafing occurs is *responsibility*. If a person's efforts are duplicated by those of another person (and if his or her individual efforts are not identifiable), the person is likely to exert less-than-maximum effort. Harkins and Petty (1982) had subjects work in groups of four on a task that required them to report whenever a dot appeared in a particular quadrant of a video screen. In one condition each subject watched an individual quadrant and was solely responsible for detecting dots that appeared there. In the other condition all four subjects watched the same quadrant; thus, the responsibility for detecting dots was shared. Subjects did not loaf when they were responsible for their own quadrant; under this condition they worked as hard as subjects working alone.

As Latané and his colleagues point out, social loafing has implications for group efforts outside the laboratory. They note that social loafing is observed in tasks that require intellectual effort as well as physical work. For example, Petty, Harkins, and Williams (1980) found that subjects who participated in a group effort to evaluate a persuasive message worked less hard at the task than did subjects who had to perform their own evaluations. Consequently, the subjects who worked alone were more persuaded by good arguments and less persuaded by poor arguments than people who worked in a group. (See *Figure 17.9.*) These results suggest that a person who wants to influence the attitudes of other people should meet with groups of people if he or she does not have good arguments. (Perhaps this phenomenon explains why politicians like to address mass rallies.)

Latané and his colleagues also point out the relevance of their studies to an observation made by Turner (1978). Apparently, achieving good quality control on the production line at pickle factories is difficult. Dill pickle halves must be stuffed into jars by hand, and only pickles of certain sizes will do; long ones will not fit, and short ones will float around in the jar, looking "cheap and crummy." Because the conveyor belt moves inexorably, workers tend to fill the

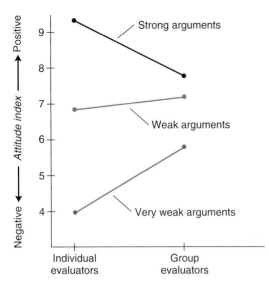

Figure 17.9 Social loafing in cognitive effort. The graphs show the attitude changes of subjects evaluating arguments individually or as members of a group after hearing strong, weak, or very weak arguments. (From Petty, R.E., Harkins, S.G., and Williams, K.D. *Journal of Personality and Social Psychology,* 1980, *38,* 81–92. Copyright 1980 by the American Psychological Association.)

jars with whatever pickles are at hand; if they stop to look for pickles of the proper size, the jars pile up. Jars that are filled with pickles of the wrong size must be culled by inspectors, and this inspection adds considerably to the cost of production. However, because there is no way to tell which worker has filled which jar, there is little incentive for a worker to choose the pickles carefully.

Reciprocity: Do unto Others

10 Another very strong social influence is **reciprocity,** the tendency to pay back favors others have done for us. When someone does something for us, we feel uncomfortable until the debt is discharged. For example, if people invite us to their house for dinner, we feel obliged to return the favor in the near future. And owing a social debt to someone we do not like is especially distasteful. Often people will suffer in silence rather than ask for help from someone they dislike.

The strong human tendency to pay back favors is almost certainly the basis for trade; we can give goods and services to other people with the assurance that we will receive something in return. In some primitive cultures people do not explicitly trade goods but make "gifts" to each other. For example, a person who obtains some food on a hunting trip will share it with other members of the tribe. Another person who is particularly skilled at making tools provides them for others. Even though the goods and services do not have prices and are not explicitly traded, people who receive them from others feel obliged to do what they can in return.

Experiments by social psychologists have confirmed the strength of reciprocity in human interactions. For example, Regan (1971) enlisted the participation of college students in an experiment that supposedly involved art appreciation. During a break some subjects were treated to a soft drink by the experimenter or by another "subject" (a confederate); others received nothing. After the experiment the confederate asked the subject to purchase some raffle tickets he was selling. Compliance with the request was measured by the number of tickets each subject bought. Figure 17.10 shows the results. The subjects treated to a soft drink by the confederate purchased the most raffle tickets. Getting a free drink from the experimenter also had an effect. Perhaps the subjects responded to the example of doing a favor for someone else. They probably thought well of the experimenter and, with this example fresh in mind, complied with the confederate's request so that they, too, would be thought well of. (See *Figure 17.10.*)

People trying to sell something often try to capitalize on the reciprocity rule by giving the

Figure 17.10 Mean number of raffle tickets purchased from a confederate when subjects received a favor or no favor from the experimenter or confederate. (Based on data from Regan, D.T. *Journal of Experimental Social Psychology,* 1971, *7,* 627–639.)

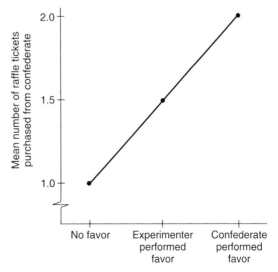

potential customer a free sample. Once the person has accepted the "gift," the sales representative tries to get him or her to return the favor by making a purchase. If you have ever accepted a piece of food from a friendly person handing out samples in a supermarket, you realize how hard it is to walk away without purchasing something. I know that I avoid accepting free samples because I dislike being manipulated into buying something I don't want.

Besides feeling obligated to pay back favors, we also feel obligations to make amends when our behavior causes someone harm or discomfort. For example, Carlsmith and Gross (1969) had subjects participate in a "learning task." The subject served as "teacher," and another student (actually, a confederate) served as "learner." Following the experimenter's instructions, the subject informed the learner when he was wrong by operating a switch that (1) purportedly delivered an electrical shock to the learner or (2) sounded a buzzer. (In the first condition the learner did not actually receive a shock.)

After the experiment appeared to be over, the learner asked the teacher whether he or she would be willing to circulate a petition to help stop the construction of a freeway through a redwood forest in California. Seventy-five percent of the subjects who believed they had shocked the learner complied with the request, whereas only 25 percent of the subjects who had simply sounded a buzzer complied. Presumably, the subjects did a favor for the victim in compensation for the pain they thought they had caused.

Making a Commitment: It's Hard to Say No Once You've Said Yes

Once people commit themselves by making a decision and acting on it, they are reluctant to renounce their commitment. For example, have you ever joined one side of an argument on an issue that you do not really care about, only to find yourself vehemently defending a position that just a few minutes ago meant almost nothing to you? I know I certainly have. This phenomenon was demonstrated in a very clever experiment by Knox and Inkster (1968). The experimenters asked people at the betting windows of a racetrack how confident they were that their horse would win. They questioned half the people just before they had made their bets, the other half just afterward. The people who had already made their bets were more confident than those who had not yet paid. Their

commitment increased the perceived value of their decision.

An experiment by Freedman and Fraser (1966) showed that commitment has a long-lasting effect on people's tendency to comply with requests. They sent a person posing as a volunteer worker to call on homeowners in a residential California neighborhood, asking them to perform a small task: to accept a 3-inch-square sign saying "Keep California Beautiful" or "Be a Safe Driver," or to sign a petition supporting legislation favoring one of these goals. Almost everyone agreed. Two weeks later, the experimenters sent another person to ask these people whether they would be willing to have a public service billboard erected in front of their house. To give them an idea of precisely what was being requested, the "volunteer worker" showed the homeowners a photograph of a house almost completely hidden by a huge, ugly, poorly lettered sign saying "DRIVE CAREFULLY." Over 55 percent of the people agreed to this obnoxious request! In contrast, less than 20 percent of householders who had not been contacted previously agreed to have such a billboard placed on their property. For obvious reasons, Freedman and Fraser referred to their procedure as the *foot-in-the-door technique*.

Needless to say, people trying to influence our purchasing behavior also use the foot-in-the-door technique. Many jurisdictions in the United States have passed "cooling off" laws that permit people to back out of contracts they have signed to purchase goods while under the influence of high-pressure tactics. These laws have had the desired effect: Many people have had second thoughts about whether they really needed the items they had been coerced into buying and have canceled their orders in a day or two. However, as Cialdini (1984) notes, many sellers have begun enlisting the power of commitment to make it difficult for people to reverse their decisions: They now have people fill out the sales contract themselves, not simply sign it. Cialdini (1984) quotes a training program for sales representatives at one firm as saying that the procedure is "a very important psychological aid in preventing customers from backing out of their contracts" (p. 86). Obviously, the "aid" in this case is perceived from the vantage point of the seller, not the buyer.

Commitment increases people's compliance even when the reason for the original commitment is removed. For example, some unscrupulous car salespeople offer to sell a car for an unusually low price. The surprised buyer agrees, thinking that he or she has gotten an especially good deal. Then after doing some preliminary paperwork—which succeeds in getting the customer to make a commitment—the salesperson disappears for a while, only to return with the sad news that the sales manager will not permit such a low price. However, the salesperson can still offer a good price, although it is not nearly as good as the first. All too often, the customer agrees to the higher price, even though it is not one he or she would have agreed to in the first place. This technique is called *low-balling.*

Commitment probably increases compliance for several reasons. First, the act of complying with a request in a particular category may change a person's self-image. Through the process of attribution people who sign a petition to support a beautiful environment may come to regard themselves as public-spirited individuals. Thus, when they hear the billboard request, they find it difficult to refuse. After all, they are public-spirited, so how can they say no? Saying no would imply that they did not have the courage of their convictions. Thus, this reason has at its root a person's self-esteem; to maintain good self-esteem, the person must say yes to the large request.

Commitment may also increase compliance because the first, smaller request changes people's perception of compliance in general. Evidence supporting this suggestion was provided by Rittle (1981). While sitting in a waiting room before participating in an experiment, some adult subjects were approached by an eight-year-old child who was having trouble operating a vending machine. Later, while answering a series of questions designed to disguise the true nature of the experiment, they were asked to rate their perception of how unpleasant it might be to provide help for other people. After the subjects had answered all the questions and the study was apparently over, the interviewer then asked them whether they would volunteer between thirty minutes and four hours of their time to participate in a research project. The results showed that subjects who had helped the child rated helping as less unpleasant and were more willing to participate in the research project than people who had not helped the child. (See *Figure 17.11.*)

The results suggest that when a person helps someone else, he or she finds that helping is not at all unpleasant; in fact, helping a young child probably increases one's self-esteem and hence reinforces helping behavior. Thus, the person's attitude toward helping behavior in general probably becomes more positive, and

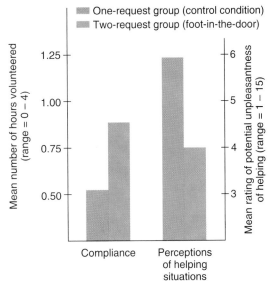

Figure 17.11 Mean number of hours volunteered and mean rating of potential unpleasantness of volunteering for control subjects and subjects who first helped a child. (Based on data from Rittle, R.H. *Personality and Social Psychology Bulletin,* 1981, *7,* 431–437.)

this changed attitude translates itself into behavior.

Attractive People: It's Hard to Refuse Them

[11] People tend to be most influenced by requests or persuasive messages from attractive people. As we will see in a later section, physical good looks are one of the most important factors in determining whether we find someone likable.

People generally find it difficult to say no to an attractive person, even though they usually deny being influenced by such a "superficial" characteristic as looks. For example, Efran and Patterson (1976) had subjects rate the attractiveness of the candidates in the 1974 Canadian federal election. They found that the most attractive candidates received two and one-half times as many votes as the least attractive ones. However, when they surveyed Canadian voters, they found that the overwhelming majority of them denied that their vote had been affected in the least by the candidates' looks. People are either not conscious of the influence of physical attractiveness or unwilling to admit to it.

Kulka and Kessler (1978) demonstrated the effect of good looks on people's behavior in a controlled experiment. They staged a mock trial of a negligence suit in which someone was suing another person for damages. The subjects served as jury members and decided how much money the plaintiff should be awarded. Physically attractive plaintiffs received an average of $10,051, but physically unattractive plaintiffs received only $5623. Who says justice is blind?

Why is attractiveness such a potent influence on people's behavior? The most likely explanation involves classical conditioning and—again—self-esteem. Classical conditioning says that when people have positive or negative reactions to some stimuli, they begin to have positive or negative reactions to other stimuli also present. Thus, as Cialdini (1988) notes, some people irrationally blame the weather forecaster for bad weather. Similarly, in ancient times a messenger bringing news about a battle to the ruler of Persia was treated to a banquet if the news was good and beheaded if it was bad.

Advertisers regularly pay tribute to the effectiveness of association when they have attractive models and celebrities appear with their products. For example, Smith and Engel (1968) showed two versions of an advertisement for a new car. One version included an attractive young woman and the other did not. When the subjects subsequently rated the car, those who saw the advertisement with the attractive young woman rated the car as faster, more appealing, more expensive looking, and better designed.

Besides making products or opinions more attractive by being associated with them, attractive people are better able to get others to comply with their requests. This phenomenon, like so many others, probably has self-esteem at its root. One of the reasons people tend to comply with the requests of attractive people is that they want to be liked by attractive people; in their minds, being liked by attractive people makes them more desirable, too. Clearly, people tend to emphasize their associations with attractive and important people; we have all encountered name-droppers who want us to think that they are part of a privileged circle of friends. This phenomenon is even demonstrated by fans of sports teams. Cialdini, Borden, Thorne, Walker, Freeman, and Sloan (1976) found that university students were more likely to wear sweatshirts featuring the university name on Mondays after the football team had won a game than after the team had lost. They also found in telephone interviews with students that the pronouns *we* and *our* (as in "our victory") were prominent after wins but that the

pronouns *they* and *their* (as in "their defeat") were prominent after losses.

Authority: We're Loyal Followers

People tend to comply with the requests of people in authority and to be swayed by their persuasive arguments, and such obedience is generally approved by society. For example, the Bible describes God's test of Abraham, who is ordered to sacrifice his beloved son Isaac. Just as he is about to plunge the knife, an angel tells him to stop; he has proved his obedience. Cohen and Davis (1981) cite a more recent, if less dramatic, example of unthinking obedience. A physician prescribed eardrops for a hospitalized patient with an ear infection. His order read "place in R ear." Unfortunately, he apparently did not put enough space between the abbreviation for *right* (R) and the word *ear,* because the nurse delivered the ear drops rectally. Neither she nor the patient thought to question such treatment for an earache.

An interesting study showed that we tend to perceive authority figures as larger than life (literally). Wilson (1968) introduced a man to his classes in an Australian college as a visitor from Cambridge University. In different classes he introduced the man as a student, a demonstrator, a lecturer, a senior lecturer, or a professor. Later, he asked the students in his classes to estimate the visitor's height. The average estimates are shown in Figure 17.12; as you can see, the "professor" was perceived as being over 3 1/2 inches taller than the "student." (See *Figure 17.12.*)

A disturbing example of mindless obedience was obtained in a series of experiments performed by Milgram (1963), who advertised for subjects in local newspapers in order to obtain as representative a sample as possible. The subjects served as "teachers" in what they were told was a learning experiment. A confederate (a middle-aged accountant) serving as the "learner" was strapped into a chair "to prevent excessive movements when he was shocked," and electrodes were attached to his wrist. (See *Figure 17.13.*) The subjects were told that "although the shocks can be extremely painful, they cause no permanent tissue damage."

The subject was then brought to a separate room housing an apparatus with dials, buttons, and a series of switches that supposedly delivered shocks ranging from 15 to 450 volts in intensity. The subject was instructed to use this apparatus to deliver shocks to the learner in the

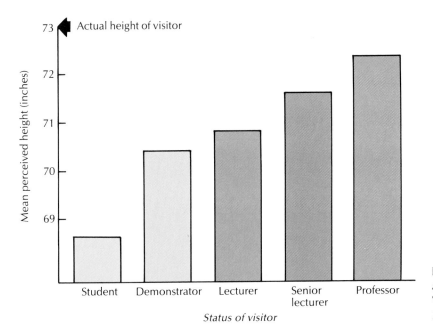

Figure 17.12 Mean perceived height of a person as a function of his status. (Based on data from Wilson, P.R. *Journal of Social Psychology*, 1968, *74*, 97–102.)

other room. Beneath the switches were descriptive labels ranging from "Slight Shock" to "Danger: Severe Shock."

The learner gave his answers by pressing the appropriate lever on the table in front of him. Each time he made an incorrect response, the experimenter told the subject to throw another switch and give a larger shock. At the 300-volt level the learner pounded on the wall and then stopped responding to questions. The experimenter told the subject to consider no answer as an incorrect answer. At the 315-volt

Figure 17.13 A "learner" (confederate) being strapped into a chair in one of Milgram's studies. (Photograph from *Obedience to Authority* by Stanley Milgram. Copyright © 1974 by Stanley Milgram. Reprinted by permission of Harper Collins Publishers.)

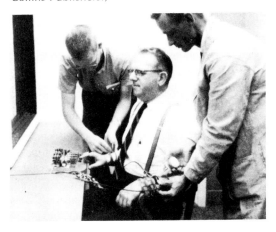

level the learner pounded on the wall again. If the subject hesitated in delivering a shock, the experimenter said, "Please go on." If this admonition was not enough, the experimenter said, "The experiment requires that you continue," then "It is absolutely essential that you continue," and finally, "You have no other choice; you *must* go on." The factor of interest was how long the subjects would continue to administer shocks to the hapless victim. A majority of subjects gave the learner what they believed to be the 450-volt shock, despite the fact that he pounded on the wall twice and then stopped responding altogether. (See *Figure 17.14.*)

In a later experiment, when the confederate was placed in the same room as the subject and his struggling and apparent pain could be observed, 37.5 percent of the participants—over a third—obeyed the order to administer further shocks (Milgram, 1974). Thirty percent were even willing to hold his hand against a metal plate to force him to receive the shock.

Milgram's experiments indicate that a significant percentage of people will blindly follow the orders of authority figures, no matter what the effects are on other people. Milgram had originally designed his experimental procedure to understand why ordinary people in Germany had participated in the murders of millions of innocent people during World War II. He had planned to perfect the technique in the United States and then travel to Germany to continue his studies. The results he obtained made it clear that he did not have to leave home.

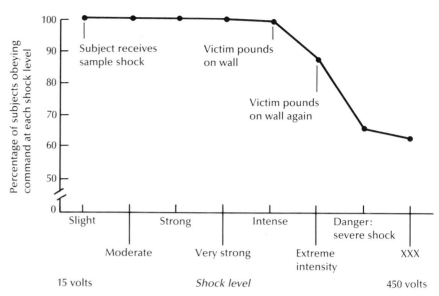

Figure 17.14   Data from one of Milgram's studies of obedience. (From Baron, R.A., and Byrne, D. *Social Psychology: Understanding Human Interaction,* 2nd ed. Boston: Allyn and Bacon, 1977. Reprinted with permission. After Milgram, 1963.)

Most people find the results of Milgram's studies surprising; they can't believe that for such a large proportion of people the social pressure to conform to the experimenter's orders is stronger than the subject's own desire not to hurt someone else. As Ross (1977) points out, this misperception is an example of the fundamental attributional error. People tend to underestimate the effectiveness of situational factors and to overestimate the effectiveness of dispositional ones. Clearly, the tendency to obey an authority figure is amazingly strong. Perhaps we should emphasize to our children the importance of doing no harm to others as least as much as we emphasize obedience.

INTERIM SUMMARY

Social Influences

You probably did not need to be told that one of the most important influences on our behavior is provided by other humans, but the experiments of social psychologists have shown us just how potent these social influences are. We tend to imitate the behavior of other people, conforming to social norms and preferring not to disagree with attitudes and judgments expressed by others. This tendency undoubtedly serves us well most of the time, but the fact that people are less likely to assist someone if other by-standers are present shows that imitation can also have unfortunate effects.

When they are part of a group or are observed by others, people act differently than when alone. In general, the presence of observers increases the likelihood that the performer will make the dominant response; depending on the complexity of the task, this effect can either facilitate or inhibit performance. When performing as part of a group, a person's efforts will usually be less vigorous if individual contribution cannot be measured. This phenomenon is called social loafing. The most important variables that affect social loafing are identifiability and responsibility. If our efforts can be detected by others, then the contingencies of social reinforcement and punishment come into play, and we tend not to loaf. Also, if we have a particular responsibility that is not duplicated by other people—if our contribution is a unique and important one—we tend to continue to work hard in support of the group effort.

When someone does us a favor, we tend to reciprocate, doing something for them when we have the opportunity. This tendency probably serves as the historical basis for trade, but the individual can sometimes be tricked into returning a small favor with a big one. When we commit ourselves to a course of action, we tend to honor these commitments. As the study with the billboards showed, we even act consistently with prior commitments when we are not conscious of having made them. And not everyone is treated equally by other people. Attractive people and people who are perceived as authority figures tend to get what they want from others; we find it difficult to say no to them. ■

INTERPERSONAL ATTRACTION

Humans are very social animals. We make friends, eat and drink together in groups, join clubs, and form close associations with our mates and children. For most of us the behavior of other people serves as our most important source of reinforcing and aversive stimuli. As we saw in Chapter 11, most of us have a need for affiliation with other people. But we are not equally attracted to all people. Why do we enjoy the company of some people and not others?

Many factors determine *interpersonal attraction*—that is, people's tendency to approach each other and evaluate each other positively. Some factors are characteristics of the individuals themselves; others are determined by the environment, as we will see in this section.

The simplest and most parsimonious explanation for interpersonal attraction is that people who serve as sources of reinforcing stimuli for each other tend to remain in each other's company. As you will recall from Chapter 6, stimuli that are regularly associated with reinforcing stimuli will themselves become reinforcing stimuli, through the process of classical conditioning. Thus, we learn to prefer the company of people who regularly provide us with social reinforcement.

The nature of social reinforcement is quite varied. Acknowledgment of our abilities and accomplishments and appreciation of our intelligence and wit are certainly desirable characteristics in a close friend. Other characteristics, such as talent and physical attractiveness, also endear others to us; having an attractive and accomplished friend suggests both to ourselves and to other people that we, too, are worthy of respect.

Positive Evaluation

12 Humans need to be evaluated positively—to be held in high regard by other people. This need is expressed in interpersonal attraction. Byrne and Rhamey (1965) studied the effects of positive personal evaluations on attraction. First, they asked subjects to express their attitudes toward twelve issues. Then they described a fictitious stranger, explaining what his

attitudes were on the twelve issues. The subjects were told that the stranger had read their attitude survey and had accordingly evaluated them positively or negatively. Finally, the experimenters asked the subjects to rate the amount of attraction they felt toward the stranger. As Figure 17.15 shows, subjects reported being more attracted if the stranger's attitudes were similar to their own. However, the most important factor was whether the stranger approved of them; subjects who were evaluated positively reported being much more attracted to the stranger than did those who were rated negatively. (See *Figure 17.15*.)

In situations involving real people the effects of evaluation are even more pronounced. Geller, Goodstein, Silver, and Sternberg (1974) had female college students individually join group discussions with two other women, confederates of the experimenter. During the discussion the confederates either treated the subject normally or ignored her, showing a lack of interest in what she said and changing the subject whenever she spoke. The subjects who were ignored found the conversations distressing; they felt very unhappy and even gave *them-*

Figure 17.15 Ratings of the description of a stranger who was said to have evaluated the subject positively or negatively, as a function of similarity in attitudes between stranger and subject. (From Baron, R.A., and Byrne, D. *Social Psychology: Understanding Human Interaction*, 2nd ed. Boston: Allyn and Bacon, 1977. Reprinted with permission. After Byrne and Rhamey, 1965.)

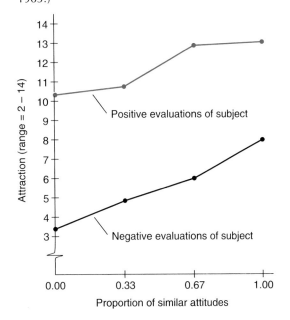

selves poor ratings. Being ignored is a form of negative evaluation by other people, and it exerts a powerful effect.

Similarity

A second factor that influences interpersonal attraction is similarity—similarity in looks, interests, and attitudes. Couples tend to be similar in attractiveness; in fact, couples who are mismatched in this respect are the most likely to break up (White, 1980). Although we might think that people would seek the most attractive partner that he or she could find, people tend to fear rejection and ridicule. Men especially tend to be afraid of approaching attractive women (Bernstein, Stephenson, Snyder, and Wicklund, 1983). Even same-sexed friends are likely to be similar in attractiveness (Cash and Derlega, 1978).

Couples (and groups of friends) also tend to hold similar opinions. This factor, too, can be explained in terms of social reinforcement. Presumably, a person who shares our opinions is likely to approve of us when we express them. Also, having friends who have similar opinions guarantees that our opinions are likely to find a consensus; we will not often find ourselves in the unpleasant position of saying something that brings disapproval from other people.

Byrne and Nelson (1965) measured various attitudes of their subjects and then had them read descriptions of the attitudes of a stranger.

Similarity of life situations can lead individuals to be attracted to one another.

After learning about this person's attitudes, the subjects rated how much they liked or disliked the stranger. Their responses indicated that the more similar the stranger's attitudes were to those of the subject, the better the stranger was liked.

In the real world similarity of attitudes is not the only factor determining the strength of interpersonal attraction. Other kinds of similarities are also important, such as age, occupational status, and ethnic background. Friends tend to have similar backgrounds as well as similar attitudes.

Physical Appearance

We *do* judge people by the characteristic that is supposed to be only skin deep. In general, we are more attracted to good-looking people than to ugly people (Albright, Kenny, and Malloy, 1988). (In fact, the word *attractive* is often used as a synonym for *good-looking*.) Again, social reinforcement provides a likely explanation for this phenomenon. Although aesthetics (such as our attraction to a beautiful painting) may account in part for our attraction to good-looking people, self-esteem probably plays a more important role. Someone who is seen in the company of an attractive person and is obviously favored by this person is likely to be well regarded by other people ("If she's so good looking and she likes him, then he must really have something going for him").

Walster, Aronson, Abrahams, and Rottman (1966) studied the effects of physical appearance at a dance at which college students were paired by a computer. Midway through the evening, the experimenters asked the subjects to rate the attraction they felt toward their partners and to say whether they thought they would like to see them in the future. For both sexes the only characteristic that correlated with attraction was physical appearance. Intelligence, grade point average, and personality variables seemed to have no significant effect. Berscheid, Dion, Walster, and Walster (1971) found that although physical appearance may be the most important variable in determining attraction between people who are randomly paired by a computer, when people choose their own partners, they tend to pick someone who is about as physically attractive as they are—a phenomenon that I discussed in the previous subsection.

When people first meet someone with a good physical appearance, they rate the person as probably holding attitudes similar to their own

(Schoedel, Frederickson, and Knight, 1975) and tend to assume that they have good personalities, successful marriages, and high occupational status (Adams and Huston, 1975; Dion, Berscheid, and Walster, 1972). In fact, physically attractive people usually *do* possess many of these characteristics, probably because they receive favorable treatment from society (Hatfield and Sprecher, 1986).

Familiarity

Fortunately for the majority of us who are not especially beautiful or handsome, the variable of exposure influences people's attitudes toward others. The more frequent the exposure, the more positive the attitude is.

In order for an attachment to form between people, they must meet each other. Festinger, Schachter, and Back (1950) found that the likelihood of friendships between people who lived in an apartment house was related to the distance between the apartments in which they lived; the closer the apartments, the more likely the friendship was. People were also unlikely to have friends who lived on a different floor, unless their apartment was next to a stairway, where they would meet people going up or down the stairs. In suburban housing developments neighbors are more likely to be friends if their driveways are adjacent to each other

(Whyte, 1956). The rule holds even in a classroom: People who sit together are more likely to become friends. Segal (1974) asked trainees in the Maryland State Police School to list classmates they would like to have for friends. Almost half the people they listed had last names that began with letters near theirs in the alphabet. (Can you guess why?)

As you have learned in other chapters, repetition generally increases our preference for a stimulus. This phenomenon applies to people as well. Even in the brief time it takes to participate in an experiment, familiarity affects interpersonal attraction. Saegert, Swap, and Zajonc (1973) had college women participate in an experiment supposedly involving the sense of taste. Groups of two students (all were subjects; no confederates this time) entered booths, where they tasted and rated various liquids. The movements of the subjects from booth to booth were choreographed so that pairs of women were together from zero to ten times. Afterward, the subjects rated their attraction to each of the other people in the experiment. The amount of attraction the subjects felt toward a given person was related to the number of interactions they had had. (See *Figure 17.16*.)

Figure 17.16 The rated likability of a fellow subject as a function of number of interactions. (Based on data from Saegert, S.C., Swap, W., and Zajonc, R.B. *Journal of Personality and Social Psychology*, 1973, 25, 234–242.)

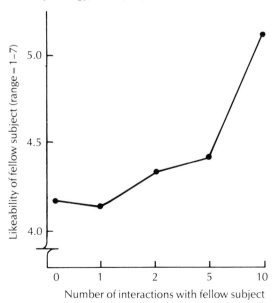

EVALUATING SCIENTIFIC ISSUES

Is Loving Fundamentally Different from Liking?

[13] The simplest explanation for the intense interpersonal relationship we call "love" is that it is merely a strong form of liking. According to this explanation, the feeling we have for the person we love is qualitatively no different from the attraction we feel for other people, except for the added feelings derived from sexual intimacy, if that occurs. However, some psychologists have suggested that love is fundamentally different from liking, because the phenomenon of reinforcement cannot explain some of the factors that affect this special kind of interpersonal attraction people feel. As Walster and Berscheid (1971) have put it, "Passion sometimes develops in conditions that would seem more likely to provoke aggression and hatred" (p. 47).

Evidence for a Fundamental Difference. Dutton and Aron (1974) had an attractive young woman interview male college students as they walked across a suspension bridge spanning a gorge 280 feet deep. The bridge was 5 feet wide and 450 feet long and had "a tendency to tilt, sway, and wobble, creating the impression that one is about to fall over the side" (p. 511). The same woman interviewed control subjects on a more conventional, sturdy bridge spanning a 10-foot drop.

The men who were interviewed on the suspension bridge appeared to find the woman more attractive than did those who were interviewed on the ordinary bridge. They were more likely to make sexually related responses to a brief personality test. Perhaps more significantly, they were much more likely to telephone the woman later. The interviewer gave her telephone number to all subjects with the suggestion that they call her if they wanted to discuss the experiment further.

The results suggest that the anxiety evoked by standing on a precarious suspension bridge increased the men's sexual attraction toward the woman. At first, this finding appears to be incompatible with the suggestion that interpersonal attraction stems from reinforcement. The subjects met the woman in the context of aversive stimuli, not reinforcing ones; therefore, she should subsequently have become an aversive stimulus herself and elicited avoidance behaviors, not telephone calls. This phenomenon does occur; when someone meets another person in an uncomfortably hot and humid room, he or she tends not to like that person (Griffitt, 1970).

Dutton and Aron (1974) explained their results in terms of attribution theory: A man experiences increased arousal in the presence of a woman; he attributes it to the most obvious stimulus—the woman—and concludes that he is attracted to her. Later, he acts on this conclusion by telephoning her.

Several researchers have shown that adversity and unpleasant arousal do tend to increase interpersonal attraction between men and women. For example, Rubin (1973) noted that couples of mixed religious background reported stronger degrees of romantic love. Presumably, the conflict that followed their choice of each other (especially among other family members) provided arousal that strengthened their mutual attraction. Similarly, an ancient Roman expert advised men to take their women to the Colosseum to see the gladiators fight, because the experience would increase their romantic ardor.

An Alternative Explanation. Kenrick and Cialdini (1977) suggested that misattributed arousal was not the best explanation for the fact that anxiety and fear can increase interpersonal attraction. To begin with, it is unlikely that a person who is standing on a swaying suspension bridge cannot identify the source of his or her arousal; most people have better insight than that into the source of their emotions. If the subjects had correctly attributed their arousal to the bridge, they would not have needed to attribute it to the woman standing on it. Furthermore, a person who is present in an aversive situation does not inevitably become an aversive stimulus by association; instead, he or she can become a *conditioned reinforcer*.

Consider what happened to the subjects. They started walking across a narrow, swaying bridge suspended above a deep gorge and met a calm, attractive young woman who stopped them and asked them to participate in an experiment. They spent several minutes talking with her, then continued on their way. Probably this encounter reduced rather than increased their fear. The woman seemed calm and reassuring and accustomed to standing on the bridge; therefore, she served as an example to the students. Her presence may also have distracted them from the view of the rocks far below. Because a stimulus that causes the reduction of an aversive stimulus becomes a reinforcer, the men's increased attraction toward the woman can be accounted for in terms of reinforcement, not misattribution. The woman's presence became a conditioned reinforcer because it was associated with reduction of fear. (Remember from Chapter 6 that the reduction of an aversive stimulus serves as a *negative reinforcer*.)

This conclusion is consistent with the results of many studies performed with other animals. For example, you will remember from Chapter 10 that infant monkeys cling to their mothers when they are frightened by novel stimuli. In addition, ethologists have noted that the presence of predators causes animals to congregate together. Undoubtedly, this tendency exists in humans too: When we are faced with danger or adversity, we seek the company of other people.

A further study by Dutton and Aron (1974) demonstrated that the presence of another person can, indeed, reduce aversive arousal. The experimenters led a group of male subjects to expect to receive a weak electrical shock, a strong and painful electrical shock, or no shock. During a delay period some subjects waited alone; others waited with a young woman. Presumably, the subjects who anticipated receiving a strong shock were unpleasantly aroused. As in the bridge experiment, subjects who were expecting a shock reported more attraction than did those who were not expecting a shock. Dutton and Aron also asked the subjects to rate their level of anxiety. Those who had waited with the young woman reported less anxiety than did control subjects who had waited alone. The fact that the woman's presence decreased the subjects' arousal provides important support for the negative reinforcement hypothesis.

What Should We Conclude? Is loving fundamentally different from liking? Is love a special phenomenon that feeds on adversity? The best explanation for a phenomenon is usually the simplest one. In this case we should probably conclude that fear and anxiety intensify interpersonal attraction because the presence of the other person can reduce these negative feelings. This explanation can account for Rubin's (1973) findings about couples of mixed religious background. The adverse feelings produced by family conflicts are decreased when the couples are together; thus, the presence of the partner is reinforcing.

Certainly, intimate relationships are very complex. People are attracted to each other because of many factors other than anxiety reduction. Knowing how adversity affects such relations does not tell us all there is to know about the nature of loving. ■

INTERIM SUMMARY

Interpersonal Attraction

Although the factors that influence interpersonal attraction are complex and not yet fully understood, they all appear to involve social reinforcement (and, in the case of lovers, physical reinforcement). In turn, people learn to act in ways that reinforce friends and lovers, to maintain and strengthen their ties with them. Attraction is increased by positive evaluation of oneself by the other person, by shared opinions, by physical good looks, and by familiarity.

Attribution undoubtedly plays an important role in interpersonal attraction; for example, our beliefs about why other people act as they do certainly affect how much we like them. Yet a careful analysis suggests that the reason romantic bonds can be strengthened by adversity involves the phenomenon of negative reinforcement. The presence of another person makes an unpleasant situation more tolerable, and this reduction in strength of an aversive stimulus confers on the other person the status of a conditioned reinforcer. ■

APPLICATION

Resisting Social Influences

Although most people believe that their behavior is controlled by a process of rational decision making, much of what we do is strongly influenced by unconscious processes. As we saw in the section on social influences, many social variables influence our behavior automatically. Perhaps in reading about them, you said to yourself, "Canned laughter doesn't make *me* laugh," or "I'd help the man having the seizure even if other people were around," or "I am influenced by a person's ideas, not by what he or she looks like," or "I'd never give a shock to someone else even if the experimenter said I had to." After all, being vulnerable to the effects of social influence means that your choices are constrained by your automatic reactions.

At first glance, instances of social influence may appear to be bad; perhaps we would be better off if all our behavior was under rational, conscious control. But as Cialdini (1988) points out, this conclusion is not warranted. Most of the

time our species profits from our tendencies to be fair in our interactions with others, to take our cues for acting from each other, and to honor our commitments. If, in every situation we encountered in our lives, we had to expend time and effort consciously deciding what to do, we would be exhausted at the end of the day and get hardly anything done. For most normal people in most situations the automatic, unconscious reaction is the best and most efficient one. We should save our cognitive efforts for the times when they count the most. However, no general rule works all the time; exceptions can occur that have bad effects. For example, an authority figure can order us to do things that hurt ourselves or others, and advertisers and sales representatives who know the rules can induce us to purchase items we do not need.

Cialdini (1988) suggests some ways to resist the attempts of people who try to profit from our automatic, reflexive tendencies. First, it is helpful to know the principles that their tricks are based on. As we saw, people trying to take advantage of us may try to obtain a commitment that we find hard to disavow; they may pay us compliments so that we will like them; they may do us "favors" so that we will feel impelled to reciprocate; and so on. If you know the principles behind their tricks (and now you do), you are more likely to detect when someone is trying to manipulate you, so that you can then engage in a carefully thought-out reaction instead of an automatic one.

Suppose that you are looking for a compact disk player for your stereo system. A salesman approaches you and says, "I see you're looking at Model X. It's a great item, and you can't beat the price. But I'm pretty sure we just sold the last one."

You probably feel disappointed and even a little angry. The salesman shrugs and says, "Well, I can go back to the stock room to see if we have another one." He looks at you inquiringly, and you say "Ok." He starts to leave and then looks back over his shoulder at you and asks, "If we do have one, you want to buy it, right?" You hesitate. You didn't really get a chance to think about whether that was the model you want. On the other hand, you don't like the idea of missing the opportunity to buy the component. And after all, you are the one who is sending him back to the stock room. You feel the pressure of having to make a quick decision. "Sure," you say. They probably don't even have another Model X in stock.

But they do. The salesman comes back with a smile on his face, a carton under his arm, and a sales form in his hand. You have just bought yourself a compact disk player. You feel just a little uncomfortable—everything seems to have happened so fast—but you tell yourself that you got a great deal and that you were lucky to have such a diligent salesman who took the trouble to check the stock room for you.

Perhaps you really did get a good deal and will be happy with the compact disk player for years. But your choice was controlled by the salesman. He made you want one particular item because you believed that it was scarce, and he created a feeling of obligation in you by walking all the way to the stock room. In addition, he made sure you committed yourself to purchase the item in the unlikely case that he was successful in finding one. With this triple whammy, you were hooked!

Cialdini suggests that the best way to defend ourselves from the unscrupulous use of social influences is to be sensitive to ourselves and to the situation. Whenever we are spending money or committing ourselves to do something that will cost us time and effort, we should ask ourselves whether we feel any discomfort. Do we feel pressured? Do we feel tense? Do we wish we were somewhere else? If so, someone is probably trying to manipulate us. We should try to relax and step back from the situation. Does the other person stand to profit from what he or she is trying to get us to do? If we could go back to the time just before we got into this situation would we put ourself where we are now, or would we avoid this situation? If we would avoid it, then now is the time to leave. The feeling that we *have to* keep going, that we *have to* live up to our commitment is exactly what the other person is counting on.

We must realize that when someone is trying to manipulate us, the rules that govern normal social interchanges are off. Of course, we should be polite and honest—just as we want other people to be with us—but we are not obliged to return "favors" from someone trying to sell us something. If they trick us into making a commitment, we should feel no compunction about breaking it. If someone tries to abuse our natural tendencies to be fair in our interactions with others, we should fight back. Otherwise, we run the risk of becoming cynical in our dealings of other people who are *not* trying to take advantage of us. Forewarned is forearmed.

A personal note: The research and writings of thousands of men and women have contributed to the information contained in this book. If this text has achieved all its purposes, not only will you now know more about human behavior than you did before, you will also have learned to be skeptical with regard to unsupported statements about human behavior; and you will be convinced that the only way to find out how we humans work is to investigate ourselves scientifically. As we have seen, even human thought and emotion are fair topics for scientific investigators.

While writing this book, I have enjoyed feeling that I have been talking with someone. If any of you would like to discuss with me what I have written (or not written), do let me hear from you. Write to me at the Department of Psychology, Tobin Hall, University of Massachusetts, Amherst, Massachusetts 01003.

KEY TERMS AND CONCEPTS

social cognition *(573)*

Attribution

attribution *(573)*
implicit psychology *(573)*
situational factor *(573)*
dispositional factor *(573)*
consensual behavior *(574)*
consistency *(574)*
distinctiveness *(574)*
fundamental attributional error *(574)*
false consensus *(576)*
personal causation *(576)*
representativeness heuristic *(577)*
base-rate fallacy *(578)*
availability heuristic *(578)*
regression fallacy *(579)*

Attitudes and Their Formation

modeling *(581)*
self-attribution *(582)*
cognitive dissonance *(582)*
dissonance reduction *(583)*
self-perception theory *(586)*

Prejudice

prejudice *(587)*
stereotype *(587)*
discrimination *(587)*
illusory correlation *(589)*
illusion of out-group homogeneity *(589)*
self-fulfilling prophecy *(589)*

Social Influences

bystander intervention *(593)*
social facilitation *(594)*
social loafing *(596)*
reciprocity *(597)*

Interpersonal Attraction

SUGGESTIONS FOR FURTHER READING

Baron, R.A., and Byrne, D. *Social Psychology: Understanding Human Interaction*, 6th ed. Boston: Allyn and Bacon, 1991.

This excellent and very readable text describes all aspects of social psychology.

Harvey, J.H., and Weary, G. *Attribution: Basic Issues and Applications.* San Diego: Academic Press, 1989.

Ross, L., and Nisbett, R.E. *The Person and the Situation: Perspectives of Social Psychology.* New York: McGraw-Hill, 1991.

These books describe the variables that influence our causal attributions and the interaction between persons and situations.

Petty, R.E., and Cacioppo, J.T. *Attitude Change: Central and Peripheral Routes to Persuasion.* New York: Springer-Verlag, 1986.

Attitude formation and the ways in which attitudes can be changed are described in Petty and Cacioppo's book.

Fiske, S.T., and Taylor, S.E. *Social Cognition.* Reading, Mass.: Addison-Wesley, 1984.

This classic book is interesting, informative, and well-written.

Cialdini, R.B. *Influence: Science and Practice,* 2nd ed. New York: Harper-Collins, 1988.

Cialdini's book was written for a general audience. It provides a fascinating and well-written account of the ways people influence each other.

APPENDIX: PSYCHOLOGISTS AT WORK

Robert Gifford *University of Victoria*

By now, you should have a good introduction to the science of psychology and some of the knowledge that psychologists have obtained. All the facts you have learned stem from the work of thousands of committed researchers and practitioners around the world. Each of the hundreds of studies mentioned in this book took several months or years of work by a team, each headed by one or more psychologists.

Who are these psychologists? What do they actually do on the job? How did they become psychologists?

PSYCHOLOGY: AN OCCUPATION

Psychologists solve problems. Science-oriented psychologists solve intellectual problems, such as finding the best model or theory to account for a certain behavior process. Most of this book describes the kind of work done by the science-oriented psychologist, who typically works in a university or government-funded laboratory.

Practitioners, or practicing applied psychologists, solve practical, everyday problems that individuals or organizations bring to them. Many of them also do research, but their primary goal is to provide useful information or assistance quickly (these problems often cannot wait months or years) when problems are brought to them. The request for help is so touching or so interesting that the practicing psychologist decides assistance really must be rendered. Either existing principles and knowledge are adapted to attack the problem, or the psychologist uses his or her stock of methods and techniques, acquired through years of training and experience, to try to solve the problem.

Every practicing psychologist can describe problems that have been solved through such efforts. Every one of them can also point to many more problems that *could have been* solved if only more time, assistance, and funds had been available. Increasingly, these resources are becoming available. The growth of applied psychology over the past century has been phenomenal, and there is room for more eager, talented young psychologists.

The science-oriented psychologist primarily cares about understanding human behavior in general, and the practice-oriented psychologist primarily cares about improving the welfare of individuals and organizations. Thus, practice- and science-oriented psychology may seem incompatible, but they are not. An important figure in the history of modern psychology, Kurt Lewin, said many years ago that there is nothing as practical as a good theory. It does not happen every day, but professional practice can contribute to theory; conversely, good professional practice is guided by knowledge of relevant theories.

Practicing psychologists dream that the solution to the problem they are solving now will help other psychologists solve similar problems; that their research, done locally, will reveal glimpses of a global set of principles by which human behavior in everyday life can be understood. Science-oriented psychologists would not be working unless they hoped that their findings might someday be applied to everyday life. Unfortunately, perhaps, psychologists are only human; as much as they might wish they could perform both roles, they must specialize in order to perform well in a particular area of psychology. There is far too much research going on in psychology for anyone to be a real expert in the whole field.

Which problems are solved by practicing psychologists? Of course, they confront problems brought to them by individuals in emotional crisis. But they also work on the concerns brought to them by office workers with chronic back pain, by governments that want to select better managers, by organizations that want better buildings, by athletes in search of better performance, by people with brain injuries who hope to regain as much of their former ability as possible, by lawyers who want an edge in the courtroom, by toy makers who wish to create desirable toys, by consumer groups who try to improve marketplace goods, and by many others.

In sum, practicing psychologists retain the goal of advancing knowledge through a scientific approach to human behavior. But they are also dedicated to ameliorating the immediate and developing problems of individuals and organizations.

THE BACKGROUND OF PSYCHOLOGY AS A PRACTICE

Modern applied psychology developed around the end of the last century. Its first manifestation was the opening, in 1896, of Lightner Witmer's psychological clinic at the University of Pennsylvania. This event signaled the beginning of both clinical psychology and school psychology, because the clients were students with learning problems or emotional disturbances. The next area to develop was consumer psychology, which was then mainly concerned with advertising. Walter Dill Scott's book *The Theory of Advertising* was published in 1903. Then came law and psychology, when Hugo Munsterberg published his book *On the Witness Stand* in 1908. Soon after, industrial psychology (later called *industrial-organizational psychology* and then simply *organizational psychology*) was established when Frederick Winslow Taylor developed an approach to work efficiency known as *scientific management*. His book, *The Principles of Scientific Management*, appeared in 1911.

Psychologists began to realize that an entire new discipline was developing. Munsterberg followed up his book on law and psychology in 1915 with a broader one, called *Psychology: General and Applied*. Finally, in 1917, an outstanding early psychologist, G. Stanley Hall, established the *Journal of Applied Psychology*, which remains one of the premier publications in the discipline. The number of practicing psychologists increased from a handful in the first decade of the century to hundreds in the 1940s to thousands today.

THE VARIETIES OF PRACTICING PSYCHOLOGISTS

Just as psychology (as a scientific discipline) examines many aspects of behavior (as represented in the titles of the chapters in this book), practicing psychologists concentrate on a wide variety of problems. It might even be said that every psychologist has a different specialty, because no two do exactly the same things. However, there is a relatively small number of "standard brands" of psychologists. In this section the most important types of working psychologists are briefly described. Some categories are larger in number and more established; others are growing but not yet as well established. (See *Tables A.1 and A.2*.) If you are interested in more detail about any of these occupations, you may want to consult a book (Gifford, 1991) that devotes a chapter to each of 12 kinds of psychologist described next.

The Professor

Having taken classes from a number of professors, some students may assume that they know all about this job. However, teaching is only one of the professor's tasks. Every professor or instructor will also be asked to help manage the psychology department or other portions of the school's administration. In many schools professors are also expected to do re-

Table A.1 Membership figures for some relevant divisions of the American Psychological Association (fellows, members, and associate members)

Division	1991 Membership
Clinical psychology	6284
Clinical neuropsychology	3099
Industrial and organizational	2481
Applied experimental and engineering	463
Consumer psychology	447
Community psychology	909
Population and environmental psychology	491
Teaching of psychology	2057
School psychology	2139
Health psychology	2980
Exercise and sport psychology	867
Psychology—law society	1418
Total APA membership[a]	72,202

Source: 1991 APA Membership Register.

[a] Total membership includes members of several divisions not listed here and those who do not belong to any division.

Table A.2 Membership figures for some relevant sections of the Canadian Psychological Association

Section	1991 Membership[a]
Clinical psychology	352
Clinical neuropsychology	170
Criminal justice systems	134
Community psychology	72
Education and school psychology	128
Environmental psychology	27
Industrial and organizational	170
Psychological gerontology	102
Health psychology	191
Sport and exercise psychology	36
Teaching of psychology	56
Total CPA membership[b]	4101

Source: CPA Central Office, December 1991.

[a] Including student members.

[b] Including members not in sections listed above.

difficult to obtain, but larger grants are very hard to get; only 10 to 30 percent of applications—even those submitted by well-qualified professors—are approved. The phrase "publish or perish" is a fact of life in many of the better schools. However, this phrase is often misunderstood. Some people who hear it think it means that professors are required to do research but would really rather not bother—that research is an undesirable chore forced upon them. Actually, most professors love to do research; to them, "perishing" is a possibility that results only from a shortage of grant funds, not from their own lack of interest or ability. Research can, and often does, take much of the free time the professor has, including evenings, weekends, and those daytime hours not spent in classrooms or meetings. Research includes designing experiments or studies, conducting them or supervising their execution, analyzing the data they produce, and communicating their findings in articles or books.

As a group, professors also administer many university functions, such as setting the curriculum of the department or college, watching over the department budget, hiring and monitoring the progress of new faculty members, and training graduate students. Although the other psychologists to be described subsequently sometimes lecture on their specialty, the professor is the only one whose main work setting is the university or college. The others work mainly in the community, in clinics, or in industry.

The Clinical Psychologist

Clinical psychologists are dedicated to improving human functioning, especially that of individuals in distress. Because this distress strikes people of different ages, and because some clearly results from injury or disease rather than nonmedical stress, four kinds of clinical psychologists will be described. The first primarily deals with adults in emotional crisis. The other three deal with children, with old persons, or with individuals with brain injuries or neurological disorders.

All clinical psychologists primarily engage in psychological assessment and psychotherapy, but sometimes, they also conduct research and teach (Halgin, 1991). Although many students wish to help others in distress, not everyone is suited to the often demanding and emotionally draining nature of this occupation. Those who are, however, find clinical practice very rewarding.

search (most students see little evidence of the professor's research or administration work). Professors spend different amounts of time on teaching, research, and administration, but every professor will do some of each in the course of a career. Once established in a career, some professors focus exclusively on one of these three activities: Some psychologists become deans or presidents, some do only research, some only teach. Professors at universities with graduate programs are most often expected to do a good deal of research; instructors at two-year or four-year schools without graduate programs often spend more time teaching, and are not expected to do as much research.

These days, the hiring of a professor shows that he or she is special; the person has emerged as the school's choice from among a long list of applicants. Once hired, the typical professor will teach between two and four courses each term. Teaching, however, is much more than lecturing. Time must be spent preparing or updating lectures, meeting students individually, reading term papers, constructing and scoring examinations, selecting textbooks, and occasionally attending seminars to enhance one's teaching.

The professor usually must seek funding to accomplish research. The research team does not come free; its supplies and salaries are paid from grants. Small grants sometimes are not

Psychotherapy, like other forms of therapy, takes several forms. Some psychotherapists are trained in and use more than one form of therapy; they are *eclectic* psychotherapists. Others prefer a single form. The major forms of psychotherapy are psychodynamic (based on original or updated ideas that originated with Freud), behaviorist (based on or developed from Skinner's ideas), humanistic-existential (which focuses on personal growth, increased awareness of oneself, and responsibility for decisions), and neuroscientific (which focuses on biological functions, particularly brain function and dysfunction).

Psychological assessment refers to the use of carefully developed tests to understand an individual's abilities, aptitudes, personality, or distress. Psychological testing is not merely a matter of giving a test; rather, it requires a highly trained set of skills that include knowledge about how the test was developed and exactly what it measures, how to administer the test, how to score it and interpret those scores, and how to properly use and deliver the test results.

Clinical psychologists work in private practice (on their own or as part of a joint practice), in hospitals and mental health clinics, as part of government services, in work organizations, and sometimes as professors. Accreditation is an important issue in clinical psychology; when a psychological crisis strikes, we want to be sure

the person entrusted with helping is well qualified. (Accreditation is discussed later, in a separate section.)

Two specialties within clinical psychology depend on which age group is of greater interest to the practitioner. The *clinical child psychologist* serves children (and their families), and the *geropsychologist* serves elderly individuals (and their families). The clinical child psychologist must be particularly interested in children, of course, but must also be an expert in developmental psychology, because understanding children's problems requires expertise in the stages of physical, cognitive, intellectual, and moral growth. Psychological tests have been developed especially for children, and therapy must be adapted to children's needs.

Like the clinical child psychologist, the geropsychologist must have a natural affinity for the population to be assisted—in this case, old people. Advancing age brings with it joys and crises that may be like those experienced by younger people, but some are unique to this stage of life.

The Clinical Neuropsychologist

Clinical neuropsychologists specialize in the identification and treatment of the behavioral consequences of nervous system disorders and injuries (Costa, 1991). When a person sustains a brain injury in an accident or from a disorder

Clinical child psychologists often work with disabled children.

A neuropsychologist administers the formboard test, which is sensitive to certain types of brain damage.

such as Alzheimer's disease, some resulting problems are medical and some are behavioral: The person's motor, sensory, verbal, cognitive or other skills may be impaired. Because much is still not known about the workings of the brain and because medical tests such as CT or MRI scans cannot always determine the exact location and severity of the damage, clinical neuropsychologists have developed tests that identify which skills have been harmed and to what degree. For example, tests are now available that help determine whether a person is in the early stages of Alzheimer's disease or has some other disorder, long before physicians can make a diagnosis from other information.

Clinical neuropsychologists typically work in a hospital, closely associated with neurologists (physicians who specialize in diseases of the nervous system), although some teach or have private practices. In cases where medical tests cannot determine whether a patient's symptoms are caused by brain damage or dysfunction, their tests often help provide a diagnosis. They also assess the patient's deficits and remaining capabilities and help design rehabilitation programs for them. Finally, they help advise and counsel the patient's family.

The Health Psychologist

Health psychology is related to clinical psychology. The field is relatively new, but it is growing very rapidly. Health psychologists use their skills to promote and maintain health, prevent and treat illness, and identify the causes of health problems (Belar, 1991). The emphasis is on psychological factors that affect health and on psychological outcomes of poor and good health. Although some forms of medical practice have downplayed these links, more medical practitioners are coming to realize that the body and the mind are inseparably linked.

Health psychologists concentrate on the consequences of certain behaviors for one's health (for example, the dangers of smoking and overeating and the use of condoms to help prevent AIDS), how stress affects health, how persons with disease cope (or fail to cope) with their illness and pain, and how physicians can communicate better with their patients. They are employed in hospitals, health maintenance organizations, government agencies, universities, and private practice.

The School Psychologist

School psychology was among the first forms of applied psychology. This field, too, is related to clinical psychology. As the name implies, it deals with students at school. For example, most school counselors were trained as school psychologists. However, school psychologists perform many more roles than vocational guidance. They design and administer tests to assess pupils' abilities and aptitudes for different subjects, they intervene with treatment programs for children who are having behavioral problems or learning difficulties, and, when necessary, they serve as a link between the school and the family (Koe, 1991).

The school psychologist deals with all aspects of school life: learning, social relations, testing, violence, substance abuse, neglect. For example, Lightner Witmer's very first case back in 1896 was a child who had exceptional difficulty with spelling. Today common problems include the diagnosis and treatment of attention deficit disorder, in which the pupil has great difficulty concentrating on a task, and dyslexia, a severe difficulty with the perception of printed words and numbers. Many graduate programs are available to train practitioners in this well-established area of psychology.

The Sports Psychologist

The remaining types of psychologists are less concerned with relieving immediate emotional or physical pain than with helping people or organizations improve their functioning on an everyday basis. The sports psychologist, for example, does a little of both. The popular image is of someone whose goal is to help elite athletes win, but that image fits only a minority of sports psychologists.

Sports psychologists specialize in physical activities that range from children's play to adult recreation to Olympic competition. They are interested in better performance, as the popular image suggests, but also in the psychological and physical benefits of merely participating in physical activity, in the reasons for taking up a sport or staying in it, in sports violence, in the role of spectators, in what people learn from taking part in a physical activity, and in social relations among teammates (Durkin, 1991). There are sports psychologists who specialize in judo, figure skating, or fencing, as well as in the more popular sports such as track and field, football, and baseball. Whatever the sport or recreational activity, the sports psychologist aims to improve safety, performance, participation rate, and other benefits to participants.

Many techniques, such as relaxation, concentration, and visualization, are used to improve performance. Relaxation and concentration are often difficult to attain under the pressure of competition. Visualization is a pro-

One of the goals of sports psychologists is to improve the stamina and performance of athletes.

cess by which the athlete carefully imagines each step of a performance in order to help weave each step of the sequence into a seamless whole.

Sports psychology is relatively new and is less well established than the other areas of applied psychology. However, graduate programs in sports psychology do exist, and someone who has the necessary ability and motivation will probably be able to find a position in this field.

The Consumer Psychologist

The consumer psychologist helps individuals and organizations who make products or who buy or sell products or services. Consumer psychologists study the motivation, perception, learning, cognition, and purchasing behavior of individuals in the marketplace and their use of products once they reach the home (Sommer and Schutz, 1991). Advertising, promotion, marketing, and study of the behavior with products are all part of consumer psychology.

Some consumer psychologists take a marketer's perspective (especially if they work for a manufacturer), some take a consumer's perspective (especially if they work for a consumer group), and some adopt a more or less neutral perspective (especially if they work in a university). Which perspective they take influences the kinds of questions they ask and the kinds of problems they try to solve. For example, if a toy is not selling well, the consumer psychologist who works for the toy company may do a study of the public's perception of the toy and recommend that it be redesigned or marketed in a different way. The consumer psychologist employed by a consumer group may, instead, do a study of how children actually play with the toy, to see what they learn (if anything) or whether the toy promotes aggression or cooperation among playmates.

The Community Psychologist

The community psychologist is concerned with the welfare of individuals in the social system—usually, disadvantaged persons. The focus is on the quality of life in the community. Typical projects of the community psychologist include understanding and helping the homeless, investigating the relations between police and citizens, and examining the stress of street life for those who have been discharged from an institution.

In general, the community psychologist favors the modification and improvement of "the system" rather than treating the individual person as a problem (Baumann and Holahan, 1991). Thus, many community psychologists are also social activists. This does not mean that the community psychologist necessarily abandons research; rather, the goal is to use the very best research methods available to demonstrate that problems exist and to find ways to solve them.

The Environmental Psychologist

The environmental psychologist acknowledges the importance of the other forms of psychology but chooses to emphasize the relation between individuals and their built surroundings (Gifford, 1991). After all, everything we do is done in one physical setting or another. Various features of those settings (their design, lighting, noise, temperature, and crowdedness, for example) have strong influences on our thinking, social relations, health, and mood. Poorly designed buildings and streets cause considerable stress and may even be dangerous.

Thus, the environmental psychologist studies how architecture and outdoor settings can harm or hinder us. However, the positive side is also considered; how a well-designed building or park can refresh, restore, or enhance our productivity and well-being. Furthermore, the relation between people and their environments is not one-directional; as individuals, we collectively have a strong influence on the environment, too. Through the overuse and misuse of resources, our behavior can spoil nature, ruin the landscape or the soundscape, cause diseases, and even change the climate. (For instance, the projected rise in skin cancer and changes in global temperature are results of the destruction of the ozone layer by CFCs—consequences of our behavior.)

Environmental psychology is one of the newer, less established fields of applied psychology. However, it is possible to find graduate training and a position as an environmental psychologist if one feels strongly that psychologists should do something about the built and natural environments around us. As Winston Churchill once said: "First we shape the environment, and then it shapes us."

The Organizational Psychologist

One of the largest and oldest fields of applied psychology deals with the workplace. Psychologists concerned with the workplace formerly concentrated on industrial work processes (such as the most efficient way to shovel coal), but they now spend more effort analyzing the modern sociotechnological office. Everything about the workplace fascinates the organizational psychologist: hiring of personnel, measuring and defining jobs, decision making, job motivation, social relations and communication patterns on the job, enhancing work performance, accident prevention, training, leadership, labor-management relations, and the analysis and design of organizations (Coutts, 1991).

Obviously, organizational psychologists have a strong interest in and curiosity about how organizations work and how employees and organizations interact. Some typical problems they try to solve are the following: Does setting goals enhance employee performance? How can employees with drug or alcohol problems be assisted? How can employees with the potential to be good managers be identified early in their careers? How does the pattern of communication in a company affect its overall efficiency?

Most organizational psychologists are employed by large companies and organizations, but almost a third are employed in universities. Many graduate programs are available, and the main task for students is to decide which is best for them.

The Engineering Psychologist

At first glance, engineering and psychology would seem to have little in common. However, the two fields complement each other (Heron, 1991). The engineering psychologist (sometimes also called an ergonomist or human factors psychologist) mainly focuses on the ways that persons and machines work together (or fail to). The machines studied range from cockpits to computers, from robots to CD players, from transportation vehicles for the disabled to telephones.

We all deal with many machines every day; the engineering psychologist examines inferior machine designs that confuse people, make them uncomfortable or ill, or even kill them. These are the problems that engineering psychologists seek to solve. To do so, they try to apply the basic psychological processes of perception, cognition, and learning. However, instead of trying to understand these processes in themselves, they attempt to determine how machine arrangements, displays, and design suit the way humans normally see, hear, think, and move. If the machine is well designed, the task can be much easier, more enjoyable, and safer.

If it is not, using the machine will be difficult, frustrating, or even dangerous. Very often, machines work reasonably well for the engineer who designed them, but are difficult for other people to use. The credo of the engineering psychologist is that machines should be designed not merely to work but to work well for anyone who needs to use them.

The engineering psychologist is someone who loves technology but understands that machines are supposed to serve people—not the other way around. Engineering psychology is well established in technology-oriented organizations such as large manufacturers and the military. There are a reasonable number of graduate programs and career opportunities in this field.

The Lawyer-Psychologist

The last psychological speciality to be described here deals with law and criminal justice. The lawyer-psychologist examines every phase of the legal process: police-community relations, criminal investigation (when the name changes to forensic psychologist), arrest, the courtroom, jail, and parole.

Law and psychology are very different in some ways (for example, the lawyer's goal is to win the client's case at virtually any cost; the psychologist's goal is to understand how the justice process works), but the two fields still intersect in several important ways (Hofer, 1991). For example, eyewitness testimony is a crucial form of evidence in court, but psychologists have demonstrated that even well-intentioned eyewitnesses often misremember key events. Other psychologists who specialize in law help lawyers select jurors who are likely to favor their clients. Lawyer-psychologists also study the effectiveness of new technologies such as electronic monitoring devices that permit convicted persons to be at large in the community yet be monitored by prison officials. Others have compared sentences for the same offense across jurisdictions.

The ideal education for the lawyer-psychologist is a law degree and a Ph.D. in psychology. A person with such training is in the best position to understand—and have the respect of—both disciplines and to do a better job. A few graduate programs combine the two types of training, but most often the two degrees are obtained separately. Depending on the problem to be solved, a law degree may not always be necessary.

Education

To independently practice psychology today, you will need a doctoral degree (Ph.D. or Psy.D.). With less than a doctoral degree, you may still be able to help people in various ways, but your work will be supervised by a qualified psychologist. Doctoral degrees are earned after a master's degree, which is earned after a bachelor's degree. The doctoral degree takes at least four years of school after the bachelor's degree. Many individuals take seven or eight years after getting their bachelor's degree to achieve this goal because they work inside or outside their school while they learn.

Although a doctoral degree takes a long time and much effort, life does not stop while you are a graduate student (working on a master's or doctoral degree). Graduate students can engage in most normal activities that do not involve spending large sums of money. In addition, many graduate students are employed in academic jobs that are interesting and are related to their field of study.

If you are unable or unwilling to pursue a doctoral degree, you can still obtain a job that will benefit from your psychological knowledge, although you will not be able to call yourself a psychologist. With some training in psychology, but without a bachelor's degree, you may be able to work in human service fields such as social welfare, corrections, agencies serving the elderly and the disabled, group homes, crisis intervention units, community mental health centers, drug and alcohol rehabilitation centers, or early childhood education. In such positions you would be supervised by someone with more advanced training, but you would be helping people.

If you obtain a bachelor's degree, more positions will be open, but the title "psychologist" will still not be available. Typical positions for employees with a bachelor's degree in psychology include psychiatric assistant, parole officer, employment interviewer, marketing specialist, administrator, teacher, and geriatric worker.

Students who earn a master's degree (but not a Ph.D.) will begin to see parts of the word *psychology* in their title. Two positions, for example, are psychometrist (someone who administers psychological tests but does not develop the tests or conduct research with them) and psychological assistant (one who assists or works under the supervision of a doctoral-level psychologist).

Are you interested? If so, take more courses in psychology with titles that reflect the specialty you prefer—clinical, organizational, health, or environmental psychology, for example. Take developmental psychology if you are interested in the child clinical specialty; take physiological psychology if you prefer clinical neuropsychology; take psychology of aging if you think you would like to know more about geropsychology.

Other courses in psychology and other disciplines are useful in broadening your horizons. For example, social psychology is a useful basis for several specialities. Relevant courses are found outside the psychology department as well; courses in English composition (good writing skill is very important in graduate school and beyond), sociology (to understand the problems the applied psychologist will deal with from a societal perspective), biology (to gain a fuller understanding of basic physiological processes), and philosophy (to sharpen your thinking) will be useful. Also, be sure to ask your professor, instructor, or adivsor which courses are best suited for someone thinking of a career in a specific field of psychology.

Do not be alarmed if your interests within psychology change. Many students start with an interest in clinical psychology, which often reflects their admirable goal to understand themselves, their family, and their friends. But many later change their interests when they encounter an area that suits them better. If you are unsure of your career direction now, don't worry! Even if you think you are certain of your career direction, keep your options open.

Graduate school is different from undergraduate education. Generally speaking, graduate students spend much less time in class, and classes are much smaller. Much (or even most) learning is self-directed. Graduate students usually have one professor as an advisor and two or three other faculty members who serve on a committee that monitors their progress. These committees help graduate students learn more about the important people, organizations, theories, and research done in their area of psychology; how to write better; how to conduct research; and how to evaluate research done by others.

Graduate students write more papers and take fewer multiple-choice exams than undergraduates. However, most of them enjoy writing the papers, because their classes are in subjects that interest them. Doctoral students, after a year or two, take a comprehensive examination that covers a wide range of topics in their specialty. Success on this exam permits them to become formal candidates for the doctoral degree. Graduate students also undertake at least two major research projects under the watchful and supportive direction of their committee: one for the master's degree and one for the doctoral degree. How demanding are these research projects? The Ph.D. dissertation usually takes at least a year, and many students need two or more years to plan, execute, analyze, write, and defend it in an oral examination.

Very good and excellent students (roughly A- or better, especially in the last two undergraduate years) have a good expectation of receiving financial assistance in their graduate program. They may receive scholarships or fellowships that free them from working while enrolled in school. Those with grades in the B to B+ range may be accepted into a graduate program (probably not one of the top programs) and may be able to work as a teaching or research assistant to pay their way. These duties, however, will slow their progress a little, unless the research they do is directly related to their own interests. Both forms of assistance depend on the student (the best are offered more) and the school (the best are more selective in whom they assist). However, the important thing to remember is that these tasks *are* accomplished by thousands of graduate students every year.

The financial assistance that graduate students receive is generally enough to keep them at a subsistence level, but no more. They may temporarily envy friends who are earning a good income in a field that does not require an advanced degree. When they finally get that first real job, at age thirty or so, they will still be earning less than many of those friends; practicing psychologists are not likely to earn as much as their colleagues who are very successful in business. But gradually, as studies have shown, their earnings will increase until they eventually earn more than most of their friends who did not go to graduate school. Their total lifetime earnings will, despite the slow start, exceed that of many occupations.

Accreditation

Accreditation is the process by which an official organization grants professional recognition. Both psychology graduate programs (that is, courses of graduate study in universities and other institutions) and individual psychologists can be accredited. Accreditation is not always required for employment, but it is increasingly important in some specialties, in certain jobs, and in some places. For example, accreditation is an important consideration in clinical psychology. A complete list of accredited graduate programs is published every December in the *American Psychologist,* a magazine that can be found in most college libraries. More information is available from the American Psychological Association or the Canadian Psychological Association. (Their addresses are listed at the end of this appendix.) However, some nonaccredited schools offer good graduate programs, and, as noted earlier, some positions do not require training in an accredited program. Nevertheless, if you wish to become a professional in an area of psychology that has an accreditation process, your goal should be to enter an accredited program.

In a few instances earning a Ph.D. degree (even from an accredited program) is not enough to obtain the right to practice. Individuals may need to be accredited, just as programs are. There are two basic forms of individual accreditation: licensing and board certification. This topic is complex because of variations across the specialities and across the states and provinces. Also, accreditation practices are still developing—very actively in some specialties. Be aware of the fact that individual accreditation exists, but you do not need to worry about the details at this stage.

Employment

Employment prospects vary among the specialties, but on the whole they are very good. The National Science Foundation produced a special report in 1988 on employment in psychology. The report notes that in the decade prior to 1988 psychology was the third-fastest-growing scientific field in the United States (after computer and mathematical specialties). The NSF estimates that between 1986 and 2000 the growth in psychology employment will be between 27% and 39% (in comparison, its estimate for all occupations is an increase of 13% to 23%). The largest increase within psychology is expected to occur in health-related areas (between 55% and 68% growth by 2000). Psychology has always been a leader in the employment of women, and by 1986 women held 45% of all psychology positions.

The American and Canadian Psychological Associations publish several books and booklets that provide further information. Your school's psychology department or counseling center may have copies of them. Or you may write to the APA or CPA at the addresses given in the section below on membership. The APA publishes the following items:

Is Psychology the Major for You? This 137-page volume is oriented toward students who wish to make a career of psychology. It tells you what careers are available, how to find a job, how to utilize career counseling, and how to survive as a new employee.

Preparing for Graduate Study in Psychology: NOT for Seniors Only! This 96-page sourcebook discusses how to plan the steps needed for graduate school, with an emphasis on students who do not have the "credentials" yet. It provides help on acquiring recommendations, writing resumes, practicing interviews and the like.

Graduate Study in Psychology and Associated Fields. This book is a comprehensive guide (over 600 pages) to graduate programs in the United States and Canada. It indicates which schools offer which specialties and discusses admission requirements, housing facilities, financial assistance, tuition, and so on.

Careers in Psychology. This brief (28-page) pamphlet describes the fields of and careers in psychology. Single copies are free to students.

The Canadian Psychological Association publishes the following book:

Graduate Guide: Description of Graduate Psychology Programs in Canadian Universities.

MEMBERSHIPS

You can join a national organization as a student affiliate. APA's annual fee for students is $25, for which you get (1) discounts on books published by APA, (2) lower prices on APA journal subscriptions, (3) the *APA Monitor* (the organization's monthly newspaper), and (4) the *American Psychologist* (its official journal) at no extra cost. Its address is 750 First Street, N. E., Washington, D.C. 20002.

The Canadian Psychological Association's student membership is only $10, for which you receive news in the field and journals. CPA's address is Vincent Road, Old Chelsea, Quebec J0X 2N0.

Another organization of interest is the International Association of Applied Psychology. This worldwide group was formed in 1920 and it holds congresses every four years The IAAP has ten divisions: organizational psychology; psychological assessment; psychology and national development; environmental psychology; educational, instruction, and school psychology; clinical and community psychology; applied gerontology; health psychology; economic psychology; and psychology and law. For more information, contact Dr. Harry C. Triandis, 603 East Daniel Street, Champaign, Illinois 61820.

GLOSSARY

absolute threshold The minimum value of a stimulus that can be detected.

accommodation 1. According to Jean Piaget, the process by which a child's behavioral schemas are altered by interaction with the environment. 2. Changes in the thickness of the lens of the eye, accomplished by the ciliary muscles, that focus images of near or distant objects on the retina.

acetylcholine A transmitter substance released by the terminal buttons of some neurons in the brain and peripheral nervous system. Acetylcholine is the transmitter substance that causes muscles to contract, and acetylcholine-secreting neurons in the brain appear to be involved in memory.

achromatopsia The inability to discriminate among different hues; caused by damage to the visual association cortex.

action potential A brief electrochemical event that is carried by an axon from the cell body of the neuron to its terminal buttons, which in turn release a transmitter substance, stimulating or inhibiting the neurons with which the terminal buttons form synapses.

activational effect (of hormone) The effect of a hormone on a physiological system that is already developed, as contrasted with an organizational effect, which influences prenatal or early postnatal development. If the effect involves the brain, it can influence behavior. Examples include breast growth, beard growth, and facilitation of sexual arousal and performance.

actuarial judgment A diagnosis of mental disorders or predictions of future behavior based on numerical formulas derived from analyses of prior outcomes.

adrenal gland An endocrine gland located just above the kidney, which secretes several kinds of hormones, including the sex hormones androstenedione and testosterone.

adrenocorticotropic hormone (ACTH) A hormone released by the anterior pituitary gland that causes the adrenal glands to secrete their hormones. See *corticosterone.*

affix A sound or group of letters that is added to the beginning of a word (prefix) or its end (suffix).

agoraphobia A mental disorder; fear of and avoidance of being alone in public places. Often accompanied by panic attacks.

agrammatism A language disturbance; difficulty in the production and comprehension of grammatical features, such as proper use of function words, word endings, and word order. Often seen in cases of Broca's aphasia.

alpha activity Rhythmical activity of the electroencephalogram with a frequency between 8 and 12 cycles per second, usually indicating a state of quiet relaxation.

Alzheimer's disease A degenerative illness in which neurons of the cerebral cortex die. The result is loss of memory and other cognitive processes and ultimately death.

amnesia A loss of memory for events that should normally be subject to recall.

amniotic sac A membrane filled with amniotic fluid that surrounds and protects the mammalian fetus.

amygdala A part of the limbic system of the brain located deep in the temporal lobe; damage causes changes in emotional and aggressive behavior.

anal stage According to Freud, the second stage of psychosexual development, during which the infant obtains gratification by passing or retaining feces.

anatomical coding A means of representing information by the nervous system; different features are coded by the activity of different neurons. For example, in the auditory system each pitch of moderate to high frequency is represented by the activity of a different set of neurons.

androgen The primary class of sex hormones in males. The most important androgen is testosterone.

animism A primitive belief that all animals, or even all moving objects, possessed spirits providing their motive force.

anorexia nervosa An eating disorder characterized by attempts to lose weight, sometimes to the point of starvation.

anterograde amnesia The inability to learn new information permanently; usually caused by brain damage resulting from chronic alcoholism or head injury. The person can typically remember information that was learned long before the injury and has an adequate short-term memory but cannot form long-term memories.

antianxiety drug A "tranquilizer," which reduces anxiety. The most common include chlordiazepoxide (Librium) and diazepam (Valium).

antibody A protein that recognizes antigens and helps kill invading microorganisms.

anticipatory anxiety A fear of having a panic attack; may lead to the development of agoraphobia.

antidepressant drugs Drugs used to treat psychotic depression, one of the affective disorders. Tricyclic antidepressant drugs, such as imipramine, are used to treat major depression; lithium carbonate is used to treat bipolar disorder.

antigen A protein found on the surface of an invading microorganism.

antipsychotic drugs Drugs used to eliminate or reduce the positive symptoms of schizophrenia, including hallucinations, delusions, and thought disorders; examples include chlorpromazine (Thorazine) and haloperidol (Haldol). The drugs apparently work by blocking dopamine receptors in the brain.

antisocial personality disorder A personality disorder characterized by a consistent pattern of such behaviors as truancy, delinquency, lying, promiscuity, drunkenness or substance abuse, theft, vandalism, and fighting.

anxiety A vague, uneasy fearfulness.

anxiety disorder A psychological disorder characterized by tension, overactivity of the autonomic nervous system, expectation of an impending disaster, and continuous vigilance for danger.

anxiolytic effect The anxiety-reducing effect of a drug.

aphasia A language disturbance caused by brain damage that manifests itself in various deficits of speech production or comprehension.

appeasement gesture A stereotyped gesture made by a submissive animal in response to a threat gesture by a dominant animal; tends to inhibit an attack.

appetitive stimulus A stimulus that an organism will attempt to approach; can be used to reinforce a response.

applied psychology A branch of psychology that applies principles discovered through research to solving practical problems.

artificial intelligence A field of study in which computer programs are designed to simulate human perception, learning, or problem solving, with the expectation that the details of such programs will help the investigator understand the nature of the relevant human brain mechanisms.

assimilation According to Jean Piaget, the process by which a new concept comes to elicit a child's behavioral schema.

association cortex Those regions of cortex that receive information from the sensory areas (sensory association cortex) or that project to the primary motor cortex (motor association cortex); plays an important role in perception, learning, and planning.

attachment The process by which parent (or caregiver) and child form a mutually reinforcing system.

attention Readiness to respond to stimuli. Selective attention involves readiness to respond to certain categories of stimuli or to stimuli in a particular location.

attribution Assigning a cause to an event, including a person's behavior, or assigning a personality characteristic to a person. Attributions can apply to others or to oneself.

auditory hair cell The receptive neuron of the auditory system; located on the basilar membrane.

autoimmune disease A disease in which the immune system attacks and damages some of the body's own tissue. Examples include multiple sclerosis, diabetes mellitus, and rheumatoid arthritis.

autonomic nervous system (ANS) The portion of the peripheral nervous system that controls the body's vegetative function. The *sympathetic division* mediates functions that accompany arousal; the *parasympathetic division* mediates functions that occur during a relaxed state.

availability heuristic See under *heuristic*.

aversive classical conditioning A form of behavior therapy in which unpleasant conditioned responses are established to stimuli that produced undesired behaviors.

aversive stimulus A stimulus that an organism will attempt to avoid or escape; can be used either to punish or to negatively reinforce a response.

avoidance response The performance of a response that prevents an aversive stimulus from occurring. See also *escape response*.

avoidant attachment A form of a child's attachment to its mother (or primary caregiver), as determined by the Strange Situation; the child avoids contact with the mother.

axon A long, thin process of a neuron that divides into a few or many branches, ending in terminal buttons. See also *action potential*.

backward masking The ability of a stimulus to interfere with the perception of a stimulus presented before it.

Balint's syndrome A syndrome caused by bilateral damage to the parieto-occipital region; includes difficulty in reaching for objects under visual guidance, difficulty in visual scanning, and difficulty in perceiving more than one object at a time.

barbiturate A drug that causes sedation; one of several derivatives of barbituric acid.

base-rate fallacy The tendency to overemphasize personal encounters and ignore statistical information in making decisions.

basic-level concept See under *concept*.

basilar membrane A membrane that divides the cochlea of the inner ear into two compartments. The receptive organ for audition resides here.

behaviorism A movement in psychology that asserts that the only proper subject matter for scientific study in psychology is observable behavior.

behavior therapy A method for treating abnormal behavior and mental disorders based on identifying inappropriate, maladaptive behaviors and replacing them with adaptive ones; utilizes the principles of instrumental and classical conditioning.

benzodiazepine A class of drug with anxiolytic ("tranquilizing") effects; examples are Librium and Valium.

beta activity The irregular, high-frequency activity of the electroencephalogram, usually indicating a state of alertness or arousal.

Binet-Simon Scale An intelligence test developed by Binet and Simon in 1905; the precursor of the Stanford Binet Scale.

bipolar cell A neuron in the retina that receives information from photoreceptors and passes it on to the ganglion cells, from which axons proceed through the optic nerves to the brain.

bipolar disorder A serious affective disorder characterized by alternating periods of mania and depression; a form of psychosis.

B lymphocyte A white blood cell produced in the bone marrow; part of the immune system.

bottom-up processing A perception based on successive analyses of the details of the stimuli present. See also *top-down processing*.

brain lesion Damage to a particular region of the brain.

brain stem The "stem" of the brain, including the medulla, pons, midbrain, and diencephalon (thalamus and hypothalamus). The cerebral hemispheres and cerebellum are not part of the brain stem.

brightness A perceptual dimension of color, most closely related to the intensity or degree of radiant energy emitted by a visual stimulus.

brightness constancy The tendency to perceive objects as having constant brightness even when they are observed under varying levels of illumination.

Broca's aphasia Severe difficulty in articulating words, especially function words, caused by damage to *Broca's area*, a region of the frontal cortex on the left (speech-dominant) side of the brain.

Broca's area   See *Broca's aphasia.*

bulimia   Periodic "binging"—excessive intake of food, often followed by forced vomiting or the use of laxatives; often accompanies anorexia nervosa.

bystander intervention   The intervention of a person in a situation that appears to require his or her aid.

case study   The observation of the behavior of particular individuals, as opposed to studies of groups; primarily encountered in studies of people with mental or neurological disorders.

cataplexy   A form of narcolepsy in which the person collapses, becoming temporarily paralyzed but not unconscious; usually triggered by anger or excitement; apparently related to the paralysis that normally accompanies REM sleep.

catatonic posture   A bizarre, stationary pose maintained by a patient with catatonic schizophrenia.

catatonic schizophrenia   A form of schizophrenia in which a person remains immobile, often in bizarre postures, or exhibits wild hyperactivity.

catharsis   According to Freud, the release, through relatively harmless means such as symbolic aggression or vigorous sports, of energy from a drive that might otherwise result in undesirable behavior.

causal event   An event that causes another event to occur.

central nervous system   The brain and spinal cord.

cerebellum   A pair of hemispheres resembling the cerebral hemispheres but much smaller and lying beneath and in back of them; controls posture and movements, especially rapid ones.

cerebral cortex   The outer layer of the cerebral hemispheres of the brain. Specialized areas include the primary sensory and motor cortex, the association cortex, and regions necessary for speech comprehension and production.

cerebral hemisphere   One of the two major portions of the forebrain, covered by the cerebral cortex.

child-directed speech   The speech of an adult directed toward a child; differs in important features from adult-directed speech; tends to facilitate learning of language by children.

chlorpromazine   A drug used to reduce or eliminate the symptoms of schizophrenia; blocks dopamine receptors.

chunking   The process by which information is simplified by rules and hence can be remembered easily once the rules are learned. For example, the sequence 1 3 5 7 9 11 13 15 is easy to remember if a person knows the rule that describes odd numbers.

cilium   A hairlike appendage of a cell; involved in movement or in transducing sensory information. Cilia are found on the receptors in the auditory and vestibular system.

cingulectomy   The destruction of the cingulum bundle, which connects the prefrontal cortex with parts of the limbic system; helps reduce intense anxiety and the symptoms of obsessive compulsive disorder.

classical conditioning   The process by which a defensive response or appetitive response, normally produced automatically by an eliciting stimulus, comes to be produced by a previously neutral stimulus. The previously neutral stimulus is followed shortly by an eliciting stimulus (unconditioned stimulus) that normally produces the response (unconditioned response) and becomes, after several pairings, a conditioned stimulus producing the conditioned response.

client-centered therapy   Carl Rogers's therapeutic method of treating mental disorders and disturbances of adjustment by providing unconditioned positive regard for the client, which permits the person's natural tendency to be healthy and productive to express itself.

clinical judgment   A diagnosis of mental disorders or predictions of future behavior by an expert based on his or her experience.

clinical psychology   The branch of psychology devoted to the investigation and treatment of abnormal behavior and mental disorders.

cochlea   A snail-shaped chamber set in bone in the inner ear, where audition takes place. See also *basilar membrane.*

cognition   The process by which individuals get to know things about themselves and their world; involves perception, learning, thinking, reasoning, and so on.

cognitive behavior therapy   A method for treating abnormal behavior and mental disorders; similar to behav-

ior therapy but emphasizes unobservable cognitive processes as well as directly observable behaviors.

cognitive disequilibrium   According to Piaget, a state produced by unexpected feedback from the environment; leads to the acquisition of new concepts and behavioral schemas.

cognitive dissonance   An unpleasant state of tension caused when a disparity exists between a person's beliefs or attitudes and behavior, especially beliefs or attitudes that are related to one's self-esteem.

cognitive psychology   A branch of psychology that deals with perception, learning and memory, concept formation, verbal behavior, and problem solving, especially of humans. Unlike behaviorism, cognitive psychology deals with unobservable mental processes that presumably are composed of particular brain functions.

cognitive restructuring   A procedure used by cognitive behavior therapists to change maladaptive patterns of cognition they believe underlie maladaptive patterns of clients' behavior.

cognitive structure   According to Piaget, the rules used for understanding and dealing with the world and for thinking about and solving problems.

color mixing   The perception of two or more lights of different wavelengths seen together as light of an intermediate wavelength.

comparative psychology   The branch of psychology that studies the behaviors of a variety of organisms, in an attempt to understand the adaptive and functional significance of the behaviors and their relation to evolution.

complementary colors   Colors that, when mixed, will produce a neutral hue (white or shades of gray). A negative afterimage is complementary to the color to which the eye was exposed.

componential intelligence   According to Sternberg, the mental mechanisms people use to plan and execute tasks; includes metacomponents, performance components, and knowledge acquisition components.

compromise formation   According to Freud, the process by which the demands of the instinctual drive are reconciled with the suppressive effects of internalized prohibitions.

compulsion   The feeling that one is obliged to perform a behavior, even if one prefers not to do so.

concept A category of objects or situations that share some common attributes. *Basic-level concepts* are distinguished from each other by the most important distinctions, *superordinate concepts* only by the most elementary distinctions, and *subordinate concepts* by the most detailed distinctions.

conditioned emotional response A classically conditioned response produced by an unconditioned stimulus that evokes an emotional response—in most cases, including behavioral and physiological components.

conditioned flavor aversion The process by which a particular flavor, followed by an unpleasant reaction such as illness, results in the organism's avoiding the stimulus.

conditioned punishment A process by which a previously neutral stimulus followed by an aversive stimulus itself becomes capable, through classical conditioning, of punishing a response.

conditioned reinforcement A process by which a previously neutral stimulus followed by an appetitive stimulus itself becomes capable, through classical conditioning, of reinforcing a response.

conditioned response (CR) After classical conditioning, the response elicited by the conditioned stimulus.

conditioned stimulus (CS) After classical conditioning, the stimulus that elicits the conditioned response, which resembles the unconditioned response.

conduction aphasia An inability to repeat words that are heard, although they can usually be understood and responded to appropriately; results from damage to the connections between Wernicke's area and Broca's area.

cone One of the photoreceptors in the retina; responsible for acute daytime vision and for color perception. See also *rod*.

confirmation bias A tendency to seek evidence that might confirm a hypothesis rather than evidence that might disconfirm it; a logical error.

confounding of variables An inadvertent alteration of more than one independent variable during an experiment. The results of an experiment with confounded independent variables permit no valid conclusions about cause and effect.

conjugate eye movement The cooperative movement of the eyes, which ensures that the image of an object falls on identical portions of both retinas.

conscience According to Freud, an internalization of the rules and restrictions of society, which determines which behaviors are permissible.

consensual behavior In attribution theory, a behavior that is also being performed by other people. A high level of consensus suggests that the behaviors are caused by external events.

conservation The tendency to perceive quantities, mass, and volume as remaining constant even if elements are moved or the shape of the substance is changed. According to Piaget, this is an important cognitive concept.

consistency The tendency to act in similar ways to a particular situation on different occasions. In attribution theory high consistency suggests that the behavior is caused by dispositional factors.

consolidation The process by which information in short-term memory is stored in long-term memory, presumably in the form of physical changes in neurons in the brain.

content reward According to Buss, a social stimulus that consists of bipolar dimensions; one end is reinforcing and the other is aversive.

content word A noun, verb, adjective, or adverb that conveys meaning. See also *function word*.

contextual intelligence According to Sternberg, consists of three forms: *adaptation*—fitting oneself into one's environment by developing useful skills and behaviors; *selection*—finding one's own niche in the environment; and *shaping*—changing the environment.

contingency An event that occurs only when certain conditions are fulfilled. If an appetitive stimulus is contingent on a particular behavior, the frequency of that behavior will usually increase.

continuous reinforcement schedule A schedule whereby every occurrence of a particular response is followed by presentation of the reinforcer.

contralateral Residing in the side of the body opposite to the reference point.

control group A comparison group used in an experiment, the members of which are exposed to the naturally occurring or zero value of the independent variable.

convergence The result of conjugate eye movements whereby the fixation point for each eye is identical.

conversion According to Freud, the transformation of an intrapsychic conflict into a physical symptom.

conversion disorder A psychological disorder in which a person experiences physical symptoms such as anesthesia, paralysis, or illness without organic cause; a type of somatoform disorder.

coping response A response that permits an animal to escape, avoid, or minimize the stressful (harmful or painful) effects of an aversive stimulus.

cornea The transparent tissue covering the front of the eye.

corpus callosum A large bundle of axons ("white matter") that connects the cortex of the two cerebral hemispheres.

correctional mechanism In a regulatory process, the mechanism that is capable of changing the value of the system variable.

correlation coefficient A measurement of the degree to which two variables are related. A correlation of zero indicates no relation; perfect relation is ± 1.0. A negative correlation indicates that large values of one variable are associated with small values of the other one.

corticosterone A hormone secreted by the adrenal gland; part of the stress response.

counterbalancing A systematic variation of conditions in an experiment, such as the order of presentation of stimuli or tasks, so that different subjects encounter the conditions in different orders. It prevents confounding of independent variables by eliminating the effects of time-dependent processes such as habituation or fatigue.

countertransference The projection of a psychoanalyst's feelings toward the client or, more generally, his or her emotional involvement in the therapeutic interaction; an undesirable phenomenon.

covert sensitization A method used by cognitive behavior therapists in which a person imagines aversive consequences of his or her inappropriate behavior.

CR See *conditioned response (CR)*.

criterion An independent measure of a

variable being assessed. For example, college grades are the criterion measure for scores on the Scholastic Aptitude Test.

criterion group A group of subjects whose behavior is used to validate a psychological test. For example, if people diagnosed by other means as extraverted tend to receive higher scores than randomly selected people on a test of extraversion, the test receives support as being valid.

critical period A time in development during which certain events must take place in order for normal development to occur.

cross-sectional study The observation of the behavior of people of different ages at approximately the same time. See also *longitudinal study.*

cross-situational consistency The consistent behavior of an individual in similar situations.

crystallized intelligence According to Raymond Cattell, that part of a person's intellectual abilities that accumulates through experience. See also *fluid intelligence.*

CS See *conditioned stimulus (CS).*

CT scanner A device that uses a special X-ray machine and a computer to produce images of the brain that appear as slices taken parallel to the top of the skull. Also called *CAT scanner.*

cyclothymic disorder A mental disorder similar to bipolar disorder but less severe.

dark adaptation The process by which the eye becomes capable of distinguishing dimly illuminated objects after going from a bright region to a dark one. This process involves chemical changes in the photoreceptors of the retina.

deductive reasoning Inferring specific instances from general principles or rules.

deep processing The study of complex characteristics of a stimulus, such as its meaning.

deep structure The essential meaning of a sentence, without regard to the grammatical features (surface structure) of the sentence that are needed to express it in words. See also *surface structure.*

defense mechanism According to Freud, one of several methods by which the ego protects itself from conflicts between the conscience and instinctual drives.

defensive reflex An innate, automatic response that tends to protect an organism from a potentially dangerous stimulus, usually by moving the threatened part away from it.

delay of gratification The ability to forgo a reinforcer in order to receive an even more desirable one later.

delta activity The rhythmical activity of the electroencephalogram, a recording of the brain's activity, with a frequency between 3 and 5 cycles per second, indicating deep (slow-wave) sleep.

delusion A belief that is held even though evidence or logic shows it to be false. Delusions are important symptoms of psychoses. A delusion of control is a false belief that one's thoughts and behaviors are being controlled by other people or other forces; a delusion of grandeur, that one is famous, powerful, or important; and a delusion of persecution, that other people conspire to harm or thwart one.

dendrite A treelike part of a neuron on which the terminal buttons of other neurons form synapses.

dependent variable The event that is observed in an experiment. Manipulation of independent variables demonstrates whether or not they affect the value of dependent variables.

depression A state of extreme sadness, usually characterized by slow thoughts and movements, but sometimes characterized by restless agitation. Psychotic depression includes major depression and the depressed phase of bipolar disorder; less serious (neurotic) depression includes dysthymic disorder.

descriptive statistics Mathematical procedures for organizing collections of data, such as mean, median, range, variance, and correlation coefficient.

detector In a regulatory process, a mechanism that signals when the system variable deviates from its set point.

deuteranopia A form of hereditary anomalous color vision, resulting from defective "green" cones in the retina.

developmental approach An approach to the study of intelligence that focuses on the development of cognitive abilities during childhood.

developmental dyslexia A specific learning disability in reading that is not caused by head injury or disease of the central nervous system; occurs in children, probably as a result of abnormal development of some systems of the brain.

developmental psychology The branch of psychology that studies the changes in behavioral, perceptual, and cognitive capacities of organisms as a function of age and experience.

deviation IQ A procedure for computing the intelligence quotient; compares a child's score with those received by other children of the same chronological age.

Diagnostic and Statistical Manual III-R (DSM-III-R) The system and manual developed by the American Psychiatric Association that provide specific criteria for the diagnosis of mental disorders.

dichotic listening A task that requires a person to listen to one of two different messages being presented simultaneously to each ear through headphones.

difference threshold An alternate name for *just-noticeable difference.* See *just-noticeable difference (jnd).*

differential approach An approach to the study of intelligence that focuses on the characterization of the ways in which people differ from each other in their knowledge and ability to solve problems.

differential classical conditioning A discrimination procedure whereby one stimulus (the CS^+) is followed by the unconditioned stimulus but another stimulus (the CS^-) never is. Eventually, the organism makes conditioned responses only when the CS^+ is presented.

differentiation The process by which the cells of a developing organism begin to differ and give rise to the various organs of the body.

discrimination The detection of differences between two stimuli or of a change in a stimulus, as shown by changes in an organism's behavior.

discriminative stimulus A stimulus that is associated with the occurrence or nonoccurrence of an appetitive or aversive stimulus; serves as a basis for instrumental conditioning.

disorganized schizophrenia A serious form of schizophrenia characterized by incoherent speech and inappropriate affect.

display rule A culturally determined rule that modifies the expression of emotion in a particular situation.

dispositional factor A cause of behavior that is related to one's personality characteristics and preferences. See also *situational factor*.

dissociative disorder A category of mental disorders that includes such disturbances as amnesia not caused by brain dysfunction, fugue, and multiple personality.

dissonance reduction The resolution of a state of cognitive dissonance, accomplished through adding consonant elements that explain away the conflict, reducing the importance of one of the dissonant elements, or changing one of the dissonant elements.

distinctive feature A characteristic of an object or a concept that helps distinguish it from other objects or concepts.

distinctiveness The tendency to act in a particular way only in a particular situation. In attribution theory high distinctiveness suggests that the behaviors are caused by external events (situational factors).

doctrine of specific nerve energies Johannes Müller's observation that different nerve fibers convey specific information from one part of the body to the brain or from the brain to one part of the body.

dopamine A transmitter substance released by the terminal buttons of some neurons in the brain. Dopamine is apparently important in reinforcement and control of movement. Dopamine-secreting neurons may be involved in producing schizophrenia.

dopamine hypothesis The hypothesis that the positive symptoms of schizophrenia are caused by overactivity of certain synapses in the brain that use dopamine as a transmitter substance.

double-blind method An experimental procedure in which the subjects and experimenter do not know the value of the independent variable for a particular subject. See also *single-blind method*.

Down syndrome A disorder caused by the presence of an extra twenty-first chromosome, characterized by moderate to severe mental retardation and often by physical abnormalities; previously called *mongolism*.

drive A condition, often caused by physiological changes or homeostatic disequilibrium, that energizes an organism's behavior.

drive reduction hypothesis The hypothesis that a drive (resulting from physiological need or deprivation) produces an unpleasant state that causes an organism to engage in motivated behaviors. Reduction of drive is assumed to be reinforcing.

DSM-III-R See *Diagnostic and Statistical Manual III-R (DSM-III-R)*.

dualism The philosophical belief that humans consist of physical bodies and nonmaterial minds or souls.

dyslexia An unusual difficulty in reading, caused by developmental factors or by brain injury.

echoic memory A form of sensory memory for sounds that have just been perceived.

ECT See *electroconvulsive therapy (ECT)*.

EEG See *electroencephalogram (EEG)*.

ego According to Freud, the structure of the mind that possesses memory and mediates the drives of the id and the internalized prohibitions of the superego.

egocentrism The tendency of young children to perceive the world solely in terms relative to themselves.

ego-ideal According to Freud, an internalization of the kind of person an individual would like to be.

EKG See *electrocardiogram (EKG)*.

elaborative rehearsal The rehearsal of verbal information by actively constructing stories that link the items together.

Electra complex According to Freud (but later dismissed by him), the desire of a girl to replace her mother as the object of her father's affections.

electrocardiogram (EKG) The measurement and graphical presentation of the electrical activity of the heart, recorded by means of electrodes attached to the skin.

electroconvulsive therapy (ECT) The induction of a seizure by passing a brief surge of electricity through a person's head; used to treat severe psychotic depression. Also called *electroshock treatment*.

electroencephalogram (EEG) The measurement and graphical presentation of the electrical activity of the brain, recorded by means of electrodes attached to the scalp.

electromyogram (EMG) The measurement and graphical presentation of the electrical activity of muscles, recorded by means of electrodes at-

tached to the skin above them.

electro-oculogram (EOG) The measurement and graphical presentation of the electrical activity caused by movements of the eye, recorded by means of electrodes attached to the skin adjacent to the eye.

electroshock treatment See *electroconvulsive therapy (ECT)*.

elevation One of the cues of depth perception; objects nearer the horizon are seen as farther from the viewer.

EMG See *electromyogram (EMG)*.

emotion The effects of the presence of a situation that is important to the organism. The term can refer to physiological and behavioral responses or to the feelings they evoke.

empirical strategy The development of psychological tests by presenting a variety of more or less randomly assembled items to a criterion group. Items that are regularly answered in one way by members of the criterion group are retained; the others are discarded.

empiricism The philosophical view that all knowledge is obtained through the senses.

endocrine gland A gland that secretes a hormone into the blood supply; for example, the adrenal gland and pituitary gland.

endorphin A chemical secreted by neurons in the brain that produces analgesia and has reinforcing effects. The action of these chemicals is simulated by opiates such as morphine and heroin.

enzyme A protein that serves as a biological catalyst, breaking certain molecules apart or causing certain molecules to be joined together.

EOG See *electro-oculogram (EOG)*.

episodic memory Memory for specific information, including the time and place in which it was first learned. See also *semantic memory*.

escape response The performance of a response that terminates an aversive stimulus. See also *avoidance response*.

estradiol The primary estrogen in mammals.

estrogen The principal class of sex hormones in females.

estrous cycle The ovulatory cycle in mammals other than primates; the sequence of physical and hormonal changes that accompany the ripening and disintegration of ova.

exemplar A memory of particular examples of objects or situations that are used as the basis of classifying objects or situations into concepts.

experiential intelligence According to Sternberg, the ability to deal effectively with novel situations and to automatically solve problems that have been encountered previously.

experimental ablation The removal or destruction of a portion of the brain of an experimental animal for the purpose of studying the functions of that region. Presumably, the functions that can no longer be performed are the ones the region previously controlled.

experimental neuropsychologist A psychologist who attempts to understand human brain functions by studying patients whose brains have been damaged through accident or disease.

experimental psychologist A general term for a psychologist who attempts to understand the causes of behavior by performing experiments.

explicit memory Memory that can be described verbally and of which a person is therefore conscious. See also *implicit memory.*

expressed emotion An expression of criticism, hostility, and emotional overinvolvement by family members toward a patient with schizophrenia.

extinction The reduction or elimination of a behavior caused by ceasing the presentation of the reinforcing stimulus.

extraversion A personality trait; the tendency to seek the company of other people and to engage in conversation and other social behaviors with them.

eye tracker A device that measures the location of a person's fixation point while observing a visual display.

face validity The appearance that a method of measuring or manipulating a variable is valid; a measure of "reasonableness," rather than one that can be objectively determined.

factor analysis A statistical technique involving study of the correlations among a large number of items in order to determine whether some common factors are responsible for the patterns of correlation.

factor loading A value derived from a factor analysis; specifies the degree a particular item is related to a factor.

false consensus The tendency of an observer to perceive his or her own response as representative of a general consensus.

fetal alcohol syndrome A disorder that adversely affects a child's brain development; caused by the mother's alcohol intake during pregnancy.

fetishism A disorder in which a person receives primary sexual stimulation and gratification from a class of inanimate objects or situations.

fight-or-flight response A physiological reaction that prepares an organism for the efforts required by fighting or fleeing.

figure A visual stimulus that is perceived as a self-contained object.

FI schedule See *fixed-interval (FI) schedule.*

five-factor model A model of personality devised by McCrae and Costa; includes the traits of neuroticism, extraversion, openness, agreeableness, and conscientiousness.

fixation 1. According to Freud, the arresting of psychosexual development in a particular stage. 2. A brief interval between saccadic eye movements during which the eye does not move; visual information is gathered during this time.

fixed-interval (FI) schedule A schedule of reinforcement in which the first response that is emitted after a fixed interval of time since the previous reinforcement (or the start of the session) is reinforced.

fixed-ratio (FR) schedule A schedule of reinforcement in which reinforcement occurs only after a fixed number of responses have been emitted since the previous reinforcement (or the start of the session).

flashbulb memory Memory of an episode that occurred at a time of intense emotional turmoil.

fluid intelligence According to Cattell, the component of general intellectual ability that determines how likely a person is to profit from experience (that is, to develop crystallized intelligence).

form constancy The tendency to perceive objects as having a constant form, even when they are rotated or moved farther from or closer to the observer.

fovea A small pit near the center of the retina containing densely packed cones; responsible for the most acute and detailed vision.

free association The method of psychoanalysis in which the client is encouraged to say whatever comes to his

or her mind; presumably, the statements will express deep-seated anxieties and conflicts.

free nerve ending An unencapsulated (naked) dendrite of somatosensory neurons.

frontal lobe The front portion of the cerebral cortex, including Broca's speech area and the motor cortex; damage impairs movement, planning, and flexibility in behavioral strategies.

FR schedule See *fixed-ratio (FR) schedule.*

frustration The prevention of an expected appetitive stimulus; said to result in aggression.

functionalism The strategy of understanding a species' structural or behavioral features by attempting to establish their usefulness with respect to survival or reproductive success.

function word A preposition, article, or other word that conveys little of the meaning of a sentence but is important in specifying its grammatical structure. See also *content word.*

fundamental attributional error The tendency to overestimate the importance of personality traits and underestimate the importance of situational variables as causes of other people's behavior.

fundamental frequency The lowest, and usually most intense, frequency of a complex sound; most often perceived as the sound's basic pitch.

gamete A germ cell; a sperm or ovum.

ganglion cell A neuron in the retina that receives information from photoreceptors by means of bipolar cells, and from which axons proceed through the optic nerves to the brain.

gene The functional unit of the chromosome; contains the information that cells need to produce proteins, which serve structural purposes or operate as enzymes. Genes encode the instructions for development of an organism and for control of its maintenance and functions.

generalization An organism's tendency, once it has learned to perform a specific behavior when one stimulus is present, to perform that behavior when a similar stimulus is present.

genital stage According to Freud, the final stage of psychosexual development, during which a person receives gratification through genital sexual contact with a person of the opposite sex.

geon According to Biederman, an elementary shape that can serve as a prototype in recognizing more complex shapes, which can be perceived as constructions of one or more individual geons.

Gestalt psychology A branch of psychology that asserts that in perception the whole is more than the sum of its parts; perceptions are produced by particular configurations of the elements of stimuli.

g factor According to Spearman, a factor of intelligence that is common to all intellectual tasks; includes apprehension of experience, eduction of relations, and eduction of correlates.

glucocorticoid A steroid hormone secreted during times of stress by the cortex of the adrenal gland.

glucostat A neuron that responds to the presence and availability of glucose in the fluid surrounding it; plays a role in measuring the body's nutrient supplies and in controlling eating.

glucostatic hypothesis The hypothesis that hunger is caused by a low level or availability of glucose, a condition that is monitored by specialized sensory neurons.

glycogen An insoluble carbohydrate that can be synthesized from glucose or converted to it; used to store nutrients.

good continuation See *Figure 5.9.*

gray matter The portions of the central nervous system that are abundant in cell bodies of neurons rather than axons. See also *white matter.*

ground A visual stimulus that is perceived as a formless background against which objects are seen.

gustation The sense of taste.

gyrus A bulge in the surface of the cerebral hemispheres; located between adjacent grooves (fissures or sulci).

habituation The gradual elimination of an unconditioned response (especially an orienting response) by the repeated presentation of the unconditioned stimulus. Habituation will not occur to especially noxious stimuli.

hallucination The perception of stimuli that are not actually present; an important positive symptom of schizophrenia.

haze One of the cues of depth perception; objects that are less distinct in their outline and texture are seen as farther from the viewer.

hebephrenic schizophrenia The obsolete term for *disorganized schizophrenia.*

heritability The degree to which the variability of a particular trait in a particular population of organisms is a result of genetic differences among those organisms.

hertz (Hz) The primary measure of the frequency of vibration of sound waves; cycles per second.

heuristic A general rule that guides decision making. The *availability heuristic* describes people's tendency to pay most attention to information they can easily think of or remember. The *representativeness heuristic* refers to the tendency to believe that if some characteristics are observed, other characteristics that often go with them are present also.

hidden observer According to Hilgard, a part of the mind that can comment on memories or perceptions of which a hypnotized person is unaware.

hippocampus A component structure of the limbic system of the brain, located in the temporal lobe; plays important roles in learning.

homeostasis The process by which important physiological characteristics (such as body temperature and blood pressure) are regulated so that they remain at their optimum level.

hormone A chemical secreted by an endocrine gland, which circulates through the blood and affects the growth or activity of cells located elsewhere in the body.

hue A perceptual dimension of color, most closely related to the wavelength of a pure light. The effect of a particular hue is caused by the mixture of lights of various wavelengths.

hypnagogic hallucination The perception of nonexistent objects and events just before sleep; a symptom of narcolepsy; presumably a premature dream.

hypochondriasis A psychological disorder characterized by excessive concern and preoccupation with one's health, along with frequent fears of suffering from serious illness.

hypothalamus A region of the brain located just above the pituitary gland; controls the autonomic nervous system and many behaviors related to regulation and survival, such as eating, drinking, fighting, shivering, and sweating.

hypothesis A statement, usually designed to be tested by an experiment, that expresses a tentative causal relationship between variables.

Hz See *hertz (Hz).*

iconic memory A form of sensory memory that holds a brief visual image of a scene that has just been perceived.

id One of Freud's three divisions of the mind (along with the ego and superego); contains the instinctual drives.

illusory contours A contour perceived where there is none in the physical stimulus. See *Figure 5.6.*

illusory correlation Seeing a relation between two distinctive elements that does not actually exist; one of the causes of social discrimination.

immunoglobulin An antibody produced by a B lymphocyte.

implicit memory Memory that cannot be described verbally and of which a person is therefore unaware; automatic memory. See also *explicit memory.*

implicit psychology A set of inferences (attributions) that people make in everyday life about the causes of people's behavior, including predictions of what they are likely to do.

implosion therapy An attempt to rid a person of fears by arousing them intensely until they diminish through habituation and insight into the fact that nothing bad happens.

incentive A goal object, the anticipation of which motivates behavior.

independent variable The variable that is manipulated in an experiment as a means of determining causal relations. Manipulation of an independent variable demonstrates whether or not it affects the value of the dependent variable.

inductive reasoning Inferring general principles or rules from specific facts.

inflection A change in the form of a word (usually by adding a suffix) to denote a grammatical feature such as tense or number.

information processing An approach used by cognitive psychologists to explain the workings of the brain; information received through the senses is processed by systems of neurons in the brain.

information-processing approach An approach to the study of intelligence that focuses on abilities and mental operations studied by cognitive psychologists.

inhibitory synapse A synapse that inhibits the postsynaptic neuron, making it fire at a slower rate.

insight psychotherapy A general approach to treating mental disorders in which the patient is helped to understand the causes of his or her maladaptive behaviors, especially those that occurred in the remote past; such understanding is presumed to lead to improvement.

instrumental conditioning Operant conditioning; increasing or decreasing the frequency of a response through contingent reinforcement or punishment.

intelligence quotient (IQ) A simplified single measure of general intelligence; by definition, the ratio of a person's mental age to his or her chronological age, multiplied by 100; often derived by other formulas.

intensity The amplitude of a physical stimulus. In audition, the intensity of a sound is closely associated with its loudness (a perceptual dimension); in vision, the intensity of a light is closely associated with its brightness (a perceptual dimension).

intermittent reinforcement A contingency whereby some, but not all, responses are reinforced. Behaviors reinforced intermittently are more resistant to extinction than behaviors reinforced on a continuous reinforcement schedule.

internalized prohibition According to Freud, a characteristic of the superego; rules of behavior learned in childhood that protect the person from the guilt that would be produced by the expression of instinctual drives.

interneuron A neuron located entirely within the central nervous system.

interposition One of the cues of depth perception; an object that partially occludes another object is perceived as closer.

interrater reliability The degree to which two or more independent observers agree in their ratings of another organism's behavior, expressed in terms of a correlation coefficient.

intraspecific aggression The attack by one animal upon another member of its species.

intrinsic motivation The ability of a particular activity to produce reinforcing effects; examples include games, puzzles, and hobbies.

introspection Literally, "looking within," in an attempt to describe one's own memories, perceptions, cognitive processes, or motivations.

introversion A personality trait; the tendency to avoid the company of other people, especially large groups of people; shyness.

IQ See *intelligence quotient (IQ)*.

iris The pigmented muscle of the eye that controls the size of the pupil.

isolation aphasia A language disturbance that includes an inability to comprehend speech or produce meaningful speech, along with the ability to repeat speech and learn new sequences of words; caused by brain damage that isolates the brain's speech mechanisms from other parts of the brain.

James-Lange theory A theory of emotion that suggests that behaviors and physiological responses are directly elicited by situations, and that feelings of emotions are produced by feedback from these behaviors and responses.

just-noticeable difference (jnd) The smallest difference between two similar stimuli that can be distinguished. Also called *difference threshold*.

language universal A characteristic feature found in all natural languages.

latency period According to Freud, one of the stages of psychosexual development during which the child experiences little sexual instinctual drive; follows the phallic stage and precedes the genital stage.

law of closure See *Figure 5.10*.

law of common fate A Gestalt law of organization; elements that move together give rise to the perception of a particular figure.

law of effect Thorndike's observation that stimuli that are contingent on a response can increase (through reinforcement) or decrease (through punishment) response frequency.

law of proximity See *Figure 5.7*.

law of similarity See *Figure 5.8*.

leakage A sign of expression of an emotion that is being masked.

learned helplessness A response to exposure to an inescapable aversive stimulus, characterized by reduced ability to learn a solvable avoidance task; thought to play a role in the development of some psychological disturbances.

lens The transparent organ situated behind the iris of the eye; helps focus an image on the retina.

libido According to Freud, the psychic energy associated with instinctual drives.

limbic cortex The phylogenetically old cortex, located at the edge ("limbus") of the cerebral hemispheres; part of the limbic system.

limbic system A set of interconnected structures of the brain, important in emotional and species-typical behavior; includes the amygdala, hippocampus, and part of the hypothalamus.

lithium carbonate A simple salt used to treat bipolar disorder.

longitudinal study The observation of the behavior of one group of people at several different stages of development.

long-term memory Relatively permanent memory. See also *short-term memory*.

loudness A perceptual dimension of sound, most closely associated with intensity (amplitude).

maintenance rehearsal The rehearsal of verbal information by repeating it subvocally, in rote fashion.

major depression A psychotic depression characterized by extreme sadness, feelings of guilt and unworthiness, and delusions.

malingering A deliberate simulation of the symptoms of a real disease, generally to avoid work or unpleasant situations or to receive compensation.

mania Extreme exuberance, characterized by rapid thoughts, restlessness, sleeplessness, and grandiose plans; seen in bipolar disorder.

masking Attempting to hide the expression of an emotion.

matching A systematic selection of subjects of groups in an experiment or (more often) an observational study to ensure that the mean values of important subject variables of the groups are similar.

materialism A philosophical belief that reality can be known only through an understanding of the physical world, of which the mind is a part.

mean A measure of central tendency; the sum of a group of values divided by their number; the arithmetical average.

means-ends analysis A general heuristic method of problem solving; involves looking for differences between the current state and the goal state and seeking ways to reduce the differences.

measure of central tendency A statistical measure used to characterize the value of items in a sample of numbers. The most common examples are the mean and the median.

measure of variability A statistical measure used to characterize the dispersion in values of items in a sample of numbers. The most common examples are the variance, the standard deviation, and the range.

median A measure of central tendency; the midpoint of a group of values arranged numerically.

mental age The measure of a person's intellectual development. A child with a mental age of eight performs as well on intelligence tests as the average child of that age.

mental model A mental construction based on physical reality that is used to solve problems of logical deduction.

mental retardation Mental development that is substantially below normal; often caused by some form of brain damage or abnormal brain development.

meta-analysis A statistical procedure by which the results of several experiments are combined to estimate the magnitude of an effect.

method of loci A mnemonic system whereby visual representations of items to be memorized are imagined in conjunction with a sequence of locations in a building (real or imaginary).

method of successive approximations See *shaping*.

Minnesota Multiphasic Personality Inventory (MMPI) An objective test of personality; consists of ten clinical scales and four validity scales.

mnemonic system A method by which information can easily be remembered, such as the method of loci.

model A mathematical or physical analogy for a physiological process; for example, computers have been used as models for various functions of the brain.

modeling Changing a person's behavior by providing an example of desirable behavior and (usually) overtly or covertly reinforcing that behavior.

modulation An attempt to exaggerate or minimize the expression of an emotion.

mood A relatively long-lasting state of affect.

mood disorder A serious psychological disorder in which a person is excessively, unrealistically sad (depression) or elated (mania). Formerly called *affective disorder*.

morality of cooperation According to Piaget, the second stage of moral development, characterized by the realization that many moral rules are social conventions.

moral realism According to Piaget, the first stage of moral development, characterized by egocentrism and blind adherence to rules.

motion parallax One of the cues of depth perception. See *Figure 5.31*.

motivation A general term for a group of phenomena that affect the nature, strength, or persistence of an individual's behavior.

motor association cortex See under *association cortex*.

motor neuron A neuron whose terminal buttons form synapses with muscle fibers. When an action potential travels down its axon, the associated muscle fibers will twitch.

multiple personality A psychological disorder in which a person displays very different behaviors at different times, giving the impression of having distinct and different personalities.

muscle spindle A muscle fiber that functions as a stretch receptor, arranged parallel to the muscle fibers responsible for contraction of the muscle, thus detecting muscle length.

myelin sheath The insulating material that encases most large axons in the nervous system.

nanometer (nm) One-billionth of a meter, or one-millionth of a millimeter.

narcolepsy A neurological disorder in which a person suffers from irresistible sleep attacks and often cataplexy and hypnagogic hallucinations.

natural killer cell A white blood cell that continuously prowls through tissue and kills cells that have become infected by a virus or have become cancerous.

need for achievement According to Murray, the tendency for people to strive to overcome obstacles—to do something difficult as well and as quickly as possible.

need for affiliation According to Murray, a need to maintain social relationships with other people.

need for power According to Murray, a need to assert authority and control the behavior of other people.

negative afterimage The image seen after a portion of the retina is exposed to an intense visual stimulus; a negative afterimage consists of colors complementary to those of the physical stimulus.

negative correlation An inverse relation between two variables; large values of one measure are associated with small values of the other.

negative feedback A process whereby the effect produced by an action serves to diminish or terminate that action. Regulatory systems are characterized by negative feedback loops.

negative hallucination The perception that a stimulus that is present is actually absent; can be induced by hypnotic suggestion.

negative reinforcement The removal or reduction of an aversive stimulus that is contingent on a particular response, with an attendant increase in the frequency of that response; the effect of an escape response.

negative symptom With respect to schizophrenia, the absence of a normal behavior, such as flattened emotional response, poverty of speech, lack of initiative and persistence, and social withdrawal.

neodissociation Hilgard's explanation for hypnosis; different aspects or components of the mind are dissociated during hypnosis.

NEO-PI The Neuroticism, Extraversion, and Openness Personality Inventory; a personality inventory devised by McCrae and Costa in conjunction with their five-factor model.

neural network A model of the nervous system based on interconnected networks of elements that have some of the properties of neurons.

neurologist A physician who treats disorders of the nervous system.

neuromodulator A naturally secreted substance that acts like a neurotransmitter except that it has more widespread effects. Presumably, it activates receptor molecules on neurons that are not located at synapses.

neuron The most important cell of the nervous system; consists of a cell body with dendrites and an axon whose branches end in terminal buttons that synapse with muscle fibers, gland cells, or other neurons.

neuropsychology A branch of psychology involved with the diagnosis and behavioral treatment of neurological disorders and the study of human brain functions through observation of people with such disorders.

neurosis A mental disorder of less severity than a psychosis. The term is not used in the new *Diagnostic and Statistical Manual III* of the American Psychiatric Association.

neuroticism According to Eysenck, a personality type characterized by anxiety, worry, and guilt.

nm See *nanometer (nm)*.

nominal fallacy The false belief that one has explained the causes of a phenomenon by identifying and naming it; for example, one does not explain lazy behavior by attributing it to "laziness."

norm Data from comparison groups that permit the score of an individual to be assessed relative to peers.

object concept The beliefs and expectancies that children have about physical objects; an important part of Piaget's theory of cognitive development.

objective test A psychological test that can be scored objectively, such as a multiple-choice or true/false test.

observational study The observation of two or more variables in the behavior or other characteristics of a group of people. Observational studies can reveal correlations but not causal relations among variables; the latter can be revealed only by experiments.

obsession Recurrent, persistent thoughts and ideas.

obsessive compulsive disorder A neurotic disorder characterized by obsessions and compulsions.

occipital lobe The rearmost portion of the cerebral cortex; contains the primary visual cortex.

Oedipus complex According to Freud, the desire of a boy to replace his father and have sexual relations with his mother.

olfaction The sense of smell.

olfactory bulb The protrusion at the end of the olfactory nerve; receives input from the olfactory receptors.

olfactory mucosa The mucous membrane lining the top of the nasal sinuses; contains the cilia of the olfactory receptors.

operant chamber An experimental chamber in which animals can be placed for instrumental (or operant) conditioning; contains a device to measure responses and provide reinforcing or punishing stimuli.

operant conditioning See *instrumental conditioning.*

operational definition The specification of a measurement or of the manipulation of a variable in terms of the operations the experimenter performs to measure or manipulate it.

opioid A neuromodulator (for example, an endorphin) whose action is mimicked by a natural or synthetic opiate, such as opium, morphine, or heroin.

optic disk A circular structure located at the exit point from the retina of the axons of the ganglion cells that form the optic nerve.

optimum-level hypothesis The hypothesis that organisms will perform behavior that restores the level of arousal to an optimal level.

oral stage According to Freud, the first stage of psychosexual development, during which an infant receives primary gratification by sucking.

orbitofrontal cortex A region of the prefrontal cortex that plays an important role in recognition of situations that produce emotional responses.

organizational effect (of hormone) An effect of a hormone that usually occurs early in development, producing permanent changes that alter the subsequent development of the organism. An example is androgenization. See also *activational effect.*

orienting response The response by which an organism orients appropriate sensory organs (such as eyes or ears) toward the source of a novel stimulus.

ossicles The three bones of the middle ear (known as the *hammer, anvil,* and *stirrup*) that transmit acoustical vibrations from the eardrum to the membrane behind the oval window of the cochlea.

oval window An opening in the bone surrounding the cochlea that permits the footplate of the stirrup to transmit acoustical vibrations to the receptive organ inside the cochlea.

overextension The use of a word to denote a larger class of items than is appropriate, for example, referring to the moon as a *ball;* commonly observed in the speech of young children.

overtone The frequencies of complex tones that occur at multiples of the fundamental frequency.

ovulation The release of a ripe ovum, which can subsequently be fertilized.

ovum The female gamete; egg.

Pacinian corpuscle A specialized, encapsulated somatosensory nerve ending, which detects mechanical stimuli, especially vibrations.

panic disorder A psychological disorder characterized by frequent panic attacks, during which a person experiences great fear and symptoms such as shortness of breath, heart palpitations, sensations of choking, dizziness, sweating, faintness, and fear of dying.

papilla A small bump on the tongue that contains a group of taste buds.

parallel processor A computing device that can perform several operations simultaneously.

paranoid schizophrenia A type of schizophrenia characterized by delusions of persecution, grandeur, or control.

paraphilia A sexual disorder such as fetishism, transvestism, pedophilia (attraction to children), zoophilia (attraction to animals), or exhibitionism.

parasympathetic branch See under *autonomic nervous system (ANS).*

parietal lobe The region of the cerebral cortex behind the frontal lobe and above the temporal lobe; contains the somatosensory cortex; is involved in spatial perception and memory for and planning of the execution of motor sequences.

passive expectation According to Piaget, the behavior of an infant who apparently knows that a hidden object still exists but does not attempt to retrieve it.

perception The detection of the more complex properties of a stimulus, including its location and nature; involves learning.

period of concrete operations According to Piaget, the period that comprises approximately ages seven to twelve, during which the ability to perform logical analysis, to empathize, and to understand complex cause-and-effect relations emerges.

period of formal operations According to Piaget, the final stage of cognitive development, characterized by an essentially adult form of logic and symbolic representation; begins at approximately twelve years.

peripheral nervous system The cranial and spinal nerves and their associated structures; that part of the nervous system peripheral to the brain and spinal cord.

permanence The concept that objects

and people continue to exist even when they are hidden from view; develops during infancy.

perseverance The tendency to continue to perform a behavior even when it is not being reinforced.

personal causation The belief that one's behavior has important effects on one's environment.

personality psychologist A psychologist who attempts to categorize and understand the causes of individual differences in patterns of behavior.

personality trait A relatively stable pattern of behavior that is at least somewhat predictable in a variety of situations.

personality type A label used to classify people according to their characteristic patterns of behavioral reactions.

person perception The study of the ways in which people perceive other people's personality characteristics.

perspective One of the cues of depth perception; the arrangement or drawing of objects on a flat surface such that the impression of a three-dimensional scene is given.

phallic stage According to Freud, the third stage of psychosexual development, during which a person receives primary gratification from touching his or her genitalia; precedes the latency period and genital stage.

phenylketonuria (PKU) A hereditary disorder caused by the absence of an enzyme that converts the amino acid phenylalanine to tyrosine. The accumulation of phenylalanine causes brain damage unless a special diet is implemented soon after birth.

phi phenomenon The perceived movement caused by the turning on of two or more lights, one at a time, in sequence; often used on theater marquees; responsible for the apparent movement of images in movies and television.

phobia An excessive, unreasonable fear of a particular class of objects or situations.

phobic disorder A mental disorder characterized by excessive and irrational fear of an object or situation.

phoneme The minimum unit of sound that conveys meaning in a particular language, such as /p/.

phonetic reading Reading by decoding the phonetic significance of letter strings, or "sound reading," as opposed to whole-word reading, or "sight reading." Brain injury can abolish one method without affecting the other.

phonological short-term memory Short-term memory for verbal information.

photopigment A protein dye bonded to a substance derived from vitamin A; when struck by light, it bleaches and stimulates the membrane of the photoreceptor in which it resides.

photoreceptor A receptive cell in the retina; rods and cones are photoreceptors.

physiological psychologist A psychologist who attempts to understand the causes of behavior by investigating physiological processes.

physiological psychology The branch of psychology that studies the physiological basis of behavior.

pitch A perceptual dimension of sound, most closely associated with frequency.

pituitary gland An endocrine gland attached to the hypothalamus at the base of the brain.

PKU See *phenylketonuria (PKU)*.

placebo An inert substance that cannot be distinguished from a real medication by the patient or subject; used to please anxious patients or as the control substance in a single-blind or double-blind experiment.

polygraph An instrument that records changes in physiological processes such as brain activity, heart rate, and breathing.

positive hallucination The perception of an object that is not actually present; can be induced by hypnotic suggestion; a frequent symptom of psychosis.

positive symptom With respect to schizophrenia, a symptom obvious by its presence, including thought disorder, hallucinations, and delusions.

posthypnotic amnesia A failure to remember what occurred during hypnosis; induced by suggestions made during hypnosis.

posthypnotic suggestibility The tendency of a person to perform a behavior suggested by the hypnotist some time after the person has left the hypnotic state.

postsynaptic neuron A neuron with which the terminal buttons of another neuron form synapses and that is excited or inhibited by that neuron.

posttraumatic stress disorder A psychological disorder caused by exposure to extremely stressful events.

preference hierarchy A rank-ordered list of behaviors that an individual would prefer to have the opportunity to perform. See *Premack principle*.

prefrontal lobotomy A surgical procedure that disconnects parts of the frontal lobe from the rest of the brain, with the intention of alleviating severe anxiety or severe, chronic pain; not currently employed.

prejudice An attitude (usually unfavorable) toward a particular group of people that affects perception of members of that group.

Premack principle The assertion that the opportunity to engage in a preferred behavior can be used to reinforce the performance of a nonpreferred behavior.

presynaptic neuron A neuron whose terminal buttons form synapses with and excite or inhibit another neuron.

primary auditory cortex The region of the cerebral cortex that receives information directly from the auditory system; located in the temporal lobes.

primary motor cortex The region of the cerebral cortex that directly controls the movements of the body; located in the back part of the frontal lobes.

primary punisher A naturally aversive stimulus, such as one that produces pain or nausea, which can be used to punish a response.

primary reinforcer A naturally appetitive stimulus, such as food, water, or warmth, which can be used to reinforce a response.

primary sex characteristics Sex organs such as genitalia, gonads, and related organs.

primary somatosensory cortex The region of the cerebral cortex that receives information directly from the somatosensory system (touch, pressure, vibration, pain, and temperature); located in the front part of the parietal lobes.

primary visual cortex The region of the cerebral cortex that receives information directly from the visual system; located in the occipital lobes.

priming A phenomenon in which exposure to a particular stimulus automatically facilitates perception of that stimulus or related stimuli.

proactive inhibition The tendency

for exposure to lists of items to make it difficult to learn subsequent lists of items, especially if the items are related.

process reward According to Buss, a social stimulus that is pleasant in moderate amounts but aversive at very high or low levels.

process schizophrenia According to Bleuler, a form of schizophrenia with a gradual onset and a poor prognosis.

projection According to Freud, an ego defense mechanism in which a prohibited drive is attributed to another person.

projective test A psychological test that attempts to determine a person's attitudes, personality, or motivation through his or her responses to ambiguous stimuli. The assumption is that because the stimuli provide few clues, the responses will characterize the subject.

prosody The use of changes in intonation and emphasis to convey meaning in speech besides that specified by the particular words; an important means of communication of emotion.

prosopagnosia A form of visual agnosia characterized by difficulty in recognizing people's faces; caused by damage to the occipital and parietal lobes.

protanopia A form of hereditary anomalous color vision, caused by defective "red" cones in the retina.

prototype In perception, a hypothetical idealized pattern used to perceive objects or shapes by a process of comparison; recognition can occur even when an exact match is not found.

pseudobulbar palsy A paralysis of the face caused by damage to the pathway between the frontal lobes and the regions of the brain stem that control movements of the facial muscles; the ability remains to make automatic facial movements such as coughing, sneezing, or expressions of emotion.

psychoanalysis A form of psychotherapy invented by Freud; aims to bring unconscious fears, motives, and conflicts to consciousness.

psychodynamic Referring to the warring factions of instinct, reason, and conscience in Freud's theory of personality.

psychogenic amnesia Amnesia caused by psychological conflicts and unpleasant situations, not by brain injury.

psychogenic fugue A conversion disorder in which a person leaves and starts a new life elsewhere; accompanied by amnesia for the previous life.

psycholinguistics A branch of psychology devoted to the study of verbal behavior.

psychometrics A branch of psychology devoted to the development of tests of personality and mental abilities.

psychoneuroimmunology Study of the interactions between the immune system and behavior.

psychophysics A branch of psychology that measures the quantitative relation between physical stimuli and perceptual experience.

psychophysiological disorder A real physical illness caused or made worse by psychological factors, especially emotional stress. Sometimes called *psychosomatic disorder.*

psychophysiological disorder An organic illness caused or made worse by psychological factors, such as gastric ulcers or asthma.

psychophysiology The measurement of peripheral physiological processes, such as blood pressure and heart rate, to infer changes in internal states, such as emotions.

psychosurgery The destruction of brain tissue in an attempt to eliminate maladaptive behavior or otherwise treat a mental disorder.

psychoticism According to Eysenck, a personality type characterized by aggressiveness, egocentrism, and antisocial tendencies.

puberty The onset of the process that leads to sexual maturity.

punishing stimulus A stimulus that reduces the frequency or strength of the response that immediately precedes it.

punishment The suppression of a response by the contingent presentation of an aversive stimulus or the contingent removal of an appetitive stimulus (response cost).

pursuit movement The movement that the eyes make to maintain an image upon the fovea.

radical behaviorism The approach to the analysis of behavior devised by Skinner; all behavior is explained in terms of the principles of operant/instrumental conditioning.

random assignment An assignment of subjects to the various groups of an experiment by random means, ensuring comparable groups.

range The difference between the highest score and the lowest score of a sample.

rapid eye movement sleep See *REM sleep.*

ratio IQ A formula for computing the intelligence quotient; mental age divided by chronological age, multiplied by 100.

rational-emotive therapy A form of cognitive restructuring developed by Ellis; stresses that people must hold realistic expectations about the behavior of other people and about their own behavior and its consequences.

rationalization According to Freud, an ego defense mechanism in which a person gives an acceptable reason for a behavior that is actually motivated by a prohibited drive.

rational strategy The development of a psychological test by means of including items that appear to be related to the trait in question; contrasts with the empirical strategy.

reaction formation According to Freud, an ego defense mechanism in which a person experiences feelings opposite to a prohibited drive, such as disgust toward sexual material that the person actually finds interesting.

reactive schizophrenia According to Bleuler, a form of schizophrenia with a rapid onset and brief duration; he assumed the cause was stressful life situations.

reality principle According to Freud, a part of the ego that permits the delay of gratification of a drive until an appropriate goal is located.

receiver operating characteristic curve See *Figure 4.4.*

receptor cell A neuron that directly responds to a physical stimulus, such as a light, vibrations, or aromatic molecules.

receptor molecule A special protein molecule located in the membrane of the postsynaptic neuron that responds to molecules of the transmitter substance. Receptors such as those that respond to opiates are sometimes found elsewhere on the surface of neurons.

reflex An automatic response to a stimulus, such as the blink reflex to the sudden approach of an object toward the eyes.

regression fallacy A fallacy in decision making in which the tendency for extreme values of events to become less extreme (to regress toward the mean) is attributed to one's own behavior.

regulatory behavior A behavior that tends to bring physiological conditions back to normal, thus restoring the condition of homeostasis.

reinforcement The presentation of an appetitive stimulus (positive reinforcement) or the reduction or removal of an aversive stimulus (negative reinforcement) that is contingent on a response; reinforcement increases the frequency of the response.

reinforcing stimulus (reinforcer) A stimulus that, when contingent on a behavior, increases the occurrence of the behavior. See also *reinforcement*.

release from proactive inhibition The improvement of retrieval of information from short-term memory produced by the identification that the items belong to particular categories.

reliability The repeatability of a measurement; the likelihood that if the measurement were made again, it would yield the same value. See also *validity*.

REM sleep A period of sleep during which dreaming, rapid eye movements, and muscular paralysis occur and the EEG shows beta activity.

replication Repetition of a particular experiment or observational study to see whether the previous results will be obtained.

representativeness heuristic The tendency to conclude that if a person, object, or situation possesses certain characteristics, then other characteristics that are often associated with them must be present, too.

repression According to Freud, an ego defense mechanism that prevents threatening material from reaching consciousness.

reserpine A drug used to treat high blood pressure; prevents the release of norepinephrine and serotonin in the brain and often causes depression.

resistance According to Freud, a discomfort shown by a patient when painful topics are being approached during psychoanalysis.

resistant attachment A form of the child's attachment to its mother (or primary caregiver), as determined by the Strange Situation; signs of tension are present, and the reaction to the return of the mother after a period of absence shows ambivalence.

response cost A form of punishment in which a response is followed by the removal of an appetitive stimulus.

retina The tissue at the back inside surface of the eye that contains the photoreceptors and associated neurons.

retinal disparity The fact that points on objects located at different distances from the observer will fall on slightly different locations on the two retinas; provides the basis for stereopsis, one of the forms of depth perception.

retrograde amnesia Lack of memory for events that occurred just before a particular event, such as chemical or physical injury to the brain.

retrospective study A research technique that requires subjects to report what happened in the past.

reuptake The process by which a terminal button retrieves the molecules of transmitter substance that it has just released; terminates the effect of the transmitter substance on the receptors of the postsynaptic neuron.

rhodopsin The photopigment contained by rods.

rod A photoreceptor that is very sensitive to light but cannot detect changes in hue. See also *cone*.

rod-cone break An abrupt transition in the dark adaptation curve; marks the change between vision mediated by cones with that mediated by rods.

rooting A reflex seen in newborn infants; when the cheek is lightly touched, the infant's head turns so that the lips contact the object.

Rorschach Inkblot Test A projective test of personality in which people describe what they see when they look at a set of ten inkblots.

saccadic movement The rapid movement of the eyes that is used in scanning a visual scene, as opposed to the smooth pursuit movements used to follow a moving object.

sample A group of items selected from a larger population; can refer to subjects, stimuli, or behaviors.

saturation A perceptual dimension of color, most closely associated with purity of a color.

scatterplot A graph of items that have two values; one value is plotted against the *x* axis and the other against the *y* axis.

schedule of reinforcement The scheme that determines the nature of

intermittent reinforcement. See also *fixed-interval (FI) schedule, fixed-ratio (FR) schedule, variable-interval (VI) schedule,* and *variable-ratio (VR) schedule.*

schema In the theory of Piaget, the set of rules that define a behavior or behavioral sequence. See also *accommodation*.

schizophrenia A serious mental disorder (psychosis) characterized by disordered thoughts, delusions, hallucinations, and often bizarre behaviors.

scientific method A set of rules that govern the collection and analysis of data gained through observational studies or experiments. See the numbered list in the first section of Chapter 2.

sclera The tough outer layer of the eye; the "white" of the eye.

script The characteristics (events, rules, and so on) that are typical of a particular situation; assists the comprehension of verbal discourse.

seasonal affective disorder A mood disorder characterized by depression, lethargy, sleep disturbances, and craving for carbohydrates; occurs during the winter season; can be treated by daily exposure to bright lights.

secondary sex characteristics The external distinguishing features of a mature male or female, such as facial hair or breasts.

secure attachment A form of the child's attachment to its mother (or primary caregiver), as determined by the Strange Situation; a distinct preference for the mother, who provides reassurance by her presence.

secure base An object (a mother or surrogate mother) that provides reassurance to an infant exploring a novel environment or encountering novel objects.

self-attribution The application of the principles of attribution theory to one's own behavior.

self-concept According to social learning theory, a person's perception of his or her own personality and ability.

self-control 1. According to social learning theory, the ability to withhold a response normally elicited by a particular situation—usually because doing so serves a more important goal. 2. A technique used by behavior therapists; the client controls his or her environment so that reinforcing stimuli follow appropriate behaviors or punishing stimuli follow inappropriate ones.

self-criticism According to social learning theory, a response a person makes after he or she performs maladaptive, unproductive behavior.

self-deception The tendency to hold contradictory beliefs with importance to the believer, one or more of which are unconscious.

self-efficacy A belief in the ability to control one's own situation; an important feature of Bandura's method of cognitive behavior therapy.

self-perception theory Bem's theory that self-knowledge comes through observing the stimuli and situations that appear to be responsible for one's own behavior.

self-praise According to social learning theory, a response a person makes after he or she performs useful, productive behavior.

self-talk The private verbal behavior that comments on what the person is doing. According to cognitive behavior therapists, changing a client's self-talk can help change the client's patterns of behavior.

semantic memory Long-term memory for information but not for the time or circumstances of learning it. See also *episodic memory*.

semantic priming A facilitating effect on the recognition of words with meanings related to a word that was presented previously.

semantics The study of the meanings represented by words.

semicircular canals A set of organs in the inner ear that respond to rotational movements of the head.

sensation The detection of the elementary properties of a stimulus.

sensorimotor period According to Piaget, the period that comprises approximately the first two years of life, during which cognition is closely tied to external stimulation.

sensory association cortex See under *association cortex*.

sensory memory A very brief memory of a stimulus that has just occurred. See also *echoic memory* and *iconic memory*.

sensory neuron A neuron that detects changes in the external or internal environment and sends information about these changes to the central nervous system.

serial device A computing device that performs its operations one at a time,

in a particular order.

serotonin A transmitter substance secreted by the terminal buttons of some neurons; appears to play a role in the control of sleep and has been implicated in the affective disorders.

set point The optimal value of the system variable in a regulatory mechanism. The set point for human body temperature, recorded orally, is approximately 37°C.

sex chromosomes The X and Y chromosomes, which determine an organism's gender. Normally, XX individuals are female, and XY individuals are male.

sex role The collection of behaviors that are identified as suitable and proper for males or females in a particular culture.

sex stereotype The beliefs about the behaviors, abilities, and personality traits of males or females held by members of a particular culture.

sexual identity An acceptance of one's status as a male or a female.

s factor According to Spearman, a factor of intelligence that is specific to a particular task.

shading One of the cues of depth perception; determines whether portions of the surface of an object are perceived as concave or convex.

shadowing The act of continuously repeating verbal material as soon as it is heard.

shallow processing The study of superficial characteristics of a stimulus, such as its shape.

shaping The training of a very low frequency response by successively reinforcing responses that are increasingly similar to the desired one; also called *method of successive approximations*.

short-term memory Memory for information that has just been presented; conceptually similar to working memory, which also includes information that has just been retrieved from long-term memory. See also *long-term memory*.

sign According to Piaget, an abstract symbol such as a word that represents a concept.

signal detection theory A mathematical theory of the detection of stimuli, which involves discriminating a signal from the noise in which it is embedded, and which takes into account the subjects' willingness to report detecting the signal.

signifier According to Piaget, a behavior that symbolically represents a particular concept.

simple phobia An excessive and irrational fear of specific objects or situations, such as snakes, darkness, or heights.

simulation An attempt to falsely express an emotion.

simultanagnosia The inability to visually perceive more than one stimulus presented in proximity to each other; caused by bilateral damage to the parietal and occipital lobes.

single-blind method An experimental method in which the experimenter but not the subject knows the value of the independent variable. See also *double-blind method*.

situational factor A cause of behavior that is related to the situation rather than to the actor's personality traits. See also *dispositional factor*.

slow-wave sleep Sleep other than REM sleep, characterized by regular, slow waves on the electroencephalograph.

social cognition The study of the inferences people make about social situations; includes the topics of attribution, attitudes, and prejudice.

social facilitation The facilitating effect of the presence of a group of people on the behavior of one or more of its members.

social loafing The tendency for people working in groups in which their contributions are not identifiable to expend less effort than they would working alone.

social phobia A mental disorder characterized by excessive and irrational fear of situations in which the person is observed by others.

social psychology A branch of psychology devoted to the study of the effects people have on each other's behavior.

soma A cell body or, more generally, the body.

somatization disorder A mental disorder characterized by numerous vague symptoms of physical disorders in the absence of obvious physical diseases; a type of somatoform disorder.

somatoform disorder A category of mental disorders characterized by symptoms of physical disorders, including conversion disorder, somatization disorder, and hypochondriasis.

somatosenses Bodily sensations; sensitivity to such stimuli as touch, pain, and temperature.

species-typical behavior A behavior seen in all or most members of a species, such as nest building, special food-getting behaviors, or reproductive behaviors.

split-brain operation A surgical procedure that severs the corpus callosum, thus abolishing the direct connections between the cortex of the two cerebral hemispheres.

spontaneous recovery The recurrence of a behavior that was previously extinguished, after a rest period.

standard deviation A statistic that expresses the variability of a measurement.

Stanford-Binet Scale A test of intelligence for children; provides the standard measure of IQ.

statistical significance The likelihood that an observed relation or difference between two variables is not due to chance factors.

stereopsis See *retinal disparity.*

stereotaxic apparatus A device used to insert an object such as a wire or hypodermic needle into a particular part of the brain for the purpose of injecting or removing a substance, recording electrical activity, stimulating the brain electrically, or producing localized damage.

stereotype A commonly held belief about the characteristics of a particular group; can be favorable or unfavorable.

stimulus A change in the environment that can be detected by the sense organs and is subsequently perceived by an organism.

Strange Situation A test devised by Ainsworth and her colleagues that determines the nature of a child's attachment to its caregiver.

stress A physiological reaction caused by the perception of aversive or threatening situations.

structural family therapy A form of family therapy devised by Minuchin; the maladaptive relationships among family members are inferred from their behavior and attempts are made to restructure these into more adaptive forms.

structuralism Wundt's system of experimental psychology; it emphasized introspective analysis of sensation and perception.

sublimation According to Freud, an ego defense mechanism in which a person finds an outlet for a prohibited drive in other behaviors, especially creative or artistic activity.

subliminal perception The perception of a stimulus, as indicated by a change in behavior, at an intensity insufficient to produce a conscious sensation.

subordinate concept See under *concept.*

subvocal articulation "Talking to oneself" without actually engaging in speech.

sucking A reflex seen in newborn infants; the means of obtaining milk from the nipple.

superego According to Freud, the part of the mind that incorporates prohibitions that a person has learned from society; includes the conscience and the ego-ideal.

superordinate concept See under *concept.*

superstitious behavior A behavior that occurs in response to regular, noncontingent administration of an appetitive stimulus to a motivated organism.

surface structure The grammatical features of a sentence. See also *deep structure.*

surrogate mother An artificial object used in experiments with isolated animal species that contains some of the characteristics of the mother.

syllogism A logical construction that contains a major premise, a minor premise, and a conclusion. Major and minor premises are assumed to be true, and the truth of the conclusion is to be evaluated by deductive reasoning.

symbolic function According to Piaget, the ability of an infant to represent things symbolically; a precursor of language ability.

sympathetic branch See under *autonomic nervous system (ANS).*

symptom substitution The hypothesis that if a maladaptive behavior is eliminated (for example, by contingent punishment or by reinforcement of competing behaviors), then the causes of the behavior will remain and will produce another maladaptive behavior.

synapse The junction between the terminal button of one neuron and the membrane of the postsynaptic neuron, which contains receptors that respond to the transmitter substance released by the terminal button.

synaptic cleft The space between a terminal button and the membrane of the postsynaptic neuron.

synaptic vesicle A submicroscopic sac located in a terminal button and containing the transmitter substance.

syntactical rule A grammatical rule of a particular language.

systematic desensitization A form of behavior therapy devised by Wolpe in which emotional responses to a feared object are replaced with the response of relaxation; presumably achieved through classical conditioning.

system variable The variable controlled by a regulatory mechanism; for example, temperature in a heating system.

tachistoscope A device that can present visual stimuli for controlled (usually very brief) durations of time.

tardive dyskinesia A serious movement disorder that can occur when a person has been treated with antipsychotic drugs for an extended period.

target behavior The final behavior that serves as the goal of the shaping procedure.

taste bud A small organ on the tongue that contains a group of receptor cells.

tectorial membrane A membrane located above the basilar membrane; serves as a shelf against which the cilia of the auditory hair cells move.

temperament A personality trait; a general pattern of behavior in particular types of situations.

template In perception, a hypothetical pattern used to perceive objects or shapes by a process of comparison.

temporal coding A means of representing information by the nervous system; different features are coded by the pattern of activity of neurons. For example, in the auditory system pitches of low frequency are represented by the rate of firing of a particular set of neurons.

temporal lobe The portion of the cerebral cortex below the frontal and parietal lobes and containing the auditory cortex. Damage to the temporal lobe produces deficits in audition, speech perception and production, sexual behavior, visual perception, and/or social behaviors.

terminal button The rounded swelling at the end of the axon of a neuron; releases transmitter substance. See also *action potential.*

testosterone The principal androgen, or male sex hormone, secreted by the testes.

texture One of the cues of depth perception; the fineness of detail present in the surface of objects or in the ground or floor of a scene.

thalamus A region of the brain near the center of the cerebral hemispheres. All sensory information except smell is sent to the thalamus and then relayed to the cerebral cortex.

Thematic Apperception Test (TAT) A projective test of personality in which people describe what they see when they look at a set of drawings of ambiguous situations, most of which involve people.

theory A set of statements designed to explain a set of phenomena; more encompassing than a hypothesis.

theta activity EEG activity of 3.5–7.5 Hz; occurs during the transition between sleep and wakefulness.

thought disorder The disorganized, irrational, illogical thinking characteristic of schizophrenia.

threat gesture A stereotyped gesture that signifies that one animal is likely to attack another member of the species. See also *appeasement gesture*.

threshold The point at which a stimulus can just be detected.

timbre A perceptual dimension of sound, determined by the complexity of the sound—for example, as shown by a mathematical analysis of the sound wave.

time out A method used by behavior therapists; an inappropriate response is punished by temporarily removing the person from a situation in which reinforcing stimuli are available.

T lymphocyte A white blood cell produced in the thymus gland; part of the immune system.

token economy A scheme within an institution whereby residents' adaptive behaviors are regularly reinforced, and maladaptive behaviors are punished or not reinforced. The typical medium of reinforcement consists of tokens that can be exchanged for desirable commodities or special privileges.

tolerance The decreased sensitivity to a drug as a result of its continued use.

top-down processing A perception based on information provided by the context in which a particular stimulus is encountered. See also *bottom-up processing*.

Tourette's syndrome A neurological disorder characterized by tics and involuntary vocalizations and sometimes by compulsive uttering of obscenities and repetition of the utterances of others.

training analysis The psychoanalysis received by a person being trained as a psychoanalyst; the goal is to lead to an understanding of the therapist's own conflicts and motivations so that they will not interfere with his or her attempts to perform psychotherapy.

transduction The conversion of physical stimuli into electrical events in cells of sensory organs.

transference neurosis According to Freud, the process by which a patient transfers his or her feelings toward a dominant childhood figure to the psychoanalyst.

transmitter substance A chemical released by the terminal buttons that causes the postsynaptic neuron to be excited or inhibited. See also *action potential*.

transsexualism Adopting the identity of the opposite gender, sometimes including surgical changes and administration of sex hormones.

transvestism Wearing the clothes of the opposite gender; almost exclusively, the wearing of women's clothes by a man.

trephining A surgical procedure in which an opening is made in the skull of a living person.

tricyclic antidepressant drug A drug (for example, imipramine) used to treat major depression; named for the shape of the molecule.

tritanopia "Third-color defect," in which people see the world in reds and greens; caused by loss of cones in the retina that are sensitive to light of short wavelengths ("blue" cones).

two-point discrimination threshold The minimum distance between two small points that can be detected as separate stimuli when pressed against a particular region of the skin.

type A pattern A behavior pattern characterized by excessive competitive drive, impatience, hostility, fast movements, and rapid speech; supposedly associated with an increased likelihood of cardiovascular disease.

type B pattern A behavior pattern characterized by low levels of competitiveness and hostility, patience, and an easygoing, slow-talking nature; supposedly associated with a decreased likelihood of cardiovascular disease.

type C pattern A behavior pattern characterized by cooperativeness, unassertiveness, patience, suppression of the expression of negative emotions, and acceptance of external authority; supposedly associated with an increased likelihood of cancer.

unconditional positive regard According to Carl Rogers, the accepting, nonjudgmental attitude that a therapist should express toward the client.

unconditioned response (UR) The response elicited by the unconditioned stimulus in classical conditioning.

unconditioned stimulus (US) The unconditioned eliciting stimulus in classical conditioning.

unconscious inference A mental computation of which we are unaware; plays a role in perception.

underextension The use of a word to denote a smaller class of items than is appropriate; for example, referring only to one particular animal as a *dog;* commonly observed in the speech of young children.

undermining of intrinsic motivation The tendency for an extrinsic reinforcer to reduce an organism's tendency to perform a particular task under certain conditions.

undifferentiated schizophrenia Schizophrenia whose symptoms do not meet the specific criteria for catatonic, paranoid, or disorganized schizophrenia.

validity The degree to which a test or measurement is related to the variable it is designed to measure. A valid test is a perfect reflection of the psychological trait that it purports to measure.

validity scale The scale of the MMPI devised to detect lying or carelessness in answering questions.

variable A measure capable of assuming any of several values. See also *independent variable* and *dependent variable.*

variable error An error caused by random differences in experimental conditions, such as the subject's mood or changes in the environment.

variable-interval (VI) schedule A schedule of reinforcement similar to a fixed-interval schedule but characterized by a variable time requirement with a particular mean.

variable-ratio (VR) schedule A schedule of reinforcement similar to a fixed-ratio schedule but characterized by a variable response requirement with a particular mean.

ventricle One of the hollow chambers in the brain that are filled with cerebrospinal fluid.

verbal access The ability to describe verbally a perception, thought, emotion, behavior, or memory.

verbal control The ability to initiate, stop, or modify a behavior by means of verbal behavior.

vertebra One of the bones that encase the spinal cord and constitute the vertebral column.

vestibular apparatus The receptive organs of the inner ear that contribute to balance and perception of head movement.

vestibular sacs A set of two receptor organs in each inner ear that detect changes in the tilt of the head.

VI schedule See *variable-interval (VI) schedule.*

visual agnosia The inability of a person who is not blind to recognize the identity or use of an object by means of vision; usually caused by damage to the brain.

voice-onset time The delay between the initial sound of a voiced consonant (such as the puffing sound of the phoneme /p/) and the onset of vibration of the vocal cords.

VR schedule See *variable-ratio (VR) schedule.*

wavelength The distance between adjacent waves of radiant energy; in vision, most closely associated with the perceptual dimension of hue.

waxy flexibility The ability of the limbs of a person with catatonic schizophrenia to be molded into a position that will be maintained for a prolonged period.

Weber fraction The ratio between a just noticeable difference and the magnitude of a stimulus; reasonably constant over the middle range of most stimulus intensities.

Wechsler Adult Intelligence Scale (WAIS) An intelligence test for adults devised by David Wechsler; contains eleven subtests divided into the categories of verbal and performance.

Wechsler Intelligence Scale for Children (WISC) An intelligence test for children devised by David Wechsler; similar in form to the Wechsler Adult Intelligence Scale.

Wernicke's aphasia A disorder caused by damage to Wernicke's area, located in the temporal lobe (usually, on the left side); characterized by deficits in the perception of speech and by the production of fluent but rather meaningless speech.

Wernicke's area See *Wernicke's aphasia.*

white matter The portions of the central nervous system that are abundant in axons rather than cell bodies of neurons. The color derives from the presence of the axons' myelin sheaths. See also *gray matter.*

withdrawal symptom An effect produced by discontinuance of a drug after a period of continued use; generally opposite to the drug's primary effects.

working memory Memory of what has just been perceived and what is currently being thought about; consists of new information and related information that has recently been "retrieved" from long-term memory.

X chromosome See *sex chromosomes.*

Y chromosome See *sex chromosomes.*

REFERENCES

Abel, E.L., and Sokol, R.J. Fetal alcohol syndrome is now a leading cause of mental retardation. *Lancet,* 1986, *2,* 1222.

Adamec, R.E., and Stark-Adamec, C. Limbic hyperfunction, limbic epilepsy, and interictal behavior: Models and methods of detection. In *The Limbic System,* edited by B.K. Doane and K.E. Livingston. New York: Raven Press, 1986.

Adams, G.R., and Huston, T.L. Social perception of middle-aged persons varying in physical attractiveness. *Developmental Psychology,* 1975, *11,* 657–658.

Adey, W.R., Bors, E., and Porter, R.W. EEG sleep patterns after high cervical lesions in man. *Archives of Neurology,* 1968, *19,* 377–383.

Ainsworth, M.D.S. *Infancy in Uganda: Infant Care and the Growth of Love.* Baltimore: Johns Hopkins University Press, 1967.

Ainsworth, M.D.S. The development of infant-mother attachment. In *Review of Child Development Research, Vol. 3,* edited by B.M. Caldwell and H.R. Ricciuti. Chicago: University of Chicago Press, 1973.

Ainsworth, M.D.S., Blehar, M.C., Waters, E., and Wall, S. *Patterns of Attachment.* Hillsdale, N.J.: Lawrence Erlbaum Associates, 1978.

Albright, L., Kenny, D.A., and Malloy, T.E. Consensus in personality judgments at zero acquaintance. *Journal of Personality and Social Psychology,* 1988, *55,* 387–395.

Allen, M.G. Twin studies of affective illness. *Archives of General Psychiatry,* 1976, *33,* 1476–1478.

Amoore, J.E. *Molecular Basis of Odor.* Springfield, Ill.: Charles C. Thomas, 1970.

Anderson, D.R., and Collins, P.A. *The Impact on Children's Education: Television's Influence on Cognitive Development.* Washington, D.C.: U.S. Department of Education, 1988.

Anderson, D.R., and Field, D. Children's attention to television: Implications for production. In *Children and the Formal Features of Television,* edited by M. Meyer. Munich: Saur, 1983.

Anderson, D.R., Field, D., Collins, P., Lorch, E., and Nathan, J. Estimates of young children's time with television: A methodological comparison of patent reports with time-lapse video home observation. *Child Development,* 1985, *56,* 1345–1357.

Anderson, D.R., and Lorch, E. Looking at television: Action or reaction? In *Children's Understanding of Television: Research on Attention and Comprehension,* edited by J. Bryant and D.R. Anderson. New York: Academic Press, 1983.

Anderson, R.H., Fleming, D.E., Rhees, R.W., and Kinghorn, E. Relationships between sexual activity, plasma testosterone, and the volume of the sexually dimorphic nucleus of the preoptic area in prenatally stressed and non-stressed rats. *Brain Research,* 1986, *370,* 1–10.

Andreasen, N.C., and Olsen, S.A. Negative vs. positive schizophrenia: Definition and validation. *Archives of General Psychiatry,* 1982, *39,* 789–794.

Angrist, B.J., Rotrosen, J., and Gershon, S. Positive and negative symptoms in schizophrenia—Differential response to amphetamine and neuroleptics. *Psychopharmacology,* 1980, *72,* 17–19.

Anonymous. Effects of sexual activity on beard growth in man. *Nature,* 1970, *226,* 869–870.

Arenberg, D. Cognition and aging: Verbal learning, memory, and problem solving. In *The Psychology of Adult Development and Aging,* edited by C. Eisdorfer and M.P. Lawton. Washington, D.C.: American Psychological Association, 1973.

Aronson, E. Personal communication, 1975, cited by Nisbett, R.E., and Wilson, T.D. Telling more than we can know: Verbal reports on mental processes. *Psychological Review,* 1977, *84,* 231–259.

Aronson, E., and Mills, J. The effects of severity of initiation on liking for a group. *Journal of Abnormal and Social Psychology,* 1959, *59,* 177–181.

Artmann, H., Grau, H., Adelman, M., and Schleiffer, R. Reversible and non-reversible enlargement of cerebrospinal fluid spaces in anorexia nervosa. *Neuroradiology,* 1985, *27,* 103–112.

Asch, S.E. Effects of group pressure upon the modification and distortion of judgment. In *Groups, Leadership, and Men,* edited by H. Guetzkow. Pittsburgh: Carnegie, 1951.

Ash, P. Honesty test scores, biographical data, and delinquency indicators. Paper presented at the annual meeting of the Academy of Criminal Justice Sciences, St. Louis, March, 1987. (Cited by Sackett, Burris, and Callahan, 1989.)

Atkinson, J.W. *An Introduction to Motivation.* New York: Van Nostrand, 1964.

Atkinson, R.C., and Shiffrin, R.M. Human memory: A proposed system and its control processes. In *The Psychology of Learning and Motivation: Advances in Research and Theory, Vol. 2,* edited by K.W. Spence and J.T. Spence. New York: Academic Press, 1968.

Ayllon, T., and Azrin, N.H. *The Token Economy: A Motivational System for Therapy and Rehabilitation.* Englewood Cliffs, N.J.: Prentice-Hall, 1968.

Baddeley, A.D. Domains of recollection. *Psychological Review,* 1982, *89,* 708–729.

Baddeley, A.D. *Working Memory.* Oxford: Clarendon Press, 1986.

Baer, D.M., Peterson, R.F., and Sherman, J.A. Development of imitation by reinforcing behavioral similarity to a model. *Journal of the Experimental Analysis of Behavior,* 1967, *10,* 405–416.

Bailey, J.M., and Pillard, R.C. A genetic study of male sexual orientation. *Archives of General Psychiatry,* 1991, *48,* 1089–1096.

Bain, J. Hormones and sexual aggression in the male. *Integrative Psychiatry,* 1987, *5,* 82–89.

Bak, M., Girvin, J.P., Hambrecht, F.T., Kufta, C.V., Loeb, G.E., and Schmidt, E.M. Visual sensations produced by intracortical microstimulation of the human occipital cortex. *Medical and Biological Engineering and Computing,* 1990, *28,* 257–259.

Baker, B.L. Symptom treatment and symptom substitution in enuresis. *Journal of Abnormal Psychology,* 1969, *74,* 42–49.

Baker, R.A. *They Call It Hypnosis.* Buffalo, N.Y.: Prometheus Books, 1990.

Baldessarini, R.J. *Chemotherapy in Psychiatry.* Cambridge, Mass.: Harvard University Press, 1977.

Baldessarini, R.J., and Tarsy, D. Dopamine and the pathophysiology of dyskinesias induced by antipsychotic drugs. *Annual Review of Neuroscience,* 1980, *3,* 23–41.

Ball, K., and Sekuler, R. A specific and enduring improvement in visual motion discrimination. *Science,* 1982, *218,* 697–698.

Ball, S., and Bogatz, G. *The First Years of Sesame Street: An Evaluation.* Princeton, N.J.: Educational Testing Service, 1970.

Ballantine, H.T., Bouckoms, A.J., Thomas, E.K., and Giriunas, I.E. Treatment of psychiatric illness by stereotactic cingulotomy. *Biological Psychiatry,* 1987, *22,* 807–819.

Balon, R., Jordan, M., Pohl, R., and Yeragani, V.K. Family history of anxiety disorders in control subjects with lactate-induced panic attacks. *American Journal of Psychiatry,* 1989, *146,* 1304–1306.

Baltes, P., and Schaie, K. Aging and IQ: The myth of the twilight years. *Psychology Today,* October 1974, pp. 35–38.

Bandura, A. *Principles of Behavior Modification.* New York: Holt, Rinehart and Winston, 1969.

Bandura, A. Psychotherapy based upon modeling principles. In *Handbook of Psychotherapy and Behavior Change,* edited by A.E. Bergin and S.L. Garfield. New York: John Wiley & Sons, 1971.

Bandura, A. *Aggression: A Social Learning Analysis.* Englewood Cliffs, N.J.: Prentice-Hall, 1973.

Bandura, A. Self-efficacy: Toward a unifying theory of behavioral change. *Psychological Review*, 1977a, *84*, 191–215.

Bandura, A. *Social Learning Theory*. Englewood Cliffs, N.J.: Prentice-Hall, 1977b.

Bandura, A., and Menlove, F.L. Factors determining vicarious extinction of avoidance behavior through symbolic modeling. *Journal of Personality and Social Psychology*, 1968, *8*, 99–108.

Bandura, A., and Mischel, W. Modification of self-imposed delay of reward through exposure to live and symbolic models. *Journal of Personality and Social Psychology*, 1965, *2*, 698–705.

Banks, M.S., Aslin, R.N., and Letson, R.D. Sensitive period for the development of human binocular vision. *Science*, 1975, *190*, 675–677.

Barber, T.X. Responding to "hypnotic" suggestions: An introspective report. *American Journal of Clinical Hypnosis*, 1975, *18*, 6–22.

Barber, T.X. Suggested ("hypnotic") behavior: The trance paradigm versus an alternative paradigm. In *Hypnosis: Developments in Research and New Perspectives*, edited by E. Fromm and R.E. Shor. Chicago: Aldine Press, 1979.

Barclay, C.D., Cutting, J.E., and Kozlowski, L.T. Temporal and spatial factors in gait perception that influence gender recognition. *Perception and Psychophysics*, 1978, *23*, 145–152.

Baron, R.A., and Byrne, D. *Social Psychology: Understanding Human Interaction*. Boston: Allyn and Bacon, 1987.

Bartlett, F.C. *Remembering: An Experimental and Social Study*. Cambridge, England: Cambridge University Press, 1932.

Bastiaans, J. Psychological factors in the development of cancer. In *Cancer Campaign. Vol. 19: The Cancer Patient—Illness and Recovery*, edited by E. Grundemann. Stuttgart: Gustav Fischer Verlag, 1985.

Baumann, D.J., and Holahan, C.J. The community psychologist. In *Applied Psychology: Variety and Opportunity*, edited by R. Gifford. Boston: Allyn and Bacon, 1991.

Baxt, W.G. Use of an artificial neural network for the diagnosis of myocardial infarction. *Annals of Internal Medicine*, 1991, *115*, 843–848.

Beck, A.T. *Depression: Clinical, Experimental, and Theoretical Aspects*. New York: Harper & Row, 1967.

Beck, A.T. *Cognitive Therapy and the Emotional Disorders*. New York: International Universities Press, 1976.

Beck, A.T., and Emery, G. *Anxiety Disorders and Phobias: A Cognitive Perspective*. New York: Basic Books, 1985.

Beckman, L. Effects of students' performance on teachers' and observers' attributions of causality. *Journal of Educational Psychology*, 1970, *61*, 75–82.

Belar, C.D. The health psychologist. In *Applied Psychology: Variety and Opportunity*, edited by R. Gifford. Boston: Allyn and Bacon, 1991.

Bell, A.P., and Weinberg, M.S. *Homosexualities: A Study of Diversity among Men and Women*. New York: Simon & Schuster, 1978.

Bell, A.P., Weinberg, M.S., and Hammersmith, S.K. *Sexual Preference: Its Development in Men and Women*. Bloomington: Indiana University Press, 1981.

Bell, S.M., and Ainsworth, M.D. Infant crying and maternal responsiveness. *Child Development*, 1972, *43*, 1171–1190.

Bellugi, U., and Klima, E.S. The roots of language in the sign talk of the deaf. *Psychology Today*, June 1972, pp. 61–76.

Belsky, J., and Rovine, M.J. Nonmaternal care in the first year of life and the security of infant-parent attachment. *Child Development*, 1988, *59*, 157–167.

Bem, D., and Allen, A. On predicting some of the people some of the time: The search for cross-situational consistencies in behavior. *Psychological Review*, 1974, *81*, 506–520.

Bem, D.J. Self-perception theory. In *Advances in Experimental Social Psychology, Vol. 6*, edited by L. Berkowitz. New York: Academic Press, 1972.

Berger, S.M. Conditioning through vicarious instigation. *Psychological Review*, 1962, *69*, 450–466.

Berk, L.E. *Child Development*. Boston: Allyn and Bacon, 1989.

Berkowitz, L. Aggressive cues in aggressive behavior and hostility catharsis. *Psychological Review*, 1964, *71*, 104–122.

Berkowitz, L. Whatever happened to the frustration-aggression hypothesis? *American Behavioral Scientist*, 1978, *21*, 691–708.

Berkowitz, L., and Frodi, A. Stimulus characteristics that can enhance or decrease aggression. *Aggressive Behavior*, 1977, *3*, 1–15.

Berlyne, D.E. Motivational problems raised by exploratory and epistemic behavior. In *Psychology: A Study of a Science, Vol. 5*, edited by S. Koch. New York: McGraw-Hill, 1966.

Bermant, G., and Davidson, J.M. *Biological Bases of Sexual Behavior*. New York: Harper & Row, l974.

Bernstein, I.L. Learned taste aversion in children receiving chemotherapy. *Science*, 1978, *200*, 1302–1303.

Bernstein, I.L. Aversion conditioning in response to cancer and cancer treatment. *Clinical Psychology Review*, 1991, *11*, 183–191.

Bernstein, I.L., Webster, M.M., and Bernstein, I.D. Food aversions in children receiving chemotherapy for cancer. *Cancer*, 1982, *50*, 2961–2963.

Bernstein, W.M., Stephenson, B.O., Snyder, M.L., and Wicklund, R.A. Causal ambiguity and heterosexual affiliation. *Journal of Experimental Social Psychology*, 1983, *19*, 78–92.

Berscheid, E., Dion, K., Walster, E., and Walster, G.W. Physical attractiveness and dating choice: A test of the matching hypothesis. *Journal of Experimental Social Psychology*, 1971, *7*, 173–189.

Best, D.L., Williams, J.E., Cloud, J.M., Davis, S.W., Robertson, L.S., Edwards, J.R., Giles, H., and Fowles, J. Development of sex-trait stereotypes among young children in the United States, England, and Ireland. *Child Development*, 1977, *48*, 1375–1384.

Biederman, I. Recognition-by-components: A theory of human image interpretation. *Psychological Review*, 1987, *94*, 115–147.

Biederman, I. Higher-level vision. In *An Invitation to Cognitive Science. Vol. 2: Visual Cognition and Action*. Cambridge, Mass.: MIT Press, 1990.

Binet, A., and Henri, V. La psychologie individuelle. *Année Psychologique*, 1896, *2*, 411–465.

Birren, J.E., and Morrison, D.F. Analysis of the WISC subtests in relation to age and education. *Journal of Gerontology*, 1961, *16*, 363–369.

Bliss, E.L. Multiple personalities: A report of 14 cases with implications for schizophrenia and hysteria. *Archives of General Psychiatry*, 1980, *37*, 1388–1397.

Bliss, E.L. Multiple personalities, related disorders, and hypnosis. *American Journal of Clinical Hypnosis*, 1983, *26*, 113–123.

Bloom, L. *Language Development: Form and Function in Emerging Grammars*. Cambridge, Mass.: MIT Press, 1970.

Bogatz, G., and Ball, S. *The Second Year of Sesame Street: A Continuing Evaluation*. Princeton, N.J.: Educational Testing Service, 1972.

Bohannon, J.N., and Stanowicz, L. The issue of negative evidence: Adult responses to children's language errors. *Developmental Psychology*, 1988, *24*, 684–689.

Bolles, R.C. Species-specific defense reactions and avoidance learning. *Psychological Review*, 1970, *77*, 32–48.

Bonvillian, J., Nelson, K.E., and Charrow, V. Languages and language-related skills in deaf and hearing children. *Sign Language Studies*, 1976, *12*, 211–250.

Bookmiller, M.N., and Bowen, G.L. *Textbook of Obstetrics and Obstetric Nursing*, 5th ed. Philadelphia: W.B. Saunders, 1967.

Borgida, E., and Nisbett, R.E. The differential viewpoint of abstract vs. concrete information on decisions. *Journal of Applied Social Psychology*, 1977, *7*, 258–271.

Borysenko, J.Z. Behavioural-physiological factors in the development and management of cancer. *General Hospital Psychiatry*, 1982, *3*, 69–74.

Botwinick, J., and Storandt, M. *Memory, Related Functions and Age*. Springfield, Ill.: Charles C. Thomas, 1974.

Bouchard, T.J., Heston, L., Eckert, E., Keyes, M., and Resnick, S. The Minnesota Study of Twins Reared Apart: Project description and sample results in the developmental domain. In *Twin Research 3: Intelligence, Personality, and Development*, edited by L. Gedda, P. Parisi, and W.E. Nance. New York: A.R. Liss, 1981.

Bower, G.H., and Clark, M.C. Narrative stories as mediators for serial learning. *Psychonomic Science*, 1969, *14*, 181–182.

Bowlby, J. *Attachment and Loss. Vol. 1: Attachment*. New York: Basic Books, 1969.

Boynton, R.M. *Human Color Vision*. New York: Holt, Rinehart and Winston, 1979.

Boysson-Bardies, B., Sagart, L., and Durand, C. Discernible differences in the babbling of infants according to target language. *Journal of Child Language*, 1984, *11*, 1–15.

Bozarth, M.A., and Wise, R.A. Toxicity associated with long-term intravenous heroin and cocaine self-administration in the rat. *Journal of the American Medical Association*, 1985, *254*, 81–83.

Brady, J.P., and Lind, D.L. Experimental analysis of hysterical blindness. *Archives of General Psychiatry*, 1961, *4*, 331–359.

Brantner, J.P., and Doherty, M.A. A review of time out: A conceptual and methodological analysis. In *The Effects of Punishment on Human Behavior,* edited by S. Axelrod and J. Apsche. New York: Academic Press, 1983.

Brecher, E.M. *Licit and Illicit Drugs.* Boston: Little, Brown, 1972.

Breckler, S.J. Empirical validation of affect, behavior, and cognition as distinct components of attitude. *Journal of Personality and Social Psychology,* 1984, *47,* 1191–1205.

Breitmeyer, B.G. *Visual Masking: An Integrative Approach.* New York: Oxford University Press, 1980.

Brickner, R.M. *The Intellectual Functions of the Frontal Lobe. A Study Based Upon Observations of a Man After Partial Frontal Lobectomy.* New York: Macmillan, 1936.

Briggs, S.R. Shyness: Introversion or Neuroticism? *Journal of Research in Personality,* 1988, *22,* 290–307.

Broberg, D.J., and Bernstein, I.L. Candy as a scapegoat in the prevention of food aversions in children receiving chemotherapy. *Cancer,* 1987, *60,* 2344–2347.

Broca, P. Remarques sur le siège de la faculté du langage articulé, suivies d'une observation d'aphémie (perte de la parole). *Bulletin de la Societe Anatomique* (Paris), 1861, *36,* 330–357.

Brody, G.H., and Shaffer, D.R. Contributions of parents and peers to children's moral socialization. *Developmental Review,* 1982, *2,* 31–75.

Brooks-Gunn, J. Pubertal processes and the early adolescent transition. In *Child Development Today and Tomorrow,* edited by W. Damon. San Francisco: Jossey-Bass, 1989.

Brooks-Gunn, J., and Furstenberg, F.F. Adolescent sexual behavior. *American Psychologist,* 1989, *44,* 249–257.

Brot, M.D., Braget, D.J., and Bernstein, I.L. Flavor, not postingestive, cues contribute to the salience of proteins as targets in aversion conditioning. *Behavioral Neuroscience,* 1987, *101,* 683–689.

Brown, G.W. The discovery of expressed emotion: Induction or deduction? In *Expressed Emotion in Families,* edited by J. Leff and C. Vaughn. New York: Guilford Press, 1985.

Brown, G.W., Bone, M., Dalison, B., and Wing, J.K. *Schizophrenia and Social Care.* London: Oxford University Press, 1966.

Brown, R., and Bellugi, U. Three processes in the child's acquisition of syntax. *Harvard Education Review,* 1964, *34,* 133–151.

Brown, R., and Fraser, C. The acquisition of syntax. *Monographs of the Society for Research in Child Development,* 1964, *29,* 43–79.

Brown, R., and Hanlon, C. Derivational complexity and order of acquisition in child speech. In *Cognition and the Development of Language,* edited by J.R. Hayes. New York: John Wiley & Sons, 1970.

Brown, R.W., and Kulik, J. Flashbulb memories. *Cognition,* 1977, *5,* 73–99.

Brownell, K.D., Greenwood, M.R.C., Stellar, E., and Shrager, E.E. The effects of repeated cycles of weight loss and regain in rats. *Physiology and Behavior,* 1986, *38,* 459–464.

Buck, R.W. Nonverbal communication of affect in children. *Journal of Personality and Social Psychology,* 1975, *31,* 644–653.

Buck, R.W. Nonverbal communication accuracy in preschool children: Relationships with personality and skin conductance. *Journal of Personality and Social Psychology,* 1977, *33,* 225–236.

Burt, C. The concept of consciousness. *British Journal of Psychology,* 1962, *53,* 229–242.

Buss, A.H. Social rewards and personality. *Journal of Personality and Social Psychology,* 1983, *44,* 553–563.

Byrne, D., McDonald, R.D., and Mikawa, J. Approach and avoidance affiliation motives. *Journal of Personality,* 1963, *31,* 21–37.

Byrne, D., and Nelson, D. Attraction as a linear function of proportion of positive reinforcements. *Journal of Personality and Social Psychology,* 1965, *1,* 659–663.

Byrne, D., and Rhamey, R. Magnitude of positive and negative reinforcements as a determinant of attraction. *Journal of Personality and Social Psychology,* 1965, *2,* 884–889.

Cadoret, R.J. Psychopathology in adopted-away offspring of biologic parents with antisocial behavior. *Archives of General Psychiatry,* 1978, *35,* 176–184.

Campos, J.J., Langer, A., and Krowitz, A. Cardiac responses on the visual cliff in prelocomotor human infants. *Science,* 1970, *170,* 196–197.

Cannon, W.B. The James-Lange theory of emotions: A critical examination and an alternative. *American Journal of Psychology,* 1927, *39,* 106–124.

Cannon, W.B., and Washburn, A.L. An explanation of hunger. *American Journal of Physiology,* 1912, *29,* 444–454.

Carlsmith, J.M., and Gross, A.E. Some effects of guilt on compliance. *Journal of Personality and Social Psychology,* 1969, *11,* 240–244.

Carlson, N.R. *Physiology of Behavior,* 4th ed. Boston: Allyn and Bacon, 1991.

Carlson, N.R. *Foundations of Physiological Psychology,* 2nd ed. Boston: Allyn and Bacon, 1992.

Caron, R.F., Caron, A.J., and Myers, R.S. Abstraction of invariant face expressions in infancy. *Child Development,* 1982, *53,* 1008–1015.

Carpenter, P.A., and Just, M.A. What your eyes do while your mind is reading. In *Eye Movements in Reading: Perceptual and Language Processes,* edited by K. Rayner. New York: Academic Press, 1983.

Carr, E.G., and Lovaas, O.J. Contingent electric shock as a treatment for severe behavior problems. In *The Effect of Punishment on Human Behavior,* edited by S. Axelrod and J. Apsche. New York: Academic Press, 1983.

Cash, T.F., and Derlega, V.J. The matching hypothesis: Physical attractiveness among same-sexed friends. *Personality and Social Psychology Bulletin,* 1978, *4,* 240–243.

Cattell, R.B. *Abilities: Their Structure, Growth, and Action.* Boston: Houghton Mifflin, 1971.

Chambless, D., Foa, E., Graves, G., and Goldstein, A. Flooding with Brevital in the treatment of agoraphobia: Countereffective. *Behavior Research and Therapy,* 1979, *17,* 243–251.

Chen, J., Paredes, W., Li, J., Smith, D., Lowinson, J., and Gardner, E.L. Delta⁹-tetrahydrocannabinol produces naloxone-blockable enhancement of presynaptic basal dopamine efflux in nucleus accumbens of conscious, freely-moving rats as measured by intracerebral microdialysis. *Psychopharmacology,* 1990, *102,* 156–162.

Cherry, E.C. Some experiments on the recognition of speech, with one and with two ears. *Journal of the Acoustical Society of America,* 1953, *25,* 975–979.

Chomsky, N. *Syntactic Structure.* The Hague: Mouton Publishers, 1957.

Chomsky, N. *Aspects of the Theory of Syntax.* Cambridge, Mass.: MIT Press, 1965.

Cialdini, R.B. *Influence: How and Why People Agree to Things.* New York: William Morrow, 1984.

Cialdini, R.B., Borden, R.J., Thorne, A., Walker, M.R., Freeman, S., and Sloan, L.R. Basking in reflected glory: Three (football) field studies. *Journal of Personality and Social Psychology,* 1976, *34,* 366–375.

Clark, R.D., and Word, L.E. Where is the apathetic bystander? Situational characteristics of the emergency. *Journal of Personality and Social Psychology,* 1974, *29,* 279–287.

Clarke-Stewart, A. And daddy makes three: the father's impact on mother and young child. *Child Development,* 1978, *49,* 466–479.

Clarke-Stewart, K.A., and Fein, G.G. Early childhood programs. In *Handbook of Child Psychology. Vol. 2: Infancy and Developmental Psychobiology,* edited by P.H. Mussen. New York: John Wiley & Sons, 1983.

Cleckley, H. *The Mask of Sanity.* St. Louis: C.V. Mosby, 1976.

Cloninger, C.R. Neurogenetic adaptive mechanisms in alcoholism. *Science,* 1987, *236,* 410–416.

Cloninger, C.R., Bohman, M., Sigvardsson, S., and von Knorring, A.-L. Psychopathology in adopted-out children of alcoholics. The Stockholm Adoption Study. *Recent Developments in Alcoholism,* 1985, *7,* 235.

Cobb, S., and Rose, R.M. Hypertension, peptic ulcer, and diabetes in air traffic controllers. *Journal of the American Medical Association,* 1973, *224,* 489–492.

Coe, W.C., Kobayashi, K., and Howard, M.L. Experimental and ethical problems in evaluating the influence of hypnosis in antisocial conduct. *Journal of Abnormal Psychology,* 1973, *82,* 476–482.

Cohen, E.A. *Human Behavior in the Concentration Camp.* New York: W.W. Norton, 1953.

Cohen, M., and Davis, N. *Medication Errors: Causes and Prevention.* Philadelphia: G.F. Stickley, 1981.

Cole, O.J., and Washington, V. A critical analysis of the assessment of the effects of Head Start on minority children. *Journal of Negro Education,* 1986, *55,* 91–106.

Colegrove, F.W. Individual memories. *American Journal of Psychology,* 1899, *10,* 228–255.

Coleman, J.C. *Abnormal Psychology and Modern Life,* 5th ed. Glenview, Ill.: Scott, Foresman, 1976.

Collins, A.M., and Quillian, M.R. Retrieval time from semantic memory. *Journal of Verbal Learning and Verbal Behavior,* 1969, *8,* 240–248.

Condry, J., and Condry, S. Sex differences: A study of the eye of the beholder. *Child Development*, 1976, *47*, 812–819.

Conley, J.J. A personality theory of adult and aging. In *Perspectives in Personality*, edited by R. Hogan and W.J. Jones. Greenwich, Conn.: JAI Press, 1985.

Conner, R.L., and Levine, S. Hormonal influences on aggressive behaviour. In *Aggressive Behaviour*, edited by S. Garattine and E.B. Sigg. New York: John Wiley & Sons, 1969.

Conrad, R. Acoustic confusions in immediate memory. *British Journal of Psychology*, 1964, *55*, 75–83.

Conrad, R. Short-term memory processes in the deaf. *British Journal of Psychology*, 1970, *61*, 179–195.

Constantian, C.A. *Attitudes, Beliefs, and Behavior in Regard to Spending Time Alone.* Doctoral dissertation, Harvard University, Cambridge, Mass., 1981. (Cited by McClelland, 1985.)

Cooper, J., and Fazio, R.H. A new look at dissonance theory. In *Advances in Experimental Social Psychology, Vol. 17*, edited by L. Berkowitz. New York: Academic Press, 1984.

Corkin, S., Sullivan, E.V., Twitchell, T.E., and Grove, E. The amnesic patient H.M.: Clinical observations and test performance 28 years after operation. *Society for Neuroscience Abstracts*, 1981, *7*, 235.

Corteen, R., and Williams, T. Television and reading skills. In *The Impact of Television: A Natural Experiment in Three Communities*, edited by T.M. Williams. New York: Academic Press, 1986.

Coryell, W. A blind family history study of Briquet's syndrome. Further validation of the diagnosis. *Archives of General Psychiatry*, 1980, *37*, 1266–1269.

Costa, L. The clinical neuropsychologist. In *Applied Psychology: Variety and Opportunity.* edited by R. Gifford. Boston: Allyn and Bacon, 1991.

Costa, P.T., and McCrae, R.R. Still stable after all these years: Personality as a key to some issues in adulthood and old age. In *Life-Span Development and Behavior*, edited by P.B. Baltes. New York: Academic Press, 1980.

Costa, P.T., and McCrae, R.R. From catalog to classification: Murray's needs and the five-factor model. *Journal of Personality and Social Psychology*, 1988, *55*, 258–265.

Cottrell, N.B., Wack, D.L., Sekerak, G.J., and Rittle, R.H. Social facilitation of dominant responses by the presence of an audience and the mere presence of others. *Journal of Personality and Social Psychology*, 1968, *9*, 245–250.

Council on Scientific Affairs, American Medical Association. Scientific status of refreshing recollection by the use of hypnosis. *Journal of the American Medical Association*, 1985, *253*, 1918–1923.

Coutts, L.M. The organizational psychologist. In *Applied Psychology: Variety and Opportunity*, edited by R. Gifford. Boston: Allyn and Bacon, 1991.

Cowart, J., and Whaley, D. Punishment of self-mutilation behavior. Unpublished manuscript cited by Whaley, D.L., and Malott,

R.W. *Elementary Principles of Behavior.* New York: Appleton-Century-Crofts, 1971.

Cowley, D.S., and Arana, G.W. The diagnostic utility of lactate sensitivity in panic disorder. *Archives of General Psychiatry*, 1990, *47*, 277–284.

Craik, F.I.M., and Lockhart, R.S. Levels of processing: A framework for memory research. *Journal of Verbal Learning and Verbal Behavior*, 1972, *11*, 671–684.

Craik, F.I.M., and Tulving, E. Depth of processing and the retention of words in episodic memory. *Journal of Experimental Psychology: General*, 1975, *104*, 268–294.

Crouse, B.B., and Mehrabian, A. Affiliation of opposite-sexed strangers. *Journal of Research in Personality*, 1977, *11*, 38–47.

Crow, T.J. Molecular pathology of schizophrenia: More than one disease process? *British Medical Journal*, 1980, *280*, 66–68.

Crowe, R.R., Noyes, R., Pauls, D.L., and Slymen, D. A family study of panic disorder. *Archives of General Psychiatry*, 1983, *40*, 1065–1069.

Crowe, R.R., Noyes, R., Wilson, A.F., Elston, R.C., and Ward, L.J. A linkage study of panic disorder. *Archives of General Psychiatry*, 1987, *44*, 933–937.

Crowne, D., and Marlowe, D. *The Approval Motive.* New York: John Wiley & Sons, 1964.

Croyle, R.T., and Cooper, J. Dissonance arousal: Physiological evidence. *Journal of Personality and Social Psychology*, 1983, *45*, 782–791.

Csikszentmihalyi, M., and Larson, R. *Being Adolescent: Conflict and Growth in the Teenage Years.* New York: Basic Books, 1984.

Culebras, A., and Moore, J.T. Magnetic resonance findings in REM sleep behavior disorder. *Neurology*, 1989, *39*, 1519–1523.

Curtiss, S. Issues in language acquisition relevant to cochlear implants in young children. In *Cochlear Implants in Young Deaf Children*, edited by E. Owens and D.K. Kessler. Boston: College-Hill Press, 1989.

Dabbs, J.M., Frady, R.L., Carr, T.S., and Besch, N.F. Saliva testosterone and criminal violence in young adult prison inmates. *Psychosomatic Medicine*, 1987, *49*, 174–182.

Dabbs, J.M., Ruback, J.M., Frady, R.L., and Hopper, C.H. Saliva testosterone and criminal violence among women. *Personality and Individual Differences*, 1988, *9*, 269–275.

Dale, P.S. *Language Development: Structure and Function*, 2nd ed. New York: Holt, Rinehart and Winston, 1976.

Damasio, A.R., Tranel, D., and Damasio, H. Face agnosia and the neural substrates of memory. *Annual Review of Neuroscience*, 1990, *13*, 89–109.

Damsma, G., Day, J., and Fibiger, H.C. Lack of tolerance to nicotine-induced dopamine release in the nucleus accumbens. *European Journal of Pharmacology*, 1989, *168*, 363–368.

Darley, J.M., and Latané, B. Bystander intervention in emergencies: Diffusion of responsibility. *Journal of Personality and Social Psychology*, 1968, *8*, 377–383.

Darwin, C. *The Expression of the Emotions in Man and Animals.* Chicago: University of Chicago Press, 1872/1965.

Darwin, C.J., Turvey, M.T., and Crowder, R.G. An auditory analogue of the Sperling partial report procedure: Evidence for brief auditory storage. *Cognitive Psychology*, 1972, *3*, 255–267.

Dasen, P.R., and Heron, A. Cross-cultural tests of Piaget's theory. In *Handbook of Cross-Cultural Psychology. Vol. 4: Developmental Psychology*, edited by H. Triandis. Boston: Allyn and Bacon, 1981.

Dashiell, J.F. Experimental studies of the influence of social situations on the behavior of individual human adults. In *A Handbook of Social Psychology*, edited by C. Murcheson. Worcester, Mass.: Clark University Press, 1935.

Davidson, J.M., Camargo, C.A., and Smith, E.R. Effects of androgen on sexual behavior in hypogonadal men. *Journal of Clinical Endocrinology and Metabolism*, 1979, *48*, 955–958.

Davis, J.D., and Campbell, C.S. Peripheral control of meal size in the rat: Effect of sham feeding on meal size and drinking rats. *Journal of Comparative and Physiological Psychology*, 1973, *83*, 379–387.

Davis, J.M. A two-factor theory of schizophrenia. *Journal of Psychiatric Research*, 1974, *11*, 25–30.

Davison, G.C., and Neale, J.M. *Abnormal Psychology: An Experimental Clinical Approach*, 3rd ed. New York: John Wiley & Sons, 1982.

Davison, G.C., and Neale, J.M. *Abnormal Psychology*, 5th ed. New York: John Wiley & Sons, 1990.

Dawes, R.M., Faust, D., and Meehl, P.E. Clinical versus actuarial judgment. *Science*, 1989, *243*, 1668–1674.

Deaux, K. Sex and gender. *Annual Review of Psychology*, 1985, *36*, 49–81.

Deci, E.L. Effects of externally mediated rewards on intrinsic motivation. *Journal of Personality and Social Psychology*, 1971, *18*, 105–115.

Deci, E.L. *Intrinsic Motivation.* New York: Plenum Press, 1975.

deGroot, A.D. *Thought and Choice in Chess.* The Hague: Mouton Publishers, 1965.

Dekaban, A. *Neurology of Early Childhood.* Baltimore: Williams & Wilkins, 1970.

Dement, W.C. *Some Must Watch While Some Must Sleep.* San Francisco: W.H. Freeman, 1974.

Dennis, W. Causes of retardation among institutional children: Iran. *Journal of Genetic Psychology*, 1960, *96*, 47–59.

Dennis, W. *Children of the Creche.* New York: Appleton-Century-Crofts, 1973.

Deutsch, J.A., Young, W.G., and Kalogeris, T.J. The stomach signals satiety. *Science*, 1978, *201*, 165–167.

deVilliers, J.G., and deVilliers, P.A. *Language Acquisition.* Cambridge, Mass.: Harvard University Press, 1978.

DiMascio, A., Weissman, M.M., Prusoff, B.A., Neu, C., Zwilling, M., and Klerman, G.L. Differential symptom reduction by drugs and psychotherapy in acute depression. *Archives of General Psychiatry*, 1979, *36*, 1450–1456.

Dimsdale, J.E. A perspective on type A behavior and coronary disease. *The New England Journal of Medicine*, 1988, *318*, 110–112.

Dion, K., Berscheid, E., and Walster, E. What

is beautiful is good. *Journal of Personality and Social Psychology,* 1972, *24,* 285–290.

Dollard, J., Doob, L., Miller, N., Mowrer, O., and Sears, R. *Frustration and Aggression.* New Haven, Conn.: Yale University Press, 1939.

Donenberg, G.R., and Hoffman, L.W. Gender differences in moral development. *Sex Roles,* 1988, *18,* 701–717.

Douvan, E., and Adelson, J. *The Adolescent Experience.* New York: John Wiley & Sons, 1966.

Dovido, J.J., Evans, N., and Tyler, R.B. Racial stereotypes: The contents of their cognitive representations. *Journal of Experimental Social Psychology,* 1986, *22,* 22–37.

Drabman, R.S., Spitalnik, R., and O'Leary, K.D. Teaching self-control to disruptive children. *Journal of Abnormal Psychology,* 1973, *82,* 10–16.

Druckman, D., and Bjork, R.A. *In the Mind's Eye: Enhancing Human Performance.* Washington, D.C.: National Academy Press, 1991.

Durkin, J. The sport psychologist. In *Applied Psychology: Variety and Opportunity,* edited by R. Gifford. Boston: Allyn and Bacon, 1991.

Dutton, D.G., and Aron, A.P. Some evidence for heightened sexual attraction under conditions of high anxiety. *Journal of Personality and Social Psychology,* 1974, *30,* 510–517.

Dyer, F.N. The Stroop phenomenon and its use in the study of perceptual, cognitive, and response processes. *Memory and Cognition,* 1973, *1,* 106–120.

D'Zurilla, T. Recall efficiency and mediating cognitive events in "experimental repression." *Journal of Personality and Social Psychology,* 1965, *1,* 253–257.

Eddy, N.B., Halbach, H., Isbell, H., and Seevers, M.H. Drug dependence: Its significance and characteristics. *Bulletin of the World Health Organization,* 1965, *32,* 721–733.

Efran, M.G., and Patterson, E.W.J. The politics of appearance. Unpublished manuscript, 1976, cited by Cialdini, R.B. *Influence: How and Why People Agree to Things.* New York: William Morrow, 1984.

Ehlers, C.L., Frank, E., and Kupfer, D.J. Social zeitgebers and biological rhythms. *Archives of General Psychiatry,* 1988, *45,* 948–952.

Eimas, P.D., Siqueland, E.R., Jusczyk, P., and Vigorito, J. Speech perception in infants. *Science,* 1971, *171,* 303–306.

Eisenberg, N. The development of reasoning regarding prosocial behavior. In *The Development of Prosocial Behavior,* edited by N. Eisenberg. New York: Academic Press, 1982.

Eisenberg, N., Lennon, R., and Pasternack, J.F. Altruistic values and moral judgment. In *Altruistic Emotion, Cognition, and Behavior,* edited by N. Eisenberg. Hillsdale, N.J.: Lawrence Erlbaum Associates, 1986.

Ekman, P. *The Face of Man: Expressions of Universal Emotions in a New Guinea Village.* New York: Garland STPM Press, 1980.

Ekman, P., and Friesen, W.V. Nonverbal leakage and clues to deception. *Psychiatry,* 1969, *32,* 88–105.

Ekman, P., and Friesen, W.V. Detecting deception from body or face. *Journal of Personality and Social Psychology,* 1974, *29,* 288–298.

Ekman, P., and Friesen, W.V. *Unmasking the Face.* Englewood Cliffs, N.J.: Prentice-Hall, 1975.

Ekman, P., Friesen, W.V., and Ellsworth, P. *Emotion in the Human Face: Guidelines for Research and a Review of Findings.* New York: Pergamon Press, 1972.

Ekman, P., Levenson, R.W., and Friesen, W.V. Autonomic nervous system activity distinguished between emotions. *Science,* 1983, *221,* 1208–1210.

Elias, M. Serum cortisol, testosterone and testosterone binding globulin responses to competitive fighting in human males. *Aggressive Behavior,* 1981, *7,* 215–224.

Elkin, I., Parloff, M.B., Hadley, S.W., and Autry, J.H. NIMH Treatment of Depression Collaborative Research Program. *Archives of General Psychiatry,* 1985, *42,* 305–316.

Elkin, I., Shea, M.T., Watkins, J.T., Imber, S.D., Sotsky, S.M., Collins, J.F., Glass, D.R., Pilkonis, P.A., Leber, W.R., Docherty, J.P., Fiester, S.J., and Parloff, M.B. National Institute of Mental Health Treatment of Depression Collaborative Research Program: General Effectiveness of Treatments. *Archives of General Psychiatry,* 1989, *46,* 971–982.

Elkind, D. *Child Development and Education.* New York: Oxford University Press, 1976.

Ellenberger, H.F. The story of "Anna O": A critical review with new data. *Journal of the History of the Behavioral Sciences,* 1972, *8,* 267–279.

Ellis, A. Rational-emotive therapy. In *Current Psychotherapies,* 2nd ed., edited by R.J. Corsini. Itasca, Ill.: R.E. Peacock, 1979.

Ellis, S.R., McGreevy, M.W., and Hitchcock, R.J. Perspective traffic display format and airline pilot traffic avoidance. *Human Factors,* 1987, *29,* 371–382.

Emmelkamp, P.M.G., Kuipers, A.C.M., and Eggeraat, J.B. Cognitive modification versus prolonged exposure *in vivo:* A comparison with agoraphobics as subjects. *Behaviour Research and Therapy,* 1978, *16,* 33–42.

Emmons, R.A., Diener, E., and Larsen, R.J. Choice and avoidance of everyday situations and affect congruence: Two models of reciprocal interactionism. *Journal of Personality and Social Psychology,* 1986, *51,* 815–826.

Entwisle, D. To dispel fantasies about fantasy-based measures of achievement motivation. *Psychological Bulletin,* 1972, *77,* 377–391.

Epstein, R. The spontaneous interconnection of three repertoires. *The Psychological Record,* 1985, *35,* 131–141.

Epstein, R. The spontaneous interconnection of four repertoires of behavior in a pigeon (*Columba livia*). *Journal of Comparative Psychology,* 1987, *101,* 197–201.

Epstein, R., Kirshnit, C., Lanza, R.P., and Rubin, L. Insight in the pigeon: Antecedents and determinants of an intelligent performance. *Nature,* 1984, *308,* 61–62.

Epstein, S. The stability of behavior. I. On predicting most of the people much of the time. *Journal of Personality and Social Psychology,* 1979, *37,* 1097–1126.

Epstein, W. The influence of syntactical structure on learning. *American Journal of Psychology,* 1961, *74,* 80–85.

Erickson, M.F., Sroufe, L.A., and Egeland, B. The relationship between quality of attachment and behavior problems in preschool in a high-risk sample. *Monographs of the Society for Research in Child Development,* 1985, *50(1–2, Serial No. 209).*

Eriksen, C.W., and Collins, J.F. Some temporal characteristics of visual pattern perception. *Journal of Experimental Psychology,* 1967, *74,* 476–484.

Ernulf, K.E., Innala, S.M., and Whitam, F.L. Biological explanation, psychological explanation, and tolerance of homosexuals: A cross-national analysis of beliefs and attitudes. *Psychological Reports,* 1989, *248,* 183–188.

Eron, L.D. A normative study of the thematic apperception test. *Psychological Monographs,* 1950, *64,* Whole No. 315.

Eslinger, P.J., and Damasio, A.R. Severe disturbance of higher cognition after bilateral frontal lobe ablation: Patient EVR. *Neurology,* 1985, *35,* 1731–1741.

Eysenck, H.J. The effects of psychotherapy: An evaluation. *Journal of Consulting Psychology,* 1952, *16,* 319–324.

Eysenck, H.J. *The Structure of Human Personality,* 3rd ed. London: Methuen, 1970.

Eysenck, H.J. Personality, stress and cancer: Prediction and prophylaxis. *British Journal of Medical Psychology,* 1988, *61,* 57–75.

Eysenck, H.J., and Eysenck, M.W. *Personality and Individual Differences: A Natural Science Approach.* New York: Plenum Press, 1985.

Fadda, F., Mosca, E., Colombo, G., and Gessa, G.L. Alcohol-preferring rats: Genetic sensitivity to alcohol-induced stimulation of dopamine metabolism. *Physiology and Behavior,* 1990, *47,* 727–729.

Fagan, J.F. Infants' recognition of invariant features of faces. *Child Development,* 1976, *47,* 627–638.

Fagot, B.I. Consequences of moderate cross-gender behavior in preschool children. *Child Development,* 1977, *48,* 902–907.

Farmer, A., McGuffin, P., and Gottesman, I. Twin concordance in DSM-III schizophrenia. *Archives of General Psychiatry,* 1987, *44,* 634–641.

Farrell, M.P. and Rosenberg, S.D. *Men at Midlife.* Boston: Auburn House, 1981.

Feigenbaum, S.L., Masi, A.T., and Kaplan, S.B. Prognosis in rheumatoid arthritis: A longitudinal study of newly diagnosed younger adult patients. *American Journal of Medicine,* 1979, *66,* 377–384.

Feldman, R.D. *Whatever Happened to the Quiz Kids?* Chicago: Chicago Review Press, 1982.

Ferster, C.B., and Skinner, B.F. *Schedules of Reinforcement.* New York: Appleton-Century-Crofts, 1957.

Feshbach, S., and Singer, R.D. *Television and Aggression.* San Francisco: Jossey-Bass, 1971.

Festinger, L. *A Theory of Cognitive Dissonance.* Stanford: Stanford University Press, 1957.

Festinger, L., and Carlsmith, J.M. Cognitive consequences of forced compliance. *Jour-*

nal of Abnormal and Social Psychology, 1959, *58*, 203–210.

Festinger, L., Schachter, S., and Back, K. *Social Pressures in Informal Groups: A Study of a Housing Community*. New York: Harper & Row, 1950.

Feynman, R.P. *Surely You're Joking, Mr. Feynman!*. New York: Bantam Books, 1985.

Field, T. Individual differences in the expressivity of neonates and young infants. In *Development of Nonverbal Behavior in Children*, edited by R.S. Feldman. New York: Springer-Verlag, 1982.

Field, T., Woodson, R., Greenberg, R., and Cohen, D. Discrimination and imitation of facial expressions in neonates. *Science*, 1982, *218*, 179–181.

Fink, M. Presidential address: Brain function, verbal behavior, and psychotherapy. In *Evaluation of Psychological Therapies: Psychotherapies, Behavior Therapies, Drug Therapies, and Their Interactions*, edited by R.L. Spitzer and D.F. Klein. Baltimore: Johns Hopkins University Press, 1976.

Fiske, S.T., and Taylor, S.E. *Social Cognition*. Reading, Mass.: Addison-Wesley, 1984.

Fix, A.J., and Haffke, E.A. *Basic Psychological Therapies: Comparative Effectiveness*. New York: Human Sciences Press, 1976.

Flaherty, J., Frank, E., Hoskinson, K., Richman, J., and Kupfer, D. Social zeitgebers and bereavement. Paper presented at the 140th Annual Meeting of the American Psychiatric Association, Chicago, May 1987.

Flavell, J.H., Everett, B.H., Croft, K., and Flavell, E.R. Young children's knowledge about visual perception: Further evidence for the level 1–level 2 distinction. *Developmental Psychology*, 1981, *17*, 99–103.

Fodor, E.M. The power motive and reactivity to power stress. *Journal of Personality and Social Psychology*, 1984, *47*, 853–859.

Foley, V.D. Family therapy. In *Current Psychotherapies*, 2nd ed., edited by R.J. Corsini. Itasca, Ill.: R.E. Peacock, 1979.

Ford, D.H., and Urban, H.B. *Systems of Psychotherapy: A Comparative Study*. New York: John Wiley & Sons, 1963.

Fouts, R.S. Chimpanzee language and elephant tails: A theoretical synthesis. In *Language in Primates: Perspectives and Implications*, edited by J. de Luce and H.T. Wilder. New York: Springer-Verlag, 1983.

Fouts, R.S., Hirsch, A., and Fouts, D. Cultural transmission of a human language in a chimpanzee mother/infant relationship. In *Psychological Perspectives: Child Nurturance Series, Vol. III*, edited by H.E. Fitzgerald, J.A. Mullins, and P. Page. New York: Plenum Press, 1983.

Frankenberg, W.K., and Dodds, J.B. The Denver Developmental Screening Test. *Journal of Pediatrics*, 1967, *71*, 181–191.

Fraser, J.G. Selection of patients. In *Cochlear Implants*, edited by R.F. Gray. London: Croom Helm, 1985.

Freedman, J.L., and Fraser, S.C. Compliance without pressure: The foot-in-the-door technique. *Journal of Personality and Social Psychology*, 1966, *4*, 195–203.

Friedman, M., and Rosenman, R.H. Association of specific overt behavior patterns with blood and cardiovascular findings—Blood cholesterol level, blood clotting time, inci-

dence of arcus senilis, and clinical coronary artery disease. *Journal of the American Medical Association*, 1959, *162*, 1286–1296.

Friedman, M.I., Tordoff, M.G., and Ramirez, I. Integrated metabolic control of food intake. *Brain Research Bulletin*, 1986, *17*, 855–859.

Fries, J.F., Bloch, D.A., Sharp, J.T., McShane, D.J., Spitz, P., Bluhm, G.B., Forrester, D., Genant, H., Gofton, P., and Richman, S. Assessment of radiologic progression in rheumatoid arthritis: A randomized, controlled trial. *Arthritis and Rheumatology*, 1986, *29*, 1–9.

Friesen, W.V. *Cultural Differences in Facial Expression in a Social Situation: An Experimental Test of the Concept of Display Rules*. Doctoral dissertation, University of California, San Francisco, 1972.

Fromkin, V. *Speech Errors as Linguistic Evidence*. The Hague: Mouton Publishers, 1973.

Fuhrman, W., Rahe, D.F., and Hartup, W.W. Rehabilitation of socially withdrawn preschool children through mixed-age and same-age socialization. *Child Development*, 1979, *50*, 915–922.

Fuller, R.G.C., and Sheehy-Skeffington, A. Effects of group laughter on responses to humorous materials: A replication and extension. *Psychological Reports*, 1974, *35*, 531–534.

Fulton, J.F. *Functional Localization in Relation to Frontal Lobotomy*. New York: Oxford University Press, 1949.

Furrow, D., and Nelson, K. A further look at the motherese hypothesis: A reply to Gleitman, Newport & Gleitman. *Journal of Child Language*, 1986, *13*, 163–176.

Furrow, D., Nelson, K., and Benedict, H. Mothers' speech to children and syntactic development: Some simple relationships. *Journal of Child Language*, 1979, *6*, 423–442.

Galaburda, A., and Kemper, T.L. Observations cited by Geschwind, N. Specializations of the human brain. *Scientific American*, 1979, *241*, 180–199.

Galaburda, A.M. The pathogenesis of childhood dyslexia. In *Language, Communication, and the Brain*, edited by F. Plum. New York: Raven Press, 1988.

Galaburda, A.M., Sherman, G.F., Rosen, G.D., Aboitiz, F., and Geschwind, N. Developmental dyslexia: Four consecutive patients with cortical anomalies. *Annals of Neurology*, 1985, *18*, 222–233.

Ganong, W.F. Phonetic categorization in auditory word perception. *Journal of Experimental Psychology: Human Perception and Performance*, 1980, *6*, 110–125.

Garcia, J., and Koelling, R.A. Relation of cue to consequence in avoidance learning. *Psychonomic Science*, 1966, *4*, 123–124.

Gardiner, J.M., Craik, F.I.M., and Birtwistle, J. Retrieval cues and release from proactive inhibition. *Journal of Verbal Learning and Verbal Behavior*, 1972, *11*, 778–783.

Gardner, H. *Frames of Mind*. New York: Basic Books, 1983.

Gardner, R.A., and Gardner, B.T. Teaching sign language to a chimpanzee. *Science*, 1969, *165*, 664–672.

Gardner, R.A., and Gardner, B.T. Early signs of language in child and chimpanzee. *Science*, 1975, *187*, 752–753.

Gardner, R.A., and Gardner, B.T. Comparative psychology and language acquisition. *Annals of the New York Academy of Sciences*, 1978, *309*, 37–76.

Garrity, L.I. Electromyography: A review of the current status of subvocal speech research. *Memory and Cognition*, 1977, *5*, 615–622.

Gatchel, R.J., Baum, A., and Krantz, D.S. *An Introduction to Health Psychology*, 2nd ed. New York: Newbery Award Records, 1989.

Gazzaniga, M.S. *The Bisected Brain*. New York: Appleton-Century-Crofts, 1970.

Gazzaniga, M.S., and LeDoux, J.E. *The Integrated Mind*. New York: Plenum Press, 1978.

Geen, R.G., Stonner, D., and Shope, G.L. The facilitation of aggression by aggression: A study in response inhibition and disinhibition. *Journal of Personality and Social Psychology*, 1975, *31*, 721–726.

Geiselman, R.E., Fisher, R.P., Firstenberg, I., Hutton, L.A., Sullivan, S., Avetissian, L., and Prosk, A. Enhancement of eyewitness memory: An empirical evaluation of the cognitive interview. *Journal of Police Science and Administration*, 1984, *12*, 74–80.

Geller, D.M., Goodstein, L., Silver, M., and Sternberg, W.C. On being ignored: The effects of the violation of implicit rules of social interaction. *Sociometry*, 1974, *37*, 541–556.

Gelman, R. Logical capacity of very young children: Number invariance rules. *Child Development*, 1972, *43*, 75–90.

Gelman, R., and Shatz, M. Appropriate speech adjustments: The operation of conversational constraints on talk to two-year-olds. In *Interaction, Conversation, and the Development of Language*, edited by M. Lewis and L.A. Rosenblum. New York: John Wiley & Sons, 1978.

Gerbino, L., Oleshansky, M., and Gershon, S. Clinical use and mode of action of lithium. In *Psychopharmacology: A Generation of Progress*, edited by M.A. Lipton, A. DiMascio, and K.F. Killam. New York: Raven Press, 1978.

Gerrard, M. Are men and women really different? In *Females, Males, and Sexuality*, edited by K. Kelley. Albany, N.Y.: SUNY Press, 1986.

Gerrard, M. Sex, sex guilt, and contraceptive use revisited: The 1980s. *Journal of Personality and Social Psychology*, 1987, *52*, 345–359.

Geschwind, N., Quadfasel, F.A., and Segarra, J.M. Isolation of the speech area. *Neuropsychologia*, 1968, *6*, 327–340.

Geschwind, N.A., and Behan, P.O. Laterality, hormones, and immunity. In *Cerebral Dominance: The Biological Foundations*, edited by N. Geschwind and A.M. Galaburda. Cambridge, Mass.: Harvard University Press, 1984.

Gibson, E.J., and Walk, R.R. The "visual cliff." *Scientific American*, 1960, *202*, 2–9.

Gifford, R. *Applied Psychology: Variety and Opportunity*. Boston: Allyn and Bacon, 1991.

Gil, T.E. Psychological etiology to cancer: Truth or myth? *Israel Journal of Psychiatry and Related Sciences,* 1989, *26,* 164–185.

Gilligan, C.F. In a different voice: Women's conceptions of self and morality. *Harvard Educational Review,* 1977, *47,* 481–517.

Gilligan, C.F. *In a Different Voice.* Cambridge, Mass.: Harvard University Press, 1982.

Girvin, J.P. Cerebral (cortical) biostimulation. *Practical and Clinical Electrophysiology,* 1986, *9,* 764–771.

Gladwin, T. *East Is a Big Bird.* Cambridge, Mass.: Harvard University Press, 1970.

Glaser, R., Rice, J., Sheridan, J., Post, A., Fertel, R., Stout, J., Speicher, C.E., Kotur, M., and Kiecolt-Glaser, J.K. Stress-related immune suppression: Health implications. *Brain, Behavior, and Immunity,* 1987, *1,* 7–20.

Glass, G.V., McGaw, B., and Smith, M.L. *Meta-analysis in Social Research.* Beverly Hills, Calif.: Sage Publications, 1981.

Goddard, G.V. Development of epileptic seizures through brain stimulation at low intensity. *Nature,* 1967, *214,* 1020–1021.

Goldberg, L.R. Simple models or simple processes? Some research on clinical judgment. *American Psychologist,* 1968, *23,* 483–496.

Goldblatt, P.B., Moore, M.E., and Stunkard, A.J. Social factors in obesity. *Journal of the American Medical Association,* 1968, *21,* 1455–1470.

Goldin-Meadow, S., and Feldman, H. The development of language-like communication without a language model. *Science,* 1977, *197,* 401–403.

Goodglass, H. Agrammatism. In *Studies in Neurolinguistics,* edited by H. Whitaker and H.A. Whitaker. New York: Academic Press, 1976.

Goodwin, D.W. *Phobias: The Facts.* London: Oxford University Press, 1983.

Goodwin, D.W., and Guze, S.B. *Psychiatric Diagnosis,* 3rd ed. New York: Oxford University Press, 1984.

Gottesman, I.I., and Bertelsen, A. Confirming unexpressed genotypes for schizophrenia. *Archives of General Psychiatry,* 1989, *46,* 867–872.

Gould, R.L. *Transformations: Growth and Change in Adult Life.* New York: Simon & Schuster, 1978.

Graf, P., and Mandler, G. Activation makes words more accessible, but not necessarily more retrievable. *Journal of Verbal Learning and Verbal Behavior,* 1984, *23,* 553–568.

Graf, P., Squire, L.R., and Mandler, G. The information that amnesic patients do not forget. *Journal of Experimental Psychology: Learning, Memory, and Cognition,* 1984, *10,* 164–178.

Graham, J.R. *MMPI-2: Assessing Personality and Psychopathology.* New York: Oxford University Press, 1990.

Granville-Grossman, K.L., and Turner, P. The effect of propranolol on anxiety. *Lancet,* 1966, *1,* 788–790.

Gray, J.A. *The Psychology of Fear and Stress,* 2nd ed. Cambridge, England: Cambridge University Press, 1987.

Green, D.M., and Swets, J.A. *Signal Detection Theory and Psychophysics.* New York: Krieger, 1974.

Green, J.G., Fox, N.A., and Lewis, M. The relationship between neonatal characteristics and three-month mother-infant interaction in high-risk infants. *Child Development,* 1983, *54,* 1286–1296.

Greenberg, R., Pillard, R., and Pearlman, C. The effect of dream (stage REM) deprivation on adaptation to stress. *Psychosomatic Medicine,* 1972, *34,* 257–262.

Greenough, W.T., and Volkmar, F.R. Pattern of dendritic branching in occipital cortex of rats reared in complex environments. *Experimental Neurology,* 1973, *40,* 491–504.

Greenspan, S.I., and White, K.R. The efficacy of preventive intervention: A glass half full? *Bulletin of the National Center for Clinical Infant Progress,* 1985, *5,* 1–5.

Greenwald, A.G., Pratkanis, A.R., Leippe, M.R., and Baumgardner, M.H. Under what conditions does theory obstruct research progress? *Psychological Review,* 1986, *93,* 216–229.

Greenwald, D.F. An external construct validity study of Rorschach personality variables. *Journal of Personality Assessment,* 1990, *55,* 768–780.

Griffiths, M., and Payne, P.R. Energy expenditure in small children of obese and nonobese mothers. *Nature,* 1976, *260,* 698–700.

Griffitt, W. Environmental effects on interpersonal affective behavior: Ambient effective temperature and attraction. *Journal of Personality and Social Psychology,* 1970, *15,* 240–244.

Grossarth-Maticek, R., Bastiaans, J., and Kanazir, D.T. Psychosocial factors as strong predictors of mortality from cancer, ischaemic heart disease and stroke: The Yugoslav prospective study. *Journal of Psychosomatic Research,* 1985, *29,* 167–176.

Grossarth-Maticek, R., and Eysenck, H.J. Personality, stress and disease: Description and validation of a new inventory. *Psychological Reports,* 1990, *66,* 355–373.

Grove, W.M., Andreasen, N.C., McDonald-Scott, P., Keller, M.B., and Shapiro, R.W. Reliability studies of psychiatric diagnosis. *Archives of General Psychiatry,* 1981, *38,* 408–413.

Grusec, J.E., Kuczynski, L., Rushton, J., and Simutis, Z. Learning resistance to temptation through observation. *Developmental Psychology,* 1979, *15,* 233–240.

Guilmette, T.J., Faust, D., Hart, K., and Arkes, H.R. A national survey of psychologists who offer neuropsychological services. *Archives of Clinical Neuropsychology,* 1990, *5,* 373–392.

Gulevich, G., Dement, W.C., and Johnson, L. Psychiatric and EEG observations on a case of prolonged (264 hours) wakefulness. *Archives of General Psychiatry,* 1966, *15,* 29–35.

Gur, R.C., and Sackheim, H.A. Self-deception: A concept in search of a phenomenon. *Journal of Personality and Social Psychology,* 1979, *37,* 147–169.

Gustafson, G.E., and Harris, K.L. Women's responses to young infants' cries. *Developmental Psychology,* 1990, *26,* 144–152.

Gustavson, C.R., and Gustavson, J.C. Predation control using conditioned food aversion methodology: Theory, practice, and implications. *Annals of the New York Academy of Sciences,* 1985, *443,* 348–356.

Guze, S.B., and Robins, E. Suicide and primary affective disorders. *British Journal of Psychiatry,* 1970, *117,* 437–438.

Guze, S.B., Wolfgram, E.D., McKinney, J.K., and Cantwell, D.P. Psychiatric illness in the families of convicted criminals. A study of 519 first-degree relatives. *Disorders of the Nervous System,* 1967, *28,* 651–659.

Guze, S.B., Woodruff, R.A., and Clayton, P.J. Secondary affective disorder: A study of 95 cases. *Psychological Medicine,* 1971, *1,* 426–428.

Haaga, D.A., and Davison, G.C. Cognitive change methods. In *Helping People Change,* 3rd ed., edited by A.P. Goldstein and F.H. Kanfer. New York: Pergamon Press, 1989.

Haan, N., Millsap, R., and Hartka, E. As time goes by: Change and stability in personality over fifty years. *Psychology and Aging,* 1986, *1,* 220–232.

Haenny, P.E., Maunsell, J.H., and Schiller, P.H. State dependent activity in monkey visual cortex. II. Retinal and extraretinal factors in V4. *Experimental Brain Research,* 1988, *69,* 245–259.

Haenny, P.E., and Schiller, P.H. State dependent activity in monkey visual cortex. I. Single cell activity in V1 and V4 on visual tasks. *Experimental Brain Research,* 1988, *69,* 225–244.

Halgin, R.P. The clinical psychologist. In *Applied Psychology: Variety and Opportunity,* edited by R. Gifford. Boston: Allyn and Bacon, 1991.

Hall, E.T. *The Hidden Dimension.* New York: Doubleday, 1966.

Halmi, K.A. Anorexia nervosa: Recent investigations. *Annual Review of Medicine,* 1978, *29,* 137–148.

Hare, R.D. Temporal gradient of fear arousal in psychopaths. *Journal of Abnormal Psychology,* 1965, *70,* 442–445.

Harkins, S.G., and Petty, R.E. Effects of task difficulty and task uniqueness on social loafing. *Journal of Personality and Social Psychology,* 1982, *43,* 1214–1229.

Harlow, H. *Learning to Love.* New York: J. Aronson, 1974.

Hartshorne, H., and May, M.A. *Studies in Deceit.* New York: Macmillan, 1928.

Hatfield, E., and Sprecher, S. *Mirror, Mirror . . . The Importance of Looks in Everyday Life.* Albany, N.Y.: SUNY Press, 1986.

Hayes, C. *The Ape in Our House.* London: Gollancz, 1952.

Hebb, D.O. *The Organization of Behaviour.* New York: Wiley-Interscience, 1949.

Hebb, D.O. Drives and the C.N.S. (conceptual nervous system). *Psychological Review,* 1955, *62,* 243–254.

Hebb, D.O., Lambert, W.E., and Tucker, G.R. A DMZ in the language war. *Psychology Today,* April 1973, pp. 55–62.

Hecht, S., and Schlaer, S. An adaptometer for measuring human dark adaptation. *Journal of the Optical Society of America,* 1938, *28,* 269–275.

Heckler, M.M. *Fifth Special Report to the U.S. Congress on Alcohol and Health.* Washington, D.C.: U.S. Government Printing Office, 1983.

Heffner, H.E., and Heffner, R.S. Role of primate auditory cortex in hearing. In *Comparative Perception. Vol. II: Complex Signals,* edited by W.C. Stebbins and M.A. Berkley. New York: John Wiley & Sons, 1990.

Heider, F. *The Psychology of Interpersonal Relations.* New York: John Wiley & Sons, 1958.

Helmer, D.C., Ragland, D.R., and Syme, S.L. Hostility and coronary artery disease. *American Journal of Epidemiology,* 1991, *133,* 112–122.

Henderson, D., and Gillespie, R.D. *A Textbook of Psychiatry for Students and Practitioners.* London: Oxford University Press, 1950.

Henderson, N.D. Human behavior genetics. *Annual Review of Psychology,* 1982, *33,* 403–440.

Henke, P.G. The telencephalic limbic system and experimental gastric pathology: A review. *Neuroscience and Biobehavioral Reviews,* 1982, *6,* 381–390.

Henningfield, J.E., and Goldberg, S.R. Nicotine as a reinforcer in human subjects and laboratory animals. *Pharmacology, Biochemistry, and Behavior,* 1983, *19,* 989–992.

Heron, R.M. The ergonomist. In *Applied Psychology: Variety and Opportunity,* edited by R. Gifford. Boston: Allyn and Bacon, 1991.

Herrnstein, R.J., and Loveland, D.H. Complex visual concept in the pigeon. *Science,* 1964, *146,* 549–551.

Higgins, E.T., Rholes, W.S., and Jones, C.R. Category accessibility and impression formation. *Journal of Experimental Social Psychology,* 1977, *13,* 141–154.

Hilgard, E.R. A neodissociation interpretation of pain reduction in hypnosis. *Psychological Review,* 1973, *80,* 396–411.

Hilgard, E.R. *Divided Consciousness: Multiple Controls in Human Thought and Action.* New York: Wiley-Interscience, 1977.

Hilgard, E.R. Divided consciousness in hypnosis: The implications of the hidden observer. In *Hypnosis: Developments in Research and New Perspectives,* edited by E. Fromm and R.E. Shor. Chicago: Aldine Press, 1979.

Hilgard, E.R., Hilgard, J.R., Macdonald, H., Morgan, A.H., and Johnson, L.S. Covert pain in hypnotic analgesia: Its reality as tested by the real-simulator design. *Journal of Abnormal Psychology,* 1978, *87,* 655–663.

Hintzman, D.L. Articulatory coding in short-term memory. *Journal of Verbal Learning and Verbal Behavior,* 1967, *6,* 312–316.

Hirsch, J., and Knittle, J.L. Cellularity of obese and nonobese human adipose tissue. *Federation Proceedings,* 1970, *29,* 1516–1521.

Hirschfeld, M.A. Comment. *Archives of General Psychiatry,* 1990, *47,* 685–686.

Hobson, J.A. *The Dreaming Brain.* New York: Basic Books, 1988.

Hofer, P. The lawer-psychologist. In *Applied Psychology: Variety and Opportunity,* edited by R. Gifford. Boston: Allyn and Bacon, 1991.

Hofling, C.K. *Textbook of Psychiatry for Medical Practice.* Philadelphia: J.B. Lippincott, 1963.

Hofman, M.A., and Swaab, D.F. Sexual dimorphism of the human brain: Myth and reality. *Experimental and Clinical Endocrinology,* 1991, *98,* 161–170.

Hogan, J., and Hogan, R. How to measure employee reliability. *Journal of Applied Psychology,* 1989, *74,* 273–279.

Hohman, G.W. Some effects of spinal cord lesions on experienced emotional feelings. *Psychophysiology,* 1966, *3,* 143–156.

Holden, C. Identical twins reared apart. *Science,* 1980, *207,* 1323–1328.

Hollander, E., Schiffman, E., Cohen, B., Rivera-Stein, M.A., Rosen, W., Gorman, J.M., Fyer, A.J., Papp, L., and Liebowitz, M.R. Signs of central nervous system dysfunction in obsessive-compulsive disorder. *Archives of General Psychiatry,* 1990, *47,* 27–32.

Hollis, K.L. Pavlovian conditioning of signal-centered action patterns and autonomic behavior: A biological analysis of function. *Advances in the Study of Behavior,* 1982, *12,* 1–64.

Hollis, K.L., Cadieus, E.L., and Colbert, M.M. The biological function of Pavlovian conditioning: A mechanism for mating success in the blue gourami *(Trichogaster trichopterus). Journal of Comparative Psychology,* 1989, *103,* 115–121.

Holyoak, K.J. Problem solving. In *An Invitation to Cognitive Science. Vol. 3: Thinking,* edited by D.N. Osherson and E.E. Smith. Cambridge, Mass.: MIT Press, 1990.

Honig, W.K., Boneau, C.A., Burstein, K.R., and Pennypacker, H.C. Positive and negative generalization gradients obtained after equivalent training conditions. *Journal of Comparative and Physiological Psychology,* 1963, *56,* 111–116.

Horn, J.L. Organization of abilities and the development of intelligence. *Psychological Review,* 1968, *75,* 242–259.

Horn, J.L. Human abilities: A review of research and theory in the early 1970s. *Annual Review of Psychology,* 1976, *27,* 437–485.

Horn, J.L. Human ability systems. In *Life Span Development, Vol. 1,* edited by P.B. Baltes. New York: Academic Press, 1978.

Horn, J.L. The theory of fluid and crystallized intelligence in relation to concepts of cognitive psychology and aging in adulthood. In *Aging and Cognitive Processes,* edited by F.I.M. Craik and S. Trehub. New York: Plenum Press, 1982.

Horn, J.L., and Cattell, R.B. Refinement and test of the theory of fluid and crystallized ability intelligences. *Journal of Educational Psychology,* 1966, *57,* 253–270.

Horne, J.A. A review of the biological effects of total sleep deprivation in man. *Biological Psychology,* 1978, *7,* 55–102.

Horne, J.A. The effects of exercise on sleep. *Biological Psychology,* 1981, *12,* 241–291.

Horne, J.A. *Why We Sleep: The Functions of Sleep in Humans and Other Mammals.* Oxford, England: Oxford University Press, 1988.

Horne, J.A., and Harley, L.J. Human SWS following selective head heating during wakefulness. In *Sleep '88,* edited by J. Horne. New York: Gustav Fischer Verlag, 1989.

Horne, J.A., and Minard, A. Sleep and sleepiness following a behaviourally "active" day. *Ergonomics,* 1985, *28,* 567–575.

Horne, J.A., and Moore, V.J. Sleep effects of exercise with and without additional body cooling. *Electroencephalography and Clinical Neurophysiology,* 1985, *60,* 347–353.

Horne, J.A., and Pettitt, A.N. High incentive effects on vigilance performance during 72 hours of total sleep deprivation. *Acta Physiologica,* 1985, *58,* 123–139.

Hornik, R. Out-of-school television and schooling: Hypothesis and methods. *Review of Educational Research,* 1981, *51,* 199–214.

Howard, J.H., Cunningham, D.A., and Rechnitzer, P.A. Health patterns associated with type A behavior: A managerial population. *Journal of Human Stress,* 1976, *2,* 24–31.

Howard, M.O., and Jenson, J.M. Chemical aversion treatment of alcohol dependence. I. Validity of current criticisms. *International Journal of the Addictions,* 1990, *25,* 1227–1262.

Hubel, D.H., and Wiesel, T.N. The period of susceptibility to the physiological effects of unilateral eye closure in kittens. *Journal of Physiology* (London), 1970, *206,* 419–436.

Hubel, D.H., and Wiesel, T.N. Functional architecture of macaque monkey visual cortex. *Proceedings of the Royal Society of London, Series B,* 1977, *198,* 1–59.

Hubel, D.H., and Wiesel, T.N. Brain mechanisms of vision. *Scientific American,* 1979, *241,* 150–162.

Humphrey, N.K. Species and individuals in the perceptual world of monkeys. *Perception,* 1974, *3,* 105–114.

Hunt, E. Verbal ability. In *Human Abilities: An Information-Processing Approach,* edited by R.J. Sternberg. New York: W.H. Freeman, 1985.

Hyde, T.S., and Jenkins, J.J. The differential effects of incidental tasks on the organization of recall of a list of highly associated words. *Journal of Experimental Psychology,* 1969, *82,* 472–481.

Ickes, W., Patterson, M.L., Rajecki, D.W., and Tanford, S. Behavioral and cognitive consequences of reciprocal versus compensatory responses to pre-interaction expectancies. *Social Cognition,* 1982, *1,* 160–190.

Inglefinger, F.J. The late effects of total and subtotal gastrectomy. *New England Journal of Medicine,* 1944, *231,* 321–327.

Institute of Medicine. *Sleeping Pills, Insomnia, and Medical Practice.* Washington, D.C.: National Academy of Sciences, 1979.

Irvine, J., Garner, D.M., Craig, H.M., and Logan, A.G. Prevalence of type A behavior in untreated hypertensive individuals. *Hypertension,* 1991, *18,* 72–78.

Isaacs, W., Thomas, J., and Goldiamond, I. Application of operant conditioning to reinstate verbal behavior in psychotics. *Journal of Speech and Hearing Disorders,* 1960, *25,* 8–12.

Isabella, R.A., and Belsky, J. Interactional synchrony and the origins of infant-mother attachment: A replication study. *Child Development,* 1991, *62,* 373–384.

Iwata, J., Chida, K., and LeDoux, J.E. Cardiovascular responses elicited by stimulation of neurons in the central amygdaloid nucleus in awake but not anesthetized rats resemble conditioned emotional responses. *Brain Research,* 1987, *418,* 183–188.

Izard, C.E. *The Face of Emotion.* New York: Appleton-Century-Crofts, 1971.

Jackson, D.N. *Personality Research Form Manual,* 3rd ed. Port Huron, Mich.: Research Psychologists Press, 1984.

Jacobs, B.L., and McGinty, D.J. Participation of the amygdala in complex stimulus recognition and behavioral inhibition: Evidence from unit studies. *Brain Research,* 1972, *36,* 431–436.

Jacobsen, C.F., Wolf, J.B., and Jackson, T.A. An experimental analysis of the functions of the frontal association areas in primates. *Journal of Nervous and Mental Disease,* 1935, *82,* 1–14.

Jaffe, J.H. Drug addiction and drug abuse. In *The Pharmacological Basis of Therapeutics, Vol. 7,* edited by L.S. Goodman and A. Gilman. New York: Macmillan, 1985.

James, W. What is an emotion? *Mind,* 1884, *9,* 188–205.

James, W. *Principles of Psychology.* New York: Henry Holt, 1890.

James, W.P.T., and Trayhurn, P. Thermogenesis and obesity. *British Medical Bulletin,* 1981, *37,* 43–48.

Javal, E. Essai sur la physiologie de la lecture. *Annales D'Oculistique,* 1879, *82,* 242–253.

Jaynes, J. The problem of animate motion in the seventeenth century. *Journal of the History of Ideas,* 1970, *6,* 219–234.

Jeffcoate, W.J., Lincoln, N.B., Selby, C., and Herbert, M. Correlations between anxiety and serum prolactin in humans. *Journal of Psychosomatic Research,* 1986, *30,* 217–222.

Jenkins, J.H., and Karno, M. The meaning of expressed emotion: Theoretical issues raised by cross-cultural research. *American Journal of Psychiatry,* 1992, *149,* 9–21.

Jensen, A.R. The nature of the black-white difference on various psychometric tests: Spearman's hypothesis. *Behavioral and Brain Sciences,* 1985, *8,* 193–263.

Jensen, T., Genefke, I., and Hyldebrandt, N. Cerebral atrophy in young torture victims. *New England Journal of Medicine,* 1982, *307,* 1341.

Jeste, D.V., Del Carmen, R., Lohr, J.B., and Wyatt, R.J. Did schizophrenia exist before the eighteenth century? *Comprehensive Psychiatry,* 1985, *26,* 493–503.

Johansson, G. Visual perception of biological motion and a model for its analysis. *Perception and Psychophysics,* 1973, *14,* 201–211.

Johnson, J.H., Butcher, J.N., Null, C., and Johnson, K.N. Replicated item level factor analysis of the full MMPI. *Journal of Personality and Social Psychology,* 1984, *47,* 105–114.

Johnson, J.S., and Newport, E.L. Critical period effects in second language learning: The influence of maturational state on the acquisition of English as a second language. *Cognitive Psychology,* 1989, *21,* 60–99.

Johnson, S.B., and Sechrest, L. Comparison of desensitization and progressive relaxation in treating test anxiety. *Journal of Consulting and Clinical Psychology,* 1968, *32,* 280–286.

Johnson, T.J., Feigenbaum, R., and Weiby, M. Some determinants and consequences of the teacher's perception of causation. *Journal of Experimental Psychology,* 1964, *55,* 237–246.

Johnson-Laird, P.N. Deductive reasoning ability. In *Human Abilities: An Information-Processing Approach,* edited by R.J. Sternberg. New York: W.H. Freeman, 1985.

Johnson-Laird, P.N., and Wason, P. *Thinking.* Cambridge, England: Cambridge University Press, 1977.

Johnston, W.A., and Dark, V.J. Selective attention. *Annual Review of Psychology,* 1986, *37,* 43–76.

Johnstone, E.C., Crow, T.J., Frith, C.D., Stevens, M., Kreel, L., and Husband, J. The dementia of dementia praecox. *Acta Psychiatrica Scandinavica,* 1978, *57,* 305–324.

Jones, A.P., and Friedman, M.I. Obesity and adipocyte abnormalities in offspring of rats undernourished during pregnancy. *Science,* 1982, *215,* 1515–1519.

Jones, E.E. *Interpersonal Perception.* New York: W.H. Freeman, 1990.

Jones, E.E., and Davis, K.E. From acts to dispositions: The attribution process in person perceptions. In *Advances in Experimental Social Psychology, Vol. 2,* edited by L. Berkowitz. New York: Academic Press, 1965.

Jones, E.E., and Nisbett, R.E. The actor and observer: Divergent perceptions of the causes of behavior. In *Attribution: Perceiving the Causes of Behavior,* edited by E.E. Jones, D.E. Kamouse, H.H. Kelley, R.E. Nisbett, S. Valins, and B. Weiner. Morristown, N.J.: General Learning Press, 1971.

Jones, M.C. Psychological correlates of somatic development. *Child Development,* 1965, *36,* 899–911.

Jones, M.C., and Bayley, N. Physical maturing among boys as related to behavior. *Journal of Educational Psychology,* 1950, *41,* 129–184.

Jouvet, M. The role of monoamines and acetylcholine-containing neurons in the regulation of the sleep-waking cycle. *Ergebnisse der Physiologie,* 1972, *64,* 166–307.

Julesz, B. Texture and visual perception. *Scientific American,* 1965, *212,* 38–48.

Julien, R.M. *A Primer of Drug Action.* San Francisco: W.H. Freeman, 1981.

Jung, C.G. The structure of the unconscious. In *Collected Works, Vol. 7.* Princeton: Princeton University Press, 1953. (First German Edition, 1916.)

Just, M.A., and Carpenter, P.A. A theory of reading: From eye fixations to comprehension. *Psychological Review,* 1980, *87,* 329–354.

Just, M.A., and Carpenter, P.A. *The Psychology of Reading and Language Comprehension.* Boston: Allyn and Bacon, 1987.

Just, M.A., Carpenter, P.A., and Wu, R. *Eye Fixations in the Reading of Chinese Technical Text* (Technical Report). Pittsburgh: Carnegie-Mellon University, 1983.

Justice, A. Review of the effects of stress on cancer in laboratory animals: Importance of time of stress application and type of tumor. *Psychological Bulletin,* 1985, *98,* 108–138.

Kagan, J., Reznick, J.S., and Snidman, N. Biological bases of childhood shyness. *Science,* 1988, *240,* 167–171.

Kahneman, D., and Tversky, A. On the psychology of prediction. *Psychological Review,* 1973, *80,* 237–246.

Kales, A., Scharf, M.B., Kales, J.D., and Soldatos, C.R. Rebound insomnia: A potential hazard following withdrawal of certain benzodiazepines. *Journal of the American Medical Association,* 1979, *241,* 1692–1695.

Kane, J., Honigfeld, G., Singer, J., Meltzer, H., and the Clozaril Collaborative Study Group. Clozapine for the treatment-resistant schizophrenic: A double-blind comparison with chlorpromazine. *Archives of General Psychiatry,* 1988, *45,* 789–796.

Kanfer, F.H., and Phillips, J.S. *Learning Foundations of Behavior Therapy.* New York: John Wiley & Sons, 1970.

Kaplan, E.L., and Kaplan, G.A. The prelinguistic child. In *Human Development and Cognitive Processes,* edited by J. Eliot. New York: Holt, Rinehart and Winston, 1970.

Kapp, B.S., Gallagher, M., Applegate, C.D., and Frysinger, R.C. The amygdala central nucleus: Contributions to conditioned cardiovascular responding during aversive Pavlovian conditioning in the rabbit. In *Conditioning: Representation of Involved Neural Functions,* edited by C.D. Woody. New York: Plenum Press, 1982.

Kasch, F.W., Wallace, J.P., and Van Camp, S.P. Effects of 18 years of endurance exercise on the physical work capacity of older men. *Journal of Cardiopulmonary Rehabilitation,* 1985, *5,* 308–312.

Katz, D. *The World of Colour.* London: Kegan, Paul, Trench, Trubner, 1935.

Keller, S.E., Weiss, J.M., Schleifer, S.J., Miller, N.E., and Stein, M. Stress-induced suppression of immunity in adrenalectomized rats. *Science,* 1983, *221,* 1301–1304.

Kelley, H.H. Attribution theory in social psychology. In *Nebraska Symposium on Motivation, Vol. 15,* edited by D. Levine. Lincoln: University of Nebraska Press, 1967.

Kelley, H.H., and Michela, J.L. Attribution theory and research. *Annual Review of Psychology,* 1980, *31,* 457–501.

Kelly, D.H., Walker, A.M., Cahen, L.A., and Shannon, D.C. Periodic breathing in siblings of SIDS victims. *Pediatric Research,* 1980, *14,* 645–650.

Kelly, E.L., and Conley, J.J. Personality and compatibility: A prospective analysis of marital stability and marital satisfaction. *Journal of Personality and Social Psychology,* 1987, *52,* 27–40.

Kenrick, D.T., and Cialdini, R.B. Romantic attraction: Misattribution versus reinforcement explanations. *Journal of Personality and Social Psychology,* 1977, *35,* 381–391.

Kertesz, A. Personal communication, 1980.

Kety, S.S., Rosenthal, D., Wender, P.H., and Schulsinger, F. The types and prevalence of mental illness in the biological and adoptive families of adopted schizophrenics. In *The Transmission of Schizophrenia,* edited by D. Rosenthal and S.S. Kety. Elmsford, N.Y.: Pergamon Press, 1968.

Khachaturian, Z.S., and Blass, J.P. *Alzheimer's Disease: New Treatment Strategies.* New York: Dekker, 1992.

Kiang, N.Y.-S. *Discharge Patterns of Single Nerve Fibers in the Cat's Auditory Nerve.* Cambridge, Mass.: MIT Press, 1965.

Kihlstrom, J.F. Hypnosis. *Annual Review of Psychology,* 1985, *36,* 385–418.

Kimura, D. Are men's and women's brains really different? *Canadian Psychology,* 1987, *28,* 133–147.

Kissen, D.M. Personality characteristics in males conducive to lung cancer. *British Journal of Medical Psychology,* 1963, *36,* 27–36.

Klein, D.F., and Howard, A. *Psychiatric Case Studies: Treatment, Drugs, and Outcome.* Baltimore: Williams & Wilkins, 1972.

Klein, D.F., Zitrin, C.M., Woerner, M.G., and Ross, D.C. Treatment of phobias. II. Behavior therapy and supportive psychotherapy: Are there any specific ingredients? *Archives of General Psychiatry,* 1983, *40,* 139–145.

Kline, M.V. The production of antisocial behavior through hypnosis: New clinical data. *International Journal of Clinical and Experimental Hypnosis,* 1972, *20,* 80–94.

Kluft, R.P. An introduction to multiple personality disorder. *Psychiatric Annals,* 1984, *7,* 9–29.

Knittle, J.L., and Hirsch, J. Effect of early nutrition on the development of rat epididymal fat pads: Cellularity and metabolism. *Journal of Clinical Investigation,* 1968, *47,* 2001–2098.

Knowlton, B.J., Ramus, S., and Squire, L.R. Normal acquisition of an artificial grammar by amnesic patients. *Society for Neuroscience Abstracts,* 1991, *17,* 4.

Knox, R.E., and Inkster, J.A. Postdecision dissonance at post time. *Journal of Personality and Social Psychology,* 1968, *8,* 310–323.

Koch, J.L.A. *Leitfaden der Psychiatrie,* 2nd ed. Ravensburg, Austria: Dorn, 1889.

Koe, G. The school psychologist. In *Applied Psychology: Variety and Opportunity,* edited by R. Gifford. Boston: Allyn and Bacon, 1991.

Kogan, N. *Categorizing and Conceptualizing Styles in Younger and Older Adults, RB-73.* Princeton, N.J.: Educational Testing Service, 1973.

Köhler, W. *The Mentality of Apes,* 2nd ed. New York: Liveright, 1927/1973.

Kolb, B., and Whishaw, I.W. *Fundamentals of Human Neuropsychology.* New York: W.H. Freeman, 1990.

Konner, M.J. Aspects of the developmental ethology of a foraging people. In *Ethological Studies of Child Behaviour,* edited by N. Blurton Jones. Cambridge, England: Cambridge University Press, 1972.

Kosslyn, S.M. Scanning visual images: Some structural implications. *Perception and Psychophysics,* 1973, *14,* 90–94.

Kosslyn, S.M. Evidence for analogue representation. Paper presented at the Conference on Theoretical Issues in Natural Language Processing, Massachusetts Institute of Technology, Cambridge, Mass., July 1975.

Kozlowski, L.T., and Cutting, J.E. Recognizing the sex of a walker from a dynamic point-light display. *Perception and Psychophysics,* 1977, *21,* 575–580.

Kral, J.G. Surgical treatment of obesity. *Medical Clinics of North America,* 1989, *73,* 251–264.

Kramer, F.M., Jeffery, R.W., Forster, J.L., and Snell, M.K. Long-term follow-up of behavioral treatment for obesity: Patterns of weight regain among men and women. *International Journal of Obesity,* 1989, *13,* 123–136.

Kroger, W.S., and Doucé, R.G. Hypnosis in criminal investigation. *International Journal of Clinical and Experimental Hypnosis,* 1979, *27,* 358–374.

Krueger, T.H. *Visual Imagery in Problem Solving and Scientific Creativity.* Derby, Conn.: Seal Press, 1976.

Kuhl, P.K., Williams, K.A., Lacerda, F., Stevens, K.N., and Lindblom, B. Linguistic experience alters phonetic perception in infants by 6 months of age. *Science,* 1992, *255,* 606–608.

Kulka, R.A., and Kessler, J.R. Is justice really blind? The effect of litigant physical attractiveness on judicial judgment. *Journal of Applied Social Psychology,* 1978, *4,* 336–381.

Kulka, R.A., Schlenger, W.E., Fairbank, J.A., Hough, R.L., Jordan, B.K., Marmar, C.R., and Weiss, D.S. *Trauma and the Vietnam War Generation: Report of Findings from the National Vietnam Veterans Readjustment Study.* New York: Brunner/Mazel, 1990.

Kupfer, D.J. REM latency: A psychobiologic marker for primary depressive disease. *Biological Psychiatry,* 1976, *11,* 159–174.

Lacey, J.I., and Lacey, B.C. The law of initial value in the longitudinal study of autonomic constitution: Reproducibility of autonomic response patterns over a four-year interval. *Annals of the New York Academy of Sciences,* 1962, *98,* 1257–1290.

Ladame, P.L. L'hypnotisme et la médecine légale. *Archives de l'Anthropologie Criminelle et des Sciences Pénales,* 1887, *2,* 293–335; 520–559.

Lakoff, G., and Turner, M. *More Than Cool Reason: The Power of Poetic Metaphor.* Chicago: University of Chicago Press, 1989.

Lange, C.G. *Über Gemüthsbewegungen.* Leipzig, East Germany: T. Thomas, 1887.

Langer, E.J. The illusion of control. *Journal of Personality and Social Psychology,* 1975, *32,* 311–328.

Langer, E.J., and Abelson, R.P. A patient by any other name . . . : Clinician group difference in labeling bias. *Journal of Consulting and Clinical Psychology,* 1974, *42,* 4–9.

Langer, E.J., Bashner, R.S., and Chanowitz, B. Decreasing prejudice by increasing discrimination. *Journal of Personality and Social Psychology,* 1985, *49,* 113–120.

Langlois, J.H., and Downs, A.C. Mothers, fathers, and peers as socialization agents of sex-typed play behaviors in young children. *Child Development,* 1980, *51,* 1237–1247.

Lankenau, H., Swigar, M.E., Bhimani, S., Luchins, S., and Quinlon, D.M. Cranial CT scans in eating disorder patients and controls. *Comprehensive Psychiatry,* 1985, *26,* 136–147.

LaPiere, R.T. Attitudes and actions. *Social Forces,* 1934, *13,* 230–237.

Larsson, L. Morphological and functional characteristics of the ageing skeletal muscle in man. *Acta Physiologica Scandinavia (Supplement),* 1978, *457,* 1–29.

Latané, B., Williams, K., and Harkins, S. Many hands make light the work: The causes and consequences of social loafing. *Journal of Personality and Social Psychology,* 1979, *37,* 823–832.

Lau, R.R., and Russell, D. Attributions in the sports pages. *Journal of Personality and Social Psychology,* 1980, *39,* 29–38.

Laurence, J.-R., and Perry, C. *Hypnosis, Will, and Memory: A Psycho-Legal History.* New York: Guilford Press, 1988.

Lazarus, A.A. Group therapy of phobic disorders by systematic desensitization. *Journal of Abnormal and Social Psychology,* 1961, *63,* 504–510.

Lazarus, R.S. Thoughts on the relations between emotion and cognition. In *Approaches to Emotion,* edited by K.R. Scherer and P. Ekman. Hillsdale, N.J.: Lawrence Erlbaum Associates, 1984.

Lazarus, R.S., and Folkman, S. *Stress, Coping, and Adaptation.* New York: Springer-Verlag, 1984.

LeDoux, J.E. Emotion. In *Handbook of Physiology: Nervous System V,* edited by F. Plum. Washington, D.C.: American Physiological Society, 1987.

Leech, S., and Witte, K.L. Paired-associate learning in elderly adults as related to pacing and incentive conditions. *Developmental Psychology,* 1971, *5,* 180.

Lefkowitz, M.M., Eron, L.D., Walder, L.O., and Huesmann, L.R. *Growing Up to Be Violent: A Longitudinal Study of the Development of Aggression.* New York: Pergamon Press, 1977.

Leli, D.A., and Filskov, S.B. Clinical detection of intellectual deterioration associated with brain damage. *Journal of Clinical Psychology,* 1984, *40,* 1435–1441.

Leon, G.R. *Case Histories of Deviant Behavior,* 2nd ed. Boston: Allyn and Bacon, 1977.

Leonard, C.M., Rolls, E.T., Wilson, F.A.W., and Baylis, G.C. Neurons in the amygdala of the monkey with responses selective for faces. *Behavioral Brain Research,* 1985, *15,* 159–176.

Leonard, H.L., Swedo, S.E., Rapoport, J.L., Koby, E.V., Lenane, M.C., Cheslow, D.L., and Hamburger, S.D. Treatment of obsessive-compulsive disorder with clomipramine and desipramine in children and adolescents: A double-blind crossover comparison. *Archives of General Psychiatry,* 1989, *46,* 1088–1092.

Lepper, M.R., Greene, D., and Nisbett, R.E. Undermining children's intrinsic interest with extrinsic rewards: A test of the "overjustification" hypothesis. *Journal of Personality and Social Psychology,* 1973, *28,* 129–137.

LeShan, L.L., and Worthington, R.E. Personality as a factor in the pathogenesis of cancer: A review of literature. *British Journal of Medical Psychology,* 1956a, *29,* 49–56.

LeShan, L.L., and Worthington, R.E. Some recurrent life history patterns observed in patients with malignant disease. *Journal of Nervous and Mental Disorders,* 1956b, *124,* 460–465.

LeVay, S. A difference in hypothalamic structure between heterosexual and homosexual men. *Science,* 1991, *253,* 1034–1037.

Levenson, R.W., Ekman, P., and Friesen, W.V. Voluntary facial action generates emotion-specific autonomic nervous system activity. *Psychophysiology,* 1990, *27,* 363–384.

Levinson, D.J., Darrow, C.N., Klein, E.B., Levinson, M.H., and McKee, B. *The Seasons of a Man's Life.* New York: Alfred A. Knopf, 1978.

Levy, L.H. *Psychological Interpretation.* New York: Holt, Rinehart and Winston, 1963.

Lewinsohn, P.H., Weinstein, M., and Alper, T. A behavioral approach to the group treatment of depressed persons: A methodological contribution. *Journal of Clinical Psychology,* 1970, *26,* 525–532.

Lewis, M., Young, G., Brooks, J., and Michalson, L. The beginning of friendship. In *Friendship and Peer Relations*, edited by M. Lewis and L.A. Rosenblum. New York: John Wiley & Sons, 1975.

Liberman, A.M., Cooper, F.S., Shankweiler, D.P., and Studdert-Kennedy, M. Perception of the speech code. *Psychological Review*, 1967, *74*, 431–461.

Liégois, J. Rapports de la suggestion et du somnambulisme avec la jurisprudence et la médicine légale: La responsabilité dans les états hypnotiques. In *Premier Congrès International de l'Hypnotisme Expérimentale et Thérapeutique: Comptes Rendus*. Paris: Octave Doin, 1889.

Linville, P.W. The complexity-extremity effect and age-based stereotyping. *Journal of Personality and Social Psychology*, 1982, *42*, 183–211.

Linville, P.W., Fischer, G.W., and Salovey, P. Perceived distributions of the characteristics of in-group and out-group members: Empirical evidence and a computer simulation. *Journal of Personality and Social Psychology*, 1989, *57*, 165–188.

Lisker, L., and Abramson, A. The voicing dimension: Some experiments in comparative phonetics. In *Proceedings of Sixth International Congress of Phonetic Sciences, Prague, 1967*. Prague: Academia, 1970.

Livingstone, M.S., and Hubel, D. Segregation of form, color, movement, and depth: Anatomy, physiology, and perception. *Science*, 1988, *240*, 740–749.

Loeb, G.E. Cochlear prosthetics. *Annual Review of Neuroscience*, 1990, *13*, 357–371.

Loehlin, J.C., and Nichols, R.C. *Heredity, Environment, and Personality: A Study of 850 Sets of Twins*. Austin: University of Texas Press, 1976.

Loftus, E.F. *Eyewitness Testimony*. Cambridge, Mass.: Harvard University Press, 1979.

Loftus, E.F., and Palmer, J.C. Reconstruction of automobile destruction: An example of the interaction between language and memory. *Journal of Verbal Learning and Verbal Behavior*, 1974, *13*, 585–589.

Loftus, E.F., and Zanni, G. Eyewitness testimony: The influence of the wording of a question. *Bulletin of the Psychonomic Society*, 1975, *5*, 86–88.

Logan, F.A. Decision making by rats: Delay versus amount of reward. *Journal of Comparative and Physiological Psychology*, 1965, *59*, 1–12.

Lombardo, R., and Carreno, L. Relationship of type A behavior pattern in smokers to carbon monoxide exposure and smoking topography. *Health Psychology*, 1987, *6*, 445–452.

Loomis, W.F. Skin pigment regulation of vitamin-D biosynthesis in man. *Science*, 1967, *157*, 501–506.

LoPiccolo, J., and Friedman, J.M. Sex therapy: An integrated model. In *Contemporary Psychotherapies: Models and Methods*, edited by S.J. Lynn and J.P. Garskee. New York: Merrill, 1985.

Lorenz, K. *On Aggression*. New York: Harcourt Brace Jovanovich, 1966.

Luborsky, L., Chandler, M., Auerbach, A.H., Cohen, J., and Bachrach, H.M. Factors influencing the outcome of psychotherapy: A review of quantitative research. *Psychological Bulletin*, 1971, *75*, 145–185.

Luborsky, L., and Spence, D.P. Quantitative research on psychoanalytic therapy. In *Handbook of Psychotherapy and Behavior Change: An Empirical Analysis*, 2nd ed. New York: John Wiley & Sons, 1978.

Lundy, A. Testing conditions and TAT validity: Meta-analysis of the literature through 1983. Paper presented at the meeting of the American Psychological Association, Toronto, August 1984. (Cited by Lundy, 1988.)

Lundy, A. Instructional set and thematic apperception test validity. *Journal of Personality Assessment*, 1988, *52*, 309–320.

Lupfer, M.B., Clark, L.F., and Hutcherson, H.W. Impact of context on spontaneous trait and situational attributions. *Journal of Personality and Social Psychology*, 1990, *58*, 239–249.

Luria, A.R. *The Working Brain*. New York: Penguin Books, 1973.

Luria, S.M., Neir, D.F., and Schlichting, C. Performance and preference with various VDT phosphors. *Applied Ergonomics*, 1989, *20*, 33–38.

Luxford, W.M., and Brackmann, D.E. The history of cochlear implants. In *Cochlear Implants*, edited by R.F. Gray. London: Croom Helm, 1985.

Lykken, D.T. *A Tremor in the Blood: Uses and Abuses of the Lie Detector*. New York: McGraw-Hill, 1981.

Lykken, D.T. The case against polygraph testing. In *The Polygraph Test: Lies, Truth and Science*, edited by A. Gale. London: Sage Publications, 1988.

Lynn, R. Ethnic and racial differences in intelligence: International comparisons. In *Human Variation: The Biopsychology of Age, Race and Sex*, edited by R.T. Osborne, C.E. Noble, and N. Weyl. New York: Academic Press, 1978.

Lytton, H., and Romney, D.M. Parents' differential socialization of boys and girls: A meta-analysis. *Psychological Bulletin*, 1991, *109*, 267–296.

Maccoby, E.E., and Jacklin, C.N. *The Psychology of Sex Differences*. Stanford: Stanford University Press, 1974.

Machon, R.A., Mednick, S.A., and Schulsinger, F. The interaction of seasonality, place of birth, genetic risk and subsequent schizophrenia in a high risk sample. *British Journal of Psychiatry*, 1983, *143*, 383–388.

Mahoney, M.J., and Thoresen, C.E. *Self-control: Power to the Person*. Monterey, Calif.: Brooks/Cole, 1974.

Maier, S.F., and Seligman, M.E. Learned helplessness: Theory and evidence. *Journal of Experimental Psychology: General*, 1976, *105*, 3–46.

Malpass, R.S., and Devine, P.G. Guided memory in eyewitness identification. *Journal of Applied Psychology*, 1981, *66*, 343–350.

Mann, A.J., Harrell, A., and Hurt, M. *A Review of Head Start Research Since 1969 and an Annotated Bibliography*. Washington, D.C.: Department of Health, Education and Welfare, 1977.

Manuck, S.B., Kaplan, J.R., and Clarkson, T.B. Behaviorally-induced heart rate reactivity and atherosclerosis in cynomolgus monkeys. *Psychosomatic Medicine*, 1983, *45*, 95–108.

Manuck, S.B., Kaplan, J.R., and Matthews, K.A. Behavioral antecedents of coronary heart disease and atherosclerosis. *Arteriosclerosis*, 1968, *6*, 1–14.

Marcel, A.J. Conscious and unconscious perception: Experiments on visual masking and word recognition. *Cognitive Psychology*, 1983, *15*, 197–237.

Marczynski, T.J., and Urbancic, M. Animal models of chronic anxiety and "fearlessness." *Brain Research Bulletin*, 1988, *21*, 483–490.

Margolin, D.I., Friedrich, F.J., and Carlson, N.R. Visual agnosia-optic aphasia: Continuum or dichotomy? Paper presented at the meeting of the International Neuropsychology Society, 1985.

Margolin, D.I., Marcel, A.J., and Carlson, N.R. Common mechanisms in dysnomia and post-semantic surface dyslexia: Processing deficits and selective attention. In *Surface Dyslexia: Neuropsychological and Cognitive Studies of Phonological Reading*. London: Lawrence Erlbaum Associates, 1985.

Marler, P. Animal communication: Affect or cognition? In *Approaches to Emotion*, edited by K.R. Scherer and P. Ekman. Hillsdale, N.J.: Lawrence Erlbaum Associates, 1984.

Martens, R. Palmar sweating and the presence of an audience. *Journal of Experimental Social Psychology*, 1969, *5*, 371–374.

Masling, J. The influence of situational and interpersonal variables in projective testing. *Psychological Bulletin*, 1960, *57*, 65–85.

Maslow, A.H. *Motivation and Personality*, 2nd ed. New York: Harper & Row, 1970.

Masters, W.H., and Johnson, V.E. *Human Sexual Response*. Boston: Little, Brown, 1966.

Masters, W.H., and Johnson, V.E. *Human Sexual Inadequacy*. Boston: Little, Brown, 1970.

Masters, W.H., and Johnson, V.E. *Homosexuality in Perspective*. Boston: Little, Brown, 1979.

Matsuda, L.A., Lolait, S.J., Brownstein, M.J., Young, A.C., and Bonner, T.I. Structure of a cannabinoid receptor and functional expression of the cloned cDNA. *Nature*, 1990, *346*, 561–564.

Mattes, R.D., Arnold, C., and Boraas, M. Learned food aversions among cancer chemotherapy patients: Incidence, nature and clinical implications. *Cancer*, 1987, *60*, 2576–2580.

Mawson, A.R. Anorexia nervosa and the regulation of intake: A review. *Psychological Medicine*, 1974, *4*, 289–308.

Mayer, J. Regulation of energy intake and the body weight: The glucostatic theory and the lipostatic hypothesis. *Annals of the New York Academy of Science*, 1955a, *63*, 15–43.

Mayer, J. The role of exercise and activity in weight control. In *Weight Control: A Collection of Papers Presented at the Weight Control Symposium*, edited by E.S. Eppright, P. Swanson, and C.A. Iverson. Ames: Iowa State College Press, 1955b.

Mazur, A., and Lamb, T. Testosterone, status, and mood in human males. *Hormones and Behavior*, 1980, *14*, 236–246.

McClelland, D.C. How motives, skills, and values determine what people do. *American Psychologist*, 1985, *40*, 812–825.

McClelland, D.C., Atkinson, J.W., Clark,

R.W., and Lowell, E.L. *The Achievement Motive*. New York: Appleton-Century-Crofts, 1953.

McClintock, M.K., and Adler, N.T. The role of the female during copulation in wild and domestic Norway rats (*Rattus norvegicus*). *Behaviour*, 1978, *67*, 67–96.

McCrae, R.R., and Costa, P.T. Updating Norman's "adequate taxonomy": Intelligence and personality dimensions in natural language and in questionnaires. *Journal of Personality and Social Psychology*, 1985, *49*, 710–712.

McCrae, R.R., and Costa, P.T. Validation of the five-factor model of personality across instruments and observers. *Journal of Personality and Social Psychology*, 1987, *52*, 81–90.

McCrae, R.R., and Costa, P.T. *Personality in Adulthood*. New York: Guilford Press, 1990.

McCrae, R.R., Costa, P.T., and Busch, C.M. Evaluating comprehensiveness in personality systems: The California Q-Set and the five-factor model. *Journal of Personality*, 1986, *54*, 430–446.

McDougall, W. *Outline of Psychology*. New York: Charles Scribner's Sons, 1924.

McKay, D.C. Aspects of the theory of comprehension, memory and attention. *Quarterly Journal of Experimental Psychology*, 1973, *25*, 22–40.

McNeal, J. Children as customers. *American Demographics*, 1990, *12(9)*, 36–39.

McNeil, E.B. *The Quiet Furies: Man and Disorder*. Englewood Cliffs, N.J.: Prentice-Hall, 1967.

McNeill, D. *The Acquisition of Language: The Study of Developmental Psycholinguistics*. New York: Harper & Row, 1970.

McReynolds, W.T. Learned helplessness as a schedule-shift effect. *Journal of Research in Personality*, 1980, *14*, 139–157.

Meddis, R., Pearson, A., and Langford, G. An extreme case of healthy insomnia. *Electroencephalography and Clinical Neurophysiology*, 1973, *35*, 213–214.

Mednick, S.A., Gabrielli, W.F., and Hutchings, B. Genetic influences in criminal behavior: Some evidence from an adoption cohort. In *Prospective Studies of Crime and Delinquency*, edited by K.T. VanDusen and S.A. Mednick. Hingham, Mass.: Martinus Nyhoff, 1983.

Mednick, S.A., Machon, R.A., Huttunen, M.O., and Bonett, D. Adult schizophrenia following prenatal exposure to an influenza epidemic. *Archives of General Psychiatry*, 1988, *45*, 189–192.

Meehl, P.E. *Clinical Versus Statistical Prediction*. Minneapolis, Minn.: University of Minnesota Press, 1954.

Meehl, P.E. When shall we use our heads instead of the formula? *Journal of Counseling Psychology*, 1957, *4*, 268–273.

Meehl, P.E. Causes and effects of my disturbing little book. *Journal of Personality Assessment*, 1968, *50*, 370–375.

Meichenbaum, D.H. *Cognitive-Behavior Modification: An Integrative Approach*. New York: Plenum Press, 1977.

Meindl, J.R., and Lerner, M.J. Exacerbation of extreme responses to an out-group. *Journal of Personality and Social Psychology*, 1985, *47*, 71–84.

Merikle, P.M. Subliminal auditory messages: An evaluation. *Psychology and Marketing*, 1988, *5*, 355–372.

Merton, R.K. The self-fulfilling prophecy. *Antioch Reviews*, 1948, *8*, 193–210.

Mervis, C.B., and Rosch, E. Categorization of natural objects. *Annual Review of Psychology*, 1981, *32*, 89–116.

Mesulam, M.-M. *Principles of Behavioral Neurology*. Philadelphia: F.A. Davis, 1985.

Mikulincer, M., and Solomon, Z. Attributional style and combat-related posttraumatic stress disorder. *Journal of Abnormal Psychology*, 1988, *97*, 308–313

Miles, H.L. Apes and language: The search for communicative competence. In *Language in Primates: Perspectives and Implications*, edited by J. de Luce and H.T. Wilder. New York: Springer-Verlag, 1983.

Milgram, S. Behavioral study of obedience. *Journal of Abnormal and Social Psychology*, 1963, *67*, 371–378.

Milgram, S. *Obedience to Authority*. New York: Harper & Row, 1974.

Millenson, J.R. *Principles of Behavioral Analysis*. New York: Macmillan, 1967.

Miller, D.T., and Turnbull, W. Expectancies and interpersonal processes. *Annual Review of Psychology*, 1986, *37*, 233–256.

Miller, G.A. The magical number seven plus or minus two: Some limits on our capacity for processing information. *Psychological Review*, 1956, *63*, 81–97.

Miller, G.A., Heise, G.A., and Lichten, W. The intelligibility of speech as a function of the context of the test materials. *Journal of Experimental Psychology*, 1951, *41*, 329–335.

Miller, G.A., and Taylor, W.G. The perception of repeated bursts of noise. *Journal of the Acoustical Society of America*, 1948, *20*, 171–182.

Miller, N.E. Behavioral medicine: Symbiosis between laboratory and clinic. *Annual Review of Psychology*, 1983, *34*, 1–31.

Miller, R.J., Hennessy, R.T., and Leibowitz, H.W. The effect of hypnotic ablation of the background on the magnitude of the Ponzo perspective illusion. *International Journal of Clinical and Experimental Hypnosis*, 1973, *21*, 180–191.

Miller, W.R., Rosellini, R.A., and Seligman, M.E.P. Learned helplessness and depression. In *Psychopathology: Experimental Models*, edited by J.D. Maser and M.E.P. Seligman. San Francisco: W.H. Freeman, 1977.

Milner, B. Memory and the temporal regions of the brain. In *Biology of Memory*, edited by K.H. Pribram and D.E. Broadbent. New York: Academic Press, 1970.

Minuchin, S. *Families and Family Therapy*. Cambridge, Mass.: Harvard University Press, 1974.

Mischel, W. *Personality and Assessment*. New York: John Wiley & Sons, 1968.

Mischel, W. Toward a cognitive social learning reconceptualization of personality. *Psychological Review*, 1973, *80*, 252–283.

Mischel, W. *Introduction to Personality*, 2nd ed. New York: Holt, Rinehart and Winston, 1976.

Mischel, W. The interaction of person and situation. In *Personality at the Crossroads: Current Issues in Interactional Psychology*, edited by D. Magnusson and N.S. Endler. Hillsdale, N.J.: Lawrence Erlbaum Associates, 1977.

Mischel, W. On the interface of cognition and personality: Beyond the person-situation debate. *American Psychologist*, 1979, *34*, 740–754.

Money, J., and Ehrhardt, A. *Man & Woman, Boy & Girl*. Baltimore: Johns Hopkins University Press, 1972.

Money, J., Schwartz, M., and Lewis, V.G. Adult erotosexual status and fetal hormonal masculinization and demasculinization: 46,XX congenital virilizing adrenal hyperplasia and 46,XY androgen-insensitivity syndrome compared. *Psychoneuroendocrinology*, 1984, *9*, 405–414.

Money, J., and Tucker, P. *Sexual Signatures: On Being a Man or a Woman*. Boston: Little, Brown, 1975.

Montemayor, R. Children's performance in a game and their attraction to it as a function of sex-typed labels. *Child Development*, 1974, *45*, 152–156.

Moody, K. *Growing Up on Television: The TV Effect*. New York: Times Books, 1980.

Moore, C.L. Interaction of species-typical environmental and hormonal factors in sexual differentiation of behavior. *Annals of the New York Academy of Sciences*, 1986, *474*, 108–119.

Moray, N. Attention in dichotic listening: Affective cues and the influence of instructions. *Quarterly Journal of Experimental Psychology*, 1959, *11*, 56–60.

Morris, T.A. "Type C" for cancer? Low trait anxiety in the pathogenesis of breast cancer. *Cancer Detection and Prevention*, 1980, *3*, 102.

Moss, C.S. *Hypnosis in Perspective*. New York: Macmillan, 1965.

Mukhametov, L.M. Sleep in marine mammals. In *Sleep Mechanisms*, edited by A.A. Borbély and J.L. Valatx. Munich: Springer-Verlag, 1984.

Murray, H.A. *Explorations in Personality*. New York: Science Editions, 1962. (Originally published 1938.)

Nafe, J.P., and Wagoner, K.S. The nature of pressure adaptation. *Journal of General Psychology*, 1941, *25*, 323–351.

National Clearinghouse for Alcohol and Drug Information. *Economic Costs of Alcohol and Drug Abuse and Mental Illness: 1985*. Rockville, Md.: U.S. Government Printing Office, 1991.

National Commission for the Protection of Human Subjects of Biomedical and Behavioral Research. *Report and Recommendations: Psychosurgery*. Washington, D.C.: U.S. Government Printing Office, 1977.

Nawas, M.M., Fishman, S.T., and Pucel, J.C. The standardized desensitization program applicable to group and individual treatment. *Behaviour Research and Therapy*, 1970, *6*, 63–68.

Neimark, E.D. Current status of formal operations research. *Human Development*, 1979, *22*, 60–67.

Neisser, U. Visual search. *Scientific American*, 1964, *210*, 94–102.

Neisser, U. Selective reading: A method for the study of visual attention. Paper presented at the 19th International Congress of Psychology, London, 1969.

Neisser, U. *Memory Observed*. San Francisco: W.H. Freeman, 1982.

Neisser, U., and Becklen, R. Selective looking: Attending to visually significant events. *Cognitive Psychology*, 1975, *7*, 480–494.

Newell, A., and Simon, H.A. *Human Problem Solving*. Englewood Cliffs, N.J.: Prentice-Hall, 1972.

Newport, E.L., Gleitman, H.R., and Gleitman, L. Mother I'd rather do it myself: Some effects and noneffects of maternal speech style. In *Talking to Children: Language Input and Acquisition*, edited by C.E. Snow and C.A. Ferguson. Cambridge, England: Cambridge University Press, 1977.

Newport, E.L., and Supalla, R. A critical period effect in the acquisition of a primary language. Unpublished manuscript cited by Johnson, J.S., and Newport, E.L. Critical period effects in second language learning: The influence of maturational state on the acquisition of English as a second language. *Cognitive Psychology*, 1989, *21*, 60–99.

Nicholl, C.S., and Russell, R.M. Analysis of animal rights literature reveals the underlying motives of the movement: Ammunition for counter offensive by scientists. *Endocrinology*, 1990, *127*, 985–989.

Nicolaus, L.K., Hoffman, T.E., and Gustavson, C.R. Taste aversion conditioning in free ranging raccoons (*Procyon lotor*). *Northwest Science*, 1982, *56*, 165–169.

Nicolaus, L.K., and Nellis, D.W. The first evaluation of the use of conditioned taste aversion to control predation by mongooses upon eggs. *Applied Animal Behaviour Science*, 1987, *17*, 329–346.

Nielsen, L.L., and Sarason, I.G. Emotion, personality, and selective attention. *Journal of Personality and Social Psychology*, 1981, *41*, 945–960.

Nisbett, R.E., and Schachter, S. Cognitive manipulation of pain. *Journal of Experimental Social Psychology*, 1966, *2*, 227–236.

Nisbett, R.E., and Wilson, T.D. Telling more than we can know: Verbal reports on mental processes. *Psychological Review*, 1977, *84*, 231–259.

Noirot, E. Selective priming of maternal responses by auditory and olfactory cues from mouse pups. *Developmental Psychobiology*, 1972, *5*, 371–387.

Norman, W.T. Toward an adequate taxonomy of personality attributes: Replicated factor structure in peer nomination personality ratings. *Journal of Abnormal and Social Psychology*, 1963, *66*, 574–583.

Novak, M.A., and Harlow, H.F. Social recovery of monkeys isolated for the first year of life. 1. Rehabilitation and therapy. *Developmental Psychology*, 1975, *11*, 453–465.

Offer, D., and Sabshin, M. *Normality and the Life Cycle: A Critical Integration*. New York: Basic Books, 1984.

Öhman, A., Erixon, G., and Löfberg, I. Phobias and preparedness: Phobic versus neutral pictures as conditional stimuli for human autonomic responses. *Journal of Abnormal Psychology*, 1975, *84*, 41–45.

O'Keefe, J., and Bouma, H. Complex sensory properties of certain amygdala units in the freely moving cat. *Experimental Neurology*, 1969, *23*, 384–398.

Oldenburg, D. Hidden messages. *The Washington Post*, April 3, 1990.

Olds, J. Commentary. In *Brain Stimulation and Motivation*, edited by E.S. Valenstein. Glenview, Ill.: Scott, Foresman, 1973.

Olton, D.S., Collison, C., and Werz, M.A. Spatial memory and radial arm maze performance in rats. *Learning and Motivation*, 1977, *8*, 289–314.

Olton, D.S., and Samuelson, R.J. Remembrance of places past: Spatial memory in rats. *Journal of Experimental Psychology: Animal Behavior Processes*, 1976, *2*, 97–116.

Orne, M.T. The nature of hypnosis: Artifact and essence. *Journal of Abnormal and Social Psychology*, 1959, *58*, 277–299.

Orne, M.T., and Evans, F.J. Social control in the psychological experiment: Antisocial behavior and hypnosis. *Journal of Personality and Social Psychology*, 1965, *1*, 189–200.

Orne, M.T., Whitehouse, W.G., Dinges, D.F., and Orne, E.C. Reconstructing memory through hypnosis. In *Hypnosis and Memory*, edited by H.M. Pettinati. New York: Guilford Press, 1988.

Overmeier, J.B., and Seligman, M.E.P. Effects of inescapable shock upon subsequent escape and avoidance responding. *Journal of Comparative and Physiological Psychology*, 1967, *63*, 28–33.

Ozer, D.J. Correlation and the coefficient of determination. *Psychological Bulletin*, 1985, *97*, 307–315.

Palmer, S.E. The effects of contextual scenes on the identification of objects. *Memory and Cognition*, 1975, *3*, 519–526.

Park, B., and Rothbart, M. Perception of outgroup homogeneity and levels of social categorization: Memory for the subordinate attributes of in-group and out-group members. *Journal of Personality and Social Psychology*, 1982, *42*, 1051–1068.

Parke, R.D., and Collmer, C.W. Child abuse: An interdisciplinary analysis. In *Review of Child Development Research, Vol. 5*, edited by E.M. Hetherington. Chicago: University of Chicago Press, 1975.

Parke, R.D., and Tinsley, B.R. The father's role in infancy: Determinants of involvement in caregiving and play. In *The Role of the Father in Child Development*, edited by M.E. Lamb. New York: John Wiley & Sons, 1981.

Parsons, T. Family structure and the socialization of the child. In *Family Socialization and Interaction Processes*, edited by T. Parsons and R.F. Bales. New York: Free Press, 1955.

Patterson, F.G., and Linden, E. *The Education of Koko*. New York: Holt, Rinehart and Winston, 1981.

Pattie, F.A. The genuineness of hypnotically produced anesthesia of the skin. *American Journal of Psychology*, 1937, *49*, 435–443.

Patton, G. The course of anorexia nervosa. *British Medical Journal*, 1989, *299*, 139–140.

Patton, J., Stinard, T., and Rough, D. Where do children study? *Journal of Educational Research*, 1983, *76*, 280–286.

Paul, G.L., and Lentz, R.J. *Psychosocial Treatment of Chronic Mental Patients: Milieu versus Social Learning Program*. Cambridge, Mass.: Harvard University Press, 1977.

Pauls, D.L., and Leckman, J.F. The inheritance of Gilles de la Tourette's syndrome and associated behaviors. *New England Journal of Medicine*, 1986, *315*, 993–997.

Penfield, W., and Jasper, H. *Epilepsy and the Functional Anatomy of the Human Brain*. Boston: Little, Brown, 1954.

People v. Kempinski. No. W80CF 352 (Circuit Court, 12th District, Will County, Illinois, 21 October 1980).

Persky, H., Lief, H.I., Strauss, D., Miller, W.R., and O'Brien, C.P. Plasma testosterone level and sexual behavior of couples. *Archives of Sexual Behavior*, 1978, *7*, 157–173.

Personnel Decisions, Inc. *Retail Department Store Evaluation of the PDI Employment Inventory*. Minneapolis: Personnel Decisions, Inc., 1987.

Pert, C.B., Snowman, A.M., and Snyder, S.H. Localization of opiate receptor binding in presynaptic membranes of rat brain. *Brain Research*, 1974, *70*, 184–188.

Pervin, L.A. *Personality: Theory, Assessment, and Research*. New York: John Wiley & Sons, 1975.

Peterson, A.C., and Ebata, A.T. Developmental transitions and adolescent problem behavior: Implications for prevention and intervention. In *Social Prevention and Intervention*, edited by K. Herrelmann. New York: De Gruyter, 1987.

Petty, R.E., and Cacioppo, J.T. Issue involvement as a moderator of the effects on attitude of advertising content and context. *Advances in Consumer Research*, 1981, *8*, 20–24.

Petty, R.E., Cacioppo, J.T., and Goldman, R. Personal involvement as a determinant of argument-based persuasion. *Journal of Personality and Social Psychology*, 1981, *41*, 847–855.

Petty, R.E., Harkins, S.G., and Williams, K.D. The effects of group diffusion of cognitive effort on attitudes: An information processing view. *Journal of Personality and Social Psychology*, 1980, *38*, 81–92.

Pfefferbaum, A., Zipursky, R.B., Lim, K.O., Zatz, L.M., Stahl, S.M., and Jernigan, T.L. Computed tomographic evidence for generalized sulcal and ventricular enlargement in schizophrenia. *Archives of General Psychiatry*, 1988, *45*, 633–640.

Phares, E.J. *Clinical Psychology: Concepts, Methods, and Profession*. Homewood, Ill.: Dorsey Press, 1979.

Piaget, J. *The Moral Judgment of the Child*. Translated by M. Gabain. New York: Harcourt, Brace & World, 1932.

Piaget, J. *The Origins of Intelligence in Children*. Translated by M. Cook. New York: International Universities Press, 1952.

Pilleri, G. The blind Indus dolphin, *Platanista indi. Endeavours*, 1979, *3*, 48–56.

Pinker, S. Language acquisition. In *An Invitation to Cognitive Science. Vol. 1: Language*, edited by D.N. Osherson and H. Lasnik. Cambridge, Mass.: MIT Press, 1990.

Plomin, R. The nature and nurture of cognitive abilities. In *Advances in the Psychology of Human Intelligence*, edited by R. Sternberg. Hillsdale, N.J.: Lawrence Erlbaum Associates, 1988.

Plomin, R., and Bergeman, C.S. The nature of nurture: Genetic influence on "environmental" measures. *Behavioral and Brain Sciences*, 1991, *14*, 373–427.

Plutchik, R. *The Emotions: Facts, Theories and a New Model*. New York: Random House, 1962.

Plutchik, R. *Emotion: A Psychoevolutionary Synthesis*. New York: Harper & Row, 1980.

Poggio, G.F., and Poggio, T. The analysis of stereopsis. *Annual Review of Neuroscience*, 1984, *7*, 379–412.

Pollack, I., and Pickett, J.M. Intelligibility of excerpts from fluent speech: Auditory vs. structural context. *Journal of Verbal Learning and Verbal Behavior*, 1964, *3*, 79–84.

Posner, M.I., Snyder, C.R.R., and Davidson, B.J. Attention and the detection of signals. *Journal of Experimental Psychology: General*, 1980, *109*, 160–174.

Potts, G.R. Information processing strategies used in the encoding of linear orderings. *Journal of Verbal Learning and Verbal Behavior*, 1972, *11*, 727–740.

Pratkanis, A.R., Breckler, S.H., and Greenwald, A.G. *Attitude Structure and Function*. Hillsdale, N.J.: Lawrence Erlbaum Associates, 1989.

Pratkanis, A.R., Eskenazi, J., and Greenwald, A.G. What you expect is what you believe, but not necessarily what you get: On the effectiveness of subliminal self-help audiotapes. Paper presented at the annual convention of the Western Psychological Association, Los Angeles, 1990. (Cited by Druckman and Bjork, 1990.)

Premack, D. Reinforcement theory. In *Nebraska Symposium on Motivation,* edited by D. Levine. Lincoln: University of Nebraska Press, 1965.

Premack, D. Language and intelligence in ape and man. *American Scientist*, 1976, *64*, 674–683.

Prichard, J.C. *A Treatise on Insanity and Other Disorders Affecting the Mind*. London: Sherwood, Gilbert, and Piper, 1835.

Propping, P., Kruger, J., and Janah, A. Effect of alcohol on genetically determined variants of the normal electroencephalogram. *Psychiatry Research*, 1980, *2*, 85–98.

Propping, P., Kruger, J., and Mark, N. Genetic disposition to alcoholism: An EEG study in alcoholics and their relatives. *Human Genetics*, 1981, *59*, 51–59.

Quattrone, G.A., and Tversky, A. Causal versus diagnostic contingencies: On self-deception and on the voter's illusion. *Journal of Personality and Social Psychology*, 1984, *46*, 237–248.

Quay, H.C. Psychopathic personality as pathological stimulus seeking. *American Journal of Psychiatry*, 1965, *122*, 180–183.

Rachman, S., and Hodgson, R.J. Experimentally-induced "sexual fetishism": Replication and development. *Psychological Record*, 1968, *18*, 25–27.

Rachman, S.J., and Wilson, G.T. Using direct and indirect measures to study perception without awareness. *Perception and Psychophysics*, 1980, *44*, 563–575.

Ragland, D.R., and Brand, R.J. Type A behavior and mortality from coronary heart disease. *New England Journal of Medicine*, 1988, *318*, 65–69.

Rajecki, D.J. *Attitudes*, 2nd ed. Sunderland, Mass.: Sinauer Associates, 1989.

Ravelli, G.-P., Stein, Z.A., and Susser, M.W.

Obesity in young men after famine exposure in utero and early infancy. *New England Journal of Medicine*, 1976, *295*, 349–353.

Ray, A., Henke, P.G., and Sullivan, R. The central amygdala and immobilization stress-induced gastric pathology in rats: Neurotensin and dopamine. *Brain Research,* 1987, *409*, 398–402.

Raybin, J.B., and Detre, T.P. Sleep disorder and symptomatology among medical and nursing students. *Comprehensive Psychiatry,* 1969, *10*, 452–467.

Reber, A.A., and Allen, R. Analogical and abstraction strategies in synthetic grammar learning: A functionalist interpretation. *Cognition,* 1978, *6*, 189–221.

Reber, A.S. *The Penguin Dictionary of Psychology*. Harmondsworth, England: Penguin Books, 1985.

Regan, D.T. Effects of a favor and liking on compliance. *Journal of Experimental Social Psychology*, 1971, *7*, 627–639.

Regan, D.T., and Fazio, R.H. On the consistency between attitudes and behavior: Look to the method of attitude formation. *Journal of Experimental Social Psychology*, 1977, *13*, 28–45.

Regier, D.A., Boyd, J.H., Burke, J.D., Rae, D.S., Myers, J.K., Kramer, M., Ropins, L.N., George, L.K., Karno, M., and Locke, B.Z. One-month prevalence of mental disorders in the United States. *Archives of General Psychiatry*, 1988, *45*, 977–986.

Reinink, E., Bouhuys, N., Wirz-Justice, A., and van den Hoofdakker, R. Prediction of the antidepressant response to total sleep deprivation by diurnal variation of mood. *Psychiatry Research*, 1990, *32*, 113–124.

Reinke, B.J., Holmes, D.S., and Harris, R.L. The timing of psychosocial changes in women's lives: The years 25 to 45. *Journal of Personality and Social Psychology*, 1985, *48*, 1353–1364.

Reiser, M., and Nielson, M. Investigative hypnosis: A developing specialty. *American Journal of Clinical Hypnosis*, 1980, *23*, 75–83.

Rest, J.R. *Development in Judging Moral Issues*. Minneapolis: University of Minnesota Press, 1979.

Review Panel. Coronary-prone behavior and coronary heart disease: A critical review. *Circulation*, 1981, *673*, 1199–1215.

Reynolds, A.G., and Flagg, P.W. *Cognitive Psychology*, 2nd ed. Boston: Little, Brown, 1983.

Rice, M.L., Huston, A.C., Truglio, R., and Wright, J. Words from "Sesame Street": Learning vocabulary while viewing. *Developmental Psychology*, 1990, *26*, 421–428.

Rideout, B. Non-REM sleep as a source of learning deficits induced by REM sleep deprivation. *Physiology and Behavior*, 1979, *22*, 1043–1047.

Riggs, L.A., Ratliff, F., Cornsweet, J.C., and Cornsweet, T.N. The disappearance of steadily fixated visual test objects. *Journal of the Optical Society of America*, 1953, *43*, 495–501.

Rips, L.J., Shoben, E.J., and Smith, E.E. Semantic distance and the verification of semantic relations. *Journal of Verbal Learning and Verbal Behavior*, 1973, *12*, 1–20.

Ritter, S., and Taylor, J.S. Capsaicin abolishes

lipoprivic but not glucoprivic feeding in rats. *American Journal of Physiology*, 1989, *256*, R1232–R1239.

Rittle, R.H. Changes in helping behavior: Self-versus situational perceptions as mediators of the foot-in-the-door effect. *Personality and Social Psychology Bulletin*, 1981, *7*, 431–437.

Robbins, L.N., Helzer, J.E., Weissman, M.M., Orvaschel, H., Gruenberg, E., Burke, J.D., and Regier, D.A. Lifetime prevalence of specific psychiatric disorders in three sites. *Archives of General Psychiatry*, 1984, *41*, 949–958.

Robinson, C.P., and Eberts, R.E. Comparison of speech and pictorial displays in a cockpit environment. *Human Factors*, 1987, *29*, 31–44.

Rock, I., and Gutman, D. The effect of inattention on form perception. *Journal of Experimental Psychology: Human Perception and Performance*, 1981, *7*, 275–285.

Rodin, J., Schank, D., and Striegel-Moore, R. Psychological features of obesity. *Medical Clinics of North America*, 1989, *73*, 47–66.

Rogers, C.T. *Client-centered Therapy*. Boston: Houghton Mifflin, 1951.

Rogers, M.P., Trentham, D.E., McCune, W.J., Ginsberg, B.I., Rennke, H.G., Reike, P., and David, J.R. Effect of psychological stress on the induction of arthritis in rats. *Arthritis and Rheumatology*, 1980, *23*, 1337–1342.

Rolls, E.T. Feeding and reward. In *The Neural Basis of Feeding and Reward,* edited by B.G. Hobel and D. Novin. Brunswick, Maine: Haer Institute, 1982.

Rolls, E.T. A theory of emotion, and its application to understanding the neural basis of emotion. In *Emotions: Neural and Chemical Control,* edited by Y. Oomura. Tokyo: Japan Scientific Societies Press, 1986.

Rosch, E.H. Cognitive representations of semantic categories. *Journal of Experimental Psychology: General*, 1975, *104*, 192–233.

Rosch, E.H., Mervis, C.B., Gray, W.D., Johnson, D.M., and Boyes-Braem, P. Basic objects in natural categories. *Cognitive Psychology*, 1976, *8*, 382–439.

Rose, G.A., and Williams, R.T. Metabolic studies of large and small eaters. *British Journal of Nutrition*, 1961, *15*, 1–9.

Rose, R.J. Genetic and environmental variance in content dimensions of the MMPI. *Journal of Personality and Social Psychology*, 1988, *55*, 302–311.

Rosenblatt, J.S., and Aronson, L.R. The decline of sexual behavior in male cats after castration with special reference to the role of prior sexual experience. *Behaviour*, l958, *12*, 285–338.

Rosenman, R.H., Brand, R.J., Jenkins, C.D., Friedman, M., Straus, R., and Wurm, M. Coronary heart disease in the Western Collaborative Group Study: Final follow-up experience of 8½ years. *Journal of the American Medical Association*, 1975, *233*, 872–877.

Rosenthal, A.M. *Thirty-eight Witnesses*. New York: McGraw-Hill, 1964.

Rosenthal, D. *Genetic Theory and Abnormal Behavior*. New York: McGraw-Hill, 1970.

Rosenthal, N.E., Genhart, M., Jacobson, F.M., Skwerer, R.G., and Wehr, T.A. Disturbances of appetite and weight regulation in seasonal affective disorder. *Annals of the New York Academy of Sciences,* 1986, *499,* 216–230.

Rosenthal, N.E., Sack, D.A., James, S.P., Parry, B.L., Mendelson, W.B., Tamarkin, L., and Wehr, T.A. Seasonal affective disorder and phototherapy. *Annals of the New York Academy of Sciences,* 1985, *453,* 260–269.

Rosenthal, T.L., and Bandura, A. Psychological modeling: Theory and practice. In *Handbook of Psychotherapy and Behavior Change: An Empirical Analysis,* 2nd ed., edited by S.L. Garfield and A.E. Bergin. New York: John Wiley & Sons, 1978.

Ross, L. The intuitive psychologist and his shortcomings: Distortions in the attribution process. In *Advances in Experimental Social Psychology,* edited by L. Berkowitz. New York: Academic Press, 1977.

Ross, L.D., Amabile, T.M., and Steinmetz, J.L. Social roles, social control, and biases in social-perception processes. *Journal of Personality and Social Psychology,* 1977, *35,* 485–494.

Roth, E.M., and Mervis, C.B. Fuzzy set theory and class inclusion relations in semantic categories. *Journal of Verbal Learning and Verbal Behavior,* 1983, *22,* 509–525.

Rothkopf, E.Z. Incidental memory for location of information in text. *Journal of Verbal Learning and Verbal Behavior,* 1971, *10,* 608–613.

Rounsaville, B.J., Harding, P.S., and Weissman, M.M. Single case study. Briquet's syndrome in a man. *Journal of Nervous and Mental Disease,* 1979, *167,* 364–367.

Rowland, L.J. Will hypnotized persons try to harm themselves or others? *Journal of Abnormal and Social Psychology,* 1939, *34,* 114–117.

Rubin, Z. *Liking and Loving: An Invitation to Social Psychology.* New York: Holt, Rinehart and Winston, 1973.

Rumelhart, D.E., McClelland, J.L., and the PDP Research Group. *Parallel Distributed Processing: Explorations in the Microstructure of Cognition.* Cambridge, Mass.: MIT Press, 1986.

Rushton, J.P. Race differences in behaviour: A review and evolutionary analysis. *Personality and Individual Differences,* 1988, *9,* 1009–1024.

Rushton, J.P. Race, brain size, and intelligence: A reply to Cernovsky. *Psychological Reports,* 1990, *66,* 659–666.

Ryan, A.M., and Sackett, P.R. Pre-employment honesty testing: Fakability, reactions of test takers, and company image. *Journal of Business and Psychology,* 1987, *1,* 248–256.

Ryback, R.S., and Lewis, O.F. Effects of prolonged bed rest on EEG sleep patterns in young, healthy volunteers. *Electroencephalography and Clinical Neurophysiology,* 1971, *31,* 395–399.

Sachs, J.S. Recognition memory for syntactic and semantic aspects of connected discourse. *Perception and Psychophysics,* 1967, *2,* 437–442.

Sackett, P.R., Burris, L.R., and Callahan, C. Integrity testing for personnel selection: An update. *Personnel Psychology,* 1989, *42,* 491–529.

Sackheim, H.A., Paulus, D., and Weiman, A.L.

Classroom seating and hypnotic susceptibility. *Journal of Abnormal Psychology,* 1979, *88,* 81–84.

Saegert, S.C., Swap, W., and Zajonc, R.B. Exposure, context, and interpersonal attraction. *Journal of Personality and Social Psychology,* 1973, *25,* 234–242.

Saffran, E.M., Schwartz, M.F., and Marin, O.S.M. Evidence from aphasia: Isolating the components of a production model. In *Language Production,* edited by B. Butterworth. London: Academic Press, 1980.

Sakai, F., Meyer, J.S., Karacan, I., Derman, S., and Yamamoto, M. Normal human sleep: Regional cerebral haemodynamics. *Annals of Neurology,* 1979, *7,* 471–478.

Salame, P., and Baddeley, A.D. Disruption of short-term memory by unattended speech: Implications for the structure of working memory. *Journal of Verbal Learning and Verbal Behavior,* 1982, *21,* 150–164.

Salapatek, P. Pattern perception in early infancy. In *Infant Perception: From Sensation to Cognition, Vol. 1,* edited by L.B. Cohen and P. Salapatek. New York: Academic Press, 1975.

Salmon, U.J., and Geist, S.H. Effect of androgens upon libido in women. *Journal of Clinical Endocrinology and Metabolism,* 1943, *172,* 374–377.

Salthouse, T.A. Effects of age and skill in typing. *Journal of Gerontology,* 1984, *113,* 345–371.

Salthouse, T.A. Cognitive aspects of motor functioning. In *Central Determinants of Age-Related Declines in Motor Function,* edited by J.A. Joseph. New York: New York Academy of Sciences, 1988.

Sanna, L.J., and Shorland, R.L. Valence of anticipated evaluation and social facilitation. *Journal of Experimental Social Psychology,* 1990, *26,* 82–92.

Sapolsky, R. Glucocorticoid toxicity in the hippocampus: Reversal by supplementation with brain fuels. *Journal of Neuroscience,* 1986, *6,* 2240–2244.

Sapolsky, R.M., Krey, L.C., and McEwen, B.S. The neuroendocrinology of stress and aging: The glucocorticoid cascade hypothesis. *Endocrine Reviews,* 1986, *7,* 284–301.

Savage-Rumbauch, E.S. Language acquisition in a nonhuman species: Implications for the innateness debate. *Development Psychobiology,* 1990, *23,* 599–620.

Scarr, S., Webber, P.L., Weinberg, A., and Wittig, M.A. Personality resemblance among adolescents and their parents in biologically related and adoptive families. *Journal of Personality and Social Psychology,* 1981, *40,* 885–898.

Scarr, S., and Weinberg, R.A. IQ Performance of black children adopted by white families. *American Psychologist,* 1976, *31,* 726–739.

Scarr, S., and Weinberg, R.A. The influence of "family background" on intellectual attainment. *American Sociological Review,* 1978, *43,* 674–692.

Schachter, S. The interaction of cognitive and physiological determinants of emotional state. In *Psychobiological Approaches to Social Behavior,* edited by P.H. Liederman and D. Shapiro. Stanford: Stanford University Press, 1964.

Schachter, S., and Singer, J.E. Cognitive, social and physiological determinants of emo-

tional state. *Psychological Review,* 1962, *69,* 379–399.

Schaie, K.W. Intellectual development in adulthood. In *Handbook of the Psychology of Aging,* 3rd ed., edited by J.E. Birren and K.W. Schaie. San Diego: Academic Press, 1990.

Schanberg, S.M., and Field, T.M. Sensory deprivation stress and supplemental stimulation in the rat pup and preterm human neonate. *Child Development,* 1987, *58,* 1431–1447.

Schank, R., and Abelson, R.P. *Scripts, Plans, Goals, and Understanding.* Hillsdale, N.J.: Lawrence Erlbaum Associates, 1977.

Schenck, C.H., Bundlie, S.R., Ettinger, M.G., and Mahowald, M.W. Chronic behavioral disorders of human REM sleep: A new category of parasomnia. *Sleep,* 1986, *9,* 293–308.

Scherschlicht, R., Polc, P., Schneeberger, J., Steiner, M., and Haefely, W. Selective suppression of rapid eye movement sleep (REMS) in cats by typical and atypical antidepressants. In *Typical and Atypical Antidepressants: Molecular Mechanisms,* edited by E. Costa and G. Racagni. New York: Raven Press, 1982.

Schiano, D.J., and Watkins, M.J. Speech-like coding of pictures in short-term memory. *Memory and Cognition,* 1981, *9,* 110–114.

Schiffman, P.L., Westlake, R.E., Santiago, T.V., and Edelman, N.H. Ventilatory control in parents of victims of the sudden infant death syndrome. *New England Journal of Medicine,* 1980, *302,* 486–491.

Schleifer, S.J., Keller, S.E., Camerino, M., Thornton, J.C., and Stein, M. Suppression of lymphocyte stimulation following bereavement. *Journal of the American Medical Association,* 1983, *15,* 374–377.

Schmauk, F.J. Punishment, arousal, and avoidance learning in sociopaths. *Journal of Abnormal Psychology,* 1970, *122,* 509–522.

Schmidt, G., and Sigusch, V. Sex differences in responses to psychosexual stimulation by films and slides. *Journal of Sex Research,* 1970, *44,* 229–237.

Schoedel, J., Frederickson, W.A., and Knight, J.M. An extrapolation of the physical attractiveness and sex variables within the Byrne attraction paradigm. *Memory and Cognition,* 1975, *3,* 527–530.

Schofield, J.W. Effects of norms, public disclosure, and need for approval on volunteering behavior consistent with attitudes. *Journal of Personality and Social Psychology,* 1975, *31,* 1126–1133.

Schwartz, R., and Schwartz, L.J. *Becoming a Couple.* Englewood Cliffs, N.J.: Prentice-Hall, 1980.

Schwarzkopf, S.B., Nasrallah, H.A., Olson, S.C., Coffman, J.A., and McLaughlin, J.A. Perinatal complications and genetic loading in schizophrenia: Preliminary findings. *Psychiatry Research,* 1989, *27,* 233–239.

Scoville, W.B., and Milner, B. Loss of recent memory after bilateral hippocampal lesions. *Journal of Neurology, Neurosurgery and Psychiatry,* 1957, *20,* 11–21.

Scribner, S. Modes of thinking and ways of speaking: Culture and logic reconsidered. In *Thinking: Readings in Cognitive Science,* edited by P.N. Johnson-Laird and P.C. Wason. Cambridge, England: Cambridge University Press, 1977.

653

Segal, M.W. Alphabet and attraction: An unobstrusive measure of the effect of propinquity in a field setting. *Journal of Personality and Social Psychology,* 1974, *30,* 654–657.

Seligman, M.E.P. *Helplessness.* San Francisco: W.H. Freeman, 1975.

Selye, H. *The Stress of Life.* New York: McGraw-Hill, 1976.

Selye, H., and Tuchweber, B. Stress in relation to aging and disease. In *Hypothalamus, Pituitary and Aging,* edited by A. Everitt and J. Burgess. Springfield, Ill.: Charles C. Thomas, 1976.

Shaffer, D.R. *Developmental Psychology: Childhood and Adolescence,* 2nd ed. Belmont, Calif.: Brooks/Cole, 1989.

Shakin, E.J., and Holland, J. Depression and pancreatic cancer. *Journal of Pain and Symptom Management,* 1988, *3,* 194–198.

Shatz, M., and Gelman, R. The development of communication skills: Modifications in the speech of young children as a function of listener. *Monographs of the Society for Research in Child Development,* 1973, *38* (Serial no. 152).

Shavit, Y., Depaulis, A., Martin, F.C., Terman, G.W., Pechnick, R.N., Zane, C.J., Gale, P.P., and Liebeskind, J.C. Involvement of brain opiate receptors in the immune-suppressive effect of morphine. *Proceedings of the National Academy of Sciences, USA,* 1986, *83,* 7114–7117.

Shavit, Y., Lewis, J.W., Terman, G.W., Gale, R.P., and Liebeskind, J.C. Opioid peptides mediate the suppressive effect of stress on natural killer cell cytotoxicity. *Science,* 1984, *223,* 188–190.

Sheehan, P.W., and Perry, C.W. *Methodologies of Hypnosis: A Critical Appraisal of Contemporary Paradigms of Hypnosis.* Hillsdale, N.J.: Lawrence Erlbaum Associates, 1976.

Shepard, R.N., and Metzler, J. Mental rotation of three-dimensional objects. *Science,* 1971, *171,* 701–703.

Sherif, M., Harvey, O.J., White, B.J., Hood, W.E., and Sherif, C.W. *Intergroup Conflict and Cooperation: The Robbers Cave Experiment.* Norman, Okla.: Institute of Group Relations, 1961.

Sherman, S.J., Presson, C.C., and Chassin, L. Mechanisms underlying the false consensus effect: The special role of threats to the self. *Personality and Social Psychology Bulletin,* 1984, *10,* 127–138.

Shipley, E.F., Smith, C.S., and Gleitman, L.R. A study in the acquisition of language: Free responses to commands. *Language,* 1969, *45,* 322–342.

Shipley, T.E., and Veroff, J. A projective measure of need for affiliations. *Journal of Experimental Psychology,* 1952, *43,* 349–356.

Shirley, M.M. The first two years: A study of 25 babies. Vol. I: Postural and locomotor development. In *Institute of Child Welfare Monographs* (series no. 6). Minneapolis: University of Minnesota Press, 1933.

Shock, N. Systems integration. In *Handbook of the Biology of Aging,* edited by C. Finch and L. Hayflick. New York: Van Nostrand Reinhold, 1977.

Shortliffe, E.H. *Computer-Based Medical Consultations: MYCIN.* New York: Elsevier/North Holland, 1976.

Shotland, R.L., and Heinold, W.D. Bystander response to arterial bleeding: Helping skills, the decision-making process, and differentiating the helping response. *Journal of Personality and Social Psychology,* 1985, *49,* 347–356.

Siegel, S., Hinson, R.E., Krank, M.D., and McCully, J. Heroin "overdose" death: Contribution of drug-associated environmental cues. *Science,* 1982, *216,* 436–437.

Siegel, S.A. Pavlovian conditioning analysis of morphine tolerance. In *Behavioral Tolerance: Research and Treatment Implications,* edited by N.A. Krasnegor. Washington, D.C.: NIDA Research Monographs, 1978.

Sigusch, V., Schmidt, G., Reinfeld, A., and Wiedemann-Sutor, I. Psychosexual stimulation: Sex differences. *Journal of Sex Research,* 1970, *6,* 10–24.

Silver, J.M., Shin, C., and McNamara, J.O. Antiepileptogenic effects of conventional anticonvulsants in the kindling model of epilepsy. *Annals of Neurology,* 1991, *29,* 356–363.

Sinclair, J.D. Drugs to decrease alcohol drinking. *Annals of Medicine,* 1990, *22,* 357–362.

Sirevaag, A.M., Black, J.E., Shafron, D., and Greenough, W.T. Direct evidence that complex experience increases capillary branching and surface area in visual cortex of young rats. *Developmental Brain Research,* 1988, *43,* 299–304.

Sivacek, J., and Crano, W.D. Vested interest as a moderator of attitude-behavior consistency. *Journal of Personality and Social Psychology,* 1982, *43,* 210–221.

Skinner, B.F. Superstition in the pigeon. *Journal of Experimental Psychology,* 1948, *38,* 168–172.

Skinner, B.F. *About Behaviorism.* New York: Vintage Books, 1974.

Sloane, R.B., Staples, F.R., Cristol, A.H., Yorkston, N.J., and Whipple, K. *Psychoanalysis Versus Behavior Therapy.* Cambridge, Mass.: Harvard University Press, 1975.

Smith, G.H., and Engel, R. Influence of a female model on perceived characteristics of an automobile. *Proceedings of the 76th Annual Convention of the American Psychological Association,* 1968, *3,* 681–682.

Smith, J.W., and Frawley, P.J. Long-term abstinence from alcohol in patients receiving aversion therapy as part of a multimodal inpatient program. *Journal of Substance Abuse Treatment,* 1990, *7,* 77–82.

Smith, M.L., Glass, G.V., and Miller, T.I. *Benefits of Psychotherapy.* Baltimore: Johns Hopkins University Press, 1980.

Snow, C.E. Mothers' speech to children learning language. *Child Development,* 1972a, *43,* 549–565.

Snow, C.E. Young children's responses to adult sentences of varying complexity. Paper presented at the Third International Congress of Applied Linguistics, Copenhagen, August, 1972b.

Snow, C.E. Mothers' speech research: From input to interaction. In *Talking to Children: Language Input and Acquisition,* edited by C.E. Snow and C. Ferguson. Cambridge, England: Cambridge University Press, 1977.

Snow, C.E. Conversations with children. In *Language Acquisition,* 2nd ed., edited by P. Fletcher and M. Garman. Cambridge, England: Cambridge University Press, 1986.

Snow, C.E., Arlman-Rupp, A., Hassing, Y., Jobse, J., Joosten, J., and Vorster, J. Mothers' speech in three social classes. *Journal of Psycholinguistic Research,* 1976, *5,* 1–20.

Snow, C.E., and Goldfield, B.A. Building stories: The emergence of information structures from conversation. In *Analyzing Discourse: Text and Talk,* edited by D. Tannen. Washington, D.C.: Georgetown University Press, 1982.

Snow, M.E., Jacklin, C.N., and Maccoby, E.E. Sex-of-child differences in father-child interaction at one year of age. *Child Development,* 1983, *54,* 227–232.

Snyder, M., Tanke, E.D., and Berscheid, E. Social perception and interpersonal behavior: On the self-fulfilling nature of social stereotypes. *Journal of Personality and Social Psychology,* 1977, *35,* 656–666.

Snyder, S.H. *Madness and the Brain.* New York: McGraw-Hill, 1974.

Sobesky, W.E. The effects of situational factors on moral judgments. *Child Development,* 1983, *54,* 575–584.

Sojourner, R.J., and Antin, J.F. The effects of a simulated head-up display speedometer on perceptual task performance. *Human Factors,* 1990, *32,* 329–339.

Solkoff, N., and Matuszak, D. Tactile stimulation and behavioral development among low-birthweight infants. *Child Psychiatry and Human Development,* 1975, *6,* 33–37.

Solkoff, N., Yaffe, S., Weintraub, D., and Blase, B. Effects of handling on the subsequent development of premature infants. *Developmental Psychology,* 1969, *4,* 765–768.

Solomon, G.F. Psychoneuroimmunology: Interactions between central nervous system and immune system. *Journal of Neuroscience Research,* 1987, *18,* 1–9.

Sommer, R., and Schutz, H.G. This consumer psychologist. In *Applied Psychology: Variety and Opportunity,* edited by R. Gifford. Boston: Allyn and Bacon, 1991.

Sorensen, R.C. *Adolescent Sexuality in Contemporary America: Personal Values and Sexual Behavior, Ages Thirteen to Nineteen.* New York: World Publishers, 1973.

Spanos, N.P., Gwynn, M.I., and Stam, H.J. Instructional demands and ratings of overt and hidden pain during hypnotic analgesia. *Journal of Abnormal Psychology,* 1983, *92,* 479–488.

Spanos, N.P., Weekes, J.R., and Bertrand, L.D. Multiple personality: A social psychological perspective. *Journal of Abnormal Psychology,* 1985, *94,* 362–376.

Spearman, C. *The Abilities of Man.* London: Macmillan, 1927.

Spears, R., van der Pligt, J., and Eiser, J.R. Illusory correlation in the perception of group attitudes. *Journal of Personality and Social Psychology,* 1985, *48,* 863–875.

Sperling, G.A. The information available in brief visual presentation. *Psychological Monographs,* 1960, *74* (no. 498).

Sperry, R.W. Brain bisection and consciousness. In *Brain and Conscious Experience,* edited by J. Eccles. New York: Springer-Verlag, 1966.

Spiegel, D., Bloom, J., and Yalom, I.D. Group

support for patients with metastatic breast cancer. *Archives of General Psychiatry,* 1981, *38,* 527–533.

Spiegel, D., Bloom, J.R., Kraemer, H.C., and Gottheil, E. Effect of psychosocial treatment on survival of patients with metastatic breast cancer. *Lancet,* 1989, *2,* 888–891.

Spinelli, D.H., and Jensen, F.E. Plasticity: The mirror of experience. *Science,* 1979, *203,* 75–78.

Spinelli, D.H., Jensen, F.E., and DiPrisco, G.V. Early experience effect on dendritic branching in normally reared kittens. *Experimental Neurology,* 1980, *62,* 1–11.

Spirduso, W.W., and MacRae, P.G. Motor performance and aging. In *Handbook of the Psychology of Aging,* 3rd ed., edited by J.E. Birren and K.W. Schaie. San Diego: Academic Press, 1990.

Spiro, R.J. Remembering information from text: The "state of schema" approach. In *Schooling and the Acquisition of Knowledge,* edited by R.C. Anderson, R.J. Spiro, and W.E. Montague. Hillsdale, N.J.: Lawrence Erlbaum Associates, 1977.

Spiro, R.J. Accommodative reconstruction in prose recall. *Journal of Verbal Learning and Verbal Behavior,* 1980, *19,* 84–95.

Squire, L.R. *Memory and Brain.* Oxford, England: Oxford University Press, 1987.

Squire, L.R., Slater, P.C., and Miller, P.L. Retrograde amnesia following ECT: Long-term follow-up studies. *Archives of General Psychiatry,* 1981, *38,* 89–95.

Staats, A.W., and Staats, C.K. Attitudes established by classical conditioning. *Journal of Abnormal and Social Psychology,* 1958, *57,* 37–40.

Staats, C.K., and Staats, A.W. Meaning established by classical conditioning. *Journal of Experimental Psychology,* 1957, *54,* 74–80.

Standing, L. Learning 10,000 pictures. *Quarterly Journal of Experimental Psychology,* 1973, *25,* 207–222.

Stebbins, W.C., Miller, J.M., Johnsson, L.-G., and Hawkins, J.E. Ototoxic hearing loss and cochlear pathology in the monkey. *Annals of Otology, Rhinology, and Laryngology,* 1969, *78,* 1007–1026.

Steele, C.M., and Liu, T.J. Making the dissonance act unreflective of self: Dissonance avoidance and the expectancy of a value-affirming response. *Personality and Social Psychology Bulletin,* 1981, *7,* 393–397.

Steen, S.N., Oppliger, R.A., and Brownell, K.D. Metabolic effects of repeated weight loss and regain in adolescent wrestlers. *Journal of the American Medical Association,* 1988, *260,* 47–50.

Steinberg, L. Impact of puberty on family relations: Effects of pubertal status and pubertal timing. *Developmental Psychology,* 1987, *23,* 451–460.

Steiner, J.E. Human facial expression in response to taste and smell stimulation. In *Advances in Child Development and Behavior, Vol. 13,* edited by H.W. Reese and L.P. Lipsett. New York: Academic Press, 1979.

Stern, J.A., Brown, M., Ulett, G.A., and Sletten, I. A comparison of hypnosis, acupuncture, morphine, Valium, aspirin, and placebo in the management of experimentally induced pain. In *Hypnosis and Relaxation: Modern Verification of an Old Equation.* New York: Wiley-Interscience, 1977.

Stern, M., and Karraker, K.H. Sex stereotyping of infants: A review of gender labeling studies. *Sex Roles,* 1989, *20,* 501–522.

Stern, W. *The Psychological Methods of Testing Intelligence.* Baltimore: Warwick and York, 1914.

Sternberg, R.J. *Beyond IQ: A Triarchic Theory of Human Intelligence.* Cambridge, England: Cambridge University Press, 1985.

Stevens, J.R. Schizophrenia and multiple sclerosis. *Schizophrenia Bulletin,* 1988, *14,* 231–241.

Stich, S.P. Rationality. In *An Invitation to Cognitive Science. Vol. 3: Thinking,* edited by D.N. Osherson and E.E. Smith. Cambridge, Mass.: MIT Press, 1990.

Stine, E.L., and Bohannon, J.N. Imitations, interactions, and language acquisition. *Journal of Child Language,* 1983, *10,* 589–603.

Stokoe, W.C. Apes who sign and critics who don't. In *Language in Primates: Perspectives and Implications,* edited by J. de Luce and H.T. Wilder. New York: Springer-Verlag, 1983.

Stone, A.A., Cox, D.S., Valdimarsdottir, H., Jandorf, L., and Neale, J.M. Evidence that secretory IgA antibody is associated with daily mood. *Journal of Personality and Social Psychology,* 1987, *52,* 988–993.

Stone, A.A., Reed, B.R., and Neale, J.M. Changes in daily event frequency precede episodes of physical symptoms. *Journal of Human Stress,* 1987, *13,* 70–74.

Stone, S. Psychiatry through the ages. *Journal of Abnormal and Social Psychology,* 1937, *32,* 131–160.

Storms, M.D. Videotape and the attribution process: Reversing actors' and observers' point of view. *Journal of Personality and Social Psychology,* 1973, *27,* 165–175.

Stroop, J.R. Studies of interference in serial verbal reactions. *Journal of Experimental Psychology,* 1935, *18,* 743–762.

Strupp, H.H., and Hadley, S.W. Specific vs. nonspecific factors in psychotherapy. *Archives of General Psychiatry,* 1979, *36,* 1125–1136.

Stunkard, A.J., Sørenson, T.I., Harris, C., Teasdale, T.W., Chakraborty, R., Schull, W.J., and Schulsinger, F. An adoption study of human obesity. *New England Journal of Medicine,* 1986, *314,* 193–198.

Stunkard, A.S., and Burt, B. Obesity and the body image. I. Age of onset of disturbances in the body image. *American Journal of Psychiatry,* 1967, *123,* 1443–1447.

Suddath, R.L., Christison, G.W., Torrey, E.F., Casanova, M.F., and Weinberger, D.R. Anatomical abnormalities in the brains of monozygotic twins discordant for schizophrenia. *The New England Journal of Medicine,* 1990, *322,* 789–794.

Sullivan, R.M., Taborsky-Barba, S., Mendoza, R., Itano, A., Leon, M., Cotman, C.W., Payne, T.F., and Lott, I. Olfactory classical conditioning in neonates. *Pediatrics,* 1991, *87,* 511–518.

Suomi, S.J., and Harlow, H.F. Social rehabilitation of isolate-reared monkeys. *Developmental Psychology,* 1972, *6,* 487–496.

Suzdak, P.D., Glowa, J.R., Crawley, J.N., Schwartz, R.D., Skolnick, P., and Paul, S.M. A selective imidazobenzodiazepine antagonist of ethanol in the rat. *Science,* 1986, *234,* 1243–1247.

Swaab, D.F., and Hofman, M.A. An enlarged suprachiasmatic nucleus in homosexual men. *Brain Research,* 1990, *537,* 141–148.

Swann, W.B., and Pittman, T.S. Initiating play activity of children: The moderating influence of verbal cues on intrinsic motivation. *Child Development,* 1977, *48,* 1128–1132.

Tanenhaus, M.K. *Psycholinguistics: An Overview.* Cambridge, England: Cambridge University Press, 1988.

Taras, H.L., Sallis, J.F., Patterson, T.L., Nader, P.R., and Nelson, J.A. Television's influence on children's diet and physical activity. *Journal of Developmental and Behavioral Pediatrics,* 1989, *10,* 176–180.

Taube, S.L., Kirstein, L.S., Sweeney, D.R., Heninger, G.R., and Maas, J.W. Urinary 3-methoxy-4-hydroxyphenyleneglycol and psychiatric diagnosis. *American Journal of Psychiatry,* 1978, *135,* 78–82.

Temoshok, L. Personality, coping style, emotion and cancer: Towards an integrative model. *Cancer Surveys,* 1987, *6,* 545–567.

Temoshok, L., Heller, B.W., Sagebiel, R.W., Blois, M.S., Sweet, D.M., DiClemente, R.J., and Gold, M.L. The relationship of psychosocial factors to prognostic indicators in cutaneous malignant melanoma. *Journal of Psychosomatic Research,* 1985, *29,* 139–153.

Terenius, L., and Wahlström, A. Morphine-like ligand for opiate receptors in human CSF. *Life Sciences,* 1975, *16,* 1759–1764.

Terrace, H.S., Petitto, L.A., Sanders, R.J., and Bever, T.G. Can an ape create a sentence? *Science,* 1979, *206,* 891–902.

Terry, R.D., and Davies, P. Dementia of the Alzheimer type. *Annual Review of Neuroscience,* 1980, *3,* 77–96.

Thayer, R.E. Measurement of activation through self-report. *Psychological Reports,* 1967, *20,* 663–678.

Thibadeau, R., Just, M.A., and Carpenter, P.A. A model of the time course and content of reading. *Cognitive Science,* 1982, *6,* 157–203.

Thibaut, J.W., and Riecken, H.W. Some determinants and consequences of the perception of social causality. *Journal of Personality,* 1955, *24,* 113–133.

Thorndike, E.L. *The Elements of Psychology.* New York: Seiler, 1905.

Thorpe, G.L., and Olson, S.L. *Behavior Therapy: Concepts, Procedures, and Applications.* Boston: Allyn and Bacon, 1990.

Thurstone, L.L. *Primary Mental Abilities.* Chicago: University of Chicago Press, 1938.

Tienari, P., Sorri, A., Lahti, I., Naarala, M., Wahlberg, K.-E., Moring, J., Pohjola, J., and Wynne, L.C. Genetic and psychosocial factors in schizophrenia: The Finnish adoptive family study. *Schizophrenia Bulletin,* 1987, *13,* 476–483.

Tiffany, S.T., Martin, E.M., and Baker, T.B. Treatments for cigarette smoking: An evaluation of the contributions of aversion and counseling procedures. *Behaviour Research and Therapy,* 1986, *24,* 437–452.

Tippin, J., and Henn, F.A. Modified leukotomy in the treatment of intractable obsessional neurosis. *American Journal of Psychiatry,* 1982, *139,* 1601–1603.

Tomkins, S.S. *Affect, Imagery, and Consciousness. Vol. 1: The Positive Affects.* New York: Springer-Verlag, 1962.

Tomkins, S.S. *Affect, Imagery, and Consciousness. Vol. 2: The Negative Affects.* New York: Springer-Verlag, 1963.

Tomkins, S.S. *Affect, Imagery, and Consciousness. Vol. 3: Cognition and Affect.* New York: Springer-Verlag, 1982.

Tong, Y.C., Busby, P.A., and Clark, G.M. Perceptual studies on cochlear implant patients with early onset of profound hearing impairment prior to normal development of auditory, speech and language skills. *Journal of the Acoustical Society of America,* 1988, *84,* 951–962.

Torgerson, S. Genetic factors in anxiety disorders. *Archives of General Psychiatry,* 1983, *40,* 1085–1089.

Torrey, E.F., Torrey, B.B., and Peterson, M.R. Seasonality of schizophrenic births in the United States. *Archives of General Psychiatry,* 1977, *34,* 1065–1070.

Tourney, G. Hormones and homosexuality. In *Homosexual Behavior,* edited by J. Marmor. New York: Basic Books, 1980.

Träskmann, L., Åsberg, M., Bertilsson, L., and Sjöstrand, L. Monoamine metabolites on CSF and suicidal behavior. *Archives of General Psychiatry,* 1981, *38,* 631–636.

Treisman, A.M. Contextual cues in selective listening. *Quarterly Journal of Experimental Psychology,* 1960, *12,* 242–248.

Triplett, N. The dynamogenic factors in pacemaking and competition. *American Journal of Psychology,* 1987, *9,* 507–533.

Tronick, E., Als, H., Adamson, L., Wise, S., and Brazelton, T.B. The infant's response to entrapment between contradictory messages in face-to-face interaction. *Journal of the American Academy of Child Psychiatry,* 1978, *17,* 1–13.

Truax, C.B. Reinforcement and nonreinforcement in Rogerian psychotherapy. *Journal of Abnormal Psychology,* 1966, *71,* 1–9.

Tulving, E. Episodic and semantic memory. In *Organization of Memory,* edited by E. Tulving and W. Donaldson. New York: Academic Press, 1972.

Tulving, E. *Elements of Episodic Memory.* Oxford, England: Oxford University Press, 1983.

Tulving, E. Precis of *Elements of Episodic Memory. The Behavioral and Brain Sciences,* 1984, *7,* 223–268.

Tupes, E.C., and Christal, R.E. Recurrent personality factors based on trait ratings. USAF ASD Technical Report, 1961, 61–97.

Turner, A.M., and Greenough, W.T. Differential rearing effects on rat visual cortex synapses. I. Synaptic and neuronal density and synapses per neuron. *Brain Research,* 1985, *329,* 195–203.

Turner, S. The life and times of a pickle packer. *Boston Sunday Globe,* January 8, 1978, pp. 10–22.

Turner, S.M., Beidel, D.C., and Nathan, R.S. Biological factors in obsessive-compulsive disorders. *Psychological Bulletin,* 1985, *97,* 430–450.

Tversky, A., and Kahneman, D. Judgment under uncertainty: Heuristics and biases. In *Judgment Under Uncertainty,* edited by D. Kahneman, P. Slovic, and A. Tversky. New York: Cambridge University Press, 1982.

Tyrell, J.B., and Baxter, J.D. Glucocorticoid therapy. In *Endocrinology and Metabolism,* edited by P. Felig, J.D. Baxter, A.E. Broadus, and L.A. Frohman. New York: McGraw-Hill, 1981.

Tyson, W. Personal communication, 1980.

Ullman, L.P., and Krasner, L. *Psychological Approach to Abnormal Behavior.* Englewood Cliffs, N.J.: Prentice-Hall, 1969.

Ungerleider, L.G., and Mishkin, M. Two cortical visual systems. In *Analysis of Visual Behavior,* edited by D.J. Ingle, M.A. Goodale, and R.J.W. Mansfield. Cambridge, Mass.: MIT Press, 1982.

Uno, H., Tarara, R., Else, J.G., Suleman, M.A., and Sapolsky, R.M. Hippocampal damage associated with prolonged and fatal stress in primates. *The Journal of Neuroscience,* 1989, *9,* 1705–1711.

U.S. Bureau of the Census. *Statistical Abstract of the United States,* 98th ed. Washington, D.C.: U.S. Government Printing Office, 1990.

Vaillant, B. *Adaptation to Life.* Boston: Little, Brown, 1977.

Valenstein, E.S. *The Psychosurgery Debate: Scientific, Legal, and Ethical Perspectives.* San Francisco: W.H. Freeman, 1980.

Valenstein, E.S. *Great and Desperate Cures: The Rise and Decline of Psychosurgery and Other Radical Treatments for Mental Illness.* New York: Basic Books, 1986.

Van de Kar, L.D., Piechowski, R.A., Rittenhouse, P.A., and Gray, T.S. Amygdaloid lesions: Differential effect on conditioned stress and immobilization-induced increases in corticosterone and renin secretion. *Neuroendocrinology,* 1991, *54,* 89–95.

Vernon, P.E. *Intelligence: Heredity and Environment.* San Francisco: W.H. Freeman, 1979.

Vogel, G.W., Thurmond, A., Gibbons, P., Sloan, K., Boyd, M., and Walker, M. REM sleep reduction effects on depression syndromes. *Archives of General Psychiatry,* 1975, *32,* 765–777.

Vogel, G.W., Vogel, F., McAbee, R.S., and Thurmond, A.G. Improvement of depression by REM sleep deprivation. *Archives of General Psychiatry,* 1980, *37,* 247–253.

von Békésy, G. *Experiments in Hearing.* New York: McGraw-Hill, 1960.

Von Wright, J.M., Anderson, K., and Stenman, U. Generalization of conditioned GSRs in dichotic listening. In *Attention and Performance, Vol. V,* edited by P.M.A. Rabbitt and S. Dornic. London: Academic Press, 1975.

Wachtel, P. *Psychoanalysis and Behavior Therapy: Toward an Integration.* New York: Basic Books, 1977.

Wade, G.N., and Gray, J.M. Gonadal effects on food intake and adiposity: A metabolic hypothesis. *Physiology and Behavior,* 1979, *22,* 583–593.

Walker, E., and Lewine, R.J. Prediction of adult-onset schizophrenia from childhood home movies of the patients. *American Journal of Psychiatry,* 1990, *147,* 1052–1056.

Walker, L.J. A longitudinal study of moral reasoning. *Child Development,* 1989, *60,* 157–166.

Walster, E., Aronson, V., Abrahams, D., and Rottman, L. Importance of physical attractiveness in dating behavior. *Journal of Personality and Social Psychology,* 1966, *4,* 508–516.

Walster, E., and Berscheid, E. Adrenaline makes the heart grow fonder. *Psychology Today,* June 1971, pp. 47–62.

Ward, I. Prenatal stress feminizes and demasculinizes the behavior of males. *Science,* 1972, *175,* 82–84.

Wason, P. Reasoning about a rule. *Quarterly Journal of Experimental Psychology,* 1968, *20,* 273–281.

Waters, E., Wippman, J., and Sroufe, L.A. Attachment, positive affect, and competence in the peer group: Two studies in construct validation. *Child Development,* 1979, *50,* 821–829.

Watson, D.L., and Tharp, R.G. *Self-directed Behavior: Self-modification for Personal Adjustment,* 4th ed. Monterey, Calif.: Brooks/Cole, 1972.

Watson, J.B. *Behaviorism,* rev. ed. New York: W.W. Norton, 1930.

Watson, J.S., and Ramey, C.T. Reactions to responsive contingent stimulation in early infancy. *Merrill-Palmer Quarterly,* 1972, *18,* 219–227.

Waugh, N.C., and Norman, D.A. Primary memory. *Psychological Review,* 1965, *72,* 89–104.

Weidner, G., Sexton, G., McLellarn, R., Connor, S.L., and Matarazzo, J.D. The role of type A behavior and hostility in an elevation of plasma lipids in adult women and men. *Psychosomatic Medicine,* 1987, *49,* 136–145.

Weigel, R.H., Vernon, D.T.A., and Tognacci, L.N. Specificity of the attitude as a determinant of attitude-behavior congruence. *Journal of Personality and Social Psychology,* 1974, *30,* 724–728.

Weinberger, D.R., Bigelow, L.B., Kleinman, J.E., Klein, S.T., Rosenblatt, J.E., and Wyatt, R.J. Cerebral ventricular enlargement in chronic schizophrenia: An association with poor response to treatment. *Archives of General Psychiatry,* 1980, *37,* 11–13.

Weinberger, D.R., and Wyatt, J.R. Brain morphology in schizophrenia: *In vivo* studies. In *Schizophrenia as a Brain Disease,* edited by F.A. Henn and G.A. Nasrallah. New York: Oxford University Press, 1982.

Weir, W. Another look at subliminal "facts." *Advertising Age,* 1984, *55,* 46.

Weiss, J.M. Effects of coping responses on stress. *Journal of Comparative and Physiological Psychology,* 1968, *65,* 251–260.

Weitzman, E.D. Sleep and its disorders. *Annual Review of Neuroscience,* 1981, *4,* 381–418.

Werner, H. Studies on contour. *American Journal of Psychology,* 1935, *37,* 40–64.

Wernicke, K. *Der Aphasische Symptomenkomplex.* Breslau, Poland: Cohn & Weigert, 1874.

Wertheimer, M. Psychomotor co-ordination of auditory-visual space at birth. *Science,* 1961, *134,* 1692.

Whitbourne, S.K. *Adult Development,* 2nd ed. New York: Praeger Publishers, 1986.

White, G.L. Physical attractiveness and courtship progress. *Journal of Personality and Social Psychology,* 1980, *39,* 660–668.

Whitehead, R.G., Rowland, M.G.M., Hutton, M., Prentice, A.M., Müller, E., and Paul, A. Factors influencing lactation performance in rural Gambian mothers. *Lancet,* 1978, *2,* 178–181.

Whitlock, F.A. The aetiology of hysteria. *Acta Psychiatrica Scandinavica,* 1967, *43,* 144–162.

Whyte, W.W., Jr. *The Organization Man.* New York: Simon & Schuster, 1956.

Wickens, D.D. Characteristics of word encoding. In *Coding Processes in Human Memory,* edited by A.W. Melton and E. Martin. Washington, D.C.: Winston, 1972.

Wiesel, T.N. Postnatal development of the visual cortex and the influence of environment. *Nature,* 1982, *299,* 583–592.

Wilcoxon, H.C., Dragoin, W.B., and Kral, P.A. Illness-induced aversions in rat and quail: Relative salience of visual and gustatory cues. *Science,* 1971, *171,* 826–828.

Williams, J.E., Bennett, S.M., and Best, D.L. Awareness and expression of sex stereotypes in young children. *Developmental Psychology,* 1975, *11,* 635–642.

Williams, K., Harkins, S., and Latané, B. Identifiability as a deterrent to social loafing: Two cheering experiments. *Journal of Personality and Social Psychology,* 1981, *40,* 303–311.

Williams, R.B., Hanel, T.L., Lee, K.L., and Kong, Y.H. Type A behavior, hostility, and coronary atherosclerosis. *Psychosomatic Medicine,* 1980, *42,* 539–549.

Wilson, G.T., and O'Leary, K.D. *Principles of Behavior Therapy.* Englewood Cliffs, N.J.: Prentice-Hall, 1978.

Wilson, P.R. The perceptual distortion of height as a function of ascribed academic status. *Journal of Social Psychology,* 1968, *74,* 97–102.

Winter, A. Depression and intractable pain treated by modified prefrontal lobotomy. *Journal of Medical Sociology,* 1972, *69,* 757–759.

Winter, D.G. *The Power Motive.* New York: Free Press, 1973.

Wise, R.A. Psychomotor stimulant properties of addictive drugs. *Annals of the New York Academy of Sciences,* 1988, *537,* 228–234.

Wise, S.P., and Rapoport, J.L. Obsessive compulsive disorder: Is it a basal ganglia dysfunction? *Psychopharmacology Bulletin,* 1988, *24,* 380–384.

Woerner, P.L., and Guze, S.B. A family and marital study of hysteria. *British Journal of Psychiatry,* 1968, *114,* 161–168.

Wolff, P.H. Observations on the early development of smiling. In *Determinants of Infant Behaviour, Vol. 2,* edited by B.M. Foss. London: Methuen, 1963.

Wolff, P.H. *The Causes, Controls and Organization of Behavior in the Neonate.* New York: International Universities Press, 1966.

Wolff, P.H. Crying and vocalization in early infancy. In *Determinants of Infant Behaviour, Vol. 4,* edited by B.M. Foss. London: Methuen, 1969.

Wood, D.L., Sheps, S.G., Elveback, L.R., and Schirder, A. Cold pressor test as a predictor of hypertension. *Hypertension,* 1984, *6,* 301–306.

Woodruff, R.A., Guze, S.B., and Clayton, P.J. Anxiety neurosis among psychiatric outpatients. *Comprehensive Psychiatry,* 1972, *13,* 165–170.

Woods, S.W., Charney, D.S., Goodman, W.K., and Heninger, G.R. Carbon dioxide–induced anxiety. *Archives of General Psychiatry,* 1988, *45,* 43–52.

Woodworth, R.S., and Schlosberg, H. *Experimental Psychology.* New York: Holt, Rinehart and Winston, 1954.

Wu, J.C., and Bunney, W.E. The biological basis of an antidepressant response to sleep deprivation and relapse: Review and hypothesis. *American Journal of Psychiatry,* 1990, *147,* 14–21.

Young, A., Stokes, M., and Crowe, M. Size and strength of the quadriceps muscles of old and young women. *European Journal of Clinical Investigation,* 1984, *14,* 282–287.

Youniss, J., and Smollar, J. Adolescent relations with mothers, fathers, and friends. Chicago: University of Chicago Press, 1985.

Yu, V.L., Fagan, L.M., and Wraith, S.M. Antimicrobial selection for meningitis by a computerized consultant: A blinded evaluation by infectious disease experts. *Journal of the American Medical Association,* 1979, *242,* 1279–1282.

Zahn-Waxler, C., Radke-Yarrow, M., and King, R.A. Child-rearing and children's prosocial initiations toward victims of distress. *Child Development,* 1979, *50,* 319–330.

Zajonc, R.B. Social facilitation. *Science,* 1965, *149,* 269–274.

Zajonc, R.B. On primacy of affect. In *Approaches to Emotion,* edited by K.R. Scherer and P. Ekman. Hillsdale, N.J.: Lawrence Erlbaum Associates, 1984.

Zajonc, R.B., and Sales, S.M. Social facilitation of dominant and subordinate responses. *Journal of Experimental Social Psychology,* 1966, *2,* 160–168.

Zeki, S., and Shipp, S. The functional logic of cortical connections. *Nature,* 1988, *335,* 311–317.

Zigler, E. Assessing Head Start at 20: An invited commentary. *American Journal of Orthopsychiatry,* 1985, *55,* 603–609.

Zigler, E., and Valentine, J. *Project Head Start: A Legacy of the War on Poverty.* New York: Free Press, 1979.

Zihl, J., von Cramon, D., Mai, N., and Schmid, C. Disturbance of movement vision after bilateral posterior brain damage: Further evidence and follow up observations. *Brain,* 1991, *114,* 2235–2252.

Zuckerman, M. *Psychobiology of Personality.* Cambridge, England: Cambridge University Press, 1991.

Zukier, H., and Pepitone, A. Social roles and strategies in prediction: Some determinants of the use of base-rate information. *Journal of Personality and Social Psychology,* 1984, *47,* 349–360.

Zvolsky, P., Jansky, L., Vyskocilova, J., and Grof, P. Effects of psychotropic drugs on hamster hibernation: Pilot study. *Progress in Neuropsychopharmacology,* 1981, *5,* 599–602.

NAME INDEX

Festinger, L., 582–583, 586, 605
Feynman, R.P., 301
Fibiger, H.C., 386
Field, D., 79, 354, 410, 415
Filskov, S.B., 503
Fink, M., 561
Fischer, G.W., 589
Fishman, S.T., 555
Fiske, S.T., 577
Fix, A.J., 566
Flagg, P.W., 273
Flaherty, J., 529
Flavell, J.H., 326
Foa, E., 546
Fodor, E.M., 363
Foley, V.D., 556
Folkman, S., 421
Ford, D.H., 540
Fouts, D., 294, 296
Fox, N.A., 331
Frady, R.L., 390
Frank, E., 529
Frankeberg, W.K., 316
Fraser, C., 128, 287, 598
Frawley, P.J., 194
Frederickson, W.A., 605
Freedman, J.L., 598
Freeman, S., 600
Friedman, M., 372, 374, 422, 557
Friedrich, F.J., 244
Fries, J.F., 503
Friesen, W.V., 409–410, 415
Frodi, A., 392
Fromkin, V., 275
Fuhrman, W., 333
Fuller, R.G.C., 592
Fulton, J.F., 404
Furrow, D., 292
Furstenberg, F.F., 342

Gabrielli, W.F., 516
Galaburda, A., 281
Ganong, W.F., 272
Garcia, J., 188
Gardiner, J.M., 204
Gardner, E.L., 293–294, 442
Garrity, L.I., 205
Gatchel, R.J., 421
Gazzaniga, M.S., 245
Geen, R.G., 393
Geiselman, R.E., 227
Geist, S.H., 378
Geller, D.M., 603
Gelman, R., 287, 326
Genefke, I., 420
Gerbino, L., 560
Gerrard, M., 342
Gershon, S., 524, 560
Geschwind, N., 243, 281
Gibson, E.J., 319
Gifford, R., 610, 611
Gil, T.E., 427

Gillespie, R.D., 512
Gilligan, C.F., 338
Girvin, J.P., 127
Gladwin, T., 442
Glaser, R., 426
Glass, D.R., 565
Gleitman, L.R., 287, 291
Glowa, J.R., 82
Goddard, G.V., 85
Goldberg, L.R., 386, 503
Goldblatt, P.B., 374
Goldfield, B.A., 287
Goldiamond, I., 536, 546
Goldin-Meadow, S., 286
Goldstein, A., 546
Goodglass, H., 277
Goodstein, L., 603
Goodwin, D.W., 506–507, 562
Gottesman, I., 521–522
Gottheil, E., 429
Gould, R.L., 349
Graf, P., 217, 219
Graham, J.R., 488
Granville-Grossman, K.L., 560
Graves, G., 546
Gray, J.A., 376, 471
Green, D.M., 94, 331
Greenberg, R., 262, 415
Greene, D., 366
Greenough, W.T., 79
Greenspan, S.I., 458
Greenwald, A.G., 97–98, 492, 503, 580
Greenwood, M.R.C., 373
Griffiths, M., 373
Griffitt, W., 606
Gross, A.E., 598
Grossarth-Maticek, R., 428
Grove, E., 218, 501
Grusec, J.E., 339
Guilmette, T.J., 504
Gulevich, G., 259
Gur, R.C., 485
Gustafson, G.E., 330
Gustavson, C.R., 194
Gutman, D., 241
Guze, S.B., 505–507, 510, 527, 562
Gwynn, M.I., 251

Haaga, D.A., 551
Haan, N., 347
Hadley, S.W., 566
Haenny, P.E., 147
Haffke, E.A., 566
Hagler, M., 532
Halbach, H., 387
Halgin, R.P., 612
Hall, E.T., 260
Hall, S.G., 611
Halmi, K.A., 375–376
Hammersmith, S.K., 379
Hanlon, C., 291
Harding, P.S., 509

Hare, R.D., 516
Harkins, S.G., 596
Harley, L.J., 259
Harlow, H., 328, 332–333
Harrell, A., 458
Harris, K.L., 330, 349
Hartka, E., 347
Hartshorne, H., 477
Hartup, W.W., 333
Hatfield, E., 605
Hawkins, J.E., 114
Hayes, C., 293
Hebb, D.O., 211, 290, 361
Hecht, S., 102
Heckler, M.M., 517
Heffner, H.E., 276
Heffner, R.S., 276
Heider, F., 572
Heinold, W.D., 594
Heise, G.A., 273
Helmer, D.C., 423
Henderson, D., 453, 512
Henke, P.G., 402
Henn, F.A., 563
Hennessy, R.T., 249
Henningfield, J.E., 386
Henri, V., 444
Heron, A., 325, 616
Herrnstein, R.J., 184
Higgins, E.T., 578
Hilgard, E.R., 249, 252
Hilgard, J.R., 249
Hintzman, D.L., 205
Hirsch, A., 296, 374
Hirschfeld, M.A., 565
Hitchcock, R.J., 160
Hobson, J.A., 261
Hodgson, R.J., 171
Hoffman, L.W., 194, 338
Hofling, C.K., 510
Hofman, M.A., 335, 380
Hofer, P., 617
Hogan, J., 493
Hogan, R., 493
Hohman, G.W., 414–415
Holahan, C.J., 616
Holden, C., 462
Holland, J., 428
Hollander, E., 509
Hollis, K.L., 168
Holmes, D.S., 349
Holyoak, K.J., 303, 305
Honig, W.K., 184
Horn, J.L., 351, 440–441
Horne, J.A., 258–259
Hornik, R., 354
Howard, M.L., 194, 254, 423, 508
Hubel, D.H., 134–135, 319
Huesmann, L.R., 391
Humphrey, N.K., 140
Hunt, E., 275
Hurt, M., 458

SUBJECT INDEX

Page numbers in *italic* type indicate illustrations.
Page numbers in **boldface** type indicate key terms and concepts.

Apraxia, 442
Aqueous humor, 99, *99*
Arousal
    attitude change and, 584
    personality and, 472
Articulation, subvocal, 205–206
Artificial intelligence, 143–144
Assessment. *See also* Test(s)
    of brain damage, 54–56
    of intelligence, 443–449
    of personality, 486–493
Assimilation, 321
Association cortex, 60–61, *61*, 63, 134–136
Attachment, 327–332
    avoidant, 331, 332
    behaviors fostering, 327–331
    crying behavior and, 330–331
    cuddling behavior and, 328–329, *328*
    day care and, 332
    Harlow's experiments in, 328–329
    looking behavior and, 329–330, *329*
    nature of, 331–332
    quality of, 331–332
    resistant, 331
    secure, 331
    smiling behavior and, 330
    sucking behavior and, 327–328
Attention
    auditory information and, 237–240
    consciousness and, 237–243
    selective, 239–243
    visual information and, 240–241
Attitude, 580–587
    changes in, 583–584
    cognitive dissonance theory and, 582–586
    components of, 580–582
    degree of specificity of, 581–582
    expenditures and, 585–586
    formation of, 580–582
    self-esteem and, 583–584
    self-perception and, 586
Attraction, interpersonal, 603–607
Attractiveness
    interpersonal interactions and, 603, 604–605
    self-esteem and, 600, 604
    social influence and, 599–600
Attribution, 573–580
    biases from, 574–577
    dispositional factors and, 573–574
    heuristics and, 577–579
    implicit psychology and, 573
    of self, 582
    situational factors and, 573–574
    sources of information for, 574
Attribution theory, 367, 413
Attributional error, fundamental, 574–575

Audition, 111–118, 127
    auditory system and, 112–117, *112*
    stimulus of sound and, 111–112
    temporal lobe and, 62–63
Auditory cortex, 60, *60*, *61*, 62–63, *62*
Auditory hair cells, 113
Auditory information, and attention, 237–240
Auditory prostheses, 127–128
Auditory system, 112–117, *112*
Authority, and social influence, 600–602
Autoimmune diseases, 425
Autonomic nervous system, 68–69
Autonomic responses, 401
Availability heuristic, 578–579
Aversive classical conditioning, 546
Aversive control, 185–187
Aversive stimulus, 172–174, *173*, 185–187, 188–189, 193–194
Avoidance response, 186
Avoidant attachment, 331, 332
Awareness and learning, 217–218
Axon, 71, *71*, 72
    of eye, 99

B lymphocytes, 424
Babbling, 285
Background, in perception, 137
Backward masking, 157–158, *158*
Balance, sense of, 125
Balint's syndrome, 136, 242
Bandura's social learning experiments, 476, *477*
Barber's social role theory, 250–252
Barbiturates, 81, 82
Base-rate fallacy, 578
Basic-level concepts, 299
Basilar membrane, 112–113, 115
Bed-wetting, 266
Behavior. *See also* Response
    adaptive, 546
    addictive, 382–388, 394–395, 516–519
    aggressive, 389–393
    antisocial, 252–255
    attachment and, 327–331
    aversive control of, 185–187
    biology of, 52–85
    classifying, 25–26
    complex, 176–177
    consensual, 574
    consistent, 574
    constraints on, 582
    control of, by brain, 59–71
    cooing, 284, 285
    crying, 284, 330–331
    cuddling, 328–329, *328*
    distinctive, 574
    drugs affecting, 81–84
    emotion and, 398–432
    explanations of, 13–15

    group, 554–559
    guided by stimuli, 182–185
    insightful, 190–192
    looking, 329–330, *329*
    maladaptive, 499, 546–547
    moral, 337–339
    motivation and, 358–395
    motivational relevance of, 576, 582
    personality and, 462–494
    puberty and, 341
    regulatory, 359
    sensation and, 90–128
    sexual, 376–382
    smiling, 330
    social, 235–237, 327–331, 341–343
    species-typical, 65, 67, 78, 185, 189
    sucking, 316, 327–328
    superstitious, 187–188
    target, 178
    type A and type B, 422–423
    type C, 427–428
    verbal, 235–236, 243–246, 270–296. *See also* Language
Behavior therapy, 544–550
    classical conditioning approach of, 544–546
    group, 554–559
    instrumental conditioning approach of, 544, 546–548
Behavioral change, maintaining, 549–550
Behavioral/cognitive approaches to personality, 474–479
    behaviorism, 474–475
    social learning theory, 475–476
    trait theories vs., 476–479
Behavioral components of attitudes, 581–582
Behaviorism, 13–15
    methodological, 15
    Pavlov's experiments in, 14
    personality and, 474–475
    radical, 474
    reactions against, 15–16
    Thorndike's experiments in, 13–14
    Watson's theory of, 14–15
Belongingness, need for, 364
Benzodiazepines, 81, 387
Beta activity, 256, *257*
Bias
    attributional, 574–577
    confirmation, 302
    motivational, 576–577
    response, 94–95
Binet-Simon Scale, 444
Binge drinking, 517–518
Binocular cues, in perception, 149–151, *149*
Biological factors in personality, 471–473
Biological needs, 359–361
Biological roots of psychology, 8–10

Commitment, 598–599
Common fate, law of, 139
Communication
  consciousness and, 236
  of emotion, in primates, 292–296, 410–411
Community psychologist, 615
Community psychology, 558–559
Comparative psychologist, 17
Competition, 588–589
Complementary colors, 109
Complex behavior, 176–177
Compliance, induced, 583–584
Componential intelligence, 440–441, 442
Comprehension
  of speech, 271–278, 286–287
  of words and sentences, 272–275, 282, 287–289
Compromise formation, 481
Compulsions, 507–509
Computer(s)
  expert systems and, 306–309
  mental functions and, 143–148, *143, 145, 148*
Computerized tomography, 54–55, *55*
Concept, 184, 297–299, 321
Conception, 313–314, 452
Concrete operations period, 325
Conditioned emotional response, 169–171, 401–403
Conditioned flavor aversion, 188–189, 193–194
Conditioned punishers, 176
Conditioned punishment, 176–178
Conditioned reinforcement, 174, 176–178, 365–366
Conditioned reinforcers, 176, 606
Conditioned response (CR), *167,* 168, *168,* 169–171
Conditioned stimulus (CS), 168, *168,* 169, 189
Conduction aphasia, 206–207, *207*
Conduction deafness, 127
Cones, of retina, 100
Confirmation bias, 302
Conflict resolution, 584–585
Conformity, 591–593
Confounding of variables, 29–32
Conjugate movements of eye, 103
Conscience, 481
Conscientiousness, 467–468, 469
Consciousness, 5–6, 234–266
  altered states of, 255, 260–263. *See also* Hypnosis; Sleep
  attention and, 237–243
  brain and, 243–247
  hypnosis and, 247–255
  loss of, 243–247
  sleep and, 255–266
  as social behavior, 235–237
Consensual behavior, 574

Consensus, false, 575–576
Conservation, in cognitive development, 324, *324, 325*
Consistency of behavior, 574
Consolidation, 211–212
Consumer psychologist, 615
Content rewards, 475
Content words, 274, 282, 287–288
Context
  effects of, in perception, 142, 146–148
  memory and, 221
  perception of speech and, 272–273
  reading and, 282
Contextual cues, 142, *142*
Contextual intelligence, 441, 442
Contingency, 171
Contours, illusory, 138, *138*
Contralateral connections, 60
Control
  aversive, 185–187
  of behavior, by brain, 59–71
  delusions of, 520
  of self, 466, 476, 550
  verbal, 235–236
Control group, 30, 564
Controlled variable, 28–33
Conventional level of morality, 338
Convergence, 149, *150*
Conversion, 482
Conversion disorder, 510–512
Conversion reaction, 539
Convulsions, 85
Cooing behavior, 284, 285
Cooperation, morality of, 337
Coping response, 402, 421–422
Cornea, 99, *99*
Corpus callosum, *70,* 245, *246*
Correct negatives, 94–95, *95*
Correctional mechanism, 359–360
Correlated variables, 34
Correlation, 34, *34,* 42–43, 444
  illusory, 589
Correlation coefficient, 43
Cortical motor map, *9*
Cortisol, 419
Counterbalancing, 30
Countertransference, 541
Couples therapy, 556–558
Covert sensitization, 547
CR (conditioned response), *167,* 168, *168,* 169–171
Crack cocaine, 82, 385, 517
Cranial nerves, 58–59, *59*
Criterion, 447
Criterion group, 487
Critical period, in development, 319–320
Cross-cultural studies. *See* Cultures.
Cross-situational consistency, 477
Crying behavior, 284, 330–331

Crystallized intelligence, 350–351, 440
CS (conditioned stimulus), 168, *168,* 169, 189
CSF (cerebrospinal fluid), 57
CT scan, *55*
CT scanner, 54–55
Cuddling behavior, 328–329, *328*
Cultural bias in intelligence tests, 447–448
Cultural definition of intelligence, 442
Cultural diversity, need for, 468
Culture
  children's two-word utterances and, 286
  expression of emotion and, 406–407, 522–523
  family environment and, 471
  food choice, and, 370
  infants' speech perception and, 285
  intelligence and, 436, 441, 447–448, 455–457
  language universals and, 290, 291, 292
  nonnutritive sucking and, 328
  prejudice and, 589
  reciprocity and, 597
  schizophrenia and, 522–523
  stereotypes and, 587
  youth, 342
Curare, 77
Cyclothymic disorder, 526

Dark adaptation of eye, 101–103
Darwin's theory of emotion, 406
Day care, 332
Daydreaming, 34
Deafness, 127
Deductive reasoning, 299–301
Deep processing, 214
Deep structure of sentences, 275
Defense mechanisms, 481–482
Definition, operational, 26–28
Degree of specificity of attitude, 581–582
Delay of gratification, 476
Delta activity, 257, *257*
Delusions, 520
Delusions of control, 520
Delusions of grandeur, 520
Delusions of persecution, 520
Dementia, 349–350, 452
Demonology, and mental disorders, 537
DENDRAL program, 308
Dendrites, 71, *71*
Dependent variable, 23–24, 25
Depression
  major, 526, 527–530
  seasonal, 529
  treatment for, 83, 528, 560–562, 565–566

Space, perception of, 149–155, 159, 319–320
Spatial ability, 438
Spatial metaphor of problem-solving process, 303–304, *304*
Spatial perception, 63
Spearman's two-factor theory of intelligence, 437–438
Species-typical behavior, 65, 67, 78, 185
Specific exploration, 361
Specific nerve energies, doctrine of, 8
Spectral colors, 105
Speech
 brain damage and, 276–277
 child-directed, 286–287
 comprehension and, 271–278, 286–287
 language and, 271–278, 286–289
 perception of, 271–273, 284
Speech sounds, recognition of, 271–272, 284
Sperm, 313, *313*
Spinal cord, 56, *56*, 58, 414
Spinal nerves, 56, 58
Split-brain operation, 245, *245*
Split-brain syndrome, 245–246, *246*
Spontaneity, loss of, 64
Spontaneous recovery
 in classical conditioning, 169
 in instrumental conditioning, 175
Sports psychologist, 614–615
Stabilized image in vision, 103, *103*
Standard deviation, 42
Stanford-Binet Scale, 445
Statistical significance, 24, 43–47
Statistics. *See* Descriptive statistics
Stereograms, 150–151, *151*
Stereopsis, 150, 319
Stereoscopic vision, 319
Stereotaxic apparatus, 53, *53*
Stereotypes, 334, 587, 589, 590
Sternberg's theory of intelligence, 440–442
Stimulants, 82–83, 384, 385
Stimuli
 appetitive, 169, 172–174, *173*, 187, 188–189
 aversive, 172–174, *173*, 185–187, 188–189, 193–194
 for behavior, 182–185
 conditioned, 168, *168*, 169, 189
 discriminative, 182–183, *183*, 189
 generalization of, 183–185, *184*, *185*
 punishing, 172
 reinforcing, 172–174, 188–189
 unconditioned, 168, *168*, 169
Strange Situation, 331–332
Stress
 cancer and, 427–429
 cardiovascular disease and, 422–423
 coping with, 421–422

health and, 418–430
 immune system and, 424–429
 lie detection and, 431–432
 physiology of, 419–420
 posttraumatic, 423–424
Stress inoculation training, 552
Stroke, 54
Stroop effect, 223, *223*
Structural family therapy, 556
Structuralism, 11
Studies on Hysteria (Freud), 480
Subject expectations, 32–33
Subject variables, confounding of, 31–32
Sublimation, 482
Subliminal perception, 96–98
Subordinate concepts, 299
Substance abuse. *See* Addiction
Subvocal articulation, 205–206
Successive approximations, method of, 178
Sucking response, 316, 327–328
Sudden infant death syndrome (SIDS), 265
Suggestibility, posthypnotic, 248
Superego, 481
Superordinate concepts, 299
Superstitious behavior, 187–188
Surface structure of sentences, 275
Surrogate mother, 328–329, *328*
Swallowing response, 316
Syllogism, 299–300
Symbolic function, 324
Symbolism in dreams, 260–261
Sympathetic branch of autonomic nervous system, 68, 69
Symptom substitution, 553
Synapse, 72–77, *72*, *73*
 effects of drugs on, 76–77
 excitatory, 72–75, *73*
 inhibitory, 72–75, *73*
 transmission of messages and, 75–76
Synaptic cleft, 75
Syntactical cues, 274–275
Syntactical rules, 273–275, 288
Syntax, 273–275, 287–288
System variable, 359–360
Systematic desensitization, 544–546

T lymphocytes, 424
Tachistoscope, 146, *147*
Tardive dyskinesia, 559
Target behavior, 178
Taste, 118–119, 121–122
Taste bud, 118, *119*
TAT (Thematic Apperception Test), 363, 491–492, *491*
Tectorial membrane, 113
Television
 aggression and, 391–392
 children and, 353–355
Temperament, 400
Temperature, sensation of, 123

Templates, 139–140
Temporal coding, 92–93
Temporal lobe, 61, *61*, 62–63
Terminal buttons, 71, *71*, *73*, 75, *75*, 76, *76*, 77
Test(s)
 for attachment, 331–332
 construction of, 486–487
 integrity, 493–494
 of intelligence, 443–449
 lie detector, 256, 431–432
 objective, 487–490
 of personality, 363, 486–493
 projective, 490–492
Testes, 68, *69*
Testosterone, 315, 340
 aggression and, 389–391
 sexual behavior and, 377–378
Texture, 152, *152*
Thalamus, 66–67, *67*
THC (tetrahydrocannibinal), 83, 386
Thematic Apperception Test (TAT), 363, 491–492, *491*
Theory, 24–25
Therapy, 536–568
 behavior, 544–550, 555
 biological, 559–564
 client-centered, 542–544
 cognitive behavior, 550–554
 drug, 81, 83, 523–524, 528, 559–560, 565–566
 early approaches to, 536–540
 electroconvulsive, 528, 561–562, *561*
 evaluation of, 541–542, 552–554, 564–567
 family, 556–558
 group, 554–559
 humanistic, 542–544
 hypnosis, 538–539
 implosion, 546
 insight, 540–544, 564–568
 nondirective, 543
 psychoanalysis, 540–542
 psychosurgery, 124, 404, 562–563
 rational-emotive, 550–551
Theta activity, 256, *257*
Thinking, 296–309. *See also* Intelligence
Thorndike's law of effect, 13–14
Thought disorder, 519–520
Threat gestures, 389
Three stages, law of, 10
Threshold, in perception, 94
Thurstone's factors of intelligence, 439–440
Timbre, of sound, 112, 116–117
Time-out, 547
Tobacco. *See* Smoking
Token economies, 548
Tolerance, 387, 394
Tomography
 computerized, 54–55, *55*
 positron emission, 55–56, *56*, *508*

Credits (*continued*)

Library of Medicine; p. 12, (margin) North Wind Picture Archives, p. 12, (bottom) Kim Hill, Department of Anthropology, University of Michigan; p. 13, National Library of Medicine; p. 14, Bob Daemmrich/The Image Works; p. 15 (top) Bettmann Archive, (margin) Archives of the History of American Psychology, University of Akron; p. 17, Michael Grecco/Stock Boston.

Chapter 2
P. 23, SuperStock, Inc.; p. 26, Seth Resnick/Stock Boston; p. 36, Bettmann Archive; p. 38, Hank Morgan/Photo Researchers, Inc.; p. 40, Ray Stott/The Image Works; pp. 47–48, Extract, Copyright © 1976 by The New York Times Company. Reprinted by permission.

Chapter 3
P. 54, FourByFive, Inc.; p. 56, Fig. 3.5, Mallinkrodt Institute of Radiology; p. 56, Fig. 3.6, *Discover*, 1989, 10(3); p. 66, Herbert Migdoll/Rainbow; p. 67, Tony Howarth/Woodfin Camp and Associates; p. 77, Jacques Jangoux/Peter Arnold, Inc.; p. 78 Shostal Associates/SuperStock, Inc.; p. 82, Steve Starr/Picture Group.

Chapter 4
P. 91, Piergiorgio Sclarandis/Black Star; p. 94, Vania Fine/Agence Vardy Stadt/Photo Researchers, Inc.; p. 102, SuperStock, Inc.; p. 117, Robert Brenner/PhotoEdit; p. 118, Omikron/Science Source/Photo Researchers, Inc.; p. 124, SuperStock, Inc.; p. 125, Dan McCoy/Rainbow.

Chapter 5
P. 133, Dan McCoy/Rainbow; p. 136, Susan Lapides; p. 141, Curtis Willocks Photography/Brooklyn Image Group; p. 150, California Museum of Photography; p. 151, Jonathan Blair/Woodfin Camp and Associates; p. 156, John Ficara/Woodfin Camp and Associates.

Chapter 6
P. 165, Frank Siteman; p. 170, Susan Lapides; p. 172, Susan Lapides; p. 173, Mark Antman/The Image Works; p. 177, Chuck Fishman/Woodfin Camp and Associates; p. 179 (left/right) U.S. Coast Guard; p. 181, Wide World Photos, Inc.; p. 188, Dion Ogust/The Image Works; p. 189, Margaretta K. Mitchell/PhotoEdit; p. 191, SuperStock International, Inc.; p. 192, from Norman Baxley/c 1984 Discover Publication; p. 194, Stan Wayman/Photo Researchers, Inc.

Chapter 7
P. 200, Bob Daemmrich/Stock Boston; p. 209, SuperStock, Inc.; p. 211, Ellis Herwig/The Picture Cube; p. 213, FourByFive, Inc.; p. 215, Leslye Borden/PhotoEdit; p. 216, David Young-Wolff/PhotoEdit; p. 217, Margot Granitsas/The Image Works; p. 225, Ellis Herwig/Stock Boston; p. 226, A. Tannenbaum/Sygma.

Chapter 8
P. 235, S. Lousada/Petit Format/Photo Researchers, Inc.; p. 239, Fujifotos/The Image Works; p. 247, North Wind Picture Archives; p. 248, Larry Kolvoord/The Image Works; p. 250, Dr. E. Hilgard, Stanford University; p. 256, Fig. 8.14, Philippe Platilly/Science Source/Photo Researchers, Inc.; p. 261, *Winter Night in Vitebsk*, Marc Chagall/SuperStock, Inc.; p. 265, Tim Hazael/BOC Group/Science Photo Library/Photo Researchers, Inc.

Chapter 9
P. 270, SuperStock, Inc.; p. 278, Photo Researchers, Inc.; p. 281, Claude Charlier/Black Star; p. 284, Fig. 9.7, Patricia Kuhl, University of Washington, Seattle; p. 285, Amy C. Etra/PhotoEdit; p. 286, James Wilson/Woodfin Camp and Associates; pp. 288–289, Tables 9.1 and 9.2: Tables adapted from *Psychology and Language: An Introduction to Psycholinguistics* by Herbert H. Clark and Eve V. Clark, copyright © 1977 by Harcourt Brace Jovanovich, Inc., reprinted by permission of the publisher. p. 289, Camilla Smith/Rainbow; p. 292, Nathan Benn/Woodfin Camp and Associates; p. 294, Paul Fusco/Magnum Photos,

Inc.; p. 304, Jocelyn Boutin/The Picture Cube. pp. 307–308, Figs. 9.14 and 9.15: Copyright 1983 by the American Association for the Advancement of Science.

Chapter 10
P. 314, David Scharf; p. 319, Nancy Rader and Associates; p. 321, Yves Debraine/Black Star; p. 322 (left/right), Doug Goodman/Monkmeyer Press; p. 323, Carol Palmer/The Picture Cube; p. 328 (top), Bob Daemmrich/The Image Works; p. 328 (bottom), Harlow Primate Laboratory, University of Wisconsin; p. 333, J. Chenet/Woodfin Camp and Associates; p. 336, Stephen McBrady/PhotoEdit; p. 343 (right), Bob Daemmrich/Stock Boston, p. 343 (left), Michael Newman/PhotoEdit; p. 345, Wide World Photos, Inc.; p. 345 (left), Wide World Photos, Inc.; p. 345 (right), Sarah Putnam/NYT Pictures; p. 351, Len Johnson/Black Star; p. 352, John Eastcott/Yva Momatiuk/The Image Works.

Chapter 11
P. 359, Mauritius-Rawi/SuperStock, Inc.; p. 365, Dilip Mehta/Contact Press Images; p. 367, Emil Muench/APSA/Photo Researchers, Inc.; p. 370, Christiana Dittman/Rainbow; p. 374, Bob Daemmrich/Stock Boston; p. 375, Bonnie Schiffman/Gamma Liaison; p. 377, Elizabeth Crews/The Image Works; p. 381, Alain Evrard/Photo Researchers, Inc.; p. 385, Stacy Pick/Stock Boston; p. 390, H. Reardon/Photo Researchers, Inc.; p. 394, Robert Brenner/PhotoEdit.

Chapter 12
P. 399, Larry Kolvoord/The Image Works; p. 411, William E. Townsend, Jr./Photo Researchers, Inc.; p. 413, Alan Oddie/PhotoEdit; p. 418, Unisys/PhotoEdit; p. 420, SuperStock, Inc.; p. 421, CNRI/SPL/Science Source/Photo Researchers, Inc.; p. 422, SuperStock, Inc.

Chapter 13
P. 437, Marc and Evelyne Bernheim/Woodfin Camp and Associates; p. 441, David Hathcox; p. 445, Reprinted with permission of The Riverside Publishing Company: *The Stanford-Binet Intelligence Scale* by R.L. Thorndike, E.P. Hagen, and J.M. Sattler. The Riverside Publishing Co., 8420 W. Bryn Mawr Ave., Chicago, IL 60631. © 1986. p. 446, Lew Merriam/Monkmeyer Press; p. 450 (left) Joe Sohm/The Image Works; p. 450 (right), John Eastcott/Yva Momatiuk/The Image Works; p. 455, Myrleen Ferguson/PhotoEdit.

Chapter 14
P. 463 (top), Frank Siteman; p. 463 (bottom) The Bettmann Archive; p. 468, Bob Daemmrich/The Image Works; p. 473, Bob Daemmrich/The Image Works; p. 477, Fig. 14.8, Dr. Albert Bandura; p. 481, Bettmann Archive; p. 487, Bob Daemmrich/The Image Works.

Chapter 15
P. 499, Scala/Art Resource; p. 507, Dan McCoy/Rainbow; p. 508, Dr. L. R. Baxter/UCLA; p. 512, AP/Wide World Photos, p. 517, Jane Schreibman/Photo Researchers, Inc.; p. 520, Grunnitus/Monkmeyer Press/The Dark Room; p. 527, Richard Sobol/Stock Boston.

Chapter 16
P. 536, Dan McCoy/Rainbow; p. 538 (left) Bettmann Archive; p. 538 (right) UPI/Bettmann; p. 539, Giraudon/Art Resource, NY; p. 542, Michael Rougier/Life Magazine © Time Inc.; p. 551, Courtesy Albert Ellis; p. 555, N. Rowan/The Image Works; p. 556, M. Siluk/The Image Works; p. 557, Will and Demi McIntyre/Photo Researchers, Inc.; p. 558, Robert McElroy/Woodfin Camp and Associates.

Chapter 17
P. 572, Dagmar Fabricius/Stock Boston; p. 577 (left), Wide World Photos, Inc.; p. 577 (right), Wally McNamee/Woodfin Camp and Associates; p. 581, Susan Lapides; p. 587, Rob Nelson/Picture Group; p. 588, Weslyan University Press and Dr. O.J. Harvey; p. 592, Gerard Chaplong/The Image Bank; p. 593, Dan Miller/Woodfin Camp and Associates; p. 604, Bob Daemmrich/Stock Boston.